Exclusion and Refoulement: Criminality in International and Domestic Refugee Law

Exclusion and Refoulement

CRIMINALITY IN INTERNATIONAL AND DOMESTIC REFUGEE LAW

Joseph Rikhof

IRWIN LAW

Published in 2023 by

Irwin Law Inc
Suite 206, 14 Duncan Street
Toronto, Ontario M5H 3G8
irwinlaw.com

ISBN 978-1-55221-679-8 (print) | ISBN 978-1-55221-680-4 (PDF)

Library and Archives Canada Cataloguing in Publication

Title: Exclusion and refoulement : criminality in international and domestic refugee law / Joseph Rikhof.
Names: Rikhof, Joseph, author.
Description: Includes bibliographical references and index.
Identifiers: Canadiana (print) 20230500749 | Canadiana (ebook) 20230500889 | ISBN 9781552216798 (softcover) | ISBN 9781552216804 (PDF)
Subjects: LCSH: Refugees — Legal status, laws, etc. | LCSH: Asylum, Right of.
Classification: LCC KZ6530 .R55 2023 | DDC 341.4/86—dc23

Printed and bound by CPI Group (UK) Ltd, Croydon, CR0 4YY

1 2 3 4 5 27 26 25 24 23

To my wife Ruth, whose unstinting support throughout my career made it possible to combine a full-time government job with increasingly exciting but time-consuming academic endeavours—and this was before the writing of this book, for which her enthusiasm knew no bounds, and during the journey of which she gave new meaning to the term "partner."

Summary Table of Contents

Detailed Table of Contents

Foreword

BY PROFESSOR DAVID CANTOR

Who deserves protection? One of the main functions of refugee law is to provide a set of criteria for distinguishing non-nationals who merit international protection from those who do not. That assessment is rooted in a fear of extreme discrimination in the refugee's own country for which national protection is not forthcoming. This enquiry, then, is fundamental to the rationale of refugee law. But refugee law also demands an answer to a second, and less comfortable, question: who, regardless of such fear, does not deserve international protection? It is here where considerations of individual character and criminality enter the ambit of refugee law. This is the vexed matter to which Dr. Joseph Rikhof turns his considerable powers of legal scholarship in the monograph *Exclusion and Refoulement*, first published in 2012 as *The Criminal Refugee: The Treatment of Asylum Seekers with a Criminal Background in International and Domestic Law* and appearing here in its second edition.

Exclusion and Refoulement gifts the reader with a clear and perceptive understanding of how key elements of this field of law deal with actual or suspected criminality by non-nationals who might otherwise qualify for international protection. That this is an ongoing practical concern in many countries, and not merely a matter for abstract legal discussion, is evidenced by major developments in the caselaw of leading jurisdictions since the first edition of this volume was published ten years ago. It is seen too in the surge of important new legal scholarship on this topic, including *Terrorism and Exclusion from Refugee Status in the UK* by Dr. Sarah Singer, *Exclusion Clauses of the Refugee Convention: Article 1F versus the Non-refoulement Principle* by Dr. Zarif Yakut-Bahtiyar, and *Exclusion from Protection as a Refugee* by Dr. Yao Li. The new edition of Dr. Rikhof's *Exclusion and Refoulement* both takes stock and builds upon these practical and scholarly advances in the field.

The strength of the book lies in how it situates a detailed study of exclusion from international protection within wider legal debates. First, it offers a persuasive argument that exclusion from refugee status under article 1F of the 1951 Convention and 1967 Protocol represents an example par excellence of a site at which different bodies of law entwine to shape the interpretative exercise. The earlier chapters of the book engagingly show the entanglements of refugee law with such diverse fields as extradition law, criminal law, public law, and human rights law. Later chapters ask how the qualified duty of *non-refoulement* in refugee law now squares with an absolute prohibition in human rights law on expulsions if there is a real risk of torture. Such linkages speak to wider foundational debates in legal studies about the coherence of law as a project of governance, the interaction between distinct legal regimes and the potential fragmentation of international law as a whole.

Second, *Exclusion and Refoulement* rightly treats "refugee law" as a field that extends beyond just the 1951 Convention and 1967 Protocol. The earlier chapters offer important insights into the development of a wider range of international instruments relevant to the topic. Those instruments also hold a central place in the analyses of contemporary approaches in later chapters. However, Dr. Rikhof also takes seriously the idea that refugee law is comprised as much by domestic law as by international law. The presentation of national jurisprudence from selected countries by those chapters complements the international law perspective in showing the breadth of sources that we must consider if we truly wish to understand refugee law. It raises far-reaching questions about how our understanding of refugee law, including exclusion and *non-refoulement*, will shift as we broaden our frame of study to other national laws and jurisprudence from around the world.

Third, the volume raises the contentious issue of what States can or should do with individuals whose criminality excludes them from refugee status but who cannot be expelled from the host State for legal or practical reasons. This trenchant policy challenge was taken up for study in 2014 by a two-year research project, "Undesirable and

Unreturnable?," funded by the UK Arts & Humanities Research Council (AH/L015463/1) and led by Professor Joris van Wijk and myself. Dr. Rikhof was a key contributor to the project and his first edition of *Exclusion and Refoulement* was crucial in helping set the agenda for that research project and for special issues in the *Refugee Survey Quarterly* and *Journal of International Criminal Justice* journals and other reports that it produced. Indeed, on this topic, the first edition of the book was genuinely ground-breaking and had a catalysing impact on scholarship and, through that growing body of work, on policy and practice in several countries.

For these reasons, the new edition of *Exclusion and Refoulement* will be a point of reference for both scholars and practitioners working on refugee law and, particularly, its intersection with concerns about criminality. Its detailed and useful commentary on the article 1F exclusion provisions, on *non-refoulement* rules in refugee and human rights law, and on alternatives to *refoulement* is balanced by a sense of connection to wider debates in our legal field. However, it also pushes us to ask more searching questions about who "deserves" refugee status; what constitutes refugee law as a field and where do its boundaries lie; and what are the moral, legal, and practical implications of excluding people from refugee status on grounds of actual or suspected criminality.

Professor David Cantor
REFUGEE LAW INITIATIVE
UNIVERSITY OF LONDON

Foreword
BY LUKE MORTON

As the second edition of this book goes to print, war is raging in Ukraine. The International Criminal Court, headquartered in The Hague, has sent teams of experts to Ukraine to investigate "allegations of war crimes, crimes against humanity or genocide committed on any part of the territory of Ukraine." Canada's House of Commons voted unanimously to approve the following motion: "That, given reports of human rights abuses and attacks on civilians in Ukraine and other parts of the world by the Russian-supported Wagner Group, the House call upon the government to immediately designate the Wagner Group as a terrorist entity." The United States has designated the Wagner Group a transnational criminal organization, citing human rights abuses in Ukraine, Mali, and the Central African Republic. A former commander of the Wagner Group is reported to have deserted, illegally crossed the border into Norway, and applied for asylum in that country. Given global events such as the war in Ukraine, the publication of this important and excellent book's second edition could not be more timely.

History—and this book—shows that although the wheels of international justice turn slowly, they do turn, and anyone found responsible for committing atrocities such as war crimes or crimes against humanity anywhere in the world can be held accountable. Although, during the time of conflict, those responsible for such atrocities are usually insulated by national borders and perhaps a sense of hubris and invincibility, history has also shown that armed conflicts end, regimes eventually change, and persecutors often become the persecuted (or the prosecuted) and flee their homeland to evade harm. Invariably, they arrive in another country and seek asylum.

The asylum seeker then usually claims that he or she will face persecution, torture, or other serious harm if deported to the country of origin and, for reasons based in law and morality, should be granted asylum. In this scenario, government officials will often maintain, before refugee adjudicators and judges, that for reasons based in law and morality, this kind of asylum seeker is not deserving of protection because of the atrocities committed and should be deported to the country of origin. It is often the case that the person seeking asylum will plead additional factors, such as being under duress ("I would be shot in the head if I didn't follow orders") or having had a low-level supporting role in the organization that committed the atrocities (such as courier, interpreter, mechanic, cook, or barber). At this point in the scenario, lawyers and judges involved in such cases should carefully read this book.

The book is a tour de force, an indispensable addition to the legal literature regarding international refugee law and international criminal law and a must-read for law students, academics, lawyers, adjudicators and judges, policy makers, and anyone with an interest in this field of law. International refugee law is a complex area of law and international criminal law is a complex area of law, but the complexities increase exponentially where these two legal spheres intersect.

To give the reader an idea of the scope of the issues dealt with in this book, imagine a Rubik's cube but where each coloured tile represents a legal principle, an international treaty, a UN resolution, a judicial decision of an international tribunal, a domestic judicial decision from one of nine countries, and so on. Imagine trying to unscramble this legal Rubik's cube to make sense of it all. Well, that is what the author has done for the reader. He makes sense of it all. To give a better idea of the magnitude and interplay of the legal tiles in this Rubik's cube, in a coherent manner, readers will learn about international refugee law, international human rights law, international humanitarian law, international criminal law, transnational criminal law, the Refugee Convention, the Convention against Torture (CAT), the International Covenant on Civil and Political Rights (ICCPR), the Convention on the Rights of the Child, the Rome Statute, the Geneva Conventions relating to war, the European Convention on Human Rights, the African Charter on Human and Peoples' Rights, the International Court of Justice, the

International Criminal Tribunal for the former Yugoslavia, the International Criminal Tribunal for Rwanda, the Human Rights Committee, the Committee against Torture, the Court of Justice of the European Union, the European Court of Human Rights, the Inter-American Court of Human Rights, jurisprudence from the domestic courts of nine countries (Australia, Belgium, Canada, France, Germany, the Netherlands, New Zealand, the United Kingdom, and the United States), extradition laws, and much more. The scholarship, comprehensive research, and meticulous attention to (important) detail will be evident to the reader.

Although the 1951 Convention relating to the Status of Refugees is primarily protection focused (i.e., to give asylum to persons facing persecution), article 1F provides three exclusion clauses concerning persons whom the framers of the convention decided were undeserving of protection. It reads as follows:

> The provisions of this Convention shall not apply to any person with respect to whom there are serious reasons for considering that:
> (a) He has committed a crime against peace, a war crime, or a crime against humanity, as defined in the international instruments drawn up to make provision in respect of such crimes;
> (b) He has committed a serious non-political crime outside the country of refuge prior to his admission to that country as a refugee;
> (c) He has been guilty of acts contrary to the purposes and principles of the United Nations.

Article 1F considerations generally apply at the beginning of the refugee process, where asylum seekers can be excluded from protection if they fall within the ambit of the three scenarios described above. However, if a person has been accepted as a refugee, there is another important provision in the Refugee Convention that can, in theory, still result in *refoulement*—or return to the country of origin—as article 33(2) states:

> [Article 33(1) reproduced here for context]
>
> 1. No Contracting State shall expel or return ("refouler") a refugee in any manner whatsoever to the frontiers of territories where his life or freedom would be threatened on account of his race, religion, nationality, membership of a particular social group or political opinion.
>
> 2. The benefit of the present provision may not, however, be claimed by a refugee whom there are reasonable grounds for regarding

> as a danger to the security of the country in which he is, or who, having been convicted by a final judgment of a particularly serious crime, constitutes a danger to the community of that country.

Those two provisions of the Refugee Convention—article 1F and article 33(2)—while seemingly simple to articulate, are often very difficult to apply to real-life cases as they involve the intersection of international refugee law and international criminal law. This intersection is thus the essence of the book, which examines who is undeserving of protection in the first place (article 1F) and when it is appropriate to apply exceptions to the principle of *non-refoulement* found in article 33(2) (i.e., a refugee cannot be returned to the country of origin except if determined to be a danger to the security or a danger to the community of the country of refuge).

The approximate 750 pages of this book comprehensively deal with articles 1F and 33(2) and include historical background, an explanation of relevant human rights and international criminal law treaties, UN resolutions, judicial interpretation, and much more. The reader will no doubt appreciate the author's expert understanding, insights, and analyses when reading this book.

As mentioned, this book is impressively comprehensive in scope. It provides a very informative history of the concept of asylum and explains how the custom of giving asylum was well known in ancient times in countries such as Egypt and Greece. Historically, asylum was granted on a religious or secular basis. Religious asylum (or sanctuary) was sought at holy places against powers within the same territory, while the secular version was given by kingdoms, republics, and free cities to protect persons from outside their territory from persecution.

Fast-forward to what is described as the "modern era of asylum" when in 1685 Louis XIV of France signed a law repealing the Edict of Nantes, which had resulted in the persecution of Huguenots in France. The granting of asylum to groups such as religious minorities was expanded upon after the French Revolution, when, as a result of both aristocrats and others opposing the various regimes in power, political asylum became much more prominent. After the First World War, we learn that hundreds of thousands of asylum seekers (primarily Armenians and Russians) sought refuge, and a few decades later, following the atrocities committed in the Second World War, the international community negotiated the 1951 Convention relating to the Status of Refugees, which is still in force to this day.

The author deftly connects all the historical, policy, and legal dots as he introduces the reader to a multitude of international conventions, UN resolutions, and other instruments that form the backdrop to the author's extensive analyses of the exclusion clauses in article 1F and the exceptions to *non-refoulement* in article 33(2). There is a detailed analysis of every relevant legal concept, including article 1F(a) crimes, such as genocide, war crimes, and crimes against humanity. The reader will find a comprehensive discussion of the extended liability concept, which includes aiding and abetting, command/superior responsibility, conspiracy, and incitement. There are also important sections covering legal defences; child soldiers; the views of the United Nations High Commissioner for Refugees (UNHCR); article 1F(b) and "serious non-political crime"; article 1F(c) and "acts contrary to the purposes and principles of the United Nations"; and article 33(2) considerations dealing with *refoulement* and "danger to the security" and "danger to the community."

In addition, there is an excellent analysis of issues related to the CAT and the ICCPR, dealing, respectively, with torture and cruel, inhuman, or degrading treatment or punishment. For those cases with legal or practical limitations to removal, there is an excellent chapter canvassing alternatives to *refoulement*, which includes discussion and analysis of alternatives such as prosecution, extradition, detention, and humanitarian solutions. Throughout the book, the reader will benefit from the insights and commentary of the author, such as the following:

> While the vicissitudes of international events influence refugee movements, they also leave a mark on the appreciation of legal developments. It is a truism that new legal concepts or even entire new legal fields find their inspiration in important political or social events. The continuing development of international instruments dealing with issues such as genocide, war crimes, crimes against humanity, organized crime, and terrorism, as well as refinements in these areas of law, can all be connected to traumatic events preceding calls to adjust the legal means to address such criminal behaviour. This is true in international and domestic areas of criminal law, and it is no less true for exclusion in the area of refugee law, which has a close connection to criminal law. (p. 582)

One of the most difficult determinations in any area of law is deciding where to draw the line that demarcates an important legal concept. In other words, it is relatively easy for a legislature to refer to terms such as "offer" (contract law), "negligence" (tort law), "income" (tax law), and "freedom" (constitutional law) but an entirely different and much more difficult task to define the parameters of such important legal concepts. Apropos the challenge of defining a legislative term, and well known to lawyers in Canada and the United States, is the dictum from a 1964 decision of the US Supreme Court in which Justice Stewart, in deciding an obscenity case, stated:

> I shall not today attempt to further define the kinds of material I understand to be embraced within that shorthand description [hard-core pornography] and perhaps I could never succeed in intelligently doing so. *But I know it when I see it*, and the motion picture involved in this case is not that.[1]

Although it is quite rare nowadays to see this type of intuitive decision making—"I know it when I see it"—explicitly referenced in a decision, it nevertheless seems to be the case, at times, that adjudicators or judges will do their best to determine what is a fair and just result in the case before them and then justify that subjective decision by drawing from a smorgasbord of legal principles and Latin maxims and weaving them into a written decision. The result may be fair and just in a particular case, but it also results in ever-shifting lines drawn to demarcate important legal concepts.

In this book, the reader will learn about important legal concepts such as persecution; torture; cruel, inhuman, and degrading treatment or punishment; war crimes; crimes against humanity; genocide; aiding and abetting; and conspiracy, to name just a few. To demonstrate the difficulty in drawing important conceptual lines or setting parameters, the term "persecution" does not include every form of minor discrimination. But drawing the line where discrimination crosses the threshold to become persecution is a difficult task.

The author of this book recognizes the complexity of the many legal terms relevant to international refugee law and international criminal law and identifies many important judicial precedents where judges demarcated the legal conceptual line on the facts being adjudicated. The

1 *Jacobellis v Ohio*, 378 US 184 (1964) p 378 [emphasis added].

practical result for an asylum claimant being on one side of the line or the other in this area of the law can often mean the difference between deportation or incarceration and asylum or freedom. To better illustrate, here are some helpful "line-drawing" examples and legal precedents that the author has researched and that should be helpful to lawyers pleading related cases.

The first example, from *Fedorenko v United States*, deals with persecution in concentration camps:

> Thus, an individual who did no more than cut the hair of female inmates before they were executed cannot be found to have assisted in the persecution of civilians. On the other hand, there can be no question that a guard who was issued a uniform and armed with a rifle and a pistol, who was paid a stipend and was regularly allowed to leave the concentration camp to visit a nearby village, and who admitted to shooting at escaping inmates on orders from the commandant of the camp, fits within the statutory language about persons who assisted in the persecution of civilians. Other cases may present more difficult *line-drawing problems*, but we need decide only this case.[2]

The second example addresses the issue of assisting in forced abortion as persecution:

> In the *Xie* case, it was decided that a person who was a driver between 1990 and 1992 for the Department of Health in Fujian Province in China, in which capacity he would transport pregnant women to hospitals where forced abortions were performed as part of the Chinese one-child policy, was *assisting in persecution*.... The same was said for a person who had been a guard at a birth control facility on an ongoing basis; a person who had guarded ten women scheduled for abortions over a period of three months; [and] a person who for over twenty years reported the identities of women with unauthorized pregnancies ....
>
> *However, another person, Weng, was found not to be involved in persecutorial acts* by the Federal Court of Appeals. She was a nurse's assistant working at a public hospital in China in which forced abortions were performed pursuant to the country's family planning policy. Regarding the question of whether she was a persecutor, the court found that her involvement had not been "active with direct

---

2 449 US 490 (1981) at 384 [emphasis added].

> consequences for the victims," as had been the case in the *Xie* judgment. Her post-surgical care did not contribute to or facilitate the victim's forced abortions in any direct or active way. While she did guard patients once who were awaiting forced abortions, *her conduct, taken as a whole, did not support a finding that the line had been crossed.* It was only one time, she was unarmed, she only guarded the patients for ten minutes, and she helped one person escape, for which she later lost her job. (p. 389–90) [Emphasis added; footnotes omitted.]

The third example deals with the threshold of cruel, inhuman, and degrading treatment or punishment:

> *In the refugee and immigration context, the court has held that expulsion can involve a degree of suffering but must reach a certain level of severity before it becomes objectionable....* Article 3 has been applied by the court where it found that ... a person would be returned to a country with an officially recognized regime of slavery; where a person could be stoned to death for committing adultery; where a person would publicly receive 100 lashes for sexual activity; where a person would be subjected to kicking, intimidation, harassment, and forced labour; where a person would be subject to female genital mutilation; or where the person might be exposed to detention incommunicado, prolonged exposure to the sun at high temperatures, and tying of hands and feet in painful positions....
>
> *The degree of suffering does not reach the objectionable level* where a child is deported as long as they are accompanied by an adult and appropriate arrangements are made upon arrival in the country of destination. The same was said in cases where a person's state of health or life expectancy might diminish sharply due to illness and a lack of resources in the receiving country, such as not being able to receive the same health treatment for HIV/AIDS. (p. 661–62) [Emphasis added; footnotes omitted.]

The quality and quantity of the legal research accomplished by the author are exceptional (over 2,000 judicial decisions referenced), and I cannot see how an experienced lawyer practising in this legal field could write a quality factum or memorandum of law without consulting this book. Lawyers rely on precedents to support a legal argument, and this book is a treasure trove of legal authorities and precedents, including decisions from the Nuremberg trials, which followed the

Second World War, up to and including recent COVID-19 pronouncements, such as the following: "The Special Rapporteur [on Torture and Other Cruel, Inhuman Treatment] has reported that COVID-19 has caused a deterioration in conditions of detention, including increased use of lethal force and unrestrained police brutality" (p. 676 [footnote omitted]). Here is an excellent example of meticulous research and practical authorities—for lawyers pleading 1F(b) "serious crime" cases—where every crime listed below has been footnoted with a relevant judicial precedent:

> The following have all been held to be serious crimes for the purposes of Article 1F(b) in Canada: murder, manslaughter, drug trafficking, human trafficking and pimping, aggravated assault, assault, assault with a deadly weapon, sexual assault, spousal assault, drunk driving causing bodily harm, bombing, *coup d'états* (including activities such as delivering weapons and seizing radio and TV stations), kidnapping, sabotage, armed robbery, arson, terrorist acts, serious crimes as an organized crime gang member, child abduction, and producing child pornography. In addition, economic crimes such as embezzlement, smuggling, tax evasion, money laundering, customs smuggling, illegal arms exports, weapons offences, taking bribes, offering bribes, usury, fraud, burglary, evading arrest, use of a forged document, forgery of a passport, forgery and identity fraud, and theft involving large amounts of money have all been found to be excludable crimes. (p. 477–79) [Footnotes omitted.]

One of the Herculean tasks accomplished in this book, which the author has made look easy, is the seamless analysis of jurisprudence emanating from international tribunals and the tribunals and courts in nine different countries. This comparative analysis is completed on eight different legal issues on difficult subject matters, such as the scope of the term "crimes against humanity." This should prove to be very practical as a reference to lawyers when pleading cases given that many of the legal issues and legal reasoning transcend national borders. Here's just one example of excellent research in the comparative analysis of jurisprudence:

> *The reasoning used to conclude that a crime should be considered serious has been different in the nine countries.* Some countries have stated in the past (*Australia and France*) or still do (*Germany*) that

Article 1F(b) applies to capital or grave crimes without utilizing a more detailed methodology, while other countries examined the maximum penalty that could be imposed for a particular crime in the criminal legislation (*older Canadian and French cases*) or what penalty would likely be imposed if a person was tried criminally (in *New Zealand*, where a tribunal concluded that this sentence should be, at a minimum, between eighteen months and two years, and in the *United Kingdom*, where a two-year minimum is set out in the legislation). A third approach has been a more contextual method, whereby a number of factors are used to determine whether a crime is serious .... *This was originally used in Canada and the United States but now has found more general acceptance.* (p. 530) [Emphasis added; footnotes omitted.]

Although this book is remarkably well researched and is, as alluded to above, a bonanza for lawyers seeking judicial precedents, the book is much more than a survey of relevant jurisprudence. Several chapters contain insightful commentary and analysis under the heading "Observations." These observations will likely have an important impact in moving the legal or policy needle in future court cases or when the international community contemplates drafting future conventions. The author's commentaries—"where the jurisprudence is lacking," "off the mark," and "puzzling"—provide red flags to astute litigation counsel that a particular area of law is far from settled and is ripe for judicial (re)consideration. Here is just one example:

The decision contains some puzzling aspects. One of them is the rejection of the Court of Appeal decision for confining "Article 1F liability essentially to just the same sort of joint criminal enterprises as would result in convictions under domestic law" since the analysis of the Court of Appeal took place completely within the realm of international law, with only one reference to British law, and not in the paragraph quoted by the Supreme Court as being problematic....

However, it also says that the *Krajišnik* Appeals Chamber judgment is not relevant as it pertains to high-level operatives. *This comment is odd as* Krajišnik *dealt specifically with [joint criminal enterprise (JCE) I] rather than the case cited by the court,* Brđanin. *Also odd is the fact that when referring to the [International Criminal Tribunal for the former Yugoslavia] caselaw to set out the requirements for JCE,*

> *the court mentions only in passing the very aspect that makes JCE unique: the common design ....*
>
> While the analysis is couched in JCE language, the test for complicity suggested by the court for not including as part of this test the common design aspect closely resembles the notion of aiding and abetting in international criminal law, especially since the court equates "significant" with "substantial." *This means that either the court has provided an incomplete definition of JCE or has collapsed all aspects of complicity known in international criminal law into only one type, aiding and abetting, a comment that was also made when discussing the* Ezokola *judgment by the Supreme Court of Canada.* (p. 382–83) [Emphasis added.]

It is not often that a legal textbook can hit the mark with a wide audience, but this book does just that. Although the subject matter is complex and multifaceted, it is written clearly, and the content is well organized. Those with limited knowledge of or experience in this field should find the book very readable and informative, while experienced lawyers, academics, and judges should find it comprehensive, insightful, and replete with practical legal precedents.

The English poet John Milton is credited with saying, "Where there is much desire to learn, there of necessity will be much arguing, much writing, many opinions; for opinion in good men is but knowledge in the making." Having read this book, I have no doubt that the author has made a significant contribution to the making of knowledge in the field of international refugee law and international criminal law. Consequently, the author's work should also have a positive impact on the quality of justice rendered in future cases before tribunals and courts at both the domestic and the international level.

Luke Morton
BARRISTER AND SOLICITOR (ONTARIO)
(RETIRED) SENIOR COUNSEL AND MANAGER,
REFUGEE LAW GROUP, DEPARTMENT OF JUSTICE, CANADA
OTTAWA, FEBRUARY 2023

Preface

TO THE SECOND BOOK

This new book is, in effect, the second edition of the original 2012 edition even though it has a new title, a new structure, and a new publisher. These changes reflect the more fundamental shifts in immigration and refugee trends in the last ten years and their effects on the approaches taken at the international and national levels with respect to criminality in refugee law—specifically, exclusion and *refoulement*.

The global asylum situation is grim. According to the United Nations High Commissioner for Refugees (UNHCR), as of mid-2022, global forced displacement had reached 103 million people, of which 53.2 million were internally displaced people, 32.5 million were refugees, 4.9 million were asylum seekers, and another 5.3 million were individuals in need of international protection.[1] While persons have fled from intolerable situations all over the world, the situation in Syria in the last ten years and the situation in Ukraine in 2022 stand out not only for the vast numbers of persons affected by the turmoil in those countries but also for the fact that in both instances the connection between war and refugees has once again been made abundantly clear.

While countries since 2012 initially welcomed refugees, public and government attitudes have been hardening over the last decade. The issue of migration has been especially at the forefront of public discussion in North America and Europe, with its subsequent effect on political debate, resulting in turn in the election of populist governments

1 See UNHCR, "Refugee Data Finder" (27 October 2022), online: www.unhcr.org/refugee-statistics.

and more restrictive policies on migration and asylum. This heightened level of attention on migration issues resulted in three profound changes in policy. First, at the international level, both the United Nations and the European Union established international agreements to ensure better cooperation between countries in the area of migration. In December 2018, the United Nations General Assembly concluded the Global Compact on Refugees, which is "a framework for more predictable and equitable responsibility-sharing, recognizing that a sustainable solution to refugee situations cannot be achieved without international cooperation."[2] In September 2020, the European Union announced the New Pact on Migration and Asylum, which "sets out improved and faster procedures throughout the asylum and migration system and sets in balance the principles of fair sharing of responsibility and solidarity. This is crucial for rebuilding trust between Member States and confidence in the capacity of the European Union to manage migration."[3] The other two developments are less laudatory. The desperation of people fleeing their countries of origin resulted in a rapid increase in the phenomenon of people smuggling, especially in Central America, with people trying to access the United States, and in the Mediterranean, with routes from Africa and the Middle East to Europe. While governments have been trying to address people smuggling by taken interdiction action against people smugglers and assisting the victims of such operations, governments have also been trying to prevent people from attempting to come to their countries by using quasi-criminal approaches as a deterrent. This policy has been generally referred to as "crimmigration" and has been described as "a legal process that involved the integration of criminal law processes, categories, and techniques into immigration control, and the use of criminal law enforcement strategies, or administrative sanctions that mimic ones, on migrants for immigration violations."[4] It has also been said, "Once a mere administrative matter, irregular migration and presence are now often made a crime in domestic laws, often with

2 See UNHCR, "The Global Compact on Refugees" (December 2018), online: www.unhcr.org/the-global-compact-on-refugees.html.

3 See EU, Migration and Home Affairs, "New Pact on Migration and Asylum, Setting Out a Fairer, More European Approach" (23 September 2020), online: https://home-affairs.ec.europa.eu/news/new-pact-migration-and-asylum-setting-out-fairer-more-european-approach-2020-09-23_en.

4 Idil Atak & James C. Simeon, "Introduction" in Idil Atak & James C. Simeon, eds, *The Criminalization of Migration: Context and Consequences* (Montreal & Kingston: McGill-Queen's University Press, 2018) at 5.

additional criminal offences such as for failure to cooperate in migration and asylum proceedings, or failure to have or produce identity documentation. In addition to criminalization, States also have meted out increasingly harsh treatment to those who breach their migration controls, irrespective of whether they are refugees or not."[5]

This development of using quasi-criminal means to curb the immigration and refugee flows by national government is one of the reasons why the title of the book has changed. The reference to criminal refugees in the first book would have given the false impression that these new forms of criminalization were part of the narrative of the text, which is most assuredly not the case. This new book continues to only examine forms of criminality, which are in set out in the Refugee Convention and which have been considered criminal in that international treaty since 1951.

Even without accounting for the concept of crimmigration, the developments of criminality in refugee law in the narrow sense have undergone some profound changes in the last decade. On the jurisprudential front, a number of issues in exclusion and *refoulement* have become more settled, especially as a result of decisions by the highest courts in the common law countries of Australia, Canada, New Zealand, and the United Kingdom (which also frequently relied on each others' judgments) and by the Court of Justice of the European Union. This more consistent approach in the jurisprudence has been followed by the courts at the lower levels in nine countries, which have been examined in detail in this book. In order to be as comprehensive as possible and arrive at conclusions with the most empirical evidence, the book makes reference to over 2,000 cases in twenty-one countries and nineteen international and regional judicial institutions in the area of public international law, refugee law, international criminal law, and international human rights law and is current as of 1 July 2022.

Not only have exclusion and *refoulement* become more prominent in the international and national jurisprudence, but academia has taken

---

5 Cathryn Costello & Yulia Ioffe, "Non-penalization and Non-criminalization" in Cathryn Costello, Michelle Foster & Jane McAdam, eds, *The Oxford Handbook of International Refugee Law* (Oxford: Oxford University Press, 2021) at 917. For other recent discussions, see Peter Billings, ed, *Crimmigration in Australia: Law, Politics and Society* (Singapore: Springer, 2019); Valsamis Mitsilegas, Stefano Zirulia & Gian Luigi Gatta, eds, *Controlling Immigration Through Criminal Law: European and Comparative Perspectives on "Crimmigration"* (London: Hart, 2021); and César Cuauhtémoc & García Hernández, "Deconstructing Crimmigration" (2018) 52 *UC Davis Law Review* 197–253.

notice as well. While the two notions of exclusion and *refoulement* were already mentioned in publications before 2012, the number of books, book chapters, and articles has rapidly increased, which have also addressed a broader range of issues of concern, especially related to exclusion. Recent updated versions of some of the best-known monographs in refugee law by Guy Goodwin-Gill and Jane McAdam,[6] James Hathaway,[7] and Andreas Zimmerman[8] have expanded and updated the examination of exclusion and *refoulement*, as have two newly published handbooks on refugee law.[9] As well, there has been important original research in the area of exclusion with four PhD dissertations on the topic.[10] Along the same lines, a major research project, entitled "Building a Global Criminal Justice System at the Domestic Level," which will be carried out by professor Elies van Sliedregt of the University of Tilburg in the Netherlands, will look at the relationship between exclusion and the prosecution for international crimes at the national level; this project, which will take five years, has started in early 2023. In addition, the European Asylum Support Organization (EASO) issued a number of guidelines for national refugee decision makers in the area of exclusion and *refoulement*,[11] while exclusion has also been a topic during international conferences and meetings, such as in the European Network for Investigation and Prosecution of Genocide (Genocide Network),

---

6 Guy S. Goodwin-Gill & Jane McAdam, *The Refugee in International Law*, 4th ed (Oxford: Oxford University Press, 2021).

7 James Hathaway, *The Rights of Refugees Under International Law*, 2d ed (Cambridge: Cambridge University Press, 2021).

8 Andreas Zimmerman, ed, *The 1951 Convention Relating to the Status of Refugees and its 1967 Protocol: A Commentary* (Oxford: Oxford University Press, 2011); a second edition is expected in late 2023, edited by Andreas Zimmerman and Terje Einarsen.

9 Satvinder Singh Juss, ed, *Research Handbook on International Refugee Law* (Cheltenham, UK & Northampton, US: Elgar, 2019), and Costello, Foster & McAdam, above note 5.

10 Three of the dissertations were subsequently published as books, namely, Sarah Singer, *Terrorism and Exclusion from Refugee Status in the UK: Asylum Seekers Suspected of Serious Criminality* (Leiden & Boston: Brill Nijhoff, 2015); Zarif Yakut-Bahtiyar, *Exclusion Clauses of the Refugee Convention in Relation to National Immigration Legislations, European Policy and Human Rights Instruments: Article 1F Versus the Non-refoulement Principle* (Nijmegen: Wolf Legal Publishers, 2016); and Yao Li, *Exclusion from Protection as a Refugee: An Approach to a Harmonizing Interpretation in International Law* (Leiden & Boston: Brill Nijhoff, 2017). The fourth dissertation, Maarten Bolhuis, *Narrowing the Impunity Gap?*, was successfully defended in 2018 and included a number of chapters, which had been published in various academic journals.

11 EASO changed its name and mandate in January 2022 and is now known as the European Union Agency for Asylum (EUAA).

which is supported by the European Union Agency for Criminal Justice Cooperation (Eurojust) as well as the International Association of Refugee and Migration Judges (IARMJ) and the International Association for the Study of Forced Migration (IASFM).

While most of this book addresses criminality as part of exclusion and *refoulement*, a small but important portion examines the dilemma of countries that have found persons involved in such activities undesirable but are unable to remove them to their country of origin because of human rights concerns. A number of international and regional human rights bodies have provided detailed and extensive jurisprudence as to the meaning of the most egregious violations of these human rights: torture and inhuman and degrading treatment or punishment. I would like to thank Supanki Kalanadan for doing the research into the massive caselaw emanating from these institutions since 2012 and for including the most relevant judicial statements into the updated text of the book; it was a very complex undertaking that she carried out with a great deal of poise and insight.

Lastly, I would like to thank Irwin Law for the excellent support when writing this book. Jeff Miller, the publisher, saw the potential for a second edition of the book and provided great encouragement from the beginning of the project. Lesley Steeve, the editor-in-chief who managed the practical aspects of taking the book from its initial stages to the final text, provided the type of cooperation of which an author can only dream by providing excellent direction and advice while still allowing sufficient independence to ensure that the views of the author are reflected in the book. Marg Anne Morrison, who edited the book, was wonderful to work with, and the book reads much better as a result of her detailed and very helpful suggestions. I am much indebted to all of them.

Ottawa, November 2022

Preface
TO THE FIRST BOOK

The book you see before you has been in the making for over twenty years. The issue of criminality, especially in the international sphere, has been of great interest to me for a long time, both professionally as well as academically. As a government lawyer for the Department of Justice of Canada, I have been fortunate to have had a front seat during major developments in the areas of international criminal law as well as exclusion law. I have also been fortunate in the opportunity to move back and forth between these two disciplines: as counsel for the Crimes against Humanity and War Crimes Section when it was established in 1987; as in-house counsel for the new War Crimes Section of the Department of Citizenship and Immigration in 1998; and then, finally, returning as senior counsel to the Department of Justice in 2003. In that last capacity, the two strands of interest were brought together under the title "manager of the law," meaning that I could provide legal advice in both international criminal law and exclusion law.

While international criminal law has been developed mostly by international institutions in the last two decades, this is changing in that national jurisdictions are now also starting to apply international law concepts to domestic processes. This national approach with respect to international crimes is even more apparent in exclusion law as national tribunals and courts relied for the most part on their innate sense of justice and logic to give meaning to terms used in the 1951 Refugee Convention, where the notion of exclusion is embedded. These national developments are gaining importance as the interplay between international manifestations of both international criminal law and exclusion law and national jurisprudence in these areas is growing, and a better understanding is required to ensure that a divergence will not occur either between the international and the national plane or even between national jurisdictions.

On a personal level, these national trends became of interest to me while working with a number of very talented investigators and prosecutors in North America and Europe and seeing how they use their national criminal statutes to give both a unique and universal meaning to the various international crimes. Similarly, as a result of having the privilege of training various specialized units dealing with exclusion in Australia, New Zealand, the Netherlands, and the United Kingdom, I became intrigued by the immigration and refugee legislation in those countries and its application to persons involved in serious crimes. Both of these aspects of national law resulted in comparative research into the work done in a number of these countries, which not only became publications in their own right but also eventually provided a solid basis to begin the work on this book.

I hope this book provides some assistance in this goal of accomplishing a consistent approach to the various concepts known in international criminal law and exclusion law, while the issue of *refoulement* for persons with a criminal background is given attention as well, with the same purpose in mind. The book is primarily written for the practitioner of criminal and refugee law, although in the conclusions of the chapters the various concepts are given a more academic treatment in order to point to some overarching trends and issues of concern. The ultimate aspiration of this book is that it be used in the same manner as practitioners, academics, and the judiciary rely on books written by two shining examples of erudition and professionalism, William Schabas and Guy Goodwin-Gill: as the initial source for any question related to the subject matters in which they excel, international criminal law and refugee law, respectively. I was very honoured to have them as the examiners for my PhD thesis, which was completed in 2011 in Galway, Ireland, and which constitutes three-quarters of this book.

As indicated above, I have been a government lawyer for almost my entire professional career, although I combined this for a number of years with a part-time teaching function at the law school of the University of Ottawa. Although this book does not represent the views of the Department of Justice or the Government of Canada, this could raise a concern of possible bias, and it would be useful to make it clear from the beginning that I am indeed biased. My motivation in writing and practising law stems from an abiding concern and sympathy for victims of international crimes. Interviewing survivors of Auschwitz as a young lawyer in preparation for a criminal case, then later meeting with victims of very serious crimes from countries such as Rwanda and Ethiopia, does not leave one unaffected and generates a strong desire to make things right for such persons. Or at least it should. It did for me, and given my legal background and employment with the government, it was only logical that I turn my attention to the perpetrators of such crimes, to try to make a small contribution to render things right. If that constitutes bias, I am guilty. However, bias does not equate to uncritical acceptance of every law or regulation passed by the countries under examination in this book, and it does not mean that court or tribunal decisions should not be scrutinized. This book has not shied away from criticism or scrutiny but within certain parameters, from a legal and policy perspective rather than from a political or sociological angle, and with its purpose to tease out inconsistencies in the practice of countries and judiciaries with a view to offering solutions to make the entire body of international criminal law, exclusion, and *refoulement* more consistent.

While the writing of a book is an insular endeavour, the process of getting to the stage whereby pen is put to paper (symbolically, of course, in this electronic era) and eventually having something people might want to read certainly is not. From the inspiration to undertake such a large project, to assistance in discovering new and exciting areas of law, to ensuring that the thesis was more than disconnected thoughts and random words, a large and dedicated team is needed. I would now like to introduce this team.

Inspiring me to even contemplate writing hundreds of pages about an esoteric area of law, knowing that it would most likely be an all-consuming effort and then continuing not only to be supportive but also proud, is my wife, Ruth Walden. As busy as she was with her own legal cases, she always had time to be there during the highs and lows of the entire project. I should also mention my daughter, Rhiannon Vader-Rikhof, whose decision to go to law school galvanized me to provide an example of what I hope is academic erudition and integrity. The fact that she became a barrister in the same year as her father obtained a PhD fills me with enormous pride.

The depth to which I was able to conduct research jurisprudence of several foreign countries would have been very difficult without the help of a large number of dedicated professionals. Without being exhaustive, I would like to mention Terje Einarsen in Norway, Kate Jastram in the United States, Gareth Ledbetter in the United Kingdom, Robert Kirkness in New Zealand, David Kosař in the Czech Republic, and Lennaert Post, Marloes de Graaff, Niels Kramer, Geerten van Zadelhoff, and Peter ten Hove in the Netherlands. I owe a debt of gratitude especially to Lennaert Post as he not only provided me with the most current jurisprudence in Dutch refugee law, but he also provided me with valuable feedback on the portions of the thesis that describe the exclusion experience in the Netherlands.

In Canada, the librarian at the Immigration and Refugee Board, Geralyne Dionne, and the staff at the Reference and Research Services Team of the Department of Justice, Sylvie Nugent, Devon Bartley, Martin McGreal, Tanya Durr, and Micheline Levesque, were able to find me the most obscure books and articles and always within days of making my requests. They still amaze me. Also in Canada, Terry Beitner and Daniel Therrien at the Department of Justice not only supported my effort to do a PhD, but they made it possible to take a six-month education leave from my office.

To stay true to form, I will keep my greatest praise for last, my thesis supervisor, Shane Darcy of the Irish Human Rights Centre. His efforts to get the thesis and a large part of this book from a general research project to a product of academic quality were remarkable. His detailed comments and his encouraging feedback, always within short time frames, made it a great pleasure to work with him. The centre is lucky to have such a dedicated, responsible, and learned academic. I certainly was.

As a concluding comment, it is difficult to complete a large project such as this without the ability to pace oneself by taking off short periods of time to take stock of the work produced and to contemplate conceptual issues in relative peace. While I thought that I had this ability, our cats, Peabody and Emerson, were of the view, forcibly expressed, that some adjustments in this area were highly desirable; invariably, they proved to be correct in their assessment when a pause in writing was required even before I realized this.

Ottawa, January 2012

CHAPTER ONE

Introduction

Crime does not pay. This is a basic tenet of both moral and legal value systems. While this adage is often substituted into the normative alternative of "crime should not pay," and while there might be historical, regional, and cultural differences in the meanings of the terms "crime" and "pay," it is still a fundamental concept that can be witnessed primarily in criminal law and more recently in international criminal law.[1] This book will examine whether criminal conduct plays a role in refugee law.

Asylum as a concept has been known since ancient times, but persons with a criminal background were always treated with suspicion and, depending on the time and place, would either not be granted asylum or only in a limited form. When amorphous notions related to asylum began to be crystallized in international treaties during the twentieth century, again, criminality, while only pertaining to a very small number of asylum seekers, caused sufficient concern to the drafters of the various instruments to warrant mention in several provisions in those agreements. At times, but not always, such provisions had some resemblance to concepts of criminality known in other areas of law, specifically, domestic criminal law and, after the Second World War, the nascent field of international criminal law. When states ratified the international treaties or when international institutions applied these

1 See, e.g., Yao Li, *Exclusion from Protection as Refugee: An Approach to a Harmonizing Interpretation in International Law* (Leiden & Boston: Brill Nijhoff, 2017) at 71–78; Jennifer Bond, "Excluding Justice: The Dangerous Intersection Between Refugee Claims, Criminal Law, and 'Guilty' Asylum Seekers" (2012) 24:1 *International Journal of Refugee Law* 37 at 47.

instruments, they had to interpret these general provisions addressing criminal behaviour while keeping in mind the purpose of asylum and ensuring that these interpretations kept pace with both international and domestic developments in regulating criminal conduct.

This book will assess how much refugee law has been in step with the international and domestic regulation of criminal conduct. At the international level, crimes such as genocide, crimes against humanity, war crimes, terrorism, and organized crime have become the subjects of international treaties and jurisprudence, while these types of criminality as well as other areas of concern have been increasingly incorporated into domestic criminal legislation. Since refugee law is used in the same countries that are at the forefront of regulating these new types of criminal behaviour, decision makers had to consider these parallel developments. This book will determine how successful this attempt has been by comparing the legislation and jurisprudence in several countries and contrasting those with the regulation of similar criminal conduct outside refugee law. As well, the approach taken with respect to refugees with a criminal background in these countries will be subjected to a comparative analysis to reveal possible discrepancies and offer possible solutions.

The issue of criminality of asylum seekers cannot be examined in isolation. The provisions in refugee instruments dealing with this aspect form only a small portion of the entire text of such treaties, while similarly only a small portion of the practice of refugee decision makers deals with criminal questions. In order to place the notion of criminality in a larger context, this introduction will set out the larger picture of protection for refugee claimants. As well, since refugee law is a specialized area within the framework of human rights law, this part of the book will begin with a general background of that area of law.

A. HUMAN RIGHTS LAW

As refugee law can be considered a subset of human rights law,[2] and since general human rights law has had an important impact on issues

2 One author views the relationship between refugee law and human rights law as one of *lex specialis;* see Jane McAdam, *Complementary Protection in International Refugee Law* (Oxford: Oxford University Press, 2007) at 17, 29–31, and 211–13, and Jane McAdam, "The Refugee Convention as a Rights Blueprint" in Jane McAdam, ed, *Forced Migration, Human Rights and Security* (Oxford & Portland, OR: Hart, 2008) 263–82 at 280; see, also, Li, above note 1 at 83–85; Spyridoula Katsoni, "Impacts of the Interpretative Interaction Between International Human

associated with refugees, notably the prohibition against *refoulement*—that is, the removal of a person to a country where this person might be subjected to persecution, torture, or inhuman or cruel punishment or treatment—it is useful to set out some general principles of human rights law. While historically the concept of human rights had emerged in a fragmentary manner at the domestic level in primarily Western European and North American states, the horrors of the Second World War provided an impetus for the international community to begin devising an international comprehensive regime for the protection of basic human rights.[3] The first steps in this direction were the 1945 Charter of the United Nations and the 1948 Universal Declaration of Human Rights. The former mentions "international co-operation ... in promoting and encouraging respect for human rights and for fundamental freedoms for all without distinction as to race, sex, language or religion"[4] as one of the main purposes of the United Nations, while the declaration, albeit in a non-binding format,[5] provides more detail in thirty articles as to what

---

Rights Law and the Refugee Convention" (2021) 11:1 *Cambridge International Law Journal* 96–120, and Vincent Chetail, "Moving Towards an Integrated Approach of Refugee Law and Human Rights Law" in Cathryn Costello, Michelle Foster & Jane McAdam, eds, *The Oxford Handbook of International Refugee Law* (Oxford: Oxford University Press, 2021) at 202–20. See, also, in general, regarding the notion of *lex specialis* and its relationship to general international law, UN Doc A/CN.4/L.682, International Law Commission, Fifty-eighth Session, 1 May–9 June and 3 July–11 August 2006, *Fragmentation of International Law: Difficulties Arising from the Diversification and Expansion of International Law*, Report of the Study Group of the International Law Commission, finalized by Martti Koskenniemi, 13 April 2006, which refers specifically to refugee law in this context at paras 8, 22, and 254. This juxtaposition between general international human rights law and a specialized area of human rights has also been recognized judicially in the field of international humanitarian law in the cases of *Legal Consequences of the Construction of a Wall in the Occupied Palestinian Territory*, Advisory Opinion, [2004], ICJ Rep 136 at para 106, and *Armed Activities on the Territory of the Congo (Democratic Republic of the Congo v Uganda)*, [2005] ICJ Rep at para 216; see, also, Walter Kälin & Jörg Künzli, *The Law of International Human Rights Protection*, 2d ed (Oxford: Oxford University Press, 2019) at 9, 30, and 146.

3 Kälin & Künzli, *ibid* at 3–12, for a historical overview of human rights until 1945 and at 18–27 for the various philosophical theories underlying the notion of human rights.

4 Charter of the United Nations, 26 June 1945, Can TS 1945 No 7, art 1.

5 The Commission on Human Rights, which was established on 16 February 1946 by the United Nations Economic and Social Council during its first session, was given the mandate for the preparation of a preliminary draft of an International Bill of Human Rights. This commission considered the preliminary draft of its drafting committee during its second session in Geneva from 2 to 17 December 1947. During this session, the commission decided on a terminology to be used in referring to the three documents that together were to constitute the *International Bill of Human Rights*: a Declaration of Human Rights, a Covenant on Human Rights, and Measures of Implementation. The commission was of the opinion that the

these fundamental human rights entail. Following these initial steps to protect human rights in the sense of creating inalienable individual rights against the power of the state and the collective rights within that state,[6] two universal (as in with global reach) and general (as in covering a bundle of rights) human rights treaties were created on 16 December 1966: the International Covenant on Civil and Political Rights[7] and the International Covenant on Economic, Social and Cultural Rights.[8]

In addition to these universal, general, and binding international instruments, some of the core rights contained in these agreements have been fleshed out and developed by the United Nations either by creating treaties to protect specific human rights or to protect specific categories of persons. Within the first category, the International Convention on the Elimination of All Forms of Racial Discrimination of 21 December 1965 should be mentioned, as well as the Convention Against Torture and Other Cruel, Inhuman or Degrading Treatment or Punishment (CAT) of 10 December 1984 and the Convention for the Protection of All Persons from Enforced Disappearance of 20 December 2006.[9]

---

declaration would be a simple statement defining human rights and fundamental freedoms and its force, upon adoption by the General Assembly, would be more of a moral rather than a legal nature; the declaration would establish and indicate goals rather than impose precise obligations upon states. The draft covenant, on the other hand, was visualized as an instrument that would legally bind the states acceding to it. Such states would undertake to make their national laws conform to its standards and would agree to the imposition of sanctions in the case of violation of the rights enumerated therein. The Measures of Implementation only related to the proposed covenant and possible future conventions (see *Yearbook of the United Nations, 1947–48* (Lake Success, NY: UN, 1949) at 572–73, online: www.unmultimedia.org/searchers/yearbook/page.jsp?volume=1947-48&page=1&search-Type=advanced, and United Nations, *Yearbook on Human Rights for 1948* (Lake Success, NY: UN, 1950) at 457, online: https://digitallibrary.un.org/record/860914?ln=en). See, also, James Hathaway, *The Rights of Refugees Under International Law,* 2d ed (Cambridge: Cambridge University Press, 2021) at 45–46.

6 Kälin & Künzli, above note 2 at 29–30, which also contains a brief description of first-generation rights (civil and political rights), second-generation rights (economic, social, and cultural rights), and third-generation rights (solidarity or group rights). See, also, Hathaway, above note 5 at 87–102.

7 This treaty has a Second Optional Protocol to the International Covenant on Civil and Political Rights (ICCPR) aiming at the abolition of the death penalty; see Kälin & Künzli, above note 2 at 38.

8 *Ibid* at 37–38, which also includes a brief description of these treaties.

9 *Ibid* at 38–40; also mentioned in this category is the Convention on the Prevention and Punishment of the Crime of Genocide of 9 December 1948 at 38, which is in keeping with the approach that both international humanitarian law and international criminal law are also manifestations of human rights law (see pages 30–33).

Treaties to protect specific categories of persons include the Convention on the Elimination of All Forms of Discrimination Against Women of 18 December 1979; the Convention on the Rights of the Child of 20 November 1989; the Convention on the Protection of the Rights of All Migrant Workers and Members of Their Families of 18 December 1990; and the Convention on the Rights of Persons with Disabilities of 13 December 2006.[10]

All the above nine treaties are in force and widely accepted given the high number of ratifications.[11] There are ten human rights treaty bodies, which are committees of independent experts that monitor implementation of these international human rights treaties. They are created in accordance with the provisions of the treaty, which they monitor, while in some cases Optional Protocols have also allowed for individual complaints or communications to be lodged with these institutions from individuals in and against their own states if those states have ratified these protocols.[12]

Not only have human rights come within the important purview of global institutions. Most regions of the world have also undertaken steps to address the protection of individuals by introducing general human rights treaties or binding instruments for specific subject matters.

---

10 See the Office of the High Commissioner of Human Rights of the United Nations (OHCHR) under "The Core International Human Rights Instruments and Their Monitoring Bodies," online: www.ohchr.org/EN/ProfessionalInterest/Pages/CoreInstruments.aspx; see, also, Kälin & Künzli, above note 2 at 40–42, which mentions at 42–43 the work of the International Labour Organization with its 189 binding conventions in the field of labour law; see, also, Hathaway, above note 5 at 85–86.

11 See the ratification status and reservations of the United Nations Treaty Collection, "Depositary," "Status of Treaties," Chapter IV, "Human Rights," and Chapter V, "Refugee and Stateless Persons," online: https://treaties.un.org/Pages/ParticipationStatus.aspx?clang=_en.

12 These are the Human Rights Committees (under the ICCPR): the Committee on Economic, Social and Cultural Rights (CESCR); the Committee on the Elimination of Racial Discrimination (CERD); the Committee on the Elimination of Discrimination Against Women (CEDAW); the Committee against Torture; the Subcommittee of Prevention of Torture (SPT); the Committee on the Rights of the Child (CRC); the Committee on Migrant Workers (CMW); the Committee on the Rights of Persons with Disabilities (CRPD); and the Committee on Enforced Disappearances (CED); see the OHCHR under "Human Rights Bodies," online: www.ohchr.org/EN/HRBodies/Pages/HumanRightsBodies.aspx. See, also, Kälin & Künzli, above note 2 at 201–5. There is also a Human Rights Council, which is a monitoring agency without an individual complaints mechanism; see the OHCHR under "Human Rights Bodies," online: www.ohchr.org/EN/HRBodies/Pages/HumanRightsBodies.aspx, and Kälin & Künzli, above note 2 at 235–43.

This has happened in Africa, the Americas, the Middle East, Asia, and especially Europe.

In Africa, the African Charter on Human and Peoples' Rights (Banjul Charter) was adopted on 26 June 1981 by the Organization of African Unity (OAU)[13] and is monitored (while also having jurisdiction to entertain individual complaints) by the African Commission on Human and Peoples' Rights and the African Court on Human and Peoples' Rights. Other human rights instruments in place are the OAU Convention Governing the Specific Aspects of Refugee Problems in Africa of 10 September 1969; the Protocol to the African Charter on Human and Peoples' Rights on the Rights of Women in Africa of 11 July 2003; the African Charter on the Rights and Welfare of the Child of 11 July 1990; and the African Union Convention on the Protection and Assistance of Internally Displaced Persons in Africa (the Kampala Convention) of 22 October 2009.[14]

In the Americas, the most important human rights treaty is the American Convention on Human Rights of 22 November 1969, pursuant to which individual complaints can be made to the Inter-American Commission on Human Rights and the Inter-American Court of Human Rights. There are also six other human rights treaties in this region, two general and four dealing with specific categories of human rights, namely, torture, forced disappearance, violence against women, and discrimination against persons with disabilities.[15] In the Middle East, the Council of the League of Arab States adopted the Arab Charter on Human Rights on 15 September 1994, which is monitored by the Arab Human Rights Committee.[16] In Asia, the Association of Southeast Asian Nations (ASEAN) adopted a charter on 20 November 2007 while establishing a monitoring agency, the ASEAN Intergovernmental Commission on Human Rights, on 23 October 2009.[17]

---

13 Since 9 July 2002, called the African Union or AU.

14 Kälin & Künzli, above note 2 at 43–44 and 206–7; see, also, Hathaway, above note 5 at 68–71; with respect to the last convention, a first in international refugee law, see Moetsi Duchatelier & Catherine Phuong, "The African Contribution to the Protection of Internally Displaced Persons: A Commentary on the 2009 Kampala Convention" in Vincent Chetail & Céline Bauloz, eds, *Research Handbook on International Law and Migration* (Cheltenham, UK & Northampton, US: Elgar, 2014) at 650–67.

15 Kälin & Künzli, above note 2 at 44–45 and 206–7; see, also, Hathaway, above note 5 at 77–81.

16 Kälin & Künzli, above note 2 at 47–48 and 207; see, also, Hathaway, above note 5 at 81–82.

17 Kälin & Künzli, above note 2 at 48–49; see, also, *ibid* at 82–84.

The most important regional human rights treaty in terms of its impact on the practice of states is the European Convention on Human Rights (ECHR), which was adopted by the Council of Europe[18] on 4 November 1950. Under this treaty, the European Court of Human Rights can issue judgments with respect to violations of this treaty. Apart from this overarching treaty, the Council of Europe has been responsible for a large body of human rights protections resulting in the issuance of another twenty-two treaties in this field, of which nine are protocols to the ECHR dealing with procedural matters, while the other thirteen deal with specific human rights issues (such as social rights, torture, minority protection, biomedicine, trafficking in human beings, and migration) or with the protection of specific persons (such as the protection of children in general as well as protection of children against sexual exploitation and the protection of women against violence).[19] As of 1 December 2009, another player in Europe has entered the field of human rights, namely, the Court of Justice of the European Union (CJEU). This court is the final legal arbiter within the European Union[20] and, because of the Treaty of Lisbon, the European Union has acceded to the ECHR with the result that this court can now also adjudicate on issues under the ECHR, albeit only by referral of a national court of final appeal as opposed to an individual complaint.[21]

Treaties do not form the only source of international human rights law according to article 38 of the Statute of the International Court of Justice. Other main sources are international custom, as evidenced by a general practice accepted as law and the general principles of law recognized by civilized nations.[22]

---

18 The Council of Europe was established in 1949 with a view to working toward European integration; it has forty-seven members.

19 Kälin & Künzli, above note 2 at 45–47 and 205–6; see, also, Hathaway, above note 5 at 72–78.

20 The European Union was established in 1993 by the Treaty on European Union (Maastricht Treaty) and has twenty-seven members, all of which are also members of the Council of Europe.

21 See Steve Peers et al, "Institutional Framework" in Steve Peers et al, eds, *EU Immigration and Asylum Law (Text and Commentary)*, 2d revised ed, Volume 3: *EU Asylum Law* (Leiden & Boston: Brill Nijhoff, 2015) 7–25 at 17–18; European Asylum Support Office (EASO), *An Introduction to the Common European Asylum System for Courts and Tribunals: A Judicial Analysis* (August 2016), online: https://op.europa.eu/en/publication-detail/-/publication/9a3edb48-4d06-41dd-a16e-5438b2916e1b/language-en..

22 See Kees Wouters, *International Legal Standards for Protection from* Refoulement (Antwerp-Oxford-Portland: Intersentia, 2009) at 7–13 regarding the interpretation of human rights treaties.

With respect to custom, which applies to countries even if they have not been involved in the development of a particular rule as opposed to treaty law, a number of general observations can be made, beginning with the fact that the two elements of general practice—general and consistent practice of states followed by them from a sense of legal obligation, *opinio juris*[23]—are not as strictly applied as they once were. The element of *opinio juris* is usually described by states as a notion that the practice followed is the result of conforming to a legal obligation and not arising out of motivations of courtesy, convenience, or tradition or, in other words, an assertion by a state that something is required by law.[24]

With respect to the objective element of general practice, it has been recognized that a custom can relate to a practice of a majority of states but also to a limited number of states or to certain areas of importance to states directly concerned in that area. The element of duration does not require a practice from time immemorial in all circumstances. It is clear that the more specialized the custom, the fewer actors on the international scene are required to establish, change, or develop this custom. The types of evidence that are normally used to point to a general practice would also suffice for a special practice, such as the external conduct of states, but also domestic legislation, judicial decisions, diplomatic dispatches, internal government memoranda, and ministerial statements in parliaments and elsewhere.[25]

The same can be said with respect to the necessity of the consistency of acts, which is required to constitute a state practice. It is generally recognized that state practice needs to be repeated before it can be considered of sufficient value to be elevated to customary international law.[26] It has been argued, however, that very few acts or even a single

---

23 See UN Doc A/73/10, *Report of the International Law Commission*, Seventieth Session, Chapter V, "Identification of Customary International Law" (2018) at 119, Conclusion 2, online (pdf): https://legal.un.org/ilc/reports/2018/english/a_73_10_advance.pdf (for more details, see 121–56), which was also noted in the refugee context in *R v Immigration Officer at Prague Airport; ex parte European Roma Rights Centre (European Rome Rights Centre)*, [2004] UKHL 55 at para 23.

24 UN Doc A/73/10, *Report of the International Law Commission*, above note 23 at 120, Conclusion 9; see, also, *R v Immigration Officer at Prague Airport; ex parte European Roma Rights Centre (European Rome Rights Centre)*, [2004] UKHL 55 at para 23. For the notion of *opinio juris* in refugee law, see Ellen F. D'Angelo, "*Non-refoulement*: The Search for a Consistent Interpretation of Article 33" (2009) 42:1 *Vanderbilt Journal of Transnational Law 279* at 288–90.

25 UN Doc A/73/10, *Report of the International Law Commission*, above note 23, conclusions at 119–21.

26 *Ibid* at 8.

act can amount to the establishment of state practice, especially where some states have the capacity to influence a certain area of customary international law or if the evidence of *opinio juris* is considered particularly strong.[27] The latter observation appears to have been confirmed by the International Court of Justice in 1986, where the court found a rule of customary international law, although there was very little, if any, state practice in this area, but found evidence of the rule to refrain from the threat or use of force against the territorial integrity or political independence of any state in statements and documents by international organizations, primarily resolutions of the United Nations' and the Organization of American States' general assemblies.[28]

As a result of this decision, it has been postulated that there is a relationship between the level of *opinio juris* and the amount of state practice required in that in areas where the stakes are high, such as in issues of armed force or human rights, little state practice is required, while this situation is reversed where the issue at hand is of an economic or political nature.[29]

Certain human rights norms have been accepted as customary international law, such as the prohibitions against genocide, torture, slavery, and systematic racial discrimination.[30] In this context, the notion of *ius cogens*, as a customary international norm from which no derogation is permitted and that can only be modified by a subsequent norm of general international law having the same character,[31] should be mentioned. Some of the regular norms of customary international law have also acquired this higher legal status, such as the prohibitions against genocide, slavery, torture, systematic racial discrimination, and

27 *Ibid* at 137–38.

28 *Military and Paramilitary Activities in and against Nicaragua (Nicaragua v United States of America), Merits*, International Court of Justice, 27 June 1986, ICJ Rep (1986) 14 at paras 189–90.

29 Frederic L. Kirgis, "Custom on a Sliding Scale" (1987) 81 *American Journal of International Law* 146 at 147–48; see, also, Theodor Meron, *Human Rights and Humanitarian Norms of Customary International Law* (Oxford: Clarendon Press, 1989) at 42–43 and 111–13; this is also alluded to in UN Doc A/73/10, *Report of the International Law Commission*, above note 23 at 138, para 9. With respect to the relationship between treaties and customary international law in the same area, see UN Doc A/73/10, *Report of the International Law Commission*, above note 23, conclusion at 11; Elihu Lauterpacht & Daniel Bethlehem, "*Non-refoulement* (Article 33 of the 1951 Convention)" in Erika Feller, Volker Türk & Frances Nicholson, eds, *Refugee Protection in International Law: UNHCR's Global Consultations on International Protection* (Cambridge: Cambridge University Press, 2003) at 141–49.

30 Kälin & Künzli, above note 2 at 59–61; see, also, Hathaway, above note 5 at 436.

31 Vienna Convention on the Law of Treaties, art 53.

arbitrary killing.[32] There has been academic debate about whether the prohibition against *refoulement*, which is generally considered a norm of customary international law,[33] has attained the status of *ius cogens*.[34]

---

32 Kälin & Künzli, above note 2 at 61–62; Maarten Den Heijer, "Whose Rights and Which Rights? The Continuing Story of *Non-refoulement* under the European Convention on Human Rights" (2008) 10:3 *European Journal of Migration and Law* 277 at 299; Li, above note 1 at 43–48; see, also, UN Doc A/CN/.4/L.747, International Law Commission, Seventy-third Session, Geneva, 18 April–3 June and 4 July–5 August 2022, Fifth Report on Peremptory Norms of General International Law *(jus cogens)* by Dire Tladi, Special Rapporteur, 24 January 2022, at 66–69 and 82–83, the latter of which refers only to the prohibitions of aggression, genocide, crimes against humanity, the basic rules of international humanitarian law, racial discrimination and apartheid, slavery, and torture as well as the rights of self-determination; *A & Ors v Secretary of State for the Home Department*, [2005] UKHL 71 at para 33; C and Director of Immigration, HCAL 132/2006, 18 February 2008 (The High Court of the Hong Kong Special Administrative Region, Court of First Instance), at paras 126–29; with a commentary on the latter case, see Kelley Loper, "Human Rights, *Non-refoulement* and the Protection of Refugees in Hong Kong" (2010) 22:3 *International Journal of Refugee Law* 404 at 416–25. For the proposition that torture has reached this status, see two judgments by the Inter-American Court of Human Rights, namely, the Case of *Miguel Castro-Castro Prison v Peru*, Judgment 25 November 2006, Series C No 160 at para 271, and the Case of *Bayarri v Argentina*, Judgment 30 October 2008, Series C No 187 at para 81; see, also, in the United States, *Cornejo-Barreto v Seifert*, 218 F 3d 1004 (9th Cir 2000).

33 Guy S. Goodwin-Gill & Jane McAdam, *The Refugee in International Law*, 4th ed (Oxford: Oxford University Press, 2021) at 300–6; Lauterpacht & Bethlehem, above note 29 at 150–58; Hathaway, above note 5 at 441–59 (casting some doubt on whether the requirement of *opinio juris* and state practice has been fulfilled); James Mansfield, "Extraterritorial Application and Customary Norm Assessment of *Non-refoulement*: The Legality of a *Refoulement*: The Legality of Australia's 'Turn-Back' Policy" (2015) 17 *The University of Notre Dame Australia Law Review* 18 at 36–52; Hélène Lambert, "Customary Refugee Law" in Costello, Foster & McAdam, above note 2 at 243–47; UNHCR, *Note on International Protection* (A/AC.96/951) (13 September 2001) at 5, para 16, online (pdf): www.unhcr.org/excom/excomrep/3bb1c6cc4/note-international-protection.html; UNHCR, *Advisory Opinion on the Extraterritorial Application of Non-refoulement Obligations Under the 1951 Convention relating to the Status of Refugees and its 1967 Protocol* (26 January 2007) at para 15, online (pdf): www.unhcr.org/4d9486929.pdf; UNHCR, *Guidance Note on Extradition and International Refugee Protection* (April 2008) at para 8, online (pdf): www.refworld.org/docid/481ec7d92.html; C and Director of Immigration, above note 32 at paras 113–16; European Court of Human Rights, *MSS v Belgium and Greece*, 21 January 2011, Application No 30696/09 at para 56.

34 In favour of *ius cogens*, see Jean Allain, "The *Jus Cogens* Nature of *Non-Refoulement*" (2001) 13:4 *International Journal of Refugee Law* 533–58, as well as Alice Farmer, "*Non-refoulement* and *Jus Cogens*: Limiting Anti-terror Measures That Threaten Refugee Protection" (2008) 23 *Georgetown Immigration Law Journal* 2–43; Chantal Marie-Jeanne Bostock, "The International Legal Obligations Owed to the Asylum Seekers on the *MV Tampa*" (2002) 14:2/3 *International Journal of Refugee Law 279* at 289, n79; and Sibylle Kapferer, *The Interface Between Extradition and Asylum* (November 2003) UNHCR Legal and Protection Policy Research Series PPLA/2003/05 at para 221, online (pdf): www.unhcr.org/3fe84fad4.pdf; against this proposition, see Aoiffe Duffy, "Expulsion to Face Torture? *Non-refoulement* in International

Judicial consideration on this point has been negative in that a Hong Kong decision, after canvassing literature and international practice in detail, indicated that

> [w]hile, on balance, I am drawn to the conclusion that the rule against *refoulement* is a rule of customary international law, I think it goes too far to hold—at this time—that the rule has acquired the status of a peremptory norm. Put another way, the ideal does not accord with present reality and, if the ideal is to prevail, it may bring the norm itself into disrepute.[35]

Regarding the third source of international law, general principles, in human rights law there have been no norms identified under this source, which, unlike customary international law, requires an examination in a comparative manner of the consistency of domestic laws across a significant range of countries.[36]

B. REFUGEE LAW AND CONCEPTS

The right to asylum was already contained in the Universal Declaration of Human Rights.[37] However, the most well-known definition of a refugee can be found in the 1951 Convention Related to the Status of

---

Law" (2008) 20:3 *International Journal of Refugee Law* 373 at 383–90; William A. Schabas, "Non-refoulement" in *Expert Workshop on Human Rights and International Co-operation in Counter-Terrorism: Final Report* (Triesenberg, Liechtenstein: OSCE Office for Democratic Institutions and Human Rights and Office of the United Nations High Commissioner for Human Rights, February 2007) at 27, n22; Goodwin-Gill & McAdam, above note 33 at 304–6; Lauterpacht & Bethlehem, above note 29 at 150–51; for an overview, see James C. Simeon, "What Is the Future of *Non-refoulement* in International Refugee Law?" in Satvinder Singh Juss, ed, *Research Handbook on International Refugee Law* (Cheltenham, UK & Northampton, US: Elgar, 2019) at 189–93, and Hélène Lambert, "Customary Refugee Law" in Costello, Foster & McAdam, above note 2 at 247.

35 C and Director of Immigration, above note 32 at para 135. This conclusion had already been reached earlier by the Supreme Court of New Zealand in *Attorney-General v Zaoui & Ors*, [2005] NZSC 38 at para 51 [*Zaoui & Ors*], while the Supreme Court of Canada implicitly came to the same finding by ruling that the prohibition against torture is a *ius cogens* norm but not extending this to deportation and torture (*Suresh v Canada (Minister of Citizenship and Immigration)*, 2002 SCC 1 at paras 61–75).

36 See, generally, regarding the concept of general principles in international law, UN Doc A/CN.4/741, International Law Commission, Seventy-second Session, Geneva, 27 April–5 June and 6 July–7 August 2020, *Second Report on General Principles of Law* by Marcelo Vázquez-Bermúdez, Special Rapporteur, 9 April 2020.

37 United Nations General Assembly, Resolution 217A (III), UN Doc A/810 at 71 (1948), art 14(1).

Refugees,[38] which states that a person who fears persecution[39] for reasons of race, religion, nationality, or membership of a particular social group or political opinion should be granted protection against a country from where this person has fled and from which the person is unwilling or unable to seek protection. If a person is recognized as a refugee, a number of benefits will follow according to this treaty, such as the rights of association (article 15), employment (articles 17–19), housing (article 21), education (article 22), social security (article 24), freedom of movement (article 26), and, most importantly, *non-refoulement*, the right not to be expelled if in the country lawfully (article 32) or even without status (article 33).

The notion of a refugee should be placed in the larger context of international migration, which can be divided into two main categories: voluntary and involuntary migration. Involuntary or forced migration refers to movement of persons who are leaving an intolerable situation in their own country and seeking protection in another country, while voluntary migration connotes situations whereby people seek better circumstances for themselves without feeling compelled to leave their country; the latter is usually the case when people go to other countries for economic reasons or family reunion.[40]

---

38 This convention also has a protocol (UN Doc A/RES/21/2198, 1966) that came into force in 1967 and clarifies some issues that had arisen since 1951.

39 Persecution is used not only in human rights instruments but also in international criminal law as one of the underlying crimes of crimes against humanity; however, the contours of the international crime are narrower than the human rights violation, as was made clear in a decision by the International Criminal Tribunal for the former Yugoslavia (ICTY), where the Trial Chamber was of the view that the interpretation of persecution in refugee law or human rights law was of little assistance to providing parameters for the crime against humanity of persecution as the purposes of human rights law and international criminal law are not the same (see *Kupreski* (IT-95-16), Trial Chamber Judgment, 14 January 2000 at paras 586–98).

40 Susan Kneebone, "Introduction: Refugees and Asylum Seekers in the International Context" in Susan Kneebone, *Refugees, Asylum Seekers and the Rule of Law: Comparative Perspectives* (Cambridge: Cambridge University Press, 2009) at 23–26. See, also, McAdam, above note 2 at 33–35; the most recent international development in this area is the *Global Compact for Safe, Orderly and Regular Migration*, UN Doc A/RES/73/195, 11 January 2019 (for a commentary, see Gillian D. Triggs & Patrick C.J. Wall, "'The Makings of a Success': The Global Compact on Refugees and the Inaugural Global Refugee Forum" (2020) 32:2 *International Journal of Refugee Law* 283–339); Goodwin-Gill & McAdam, above note 33 at 566–70. All of these concepts should be distinguished from the notion of "irregular migration," which is migration that takes place outside the norms and procedures established by states to manage the orderly flow of migrants into, through, and out of their territories and is often associated with migrant smuggling and trafficking in persons; international legal

On the forced migration side, three concepts need to be distinguished: the notions of internally displaced persons,[41] asylum seekers, and refugees. Internally displaced persons are defined as "persons or groups of persons who have been forced or obliged to flee or to leave their homes or places of habitual residence, in particular as a result of or in order to avoid the effects of armed conflict, situations of generalized violence, violations of human rights or natural or human-made disasters, and who have not crossed an internationally recognized State border."[42] While *refoulement* is technically not possible in internally

---

efforts to counter these phenomena are contained in the *Protocol to Prevent, Suppress and Punish Trafficking in Persons, Especially Women and Children* and the *Protocol against the Smuggling of Migrants by Land, Sea and Air*, which are part of the *United Nations Convention against Transnational Organized Crime* (*Palermo Convention*); for a background of these two protocols, see Robert J. Currie & Joseph Rikhof, *International & Transnational Criminal Law*, 3d ed (Toronto: Irwin Law, 2020) at 387–89 and 393–95; for discussions about these forms of migration, see Catherine Dauvergne, "Irregular Migration, State Sovereignty and the Rule of Law" in Chetail & Bauloz, above note 14 at 75–92; Ryszard Piotrowicz, "Smuggling and Trafficking of Human Beings" in Chetail & Bauloz, above note 14 at 132–47; Steve Peers, "Irregular Migrants: Can Humane Treatment Be Balanced Against Efficient Removal?" (2015) 17:4 *European Journal of Migration and Law* 289–304; Ioannis Kalpouzos, "International Criminal Law and the Violence Against Migrants" (supp, 2020) 21 *German Law Journal* 571–97 (as part of a special issue entitled "Border Justice: Migration and Accountability for Human Rights Violations"); Flavia Patanè et al, "Asylum-Seekers Prosecuted for Human Smuggling: A Case Study of *Scafisti* in Italy" (2020) 39:2 *Refugee Survey Quarterly* 123–52; Council of Europe, Group of Experts on Action against Trafficking in Human Beings (GRETA), *Guidance Note on the Entitlement of Victims of Trafficking, and Persons at Risk of Being Trafficked to International Protection* (June 2020), online (pdf): https://rm.coe.int/guidance-note-on-the-entitlement-of-victims-of-trafficking-and-persons/16809ebf44; Idil Atak & François Crépeau, "Refugees as Migrants" in Costello, Foster & McAdam, above note 2 at 134–51; Andreas Schloenhardt, "Smuggling of Migrants and Refugees," *ibid* at 535–52; Catherine Briddick & Vladislava Stoyanova, "Human Trafficking and Refugees," *ibid* at 553–68; and Elspeth Guild, "When Border Control Operations Become Crimes Against Humanity" in James C. Simeon, ed, *Serious International Crimes, Human Rights, and Forced Migration* (London: Routledge, 2022) at 329.

41 Regarding the use and evolution of the terms "displaced person" and "externally displaced person" for asylum seekers, see Ivor C. Jackson, *The Refugee Concept in Group Situations* (The Hague/London/Boston: Martinus Nijhoff, 1999) at 416–54; in general, see Brid Ni Ghráinne, "Internally Displaced Persons and International Refugee Law" in Singh Juss, above note 34 at 31–43; see, also, a number of articles in the "Special Issue on the 20th Anniversary of the Guiding Principles on Internal Displacement" (supp, 2018) 30:2 *Journal of International Refugee Law*, as well as David James Cantor, *Returns of Internally Displaced Persons During Armed Conflict, International Law and Its Application in Colombia* (Leiden & Boston: Brill Nijhoff, 2018), especially chs 2 & 3 at 41–120; and Romola Adeola, *The Internally Displaced Person in International Law* (Cheltenham, UK & Northampton, US: Elgar, 2020).

42 See the first binding instrument regulating internally displaced persons, namely, the African Union Convention for the Protection and Assistance of Internally Displaced Persons in

displaced person situations as such persons have not crossed any borders, the Kampala Convention obligates state parties not to engage in serious criminal activities against such persons, including genocide, war crimes, crimes against humanity, torture, and other forms of cruel, inhuman, or degrading treatment or punishment.[43]

The terms "asylum seeker" and "refugee" pertain to people who have left their own country for another country to seek protection. The difference between asylum and refugee is twofold: First, asylum, as opposed to refugee status, is used to refer to the right of a state to grant asylum against the exercise of jurisdiction of another state with the corresponding duty of states not to retaliate against states that have granted asylum.[44] The parameters of the exercise of the right of asylum by a state have been traditionally described to include the right to admit a person to the state's territory; the right to allow a person to remain in the state; the right to refuse to expel a person; the right to refuse to extradite a person to another state; and the right not to prosecute or punish the person.[45]

Second, like refugee status, asylum also operates at the individual level in the sense that it relates to protection against harm, specifically violations of human rights.[46] There have been long-standing efforts to incorporate into the notion of asylum not only a state obligation to allow people to seek asylum but also a further obligation to grant such a status as part of a more durable solution in the sense of admission to residence and lasting protection against persecution, but these efforts

---

Africa (Kampala Convention), art 1. Regarding internally displaced persons in general, see Goodwin-Gill & McAdam, above note 33 at 30–39 and 640–42; Elisabeth Ferris, "Internal Displacement and the Right to Seek Asylum" (2008) 27:3 *Refugee Survey Quarterly 76* at 76–79, and Kneebone, above note 40 at 20–22; James Hathaway & Michelle Foster, *The Law of Refugee Status*, 2d ed (Cambridge: Cambridge University Press, 2014) at 17–19.

43 Article 9.1(b) & (c).

44 Goodwin-Gill & McAdam, above note 33 at 400–3; Atle Grahl-Madsen, *The Status of Refugee in International Law, Volume 2, Asylum, Entry and Sojourn* (Leiden: AW Sijthoff, 1972) at 6–7; Li, above note 1 at 19–26; María-Teresa Gil-Bazo & Ispeth Guild, "The Right to Asylum" in Costello, Foster & McAdam, above note 2 at 868–82; Stephen Meili, "National Constitutions and the Right to Asylum," *ibid* at 883–98; see, also, the 1967 United Nations Declaration on Territorial Asylum, Preamble, para 4; the 1969 Convention on the Specific Aspects of Refugee Problems in Africa, art II, 2; and the 1984 Cartagena Declaration, Conclusion 4.

45 Grahl-Madsen, above note 44 at 23.

46 Goodwin-Gill & McAdam, above note 33 at 400–3; Grahl-Madsen, above note 44 at 356. One international instrument sets out both concepts of refugee and asylum, the 1969 Convention on the Specific Aspects of Refugee Problems in Africa, arts I & II.

have not come to fruition so far.[47] Apart from the fact that asylum does not include the right to be granted a permanent solution compared with granting of refugee status, asylum rights are typically fewer or more limited than the ones granted under the Refugee Convention.[48] For instance, under German law it is possible to claim asylum under its *Basic Law* (in addition to refugee protection), but this is only possible for political persecution,[49] while the French Constitution allows asylum for the persecuted person in relation to their actions in pursuit of liberty.[50] The Italian Constitution states that "an alien who is denied the effective exercise of the democratic liberties guaranteed by the Italian Constitution in his or her own country has the right of asylum in the territory of the Italian Republic in accordance with the conditions established by law."[51]

While asylum will not play an important role in countries that are party to the Refugee Convention, there remains a need for this concept where no other international or regional refugee instrument can be

---

47 Grahl-Madsen, above note 44 at 79–81 and 107–9, as well as Goodwin-Gill & McAdam, above note 33 at 400 and 415. The only exceptions are two regional conventions, the first of which is the American Convention on Human Rights, which contains a limited form of asylum in art 22.7, which says: "Every person has the right to seek and be granted asylum in a foreign territory, in accordance with the legislation of the state and international conventions, in the event he is being pursued for political offenses or related common crimes." Article 22.8 addresses the issue of *refoulement* in the following terms: "In no case may an alien be deported or returned to a country, regardless of whether or not it is his country of origin, if in that country his right to life or personal freedom is in danger of being violated because of his race, nationality, religion, social status, or political opinions." The second is the African Charter on Human and Peoples' Rights, which says in art 12.3 that "[e]very individual shall have the right, when persecuted, to seek and obtain asylum in other countries in accordance with laws of those countries and international conventions," while art 12.4 adds: "A non-national legally admitted in a territory of a State Party to the present Charter, may only be expelled from it by virtue of a decision taken in accordance with the law."

48 One author indicates that apart from the right to *non-refoulement*, asylum would also include basic rights, such as freedom of thought, expression, assembly, movement, and privacy; see Grahl-Madsen, above note 44 at 107–8 and 148–49.

49 Intergovernmental Consultations on Migration, Asylum and Refugees, *Asylum Procedures: Report on Policies and Practices in IGC Participating States* (Geneva: IGC, December 2015; also called the *Blue Book*) at 196 [*Asylum Procedures*]; see, also, Hélène Lambert, Francesco Massineo & Paul Tiedemann, "Comparative Perspectives of Constitutional Asylum in France, Italy, and Germany: *Requiescat in Pace?*" (2008) 27:3 *Refugee Law Quarterly* 16 at 26–32.

50 Intergovernmental Consultations on Migration, Asylum and Refugees, *Asylum Procedures: Report on Policies and Practices in IGC Participating States* (Geneva: IGC, December 2012) at 191; Lambert, Massineo & Tiedemann, above note 49 at 17–21.

51 *Ibid* at 22.

relied upon, specifically in Asia.[52] The Supreme Court of India recognized this in 1996 when it was called upon to determine whether persons who had been displaced from Bangladesh to India could be forcibly removed back to their country of origin. The court was of the view that the right to life and liberty enshrined in the Indian Constitution also applies to persons who are not citizens of India, and, as a result, non-citizens cannot be expelled.[53]

While the 1951 Refugee Convention is the most widely used instrument for refugee protection, there are also three regional arrangements[54] that have expanded on the convention's definition of refugee. These are the 1966 Bangkok Principles on Status and Treatment of Refugees (Bangkok Principles),[55] which is a non-binding document adopted by the Asian-African Legal Consultative Organization (AALCO), applicable in Asia; the 1969 Convention on the Specific Aspects of Refugee Problems in Africa; and the 1984 Cartagena Declaration on Refugees (Cartagena Declaration), applicable in Latin America.

The Bangkok Principles use the Refugee Convention definition while adding as affected groups those defined by colour, ethnic origin, and gender in article 1. Article 2 states that

> the term "refugee' shall also apply to every person, who, owing to external aggression, occupation, foreign domination or events seriously disturbing public order in either part or the whole of his country of origin or nationality, is compelled to leave his place of habitual residence in order to seek refuge in another place outside his country of origin or nationality.

---

52 One-hundred-and-forty-six countries have ratified the convention; see United Nations Treaty Collection, "Depository," "Status of Treaties," ch V.2, while 147 countries are parties to its protocol, ch V.5 (the United States has ratified the protocol but not the convention). More recently, a non-treaty arrangement was established under the United Nations auspices, namely, the *Global Compact on Refugees*, UN Doc A/73/12 (part II), 2 August 2018.

53 *National Human Rights Commission v Respondent: State of Arunachal Pradesh & ANR*, 9 January 1996 at 8, 1996 AIR 1234.

54 The European Union has also recognized the right of asylum in its Charter of Fundamental Rights of the European Union, art 18, which refers to the 1951 Refugee Convention and its 1967 protocol. For an overview of regional regimes, see Costello, Foster & McAdam, above note 2, Part III, "Regional Regimes," at 279–459.

55 Asian-African Legal Consultative Organization (AALCO), Bangkok Principles on the Status and Treatment of Refugees ("Bangkok Principles"), 31 December 1966, online: www.refworld.org/docid/3de5f2d52.html [Bangkok Principles].

The 1969 African Convention gives in article I.1 the same definition as the Refugee Convention but then includes in article I.2 the same description as article 2 of the Bangkok Principles.[56] The Cartagena Declaration, while not a binding treaty, has considerable moral authority in Latin America[57] and recommends the following to be included in Conclusion 3 as part of the definition of refugee, again in addition to the Refugee Convention parameters: "[p]ersons who have fled their country because their lives, safety or freedom have been threatened by generalized violence, foreign aggression, internal conflicts, massive violation of human rights or other circumstances which have seriously disturbed public order."[58]

So far, the overview of refugee protection has centred on the obligation of providing persons fleeing persecution (both nationals of a country of refuge or stateless persons who can also obtain protection under

56 For a historical overview of this definition, see Jackson, above note 41 at 191–94. For an analysis of the purpose of this convention, see Jean-François Durieux & Jane McAdam, "*Non-refoulement* Through Time: The Case for a Derogation Clause to the Refugee Convention in Mass Influx Emergencies" (2004) 16:1 *International Journal of Refugee Law* 4 at 9–13; see, also, in general, Marina Sharpe, *The 1969 OAU Refugee Convention and the Protection of People Fleeing Armed Conflict and Other Situations of Violence in the Context of Individual Refugee Status Determination*, UNHCR Legal and Protection Policy Research Series No 30 (January 2013), online (pdf): www.unhcr.org/protection/globalconsult/50f9652e9/30-1969-oau-refugee-convention-protection-people-fleeing-armed-conflict.html; Tamara Wood, "The 1969 OAU Convention Governing the Specific Aspects of Refugee Problems in Africa" in Singh Juss, above note 34 at 16–30; David Cantor & Farai Chikwanha, "Reconsidering African Refugee Law" (2019) 31:2–3 *International Journal of Refugee Law* 182–260; Sanjula Weerasinghe, *Refugee Law in a Time of Climate Change, Disaster and Conflict*, UNHCR Legal and Protection Policy Research No 40 (January 2020) at 11–37, online (pdf): www.unhcr.org/en-in/protection/globalconsult/5fdc70eb4/40-refugee-law-time-climate-change-disaster-conflict.html.

57 Goodwin-Gill & McAdam, above note 33 at 42–43; see, also, in general, Michael Reed-Hurtado, *The Cartagena Declaration on Refugees and the Protection of People Fleeing Armed Conflict and Other Situations of Violence in Latin America*, UNHCR Legal and Protection Policy Research Series No 32 (June 2013), online (pdf): www.unhcr.org/protection/globalconsult/51c800fe9/32-cartagena-declaration-refugees-protection-people-fleeing-armed-conflict.html; David James Cantor & Diana Trimiño Mora, "A Simple Solution to War Refugees? The Latin American Expanded Definition and Its Relationship to IHL" in David Cantor & Jean-François Durieux, eds, *Refuge from Inhumanity? War Refugees and International Humanitarian Law* (Leiden & Boston: Brill Nijhoff, 2014) at 204–24; Weerasinghe, above note 56 at 37–55; Javier Gamarro González, *Estudio sobre los estatutos de protección internacional en América Latina* (Hungarian Helsinki Committee, 2022).

58 For a historical overview of this definition, see Jackson, above note 41 at 395–404 and 414–15.

the Refugee Convention)[59] with a permanent solution by granting refugee status. However, as not all issues arising out of situations of turmoil causing refugee movements are covered by the Refugee Convention, new concepts, such as complementary, temporary, and subsidiary protection, have been developed to fill the gap between new realities and the existing convention's legal regime.[60] "Complementary protection" is an umbrella term that connotes protection granted by states based on an international protection need, which cannot be granted under the Refugee Convention. The main components of complementary protection are temporary protection, subsidiary protection, and international human rights protection from *refoulement*.[61]

---

59 The Refugee Convention (art 1A(2)), as well as the regional instruments in Asia and Africa, extends refugee protection to a person "who, not having a nationality and being outside the country of his former habitual residence as a result of such events, is unable or, owing to such fear, is unwilling to return to it." Two conventions have regulated the status of such persons: the 1961 Convention on the Reduction of Statelessness and the 1964 Convention Related to the Status of Stateless Persons. For further information on this issue, see Atle Grahl-Madsen, *The Status of Refugees in International Law*, vol 1 (Leiden: AW Sijthoff, 1966) at 93–94 and 315–17; Goodwin-Gill & McAdam, above note 33 at 669–704; UNHCR, *Expert Meeting, The Concept of Stateless Persons under International Law, Summary Conclusion*, Expert Meeting organized by the Office of the United Nations High Commissioner for Refugees, Prato, Italy, 27–28 May 2010; Hélène Lambert, *Refugee Status, Arbitrary Deprivation of Nationality, and Statelessness within the Context of Article 1A(2) of the 1951 Convention and its 1967 Protocol relating to the Status of Refugees*, UNHCR Legal and Protection Policy Research Series No 33 (October 2014), online (pdf): www.unhcr.org/protection/globalconsult/5433f0f09/33-refugee-status-arbitrary-deprivation-nationality-statelessness-context.html; Laura Van Waas, "The Intersection of International Refugee Law and International Statelessness Law" in Costello, Foster & McAdam, above note 2 at 152–68.

60 The Supreme Court of Canada, in the case of *Canada (Attorney General) v Ward*, [1993] 2 SCR 689, used the term "surrogate" protection in the sense that international protection will be provided when national protection is not available to an individual. Despite criticism of this terminology (see Goodwin-Gill & McAdam, above note 33 at 8), the lower court levels in Canada still used this notion as recently as 2016 (at the Federal Court, see *Canada (Citizenship and Immigration) v Kabunda*, 2016 FC 848, while at the Federal Court of Appeal, see *Tretsetsang v Canada (Citizenship and Immigration)*, 2016 FCA 175.

61 McAdam, above note 2 at 21–23 and 49–52; this writer also includes the concept of "the best interest of the child" as set out in the 1989 Convention on the Rights of the Child within the notion of complementary protection at 173–96; see, also, Goodwin-Gill & McAdam, above note 33 at 353–99; Hemme Battjes, "Subsidiary Protection and Other Alternative Forms of Protection" in Chetail & Bauloz, above note 14 at 541–61 and 542–44, and Jane McAdam, "Complementary Protection" in Costello, Foster & McAdam, above note 2 at 661–77. It should be pointed out that the notions of complementary and subsidiary protection are not used in a consistent manner by academics and governments; an examination of the sixteen countries of the Intergovernmental Consultations on Migration, Asylum and Refugees (IGC) (in *Asylum Procedures*, above note 49) reveals that while the term

Temporary protection was already mentioned as a concept by the scholar Grahl-Madsen in 1972 when he said that this type of protection could only be given "in times of civil unrest or other upheavals, and only as a protection against violent mobs, groups of insurgents, guerrilla units, marauding bands, etc., or against unauthorized pursuit by local authorities, local military commanders, or their like, acting on their own; but not as a protection against the duly authorized agents of a government exercising effective authority."[62] This type of protection has not undergone major changes and is still considered an "exceptional, emergency, time-bound response of granting protection to a mass influx of asylum seekers fleeing armed conflict, endemic violence, or a serious risk of systematic or generalized violations of human rights."[63] In the European Union,[64] the details of temporary protection are set out in

---

"complementary" is used often in the European Union context as an overarching concept (although Germany uses the two terms interchangeably), non-EU countries such as Australia, Canada, New Zealand, and the United States connote this term with *non-refoulement* obligations under international treaties such as the CAT and the ICCPR, while Norway uses the term "subsidiary protection" for the same purpose, and Denmark calls this "protected status"; Spain uses the term "subsidiary protection" to indicate forms of risk not contained in the 2004 European Qualification Directive (recast in 2011); countries such as Belgium and Sweden use subsidiary protection for the same terminology as in the Qualification Directive and nothing more, while Finland, Germany, Greece, the Netherlands, and the United Kingdom use the concepts from the Qualification Directive and add other forms of protection while calling the added portion either complementary or humanitarian protection; neither Ireland nor Switzerland mentions any type of added protection; for forms of complementary protection in other countries, see Goodwin-Gill & McAdam, above note 33 at 361–62.

62 Grahl-Madsen, above note 44 at 6; see, also, Guy Goodwin-Gill, "*Non-refoulement*, Temporary Refuge, and the 'New' Asylum Seekers" in David Cantor & Jean-François Durieux, above note 57 at 433–59; Jean-François Durieux, "Temporary Protection and Temporary Refuge" in Costello, Foster & McAdam, above note 2 at 678–94.

63 Goodwin-Gill & McAdam, above note 33 at 292–98 and 360–61; McAdam, above note 2 at 3 and 41–44.

64 As a result of the Treaty of Amsterdam, which came into force in 1999, asylum and immigration matters were moved from the jurisdiction of the individual states of the European Union and became the subject of legally binding instruments of harmonization by one of the legislative organs of the European Union, the Council of the European Union, as part of a Common European Asylum System (CEAS); as part of this asylum harmonization, the council has adopted five measures that set out minimum standards for members of the European Union, namely, the Temporary Protection Directive in 2001, the Receptions Conditions Directive in 2003 (recast in 2013 and dealing with conditions and rights for asylum seekers pending the asylum procedure), the Dublin Regulation in 2003 (recast in 2013 and regulating which member state is responsible for examining an asylum claim), the Qualification Directive in 2004 (recast in 2011 and addressing eligibility for protection), and the Asylum Procedures Directive in 2005 (recast in 2013 and dealing with the rules of procedure during examination of asylum claims); see Goodwin-Gill & McAdam, above

the Temporary Protection Directive, including the fact that it will only come into effect when the Council of the European Union designates a particular flow of refugees as a mass influx,[65] which did not occur until March 2022,[66] and the fact that the duration of temporary protection is for one year with a possible extension of two more years.[67]

In countries outside the European Union, the use of temporary protection varies. Two Western European countries, Norway and Switzerland, which are not part of the European Union, have a form of temporary protection.[68] In the five main refugee-receiving common law countries, South Africa does not have this status in its *Refugees Act* of 1998, while neither New Zealand nor Canada has a temporary refugee protection possibility in their legislation, but the highest executive organs can provide such protection on an individual basis in extreme circumstances under other provisions of their legislation.[69] Australian immigration law has the possibility to issue a temporary safe haven visa for persons who have been displaced by upheaval in their country of origin. This visa is provided for a temporary stay on the understanding that holders return to their home country when the Australian government considers it safe to do so.[70] In the United Kingdom, the *Immigration Rules* allow temporary protection in the same circumstances as the Temporary Protection Directive.[71] In the United States, the secretary of homeland security can designate a country or a part of a country for

---

note 33 at 44; Peers et al, above note 21 at 1–5; Zarif Yakut-Bathiyar, *Exclusion Clauses of the Refugee Convention in Relation to National Immigration Legislations, European Policy and Human Rights Instruments: Article 1F Versus the Non-refoulement Principle* (Oisterwijk, the Netherlands: Wolf Legal Publishers, 2016) at 51–58.

65 Article 5.1 of the Temporary Protection Directive; for further information, see Peers et al, above note 21 at 571–615; Battjes, above note 61 at 557–58; Bathiyar, above note 64 at 58–59.

66 See European Council Implementing Decision (EU) 2022/382 of 4 March 2022 establishing the existence of a mass influx of displaced persons from Ukraine within the meaning of art 5 of Directive 2001/55/EC and having the effect of introducing temporary protection.

67 Articles 4.1 & 4.2 of the directive; see, also, Meltem Ineli-Ciger, "Temporary Protection of Forced Migrants" in Singh Juss, above note 34 at 58–60.

68 *Asylum Procedures*, above note 49 at 319 and 390–91.

69 *Ibid* at 120 for Canada (although art 230 of the *Immigration and Refugee Protection Regulations*, SOR/2002-227, allows the minister to impose a stay on removal orders with respect to a country or a place if the circumstances in that country or place pose a generalized risk to the entire civilian population as a result of an armed conflict within the country or place, an environmental disaster resulting in a substantial temporary disruption of living conditions, or any situation that is temporary and generalized) and at 324 for New Zealand.

70 *Asylum Procedures*, above note 49 at 36; Ineli-Ciger, above note 67 at 59–68.

71 *Immigration Rules*, ss 354–356B.

temporary protected status if there is an ongoing armed conflict in that country or an environmental disaster and that country requests designation while it is temporarily unable to adequately handle the return of its nationals.[72]

As another form of complementary protection, the European Qualification Directive provides additional or subsidiary protection (in addition to refugee protection) to persons who are subjected to serious harm, identified as follows:

(a) death penalty or execution; or
(b) torture or inhuman or degrading treatment or punishment of an applicant in the country of origin; or
(c) serious and individual threat to a civilian's life or person by reason of indiscriminate violence in situations of international or internal armed conflict.[73]

The international human rights protection from *non-refoulement* is a form of alternative protection that goes beyond the protection

72 *Asylum Procedures*, above note 49 at 437; Ineli-Ciger, above note 67 at 59–68.

73 For more information regarding the directive as a whole, see Goodwin-Gill & McAdam, above note 33 at 44–45 and 387–92; McAdam, above note 2 at 53–110; Hugo Storey, "EU Refugee Qualification Directive: A Brave New World? (2008) 20:1 *International Journal of Refugee Law 1* at 1–23; Peers et al, above note 21 at 65–182; Bathiyar, above note 64 at 66–91. With respect to art 15 of the directive, which has been for the most part inspired by the CAT, the ICCPR, and the ECHR, see Battjes, above note 61 at 551–56; Peers et al, above note 21 at 135–36. The second sentence of this article has been interpreted by the CJEU in the case of *MP v Secretary of State for the Home Department*, C-353/16, 24 April 2018 (see, also, EASO, *Qualification for International Protection (Directive 2011/95/EU): A Judicial Analysis* (December 2016) at 106–10, online (pdf): https://euaa.europa.eu/sites/default/files/QIP%20-%20JA.pdf), while the last sentence of this article has been given meaning by the same court in the cases of *M Elgafaji, N Elgafaji v Staatssecretaris van Justitie*, C-465/07, 17 February 2009; *Aboubacar Diakité v Commissaire général aux réfugiés et aux apatrides*, C-285/12, 30 January 2014, and *CF, DN v Bundesrepublik Deutschland*, C901/19, 10 June 2021; see, also, with respect to art 15(c), Peers et al, above note 21 at 136–47; Hugo Storey, "The 'War Flaw' and Why It Matters" in David Cantor & Jean-François Durieux, above note 57 at 39–56; Céline Bauloz, "The (Mis)Use of International Humanitarian Law Under Article 15(C) of the EU Qualification Directive" in David Cantor & Jean-François Durieux, above note 57 at 247–69; EASO, *Article 15(c) Qualification Directive (2011/95/EU): A Judicial Analysis* (December 2014), online (pdf): https://euaa.europa.eu/sites/default/files/public/Article-15c-Qualification-Directive-201195EU-A-judicial-analysis.pdf; Peers et al, above note 21 at 135–47; Satvinder Singh Juss & Jeni Mitchell, "Gatekeepers of Asylum: UK Country Guidance, Indiscriminate Violence and Internal Relocation" in Singh Juss, above note 34 at 147–58; for a general overview of the interaction between international humanitarian law and refugee law, see Reuven Ziegler, "International Humanitarian Law and Refugee Protection" in Costello, Foster & McAdam, above note 2 at 222–39.

envisaged in the Refugee Convention and finds its inspiration in other sources of human rights, including treaties dealing with *non-refoulement*. The Refugee Convention says the following about *refoulement*: "No Contracting State shall expel or return ('*refouler*') a refugee in any manner whatsoever to the frontiers of territories where his life or freedom would be threatened on account of his race, religion, nationality, membership of a particular social group or political opinion."[74]

The limitation in the last portion of this article leaves open the possibility of people being removed who might be exposed to other human rights abuses or who fall outside the groups mentioned in this provision. As a result, reliance has been placed on three general international treaties and one regional treaty[75] to fill this gap. The three international treaties[76] are the International Covenant on Civil and Political Rights (ICCPR), the CAT,[77] and the International Convention for the Protection of All Persons from Enforced Disappearance, while the regional treaty is the ECHR.

The operative section in the ICCPR is article 7,[78] which states that "no one shall be subjected to torture or to cruel, inhuman or degrading

---

74 Article 33.1; art 32.1 serves a similar purpose by stating that "the contracting party shall not expel a refugee lawfully in their territory." Article 22.8 of the American Convention on Human Rights has very similar wording, as does art II.3 of the 1969 Convention on the Specific Aspects of Refugee Problems in Africa, although the latter ties the instances of *refoulement* to its wider definition of refugee; the Bangkok Principles use the same terminology as the Refugee Convention.

75 There also exists the Inter-American Convention to Prevent and Punish Torture, which prohibits *refoulement* in art 13 "when there are grounds to believe that his life is in danger, that he will be subjected to torture or to cruel, inhuman or degrading treatment, or that he will be tried by special or ad hoc courts in the requesting States," but this provision only applies to extradition.

76 While the International Convention on the Elimination of All Forms of Racial Discrimination does not mention the issue of *refoulement*, the Committee on the Elimination of Racial Discrimination mentions in its *General Recommendation No 30: Discrimination Against Non-Citizens*, 10 January 2004, para 27, that "non-citizens are not returned or removed to a country or territory where they are at risk of being subject to serious human rights abuses, including torture and cruel, inhuman or degrading treatment or punishment."

77 For a judicial consideration of the overlap between the Refugee Convention and the CAT in a situation where only the latter applies, see Secretary for Security and Prabakar, [2004] HKCA 43, 24 June 2004 (Court of Final Appeal of the Hong Kong Special Administrative Region), paras 14–17; for a commentary on this case, see Loper, above note 32 at 414–16.

78 The imposition of the death penalty and some manners of execution are not prohibited under art 6 of this instrument, but extradition to a country that employs this type of punishment without seeking assurances that it will not carry out this penalty could amount to prohibited *refoulement* under art 6, the right to life; see Wouters, above note 22 at 377–79 & 380.

treatment or punishment. In particular, no one shall be subjected without his free consent to medical or scientific experimentation." This article has been interpreted by the Human Rights Committee of the United Nations, the monitoring body of the ICCPR, also to include a prohibition against *refoulement*.[79] Similarly, article 3 of the CAT, which was given further meaning by the Committee against Torture of the United Nations, indicates that "no State Party shall expel, return ('*refouler*') or extradite a person to another State where there are substantial grounds for believing that he would be in danger of being subjected to torture." Along the same lines, the Enforced Disappearance Convention states in article 16.1 that "no State Party shall expel, return ('*refouler*'), surrender or extradite a person to another State where there are substantial grounds for believing that he or she would be in danger of being subjected to enforced disappearance."

The ECHR, article 3, in very similar words stipulates that "no one shall be subjected to torture or to inhuman or degrading treatment or punishment," which has also been developed jurisprudentially as a *non-refoulement* principle.[80] The latter provision has application within the forty-seven countries of the Council of Europe and has been the subject of extensive interpretation by the European Court of Human Rights.[81] In addition, the Qualification Directive has a similar provision specifically for the refugee context, which states: "Member States shall respect the principle of *non-refoulement* in accordance with their international obligations."[82]

---

79 See Chapter 6, Section E(2)(b)(i).

80 See Chapter 6, Section E(2)(c)(i); see, also, Peers et al, above note 21 at 160–63. Other articles in this instrument have been sporadically used in the *refoulement* context, such as the right to a fair trial (art 6), right to private life (art 8), and right to religion; Wouters, above note 22 at 348–53.

81 See Chapter 6, Section E(2)(a)(i).

82 Article 21(1), while art 21(2) says: "Where not prohibited by the international obligations mentioned in paragraph 1, Member States may *refoule* a refugee, whether formally recognised or not, when: (a) there are reasonable grounds for considering him or her as a danger to the security of the Member State in which he or she is present; or (b) he or she, having been convicted by a final judgment of a particularly serious crime, constitutes a danger to the community of that Member State." This provision was interpreted and contrasted with art 33(2) of the Refugee Convention by the CJEU in *M v Ministerstvo vnitra, X and X v Commissaire général aux réfugiés et aux apatrides*, C-319/16, C-77/17, and C-78/17, 14 May 2019 at paras 94 and 110, which indicated that EU law provides more protection because of these international obligations than art 33(2).

Outside Europe, South Africa does not have any provisions preventing the removal of persons beyond the Refugee Convention grounds, while Canada has extended protection against *refoulement* to persons who are at risk of torture or cruel and unusual treatment or punishment.[83] The United States, which has not ratified the Refugee Convention but has done so with its 1967 protocol, will not remove a refugee to their country of origin if the life or freedom of that person would be threatened in that country because of that person's race, religion, nationality, membership in a particular social group, or political opinion.[84] Also, a person can obtain protection from removal if the person fears torture in the country of origin.[85]

In New Zealand, the *Immigration Act 2009* has the following two provisions: "A person must be recognised as a protected person in New Zealand under the Convention Against Torture if there are substantial grounds for believing that he or she would be in danger of being subjected to torture if deported from New Zealand"[86] and "a person must be recognised as a protected person in New Zealand under the Covenant on Civil and Political Rights if there are substantial grounds for believing that he or she would be in danger of being subjected to arbitrary deprivation of life or cruel treatment if deported from New Zealand."[87]

Australia has a number of provisions with respect to human rights obligations but specifically a provision that would entitle a person to a protection visa if there are "substantial grounds for believing that, as a necessary and foreseeable consequence of the non-citizen being removed from Australia to a receiving country, there is a real risk that the non-citizen will suffer significant harm";[88] significant harm means:

(a) the non-citizen will be arbitrarily deprived of his or her life; or
(b) the death penalty will be carried out on the non-citizen; or

83 *Immigration and Refugee Protection Act*, SC 2001, c 27, s 115(1) [*IRPA*].

84 *Immigration and Nationality Act*, § 241(b)(3)(A) [*INA*, which can also be found as 8 *United States Code* or *USC* 1231].

85 *Ibid*, in conjunction with para 208.16(c) of Title 8 of the *Code of Federal Regulations*.

86 *Immigration Act 2009* (New Zealand), 2009/51, s 130(1).

87 *Ibid*, § 131(1). While this protection is contained in legislation for the first time, these international obligations had already been recognized judicially by the Supreme Court of New Zealand in *Zaoui & Ors*, above note 35 at para 93; for a review of this case, see Roger Haines, "National Security and *Non-refoulement* in New Zealand: Commentary on *Zaoui v Attorney-General (No. 2)*" in Jane McAdam, ed, *Forced Migration, Human Rights and Security* (Oxford & Portland, OR: Hart, 2008) at 63–92.

88 *Migration Act 1958*, s 36(2)(aa).

(c) the non-citizen will be subjected to torture; or
(d) the non-citizen will be subjected to cruel or inhuman treatment or punishment; or
(e) the non-citizen will be subjected to degrading treatment or punishment.[89]

Two observations can be made with respect to the issue of *non-refoulement*, both at the international and the domestic level. First, apart from the fact that this type of removal is universally prohibited, the contents of what constitutes *non-refoulement* in the refugee context is also becoming clearer in that a consistent pattern is emerging in the types of activities feared upon return to the country of refuge. All jurisdictions examined, except for South Africa, have moved beyond the concept contained in article 33 of the Refugee Convention and have recently added human rights *non-refoulement* notions borrowed from the CAT and the ICCPR, although the United States has only incorporated a prohibition to torture. There are some differences in the way and in how much detail these human rights precepts have been incorporated legislatively. For instance, New Zealand expresses this prohibition by a direct reference to the international instruments, while Australia tracks the wording of them very closely without specifically mentioning them. Canada and the United States use a more general wording, while the word "degrading" has been deleted from the *non-refoulement* provision in the former's legislation.

Second, there is at times a very close connection between the grounds for protection, which allows a person to stay in the country of refuge, and the reasons why a person should not be removed. This stands to reason since although there might be legal differences between these concepts for a refugee claimant, the consequences of each would ultimately be illusory (having certain benefits as a refugee but still subject to *refoulement*) if there was not some congruency between the two

---

89 *Ibid*, s 36(2A); "cruel or inhuman treatment or punishment," "degrading treatment or punishment," and "torture" are defined in s 5 of the Act; however, s 197C limits these rights by saying: "it is irrelevant whether Australia has non-refoulement obligation in respect of an unlawful citizen"; for commentaries regarding this latter provision, see Savitri Taylor, "Australia and the Refugee Convention" in Singh Juss, above note 34 at 244–45 and 248–50, and Chantal Bostock & Jason Cabarrús, "Short Shrift to International *Non-refoulement* Obligations? Australia's Approach to Criminal Deportation" (2020) 32:4 *International Journal of Refugee Law* 597 at 602–4 and 617–18.

notions.[90] While under the Refugee Convention the grounds for these two types of concepts are identical,[91] this connection has been lost in other international instruments, which extend protection beyond what is contained in the Refugee Convention while at the same time using the wording of the Refugee Convention for *non-refoulement*. This is the case in the Bangkok Principles,[92] while neither the Convention on the Specific Aspects of Refugee Problems in Africa nor the Cartagena Declaration contains a provision regarding *refoulement*, and the Qualification Directive only says that "states shall respect the principle of *non-refoulement* in accordance with their international obligations."[93]

The same discrepancy, albeit at a less fundamental level, can also be seen at the domestic level in Canada and the United States. In Canada, protection is given on the basis of torture, a risk to life, or a risk of cruel and unusual treatment or punishment, but the reference to life is omitted in the *non-refoulement* provision. Similarly, in the United States, a refugee is defined as a person subject to "persecution or a well-founded fear," only to be replaced in the *refoulement* language by "threat to life or freedom."[94]

C. CRIMINALITY IN REFUGEE AND REFUGEE-TYPE INSTRUMENTS

While the above refugee and human rights instruments provide protection and benefits to persons seeking asylum, none of them do this in an absolute fashion. The main treaty in this area, the Refugee Convention, sets limits on the circumstances where protection can be extended. These limits fall into two distinct categories, the first being that a person is not entitled to refugee protection *ab initio*, while the second pertains to a situation where persons have been granted refugee status but despite this status can still lose their benefits or be forced to leave the country of refuge.

---

90 See Hathaway, above note 5 at 343–47; Goodwin-Gill & McAdam, above note 33 at 266–67.

91 See, for instance, in Australia, the case of *Shahrooie v Minister for Immigration & Multicultural & Indigenous Affairs*, [2003] FCA 996 at para 25, and in the United States, the case of *Castellano-Chacon v Ashcroft*, 341 F3rd 533 (6th Cir 2003), although in the latter a higher standard of proof for *refoulement* is required.

92 Bangkok Principles, above note 55, art III.1.

93 Qualification Directive, above note 61, art 21.1.

94 Compare § 1101(a)(42) and § 241(b)(3)(A) of the *INA*, above note 84.

These two categories can in turn be further subdivided with a criminal and a non-criminal component in each category.[95] Regarding the latter sub-category, the convention says with respect to *ab initio*–type disentitlement, called exclusion, that persons are not entitled to protection if they receive assistance from other United Nations agencies or organs other than the United Nations High Commissioner for Refugees (UNHCR).[96] As well, a person who "is recognized by the competent authorities of the country in which he has taken residence as having the rights and obligations which are attached to the possession of the nationality of that country" cannot obtain refugee status either.[97] The convention employs the concept of cessation, which is applied to persons who have obtained refugee status but can be returned to their country of origin in the following circumstances:

---

95 See James C. Hathaway & Colin J. Harvey, "Framing Refugee Protection in the New World Disorder" (2001) 34:2 *Cornell International Law Journal* 257 at 287–89; Lauterpacht & Bethlehem, above note 29 at 129–30, while at the judicial level, the Supreme Court of Canada has made the same observation in *Pushpanathan v Canada (Minister of Citizenship and Immigration)*, [1998] 1 SCR 982 at paras 6–9 and 13, as has the Conseil d'État in France in the case of Pariola (CE, 28 July 2000, 205619).

96 Refugee Convention, art 1D; see UNHCR, *Guidelines on International Protection No. 13: Applicability of Article 1D of the 1951 Convention relating to the Status of Refugees to Palestine Refugees*, HCR/GIP/17/13 (December 2017), online (pdf): www.unhcr.org/publications/legal/5ddfca844/guidelines-international-protection-13-applicability-article-1d-1951-convention.html; Hathaway & Foster, above note 42 at 509–23; Kate Ogg, "New Directions in Article 1(D) Jurisprudence: Greater Barriers for Palestinian Refugee Seeking the Benefits of the Refugee Convention" in Singh Juss, above note 34 at 358–73; for more recent cases, see, in New Zealand, AE (Lebanon), [2019] NZIPT 801588, 28 May 2019; the Netherlands, Rb, The Hague, NL 20.6600, 2 August 2020 (overruled on appeal in AbRS, 14 July 2021, nr 202004766/1/V1) and Rb, The Hague, NL 20.17791, 4 June 2021; Belgium, CCE No 243.517, 30 October 2020; France, CNDA, 14 September 2020, 19055889, Mme A as well as CNDA, 9 December 2020, 20016437/20005472, ME; and Switzerland, Urteil (des Bundesgerichts) 2C_330/2020, 6 August 2021 and Urteil (des Bundesgerichts) 2C_587/2021, 16 February 2022; and the UK Home Office's *Asylum Policy Instruction: Article 1D of the Refugee Convention: Palestinian Refugees Assisted by the United Nations Relief and Works Agency (UNRWA)*, version 2 (9 May 2016), online (pdf): https://assets.publishing.service.gov.uk/government/uploads/system/uploads/attachment_data/file/524502/A-on-Article-1D-and-Palestinians-v2_0.pdf.

97 Refugee Convention, art 1E; Hathaway & Foster, above note 42 at 500–9; for an example of national jurisprudence, see Immigration and Refugee Board of Canada (IRB), *Interpretation of Convention Refugee and Person in Need of Protection in the Case Law*. Chapter 10 — Exclusion Clauses — Article 1E (31 December 2020), online (pdf): https://irb.gc.ca/en/legal-policy/legal-concepts/Documents/Interpretation%20of%20Convention%20Refugee%20and%20Person%20in%20Need%20of%20Protection%20in%20the%20Case%20Law%20(31%20Dec%202020).pdf.

> (1) he has voluntarily re-availed himself of the protection of the country of his nationality; or
> (2) having lost his nationality, he has voluntarily reacquired it; or
> (3) he has acquired a new nationality, and enjoys the protection of the country of his new nationality; or
> (4) he has voluntarily re-established himself in the country which he left or outside which he remained owing to fear of persecution; or
> (5) he can no longer, because the circumstances in connection with which he has been recognized as a refugee have ceased to exist, continue to refuse to avail himself of the protection of the country of his nationality.[98]

Criminal conduct also has consequences in the Refugee Convention. Article 1F is the key section of the convention and contains three types of criminal exclusionary provisions:

> The provisions of this Convention shall not apply to any person with respect to whom there are serious reasons for considering that:
> (a) he has committed a crime against peace, a war crime, or a crime against humanity, as defined in the international instruments drawn up to make provision in respect of such crimes;
> (b) he has committed a serious non-political crime outside the country of refuge prior to his admission to that country as a refugee;
> (c) he has been guilty of acts contrary to the purposes and principles of the United Nations.

Forcible removal for criminality of persons who have obtained refugee status is regulated in articles 32 and 33 of the convention. Article 32 pertains to refugees who are lawfully present in the country of refuge and allows expulsion on grounds of national security or public order.

---

98 Refugee Convention, art 1C; see Hathaway & Foster, above note 42 at 465–500; Maria O'Sullivan, *Refugee Law and Durability of Protection: Temporary Residence and Cessation of Status* (Abingdon & New York: Routledge, 2019); Goodwin-Gill & McAdam, above note 33 at 159–78; Georgia Cole, "Cessation" in Costello, Foster & McAdam, above note 2 at 1029–45. Although the concept is not contained in the Refugee Convention, refugee law also knows the device of vacation or cancellation, whereby a person who made misrepresentations during the refugee process can have this status removed, and if the misrepresentation included criminal activities, exclusion can be applied as part of the vacation/cancellation process; see Sibylle Kapferer, *Cancellation of Refugee Status*, PPLA/2003/02 (March 2003), at 11–12, online (pdf): www.unhcr.org/3e9418df4.pdf, and UNHCR, *Unit 10: Procedures for Cancellation and Revocation of Refugee Status* (August 2020), online (pdf): www.refworld.org/docid/5e8707583.html; at the regional level, see the Qualification Directive, arts 14 and 19.

Article 33 deals with *refoulement* and makes an exception to the principle of non-removal if "there are reasonable grounds for regarding as a danger to the security of the country in which he is, or who, having been convicted by a final judgement of a particularly serious crime, constitutes a danger to the community of that country."[99]

Such crime-related exceptions from the benefits in refugee-type instruments are by no means unique. The Universal Declaration of Human Rights granted the right to asylum on the one hand but at the same time restricted it by saying that this right "may not be invoked in the case of prosecutions genuinely arising from non-political crimes or from acts contrary to the purposes and principles of the United Nations."[100] The statute of the UNHCR, which provides it with the authority to carry out refugee status determination in countries that have ratified the Refugee Convention but are not willing or able to engage in this work themselves, allows for the exclusion of a person: "In respect of whom there are serious reasons for considering that he has committed a crime covered by the provisions of treaties of extradition or a crime mentioned in article VI of the London Charter of the International Military Tribunal or by the provisions of article 14, paragraph 2, of the Universal Declaration of Human Rights."[101]

A slightly different pattern with respect to criminal exceptions can be seen in the regional refugee instruments. While the Bangkok Principles have the same wording regarding exclusion,[102] *refoulement*, and expulsion[103] as the Refugee Convention, the 1969 Convention on the Specific Aspects of Refugee Problems in Africa has only similar exclusionary wording as the convention in its definition of refugees[104] but no provision for *refoulement* based on criminality. The Cartagena Declaration is silent on criminality.

Instruments dealing with issues such as internally displaced persons, asylum, and statelessness also contain provisions regarding criminality. The 1967 United Nations Declaration on Territorial Asylum

---

99 Refugee Convention, article 33.2.

100 Article 14(2).

101 Article 7(d).

102 Article I.7.

103 Articles III.1 and V.4, although the latter only applies for situations of national security.

104 Article I.5, although it adds a clause excluding persons who are guilty of acts contrary to the purposes and principles of the OAU. Furthermore, art III contains a prohibition to carry out subversive activities while in the country of refuge.

repeats article 1F in its entirety,[105] as does the Convention Related to the Status of Stateless Persons.[106] The Kampala Convention, which deals with internally displaced persons, also contains a prohibition against protection on the basis of criminality, although it is framed as a state obligation to ensure that internally displaced persons do not engage in subversive activities.[107]

The situation is no different in complementary protection, at both regional and national levels. The Temporary Protection Directive of the European Union excludes persons from benefits for the same reasons as article 1F of the Refugee Convention, while adding the following for serious political crimes: "The severity of the expected persecution is to be weighed against the nature of the criminal offence of which the person concerned is suspected. Particularly cruel actions, even if committed with an allegedly political objective, may be classified as serious non-political crimes. This applies both to the participants in the crime and to its instigators."[108] It then goes on to incorporate the wording of article 33.2 of the Refugee Convention as a further ground for exclusion.[109] This directive also refers to *non-refoulement* twice by a general reference to the member states' obligations in this regard.[110]

The Qualification Directive (recast) of the European Union follows a similar approach with respect to exclusion as the Temporary Protection Directive for both refugee status and subsidiary protection with some differences:

- It adds the wording of cessation clause 1C of the Refugee Convention[111]
- It refers to exclusion 1D of the Refugee Convention[112]

105 Article I.2.

106 Article 2.iii.

107 Article 3.1(f).

108 Article 28.1(a)(ii).

109 Article 28.1(b); it also says in art 28.2: "The grounds for exclusion referred to in paragraph 1 shall be based solely on the personal conduct of the person concerned. Exclusion decisions or measures shall be based on the principle of proportionality."

110 Articles 3.2 and 6.2.

111 Article 11; see Peers et al, above note 21 at 116–20; EASO, *Ending International Protection: Articles 11, 14, 16 and 19 Qualification Directive (2011/95/EU): A Judicial Analysis* (December 2016) at 23–40, online (pdf): https://euaa.europa.eu/sites/default/files/Ending%20International%20Protection_Articles%2011_14_16%20and%2019%20QD%20EASO%20Judicial%20Analysis%20FINAL.pdf [EASO, *Ending International Protection*].

112 Refugee Convention, art 12.1(a); this provision has been the subject of four judgments by the CJEU: *Nawras Bolbol v Bevándorlási és Állampolgársági Hivatal* C-31/09, 17 June 2010;

- It uses the wording of exclusion ground 1E of the Refugee Convention[113]
- With respect to the serious non-political crime component, the reference to participants and instigators in the crime has been removed and has become a separate paragraph that now applies to all forms of criminality; this applies to both refugee and subsidiary protection status[114]
- With respect to the same crime, this has been reduced to only "serious crime" for subsidiary protection[115]
- The reference to acts contrary to the purposes and principles of the United Nations has been augmented by the words "as set out in the Preamble and Articles 1 and 2 of the Charter of the United Nations" for both types of protection[116]
- The article 33.2 convention wording only applies to subsidiary protection as part of exclusion and is reframed as follows: "he or she constitutes a danger to the community or to the security"[117]
- For the subsidiary part, the following is added:

> Member States may exclude a third country national or a stateless person from being eligible for subsidiary protection, if he or she prior to his or her admission to the Member State has committed one or more crimes, outside the scope of paragraph 1, which would be punishable by imprisonment, had they been committed in the Member State concerned, and if he or she left his or her country of origin solely in order to avoid sanctions resulting from these crimes[118]

Karem El Kott v Bevándorlási és Állampolgársági Hivatal, C-364/11, 19 December 2012; *Serin Alheto v Zamestnik-predsedatel na Darzhavna agentsia za bezhantsite*, C-585/16, 25 July 2018; *Bundesrepublik Deutschland v XT*, C507/19, 13 January 2021, and *NB and AB v SSHD (UK)*, C-349/20, 3 March 2022. See, also, Peers et al, above note 21 at 120–25; EASO, *Judicial Analysis: Exclusion: Articles 12 and 17 Qualification Directive*, 2d ed (2020) at 31–39, online (pdf): https://euaa.europa.eu/sites/default/files/EASO_Exclusion_second_edition_JA_EN.pdf [EASO, *Exclusion*].

113 Refugee Convention, art 12.1(b); see Peers et al, above note 21 at 125; EASO, *Exclusion*, *ibid* at 41–44.

114 Refugee Convention, art 12.2(b) in conjunction with art 12.3 for refugees; art 17.1 in conjunction with art 17.2 for subsidiary protection.

115 Article 17.1(b); see *Shajin Ahmed v Bevándorlási és Menekültügyi Hivatal*, C-369/17, 13 September 2018 at para 47.

116 Articles 12.2(c) and 17.1(c).

117 Article 17.1(d).

118 Article 17.3.

- Article 28.2 of the Temporary Protection Directive regarding the requirements for personal conduct and proportionality is not repeated

This directive, which is narrower than the Temporary Protection Directive and the Refugee Convention with respect to criminal exclusion and refoulement, also uses criminal behaviour to allow member states to revoke, end, or refuse an already granted status. This ending of refugee status is mandatory if this status should not have been granted pursuant to the above exclusion clauses[119] but discretionary only in situations described in article 33.2 of the Refugee Convention.[120] It is mandatory for all types of exclusion for subsidiary status.[121] In addition, the *refoulement* provision for both types of protection has the same contents as article 33.2 of the Refugee Convention.[122]

While in international human rights law there are exceptions in the ICCPR and ECHR, they only allow derogation in a state of emergency, and even then these exceptions do not apply to the articles dealing with *non-refoulement*.[123] The CAT does not allow any exception at any level.[124]

At the domestic level, countries generally tend to reflect the wording of the exclusion and *refoulement* provisions of the Refugee Convention, more or less faithfully, in their legislation, with some exceptions. Switzerland, while not being a member of the European Union, has also added the *refoulement* provisions of the Refugee Convention to the regular exclusion provisions,[125] while the United States has used

---

119 Articles 14.3(a) and 19.3(a); EASO, *Ending International Protection*, above note 111 at 41–45; article 14(6) indicates that even after such a revocation, the person continues to have rights associated with being a refugee, which was confirmed by the CJEU in *M v Ministerstvo vnitra, X and X v Commissaire général aux réfugiés et aux apatrides*, C-319/16, C-77/17 and C-78/17, 14 May 2019 at paras 99 and 110.

120 Refugee Convention, art 14.4 as well as 14.5, where no status has been conferred yet; see, also, Peers et al, above note 21 at 129–35; EASO, *Ending International Protection*, above note 111 at 46–49.

121 Refugee Convention, art 18.3(a) with the exception for unique type of exclusion set out in art 17.3 (as indicated by art 18.2), which makes this type of ending the subsidiary status discretionary.

122 Article 21.2.

123 Articles 4 and 15, respectively.

124 Article 2.

125 *Asylum Procedures*, above note 49 at 391; see, also, Nula Frei & Constantin Hruschka, "Caught Between Unworthiness and Exclusion: Asylum Applicants and Refugees Suspected of Terrorism in Swiss Law and Practice" in James C. Simeon, ed, *Terrorism and Asylum* (Leiden & Boston: Brill Nijhoff, 2020) at 311–41.

a similar approach to exclusion by combining article 1F(b) activities (serious non-political crimes) with article 33.2 offences (including, specifically, activities related to terrorism) as well as participation in the persecution of others,[126] the latter of which is defined as "ordering, inciting, assisting or otherwise participating in the persecution of any person on account of race, religion, nationality, membership in a particular social group, or political opinion."[127] With respect to *refoulement*, the same activities used for exclusion can be used for this purpose as well as participation in Nazi persecution and genocide.[128]

In Canada, the *refoulement* provision, which applies not only to the refugee-type *non-refoulement* but also to human rights prohibitions,[129] also includes a third category, "the nature and severity of acts committed,"[130] while it has mixed the application of *refoulement* and exclusion provisions by introducing an eligibility provision that could prevent refugee claimants from accessing the refugee determination system if they have committed the Canadian equivalent of immigration inadmissibility provisions that bear a close resemblance to exclusion and article 33.2 activities.[131]

As with the above discussion of *non-refoulement*, two observations can be made here. The first one is that some of the incongruence

---

126 *INA*, § 208(b)(2)(A); see Dree K. Collopy, *AILA Asylum Primer: A Practical Guide to U.S. Asylum Law and Procedure,* 8th ed (Washington, DC: American Immigration Lawyers Association, 2019) at 196–208. Exclusion is called mandatory bar to asylum, while *refoulement* is called mandatory bar to withholding of removal; both are usually argued at the same time during the refugee claim procedure.

127 *INA*, § 208(b)(2)(A)(i).

128 *INA*, § 241(b)(3)(B); § 244(c)(2)(A)(iii) of the *INA* also disallows temporary protection for the same grounds.

129 As a result of a combination of ss 115(1) and (2) of the *IRPA*, above note 83, even though it had already been recognized by the Supreme Court of Canada before the *IRPA* came into force in June 2002 that the prohibition for *refoulement* to torture was absolute in international law in *Suresh v Canada (Minister of Citizenship and Immigration)*, 2002 SCC 1 at para 75, although it allowed for a narrow exception for such a possibility in Canadian domestic law in exceptional circumstances at paras 58 and 78. The decision has been criticized for that reason; see François Crépeau, "Anti-terrorism Measures and Refugee Law Challenges in Canada" (2011) 29:4 *Refugee Survey Quarterly* 31 at 35–36; Asha Kaushal & Catherine Dauvergne, "The Growing Culture of Exclusion: Trends in Canadian Refugee Exclusions" (2011) 23:1 *International Journal of Refugee Law* 54 at 70–71.

130 *IRPA*, above note 83, s 115(2)(b).

131 *Ibid*, s 101(1)(f); for a criticism, see Jennifer Bond, Nathan Benson & Jared Porter, "Guilt by Association: Ezokola's Unfinished Business in Canadian Refugee Law" (2020) 39:1 *Refugee Survey Quarterly* 1–25.

between the wording pertaining to protection and *non-refoulement* can be seen here as well when describing exclusion and criminal behaviour as part of *refoulement*. However, this gap in defining the contours of criminality in articles 1F and 33.2 is diminishing in Europe due to the Temporary Protection Directive and the Qualification Directive, as well as in the United States and Canada. Even when the traditional distinction between exclusion and *refoulement* is applied (taking into account that exclusion still tends to be applied in practice to acts committed before coming to and outside the country of refuge, while *refoulement* typically is used for criminal behaviour carried out in the country of refuge after having obtained refugee status), there always was and still is some overlap in practice between exclusionary and *refoulement* crimes.

Second, while there has been some experimenting with the application and overlapping of these two concepts, the main features of both exclusion and *refoulement* as used in the Refugee Convention have remained remarkably constant, and as such, an examination based on the interpretation of these notions can provide useful conclusions not only in the context of the Refugee Convention but also as part of a more general approach.

D. METHODOLOGY AND STRUCTURE

The methodology of this book consists of a historical and comparative analysis of the two main tenets of the treatment of persons with criminal backgrounds who have claimed asylum either internationally or in countries of refuge: the concepts of exclusion and *refoulement*. The historical analysis in Chapter 2 will examine the reasons why the drafters of the three most important documents, the Statute of the International Refugee Organization, the Universal Declaration of Human Rights, and the Refugee Convention, deemed it necessary after the Second World War to limit the rights of persons in the refugee context if they had been involved in criminal activities.

The comparative analysis will focus primarily on the interpretation of the two sections in the Refugee Convention that deal with criminality, article 1F and article 33.2, by the main international agency in this area, the UNHCR, as well as by national refugee tribunals and courts. This comparative analysis will by necessity include forays into other areas of law, such as international criminal law (for exclusion ground 1F(a)), domestic extradition law (for exclusion ground 1F(b)), public international law (for exclusion ground 1F(c)), domestic criminal law (for the *refoulement* provision in article 33.2), and human rights law for the notions of torture and inhumane treatment, thereby providing an overarching and comprehensive treatment of the law.

The emphasis in examining these areas of law at the domestic level will be on court decisions rendered in refugee cases as refugee law provides a more fertile and consistent research environment since, as noted, virtually all major aspects dealing with criminality eventually trace their way back to articles 1F and 33.2. On the other hand, the immigration laws of domestic jurisdictions in the area of criminality have many more permutations, thereby making it difficult to discern patterns that can be used to reach meaningful conclusions.[132] At times it will be necessary to use some immigration jurisprudence in order to elucidate a point with respect to refugee criminality, as, for instance, will be the case when relying on Australian immigration caselaw regarding criminal associations,[133] on inadmissibility based on membership in terrorist and criminal organizations in Canada,[134] and on article 1F in the Netherlands, where it is not only applied in exclusion but is also one of the grounds for immigration inadmissibility.[135] This book will examine the refugee status determination processes of the UNHCR and, at the national level, primarily in the European Union and the common law countries of Australia, Canada, New Zealand, the United Kingdom, and the United States. According to the UNHCR,[136] of the 173 countries for which data were available for 2014, governments were solely responsible for carrying out refugee status determination in 103 countries, the UNHCR was the only responsible body for status determination processing in fifty-one countries, and a shared responsibility occurred in nineteen countries. Most of the refugee claims were submitted in European Union and common law countries,[137] while the development of the legal issues

132 As an example of this problem, see Joseph Rikhof, "War Criminals Not Welcome: How Common Law Countries Approach the Phenomenon of International Crimes in the Immigration and Refugee Context" (2009) 21:3 *International Journal of Refugee Law* 453–507.

133 *Haneef v Minister for Immigration & Citizenship*, [2007] FCA 1273 (21 August 2007), and *Minister for Immigration & Citizenship v Haneef*, [2007] FCAFC 203 (21 December 2007).

134 *IRPA*, above note 83, ss 34(1)(f) and 37(1)(a).

135 Bathiyar, above note 64 at 156–57.

136 *UNHCR Statistical Yearbook 2014*, (8 December 2015), ch 4 at 51, online (pdf): www.unhcr.org/statistics/country/56655f4d8/statistical-yearbook-2014-complete.html.

137 UNHCR, *Global Trends: Forced Displacement in 2021* (Copenhagen, Denmark: UNHCR Global Data Service, 16 June 2022), online: www.unhcr.org/62a9d1494/global-trends-report-2021.

surrounding exclusion and *refoulement* has taken place for the most part in the same jurisdictions.[138] The countries investigated in depth that have contributed the most to the concepts of exclusion and *refoulement* are Australia, Belgium, Canada, France, Germany, the Netherlands, New Zealand, the United Kingdom, and the United States, while others will be mentioned in passing.[139]

In most situations, it will be sufficient to rely on decisions by the courts in the above countries given the volume of jurisprudence. This is the case in Canada, the Netherlands, Germany, and the United States. Where there is a paucity of judicial decision making, administrative tribunals will also be relied upon to determine trends in exclusion and *refoulement*, as is the case in Australia, Belgium, France, New Zealand, and the United Kingdom.

While there is a correlation between protection and *non-refoulement* in the sense that persecution, torture, and inhuman or cruel punishment and treatment can result in a person becoming a refugee while at the same time prohibiting removal on these same grounds, this book will not examine the concept of persecution. This approach is taken for two reasons. The first is that, compared to the human rights grounds, there is a plethora of academic work on this issue and a much-lesser volume in the torture and inhuman treatment areas.[140] Second, when courts and administrative tribunals have examined the protection aspect of refugee law, invariably the discussion and the result tend to concentrate on the issue of persecution rather than torture or ill treatment; as a matter of fact, while a protection decision might refer to both persecution and torture/ill treatment in the conclusion, the analysis in that same decision deals only with persecution. The situation tends to be reversed at the *refoulement* stage, where a legal discussion is primarily about torture/ill treatment, especially where there is a tension between a positive

---

138 For an overview of the work of the UNHCR in refugee status determination, see Goodwin-Gill & McAdam, above note 33 at 55–56 and 487–97; for a historical overview of the UNHCR work, see Jackson, above note 41 at 143–228 and 235–39 for the period 1961–75 and at 243–415 for the period 1975–85; for a critical examination of the UNHCR in the wake of the 1994 Rwanda genocide, see Kristen Wagner, "UNHCR's Involvement in the Great Lakes Refugee Crisis" (2009) 21:1 *Pace International Law Review* 365 at 375–78.

139 For brief overviews of the exclusion procedures for some other European countries, see *Asylum Procedures*, above note 49 at 142 (Denmark), 169 (Finland), 222 (Greece), 241 (Ireland), 321 (Norway), 343 (Spain), 365 (Sweden), and 391 (Switzerland).

140 For some recent comprehensive overviews of persecution, see Hathaway & Foster, above note 42 at 91–181; EASO, *Qualification for International Protection*, above note 73 at 26–54.

article 33.2 finding (indicating that *refoulement* would be possible for danger to the public or security reasons) and human rights imperatives mandating against such a removal. In such situations, the question of whether torture or deplorable treatment would occur upon removal to the country of origin assumes a much larger dimension and has been the subject of a great number of decisions in that context.

Chapter 2 provides a historical overview, canvassing the concepts of asylum, including its exceptions from early days, tracing multinational efforts to address refugee situations between the First World War and the Second World War, and examining in detail the work of the International Refugee Organization in its efforts to resettle large numbers of displaced persons in Europe immediately after the Second World War. From this practical work, the book will turn to the world of diplomacy and will provide an insight into the negotiations of the Universal Declaration of Human Rights and the Refugee Convention, both of which took place within a short time of each other and provide valuable insight into the decision of the delegations to include criminality provisions in both documents. The negotiation records of the CAT, the ICCPR, and the ECHR will also be examined. A brief foray will be made into the significance of the *travaux préparatoires* on treaties in general and these five instruments in particular.

Chapters 3, 4, and 5 are concerned with exclusion. They begin by addressing some overarching issues common to all three exclusion clauses, such as the standard of proof and the balancing between the level of persecution a person might face upon return (inclusion) and exclusion. Both the UNHCR's practice, as evidenced by its handbook and guidelines, as well as national jurisprudence, will be reviewed.

The approach to each of the three exclusion clauses will be different. For article 1F(a), which, in the words of the Refugee Convention, deals with crimes against peace, war crimes, and crimes against humanity, it is felt that for a better understanding of these crimes and their surrounding elements an overview of the main concepts of international criminal law would be useful. As a result, there will be separate discussions of these three crimes (as well as genocide, even though it is not mentioned in article 1F(a)), their contextual or international elements, and their underlying crimes in Chapter 3, followed in Chapter 4 by an examination of the parameters of extended liability and available defences for persons who have met both the *actus reus* and *mens rea* requirements of the crimes in question. The structure of these two chapters will be the same:

an overview of international criminal law in this area, then the views of the UNHCR on that aspect, and, finally, the jurisprudence in the nine domestic jurisdictions on the issues of international crimes, extended liability, and defences. Under the last issue, defences, the topic of child soldiers will find a home as often the liability of child soldiers, as discussed at the national level, involves an interplay between *actus reus* and a defence. These two chapters will conclude with a comparison of the tenets of international criminal law and their adoption into refugee law while teasing out discrepancies and the impact of these discrepancies.

The examination in Chapter 5 of the exclusion ground in article 1F(b) of serious non-political crimes will canvass both UNHCR practice and national court and administrative tribunal decisions. The areas of interest are the meaning of each word in the phrase: "serious," "non-political," and "crime." As some of these concepts had their origins in extradition law, since domestic refugee cases have sought inspiration in extradition law, and since political crimes are still an important issue in both extradition and refugee law, a detour into that legal territory will be necessary. As well, article 1F(b) (as well as article 1F(c)) has been used to counter the phenomenon of refugee claimants being involved in terrorism, so an inquiry into the international and domestic regimes dealing with such activities will need to be carried out to ascertain the interplay between them. The conclusion of this aspect of the chapter will be a comparative analysis of the UNHCR and domestic practice with a view to determining whether this practice is consistent and which reasons can be found to explain any fault lines.

While exclusion clause 1F(c), which is also discussed in Chapter 5 and addresses acts against the purposes and principles of the United Nations, looks difficult to apply at the surface because of its very broad wording and the caution of the UNHCR to use it sparingly, it has found unexpected uses in some quarters, such as in Canada, for serious crimes committed within that country (and that were not part of 1F(b) as that clause has a requirement that a crime has to be committed outside of and before coming to the country of refuge), and in France, where it has been the primary vehicle to penalize perpetrators of international crimes in addition to 1F(a), while in a number of countries, especially the United Kingdom, clause 1F(c) has also been used in relation to terrorist offences.

Chapter 6 is concerned with *refoulement*, specifically the application of articles 32 and 33.2 of the Refugee Convention and the prohibition of removing a person to torture, death, or inhuman or cruel punishment or treatment contained in several of the human rights treaties, primarily the ICCPR, the CAT, and the ECHR. Since there is no provision in the Refugee Convention for an international treaty body with an individual complaints mechanism,[141] such as the Human Rights Committee, the Committee against Torture, or the European Court of Human Rights, the interpretation of these two articles has taken place in UNHCR guidelines and state practice as set out in court and tribunal decisions. As a mirror vision, virtually all the interpretation regarding the prohibition of *refoulement* stems from the just-mentioned three institutions and will, therefore, be examined in some depth, while the jurisprudence of the Inter-American Court of Human Rights with respect to the notions of torture and inhuman treatment will also be given attention. The contours of the various aspects of elements contained in these provisions, such as "danger to the public," "danger to the security," "torture," and "unusual treatment or punishment," will be sketched out with another foray into international criminal law, where some of these concepts have been raised to the level of international crimes, and as such, international criminal jurisprudence could provide another point of view. The conclusion will take all these various approaches and meld them into one cohesive picture.

In Chapter 7, the question is broached of how to deal with situations after a determination of *refoulement* of an excluded person. It may be asked, "What should one do with a torturer who faces torture?" As a result of the implementation of international jurisprudence of the human rights prohibition of *refoulement*, recently the circle of people who cannot be removed has expanded. Countries have attempted to resolve this issue in various manners, from criminal prosecutions, to extraditions, to long-term detentions, to allowing these persons to remain in their country with or without status. This chapter will examine the legal framework in this regard, especially the *aut dedere aut judicare* obligation in international law, as well as practical considerations associated with some of the solutions proposed for this dilemma.

The academic literature, legislation, and jurisprudence are current as of 1 July 2022.

The conclusion of this book, Chapter 8, is designed to identify trends arising out of the historical and comparative analysis. It proposes

141 Article 35 of the Refugee Convention only contains an obligation for state parties to cooperate with the UNHCR and facilitate its duty of supervising the application of its provisions.

solutions to address possible divergent trends as well as determining whether the balance arrived at so far in the international and domestic practice, between the individual rights of the criminal refugee and the collective rights of the society in which they have claimed asylum, is an appropriate one, with suggestions for improvement if the answer to that question is negative. One element in this analysis will be to see whether the political climate surrounding the drafting of the Refugee Convention bears any resemblance to present circumstances. Any comparison in that regard will need to keep in mind that the greatly increased application of the exclusion clause has been seen as connected with the advent and explosive developments of international criminal law in the last thirty years, as well as the grave concern with terrorism, especially since 9/11. This could be usefully contrasted to the situation shortly after the Second World War with the then-renewed interest on the part of the international community in international humanitarian law culminating in the adoption of four Geneva Conventions only two years after the Refugee Convention saw the light of day. Similarly, it had not been that long since the concerns of the international community about terrorism had seen the introduction of the comprehensive 1937 Convention for the Prevention and Punishment of Terrorism.

Comparing this larger framework at the time of the Refugee Convention to the present situation might provide a better insight into whether the main precepts regarding criminality, which underlie exclusion and *refoulement*, are still valid or whether new solutions are necessary. One question that threads its way throughout this book is the nature of criminality in refugee law compared to domestic criminal law or international criminal law.

CHAPTER TWO

A Legal History of Human Rights and Asylum

A. EARLY PRACTICE AND WRITINGS

The custom of giving asylum was well known in antiquity, in the Middle East, Greece, and several other countries,[1] and it could be granted on a religious or secular basis. Religious asylum or sanctuary was sought internally at holy places against powers within the same territory as the place of asylum and was allowed because of the respect of the seeker for a particular deity or church. The secular version, external asylum, was given by kingdoms, republics, and free cities to protect persons from outside their territory from persecution.[2] Territorial asylum can also be seen as part of a larger immigration movement since time immemorial, where aliens with well-established skills and talents were welcomed by political entities. Such aliens were given limited rights, partially in recognition of the fact that the subjects of these same entities required protection when engaged in trade and commerce elsewhere.[3]

These practices became the subject of debate by writers from the fifteenth century on, such as Franciscus de Vitoria, Franciscus Suarez, Hugo Grotius, Samuel von Pufendorf, Christian Wolff, and Emerich

1 Terje Einarsen, "Drafting History of the Convention/New York Protocol" in Andreas Zimmermann, ed, *The 1951 Convention Relating to the Status of Refugees and its 1967 Protocol: A Commentary* (Oxford: Oxford University Press, 2011) at marginal note 4.

2 Atle Grahl-Madsen, *The Status of Refugee in International Law*, vol 2 (Leiden: AW Sijthoff, 1972) at 7–8.

3 James Hathaway, *The Rights of Refugees Under International Law*, 2d ed (Cambridge: Cambridge University Press, 2021) at 10–17.

de Vattel.[4] The writings of Grotius, Pufendorf, and Vattel are especially useful in understanding the various approaches taken to the issues of asylum and refuge in the legal and philosophical literature over these years.

Grotius, who had been a refugee himself and was therefore sympathetic to the plight of asylum seekers, was of the view that "victims of unmerited persecution," or suppliants, had a right to asylum and favourable treatment under certain conditions, including submission to established law and order and any regulations that were necessary to avoid strife. Furthermore, he argued that refugees had no right to demand a share in the government. The inviolable nature of asylum was, however, not designed for those who had committed crimes injurious to humankind and destructive to society.[5]

Pufendorf, on the other hand, was of the view that each state is first and foremost an agent of its own interests. The grant of asylum to non-criminal strangers driven from their homes might well be a commendable "act of humanity" but not something the state should be obliged to do. As well, he felt that refugees should keep quiet and be content with what they had received in the state of reception. Consequently, while Grotius advocated that states should follow common principles of law in their reception of refugees, Pufendorf reduced the notion of asylum to an issue of governmental discretion where the balance of self-interest and reasonableness had to be struck exclusively by the state itself.[6]

Vattel recognized the natural rights of a banished or an exiled person to live elsewhere. He was of the view that there was neither an absolute right for the individual to seek asylum nor a complete discretion for the receiving state to refuse such a person when they were forced to flee their country. Vattel concluded that a person has a conditional right to seek asylum and that only if a state had justifiable reasons could it reject a claim for asylum. In addition, he made an exception to the right of asylum for those criminals who, by the character and frequency of

---

4 Grahl-Madsen, above note 2 at 12.

5 Hugo Grotius, *The Law of War and Peace in Three Books* (1625), translated by Francis W. Kelsey (1925), Book 2, ch 2 at § XVI and ch 21 at § IV at 8; Grahl-Madsen, above note 2 at 13; Einarsen, above note 1 at marginal note 5. This limitation for asylum in Grotius's work was also noted in Germany by the Bundesverwaltungsgericht (Federal Administrative Court), BverwG 10 C 24.08, 11 November 2009, para 24, and in the United Kingdom in *Gurung v Secretary of State for the Home Department*, [2002] UKIAT 04870, para 30.

6 Samuel von Pufendorf, *On the Law of Nature and Nations, Eight Books* (1672), translated by Basil Kennett (1703), Book VIII, ch 11 at §§ 3 and 5; Einarsen, above note 1 at marginal note 5.

their crimes, are a menace to public security everywhere and proclaim themselves enemies of the whole human race. He considered poisoners, assassins, incendiaries, and pirates to fall within this category.[7]

In canvassing these doctrines, it becomes clear that writers such as Grotius and Vattel, who are most disposed toward a state obligation to grant asylum in deserving cases, do not consider such a right absolute, requiring refugees to obey the laws of the country of refuge and being of the view that serious criminals should not be given such a right.

State practice continued to evolve throughout the period of these writings and quite possibly because of them. It was said that the modern era of asylum began in 1685 when Louis XIV of France signed a law repealing the earlier Edict of Nantes, which had resulted in the persecution of Huguenots in France. This example of allowing Huguenots to establish themselves was followed by almost a dozen non-Catholic countries by 1708.[8] This granting of asylum to religious minorities was expanded upon after the French Revolution, when, as a result of the persecution of both aristocrats and others opposed to the various regimes in power, political asylum became much more prominent. The contours of political asylum became intertwined with the concept of sending people back to the country of origin because of crimes committed there. This nascent extradition law fluctuated from sending back political refugees, to refusing to return any asylum seekers, to finding the compromise, first reached in 1833 in Belgium, of not extraditing persons for political crimes. This approach was soon followed by several European countries between 1833 and 1849.[9]

B. THE PERIOD BETWEEN THE FIRST AND SECOND WORLD WARS

As a result of the very large number of people displaced after the First World War and the difficulty of returning them, especially 800,000 Russians, to their countries of origin due to changes in the political climate, the council of the recently established League of Nations decided to

---

7 Emerich de Vattel, *The Law of Nations or the Principles of Natural Law Applied to the Conduct and Affairs of Nations and Sovereigns* (1758), translated by Joseph Chitty, Esq, based on the 1797 edition, Book I: "Of Nations Considered in Themselves," ch 19 at, §§ 231–33; Grahl-Madsen, above note 2 at 14–15.

8 Grahl-Madsen, *ibid* at 8–10.

9 *Ibid.*

convoke a conference on 21 June 1921 on the question of Russian refugees and to authorize the president of the council to appoint Dr. Fridjof Nansen as the first League of Nations High Commissioner for Russian Refugees.[10] In 1922, the first League of Nations' international arrangement to alleviate the situation of postwar refugees was put in place, the Arrangement with Regard to Issue of Certificates of Identity to Russian Refugees.[11] This was followed two years later by a similar arrangement for Armenian refugees.[12] The provisions of these two instruments were expanded and strengthened by the Arrangement Relating to the Issue of Identity Certificates to Russian and Armenian Refugees of 12 May 1926,[13] which applied to the following categories of persons:

> Russian: Any person of Russian origin who does not enjoy or who no longer enjoys the protection of the Government of the Union of Socialist Soviet Republics and who has not acquired another nationality.
>
> Armenian: Any person of Armenian origin formerly a subject of the Ottoman Empire who does not enjoy or who no longer enjoys the protection of the Government of the Turkish Republic and who has not acquired another nationality.[14]

The purpose of this and the previous arrangements was to have states recognize the so-called Nansen certificate or passport as an identity document, which was valid for one year but could be extended by the Office of the High Commissioner, and to issue a return visa to these refugees if they wanted to leave and then come back to their country of refuge.[15]

---

10 Atle Grahl-Madsen, *The Status of Refugee in International Law,* vol I at 12 and 122–27; Alessandra Roversi, "The Evolution of the Refugee Regime and Institutional Responses: Legacies from the Nansen Period" (2003) 22:1 *Refugee Survey Quarterly* 21 at 22–26. For more detail on the political background in that period, see Louise W. Holborn, *The International Refugee Organization: A Specialized Agency of the United Nations, Its History and Work 1946–1952* (London, New York, & Toronto: Oxford University Press, 1956) at 3–7; Louise W. Holborn, *Refugees: A Problem of Our Time: The Work of the United Nations High Commissioner for Refugees, 1951–1972,* vol I (Metuchen, NJ: The Scarecrow Press, 1975) at 3–8; Ivor C. Jackson, *The Refugee Concept in Group Situations* (The Hague/London/Boston: Martinus Nijhoff, 1999) at 11–15; and Hathaway, above note 3 at 19–26.

11 Thirteen League of Nations Treaty Series 237, ratified by fifty-four countries.

12 Plan for the Issue of a Certificate of Identity to Armenian Refugees (*League of Nations Official Journal,* No 7-10, 1924, 969–70), ratified by thirty-eight states; see Holborn, *Refugees,* above note 10 at 9.

13 Eighty-nine League of Nations Treaty Series 47.

14 *Ibid,* art 2.

15 *Ibid,* art 3; this article allowed for exceptions to returning in special cases.

This identity document allowed this category of refugees to travel and resettle in other countries.[16]

As a result of the Intergovernmental Conference on the Legal Status of Refugees on 28 June 1928,[17] similar arrangements were made for refugees of Assyrian, Assyro-Chaldean, Syrian, Kurdish, and Turkish origin,[18] while there were also the beginnings of efforts to regulate the legal status of Russian and Armenian refugees with respect to some civil rights in the country of refuge.[19] As all these arrangements were ad hoc and did not set out in any detail the status of the persons who had been given a Nansen certificate, and because *refoulement* became more prominent due to the economic crisis at the time, the Intergovernmental Conference in October 1933 was instrumental in creating the more general Convention relating to the International Status of Refugees of 28 October 1933.[20] This treaty does not give a definition of refugee but makes reference to holders of Nansen certificates.[21] It provides that such persons are entitled to the most favourable treatment given to nationals of a foreign country residing in the country of refuge.[22] As well, such persons have a right not to be expelled or *refouled*,[23] except "by reasons of national security or public order."[24] Regarding the notion of public order, the drafters of the convention were of the view that it should not be applied to trivial matters but only in extreme cases and that a

16 The technical aspects of the main benefit of resettlement, the finding of employment, were carried out by the International Labour Organization; see Holborn, *Refugees*, above note 10 at 16.

17 Grahl-Madsen, above note 10 at 127–30.

18 The instrument is called the Arrangement concerning the Extension to other Categories of Refugees of certain Measures taken in favour of Russian and Armenian Refugees of 28 June 1928 (89 League of Nations Treaty Series 63), which was recognized by thirteen governments; for more detail, see Jackson, above note 10 at 15–18, and Guy S. Goodwin-Gill & Jane McAdam, *The Refugee in International Law*, 4th ed (Oxford: Oxford University Press, 2021) at 16–18.

19 Arrangement relating to the Legal Status of Russian and Armenian Refugees of 30 June 1928 (89 League of Nations Treaty Series 53).

20 159 League of Nations Treaty Series 199; see Grahl-Madsen, above note 10 at 130–31; Roversi, above note 10 at 27–28, and UNHCR, *Commentary on the Refugee Convention 1951 Articles 2–11, 13–37* October 1997 (written by Professor Atle Grahl-Madsen in 1963; republished by the UNHCR Division of International Protection in October 1997) at 109–11. It was ratified by eight countries; see Holborn, *Refugees*, above note 10 at 15–16, and Grahl-Madsen, above note 2 at 96, n38.

21 Article 2.

22 Articles 4–10.

23 Hathaway, above note 3 at 19–26.

24 Article 3.

criminal conviction in itself should not automatically result in expulsion or *refoulement*.[25] This is reflected in the following commentary:

> Taking into consideration that refugees as a rule had nowhere to go, once they were expelled, it was obviously the intention of the drafters that expulsion should only be resorted to in those extreme cases where the continued presence of the refugee would to some extent upset the very equilibrium of society.[26]

The Nansen certificate approach was extended to refugees from the Saar in 1935,[27] from Germany in 1938,[28] and from Austria in 1939.[29] The Convention Related to German Refugees (implicitly followed by the Austrian Protocol) reflected the most recent developments in international refugee law at that time in that it was the most extensive instrument and incorporated elements of earlier arrangements. On the one hand, it followed the description in earlier treaties of what constitutes a refugee by an evaluation of an objective situation in a given country plus the two requirements of being a national of that country and not being able to find protection in that country, while, on the other hand, it included the 1933 benefits, including the prohibition against *refoulement* taken from the 1933 Refugee Convention.[30] This prohibition contains an exception, like the 1933 convention, for national security or public order.[31]

C. THE UNITED NATIONS RELIEF AND REHABILITATION AGENCY

In 1943, during the Second World War, the governments of forty-four allied nations created the United Nations Relief and Rehabilitation

25 UNHCR, *Commentary on the Refugee Convention 1951*, above 20 at 123–24.

26 *Ibid* at 124.

27 Called the Arrangement for the Issue of a Certificate of Identity to Refugees from the Saar (1935 League of Nations Official Journal 1681).

28 Called the Convention concerning the Status of Refugees Coming from Germany (192 League of Nations Treaty Series 59), ratified by three states (see Grahl-Madsen, above note 2 at 96, n38). For the negotiation background, see UNHCR, *Commentary on the Refugee Convention 1951*, above note 20 at 111–12.

29 Called the Additional Protocol to the Provisional Arrangement and to the Convention concerning the Status of Refugees Coming from Germany (198 League of Nations Treaty Series 141) [Austrian Protocol]; see Grahl-Madsen, above note 2 at 131–33; Jackson, above note 10 at 18–21; and Goodwin-Gill & McAdam, above note 18 at 17–18.

30 Articles 1 and 6-16.

31 Article 5.2.

Agency (UNRRA) to deal with the issue of displaced persons in Europe. It was designed as a temporary agency with the limited goal of assisting the return of people belonging to allied countries. It had a council as its policy-making body and a director general with executive authority.[32] It ceased activities in 1947.[33]

In August 1945, the council adopted a resolution, which stated:

> [T]he Administration will not assist displaced persons who may be detained in the custody of the military or civilian authorities of any of the United Nations on charges of having collaborated with the enemy or having committed other crimes against the interests or nationals of the United Nations.[34]

This resolution was amended in May 1946 to the effect that merely a determination of being a collaborator by military authorities was sufficient to deny assistance irrespective of being in custody.[35]

D. THE INTERNATIONAL REFUGEE ORGANIZATION

The idea of creating an international refugee organization was first discussed on 7 May 1945 during the San Francisco conference at which the Charter of the United Nations was drafted. Because of the importance of refugee issues, a considerable amount of time was devoted to a discussion of this problem during the first session of the General Assembly of the United Nations on 15 December 1945. This led to a resolution accepting an agreement for interim measures to establish an international refugee organization and referring the matter on 19 January 1946 for further debate to the Third Committee given its mandate over social, humanitarian, and cultural questions.[36]

---

32 Agreement for United Nations Relief and Rehabilitation Administration, 9 November 1943, arts III & IV.

33 Roversi, above note 10 at 30; Holborn, *Refugees*, above note 10 at 23–26; and Holborn, *The International Refugee Organization*, above note 10 at 12–27.

34 Resolution 71, para 2(a); see Grahl-Madsen, above note 10 at 271.

35 Resolution 92, para 5; see Grahl-Madsen, above note 10 at 271.

36 Holborn, *The International Refugee Organization*, above note 10 at 30–31; see, also, Einarsen, above note 1 at marginal notes 12–17.

1) Drafting the Constitution of the International Refugee Organization

The very first debate in the Third Committee showed differences of approach between Western nations and Eastern bloc countries. For example, the Netherlands proposed that the resettlement of refugees should be the responsibility of an international organization, while the former Union of Soviet Socialist Republics (USSR or Soviet Union) wanted to make such resettlement conditional on the consent of the country of origin. The Soviet Union also introduced a draft resolution on 4 February 1946 to the effect that

> quislings, traitors and war criminals, as persons dishonoured for the collaboration with the enemies of the United Nations in any form, should not be regarded as refugees who are entitled to get protection from the United Nations, and that quislings, traitors and war criminals who are still hiding, under the guise of refugees, should be immediately returned to their countries.[37]

The United States proposed a compromise, indicating that forcible repatriation should not occur, but there should be no interference with the surrender and punishment of war criminals, quislings, and traitors in conformity with international arrangements.[38]

On 12 February 1946, after a report by the Third Committee, the General Assembly passed a resolution in which it was recognized that the problem of refugees and displaced persons was one of immediate urgency and that there was a necessity to distinguish between genuine refugees and displaced persons on the one hand and war criminals, quislings, and traitors on the other. The assembly also recommended that the Economic and Social Council (ECOSOC) establish the Special Committee on Refugees and Displaced Persons to examine all aspects of this issue.[39]

This special committee's deliberations resulted in a report with a draft constitution for a non-permanent organization to be called the International Refugee Organization (IRO) and established as a specialized agency of the United Nations. Its report was considered by the ECOSOC at its second session in June 1946; the ECOSOC approved

---

37 Holborn, *The International Refugee Organization*, above note 10 at 32.

38 *Ibid* at 32–33.

39 Jackson, above note 10 at 26; see, also, Sibylle Kapferer, "Article 14(2) of the Universal Declaration of Human Rights and Exclusion from International Refugee Protection" (2008) 27 *Refugee Survey Quarterly* 53 at 56–58.

the draft constitution on 21 June 1946, submitted it to governments for comments, approved an amended version of it on 3 October 1946, and transmitted the document to the General Assembly via the Third Committee for final adoption the same day.[40] The General Assembly accepted the proposal on 15 December 1946.[41]

During the debates in the Third Committee in November 1946, the concern that war criminals, quislings, and traitors should not be assisted by the IRO was repeated by many countries, such as Brazil, Belgium, France, the Netherlands, and Argentina, while the USSR went further and suggested the addition of a paragraph that would name certain military formations that had "the blood of thousands of people on their hands." This proposal was supported by other Eastern bloc countries, such as Yugoslavia, Ukraine, Byelorussia, and Poland, but was rejected by the majority, which were of the view that those groups were already covered by the Constitution.[42]

The earlier debates in the Special Committee dealt mainly with the nature of the organization, the definition of refugees, and the distinction between genuine refugees and objectionable persons. With respect to the first question, the discussion centred on the options of making this organization a permanent body integrated within the United Nations or a temporary agency with a special arrangement with the United Nations. The latter view carried the day.[43] The issue of definition was related to the desire of certain countries to go beyond the pre–Second World War arrangements, which only defined objective categories of refugees without identifying the subjective element of fear of persecution. The compromise reached was to include "victims of persecution for reasons of race, religion, nationality or political opinions" as one category among five, of which the other four were still objectively oriented by, for instance, stating "victims of Nazi or fascist regimes" or "Spanish Republicans or other victims of the Falangist regime in Spain."[44] The definition in the Constitution of the IRO as finally adopted by the General Assembly maintained this approach by only including the above three instances within the definition of refugee (and eliminating the words "victims of persecution"). As a result, the definition of refugee read:

---

40 *Ibid* at 60.

41 Jackson, above note 10 at 30–31, and Holborn, *The International Refugee Organization*, above note 10 at 43–46.

42 Kapferer, above note 39 at 60.

43 Holborn, *The International Refugee Organization*, above note 10 at 35–36.

44 Jackson, above note 10 at 30 and 33–39.

> [T]he term "refugee" applies to a person who has left, or who is outside of, his country of nationality or of former habitual residence, and who, whether or not he had retained his nationality, belongs to one of the following categories:
>
> (a) victims of the nazi or fascist regimes or of regimes which took part on their side in the second world war, or of the quisling or similar regimes which assisted them against the United Nations, whether enjoying international status as refugees or not;
>
> (b) Spanish Republicans and other victims of the Falangist regime in Spain, whether enjoying international status as refugees or not;
>
> (c) persons who were considered refugees before the outbreak of the second world war, for reasons of race, religion, nationality or political opinion.[45]

The clarification of the distinction between genuine refugees and war criminals was related to the issue of whether political dissidents who had not actively assisted the enemy during the war but who opposed the new regimes after the war should come within the mandate of the new refugee organization. Western states were of the view that political dissidents were entitled to protection, although leaders of groups of dissidents should be denied assistance, while the Eastern bloc countries indicated that only persons who wanted to return to their home countries were entitled to assistance, with the result that any other person was a quisling, war criminal, collaborator, or traitor.[46] This issue was resolved by including a limited form of exclusion from the mandate of the IRO, applicable to people who after the war

> (a) have participated in any organization having as one of its purpose the overthrow by armed force of the country of their origin, being a Member of the United Nations; or the overthrow by armed force of the Government of any other Member of the United Nations, or have participated in any terrorist organization;
>
> (b) have become leaders of movements hostile to the government of their country of origin being a Member of the United Nations or sponsors of movements encouraging refugees not to return to their country of origin.[47]

45 Annex I to the IRO Constitution, Part I, Section A, para 1.

46 Holborn, *The International Refugee Organization*, above note 10 at 37–39.

47 Annex I to the IRO Constitution, Part II, art 6, which also has this non-criminal portion in paragraph c: "at the time of application for assistance, are in the military or civil service of a foreign state."

2) The International Refugee Organization Mandate in Practice

The IRO, which operated between 1947 and 1952[48] and dealt with the urgent needs of more than 1.5 million persons, based its mandate in its Constitution. The structure of Annex I of the Constitution,[49] which sets out the manner in which assistance is to be provided to refugees and displaced persons, starts with the principle that the organization will provide assistance in the repatriation of such persons unless they had expressed a valid objection against their countries of nationality or former habitual residence to returning to those countries. The main valid objection to returning was "persecution, or fear, based on reasonable grounds of persecution because of race, religion, nationality or political opinions, provided these opinions are not in conflict with the principles of the United Nations, as laid down in the Preamble of the Charter of the United Nations."[50]

The IRO would not provide assistance to certain persons as set out in six categories, four of which pertain to criminal activities,[51] including the members of organizations mentioned above, as well as

---

48 The IRO was operational between 1 July 1947 and February 1952, while it spent another year and a half, until September 1953, liquidating its operations (see Holborn, *The International Refugee Organization*, above note 10 at 68); at its peak, it employed between 2,500 and almost 3,000 personnel, assisted by another 3,200 local staff and so-called indigenous labour for the maintenance of camps and other IRO installations in allied occupied countries, which in Germany alone numbered over 90,000 (*ibid* at 87); as of 31 December 1951, the organization had registered 1,619,008 persons, of which 1,208,586 were resettled or repatriated (*ibid* at 202).

49 The Constitution itself is primarily organizational, while the criteria for which persons come within its mandate are contained in Annex I to this constitution; see, also, Holborn, *The International Refugee Organization,* above note 10, at 47–53.

50 Annex I to the IRO Constitution, Part I, Section C, para 1(a)(i).

51 The non-criminal categories are:

> 4. Persons of German ethnic origin, whether German nationals or members of German minorities in other countries, who:
> (a) have been or may be transferred to Germany from other countries;
> (b) have been, during the second world war, evacuated from Germany to other countries;
> (c) have fled from, or into, Germany, or from their places of residence into countries other than Germany in order to avoid falling into the hands of Allied armies.
>
> 5. Persons who are in receipt of financial support and protection from their country of nationality, unless their country of nationality requests international assistance for them.

The annex also contains a cessation clause in Part I, Section D, which is very similar to the one in the later Refugee Convention, mentioned in Chapter 1.

1. war criminals, quislings, and traitors.
2. any other persons who can be shown:
   (a) to have assisted the enemy in persecuting civil populations of countries, Members of the United Nations; or
   (b) to have voluntarily assisted the enemy forces since the outbreak of the second world war in their operations against the United Nations.
3. ordinary criminals who are extraditable by treaty.[52]

The annex itself contains one interpretative note with respect to the criminal exclusion, in respect to paragraph 2(b), and states:

> Mere continuance of normal and peaceful duties, not performed with the specific purpose of aiding the enemy against the Allies or against the civil population of territory in enemy occupation, shall not be considered to constitute "voluntary assistance." Nor shall acts of general humanity, such as care of wounded or dying, be so considered except in cases where help of this nature given to enemy nationals could equally well have been given to Allied nationals and was purposely withheld from them.

A more detailed interpretation of the contents of these provisions can be found in an internal manual, which was used in the field.[53] This manual considers that the expression "war criminals" applies to persons who have committed crimes against peace (that is, those who have planned aggressive war); violations of the accepted rules of warfare, which, according to the manual, includes "murder of prisoners, murder of hostages and other crimes of which there is a list of about 20"; and crimes against humanity, which includes "internment of civilians in inhuman conditions, extermination of Jews in gas chambers."[54] The manual also makes it clear that a conviction for such crimes is not a requirement for

52 Annex I to the IRO Constitution, Part II; see, also, Grahl-Madsen, above note 10 at 271–72; Kapferer, above note 39 at 58–61. The exclusion of war criminals in this document has been noted in Germany by the Bundesverwaltungsgericht (Federal Administrative Court), BverwG 10 C 24.08, 11 November 2009, para 25.

53 International Refugee Organization, *Manual for Eligibility Officers* (Genève: Imprimeries Populaires, 1950); this manual also interpreted the other provisions of Annex I. See Holborn, *Refugees*, above note 10 at 207. It has been referred to in the United States in the cases of *INS v Cardoza-Fonseca*, 480 US 421 (1987), and *United States v Kowalchuk*, 773 F2d 488 (3rd Cir 1985), as well as in Canada in the case of *Minister of Citizenship and Immigration and Vitols*, T-310-97, 23 September 1998, while Annex I itself was mentioned by the US Supreme Court in *Negusie v Holder*, 129 S Ct 1159 (2009) and *Fedorenko v United States*, 499 US 490 (1981).

54 International Refugee Organization, above note 53 at 31, para 5.

excluding a person, but people who are accused or suspected can also fall within the ambit of that provision, although it is not clear in which circumstances such an accusation or a suspicion would result in exclusion or what process is required to make such a determination.[55]

According to this document,

> quislings are generally understood to be persons who, while occupying high public office, have committed acts which amount to treason under the laws of their respective countries of origin, and in doing so, have acted in that office under the direction of—or in coordination with—the enemy. In other words, quislings were leaders or key men of governments or semi-governmental organizations, which were in sympathy with and actually helped the Nazis.[56]

This is further expanded upon by indicating when considering a case file that it also includes a government whose creation had been sponsored by the enemy, that the policy of that government resulted in assistance to the enemy, and that government officials had accepted their positions without compulsion or duress.[57] Traitors are persons who have been convicted or charged for high treason, but this does not include desertion from military forces.[58]

The terms "assistance" and "voluntary" are the subjects of detailed instructions. Assistance needs to be substantial and given with the intention of helping the enemy.[59] It could fit within three categories: military, administrative, and economic. Military assistance included voluntary enlistment in the German army or other forces or other acts designed to help the German army.[60] Administrative assistance is considered support given by members of the local administration to the occupying army with the specific intent of helping them win the war, but mere continuance of normal or peaceful duties does not fall within this rubric.[61] Similarly, not all forms of economic assistance are seen as negative, only those types that aided the enemy forces in their operations. It was primarily directed at the arms manufacturer segment of society.[62]

---

55 *Ibid* at 31, para 6.
56 *Ibid* at 32, para 12.
57 *Ibid* at 32(1).
58 *Ibid* at 32, para 14.
59 *Ibid* at 34, para 32.
60 *Ibid* at 33, para 24.
61 *Ibid* at 34, para 30.
62 *Ibid* at 34, para 31.

While motivation is irrelevant, other factors, such as age, sex, degree of education and intelligence, rank, social condition, and the amount of pressure put on the person and the ability to resist such pressure, were to be taken into account as part of a determination of whether a person assisted enemy forces.[63] These latter factors also played a role in the examination of the voluntariness of the assistance by indicating that members of armies of satellite states such as Hungary or Romania were generally not seen as having assisted voluntarily unless they were very high officers in decision-making positions or unless they undertook special service indicating their pro-Nazi stance.[64] Conscription is usually connoted with involuntary assistance with the exception of initial conscription in the general German army but then opting to serve in organizations specifically designed to uphold the Nazi regime, such as SS units, the Gestapo, and especially dangerous military formations such as commandos or paratroopers.[65]

The category of ordinary criminals extraditable by treaty was not often applied, "since the majority of crimes are committed by refugees in the country of haven, the use of this clause is restricted."[66] The manual allows for personal circumstances to play a role in determining whether to provide IRO assistance in two aspects. First, a distinction is made between habitual criminals who should not be within the mandate of the IRO as opposed to persons who committed one crime of little importance.[67] Second, it is emphasized that in the same manner in which a criminal court balances the nature of the crime against the punishment to be imposed, so should the IRO.[68]

As to the seriousness of the crimes that should be included in this category, a lengthy list is provided, varying from crimes against persons (murder, rape, arson, assault, and causing grave injury), crimes against property (malicious destruction), and crimes against public morals (bigamy and perjury) to economic crimes such as forgery, issuing of counterfeit money, theft, bankruptcy, receiving stolen goods, and embezzlement.[69]

---

63 *Ibid* at 34, para 32.

64 *Ibid* at 34, para 25.

65 *Ibid* at 33–34, paras 27–28. The manual provides more detail about smaller units in the SS, the German army, and other nefarious organizations at 104–15.

66 *Ibid* at 35, para 36.

67 *Ibid* at 35, para 37.

68 *Ibid* at 35, para 38.

69 *Ibid* at 34–35, para 34.

The last exclusion for criminal activities, subversion and terrorism, is not directed at people involved in the overthrow of government by legal or peaceful means but only those who want to accomplish this result by armed force.[70] However, the manual interprets the term "participated" as meaning "membership or participation" in an organization, while participation can include financial support.[71]

E. THE UNIVERSAL DECLARATION OF HUMAN RIGHTS

The first step toward the seminal Universal Declaration of Human Rights (UDHR) began with the establishment of the United Nations' Commission on Human Rights on 16 February 1946 by the ECOSOC during its first session.[72] This commission established a drafting committee, which received its terms of reference on 24 March 1947.[73] The function of the Drafting Committee was to prepare, on the basis of documentation supplied by the United Nations Secretariat, a preliminary draft of an International Bill of Human Rights.[74] This committee had its first meeting from 9 June to 25 June 1947.[75]

Apart from the documentation prepared by the Secretariat, the Drafting Committee also had before it proposals by the United Kingdom and the United States, none of which contained a reference to asylum or refugees.[76] The committee formed a temporary working group, whose purpose was to rearrange the draft articles suggested and to redraft certain articles based on discussions in the committee.[77] This working group produced a draft, which included the following article 33: "Every State has

---

70 *Ibid* at 39, para 64.

71 *Ibid*. The manual also included ineligibility for membership in certain groups outside Germany, such as the Hlinka Guard in Slovakia (at 63), the Hunyadi Division in Hungary (at 74), the Iron Guard in Romania (at 78), the State Security Police and the Military Police in Bulgaria (at 82), and the Ustas in Croatia (at 89).

72 United Nations, *Yearbook on Human Rights for 1947* (Lake Success, NY: UN, 1949) at 421, online: https://digitallibrary.un.org/record/860913?ln=en.

73 *Ibid* at 482.

74 *Ibid*.

75 *Yearbook of the United Nations, 1946–47* (Lake Success, NY: UN, 1947) at 525, online: www.unmultimedia.org/searchers/yearbook/page.jsp?bookpage=4&volume=1946-47.

76 *Yearbook on Human Rights for 1947*, above note 72 at 484–86 for the draft prepared by the Secretariat, at 487–92 for the UK proposal, and at 492–95 for the US proposal.

77 Ibid at 485.

the right to grant asylum to political refugees."[78] The Drafting Committee agreed that the right of asylum should be included in the draft bill.[79]

During the debates of the Drafting Committee, the French representative made the comment that common criminals should be excluded from the right to asylum.[80] On 20 June 1947, the USSR representative echoed statements by that country on 4 February 1946 during the deliberations regarding the establishment of the IRO, to the effect that quislings, traitors, and war criminals should not be regarded as refugees, by observing that the Moscow Declaration[81] was being neglected and asking if some sort of reservation to that effect would be made.[82] The French representative answered by saying that he wanted to reserve the question of criminals in general and of the obligations of extradition incumbent on states, which might also apply to war criminals.[83] No further steps were undertaken to follow up on these suggestions.

The Commission on Human Rights considered the preliminary draft of its drafting committee during its second session in Geneva from 2 to 17 December 1947.[84] During this session, the commission decided on a terminology to be used in referring to the three documents, which together were to constitute the International Bill of Human Rights: a Declaration of Human Rights, a Covenant on Human Rights, and Measures of Implementation.[85]

The commission decided that the declaration would be a simple statement defining human rights and fundamental freedoms, and its force, upon adoption by the General Assembly, would be more of a

---

78 *Ibid* at 497.

79 *Ibid* at 483; *Yearbook of the United Nations, 1946–47*, above note 75 at 526. For more detail regarding the concept of refugee in the declaration, see Einarsen, above note 1 at marginal notes 18–20, and Kapferer, above note 39 at 61–62.

80 UN Doc E/CN.4/AC.1/SR.9 at 8.

81 The Moscow Declaration was signed during the Moscow Conference on 30 October 1943; the formal name of the declaration was Declaration of the Four Nations on General Security, and it had, among other topics, a "Statement of Declaration," which led to the London Charter of the International Military Tribunal in Nuremberg on 8 August 1945 [London Charter].

82 UN Doc E/CN.4/AC.1/SR.13 at 11; see, also, Mary Ann Glendon, *A World Made New: Eleanor Roosevelt and the Universal Declaration of Human Rights* (New York: Random House, 2001) at 92, and Johannes Morsink, *The Universal Declaration of Human Rights* (Philadelphia: University of Pennsylvania Press, 1999) at 76.

83 UN Doc E/CN.4/AC.1/SR.13 at 11.

84 *Yearbook of the United Nations, 1947–48* (Lake Success, NY: UN, 1949) at 572 , online: www.unmultimedia.org/searchers/yearbook/page.jsp?volume=1947-48&page=1.

85 United Nations, *Yearbook on Human Rights for 1948* (Lake Success, NY: UN, 1950) at 457, online: https://digitallibrary.un.org/record/860914?ln=en.

moral rather than a legal nature. The declaration would establish and indicate goals rather than impose precise obligations upon states. The covenant, on the other hand, was visualized as an instrument that would legally bind the states acceding to it. Such states would undertake to make their national laws conform to its standards and would agree to the imposition of sanctions in the case of violation of the rights enumerated therein. The Measures of Implementation were only related to the proposed covenant and possible future conventions.[86]

With respect to asylum, some members of the newly established Working Group on a Declaration of Human Rights requested that ordinary criminals, who were generally the subject of extradition law, and all those whose acts were contrary to the principles and purposes of the United Nations be explicitly excluded from the right of asylum.[87] The working group agreed on the following sentence: "This right will not be accorded to criminals nor to those whose acts are contrary to the principles and aims of the United Nations."[88] The commission decided during the first week of January 1948 that the above documents should be forwarded to governments for their comments and requested that the secretary-general fix 3 April 1948 as the date for governments to send replies.[89] As a result of comments received, the Drafting Committee of the Commission on Human Rights held its second session from 3 to 21 May 1948.[90]

The first comment with respect to asylum during this session was made on 7 May 1948 when the French representative stated that France would reserve its right to expel foreigners who disturbed public order and morality.[91] The Chilean representative, responding to a comment by the USSR representative that the article on asylum should have a paragraph two excluding war criminals from the benefit of asylum, stated that it would be unwise to include such a paragraph, which attempted to cover cases of special criminals and did not clearly state these cases as an exception, the result of which would be that persons would be condemned *à posterior*. He felt that war criminals should be covered by other conventions.[92]

86 *Yearbook of the United Nations, 1947–48*, above note 84 at 573.
87 Kapferer, above note 39 at 62.
88 *Ibid*; Morsink, above note 82 at 76–77.
89 *Yearbook of the United Nations, 1947–48*, above note 84 at 573.
90 *Ibid* at 574.
91 UN Doc E/CN.4/AC.1/SR 25 at 7.
92 *Ibid* at 9.

On 12 May 1948, the Chilean representative made the same comment as five days earlier. As a result, it was agreed that article 14 on asylum should be accepted as it stood, with the deletion of paragraph two, and that a new article should be drafted to deal with war criminals.[93] The next day, this issue was revisited when the British representative indicated that he wanted to retain paragraph two, and the USSR representative agreed. The Chilean representative then indicated that although he felt that war criminals should be dealt with separately, this would cause more problems than retaining this paragraph; therefore, he would be in favour of the United Kingdom's suggestion. The chair, on behalf of the United States, felt that retaining this paragraph on war criminals would usurp the work of another United Nations organ, the International Law Commission, which had recently been given a mandate to look at the issue of war criminals in the context of developing international law. The French representative, however, also agreed with the United Kingdom, and as a result, paragraph two dealing with the exemption of war criminals was accepted as part of the article on asylum.[94]

On 18 May 1948, the Drafting Committee discussed new text for paragraph two, which was drawn up by its Drafting Sub-Committee and constituted of the representatives of China, France, and the United Kingdom. The new text read: "[P]rosecutions genuinely arising from non-political crimes or acts contrary to the purposes and principles of the United Nations do not constitute persecution."[95]

The USSR wanted to add that asylum would not be granted to fascists and Nazis who had been prosecuted for their activities.[96] The United Kingdom believed these activities formed part of acts against the purposes and principles of the United Nations, in response to which the USSR representative asked whether that would be the correct interpretation. Both the French and Chilean representatives agreed that that was indeed the case.[97] Consequently, the whole committee accepted this wording.[98]

93 UN Doc E/CN.4/AC.1/SR 30 at 11.
94 UN Doc E/CN.4/AC.1/SR 31 at 1–5.
95 UN Doc E/CN.4/AC.1/SR 37 at 8.
96 UN Doc E/CN.4/AC.1/SR 37 at 11.
97 *Ibid* at 12.
98 *Ibid* at 14.

The Drafting Committee presented the report of its second session to the Commission on Human Rights on 21 May 1948,[99] attaching a redraft of the proposed International Declaration of Human Rights, which contained the following article 11:

1. Everyone has the right to seek and may be granted, in other countries, asylum from persecution;
2. Prosecutions genuinely arising from non-political crimes or acts contrary to the purposes and principles of the United Nations do not constitute persecution. [*Note.* The representative of the Soviet Union proposed that the following text be submitted for the above text of article 11 (unofficial translation): "The right of asylum shall be granted to everyone persecuted because of his activity in defense of democratic interests, because of his activity in the field of science, or because of his participation in the struggle for national liberty."][100]

During the third session of the Commission on Human Rights in May and June 1948, India and the United Kingdom proposed deleting the limitation in article 11 as part of a wider proposal to streamline the draft declaration to general statements of principle. This was supported by the United States and Belgium but opposed by communist countries.[101] The Byelorussian representative was of the view that he was unable to accept this deletion, bearing in mind the suffering of the people in Byelorussia and of Byelorussian and Western European Jews in a ghetto in Minsk, while the Ukrainian delegate found it impossible to avoid reference to activities against the United Nations and against democracy. Lastly, the USSR made it clear that without paragraph 2, even if it was not entirely acceptable, this article would have no value whatsoever. The motion to delete the second paragraph was defeated.[102]

The Commission on Human Rights examined the text of the draft declaration of the Drafting Committee and adopted a new text on 28 June 1948, while the article dealing with asylum (now article 12) remained virtually the same (only the word "may" in the first paragraph had been

99 *Yearbook on Human Rights for 1948*, above note 85 at 457.
100 *Ibid* at 459; this proposal was referred to in the Third Committee meetings as UN Doc E/800 at 33.
101 Kapferer, above note 39 at 63.
102 *Ibid.*

deleted), then transmitted the text to the ECOSOC.[103] The ECOSOC, in turn, on 26 August 1948, during its seventh session, transmitted the draft declaration to the General Assembly without changes but with comments made by several representatives during its meetings.[104]

On 24 September 1948, the General Assembly referred consideration of the draft declaration to its Third Committee,[105] where the article on asylum was debated on 3–4 November 1948.[106] The only change to this article was made in paragraph 1, where the words "and be granted" were changed to "and to enjoy" as a result of a British proposal.[107] This text was accepted a day later.[108]

During the deliberations in the Third Committee, several comments were made with respect to paragraph 2 of the article. The USSR representative stated that the article should be framed in a way that war criminals, fascists, and Nazis hiding abroad, particularly in occupied Germany, could not claim to be persecuted persons.[109] The representative of the Philippines agreed with this statement.[110] The representative of Yugoslavia also felt that the limitations in paragraph 2 were insufficient in that they ignored the new provisions established in postwar international documents, all of which related to the prosecution and punishment of war criminals. He was, therefore, unable to agree to a provision drafted in too general terms, which could result in the benefit of asylum being extended to war criminals and traitors. He would therefore vote for the USSR amendment.[111]

The next day, the Polish representative expressed the same sentiments, as did the representative of the Ukraine,[112] while the French representative warned of overexpansion and overrestriction of paragraph 2 and defended the wording as submitted.[113] The French delegate opposed the Soviet proposal, saying that paragraph 2 contained all the necessary

103 *Yearbook on Human Rights for 1948*, above note 85 at 462–63.

104 *Ibid* at 464; see, also, *Yearbook of the United Nations, 1947–48*, above note 84 at 576–78.

105 *Yearbook on Human Rights for 1948*, above note 85 at 465.

106 UN Doc, Official Records of the Third Session of the General Assembly, Part I, Social, Humanitarian and Cultural Questions, Third Committee, Summary Records of Meetings, 21 September–8 December at 327–48; see also, UN Doc A/C.3/SR 121 & 122.

107 UN Doc, Official Records of the Third Session of the General Assembly, above note 106 at 330.

108 *Ibid* at 344.

109 *Ibid* at 327.

110 *Ibid* at 335.

111 *Ibid* at 339.

112 *Ibid* at 341.

113 *Ibid* at 342.

limitations and reservations, while the United States indicated that it saw no reason to change what it considered to be a very reasonable limitation in that article.[114] The representative of Pakistan argued that by denying the right of asylum to all those guilty of acts contrary to the purposes and principles of the United Nations, the provisions of paragraph 2 denied asylum to the Nazis and fascists, which the USSR wanted to exclude from the benefits of this article 12.[115]

The USSR representative believed that his amendment was not covered by paragraph 2 of the proposed article, as suggested by the United States and Chile, and would, as a result, provide a loophole for war criminals.[116] The USSR amendment was rejected after taking a roll call,[117] while the entire article 12 was adopted the same day.[118] In explanation, the USSR representative stated that he had been able to vote in favour of paragraph 2 of article 12 on the understanding that no country would give shelter to war criminals on the grounds that their crimes were committed before the United Nations had come into being since the purposes and principles of the United Nations had at that time already been recognized by all democratic peoples and that no objection had been raised to that interpretation by any member of the committee.[119]

As a result of a considerable number of amendments adopted during the meetings of the Third Committee, a sub-committee was set up to consider the Declaration of Human Rights as a whole, from the point of view of arrangement, consistency, uniformity, and style.[120] As a result of the work of this sub-committee, the commas disappeared in the first paragraph of the article dealing with asylum, while the first word and the last four words of paragraph 2, "prosecutions . . . do not constitute persecution," were reworked to read: "This right might not be invoked in the case of prosecutions."

The representative of the USSR said "that he was not opposed to paragraph 2 but noted that the Sub-Committee had not merely altered the wording of the original text but rather had touched upon the substance

114 Kapferer, above note 39 at 64.

115 *Ibid.*

116 UN Doc, Official Records of the Third Session of the General Assembly, above note 106 at 342–43.

117 *Ibid* at 343.

118 *Ibid* at 346.

119 *Ibid* at 347.

120 *Yearbook on Human Rights for 1948*, above note 85 at 465.

of the question."[121] No response to this comment was received,[122] and, finally, the article was renumbered as article 14 and now read: "This right may not be invoked in the case of prosecutions genuinely arising from non-political crimes or from acts contrary to the purposes and principles of the United Nations." The report of the sub-committee was adopted by the Third Committee, resulting in the adoption of the draft UDHR by the Third Committee and its submission to the General Assembly.[123] The General Assembly adopted the report of the Third Committee on 10 December 1948 after voting on each article and the declaration as a whole. Only one article was deleted, while virtually all the other articles, including article 14,[124] were adopted unanimously.[125]

F. THE 1951 CONVENTION RELATING TO THE STATUS OF REFUGEES

1) Introduction

Less than a year after its adoption of the UDHR, the General Assembly of the United Nations, on 3 December 1949, decided to establish the High Commissioner's Office for Refugees, to be functional as of 1 January 1951, the date when the IRO would cease to operate. At the same time, it requested that the ECOSOC prepare a resolution setting out the functions of this office while also providing recommendations with respect to the definition of "refugee" to be used by that same office.[126]

ECOSOC established the Ad Hoc Committee on Statelessness and Related Problems, which examined draft resolutions from various countries, as well as its Secretariat, during its first meeting, held

121 *Ibid.*

122 Kapferer, above note 39 at 65.

123 *Yearbook on Human Rights for 1948*, above note 85 at 465.

124 *Ibid* at 465.

125 *Ibid* at 465–66.

126 UN Doc A/RES/319(IV)A. This resolution had been preceded by work in the ECOSOC and the Third Committee earlier that year about issues such as the relation of the new agency to other organs of the United Nations, the selection of the high commissioner, the lifespan of the agency, and the persons who should receive assistance; the latter issue caused a disagreement between some European countries, which expressed concern about the great financial burden they would face as a result of the large number of refugees on their territories, on the one hand, and countries such as Australia, the United States, and the United Kingdom that wanted to have as many refugees settled as possible on the other; for more detail, see Holborn, *Refugees*, above note 10 at 65–75.

from 16 January to 16 February 1950, and drew up a draft convention related to the status of refugees, which was submitted to ECOSOC. The Social Committee of the ECOSOC discussed the work in relation to the proposed convention between 31 July and 10 August 1950, after which it submitted its report, which included a preamble and a definition of "refugee," as well as a recommendation for the Ad Hoc Committee to continue its work.[127] ECOSOC examined the report of its Social Committee and accepted its recommendation on 16 August 1950. The Ad Hoc Committee, under its new name, the Ad Hoc Committee on Refugees and Stateless Persons, resumed its work during its second session, held from 14 to 25 August 1950. Work during this session resulted in a revised draft convention, except for the definition of refugee. The Ad Hoc Committee submitted the draft convention to ECOSOC,[128] as well as the draft statute of the United Nations High Commissioner for Refugees (UNHCR). The ECOSOC concluded that the contents of the notion of exclusion, which was contained in the draft statute, should be the same as was being proposed for the future refugee convention.[129]

Both proposals were forwarded to the Third Committee, which discussed them during its 1950 November/December meeting.[130] An exclusion clause in the draft statute was adopted during this session, but the definition of "refugee," including its exclusion clause in the draft convention, did not go any further than agreeing that the document would be considered a draft document only. The Third Committee submitted both the statute and the draft convention to the General Assembly, which accepted these documents on 14 December 1950. The draft convention became the basis of discussion during the Conference of Plenipotentiaries held in Geneva from 2 to 25 July 1951. This conference adopted the Convention relating to the Status of Refugees on 25 July 1951, while the Final Act was signed three days later.[131]

---

127 UN Doc E/1814.

128 Paul Weis, *The Refugee Convention, 1951: The Travaux Préparatoires Analysed, with a Commentary by the Late Dr. Paul Weis* (Cambridge, New York: Cambridge University Press, 1995) at 1–3.

129 Kapferer, above note 39 at 66.

130 *Ibid* at 66.

131 Weis, above note 128 at 3–4. See also United Nations, Final Act of the United Nations Conference of Plenipotentiaries on the Status of Refugees and Stateless Persons, 25 July 1951, 2545 UNTS 138 (entered into force April 1954), online: www.refworld.org/docid/3e2becbb4.html.

2) The Debates in the Social Committee of the Economic and Social Council and the Third Committee of the General Assembly[132]

The first reference to a possible exclusion of certain persons can be found in article 1(2) of the draft Refugee Convention text proposed by France on 17 January 1950. This document stated, in reference to the UDHR, that "[n]o person to whom Article 14, paragraph 2 of the aforesaid Declaration is applicable shall be recognised as a refugee."[133] During the deliberations in the Ad Hoc Committee on Statelessness and Related Problems, the following definition of exclusion was produced in its report of 17 February 1950:

> No contracting State shall apply the benefits of this Convention to any person who in its opinion has committed a crime specified in Article VI of the London Charter of the International Military Tribunal or any other act contrary to the purposes and principles of the Charter of the United Nations.[134]

The Social Committee of the ECOSOC discussed the entire text of the proposed convention between 31 July and 10 August 1950, while the above provision (or an identical text based on a French proposal of 29 July 1950)[135] was the subject of debate between 2 and 7 August 1950.

On 2 August, the discussion was mostly devoted to voicing concerns over whether the wording was too vague, such that it could be open to abuse,[136] and to giving examples of what acts could be cov-

132 The *travaux préparatoires* of the ECOSOC and of the next phase, the Conference of Plenipotentiaries, can be found in Alex Takkenberg & Christopher C. Tahbaz, *The Collected Works of the 1951 Geneva Convention Relating to the Status of Refugees* (Amsterdam: Dutch Refugee Council under the auspices of the European Legal Network on Asylum, 1989). For general comments on the drafting of the Refugee Convention, specifically the meaning of refugee, see Einarsen, above note 1 at marginal notes 31–59; Jackson, above note 10 at 40–81. For a discussion of these *travaux préparatoires* as they relate to exclusion, see Goodwin-Gill & McAdam, above note 18 at 198–99, 207–8, and 219–20, and Kapferer, above note 39 at 67–70, while for a judicial consideration, see Bundesverwaltungsgericht (Federal Administrative Court), BverwG 10 C 24.08, 11 November 2009, at paras 26–28 (Germany) and *Pushpanathan v Canada (Minister of Citizenship and Immigration)*, [1998] 1 SCR 982 at paras 59–60 (Canada) [*Pushpanathan*].

133 UN Doc E/AC.32/L3.

134 Annex I, article 1(C) in UN Doc E/1618 and Corr 1 [UN Doc E/AC.32/5 and Corr 1].

135 UN Doc E/L.82 together with UN Doc E/AC.7/SR 160 at 10.

136 Countries that found the provision too vague were Canada (UN Doc E/AC.7/SR 160 at 15), Pakistan (at 16), and the United Kingdom (at 19); Mexico thought that the provision

ered by the provision; collaborators, those responsible for genocide, and persons practising racial discrimination were mentioned. The day ended with the Canadian representative suggesting (after reconsidering her original position that the provision was too vague and indicating that the French proposal had merit) that this provision be referred to a drafting committee to make it clearer. This suggestion was accepted.[137]

By the 7 August meeting, the French delegation had amended its original proposal by changing the words "or any other act contrary to the purposes and principles of the United Nations" to a general reference to article 14(2) of the UDHR. France's delegate started the discussion that day by saying that

> his delegation held that the phrase in question applied to—and hence excluded—war criminals, ordinary criminals and certain individuals who, though not guilty of war crimes, might have committed acts of similar gravity against the principles of the United Nations, in other words, crimes against humanity.[138]

Later, he elaborated on this statement in the following way:

> [P]ut differently, the question was whether an ex-Hitler, who was not guilty of any war crimes, merely because there had been no war, would have the right to be classified as a refugee after torturing, persecuting and reducing a people to slavery. That was the extreme case of the great tyrant. There might, however, be a larger number of more petty tyrants likewise guilty of acts contrary to the purposes and principles of the Charter, who had by such acts helped create fear which the refugees had fled .... [T]he provision was not aimed at the man-in-the-street, but at persons occupying government posts, such as head of States, Ministers, and high officials.[139]

Mr. Giraud of the United Nations Secretariat responded to the latter statement of France by saying that

---

could lead to abuse (at 19), while Chile felt that it was difficult to see how an individual could commit acts contrary to the purposes and principles of the *Charter*; the example of collaborators was given by the United States (at 16) and the United Kingdom (at 19), the example of genocide originated from the French delegation (at 15), while India mentioned the situation of discrimination (at 15).

137 UN Doc E/AC.7/SR 160 at 19.

138 UN Doc E/AC.7/SR 166 at 4.

139 *Ibid* at 6.

> it was a fact that an individual could violate the provisions of the United Nations Charter. According to the terms of the Charter and the judgement of the Nuremberg Tribunal and by virtue of the provisions of the Genocide Convention an individual could nowadays be held liable under international law and could be called upon to answer for crimes constituting a violation of such international law.[140]

France was in entire agreement with this explanation.[141] Mr. Giraud also suggested that "an individual who, without having committed a crime against humanity, had violated human rights, for instance by the exercise of discrimination, could be considered to have committed acts contrary to the purposes and principles of the United Nations."[142] Canada then stated that

> the Canadian government would certainly not wish the persons envisaged in the amendment to benefit from the Convention. As has been said, they would be persons who had abused positions of authority by committing crimes against humanity, other than war crimes.[143]

The delegate of Chile indicated that "he was glad to see his French colleague had modified his original wording; he was glad to see, too, that for the first time an article proclaiming human rights was to take a contractual form."[144] The chair put the French amendment to a vote, as a result of which (7:0, with 8 abstentions), the following text for the last portion of the exclusion ground was arrived at:

> No contracting State shall be obliged under the provisions of this Convention, to grant refugee status to any person whom it has serious reasons to consider, as falling under the provisions of article 14(2) of the Universal Declaration of Human Rights.[145]

This proposal (together with the original text regarding crimes specified in the London Charter) was adopted by the ECOSOC and forwarded to the Third Committee of the General Assembly for its November/December 1950 session. In that forum, on 24 November,

---

140 *Ibid* at 7.
141 *Ibid* at 8.
142 *Ibid* at 9.
143 *Ibid* at 10.
144 *Ibid*.
145 *Ibid* at 11; the same text is also contained in the Second Report of the Social Committee, UN Doc E/1814, para C of the definition of "refugee."

Yugoslavia submitted a proposal to change this definition but only for the Statute of the Office of the United Nations High Commissioner for Refugees, which retained the ECOSOC definition but had added the category of "persons who have committed non-political crimes."[146] An informal working party examined the various drafts and proposals and suggested that for the purposes of the Statute, the mandate of the high commissioner should not extend to

> a person in respect of whom there are serious reasons for considering that he has committed a crime covered by the provisions of extradition or a crime mentioned in article VI of the London Charter of the International Military Tribunal or by the provisions of article 14, paragraph 2, of the Universal Declaration of Human Rights.[147]

The Australian representative, during the subsequent debate in the Third Committee, was concerned that the language of the UDHR was too vague to be part of both instruments under consideration and proposed to delete all words after "extradition." The French delegate pointed out that "the paragraph proposed by the informal working party applied to war criminals, common criminals and those responsible for crimes against the United Nations" and was opposed to deleting the latter two categories. Yugoslavia also opposed the Australian proposal, with the result that it was rejected. Consequently, the definition originally proposed by the informal working group became part of the Statute as it was also approved by the General Assembly.[148]

This same wording, but with the deletion of the reference to common criminals, appeared as article 1(E) in the text of the Draft Convention relating to the Status of Refugees, which was annexed to the Official Records of the United Nations General Assembly 325th Plenary Meeting of 14 December 1950. The entire text read:

> The provisions of the present Convention shall not apply to any person with respect to whom there are serious reasons for considering that (a) he has committed a crime specified in article VI of the London Charter of the International Military Tribunal; or (b) he falls under the provisions of article 14, paragraph 2, of the Universal Declaration of Human Rights. [Citations omitted.]

146 Kapferer, above note 39 at 66.

147 *Ibid* at 66.

148 *Ibid* at 66–67.

3) The Debates During the Conference of Plenipotentiaries on the Status of Refugees and Stateless Persons

Since no agreement on a convention could be reached in the context of the ECOSOC, the United Nations Conference of Plenipotentiaries on the Status of Refugees and Stateless Persons was called in Geneva from 2 to 25 July 1951 in order to reach such an agreement. The draft text of article 1 with respect to exclusion was the same as the one in the above draft convention.[149]

Since the definition of refugees, in which this exclusion clause appeared, was of great importance to the conference, and since it was difficult to come to a consensus with respect to the exclusion grounds, it was decided to appoint a working group to study Section E of article 1 of the draft convention. This working group was able to achieve a consensus on the wording with respect to the war crimes exclusion but not on the other exclusion grounds, so the discussion on what was to become sections (b) and (c) of article F continued in plenary session.

The debate on the issue of exclusion for war crimes had begun in the working group with the following amendment to the definition in the draft convention on exclusion put forward by Germany:

> The provisions of the present Convention shall not apply to any person to whom there are serious reasons for considering that (a) he has committed a war crime or crime against humanity as specified in article 147 of the Geneva Convention of 12 August 1949 relative to the Protection of Civilian Persons in Time of War and in the corresponding articles of the three other Geneva Conventions of the same date and in article III of the Convention on the Prevention and Punishment of the Crime of Genocide of 9 December 1948; or (b) he has committed a crime against peace, namely planning, preparation, initiation or waging of a war of aggression, or a war in violation of international treaties, agreements or assurances, or participation in common plan or conspiracy for the accomplishment of any of the foregoing; or (c) he falls under the provisions of article 14, paragraph 2 of the Universal Declaration of Human Rights.[150]

The main reason for this amendment, as stated by the German representative, was to have a more appropriate reference to recent

149 UN Doc A/Conf.2/4 at 6.
150 UN Doc A/Conf. 2/76.

developments in the area of international crimes than the *London Charter* as that document had only been approved by a limited number of states.[151]

Mr. Meyrowitz of the Consultative Council of Jewish Organizations objected to the German proposal for two reasons, the first of which was that the principles of the London Charter had transcended the institution for which they were created and had already been the subject of the work of the International Law Commission. Second, the suggested definition would not apply to crimes against humanity.[152]

In response to this comment, the German representative stated that, while not being opposed to using the London Charter, he wanted to point out that the Charter did not cover crimes against humanity committed after the Second World War due to its restrictive wording. As well, he was also fully cognizant of the fact that war crimes, crimes against humanity, and crimes against peace could very well fall within the other proposed exclusion clauses as such crimes were both common crimes and acts against the United Nations.[153] However, the delegate of Israel agreed with the comments of Mr. Meyrowitz that the Nuremberg principles provided a more comprehensive body of international criminal law than the German proposal and urged its rejection.[154] Further discussion on this issue was referred to a working group.[155]

The working group held two meetings between 17 and 19 July 1951 and proposed that a person be excluded where "(a) he has committed a crime against peace, a war crime, or a crime against humanity, as defined in the international instruments drawn up to make provision in respect of such crimes."[156] This was accepted by the conference, although Israel was unable to vote for this definition.[157]

151 UN Doc A/Conf.2/SR 19 at 26.

152 UN Doc A/Conf. 2/SR 21 at 7–11.

153 UN Doc A/Conf.2/SR 24 at 6–8.

154 *Ibid* at 14–16.

155 *Ibid* at 16.

156 UN Doc A/Conf.2/92; there are no summary records of the meeting of the working group, only a report, which indicated that during the drafting of this exclusion ground, the relationship between the work of the International Law Commission and the breadth of this ground was discussed, although no conclusive agreement was reached (UN Doc A/Conf.2/SR 21 at 7–10). Grahl-Madsen states that this ground was couched (especially the term "international instruments") in more general terms as a result of the fact that it was felt by the drafters that the work of the International Law Commission on its Code of Crimes against the Peace and Security of Mankind should be encompassed by the provision contained in F(a) (Grahl-Madsen, above note 10 at 276).

157 UN Doc A/Conf. 2/SR 29 at 10.

Before setting out in some detail the debates with respect to the ground for exclusion dealing with other forms of criminality, it is useful to point out that this discussion can be traced back to the positions of the British and French delegations, which at the beginning were diametrically opposed. The French delegation was very concerned that France, which had been absorbing large numbers of refugees, would face severe problems with the entry of criminals among genuine refugees. Britain, on the other hand, had great difficulties with the notion that refugees who had been admitted to a country could afterward be removed for having committed only relatively minor offences in the country of refuge.

The debate began on 11 July 1951 in plenary when Mr. Hoare of the UK delegation stated that he presumed that article 14 of the UDHR meant to exclude common criminals, and if that was the intention of the conference, he had difficulty with such an approach.[158] Two days later, the same representative stated that "it was difficult to define what acts were contrary to the purposes and principles of the United Nations though he presumed that what was meant was such acts as war crimes, genocide and the subversion or overthrow of democratic regimes."[159] He also stated that he was of the view that people who committed minor crimes in the country of refuge should not be excluded from the benefits of the convention.[160] France's representative responded that it was

> observed that the divergence between two standpoints arose from the fact that certain delegations wished their governments to be able to return and expel refugees who were common-law criminals, whereas the French government wanted to be able, under certain circumstances, to receive them, without, however, being compelled to apply to such individuals the benefits accorded by the Convention. For France, the definition was the criterion for the right of asylum, and that was why she attached fundamental importance to it.[161]

The Belgian representative replied that in his view this exclusion ground should apply in both the country of origin and the country of refuge.[162] The delegate of the UNHCR noted that there was a

158 UN Doc A/Conf. 2/SR 3 at 15.

159 UN Doc A/Conf.2/SR 24 at 5.

160 *Ibid* at 8.

161 *Ibid* at 12.

162 *Ibid* at 9.

discrepancy between the UNHCR Statute, which excluded persons who had committed crimes envisaged by extradition treaties, and the draft convention, which did not.[163] This sparked a general debate about this discrepancy and the relationship between extradition treaties and the proposed Refugee Convention,[164] resulting in this area of exclusion also being referred to the working group.[165]

163 *Ibid* at 9–10.

164 The concern, as voiced by the Belgium representative, was that a refugee under an international treaty who had committed a common law crime could be handed over under a bilateral treaty to the country where they feared persecution (UN Doc A/Conf.2/SR 24 at 9); the UK delegate recognized this concern but felt that extradition treaties should prevail and that the exclusion article should reflect this (UN Doc A/Conf.2/SR 24 at 10–11). Both Israel and Belgium agreed with the United Kingdom (UN Doc A/Conf.2/SR 24 at 11), while Denmark stated that "states who had received a request for extradition of a refugee who had committed a crime of no great consequence from the government that was likely to persecute him, would be faced with a very difficult decision. On the other hand, states could not be expected to grant asylum to persons committing capital crimes merely because they happened to be exposed at the same time to relatively minor dangers on account of some unimportant political activity. A proper balance must be struck between all the considerations involved." (UN Doc A/Conf.2/SR 24 at 13.) The Belgium and Dutch representatives, in order to resolve this issue, suggested a couple of days later making a reservation regarding extradition in the provision dealing with *refoulement* (UN Doc A/Conf.2/SR 29 at 14), which was given reluctant support by the United Kingdom (UN Doc A/Conf.2/SR 29 at 15). However, the debate on the *refoulement* provision hardly touched upon extradition, with the exception of a comment by the UK delegate to the effect that "extradition treaties between countries of refuge and countries of persecution were outside the purview of the Convention. Most treaties of that kind specified that not only the facts should be established *prima facie* to the satisfaction of the country receiving the request for extradition but also that the crime for which the criminal was to be returned should not be of a political nature." This statement was echoed by France, saying that "Article 33 was without prejudice to the rights of extradition." (See Weis, above note 128 at 332 and 334.) Weis, in his commentary, makes the observation: "As to extradition it would also seem to be covered by the words 'in any manner whatsoever,'" and goes on to say that, with respect to the comment given by the United Kingdom, "these arguments are hardly convincing. The question arises in cases where extradition is requested for a non-political offence and the requested person is in fear of disproportionate punishment or of persecution apart from punishment for one of the reasons mentioned in Article 1 of the Convention. The Convention supersedes, in any case, extradition treaties concluded previously by the same parties. It appears that the question has been clarified by the European Convention on Extradition and by court decisions. Article 33 should be applied to extradition, at least by analogy." (See Weis, above note 128 at 342; for the same views, see UNHCR, *Commentary on the Refugee Convention 1951*, above note 20 at 135; see, also, James Hathaway & Michelle Foster, *The Law of Refugee Status*, 2d ed (Cambridge: Cambridge University Press, 2014) at 538–42.)

165 UN Doc A/Conf.2/SR 24 at 10–13 and 16. See, also, Nadia Yakoob, "Political Offender or Serious Criminal? Challenging the Interpretation of 'Serious, Nonpolitical Crimes' in *INS v Aquirre-Aguirre*" (2000) 14 *Georgetown Immigration Law Journal* 545 at 546–49.

The same day, a formal proposal was put forward that suggested deleting paragraph (b) entirely from article 1(E) or, in the alternative, substituting the wording in (b) with the following: "that he has committed an act contrary to the purposes and principles of the United Nations."[166]

On 19 July 1951, after the working group and the conference had not been able to reach a consensus on exclusion other than with respect to crimes against peace, war crimes, and crimes against humanity, the discussion regarding this ground for exclusion resumed. The UK delegate was quick to reiterate his concern about the vagueness of the words "against the purposes and principles of the United Nations" and its exact meaning since governments would use this wording to exclude people they should not.[167] In response to the comment by the Dutch representative that some criminals should be excluded,[168] Mr. Hoare of the United Kingdom stated that

> article 14(2) seems intended to apply to persons who were fugitives from prosecution in another country for non-political crimes. He could not imagine that those who had drafted it had intended that article 14(2) should apply to a person who having been granted asylum subsequently committed a crime in the country of refuge.[169]

The Swiss representative stated that article 14(2) simply referred to serious crimes as a reason for exclusion,[170] while the Yugoslavian representative suggested inserting the words "in common law" after the word "crime" and adding a subparagraph (c) that would comprise the words of the original amendment suggested above.[171] The French delegate still had concerns related to crimes committed before entering the country of refuge; in addition, he assumed that crimes meant "serious crimes."[172] The UK delegate had no objection to excluding persons who had committed crimes before entering the country of refuge.[173] The French delegate then suggested adding the word "serious" to the word "crime."[174]

166 UN Doc A/Conf.2/74.

167 UN Doc A/Conf. 2/SR 29 at 12.

168 *Ibid* at 12.

169 *Ibid* at 14–15.

170 *Ibid* at 17.

171 *Ibid.*

172 *Ibid* at 18.

173 *Ibid* at 19.

174 *Ibid* at 20.

At this point, the president of the conference adjourned the meeting to give delegations an opportunity to draft a text on which they could agree.[175] As a result of this intervention, the text read as follows:

> (b) he has committed a serious crime under common law outside the country of reception; (c) he has committed acts contrary to the purposes and principles of the United Nations.[176]

The British delegate stated that this amendment removed his main objection to the text as originally drafted, which would have made it too easy for states to withdraw the status of refugee from many persons who had been granted asylum from persecution.[177] At this point, the president took the opportunity to say that

> [w]hen a person with a criminal record sought asylum as a refugee, it was for the country of refuge to strike a balance between the offences committed by that person and the extent to which his fear of persecution was well founded.
>
> He would simply ask representatives to keep in mind the hypothetical case of some minor official of an outlawed political party who had a criminal record. [The president] was convinced that all countries, both in Europe and overseas, had, even under the earlier [refugee] Conventions, always dealt with such cases fairly.[178]

The Belgian delegate suggested the following wording: "that he has committed a serious crime under common law outside the receiving country before being admitted to it as a refugee."[179] The Dutch representative wanted to know whether the new definition applied to the following two situations: (1) a person guilty of crimes committed before the guilty person acquired the status of refugee and (2) a person who had committed crimes outside the receiving country.[180] The Yugoslavian delegate was of the opinion that both situations were covered by paragraph (b).[181] The president put the Belgian proposal to a vote, and the proposal was accepted,[182] after which the remainder of the original

175 *Ibid.*
176 *Ibid* at 21.
177 *Ibid.*
178 *Ibid* at 23.
179 *Ibid* at 25.
180 *Ibid* at 26.
181 *Ibid.*
182 *Ibid.*

amendment, subparagraph (c), was also accepted by vote,[183] and, finally, the complete text of paragraph E was adopted.[184]

The text of subparagraph (b) was slightly altered by the Style Committee to make the text clearer,[185] and this was the wording that found its way into the Final Act of the conference and into the Convention relating to the Status of Refugees, although paragraph E was now paragraph F:

> F. The provisions of this Convention shall not apply to any person with respect to whom there are serious reasons for considering that:
> a) he has committed a crime against peace, a war crime, or a crime against humanity, as defined in the international instruments drawn up to make provision in respect of such crimes;
> b) he has committed a serious non-political crime outside the country of refuge prior to his admission to that country as a refugee;
> c) he has been guilty of acts contrary to the purposes and principles of the United Nations.

G. THE WORK OF THE UNITED NATIONS IN THE AREA OF EXPULSION AND *REFOULEMENT*, 1949–51

1) Introduction

Articles 32 and 33 of the Refugee Convention prohibit the expulsion of refugees lawfully in the country of refuge and the *refoulement* of refugees, respectively. Article 32 says, with respect to the general prohibition, that "the Contracting States shall not expel a refugee lawfully in their territory," while article 33 states that "no Contracting State shall expel or return (*refouler*) a refugee in any manner whatsoever to the frontiers of territories where his life or freedom would be threatened on account of his race, religion, nationality, membership of a particular social group or political opinion." Both articles contain exceptions to this general rule, which were subject to extensive debate during the negotiations of this convention.

The exception contained in article 32.1 states the exception as "save on grounds of national security or public order and in pursuance of a

183 *Ibid* at 27.

184 *Ibid.*

185 UN Doc A/Conf.2/L.1/Add 10.

decision reached in accordance with the process of law," while article 32.2 indicates that "except where compelling reasons of national security otherwise require, the refugee shall be allowed to submit evidence to clear himself, and to appeal to and be represented for the purpose before competent authority or a person or persons specially designated by the competent authority."

Article 33.2 makes it clear that "the benefit of the present provision may not, however, be claimed by a refugee of whom there are reasonable grounds for regarding as a danger to the security of the country in which he is, or who, having been convicted by a final judgment of a particularly serious crime, constitutes a danger to the community of that country."

The term "national security" is also used in article 9, which says: "Nothing in this Convention shall prevent a Contracting State, in time of war or other grave and exceptional circumstances, from taking provisionally measures which it considers to be essential to the national security in the case of a particular person, pending a determination by the Contracting State that that person is in fact a refugee and that the continuance of such measures is necessary in his case in the interests of national security," while article 28.1 uses both terms of article 32.1 to ensure that "the Contracting States shall issue to refugees lawfully staying in their territory travel documents for the purpose of travel outside their territory, unless compelling reasons of national security or public order otherwise require." Finally, the concept of public order is also used in article 2 in the following manner: "Every refugee has duties to the country in which he finds himself, which require in particular that he conform to its laws and regulations as well as to measures taken for the maintenance of public order."

2) Exceptions in the Articles with No Reference to Expulsion or *Refoulement*

The debates regarding articles 2 and 9 were brief. The discussion in respect to article 2 started with a proposal of the Secretariat, saying that "refugees authorized to reside in a country must conform to the laws in force," on which some variations, such as "maintenance of public order and also to the laws and regulations of the country," "public order and morality," and "guilty of grave dereliction of duty and who constitutes a danger to the internal or external security," were proposed before a working group settled on the final text.[186] The debates regarding the issue of national security in article 9 centred primarily on whether this term should be more precisely defined in order to avoid a broad interpretation by states, on the one hand, while on the other hand, some delegates were looking for a wider exception beyond national security, such as public order.[187]

The notion of national security in the article dealing with travel documents (article 28.1) was introduced quite late, at the end of the first week of the Conference of Plenipotentiaries as part of a more general discussion about whether the issuance of a travel document could be refused on the same grounds as refusal to grant a citizen a passport. The debate regarding national security began with the introduction of two amendments, one by Belgium, which wanted to add in general terms that granting of a document could be refused "subject to the requirements of national security or public order," while Australia and Canada submitted a joint amendment with the following text: "As an exceptional measure a Contracting State may withhold the issue of a travel document to a refugee if the circumstances are such that the issue of a passport would be withheld from a national of that State."[188]

Belgium explained that "the limiting clause in the Belgian amendment did not mean that the issue of a travel document would categorically be refused. It was merely intended to allow for the temporary discontinuance of the issue of such documents. That action would no longer be necessary once the considerations of national security or public order which had led States to suspend the issue of travel documents, had ceased to hold."[189]

Initially, the Danish, Norwegian, and UK representatives were in favour of the Australian-Canadian proposal, while France and Sweden found the Belgian amendment more palatable. The Belgian delegate indicated that he found the Australian-Canadian proposal too broad as a passport could be refused for arrears in tax payments or for not complying with a military service obligation. The Swiss representative tried a compromise approach by suggesting that the words "public order" be deleted from the Belgian proposal, but this was not acceptable to

186 Weis, above note 128 at 36–37.

187 *Ibid* at 63–69.

188 *Ibid* at 248–49; Hathaway, above note 3 at 860–61.

189 Weis, above note 128 at 250.

Belgium as it had intended to cover in its proposal the situation of a refugee who was being prosecuted "for an offence under civil law; he would be refused a travel document for reasons of public order."[190]

The Danish representative said, in agreeing with the concept of public order,

> that it might well be that a refugee suspected of having committed a crime in a particular country would be able to obtain a visa from the Consul of another country without the Consul being aware of the facts of the case. It would consequently be undesirable to issue a travel document to such a person before the alleged offence had been fully investigated. Such cases were admittedly covered by the Belgian amendment, but the latter appeared to go much further than was necessary in actual practice.[191]

Australia explained that the joint amendment was introduced to limit exceptions to a minimum as that was the case with passport refusals, while the French representative indicated that expressing extremist views was not a reason to withhold a passport in France but that it might be necessary to treat refugees differently. The UK delegate felt that

> to refuse a travel document to a refugee on the grounds mentioned by the French representative would be tantamount to discrimination on the grounds of political opinion .... He was mainly concerned with the question of principle. If the holding of extremist views was accepted as valid ground for not issuing travel documents, certain States might take advantage of that facility in order to put obstacles in the way of legitimate travel on the part of the refugees.[192]

This debate came to an end when the president observed

> that for the past twenty years arrangements had existed for the issue of travel documents to refugees. He was sure that all States had delivered such documents, and also that, when the exceptional case had turned up, the competent authorities had known what action to take. He was reluctant to see the Conference give world public opinion the impression that it was seeking to deprive refugees of facilities

---

190 *Ibid.*

191 *Ibid* at 251.

192 *Ibid.*

> that had been accorded by all previous agreements, and consequently wondered whether any amendment . . . was necessary.[193]

The UK representative suggested, in order to avoid any abuse of the formula finally adopted, that the phrase in the Belgian amendment should be replaced by the words "except when imperative reasons of national security of public order otherwise require." The Belgian representative accepted the suggestion, while the Australian and Canadian representatives withdrew their amendment in favour of the Belgian proposal, as did the French delegate.[194] The Style Committee changed the word "imperative" to "compelling."[195]

One commentator summarized the debate as follows:

> [T]hus, not any grounds of national security or public order may be invoked but only compelling grounds. The wording was adopted after much discussion. The proposal that the travel document may be refused on the same grounds on which a national passport may be refused was not adopted. It would seem to cover cases where a refugee seeks to escape prosecution or punishment for a criminal offence or where the refugee is suspected of travelling in order to engage in criminal or espionage activities. It does not cover, according to the debate, cases in which a national passport may be refused, such as insolvency, failure to pay taxes or to comply with military obligations.[196]

3) Exceptions in the Expulsion Article

The discussions with respect to the exceptions contained in articles 32 and 33 cannot be understood without also considering the debates of what is now article 31 of the convention (dealing with refugees unlawfully in the country of refuge).[197] The reason is that the original draft by the Secretariat submitted to the Ad Hoc Committee combined provisions

---

193 *Ibid.*

194 *Ibid* at 251–52.

195 *Ibid* at 266.

196 *Ibid.*

197 It says:

> 1. The Contracting States shall not impose penalties, on account of their illegal entry or presence, on refugees who, coming directly from a territory where their life or freedom was threatened in the sense of Article 1, enter or are present in their territory without authorization, provided they present themselves without delay to the authorities and show good cause for their illegal entry or presence.

dealing with all aspects now in articles 31–33 in one document, which were only separated at the end of the first meeting of this committee in February 1950 and subsequently revisited during its second meeting as three distinct provisions.

This draft stated the following:

> 1. Each of the High Contracting Parties undertakes not to remove or keep from the territory, by application of police measures, such as expulsions or non-admittance at the frontier *(refoulement)*,[198] refugees (and stateless persons) who have been authorized to reside there regularly, unless the said measures are dictated by reasons of national security or public order.

> 2. The Contracting States shall not apply to the movements of such refugee restrictions other than those which are necessary and such restrictions shall only be applied until their status in the country is regularized or they obtain admission into another country. The Contracting States shall allow such refugees a reasonable period and all the necessary facilities to obtain admission into another country.

198 At the beginning of the debates in the Ad Hoc Committee, there was some confusion as to the notion of the term *refoulement*, which was seen by some delegates (as well as the Secretariat) as a concept used upon entry rather than removal; see the following exchange reflected by Weis, above note 128 at 289–90: "The representative of the Secretariat explained that the original draft of Article 24 had been based on Article 3 of the 1933 Convention. The reference to non-admittance at the frontier in paragraph 1 *(refoulement)* applied only to refugees who had already been authorized to reside in the territory in question. The practice known as *refoulement* in French did not exist in the English-speaking countries. In Belgium and France, however, there was a definite distinction between expulsion, which could only be carried out in pursuance of a decision of a judicial authority, and *refoulement*, which meant either deportation as a police measure or non-admittance at the frontier. The Belgian representative agreed and added that the term 'expulsion' was used when the refugee had committed a criminal offence, whereas the term '*refoulement*' was used in cases where a refugee was deported or refused admittance because his presence in the country was considered undesirable, even though he was a person of good character. The UK representative concluded from the discussion that the term '*refoulement*' would apply to (a) refugees seeking admission; (b) refugees illegally in the country; (c) refugees admitted temporarily or conditionally. In the UK refugees who had been allowed to enter the UK could be sent out only by expulsion or deportation. There was no concept in these cases corresponding to that of '*refoulement*.'" This debate also occurred again later during the discussions of art 33 during the Conference of Plenipotentiaries, where Switzerland expressed as its view that the term "expel" applied to a refugee who had already been admitted to the territory of a country, while *refoulement* was a vaguer concept that could not apply to a refugee who had not entered the territory of a country (Weis, above note 128 at 329); the Netherlands clarified this by saying that *refoulement* was used for refugees within the country but not yet resident there (*ibid* at 334).

2. The penalties enacted against foreigners entering the territory of the Contracting Party without prior permission shall not be applied to refugees seeking to escape from persecution, provided that such refugees present themselves without delay to the authorities of the reception country and show good cause for their entry.
3. Each of the High Contracting Parties undertakes in any case not to turn back refugees to the frontiers of their country of origin, or to territories where their life or freedom would be threatened on account of their race, religion, nationality or political opinions.
4. A refugee (or stateless person) authorized to reside regularly in the territory of any of the High Contracting Parties may not be expelled save in pursuance of the decision of a judicial authority.
5. Each of the High Contracting Parties reserves the right to apply such internal measures as it may deem necessary to refugees (or stateless persons) whose expulsion has been ordered and who are unable to leave its territory because they have not received, at their request or through the intervention of Governments or through the High Commissioner for Refugees or non-governmental agencies, the necessary authorizations and visas permitting them legally to proceed to another country.[199]

The debate regarding paragraph 1 started with a lengthy comment by the Observer of the Agudas Israel World Organization, who said in part:

> [E]xpulsion was to be permitted if it was dictated by reasons of national security or public order. In the French draft, the words "public order" were omitted, but even so the expression "dictated by reasons of national security" was extremely broad.[200] The Nazis might quite well have claimed that their national security had necessitated the expulsion of the Jews, although the whole world had been shocked at that brutal act. Thus, the inclusion of such a phrase would leave all refugees open to expulsion at the slightest provocation. If a refugee were suspected of spying it would surely serve the interests of national security better to imprison him rather than to expel him. If he committed criminal acts, he should be punished according to the normal laws of the country. He should not, however, be additionally penalized by the terrible threat of expulsion. In his opinion, the best way to safeguard both the

199 Weis, above note 128 at 278.

200 Incidentally, the French draft to which this statement refers did not contain any reference to national security; see Weis, above note 128 at 280.

> national security and the rights of the refugee would be to state that a refugee could not be expelled save in pursuance of the decision of a judicial authority. That provision was contained in paragraph 4 of the Secretariat draft and he did not think it necessary to include the special provisions contained in paragraph 1. If the Committee decided that it was essential to mention national security, the words "on guards of national security" could be added at the end of paragraph 1.[201]

Most of the observations made by delegates related to the concept of public order rather than national security, apart from some general comments to the effect that refugees should not be returned to countries where their life or freedom would be threatened, even for reasons of national security of public order.[202] The first delineation of the concept of public order was that this concept should not apply to situations involving economic or social reasons, such as destitution, but primarily to offences against the law.[203]

To provide more clarity to the meaning of public order, a number of suggestions were made, such as "save on grounds of national security or public order and in pursuance of a final decision reached by due process of law"[204] and "for reasons of national security or if the refugees concerned have been convicted for a criminal offence,"[205] by adding the words "for a violation of the law,"[206] by replacing the public order reference to "internal and external national security,"[207] or by deleting this term altogether.[208]

---

201 *Ibid* at 280–81.

202 *Ibid* at 282–83 (Belgium), 283 (United States), and 285 (United States and the Secretariat). Alternatives in resolving the dilemma of having a person in a country of refuge who posed a security or public risk but would also face a very serious risk upon return to the country of origin could be removal to a third country (Belgium at 283; United States at 285) or placement in an internment camp (United States at 285).

203 *Ibid* at 286 (Denmark and Belgium) and 287 (United States and United Kingdom).

204 *Ibid* at 287 (the chair); France suggested adding the word "final" so that a person could not be expelled by "a decision of a mere policeman."

205 *Ibid* at 287 (the representative of the International Labour Organization).

206 *Ibid* at 287 (United States).

207 *Ibid* at 287 (Israel).

208 *Ibid* at 287 (France); France was concerned that the term "public order" was not given the same meaning in all countries and found the term "national security" to be more precise; in response, the Venezuelan representative expressed a preference for "public order." In his country, "public order" was synonymous with "internal order," while "national security" implied "international order," for the two ideas complemented each other and were closely linked. See, also, Hathaway, above note 3 at 844–55.

Since Turkey and Venezuela, as well as Belgium, preferred the term "save on grounds of national security or public order," this terminology was accepted by the committee, while also adding the words "and in pursuance of a decision reached in accordance with due process of law."[209] A late reference to national security was proposed for what became the present article 31 by Sweden, but this suggestion was ignored.[210]

The discussions regarding national security and public order were revived during the debates of the second meeting of the Ad Hoc Committee regarding article 32. As had been the case during the first session, it was emphasized that the notion of public order did not include "social cases,"[211] although an amendment to make that clear in the text was rejected.[212] It was also generally agreed that the guarantee of due process should be maintained.[213]

Attempts to clarify the notion of public order were not successful, as was evident, for instance, with the proposal of the United States to change the text to "national security or based on the commission of illegal acts," but the chair objected to this, saying:

> [I]llegal acts ranged from riding bicycles the wrong way on footpaths, to the gravest of crimes. It might be better to change the term "public order" to "public safety" which would not cover both extremes and would permit the deportation of any refugee who had committed the smallest illegal act.[214]

The issue of public order was referred to the Drafting Committee of the Ad Hoc Committee, which retained the exception for national security or public order but included the due process provision in a separate article with the text: "the expulsion of such refugee shall be only in pursuance of a decision reached in accordance with due process of law. The refugee shall have the right to submit evidence to clear himself and the right to appeal to and be represented before competent authority."[215]

---

209 Weis, above note 128 at 291 & 292.

210 *Ibid* at 296.

211 *Ibid* at 308 (United States and Israel), 309 (United States), and 310 (France and the Secretariat).

212 *Ibid* at 310.

213 *Ibid* at 305 (Austria), 308 (Israel), 309 (France), and 310 (China). See, also, Hathaway, above note 3 at 845–46.

214 Weis, above note 128 at 309.

215 *Ibid* at 311.

The Drafting Committee also had the following comment:

> [T]he Committee decided, after long discussion, to maintain the present text of the first paragraph. While several members expressed dissatisfaction with the vagueness of the term "public order," and with the different interpretations given to the term in different countries, it was felt necessary to take into account the jurisprudence, which this term had acquired in certain systems of law. The Committee felt that this provision would permit the deportation of aliens who had been convicted of certain serious crimes where in that country such crimes are considered violations of "public order." The phrase "public order" would not, however, permit the deportation of aliens on "social grounds" such as indigence or illness. The procedural safeguards accorded to refugees were clarified and are now contained wholly in paragraph 2.[216]

This draft was submitted to the Conference of Plenipotentiaries, together with a detailed amendment by Egypt, as well as a memorandum prepared by the Secretariat on the notion of public order.

The Egyptian amendment read:

> Delete paragraphs 1 and 2 of this Article and substitute the following text:
>
> (1) The Contracting States shall not expel a refugee lawfully in their territory save on one of the following grounds:
>   (a) because he has been convicted of a crime or offence punishable by more than three months' imprisonment;
>   (b) because he has engaged in activities of a subversive nature or which are prejudicial to public order, the internal or external security of the State, public morals or health;
>   (c) because he is indigent and is a charge on the State.
>
> (2) In every case, expulsion shall apply solely to individuals. Expulsion may only be effected by a ministerial order communicated to the person to be expelled.[217]

The memorandum explained:

> First, it should be observed that the English expression "public order" is not the equivalent and is indeed substantially different from the

216 *Ibid.*

217 *Ibid* at 312.

> French expression *"l'ordre publique"* (or in Spanish, "*orden publico"*). In civil law countries the concept of "*l'ordre publique" is* a fundamental legal notion used principally as a basis for negating or restricting private agreements, the exercise of police power, or the application of foreign law. The common law counterpart of *"l'ordre publique"* is not "public order" but rather "public policy." It is this concept, which is employed in common law countries to invalidate or limit private agreements of the application of law. In contrast to this concept of public policy, the English expression "public order" is not a recognized legal concept. In its ordinary English sense it would presumably mean merely the absence of public disorder. This notion is obviously far removed from the concept of *"l'ordre publique"* or "public policy." Since the Covenant should undoubtedly contain equivalent concepts in English and French, the question arises as to whether the notion of *"l'ordre publique"* or, in English, "public policy" should be retained as an exception to the rights in Articles 13–16. In the Secretary-General's opinion, this is a most important question since the concept of *"l'ordre publique*/public policy" is in most jurisdictions, a broad and flexible principle, often characterized by legal commentators as vague and indefinite. It is true that in regard to certain situations public policy or *"l'ordre publique"* has been given a technical and fairly well-defined meaning, but at the same time the concept is sufficiently wide and fluid to permit its application in a variety of new situations. Accordingly, it could hardly be doubted that by introducing it as an exception to fundamental human rights, it may well constitute a basis for far reaching derogations from the rights granted.[218]

After objections, the Egyptian proposal was withdrawn. The UK representative expressed concerns with the expression "public order" as it did not have the same meaning in common law countries as in civil law countries, although it was felt that the expression "public policy" was too narrow in scope as it did not cover police measures or criminal legislation.[219]

Caritas International, present as an observer organization, took the view that

218 *Ibid* at 313; see, also, Hathaway, above note 3 at 853.

219 Weis, above note 128 at 314–15.

> a refugee should only be liable to expulsion if he made himself unworthy of asylum, by becoming truly dangerous either to the State which had received him or to the community of which he formed part. It should be borne in mind that a refugee could not return to his country of origin and that a refugee might sometimes be treated more severely than his case deserved. If an expulsion order was made against him, he would be unable to find any country that was prepared to grant him the necessary entry visa. He would have to choose between staying in the country and going underground, and returning to his own country and facing the certain death that awaited him there. The proviso relating to "national security" and especially that relating to "public order" seemed to his organization far too vague, and consequently harmful to the interests of refugees. Those provisions should be very clearly defined; it was capable of serving as justification for glaring abuse.[220]

The debate regarding social cases raised its head again as a result of the Canadian delegate indicating that Canadian immigration law contained provisions to deport public charges such as inmates of a mental asylum or of public charitable institutions. After strong objections by France, other countries, such as Belgium and the United Kingdom, agreed that expulsion based in indigence should not be part of this provision.[221]

One commentator summarized the debates as follows:

> As to the grounds of national security and public order, it results from the discussions that they do not include "social causes" such as indigence, illness or disability. They include convictions for criminal offences but the offence must be sufficiently serious as to constitute a violation of public order. Minor offences and, in particular, infractions of the aliens legislation, are not included. The principle of proportionality must be observed, that is, the expulsion must, in the circumstances, be the appropriate measure; the seriousness of the measure has to be weighed against the interests of public order and national security .... Compelling reasons of national security has a similar meaning as in Article 28 of the Convention. The exception

220 *Ibid* at 315.

221 *Ibid* at 316–17; see, also, Hathaway, above note 3 at 852. As well, the Netherlands suggested adding the word "imperative" to qualify the reference to national security in art 33.2 dealing with evidence, which was accepted (Weis, about note 128 at 318), leading to the present text with the substitution of "imperative" for "compelling" by the Style Committee along the same lines as for art 28.

> may be invoked, in particular, when it is not in the public interest that the reasons for the decisions should be divulged, for example, in espionage cases.[222]

With respect to due process, he reached the conclusion that

> it means a decision reached in accordance with a procedure established by law, and containing the safeguards which the law provides for the class of cases in question, in particular equality before the law and the right to a fair hearing. Substantially, it means that the decision must be based on law, that it may not be unreasonable, arbitrary or capricious and must have a real and substantive relation to its object.[223]

Another commentator was of the view that national security as set out in this article means "anything that threatens a country's sovereignty, independence, territorial integrity, constitution, government, external peace, war potential, armed forces or military installations may be construed as a threat to the national security,"[224] and

> it must also be stressed that an alien may offend against national security even if he cannot be considered guilty of any crime. If for example a refugee persists in producing or disseminating propaganda against a foreign government, the case may be such as to justify expulsion under the terms of Article 32.[225]

He went on to say:

> On the other hand, there was general agreement at the Conference of Plenipotentiaries to the effect that a refugee should not be considered as a danger to national security only because he was wanted by another State, notably the one from which he has fled. As a general rule it is the acts and behaviour of the refugee in his country of refuge—not the public image of his personality—which may justify expulsion under the provisions of Article 32. In general terms, a person may be said to offend against "national security" if he engages in activities directed at the overthrow by external or internal force or other illegal means of the government of the country concerned, or in activities which are directed against a foreign government, which as a result threatens the

222 Weis, above note 128 at 322.

223 *Ibid.*

224 UNHCR, *Commentary on the Refugee Convention 1951*, above note 20 at 119.

225 *Ibid* at 120.

former government with intervention of a serious nature. In short, the concept of "national security" may be invoked in the case of acts of a rather serious nature threatening directly or indirectly the government, the integrity, the independence or the external peace of the country.[226]

With respect to public order, the same commentator reflected:

> [T]his does not, however, necessarily amount to giving each State an entirely free hand to decide what it considers a violation of "public order" in the sense in which it is used in Article 32. The statement may rather serve as a warning to the effect that the committal of and conviction for even "certain serious crimes" does not automatically give the State a right to expel a refugee by virtue of Article 32 . . . . There can be no doubt, therefore, that the term "public order" as used in Article 32 of the Refugee Convention is an international, technical term, the meaning of which has to be delimitated by international criteria.[227]

He concludes that the Refugee Convention does not automatically justify the expulsion of any refugee who has committed or been convicted for a crime, however serious, but that a separate finding is required, namely, that the continued presence of the offender is prejudicial to the maintenance of public order, "that is to say the preservation of peace and tranquility in the society at large."[228]

Last, he makes it clear that the lapse of time between the committing of a crime or a conviction and the time when an order of expulsion is considered is not irrelevant by saying:

> [I]f a refugee who has committed an offence has behaved well for a considerable period after the deed, the chances that he will cause trouble again will normally be so reduced, that maintenance of public order will not be promoted by expelling him. It is also hardly reconcilable with the notion of the rule of law to let the threat of expulsion hang like a sword of Damocles over the head of a refugee who once upon a time has offended against the law or the established order.[229]

---

226 *Ibid* at 121.

227 *Ibid* at 122; see, also, Hathaway, above note 3 at 855–66.

228 UNHCR, *Commentary on the Refugee Convention 1951*, above note 20 at 129.

229 *Ibid* at 129.

4) Exceptions in the *Refoulement* Article

The draft convention as adopted by the Ad Hoc Committee at its first session did not contain any exceptions to the expulsion of refugees who might face threats to life or freedom, although the United Kingdom made it clear that it would continue to expel a person who

> despite warning, persists in conduct prejudicial to good order and government and the ordinary sanctions of the law have failed to stop such conduct; or those in which an alien, although technically a refugee within the meaning of Article 1 of the Convention is known to be a criminal.[230]

During the second meeting of the Ad Hoc Committee, the United Kingdom again took the lead on this issue by asking how to deal with cases where a refugee was disturbing the public order of the United Kingdom by being engaged not in ordinary crimes but acts "inviting disorder," to which the United States responded "that it would be highly undesirable to suggest in the text of that article that there might be cases, even highly exceptional cases, where a man might be sent to death or persecution,"[231] a sentiment with which France agreed. As a result, the original text was not changed, and no exception was made to the principle of *refoulement*, emphasized by this comment of the committee as a whole: "While some question was raised as to the possibility of exceptions . . . , the Committee felt strongly that the principle here expressed was fundamental and that it should not be impaired."[232]

This changed by the time the Conference of Plenipotentiaries convened a year later. A proposal by Sweden and a joint submission by France and the United Kingdom both contained exceptions, the Swedish one by saying to "where the presence of a refugee . . . would constitute a danger to national security or public order" and the joint France/UK text limiting this measure, where "there are reasonable grounds for regarding as a danger to the security of the country in which he is residing, or who, having been lawfully convicted in that country of particularly serious crimes or offences, constitutes a danger to the community thereof."[233]

---

230 Weis, above note 128 at 325.

231 *Ibid* at 326.

232 *Ibid* at 327.

233 *Ibid* at 328.

France explained its position by saying that the right of asylum was "sacred but people should not be allowed to abuse it" and that the right of asylum rested on moral and humanitarian grounds but with "certain essential limitations," while the UK representative alluded to the fact "that the climate of opinion had altered" since this article had first been drafted and that "each government had become more keenly aware of the current dangers to its national security." The UK government was also of the view that given the large numbers of refugees, it would be inevitable that some would engage against activities against the country of refuge, which should be able to protect itself, without having to resort to "lifelong imprisonment."[234] The UK delegate, in response to a question of the representative of the Holy See as to the meaning of "reasonable grounds" (who had preferred the exception to read "a refugee who constitutes a danger to the security"), said that this formulation was used because he felt that "it must be left to States to determine whether there were sufficient grounds for regarding a refugee as a danger to the security of the country."[235]

The only reference to national security was a comment by Sweden that its amendment was intended to deal with refugees engaged in subversive activities, which would threaten the security of the country of refuge.[236] Most of the debate dealt with the notion of crime and the relationship of this article with exclusion 1F(b). Substantively, with respect to the issue of crimes, Italy proposed to add the words "or having been declared by a court an habitual offender." This was deemed to be too broad by the UK representative, who was of the view that a person who was seen as a habitual or hardened criminal had either committed serious crimes or a number of petty crimes and that the former was covered by the amendment, while he saw no reason to bring the second within the purview of the article.[237]

In terms of the meaning of the words used in the original joint French/UK amendment, it had contained the words "crimes or offences" in the English text, while the French text read "*crimes ou délits*." Later, during the debates, the UK representative was of the view that the term "offences" could be deleted, while for the French text, the Belgian delegate

234 *Ibid* at 329–30; Canada agreed with the United Kingdom that the international situation had deteriorated (at 330).

235 *Ibid* at 329–30.

236 *Ibid* at 330.

237 Weis, above note 128 at 333–34.

preferred both terms. Responding to a comment by the chair that both the French and English words might be interpreted differently in other languages, France suggested using the term "convicted because of particularly serious acts," but Belgium did not think this was helpful. The Netherlands suggested using "infraction" in French.[238] Eventually, the original text was maintained, with one change: "lawful" became "final" as a result of an exchange between Belgium and the United Kingdom in which the UK representative agreed to make the change with this explanation: "It was, in fact, 'final conviction' that was meant, that was after any appeal had been heard and after the time of appeal had expired."[239]

After the Style Committee had worked on the proposal, which had been accepted by the delegates, the United Kingdom wanted to clarify that

> convicted by a final judgment in that country meant the country of refuge, as the commission of serious crimes before coming to and outside the country of refuge would be covered by article 1F(b) and therefore outside the scope of article 33, in the sense that, if a person had committed such a crime, he would be disqualified from protection of refugee status of both article 1 and article 33.

The delegates of both Sweden and France thought that the text was clear as it stood, with the latter indicating that

> once the possibility had been recognized by Article 1 that the status of refugee could be denied to a person who had committed a crime in his country of origin, there could be no objection to allowing the expulsion of a refugee if it transpired that after his admission to the country of asylum that he had committed a crime in his country of origin. Moreover, the possibility of a refugee committing a crime in a country other than his country of origin or his country of asylum could not be ignored. No matter where a crime was committed, it reflected upon the personality of the guilty individual and the perpetrator was always a criminal. What was required was that a distinction should be made between real criminals and genuine refugees.[240]

The text remained the same. One commentator was of the view that the above debate stands for the following propositions:

---

238 *Ibid* at 333.

239 *Ibid* at 331, 332, & 333. A similar exchange with the same result had occurred during the discussions of art 32; see at *ibid* 318.

240 *Ibid* at 335–36.

> As to paragraph 2 it constitutes an exception to the general principle embodied in paragraph 1 and has, like all exceptions, to be interpreted restrictively. Not every reason of national security may be invoked, the refugee must constitute a danger to the national security of the country. The principle of proportionality has to be observed, that is, in the words of the UK representative at the Conference, whether the danger entailed to the refugee by expulsion or return outweighs the menace to public security that would arise if he were permitted to stay.[241]

Another commentator said:

> It seems to be a fair interpretation that the word "danger" must mean a "present or future danger" apart from the fact that a conviction is not necessary for expulsion for reasons of national security, a conviction for espionage or some other activity which is traditionally considered as a threat to the national security, will not in itself warrant the application of Article 33(2). This is particularly true if the act for which he is convicted has been committed in a distant past. Only if his continued presence is regarded as a danger to the security of the country, the authorities may expel him to a country of persecution.[242]

With respect to the notion of danger to the community, Atle Grahl-Madsen gave the following explanation:

> [I]t will seem that the word "community" as used in Article 33(2) denotes the population at large, and that a "danger to the community" means a danger to the peaceful life of the population in its many facets. In this sense a man will be a danger to the community if he sabotages means of communication, blows up or sets fire to houses and other constructions, assaults or batters peaceful citizens, commits burglaries, holdups or kidnapping etc., in short if he disrupts or upsets civil life, and particularly if this is done on a large scale, so that the person concerned actually becomes a public menace.[243]

5) Observations

Comparing the three main articles that set out exceptions based on security or other serious concerns—articles 28, 32, and 33—it is striking

241 *Ibid* at 342.

242 UNHCR, *Commentary on the Refugee Convention 1951*, above note 20 at 140.

243 *Ibid* at 143.

that the highest standard in the sense of non-deviation of such benefits is not found in the provisions prohibiting expulsion or *refoulement* but rather the one dealing with travel documents. Article 28 makes it mandatory for states to issue travel documents to refugees unless there are compelling reasons of national security or public order. The word "compelling" cannot be found in article 32 or 33, except in article 32.2, which is of a procedural character in that a refugee can submit evidence during the court process, which is required to validate an expulsion under article 32.1.

The standards in article 32 ("grounds") and article 33 ("reasonable grounds") are considerably lower, which is rather puzzling given the fact that in 1950 it had been very clear during the debates in the Ad Hoc Committee that exceptions to *refoulement* were rather reprehensible; the discussions about this aspect of all three provisions took place late in the Conference of Plenipotentiaries; and the UK delegate suggested this wording for section 28 and was the co-drafter of the joint UK/France amendment for section 33, the text of which was eventually accepted. It is possible that the circumstance of travel documents having been issued at the time of the negotiations for almost thirty years without exception might have played a role in this discrepancy.

As regards the substantive differences among these three sections, they all refer to either national security or the security of the country, which, according to a commentator, have the same meaning. However, the second exception in article 33 is of a more limited nature than the limitations in articles 28 and 32 as it speaks of the commission of a particularly serious crime in conjunction with a conviction by a final judgment for that crime and also has the requirement of a person being a danger to the community. Section 28 only requires a public order concern, while article 32 goes slightly further than section 28 by insisting on public order in combination with a due process decision to expel (rather than a conviction for the act underlying the expulsion). This would be more in line with the implied hierarchy of the norms during the discussions of the convention, whereby *refoulement* should be the most sacrosanct, followed by expulsion and then the issuance of travel documents.

Another overarching observation is related to the embryonic understanding of the relationship between *refoulement* and exclusion, as can be seen from the discussion during the later days of the conference with respect to article 33. The debate suggests that exclusion applies to acts committed before coming to and outside of the country of refuge, while *refoulement* is relevant to crimes committed while in such a country, although at times the language is imprecise in this regard. As well, the overlap between *refoulement* and exclusion was only stated with respect to one exclusion clause, article 1F(b), in the possibly mistaken belief that since article 1F(b) refers specifically to crimes, it is more naturally connected to *refoulement* and its reference to security and convictions. This could be an impoverished and inconsistent view of the limited reach of article 33 compared to article 1F(b) as the latter is considerably broader for criminal offences in that it does not require a conviction or an assessment with respect to the danger to the community. At the same time, not referring to exclusion clauses, article 1F(a) or 1F(c) might also be a disservice to the overlap between exclusion and *refoulement* given that especially article 1F(c) and the understanding that subversion and the overthrow of governments fall within its reach can be considered similar to national security activities, which are within the purview of article 33. In this context, it is clear that the changed international political climate mentioned by both the United Kingdom and Canada as a justification for abandoning the absolute character of *non-refoulement* is related to the intensification of the Cold War as all the references during the national security debates and commentaries refer to subversion or espionage rather than terrorism.

As to the meaning of the various terms used to describe the exceptions to expulsion and *non-refoulement*, national security concerns are related to serious activities directly or indirectly threatening the government and its integrity, as well as the independence and external peace of a country, and can involve acts such as subversion, espionage, or the overthrow of a government. With respect to public order or danger to the community, it would appear from examples given that while both concepts refer to criminal activities, the latter is of a more limited nature in that it involves activities affecting the peaceful life of the population, such as certain forms of terrorism, including sabotaging means of communication, blowing up structures, and kidnappings. Although public order has on one occasion been referred to as related to the peace and stability of a state, there is virtually no indication of what the substantive contents of this expression are, apart from the fact that it deals with criminal convictions of serious offences.

H. THE *TRAVAUX PRÉPARATOIRES* OF THREE HUMAN RIGHTS TREATIES

1) Introduction

Three human rights treaties have had an impact on this issue of *refoulement* of refugees. One, the Convention against Torture, has such a prohibition contained in the treaty itself, article 3, while the other two conventions do not allow conduct such as unlawful killing, torture, or inhuman or degrading treatment or punishment on the territory of state parties, but a prohibition against *refoulement* to such treatment has been read into these provisions as well. These instruments are the International Covenant on Civil and Political Rights (ICCPR), articles 6 and 7, and the European Convention on Human Rights (ECHR), article 3. As well, the parameters of the notions of torture and other maltreatment are important in this context since *refoulement* can occur only if the threshold of these specific types of suffering has not been met.

2) The International Covenant on Civil and Political Rights

The ICCPR was part of the United Nations project that began in 1947 and was to constitute the International Bill of Human Rights with three components: a Declaration of Human Rights, a Covenant on Human Rights, and Measures of Implementation. The declaration became the UDHR, while the Covenant on Human Rights turned into the ICCPR. The drafting process of the ICCPR was difficult and took almost twenty years to complete. The same Commission on Human Rights, which had worked on the UDHR, turned its attention to the drafting of a binding human rights instrument and submitted a report with its first draft of the Covenant on Human Rights to the ECOSOC in 1950 and then to the General Assembly. The General Assembly considered the report at its fifth session and adopted Resolution 421(V) of 4 December 1950, deciding that the covenant should include economic, social, and cultural rights. This decision, on the advice of the Commission on Human Rights, was reversed two years later when the General Assembly decided, in Resolution 543(VII) of 5 February 1952, that the Commission on Human Rights should draft two separate covenants. A text for the two documents was submitted to the General Assembly in 1954, which asked its Third Committee to study the proposals, done between 1955 and 1962. After the Third Committee adopted the substantive provisions in 1963, the General Assembly on 12 December 1963 invited all governments to consider the text of the articles adopted by the Third Committee and decided to make a special effort to adopt the entire texts of the draft covenants the following year.[244] In 1966, the Third Committee completed the drafting of the covenants, adopting final clauses and articles relating to measures of implementation. The two draft covenants and the Optional Protocol to the Covenant on Civil and Political Rights were submitted to the General Assembly. After discussions in plenary, the General Assembly unanimously adopted the recommendation of the Third Committee on 16 December 1966.[245] The International Covenant on Civil and Political Rights came into force on 23 March 1976.[246]

Article 6.1 of the ICCPR states that "every human being has the inherent right to life. This right shall be protected by law. No one shall be arbitrarily deprived of his life." Article 7 states that "no one shall be subjected to torture or to cruel, inhuman or degrading treatment or punishment. In particular, no one shall be subjected without his free consent to medical or scientific experimentation."

The contours of these articles had already been formed during the debates on the UDHR, which had these equivalents in articles 3 and 5: "Everyone has the right to life, liberty and security of person" and "no one shall be subjected to torture or to cruel, inhuman or degrading treatment or punishment." The Drafting Committee of the Commission on Human Rights had the following two alternative texts before it during its first session: "It shall be unlawful to deprive any person of his life save in the execution of a sentence of a court following on his conviction of a crime for which this penalty is provided by law," as well as "it shall be unlawful to deprive any person, from the moment of conception of his life or bodily integrity, save in the execution of a sentence of a court following on his conviction of a crime for which this

---

244 Resolution 1960 (XVIII).

245 Resolution 220A (XXI).

246 UN Office of Legal Affairs, Codification Division, International Covenant on Civil and Political Rights, New York, 16 December 1966, "Procedural History," online: Audiovisual Library of International Law https://legal.un.org/avl/ha/iccpr/iccpr.html. The other covenant was the International Covenant on Economic, Social and Cultural Rights, which came into force on the same date.

penalty is provided by law."[247] During its second session in 1948, the Commission on Human Rights adopted the first version.[248]

Between 1948 and 1950, the debates in the commission varied from delegates expressing the view that the principle of the right to life should be enunciated without any exception to the contention that this was not realistic and that the provision should contain exceptions, such as the execution of a death sentence; killing in self-defence; death as a result of suppression, rebellion, or insurrection; killing during lawful enforcement actions; or even killing for violation of honour.[249] Eventually, the text of the first draft was adopted in the document.

In 1957, during the debates in Third Committee, Colombia and Uruguay submitted an amendment, which read: "Every human being has the inherent right to life. The death penalty shall not be imposed on any person." The first sentence met the approval of most members of the committee and was adopted.[250]

With respect to article 7 of the ICCPR, during the UDHR phase, the Drafting Committee began the first session with a proposal of its Secretariat with the text "no one shall be subjected to torture, or to any unusual punishment or indignity." The United Kingdom proposed the following formulation:

> [N]o person shall be subjected to:
> (a) torture in any form;
> (b) any form of physical mutilation or medical or scientific experimentation against his will;
> (c) cruel or inhuman punishments.[251]

During its second session, the United States and the United Kingdom had crystallized some of the original ideas into new, more focused proposals. The American one read: "It shall be unlawful to subject any person to torture, or to cruel and inhumane punishment, or to cruel or inhumane indignity," while the United Kingdom provided a variation to its earlier proposal by saying, "it shall be illegal for any person to be subjected to:

---

247 Marc J. Bossuyt, *Guide to the "Travaux Préparatoires" of the International Covenant on Civil and Political Rights* (Dordrecht/Boston/Lancaster: Martinus Nijhoff, 1987) at 113.

248 *Ibid* at 114.

249 *Ibid* at 115–16.

250 *Ibid* at 119.

251 *Ibid* at 147.

(a) torture;
(b) any form of physical mutilation or medical or scientific treatment or experimentation against his will.[252]

At the end of the second session, the Drafting Committee wrote in its report to the commission:

> [N]o one shall be subjected to any form of physical mutilation or medical or scientific treatment or experimentation against his will.
>
> (Note. The Drafting Committee decided to forward this text to the Commission together with a list of possible limitations. This list follows.)
> 1. Compulsory vaccination (United States of America);
> 2. Legitimate medical and scientific experimentation in hospitals for the insane, with the consent of parent or guardian of the patient (United States of America);
> 3. Emergency operations undertaken to save the life of a patient, where the patient is unable to give his consent or where a person empowered to give consent on behalf of the patient gives such consent (United States of America);
> 4. Other limitations might be developed later (United States of America). No one shall be subjected to torture or to cruel or inhuman treatment or to cruel and inhuman indignity.[253]

The Commission on Human Rights accepted this text without the note during its second session, but a year later the first clause regarding medical experimentation had disappeared from the text prepared in its third session.[254] During debates in the Third Committee of the General Assembly, the word "degrading" was added, while the word "indignity" was replaced by the word "punishment," with the result that the final text of article 5 of the UDHR became: "No one shall be subjected to torture or to cruel, inhuman or degrading treatment or punishment."

The basis of discussion during the fifth session of the Human Rights Commission in 1949 was this article 5 of the UDHR in which the commission reinserted the medical experimentation clause for debate, although there had been some proposals to continue with the same text agreed upon by the commission the year before.[255]

---

252 *Ibid.*

253 *Ibid* at 148–49.

254 *Ibid* at 149.

255 *Ibid* at 150.

During the commission's discussions regarding the concepts of torture and inhuman treatment, clarifications as to the meaning of these concepts were made. The chair indicated that torture could be both physical and mental torture, while it was generally agreed that the term "treatment" was broader than "punishment," but not so broad that it should be applied to degrading situations due to general economic and social factors.[256] When the Third Committee met in 1952, there was concern raised about the fact that the word "unusual," which was proposed by the Philippines as an addition to the other qualifiers, was too vague according to some representatives, while other delegates were of the view that there were actual practices that might not be cruel, inhuman, or degrading but still affected the physical and moral integrity of the person, and as such, the word "unusual" should be included. After debate, the representative of the Philippines withdrew his amendment.[257]

With respect to the medical experimentation clause, it was included as a result of the abhorrent practices in Nazi concentration camps during the Second World War. Some delegates indicated during the debates of the Human Rights Commission that they thought this type of behaviour was implied in the general prohibition in the first part of the provision, while others were of the view that the general part was not sufficiently precise to prevent future experiments. It was finally agreed that the matter was so important that it justified a specific inclusion, even at the risk of repetition.[258] The notion of free consent to medical treatment was the subject of some debate as well in that some countries were of the view that there might be exceptions to this principle where the health of the individual or the community was involved, while others felt it would be very difficult to draw up a precise list of such exceptions. There was agreement that the lack of consent from a sick or an unconscious person to carry out a dangerous medical treatment would not make the intervention illegal if it was required for a patient's physical or mental health. However, a proposal to allow compulsory measures in the interests of community health was rejected on the ground that it could lead to abuse.[259] Other proposals that tried to introduce exceptions, such as compulsory vaccinations, emergency operations to save the life of a patient, castration or sterilization of dangerous sexual offenders or

---

256 *Ibid* at 149–50.

257 *Ibid* at 151.

258 *Ibid* at 151–52.

259 *Ibid* at 152.

persons with mental deficiencies in the interests of the community,[260] and the use of drugs to induce confessions with the consent of the individual involved,[261] were all rejected or withdrawn.

Eventually, in 1952 the commission adopted the following text for the medical experimentation clause: "In particular, no one shall be subjected without his free consent to medical or scientific experimentation involving risk where such is not required by his state of physical or mental health."[262]

In the Third Committee in 1958, most of the debate centred again on whether the medical experiment clause should be included. Some delegates indicated that this clause was not only superfluous but actually weakened the entire article by diverting attention to only one form of torture: cruel and degrading treatment. Most representatives were of the view, however, that this sentence was meant to prevent the occurrences of the Second World War and in that sense complemented the first part of the provision.[263] It was agreed that it would be difficult to find a balance in the text between legitimate medical treatment and illegal medical experimentation and that the covenant should not attempt to lay down specific rules in this regard; that should be left to national legislation and the medical profession.[264]

They also agreed to delete the words "involving risk where such is not required by his state of physical or mental health" as they were confusing. Some doubts were raised about retaining the phrase "free consent" as it might open the door to abuse on the pretext that consent had been given and medical experimentation should not be allowed in any event, whether consent was given or not.[265] These doubts did not displace the wording as originally suggested.

---

260 *Ibid.*

261 *Ibid* at 153.

262 *Ibid* at 159.

263 *Ibid* at 155.

264 *Ibid* at 156.

265 *Ibid* at 157.

3) The European Convention on Human Rights

While it was acknowledged by the European Court of Human Rights that several articles in the ECHR[266] can contribute to an obligation of member states not to *refoule* a person,[267] the most important provision in this regard by far is article 3, the torture prohibition, which reads as follows: "No one shall be subjected to torture or to inhuman or degrading treatment or punishment." This language is very similar to the first sentence used in the ICCPR, with the exception of the word "cruel," which is added in the ICCPR after the word "torture." While the consideration of the ECHR began later than the debates in the United Nations for the ICCPR, the European treaty was concluded much earlier, in 1950, but the influence of the United Nations Commission on Human Rights in drafting the UDHR and the Draft Convention on Human Rights can be clearly detected.

In August 1949, the Consultative Assembly of the Council of Europe, in the context of furthering and safeguarding the human rights and fundamental freedoms in the territory of the states belonging to the Council of Europe, submitted proposals to the Assembly Committee on Legal and Administrative Questions of the same organization to draft a human rights convention. These proposals included a suggestion drafting a provision with respect to the safety of the person in accordance with articles 3, 5, and 8 of the UDHR.[268] On 29 August 1949, the committee submitted a draft to the assembly, which contained an article with the same wording as originally suggested by the assembly.[269]

This provision was debated at length in the assembly on 8 September 1949 after an assembly representative of the United Kingdom had submitted two amendments the day before. The first one added some more details to the proposal and read:

---

266 There is another Council of Europe instrument, the European Convention for the Prevention of Torture and Inhuman or Degrading Treatment or Punishment, which came into force in 1989 and established a European Committee for the Prevention of Torture and Inhuman or Degrading Treatment or Punishment with a mandate to visit places of detention.

267 Article 2, the right to life, and art 6, the right to a fair trial, have been mentioned in this context; see Kees Wouters, *International Legal Standards for Protection from Refoulement* (Antwerp-Oxford-Portland: Intersentia, 2009) at 188 and 345–50.

268 Council of Europe, *Collected Edition of the "Travaux Préparatoires" of the European Convention on Human Rights* (The Hague: Martinus Nijhoff, 1976) vol 1, at 36–38, 116–18, and 154 [*Collected Edition*].

269 *Ibid* at 166–72, 192–96, and 206.

> [I]n particular no person shall be subjected to any form of mutilation or sterilization, or to any form of torture or beating. Nor shall he be forced to take drugs nor shall they be administered to him without his knowledge and consent. Nor shall he be subjected to imprisonment with such an excess of light, darkness, noise or silence as to cause mental suffering.[270]

The second amendment intended to provide some clarification to the proposal by saying:

> [T]he Consultative Assembly takes this opportunity of declaring that all forms of physical torture, whether inflicted by the police, military authorities, members of private organizations or any other persons, are inconsistent with civilized society, are offences against Heaven and Humanity and must be prohibited. They declare that this prohibition must be absolute and that torture cannot be permitted for any purpose whatsoever, either for extracting evidence, for saving life or even for the safety of the State. They believe that it would be better even for Society to perish than for it to permit this relic of barbarism to remain.[271]

The UK representative of the committee, referring to the second amendment, was of the view that emphasizing one particular form of abhorrent behaviour would upset the delicate balance achieved in the provision,[272] which was echoed by his French colleague, who also preferred the original text since mentioning one form of torture would carry the risk that other forms might not be considered prohibited.[273] As a result, both amendments were withdrawn,[274] and the original article with its reference to the UDHR was adopted on the same day.[275] Later that day, the UK representative submitted a variation of his first amendment as a draft assembly resolution with this text:

> The Consultative Assembly solemnly declares that any use of torture by public authorities or individuals is a crime against humanity and can never be justified on the grounds that it is being used for extracting information. To save life or to protect the interest of the State or on

270 *Ibid* at 252.

271 *Ibid* at 252–54.

272 Council of Europe, *Collected Edition*, vol 2, above note 268 at 42.

273 *Ibid* at 44.

274 *Ibid* at 46.

275 *Ibid*.

> any other grounds whatsoever. The Assembly records its abhorrence at the subjection of any person to any form of mutilation or sterilization or beating.[276]

The last sentence of this motion became controversial when the representatives of Denmark, Sweden, and Norway objected to the term "sterilization" because their countries used this practice on sexual criminals,[277] while another UK assembly representative wanted the reference to beating removed as corporal punishment was still lawful in the United Kingdom.[278] In the end, the chair suggested having the entire text of the article, as well as the motion, referred back to the committee for further deliberations.[279]

At the end of its first session in 1949, the assembly adopted the text of the article originally proposed by the committee and submitted it as a recommendation to the Committee of Ministers of the Council of Europe,[280] which in turn referred the draft to the Committee of Experts on Human Rights, convened for this purpose.[281] The Committee of Experts had before it a document with this revised text: "No one shall be subjected to torture or to cruel, inhuman or degrading treatment or punishment," to which the UK Committee of Experts' representative suggested an amendment with the following wording: "No one shall be subjected to any form of physical mutilation or medical or scientific experimentation against his will."[282] It was observed that the initial revised text was identical to article 5 of the UDHR and article 6 of the 1949 version of the draft international covenant on human rights, while the amendment followed the wording of a proposed article 7 in the same United Nations draft covenant.[283]

At the second session of the Committee of Experts in March 1950, the same UK representative suggested an amendment to the article

---

276 *Ibid* at 238. Although the UK representative presented this motion to the assembly, it had been drafted by him and the two members of the committee, who had opposed his original amendment (*ibid* at 240). One of these two persons was Sir David Maxwell-Fyfe, who had been one of the British prosecutors during the trial of the International Military Tribunal in Nuremberg, which would explain the reference to a crime against humanity in this motion.

277 *Ibid* at 238 and 242.

278 *Ibid* at 244.

279 *Ibid*.

280 *Ibid* at 274–76 and 282.

281 *Ibid* at 288 and 296.

282 Council of Europe, *Collected Edition*, vol 3, above note 268 at 206.

283 *Ibid* at 254–58.

dealing with torture, which deleted the words "cruel" and "degrading."[284] This committee submitted a draft convention at the end of the session with no specific comments on this article in its report but proposed two alternatives to it: one with and one without those two words.[285] Three months later, in June 1950, the Conference of Senior Officials combined the two alternatives by keeping the word "degrading" and omitting the word "cruel," without any discussion.[286] No further amendments were made to this text.[287]

4) The Convention against Torture and Other Cruel, Inhuman or Degrading Treatment or Punishment

The Convention against Torture (CAT) was adopted by the United Nations General Assembly on 10 December 1984[288] and entered into force on 26 June 1987. The work on the CAT was initiated soon after the adoption of the Declaration on the Protection of All Persons from Being Subjected to Torture and Other Cruel, Inhuman or Degrading Treatment or Punishment (the Torture Declaration) by the General Assembly on 9 December 1975.[289] In fact, the Torture Declaration was intended to be the starting point for further work against torture. In a second resolution, also adopted on 9 December 1975, the General Assembly asked the Commission on Human Rights to study the question of torture and suggest any necessary steps for ensuring the effective observance of the Torture Declaration.[290] Two years later, on 8 December 1977, the General Assembly specifically requested that the Commission on Human Rights draw up a draft convention against torture and other cruel, inhuman, or degrading treatment or punishment in light of the principles embodied in the Torture Declaration.[291] The commission began its work on this subject in February/March 1978. A working group was set up to deal with this item, and the main basis for their discussions was a draft convention presented by Sweden. Every

284 *Ibid* at 282.

285 *Ibid* at 314 and 320.

286 Council of Europe, *Collected Edition*, vol 4, above note 268 at 184 and 218.

287 *Ibid* at 258–60 and 274.

288 Resolution 39/46.

289 Resolution 3452 (XXX).

290 Resolution 3453 (XXX).

291 Resolution 32/62.

year until 1984, a similar group was set up to continue the work on the draft convention.[292]

Article 1 of the Torture Declaration stated:

> 1. For the purpose of this Declaration, torture means any act by which severe pain or suffering, whether physical or mental, is intentionally inflicted by or at the instigation of a public official on a person for such purposes as obtaining from him or a third person information or confession, punishing him for an act he has committed or is suspected of having committed, or intimidating him or other persons. It does not include pain or suffering arising only from, inherent in or incidental to, lawful sanctions to the extent consistent with the Standard Minimum Rules for the Treatment of Prisoners.
> 2. Torture constitutes an aggravated and deliberate form of cruel, inhuman or degrading treatment or punishment.

This definition was part of the Swedish proposal, which also added, for the first time, because of the developing jurisprudence related to the ECHR, that it should not be allowed to expel or extradite a person "where there are reasonable grounds to believe that he may be in danger of being subjected to torture or other cruel, inhuman or degrading treatment or punishment."[293]

With respect to the definition of torture, many governments proposed alternative wordings during the meetings of the working group in 1979. The United States suggested:

> 1. [T]he offence of torture includes any act by which extremely severe pain or suffering, whether physical or mental, is deliberately and maliciously inflicted on a person by or with the consent or acquiescence of a public official.

---

292 UN Office of Legal Affairs, Codification Division, Convention against Torture and Other Cruel, Inhuman or Degrading Treatment or Punishment, New York, 10 December 1984, "Procedural History," Audiovisual Library of International Law online: https://legal.un.org/avl/ha/catcidtp/catcidtp.html. For more details on the Declaration on the Protection of All Persons from Being Subjected to Torture and Other Cruel, Inhuman or Degrading Treatment or Punishment, see J. Hermann Burgers & Hans Danelius, *The United Nations Convention against Torture; A Handbook on the Convention against Torture and Other Cruel, Inhuman or Degrading Treatment or Punishment* (Dordrecht/Boston/London: Martinus Nijhoff, 1988) at 13–18.

293 *Ibid* at 35 and 41.

2. Torture does not include pain or suffering arising only from, inherent in or incidental to sanctions lawfully imposed; but does include sanctions imposed under colour of law but in flagrant disregard of accepted international standards.[294]

As well, the United States proposed that the term "public official" be defined as follows:

1. A public official is any person vested with exercise of some official power of the state, either civil or military.
2. Any public official who (a) consents to an act of torture, (b) assists, incites, solicits, commands, or conspires with others to commit torture, or (c) fails to take appropriate measures to prevent or suppress torture when such person has knowledge or should have knowledge that torture has or is being committed and has the authority or is in a position to take such measures, also commits the offence of torture within the meaning of this Convention.[295]

Switzerland and Portugal suggested amendments dealing with medical practices, whereby Switzerland tracked the language of the ICCPR in this regard, while Portugal had in mind the abuse of psychiatry. Denmark wanted to generalize the sentence referring to the treatment of prisoners.[296]

The debate on this article provided some insight into the thinking behind the amendments. The United States indicated that permanent impairment of physical and mental faculties is indicative but not an essential element of torture, while the United Kingdom wanted to restrict the definition of torture by requiring systematic and intentional infliction of extreme pain. Barbados wanted to make it clear that the use of truth drugs was always torture even if no physical or mental suffering was apparent. Some delegates, such as France, wanted to expand the definition of torture from public officials to private persons as well, and while this broad suggestion was not generally accepted, there was consensus that the definition should also include acts of public authorities who had responsibility for people carrying out torture by using the wording, as Austria suggested, "persons, acting in an official capacity." In the end, it was agreed that acts by public officials should be expanded

---

294 *Ibid* at 41.

295 *Ibid* at 42.

296 *Ibid.*

to include acts committed by, or at the instigation of, or with the consent or acquiescence of a public official.[297] This discussion ended in the acceptance of the second US proposal, above.

There were also debates about whether torture should be carried out for specific purposes, for which an act of torture was committed, and whether a possible exception for lawful sanctions should be included. As to the issue of lawful sanctions, it was pointed out that the convention was not meant to make criminal sanctions more inhumane but to outlaw torture, to which France replied that a distinction should be made between punishment affecting the person and honour of a person, which was legitimate, and the treatment, which, by causing violent physical pain or extreme mental suffering, would alter the capacity of the victim or make the victim an object of derision or hate.[298]

No agreement was reached on the meaning of cruel, inhuman, or degrading treatment or punishment, with some delegations being of the view that this notion was too vague, while others pointed out that these words were contained in the ICCPR.[299] The working group agreed at the end of the session to this text:

> 1. For purposes of this Convention, torture means any act by which severe pain or suffering, whether physical or mental, is intentionally inflicted on a person for such purposes as obtaining from him or a third person information or a confession, punishing him for an act he or a third person has committed or is suspected of having committed, or intimidation or coercing him or a third person, or for any reason based on discrimination of any kind, when such pain or suffering is inflicted by or at the instigation of or with the consent or acquiescence of a public official or other person acting in an official capacity. It does not include pain or suffering arising from, inherent in or incidental to lawful sanctions.
>
> [2. Torture is an aggravated and deliberate form of cruel, inhuman or degrading treatment or punishment.]
>
> 3. This Article is without prejudice to any international instrument or national legislation which does or may contain provisions of wider application relating to the subject matter of this Convention.[300]

297 *Ibid* at 44–46.
298 *Ibid* at 46.
299 *Ibid* at 47.
300 *Ibid* at 44.

During the meeting of the working group in 1980, the definition of torture was not discussed, apart from some debate about the notion of cruel, inhuman, or degrading treatment or punishment. Again, no consensus could be reached on the question of whether these forms of torture should be in a separate article, which would exclude a reference to purposes, nor on the question of whether the prohibition on expulsion and extradition should apply to these forms of maltreatment.[301] This situation did not improve during the 1981,[302] 1982, or 1983[303] meetings, although during the 1982 meeting it was agreed to delete the bracketed sentence, which declared that torture was an aggravated form of cruel, inhuman, or degrading treatment or punishment.[304]

This provision was not discussed during its 1984 meeting, and the working group submitted a report to the plenary Commission on Human Rights, in which the 1979 text was included minus the bracketed portion. The commission discussed the report in March 1984, and while there were some reservations regarding the lawful sanction portion of the definition, the report was accepted on 6 March 1984 and submitted to the General Assembly.[305] The General Assembly forwarded the report of the commission to the governments of the members of the United Nations on 26 March 1984. After receiving their comments, the General Assembly forwarded the draft convention and comments to its Third Committee for deliberations, which were held on 19–28 November 1984 after informal meetings between the committee chair and the delegations earlier in the month.[306]

During these debates, the Soviet Union and Byelorussia submitted an amendment with respect to article 1, which contained the definition of torture, proposing to delete the word "severe" before "pain or suffering," the words "based on discrimination of any kind," and the entire second sentence dealing with lawful sanctions.[307] However, after intense discussions, this amendment was withdrawn.[308] As well, several Islamic countries sought assurances that the death penalty and certain

301 *Ibid* at 71.

302 *Ibid* at 73.

303 *Ibid* at 85.

304 *Ibid* at 80.

305 *Ibid* at 101.

306 *Ibid* at 102–3.

307 *Ibid* at 104.

308 *Ibid* at 106.

other forms of punishment by Islamic law were compatible with the convention.[309]

With respect to the *non-refoulement* article, the discussions focused on three main issues. The first issue was about the level of proof required to allow expulsion or extradition as some delegations wanted more precision than the Swedish proposal. For that reason, the words "reasonable grounds to believe" were subject to proposals with terms such as "substantial ground for believing," "substantial evidence indicating," and "substantial indications."[310]

A second debate had to do with the extradition reference because some countries wanted to include a further article suggesting that states should re-examine their extradition treaties already in force to avoid conflict in existing arrangements.[311]

The third item involved the advisability of a provision prohibiting the expulsion of refugees. Some delegates were of the view that since there was already a provision dealing with *refoulement* in the Refugee Convention, there were strong humanitarian reasons to expand upon this concept. On the other hand, there were comments to the effect that such a widening of the concept was inadvisable as the Refugee Convention dealt with a different subject matter and was, furthermore, not broadly accepted. It was also suggested that the inclusion of this concept might require a state to accept a mass influx of persons when it was not in a position to do so.[312]

The Soviet Union proposed an amendment with some serious exceptions to general principle by saying:

1. No State party shall expel or extradite a person to another state where substantial evidence indicates that he may be in danger of being subjected to torture.
2. The evidence referred to in the preceding paragraph of this article includes above all situations characterized by flagrant and massive violations of human rights brought about when apartheid, racial discrimination or genocide, the suppression of national liberation movements, aggression or the occupation of foreign territory are made State policy.

309 *Ibid* at 103 and 106.
310 *Ibid* at 50.
311 *Ibid.*
312 *Ibid.*

3. The provisions of this article shall not be invoked as grounds for refusing to institute proceedings against persons who have committed crimes against peace or mankind, or war crimes as defined in the relevant international instruments.[313]

Some of the delegations could not accept this proposal as a listing of specific situations would imply that in other situations torture could be acceptable, leading to misinterpretation of the article. As well, the article was meant to deal with individual cases, and a reference to general situations was not helpful. While only one delegation wanted to delete this article altogether, most countries were in favour of retaining it, although no final agreement could be reached as to its wording,[314] even after Sweden presented a revised draft with the following text: "No State party shall expel, return ('*refouler*') or extradite a person where there are substantial grounds for believing that he may be in danger of being subjected to torture."[315]

During the 1980 meeting, the Soviet Union reintroduced the second paragraph of its 1979 proposal, while Argentina submitted a second paragraph as well, after the Swedish 1979 proposal had been accepted as a first paragraph for the *non-refoulement* article, which said: "If a State which would otherwise be obliged to extradite did not do so for the reasons mentioned, it shall take the necessary measures to bring the person, whose extradition it refuses to grant, to trial."[316]

The Argentine proposal caused difficulties with some of the delegations on the ground that not every country had the jurisdiction to try offences for which extradition was requested, and although compromise was sought by including the words "if its national legislation so permits," no agreement could be reached on this issue. As to the Soviet proposal, some delegations felt that the proposal had political overtones and should be deleted for that reason. Others were of the view that more examples should be included, such as colonialism or religious persecution, denial of free speech, suppression of political dissent and the free flow of information, and armed intervention in the affairs of a sovereign state. Again, no agreement on this proposal could be found.[317]

---

313 *Ibid* at 51.

314 *Ibid*.

315 *Ibid* at 50.

316 *Ibid* at 54–55.

317 *Ibid* at 55–56.

Agreement on a final text of a second paragraph remained elusive during the meetings of the working group in 1981,[318] 1982,[319] and 1983.[320] In 1984, some delegations had reservations regarding paragraph 1, which had already been adopted, by saying that their governments might not consider themselves bound by this article insofar as it was not compatible with their obligations under extradition treaties.[321]

As to paragraph 2, divisions remained, primarily based on the objections from Western delegations to having a listing of situations. This resulted in a number of compromise suggestions, of which the Indian proposal to replace all formulations so far with the text "a consistent pattern of gross, flagrant or mass violations of human rights" was accepted. The Soviet delegate was prepared to accept this compromise text, although he preferred its original amendment but indicated that he placed great importance on the concept of mass violations of human rights, which in his understanding implied that they occurred on a massive scale, and as such, the concepts of "gross" and "mass" should be seen as complementary. And last, with respect to paragraph 2, the United Kingdom wanted to make it clearer who should take these considerations into account and suggested adding the words "the competent authorities," which was accepted.[322]

During the debate in plenary in 1984, there was only one comment regarding article 3, by the Soviet Union's representative, who said that improvements to this article were possible and that he would prefer more work to be done by the working group but, on the other hand, would not stand in the way of transmitting the present text to the General Assembly.[323] The text as proposed earlier in the year by the working group was accepted in Third Committee.

5) Observations

A few observations can be made about the negotiations and drafting of these three human rights treaties. The first one is that strong connections exist between them. The ICCPR negotiations began before

318 *Ibid* at 73.
319 *Ibid* at 80.
320 *Ibid* at 85.
321 *Ibid* at 92.
322 *Ibid* at 93.
323 *Ibid* at 101.

the Council of Europe decided to embark on its human rights project, and when it did, those involved in the drafting were keenly aware of the work already done at the United Nations. It is no coincidence that the wording between the ICCPR and ECHR articles are virtually identical, with the only exception being the deletion of the word "cruel" in the ECHR. Similarly, the drafters of the CAT specifically decided to include a provision addressing the problem of *refoulement* because of the jurisprudence developed under the ECHR, which had read in such a prohibition in the substantive prohibition against torture.[324]

Second, the issue of how to incorporate odious medical practices within the parameters of torture and distinguish them from legitimate medical interventions was of concern to the drafters of all three instruments, in which the administration of sterilization of sexual offenders was raised specifically during the two older, general agreements. Only one of the three treaties, however, included a provision to that effect, the ICCPR.

Third, it was made clear, either in proposals, such as during the CAT negotiations, or during the debates, that torture is a more serious form of cruel, inhuman, or degrading treatment or punishment. However, none of the three instruments have a definition of the latter forms of maltreatment, prompting delegates at times to delete such a provision.

The ICCPR and the ECHR, as overarching treaties, only provide the skeleton of the prohibition against torture and similar practices, while the CAT, as a specialized subject matter treaty, provides the most detail. It has a definition of torture, indicates that it only applies to officials, sets out the purposes for which torture cannot be used, makes provision for a lawful exception, and includes the concept of *non-refoulement* within its framework.

I. CONCLUSION

1) The Role of *Travaux Préparatoires*

While the *travaux préparatoires* of treaties can "provide a fascinating insight into the politics of a highly sensitive and emotive issue,"[325]

---

324 There had been a similar but weaker connection during the negotiations of the Refugee Convention, where there had been some reference to the Draft Covenant on Human Rights during the debates of art 32; see Weis, above note 128 at 307–10.

325 Goodwin-Gill & McAdam, above note 18 at 6–7.

they do fulfill another, more important role in the interpretation of international instruments. The Vienna Convention on the Law of Treaties (Vienna Convention)[326] has this to say about interpretation of international agreements:

> Article 31
>
> *General rule of interpretation*
>
> 1. A treaty shall be interpreted in good faith in accordance with the ordinary meaning to be given to the terms of the treaty in their context and in the light of its object and purpose.
> 2. The context for the purpose of the interpretation of a treaty shall comprise, in addition to the text, including its preamble and annexes:
>   a. Any agreement relating to the treaty which was made between all the parties in connexion with the conclusion of the treaty;
>   b. Any instrument which was made by one or more parties in connexion with the conclusion of the treaty and accepted by the other parties as an instrument related to the treaty.
> 3. There shall be taken into account, together with the context:
>   a. Any subsequent agreement between the parties regarding the interpretation of the treaty or the application of its provisions;
>   b. Any subsequent practice in the application of the treaty which establishes the agreement of the parties regarding its interpretation;
>   c. Any relevant rules of international law applicable in the relations between the parties.
> 4. A special meaning shall be given to a term if it is established that the parties so intended.[327]

---

326 For a discussion on the *travaux préparatoires* of this treaty, see *ibid* at 8 and Jan Klabbers, "International Legal Histories: The Declining Importance of *Travaux Préparatoires* in Treaty Interpretation?" (2003) 50:3 *Netherlands International Law Review* 267 at 272–88.

327 For a general overview of art 31 in the context of refugee law, see Sarah Singer, *Terrorism and Exclusion from Refugee Status in the UK: Asylum Seekers Suspected of Serious Criminality* (Leiden & Boston: Brill Nijhoff, 2015) at 28–36; Yao Li, *Exclusion from Protection as Refugee: An Approach to a Harmonizing Interpretation in International Law* (Leiden & Boston: Brill Nijhoff, 2017) at 118–62; Guy S. Goodwin-Gill, "The Office of the United Nations High Commissioner for Refugees and the Sources of International Refugee Law" (2020) 69:1 *International & Comparative Law Quarterly* 1 at 37–39; and Hathaway, above note 3 at 148–56. For an application of arts 31 & 32 in the context of exclusion, see, for instance, in Canada, for

Article 32

Supplementary means of interpretation
Recourse may be had to supplementary means of interpretation, including the preparatory work of the treaty and the circumstances of its conclusion, in order to confirm the meaning resulting from the application of article 31, or to determine the meaning when the interpretation according to article 31:

a. Leaves the meaning ambiguous or obscure; or
b. Leads to a result which is manifestly absurd or unreasonable.

Given its status of supplementary means of interpretation, some writers dismiss the use of the *travaux préparatoires* out of hand,[328] while others urge caution when employing these types of documentation, either because the "living instrument" theory is seen as preferable[329] or because of the quite often political character of the negotiations leading up to the conclusion of a treaty.[330] One author is trying to combine both the living instrument approach with the use of *travaux* by saying that "it follows that treaty interpretation must be open to context, and there is no good reason (bar the text of the Vienna Convention itself) to exclude the *travaux préparatoires* from a treaty's context."[331] This is exactly the approach taken by the highest courts in Canada, Germany, New Zealand, and the United Kingdom,[332] including in the areas of exclusion and *refoulement*. In respect to the general interpretation of

---

all three exclusion clauses, *Ezokola v Canada (Citizenship and Immigration)*, 2013 SCC 40 at para 31 (for 1F(a)); *Febles v Canada (Citizenship and Immigration)*, 2014 SCC 68 at para 12 (for 1F(b)) [*Febles*]; and *Pushpanathan*, above note 132 at para 52 (for 1F(c)).

328 Wouters, above note 267 at 10–11, and Einarsen, above note 1 at marginal note 19.

329 Guy S. Goodwin-Gill, "The Search for the One, True Meaning . . ." in Guy S. Goodwin-Gill & Hélène Lambert, eds, *The Limits of Transnational Law, Refugee Law, Policy Harmonization and the Judicial Dialogue in the European Union* (Cambridge: Cambridge University Press, 2010) at 232; Goodwin-Gill, above note 327 at 35–37.

330 Goodwin-Gill & McAdam, above note 18 at 6–7.

331 Klabbers, above note 326 at 288; see, also, James C. Hathaway & Colin J. Harvey, "Framing Refugee Protection in the New World Disorder" (2001) 34:2 *Cornell International Law Journal* 257 at 261; Geoff Gilbert, "Current Issues in the Application of Exclusion Clauses" in Erika Feller, Volker Türk & Frances Nicholson, eds, *Refugee Protection in International Law: UNHCR's Global Consultations on International Protection* (Cambridge: Cambridge University Press, 2003) at 452.

332 The Supreme Court of the United States has not specifically referred to the *travaux préparatoires* of the convention but does rely on other historical documents to assist in interpretation of its immigration legislation, such as the IRO Statute and manual; see *Fedorenko v United States*, 499 US 490 (1981), and *Negusie v Holder*, 129 S Ct 1159 (2009).

the Refugee Convention, some members of the House of Lords have given great weight to the *travaux préparatoires*,[333] while others have preferred the living instrument approach.[334]

The Supreme Court of Canada, in interpreting exclusion in article 1F(c),[335] rejected the living instrument approach, which had been adopted by the Federal Court of Appeal in a number of decisions in exclusion,[336] and instead opted for an analysis of the *travaux* to give meaning to the words "acts against the purposes and principles of the United Nations," by saying after a reference to the Vienna Convention:

> [T]he legislative history of Article 1F indicates that the signatories to the Convention wished to ascribe a special meaning to the words "purposes and principles of the United Nations" in the context of the Convention. . . . The extremely general words in Article 1F(c) are not so unambiguous as to foreclose examination of other indications of the proper scope of the provision. An examination of the purpose and context of the treaty as a whole, as well as the purpose of the individual provision in question as suggested by the *travaux préparatoires*, provide helpful interpretative guidelines.[337]

This statement was slightly tempered in a more recent decision of the Supreme Court of Canada dealing with exclusion 1F(b), where it was said:

> Article 31(1) of the *Vienna Convention* provides for interpretation of treaty provisions in accordance with the ordinary meaning of the terms in their context and in light of the treaty's object and purpose. Article 32 only allows for recourse to "supplementary means of interpretation"—including the *Travaux préparatoires* — in order to confirm the meaning resulting from the application of Article 31, or to determine the meaning when the interpretation according to Article 31 leaves the meaning ambiguous or obscure; or leads to a result which is manifestly absurd or unreasonable. These conditions for use

---

333 Hathaway & Harvey, above note 331 at 261, referring to Lord Lloyd of Berwick in the case of *Adan v Home Secretary*, [1999] 1 AC 293 at 305.

334 Goodwin-Gill, "The Search for the One, True Meaning . . . ," above note 329 at 232, referring to Lord Bingham in the *R v Secretary of State for the Home Department, ex parte Adan*, [2001] 2 AC 477 at 500.

335 *Pushpanathan*, above note 132.

336 *Ibid* at paras 54–55.

337 *Ibid* at para 55.

> of the *Travaux préparatoires* are not present in this case. . . . [T]he meaning of Article 1F(*b*) is clear, and admits of no ambiguity, obscurity or absurd or unreasonable result. Therefore, the *Travaux préparatoires* should not be considered.[338]

In Germany, the Federal Administrative Court also examined the *travaux* in the context of 1F(c), while at the same time keeping in mind the practice of other states in this area. With respect to the *travaux*, it said:

> This reason for exclusion likewise already appears in the Geneva Refugee Convention [GRC]. From the *Travaux Préparatoires* one finds that during the deliberations it was unclear which acts are included under the reason for exclusion incorporated into Article 1 F (c) of the GRC on the basis of Article 14 (2) of the United Nations Universal Declaration of Human Rights of 10 December 1948.[339]

In New Zealand, the Supreme Court was called upon to determine whether there existed an obligation in international law for New Zealand not to return a person with a criminal background to possible torture even though New Zealand was at that time not a party to the CAT. In its decision, the court had an opportunity to comment on the *refoulement* provision in the Refugee Convention and how it came into existence and concluded:

> We now turn to the passage in the drafting history of the Convention . . . . In terms of article 32 of the Vienna Convention, the drafting history of a treaty is to be invoked only to confirm a meaning reached by the means set out in article 31 or to dispel an ambiguity or a manifestly unreasonable or absurd meaning arising from those other means. Given that the passage from the negotiating history is cited in support of the proportionality reading, the unreasonableness or absurdity ground would have to be invoked. But as already indicated, the ordinary meaning of the terms of article 33 read in context by reference to purpose and supported by subsequent practice is not absurd; to the contrary it is perfectly reasonable. There is the further

338 *Febles*, above note 327 at paras 38–39.

339 Bundesverwaltungsgericht (Federal Administrative Court), BverwG 10 C 48.07, 14 October 2008, at para 24, while para 30 does the same for the principle of *refoulement*; see, also, Bundesverwaltungsgericht (Federal Administrative Court), BverwG 10 C 24.08, 11 November 2009.

difficulty that the drafting history does not in fact support a proportionality or balancing proposition. The relevant statement was made by the United Kingdom representative when he spoke in support of the French/United Kingdom amendment proposing the addition to the text of what became para (2) of article 33.[340]

2) Final Observations

The regulation of refuge and asylum at the international level did not begin until after the First World War, with the first tentative attempt in 1922 and culminating in a number of conventions in the 1930s. Three observations about the work in this period can be made. To begin, it was the first time the issue of refugees had risen beyond the concern of individual states and become the subject of international efforts and regulation. Second, after the ad hoc arrangements of the 1922–28 period, which dealt with the aftermath of the chaos of the First World War, the conventions of the 1933–39 period dealt with new situations in Europe, which had resulted in large, new refugee flows. Possibly as a result, these new arrangements attempted to create a more comprehensive regime for the treatment of refugees. Third, while these new arrangements did not yet attempt to create a definition of what constitutes an individual refugee but rather repeated the collective objective approach from the earlier arrangements by referring to specific groups, they do already contain embryonic rights, which should be granted to refugees. They also already contain limits on one of these rights, the right of *non-refoulement*, which could be adjusted in situations of national security or public order.

After the Second World War, the IRO became the primary international vehicle to address the urgent issue of massive displacement of persons in Europe. With respect to the drafting of its constitution, it is interesting, albeit not surprising given the timing of the establishment of the organization, that the exclusion from refugee status of war criminals was quickly and readily accepted and that it was equally and readily extended to collaborators of all stripes. This acceptance was not only forthcoming from the two major powers involved in the negotiations at the time, the United States and the USSR, but also from several erstwhile occupied countries and from South American countries that were

340 *Attorney-General v Zaoui & Ors*, [2005] NZSC 38 at para 36.

in danger of becoming safe havens for Nazi perpetrators of such crimes. Another comment regarding the constitution is the fact that the drafters had serious concerns about subversive and terrorist activities, although unlike in later eras, these concerns did not come from Western states but from Eastern bloc countries, which were afraid that their relatively fragile governments could be easily overthrown by political opponents who had fled their countries during the war.[341]

Regarding the practice of the IRO as exemplified by its manual, it is remarkable how much detail is provided about what constitutes crimes against peace, war crimes, crimes against humanity, and common crimes, as well as in the examples of extended liability (including an embryonic version of what was later to become an approach used in several countries by relying on a number of factors). In this context, it is not clear how far the writers of the manual relied on the developing jurisprudence in Europe with respect to war crimes–related concepts.[342] The manual was written in 1951, by which time many cases had been heard and reported, although no caselaw is set out in the manual. It is also known that this was the third version of a field guide, a rudimentary version of which was in place in January 1947, soon after the IRO started to operate.[343] At that time, there were very few decisions in war crimes cases, although the decision of the International Military Tribunal (IMT) at Nuremberg had already been handed down, which could explain why the manual excluded mere members of some notorious organizations, although with a different reasoning and a different number of organizations than the IMT had decided upon in 1946.[344]

The next historical event of importance in the development of the concept of asylum was the creation of the UDHR, about which some comments can be made. The first is that earlier work in defining which persons should not be given assistance by international aid organizations, such as the UNRRA and the IRO, was now carried through in

341 Holborn, *The International Refugee Organization*, above note 10 at 37–39.

342 See, for an overview of this jurisprudence, Joseph Rikhof, "War Crimes, Crimes Against Humanity and Immigration Law" (1993) 19 *Immigration Law Reporter* (2d) at 23–36; see, also, United Nations War Crimes Commission, *Law Reports of Trials of War Criminals, Volume XV, Digest of Laws and Cases* (London: His Majesty's Stationary Office, 1949) at 49–79 and 89–154.

343 Holborn, *The International Refugee Organization*, above note 10 at 207.

344 The manual mentions the SS and the Gestapo, while the IMT designated the Leadership Corps of the Nazi Party, the Gestapo, the SD, and the SS as criminal organizations (see Shane Darcy, *Collective Responsibility and Accountability Under International Law* (Leiden: Transnational Publishers, 2007) at 273–78, and Rikhof, above note 342 at 40–41).

general terms to an exclusion from entitlement to asylum. This can be seen in the development of the mandates of the UNRRA and the IRO, from denying collaborators any benefits and the reference to war criminals in the Constitution of the IRO to the extensive discussion regarding article 14(2) of the UDHR with respect to persons involved in war crimes. Along the same vein, the reference in UNRRA documents to persons committing crimes against the interests and nationals of the United Nations is echoed in the phrase "purposes and principles of the United Nations" in the UDHR. As well, while the IRO's exclusion of "ordinary criminals who are extraditable by treaty" has given way to more general language in the UDHR, the phrase "prosecutions genuinely arising from non-political crimes" has a direct lineage to the Constitution of the IRO, especially when considering the interpretation in the manual. Last, with respect to the words "acts contrary to the purposes and principles of the United Nations," two other conclusions can be drawn. The first is that the implicit reference to war crimes would also include the commission of crimes against humanity and crimes against peace.[345] In this context, it is also significant that in the same time period the United Nations appears to have equated the violation of human rights with crimes against humanity.[346] The second conclusion is that, as a result of references to fascists, Nazis, and traitors, these words appear to include more than just war criminals, even in the broadest sense.

The final stage in crystallizing the notion of exclusion in international refugee law came in 1950–51 during the work done to draft a refugee convention. In general, it was said that the negotiations reflected a sense of international morality in which the protection of perpetrators of atrocities was seen as repugnant, while the humanitarian objective

345 UN Doc, United Nations Economic and Social Council, Commission on Human Rights, Drafting Committee, International Bill of Rights, First Session, Summary Record of Thirteenth Meeting (20 June 1947), where a reference is made to the Moscow Declaration (which has the same contents as the London Agreement or London Charter).

346 This is confirmed by Annex I of the IRO Constitution, but see, also, the *Yearbook of the United Nations, 1946–47*, above note 75 at 523; Nehemiah Robinson, *The Universal Declaration of Human Rights: Its Origin, Significance, Application and Interpretation* (New York: Institute of Jewish Affairs, World Jewish Congress, 1958) at 122; UN Doc, Report of the International Law Commission on the Work of its Forty-eighth Session, Official Records of the General Assembly, Fifty-first Session, Supp No 10, ch 2 at 98–99.

of protecting refugees should only be extended to those who deserve such protection.[347]

Regarding article 1F(a), it was clear from the beginning that the drafters wanted this exclusion ground to be framed as broadly as possible and that any formulation of the concepts included in this provision was to take into account both the jurisprudence developed after the Second World War and recent attempts to bring both international humanitarian law and criminal law up to date as a result of some of the shortcomings in this area. The debate in the various fora of the diplomatic conference established to finalize the Refugee Convention focused primarily on how to meaningfully achieve this result. This was done by using the term "international instruments" to exclude persons involved in crimes against peace, war crimes, and crimes against humanity as defined by both recent international treaties, such as the 1949 Geneva Convention and the 1948 Genocide Convention (which was seen during the debates as an adjunct to crimes against humanity), and other, less binding sources of international law, such as the work of the International Law Commission. The even broader concept proposed by the Eastern bloc countries, which also wanted to include traitors,[348] was rejected.

With respect to article 1F(b), a version of which was included in the Statute of the Office of the United Nations High Commissioner for Refugees but not in the 1950 draft Refugee Convention, the main disagreement had to do with the differences in approaches among delegations. Some states had no problem allowing persons into their countries who had committed minor crimes, whereas other countries took a more absolute stance without exceptions. This was eventually resolved by including the notion of serious criminality. While extradition was mentioned many times, it was mostly in the context of the relationship between the Refugee Convention and extradition treaties, in which most delegations favoured the latter in cases of conflict during a possible removal. This issue later became part of the discussions surrounding article 33, the *non-refoulement* provision. While there had been some mention of non-political crimes, and this wording found its way into the final text, the drafting history does not provide any guidance

347 See Matthew Zagor, "Persecutor or Persecuted: Exclusion Under Article 1F(A) and (B) of the Refugees Convention" (2000) 23:3 *University of New South Wales Law Journal* 164 at 167.

348 See, also, Kapferer, above note 39 at 71.

as to whether extradition concepts could be automatically transferred to the exclusion context.[349]

Although the debates about the meaning of the exclusion ground in article 1F(c)[350] are not exactly paragons of clarity, it can be deduced that this exclusion ground was meant to be a residual one to the two preceding grounds, and as such, it should be interpreted restrictively.[351] The acts committed must be criminal in nature,[352] and the exclusion ground appears to be capable of including acts committed in both the country of refuge and the country of origin. As well, from the statements and examples given by the various delegates of what would constitute acts contrary to the purposes and principles of the United Nations, it appears that acts that can be committed by private individuals and acts that can only be committed by individuals in the exercise of government functions were both contemplated.[353]

In examining the history of refuge and asylum, it is clear that the concern with criminality has permeated all discussions related to the rights of refugees. This started with legal philosophers, such as Grotius and Vattel, who advocated states' obligations to protect persons fleeing persecution but who were not inclined to extend these rights to serious criminals. This trend has not abated in modern times. Very soon after

---

349 *Ibid* at 74.

350 Hathaway, above note 3 at 227.

351 Grahl-Madsen, above note 10 at 286.

352 The UK delegate during the Conference of Plenipotentiaries referred to acts such as war crimes, genocide, and the subversion or overthrow of democratic regimes, while other indications were given earlier during the debate in the Social Committee, where the French delegate referred to both people who have committed crimes against humanity other than war crimes (UN Doc E/AC.7/SR 166 at 4, which was mirrored by the Canadian delegation at 10) or who are guilty of genocide (UN Doc E/AC.7/SR 160 at 15).

353 In addition to persons who occupy government posts, such as heads of state, ministers, and high officials (UN Doc E/AC.7/SR 166 at 6), the US and UK delegates mentioned collaborators (UN Doc E/AC/SR 166 at 16 and 19), and the United Nations Secretariat submitted a proposal saying that persons violating human rights without committing a crime against humanity, such as discrimination should be included (UN Doc E/AC.7/SR 166 at 9) even when committed by individuals (UN Doc E/AC.7/SR 166 at 8), a notion also expressed by India (UN Doc E/AC.7/SR 160 at 17). Grahl-Madsen appears to be in favour of a combination of the above approaches by suggesting that art 1F(c) should be limited to persons occupying government posts, such as heads of state, Cabinet members, officials, and agents of a government, who are guilty of persecutory measures and atrocities in defiance of human rights or who have instigated, committed, or abetted acts of state contrary to the maintenance of a just peace, with the possible addition of persons who, although acting in an individual capacity, are guilty of especially flagrant violations of human rights, such as those mentioned above (Grahl-Madsen, above note 10 at 286).

the issue of refugees became a concern of the international community and international agreements were drawn up to provide protection to displaced persons (in addition to the regulation of the use of identity cards), criminality in the form of a *refoulement* provision for persons granted refugee status found a place in the first comprehensive refugee arrangement, the 1933 Refugee Convention. This convention included exceptions for *non-refoulement* for situations of national security or public order.

The first instruments after the Second World War were less concerned with criminality as an exception to *refoulement* but more with ensuring that certain criminal elements would not be entitled to any benefit normally associated with refugees. The Statute of the UNRRA and the Constitution of the IRO, two organizations with a temporary mandate to deal with refugees both in terms of repatriation to their home countries and resettlement in third countries, specifically barred assistance to serious criminals. This exclusionary practice became permanent with the Statute of the UNHCR. In the meantime, in the human rights area, the very first instrument cataloguing basic human rights, the UDHR, contained an exception for criminality in its provision dealing with asylum, the only specific provision to do.[354] The drafting of the Refugee Convention brought these two strands of criminality together for the first time by having both an exclusion ground and an exception to the *non-refoulement* provision.

In terms of what types of criminal activities should limit the benefits to asylum seekers, the basic parameters as sketched out by Grotius and Vattel do not differ conceptually from what was considered to be nefarious in later centuries, taking into account the political and legal context of the times those instruments were conceived. After all, crimes injurious to humankind and destructive to society or menaces to public security everywhere and enemies of the whole human race, as stated by those two scholars, are not all that far removed from concepts such as national security, public order, crimes against peace, war crimes, crimes against humanity, or acts against the purposes and principles of the United Nations. Similarly, an elucidation of what constitutes a danger to security, by a commentator on the 1933 Refugee Convention on the

354 The UDHR has thirty articles; arts 29 & 30 contain general limitations, which apply to all previous articles, including art 29(3), which says: "These rights and freedoms may in no case be exercised contrary to the purposes and principles of the United Nations," which mirrors part of the asylum exception.

effect of activities that upset the very equilibrium of society, resonates quite clearly with the comments made about the 1951 Refugee Convention, that such a concept involves acts of a rather serious nature threatening directly or indirectly the government or the integrity, the independence, or the external peace of the country.[355]

What changed after the Second World War was, first, attempts to provide more detail for those universally known criminal concepts, especially due to the debates on the 1951 Refugee Convention. Second, because of concerns about *refoulement* to unacceptable situations from a human rights perspective, the limitations on the benefits for refugees were restricted and further clarified. In examining the history of the institution of asylum, it is clear that the issue of possible criminals within refugee movements was a concern for the drafters of international instruments dealing with asylum for a long time. These instruments set out concepts of exceptions to the right of asylum only in general terms and often due to political compromises arrived at during its negotiations. As such, they only provide a limited understanding of the various notions contained in them even when such an instrument was operationalized, as with the IRO. The next chapters will flesh out these general concepts as they developed in domestic legislation and jurisprudence while also examining how much the work of international institutions has influenced national decision makers in providing their interpretation of the elements of exclusion and *refoulement* with an international component, such as the international crimes in article 1F(a) and the parameters of the phenomenon of terrorism, which have been used for exclusion purposes in both articles 1F(b) and 1F(c) and in article 33.2.

355 UNHCR, *Commentary on the Refugee Convention 1951*, above note 20 at 124.

CHAPTER THREE

Exclusion — Introduction and 1F(a) Crimes

A. INTRODUCTION

As we saw in the previous chapter, the international community had grave concerns about the atrocities committed during the Second World War and was determined to address the issue of impunity of the persons who had perpetrated such acts. Most of the law of crimes against peace, war crimes, and crimes against humanity was developed in the immediate aftermath of the Second World War and consisted of the instruments setting up the two international military tribunals (IMTs) in Nuremberg and Tokyo, the legislative authority enabling domestic courts to deal with war criminals in Europe and Asia, the caselaw developed by these tribunals and courts,[1] the adoption of the 1948 Genocide Convention,

1 The most important cases have been described in a variety of law reports; the proceedings and the verbatim judgments of the military tribunals in Nuremberg have been reported very extensively in the fifteen volumes of the *Trials of War Criminals Before the Nuremberg Military Tribunals*, the so-called Green Series. There has also been the Law Reports of Trials of War Criminals for all proceedings, including the Nuremberg tribunals, which is a fifteen-volume compilation of summaries and case comments of important decisions selected and prepared by the United Nations War Crimes Commission. The judgment of the Nuremberg IMT is reported in Volume XXII of the *Trial of the Major War Criminals Before the International Military Tribunal, Nuremberg, 14 November 1945–1 October 1946*, which was published in Nuremberg in 1949 and is also known as the Blue Series. There has also been some reporting of war crimes trials in *Annual Digest and Reports of Public International Law Cases*, which changed its name in 1950 to *International Law Reports*.

and the passing of the Geneva Conventions, which regulated the conduct of war, including its violations.[2]

Another main issue facing the international community, in addition to bringing war criminals to justice and the strengthening of human rights norms, in times of both peace and war through human rights instruments and improved rules of war, was a new framework for dealing with the large number of refugees. While the main treaty in this area, the Refugee Convention, was primarily a vehicle for the protection of people seeking asylum status, it was felt that persons who had been involved in criminal activity should not benefit from such generosity. With the memory of the Second World War still fresh in the mind of the drafters of the Refugee Convention, a clause denying asylum rights to criminals did not take long to become embedded in the text of this instrument, resulting in the exclusion clause, which reads:

> F. The provisions of this Convention shall not apply to any person with respect to whom there are serious reasons for considering that:
> a) he has committed a crime against peace, a war crime, or a crime against humanity, as defined in the international instruments drawn up to make provision in respect of such crimes;
> b) he has committed a serious non-political crime outside the country of refuge prior to his admission to that country as a refugee;
> c) he has been guilty of acts contrary to the purposes and principles of the United Nations.

While there are legal differences between the three exclusion grounds, similarities do exist between them, from both a legal perspective as well as arising from factual situations, which do not tend to divide themselves up along neat legal principles. For instance, a bombing attack with a large number of victims during an armed conflict and designed to terrorize people, which was committed before the perpetrator came to a country of refuge, could fall within the parameters of all three exclusion

---

2 There are four Geneva Conventions: Geneva Convention for the Amelioration of the Condition of the Wounded and Sick in Armed Forces in the Field (Geneva Convention I); Geneva Convention for the Amelioration of the Condition of Wounded, Sick and Shipwrecked Members of Armed Forces at Sea (Geneva Convention II); Geneva Convention relative to the Treatment of Prisoners of War (Geneva Convention III); and Geneva Convention relative to the Protection of Civilian Persons in Time of War (Geneva Convention IV). Each has one article dealing with grave breaches or war crimes (arts 50, 51, 130, and 147, respectively). The 1977 Additional Protocol I has supplemented the war crimes provisions of the 1949 Geneva Convention in arts 11 and 85.

grounds.[3] This overlap in the use of the different aspects of article 1F is echoed in the jurisprudence of the countries under consideration. For instance, several decisions in New Zealand and the United Kingdom combined the use of articles 1F(b) and 1F(c) for the same underlying fact pattern, while in Australia, article 1F(a) is regularly used in combination with article 1F(b), as is also the case at times in New Zealand. In Canada, the administrative tribunal dealing with refugee matters used to combine article 1F(a) with article 1F(c) in Quebec and in some cases has used all three exclusion grounds for one situation, as have Australia and the Netherlands. In this context, France tends to use article 1F(c) almost exclusively for cases that are, for all intents and purposes, crimes against humanity.

This chapter will focus on some procedural issues with respect to exclusion in general as well as the crimes in article 1F(a) and will discuss regarding the latter the relevant jurisprudence sequentially in relation to each of the categories of crimes in that provision while also examining the one international crime not mentioned in article 1F, genocide.

1) The Work of the UNHCR in Exclusion

The United Nations High Commissioner for Refugees (UNHCR) plays an important role in refugee law and refugee determinations, not only as the United Nations agency that provides guidance internationally[4] in

3 They can also be more than one crime within the parameters of art 1F(a); see, also, European Asylum Support Office (EASO), *Judicial Analysis, Exclusion: Articles 12 and 17 Qualification Directive*, 2d ed (2020) at 54, online (pdf): https://euaa.europa.eu/sites/default/files/EASO_Exclusion_second_edition_JA_EN.pdf.

4 Governments also issue internal guidelines for the application of exclusion-related issues, such as the *Operations Manual, Enforcement 18 — Human or International Rights Violations*, ch 8 (2020), online (pdf): www.canada.ca/content/dam/ircc/migration/ircc/english/resources/manuals/enf/enf18-eng.pdf, issued by the UK Home Office, "Exclusion (Article 1F) and Article 33(2) of the Refugee Convention" (28 June 2022), online: www.gov.uk/government/publications/asylum-instruction-exclusion-article-1f-of-the-refugee-convention/exclusion-article-1f-and-article-332-of-the-refugee-convention-accessible-version#relevant-legislation, of UK Visas and Immigration by the UK Home Office. In Europe, the Commission of the European Communities (now called the Commission of the EU) issued a working document entitled *The relationship between safeguarding internal security and complying with international protection obligations and instruments*, Document COM 743 (5 December 2001), which talks about exclusion in the context of terrorism, while the Council of Europe issued *Joint Position of 4 March 1996 defined by the Council on the basis of Article K.3 of the Treaty on European Union on the harmonized application of the definition of the term "refugee" in Article 1 of the Geneva Convention of 28 July 1951 relating to the status of refugees*, 96/196/JHA (4 March 1996) at para 13; other instruments in the context of the European Union with respect to

all matters related to asylum but also in a more direct manner, by being involved in the actual refugee determination process in countries that have not established their own national refugee determination systems.

The UNHCR has had a long and abiding interest in exclusion. This had already started in 1979 when it issued the first version of its handbook.[5] Exclusion 1F was discussed in broad terms, in which 1F(b) was given the most attention,[6] as part of a general, all-encompassing guideline for the interpretation of article 1 of the convention, by dealing with inclusion, cessation, exclusion, and family unity.

The general overview of the handbook was followed in December 1996 by a detailed document called "The Exclusion Clauses: Guidelines on their Application," which, according to its introduction, had as its purpose to be a "detailed analysis and review of the exclusion clauses, taking into account the practice of states, UNHCR and other relevant actors, UNHCR's Handbook on Procedures and Criteria for Determining Refugee Status (the Handbook), caselaw, the *travaux préparatoires* of the relevant international instruments, and the opinions of commentators."[7] The crimes set out in 1F(a), as well as extended liability and defences applicable in international criminal law, were discussed as well as various issues under 1F(b), such as what constitutes a crime and a serious crime, plus some emerging crimes of interest to the application of 1F, such as terrorism, hijacking, and torture.

---

terrorism have been the *Council Framework Decision on combating terrorism* (2002/475/JHA), the *Council Framework Decision on the European arrest warrant and the surrender procedures between member states* (2002/584/JHA), and *Directive (EU) 2017/541 of the European Parliament and of the Council of 15 March 2017 on combating terrorism and replacing Council Framework Decision 2002/475/JHA and amending Council Decision 2005/671/JHA*; there is also a document prepared by the Committee of Ministers of the Council of Europe of 23 March 2005, *Recommendation Rec(2005)6 on exclusion from refugee status in the context of Article 1 F of the Convention relating to the Status of Refugees of 28 July 1951*, provided 23 March 2005, online: www.refworld.org/docid/4278d27c4.html which sets out briefly (in seven short paragraphs) the essence of exclusion 1F; in this context, it is also useful to mention the detailed "Position on Exclusion from Refugee Status PP1/03/2004/Ext/CA, March 2004" from the European Council on Refugees and Exiles (ECRE), in which 65 paragraphs discuss all aspects of exclusion 1F (see (2004) 16:2 *International Journal of Refugee Law* 257–85).

5 UNHCR, *Handbook on Procedures and Criteria for Determining Refugee Status Guidelines on International Protection Under the 1951 Convention and the 1967 Protocol relating to the Status of Refugees*, HCR/1P/4/Eng/Rev.4 (February 2019), online (pdf): www.unhcr.org/publications/legal/5ddfcdc47/handbook-procedures-criteria-determining-refugee-status-under-1951-convention.html [*Handbook*].

6 *Guidelines*, below note 8 at paras 147–63, of which ten paragraphs were devoted to 1F(b), while at paras 164–80 also refer to the exclusion clauses as part of the chapter dealing with special cases, such as "persons having resorted to force or committed acts of violence."

7 *Ibid* at para 2. The guidelines consisted of 28 pages and 86 paragraphs.

The 1996 guidelines were updated and reissued on 4 September 2003 and consisted of two documents: the *Guidelines* themselves[8] and a more detailed *Background Note*.[9] These documents were the result of the "Global Consultations on International Protection" process, which examined this subject at its expert meeting in Lisbon, Portugal, in May 2001,[10] while "an update of these Guidelines was also deemed necessary in light of contemporary developments in international law."[11] While the subject matters discussed in the 2003 documents are very similar to the 1996 guidelines (the issue of torture has been deleted from the special cases section, but the application of the exclusion clause to the special situations of minors and mass influx has been added), there is a much heavier emphasis on international and national jurisprudence than in the previous guidelines.

The UNHCR has not only addressed exclusion in guidelines[12] specific to this provision, it has also taken the opportunity to state and

---

8 UNHCR, *Guidelines on International Protection: Application of the Exclusion Clauses: Article 1F of the 1951 Convention relating to the Status of Refugees*, HCR/GIP/03/05 (4 September 2003), online (pdf): www.unhcr.org/publications/legal/3f7d48514/guidelines-international-protection-5-application-exclusion-clauses-article.html [*Guidelines*].

9 UNHCR, *Background Note on the Application of the Exclusion Clauses: Article 1F of the 1951 Convention relating to the Status of Refugees* (4 September 2003), online: www.refworld.org/docid/3f5857d24.html [*Background Note*].

10 See the introductory paragraph of the *Guidelines*, above note 8. The result of the Lisbon expert meeting can be found as "Summary Conclusions: Exclusion from Refugee Status" in Erika Feller, Volker Türk & Frances Nicholson, eds, *Refugee Protection in International Law: UNHCR's Global Consultations on International Protection* (Cambridge: Cambridge University Press, 2003) at 479–85.

11 See the introductory paragraph of the *Guidelines*, above note 8. While the *Guidelines* are relatively short (9 pages and 36 paragraphs), the *Background Note* has been expanded considerably from the 1996 guidelines and has 45 pages and 113 paragraphs.

12 While the UNHCR makes it clear that its handbook and guidelines are indeed meant for guidance (UNHCR, *Handbook*, above note 5 at Foreword at para VII), the persuasive value of the handbook and guidelines has varied in national jurisprudence. In the United Kingdom, the handbook and guidelines have found, in general, support with the courts but less so at the tribunal level, especially in the context of exclusion, where some UNHCR interpretations have been specifically rejected (see Guy S. Goodwin-Gill, "The Search for the One, True Meaning . . ." in Guy S. Goodwin-Gill & Hélène Lambert, eds, *The Limits of Transnational Law, Refugee Law, Policy Harmonization and the Judicial Dialogue in the European Union* (Cambridge: Cambridge University Press, 2010) 204 at 224–25; Sarah Singer, *Terrorism and Exclusion from Refugee Status in the UK: Asylum Seekers Suspected of Serious Criminality* (Leiden & Boston: Brill Nijhoff, 2015) at 46–47 (for UK cases); and Guy S. Goodwin-Gill, "The Office of the United Nations High Commissioner for Refugees and the Sources of International Refugee Law" (2020) 69:1 *International & Comparative Law Quarterly* 1 at 22); see, also, specifically, *Al-Sirri (FC) (Appellant) v Secretary of State for the Home Department (Respondent)*, [2012] UKSC 54 at para 36 [*Al-Sirri*], and *El-Sayed El-Sebai Youssef v Secretary of State for the Home Department*,

restate its position on exclusion matters as part of guidelines related to other topics or when it issued statements related to judicial proceedings. One of the more elaborate guidelines that expanded on one issue raised in the 2003 *Guidelines* was the "UNHCR Guidelines on the Application in Mass Influx Situations of the Exclusion Clauses of Article 1F of the 1951 Convention relating to the Status of Refugees,"[13] which discusses almost exclusively procedural issues related to exclusion rather than substantive matters. Also of interest are the documents "Procedural Standards for Refugee Status Determination under UNHCR's Mandate,"[14] "Guidelines on International Protection: Child Asylum Claims Under Articles 1(A)2 and 1(F) of the 1951 Convention and/or 1967 Protocol relating to the Status of Refugees,"[15] and "Guidance Note on Refugee Claims relating to Victims of Organized Gangs,"[16] with their

---

[2018] EWCA Civ 933 at paras 60–61. In New Zealand, the Supreme Court did not find the handbook persuasive with respect to its position on *refoulement* in *Attorney-General v Zaoui & Ors*, [2005] NZSC 38 at para 30, while the High Court of Australia, in *Minister for Immigration and Multicultural and Indigenous Affairs v QAAH of 2004*, [2006] HCA 53 at para 76, said: "[D]eciding an appeal such as this, due weight should therefore be given to the guidance provided by relevant UNHCR publications, including the UNHCR *Handbook* and the *Guidelines*. This does not mean that such sources are binding on this or any other court. But it does mean that, like other final courts, this Court will often derive great assistance by having access to such materials." (See, also, along the same lines, *FTZK v MIBP*, [2014] HCA 26 at para 73) [*FTZK*]. In Canada, the Supreme Court, in the case of *Pushpanathan v Canada (Minister of Citizenship and Immigration)*, [1998] 1 SCR 982 at para 54 [*Pushpanathan*], did not specifically mention the handbook but in the end disagreed with it in respect to exclusion 1F(c), while the Federal Court of Appeal, in *Jayasekara v Canada (Minister of Citizenship and Immigration)*, 2008 FCA 404 at para 39, with respect to a 1F(b) case, was of the view that neither the handbook nor the guidelines are binding but can be relied upon by the court for guidance without overriding "the functions of the court in determining the words of the Convention." A similar sentiment was expressed at the Federal Court level in the 1F(a) case of *Carrasco v Canada (Minister of Citizenship and Immigration)*, 2008 FC 436 at para 41, but was more generous by saying that the exclusion guidelines "cannot simply be ignored." In the United States, the Supreme Court in *INS v Cardoza-Fonseca*, 480 US 421 (1987), n22, follows the same approach by giving the handbook credence but not to the extent that it has the force of law or is binding. Lastly, in the Netherlands, the Rechtbank (District Court) in The Hague in the case of Awb 02/17771, 11 July 2003 at para 4.8, was also of the view, in the context of exclusion, that the handbook and guidelines are not persuasive. For an overview of the jurisprudence with respect to UNHCR guidelines in general, see Guy S. Goodwin-Gill, "The Office of the United Nations High Commissioner for Refugees and the Sources of International Refugee Law" (2020) 69:1 *International & Comparative Law Quarterly* 1 at 18–23, and James Hathaway, *The Rights of Refugees Under International Law*, 2d ed (Cambridge: Cambridge University Press, 2021) at 60–67.

13 February 2006.

14 1 September 2005, ch 4.8.

15 HCR/GIP/09/08, 22 December 2009 at 22–24 at paras 58–64.

16 March 2010 at 22–23 at paras 55–61.

short references to exclusion. This notion also figures in the various eligibility guidelines for individual countries of which the "UNHCR Eligibility Guidelines for Assessing the International Protection Needs of Members of Religious Minorities from Pakistan,"[17] the "Eligibility Guidelines for Assessing the International Protection Needs of Asylum-seekers from Guatemala,"[18] and "Eligibility Guidelines for Assessing the International Protection Needs of Asylum-seekers from Afghanistan"[19] are the most recent ones.

Another example of reference to exclusion in other subject matter guidelines is the UNHCR Resettlement Handbook, which was first issued 1997 and updated in 1998, 2002, 2004, and 2011. The latest version has special chapters on exclusion,[20] which repeat in some detail the 2003 *Guidelines*, as well as some of the other specialized documents just mentioned.

Examples of positions issued during an ongoing judicial proceeding are the July 2009 UNHCR's *Statement on Article 1F of the 1951 Convention*[21] in the context of a reference from the German Federal Administrative Court to the Court of Justice of the European Communities regarding exclusion ground 1F(b) and 1F(c), the UNHCR interventions before the Supreme Court of Canada regarding exclusion grounds 1F(a)[22] and 1F(b),[23] and the intervention before the Supreme Court of the United Kingdom with respect to exclusion ground 1F(c).[24] These documents, discussing in detail the application of those provisions to the respective exclusion grounds, in some respects represent an updated view of the 2003 *Guidelines* on exclusion 1F.

---

17 HCR/EG/PAK/17/01, January 2017 at 67.

18 HCR/EG/GTM/18/01, January 2018 at 58–59.

19 HCR/EG/AFG/18/02, 30 August 2018 at 114–18.

20 UNHCR, UNHCR Resettlement Handbook (2011), chs 3.5–3.7, online (pdf): www.unhcr.org/46f7c0ee2.pdf.

21 UNHCR, *Statement on Article 1F of the 1951 Convention* (July 2009), online (pdf): www.unhcr.org/protection/operations/4a5edac09/unhcr-statement-article-1f-1951-convention.html, issued in the context of the preliminary ruling references to the Court of Justice of the European Communities from the German Federal Administrative Court regarding the interpretation of arts 12(2)(b) & (c) of the Qualification Directive.

22 UNHCR Intervention before the Supreme Court of Canada in the case of *Ezokola v Canada (Minister of Citizenship and Immigration)*, 15 December 2012.

23 *Luis Alberto Hernandez Febles v Minister of Citizenship and Immigration*: Factum of the Intervener (UNHCR), 11 March 2014.

24 UNHCR Intervention before the Supreme Court of the United Kingdom in the cases of *Yasser al-Sirri (Appellant) v Secretary of State for the Home Department (Respondent)* and *DD (Afghanistan) (Appellant) v Secretary of State for the Home Department (Respondent)*, 23 March 2012.

The above documents were all issued by the Office of the High Commissioner of the UNHCR. The UNHCR also has another institution, the Executive Committee. The Executive Committee of the High Commissioner's Programme (ExCom) was established in 1958 and functions as a subsidiary organ of the United Nations General Assembly.[25] It has both executive and advisory functions. These functions include issuing Conclusions on International Protection (often referred to as "ExCom Conclusions"), which address issues in the field of refugee protection and serve as international guidelines to be drawn upon by states, the UNHCR, and others when developing or orienting their policies on refugee issues. ExCom Conclusions are adopted by consensus by the states that are members of the ExCom and can therefore be considered as reflecting their understanding of legal standards regarding the protection of refugees,[26] or "although not formally binding, they are relevant to the interpretation of the international protection regime. ExCom Conclusions constitute expressions of opinion, which are broadly representative of the views of the international community. The specialist knowledge of ExCom and the fact that its Conclusions are taken by consensus add further weight."[27] At present, 106 states are members of ExCom.

This institution issued a number of conclusions between 1975 and 2017, some of which also mention the issue of exclusion.[28] Compared to the UNHCR guidelines, the conclusions are much shorter, do not provide substantive details, address a number of issues, and are in the nature of resolutions. One consistent theme in exclusion is an exhortation to states that it

25 See Goodwin-Gill, "The Search for the One, True Meaning . . . ," above note 12 at 6–8.

26 UNHCR, *Statement on Article 1F of the 1951 Convention*, above note 21 at 5, n24.

27 See UNHCR, Conclusions on International Protection (October 2017), online (pdf): www.refworld.org/type,EXCONC,UNHCR,,5a2ead6b4,0.html [UNHCR, Conclusions]; see, also, Guy S. Goodwin-Gill & Jane McAdam, *The Refugee in International Law*, 4th ed (Oxford: Oxford University Press, 2020) at 489–97, indicating that they might contribute to the formulation of *opinio juris* in the development of customary international law (at 491).

28 There have been seven conclusions that mention exclusion: Conclusion No 12 (XXIX) 1978 at paras (d) and (g); No 17 (XXXI) 1980 at para 9; No 82 (XLVIII) 1997 at para (d); No 94 (LIII) 2002 at para (c) (which is referred to in the *Global Compact on Refugees*, UN Doc A/73/12 (part II), 2 August 2018 at para 57, n22); No 100 (LV) 2004 at para (j); No 102 (LVI) 2005 at para (i); and No 103 (LVI) 2005 at para (d). See UNHCR, *A Thematic Compilation of Executive Committee Conclusions*, 7th ed (June 2014) at 214–15, online (pdf): www.unhcr.org/53b26db69.pdf, as well as UNHCR, *Conclusions*, above note 27.

> *reiterates*, in light of these challenges, the need for full respect to be accorded to the institution of asylum in general, and considers it timely to draw attention to the following particular aspects: (v) the need to apply scrupulously the exclusion clauses stipulated in Article 1 F of the 1951 Convention and in other relevant international instruments, to ensure that the integrity of the asylum institution is not abused by the extension of protection to those who are not entitled to it.[29]

When the UNHCR Office of the High Commissioner issues guidelines in which exclusion is discussed, it tends to quote or refer to this political statement but also incorporates the following caveat: "at the same time, given the possible serious consequences of exclusion, it is important to apply the exclusion clauses with great caution and only after a full assessment of the individual circumstances of the case. The exclusion clauses should, therefore, always be interpreted in a restrictive manner."[30]

2) Procedural Issues

Before beginning the discussion regarding substantive crimes, it is useful to explain procedural issues related to exclusion, such as the standard of proof required in exclusion proceedings and how that standard compares with international criminal procedure, as well as the concept of inclusion versus exclusion and the related question of balancing.

a) The Standard of Proof

The standard of proof[31] in article 1F is "serious reasons for considering." This is an unusual standard as it is not known in these terms in other areas of law.[32] The *travaux préparatoires* are silent on the reasons for

29 Conclusion 82; this same language is repeated in conclusions 102 & 103.

30 See, for instance, UNHCR, *Guidelines on International Protection*, above note 8 at para 2.

31 The burden of proof, as in where the obligation lies to provide evidence of exclusion, has generally been accepted as to be borne by the state as opposed to the refugee claimant; see *Background Note*, above note 9 at 38 at para 105; James Hathaway & Michelle Foster, *The Law of Refugee Status*, 2d ed (Cambridge: Cambridge University Press, 2014) at 534; Yao Li, *Exclusion from Protection as Refugee: An Approach to a Harmonizing Interpretation in International Law* (Leiden & Boston: Brill Nijhoff, 2017) at 205–6; for the related question of presumption of innocence, see Boštjan Zalar, "Legal Implications of the 'Presumption of Innocence' and the Exclusion Clauses in International Protection Cases: The European Law Perspective" in James C. Simeon, ed, *Serious International Crimes, Human Rights and Forced Migration* (London: Routledge, 2022) at 55–75 [*Serious International Crimes*].

32 *Background Note*, above note 9 at 38 at para 107.

including this phrase or the meaning to be attributed to it. In Canada, it has been equated to the better-known concept of reasonable grounds to believe, a notion also used in article 33.2 of the Refugee Convention dealing with the *refoulement* of persons who are a danger to the community or the security of a country where they have received refugee status.[33] The UNHCR has consistently argued for a relatively high standard of proof, somewhere between the civil standard of balance of probabilities and the criminal one of beyond reasonable doubt, expressed in the Background Note as "clear and credible evidence."[34]

On the national level, there have been a number of formulations to express the evidence required for exclusion.[35] In the United Kingdom in *R (on the application of JS) (Sri Lanka) (Respondent) v Secretary of State for the Home Department (Appellant)*, the Supreme Court originally had this to say about "serious reasons for considering":

> It would not, I think, be helpful to expatiate upon article 1F's reference to there being "serious reasons for considering" the asylum-seeker to have committed a war crime. Clearly the Tribunal in *Gurung* . . . was right to highlight "the lower standard of proof applicable in exclusion clause cases"—lower than that applicable in actual war crimes trials. That said, "serious reasons for considering" obviously imports a higher test for exclusion than would, say, an expression like "reasonable grounds for suspecting." "Considering" approximates rather to "believing" than to "suspecting." I am inclined to agree . . . "it sets a standard above mere suspicion. Beyond this, it is a mistake to try to

---

33 This trend in Canada began with the seminal decision in Canadian jurisprudence regarding exclusion, *Ramirez v Canada (Minister of Employment and Immigration)*, [1992] 2 FC 306.

34 *Background Note*, above note 9 at 39 at para 108; this test was advocated more recently in the UNHCR intervention in *Febles*, above note 23 at 6–7 at para 15(iv).

35 For commentaries on this standard of proof and national jurisprudence, see Michael Bliss, "'Serious Reasons for Considering': Minimum Standards of Procedural Fairness in the Application of the Article 1F Exclusion Clauses" (supp, 2000) 12 *International Journal of Refugee Law* at 115–17; Sibylle Kapferer, "Exclusion Clauses in Europe: A Comparative Overview of State Practice in France, Belgium and the United Kingdom" (supp, 2000) 12 *International Journal of Refugee Law* at 207–10; Catherine Dauvergne, "The Troublesome Intersections of Refugee Law and Criminal Law" in Katla Franko Aas & Mary Bosworth, eds, *The Borders of Punishment: Migration, Citizenship and Social Exclusion* (Oxford: Oxford University Press, 2013) at 80–81; Hathaway & Foster, above note 31 at 532–37; Mathias Holvoet, "Harmonizing Exclusion Under the Refugee Convention by Reference to the Evidentiary Standards of International Criminal Law" (2014) 12:5 *Journal of International Criminal Justice* 1039 at 1041–46; Li, above note 31 at 208–9 and 226–27.

> paraphrase the straightforward language of the Convention: it has to be treated as meaning what it says."[36]

However, only two years later, the same court decided to set the standard of proof higher by saying:

> We are, it is clear, attempting to discern the autonomous meaning of the words "serious reasons for considering." We do so in the light of the UNHCR view, with which we agree, that the exclusion clauses in the Refugee Convention must be restrictively interpreted and cautiously applied. This leads us to draw the following conclusions:
> (1) "Serious reasons" is stronger than "reasonable grounds."
> (2) The evidence from which those reasons are derived must be "clear and credible" or "strong."
> (3) "Considering" is stronger than "suspecting." In our view it is also stronger than "believing." It requires the considered judgment of the decision-maker.
> (4) The decision-maker need not be satisfied beyond reasonable doubt or to the standard required in criminal law.
> (5) It is unnecessary to import our domestic standards of proof into the question. The circumstances of refugee claims, and the nature of the evidence available, are so variable. However, if the decision-maker is satisfied that it is more likely than not that the applicant has not committed the crimes in question or has not been guilty of acts contrary to the purposes and principles of the United Nations, it is difficult to see how there could be serious reasons for considering that he had done so. The reality is that there are unlikely to be sufficiently serious reasons for considering the applicant to be guilty unless the decision-maker can be satisfied on the balance of probabilities that he is.[37]

---

36 *R (on the application of JS) (Sri Lanka) (Respondent) v Secretary of State for the Home Department (Appellant)*, [2010] UKSC 15 at para 39 [*JS*].

37 *Al-Sirri*, above note 12 at para 75; the UK Home Office manual "Exclusion (Article 1F) and Article 33(2) of the Refugee Convention" (28 June 2022), online: www.gov.uk/government/publications/asylum-instruction-exclusion-article-1f-of-the-refugee-convention/exclusion-article-1f-and-article-332-of-the-refugee-convention-accessible-version#relevant-legislation, states, after referring to the *Al-Sirri* case (under "Defining 'serious' reasons"), "In practice, the standard of proof will not be reached unless the decision maker is satisfied that it is more likely than not that the claimant was responsible for the crimes or acts"; see, also, Singer, above note 12 at 232–33, and Mark Symes, "Exclusion from Asylum on the Basis of Criminality — The United Kingdom's Response and Its Broader International Law Context" in James C. Simeon, ed, *Terrorism and Asylum* (Leiden & Boston: Brill Nijhoff, 2020) at 271–72. A

In Canada, the standard of proof has been expressed in a number of ways at different court levels. The Supreme Court of Canada has indicated that this phrase "requires something more than mere suspicion, but less than the standard applicable in civil matters of proof on the balance of probabilities. In essence, reasonable grounds will exist where there is an objective basis for the belief which is based on compelling and credible information."[38] The Federal Court of Appeal added to this understanding by saying that this "standard requires more than suspicions. It also requires more than a mere subjective belief on the part of the person relying on them. The existence of reasonable grounds must be established objectively, that is, that a reasonable person placed in similar circumstances would have believed that reasonable grounds existed."[39] Last, it has also been expressed as meaning "a serious possibility based on credible and trustworthy evidence."[40]

The Federal Court of Australia, Full Court (FCAFC), indicated initially that neither a charge nor a conviction for an international crime is necessary but that the only requirement in this test is clear and convincing evidence that may fall below the civil standard of proof.[41] More recently, the High Court was of the view that this standard indicates that there has to be a rational foundation for inferences from the evidence before the decision maker[42] and that such an inference must

similar standard was used in South Africa, namely, clear and credible evidence; see *Gavrić v Refugee Status Determination Officer, Cape Town and Others*, [2018] ZACC 38 at para 89.

38 *Mugesera v Canada (Minister of Citizenship and Immigration)*, 2005 SCC 40 at para 114 [*Mugesera*]; the same court set the same standard in *Ezokola v Canada (Citizenship and Immigration)*, 2013 SCC 40 at para 101, by following and quoting the UK Supreme Court decision in *JS*, above note 36, even though by the time of its decision the UK Supreme Court had already changed its mind in the *Al-Sirri* judgment, above note 12; for a discussion of this issue, see Camille Lefebvre & Fannie Lafontaine, "The Exclusion Clause in Canada: Prioritizing Practical Expediency" (2021) 33:3 *International Journal of Refugee Law* 405 at 414–18.

39 *Charkaoui v Canada (Minister of Citizenship and Immigration)*, 2004 FCA 421 at para 103; the court draws a comparison with the same concept used in Canadian criminal law where this standard is used for preventative police powers.

40 *Demaria v Canada (Citizenship and Immigration)*, 2019 FC 489 at para 64; see, also, Immigration and Refugee Board of Canada (IRB), *Interpretation of Convention Refugee and Person in Need of Protection in the Case Law*, Chapter 11 — Article 1F (31 December 2020) at 11.1.1, online (pdf): https://irb.gc.ca/en/legal-policy/legal-concepts/Documents/Interpretation%20of%20Convention%20Refugee%20and%20Person%20in%20Need%20of%20Protection%20in%20the%20Case%20Law%20(31%20Dec%202020).pdf.

41 *Arquita v Minister for Immigration & Multicultural Affairs* (2000), FCA 1889; *SRYYY v Minister for Immigration and Multicultural and Indigenous Affairs*, [2005] FCAFC 42 [*SRYYY*]; and *VWYJ v Minister for Immigration and Multicultural and Indigenous Affairs*, [2006] FCAFC 1 [*VWYJ*].

42 *FTZK*, above note 12 at para 13.

be strong,[43] indicating that it must meet the balance of probabilities standard.[44] The Supreme Court of New Zealand came to the same conclusion as its UK counterpart in the 2010 *JS* case while referring to the passage above.[45]

While the United States does not have an exclusion clause in its legislation as it has not ratified the 1951 Refugee Convention, its courts, including at the highest level, have indicated that the standard of proof to deny persons asylum benefits if they have been involved in persecution-type activities, for which the legislation sets no standard, is clear, unequivocal, and convincing evidence of assistance in persecution.[46] However, where the legislation uses the terminology of "reasonable grounds to believe,"[47] then this should be equated with the probable cause standard,[48] which means "if there is information that would permit a reasonable person to believe."[49]

In comparing the national common law jurisprudence, it seems that the notion of serious grounds for considering has been in flux. Australia, Canada, New Zealand, and the United Kingdom all started

---

43 *Ibid* at paras 14 and 80–84, referring to the UK *Al-Sirri* case, above note 12 at para 82; it also said at para 97 that the standard is below the criminal standard of beyond reasonable doubt; see, also, *MRWF v Minister for Immigration & Border Protection*, [2018] FCA 504 at paras 77 and 80.

44 This was confirmed by the Federal Court of Australia in *ZYVZ v Minister for Immigration, Citizenship, Migrant Services and Multicultural Affairs (MICMSMA)*, [2020] FCA 28 at paras 20–23; and *GZCK v Minister for Home Affairs*, [2021] FCA 1618, which summarized the jurisprudence by saying at para 149: "the requirement of 'serious reasons for considering' requires that there is a rational foundation for a strong inference of guilt; the evidence must be clear and credible or strong; a considered judgment, or meticulous investigation, by and actual persuasion of the decision-maker is required." See, also, Administrative Appeals Tribunal, "Guide to Refugee Law in Australia" (2023) at 7.31–7.32, online: www.aat.gov.au/guide-to-refugee-law-in-australia.

45 *The Attorney-General (Minister of Immigration) v Tamil X and the RSAA* [2010] NZSC 107 at para 39; the higher standard of proof of the UK *Al-Sirri* judgment above note 12, was noted at the tribunal level in *AH (Mexico)*, [2020] NZIPT 801631, 11 June 2020, but the decision maker concluded that it needed to follow the New Zealand precedent over the UK jurisprudence.

46 *Federenko v United States*, 499 US 490 (United States Supreme Court, 1981); *United States v Szehinskyj*, 277 F3d 331 (3d Cir 2002).

47 As is the case for exclusions from asylum in s 208(b)(2)(A)(iii) of the *Immigration and Nationality Act*, 8 USC, when "there are serious reasons for believing that the alien has committed a serious non-political crime outside the United States prior to the arrival of the alien in the United States," and s 208(b)(2)(A)(iv), when "there are reasonable grounds to believe that the alien is a danger to the security of the United States."

48 *Khouzam v Ashcroft*, 361 F3d 161 (2d Cir 2004); *Yusupov v Attorney General of US*, 518 F3d 185 (3d Cir 2008); *Barahona v Wilkinson*, Docket No 20-1546 (8th Cir 2021).

49 *Yusupov v Attorney General of US*, above note 48.

with a standard of proof that was lower than the civil standard of balance of probabilities, although the contents of the standard still require objective, compelling, and credible evidence (Canada) or strong or clear and convincing evidence (Australia), while the standard in the United States appears to be higher in some instances—clear, unequivocal, and convincing evidence—but lower when the legislation has used language similar to what can be found in the 1951 Refugee Convention if there is information that would permit a reasonable person to believe. However, this picture became more complicated after 2012 when the UK Supreme Court in *Al-Sirri* raised this standard to the balance of probabilities, which was followed in Australia by its highest court, both with persuasive reasoning, but not in Canada and New Zealand, where the original standard was maintained, while in both cases the judges relied on the 2010 UK Supreme Court decision in *JS*, even though in the case of Canada, its Supreme Court issued its decision after the *Al-Sirri* judgment.

With respect to civil law countries, in the Netherlands, the standard of proof falls below the criminal standard of proof[50] but should be more than *prima facie* evidence,[51] while in Belgium[52] and France,[53] their councils of state used the same formulation with respect to the criminal standard.[54] As well, in France, the Council of State overturned a decision of a lower tribunal that had refused to take into consideration that a claimant from Rwanda had been mentioned in both an international commission of inquiry and a government of Rwanda list of genocide suspects in the application of article 1F(a) by saying that the tribunal had used not the serious considering test but the higher test of "démonstration de leur implication dans ces crimes,"[55] while in a later case, it said that this test requires corroboration as well as a "vérité juridique irrefutable."[56]

---

50 Rb, Utrecht, Awb 14/12595, 10 July 2014; Rb, The Hague, Awb, 17/2027, 15 August 2017; Rb, The Hague, Awb 17/5689, 13 March 2018.

51 Rb, The Hague, Awb 15/3802, 16 March 2016, comparing the standard with the lower standard in extradition proceedings.

52 CE No 94.321, 27 March 2001 at para 2.4.2 and CE No 186.913, 8 October 2008 at para 2.4.

53 See Nicole Michel, "Purpose and Principles of the United Nations: The Way in Which France Applies 1F(c)" in Peter J. van Krieken, ed, *Refugee Law in Context: The Exclusion Clause* (The Hague: TMC Asser Press, 1999) at 298.

54 As was the case in Switzerland; see Sibylle Kapferer, *The Interface Between Extradition and Asylum* (November 2003) UNHCR Legal and Protection Policy Research Series PPLA/2003/05 at 108 at para 329, online (pdf): www.unhcr.org/3fe84fad4.pdf.

55 CE, 18 January 2006, 255091, Office français de protection des réfugies et apatrides c/Tegera.

56 CE, 24 June 2015, 370417, OFPRA c/MC; see, also, CE, 2 December 2015, 387162, OFPRA c/MO; this same court also implicitly indicated that a *prima facie* standard is too low by

In Germany, the similar standard of the national legislation, "good reasons," indicates a standard below the criminal threshold,[57] while the court says that this level of proof corresponds to "clear, credible evidence that such crimes have been committed."[58] In the Czech Republic, it has been said that the standard of "serious grounds for considering" is to be limited by the minimal level of approximately 50 percent probability and that to meet this standard, clear, persuasive, and credible evidence must be available, not just assumptions.[59]

It would appear that in examining the national jurisprudence, there is a range of standards expressed by the various courts, varying from reasonable grounds to believe to the balance of probabilities as used in civil proceedings, with the only consensus being that the standard does not reach the criminal level of beyond reasonable doubt and that in terms of contents, the evidence has to be credible, clear, and objective no matter what level of standard is used. It might very well be that decision makers will take a pragmatic approach given the sometimes subtle differences between the various tests, with a trend moving toward a higher standard, the different meaning given to the same concepts, and the type of evidence used (often only the statement of the person concerned and documentary evidence and, as such, often amounting to a finding of credibility of the person) and will use the medium civil standard of balance of probabilities, which can also be expressed more simply by saying that it is more likely than not that a person committed excludable crimes.[60]

The only possible issue with this approach would be that using a standard higher than reasonable grounds to believe would mean that excluding a person whose only status is of a person seeking refuge would be determined at a higher level of proof than the possible *refoulement* pursuant to article 33.2 of the Refugee Convention of a person who has obtained refugee status in the country of refuge but has committed serious crimes as that latter provision specifically refers to reasonable

---

indicating that extradition evidence by itself does not meet the refugee standard; see CE, 28 November 2016, 389733.

57 Bundesverwaltungsgericht (Federal Administrative Court), BverwG 10 C 26.12, 19 November 2013 at para 13.

58 Bundesverwaltungsgericht (Federal Administrative Court), BverwG 10 C 2.10, 31 March 2011 at para 26.

59 Judgment of the Supreme Administrative Court, Case No 4 Azs 60/2007-136 (*AS v Ministry of Interior*), 31 March 2011 at 18, quoted in EASO, *Judicial Analysis*, above note 3 at 57, n160.

60 This is already the case in the Czech Republic and in the United Kingdom, as indicated in *Singer*, above note 12 at 234–35, and acknowledged by the Supreme Court in the United Kingdom in *Al-Sirri*, above note 37, as well as in Australia in the *FTZK* case, above note 42.

grounds to believe (although in the French text version of the Refugee Convention, very similar words are used for both provisions).[61] None of the court decisions regarding the standard of proof mentioned above refer to this distinction, and when faced with this issue, courts might conclude that such a result would not be desirable.

Given the connection between exclusion (especially 1F(a)) and international criminal law, and since that area of international law also contains reference to standards of proof, some insights might be gleaned from its jurisprudence. The International Criminal Tribunal for the former Yugoslavia (ICTY) and the International Criminal Tribunal for Rwanda (ICTR) use the reasonable grounds approach when the prosecutor wants to indict a suspect.[62] The parameters of this concept were described in an early ICTR decision as follows:

> The term "prima facie" . . . is defined as sufficient information which justifies a reasonable suspicion that the suspect did in fact commit the crime or crimes for which he is charged and the term "sufficient evidence" . . . is interpreted to mean essential facts, that when supported by evidence, could result in a conviction. This does not mean conclusive evidence or evidence beyond a reasonable doubt.[63]

This language was slightly sharpened over time in determining whether the supporting material submitted by the prosecutor with the indictment was sufficient to meet the *prima facie* test by asking whether it provides "a credible case which would (if not contradicted by the Defence) be a sufficient basis to convict the accused on the charge."[64]

---

61 This is *refoulement* to persecution; *refoulement* for serious human rights violations, specifically, torture, is set at the higher standard of substantial grounds for believing (art 3.1 of the Torture Convention), resulting in less of a conflict. The French equivalent for "serious grounds for considering" is "raisons sérieuses de penser," while "reasonable grounds to believe" is "raisons sérieuses de considerer."

62 The statutes of both institutions use the language of *prima facie* case (art 18.4 for the ICTY and art 17.4 for the ICTR), but the term "reasonable grounds" can be found in the Rules of Procedure and Evidence of both tribunals, namely, in art 47(B) of the ICTY's, which begins with "the Prosecutor, if satisfied in the course of an investigation that there is sufficient evidence to provide reasonable grounds for believing that a suspect has committed a crime." The ICTR's Rules of Procedure and Evidence uses the same words in its art 47(B). Both statutes require an indictment to be confirmed by a judge before a trial can commence on the same *prima facie* test (art 19.1 in the ICTY Statute and art 18.1 in the ICTR Statute).

63 *Nyiramasuhuko and Ntahobali* (ICTR-96-17-T), Decision on the Preliminary Motion by Defence Counsel on Defects in the Form of Indictment, Trial Chamber, 4 September 1998 at para 3.

64 Most recently, *Karadžić* (IT-95-5/18-PT), Decision on Prosecution Motion to Reconsider the Trial Chamber's Decision on the Motion to Amend the First Amended Indictment, 26 February 2009 at para 12; see, also, Li, above note 31 at 218–20.

While the Rome Statute of the International Criminal Court has provided more oversight of the work of the prosecutor than in the ICTY/ICTR statutes, and it is the Pre-Trial Chamber of the court rather than the prosecutor who takes the first step in the trial process by issuing a warrant of arrest for a suspect after an investigation has commenced, the grounds for doing so are again based on reasonable grounds to believe that a person has committed a crime.[65] Unlike in the ICTY and ICTR, however, the confirmation of the charges after the initial step of the warrant issuance has to be done at a higher level of proof, "whether there is sufficient evidence to establish substantial grounds to believe that the person committed each of the crimes charged."[66]

Both the Pre-Trial Chamber and the Appeals Chamber of the ICC have examined the reasonable grounds test. The majority of one of the Pre-Trial Chambers equated this standard with the reasonable suspicion test as set out in the European Convention on Human Rights for the arrest or detention of a person,[67] as well as by reference to article 7 of the American Convention on Human Rights.[68] The Appeals Chamber noted this approach of the Pre-Trial Chamber without criticism and then went on to provide the contours of this standard of proof by recalling the jurisprudence of the European Court of Human Rights on this point, saying:

> It is instructive to recall that the European Court of Human Rights has interpreted "reasonable suspicion" under article 5(1)(c) of the European Convention on Human Rights as "presuppos[ing] the existence of facts or information which would satisfy an objective observer that the person concerned may have committed the offence." Thus, at

---

65 Rome Statute, art 58.1(a). This is a higher test than the one for opening an investigation by the ICC prosecutor as set out in art 53.1, which is "reasonable basis to proceed"; for an analysis of this test, see Matthew E. Cross, "The Standard of Proof in Preliminary Examinations" in Morten Bergsmo & Carsten Stahn, eds, *Quality Control in Preliminary Examination*, vol 2 (Brussels: Torkel Opsahl Academic EPublisher, 2018) at 213–53.

66 Rome Statute, art 61.7. This higher standard has been said to mean that the prosecutor must offer "concrete and tangible proof demonstrating a clear line of reasoning underpinning its specific allegations" (see, most recently, in *Yekatom and Ngaïssona* (ICC-01/14-01/18), Decision on the Confirmation of Charges, 20 December 2019 at para 17), which appears to be higher than a balance of probabilities.

67 Article 5(1)(c), which says: "the lawful arrest or detention of a person effected for the purpose of bringing him before the competent legal authority on reasonable suspicion of having committed an offence or when it is reasonably considered necessary to prevent his committing an offence or fleeing after having done so."

68 *Al Bashir* (ICC-02/05-01/09), Decision on the Prosecution's Application for a Warrant of Arrest against Omar Hassan Ahmad Al Bashir, Pre-Trial Chamber I, 4 March 2009 at para 160.

this preliminary stage, it does not have to be certain that that person committed the alleged offence.[69]

Following the Appeals Chamber, another Pre-Trial Chamber has stated that "the evidence need only establish a reasonable conclusion that the person committed a crime within the jurisdiction of the Court, and it is not required that this be the only reasonable conclusion that can be drawn from the evidence."[70]

Two conclusions can be drawn from this examination of international criminal law. The first one is that if international criminal law is to play a role in the interpretation of article 1F, and if the term "serious reasons for considering" can be given the same meaning as "reasonable grounds to believe" (which national courts initially had no difficulty in accepting), then the original equation of reasonable grounds with reasonable suspicion replaced later with reasonable conclusion would result in a renewed relaxation of the trend of the standard of proof toward a balance of probabilities and the evidence required to meet this test.

Both the ICTR and ICC cases discuss the contents of their test, which is enunciated by the Appeals Chamber of the ICC by setting out two elements: an objective observer of the evidence and the conclusion by that observer that a person may have committed an offence. The objective standard has been used in national jurisprudence, but that caselaw uses terminology along the lines of "strong," "clear," "compelling," and "unequivocal," which is stricter than "may have." While

---

69 *Al Bashir* (ICC- 02/05-01/09-OA), Judgment on the appeal of the Prosecutor against the Decision on the Prosecution's Application for a Warrant of Arrest against Omar Hassan Ahmad Al Bashir, Appeals Chamber, 3 February 2010 at paras 30–31; Pre-Trial Chamber II followed the decision of the Appeals Chamber a month later, although it was of the view that the reliance on the caselaw in the context of arrest warrants might not be the most appropriate for the situation at hand, which was an art 15(3) commencement investigation *proprio motu* by the prosecutor and was of the view that the test of "reasonable basis to proceed" in that article or that of "reasonable grounds to believe" in art 53(1)(a) was lower than that for an arrest warrant, which is "sensible or reasonable justification for a belief"; see Decision Pursuant to Article 15 of the Rome Statute on the Authorization of an Investigation into the Situation in the Republic of Kenya, ICC-01/09, 31 March 2010 at paras 30–35.

70 *Prosecutor v Mudacumura* (ICC-01/04-01/12-1-RedtFRA), Decision on the Prosecutor's Application under Article 58, 13 July 2012 at para 19; see, also, *Situation on the Registered Vessels of the Union of the Comoros, the Hellenic Republic and the Kingdom of Cambodia* (ICC-1/13), Decision on the "Application for Judicial Review by the Government of the Comoros," Pre-Trial Chamber, 16 September 2020 at paras 15–16; for a more in-depth analysis, see Li, above note 31 at 212–18 and 220–21.

commentators have advocated utilizing one of the internationally developed tests to overcome such different approaches, it would appear that this would not be necessary because the international tests are still more vague than the various national enunciations, while more recently there seems to be a trend at the national level toward the balance of probabilities test, which is not known in international criminal law and might very well become the standard test in the future, especially at a practical level.[71]

The second conclusion is that there is an argument at the national level that if a person under indictment or arrest warrant by an international institution flees to another country and claims refugee status, such an indictment or arrest warrant could be viewed as conclusive regarding the question of exclusion given the similar standard of proof for such an international document and a substantive decision on exclusion. This approach might very well be strengthened by the fact that an international indictment or arrest warrant in most cases contains more and stronger evidence than is typically necessary or used in refugee determination processes, including exclusion. If the national trend to a higher standard of proof continues, the same argument would then apply with respect to the ICC, the only surviving international institution, to the confirmation of charges document with more extensive evidence and the higher standard of proof of substantial grounds to believe.

This might not be a problem when the international institution, which issued these documents, seeks to have this person transferred and a speedy resolution of the asylum claim can be obtained. However, it could (and has) become a serious issue if an international institution has acquitted a person. In that situation, such a person will be released from detention but might not be able to return to his home country or go to a third country because an acquittal does not mean that his innocence has been proven.[72] The third country can still be of the view

---

71 Li, above note 31, advocates at 227 that the ICTY *prima facie* test should be adopted for exclusion purposes, while Holvoet, above note 35 at 1055–56, is of the view that the ICC reasonable grounds test is the more appropriate one, although it can be observed that these two tests appear to be quite similar.

72 This scenario is not hypothetical as there are a number of persons who have been acquitted by the ICTR but whom that institution has not been able to resettle because of considerations mentioned above; see Emma Irving, "When International Justice Concludes: Undesirable but Unreturnable Individuals in the Context of the International Criminal Court" (2017) 15:1 *Journal of International Criminal Justice* 115 at 119–20; Elies van Sliedregt, "International Outlaws" (2020) 33:3 *Leiden Journal of International Law* 535 at 535–36.

that there was sufficient evidence in the indictment or the confirmation of the charges to warrant exclusion and refuse to admit such a person. It is incumbent upon states placed in such a situation to examine both the indictment or confirmation and the trial record to determine exactly on what basis an acquittal was entered by the institution and whether that record can overcome the initial allegation.[73]

b) Inclusion Versus Exclusion and Proportionality

With respect to the issue of whether the risk of persecution should be considered before or together with exclusion and the connected issue, whether the persecution should be balanced against the seriousness of the exclusion act committed if inclusion takes place before exclusion, there is a difference in views among the UNHCR, a number of commentators,[74] and the jurisprudence in some civil law countries on the

---

73 This has happened in three cases: in the Netherlands in AbRS, 15 October 2014, nr 201405219/1/V1 (where information from the trial before the ICC as well as new evidence was used; for a commentary on this case, see Irving, above note 72 at 121–22); in Belgium (where the decision of a person who originally had been excluded was changed as a result of new evidence having been submitted, primarily the fact that his former superior had been acquitted by the ICTR) in CCE No 76.004, 28 February 2012; and in France in CE, 28 February 2019, 414821, MA. This same sentiment has been expressed for an acquittal in a national court in the United Kingdom in *AAS and Others v Secretary of State for the Home Department*, UKUT, AA/08375/2011, 14 May 2019 (as summarized in EASO, *Judicial Analysis*, above note 3 at 57), and in Canada in *Mungwarere v Canada (Public Safety and Emergency Preparedness)*, 2017 FC 708; see, also, Elies van Sliedregt, "International Crimes, International Outlaws and the Interface Between ICL and IRL" in Simeon, *Serious International Crimes*, above note 31 at 47–54.

74 In support of inclusion before exclusion and balancing, see Atle Grahl-Madsen, *The Status of Refugee in International Law*, vol I (Leiden: A.W. Sijthoff, 1966) at 297–98; Bliss, above note 35 at 108–12; Kapferer, "Exclusion Clauses," above note 35 at 217; Walter Kälin & Jörg Künzli, "Article 1F(b): Freedom Fighters, Terrorists, and the Notion of Serious Non-Political Crimes" (supp, 2000) 12 *International Journal of Refugee Law* at 71–74; Michael Kingsley Nyinah, "Exclusion Under Article 1F: Some Reflections on Context, Principles and Practice" (suppl, 2000) 12 *International Journal of Refugee Law* 295 at 306–9; Thomas Spijkerboer & B.P. Vermeulen, *Vluchtelingenrecht* (Nijmegen: Ars Aequi Libri, 2005) at 97; Geoff Gilbert, "Current Issues in the Application of Exclusion Clauses" in Feller, Türk & Nicholson, above note 10 at 466 (confirmed in David Kosar, "Inclusion Before Exclusion or Vice Versa: What the Qualification Directive and the Court of Justice Do (Not) Say" (2013) 25:1 *International Journal of Refugee Law* 87 at 103, n111), but changing his mind in Geoff Gilbert, "Exclusion" in Cathryn Costello, Michelle Foster & Jane McAdam, eds, *The Oxford Handbook of International Refugee Law* (Oxford: Oxford University Press, 2021) at 722; Jennifer Bond, "Excluding Justice: The Dangerous Intersection Between Refugee Claims, Criminal Law, and 'Guilty' Asylum Seekers" (2012) 24:1 *International Journal of Refugee Law* 37 at 57–59; Singer, above note 12 at 226; and Elif Gökşen, "Proportionality in Refugee Exclusion: An Underestimated Analysis" (2020) 18:5 *Journal of International Criminal Justice* 1131–56. Other academics are cautiously

one hand and court decisions in common law countries and other civil law countries on the other.

The UNHCR has always maintained that inclusion should be considered at the same time as exclusion and that a balancing, also called proportionality, should occur, especially in exclusion 1F(b) cases, although its position has softened over time with respect to the other two exclusion grounds. This can be seen in the 2003 *Exclusion Guidelines*[75] and its *Background Note*,[76] as well as in the 2009 submission to the European Court of Justice.[77] Of these three documents, the *Background Note* is the most comprehensive in stating:

> In reaching a decision on exclusion, it is therefore necessary to weigh up the gravity of the offence for which the individual appears to be responsible against the possible consequences of the person being excluded, including notably the degree of persecution feared. If the applicant is likely to face severe persecution, the crime in question must be very serious in order to exclude the applicant. This being said, such a proportionality analysis would normally not be required in the case of crimes against peace, crimes against humanity, and acts contrary to the purposes and principles of the United Nations, as the acts covered are so heinous that they will tend always to outweigh the degree of persecution feared. By contrast, war crimes and serious non-political crimes cover a wider range of behaviour. For those activities which fall at the lower end of the scale, for example, isolated incidents of looting by soldiers, exclusion may be considered disproportionate if subsequent return is likely to lead, for example, to the individual's torture in his or her country of origin. Where, however, persons have intentionally caused death or serious injury to civilians

---

in favour of this approach but do not advocate an absolute application of this principle; see Matthew Zagor, "Persecutor or Persecuted: Exclusion Under Article 1F(A) and (B) of the Refugees Convention" (2000) 23:3 *University of New South Wales Law Journal* (2000) 164 at 186, and Akbar Rusalov, "Criminals as Refugees: The 'Balancing Exercise' and Article 1F(B) of the Refugee Convention" (2002) 16:4 *Georgetown Immigration Law Journal* 815 at 833–34. Hathaway & Foster, above note 31 at 531 and 562–67, always prefer exclusion before inclusion, as do Goodwin-Gill & McAdam, above note 27, although with some hesitation at 213–17.

75 UNHCR, *Guidelines*, above note 8 at para 24.

76 UNHCR, *Background Note*, above note 9 at paras 76–78.

77 UNHCR, *Statement on Article 1F*, above note 21 at 9–10 and 31–33; see, also, more recently, UNHCR Intervention in Febles, above note 23 at 6–7 at para 15(iii), and UNHCR, *UNHCR Comments on on the European Commission Proposal for a Qualification Regulation — COM* (2016) 466, February 2018 at 21–22.

as a means of intimidating a government or a civilian population, they are unlikely to benefit from proportionality considerations.

In continental Europe, inclusion is applied in France even when exclusion is raised as well,[78] while inclusion before exclusion and balancing has been applied in Switzerland for 1F(b) cases.[79] An early German case indicated that a person can be excluded despite facing persecution in their country of origin,[80] but this was later reversed by the highest administrative court.[81]

In Belgium, exclusion can be applied without a need to look at the persecution faced in the country upon return,[82] as is the case in Austria.[83]

In the Netherlands,[84] the District Court in The Hague examined the issue of balancing in detail and came to the conclusion that while the *travaux préparatoires* did not shed light on this issue, and while the UNHCR's views on this issue were not binding on the court, a balancing between the reasons for fleeing the country of origin as well as the

---

78 Kapferer, "Exclusion Clauses," above note 35 at 216; Michel, above note 53 at 294–95. This is confirmed at the highest judicial level (see CE, 15 May 2000, 190059, Hamid), while it has been the practice ever since at the tribunal level (see CNDA, Recueils de jurisprudence, under "Exclusion du Droit au Bénéfice de l'Asile," in which it is apparent that the balancing exercise is rarely resolved in favour of inclusion, an exception being the case of CNDA, 2 October 2019, 19009183—19009184, MA et Mme K épouse A, while it has also been said that if exclusion is not raised by the parties, there is no need for the tribunal to address it (see CE, 18 March 2019, 414740); Kosar, above note 74 at 99–100, is of the view that with respect to the jurisprudence, "it is difficult to reach an unequivocal conclusion."

79 Rusalov, above note 74 at 824, and UNHCR, *Background Note*, above note 9 at n71; Nula Frei & Constantin Hruschka, "Caught Between Unworthiness and Exclusion: Asylum Applicants and Refugees Suspected of Terrorism in Swiss Law and Practice" in Simeon, *Terrorism and Asylum*, above note 37 at 316 and 318–19.

80 Rusalov, above note 74 at 831.

81 Bundesverwaltungsgericht (Federal Administrative Court), BverwG 10 C 48.07, 14 October 2008, at paras 31–33; see, also, Bundesverwaltungsgericht (Federal Administrative Court), BverwG 10 C 26.10, 7 July 2011 at para 26.

82 CE No 93.579, 27 February 2001 at para 2.3.4.3, and while some doubts were placed on this by a lower tribunal in CCE No 47.223, 12 August 2010, the original approach was confirmed more recently; see, for instance, CCE No 239.570, 11 August 2020 at para 2.7; in practice, since 2010, the administrative tribunal typically applies inclusion before exclusion; see Le Conseil du Contentieux des Etrangers, under "Arrêts" with keyword "1F," online: www.rvv-cce.be/fr/arr.

83 See Kosar, above note 74 at 96.

84 For two early cases that touched upon balancing indirectly, see Rusalov, above note 74 at 825, and Hinde Chergui & Helen Oosterom-Staples, "The Impact on Immigration and Asylum Law in the Netherlands" in Anneliese Baldaccini & Elspeth Guild, eds, *Terrorism and the Foreigner: A Decade of Tension Around the Rule of Law in Europe* (Leiden & Boston: Martinus Nijhoff, 2007) at 274–75.

consequences upon return and the excludable acts committed by a refugee claimant should occur. According to the court, this was especially important for exclusion 1F(b), but even for 1F(a) and 1F(c) cases, and information provided by the claimant as part of the inclusion narrative can be relevant and should be considered by the decision maker in an exclusion determination.[85] However, the Council of State later the same year took a different approach: that the minister can decide whether to apply inclusion before exclusion or vice versa, and using only exclusion is not an error of law,[86] while more recently, other district courts were more unequivocal in favour of exclusion before inclusion,[87] although some doubt still lingers for 1F(b) cases.[88]

In the Czech Republic, the Grand Chamber of the Supreme Administrative Court opted in 2010 for the exclusion before inclusion approach.[89] The reasons given are that the Refugee Convention as a whole does not apply to a person who is excludable, which is enforced by the *refoulement* provision, while in addition it is not the purpose of the convention to protect persons who have engaged in 1F activities. As well, neither the European Convention on Human Rights nor other EU law prohibits an exclusion before inclusion approach.[90]

In common law countries, the balancing issue was first addressed in Canada in the context of exclusion ground 1F(a) in 1993, where the Federal Court of Appeal in the *Moreno* decision reached the conclusion *in obiter* that balancing was legally not required but could be advantageous from a practical perspective by saying:

> I think it helpful to point out that it would have been preferable had the Board made a determination with respect to the appellant's refugee

---

85 Rb, The Hague, Awb 02/17771, 11 July 2003 at para 4.8. Earlier, the policy of the government had been that there was no need to do inclusion before exclusion; see the Netherlands' State Secretary of Justice, "Note on Article 1F to Parliament, November 1997" in Van Krieken, ed, above note 53 at 305.

86 AbRS, 27 Oktober 2003, nr 200305116/1, which was confirmed the next year later in AbRS, 2 June 2004, nr 200308845/1.

87 Rb, Utrecht Awb 14/12595, 10 July 2014; Rb, The Hague, NL 20.13885, 2 September 2021; and Rb, The Hague, NL 21.16506, 7 March 2022.

88 See AbRS, 14 September 2015, nr 201407968/1.

89 Judgment of the Supreme Administrative Court (Grand Chamber), No 4 Azs 60/2007, 7 September 2010.

90 This analysis has been provided to the author by David Kosař, law clerk to the judge of the Supreme Administrative Court.

> claim notwithstanding its decision to apply the exclusion clause. There are three reasons for this view.
>
> First, as a practical matter it is extremely difficult to separate the grounds on which a claimant bases his or her refugee claim from the circumstances which might give rise to the application of the exclusion clause. In most cases, the claimant gives some evidence of complicity in crimes against humanity and then claims to have a well-established fear of persecution after deserting a military regime or police force which remains impervious to international conventions governing human rights . . . .
>
> Second, in the event that the Board errs with respect to the application of the exclusion clause but has also ruled on the application of the inclusion clause, it may be unnecessary to refer the matter back to the Board. The same holds true if the Board rules on the inclusion clause, reaches a negative determination and dismisses the claim without turning to the exclusion criteria. Considerations of time and expense are always persuasive when establishing practical guidelines . . . . Finally, aside from any practical considerations, it may well be that in certain cases the Board will be legally obligated to rule on the refugee claim irrespective of the applicability of the exclusion clause. That possibility arises in the context of spousal and dependent refugee claims and is discussed below.[91]

In May 1994, the same court addressed balancing again in the context of exclusion 1F(a), and, while following the reasoning in the *Moreno* decision, on the practical side it did make it clear that from a legal perspective there is nothing in the convention that would permit a decision maker to weigh persecution against exclusion because "the exclusion of Article 1F(a) is, by statute, integral to the definition. Whatever merit there might otherwise be to the claim, if the exclusion applies, the claimant simply cannot be a Convention refugee."[92]

With respect to exclusion ground 1F(b), the Federal Court of Appeal rejected a balancing between the gravity of the offence and the persecution feared by the claimant, but it did indicate that it would be appropriate to use such a proportionality test in the weighing of the gravity of the crime in limited circumstances as part of the process of determining whether the crime was political, in that a very serious crime

91 *Moreno v Canada (Minister of Employment and Immigration) (CA)*, [1994] 1 FC 298 [*Moreno*].

92 *Gonzalez v Canada (Minister of Employment and Immigration) (CA)*, [1994] 3 FC 646.

might be accepted as political if the regime against which the crime is directed is repressive and offers no scope for freedom of expression and the peaceful change of government or government policy, assuming that the other requirements with respect to political offences, such as sufficient nexus and the means employed, are fulfilled.[93] The rejection of a general balancing approach for 1F(b) was confirmed later in two other Federal Court of Appeal decisions, *Xie* and *Lai*. In *Xie*, the court added another reason for not applying this principle by saying that exclusion does not directly lead to removal but has a function to deny claimant benefits under the Refugee Convention. As a result, issues of persecution can be raised at the stage where removal of an excluded person is contemplated.[94] Almost a year later, the court in *Lai* did agree with the general proposition of no balancing but also confirmed the earlier exception stated in *Moreno*, that in a situation when derivative claims, such as for children, need to be assessed, inclusion needs to be examined for all claimants, parents and children alike.[95]

With respect to the issue of inclusion versus exclusion and balancing for exclusion ground 1F(c), the Supreme Court of Canada in the *Pushpanathan* judgment did not address this issue squarely, but the following passage can be seen as a rejection of examining the level of persecution against the seriousness of the acts carried out by a refugee claimant:

> Given the precisely drawn scope of Article 1F(b), limited as it is to "serious" "non-political crimes" committed outside the country of refuge, the unavoidable inference is that serious non-political crimes are not included in the general, unqualified language of Article 1F(c).... Article 1F(b) contains a balancing mechanism in so far as the specific adjectives "serious" and "non-political" must be satisfied.[96]

In other common law countries, balancing has generally been rejected, although it was mostly addressed in the context of 1F(b).

---

93 *Gil v Canada (Minister of Employment and Immigration) (CA)*, [1995] 1 FC 508. This approach was confirmed at the same court level in *Malouf v Canada (Minister of Citizenship and Immigration)* (1995), 190 NR 230.

94 *Xie v Canada (Minister of Citizenship and Immigration)*, 2004 FCA 250 at paras 35–39 [*Xie*].

95 *Lai v Canada (Minister of Citizenship and Immigration)*, 2005 FCA 125 at para 70 [*Lai*].

96 *Pushpanathan*, above note 12 at para 73. The excerpt is from the majority judgment; the minority is more unequivocal by saying at para 156: "It was suggested to the Court that these concerns could be dealt with by adopting a 'balancing' approach to the exclusion clauses in Article 1F. Such an approach would not be appropriate in light of the nature and wording of that article."

In the United Kingdom, the Court of Appeal dismissed a balancing approach in 1994 in no uncertain terms:

> [I]f a person has committed a non-political crime outside the United Kingdom prior to his arrival here, the provisions of the convention do not apply to him. We can find nothing in the convention which supports the view that, in deciding whether a non-political crime is "serious" and therefore within article 1F, the Secretary of State of the appeal tribunal is obliged to weigh the threat of persecution if asylum is refused against the gravity of the crime.[97]

The House of Lords confirmed this approach a year and a half later, saying, "but the crime either is or is not political when committed, and its character cannot depend on the consequences which the offender may afterwards suffer if he is returned."[98] Any doubt about the issue of balancing has been removed by a legislative action, which now declares:

> Articles 1(F) and 33(2) of the Refugee Convention (exclusions: war criminals, national security, &c.) shall not be taken to require consideration of the gravity of—
> (a) events or fear by virtue of which Article 1(A) would or might apply to a person if Article 1(F) did not apply, or
> (b) a threat by reason of which Article 33(1) would or might apply to a person if Article 33(2) did not apply.[99]

In Australia, the Federal Court already concluded in 1995[100] that there is no balancing test to be read into the provisions of the Refugee Convention. This was confirmed almost a decade later at the appeal level by the FCAFC after canvassing UNHCR materials, academic writings, and the jurisprudence in Canada, the United Kingdom, New Zealand, and the United States.[101] They maintained this proposition

97 *T v The Secretary of State for the Home Department*, [1995] 2 All ER 1042.

98 *T v Immigration Officer*, [1996] AC 742 at 768 (Lord Mustill).

99 *Anti-terrorism, Crime and Security Act 2001*, s 34; see, also, a manual from the Home Office, "Exclusion (Article 1F) and Article 33(2) of the Refugee Convention," above note 37 at 21, as well as *AS (s 55 "exclusion" certificate—process) Sri Lanka*, [2013] UKUT 00571 (IAC) at paras 19–31.

100 *Dhayakpa v Minister for Immigration and Ethnic Affairs* (1995), 62 FCR 556.

101 *Applicant NADB of 2001 v Minister for Immigration & Multicultural Affairs*, [2002] FCAFC 326 at paras 29–41. The court comments on the fact that Canada had been the only jurisdiction that was less definitive on the non-application of a balancing test at para 40. The court also applied a decision of the Australian High Court, which had come to the same conclusion

in very much the same words as the House of Lords earlier by saying, "however, there is no textual or contextual basis for reading into Art 1F(b) an additional requirement of a balancing test nor would such a requirement be justified on the basis that it is giving effect to a purpose or object of Art 1F(b) of the Refugee Convention."[102]

This result was also arrived at in New Zealand by the Court of Appeal, which had examined other common law jurisprudence in this regard and had not seen any reason to depart from the same approach used in those countries,[103] with the same result in Ireland[104] and South Africa.[105]

Finally, the Supreme Court in the United States followed this approach as well and, having cited the House of Lords' decision with approval, felt that "as a matter of plain language, it is not obvious that an already-completed crime is somehow rendered less serious by considering the further circumstance that the alien may be subject to persecution if returned to his home country."[106]

The fundamental differences between adopting a balancing approach as opposed to solely relying on exclusion without any mitigating circumstances are grounded in larger conceptual issues surrounding refugee claimants. The UNHCR and commentators, which advocate a balancing approach, especially in regard to 1F(b), point

---

earlier in the same year in *Minister for Immigration and Multicultural Affairs v Singh*, [2002] HCA 7 at para 141.

102 *Applicant NADB of 2001 v Minister for Immigration & Multicultural Affairs*, [2002] FCAFC 326 at para 41.

103 *S v Refugee Status Appeals Authority*, [1998] 2 NZLR 291 at 297–300, which was followed at the tribunal level in RSAA Appeal Nos 74796 & 74797, 19 April 2006; as a practical matter, the New Zealand Immigration and Protection Tribunal will assess inclusion before exclusion in its decisions.

104 *HO v Refugee Appeals Tribunal & anor*, [2014] IEHC 494 at paras 68–70; for a discussion, see Hillka Becker, "The Application of Article 1F UNCSR in International Protection Decision Making in Ireland in the Context of EU and International Law" in Simeon, *Serious International Crimes*, above note 31 at 225–27.

105 *Gavrić v Refugee Status Determination Officer, Cape Town and Others*, [2018] ZACC 38 at paras 34–39.

106 *INS v Aguirre-Aguirre*, 526 US 415 (1999) at 426. For a commentary on the case, see Nadia Yakoob, "Political Offender or Serious Criminal? Challenging the Interpretation of 'Serious, Nonpolitical Crimes' in INS v Aquirre-Aguirre" (2000) 14 *Georgetown Immigration Law Journal* (2000) 54 at 573–85, and Kelly Ryan, "The Serious Non-Political Crimes Bar (the United States Supreme Court Decision in INS v Aguirre-Aguirre" in Van Krieken, ed, above note 53 at 313–19; as a practical matter, the US immigration tribunals will address inclusion, exclusion, and *refoulement* in the same decision.

to the overarching human rights purpose of the Refugee Convention, which should inform all aspects of these instruments, including exclusion.[107] It has also been pointed out that the notion of proportionality is not unique to refugee law but can also be found in other areas of international law, while a more practical reason has been found in the fact that often the only route to change in repressive societies is by resorting to criminal means.[108] Another element, which applies more to the notion of inclusion before exclusion, is related to the fact that a persecution perspective can actually inform a decision maker of a circumstance relevant to exclusion.[109]

Where balancing is rejected, it is done either for the legal reason that nothing can be found in the text of the convention, which obliges a decision maker to engage in comparing persecution to crime,[110] or because those considerations are better addressed at the end of the process dealing with a criminal refugee, at the removal stage when other human rights treaties come into play.[111]

Most of the discussion, both academically and jurisprudentially, has taken place in the context of 1F(b), with the exception of the Canadian, Belgian, Czech, and Dutch caselaw. Where the debate has centred on 1F(a) and 1F(c), as in UNHCR statements and in Canadian jurisprudence, the positions are not all that far apart in that the UNHCR is willing to accept that it is in practice difficult to conceive of situations where, after a balancing, those situations (apart from minor war crimes) could result in favour of the refugee claimant, and the Canadian courts have indicated that such balancing should simply not take place. Another observation is that the initial apparent stark contrast between common law and civil law countries on the issue of balancing is starting to move across a spectrum from a clear rejection in common law countries to some exceptions in non-balancing in common law countries (such as Canada, where balancing can occur between the political aspect of 1F(b) and persecution), to exceptions to balancing (in Austrian, Belgian, Czech, Dutch, and German jurisprudence), to wholesale balancing in

107 See UNHCR, *Background Note*, above note 9 at para 77.

108 Yakoob, above note 106 at 584.

109 See "Summary Conclusions: Exclusion from Refugee Status" in Feller, Türk & Nicholson, eds, above note 10 at 482, as well as Rb, The Hague, Case 02/17771, 11 July 2003 at 4.8.

110 The jurisprudence in Australia, Canada, New Zealand, the United Kingdom, and the United States.

111 Canadian caselaw, as well as UNHCR, *Background Note*, above note 9 at para 76, and Hathaway & Foster, above note 31 at 565.

some other, but fewer, European countries (such as Belgium and possibly France and Switzerland).[112]

The distinction made by the UNHCR between 1F(b), on the one hand, and 1F(a) and 1F(c), on the other hand, where no balancing will be required for the latter, combined with the strict approach in the United Kingdom embedded not only in jurisprudence but also legislation, provided some powerful incentives in the EU context to review this approach in the context of the implementation of the Qualification Directive.[113] As a matter of fact, this issue was laid to rest in the context of the European Union by a decision of the Court of Justice of the European Union (CJEU), which said:

> Since the competent authority has already, in its assessment of the seriousness of the acts committed by the person concerned and of that person's individual responsibility, taken into account all the circumstances surrounding those acts and the situation of that person, it cannot—as the German, French, Netherlands and United Kingdom Governments have submitted—be required, if it reaches the conclusion that Article 12(2) applies, to undertake an assessment of proportionality, implying as that does a fresh assessment of the level of seriousness of the acts committed.[114]

It is unlikely that common law countries will revisit their approach given the fact that the rejection of inclusion before exclusion, which includes balancing, has been part of their jurisprudence for over two decades at the highest court levels. As well, there is the additional factor that if more attention will be given to human rights prohibitions during *refoulement*, a stricter approach at the earlier exclusion phase might become more palatable since that exclusion will not be as dramatic as previously might have been the case. It would seem that, as a result of the above factors and the jurisprudential trends, there are very few opportunities left to argue that inclusion with balancing before exclusion should prevail.

---

112 See, also, Kosar, above note 74 at 96–101 and 119.

113 "Exclusion (Article 1F) and Article 33(2) of the Refugee Convention" of the UK Home Office, above note 4, states that this directive prohibits balancing.

114 *Joined Cases C-57/09 and C-101/09 B and D*, 9 November 2010 at para 109; see, also, *Commissaire général aux réfugiés et aux apatrides v Mostafa Lounani*, Case C573/14, 31 January 2017 at para 72, and *Shajin Ahmed v Bevándorlási és Menekültügyi Hivatal*, Case C369/17, 13 September 2018 at paras 48–49.

c) Methodology

The general methodology in this chapter with respect to the development of the parameters of exclusion at the national level will be to examine the jurisprudence in countries with a sufficient number of publicly available cases, either at the court or the tribunal level, to be able to discern trends in the application of exclusion clauses. In some countries, the sample of cases that can be accessed is too small to do meaningful analysis,[115] while in other countries, such as Norway, there have been a larger number of cases, and while in these cases exclusion had been a theme, it had not necessarily been an important theme; furthermore, these cases were only set out in a summary format.[116]

The countries that fit these criteria are Australia and New Zealand, and in Europe and North America.[117] In Europe, Belgium, France, Germany, the Netherlands, and the United Kingdom will be examined, while Canada and the United States will be the subject of inquiry in North America. Preference will be given to an analysis of court jurisprudence (such as Canada, Germany, the Netherlands, and the United States), but where sufficient court cases are not available, resort will be had to administrative tribunal caselaw as well (such as Australia,

---

115 UNHCR, *Asylum in the European Union: A Study of the Implementation of the Qualification Directive* (November 2007), online (pdf): www.unhcr.org/protection/operations/47302b6c2/asylum-european-union-study-implementation-qualification-directive-2007.html,which examined five EU countries — France, Germany, Greece, Slovak Republic, and Sweden — and came to the conclusion with respect to exclusion that only Germany had generated a sufficient number of cases for analysis (at 91). Similarly, answers provided to a questionnaire issued by the Netherlands in 2007 in the context of the Strategic Committee on Immigration, Frontiers and Asylum (SCIFA) of the European Union indicated that most of the countries that had responded (Belgium, Czech Republic, Cyprus, Denmark, Estonia, Finland, France, Hungary, Ireland, Lithuania, Luxemburg, Malta, and Switzerland) use exclusion 1F sparingly; see the letter from the minister of justice to the House of Commons, 2006–7 Session, 30 800 VI, nr 12313, August 2007.

116 European Council on Refugees and Exiles (ECRE), *The Impact of the EU Qualification Directive on International Protection* (October 2008) at 148, online (pdf): https://ecre.org/wp-content/uploads/2016/07/ECRE-The-Impact-of-the-EU-Qualification-Directive-on-International-Protection_October-2008.pdf.

117 Exclusion has been applied in Africa. For a description of the process in the Great Lakes area after the 1994 genocide experience in Rwanda, see William O'Neill, Bonaventure Rutinwa & Guglielmo Verdirame, "The Great Lakes: A Survey of the Application of the Exclusion Clauses in the Central African Republic, Kenya and Tanzania" (supp, 2000) 12 *International Journal of Refugee Law* 135 at 136–70, and for this process after the civil wars in Sierra Leone and Liberia in the late 1990s, see William O'Neill, "Conflict in West Africa: Dealing with Exclusion and Separation" (supp, 2000) 12 *International Journal of Refugee Law* 171–94.

Belgium, France, New Zealand, and the United Kingdom); at times, reference will be made to the jurisprudence of other countries (as was done above) in order to illustrate a particular point or confirm a trend.

There has been some sporadic reporting of exclusion applications in European countries other than the ones just mentioned, as well as in South Africa. The following countries have been mentioned in the European Database of Asylum Law, in addition to the ones mentioned earlier, when discussing the standard of proof and inclusion before exclusion (Austria, the Czech Republic, Ireland, and Switzerland): Denmark, Finland, Greece, Spain, and Sweden.[118] In addition, Portugal has used 1F,[119] as have Italy,[120] Luxembourg, [121] Norway,[122] and Slovakia.[123]

B. EXCLUSION 1F(A) — THE CRIMES

1) International Criminal Law

a) Historical and International Context

Both the development of the legal parameters of law dealing with international crimes and the application of this law by international and national institutions have known historical ebbs and flows. A major impetus was received after the Second World War until about 1950,[124] after which very little happened until the mid-1990s, even though conflicts in which international crimes occurred continued unabated during this time.

---

118 See the European Database of Asylum Law (EDAL) website under "EDAL case summaries," then the keyword "Exclusion from protection," then "Filter by country of decision," online: www.asylumlawdatabase.eu,

119 United Nations Human Rights Committee, Concluding Observations on Portugal, 5 July 2003, UN Doc CCPR/CO/78/PRT at para 12.

120 Flavia Patanè et al, "Asylum-Seekers Prosecuted for Human Smuggling: A Case Study of *Scafisti* in Italy" (2020) 39:2 *Refugee Survey Quarterly* 123 at 145–47.

121 ECRE, above note 4 at 146.

122 See Maarten Bolhuis & Joris van Wijk, *Study on the Exchange of Information Between European Countries Regarding Persons Excluded from Refugee Status in Accordance with Article 1F Refugee Convention* (VU, Amsterdam & UDI, Oslo, 2015) at 17–19; Joris van Wijk & Maarten Bolhuis, *Case Management, Identity Controls and Screening on National Security and 1F Exclusion: A Comparative Study on Syrian Asylum Seekers in Five European Countries* (UDI, Oslo & VU, Amsterdam, 2018) at 105.

123 UNHCR, *Asylum in the European Union*, above note 115 at 98.

124 Robert J. Currie & Joseph Rikhof, *International & Transnational Criminal Law*, 3d ed (Toronto: Irwin Law, 2020) at 193–98.

Virtually all the important principles for this area of law can be traced back to this time period with some other important cases, such as the *Menten* case in the Netherlands;[125] the *Barbie*,[126] *Papon*, and *Touvier*[127] cases in France; and the Eichmann trial in Israel,[128] adding refinements to those principles. When international criminal law was examined by Canadian,[129] Australian,[130] and British criminal courts[131] in the 1980s and 1990s, a direct linkage was made between the post–Second World War law and the cases before them. This was not only done because the persons who had been investigated by the Canadian, British, and Australian governments had committed their acts during the Second World War but also because there was no new law to speak of in the interim.

However, there has been an explosion of new developments internationally in war crimes law in the last thirty years. There have been the ICTY[132] and the ICTR,[133] which were established in 1994 and 1995, respectively. These tribunals have their own Trial Chambers and a shared Appeals Chamber.[134] The decisions of the chambers of the two tribunals have greatly contributed to the development of the

125 75 *International Law Reports* 331.

126 78 *International Law Reports* 123.

127 100 *International Law Reports* 358.

128 36 *International Law Reports* 1.

129 The *Finta* case; for the Supreme Court of Canada decision, see *R v Finta*, [1994] 1 SCR 701 [*Finta*].

130 There have been three criminal prosecutions in Australia, in the cases of *Berezovsky*, *Wagner*, and *Polyukhovich*; the decisions in the first two cases can be found in Boas, Gideon & Pascale Chifflet, "Suspected War Criminals in Australia: Law and Policy" (2016) 40 *Melbourne University Law Review* 46 at 54; the decision of the High Court of Australia in the last case can be found in 101 *Australian Law Reports* 545 and 91 *International Law Reports* 1.

131 There has been one prosecution in the United Kingdom, the Sawoniuk trial, which has been the only successful prosecution of a Second World War perpetrator based on universal jurisdiction: *R v Anthony Sawoniuk*, [2000] EWCA Crim 9.

132 The official name is "The International Tribunal for the Prosecution of Persons Responsible for Serious Violations of International Humanitarian Law Committed in the Territory of the Former Yugoslavia since 1991," which was established on 25 May 1993 as the result of Security Council Resolution 837 (UN Doc S/RES/827) (1993).

133 The official name of the tribunal is "The International Criminal Tribunal for the Prosecution of Persons Responsible for Genocide and Other Serious Violations of International Humanitarian Law Committed in the Territory of Rwanda and Rwandan Citizens Responsible for Genocide and Other Such Violations in the Territory of Neighbouring States, between 1 January 1994 and 31 December 1994," and it was established by Security Council Resolution UN Doc S/RES/955 (1994) on 8 November 1994.

134 For more details, see Currie & Rikhof, above note 124 at 198–209.

international law of war crimes, genocide, and crimes against humanity and will be mentioned frequently in this chapter.

Apart from the activities of the two ad hoc tribunals, much work has been done under the auspices of the United Nations to establish a permanent international criminal court (ICC). The Statute of the ICC, which was adopted on 17 July 1998,[135] contains definitions of aggression, genocide, crimes against humanity, and war crimes, which can be considered the most contemporary formulation of the international law pertaining to these crimes, while its jurisprudence has become increasingly important and will also be referenced frequently in this chapter.[136]

The United Nations has also been instrumental in establishing five hybrid tribunals for dealing with international crimes: the Special Panel for Serious Crimes of the Dili District Court in East Timor (and its Court of Appeal); the Special Court for Sierra Leone (SCSL, with a Trial Chamber and an Appeals Chamber); the Extraordinary Chambers in the Courts of Cambodia (ECCC); the War Crimes Chamber of the state court of Bosnia and Herzegovina; and the courts in Kosovo. These courts had a mixed membership of local and international judges.[137]

b) The Prerequisites for Aggression, War Crimes, Crimes Against Humanity, and Genocide

While aggression and genocide can be considered *sui generis* crimes in international criminal law, many of the activities considered to be objectionable from an international criminal perspective are also known as offences in domestic criminal statutes. To differentiate war crimes and crimes against humanity from national crimes and elevate them to the international plane, some overarching requirements have been introduced to distinguish them from domestic crimes. The requirement for war crimes is the existence of an armed conflict, while for crimes against humanity, it is primarily the fact that the acts must be committed in a systematic or widespread manner. This part of the chapter will examine the specific requirements for aggression and genocide (which has been considered a particularly odious form of crimes against humanity) and the overarching elements of war crimes and crimes against humanity.

135 UN Doc A/CONF.183/9; 123 countries have ratified the Statute. See Rome Statute, above note 65.

136 For more details, see Currie & Rikhof, above note 124 at 209–24.

137 For more details regarding these and other international criminal institutions, see Currie & Rikhof, above note 124 at 243–61.

i) Aggression

The crime of aggression was previously known as crimes against peace in the trials after the Second World War and in the Refugee Convention itself. None of the statutes of the ad hoc international or internationalized tribunals created since the 1990s have this crime included within their mandate, and while the ICC has had a reference to aggression in its Statute since 1998,[138] the parameters of this crime were only firmly established in June 2010 during the first Review Conference of the Rome Statute in Kampala, Uganda.

The crime of aggression is of a different character than the other three crimes in several aspects. First, aggression is part of *jus ad bellum*, the law governing recourse to conflict or going to war, rather than *jus in bello*, the law that operates when war or armed conflict has begun, and, as such, can be seen as the initial cause for the commission of other international crimes. As a result of this different perspective, the crime of aggression contains some unique features not shared with war crimes, crimes against humanity, or genocide. These features are that aggression can only be committed by or on behalf of a state and as part of a state plan or policy, while the other crimes, as will be seen, can be carried out by state and non-state-like entities alike. Furthermore, while the perpetrators of the other crimes can be found anywhere in a hierarchy, the crime of aggression is a leadership crime confined to the actions of persons in high-policy decision-making positions in a state.

Because of the unusual character of this crime, it has only been prosecuted immediately after the Second World War, and even then the inclusion of this crime into the constituting documents of the IMTs in Nuremberg and Tokyo was controversial. This controversy continued from these trials until the conference to establish the ICC in 1998 in Rome. The only accomplishments in that time period had been a definition of aggression in 1974 in a resolution of the United Nations General Assembly[139] and the inclusion of the crime of aggression without an agreement as to the elements of this crime in the Rome Statute.[140] This finally changed with the 2010 Kampala Review Conference, while it was decided during the December 2017 meeting of the Assembly of

138 Articles 5.1(d) and 5.2.

139 UN Doc A/RES/3314 (XXIX) (1974).

140 For the delicate balance between the role of the Security Council and that of the ICC with respect to aggression, see Currie & Rikhof, above note 124 at 189–90.

State Parties that the jurisdiction with respect to aggression would be activated on 17 July 2018.[141]

The 2010 review conference[142] established the contours of this crime by delineating two concepts: one with respect to the type of activities that can amount to aggression and one regarding the level of functionaries that has the ability to carry out such crimes.

The crime of aggression is defined as follows:

1. For the purpose of this Statute, "crime of aggression" means the planning, preparation, initiation or execution, by a person in a position effectively to exercise control over or to direct the political or military action of a State, of an act of aggression which, by its character, gravity and scale, constitutes a manifest violation of the Charter of the United Nations.
2. For the purpose of paragraph 1, "act of aggression" means the use of armed force by a State against the sovereignty, territorial integrity or political independence of another State, or in any other manner inconsistent with the Charter of the United Nations. Any of the following acts, regardless of a declaration of war, shall, in accordance with United Nations General Assembly resolution 331 (XXIX) of 14 December 1974, qualify as an act of aggression:
   a) The invasion or attack by the armed forces of a State of the territory of another State, or any military occupation, however temporary, resulting from such invasion or attack, or any annexation by the use of force of the territory of another State or part thereof;
   b) Bombardment by the armed forces of a State against the territory of another State or the use of any weapons by a State against the territory of another State;
   c) The blockade of the ports or coasts of a State by the armed forces of another State;
   d) An attack by the armed forces of a State on the land, sea or air forces, or marine and air fleets of another State;

141 UN Doc Resolution ICC-ASP/16/Res.5.

142 See Claus Kreß & Leonie von Holtzendorff, "The Kampala Compromise on the Crime of Aggression" (2010) 8:5 *Journal International Criminal Justice* at 1179–217; see, also, Noah Weisbord, *The Crime of Aggression: The Quest for Justice in an Age of Drones, Cyberattacks, Insurgents, and Autocrats* (Princeton & Oxford: Princeton University Press, 2019).

e) The use of armed forces of one State which are within the territory of another State with the agreement of the receiving State, in contravention of the conditions provided for in the agreement or any extension of their presence in such territory beyond the termination of the agreement;
f) The action of a State in allowing its territory, which it has placed at the disposal of another State, to be used by that other State for perpetrating an act of aggression against a third State;
g) The sending by or on behalf of a State of armed bands, groups, irregulars or mercenaries, which carry out acts of armed force against another State of such gravity as to amount to the acts listed above, or its substantial involvement therein.[143]

The level of functionaries is described in article 1, above, and repeated in an amendment to the ICC *Elements of Crimes* document, saying, "the perpetrator was a person in a position effectively to exercise control over or to direct the political or military action of the State which committed the act of aggression."[144]

ii) War Crimes

The notion of war crimes as a means to hold individuals liable for certain violations of the rules of war or international humanitarian law had its genesis shortly after the First World War in the report of the 1919 Commission on the Responsibility of the Authors of the War and on Enforcement of Penalties, followed by actual trials for such crimes after the Second World War, including for the persons most responsible in the proceedings of the IMTs in Nuremberg and Tokyo.[145] War crimes have figured prominently in the statutes of the ICTY, ICTR, and the ICC, as well as the internationalized tribunals, the SCSL, and the ECCC.

From the inception of international criminal law, it was acknowledged that in order for a person to have committed a war crime, two

143 UN Doc Resolution RC/Res.6, Annex I, "Amendments to the Rome Statute of the International Criminal Court on the Crime of Aggression," which has inserted this text as article 8 *bis*.

144 UN Doc Resolution RC/Res.6, Annex II, "Amendments to the Elements of Crimes."

145 Shane Darcy, "The Reinvention of War Crimes by the International Criminal Tribunals" in Shane Darcy & Joseph Powderly, eds, *Judicial Creativity at the International Criminal Tribunals* (Oxford: Oxford University Press, 2010) at 106.

requirements needed to be fulfilled: the conduct needed to have taken place during a war and the activity in which the person had been engaged was one specifically prohibited by international law. Both have been the subject of a great deal of debate.

The requirement that there had to be a war has slowly expanded by dispensing with the notion that certain formalities, such as a declaration of war, had to be taken into account and by no longer insisting that war crimes could only be committed during an international armed conflict or war between states but not during a civil war. The Appeals Chamber of the ICTY laid to rest both questions in the *Tadić* case, first by applying a broad definition of the term "armed conflict" and second by specifically stating that war crimes could be committed in any type of armed conflict[146] by indicating that under customary international law "an armed conflict exists whenever there is a resort to armed force between States or protracted armed violence between governmental authorities and organized armed groups or between such groups within a State."[147]

A similar but more detailed definition can also be found in the Rome Statute, which

146 *Tadić* (IT-94-1), Appeals Chamber, Decision on the Defence Motion for Interlocutory Appeal on Jurisdiction, 2 October 1995 at paras 128–34. See, also, *Mucić et al (Čelebići Camp)* (IT-96-21), Appeals Chamber Judgment, 20 February 2001 at paras 168–74; this would suggest that the ICTY supports the so-called first shot theory, in which any use of force (or even the mere detention of foreign military personnel) is sufficient to constitute an international armed conflict; in contrast, there is the view of the International Court of Justice where small-scale "frontier incidents" (for example, where a soldier fires across an international border) do not constitute an international armed conflict (ICJ, *Case Concerning Military and At paramilitary Activities in and against Nicaragua Judgment (Merits)*, 27 June 1986 at para 195); see, also, Situation in the Republic of Korea, Article 5 Report, ICC OTP, June 2014 at 12–14.

147 *Tadić*, Appeals Chamber, Decision on the Defence Motion for Interlocutory Appeal on Jurisdiction, 2 October 1995 at para 70; *Lubanga* (ICC-01/04-01/06), Trial Chamber Judgment, 14 March 2012 at para 533; *Taylor* (SCSL-03-01-T), Trial Chamber Judgment, 18 May 2012 at para 563; *Stanišić and Simatović* (IT-03-69-T), Trial Chamber Judgment, 30 May 2013 at para 953; *Ntaganda* (ICC-01/04-02/06), Trial Chamber Judgment, 8 July 2019 at para 700.

In terms of the temporal aspects of the armed conflict, the *Tadić* decision goes on to say the same at para 70: "[I]nternational humanitarian law applies from the initiation of such armed conflicts and extends beyond the cessation of hostilities until a general conclusion of peace is reached; or, in the case of internal conflicts, a peaceful settlement is reached"; see, also, *Kunarac et al* (IT-96-23/IT-96-23/1), Appeals Chamber Judgment, 12 June 2002 at para 56 [*Kunarac*, 2002]; *Katanga* (ICC-01/04-01/07), Trial Chamber Judgment, 7 March 2014 at para 1173; *Mladić* (IT-09-92-T), Trial Chamber Judgment, 22 November 2017 at para 3013; see, also, the Rome Statute, art 8.2(f); see, also, *Ongwen* (ICC-02/0401/15), Trial Chamber Judgment, 4 February 2021 at para 2683.

> applies to armed conflicts not of an international character and thus does not apply to situations of internal disturbances and tensions, such as riots, isolated and sporadic acts of violence or other acts of a similar nature. It applies to armed conflicts that take place in the territory of a State when there is protracted armed conflict between governmental authorities and organized armed groups or between such groups.[148]

The *Tadić* decision described a situation in 1991, and given the fact that the 1977 Protocol II to the Geneva Conventions, which regulates non-international armed conflicts and which does not have a provision making individuals liable for violations of Protocol II (i.e., war crimes), it is unlikely that under international criminal law a person can commit war crimes in non-international armed conflicts much before 1990, unless such a conflict can be characterized as an internationalized non-international armed conflict. In such a situation, the conflict between two parties within one state is elevated legally to an international armed conflict, and individual liability is derived from international criminal law regulating war crimes in international armed conflicts. This is derived from the acknowledgement that an international armed conflict can take place not only directly between two states[149] but also within the confines of one state if one or more of the parties within that state stand in less than an arm's-length relationship with another state.[150] In the words of the ICTY Appeals Chamber when describing the relationship between the Bosnian Serbs and Yugoslavia:

> It follows that in the circumstances of the case it was not necessary to show that those specific operations carried out by the Bosnian Serb forces which were the object of the trial had been specifically ordered or planned by the Yugoslav Army. It is sufficient to show that this Army exercised overall control over the Bosnian Serb Forces. This showing has been made by the Prosecution before the Trial Chamber.

---

148 Article 8.2(f).

149 *Katanga and Chui* (ICC-01/04- 01/07), Pre-Trial Chamber, Decision of the Confirmation of the Charges, 30 September 2008 at paras 239–44, and *Kaing Guek Eav alias Duch* (Case File 001/18-07-2007/ECCC/TC), Trial Chamber Judgment, 26 July 2010 at paras 413–14.

150 *Tadić* (IT-94-1), Appeals Chamber, Decision on the Defence Motion for Interlocutory Appeal on Jurisdiction, 2 October 1995 at para 156. See, also, *Aleksovski* (IT-95-14/1-A), Appeals Chamber Judgment, 24 March 2000 at paras 122–36; *Kordić and Čerkez* (IT-95-14/2-A), Appeals Chamber Judgment, 17 December 2004 at paras 229–313; *Lubanga* (ICC-01/04-01/06), Pre-Trial Chamber I, Decision on the Confirmation of Charges, 29 January 2007 at paras 209–11.

> Such control manifested itself not only in financial, logistical and other assistance and support, but also, and more importantly, in terms of participation in the general direction, coordination and supervision of the activities and operations of the VRS. This sort of control is sufficient for the purposes of the legal criteria required by international law.[151]

With respect to indicators of protracted armed violence, the ICTY was of the view that

> [t]he two determinative elements of an armed conflict, intensity of the conflict and level of organisation of the parties, are used "*solely for the purpose*, as a minimum, of distinguishing an armed conflict from banditry, unorganized and short-lived insurrections, or terrorist activities, which are not subject to international humanitarian law." Therefore, some degree of organisation by the parties will suffice to establish the existence of an armed conflict....
>
> By way of example, in assessing the intensity of a conflict, other Chambers have considered factors such as the seriousness of attacks and whether there has been an increase in armed clashes, the spread of clashes over territory and over a period of time, any increase in the number of government forces and mobilisation and the distribution of weapons among both parties to the conflict as well as whether the conflict has attracted the attention of the United Nations Security Council, and, whether any resolutions on the matter have been passed. With respect to the organisation of the parties to the conflict Chambers of the Tribunal have taken into account factors including the existence of headquarters, designated zones of operation, and the ability to procure, transport, and distribute arms.[152]

---

151 *Tadić* (IT-94-1-A), Appeals Chamber Judgment, 15 July 1999 at para 156; see, also, *Kordić and Čerkez* (IT-95-14/2-A), Appeals Chamber Judgment, 17 December 2004 at paras 297–313; *Lubanga* (ICC-01/04-01/06), Trial Chamber Judgment, 14 March 2012 at para 541; *Stanišić and Simatović* (IT-03-69-T), Trial Chamber Judgment, 30 May 2013 at paras 954–55; *Ongwen* (ICC-02/0401/15), Trial Chamber Judgment, 4 February 2021 at paras 2686–87.

152 *Limaj et al* (IT-03-66-T), Trial Chamber Judgment, 30 November 2005 at paras 89–90; see, also, *Haradinaj et al* (IT-04-84-T), Trial Chamber Judgment, 3 April 2008 at paras 89, 99, & 100); *Boškoski and Tarčulovski* (IT-04-82-T), Trial Chamber Judgment, 10 July 2008 at paras 175–206 (including differences between armed conflict and terrorism); *Bemba* (ICC-01/05-01/08), Trial Chamber Judgment, 21 March 2016 at paras 131–41; *Ntaganda* (ICC-01/04-02/06), Trial Chamber Judgment, 8 July 2019 at paras 704 and 716–17; *Ongwen* (ICC-02/0401/15), Trial Chamber Judgment, 4 February 2021 at paras 2684–85.

The rules of armed conflict apply throughout the territories of the parties to the conflict and not only where actual combat operations are being carried out.[153] A person would be responsible for war crimes if their acts were closely related to the armed conflict, which means whether the existence of such a conflict played a substantial part in the perpetrator's ability to commit a crime, the decision to commit it, the manner in which it was committed, or the purpose for which it was committed.[154]

The number of activities that can amount to war crimes has also steadily increased from about a dozen specifically named in the Tokyo and Nuremberg charters to sixty such crimes in the Rome Statute.[155]

In addition to these two essential requirements, it should also be noted that war crimes can only be committed against civilians who do not have the nationality of the party to the armed conflict in whose hands they find themselves. While the term "national" seems to connote a restrictive interpretation along the lines of citizens of a country, the ICTY Appeals Chamber in *Tadić* loosened this notion by tying it to the allegiance of persons to a party to the conflict and the control of that party over such persons rather than a formal bond.[156] As well, more recently, this notion has been further circumscribed in the ICC context, where it was held that being made subject to rape or sexual enslavement

---

153 *Tadić* (IT-94-1), Appeals Chamber, Decision on the Defence Motion for Interlocutory Appeal on Jurisdiction, 2 October 1995 at para 69; *Prlić et al* (IT-04-74-A), Appeals Chamber Judgment, 29 November 2017 at paras 230–32. The same was said for non-international armed conflicts in *Kunarac*, 2002, above note 147 at para 57. For the related notion of "occupation" and its consequences, see n34 of the ICC *Elements of Crimes*, UN Doc ICC-ASP/1/3 (part II-B), online: https://www.icc-cpi.int/sites/default/files/Publications/Elements-of-Crimes.pdf; *Naletilić & Martinović* (IT-98-34-T), Trial Chamber Judgment, 31 March 2003 at paras 210–23; *Prlić et al* (IT-04-74-A), Appeals Chamber Judgment, 29 November 2017 at paras 316–23; *Lubanga* (ICC-01/04-01/06), Trial Chamber Judgment, 14 March 2012 at para 542; *Katanga* (ICC-01/04-01/07), Trial Chamber Judgment, 7 March 2014 at paras 1179–82; and *Situation on Registered Vessels of Comoros, Greece and Cambodia, Article 53(1) Report*, ICC OTP, 6 November 2014, at paras 22–29, 43–45.

154 *Kunarac*, 2002, above note 147 at paras 58–59; *Rutaganda* (ICTR-96-3-A), Appeals Chamber Judgment, 26 May 2003 at paras 569–75; *Ndindiliyimana et al* (ICTR-00-56-A), Appeals Chamber, 11 February 2014 at para 271; *Mladić* (IT-09-92-T), Trial Chamber Judgment, 22 November 2017 at para 3016; *Ntaganda* (ICC-01/04-02/06), Trial Chamber Judgment, 8 July 2019 at paras 731–33; *Ongwen* (ICC-02/0401/15), Trial Chamber Judgment, 4 February 2021 at para 2689.

155 Rome Statute, art 8.

156 *Tadić* (IT-94-1-A), Appeals Chamber Judgment, 15 July 1999 at paras 164–66; *Aleksovski* (IT-95-14/1-A), Appeals Chamber Judgment, 24 March 2000 at para 152; *Blaškić* (IT-95-14-A), Appeals Chamber Judgment, 29 July 2004 at paras 170–82; *Kordić and Čerkez* (IT-95-14/2-A), Appeals Chamber Judgment, 17 December 2004 at paras 322–31; *Ntaganda* (ICC-01/04-02/06), Trial Chamber Judgment, 8 July 2019 at para 1160.

negates active participation in hostilities and therefore being a combatant due to the coercion involved[157] and because such activities are prohibited no matter when and against whom committed under international law and the Rome Statute.[158]

As well, from the early cases onward, anybody could be a perpetrator of war crimes, not only persons with a connection to a state or government.

In conclusion, the notion of war crimes has undergone a substantial expansion between the Second World War and the present in two principal areas: by extending the scope of application from international armed conflicts to include non-international armed conflicts and by the ability to hold persons responsible for a greater number of activities considered undesirable by the international community.

iii) Crimes Against Humanity

The term "crimes against humanity" was first used prominently in the context of the 1915 Armenian massacres and became part of the jurisdiction after the Second World War in the charters of the IMTs in Nuremberg and Tokyo in order to criminalize crimes against citizens of their own countries, specifically Jewish nationals in Germany. While the development of the parameters of this crime was still hesitant in the post–Second World War tribunals and courts, this crime became one of the main vehicles to hold persons responsible in the jurisprudence of both the international and internationalized tribunals as well as the ICC.

Like war crimes, crimes against humanity have two basic requirements and a number of subsidiary elements. The main requirement to elevate a domestic crime to the international level is the fact that an act has to be committed in a systematic or widespread fashion. The caselaw of the ICTY and the ICTR has expanded on the historical expression of crimes against humanity by requiring five elements: (1) there must be an attack; (2) the acts of the perpetrator must be part of the attack; (3) the attack must be directed against any civilian population; (4) the attack

---

157 *Ntaganda* (ICC-01/04-02/06), Pre-Trial Chamber, Decision of the Confirmation of the Charges, 9 June 2014 at paras 76–80.

158 *Ntaganda* (ICC-01/04-02/06), Trial Chamber, Second decision on the Defence's challenge to the jurisdiction of the Court in respect of Counts 6 and 9, 4 January 2017 at paras 34–54, upheld on appeal by *Ntaganda* (ICC-01/04-02/06 OA5), Appeals Chamber, Judgment on the appeal of Mr. Ntaganda against the "Second decision on the Defence's challenge to the jurisdiction of the Court in respect of Counts 6 and 9," 15 June 2017 at paras 46–70.

must be systematic or widespread; and (5) the perpetrator must know that their acts constitute part of a pattern of widespread or systematic crimes directed against a civilian population and know that their acts fit into such a pattern.[159]

The Rome Statute defines the requirement as "acts when committed as part of a widespread or systematic attack directed against any civilian population, with knowledge of the attack,"[160] while further describing an attack against a civilian population as "a course of conduct involving the multiple commission of acts[161] . . . against any civilian population, pursuant to or in furtherance of a State or organizational policy to commit such attack."[162]

---

159 *Akayesu* (ICTR-96-4-T), Trial Chamber Judgment, 2 September 1998 at para 579 [*Akayesu*]; *Blaškić* (IT-95-14-A), Appeals Chamber Judgment, 29 July 2004 at paras 96–102; *Nahimana, Barayagwiza and Ngeze ("Media")* (ICTR-99-52-A), Appeals Chamber Judgment, 28 November 2007 at paras 915–24; *Katanga* (ICC-01/04-01/07), Trial Chamber Judgment, 7 March 2014 at paras 1097–98; *Case 002/01* (Case File No 002/19-09-2007-ECCC/SC), Supreme Court Chamber Judgment, 23 November 2016 at paras 744–49; *Ntaganda* (ICC-01/04-02/06), Trial Chamber Judgment, 8 July 2019 at para 660; *Ongwen* (ICC-02/0401/15), Trial Chamber Judgment, 4 February 2021 at para 2674.

160 Rome Statute, art 7.1. There had been some debate during the Rome Conference about whether the requirement was widespread *and* systematic rather than *or*, but it was decided that the latter was more appropriate; see Darryl Robinson, "Defining 'Crimes Against Humanity' at the Rome Conference" (1999) 93:1 *American Journal of International Law* 43 at 47–48.

161 Multiple commission of acts sets a quantitative threshold involving a certain number of acts. Each of the acts must fall within the course of conduct, and cumulatively they must satisfy the required quantitative threshold. To demonstrate the multiple commission of acts, only those acts enumerated in arts 7(1)(a) to (k) may be relied upon, but acts not listed in art 7(1) may nevertheless be considered for other purposes. For instance, they can assist the determination of whether the attack was directed against a civilian population or whether it was pursuant to, or in furtherance of, a state or organizational policy; *Ntaganda* (ICC-01/04-02/06), Trial Chamber Judgment, 8 July 2019 at para 663; *Ongwen* (ICC-02/0401/15), Trial Chamber Judgment, 4 February 2021 at para 2674; *Ntaganda* (ICC-01/04-02/06-2666-Anx3 30-03-2021 1/163 SL A A2), Appeals Chamber Judgment, Separate Opinion of Judge Luz Del Carmen Ibáñez Caranza on Mr. Ntaganda's appeal, 30 March 2021 at paras 170–77 .

162 *Akayesu*, above note 159 at para 579; *Blaškić* (IT-95-14-A), Appeals Chamber Judgment, 29 July 2004 at paras 96–102; *Nahimana, Barayagwiza and Ngeze ("Media")* (ICTR-99-52-A), Appeals Chamber Judgment, 28 November 2007 at paras 915–24; *Katanga* (ICC-01/04-01/07), Trial Chamber Judgment, 7 March 2014 at paras 1097–98; *Case 002/01* (Case File No. 002/19-09-2007-ECCC/SC), Supreme Court Chamber Judgment, 23 November 2016 at paras 744–49; *Case 002/02* (Case File No 002/19-09-2007/ECCC/TC), Trial Chamber Judgment, 16 November 2018 at para 301; *Ntaganda* (ICC-01/04-02/06), Trial Chamber Judgment, 8 July 2019 at para 660; *Ongwen* (ICC-02/0401/15), Trial Chamber Judgment, 4 February 2021 at paras 2676–78 and 2679; *Ntaganda* (ICC-01/04-02/06-2666-Anx3 30-03-2021 1/163 SL A A2), Appeals Chamber Judgment, Separate Opinion of Judge Luz Del Carmen Ibáñez Caranza on Mr. Ntaganda's appeal, 30 March 2021 at paras 42–66, 65, and 380(a) regarding organization and at paras 81–156, 150–56, and 380(b) regarding policy.

Activities committed in an isolated fashion do not fall within these parameters.[163]

"Widespread" has been defined as "massive, frequent, large scale action, carried out collectively with considerable seriousness and directed against a multiplicity of victims," while "systematic" has been defined as "thoroughly organised action, following a regular pattern on the basis of a common policy and involving substantial public or private resources," "organised nature of the acts of violence and the improbability of their random occurrence," or "patterns of crimes, in the sense of the non-accidental repetition of similar criminal conduct on a regular basis."[164]

With respect to the notion of civilian population, the term "population" does not mean that the "entire population of the geographical entity in which the attack took place must be subjected to that attack." It is sufficient to show that enough individuals were targeted in the attack or that they were targeted in such a way as to satisfy the chamber that the attack was in fact directed against a civilian "population" as opposed to a limited and randomly selected number of individuals.[165]

---

163 *Kunarac*, 2002, above note 147 at paras 98–101; *Ntaganda* (ICC-01/04-02/06), Trial Chamber Judgment, 8 July 2019 at para 662; *Ongwen* (ICC-02/0401/15), Trial Chamber Judgment, 4 February 2021 at para 2674.

164 *Kunarac*, 2002, above note 147 at paras 93–97; *Blaškić* (IT-95-14-A), Appeals Chamber Judgment, 29 July 2004 at paras 99–102 (as well as 117–20, indicating that a plan or policy is not a legal ingredient for a crime against humanity); *Limaj et al* (IT-03-66-T), Trial Chamber Judgment, 30 November 2005 at paras 180–228 (regarding crimes against humanity committed by non-state actors on a small scale and the concept of population); *Bagosora and Sengiyumva* (ICTR-98-41-A), Appeals Chamber Judgment, 14 December 2011 at para 389; *Katanga* (ICC-01/04-01/07), Trial Chamber Judgment, 7 March 2014 at paras 1102, 1105, and 1123; *Bemba* (ICC-01/05-01/08), Trial Chamber Judgment, 21 March 2016 at paras 162–63; *Mladić* (IT-09-92-T), Trial Chamber Judgment, 22 November 2017 at para 3025; *Ntaganda* (ICC-01/04-02/06), Trial Chamber Judgment, 8 July 2019 at paras 691–93; *Gbagbo and Blé Goudé* (ICC-02/11-01/15-1263-AnxC-Red), Trial Chamber, Reasons for oral decision of 15 January 2019 on the *Requête de la Défense de Laurent Gbagbo afin qu'un jugement d'acquittement portant sur toutes les charges soit prononcé en faveur de Laurent Gbagbo et que sa mise en liberté immédiate soit ordonnée*, and on the Blé Goudé Defence no case to answer motion, Public Redacted Version of Dissenting Opinion Judge Herrera Carbuccia, 16 July 2019 at paras 65–69; *Ongwen* (ICC-02/0401/15), Trial Chamber Judgment, 4 February 2021 at paras 2680–82; *Ntaganda* (ICC-01/04-02/06-2666-Anx3 30-03-2021 1/163 SL A A2), Appeals Chamber Judgment, Separate Opinion of Judge Luz Del Carmen Ibáñez Caranza on Mr. Ntaganda's appeal, 30 March 2021 at paras 168–87; with respect to the notion of widespread in relation to a large geographical area or large number of victims, see *Mladić* (IT-09-92-T), Trial Chamber Judgment, 22 November 2017 at para 3025.

165 *Kunarac*, 2002, above note 147 at para 90; *Sesay, Kallon and Gbao ("RUF")*, SCSL-04-14-A, Appeals Chamber Judgment, 26 October 2009 at para 719; *Ndindiliyimana et al* (ICTR-00-56-A),

The civilian population includes all persons who are not members of the armed forces or otherwise recognized as combatants. Even members of the armed forces who were not engaged in combat at the time of their capture are not considered civilians. As well, soldiers *hors de combat* do not qualify as civilians for this purpose, but the armed law enforcement agencies of a state can be considered civilians. A civilian population does not have to be exclusively civilian as long as it is "predominantly civilian" and "the primary object of the attack." The presence within the civilian population of individuals who do not come within the definition of civilians does not deprive the entire population of its civilian character. The civilian status of the victims, the number of civilians, and the proportion of civilians within a population are factors relevant to the determination of whether the requirement that an attack be directed against a civilian population is fulfilled.[166]

Appeals Chamber Judgment, 11 February 2014 at para 260; *Bemba* (ICC-01/05-01/08), Trial Chamber Judgment, 21 March 2016 at paras 152–56; *Mladić* (IT-09-92-T), Trial Chamber Judgment, 22 November 2017 at paras 3026–27; *Case 002/02* (Case File No 002/19-09-2007/ECCC/TC), Trial Chamber Judgment, 16 November 2018 at para 305; *Ntaganda* (ICC-01/04-02/06), Trial Chamber Judgment, 8 July 2019 at para 667; *Ongwen* (ICC-02/0401/15), Trial Chamber Judgment, 4 February 2021 at para 2675.

166 *Blaškić* (IT-95-14-A), Appeals Chamber Judgment, 29 July 2004 at paras 103–16; *Kordić and Čerkez* (IT-95-14/2-A), Appeals Chamber Judgment, 17 December 2004 at paras 95–97; *Martić* (IT-95-11-A), Appeals Chamber Judgment, 8 October 2008 at paras 291–314; *Mrkšić et al* (IT-95-13/1-A), Appeals Chamber Judgment, 5 May 2009 at paras 28–35 and 41–44; *Milošević* (IT-98-29/1-A), Appeals Chamber Judgment, 12 November 2009 at paras 50–61; *Kaing Guek Eav alias Duch* (Case File 001/18-07-2007/ECCC/TC), Trial Chamber Judgment, 26 July 2010 at paras 302–12; *Tolimir* (IT-05-88/2-A), Appeals Chamber Judgment, 8 April 2015 at para 142; *Case 002/01* (Case File No 002/19-09-2007-ECCC/SC), Supreme Court Chamber Judgment, 23 November 2016 at paras 737–40; *Case 002/02* (Case File No 002/19-09-2007/ECCC/TC), Trial Chamber Judgment, 16 November 2018 at paras 306–307 and 310; *Ntaganda* (ICC-01/04-02/06), Trial Chamber Judgment, 8 July 2019, at paras 668–69. Earlier, the ICTY caselaw had considered *hors de combat* military personnel to be civilian, but this concept was narrowed starting with the *Blaškić* case above. Unarmed peacekeepers were considered civilians in *Bagosora, Kabiligi, Ntabakuze and Nsengiyumva* (ICTR-98-41-T), Trial Chamber Judgment, 18 December 2008 at para 2175 (crimes against peacekeepers are considered war crimes in the *Rome Statute* in both international and non-international armed conflicts), as were police forces during an armed conflict in *Sesay, Kallon and Gbao ("RUF")* (SCSL-04-15-T), Trial Chamber Judgment, 25 February 2009 at paras 87–88, but not during peacetime in *Kayishema and Ruzindana* (ICTR-95-1-T), Trial Chamber Judgment, 21 May 1999 at para 127. The ICC has stated that persons involved in combat cannot be considered civilians, *Al Bashir* (ICC-02/05-01/09), Pre-Trial Chamber, Decision on the Prosecution's Application for a Warrant of Arrest against Omar Hassan Ahmad Al Bashir, 4 March 2009 at para 92, while in *Katanga* (ICC-01/04-01/07), Trial Chamber Judgment, 7 March 2014 at para 1105, it was said that the presence of non-civilians within the population does not deprive the collectivity of its protection as civilian, which was confirmed on appeal in *Ntaganda*

The second essential part of the definition is that, as with war crimes, only certain enumerated activities will amount to crimes against humanity. These would include murder, torture, rape, deportation, imprisonment, inhumane acts, and persecution. Unlike war crimes, however, there has been either no increase or only a small increase since the Second World War in the number of acts that were and are considered to be crimes against humanity,[167] and, also unlike war crimes, some crimes, even in the Rome Statute, are framed in a fairly wide manner. It can be said that conceptually crimes against humanity and violations of basic human rights are similar; in some ways, crimes against humanity are seen from the perspective of bringing the perpetrator to justice, while violations of human rights are seen from a victim's view.

As with war crimes, the term "perpetrators" has broadened over time in the context of crimes against humanity, albeit more recently than was the case for perpetrators of war crimes, by including not only persons who committed crimes against humanity while in the employ of a government or on behalf of a state but also individuals who were acting in a private capacity but pursuant to an organizational plan or policy.[168] Last, the confusion surrounding the question of whether crimes against humanity are a crime in their own right or need to be connected to an armed conflict has been resolved in favour of the former; crimes against humanity can be committed even in a time of peace.[169]

(ICC-01/04-02/06 A A2), Appeals Chamber Judgment, 30 March 2021 at paras 416–25, by saying that an attack against a civilian population does not include the requirement that the civilian population is the primary target.

167 There is virtually no difference between crimes against humanity as defined by the post–Second World War instruments and the statutes of the ICTY and ICTR. The Rome Statute seems to expand the range of activities that are considered crimes against humanity by adding the crimes of apartheid and enforced disappearance of persons (arts 7.1(i) and (j)); this is not the case since the crime of apartheid had already been specified as a crime against humanity in art 1 of the 1973 Convention on the Suppression and Punishment of the Crime of Apartheid (1015 UNTS 243), while an equivalent of forced disappearance had already been condemned by the IMT when discussing the "Nacht und Nebel" Decree instituted by the Nazi regime in occupied Europe during the Second World War (*Trial of the Major War Criminals Before the International Military Tribunal, Nuremberg, 14 November 1945–1 October 1946*, vol XXII at 475–76).

168 *Kunarac*, 2002, above note 147 at paras 83 and 86.

169 Although art 5 of the ICTY Statute makes a connection between crimes against humanity and an armed conflict, the Appeals Chamber has made it clear that this is a jurisdictional requirement for the ICTY only and is not to be considered a reflection of general international criminal law; see *Tadić* (IT-94-1), Appeals Chamber, Decision on the Defence Motion for Interlocutory Appeal on Jurisdiction, 2 October 1995 at para 141; *Kunarac*, 2002, above note 147 at para 83. The *Kaing Guek Eav alias Duch* (Case File 001/18-07-2007/ECCC/

iv) Genocide

Genocide was first defined by the 1948 Genocide Convention in article II:

> Genocide means any of the following acts committed with intent to destroy, in whole or in part, a national, ethnical, racial or religious group, as such:
> (a) Killing members of the group;
> (b) Causing serious bodily or mental harm to members of the group;
> (c) Deliberately inflicting on the group conditions of life calculated to bring about its physical destruction in whole or in part;
> (d) Imposing measures intended to prevent births within the group;
> (e) Forcibly transferring children of the group to another group.

Unlike war crimes and crimes against humanity, this is a *sui generis* crime without a distinction between contextual elements and underlying crimes. This definition of the Genocide Convention was maintained in its exact form in the statutes of the ICTY, ICTR, and ICC.

There is no numerical threshold with respect to the number of killings.[170] The concept of killing members of the group does not only mean physical killing. Other acts can also "constitute direct participation in the *actus reus* of the crime. The question is whether an accused's conduct was as much an integral part of the genocide as were the killings which it enabled,"[171] in the sense that the accused approved and embraced as their own the decision to commit the crime.[172] The harm within the term "causing serious bodily or mental harm" must go "beyond temporary unhappiness, embarrassment or humiliation" and inflict "grave and long-term disadvantage to a person's ability to lead a normal and

---

TC), Trial Chamber Judgment, 26 July 2010 at paras 291–92, and *Case 002/01* (Case File No 002/19-09-2007-ECCC/SC), Supreme Court Chamber Judgment, 23 November 2016 at paras 711–21, make it clear that such a connection was not part of international law in the 1970s, while the same is said for the 1950s by a decision of the European Court of Human Rights in the case of *Korbely v Hungary*, 19 September 2008, Application No 9174/02 at para 82.

170 *Karadžić* (IT-95-5/18-AR98bis.1), Appeals Chamber Judgment (Rule 98bis), 11 July 2013 at para 23, as long as there is evidence of acts on a scale that establishes an intent not only to target certain individuals because of their membership of a particular group but also to destroy the group itself in whole or in part; *Application of the Convention on the Prevention and Punishment of the Crime of Genocide (Croatia v Serbia)*, International Court of Justice, 3 February 2015, ICJ Rep (2015) ICJ General List No 118 at para 139; *Case 002/02* (Case File No 002/19-09-2007/ECCC/TC), Trial Chamber Judgment, 16 November 2018 at para 796.

171 *Kalimanzira* (ICTR-05-88-A), Appeals Chamber Judgment, 20 October 2010 at para 219; *Munyakazi* (ICTR-97-36A-A), Appeals Chamber Judgment, 28 September 2011 at para 135.

172 *Seromba* (ICTR-2001-66-I), Trial Chamber Judgment, 13 December 2006 at para 161.

constructive life."[173] Examples of acts that meet this threshold are bodily or mental torture, inhumane or degrading treatment, rape, and sexual violence,[174] as are interrogations combined with beatings, threats of death, and harm that damages health or causes disfigurement or serious injury.[175] In some circumstances, forcible displacement can also amount to genocide.[176]

Subjecting a group of people to a subsistence diet, systematic expulsion from their homes, and deprivation of essential medical supplies below a minimum vital standard would fall within the parameters of "deliberately inflicting on the group conditions of life calculated to bring about its physical destruction,"[177] as would "the creation of circumstances that would lead to a slow death, such as lack of proper housing, clothing and hygiene or excessive work or physical exertion"[178] and "acts of contamination of water pumps and forcible transfer coupled by

---

173 *Tolimir* (IT-05-88/2-A), Appeals Chamber Judgment, 8 April 2015 at paras 203–4; *Karadžić* (IT-95-5/18-T), Trial Chamber Judgment, 24 March 2016 at para 543.

174 *Application of the Convention on the Prevention and Punishment of the Crime of Genocide (Croatia v Serbia)*, International Court of Justice, 3 February 2015, ICJ Rep (2015) ICJ General List No 118 at paras 157–60; *Karadžić* (IT-95-5/18-T), Trial Chamber Judgment, 24 March 2016 at para 545; *Mladić* (IT-09-92-T), Trial Chamber Judgment, 22 November 2017 at para 3434.

175 *Case concerning the Application of the Convention on the Prevention and Punishment of the Crime of Genocide (Bosnia and Herzegovina v Serbia and Montenegro)*, International Court of Justice, 26 February 2007, ICJ Rep (2007) ICJ General List No 91 at para 319; *Tolimir* (IT-05-88/2-T), Trial Chamber Judgment, 12 December 2012 at para 737; *Mladić* (IT-09-92-T), Trial Chamber Judgment, 22 November 2017 at para 3434.

176 *Tolimir* (IT-05-88/2-A), Appeals Chamber Judgment, 8 April 2015 at paras 208–9. The same was said about ethnic cleansing, which by itself is not mentioned as an international crime but can be seen as an accumulation of other activities that are prohibited by international criminal law; see *Case concerning the Application of the Convention on the Prevention and Punishment of the Crime of Genocide (Bosnia and Herzegovina v Serbia and Montenegro)*, International Court of Justice, 26 February 2007, ICJ Rep (2007) ICJ General List No 91 at para 190; *Application of the Convention on the Prevention and Punishment of the Crime of Genocide (Croatia v Serbia)*, International Court of Justice, 3 February 2015, ICJ Rep (2015) ICJ General List No 118 at paras 162, 477, and 510; *Karadžić* (IT-95-5/18-T), Trial Chamber Judgment, 24 March 2016 at para 545.

177 *Akayesu*, above note 159 at paras 500–9; *Tolimir* (IT-05-88/2-T), Trial Chamber Judgment, 12 December 2012 at para 740; *Karadžić* (IT-95-5/18-T), Trial Chamber Judgment, 24 March 2016 at para 546; see, also, ICC, *Elements of Crimes*, above note 153, n4.

178 *Application of the Convention on the Prevention and Punishment of the Crime of Genocide (Croatia v Serbia)*, International Court of Justice, 3 February 2015, ICJ Rep (2015) ICJ General List No 118 at paras 161–63 (which indicates that forced displacement could fall under this heading); *Tolimir* (IT-05-88/2-A), Appeals Chamber Judgment, 8 April 2015 at paras 225–35; *Karadžić* (IT-95-5/18-T), Trial Chamber Judgment, 24 March 2016 at para 547; *Mladić* (IT-09-92-T), Trial Chamber Judgment, 22 November 2017 at para 3434.

resettlement."[179] Sexual mutilation, enforced sterilization, forced birth control, forced separation of males and females, and prohibition of marriages can be construed as "measures intended to prevent births within the group."[180]

The subcategory of "forcibly transferring children of the group to another group" has received scant judicial attention, but the ICC *Elements of Crimes* document clarifies the notion of "forcibly" by saying that "the term 'forcibly' is not restricted to physical force, but may include threat of force or coercion, such as that caused by fear of violence, duress, detention, psychological oppression or abuse of power, against such person or persons or another person, or by taking advantage of a coercive environment."[181]

The words "as such," used in the preamble in relation to the protected groups, have been interpreted to mean that the acts must be committed against an individual because the individual was a member of a specific group and "specifically because he belonged to this group, so that the victim is the group itself, not merely the individual."[182] The term "in part" in the preamble of the definition has been interpreted as requiring a "substantial number" as well as a "significant section" of the intended group. In assessing whether the targeted part of the group is substantial, the numerical size of the part of the group targeted, evaluated in absolute terms and relative to the overall group size, "is the necessary and important starting point."[183] Other factors can include the prominence within the group of the targeted part, whether the targeted part of the group "is emblematic of the overall group, or is

---

179 *Al Bashir* (ICC-02/05-01/09), Pre-Trial Chamber, Second Decision on the Prosecution's Application for a Warrant of Arrest, 12 July 2010 at para 38.

180 *Akayesu*, above note 159 at paras 500–9; *Popović et al* (IT-05-88-T), Trial Chamber Judgment, 10 June 2010 at para 818; *Tolimir* (IT-05-88/2-T), Trial Chamber Judgment, 12 December 2012 at para 743; *Application of the Convention on the Prevention and Punishment of the Crime of Genocide (Croatia v Serbia)*, International Court of Justice, 3 February 2015, ICJ Rep (2015) ICJ General List No 118 at para 166.

181 ICC, *Elements of Crimes*, above note 153, n5.

182 *Akayesu* (ICTR-96-4-A), Appeals Chamber Judgment, 1 June 2001 at para 521, and *Niyitegeka* (ICTR-96-4-A), Appeals Chamber Judgment, 9 July 2004 at paras 47–55; *Karadžić* (IT-95-5/18-T), Trial Chamber Judgment, 24 March 2016 at paras 552–53; *Case 002/02* (Case File No 002/19-09-2007/ECCC/TC), Trial Chamber Judgment, 16 November 2018 at para 798.

183 *Krstić* (IT-98-33-A), Appeals Chamber Judgment, 19 April 2004 at para 6; *Popović et al* (IT-05-88-A), Appeals Chamber Judgment, 30 January 2015 at paras 419–25; *Tolimir* (IT-05-88/2-A), Appeals Chamber Judgment, 8 April 2015 at para 186; *Mladić* (MICT-13-56-A), Appeals Chamber Judgment, 8 June 2021 at paras 576–78.

essential to its survival," and the area of the perpetrators' activity and control and limitations on the possible extent of their reach.[184]

Only a person belonging to the four types of groups mentioned in the preamble of the above definition would fall within the class of victims of genocide.[185] What amounts to a group has been resolved in the jurisprudence by relying not only on objective factors, such as the permanency or stability of a group, but also on subjective factors and should be assessed on a "case-by-case basis by reference to the objective particulars of a given social or historical context, and by the subjective perceptions of the perpetrators."[186]

When comparing the definitions of genocide and crimes against humanity, it becomes clear that the crime of genocide is subsumed within the larger category of crime against humanity so that every act of genocide is also a crime against humanity but not vice versa.[187] Only four

---

184 *Application of the Convention on the Prevention and Punishment of the Crime of Genocide (Croatia v Serbia)*, International Court of Justice, 3 February 2015, ICJ Rep (2015) ICJ General List No 118 at para 142; *Karadžić* (IT-95-5/18-T), Trial Chamber Judgment, 24 March 2016 at para 555; *Case 002/02* (Case File No 002/19-09-2007/ECCC/TC), Trial Chamber Judgment, 16 November 2018 at para 802

185 *Krstić* (IT-98-33), Trial Chamber Judgment, 2 August 2001 at paras 554–57 and 575–80, makes it clear that the destruction of groups with other characteristics than the ones mentioned in the definition does not amount to genocide; see, also, *Stakić* (IT-97-24), Trial Chamber Judgment, 22 March 2003 at paras 23–24; *Nahimana, Barayagwiza and Ngeze ("Media")* (ICTR-99-52-A), Appeals Chamber and Judgment, 28 November 2007 at paras 496–97; regarding the issue of groups in the Genocide Convention in a historical context, see, also, the European Court of Human Rights cases of *Vasiliauskas v Lithuania*, 22 October 2015, Application No 35343/05, and *Drėlingas v Lithuania*, 12 March 2019, Application No 28859/16.

186 *Semanza* (ICTR-97-20-T), Trial Chamber Judgment, 15 May 2003 at para 317; *Gacumbitsi* (ICTR-2001-64-T), Trial Chamber Judgment, 17 June 2004 at para 254; *Al Bashir* (ICC-02/05-01/09), Pre-Trial Chamber, Separate and Partly Dissenting Opinion of Judge Anita Ušacka, Decision on the Prosecution's Application for a Warrant of Arrest against Omar Hassan Ahmad Al Bashir, 4 March 2009 at para 23. Negative criteria, such as "non-Serbs," are not appropriate in this context; see *Stakic* (IT-97-24), Trial Chamber Judgment, 22 March 2006 at paras 16–36, and *Popović et al* (IT-05-88-T), Trial Chamber Judgment, 10 June 2010 at para 809; *Tolimir* (IT-05-88/2-T), Trial Chamber Judgment, 12 December 2012 at para 735; *Karadžić* (IT-95-5/18-T), Trial Chamber Judgment, 24 March 2016 at para 541; *Case 002/02* (Case File No 002/19-09-2007/ECCC/TC), Trial Chamber Judgment, 16 November 2018 at paras 792–94; *Ao An* (Case File No 004/02/07-09-2009-ECCC/OCIJ (PTC60)), Pre-Trial Chamber, Considerations on Appeals against Closing Orders, Opinion of Judges Baik and Bauvallet, 19 December 2019 at paras 619–22; *Mladić* (MICT-13-56-A), Appeals Chamber Judgment, 8 June 2021 at paras 578–89; for a different view, see the Joint Partially Dissenting Opinion of Judge N'Gum and Judge Panton in the same judgment at paras 759–80.

187 This is not surprising given the fact that the crime of genocide originated in the context of post–Second World War international criminal law. Genocide as a war crime or crime against humanity was recognized by various tribunals after the Second World War, such as the IMT

situations have been judicially recognized at the international level[188] since the Second World War as genocide: the events between 6 April and 17 July 1994 in Rwanda with the Tutsi ethnic group as the primary target;[189] the killing of over 7,000 Muslim men and boys at Srebrenica in the former Yugoslavia around 13 July 1995;[190] the situation in Darfur from March 2003 until at least 14 July 2008 against the Fur, Masalit, and Zaghawa ethnic groups;[191] and the acts between 17 April 1975 and 6 January 1979 against the ethnic and religious Cham group and the Vietnamese, an ethnic, national, and religious group, living in Cambodia.[192]

---

at Nuremberg, where it was included in the indictment as part of murder and ill-treatment of the civilian population. In the *Justice Trial, Trial of Josef Altstötter and Others*, United States Military Tribunal, Nuremberg, *Law Reports of Trials of War Criminals*, vol VI at 99, the accused, Rothaug, was actually convicted of this crime and also found guilty of the charges of crimes against humanity. Other examples where the crime of genocide was recognized can be found in the *Trial of Hauptsturmfuhrer Amon Leopold Goeth*, Supreme National Tribunal of Poland, *Law Reports of Trials of War Criminals*, vol VII at 7–9; *Trial of Ulrich Greifelt and others*, United States Military Tribunal, Nuremberg, *Law Reports of Trials of War Criminals*, vol XIII at 37–42; and *Trial of Obersturmbannfuhrer Rudolf Fanz Ferdinand Hoess*, Supreme National Tribunal of Poland, *Law Reports of Trials of War Criminals*, vol VII at 24–26. It appears that the tribunals treated genocide as the end result of a series of war crimes and crimes against humanity rather than an independent crime. This was probably done in order to achieve a balance between recognizing genocide as a crime on the one hand and fitting the crime within the confines of their constituting instruments on the other. See, also, *Sikirica* (IT- 95-8-T), Trial Chamber Judgment, 3 September 2001 at para 58. For the differences between genocide and crimes against humanity, see *Musema* (ICTR-96-13-A), Appeals Chamber Judgment, 16 November 2001 at para 366, and *Krstić* (IT-98-33-A), Appeals Chamber Judgment, 19 April 2004 at paras 220–29, although the latter decision recognized that these differences have been all but eliminated in the ICC *Elements of Crimes* document.

188 At the national level, a number of states have expanded on the number of groups that can be victimized when incorporating the Rome Statute into their national legislation, while national judiciaries have done the same; see Joseph Rikhof & Ashley Geerts, "Protected Groups in Refugee Law and International Law" (2019) 8:4 *Laws* at 22–23, online: www.mdpi.com/2075-471X/8/4/25.

189 This has been recognized in all the ICTR jurisprudence since 1998, with the clearest statement on this point by the Appeals Chamber in saying that judicial notice could be taken that genocide had taken place; see Decision on Prosecutor's Interlocutory Appeal of Decision on Judicial Notice (ICTR-98-44-AR73(C)), Appeals Chamber, 16 June 2006 at para 35.

190 *Case concerning the Application of the Convention on the Prevention and Punishment of the Crime of Genocide (Bosnia and Herzegovina v Serbia and Montenegro)*, International Court of Justice, 26 February 2007, ICJ Rep (2007) ICJ General List No 91 at para 297.

191 Second Decision on the Prosecution's Application for a Warrant of Arrest, *Al Bashir* (ICC-02/05-01/09), Pre-Trial Chamber I, 12 July 2010 at paras 9 and 30–31.

192 Closing Order (Case File 002/19-09-2007-ECCC-OCIJ), Office of the Co-Investigating Judges, 15 September 2010 at paras 1336–49, confirmed by *Case 002* (Case file 002/19-09-2007-ECCC-TC/SC(28)), Supreme Court Chamber, Decision on Immediate Appeals against Trial Chamber's Second Decision on Severance of Case 002, 23 July 2013 at paras 10–11.

c) The *Mens Rea* of the International Crimes

Apart from the fact that a crime has to fall within the parameters of international law in order to consider such activity a war crime, crime against humanity, genocide, or crime of aggression, a person who was involved in such a crime is only liable if they had the required *mens rea* or mental element to commit such a crime.[193] As a result of the caselaw at the ICTY and ICTR and the discussions surrounding the ICC, culminating in the ICC *Elements of Crimes* document,[194] it has been established that the *mens rea* extends to the contextual element of war crimes and crimes against humanity.[195] This would mean, for instance, that in order for a prosecutor to prove the crime against humanity of murder, they would need to show that a person caused the death of certain persons and intended to do so as part of widespread or systematic activity[196] and that the accused knew that the murder committed was part of the widespread or systematic activity[197] or was wilfully blind

---

193 *Mens rea* is different from motive, and the latter is not an element of any crime; see *Kanyarukiga* (ICTR-02-78-A), Appeals Chamber Judgment, 8 May 2012 at para 262; *Popović et al* (IT-05-88-A), Appeals Chamber Judgment, 30 January 2015 at para 1027; *Stanišić and Župljanin* (IT-08-91-T), Trial Chamber Judgment, 27 March 2013 at para 30.

194 See ICC, *Elements of Crimes*, above note 153, "Introduction" to the Crimes against Humanity portion at 5 at para 2, which goes on to say: "However, the last element should not be interpreted as requiring proof that the perpetrator had knowledge of all characteristics of the attack or the precise details of the plan or policy of the State or organization. In the case of an emerging widespread or systematic attack against a civilian population, the intent clause of the last element indicates that this mental element is satisfied if the perpetrator intended to further such an attack."

195 *Tadić* (IT-94-1-A), Appeals Chamber Judgment, 15 July 1999 at paras 248–50; *Kordić and Čerkez* (IT-95-14/2-A), Appeals Chamber Judgment, 17 December 2004 at paras 299–313; *Naletilić & Martinović* (IT-98-34), Appeals Chamber Judgment, 3 May 2006 at paras 109–22; *Kaing Guek Eav alias Duch* (Case File 001/18-07-2007/ECCC/TC), Trial Chamber Judgment, 26 July 2010 at paras 420–22; *Bemba* (ICC-01/05-01/08), Trial Chamber Judgment, 21 March 2016 at paras 166–69; *Mladić* (IT-09-92-T), Trial Chamber Judgment, 22 November 2017 at para 3029; *Prlić et al* (IT-04-74-A), Appeals Chamber Judgment, 29 November 2017 at para 389; *Ongwen* (ICC-02/0401/15), Trial Chamber Judgment, 4 February 2021 at paras 2691–92.

196 See *Lukić* (IT-98-32/1), Trial Chamber Judgment, 20 July 2009 at para 900; *Gotovina et al* (IT-06-90-T), Trial Chamber Judgment, 15 April 2011 at para 1707.

197 For the specific *mens rea* of the crime against humanity, see *Blaškić* (IT-95-14-A), Appeals Chamber Judgment, 29 July 2004 at paras 124–28, and *Kordić and Čerkez* (IT-95-14/2-A), Appeals Chamber Judgment, 17 December 2004 at paras 98–100; see, also, *Brima, Kamara and Kanu ('AFRC')* (SCSL-2004-16-T), Trial Chamber Judgment, 20 June 2007 at paras 221–22; *Kaing Guek Eav alias Duch* (Case File 001/18-07-2007/ECCC/TC), Trial Chamber Judgment, 26 July 2010 at para 319; *Taylor* (SCSL-03-01-T), Trial Chamber Judgment, 18 May 2012 at para 515; *Tolimir* (IT-05-88/2-T), Trial Chamber Judgment, 12 December 2012 at para 700; *Ongwen* (ICC-02/0401/15), Trial Chamber Judgment, 4 February 2021 at para 2695.

in this respect. The latter type of *mens rea* has been expressed by the ICTY as follows:

> In addition to the intent to commit the underlying offence, the accused must know that there is an attack directed against the civilian population and he must know that his acts are part of that attack, or at least take the risk that they are part thereof. This, however, does not entail knowledge of the details of the attack. It is sufficient that, through his acts or the function which he willingly accepted, he knowingly took the risk of participating in the implementation of that attack.[198]

---

198 *Kunarac*, 2002, above note 147 at para 102; *Blaškić* (IT-95-14-A), Appeals Chamber Judgment, 29 July 2004 at para 126; *Stanišić and Župljanin* (IT-08-91-T), Trial Chamber Judgment, 27 March 2013 at paras 30 and 1258, n2193 (which equates recklessness with *dolus eventualis*); *Prlić et al* (IT-04-74), Trial Chamber Judgment, 29 May 2013 at para 45; Šainović *et al* (IT-05-87-A), Appeals Chamber Judgment, 23 January 2014 at paras 270–71; see, also, *Taylor* (SCSL-04-01-T), Appeals Chamber Judgment, 26 September 2013 at para 438, where this form of knowledge is called "awareness of the substantial likelihood" for aiding and abetting. For a discussion of the various types of *mens rea* in international criminal law, see *Lubanga* (ICC-01/04-01/06), Pre-Trial Chamber, Decision on the Confirmation of Charges, 29 January 2007 at paras 349–60; *Bemba* (ICC-01/05-01/08), Pre-Trial Chamber, Decision of Confirmation of Charges, 15 June 2009 at paras 352–69. In the latter decision, art 30 of the Rome Statute, setting out the general *mens rea* concept applicable to crimes, which do not include their own *mens rea*, is analyzed, and the court makes the following distinctions between types of mental elements: (a) intent if the consequences of action were meant (*dolus directus* of the first degree in civil law) or certain to follow (*dolus directus* of the second degree in civil law); (b) *dolus eventualis* (in civil law) when a person is aware of the risk that the objective elements of the crime may result from his actions and accepts such an outcome by reconciling himself with it or consenting to it; this concept has two sublevels: the risk is a substantial one or the risk is low, but the person has clearly or expressly accepted the idea that such elements will follow from his actions; and (c) if an action followed after information was acquired in the mind of the particular person (subjective) and the risk of the consequences was high, and a decision was taken in spite of that consequence (in civil law a form of culpa or conscientious negligence); the court comes to the conclusion that only the first form of *mens rea* is part of art 30, which is a narrower interpretation than was reached by the pre-trial chamber in the *Lubanga* case on this issue and which was followed by *Lubanga* (ICC-01/04-01/06), Trial Chamber Judgment, 14 March 2012 at para 1011; see, also, *Chui* (ICC-01/04-02/12), Trial Chamber Judgment, Concurring Opinion of Judge Christine Van den Wyngaert, 18 December 2012 at paras 15, 36–38; *Katanga* (ICC-01/04-01/07), Trial Chamber Judgment, 7 March 2014 at paras 770–79; *Jean-Pierre Bemba Gombo, Aimé Kilolo Musamba, Jean-Jacques Mangenda Kabongo, Fidèle Babala Wandu and Narcisse Arido* (ICC-01/05-01/13), Trial Chamber Judgment, 19 October 2016 at paras 27–31. It has been said that the default *mens rea* at the ICTY/ICTR is recklessness; see Elies van Sliedregt, *Individual Criminal Responsibility in International Law* (Oxford: Oxford University Press, 2012) at 50–52, as well as *Prlić et al* (IT-04-74), Trial Chamber Judgment, 29 May 2013 at para 192.

What has been said about war crimes[199] and crimes against humanity is also the case for genocide, although it has been established that in general the *mens rea* of the crime of genocide is of a higher level than knowledge and includes a special intent or *dolus specialis* to destroy, in whole or in part, a national, ethnical, racial, or religious group, which has been explained as follows:

> [T]he *mens rea* requirement for persecution is higher than for ordinary crimes against humanity, although lower than for genocide. In this context the Trial Chamber wishes to stress that persecution as a crime against humanity is an offence belonging to the same *genus* as genocide. Both persecution and genocide are crimes perpetrated against persons that belong to a particular group and who are targeted because of such belonging. In both categories what matters is the intent to discriminate: to attack persons on account of their ethnic, racial, or religious characteristics (as well as, in the case of persecution, on account of their political affiliation). While in the case of persecution the discriminatory intent can take multifarious inhumane forms and manifest itself in a plurality of actions including murder, in the case of genocide that intent must be accompanied by the intention to destroy, in whole or in part, the group to which the victims of the genocide belong. Thus, it can be said that, from the viewpoint of *mens rea*, genocide is an extreme and most inhuman form of persecution. To put it differently, when persecution escalates to the extreme form of wilful and deliberate acts designed to destroy a group or part of a group, it can be held that such persecution amounts to genocide.[200]

199 *Kaing Guek Eav alias Duch* (Case File 001/18-07-2007/ECCC/TC), Trial Chamber Judgment, 26 July 2010 at paras 420–22.

200 *Kupreškić et al* (IT-95-16), Trial Chamber Judgment, 14 January 2000 at para 636. See, also, *Nahimana, Barayagwiza and Ngeze ("Media")* (ICTR-99-52-A), Appeals Chamber Judgment, 28 November 2007 at paras 523–25 and 561; *Popović et al* (IT-05-88-T), Trial Chamber Judgment, 10 June 2010 at paras 820–24, as well as *Case concerning the Application of the Convention on the Prevention and Punishment of the Crime of Genocide (Bosnia and Herzegovina v Serbia and Montenegro)*, International Court of Justice, 26 February 2007, ICJ Rep (2007) ICJ General List No 91 at paras 186–89; *Application of the Convention on the Prevention and Punishment of the Crime of Genocide (Croatia v Serbia)*, International Court of Justice, 3 February 2015, ICJ Rep (2015) ICJ General List No 118 at paras 132 and 148; *Tolimir* (IT-05-88/2-A), Appeals Chamber Judgment, 8 April 2015 at paras 246–47; *Karadžić* (IT-95-5/18-T), Trial Chamber Judgment, 24 March 2016 at para 549; *Case 002/02* (Case File No 002/19-09-2007/ECCC/TC), Trial Chamber Judgment, 16 November 2018 at paras 800–1; *Ao An* (Case File No 004/02/07-09-2009-ECCC/OCIJ (PTC60)), Pre-Trial Chamber, Considerations on Appeals against Closing Orders, Opinion of Judges Baik and Bauvallet, 19 December 2019 at paras

While the special intent is high for genocide, it does not go as far as to insist that the existence of a plan or policy is a legal ingredient,[201] nor is long meditation,[202] a prior intent,[203] or personal motivation[204] necessary to carry out a genocidal plan. On the other hand, ICC judges appear to be looking for some form of collective intent rather than individual intent.[205] The intent to destroy a group only in part amounts to genocide even if the group whose destruction is desired consists only of a local segment of the larger group or, as was said in the *Krstić* case, "the Chamber concludes that the intent to kill all the Bosnian Muslim men of military age in Srebrenica constitutes an intent to destroy in part the Bosnian Muslim group … and therefore must be qualified as a genocide."[206]

Some specific crimes against humanity also have a *dolus specialis*, such as enforced disappearance,[207] persecution,[208] and apartheid,[209] as

---

623–26. As to evidence to show such intent, see *Mladić* (MICT-13-56-A), Appeals Chamber Judgment, Joint Partially Dissenting Opinion of Judge N'Gum and Judge Panton, 8 June 2021 at paras 775–96.

201 *Jelisić* (IT-95-10), Appeals Chambers Judgment, 5 July 2001 at para 48; *Simba* (ICTR-01-76-A), Appeals Chamber Judgment, 27 November 2007 at para 260; *Popović et al* (IT-05-88-A), Appeals Chamber Judgment, 30 January 2015 at paras 430–41.

202 *Krstić* (IT-98-33), Trial Chamber Judgment, 2 August 2001 at para 572.

203 *Simba* (ICTR-01-76-A), Appeals Chamber Judgment, 27 November 2007 at para 266; *Karera* (ICTR-01-74-T), Trial Chamber Judgment, 7 December 2007 at para 534.

204 *Tadić* (IT-94-1-A), Appeals Chamber Judgment, 15 July 1999 at para 269; *Jelisić* (IT-95-10), Appeals Chambers Judgment, 5 July 2001 at para 49; *Tolimir* (IT-05-88/2-T), Trial Chamber Judgment, 12 December 2012 at para 700; *Karadžić* (IT-95-5/18-T), Trial Chamber Judgment, 24 March 2016 at para 554. However, personal motivation does not necessary preclude special intent; see *Đorđević* (IT-05-87/1-A), Appeals Chamber Judgment, 27 January 2014 at para 887.

205 *Al Bashir* (ICC-02/05-01/09), Pre-Trial Chamber, Decision on the Prosecution's Application for a Warrant of Arrest against Omar Hassan Ahmad Al Bashir, 4 March 2009 at paras 150–51.

206 *Krstić* (IT-98-33), Trial Chamber Judgment, 2 August 2001 at para 598, while for the reasoning, see at paras 581–97; see, also, *Jelisić* (IT-95-10), Appeals Chamber Judgment, 5 July 2001 at para 83; *Stakić* (IT-97-24), Trial Chamber Judgment, 22 March 2003 at paras 521–26; *Brđanin* (IT-99-36), Trial Chamber Judgment, 1 September 2004 at paras 700–3; *Karadžić* (IT-95-5/18-T), Trial Chamber Judgment, 24 March 2016 at paras 549–50. For other modalities of intent in respect to genocide, such as joint criminal enterprise and superior responsibility, see *Brđanin* (IT-99-36), Trial Chamber Judgment, 1 September 2004 at paras 708–21; *Karadžić* (IT-95-5/18-T), Trial Chamber Judgment, 24 March 2016 at para 549.

207 ICC, *Elements of Crimes*, above note 153, art 7(1)(i), Element 6.

208 Special Tribunal for Lebanon, Interlocutory Decision on the Applicable Law: Terrorism, Conspiracy, Homicide, Perpetration, Cumulative charging, STL-II-OI/I/AC/RI76bis, Appeals Chamber, 16 February 2011 at para 249.

209 ICC, *Elements of Crimes*, above note 153, art 7(1)(j), Element 5.

do war crimes such as attacking protected objects,[210] treacherously killing or wounding,[211] and depriving the nationals of the hostile power of rights or actions.[212]

d) The Underlying Crimes of War Crimes and Crimes Against Humanity

i) Introduction

The Rome Statute, which could be considered the most comprehensive instrument in describing war crimes and crimes against humanity at the time of its adoption in July 1998, makes mention of eleven crimes against humanity and fifty war crimes, both in international and non-international armed conflict, of which thirty-four are applicable in international armed conflicts, with the remainder (almost all with the same characteristics)[213] in non-international armed conflicts. This number is not static as international criminal law continues to develop, which is apparent as the number of especially war crimes mentioned in post–Second World War instruments was substantially smaller than in the Rome Statute. The number of war crimes in the Rome Statute has seen an increase as a result of a decision at the Kampala Review Conference to add three more crimes to the non-international armed conflict regime. These crimes are already known for international armed conflicts. They are:

> (xiii) Employing poison or poisoned weapons;
> (xiv) Employing asphyxiating, poisonous or other gases, and all analogous liquids, materials or devices;
> (xv) Employing bullets which expand or flatten easily in the human body, such as bullets with a hard envelope which does not entirely cover the core or is pierced with incisions.[214]

---

210 *Ibid*, art 8(2)(b)(ix), Element 3.

211 *Ibid*, art 8(2)(b)(xi), Element 2.

212 *Ibid*, art 8(2)(b)(xiv), Element 3.

213 Article 8.2(e)(iii), dealing with attacks against people and material involved in a humanitarian or peacekeeping mission, is an exception.

214 UN Doc Resolution RC/Res 5, Annex I, "Amendments to Article 8 of the Rome Statute." It appears from the Rome Statute that new types of war crimes can also be found outside the Assembly of States decision-making process as a result of the wording in the preamble of the enumeration of war crimes in both international armed conflicts (art 8.2(b)) and non-international armed conflicts (art 8.2(e)), which reads: "within the established framework of international law."

In December 2017, the Rome Statute was amended by adding three more war crimes each for international and non-international armed conflicts: employing microbial, biological, or toxin weapons; employing weapons that injure by fragments undetectable by X-rays; and employing laser weapons.[215] Two years later, the war crime of starvation was added to non-international armed conflicts.[216]

The ICTY and ICTR also recognized early on that the number and type of war crimes in their statutes, which were based on the 1949 Geneva Conventions and their additional protocols, might not reflect the realities of modern warfare. Therefore, a method was developed to ensure that nefarious activities could become war crimes if several requirements were met. These conditions are as follows:

(i) the violation must constitute an infringement of a rule of international humanitarian law;
(ii) the rule must be customary in nature, or, if it belongs to treaty law, the required conditions must be met;
(iii) the violation must be serious, that is to say, it must constitute a breach of a rule protecting important values, and the breach must involve grave consequences for the victim; and
(iv) the violation of the rule must entail, under customary or conventional law, the individual criminal responsibility of the person breaching the rule.[217]

---

215 UN Doc Resolution ICC-ASP/16/Res 4.

216 UN Doc Resolution ICC-ASP/18/Res 5.

217 *Tadić* (IT-94-1), Appeals Chamber, Decision on the Defence Motion for Interlocutory Appeal on Jurisdiction, 2 October 1995 at para 94; *Kunarac*, 2002, above note 147 at para 66; *Aleksovski* (IT-95-14/1-A), Appeals Chamber Judgment, 24 March 2000 at para 20; *Prlić et al* (IT-04-74), Trial Chamber Judgment, 29 May 2013 at para 142; *Karadžić* (IT-95-5/18-T), Trial Chamber Judgment, 24 March 2016 at para 443; *Mladić* (IT-09-92-T), Trial Chamber Judgment, 22 November 2017 at paras 3009 and 3184–88.

Based on this approach, the ICTY added the war crimes of causing terror[218] and sniping and shelling[219] to its arsenal of prosecutable acts.

The underlying crimes that share similarities, in that their essential elements are the same whether they are war crimes or crimes against humanity, will be discussed first.[220] Those are the crimes of torture, rape, and other forms of sexual violence; inhuman acts/cruel treatment;

218 *Galić* (IT-98-29-A), Appeals Chamber Judgment, 30 November 2006 at paras 99–104; *Milošević* (IT-98-29/1-A), Appeals Chamber Judgment, 12 November 2009 at paras 30–38; see, also, *Fofana and Kondewa ("CDF")* (SCSL-04-14-A), Appeals Chamber Judgment, 28 May 2008 at paras 350–58; *Sesay, Kallon and Gbao ("RUF")* (SCSL-04-15-T), Trial Chamber Judgment, 25 February 2009 at paras 113–21; *Taylor* (SCSL-03-01-T), Trial Chamber Judgment, 18 May 2012 at paras 402–10 and 1963–2192 (tying a number of other crimes, such as killing and sexual violence, to the purpose of causing terror); *Tolimir* (IT-05-88/2-T), Trial Chamber Judgment, 12 December 2012 at paras 855–57; *Prlić et al* (IT-04-74), Trial Chamber Judgment, 29 May 2013 at paras 194–97; *Popović et al* (IT-05-88-A), Appeals Chamber Judgment, 30 January 2015 at paras 737–38; *Karadžić* (IT-95-5/18-T), Trial Chamber Judgment, 24 March 2016 at paras 458–66; *Mladić* (IT-09-92-T), Trial Chamber Judgment, 22 November 2017 at para 3011; *Prlić et al* (IT-04-74-A), Appeals Chamber Judgment, 29 November 2017 at paras 424 and 563–64; see, also, *R v Khawaja*, 2012 SCC 69 at para 102. For the related notion of siege, see *Milošević* (IT-98-29/1-T), Trial Chamber Judgment, 12 December 2007 at para 571; *Milošević* (IT-98-29/1-A), Appeals Chamber Judgment, 12 November 2009 at paras 130–33; *Mladić* (MICT-13-56-A), Appeals Chamber Judgment, 8 June 2021 at paras 283–313.

219 *Galić* (IT-98-29-A), Appeals Chamber Judgment, 30 November 2006 at para 106.

220 Except the crime of killing as international law jurisprudence has not added any major new element to the parameters of this crime as known in domestic law except by saying that the terms "murder" and "killing" have been defined as "causing death" in the ICC *Elements of Crimes* document, above note 153, n2 and n7; for an explanation, see *Katanga* (ICC-01/04-01/07), Trial Chamber Judgment, 7 March 2014 at paras 765–69 and 780–94; see, also, *Tolimir* (IT-05-88/2-T), Trial Chamber Judgment, 12 December 2012 at paras 715–16; *Đorđević* (IT-05-87/1-A), Appeals Chamber Judgment, 27 January 2014 at paras 546–52; *Case 002/01* (Case File No 002/19-09-2007/ECCC/TC), Trial Chamber Judgment, 7 August 2014 at paras 411–13; *Popović et al* (IT-05-88-A), Appeals Chamber Judgment, 30 January 2015 at para 794; *Bemba* (ICC-01/05-01/08), Trial Chamber Judgment, 21 March 2016 at paras 87–97; *Karadžić* (IT-95-5/18-T), Trial Chamber Judgment, 24 March 2016 at paras 445–48; *Case 002/01* (Case File No 002/19-09-2007-ECCC/SC), Supreme Court Chamber Judgment, 23 November 2016 at paras 387–410 and 418–21; *Mladić* (IT-09-92-T), Trial Chamber Judgment, 22 November 2017 at para 3049; *Case 002/02* (Case File No 002/19-09-2007/ECCC/TC), Trial Chamber Judgment, 16 November 2018 at paras 627–50 (which also indicated that *dolus eventualis* is included in the *mens rea* of this crime); *Ntaganda* (ICC-01/04-02/06), Trial Chamber Judgment, 8 July 2019 at paras 738 and 858–62; *Gbagbo and Blé Goudé* (ICC-02/11-01/15-1263-AnxC-Red), Trial Chamber, Reasons for oral decision of 15 January 2019 on the *Requête de la Défense de Laurent Gbagbo afin qu'un jugement d'acquittement portant sur toutes les charges soit prononcé en faveur de Laurent Gbagbo et que sa mise en liberté immédiate soit ordonnée, and on the Blé Goudé Defence* no case to answer motion, Public Redacted Version of Dissenting Opinion Judge Herrera Carbuccia, 16 July 2019 at paras 383–85; *Ongwen* (ICC-02/0401/15), Trial Chamber Judgment, 4 February 2021 at paras 2696–99.

imprisonment/unlawful confinement; and deportation/transfer,[221] followed by the remaining crimes against humanity of enslavement[222] and persecution and extermination[223] and ending with brief overviews of the other war crimes (especially the crimes that are distinct from crimes against humanity, such as crimes involving objects and the use of prohibited weapons) mentioned in the Rome Statute that have been the subject of interpretation by international judicial institutions.[224]

---

221 While the crimes of unlawful deportation and transfer are considered independent crimes against humanity and war crimes in the Rome Statute (arts 7.1(d), 8.2(a)(vii), and 8.2(e)(viii), although in the last instance it is called displacement), under the ICTY and ICTR statutes, the crime of humanity of forcible transfer was not included as a separate crime, but the jurisprudence of the ICTY has held that this crime could be brought within the parameters of the crime against humanity of inhumane acts (see *Krajišnik* (IT-00-39-A), Appeals Chamber Judgment, 17 March 2009 at paras 330–31; *Popović et al* (IT-05-88-T), Trial Chamber Judgment, 10 June 2010 at paras 888–89; *Gotovina et al* (IT-06-90-T), Trial Chamber Judgment, 15 April 2011 at para 1737; *Perišić* (IT-04-81-T), Trial Chamber Judgment, 6 September 2011 at para 113; *Tolimir* (IT-05-88/2-T), Trial Chamber Judgment, 12 December 2012 at para 803).

222 The ICTY jurisprudence has held that enslavement can amount to both crimes against humanity and war crimes, even though the latter offence was not mentioned in its statute; see *Krnojelac* (IT-97-25), Trial Chamber Judgment, 15 March 2002 at paras 357–60; *Simić* (IT-95-9-T), Trial Chamber Judgment, 17 October 2003 at paras 85–90.

223 The crimes against humanity of enforced disappearance and apartheid (arts 7.1(i) /7.2(i), and 7.1(j)/7.2(h), respectively, in the Rome Statute) will not be discussed as they are not known in the ICTY and ICTR statutes and since there has been no judicial consideration of them in the ICC context. (A Trial Chamber of the ICTY discussed enforced disappearance in the context of persecution in the *Gotovina* decision, while another judgment, a decision by the ECCC, considered this situation as the crime of inhumane acts; these decisions will be discussed under those headings below. The Extraordinary African Chambers (EAC) did consider enforced disappearance in *Habré*, EAC, Trial Chamber Judgment, 30 May 2016 at paras 1457–71, as did the Kosovo Specialist Chamber in the Public Redacted Version of the decision on the Confirmation of the Indictment against Hashim Thaçi, Kadri Veseli, Rexhep Selimi, and Jakup Krasniqi (KSC-BC-2020-06), Pre-Trial Judge, 26 October 2020 at paras 72–77.)

224 There are a number of war crimes set out in the Rome Statute that have not been judicially examined yet, the ones found in arts 8.2(b)(iv)–(vii), (x)–(xii), (xiv)–(xv), (xvii)–(xx), and (xxiii)–(xxv), while the same can be said for arts 8.2(e)(ii) and (x)–(xi); however, art 8.2(b)(iv) (targeting of a military objective in the knowledge that the incidental civilian injury would be clearly excessive in relation to the anticipated military advantage) was addressed in *Situation on Registered Vessels of Comoros, Greece and Cambodia, Article 53(1) Report*, ICC OTP, 6 November 2014 at paras 100–10, while the same article as well as art 8.2(b)(xi) (perfidy or killing or wounding treacherously individuals belonging to the hostile nation or army) was interpreted by the prosecutor in *Situation in the Republic of Korea, Article 5 Report*, ICC OTP, June 2014 at paras 47–57 and 71–81. The ICC *Elements of Crimes* document, above note 153, sets out some more details of the crimes contained in the Statute, including in its sixty-eight footnotes, which on a number of occasions reflect the jurisprudence of the ICTY/ICTR regarding these crimes. For an overview of elements of all the war crimes set out in the Rome Statute, see Knut Dörman, *Elements of War Crimes Under the Rome Statute*

e) Crimes Against Humanity and War Crimes with the Same Elements

i) Torture

With respect to torture, it is important to point out that the definition of torture as set out in the Convention against Torture is not identical to the international crime of torture as understood in customary international law. The definition of the international crime of torture, according to the ICTY caselaw, is as follows:

> (i) torture consists of the infliction, by act or omission, of severe pain or suffering, whether physical or mental;
> (ii) the act or omission must be intentional; and
> (iii) the act or omission must be for a prohibited purpose, such as obtaining information or a confession, punishing, intimidating, humiliating, or coercing the victim or a third person, or discriminating, on any ground, against the victim or a third person.[225]

The differences between international human rights law and international criminal law, as expressed by the ICTY jurisprudence, are twofold: for an international crime, no involvement of a state official or any other authority wielding person is required,[226] and the prohibited purposes for which the crime of torture is carried out are not limited to the ones set out in international human rights law.[227] The Rome Statute

---

of the International Criminal Court, Sources and Commentary (Cambridge: Cambridge University Press, 2003).

225 *Kunarac*, 2002, above note 147 at para 142; *Karadžić* (IT-95-5/18-T), Trial Chamber Judgment, 24 March 2016 at para 506; *Habré*, EAC, Trial Chamber Judgment, 30 May 2016 at paras 1539–57; *Case 002/02* (Case File No 002/19-09-2007/ECCC/TC), Trial Chamber Judgment, 16 November 2018 at paras 701 and 709. The first two parts of this definition are similar to the description of torture in the Rome Statute, art 7.2(e), which says: "'Torture' means the intentional infliction of severe pain or suffering, whether physical or mental, upon a person in the custody or under the control of the accused; except that torture shall not include pain or suffering arising only from, inherent in or incidental to, lawful sanctions." The Appeals Chamber confirmed in 2007 that the level of pain is indeed "severe" and not "extreme": *Brđanin* (IT-99-36-A), Appeals Chamber Judgment, 3 April 2007 at paras 244–52.

226 *Kunarac*, 2002, above note 147 at para 148; *Stanišić and Župljanin* (IT-08-91-T), Trial Chamber Judgment, 27 March 2013 at para 49; *Karadžić* (IT-95-5/18-T), Trial Chamber Judgment, 24 March 2016 at para 508. In *Kaing Guek Eav alias Duch* (Case File 001/18-07-2007/ECCC/TC), Trial Chamber Judgment, 26 July 2010, the Trial Chamber was of the view that this was still a requirement in 1975 at para 357.

227 *Kvočka* (IT-98-30/1), Trial Chamber Judgment, 2 November 2001 at para 140 indicates that humiliation is a prohibited purpose, which is not included in the Convention against Torture.

has taken an even wider approach by not requiring official capacity and by eliminating any of the purposes set out in the Torture Convention and developed by the ICTY/ICTR caselaw.[228]

In general, the ICTY/ICTR caselaw has indicated that the seriousness of the pain or suffering sets torture apart from other forms of mistreatment but has not specifically set the threshold level of suffering or pain required. The facts will be assessed depending on the individual circumstances of each case in which the seriousness of any mistreatment, the objective severity of the harm inflicted, including the nature, purpose, and consistency of the acts committed, will be considered. Subjective criteria, such as the physical or mental condition of the victim, the effect of the treatment, and, in some cases, factors such as the victim's age, sex, state of health, and position of inferiority, will also be relevant in assessing the gravity of the harm. In particular, to the extent that an individual has been mistreated over a prolonged period of time or that they have been subjected to repeated or various forms of mistreatment, the severity of the acts should be assessed as a whole to the extent that it can be shown that this lasting period or the repetition of acts are interrelated follow a pattern or are directed toward the same prohibited goal.[229] Permanent injury is not a requirement for torture; evidence of the suffering need not even be visible after the commission of the crime.[230]

---

228 Footnote 14 in the ICC *Elements of Crimes* document, above note 153, specifically states that "it is understood that no specific purpose need be proved for this crime"; the crime in this context is a crime against humanity as the war crime of torture in the Rome Statute still maintains the purpose requirement, while the war crime of inhumane treatment/cruel treatment has abandoned this element, so in the ICC context, the *actus reus* of the crime against humanity of torture is the same as the war crime of inhumane treatment/cruel treatment, both of which are broader than the equivalent crimes under ICTY/ICTR jurisprudence; on the other hand, the war crime of torture in the Rome Statute has the same *actus reus* as both types of torture under the ICTY/ICTR caselaw (see ICC, *Elements of Crimes*, above note 153, arts 7(1)(f), 8(2)(a)(ii)-1, 8(2)(a)(ii)-2, 8(2)(c)(i)-3, and 8(2)(c)(i)-4, as well as *Mbarushimana* (ICC-01/04-01/10), Pre-Trial Chamber, Decision of the Confirmation of Charges, 16 December 2011 at para 169).

229 *Naletilić & Martinović* (IT-98-34), Appeals Chamber Judgment, 3 May 2006 at para 299; *Martić* (IT-95-11-T), Trial Chamber Judgment, 12 June 2007 at para 75.

230 *Brđanin* (IT-99-36), Trial Chamber Judgment, 1 September 2004 at paras 483–84; *Haradinaj et al* (IT-04-84*bis*-T), Trial Chamber, 29 November 2012 at para 417; *Stanišić and Župljanin* (IT-08-91-T), Trial Chamber Judgment, 27 March 2013 at para 48; *Karadžić* (IT-95-5/18-T), Trial Chamber Judgment, 24 March 2016 at para 507; *Case 002/02* (Case File No 002/19-09-2007/ECCC/TC), Trial Chamber Judgment, 16 November 2018 at para 703; *Ongwen* (ICC-02/0401/15), Trial Chamber Judgment, 4 February 2021 at paras 2700–7.

Both mutilation of body parts[231] and rape have been considered torture since these crimes imply severe pain and suffering;[232] other forms of sexual violence, such as touching of sexual organs and threats of rape,[233] forcing someone to watch serious sexual attacks on an acquaintance or a relative,[234] and forced mutual masturbation[235] also amount to torture.[236] On the other hand, interrogation, minor contempt for the physical integrity of the victim, imprisonment, and deprivation of food by themselves are not considered torture.[237]

ii) Rape

With respect to the crime of rape,[238] the ICTY/ICTR jurisprudence has adopted two definitions, which are not necessarily incompatible but emphasize different aspects of this crime. In the ICTR, rape was described as "a physical invasion of a sexual nature, committed on a person under circumstances which are coercive."[239] However, the ICTY Trial Chamber decided that a more precise definition would better accord with the criminal law principle of specificity and so adopted the more technical definition of "rape is the sexual penetration, however slight, of the vagina or anus of the victim by the penis of the perpetrator or any other object used by the perpetrator; or the mouth of the victim by the penis of the perpetrator, where such sexual penetration occurs without the consent of the victim."[240]

---

231 *Kvočka* (IT-98-30/1), Trial Chamber Judgment, 2 November 2001 at para 144.

232 *Kunarac*, 2002, above note 147 at para 150; *Brđanin* (IT-99-36), Trial Chamber Judgment, 1 September 2004 at para 485; *Stanišić and Župljanin* (IT-08-91-T), Trial Chamber Judgment, 27 March 2013 at para 48; *Bemba* (ICC-01/05-01/08), Pre-Trial Chamber, Decision of Confirmation of Charges, 15 June 2009 at para 205; *Kaing Guek Eav alias Duch* (Case File 001/18-07-2007-ECCC/SC), Supreme Court Chamber Judgment, 3 February 2012 at paras 205–8.

233 *Kvočka*, above note 159 at paras 560–61.

234 *Furundžija* (IT-95-17/1), Trial Chamber Judgment, 19 December 1998 at paras 267–68.

235 *Martić* (IT-95-11-T), Trial Chamber Judgment, 12 June 2007 at paras 288 and 413.

236 For other examples, see *Situation in Iraq/UK*, Final Report, ICC OTP, 9 December 2020 at para 82 as well as ch 4.3.

237 *Case 002/02* (Case File No 002/19-09-2007/ECCC/TC), Trial Chamber Judgment, 16 November 2018 at para 705.

238 Incidentally, the notion of the crime of rape as a distinct crime against humanity was rejected by the ECCC during the period for which it had jurisdiction; see *Kaing Guek Eav alias Duch* (Case File 001/18-07-2007-ECCC/SC), Supreme Court Chamber Judgment, 3 February 2012 at paras 174–83.

239 *Akayesu*, above note 159 at para 598; *Hategekimana* (ICTR-00-55B-T), Trial Chamber Judgment, 6 December 2010 at paras 723–24.

240 *Furundžija* (IT-95-17/1), Trial Chamber Judgment, 19 December 1998 at para 177.

The Appeals Chamber in the case of *Kunarac* agreed with the latter definition,[241] which has also been incorporated into the ICC *Elements of Crimes* document, while the ICC document adds the refinement that the crime can be committed against both women and men.[242] Another debate with respect to the crime of rape dealt with the surrounding situation of this form of sexual violence, where some decisions focused on coercive circumstances during the commission of the crime, while others instead found that the essential feature was the lack of consent of the victim. Again, the *Kunarac* decision provided some clarification on this issue by saying:

> with regard to the role of force in the definition of rape, the Appeals Chamber notes that the Trial Chamber appeared to depart from the Tribunal's prior definitions of rape. However, in explaining its focus on the absence of consent as the *conditio sine qua non* of rape, the Trial Chamber did not disavow the Tribunal's earlier jurisprudence, but instead sought to explain the relationship between force and consent. Force or threat of force provides clear evidence of nonconsent, but force is not an element *per se* of rape .... A narrow focus on force or threat of force could permit perpetrators to evade liability for sexual activity to which the other party had not consented by taking advantage of coercive circumstances without relying on physical force .... While it is true that a focus on one aspect gives a different shading to the offence, it is worth observing that the circumstances giving rise to the instant appeal and that prevail in most cases charged as either war crimes or crimes against humanity will be almost universally coercive. That is to say, true consent will not be possible.[243]

---

241 *Kunarac*, 2002, above note 147 at para 128; *Ngirabatware* (ICTR-99-54-T), Trial Chamber Judgment, 20 December 2012 at para 1381; *Prlić et al* (IT-04-74), Trial Chamber Judgment, 29 May 2013 at para 69; *Karadžić* (IT-95-5/18-T), Trial Chamber Judgment, 24 March 2016 at para 511; *Habré*, EAC, Trial Chamber Judgment, 30 May 2016 at paras 1508–12.

242 The ICC *Elements of Crimes* document, above note 153, describes the *actus reus* of rape as follows at 8: "The perpetrator invaded the body of a person by conduct resulting in penetration, however slight, of any part of the body of the victim or of the perpetrator with a sexual organ, or of the anal or genital opening of the victim with any object or any other part of the body." Footnote 15 in this description says: "The concept of invasion is intended to be broad enough to be gender-neutral"; see, also, *Katanga* (ICC-01/04-01/07), Trial Chamber Judgment, 7 March 2014 at para 963.

243 *Kunarac*, 2002, above note 147 at para 129–30; *Gacumbitsi* (ICTR-2001-64-A), Appeals Chamber Judgment, 7 July 2006 at paras 147–57; *Taylor* (SCSL-03-01-T), Trial Chamber Judgment, 18 May 2012 at paras 415–17; *Ngirabatware* (ICTR-99-54-T), Trial Chamber Judgment, 20 December 2012 at para 1381; *Prlić et al* (IT-04-74), Trial Chamber Judgment, 29 May 2013 at para 69.

The ICC *Elements of Crimes* document has a similar approach to the one used by the ICTY Appeals Chamber and states:

> The invasion was committed by force, or by threat of force or coercion, such as that caused by fear of violence, duress, detention, psychological oppression or abuse of power, against such person or another person, or by taking advantage of a coercive environment, or the invasion was committed against a person incapable of giving genuine consent.[244]

The ICTY has also recognized other forms of sexual assault than rape, but in the context of persecution for which the essence has been described as "all serious abuses of a sexual nature inflicted upon the physical and moral integrity of a person by means of coercion, threat of force or intimidation in a way that is humiliating and degrading for the victim's dignity."[245]

The Rome Statute has the following sexual crimes in addition to rape as crimes against humanity: "sexual slavery, enforced prostitution, forced pregnancy, enforced sterilization, or any other form of sexual violence of comparable gravity."[246] Child soldiers can also be the sub-

---

244 ICC, *Elements of Crimes*, above note 153 at 8, 28, and 37. See, also, *Katanga* (ICC-01/04-01/07), Trial Chamber Judgment, 7 March 2014 at para 965 (while regarding the *mens rea* of the crime, see *ibid* at para 970); *Ntaganda* (ICC-01/04-02/06), Pre-Trial Chamber, Decision of the Confirmation of the Charges, 9 June 2014 at para 49; *Bemba* (ICC-01/05-01/08), Trial Chamber Judgment, 21 March 2016 at paras 99–112; *Ntaganda* (ICC-01/04-02/06), Trial Chamber Judgment, 8 July 2019 at paras 932–35, *Gbagbo and Blé Goudé* (ICC-02/11-01/15-1263-AnxC-Red), Trial Chamber, Reasons for oral decision of 15 January 2019 on the *Requête de la Défense de Laurent Gbagbo afin qu'un jugement d'acquittement portant sur toutes les charges soit prononcé en faveur de Laurent Gbagbo et que sa mise en liberté immédiate soit ordonnée, and on the Blé Goudé Defence no case to answer motion,* Public Redacted Version of Dissenting Opinion Judge Herrera Carbuccia, 16 July 2019 at paras 426–27; *Ongwen* (ICC-02/0401/15), Trial Chamber Judgment, 4 February 2021 at paras 2708–10.

245 *Đorđević* (IT-05-87/1-A), Appeals Chamber Judgment, 27 January 2014 at paras 850–52 and 901; *Karadžić* (IT-95-5/18-T), Trial Chamber Judgment, 24 March 2016 at para 512.

246 Rome Statute, art 7.1(g). The same crimes, as well as rape, are repeated as war crimes in art 8.2(b)(xxii) for international armed conflicts and art 8.2(e)(vi) for non-international armed conflicts. Some explanations as to the nature and difference between these crimes are given in the Statute itself, which states for "forced pregnancy" in art 7.2(f) that it "means the unlawful confinement of a woman forcibly made pregnant, with the intent of affecting the ethnic composition of any population or carrying out other grave violations of international law (see, also, *Ongwen* (ICC-02/04-01/15), Pre-Trial Chamber, Decision on the confirmation of charges against Dominic Ongwen, 23 March 2016 at paras 96–101; *Ongwen* (ICC-02/0401/15), Trial Chamber Judgment, 4 February 2021 at paras 2717–29). This definition shall not in any way be interpreted as affecting national laws relating to pregnancy." The ICC *Elements of*

ject of rape and other sexual crimes as they are entitled to protection under international law.[247]

iii) Inhumane Acts/Treatment

The crime against humanity of inhumane acts and the war crime of inhumane treatment are seen as residual crimes,[248] and both envisage physical or mental suffering at a lower level than the crime of torture—for example, serious or great suffering rather than severe pain or suffering.[249]

Crimes document, above note 153 at 9–10 (for crimes against humanity), elaborates on some essential elements of the other sexual crimes, such as sexual enslavement ("exercised any or all of the powers attaching to the right of ownership over one or more persons, such as by purchasing, selling, lending or bartering such a person or persons, or by imposing on them a similar deprivation of liberty"; see, also, *Brima, Kamara and Kanu ("AFRC")* (SCSL-2004-16-T), Trial Chamber Judgment, 20 June 2007 at paras 708–9; *Katanga and Chui* (ICC-01/04-01/07), Pre-Trial Chamber, Decision of the Confirmation of the Charges, 30 September 2008 at paras 429–32; *Katanga* (ICC-01/04-01/07), Trial Chamber Judgment, 7 March 2014 at paras 975–84; *Ntaganda* (ICC-01/04-02/06), Pre-Trial Chamber, Decision of the Confirmation of the Charges, 9 June 2014 at para 53; *Ntaganda* (ICC-01/04-02/06), Trial Chamber Judgment, 8 July 2019 at para 952; *Ongwen* (ICC-02/0401/15), Trial Chamber Judgment, 4 February 2021 at paras 2715–16; *Taylor* (SCSL-03-01-T), Trial Chamber Judgment, 18 May 2012 at paras 418–30 for this particular crime, for which the latter case indicates that the term "conjugal slavery" is a subset of sexual slavery at paras 429–30; see, also, *Habré*, EAC, Trial Chamber Judgment, 30 May 2016 at paras 1482–507), enforced prostitution ("the perpetrator or another person obtained or expected to obtain pecuniary or other advantage in exchange for or in connection with the acts of a sexual nature"), and enforced sterilization ("the perpetrator deprived one or more persons of biological reproductive capacity and the conduct was neither justified by the medical or hospital treatment of the person or persons concerned nor carried out with their genuine consent," while adding n19, saying, "the deprivation is not intended to include birth-control measures which have a non-permanent effect in practice"); for a discussion of other sexual crimes, see *Francis Kirimi Muthaura, Uhuru Muigai Kenyatta and Mohammed Hussein Ali* (ICC-01/09-02/11), Pre-Trial Chamber, Decision on the Confirmation of Charges, 23 January 2012 at paras 264–66.

247 *Ntaganda* (ICC-01/04-02/06), Pre-Trial Chamber, Decision of the Confirmation of the Charges, 9 June 2014 at paras 76–80.

248 *Francis Kirimi Muthaura, Uhuru Muigai Kenyatta and Mohammed Hussein Ali* (CC-01/09-02/11), Pre-Trial Chamber, Decision on the Confirmation of Charges, 23 January 2012 at para 269; *Stanišić and Župljanin* (IT-08-91-T), Trial Chamber Judgment, 27 March 2013 at para 58; *Case 002/01* (Case File No 002/19-09-2007/ECCC/TC), Trial Chamber Judgment, 7 August 2014 at paras 436–37; *Case 002/01* (Case File No 002/19-09-2007-ECCC/SC), Supreme Court Chamber Judgment, 23 November 2016 at paras 576–80; *Case 002/02* (Case File No 002/19-09-2007/ECCC/TC), Trial Chamber Judgment, 16 November 2018 at para 724.

249 The war crime for inhumane treatment is related to international armed conflicts, and the equivalent for non-international armed conflicts is called cruel treatment; both are considered similar in gravity to another war crime called "wilfully causing great suffering or serious injury to body or health"; see *Karadžić* (IT-95-5/18-T), Trial Chamber Judgment, 24

The seriousness of the harm or injury must be assessed on a case-by-case basis, taking into consideration various factors, including the nature of the act or omission, the context in which it occurs, its duration and/or repetition, its physical and mental effects on the victim, and, in some instances, the personal circumstances of the victim, including age, gender, and health. The harm inflicted does not need to be permanent and irremediable; it must, however, have more than a short-term or temporary effect on the victim.[250]

Several cases have examined these crimes in the context of detention camps and looked at a number of acts, often in combination, to come to the conclusion that they reached the level of suffering required. In one case, being used as human shields, beaten, subjected to physical or psychological abuse and intimidation, and deprived of adequate food and water was sufficient,[251] while in another, inhumane conditions in which detainees were forced to live, such as overcrowded conditions; deprivation of food, water, and sufficient air; exposure to extreme heat or cold; and random beatings of detainees as a general measure to instil terror among them reached the required level of suffering as well.[252]

One case describes in more detail conditions of detention amounting to inhumane acts by saying:

March 2016 at para 504; *Habré*, EAC, Trial Chamber Judgment, 30 May 2016 at paras 1590–93; *Case 002/01* (Case File No 002/19-09-2007-ECCC/SC), Supreme Court Chamber Judgment, 23 November 2016 at para 580; *Mladić* (IT-09-92-T), Trial Chamber Judgment, 22 November 2017 at para 3233; *Case 002/02* (Case File No 002/19-09-2007/ECCC/TC), Trial Chamber Judgment, 16 November 2018 at para 724; the situation is slightly different under the Rome Statute, where the war crimes of inhumane treatment and cruel treatment have the same level of suffering as torture — severe — while the war crime (in international armed conflicts) of wilfully causing great suffering had the lower level of suffering — great; see ICC, *Elements of Crimes*, above note 153, arts 8(2)(a)(ii)-2, 8(2)(a)(iii), and 8(2)(c)(i)-3.

250 *Blagojević & Jokić* (IT-02-60-T), Trial Chamber Judgment, 17 January 2005 at para 586; *Tolimir* (IT-05-88/2-T), Trial Chamber Judgment, 12 December 2012 at para 854; *Stanišić and Župljanin* (IT-08-91-T), Trial Chamber Judgment, 27 March 2013 at para 59; *Prlić et al* (IT-04-74), Trial Chamber Judgment, 29 May 2013 at paras 78 and 119; *Case 002/01* (Case File No 002/19-09-2007/ECCC/TC), Trial Chamber Judgment, 7 August 2014 at paras 438–39; *Case 002/02* (Case File No 002/19-09-2007/ECCC/TC), Trial Chamber Judgment, 16 November 2018 at paras 725, 761.

251 *Blaškić* (IT-95-14-A), Appeals Chamber Judgment, 29 July 2004 at para 155; *Prlić et al* (IT-04-74), Trial Chamber Judgment, 29 May 2013 at paras 117–18.

252 *Brđanin* (IT-99-36), Trial Chamber Judgment, 1 September 2004 at para 1005; *Case 002/01* (Case File No 002/19-09-2007/ECCC/TC), Trial Chamber Judgment, 7 August 2014 at para 457; *Karadžić* (IT-95-5/18-T), Trial Chamber Judgment, 24 March 2016 at para 514; *Case 002/02* (Case File No 002/19-09-2007/ECCC/TC), Trial Chamber Judgment, 16 November 2018 at paras 734–39.

> The conditions in which people were transported to and from camps bear a resemblance to the transportation of livestock. In the camps and other places of detention, it was commonplace that detainees had no choice but to relieve themselves in the room in which they were detained. During interrogations, detainees were made to adopt uncomfortable postures while being held at gunpoint. Once, a Bosnian Muslim was forced to drink whisky. A Bosnian Croat was made to eat the piece of paper on which he had written a statement because he had used Latin, not Cyrillic script. As part of the ill-treatment by camp guards, Bosnian Muslims and Bosnian Croats were also forced to beat and perform sexual acts on each other. It was announced that their mothers and sisters would be raped in front of them. Bosnian Muslims and Bosnian Croats were forced to watch other members of their group being killed, raped, and beaten. Detainees were provided with totally inadequate food over long periods. On one occasion, when some bread was thrown into their room, they started to fight over it like animals. People licked walls in order to get water from condensation. Some detainees started to hallucinate or became mentally disturbed as a result of the conditions.[253]

Yet another case described

> the conditions of detention prevailing in the camp such as the gross overcrowding in small rooms without ventilation, requiring the detainees to beg for water, and forcing them to relieve bodily functions in their clothes, a form of abuse intended to harass, humiliate, and inflict mental harm on the detainees. The constant berating, demoralizing, and threatening of detainees, including the guards' coercive demands for money from detainees, and the housing of detainees in lice-infected and cramped facilities were calculated by participants in the operation of the camp to inflict psychological harm upon detainees.[254]

The crime of inhumane acts was also found to exist in certain instances of forced labour,[255] as well as in a situation involving the forced undressing of a woman outside a communal building after making her sit in the mud and the forced undressing of three women and forcing

253 *Brđanin* (IT-99-36), Trial Chamber Judgment, 1 September 2004 at paras 1015–20.

254 *Kvočka* (IT-98-30/1-A), Appeals Chamber Judgment, 28 February 2005 at paras 324–25.

255 *Simić* (IT-95-9-T), Trial Chamber Judgment, 17 October 2003 at paras 91–93; *Prlić et al* (IT-04-74), Trial Chamber Judgment, 29 May 2013 at paras 115 and 149–50; *Karadžić* (IT-95-5/18-T), Trial Chamber Judgment, 24 March 2016 at paras 523–26.

them to perform exercises naked in public,[256] while third parties could suffer serious mental harm by witnessing very serious criminal acts committed against others, particularly against family or friends.[257] As well, mutilation[258] and sexual and physical violence perpetrated upon dead human bodies have been included in this crime,[259] as have forced prostitution, forcible transfer, and enforced disappearance.[260] The SCSL and the ECCC have also recognized the phenomenon of forced marriage as a crime of inhumane acts,[261] as has the

---

256 *Akayesu*, above note 159 at paras 688, 697.

257 *Kayishema and Ruzindana* (ICTR-95-1-T), Trial Chamber Judgment, 21 May 1999 at para 153; *Francis Kirimi Muthaura, Uhuru Muigai Kenyatta and Mohammed Hussein Ali* (CC-01/09-02/11), Pre-Trial Chamber, Decision on the Confirmation of Charges, 23 January 2012 at para 277.

258 *Kajelijeli* (ICTR-98-44A-T), Trial Chamber Judgment, 1 December 2003 at para 936; *Taylor* (SCSL-03-01-T), Trial Chamber Judgment, 18 May 2012 at para 435; *Francis Kirimi Muthaura, Uhuru Muigai Kenyatta and Mohammed Hussein Ali* (CC-01/09-02/11), Pre-Trial Chamber, Decision on the Confirmation of Charges, 23 January 2012 at para 270 (with the comment at para 279 that destruction of property on the facts of this case did not amount to mental suffering); *Mbarushimana* (ICC-01/04-01/10), Pre-Trial Chamber, Decision of the Confirmation of Charges, 16 December 2011 at paras 152–60.

259 *Niyitegeka* (ICTR-96-14-T), Trial Chamber Judgment, 16 May 2003 at paras 462–65; *Bagosora and Sengiyumva* (ICTR-98-41-A), Appeals Chamber Judgment, 14 December 2011 at paras 728–29.

260 *Prlić et al* (IT-04-74), Trial Chamber Judgment, 29 May 2013 at para 79; *Case 002/01* (Case File No 002/19-09-2007/ECCC/TC), Trial Chamber Judgment, 7 August 2014 at paras 444–48 (with respect to enforced disappearance) and at paras 450–55 (with respect to forcible transfer); *Karadžić* (IT-95-5/18-T), Trial Chamber Judgment, 24 March 2016 at para 494 (regarding forcible transfer, but for a contrary view in the 1970s, see *Case 002/01* (Case File No 002/19-09-2007-ECCC/SC), Supreme Court Chamber Judgment, 23 November 2016 at para 589); for a comprehensive listing, see *Case 002/01* (Case File No 002/19-09-2007-ECCC/SC), Supreme Court Chamber Judgment, 23 November 2016 at paras 581–85; Decision on the "Prosecution's Request for a Ruling on Jurisdiction under Article 19(3) of the Statute," Pre-Trial Chamber (ICC-RoC46(3)-01/18), 6 September 2018 at para 77; *Case 002/02* (Case File No 002/19-09-2007/ECCC/TC), Trial Chamber Judgment, 16 November 2018 at paras 752–55.

261 *Brima, Kamara and Kanu ("AFRC")* (SCSL-2004-16-A), Appeals Chamber Judgment, 22 February 2008 at paras 195–202; *Sesay, Kallon and Gbao ("RUF")*, SCSL-04-14-A), Appeals Chamber Judgment, 26 October 2009 at paras 732–40; *Taylor* (SCSL-03-01-T), Trial Chamber Judgment, 18 May 2012 at paras 425–30 (although in this case, it is said that the term "conjugal slavery" describes the phenomenon of "bush wives" better than the notion of forced marriage while an ICTY Trial Chamber had made a reference to this crime as a crime of sexual violence; see *Kvočka* (IT-98-30/1), Trial Chamber Judgment, 2 November 2001 at para 180, n343); see, also, Closing Order (Case File 002/19-09-2007-ECCC-OCIJ), Office of the Co-Investigating Judges, 15 September 2010 at para 1443; *Ongwen* (ICC-02/04-01/15), Pre-Trial Chamber, Decision on the confirmation of charges against Dominic Ongwen, 23 March 2016 at paras 88–95; *Case 002/02* (Case File No 002/19-09-2007/ECCC/TC), Trial Chamber Judgment, 16 November 2018 at paras 741–49; *Ao An* (Case File No 004/02/07-09-2009-ECCC/OCIJ (PTC60)), Pre-Trial Chamber, Considerations on Appeals against Closing Orders, Opinion of Judges Baik and Bauvallet, 19 December 2019 at paras 606–12.

ICC.[262] However, bodily assault amounting to beatings or slapping does not by itself establish that inhumane treatment has occurred, unless such beatings reach the same level of gravity as other crimes against humanity or war crimes.[263] Similarly, interrogations alone have not been considered in the jurisprudence to be of sufficient gravity to constitute such crimes.[264]

iv) Deportation/Transfer

The elements of forcible deportation or transfer are similar in that both require the forced displacement of persons by expulsion or other forms of coercion from an area where they are lawfully present, without grounds permitted under international law.[265] However, the difference between deportation and transfer lies in the fact that deportation has to occur across de jure or de facto state borders, while transfer takes place within national borders.[266] The notion of de jure or de facto borders

---

262 *Ongwen* (ICC-02/0401/15), Trial Chamber Judgment, 4 February 2021 at paras 2748–53.

263 *Simić* (IT-95-9-T), Trial Chamber Judgment, 17 October 2003 at paras 77–78, 83; *Lukić* (IT-98-32/1-A), Appeals Chamber Judgment, 4 December 2012 at para 634; *Karadžić* (IT-95-5/18-T), Trial Chamber Judgment, 24 March 2016 at para 509; for an example of beatings that reached this threshold, see *Boškoski and Tarčulovski* (IT-04-82-T), Trial Chamber Judgment, 10 July 2008 at paras 383–90.

264 *Simić* (IT-95-9-T), Trial Chamber Judgment, 17 October 2003 at paras 67, 69.

265 *Krajišnik* (IT-00-39-A), Appeals Chamber Judgment, 17 March 2009 at para 304; *Popović et al* (IT-05-88-T), Trial Chamber Judgment, 10 June 2010 at para 891; *Gotovina et al* (IT-06-90-T), Trial Chamber Judgment, 15 April 2011 at para 1738; *Perišić* (IT-04-81-T), Trial Chamber Judgment, 6 September 2011 at para 113; *Stanišić and Župljanin* (IT-08-91-T), Trial Chamber Judgment, 27 March 2013 at para 61; *Stanišić and Simatović* (IT-03-69-T), Trial Chamber Judgment, 30 May 2013 at para 992; *Đorđević* (IT-05-87/1-A), Appeals Chamber Judgment, 27 January 2014 at para 705; *Case 002/01* (Case File No 002/19-09-2007/ECCC/TC), Trial Chamber Judgment, 7 August 2014 at paras 450–51; *Karadžić* (IT-95-5/18-T), Trial Chamber Judgment, 24 March 2016 at para 488; *Mladić* (IT-09-92-T), Trial Chamber Judgment, 22 November 2017 at para 3118; *Case 002/02* (Case File No 002/19-09-2007/ECCC/TC), Trial Chamber Judgment, 16 November 2018 at para 674; see, also, the Rome Statute, art 7.2(d), and *William Samoei Ruto, Henry Kiprono Kosgey and Joshua Arap Sang* (ICC-01/09-01/11), Pre-Trial Chamber, Decision on the Confirmation of Charges, 23 January 2012 at paras 244–45; *Ntaganda* (ICC-01/04-02/06), Trial Chamber Judgment, 8 July 2019 at para 1047.

266 *Stakić* (IT-97-24-A), Appeals Chamber Judgment, 22 March 2006 at paras 289–300 (which was of the view that forcible transfer should be brought under the crime of inhumane acts, which is made much clearer in the dissent of Judge Shahabudden, in this case at paras 72–76, but who agrees with this approach, as do *Case 002/01* (Case File No 002/19-09-2007/ECCC/TC), Trial Chamber Judgment, 7 August 2014 at para 453); *Krajišnik* (IT-00-39-A), Appeals Chamber Judgment, 17 March 2009 at para 305; *Stanišić and Simatović* (IT-03-69-T), Trial Chamber Judgment, 30 May 2013 at para 992; *Đorđević* (IT-05-87/1-A), Appeals Chamber Judgment, 27 January 2014 at paras 532–37; Decision on the "Prosecution's Request

entails a degree of permanency, and, consequently, constantly changing front lines would not fall within the parameters of the crime of deportation, although it could amount to a forcible transfer.[267] Displacement of civilians as a war crime does not require territorial control in non-international armed conflicts as opposed to national ones.[268] There is no requirement of a numerical minimum of displaced persons to constitute this crime; a small number of people or even one person who was forced from his home could be sufficient to incur criminal responsibility.[269]

It is a requirement for both forcible transfer and deportation that the displacement of persons is carried out by expulsion or other forms of coercion. The forced character of the displacement is determined by an absence of genuine choice. While those displaced may consent to or even request to be removed, that consent must be given voluntarily and from the individual's free will, assessed in light of the surrounding circumstances. The term "forced" is not restricted to physical force but may include threat of force or coercion, such as that caused by fear of violence, duress, detention, psychological oppression, or abuse of power or by taking advantage of a coercive environment. Acts of coercion can include the shelling of civilian objects, the burning of civilian property, and the commission of or the threat to commit other crimes calculated to terrify the population and make them flee the area.[270] There is no need for forced displacement to be the result of a specific order.[271]

---

for a Ruling on Jurisdiction under Article 19(3) of the Statute," Pre-Trial Chamber (ICC-RoC46(3)-01/18), 6 September 2018 at paras 50–72.

267 *Stakić* (IT-97-24-A), Appeals Chamber Judgment, 22 March 2006 at paras 300–303; *Stanišić and Župljanin* (IT-08-91-T), Trial Chamber Judgment, 27 March 2013 at para 62; *Tolimir* (IT-05-88/2-A), Appeals Chamber Judgment, 8 April 2015 at para 173; *Karadžić* (IT-95-5/18-T), Trial Chamber Judgment, 24 March 2016 at para 488; *Mladić* (IT-09-92-T), Trial Chamber Judgment, 22 November 2017 at para 3118; *Case 002/02* (Case File No 002/19-09-2007/ECCC/TC), Trial Chamber Judgment, 16 November 2018 at paras 678–81.

268 *Ntaganda* (ICC-01/04-02/06 A A2), Appeals Chamber Judgment, 30 March 2021 at paras 546–64.

269 *Krajišnik* (IT-00-39-A), Appeals Chamber Judgment, 17 March 2009 at para 309; *Prlić et al* (IT-04-74), Trial Chamber Judgment, 29 May 2013 at paras 55–56.

270 *Stakić* (IT-97-24-A), Appeals Chamber Judgment, 22 March 2006 at paras 279–83; *William Samoei Ruto, Henry Kiprono Kosgey and Joshua Arap Sang* (ICC-01/09-01/11), Pre-Trial Chamber, Decision on the Confirmation of Charges, 23 January 2012 at paras 260–61; *Tolimir* (IT-05-88/2-A), Appeals Chamber Judgment, 8 April 2015 at para 158; *Prlić et al* (IT-04-74-A), Appeals Chamber Judgment, 29 November 2017 at para 495; *Case 002/02* (Case File No 002/19-09-2007/ECCC/TC), Trial Chamber Judgment, 16 November 2018 at paras 682–85.

271 *Ntaganda* (ICC-01/04-02/06), Pre-Trial Chamber, Decision of the Confirmation of the Charges, 9 June 2014 at para 64; however, ordering the displacement of the civilian population is a separate war crime in the Rome Statute, art 8(2)(e)(viii); see *Ntaganda* (ICC-01/04-02/06), Trial Chamber Judgment, 8 July 2019 at para 1076.

Furthermore, an agreement concluded by military commanders or other representatives of the parties in a conflict per se cannot make a displacement lawful. Such an agreement does not necessarily have any consequences on the question of whether such a transfer is lawful; military commanders or political leaders cannot consent on behalf of individuals. Similarly, the assistance of humanitarian agencies, such as the International Committee of the Red Cross or civil societies, in facilitating displacements does not of itself render an otherwise unlawful transfer lawful. The determination as to whether a transferred person had a genuine choice is one to be made within the context of the particular case being considered.[272]

With respect to the element of being lawfully present, the Trial Chamber of the ICTY in the *Popović* case indicated that

> the clear intention of the prohibition against forcible transfer and deportation is to prevent civilians from being uprooted from their homes and to guard against the wholesale destruction of communities. In that respect, whether an individual has lived in a location for a sufficient period of time to meet the requirements for residency or whether he or she has been accorded such status under immigration laws is irrelevant. Rather, what is important is that the protection is provided to those who have, for whatever reason, come to "live" in the community—whether long term or temporarily. Clearly the protection is intended to encompass, for example, internally displaced persons who have established temporary homes after being uprooted from their original community. In the view of the Trial Chamber, the requirement for lawful presence is intended to exclude only those situations where the individuals are occupying houses or premises unlawfully or illegally and not to impose a requirement for "residency" to be demonstrated as a legal standard.[273]

---

272 *Stakić* (IT-97-24-A), Appeals Chamber Judgment, 22 March 2006 at paras 284–87; *Popović et al* (IT-05-88-T), Trial Chamber Judgment, 10 June 2010 at para 897; *Gotovina et al* (IT-06-90-T), Trial Chamber Judgment, 15 April 2011 at para 1739; *Perišić* (IT-04-81-T), Trial Chamber Judgment, 6 September 2011 at para 114; *Tolimir* (IT-05-88/2-T), Trial Chamber Judgment, 12 December 2012 at para 796; *Stanišić and Župljanin* (IT-08-91-T), Trial Chamber Judgment, 27 March 2013 at para 64; *Prlić et al* (IT-04-74), Trial Chamber Judgment, 29 May 2013 at paras 52–54; *Karadžić* (IT-95-5/18-T), Trial Chamber Judgment, 24 March 2016 at para 49.

273 *Popović et al* (IT-05-88-T), Trial Chamber Judgment, 10 June 2010 at para 900; *Tolimir* (IT-05-88/2-T), Trial Chamber Judgment, 12 December 2012 at para 798; *Case 002/02* (Case File No 002/19-09-2007/ECCC/TC), Trial Chamber Judgment, 16 November 2018 at paras 676–77.

With respect to the last *actus reus* element, grounds permitted under international law, the displacement of civilians during armed conflict is allowed under limited circumstances if it is carried out for the security of the persons involved or for imperative military reasons. Such an evacuation is an exceptional measure, which is permitted only when, for example, an area is in danger as a result of military operations or is liable to be subjected to intense bombing or when the presence of persons in an area hampers military operations.[274] However, the displacement for such reasons is not justifiable if the humanitarian crisis that caused such displacement is itself the result of the perpetrator's own unlawful activity.[275] Even during a lawful evacuation, the displacement must be only temporary and must be carried out in such a manner as to ensure that displaced persons are returned to their homes as soon as the situation allows,[276] while during such an evacuation, adequate accommodation, hygiene, health, safety, and nutrition must be provided.[277]

The *mens rea* of deportation and transfer is related to the *actus reus* of each crime in that for the latter there needs to be an intention to forcibly displace people, while for the former the additional element of transborder displacement is reflected in the mental element in that the intention to displace includes the animus to do so across a de jure

---

274 *Popović et al* (IT-05-88-T), Trial Chamber Judgment, 10 June 2010 at paras 901–2; *Tolimir* (IT-05-88/2-T), Trial Chamber Judgment, 12 December 2012 at paras 798–99; *Stanišić and Simatović* (IT-03-69-T), Trial Chamber Judgment, 30 May 2013 at para 994; *Karadžić* (IT-95-5/18-T), Trial Chamber Judgment, 24 March 2016 at para 492; *Mladić* (IT-09-92-T), Trial Chamber Judgment, 22 November 2017 at para 3120; with respect to the displacement of prisoners of war, broader considerations apply; see *Habré*, EAC, Trial Chamber Judgment, 30 May 2016 at paras 1170–82.

275 *Popović et al* (IT-05-88-T), Trial Chamber Judgment, 10 June 2010 at para 903; *Tolimir* (IT-05-88/2-A), Appeals Chamber Judgment, 8 April 2015 at para 158; *Karadžić* (IT-95-5/18-T), Trial Chamber Judgment, 24 March 2016 at para 492; *Mladić* (MICT-13-56-A), Appeals Chamber Judgment, 8 June 2021 at para 358.

276 *Popović et al* (IT-05-88-T), Trial Chamber Judgment, 10 June 2010 at para 901; *Gotovina et al* (IT-06-90-T), Trial Chamber Judgment, 15 April 2011 at para 1740; *Perišić* (IT-04-81-T), Trial Chamber Judgment, 6 September 2011 at para 115; *Stanišić and Simatović* (IT-03-69-T), Trial Chamber Judgment, 30 May 2013 at para 994; *Case 002/01* (Case File No 002/19-09-2007/ECCC/TC), Trial Chamber Judgment, 7 August 2014 at para 450; *Mladić* (IT-09-92-T), Trial Chamber Judgment, 22 November 2017 at para 3120.

277 *Popović et al* (IT-05-88-T), Trial Chamber Judgment, 10 June 2010 at para 902; *Case 002/01* (Case File No 002/19-09-2007/ECCC/TC), Trial Chamber Judgment, 7 August 2014 at para 450.

or de facto border.[278] The *mens rea* for these crimes does not include the intention to displace individuals on a permanent basis.[279]

v) Imprisonment

Initially, the elements of the deprivation of liberty were determined by reference to articles 42 and 43 of Geneva Convention IV which allow restrictions on the rights of civilian-protected persons, such as deprivation of their liberty by confinement, and are permissible only where there are reasonable grounds to believe that the security of the state is at risk.[280]

However, the Trial Chamber in the *Kordić and Čerkez* case determined that the definition of imprisonment is not restricted to the grave breaches provisions. Both as a war crime and as a crime against humanity, imprisonment is a crime if the following elements are present:

- an individual is deprived of their liberty
- the deprivation of liberty is imposed arbitrarily—that is, no legal basis can be invoked to justify the deprivation of liberty
- the act or omission by which the person is deprived of their liberty is performed by the accused or a person or persons for whom the accused bears responsibility, with the intent to deprive the individual arbitrarily of their physical liberty or in the reasonable knowledge that their act or omission is likely to cause arbitrary deprivation of physical liberty[281]

---

278 *Popović et al* (IT-05-88-T), Trial Chamber Judgment, 10 June 2010 at para 904; *Gotovina et al* (IT-06-90-T), Trial Chamber Judgment, 15 April 2011 at para 1741; *Perišić* (IT-04-81-T), Trial Chamber Judgment, 6 September 2011 at para 116; *Prlić et al* (IT-04-74-A), Appeals Chamber Judgment, 29 November 2017 at para 524; *Case 002/02* (Case File No 002/19-09-2007/ECCC/TC), Trial Chamber Judgment, 16 November 2018 at para 686.

279 *Stakić* (IT-97-24-A), Appeals Chamber Judgment, 22 March 2006 at paras 304–307; *Popović et al* (IT-05-88-T), Trial Chamber Judgment, 10 June 2010 at para 905; *Gotovina et al* (IT-06-90-T), Trial Chamber Judgment, 15 April 2011 at para 1741; *Perišić* (IT-04-81-T), Trial Chamber Judgment, 6 September 2011 at para 116; *Tolimir* (IT-05-88/2-T), Trial Chamber Judgment, 12 December 2012 at para 801; *Mladić* (IT-09-92-T), Trial Chamber Judgment, 22 November 2017 at para 3121.

280 *Kordić and Čerkez* (IT-95-14/2), Trial Chamber Judgment, 26 February 2001 at para 302; *Kordić and Čerkez* (IT-95-14/2-A), Appeals Chamber Judgment, 17 December 2004 at para 72; *Prlić et al* (IT-04-74), Trial Chamber Judgment, 29 May 2013 at para 61.

281 *Krnojelac* (IT-97-25-A), Trial Chamber Judgment, 15 March 2002 at para 115; *Kordić and Čerkez* (IT-95-14/2-A), Appeals Chamber Judgment, 17 December 2004 at para 73; *Martić* (IT-95-11-T), Trial Chamber Judgment, 12 June 2007 at paras 87–88; *Stanišić and Župljanin* (IT-08-91-T), Trial Chamber Judgment, 27 March 2013 at paras 78–79; *Karadžić* (IT-95-5/18-T), Trial

The arbitrariness of the deprivation of liberty will be based on a finding of whether a legal basis can be called upon to justify the initial deprivation of liberty. If national law is relied upon as justification, then those relevant provisions must not violate international law. Furthermore, the legal basis must apply throughout the individual's period of imprisonment.[282] There is no blanket power to detain the entire civilian population of a party to a conflict. There must be an assessment that each civilian detained poses a particular risk to the security of the state. Once detained, the detaining power is allowed a reasonable time to perform an assessment of whether the detainee poses a threat.[283] Some of the other elements that would render a deprivation of liberty to become arbitrary include the following:

- no valid warrant for arrest
- no reason or no valid reason for the arrest or detention
- no information as to the possible length of detention or possibility of release
- length of incarceration
- mistratment or threats of mistreatment during interrogations while detained
- no release from detention following interrogation regardless of the outcome of the interview
- not being charged, tried, or convicted for any crime either before or during detention
- not being advised of procedural rights during the detention[284]

The *mens rea* of imprisonment requires that the perpetrator intended to arbitrarily deprive the individual of liberty or that the perpetrator

---

Chamber Judgment, 24 March 2016 at para 519; *Habré*, EAC, Trial Chamber Judgment, 30 May 2016 at paras 1787–96; *Mladić* (IT-09-92-T), Trial Chamber Judgment, 22 November 2017 at paras 3238–39; *Prlić et al* (IT-04-74-A), Appeals Chamber Judgment, 29 November 2017 at paras 471 and 513–14.

282 *Kordić and Čerkez* (IT-95-14/2), Trial Chamber Judgment, 26 February 2001 at para 295; *Case 002/02* (Case File No 002/19-09-2007/ECCC/TC), Trial Chamber Judgment, 16 November 2018 at para 689.

283 *Kordić and Čerkez* (IT-95-14/2), Trial Chamber Judgment, 26 February 2001 at para 288; *Prlić et al* (IT-04-74), Trial Chamber Judgment, 29 May 2013 at paras 63–68 and 134–35; *Prlić et al* (IT-04-74-A), Appeals Chamber Judgment, 29 November 2017 at paras 375 and 479.

284 *Krnojelac* (IT-97-25-A), Trial Chamber Judgment, 15 March 2002 at paras 118–21; *Prlić et al* (IT-04-74), Trial Chamber Judgment, 29 May 2013 at para 136; *Situation in Honduras*, art 5 Report, ICC OTP, 28 October 2015 at para 99; *Case 002/02* (Case File No 002/19-09-2007/ECCC/TC), Trial Chamber Judgment, 16 November 2018 at paras 692–94.

acted the reasonable knowledge that their actions were likely to cause the arbitrary deprivation of physical liberty.[285]

In addition to the fact that imprisonment by itself can be a war crime or crime against humanity, another crime—the crime of inhumane acts or inhumane treatment—can be used if the treatment of inmates in a detention facility falls below certain international human rights standards.[286] The parameters of that crime have been discussed above.

f) Crimes Against Humanity

i) Extermination

This crime against humanity shares elements both with the crime against humanity of murder as well as the crime of genocide, especially the form of killing members of a group. Both types require the commission of killing,[287] but for genocide, the additional elements of the specific intent and the victim belonging to one of the four mentioned groups are required,[288] while for extermination, killing on a larger scale than one murder is a prerequisite.[289]

The *actus reus* element of extermination has been described as an act, an omission, or a combination thereof that contributes directly or indirectly to the killing of "persons on a massive scale or to subject a large number of people to conditions of living that would lead to their death in a widespread or systematic manner."[290] It is not required that

285 *Case 002/02* (Case File No 002/19-09-2007/ECCC/TC), Trial Chamber Judgment, 16 November 2018 at para 697.

286 *Prlić et al* (IT-04-74), Trial Chamber Judgment, 29 May 2013 at para 137.

287 The terms "murder" and "killing" have been defined as "causing death" in the ICC *Elements of Crimes* document, above note 153, n2 and n7.

288 *Munyakazi* (ICTR-97-36A-A), Appeals Chamber Judgment, 28 September 2011 at para 141.

289 *Popović et al* (IT-05-88-T), Trial Chamber Judgment, 10 June 2010 at para 799; *Perišić* (IT-04-81-T), Trial Chamber Judgment, 6 September 2011 at para 106; *Nyiramasuhuko et al* (ICTR-98-42-A), Appeals Chamber Judgment, 14 December 2015 at paras 2123, 3309, and 3492; *Case 002/01* (Case File No 002/19-09-2007-ECCC/SC), Supreme Court Chamber Judgment, 23 November 2016 at paras 525–28.

290 *Bagosora and Sengiyumva* (ICTR-98-41-A), Appeals Chamber Judgment, 14 December 2011 at para 394; *Lukić* (IT-98-32/1-A), Appeals Chamber Judgment, 4 December 2012 at para 536; *Case 002/01* (Case File No 002/19-09-2007/ECCC/TC), Trial Chamber Judgment, 7 August 2014 at paras 416 and 421–22; *Karemera* (ICTR-98-44-A), Appeals Chamber Judgment, 29 September 2014 at para 660; *Mladić* (IT-09-92-T), Trial Chamber Judgment, 22 November 2017 at para 3067; *Case 002/02* (Case File No 002/19-09-2007/ECCC/TC), Trial Chamber Judgment, 16 November 2018 at para 665; art 7.2(b) of the Rome Statute includes the deprivation of access to food and medicine, calculated to bring about the destruction of part of a population, into the element infliction of conditions of life.

the mass murder occurred in a concentrated manner or over a short period, while on the other hand, a finding of extermination may result from an aggregate of all killing incidents charged in an indictment.[291] A numerical number to determine what amounts to a massive killing is not an element of this crime,[292] nor is a "vast scheme of collective murder,"[293] but this issue should be assessed on a case-by-case basis, with analysis of all relevant factors, such as the time and place of the killings, the selection of the victims and the manner in which they were targeted, and whether the killings were aimed at the collective group rather than victims in their individual capacity.[294]

The *mens rea* of extermination is intent to kill persons on a massive scale or to subject a large number of people to conditions of living that would lead to their death.[295]

---

291 *Brima, Kamara and Kanu ("AFRC")* (SCSL-2004-16-T), Trial Chamber Judgment, 20 June 2007 at para 686; *Karemera* (ICTR-98-44-A), Appeals Chamber Judgment, 29 September 2014 at para 661; *Tolimir* (IT-05-88/2-A), Appeals Chamber Judgment, 8 April 2015 at para 147; *Karadžić* (IT-95-5/18-T), Trial Chamber Judgment, 24 March 2016 at para 484; *Case 002/01* (Case File No 002/19-09-2007-ECCC/SC), Supreme Court Chamber Judgment, 23 November 2016 at paras 551–52; *Case 002/02* (Case File No 002/19-09-2007/ECCC/TC), Trial Chamber Judgment, 16 November 2018 at para 656.

292 *Lukić* (IT-98-32/1-A), Appeals Chamber Judgment, 4 December 2012 at paras 537–38; *Stanišić and Župljanin* (IT-08-91-T), Trial Chamber Judgment, 27 March 2013 at paras 44 and 219 (mentioning twenty victims in one day as being sufficient but not seventeen, at para 1038); *Case 002/01* (Case File No 002/19-09-2007/ECCC/TC), Trial Chamber Judgment, 7 August 2014 at para 416; *Karadžić* (IT-95-5/18-T), Trial Chamber Judgment, 24 March 2016 at para 483; *Stanišić and Župljanin* (IT-08-91-A), Appeals Chamber Judgment, 30 June 2016 at para 1022 (upholding the same numbers mentioned above at paras 1024–25); *Case 002/01* (Case File No 002/19-09-2007-ECCC/SC), Supreme Court Chamber Judgment, 23 November 2016 at paras 551 (referring to sixty victims as an example) and 553; *Mladić* (IT-09-92-T), Trial Chamber Judgment, 22 November 2017 at para 3067.

293 *Popović et al* (IT-05-88-T), Trial Chamber Judgment, 10 June 2010 at para 800; *Perišić* (IT-04-81-T), Trial Chamber Judgment, 6 September 2011 at para 107; *Tolimir* (IT-05-88/2-T), Trial Chamber Judgment, 12 December 2012 at para 724; *Stanišić and Župljanin* (IT-08-91-T), Trial Chamber Judgment, 27 March 2013 at para 44.

294 *Lukić* (IT-98-32/1-A), Appeals Chamber Judgment, 4 December 2012 at paras 538–39, 542, and 544; *Stanišić and Župljanin* (IT-08-91-A), Appeals Chamber Judgment, 30 June 2016 at para 1022; *Mladić* (IT-09-92-T), Trial Chamber Judgment, 22 November 2017 at para 3067; *Case 002/02* (Case File No 002/19-09-2007/ECCC/TC), Trial Chamber Judgment, 16 November 2018 at para 655.

295 *Popović et al* (IT-05-88-T), Trial Chamber Judgment, 10 June 2010 at para 801; *Nyiramasuhuko et al* (ICTR-98-42-T), Trial Chamber Judgment, 24 June 2011 at para 6048; *Stanišić and Župljanin* (IT-08-91-A), Appeals Chamber Judgment, 30 June 2016 at para 1036; *Case 002/01* (Case File No 002/19-09-2007-ECCC/SC), Supreme Court Chamber Judgment, 23 November 2016 at paras 516–22; *Mladić* (IT-09-92-T), Trial Chamber Judgment, 22 November 2017 at para 3067; *Case 002/02* (Case File No 002/19-09-2007/ECCC/TC), Trial Chamber

ii) Enslavement

For a conviction for the crime of enslavement, it needs to be shown that any or all of the powers attaching to the right of ownership have been exercised over persons,[296] which has been further defined by stating:

> this definition, indications of enslavement include elements of control and ownership; the restriction or control of an individual's autonomy, freedom of choice or freedom of movement; and, often, the accruing of some gain to the perpetrator. The consent or free will of the victim is absent. It is often rendered impossible or irrelevant by, for example, the threat or use of force or other forms of coercion; the fear of violence, deception or false promises; the abuse of power; the victim's position of vulnerability; detention or captivity, psychological oppression or socio-economic conditions. Further indications of enslavement include exploitation; the exaction of forced or compulsory labour or service, often without remuneration and often, though not necessarily, involving physical hardship; sex; prostitution; and human trafficking.[297]

Lack of resistance or the absence of a clear and constant lack of consent during the entire time of the enslavement is not an element of the crime since enslavement flows from claimed rights of ownership. Along the same lines, the duration of the enslavement is not an element of the crime since the establishment of enslavement turns on the quality of the relationship between the perpetrator and the victim, of which only one element is the duration of the relationship.[298]

To elucidate the notion of enslavement in the above requirements, the Appeal Chamber in the *Kunarac* case found it helpful to quote the

---

Judgment, 16 November 2018 at paras 657–58; see, also, ICC, *Elements of Crimes*, above note 153, art 7(1)(b), element 4.

296 *Kunarac et al* (IT-96-23/IT-96-23/1), Trial Chamber Judgment, 22 February 2001 at para 540 [*Kunarac*, 2001]; *Taylor* (SCSL-03-01-T), Trial Chamber Judgment, 18 May 2012 at para 446; *Case 002/02* (Case File No 002/19-09-2007/ECCC/TC), Trial Chamber Judgment, 16 November 2018 at paras 662–63. The Rome Statute has a similar definition in art 7.2(c).

297 *Kunarac*, 2001, above note 296 at para 542, aproved by *Kunarac*, 2002, above note 147 at para 119; see, also, *Kaing Guek Eav alias Duch* (Case File 001/18-07-2007-ECCC/SC), Supreme Court Chamber Judgment, 3 February 2012 at paras 152–58; *Ongwen* (ICC-02/0401/15), Trial Chamber Judgment, 4 February 2021 at paras 2711–14.

298 *Kunarac*,2002, above note 147 at paras 120–22; *Taylor* (SCSL-03-01-T), Trial Chamber Judgment, 18 May 2012 at para 447; see, also, *Katanga and Chui* (ICC-01/04-01/07), Pre-Trial Chamber, Decision of the Confirmation of the Charges, 30 September 2008 at paras 343–46.

following excerpt from a case decided immediately after the Second World War:

> Slavery may exist even without torture. Slaves may be well fed, well clothed, and comfortably housed, but they are still slaves if without lawful process they are deprived of their freedom by forceful restraint. We might eliminate all proof of ill-treatment, overlook the starvation, beatings, and other barbarous acts, but the admitted fact of slavery—compulsory uncompensated labour—would still remain. There is no such thing as benevolent slavery. Involuntary servitude, even if tempered by humane treatment, is still slavery.[299]

The *mens rea* of the crime of enslavement consists of the intentional exercise of a power attaching to the right of ownership. It is not required to prove that the accused intended to detain the victims under constant control for a prolonged period.[300]

The crime of enslavement has been applied to the specific situations of sexual slavery and forced labour, neither of which constitutes a specific crime in the statutes of the ICTY and the ICTR and of which only the first manifestation has been incorporated as a distinct crime in the Rome Statute.[301]

With respect to the phenomenon of forced labour, it should be noted that in the ICTY caselaw the notion of forced labour is most often discussed as a violation of the laws of war, which have regulated the employment of prisoners of war and civilians in some detail. The general principle under the laws of war is that forced labour in itself is not necessarily illegal but that only certain types of labour are prohibited, such as work with a military character or unhealthy or dangerous work.[302] It has also been pointed out in the caselaw that the situation of civilians outside detention facilities doing similar work under similar circumstances

---

299 *Kunarac*, 2002, above note 147 at para 123; *Case 002/02* (Case File No 002/19-09-2007/ECCC/TC), Trial Chamber Judgment, 16 November 2018 at para 665.

300 *Kunarac*, 2002, above note 147 at para 122; *Case 002/02* (Case File No 002/19-09-2007/ECCC/TC), Trial Chamber Judgment, 16 November 2018 at para 670.

301 Article 7.1(g), the second form of sexual violence; see, also, above under the discussion of the crime of rape.

302 *Naletilić & Martinović* (IT-98-34-T), Trial Chamber Judgment, 31 March 2003 at paras 251–61, *Krnojelac* (IT-97-25), Trial Chamber Judgment, 15 March 2002 at paras 359–60; *Simić* (IT-95-9-T), Trial Chamber Judgment, 17 October 2003 at paras 85–93; *Mladić* (IT-09-92-T), Trial Chamber Judgment, 22 November 2017 at paras 3243–44; see, also, *Sesay, Kallon and Gbao ("RUF")*, (SCSL-04-15-T), Trial Chamber Judgment, 25 February 2009 at paras 195–203.

as detainees should be taken into account for a determination whether the forced labour of the prisoners can be characterized as a war crime.[303] Forced labour is not mentioned in international instruments as a crime against humanity; as a result, specific manifestations of forced labour will have to fit within the parameters of other enumerated crimes against humanity, such as inhumane acts or enslavement.

It has been held that inhumane acts were committed if prisoners were injured while involved in forced labour, specifically digging of trenches,[304] either as a result of mistreatment or being exposed to hazardous situations.[305]

The most important determination that forced labour as slavery occurs depends on whether a detainee has no real choice as to whether to work. Relevant factors in such an assessment are:

- the substantially uncompensated aspect of the labour performed
- the vulnerable position in which the detainees find themselves (being under guarded supervision, for instance, or performing dangerous work)
- the fact that detainees who are unable or unwilling to work are either forced to or are put in solitary confinement
- longer-term consequences of the labour (such as health problems)
- whether there are inhumane conditions during the carrying out of the work[306]

iii) Persecution

The crime of persecution is defined by the jurisprudence of the ICTY and the ICTR as an act or omission that discriminates in fact and that denies or infringes upon a fundamental right laid down in international customary or treaty law and was carried out deliberately with the intention to discriminate on one of the ground listed in their statutes,

303 *Krnojelac* (IT-97-25), Trial Chamber Judgment, 15 March 2002 at para 360; *Case 002/02* (Case File No 002/19-09-2007/ECCC/TC), Trial Chamber Judgment, 16 November 2018 at para 669.

304 *Naletilić & Martinović* (IT-98-34-T), Trial Chamber Judgment, 31 March 2003 at para 271.

305 *Aleksovski* (IT-95-14/1), Trial Chamber Judgment, 25 June 1999 at paras 128–29 and 228–29.

306 *Krnojelac* (IT-97-25), Trial Chamber Judgment, 15 March 2002 at paras 372–73, 374, 378, and 408; this case provides a number of detailed situations of what (in most cases) does not amount to forced labour at paras 371–421; see, also, *Taylor* (SCSL-03-01-T), Trial Chamber Judgment, 18 May 2012 at paras 448–50.

specifically political, racial, and religious grounds.[307] An act or omission is considered discriminatory when a victim is targeted because of their membership in a group defined by the perpetrator on a political, racial, or religious basis.[308] Not every denial of a human right is serious enough to constitute a crime against humanity of persecution, but it must be a gross or blatant denial of a fundamental right reaching the same level of gravity as the other crimes against humanity prohibited by the statutes of the ICTY and the ICTR.[309]

The *mens rea* for this crime has been described as higher than the other crimes against humanity but lower than the intent required for genocide.[310]

---

307 *Krnojelac* (IT-97-25-A), Appeals Chamber Judgment, 17 September 2003 at para 185; *Nahimana, Barayagwiza and Ngeze ("Media")* (ICTR-99-52-A), Appeals Chamber Judgment, 28 November 2007 at para 985; *Kaing Guek Eav alias Duch* (Case File 001/18-07-2007/ECCC/TC), Trial Chamber Judgment, 26 July 2010 at paras 376–77; *Kaing Guek Eav alias Duch* (Case File 001/18-07-2007-ECCC/SC), Supreme Court Chamber Judgment, 3 February 2012 at paras 236–40 regarding the *mens rea* of persecution and at paras 257–62 and 266–67 for the *actus reus*; *Šainović et al* (IT-05-87-A), Appeals Chamber Judgment, 23 January 2014 at para 579. Ethnicity has also been accepted as a ground in the ICTY jurisprudence; see *Stanišić and Župljanin* (IT-08-91-T), Trial Chamber Judgment, 27 March 2013 at para 68; *Nyiramasuhuko et al* (ICTR-98-42-A), Appeals Chamber Judgment, 14 December 2015 at paras 2129, 2138; *Karadžić* (IT-95-5/18-T), Trial Chamber Judgment, 24 March 2016 at para 497; *Mladić* (IT-09-92-T), Trial Chamber Judgment, 22 November 2017 at para 3228; *Prlić et al* (IT-04-74-A), Appeals Chamber Judgment, 29 November 2017 at para 422; *Case 002/02* (Case File No 002/19-09-2007/ECCC/TC), Trial Chamber Judgment, 16 November 2018 at para 713.

308 *Perišić* (IT-04-81-T), Trial Chamber Judgment, 6 September 2011 at paras 118–19; *Kaing Guek Eav alias Duch* (Case File 001/18-07-2007-ECCC/SC), Supreme Court Chamber Judgment, 3 February 2012 at paras 272–77; *Đorđević* (IT-05-87/1-A), Appeals Chamber Judgment, 27 January 2014 at para 876; *Case 002/01* (Case File No 002/19-09-2007/ECCC/TC), Trial Chamber Judgment, 7 August 2014 at paras 427–33 (for the notion of political group, see at para 430); *Karadžić* (IT-95-5/18-T), Trial Chamber Judgment, 24 March 2016 at para 500; *Case 002/01* (Case File No 002/19-09-2007-ECCC/SC), Supreme Court Chamber Judgment, 23 November 2016 at paras 667–80; *Case 002/02* (Case File No 002/19-09-2007/ECCC/TC), Trial Chamber Judgment, 16 November 2018 at paras 714, 718, and 720–21.

309 *Popović et al* (IT-05-88-T), Trial Chamber Judgment, 10 June 2010 at para 966; *Đorđević* (IT-05-87/1-A), Appeals Chamber Judgment, 27 January 2014 at paras 565–68 (in the context of religious or culturally significant property); *Karadžić* (IT-95-5/18-T), Trial Chamber Judgment, 24 March 2016 at para 499; *Mladić* (IT-09-92-T), Trial Chamber Judgment, 22 November 2017 at para 3229. This notion of persecution is more stringent than this concept in either international human rights law or refugee law; see *Kupreškić et al* (IT-95-16), Trial Chamber Judgment, 14 January 2000 at paras 588–89.

310 *Kupreškić et al* (IT-95-16), Trial Chamber Judgment, 14 January 2000 at para 636; *Perišić* (IT-04-81-T), Trial Chamber Judgment, 6 September 2011 at para 121; *Kaing Guek Eav alias Duch* (Case File 001/18-07-2007-ECCC/SC), Supreme Court Chamber Judgment, 3 February 2012 at para 268; *Popović et al* (IT-05-88-A), Appeals Chamber Judgment, 30 January 2015

Persecution can include murder, extermination, and torture; violations of political, social, and economic rights;[311] physical or mental harm or infringements on individual freedom;[312] unlawful detention of civilians; the deportation or forcible transfer of civilians, depending upon the circumstances; violations of the right to life, liberty, and the security of the person; the right not to be held in slavery or servitude; the right not to be subjected to torture or cruel, inhuman, or degrading treatment or punishment; and the right not to be subjected to arbitrary arrest, detention, or exile;[313] harassment, humiliation, and psychological abuse;[314] imprisonment, unlawful detention of civilians, or infringement upon individual freedom; seizure, collection, segregation, and forced transfer of civilians to camps; forced labour, such as trench digging, and the use of hostages as human shields, and sexual violence;[315] imposition of restrictive and discriminatory measures;[316] as well as enforced disappearance,[317] sexual assault,[318]and causing terror.[319] Since the severity of the persecution has to be similar to the other types of crimes against humanity, certain activities have been found not to reach that level of seriousness in terms of the violation of human rights, such as restrictions

at paras 723 and 727; *Case 002/02* (Case File No 002/19-09-2007/ECCC/TC), Trial Chamber Judgment, 16 November 2018 at para 715.

311 *Kupreškić et al* (IT-95-16), Trial Chamber Judgment, 14 January 2000 at paras 600 and 615.

312 *Vasiljević* (IT-98-32), Trial Chamber Judgment, 29 November 2002 at para 246.

313 *Blaškić* (IT-95-14), Trial Chamber Judgment, 3 March 2000 at paras 220 and 234; *Gotovina et al* (IT-06-90-T), Trial Chamber Judgment, 15 April 2011 at paras 1811, 1813, and 1817; *Stanišić and Župljanin* (IT-08-91-T), Trial Chamber Judgment, 27 March 2013 at paras 70–76; *Stanišić and Simatović* (IT-03-69-T), Trial Chamber Judgment, 30 May 2013 at para 1243; *Mladić* (IT-09-92-T), Trial Chamber Judgment, 22 November 2017 at para 3233.

314 *Kvočka* (IT-98-30/1), Trial Chamber Judgment, 2 November 2001 at para 190; *Mladić* (IT-09-92-T), Trial Chamber Judgment, 22 November 2017 at paras 3235 and 3238.

315 *Kvočka* (IT-98-30/1), Trial Chamber Judgment, 2 November 2001 at para 186; *Karadžić* (IT-95-5/18-T), Trial Chamber Judgment, 24 March 2016 at paras 523–26; *Mladić* (IT-09-92-T), Trial Chamber Judgment, 22 November 2017 at paras 3243–46 (regarding forced labour and the use of human shields); Decision on the "Prosecution's Request for a Ruling on Jurisdiction under Article 19(3) of the Statute," Pre-Trial Chamber (ICC-RoC46(3)-01/18), 6 September 2018 at para 76 (re deportation).

316 *Stanišić and Župljanin* (IT-08-91-T), Trial Chamber Judgment, 27 March 2013 at paras 91–92; *Mladić* (IT-09-92-T), Trial Chamber Judgment, 22 November 2017 at paras 3264–66.

317 *Gotovina et al* (IT-06-90-T), Trial Chamber Judgment, 15 April 2011 at paras 1831–39.

318 *Đorđević* (IT-05-87/1-A), Appeals Chamber Judgment, 27 January 2014 at paras 899–900.

319 *Popović et al* (IT-05-88-A), Appeals Chamber Judgment, 30 January 2015 at paras 738 and 762.

placed on a particular group in particular aspects of social life[320] or dismissing and removing persons from government.[321]

The crime against humanity of persecution has also been extended to two areas, which are expansions of the original notion of this crime that such a crime had to be related to violations of the integrity or well-being of a person, by also including certain crimes against property as well as certain hate crimes within its parameters.

There is an apparent discrepancy between the ICTY and the ICTR caselaw regarding the application of the crime of persecution to hate crimes in that the ICTY courts have rejected this notion,[322] while it has been accepted by the ICTR.[323] The difference lies in the fact that the ICTR does not consider all hate speech to fall within the crime of persecution but only speech with a cumulative effect and inciting violence, while it also stipulates that this violence does not have to result from the speech.[324]

The ICTY caselaw has included as part of persecution a number of property offences, such as certain types of attacks on property if they have the effect of the destruction of the livelihood of a certain

---

320 *Kupreškić et al* (IT-95-16), Trial Chamber Judgment, 14 January 2000 at para 615; *Gotovina et al* (IT-06-90-T), Trial Chamber Judgment, 15 April 2011 at para 1805; *Karadžić* (IT-95-5/18-T), Trial Chamber Judgment, 24 March 2016 at paras 535–36.

321 *Kordić and Čerkez* (IT-95-14/2), Trial Chamber Judgment, 26 February 2001 at para 210; *Karadžić* (IT-95-5/18-T), Trial Chamber Judgment, 24 March 2016 at paras 535–36.

322 *Kordić and Čerkez* (IT-95-14/2), Trial Chamber Judgment, 26 February 2001 at para 209. This aspect of the case was not appealed.

323 *Nahimana, Barayagwiza and Ngeze ("Media")* (ICTR-99-52-A), Appeals Chamber Judgment, 28 November 2007 at paras 986–88; *Bikindi* (ICTR-01-72-T), Trial Chamber Judgment, 2 December 2008 at paras 393–95 (see, also, for the connection between freedom of speech and hate speech at paras 379–89 and songs as falling within this crime at para 395).

324 *Nahimana, Barayagwiza and Ngeze ("Media")* (ICTR-99-52-T), Trial Chamber Judgment, 3 December 2003 at para 1073; *Nahimana, Barayagwiza and Ngeze ("Media")* (ICTR-99-52-A), Appeals Chamber Judgment, 28 November 2007 at para 988; the original disagreement was between the trial chambers of the ICTY and ICTR where the ICTR had applied a broader notion of hate speech than was eventually accepted by the Appeals Chamber; the Trial Chamber did not require a causal connection between the speech and subsequent violence, while the level of hate speech was "a discriminatory form of aggression that destroys the dignity of those in the group under attack. It creates a lesser status not only in the eyes of the group members themselves but also in the eyes of others who perceive them as less than human." (*Nahimana, Barayagwiza and Ngeze ("Media")* (ICTR-99-52-T), Trial Chamber Judgment, 3 December 2003 at para 1072; *Nahimana, Barayagwiza and Ngeze ("Media")* (ICTR-99-52-A), Appeals Chamber Judgment, 28 November 2007 at para 986); *Šešelj* (MICT-16-99-A), Appeals Chamber Judgment, 11 April 2018 at para 159.

population,[325] which includes comprehensive destruction of homes and property; the destruction of towns, villages, and other public or private property; the plunder of property; and the destruction and damage to religious or educational institutions.[326] The ICC jurisprudence has cast doubt on this expansion into property crimes.[327]

The Rome Statute has both narrowed and broadened the crime of persecution. It has been broadened by extending the groups that can be victimized while narrowing it by insisting that this crime is only justiciable if it has been committed in connection to another crime in the Statute or in the words of the Statute:

> persecution against any identifiable group or collectivity on political, racial, national, ethnic, cultural, religious, gender as defined in paragraph 3, or other grounds that are universally recognized as impermissible under international law, in connection with any act referred to in this paragraph or any crime within the jurisdiction of the Court.[328]

---

325 *Blaškić* (IT-95-14), Trial Chamber Judgment, 3 March 2000 at paras 227, 233, and 234; *Gotovina et al* (IT-06-90-T), Trial Chamber Judgment, 15 April 2011 at paras 1822–23 and 1829; *Tolimir* (IT-05-88/2-T), Trial Chamber Judgment, 12 December 2012 at para 859; *Stanišić and Župljanin* (IT-08-91-T), Trial Chamber Judgment, 27 March 2013 at paras 84–85; *Mladić* (IT-09-92-T), Trial Chamber Judgment, 22 November 2017 at paras 3248–54; see, also, indirectly, *William Samoei Ruto, Henry Kiprono Kosgey and Joshua Arap Sang* (ICC-01/09-01/11), Pre-Trial Chamber, Decision on the Confirmation of Charges, 23 January 2012 at para 277.

326 *Kordić and Čerkez* (IT-95-14/2), Trial Chamber Judgment, 26 February 2001 at paras 202–7; *Stanišić and Župljanin* (IT-08-91-T), Trial Chamber Judgment, 27 March 2013 at paras 89–90; *Stanišić and Župljanin* (IT-08-91-A), Appeals Chamber Judgment, 30 June 2016 at paras 1074–77; *Mladić* (IT-09-92-T), Trial Chamber Judgment, 22 November 2017 at paras 3256–62; *Prlić et al* (IT-04-74-A), Appeals Chamber Judgment, 29 November 2017 at para 422; specifically, regarding the latter form of persecution regarding religious property; see *Đorđević* (IT-05-87/1-A), Appeals Chamber Judgment, 27 January 2014 at paras 565–68.

327 *Bemba* (ICC-01/05-01/08A), Appeals Chamber Judgment, Separate Opinion of Judge Van den Wyngaert and Judge Morrison, 8 June 2018 at para 72.

328 Rome Statute, art 7.1(h), while art 7.2(g) says, "Persecution means the intentional and severe deprivation of fundamental rights contrary to international law by reason of the identity of the group or collectivity"; see *Francis Kirimi Muthaura, Uhuru Muigai Kenyatta and Mohammed Hussein Ali* (CC-01/09-02/11), Pre-Trial Chamber, Decision on the Confirmation of Charges, 23 January 2012 at paras 282–83; *Ntaganda* (ICC-01/04-02/06), Trial Chamber Judgment, 8 July 2019 at paras 749–50 and 988; *Ongwen* (ICC-02/0401/15), Trial Chamber Judgment, 4 February 2021 at paras 2730–40.

g) War Crimes

i) Directing Attacks Against the Civilian Population

The crime of directing attacks against the civilian population is set out in the Rome Statute in article 8(2)(b)(i) for international armed conflicts and article 8(2)(e)(i) for situations of a non-international character.[329] Attacks against the civilian population as such, as well as attacks against individual civilians not taking direct part in hostilities, are prohibited.[330]

The crime is made up of the following elements:

1) The perpetrator directed an attack.
2) The object of the attack was a civilian population as such or individual civilians not taking part in hostilities.
3) The perpetrator intended the civilian population as such or individual civilians not taking part in hostilities to be the object of the attack.
4) The conduct took place in the context of and was associated with an armed conflict.
5) The perpetrator was aware of factual circumstances that established the existence of an armed conflict.

According to the ICC jurisprudence, this crime is made out by the mere launching of the attack against a civilian population or individual civilians not taking direct part in hostilities who have not fallen yet into the hands of the attacking party. This caselaw has also held that it is not required that the civilian population suffers any material results, including any sort of harmful impact,[331] but whether such consequences were intended or foreseeable.[332] This is distinct from article 85(3) of the Protocol Additional to the Geneva Conventions of 12 August 1949, and Relating to the Protection of Victims of Armed International Conflicts (Protocol I), which does require harm or serious injury to body or health. It is also distinct from ICTY caselaw, which has held that

329 *Katanga* (ICC-01/04-01/07), Trial Chamber Judgment, 7 March 2014 at para 800.

330 *Ibid* at para 801; *Karadžić* (IT-95-5/18-T), Trial Chamber Judgment, 24 March 2016 at para 449.

331 *Katanga and Chui* (ICC-01/04-01/07), Pre-Trial Chamber, Decision of the Confirmation of the Charges, 30 September 2008 at para 37; *Katanga* (ICC-01/04-01/07), Trial Chamber Judgment, 7 March 2014 at para 799; *Ntaganda* (ICC-01/04-02/06), Trial Chamber Judgment, 8 July 2019 at paras 744 and 904.

332 *Ntaganda* (ICC-01/04-02/06), Pre-Trial Chamber, Decision of the Confirmation of the Charges, 9 June 2014 at paras 46–47; *Ntaganda* (ICC-01/04-02/06), Trial Chamber Judgment, 8 July 2019 at para 921.

the attack must have caused death or serious bodily injury within the civilian population.[333] In *Katanga*, the ICC adopted the meaning of the term attack from article 49(1) of the Protocol I Additional to the Geneva Conventions. Attack is defined as an "act of violence against the adversary, whether in offence or defence."[334]

According to the ICTY jurisprudence, a civilian population includes all persons who are not members of the armed forces or otherwise recognized as combatants. Members of the armed forces are not considered civilians merely because they were not engaged in combat at the time of their arrests. As well, soldiers *hors de combat* do not qualify as civilians for this purpose, but the armed law enforcement agencies of a state are considered to be civilians. A civilian population does not have to be exclusively civilian as long as it is "predominantly civilian" and "the primary object of the attack." The presence within the civilian population of individuals who do not come within the definition of civilians does not deprive the entire population of its civilian character. The civilian status of the victims, the number of civilians, and the proportion of civilians within a population are factors relevant to the determination of whether the requirement that an attack be directed against a civilian population is fulfilled.[335]

---

333 *Blaškić* (IT-95-14), Trial Chamber Judgment, 3 March 2000 at para 180; *Perišić* (IT-04-81-T), Trial Chamber Judgment, 6 September 2011 at para 99; *Mladić* (IT-09-92-T), Trial Chamber Judgment, 22 November 2017 at para 3208.

334 *Katanga and Chui* (ICC-01/04-01/07), Pre-Trial Chamber, Decision of the Confirmation of the Charges, 30 September 2008 at para 266; *Perišić* (IT-04-81-T), Trial Chamber Judgment, 6 September 2011 at para 91; *Katanga* (ICC-01/04-01/07), Trial Chamber Judgment, 7 March 2014 at para 798; *Ntaganda* (ICC-01/04-02/06), Pre-Trial Chamber, Decision of the Confirmation of the Charges, 9 June 2014 at para 45.

335 *Blaškić* (IT-95-14-A), Appeals Chamber Judgment, 29 July 2004 at paras 103–16; *Kordić and Čerkez* (IT-95-14/2-A), Appeals Chamber Judgment, 17 December 2004 at paras 95–97; *Martić* (IT-95-11-A), Appeals Chamber Judgment, 8 October 8 2008 at paras 291–314; *Mrkšić et al* (IT-95-13/1-A), Appeals Chamber Judgment, 5 May 2009 at paras 28–35 and 41–44; *Milošević* (IT-98-29/1-A), Appeals Chamber Judgment, 12 November 2009 at paras 50–61; *Perišić* (IT-04-81-T), Trial Chamber Judgment, 6 September 2011 at paras 92–95; *Kaing Guek Eav alias Duch* (Case File 001/18-07-2007/ECCC/TC), Trial Chamber Judgment, 26 July 2010 at paras 302–12; *Mbarushimana* (ICC-01/04-01/10), Pre-Trial Chamber, Decision of the Confirmation of Charges, 16 December 2011 at paras 142 and 218; *Mudacumura* (ICC-01/04-01/12), Pre-Trial Chamber, Decision on the Prosecutor's Application under Article 58, 13 July 2012 at para 38; *Prlić et al* (IT-04-74), Trial Chamber Judgment, 29 May 2013 at para 187; *Karadžić* (IT-95-5/18-T), Trial Chamber Judgment, 24 March 2016 at paras 451–53; *Ntaganda* (ICC-01/04-02/06), Trial Chamber Judgment, 8 July 2019 at para 921; *Ongwen* (ICC-02/0401/15), Trial Chamber Judgment, 4 February 2021 at paras 2758–61. Earlier, the ICTY caselaw had considered *hors de combat* military personnel to be civilian, but this concept was narrowed starting with *Blaškić*.

An essential element of the crime is that it must be carried out during the conduct of hostilities. As such, it is a crime of directing attacks against individual civilians not taking direct part in hostilities or a civilian population that has not yet fallen into the hands of the adverse or hostile party or armed forces or organized armed groups of the conflict to which the perpetrator belongs. However, while the armed conflict does have to be a substantial reason for the perpetrator's decision, it does not have to be the ultimate reason for the conduct, and the conduct does not have to take place during the battle.[336] Taking direct part in hostilities has been defined by the ICTY as actions including the following: bearing, using, or taking up arms; taking part in military or hostile acts, activities, conduct, or operations; armed fighting or combat; participating in attacks against enemy personnel, property, or equipment; transmitting military information; or transporting weapons.[337] The ICTY has held that an individual civilian, or a civilian population, falls into the hands of an adverse or a hostile party to the conflict when it comes under the control of its members.[338] "In the hands of a party" should not be interpreted literally but includes persons who find themselves in a territory that is under the control of an occupying power.[339]

There is an absolute prohibition against targeting of civilians, which may not be derogated from due to military necessity. However, this does not exclude the possibility of civilian casualties incidental to an attack aimed at legitimate military targets provided that they are proportionate to the concrete and direct military advantage anticipated prior to the attack. Indiscriminate attacks—that is to say, attacks that strike civilians or civilian objects and military objectives without distinction—may qualify as direct attacks on civilians. Military objectives are those objects that by their nature, location, purpose, or use make an effective contribution to military action and whose total or partial

---

336 *Lubanga* (ICC-01/04-01/06), Pre-Trial Chamber, Decision on the Confirmation of Charges, 29 January 2007 at para 287; see, also, *Boškoski and Tarčulovski* (IT-04-82-T), Trial Chamber Judgment, 10 July 2008 at para 358.

337 *Strugar* (IT-01-42A), Appeals Chamber Judgment, 17 July 2008 at para 177; *Mbarushimana* (ICC-01/04-01/10), Pre-Trial Chamber, Decision of the Confirmation of Charges, 16 December 2011 at para 148; *Katanga* (ICC-01/04-01/07), Trial Chamber Judgment, 7 March 2014 at para 790; *Situation on Registered Vessels of Comoros, Greece and Cambodia, Article 53(1) Report*, ICC OTP, 6 November 2014 at paras 44–55; see, also, below under the crime of child recruitment.

338 *Natetilić & Martinović* (IT-98-34-T), Trial Chamber Judgment, 23 March 2003 at para 203.

339 *Aleksovski* (IT-95-14/1-A), Appeals Chamber Judgment, 24 March 2000 at paras 147–52.

destruction, capture, or neutralization, in the circumstances ruling at the time, offers a definite military advantage.[340]

In this regard, a direct attack against civilians can be inferred from the indiscriminate character of the weapon used. An attack that may cause civilian casualties disproportionate to the concrete and direct military advantage anticipated is to be considered indiscriminate. Such an attack may also give rise to the inference that civilians were the objects of attack. The parties to a conflict have an obligation to remove civilians, to the maximum extent feasible, from the vicinity of military objectives and to avoid locating military objectives within or near densely populated areas. However, the failure of a party to abide by this obligation does not relieve the attacking side of its duty to follow the principles of distinction and proportionality when launching an attack.[341]

The *mens rea* element is fulfilled if the perpetrator intended to make individual civilians not taking direct part in the hostilities or the civilian population the object of the attack and whether the attacker could have reasonably believed that the target was a legitimate military objective, and a useful standard by which to assess the reasonableness of such belief is that of a reasonable commander in the position of the attacker. Thus, "once the perpetrators launch the attack with the intent to target individual civilians not taking direct part in the hostilities or the civilian population, the offence is completed."[342]

---

340 *Perišić* (IT-04-81-T), Trial Chamber Judgment, 6 September 2011 at paras 96–97; *Mbarushimana* (ICC-01/04-01/10), Pre-Trial Chamber, Decision of the Confirmation of Charges, 16 December 2011 at para 142 (which also indicates at para 143 that such an attack as an act of reprisal is prohibited in all circumstances); *Prlić et al* (IT-04-74), Trial Chamber Judgment, 29 May 2013 at paras 189–90; *Katanga* (ICC-01/04-01/07), Trial Chamber Judgment, 7 March 2014 at para 803; *Karadžić* (IT-95-5/18-T), Trial Chamber Judgment, 24 March 2016 at para 454; *Karadžić* (MICT-13-55-A), Appeals Chamber Judgment, 20 March 2019 at paras 486–88; *Ntaganda* (ICC-01/04-02/06), Trial Chamber Judgment, 8 July 2019 at para 921.

341 *Perišić* (IT-04-81-T), Trial Chamber Judgment, 6 September 2011 at paras 97–98; for a detailed factual analysis, see *Gotovina and Markač* (IT-06-90-A), Appeals Chamber Judgment, 16 November 2012 at paras 58–63; *Karadžić* (MICT-13-55-A), Appeals Chamber Judgment, 20 March 2019 at para 489; *Ntaganda* (ICC-01/04-02/06), Trial Chamber Judgment, 8 July 2019 at para 921.

342 *Katanga and Chui* (ICC-01/04-01/07), Pre-Trial Chamber, Decision of the Confirmation of the Charges, 30 September 2008 at para 272; *Prlić et al* (IT-04-74), Trial Chamber Judgment, 29 May 2013 at paras 192–93; *Katanga* (ICC-01/04-01/07), Trial Chamber Judgment, 7 March 2014 at paras 804–8; *Karadžić* (IT-95-5/18-T), Trial Chamber Judgment, 24 March 2016 at paras 456–57; *Karadžić* (MICT-13-55-A), Appeals Chamber Judgment, March 20, 2019 at para 489.

ii) Directing Attacks Against Civilian Objects

The crime of directing attacks against civilian objects, meaning objects that are not military objects, is set out in the Rome Statute, article 8(2)(b)(ii). This provision is closely related to article 8(2)(b)(i), discussed in the previous section, in that it is also an expression of the principle of distinction.[343] It should be noted that civilian objects, while protected in international conflicts, are not given as much protection in non-international conflicts. The Rome Statute prohibits attacks against civilians in non-international conflicts but not civilian objects in general (unless they are protected objects). Similarly, while article 52 of the Additional Protocol I to the Geneva Conventions provides for "general protection of civilian objects during an international armed conflict."[344] Additional Protocol II relating to non-international conflicts only provides protection to "objects indispensable to the survival of the civilian population."[345]

Article 3 of the ICTY Statute has a wider scope for addressing attacks on civilian objects. It prohibits destruction of cities not justified by military necessity; attacks on dwellings or buildings; and destruction of institutions dedicated to religion, charity and education, the arts and sciences, historical monuments, and works of art and science. Article 18 of Geneva Convention IV also addresses the protection that is to be accorded to certain civilian objects, such as civilian hospitals. These may not, in any circumstances, be the object of attack and should always be respected and protected by the parties to the conflict.[346]

The Rome Statute has incorporated all the above objects in separate articles, article 8(2)(b)(ix) and article 8(2)(e)(iv). The ICC *Elements of Crimes* document indicates that this crime consists of the following:

1) The perpetrator directed an attack.
2) The objects of the attack were civilian objects, that is, objects that are not military objectives.
3) The perpetrator intended such civilian objects to be the object of the attack.
4) The conduct took place in the context of and was associated with an international armed conflict.

---

343 Articles 48 and 51(2) of Additional Protocol I to the Geneva Conventions.

344 Article 52 of Additional Protocol I to the Geneva Conventions.

345 Article 14 of Additional Protocol II to the Geneva Conventions.

346 *Kordić and Čerkez* (IT-95-14/2), Trial Chamber Judgment, 26 February 2001 at para 326.

5) The perpetrator was aware of factual circumstances that established the existence of an armed conflict.

Civilian objects have been defined as all objects that are not military objectives. "Military objectives are limited to those objects which by their nature, location, purpose or use make an effective contribution to military action and whose total or partial destruction, capture or neutralization, in the circumstances ruling at the time, offers a definite military advantage."[347] The ICTY has adopted this definition, noting that "civilian property covers any property that could not be legitimately considered a military objective."[348] In situations of doubt whether an object is a civilian object, Protocol I to the Geneva Conventions states that the presumption is that objects normally dedicated to civilian purposes (such as a place of worship, a house or other dwelling, or a school) are not used to make an effective contribution to military action.[349] Attacks on civilian objects must have caused extensive damage.[350] Whether damage is extensive is evaluated on a case-by-case basis. A single act, such as the destruction of a hospital, may suffice to characterize an offence under this count.[351] Judges at the ICC have held that installations, material, units, or vehicles involved in a peacekeeping mission in the context of an armed conflict not of an international character are not to be considered military objectives and shall be accorded protection given to civilian objects.[352] The ICTY jurisprudence has held that the attack on objects must have been conducted intentionally with the knowledge, or when it was impossible not to know, that civilians or civilian property were being targeted not through military necessity.[353] Furthermore, an ICC case has held that an armed conflict must play a substantial role in the perpetrator's decision to commit the crime.[354]

---

347 Geneva Convention IV, art 52(2).

348 *Blaškić* (IT-95-14), Trial Chamber Judgment, 3 March 2000 at para 180; *Strugar* (IT-01-42T), Trial Chamber Judgment, 31 January 2005 at para 282.

349 Article 52(3) of Additional Protocol I to the Geneva Conventions.

350 *Kordić and Čerkez* (IT-95-14/2), Trial Chamber Judgment, 26 February 2001 at para 328.

351 *Blaškić* (IT-95-14), Trial Chamber Judgment, 3 March 2000 at para 157.

352 *Garda* (ICC-02/05-02/09), Pre-Trial Chamber, Decision of the Confirmation of the Charges, 8 February 2010 at para 89; see, also, *Situation on Registered Vessels of Comoros, Greece and Cambodia, Article 53(1) Report*, ICC OTP, 6 November 2014 at paras 111–25.

353 *Blaškić* (IT-95-14), Trial Chamber Judgment, 3 March 2000 at para 180.

354 *Garda* (ICC-02/05-02/09), Pre-Trial Chamber, Decision of the Confirmation of the Charges, 8 February 2010 at para 90.

iii) Destruction Not Justified by Military Necessity

Even if an object is not civilian, it does not mean that it can be destroyed in all circumstances; the destruction of an object still must be for a proper military purpose, and if this requirement is not met, the war crime of destruction not justified by military necessity comes into play. This crime can be broken into two categories: destruction of enemy property and extensive destruction and appropriation.

Article 3(b) of the ICTY Statute and articles 8.2(b)(xiii) and 8.2(e)(xii) of the Rome Statute prohibit the destruction and seizure of enemy property unless it is imperatively demanded by the necessities of war.[355] All property in the territory involved in the conflict, including property located in enemy territory and in territory that is not under effective occupation, is covered by the crime of wanton destruction.[356] The elements of this crime were laid out by the Trial Chamber in the *Kordić* judgment as follows:

- the destruction occurred on a large scale;
- the destruction was not justified by military necessity; and
- the perpetrator acted with the intent to destroy the property in question or acted in reckless disregard of the likelihood of the property's destruction.[357]

Only destruction that is related to immovable property is covered by article 3(b).[358] To be considered on a large scale, the destruction must be both serious in relation to an individual object and cover a substantial range of a particular city, town, or village.[359] Destruction must be evaluated on a case-by-case basis to determine its scale. Destruction is large scale when a large quantity of property has been destroyed or

---

355 *Orić* (IT-03-68-T), Trial Chamber Judgment, 30 June 2006 at paras 262 and 580; *Tolimir* (IT-05-88/2-T), Trial Chamber Judgment, 12 December 2012 at para 858.

356 *Orić* (IT-03-68-T), Trial Chamber Judgment, 30 June 2006 at para 582.

357 *Kordić and Čerkez* (IT-95-14/2-A), Appeals Chamber Judgment, 17 December 2004 at para 74; *Gotovina et al* (IT-06-90-T), Trial Chamber Judgment, 15 April 2011 at para 1765; *Stanišić and Župljanin* (IT-08-91-T), Trial Chamber Judgment, 27 March 2013 at para 87; *Prlić et al* (IT-04-74), Trial Chamber Judgment, 29 May 2013 at paras 124 and 166–69; *Mladić* (IT-09-92-T), Trial Chamber Judgment, 22 November 2017 at para 3256; *Prlić et al* (IT-04-74-A), Appeals Chamber Judgment, 29 November 2017 at para 411.

358 *Orić* (IT-03-68-T), Trial Chamber Judgment, 30 June 2006 at para 581.

359 *Ibid* at para 583; *Prlić et al* (IT-04-74), Trial Chamber Judgment, 29 May 2013 at para 126.

when the value of a single destroyed object is sufficiently great.[360] An example of the latter is the destruction of a hospital.[361]

There is no requirement in international humanitarian law that settlements must be destroyed in their entirety for the crime of wanton destruction to be made out. To have such a requirement of total destruction would amount to an overly narrow reading of the prohibition against wanton destruction.[362] The ICTY determined that, based on national practice, partial destruction falls within the ambit of article 3(b).[363] As a result, the requirement of destruction on a large scale is usually met when acts of partial destruction are committed on a large scale.[364]

The Trial Chamber in the *Orić* judgment indicated that "an object shall not be attacked when it would be unreasonable to believe, in the circumstances of the person contemplating the attack, including the information available to that person, that the object is being used to make an effective contribution to military action."[365] The definition of a military object can also be found in article 52 of Additional Protocol I, which states: "Military objectives are limited to those objects which by their nature, location, purpose or use make an effective contribution to military action and whose total or partial destruction, capture or neutralisation, in the circumstances ruling at the time, offers a definite military advantage."[366] As a rule, destruction carried out before fighting begins or after fighting has ceased cannot be justified by military necessity.[367]

The mental state required is the intent to destroy the property in question. This includes indirect intent where the perpetrator had

---

360 *Hadžihasanović and Kubura* (IT-01-47-T), Trial Chamber Judgment, 15 March 2006 at para 43; *Gotovina et al* (IT-06-90-T), Trial Chamber Judgment, 15 April 2011 at para 1766; *Mladić* (IT-09-92-T), Trial Chamber Judgment, 22 November 2017 at para 3257.

361 *Hadžihasanović and Kubura* (IT-01-47-T), Trial Chamber Judgment, 15 March 2006 at para 43, referring to *Blaškić* (IT-95-14-T), Trial Chamber Judgment, 3 March 2000 at para 157; *Prlić et al* (IT-04-74), Trial Chamber Judgment, 29 May 2013 at para 125.

362 *Orić* (IT-03-68-T), Trial Chamber Judgment, 30 June 2006 at paras 584 & 585.

363 *Hadžihasanović and Kubura* (IT-01-47-T), Trial Chamber Judgment, 15 March 2006 at para 44.

364 *Ibid.*

365 *Orić* (IT-03-68-T), Trial Chamber Judgment, 30 June 2006 at para 587; *Gotovina et al* (IT-06-90-T), Trial Chamber Judgment, 15 April 2011 at para 1766.

366 *Orić* (IT-03-68-T), Trial Chamber Judgment, 30 June 2006 at para 587; *Prlić et al* (IT-04-74), Trial Chamber Judgment, 29 May 2013 at para 123; see, also, *Katanga* (ICC-01/04-01/07), Trial Chamber Judgment, 7 March 2014 at para 893.

367 *Orić* (IT-03-68-T), Trial Chamber Judgment, 30 June 2006 at para 588; *Martić* (IT-95-11-T), Trial Chamber Judgment, 12 June 2007 at para 93; *Gotovina et al* (IT-06-90-T), Trial Chamber Judgment, 15 April 2011 at para 1766.

knowledge that destruction was a probable consequence of their actions.[368]

The *Katanga* decision at the ICC identified five elements of the crime of this type of destruction:[369]

- the perpetrator destroyed certain property;
- the property was the property of a hostile party;
- the property was protected from destruction under the international law of armed conflict;
- the perpetrator was aware of the factual circumstances that established the status of the property; and
- the destruction was not justified by military necessity.[370]

Under these elements, destruction includes both movable and immovable property,[371] while it also applies to any degradation of the property and can include partial destruction,[372] as well as torching, burning, and demolishing.[373] Incidental destruction of civilian property during an attack specifically directed at a military objective is not allowed[374] unless it is collateral damage.[375] The additional factor that the destruction had to occur on a large scale introduced by the ICC Pre-Trial Chamber was not followed by the Trial Chamber.[376] The *mens rea* element requires that the perpetrator had intent to destroy the property

---

368 *Boškoski and Tarčulovski* (IT-04-82-T), Trial Chamber Judgment, 10 July 2008 at para 358; *Prlić et al* (IT-04-74), Trial Chamber Judgment, 29 May 2013 at para 127.

369 In this decision, the historical war crime of extensive destruction was conflated with the war crime of destroying or seizing the enemy's property (*Katanga and Chui* (ICC-01/04-01/07), Pre-Trial Chamber, Decision on the Confirmation of Charges, 30 September 2008 at paras 311 and 314), but the trial decision in the same case applied these elements only to the latter crime (*Katanga* (ICC-01/04-01/07), Trial Chamber Judgment, 7 March 2014).

370 *Katanga and Chui* (ICC-01/04-01/07), Pre-Trial Chamber, Decision on the Confirmation of Charges, 30 September 2008 at para 309; *Mbarushimana* (ICC-01/04-01/10), Pre-Trial Chamber, Decision of the Confirmation of Charges, 16 December 2011 at para 172; *Katanga* (ICC-01/04-01/07), Trial Chamber Judgment, 7 March 2014 at para 888; *Ntaganda* (ICC-01/04-02/06), Trial Chamber Judgment, 8 July 2019 at paras 1150–52; *Ongwen* (ICC-02/0401/15), Trial Chamber Judgment, 4 February 2021 at paras 2774–79.

371 *Ntaganda* (ICC-01/04-02/06), Trial Chamber Judgment, 8 July 2019 at para 1152

372 *Katanga* (ICC-01/04-01/07), Trial Chamber Judgment, 7 March 2014 at para 890.

373 *Ntaganda* (ICC-01/04-02/06), Trial Chamber Judgment, 8 July 2019 at paras 1152–53.

374 *Katanga and Chui* (ICC-01/04-01/07), Pre-Trial Chamber, Decision on the Confirmation of Charges, 30 September 2008 at para 313.

375 *Katanga* (ICC-01/04-01/07), Trial Chamber Judgment, 7 March 2014 at para 895.

376 *Ibid* at para 896.

as well as knowledge that his action or omission would cause destruction of the protected property.[377]

With respect to the second category mentioned above, the war crime of extensive destruction and appropriation of property not justified by military necessity and carried out unlawfully and wantonly is set out in article 2(d) of the ICTY Statute, which finds its origin in the Geneva Conventions. Article 53 of Geneva Convention IV prohibits extensive destruction of property by an occupying power that is not justified by military means. This article restricts the prohibition to property that is within occupied territory.[378] The occupying power is prohibited from destroying both movable and non-movable property. The only exception is when the destruction is made absolutely necessary by military operations.[379] Article 2 of the ICTY Statute only applies when the conflict is international in nature, and the grave breaches under this article must be perpetrated against persons or property covered by the protections found in the Geneva Conventions.[380] Destruction in this article constitutes a crime when it is extensive, unlawful, and wanton.[381]

iv) Attacks Against Religious, Cultural, and Historical Buildings and Other Protected Objects

The Appeals Chamber of the ICTY in the *Kordić* judgment noted that there are two types of protection for cultural, historical, and religious monuments.[382] The first type is a general protection found under article 52 of Additional Protocol I with respect to civilian objects, as discussed above. Under this provision, a building or monument cannot be destroyed unless it is turned into a military object by offering the attacking side a definite military advantage at the time of the attack.[383] The second type of protection is a special one under article 53 of Addi-

377 *Katanga and Chui* (ICC-01/04-01/07), Pre-Trial Chamber, Decision on the Confirmation of Charges, 30 September 2008 at para 315; *Katanga* (ICC-01/04-01/07), Trial Chamber Judgment, 7 March 2014 at paras 898–901.

378 *Blaškić* (IT-95-14-T), Trial Chamber Judgment, 3 March 2000 at para 148.

379 *Ibid* at para 157; *Prlić et al* (IT-04-74), Trial Chamber Judgment, 29 May 2013 at para 172; *Karadžić* (IT-95-5/18-T), Trial Chamber Judgment, 24 March 2016 at para 533; see, also, *Katanga* (ICC-01/04-01/07), Trial Chamber Judgment, 7 March 2014 at para 894; *Ntaganda* (ICC-01/04-02/06), Trial Chamber Judgment, 8 July 2019 at paras 1164–66.

380 *Blaškić* (IT-95-14-T), Trial Chamber Judgment, 3 March 2000 at para 74.

381 *Ibid* at para 157; *Situation on Registered Vessels of Comoros, Greece and Cambodia, Article 53(1) Report*, ICC OTP, 6 November 2014 at paras 83–89.

382 *Kordić and Čerkez* (IT-95-14/2-A), Appeals Chamber Judgment, 17 December 2004 at para 89.

383 *Ibid*; *Prlić et al* (IT-04-74), Trial Chamber Judgment, 29 May 2013 at para 172.

tional Protocol I, which applies to, *inter alia*, places of worship that constitute the cultural or spiritual heritage of a people.[384] Cultural or spiritual heritage covers objects whose value transcends geographical boundaries, are unique in character, and are intimately associated with the history and culture of a people.[385] The special protection for these objects is reflected in the fact that any damage to them amounts to a war crime, as opposed to the requirement of extensive damage for other regular civilian objects.

The elements for the crime of destruction or wilful damage done to institutions dedicated to education or religion are as follows:

- the act caused damage to, or destruction of, an institution dedicated to religion or education;
- the damages or destroyed institutions were not used for military purposes at the time of the act; and
- the act was carried out with intent to destroy or damage or in reckless disregard of the likelihood of the destruction or damage to the institution in question.[386]

The Trial Chamber has held that in terms of protection being lost if the institution is used for military purposes, the decisive factor is the use of the institution for such purposes and not its location.[387] Therefore, if military activities are located in the immediate vicinity of the institution, protection will not be lost.

At the ICC, a majority of the Appeals Chamber held that where, after the main attack had been completed, mob-up or *rattisage* operations on a hospital, involving looting, and on a church involving soldiers breaking into the church, removing furniture, digging trenches around the church, and starting a fire inside it to prepare food, was

---

384 *Kordić and Čerkez* (IT-95-14/2-A), Appeals Chamber Judgment, 17 December 2004 at para 90; *Prlić et al* (IT-04-74), Trial Chamber Judgment, 29 May 2013 at para 173; see, also, *Al Mahdi* (ICC-01/12-01/15), Pre-Trial Chamber I, Decision on the Confirmation of Charges, 24 March 2016 at para 43.

385 *Kordić and Čerkez* (IT-95-14/2-A), Appeals Chamber Judgment, 17 December 2004 at para 91, referring to the *Commentary on the Additional Protocols*.

386 *Martić* (IT-95-11-T), Trial Chamber Judgment, 12 June 2007 at para 96; *Hadžihasanović and Kubura* (IT-01-47-T), Trial Chamber Judgment, 15 March 2006 at para 58; *Stanišić and Župljanin* (IT-08-91-T), Trial Chamber Judgment, 27 March 2013 at para 88; *Prlić et al* (IT-04-74), Trial Chamber, Judgment, 29 May 2013 at para 178.

387 *Martić* (IT-95-11-T), Trial Chamber Judgment, 12 June 2007 at para 98; *Prlić et al* (IT-04-74), Trial Chamber Judgment, 29 May 2013 at para 59; *Prlić et al* (IT-04-74-A), Appeals Chamber Judgment, 29 November 2017 at para 411.

sufficiently linked to the original combat operations that it could be considered one attack.[388]

The *mens rea* for this crime is that the perpetrator acted with a direct or an indirect intent to damage or to destroy the institutions.[389] The *Hadžihasanović* Trial Judgment laid out that the wilful nature of the perpetrator will be established when it is shown that the perpetrator acted (1) intentionally; (2) with knowledge of the proscribed result; and (3) in reckless disregard of the likelihood of destruction.[390]

For religious institutions specifically, there is no need to establish whether the building in question represented the cultural heritage of a people as it is sufficient for the damaged institution to be one dedicated to religion.[391] When determining grave consequences for the victim in the context of the gravity of the offence, "victim" refers to a social group or community rather than an individual given the spiritual value of the religious building that has been damaged or destroyed.[392]

Spiritual value is also important in determining whether the destruction or damage constitutes a grave breach of international law as the question to determine the breach is whether the destruction or damage is sufficiently serious to constitute desecration.[393] This seriousness is decided on a case-by-case basis and takes much greater account of the spiritual value of the damage or destruction to the religious institution than the material extent of the damage or destruction.[394]

The Rome Statute has extended the number of protected objects by including hospitals, while it also eliminated the requirement that a

---

388 *Ntaganda* (ICC-01/04-02/06 A A2), Appeals Chamber Judgment, 30 March 2021 at paras 1163–64; the judgment is confusing as this question was part of the prosecutor's appeal, which was rejected by a different majority on other grounds; however, the conclusion on this legal question can be arrived at by comparing the dissenting opinion of Judge Luz Del Carmen Ibáñez Caranza in the same judgment at paras 1165–68, as well as following separate opinions agreeing with her, the Separate Opinion of Judge Solomy Balungi Bossa on the Prosecutor's appeal at paras 8 and 18 and the Partly Concurring Opinion of Judge Chile Eboe-Osuji at paras 103–37, while two judges disagreed with that view; see Separate Opinion of Judge Howard Morrison and Judge Piotr Hofmański on the prosecutor's appeal at paras 4–45.

389 *Martić* (IT-95-11-T), Trial Chamber Judgment, 12 June 2007 at para 99.

390 *Hadžihasanović and Kubura* (IT-01-47-T), Trial Chamber Judgment, 15 March 2006 at para 59; see, also, *Đorđević* (IT-05-87/1-A), Appeals Chamber Judgment, 27 January 2014 at para 559.

391 *Hadžihasanović and Kubura* (IT-01-47-T), Trial Chamber Judgment, 15 March 2006 at para 60.

392 *Ibid* at para 63.

393 *Ibid.*

394 *Ibid.*

cultural, historical, or religious building needs to be damaged.[395] As well, in the ICC context, for this crime there is no distinction as to whether it was carried out in the conduct of hostilities or after the object had fallen under the control of an armed group.[396] However, pillaging of a protected object does not fall within the meaning of attack in this context.[397]

v) Taking of Hostages

The war crime of the taking of hostages is provided for in the context of non-international conflict in article 4(c) of the ICTR Statute, article 3(c) of the Statute of the SCSL, and article 8.2(a)(viii) of the Rome Statute,[398] but this provision has primarily been judicially considered substantially[399] by the SCSL.

The Trial Chamber of the SCSL identified three elements of the crime of taking of hostages:

- the accused seized, detained, or otherwise held hostage one or more persons;
- the accused threatened to kill, injure, or continue to detain the hostage(s); and
- the accused intended to compel a state, an international organization, a natural or legal person or group of persons to act or refrain from acting as an explicit or implicit condition for the safety or release of the hostage(s).[400]

In addition to the element of confinement, there must be a threat made against the hostage, which will be realized if a particular condition

---

395 Articles 8.2(b)(ix) and 8.2(e)(iv); see, also, *Al Mahdi* (ICC-01/12-01/15), Pre-Trial Chamber, Decision on the Confirmation of Charges, 24 March 2016 at para 43, and *Al Mahdi* (ICC-01/12-01/15), Trial Chamber Judgment, 27 September 2016 at para 16; *Ntaganda* (ICC-01/04-02/06), Trial Chamber Judgment, 8 July 2019 at para 1136.

396 *Al Mahdi* (ICC-01/12-01/15), Trial Chamber Judgment, 27 September 2016 at para 15; however, see *Ntaganda* (ICC-01/04-02/06), Trial Chamber Judgment, 8 July 2019 at para 1108, which states that this offence can only be committed during actual conduct of hostilities.

397 *Ntaganda* (ICC-01/04-02/06), Trial Chamber Judgment, 8 July 2019 at para 761.

398 The ICTY Statute has the crime of the taking of civilian hostages in art 2(h).

399 The ICTY has answered the question of whether peacekeepers can be hostages affirmatively; see *Karadžić* (IT-95-5/18-AR73.9), Appeals Chamber Decision, 11 December 2012 at paras 15–22; *Karadžić* (MICT-13-55-A), Appeals Chamber Judgment, 20 March 2019 at para 659; *Mladić* (MICT-13-56-A), Appeals Chamber Judgment, 8 June 2021 at para 489.

400 *Sesay, Kallon and Gbao ("RUF")* (SCSL-04-15-T), Trial Chamber Judgment, 2 March 2009 at para 240; *Karadžić* (IT-95-5/18-T), Trial Chamber Judgment, 24 March 2016 at para 468; *Mladić* (IT-09-92-T), Trial Chamber Judgment, 22 November 2017 at paras 3215–16.

is not fulfilled. This threat can be explicit or implicit.[401] Communication of this threat to a third party does not comprise an element that needs proof; it is just a means by which to evidence the second element of the offence.[402]

This crime involves a specific intent *mens rea* since the threat to the hostage(s) must be intended as a coercive measure to achieve the fulfilment of a condition.[403] The requisite intent may be present when the hostage is first detained, or it may be formed some time thereafter while the individual is being held.[404]

vi) Pillaging

The terms "pillage," "plunder," and "spoliation" have been used varyingly to describe the unlawful appropriation of private or public property during an armed conflict in all the international criminal institutions. While the caselaw either dealt with pillage or plunder, the terms ultimately refer to the same crime.[405] A general prohibition against pillage is found in article 33 of Geneva Convention IV, is general in application, and is not limited to occupied territories.[406]

The elements of this crime, which applies to all kinds of property, public or private, movable or immovable,[407] are:

- the perpetrator appropriated certain property;
- the perpetrator intended to deprive the owner of the property and to appropriate it for private or personal use; and
- the appropriation was without the consent of the owner.[408]

---

401 *Sesay, Kallon and Gbao ("RUF")* (SCSL-04-15-T), Trial Chamber Judgment, 2 March 2009 at para 242.

402 *Ibid* at para 580.

403 *Ibid* at para 243, quoting *Kordić and Čerkez* (IT-95-14/2), Trial Chamber Judgment, 26 February 2001 at para 313.

404 *Sesay, Kallon and Gbao ("RUF")* (SCSL-04-15-A), Appeals Chamber Judgment, 26 October 2009 at para 597; *Karadžić* (IT-95-5/18-T), Trial Chamber Judgment, 24 March 2016 at para 468.

405 *Bemba* (ICC-01/05-01/08), Trial Chamber Judgment, 21 March 2016 at para 114.

406 *Kordić and Čerkez* (IT-95-14/2-A), Appeals Chamber Judgment, 17 December 2004 at para 78; *Prlić et al* (IT-04-74), Trial Chamber Judgment, 29 May 2013 at paras 128–29.

407 *Naletilić & Martinović* (IT-98-34-T), Trial Chamber Judgment, 31 March 2003 at para 612; *Katanga* (ICC-01/04-01/07), Trial Chamber Judgment, 7 March 2014 at para 904; *Bemba* (ICC-01/05-01/08), Trial Chamber Judgment, 21 March 2016 at para 115.

408 ICC, *Elements of Crimes*, above note 153, art 8.2(b)(xvi); see, also, *Mbarushimana* (ICC-01/04-01/10), Pre-Trial Chamber, Decision of the Confirmation of Charges, 16 December 2011 at para 176; *Taylor* (SCSL-03-01-T), Trial Chamber Judgment, 18 May 2012 at paras 452–53; *Katanga* (ICC-01/04-01/07), Trial Chamber Judgment, 7 March 2014 at para 904; *Ntaganda*

The jurisprudence of the ICTY and the ICC has noted that the appropriated property must be of sufficient value to entail grave consequences for the victim.[409] The assessment of when a piece of property reaches the threshold level of a certain value can only be made on a case-by-case basis in conjunction with the general circumstances of the case.[410] A case-by-case analysis is required as appropriation need not be extensive or involve a large economic value to constitute the elements of the crime of pillage.[411] In terms of the consequence for the victims, a serious violation could be assumed in circumstances where appropriations take place vis-à-vis a large number of people, even though there are no grave consequences for each individual.[412] All forms of seizure, including acts committed by individual soldiers for private gain and acts committed as part of a systematic campaign to economically exploit a targeted area, constitute acts of appropriation.[413]

There are a few exceptions to the principle of protection against the taking of property in the context of an international armed conflict. War booty and the requisition of property for military use may constitute a limitation, and the personal effects belonging to prisoners of war are also an exception.[414] In non-international armed conflicts, regulations

---

(ICC-01/04-02/06), Pre-Trial Chamber, Decision of the Confirmation of the Charges, 9 June 2014 at para 59; *Bemba* (ICC-01/05-01/08), Trial Chamber Judgment, March 21, 2016 at paras 113–17; *Ntaganda* (ICC-01/04-02/06), Trial Chamber Judgment, 8 July 2019 at para 1029; *Ongwen* (ICC-02/0401/15), Trial Chamber Judgment, 4 February 2021 at paras 2762–67.

409 *Hadžihasanović and Kubura* (IT-01-47-T), Trial Chamber Judgment, 15 March 2006 at para 56; *Prlić et al* (IT-04-74), Trial Chamber Judgment, 29 May 2013 at para 182; *Katanga* (ICC-01/04-01/07), Trial Chamber Judgment, 7 March 2014 at para 909; *Bemba* (ICC-01/05-01/08), Trial Chamber Judgment, 21 March 2016 at para 117; *Mladić* (IT-09-92-T), Trial Chamber Judgment, 22 November 2017 at para 3252.

410 *Kordić and Čerkez* (IT-95-14/2-A), Appeals Chamber Judgment, 17 December 2004 at para 82.

411 *Sesay, Kallon and Gbao ("RUF")* (SCSL-04-15-T), Trial Chamber Judgment, 2 March 2009 at para 209.

412 *Kordić and Čerkez* (IT-95-14/2-A), Appeals Chamber Judgment, 17 December 2004 at para 83; *Karadžić* (IT-95-5/18-T), Trial Chamber Judgment, 24 March 2016 at para 529; *Bemba* (ICC-01/05-01/08), Trial Chamber Judgment, 21 March 2016 at para 117; *Ntaganda* (ICC-01/04-02/06), Trial Chamber Judgment, 8 July 2019 at para 1044.

413 *Gotovina et al* (IT-06-90-T), Trial Chamber Judgment, 15 April 2011 at para 1778; *Prlić et al* (IT-04-74), Trial Chamber Judgment, 29 May 2013 at para 130; *Katanga* (ICC-01/04-01/07), Trial Chamber Judgment, 7 March 2014 at para 905, referring to n62 of the ICC *Elements of Crimes* document, above note 153.

414 *Hadžihasanović and Kubura* (IT-01-47-T), Trial Chamber Judgment, 15 March 2006 at para 51; *Prlić et al* (IT-04-74), Trial Chamber Judgment, 29 May 2013 at para 128; *Ntaganda* (ICC-01 04-02/06), Pre-Trial Chamber, Decision of the Confirmation of the Charges, 9 June 2014 at para 59; *Bemba* (ICC-01/05-01/08), Trial Chamber Judgment, 21 March 2016 at paras 122–25.

authorizing or prohibiting war booty and requisition have not been identified, and it is up to national law to settle these issues.[415] A state of necessity may also be an exception to the prohibition on appropriation provided that the following circumstances are found:

- there must be a real and imminent threat of severe and irreparable harm to life existence;
- the acts of appropriation must have been the only means to avoid such harm;
- the acts of appropriation were not disproportionate; and
- the situation was not voluntarily brought about by the perpetrator.[416]

The *mens rea* element of this crime is established when the perpetrator acts with knowledge and intent to acquire property unlawfully or when the consequences of their actions are foreseeable.[417]

vii) Rights of Fair Trial

The statutes of all the international criminal institutions contain a provision making wilfully depriving a protected person during an armed conflict of the rights of a fair and regular trial a war crime, but only the ECCC have examined this provision.

The deprivation of the rights of fair trial is expressly prohibited as a grave breach in Geneva Convention III, which deals with prisoners of war, and Geneva Convention IV, which deals with civilians.[418] The perpetrator must have deprived one or more individuals of a fair and regular trial by denying the judicial guarantees as defined in these conventions. These include:

- the right to be judged by an independent and impartial court
- the right to be promptly informed of charges
- the right to protection against collective penalty
- the right to protection under the principle of legality

415 *Hadžihasanović and Kubura* (IT-01-47-T), Trial Chamber Judgment, 15 March 2006 at para 52.

416 *Ntaganda* (ICC-01/04-02/06), Trial Chamber Judgment, 8 July 2019 at para 1030.

417 *Hadžihasanović and Kubura* (IT-01-47-T), Trial Chamber Judgment, 15 March 2006 at para 50; *Prlić et al* (IT-04-74), Trial Chamber Judgment, 29 May 2013 at para 131; *Katanga* (ICC-01/04-01/07), Trial Chamber Judgment, 7 March 2014 at paras 911–14; *Bemba* (ICC-01/05-01/08), Trial Chamber Judgment, 21 March 2016 at paras 118–21.

418 *Kaing Guek Eav alias Duch* (Case File No 001/18-07-2007/ECCC/TC), Trial Chamber Judgment, 26 July 2010 at para 458.

- the right not to be punished more than once for the same act or on the same count
- the right to be informed of the right to appeal
- the right not to be sentenced or executed without previous judgment pronounced by a regularly constituted court[419]
- the right not to be subjected to undue delay in proceedings, whether due to the complexity of the case or the conduct of the parties and relevant authorities[420]

viii) Outrages upon Personal Dignity

The elements of this particular crime have been expressed in a very similar fashion in the jurisprudence of the ICTR, the SCSL, and the ICC. These institutions have defined outrages upon the personal as any act or omission that would be generally considered to cause serious humiliation or degradation or otherwise be a serious attack on human dignity. The *mens rea* requires only knowledge of the possible consequences of the charged act or omission.[421] Examples in the jurisprudence have been compelling victims to dance naked on a table;[422] a situation where a combatant cut off a woman's underwear with his knife, thus leaving her wearing only her blouse;[423] sexual slavery;[424] using detainees as human shields or trench diggers; forcing detainees to relieve bodily functions in their clothing; imposing conditions of constant fear of being subjected to physical, mental, or sexual violence on detainees; forced incest;

---

419 *Kaing Guek Eav alias Duch* (Case File No 001/18-07-2007/ECCC/TC), Trial Chamber Judgment, 26 July 2010 at para 459; *Case 002/02* (Case File No 002/19-09-2007/ECCC/TC), Trial Chamber Judgment, 16 November 2018 at para 770.

420 *Nyiramasuhuko et al* (ICTR-98-42-A), Appeals Chamber Judgment, 14 December 2015 at paras 360 and 363.

421 *Bagosora et al* (ICTR-98-41-T), Trial Chamber Judgment, 18 December 2008 at para 2250; *Sesay, Kallon and Gbao ("RUF")*, (SCSL-04-15-T), Trial Chamber Judgment, 25 February 2009 at paras 174–77; *Nyiramasuhuko et al* (ICTR-98-42-T), Trial Chamber Judgment 24 June 2011 at para 6179; *Bemba* (ICC-01/05-01/08), Pre-Trial Chamber, Decision of Confirmation of Charges, 15 June 2009 at paras 303–4; *Taylor* (SCSL-03-01-T), Trial Chamber Judgment, 18 May 2012 at para 431; *Situation on Registered Vessels of Comoros, Greece and Cambodia, Article 53(1) Report*, ICC OTP, 6 November 2014 at paras 70–71; *Ongwen* (ICC-02/0401/15), Trial Chamber Judgment, 4 February 2021 at paras 2755–57.

422 *Kunarac*, 2001, above note 296 at paras 766–74.

423 *Katanga and Chui* (ICC-01/04-01/07), Pre-Trial Chamber, Decision of the Confirmation of the Charges, 30 September 2008 at para 375.

424 *Taylor* (SCSL-03-01-T), Trial Chamber Judgment, 18 May 2012 at para 432.

burying dead corpses in latrine pits; and leaving infants without care after killing their guardians.[425]

ix) Directing Attacks Against Peacekeeping Missions and Materials

The *Sesay, Kallon, and Gbao ("RUF")* Trial Judgment of the SCSL was the first to specifically address the nature and scope of the offence of directing attacks against peacekeeping missions and materials.[426] This offence does not represent a new crime but rather can be seen as the particularization of the general and fundamental prohibition in international humanitarian law against attacks on civilians and civilian objects.[427]

The Rome Statute was the first explicit identification of directing attacks against peacekeeping missions and materials as a war crime,[428] but prior to the Rome Statute, the Convention on the Safety of United Nations and Associated Personnel specifically criminalized attacks against the United Nations and associated personnel as an offence subject to universal jurisdiction.[429]

The elements of this crime, as laid out by the ICC *Elements of Crimes* document, are as follows:

1. The perpetrator directed an attack;
2. The object of the attack was personnel, installations, material, units, or vehicles involved in humanitarian assistance or a peacekeeping mission in accordance with the *Charter of the United Nations*;
3. The perpetrator intended such personnel, installations, material, units, or vehicles to be the object of the attack;
4. The personnel, installations, material, units, or vehicles were entitled to protection given to civilians and civilian objects under the international law of armed conflicts;
5. The perpetrator was aware of the factual circumstances that established protection;

---

425 *Bagosora* (ICTR-94-1-T), Trial Chamber, Decision on Motions for Judgment of Acquittal, 2 February 2005 at para 40; *Aleksovski* (IT-95-14/1), Trial Chamber Judgment, 25 June 1999 at para 299; *Kvočka* (IT-98-30/1), Trial Chamber Judgment, 2 November 2001 at para 173; *Kunarac*, 2001, above note 296 at para 157.

426 *Sesay, Kallon and Gbao ("RUF")* (SCSL-04-15-T), Trial Chamber Judgment, 2 March 2009 at para 214.

427 *Ibid* at para 215.

428 *Ibid* at para 214.

429 *Ibid* at para 217.

6. The conduct took place in the context of and was associated with an armed conflict; and
7. The perpetrator was aware of the factual circumstances that established the existence of an armed conflict.[430]

There is no jurisprudence defining a peacekeeping mission in accordance with the *Charter of the United Nations*.[431] However, there are three basic principles that have been accepted as determining whether a given mission constitutes a peacekeeping mission:

(a) consent of the parties;
(b) impartiality; and
(c) non-use of force except in self-defence and defence of their mandate.[432]

Peacekeepers are considered to be civilians only insofar as they fall within the definition of civilians laid down for non-combatants in customary international law and under Additional Protocol II.[433] This protection does not cease if the peacekeepers use armed force in the exercise of their right of self-defence.[434] The determination of whether peacekeepers are directly participating in hostilities (one of the requirements is to be a non-combatant) is done on a case-by-case basis.[435] The Trial Chamber in the *Sesay, Kallon and Gbao ("RUF")* case laid out a number of circumstances existing at the time of the alleged offence to consider when determining whether the peacekeepers involved in hostilities were entitled to civilian protection:

- relevant Security Council resolutions for operation;
- the specific operational mandate;

---

430 ICC, *Elements of Crimes*, above note 153 at 18–19; see, also, *Garda* (ICC-02/05-02/09), Pre-Trial Chamber, Decision on the Confirmation of Charges, 8 February 2010 at para 62.

431 *Sesay, Kallon and Gbao ("RUF")* (SCSL-04-15-T), Trial Chamber Judgment, 2 March 2009 at para 221.

432 *Garda* (ICC-02/05-02/09), Pre-Trial Chamber, Decision on the Confirmation of Charges, 8 February 2010 at para 71; *Sesay, Kallon and Gbao ("RUF")* (SCSL-04-15-T), Trial Chamber Judgment, 2 March 2009 at para 225.

433 *Ibid* at para 233; *Garda* (ICC-02/05-02/09), Pre-Trial Chamber, Decision on the Confirmation of Charges, 8 February 2010 at para 83.

434 *Ibid* at para 83; *Sesay, Kallon and Gbao ("RUF")* (SCSL-04-15-T), Trial Chamber Judgment, 2 March 2009 at para 233.

435 *Garda* (ICC-02/05-02/09), Pre-Trial Chamber, Decision on the Confirmation of Charges, 8 February 2010 at para 83.

- the role and practice actually adopted by the peacekeeping mission during the particular conflict;
- the rules of engagement and operational orders;
- the nature of the arms and equipment used by the peacekeeping force;
- the interaction between the peacekeeping force and the parties involved in the conflict;
- any use of force between the peacekeeping force and the parties in the conflict;
- the nature and frequency of such force; and
- the conduct of the alleged victims and their fellow personnel.[436]

Any installations, material, units, or vehicles involved in the peacekeeping mission in the context of non-international armed conflict are not to be considered military objects. This will entitle such objects to the protection given to civilian objects, unless and for such time as their nature, location, purpose, or use make an effective contribution to the military action of a party to a conflict and insofar as their total or partial destruction, in circumstances ruling at the time, offers any definite military advantage.[437]

The intention requirement for the crime of directing attacks against peacekeeping missions and materials is similar to the intent requirement for attacks against civilians and civilian objects.[438] The perpetrator must have intended to make, as the object of the attack, individual civilians not taking direct part in hostilities (peacekeepers) or the civilian population.[439] It is not necessary to establish that the perpetrator actually had legal knowledge of the protection.[440] This excludes the defence of mistake of law since only knowledge in relation to the facts establishing that personnel, installations, material, units, or vehicles were involved in the peacekeeping mission is necessary.[441]

---

436 *Sesay, Kallon and Gbao ("RUF")* (SCSL-04-15-T), Trial Chamber Judgment, 2 March 2009 at para 234.

437 *Garda* (ICC-02/05-02/09), Pre-Trial Chamber, Decision on the Confirmation of Charges, 8 February 2010 at para 89.

438 *Ibid* at para 93.

439 *Ibid.*

440 *Sesay, Kallon and Gbao ("RUF")* (SCSL-04-15-T), Trial Chamber Judgment, 2 March 2009 at para 235.

441 *Garda* (ICC-02/05-02/09), Pre-Trial Chamber, Decision on the Confirmation of Charges, 8 February 2010 at para 94.

x) Child Recruitment

The war crime of child recruitment in the sense of "conscripting or enlisting children under the age of fifteen years into the national armed forces or using them to participate actively in hostilities" is not found in the statutes of the ICTY and the ICTR but is part of the mandates of the SCSL and the ICC.[442]

The distinction between conscripting and enlisting is that both notions are forms of recruitment, conscripting being forcible recruitment, while enlisting pertains more to voluntary recruitment.[443] Conscription includes all forms of coercion, such as abductions and forced recruitment,[444] while enlistment in an armed group, which is not a conventional military organization, is not a formal process but connotes any conduct accepting a child as part of the militia.[445] A child's consent is not a legitimate defence to the charge of enlistment.[446] There is no need to establish the exact age of the child soldier, only that they were under fifteen years of age.[447]

In the Rome Statute, participating actively in hostilities does not have to be given the same interpretation as the term "active" or "direct

---

442 Article 8.2(b)(xxvi) in international armed conflicts and art 8.2(e)(vii) for non-international armed conflicts. The SCSL has indicated that this crime was already part of international law before the Rome Statute was negotiated by saying that "child recruitment was criminalised before it was explicitly set out as a criminal prohibition in treaty law and certainly by November 1996"; see *Norman* (SLSC-2004-14-AR72(E)), Appeals Chamber, Decision on Preliminary Motion on Lack of Jurisdiction (Child Recruitment), 31 May 2004 at para 53.

443 *Lubanga* (ICC-01/04-01/06), Pre-Trial Chamber, Decision on the Confirmation of Charges, 29 January 2007 at para 246; *Katanga and Chui* (ICC-01/04-01/07), Pre-Trial Chamber, Decision of the Confirmation of the Charges, 30 September 2008 at para 250; *Lubanga* (ICC-01/04-01/06), Trial Chamber Judgment, 14 March 2012 at paras 607–18; *Ntaganda* (ICC-01/04-02/06), Pre-Trial Chamber, Decision of the Confirmation of the Charges, 9 June 2014 at paras 83–84; *Lubanga* (ICC-01/04-01/06 A5), Appeals Chamber Judgment, 1 December 2014 at para 38; *Ntaganda* (ICC-01/04-02/06), Trial Chamber Judgment, 8 July 2019 at paras 1105–6; *Ongwen* (ICC-02/0401/15), Trial Chamber Judgment, 4 February 2021 at para 2769.

444 *Brima, Kamara and Kanu ("AFRC")* (SCSL-2004-16-T), Trial Chamber Judgment, 20 June 2007 at para 734; *Fofana and Kondewa ("CDF")* (SCSL-04-14-T), Trial Chamber Judgment, 2 August 2007 at paras 190–92; *Sesay, Kallon and Gbao ("RUF")* (SCSL-04-15-T), Trial Chamber Judgment, 25 February 2009 at paras 1695 and 1700; *Taylor* (SCSL-03-01-T), Trial Chamber Judgment, 18 May 2012 at para 441; *Lubanga* (ICC-01/04-01/06 A5), Appeals Chamber Judgment, 1 December 2014 at paras 278–86, 295, and 301–2.

445 *Fofana and Kondewa ("CDF")* (SCSL-04-14-T), Trial Chamber Judgment, 2 August 2007 at para 144; *Taylor* (SCSL-03-01-T), Trial Chamber Judgment, 18 May 2012 at para 442; *Ntaganda* (ICC-01/04-02/06), Trial Chamber Judgment, 8 July 2019 at para 1107.

446 *Ntaganda* (ICC-01/04-02/06), Trial Chamber Judgment, 8 July 2019 at para 1107.

447 *Lubanga* (ICC-01/04-01/06 A5), Appeals Chamber Judgment, 1 December 2014 at para 198.

participation" in the context of the principle of distinction between combatants and civilians.[448] Active participation in hostilities goes beyond direct participation in hostilities or combat and also includes activities such as scouting, spying, and the use of children as decoys, as couriers, or at military checkpoints.[449]

In addition, activities further removed from the area of combat, such as guarding military objectives, including military quarters, or safeguarding the physical safety of military commanders, especially when used as body guards, can be considered activities related to hostilities insofar as the military commanders in question are in a position to take all the necessary decisions regarding the conduct of hostilities and these activities have a direct impact on the level of logistic resources and the organization of the operations in attacking military objectives.[450] The decisive factor in deciding if an indirect role is to be treated as active participation in hostilities is to analyze the link between the activity for which the child is used and the combat in which the armed force or group of the perpetrator is engaged[451] and whether the support provided by the child to the combatants exposed them to real danger as a potential target.[452]

Providing logistical support in the sense of labour or support that gives effect to or helps maintain operations in a conflict is included within this concept as well, and the jurisprudence gives the following examples of such support: carrying loads, finding and acquiring food, making trails or finding routes, acting as human shields,[453] gathering information,

448 *Ibid* at paras 324–28; in the latter context, it has been said that being made subject to rape or sexual enslavement negates active participation in hostilities due to the coercion involved; see *Ntaganda* (ICC-01/04-02/06), Pre-Trial Chamber, Decision of the Confirmation of the Charges, 9 June 2014 at paras 76–80.

449 *Lubanga* (ICC-01/04-01/06), Pre-Trial Chamber, Decision on the Confirmation of Charges, 29 January 2007 at para 261.

450 *Lubanga* (ICC-01/04-01/06), Trial Chamber Judgment, 14 March 2012 at para 622; *Katanga* (ICC-01/04-01/07), Trial Chamber Judgment, 7 March 2014 at para 1044; *Ntaganda* (ICC-01/04-02/06), Trial Chamber Judgment, 8 July 2019 at para 1108.

451 *Lubanga* (ICC-01/04-01/06 A5), Appeals Chamber Judgment, 1 December 2014 at para 335, 340; *Ntaganda* (ICC-01/04-02/06), Trial Chamber Judgment, 8 July 2019 at para 1108; *Ongwen* (ICC-02/0401/15), Trial Chamber Judgment, 4 February 2021 at para 2770.

452 *Lubanga* (ICC-01/04-01/06), Trial Chamber Judgment, 14 March 2012 at para 628; *Katanga* (ICC-01/04-01/07), Trial Chamber Judgment, 7 March 2014 at para 1045; however, see *Lubanga* (ICC-01/04-01/06 A5), Appeals Chamber Judgment, 1 December 2014 at paras 332–33 and 340.

453 *Brima, Kamara and Kanu ("AFRC")* (SCSL-2004-16-T), Trial Chamber Judgment, 20 June 2007 at para 737; the conviction regarding child recruitment was upheld in general terms by the Appeals Chamber, *Brima, Kamara and Kanu ("AFRC")* (SLSC-2004-16-A), Judgment, 22 February 2008 at para 306; see, also, *Fofana and Kondewa ("CDF")* (SCSL-04-14-T), Trial

transmitting orders, transporting ammunition and foodstuff, and acts of sabotage.[454] On the other hand, activities clearly not related to hostilities, such as food deliveries to an airbase or the use of domestic staff in married officers' quarters, are not considered active participation.[455]

2) The Meaning of International Instruments in 1F(a)

With respect to the words "international instruments" in exclusion ground 1F(a), the intention of the drafters of the Refugee Convention in 1950–51 had been to ensure that the crimes mentioned in that clause would not be hampered by new developments in international criminal law, which was in its infancy. As a result, both the UNHCR and commentators are of the view that this wording calls for a dynamic interpretation of this clause, which can go beyond one of the main sources of international law: treaties.[456] This approach was recently confirmed in a different context by the International Law Commission, which said:

> "International instrument" is to be understood as being broader than just a legally binding international agreement, but as being limited to instruments developed by States or international organizations, such as the United Nations.[457]

Chamber Judgment, 2 August 2007 at para 193, as well as *Sesay, Kallon and Gbao ("RUF")*, (SCSL-04-15-T), Trial Chamber Judgment, 25 February 2009 at paras 1714, 1718, 1724, 1725, 1729, and 1731; *Taylor* (SCSL-03-01-T), Trial Chamber Judgment, 18 May 2012 at para 444; however, as to the question of whether food-finding missions fall under direct participation, see, to the contrary, *Sesay, Kallon and Gbao ("RUF")*, (SCSL-04-15-T), Trial Chamber Judgment, 25 February 2009 at para 1743.

454 *Ntaganda* (ICC-01/04-02/06), Trial Chamber Judgment, 8 July 2019 at para 1108.

455 *Lubanga* (ICC-01/04-01/06), Pre-Trial Chamber, Decision on the Confirmation of Charges, 29 January 2007 at para 262; *Sesay, Kallon and Gbao ("RUF")*, (SCSL-04-15-T), Trial Chamber Judgment, 25 February 2009 at para 1730; *Lubanga* (ICC-01/04-01/06), Trial Chamber Judgment, 14 March 2012 at para 623; the Separate and Dissenting Opinion of Judge Odio Benito in the same case was of the view that being the victim of sexual violence in the context of being a bush wife should have been included within the concept of actively participating as this role provides essential support to the armed groups at paras 15–21.

456 See Andreas Zimmermann & Philipp Wennholz, "Article 1F (Definition of the Term 'Refugee')" in Andreas Zimmerman, ed, *The 1951 Convention Relating to the Status of Refugees and its 1967 Protocol: A Commentary* (Oxford: Oxford University Press, 2011) 596; David McKeever, "Evolving Interpretation of Multilateral Treaties: Acts Contrary to the Purposes and Principles of the United Nations in the Refugee Convention" (2015) 64:2 *International and Comparative Law Quarterly* 405 at 409–14. See, also, UNHCR, *Background Note*, above note 9, 10 at para 25.

457 International Law Commission, *Draft Articles on Prevention and Punishment of Crimes Against Humanity, with Commentaries 2019*, UN Doc A74/10, 47 at para 44.

One commentator is of the view that

> [t]he reference to "instruments" rather than e.g., treaties allows us to resort to non-binding documents, including ILC documents or General Assembly resolutions; their application, however, should be restricted to supplementary assistance and not lead to the establishment of a crime not supported by a primary source of International Law. As stated above, due to the explicit wording, only treaties or other written sources should be employed as basis for defining the international crimes as stipulated in Article 1F(a) CSR51.[458]

3) The Views of the UNHCR

The most comprehensive description of 1F(a) concepts stated by the UNHCR can be found in the 2003 Background Note on the Application of the Exclusion Clauses: Article 1F of the 1951 Convention relating to the Status of Refugees, which refers primarily to the Rome Statute for the international elements, such as armed conflict and the systematic and widespread nature of crimes against humanity, as well as the underlying crimes.[459] The only reference to international jurisprudence is to the seminal ICTY decision of *Tadić* in respect to the international elements.[460] The note makes it clear that genocide, while a separate crime, can be included within the notion of crimes against humanity in 1F(a).[461]

---

458 See Yao Li, *Exclusion from Protection as a Refugee: An Approach to a Harmonizing Interpretation in International Law* (Leiden & Boston: Brill Nijhoff, 2017) at 306–7. See, also, Colloquium on Challenges in International Refugee Law, "The Michigan Guidelines on the Exclusion of International Criminals" (2013) 35:1 *Michigan Journal of International Law* 3 at 7–9, paras 5–7, which says in the last paragraph: "In addition to analysis of the text of relevant international criminal law instruments, account should be taken of persuasive interpretations of such instruments rendered by both international tribunals and national courts. Interpretations that offer an authoritative and cogent understanding of how international criminal norms apply in comparable factual circumstances are of particular value." See, also, Zoë Egelman. "Punishment and Protection, Two Sides of the Same Sword: The Problem of International Criminal Law Under the Refugee Convention" (2018) 59:2 *Harvard International Law Journal* 461 at 478–85.

459 UNHCR, *Background Note*, above note 9 at paras 30–36.

460 *Ibid* at n22, 23, n25, and n27.

461 *Ibid* at n27.

4) National Refugee Jurisprudence

a) Australia

Australia[462] has incorporated the wording of article 1 of the Refugee Convention as part of a general provision dealing with ineligibility to receive protection.[463] In terms of procedure with respect to exclusion, the

---

462 For a general overview of efforts in Australia to address the issue of war criminals, see Boas & Chifflet, above note 130 at 46–86.

463 Section 36(2C)(a) of the *Migration Act 1958* (which is a repeat of the definitional s 5H(2); s 36(2C)(b) uses the language of art 33(2) of the Refugee Convention; see, also, Peter Billings & Rebecca Ananian-Welsh, "Counterterrorism and the Exclusion of Refugees and Refugee-Citizens from Australia" in Simeon, *Terrorism and Asylum*, above note 37 at 184–86, who make the following comment at 184: "In fact, Art 1F may be viewed as of secondary, and comparatively minor, importance as a foundation for exclusion under Australian migration law." This is because of the fact that the *Immigration Regulations* may prescribe criteria for a visa or for a visa of a specified class; among the primary criteria that must be satisfied for any visa is that, at the time the decision is made, the person satisfies the requirements of public interest criterion, which is set out in Schedule 4 of the regulation, which sets out the public interest criteria, of which criterion 4001 provides that a person has to pass a character test; s 501 of the *Migration Act* refers to refusal or cancellation of a visa on character grounds, which is set out in general in ss 501(1) in the following terms: "The Minister may refuse to grant a visa to a person if the person does not satisfy the Minister that the person passes the character test." This character test has a large number of permutations, of which the following ones are relevant with respect to international crimes:

- at para 501(6)(ba)(iii), which states: "The Minister reasonably suspects that the person has been or is involved in conduct constituting one or more of the following: . . . the crime of genocide, a crime against humanity, a war crime, a crime involving torture or slavery or a crime that is otherwise of serious international concern" while this is followed by "whether or not the person, or another person, has been convicted of an offence constituted by the conduct";
- at para 501(6)(f) with the following wording: "The person has, in Australia or a foreign country, been charged with or indicted for one or more of the following:
  - » the crime of genocide;
  - » a crime against humanity;
  - » a war crime;
  - » a crime involving torture or slavery;
  - » a crime that is otherwise of serious international concern"
- at para 501(6)(b) with these parameters: "The Minister reasonably suspects
  - » that the person has been or is a member of a group or organisation, or has had or has an association with a group, organisation or person; and
  - » that the group, organisation or person has been or is involved in criminal conduct."

In order to provide further clarification to the various aspects of the *Migration Act*, the minister of home affairs, who administers this statute, has been given authority under s 499 of the Act to issue ministerial directions. The minister has issued a number of such directions setting further details for the character test, the most recent one of which is Direction No 90, entitled "Visa refusal and cancellation under s 501 and revocation of a mandatory cancellation of a visa under s 501CA," which came into force on 8 March 2021; nothing has

Federal Court of Australia (FCA) sits in judicial review of two administrative tribunals. These tribunals are the Administrative Appeals Tribunal (AAT), in operation since 1998, and the Refugee Review Tribunal (RRT), which was active between 1994 and 1997. Decisions of the Federal Court of Australia can be appealed to the FCAFC and further to the High Court of Australia (HCA).

The sources of war crimes and crimes against humanity have evolved depending on the timing of the decisions and the legal developments in the international sphere. The earliest decisions at the RRT and the AAT referred mostly to the Statute of the IMT, while later decisions examined the statutes of the ICTY and ICTR, and, most recently, the Statute of the ICC has been found to be the most useful in this regard.[464]

---

been added by way of explanation to s 501(6)(ba) or 501(6)(f), but s 501(6)(b) has been given further meaning. See, also, Chantal Bostock & Jason Cabarrús, "Short Shrift to International Non-refoulement Obligations? Australia's Approach to Criminal Deportation" (2020) 32:4 *International Journal of Refugee Law* 597 at 607–10.

464 See, for references to the IMT at the RRT level, N96/12101 [1996] RRTA 3349 (which also makes reference to the Draft Code of Crimes against the Peace and Security of Mankind of the International Law Commission [Draft Code]); V94/02580, [1995] RRTA 1918 (which also talks about the draft Rome Statute); V94/01334 [1995] RRTA 1626; N95/08964 [1996] RRTA 691; V95/03373, [1996] RRTA 2452; V95/03351, [1995] RRTA 1952; V96/04174, [1997] RRTA 2507 (while also referring to the ICTY and its *Tadić* decision); V95/03566, [1997] RRTA 334; and N96/12254 [1997] RRTA 492 (which also refers to the Draft Code). The AAT refers to the IMT in the cases of *N96/1441 and Minister for Immigration and Multicultural Affairs*, [1998] AATA 619 (which also refers to the ICTY *Tadić* decision regarding the issue of retroactivity); *N1998/532 and Minister for Immigration and Multicultural Affairs*, [1999] AATA (which also refers to the Draft Code); *W97/164 and Minister for Immigration and Multicultural Affairs*, [1998] AATA 618; *W98/45 and Minister for Immigration and Multicultural Affairs*, [1998] AATA 948; *SRL and Minister for Immigration and Multicultural Affairs*, [2000] AATA 128; *SRLLL and Minister for Immigration Multicultural and Indigenous Affairs*, [2002] AATA 795; *VAG and Minister for Immigration and Multicultural and Indigenous Affairs*, [2002] AATA 1332 (although the latter also refers to the ICC); *SRHHH and Minister for Immigration and Multicultural and Indigenous Affairs*, [2005] AATA 1020 (together with a reference to the ICC); *SROOOO and Minister for Immigration and Multicultural and Indigenous Affairs*, [2006] AATA 91 (together with a reference to the ICTY); *WBV and Minister for Immigration and Citizenship*, [2007] AATA 2046 (together with the Rome Statute). The AAT has referred to all four international institutions in the following cases: *WBR and Minister for Immigration and Multicultural Affairs*, [2006] AATA 75; *SAH and Minister for Immigration and Multicultural and Indigenous Affairs*, [2002] AATA 263; and *SAL and Minister for Immigration and Multicultural and Indigenous Affairs*, [2002] AATA 1164, while referring only to the Rome Statute in *SRDDDD and Minister for Immigration and Multicultural and Indigenous Affairs*, [2004] AATA 150, and *SRYYY and Minister for Immigration and Multicultural Affairs*, [2006] AATA 320 cases. At the moment, legislation has defined what amounts to international instruments by identifying

At the federal court level, the Rome Statute has been held to be the most authoritative in the context of international crimes,[465] although a reference to the IMT by the AAT was not found to have been in error.[466]

In two cases, the issue of retroactivity was raised in the sense of whether the ICTY Statute, which came into force in 1994, or the Rome Statute, which was concluded in 1998 but came into force in 2002, could be used for fact situations preceding these dates. In the *VWYJ* case, the person concerned had been an officer in the Lebanese Christian Phalange Militia, which had massacred hundreds of civilians in the refugee camps of Sabra and Shatilla in Beirut in 1982, and the AAT had used the IMT, ICTY, ICTR, and ICC statutes as sources for war crimes and crimes against humanity. The FCAFC was of the view that reference to the latter three was inappropriate but that the IMT could be used for this situation.

The same court had to assess a similar issue in the *SRYYY* case with respect to the application of the Rome Statute for the situation of a Sri Lankan applicant who served as a soldier in the Sri Lankan army between 1997 and 2000, against whom there were allegations that he was involved in the interrogation, assault, and torture of civilians, including children. The court concluded that the fact that the Rome Statute was not in place at the time did not bar the AAT from using it to define the crimes in question.[467] The court concluded that article 1F(a) was designed to recognize the continuing evolution of international law; thus, recourse to the most contemporary instrument was consistent

---

twelve treaties: the four 1949 Geneva Conventions and its two 1977 protocols, the Genocide Convention and the statutes of the IMT, the International Military Tribunal for Far East, ICTY, ICTR, and ICC; see Migration Regulations 1994, s 2.03B.

465 The cases of *SHCB v Minister for Immigration and Multicultural and Indigenous Affairs*, [2003] FCA 229; *SZCWP v Minister for Immigration and Multicultural and Indigenous Affairs*, [2006] FCAFC 9; *SRYYY*, above note 41; *SZITR v Minister for Immigration and Multicultural Affairs*, [2006] FCA 1759; *GZCK and Minister for Home Affairs (Migration)*, [2019] AATA 656, which also referred to the ICC, *Elements of Crimes* document, above note 153, as did the Federal Court in the appeal decision; see *GZCK v Minister for Home Affairs*, [2021] FCA 1618.

466 The cases of *SRYYY*, above note 41, and *VWYJ*, above note 41.

467 The AAT had come to the same conclusion in 2000 in *SRNN and Department of Immigration and Multicultural Affairs*, [2000] AATA 983; for a commentary on the *SRYYY* case, see Catherine Drummond, "Different Sources of International Criminal Law and Exclusion: How the Federal Court of Australia Got It Wrong and Why It Matters in *SRYYY v Minister for Immigration and Multicultural and Indigenous Affairs*" (2013) 3 *Oxford Monitor of Forced Migration* at 35–42.

with that purpose, and as such, the Rome Statute was the most relevant current instrument.[468]

The FCAFC in the *SRYYY* decision provided context for the concepts of war crimes and crimes against humanity. While examining the historical development of these two crimes, the court found that the definitions of the crimes in article 1F(a) were different in the various international instruments and that, as a result, it was difficult to apply article 1F(a). The court gave the example that in early international instruments, there was a requirement that a crime against humanity be committed in the context of an armed conflict, a requirement that was no longer followed in the ICTY caselaw, citing the *Tadić* case. A further example was that, more recently, war crimes were considered to include acts committed during both international and internal armed conflicts, again by referring to *Tadić*.

With respect to war crimes, a tribunal was of the view, without the analysis conducted in the United Kingdom, that a "concerted lengthy and coordinated campaign led by the Oodua Peoples Congress (OPC) from at least 1996 to 2003 and beyond that time, albeit to a lesser extent, involved an ongoing sequence of large-scale rallies and protests and the sophisticated monitoring of the army and the Nigerian police force, often involving violence," amounted to a non-international armed conflict as it did not fall within situations of internal disturbances and tension, which are the exceptions to non-international armed conflicts in articles 8.2(d) and (f) of the Rome Statute, but was in the nature of protracted armed conflict between governmental authorities and organized armed groups as set out in articles 8.2(c) and (e) of the same statute.[469]

In an application of the parameters of crimes against humanity, the AAT examined the situation of a claimant who had been a prison officer at the Pul-e-Charkhi Prison in Kabul, Afghanistan, between 1981 and 1988. The main part of Pul-e-Charkhi Prison was run as an ordinary prison by officers who were employed as police officers by the Ministry

468 The *SZITR v Minister for Immigration and Multicultural Affairs*, [2006] FCA 1759, which is the continuation of the same case as the *SRYYY* decision, above note 41, after the FCAFC had remitted the case back to the AAT for further consideration and of which, again, judicial review was sought, came to the same conclusion as the FCAFC but also noted that the Australian *International Criminal Court Act* of 2002 had as its objective the fulfillment of its obligations under the Rome Statute, which was of the type referred to in art 1F(a).

469 *Adekoya and Minister for Immigration and Border Protection (Migration)*, [2017] AATA 2028 at para 66.

of the Interior. The inmates of this section of Pul-e-Charkhi Prison were sentenced prisoners who comprised both ordinary criminals and those convicted of terrorism, sabotage, and other crimes against the government.[470] KhAD, the state intelligence service, ran a separate area of the prison, but the claimant had no contact with that part. The AAT was of the view that no crimes against humanity were committed in this prison as "the appalling conditions at the prison were not so much part of a systematic process of degradation of prisoners involving the applicant and others but were more probably the product of the generally primitive conditions one might expect in an impoverished country after years of war and internecine bloodshed."[471]

The FCAFC had been called in the *SZCWP* case[472] to determine whether police officers could be considered a civilian population in the context of crimes against humanity. The majority of the court found that the finding of the AAT that the attacks had been against civilians was correct because the police, as non-military actors, were considered civilian, and as such, the group had engaged in both war crimes and crimes against humanity and the applicant had been properly excluded.

With respect to the underlying crimes, most decisions have dealt with the crimes of murder or torture without making any further comments.[473] However, in 2006, the Federal Court of Australia in the case of *SZITR* examined the elements of the crime of torture as a crime against humanity in the context of Sri Lanka.[474] The AAT had assessed the conduct of the accused using the five elements of torture (severe pain, the custody or control of the victim, unlawful sanction, part of a widespread attack against the civilian population, and knowledge on the part of the accused of the conduct forming part of the attack) as defined in the ICC *Elements of Crimes* document. The tribunal had said that legal control over the detainee was not necessary but that the test for control required that in practical terms the victim was at the mercy of the accused. The court

470 *WAV and Minister for Immigration and Multicultural Affairs*, [2002] AATA 463 at para 42.

471 *Ibid.*

472 *SZCWP v Minister for Immigration & Multicultural & Indigenous Affairs*, [2006] FCAFC 9.

473 There is some discussion of a number of underlying crimes amounting to war crimes in the minority judgment of *SZCWP v Minister for Immigration & Multicultural & Indigenous Affairs*, [2006] FCAFC 9.

474 The RRT had also examined the crime of torture in 1995 in the case of V94/01334 [1995] RRTA 1626.

agreed. A court has also held that severe sleep deprivation can amount to torture but not beatings with a stick.[475]

At the AAT level, the actions by the Saddam Hussein regime against the Kurds during the Anfal campaign in northern Iraq between 1986 and 1989, resulting in massive killing of the population, the repression of the uprising by Shi'a Moslems after the 1991 Gulf War, and the draining of the marshes and the driving out of the Marsh Arabs in southern Iraq between 1991 and 1993, were considered crimes against humanity. In respect to the latter event, it was said that the Iraqi army was engaged in the drainage of the marshes and, in doing so, forced the inhabitants out of the marshes, resulting in the loss of their homeland.[476]

On the other hand, the same tribunal was of the view that crowd-dispersing techniques involving batons as used in Zimbabwe in 2002 did not amount to an underlying act for crimes against humanity. Nor did the 2005 Operation Murambatsvina, a campaign to demolish illegal dwellings and remove their inhabitants to various parts of the country. With respect to the latter activity, the tribunal was of the view (without giving an explanation) that none of the crimes against humanity of deportation, forcible transfer, or inhumane acts were engaged.[477]

An earlier decision by the predecessor tribunal, the RRT, had concluded that a street gang in Turkey, which frequently engaged in premeditated and savage assaults on Kurds as members of a particular racial group, had committed crimes against humanity.[478]

The Australian courts and tribunals have been fairly successful in applying international criminal law to the situations before them, especially in using the international elements of crimes against humanity, the crime most often considered. While the federal court has lamented the fact that the requirements of the international aspects of the international crimes have changed over time, this has not affected the use of international criminal law in a consistent manner. Still, with respect to the international elements of crimes against humanity, when the court had been called upon to go to determine the parameters of civilian population, it showed no hesitation to include police officers within that category. It anticipated international criminal law where the same solution was found by the SCSL in 2009, thereby showing that the

---

475 *GZCK v Minister for Home Affairs*, [2021] FCA 1618.

476 *SAH and Minister for Immigration and Multicultural and Indigenous Affairs*, [2002] AATA 263.

477 *WBV and Minister for Immigration and Citizenship*, [2007] AATA 2046.

478 V96/04174, [1997] RRTA 2507.

judges in Australia had the same innate sense of the concept of civilian population.

This positive assessment of the Australian jurisprudence with respect to the overarching elements of crimes against humanity cannot be extended to the specific crimes, which are part of crimes against humanity. While the federal court was of the view that a narrow approach for the element of control for the ICC crime of torture, namely, legal control, was not desirable, this forward thinking has not been followed consistently at the tribunal level. The fact that removing people from places of inhabitation amounted to the crime against humanity of forcible transfer in the situation of Iraq but not in Zimbabwe appears to be inconsistent on the surface. The latter case could have benefited from a more in-depth analysis, especially since that case was decided in 2007, at a time when international jurisprudence was available on that point. However, it is clear that for tribunals and courts, which only examine international crimes on an infrequent basis, it is difficult to go beyond the most basic international criminal law documentation and jurisprudence.

b) Belgium[479]

The Office of the Commissioner General for Refugees and Stateless Persons (CGRS) or Commissariat général aux réfugiés et aux apatrides (CGRA)[480] has been the central body responsible for the adjudication of asylum claims since 1988. Appeals can be taken to the Aliens Litigation Council (Conseil du Contentieux des Etrangers or CCE)[481] with a final appeal to the Council of State (Conseil d'État or CE).[482]

The issue of internal armed conflict was discussed in one case in the context of the Qualification Directive, an instrument that sets out a uniform approach for members of the European Union in providing

---

479 Section 55/4 of the *Aliens Act* sets out the exclusion provisions.

480 In Dutch, it is called Commissariaat-generaal voor de Vluchtelingen en de Staatlozen (CGVS).

481 In Dutch, it is called the Raad voor Vreemdelingenbetwistingen or RvV. This is as of 1 June 2007. Before that date, the appeal body was known as the Permanent Refugee Appeals Commission (Commission permanente de recours des réfugiés or CPRR/Vaste Beroepscommissie or VBC).

482 See *AIDA Country Report: Belgium, Asylum Procedure, List of Authorities Intervening in Each State of the Procedure*; see, also, Jean-Yves Carlier & Dirk Vanheule, "Where Is the Reference? On the Limited Role of Transnational Dialogue in Belgian Refugee Law" in Guy G. Goodwin-Gill & Hélène Lambert, eds, *The Limits of Transnational Law, Refugee Law, Policy Harmonization and the Judicial Dialogue in the European Union* (Cambridge: Cambridge University Press, 2010) at 17–24.

persons with subsidiary protection when they do not qualify for refugee protection. While article 12.2(a) of the directive excludes people who have committed crimes against peace, war crimes, or crimes against humanity, the discussion of what amounts to an internal armed conflict has taken place in regard to article 15(c), which provides subsidiary protection as a result of indiscriminate violence in situations of international or internal armed conflict.

The Aliens Litigation Council defined internal armed conflict by reference to article 1 of the 1977 Protocol II to the 1949 Geneva Conventions. The protocol defines non-international armed conflicts as those taking place on the territory of a state party "between its armed forces and dissident armed forces or other organized armed groups which, under responsible command, exercise such control over a part of its territory as to enable them to carry out sustained and concerted military operations." This "shall not apply to situations of internal disturbances and tensions, such as riots, isolated and sporadic acts of violence and other acts of a similar nature, as not being armed conflicts."[483] The tribunal came to the conclusion that this threshold had not been met in the Ivory Coast in the fall of 2006[484] or in Lebanon in the 1980s[485] but was present in Burundi in 2008.[486] It also provided guidance with respect to the issue of civilian population and civilian objects. The case was concerned with a person involved in the training of several security forces belonging to the Fatah organization in Gaza, which were involved in a power struggle with groups belonging to Hamas. The evidence showed that these security organizations were involved in a systematic manner in the torture or killing of persons who had no connection with Hamas and, as such, could be considered civilians, as set out in the Rome Statute. The tribunal was also of the view that the power struggle between these two groups amounted to a non-international armed conflict resulting in the commission of war crimes such as extrajudicial

---

483 CCE Case No 3380, 31 October 2007 at para 4.8. The Swedish Migration Court of Appeal in 2007 used the same source to conclude that there was no internal armed conflict in Iraq; see UNHCR, *Asylum in the European Union: A Study of the Implementation of the Qualification Directive* (November 2007) at 77–78, online (pdf): www.unhcr.org/protection/operations/47302b6c2/asylum-european-union-study-implementation-qualification-directive-2007.html, and Correspondent's Report, Sweden (2009) 12 *Yearbook of International Humanitarian Law* at 644–46.

484 CCE No 3380, 31 October 2007 at para 4.9.

485 CCE No 37.011, 14 January 2010 at para 2.17.

486 CCE No 17.522, 23 October 2008 at para 4.14; see, also, Correspondent's Report, Belgium (2009) 12 *Yearbook of International Humanitarian Law* at 486–87.

killing of fighters who have laid down their weapons, the killing of such fighters in hospitals, carrying out torture, and using civilian objects for military purposes in violation of article 3 of the Geneva Conventions and article 8 of the Rome Statute.[487]

In general, the concept of crimes against humanity has been applied in Belgium to situations where crimes were committed in the context of a policy aimed at terrorizing a population and obstructing the process of democratization and the free expression of opinions by systematic use of violence, torture, and executions.[488] In older cases, crimes against humanity were usually identified by reference to the *Charter* of the IMT,[489] but more recently the Rome Statute has become the preferred source.[490] In older cases, the following acts had been determined to be underlying crimes for crimes against humanity: fundamental inhumane conduct, such as slavery, torture, assassination, or persecution of population groups targeted for religious, racial, or political motives; the execution of prisoners and hostages, both civilian and military; and activities within secret services, including the kidnapping, torture, and execution of opponents.[491]

Belgium is one of the few countries where the concept of crimes against peace has been applied. This occurred in a case involving a person who was one of five members of the Politburo of the ruling party in Somalia during the Barre government between 1969 and 1991. As such, he was involved in all important policy decisions of this regime. One of these decisions was the aggression against Ethiopia over the control of the Ogaden region in 1982, in which this person was involved while also being responsible specifically for the purchase of military material in preparation for this armed conflict. The tribunal relied on the *Charter* of the IMT and its judgment in deciding that the prohibition against aggression had entered the realm of customary international law. As to the factual underpinnings of the decision, the tribunal referred to the international condemnation of Somalia for initiating the war against Ethiopia.[492]

487 CCE No 80.570, 2 May 2012 at para. 2.1.4.2.

488 Kapferer, above note 35 at 198.

489 *Ibid.*

490 CE No 184.647, 24 June 2008; CE No 186.913, 8 October 2008; CCE No 49.298, 10 October 2010; see, most recently, CCE No 264.267, 25 November 2021; CCE No 265.735, 16 December 2021.

491 Kapferer, above note 35 at 198.

492 CPRR No 99-1280/W7769, 6 August 2002 at para 4.2.4.

In the same caase the concept of war crimes was introduced in the context of an internal armed conflict, in this case one between the government of Somalia and rebel groups in northern Somalia from 1988 to 1990. The tribunal makes it clear that while the reasons and justification for the armed conflict are obscure, and while international humanitarian law allows certain types of violence, the bombardment of refugees trying to flee the conflict zones; the killing of non-combatants, such as women, children, and old men; and the destruction of water reservoirs all amount to war crimes.[493] Along the same lines, while being members of a commando unit in the Afghani army and involved in daily raids, not distinguishing civilians from Taliban fighters during those raids amounted to a war crime, in violation of articles 8(2)(e)(i) and (xii) of the Rome Statute.[494] Last, with respect to underlying crimes, the forcible recruitment of children was found to be a war crime with a reference to the Rome Statute.[495]

c) Canada[496]

Refugee determinations, including assessments regarding exclusion, are made by an administrative tribunal called the Refugee Protection Division (RPD)[497] of the Immigration and Refugee Board. Judicial review can be sought at the Federal Court,[498] with an appeal to the Federal Court of Appeal and then the Supreme Court of Canada.[499]

The question of the retroactivity of the provisions of the Rome Statute, which was negotiated in 1998 and came into force in 2002, been dealt with by the Federal Court of Appeal in 2003, which made it clear that

493 *Ibid* at para 4.2.3.

494 CCE No 228260, 30 October 2019.

495 CCE No 150.989, 18 August 2015.

496 Section 98 of *the Immigration and Refugee Protection Act*, SC 2001, c 27, refers to art 1F of the 1951 Refugee Convention.

497 The Convention Refugee Determination Division or CRDD, before 2002.

498 Federal Court, Trial Division, before 2003.

499 Before 1995, the Federal Court of Appeal sat also in direct appeal of decisions of the Immigration and Refugee Board. The interpretation of 1F(a)-related concepts has increasingly been taking place outside the refugee context and instead in the immigration context, where an equivalent provision to 1F(a), s 35(1)(a) of the *Immigration and Refugee Protection Act*, has become more prevalent (see Joseph Rikhof, "Update on Exclusion and Inadmissibility Jurisprudence: New Developments Since the Decisions of the Supreme Court of Canada in Ezokola and Febles," Canadian Association for Refugee and Forced Migration Studies (CARFMS/ACERMF) Working Paper No 2017/2, April 2017 [at 11–14], online (pdf): https://carfms.org/wp-content/uploads/2017/04/CARFMS-WPS-No10-Joseph-Rikhof.pdf). Both types of jurisprudence will be considered.

this document can be used for situations before its adoption as it reflects international law from before 1998.[500] More recently, a court determined that torture is a crime against humanity, as set out in the Rome Statute, and that this concept can be applied before the Rome Statute became part of Canadian law because torture as such a crime had already been recognized in international law long before the Rome Statute.[501]

With respect to the parameters of international crimes, the Supreme Court of Canada issued a significant decision in 2005 in the context of the case of a person who had made an inflammatory speech in 1992 in Rwanda, exhorting Hutus to kill Tutsis.[502] The Court followed closely the international jurisprudence of the ICTY and the ICTR by indicating that crimes against humanity consist of four essential elements: the commission of one of the enumerated proscribed acts; the act is committed as part of a widespread or systematic attack; the attack is directed against any civilian population or any identifiable group; and the accused must have knowledge of the attack and must know that their acts comprise part of it or take the risk that their acts will comprise part of it.[503] The civilian population must be the primary object of the attack, not merely a collateral victim of it, and the attack must be directed against a relatively large group of people who share distinctive features, which identify them as targets of the attack.[504]

---

500 *Harb v Canada (Minister of Citizenship and Immigration)*, 2003 FCA 39. The Federal Court has been more ambiguous in taking this position in that *Ventocilla v Canada (Citizenship and Immigration)*, 2007 FC 575 did not apply this reasoning for war crimes, while the *Carrasco v Canada (Minister of Citizenship and Immigration)*, 2008 FC 436 followed *Harb* for crimes against humanity. More recently, the Federal Court indicated that in the context of immigration inadmissibility, all overarching aspects of the Rome Statute, including the policy element for state and other organizations, were part of immigration law, see *Canada (Public Safety and Emergency Preparedness) v Verbanov*, 2021 FC 507.

501 *Elve v Canada (Citizenship and Immigration)*, 2020 FC 454.

502 *Mugesera*, above note 38.

503 *Ibid* at paras 128 and 173; it provides more details of these elements at paras 153–58. There have been cases where an exclusion finding by the tribunal was overruled by the court because of a lack of analysis with respect to crimes against humanity, such as in *Tilus v Canada (Minister of Citizenship and Immigration)*, 2005 FC 1738, and *Ruiz Blanco v Canada (Minister of Citizenship and Immigration)*, 2006 FC 623.

504 *Mugesera*, above note 38 at paras 161–62. The Court clarified some confusion in earlier jurisprudence with respect to the general notion of crimes against humanity, where it corrected its earlier decision in *Finta*, above note 129, a criminal case (which had said that the main element of the crime against humanity was the additional component of barbaric cruelty), while it did the same indirectly with the Federal Court of Appeal case of *Equizabal v Canada (Minister of Employment and Immigration)* (CA), [1994] 3 FC 514, which relied on the *Finta* case.

On three occasions since this decision, the Federal Court has made it clear that prisoners convicted of regular crimes are included in the notion of civilian population.[505] As well, the Federal Court of Appeal has rejected the argument that proof is required of specific instances of the victimization of persons belonging to the civilian population but instead indicated that documentary information as to what generally happens to such persons is sufficient.[506] In the Canadian context, war crimes have been addressed only sporadically and then only with the observation that war crimes in internal armed conflicts were not part of international criminal law before 1990.[507] In one case, the forcible recruitment of children was determined to be a war crime, while saying "[T]he *actus reus* of the particular war crime in question is that of participating in conscripting child soldiers to participate in hostilities. It does not require the use of intimidation or force to conscript the children, merely the act of participating in a voluntary conscription program meets the requirements to be a war crime."[508]

Crimes against peace or aggression were addressed by the Federal Court, not in the context of exclusion but rather in a decision dealing with an American soldier who had deserted the US army because he did not want to fight in Iraq, on the basis that the 2003 invasion of Iraq was an act of aggression. The court concluded in the *Hinzman* case,[509] relying on UK jurisprudence, that the notion of acts that have received

505 *Carrasco v Canada (Minister of Citizenship and Immigration)*, 2008 FC 436; *Liqokeli v Canada (Citizenship and Immigration)*, 2009 FC 530; and *Khachatryan v Canada (Citizenship and Immigration)*, 2020 FC 167.

506 *Sumaida v Canada*, [2000] 3 FC 66, and *Pushpanathan v Canada (Minister of Citizenship and Immigration)*, 2002 FCT 867.

507 By the Federal Court in the cases of *Bermudez v Canada (Minister of Citizenship and Immigration)*, 2005 FC 286, for the situation in Honduras in 1989 and *Ventocilla v Canada (Citizenship and Immigration)*, 2007 FC 575, for a situation in Peru between 1985 and 1992, while passing in *Howbott v Canada (Citizenship and Immigration)*, 2007 FC 911, for Liberia between 1995 and 2003 and *Bonilla v Canada (Citizenship and Immigration)*, 2009 FC 881, for Colombia between 1984 and 1993. An earlier Federal Court of Appeal decision, *Gonzalez v Canada (Minister of Employment and Immigration)* (CA), [1994] 3 FC 646 at para 24, had said in the context of war crimes where an asylum seeker as a member of the Nicaraguan army had been involved in a battle with a Contra unit, as a result of which three peasant women and six children were killed along with about ten Contras, that this action was not culpable as "[t]ragic and appalling as its inevitable result, what the applicant admitted to was participation in a military action that does not reach the concepts of war crime or crime against humanity. It was war, not war crime."

508 *Kamanzi v Canada (Citizenship and Immigration)*, 2013 FC 1261.

509 *Hinzman v Canada (Minister of Citizenship and Immigration)*, 2006 FC 420.

condemnation by the international community as contrary to basic rules of human conduct (which is the threshold for conscientious objectors to meet) is equivalent to the conduct prescribed in article 1F(a). The court was of the view that crimes against peace, as established by the *Charter* of the IMT, were considered as leadership crimes,[510] and since Hinzman was a foot soldier, he could not have committed such a crime.

d) France[511]

Asylum decisions are made by the French Office for the Protection of Refugees and Stateless Persons (Office Français de Protection des Réfugiés et Apatrides, OFPRA) with an appeal to the National Court of Asylum (Cour Nationale du Droit d'Asile, CNDA), from which a final appeal lies to the Council of State (Conseil d'État).[512]

There have only been a few decisions in France addressing the characteristics of war crimes or crimes against humanity. With respect to war crimes, a 2006 case at the commission level relied on the definitions of war crimes in the statutes of both the IMT and the ICTY to provide context for this notion as it pertained to the 1999 conflict in Kosovo.[513]

The same authority, in the context of article 15(c) of the Qualification Directive, equated the parameters of non-international armed conflict with the description for such a conflict set out in common article 3 of the Geneva Conventions and found that the situation in Darfur corresponded to a non-international armed conflict.[514] This approach of referring to international humanitarian law has not been followed since 2005.[515] More recently, the Rome Statute has become the source

---

510 *Ibid* at paras 141–42 and 155–60.

511 Section 511-6 of the *Code for Entry and Residence of Foreigners and Right of Asylum* (*CESEDA*) refers to the 1951 Refugee Convention while using forms of extended liability as set out in the Qualification Directive, while s 512-2 incorporates the exceptions to subsidiary protection from the Qualification Directive.

512 See *AIDA Country Report: France, Asylum Procedure, List of Authorities Intervening in Each State of the Procedure* (8 April 2022), online: https://asylumineurope.org/reports/country/france/asylum-procedure/general/list-authorities-intervening-each-stage-procedure; see, also, Hélène Lambert & Janine Silga, "Transnational Refugee Law in the French Courts: Deliberate or Compelled Change in Judicial Attitudes?" in Goodwin-Gill & Lambert, above note 482 at 37–41. Before 2007, the National Court of Asylum was called the Refugee Appeal Commission (Commission des Recours des Réfugiés, CRR).

513 CRR, 18 May 2006, 548090, Kurta.

514 CRR, 22 November 2005, 538807, A; CNDA, 1 September 2010, 09016633.

515 CRR, 10 July 2007, 596407, Mlle S; CRR, 16 March 2007, 581135, M; CNDA, 27 June 2008, 581505, B; CNDA, 24 April 2009, 625816, G; and CNDA, 9 June 2009, 639474, H.

to determine the parameters of international crimes,[516] especially in the context of the war crime of child recruitment.[517]

With respect to crimes against humanity, the characteristics of this crime were described by the Council of State in 1996 as acts that were part of a coherent whole and a series of repeated acts inspired by a political, racial, or cultural motive.[518]

Regarding underlying crimes, in addition to child recruitment, human trafficking was also seen as an excludable offence,[519] which mirrors the fact that this crime was recognized as a crime against humanity by the drafters of the Rome Statute.[520]

e) Germany[521]

The office in charge of making refugee decisions is the Federal Office for Migration and Refugees (Bundesamt für Migration and Flüchtlinge, BAMF). There are three avenues for appeal: to the state Administrative Court (Verwaltungsgerichtshof), the state Higher Administrative Court (Oberverwaltungsgerichtshof), and, finally, the Federal Administrative Court (Bundesverwaltungsgericht).[522]

With respect to the issue of war crimes, the Federal Administrative Court, like the courts in Belgium, France, and the United Kingdom, had to decide whether article 15(c) of the Qualification Directive, which refers to international or internal armed conflicts, should be construed with a reference to international humanitarian law. In a decision

516 CNDA, 5 July 2019, 17040984.

517 CNDA, 29 April 2013, 12018386, MG, while also referring to Additional Protocol II, art 4(3)(c), as well as CNDA, 28 July 2016, 16011229, with respect to Sri Lanka and CNDA, 1 February 2017, 16027532, MT regarding Chad.

518 Kapferer, above note 35 at 198.

519 CNDA, 30 August 2019, MA, 18052314, for a situation in Nigeria.

520 See the ICC *Elements of Crimes* document, above note 153, connected to the Rome Statute, at 8, under the crime against humanity of sexual slavery, n18, which states: "It is also understood that the conduct described in this element includes trafficking in persons, in particular women and children." See, also, Idil Atak & James C. Simeon, "Human Trafficking: Mapping the Legal Boundaries of International Refugee Law and Criminal Justice" (2014) 12:5 *Journal of International Criminal Justice* 1019–38.

521 *Asylum Act*, s 3(2) sets out the exclusion provisions.

522 *AIDA Country Report: Germany, Asylum Procedure, List of Authorities Intervening in Each State of the Procedure* (21 April 2022), online: https://asylumineurope.org/reports/country/germany/asylum-procedure/general/list-authorities-intervening-each-stage-procedure; see, also, Paul Tiedemann, "The Use of Foreign Asylum Procedure in the German Administrative Court" in Goodwin-Gill & Lambert, above note 482 at 57–62.

rendered in 2008, it was of the view that this should be the correct manner of interpreting this article, and in doing so, it relied on the Geneva Conventions and their protocols, ICTY jurisprudence, and UK tribunal decisions.[523] It also indicated, relying on these authorities, that an internal armed conflict can occur in part of a country as opposed to a nationwide situation of conflict and, as a result, came to the conclusion that there was such a conflict in Iraq.[524] The same conclusion was reached for the situation in Afghanistan.[525] The Federal Administrative Court followed the same interpretative approach, relying on the same international materials as well as the Rome Statute a year later when giving a general meaning to the terms "war crimes"[526] and "crimes against humanity," pursuant to article 1F(a).[527]

The same court addressed the issue of internal armed conflict in the context of Afghanistan again in 2010,[528] where it was faced with an argument that its earlier decision should be adjusted in view of the developing UK trend in jurisprudence to seek the meaning of what constitutes such a conflict outside international humanitarian and criminal law. The judges were of the view that there is no principal reason for them to digress from their original point of view, despite a change of heart in the United Kingdom,[529] but do acknowledge that since the purpose of article 15(c) is different than the underlying reasons for international humanitarian law, there can be situations in 15(c) that are not covered by humanitarian law. This can be the case, especially in situations where the requirements of intensity of the conflict or the organization of the parties to the conflict, both of which are hallmarks

---

523 Bundesverwaltungsgericht (Federal Administrative Court), BverwG 10 C 43.07, 24 June 2008 at paras 19–24.

524 *Ibid* at para 26; the same conclusion was reached in Bundesverwaltungsgericht (Federal Administrative Court), BverwG 10 C 4.09, 27 April 2010 at para 25; it rejected the proposition that such a conflict existed in the whole of Iraq in the cases of Bundesverwaltungsgericht (Federal Administrative Court), BverwG 10 C 42.07, 24 June 2008 at para 4; Bundesverwaltungsgericht (Federal Administrative Court), BverwG 10 C 44.07, 24 June 2008 at para 4; and Bundesverwaltungsgericht (Federal Administrative Court), BverwG 10 C 45.07, 24 June 2008.

525 Bundesverwaltungsgericht (Federal Administrative Court), BverwG 10 C 9.08, 14 July 2009 at para 17.

526 Bundesverwaltungsgericht (Federal Administrative Court, Germany), 10 C 24.08, 24 November 2009 at paras 32–34.

527 *Ibid* at para 39.

528 Bundesverwaltungsgericht (Federal Administrative Court), BVerwG 10 C 4.09, 27 April 2010.

529 *Ibid* at para 22.

of protracted violence required to meet the international humanitarian or criminal law threshold of internal conflict, are not met.[530]

This issue was laid to rest in 2014 when the CJEU wrote:

> The answer to the question referred is that, on a proper construction of Article 15(c) of Directive 2004/83, it must be acknowledged that an internal armed conflict exists, for the purposes of applying that provision, if a State's armed forces confront one or more armed groups or if two or more armed groups confront each other. It is not necessary for that conflict to be categorised as "armed conflict not of an international character" under international humanitarian law; nor is it necessary to carry out, in addition to an appraisal of the level of violence present in the territory concerned, a separate assessment of the intensity of the armed confrontations, the level of organisation of the armed forces involved or the duration of the conflict.[531]

In terms of the notions of war crimes and crimes against humanity, the Federal Administrative Court felt that a connection should be sought with the definitions set out in the Rome Statute, which meant that crimes against humanity are crimes carried out in a sustained, systematic attack against civilians.[532]

This same court has made some findings that expand on the nature of war crimes in general and, with respect to one specific war crime, treacherous killing in the context of exclusion. The situation involved a person who "had shot to death two people in Chechnya and taken a Russian officer prisoner to obtain through an exchange the release of his brother, who had been taken captive in a 'cleanup' operation."[533] After a finding that the situation in Chechnya amounted to an internal armed conflict along the lines of the Rome Statute, the court then relied on ICTY and ICTR jurisprudence to opine that both civilians and combatants can commit war crimes.[534] In order to hold a person liable for war crimes, a nexus needs to be shown between the acts and the armed conflict, or, according to the court, "the existence of an armed

530 *Ibid* at para 23.

531 *Aboubacar Diakité v Commissaire général aux réfugiés et aux apatrides*, C-285/12, 30 January 2014 at para 35

532 Bundesverwaltungsgericht (Federal Administrative Court), BverwG 10 C 2.10, 31 March 2011 at para 28.

533 Bundesverwaltungsgericht (Federal Administrative Court), BverwG 10 C 7.09, 10 February 2010 at para 2.

534 *Ibid* at paras 26–31.

conflict must be of material significance to the actor's ability to commit the crime, his decision to commit the act, the manner in which it was committed, or the purpose of the act." This was found to exist in the present case.[535]

The court proceeded with a detailed examination of the contours of the war crime of killing or wounding treacherously, which is contained in the Rome Statute but has not yet received judicial consideration by the ICC,[536] and indicated that, in general, "not every misleading of an adversary is prohibited, but rather only the exploitation of a confidence obtained under false pretenses through specific acts contrary to international law."[537] Even in an internal armed conflict where there is no obligation to wear a uniform, "combatants do not violate the prohibition on perfidy if they carry their arms openly during each military engagement, including during the preparation of attacks. This assessment must also be considered in the application of the prohibition of perfidy in an internal armed conflict."[538] It concluded that this crime might have been committed since

> carrying a concealed weapon might have deceived the Russian soldiers that they need expect no attack from the resistance fighter and the Complainant working with him, and that therefore they were not allowed to attack the two of them. The fact that the soldiers extended confidence to the Complainant and his companion could possibly be deduced from the fact that according to the Complainant, the soldiers had turned their backs as they were struck by the shots.[539]

As this finding and its underlying reasoning represent a good understanding of international humanitarian and criminal law, other decision makers, at both the national and the international level, when dealing with this specific crime, might very well benefit from using this judgment in developing their own understanding of this war crime. As a matter of fact, this reasoning was persuasive enough that the prosecutor of the ICC used this judgment in one report when assessing the parameters of this particular war crime.[540]

---

535 *Ibid* at paras 32–33.
536 *Ibid* at paras 37–41.
537 *Ibid* at para 39.
538 *Ibid* at para 40.
539 *Ibid* at para 41.
540 *Situation in the Republic of Korea, Article 5 Report*, ICC OTP, June 2014 at para 50.

f) The Netherlands

The Immigration and Naturalisation Service (Immigratie en Naturalisatiedienst, IND) is the decision maker for refugee claims in the Netherlands.[541] Appeals can be made to the District Court (Rechtbank, Rb), with a further appeal to the Administrative Jurisdiction Division of the Council of State (Afdeling Bestuursrechtspraak, Raad van State, AbRS).[542]

Only the notion of crimes against peace is briefly described in the *Aliens Manual* by saying that such a crime can be used against the highest civilian or military authorities in a country and that the seriousness of the crime is determined by the nature and the seriousness of the consequences of the act in question.[543]

According to the jurisprudence, the Rome Statute can be used for activities that occurred before the coming into force of this instrument.[544] There have been three decisions by a Dutch court that examined the issue of war crimes in an international armed conflict. The first situation dealt with an oil tanker sailing in 1986 under the Liberian flag, but for and from Iran, during the Iran-Iraq war, which was attacked by a rocket launched from a helicopter on which the person concerned had been a navigation officer. The District Court was of the view that such an attack did not amount to a violation of international humanitarian law pursuant to articles 67 and 85 of Protocol I, nor a war crime pursuant to article 147 of Geneva Convention IV or article 8 of the Rome Statute, as the ship was not a civilian object. This was based on the consideration of the court that while the crew of the ship was civilian, and it was attacked without specific warning (which could lead, in general, to a possible conclusion of war crimes), in this specific situation the ship was, as part of an oil-export system, in the exclusive service for

541 Section 29(1)(a) of the *Aliens Act* 2000 refers to the 1951 Refugee Convention; for a historical background of the exclusion provisions, see Zarif Yakut-Bahtiyar, *Exclusion Clauses of the Refugee Convention in Relation to National Immigration Legislations, European Policy and Human Rights Instruments: Article 1F Versus the Non-refoulement Principle* (Nijmegen: Wolf Legal Publishers, 2016) at 149–57.

542 See *AIDA Country Report: The Netherlands, Asylum Procedure, List of Authorities Intervening in Each State of the Procedure*, online: https://asylumineurope.org/reports/country/netherlands/asylum-procedure/general/list-authorities-intervening-each-stage-procedure.

543 *Vreemdelingencirculaire* 2000 (C), art C2/7.10.2.1; in a previous version of this document, the reference to crimes against peace was more elaborate; see *Vreemdelingencirculaire* 2000 (C), art C4/3.11.3.2.

544 AbRS, 18 April 2005, nr 200408765/1, and Rb, The Hague, Awb 10/28846, 23 June 2011.

the Iranian government, one of the parties to an international armed conflict. As well, Iraq had announced an exclusion zone in the waters where the ship was travelling, amounting to a more general warning to the crew and the ship, which had been subject to attacks before, leading to the conclusion that it had some warning of Iraq's intention.[545] It would appear that this appreciation of what constitutes a non-civilian object might have been construed too narrowly, as IHL[546] and ICTY jurisprudence require in that context that military objectives are limited to those objects that, by their nature, location, purpose, or use, make an effective contribution to military action and whose total or partial destruction, capture, or neutralization, in the circumstances ruling at the time, offers a definite military advantage.[547]

Second, the armed conflict between Israel and Hezbollah on the territory of Lebanon in July and August 2006 was considered twice by a Dutch District Court to be an international armed conflict, although it relied on a conclusion in a 2006 report of the United Nations Human Rights Council for this determination rather than doing its own analysis.[548]

The Council of State indicated that with respect to non-international armed conflicts, the factors set out in article 1 of Protocol II regarding the organization of the parties to the conflict and the ability to control territory must be present. As well, in its view, it is possible, pursuant to common article 3 of the Geneva Conventions, in conjunction with article 4 of Geneva Convention IV, which deals with the protection of civilians during occupation, that occupation can occur in a non-international armed conflict setting. However, in the case before it, the Council of State held that the requirements for occupation were not fulfilled in the situation of armed clashes between the Kurdistan Workers' Party (PKK) and the Turkish government in southeast Turkey between 1995 and 1998, but they should be characterized as acts of war. Activities set out in article 13(2) of Protocol II, which states that "acts or threats of violence the primary purpose of which is to spread terror among the civilian population are prohibited" are to be considered war crimes.[549]

---

545 Rb, Den Bosch, Awb 10/32882, 14 November 2011.

546 Geneva Convention IV, art 52(2), as well as the *San Remo Manual on International Law Applicable to Armed Conflicts at Sea*, art 67.

547 *Blaškić* (IT-95-14), Trial Chamber Judgment, 3 March 2000 at para 180; *Strugar* (IT-IT-01-42T), Trial Chamber Judgment, 31 January 2005 at para 282.

548 Rb, The Hague, Awb 16/12591, 18 August 2016, and Rb, The Hague, NL 18.10336, 7 November 2018.

549 AbRS, 23 July 2004, nr 200402639/1 and 200402651/1.

Following this reasoning, the Anfal campaign by the Iraqi government of Saddam Hussein against the Kurdish population in northern Iraq between 1986 and 1989 was considered to be an internal armed conflict during which war crimes were committed.[550] Similarly, the conflict between Maoist groups and the government of Nepal in 1998 was considered to be an internal armed conflict in which the ill-treatment of a village head by members of the Maoist groups was a war crime given that he was a civilian. The fact that, according to the claimant, this village head was a representative of an exploitative government against which armed attacks were directed was not relevant to the status as non-combatant of the victim, nor was the argument that village heads were not unarmed as they could invoke the assistance of the Nepalese army.[551]

According to the Council of State, it is clear with respect to crimes against humanity that, based on the Rome Statute and the ICTR case of *Akayesu*, such crimes must have been committed in a systematic or widespread fashion. There is no need for a great number of acts to consider the systematic nature of a crime against humanity as long as these acts have been repetitive.[552] Crimes against humanity can also be committed by non-governmental entities, which operate in an organized fashion as set out by the Rome Statute, article 7.2(d).[553]

Following the seminal decisions of the ICTR in *Akayesu* and the ICTY in *Tadić*, the Council of State was also of the view that the notion of a civilian population as victims of crimes against humanity stands in contrast to military personnel, and the term "population" is used to indicate the collective nature of the attack. There is no requirement that the attack is carried out against the entire population.[554] While genocide can be considered part of crimes against humanity, according to a Dutch commentator,[555] it is also a crime in itself.[556]

---

550 AbRS, 9 July 2004, nr 200401181/1; AbRS, 7 October 2010, nr 201006259/1/V1; AbRS, 14 December 2010, nr 200909884/1/V3. Dutch courts, including the Supreme Court of the Netherlands, are of the view that under Dutch law crimes committed during non-international armed conflicts between 1979 and 1989 are punishable as war crimes; see Joseph Rikhof, "Fewer Places to Hide? The Impact of Domestic War Crimes Prosecutions on International Impunity" (2009) 20 *Criminal Law Forum* 1 at 47–49.

551 Rb, The Hague, Awb 02/93493, 28 October 2004.

552 AbRS, 31 August 2005, nr 200502650/1; Rb, The Hague, Awb 09/40819, 9 April 2010.

553 Rb, The Hague, Awb 00/7608, 1 March 2004.

554 AbRS, 31 August 2005, nr 200502650/1.

555 Spijkerboer & Vermeulen, above note 74 at 99.

556 Rb, The Hague, Awb 10/4388, 23 December 2010.

With respect to the underlying crimes, most cases have dealt with crimes such as murder, torture, and inhumane acts. However, more recently, a Dutch court was called upon to determine the parameters of a war crime, in particular, the use of chemical weapons in Syria in 2012–14 during a non-international conflict. Without resort to international instruments or an analysis of the nature of the conflict (as this was agreed upon between the parties, and the only issue of discussion was whether the person in question had been complicit), the court concluded that the use of such weapons was a war crime because it had resulted in wilful killing, wilfully causing great suffering, or serious injury to body or health and intentionally directing attacks against the civilian population as such or against individual civilians not taking direct part in hostilities.[557] While the judgment is a bit inconsistent by using the text of the Rome Statute for the underlying crimes as it relates to both international and non-international armed conflict, while it determined that the conflict was non-international,[558] it should be commended for calling attention to the use of such weapons and their consequences in non-international armed conflicts when this had not yet been interpreted internationally.[559]

Along the same lines, a Dutch court also stipulated that the use of human shields amounted to a war crime in the armed conflict between Israel and Hezbollah on the territory of Lebanon during July and August 2006 without any further discussion.[560] This war crime cannot be found in the Rome Statute but has been seen as an example of the war crime of inhumane treatment[561] or was included in the war crime of child recruitment.[562] Last, again without any reference to international criminal law, another Dutch court found the director of a water supply company in Syria, who had withheld water from the population of cities under siege

557 Rb, The Hague, Awb 15/15728, 21 September 2015, upheld on appeal in AbRS, 24 June 2016, nr 201507522/1/V1.

558 Specifically, the reference to great suffering and serious injury comes from art 8(2)(a)(iii).

559 While the Rome Statute had the use of chemical weapons for international armed conflicts since its inception in 1998 in arts 8(2)(b)(xvii) and (xix), they are only added for non-international armed conflicts in 2010 as a result of UN Doc Resolution RC/Res 5, Annex I, "Amendments to Article 8 of the Rome Statute," adding arts 8(2)(e)(xiii) & (xiv).

560 Rb, The Hague, Awb 16/12591, 18 August 2016, and Rb, The Hague, NL 18.10336, 7 November 2018.

561 *Blaškić* (IT-95-14-A), Appeals Chamber Judgment, 29 July 2004 at para 155; *Prlić et al* (IT-04-74), Trial Chamber Judgment, 29 May 2013 at paras 117–18.

562 *Brima, Kamara and Kanu ("AFRC")* (SCSL-2004-16-T), Trial Chamber Judgment, 20 June 2007 at para 737.

by the Syrian army, was complicit in war crimes and crimes against humanity as the lack of water supply was part of a policy of starvation, an international crime.[563]

The Dutch courts have sought, from early on, a connection between exclusion and international humanitarian and criminal law in which the reliance on international criminal law in setting out the overarching elements of war crimes and crimes against humanity has been more successful than the use of international humanitarian law. The earlier decisions of the Council of State around war crimes, where non-international armed conflicts were based on the definition in Protocol II, might not have yielded a different result, but it would have been more persuasive if the jurisprudence of the ICTY had been utilized instead as Protocol II does not refer to war crimes. Plus, the way international criminal law has specified the requirements of a non-international armed conflict is broader than in international humanitarian law in that the control of a territory is not an essential element in the former area of law, resulting in the possibility of more situations being characterized as non-international armed conflict in exclusion situations.

On the other hand, the same judicial institution was prescient in finding that causing terror could amount to a war crime even without the benefit of the ICTY jurisprudence,[564] although its reasoning could have been improved upon by explaining why an international humanitarian law norm could be transformed into a crime with individual responsibility. The Dutch courts have also identified war crimes that have not been considered at the international level, such as the use of chemical weapons and human shields.

---

563 Rb, The Hague, Awb 16/22445, 6 February 2017; starvation is mentioned as a war crime in international armed conflicts in the Rome Statute in art 8(2)(b)(xxv), while for non-international armed conflicts, it is mentioned (since 6 December 2019 by virtue of UN Doc Resolution ICC-ASP/18/Res 5, "Resolution on amendments to article 8 of the Rome Statute of the International Criminal Court," Annex I) in art 8(2)(e)(xix). Incidentally, the deprivation of water has been seen as inhumane treatment, which can be both a war crime and a crime against humanity; see *Blaškić* (IT-95-14-A), Appeals Chamber Judgment, 29 July 2004 at para 155.

564 The case of *Galić* (IT-98-29-T), Trial Chamber Judgment, 5 December 2003 at paras 133–38, had set out the basis of this crime in customary international law and its elements almost eight months before the decision of the Council of State.

g) New Zealand[565]

As of 29 November 2010, the Immigration and Protection Tribunal (NZIPT) is the authority entrusted with making exclusion decisions.[566] Judicial review is possible at the High Court of New Zealand, with appeals coming before the Court of Appeal and the Supreme Court. There has been one Supreme Court and one Court of Appeal decision of relevance, as well as two judgments from the High Court of New Zealand.

At the court level, the first decision was the 1997 *Sequeiros Garate* case involving a policeman from Peru who was a member of an anti-terrorist squad in 1991–92.[567] He was responsible for the capture and interrogation of members of the Shining Path, a terrorist organization, and in that capacity, he arrested between thirty and forty suspected members and personally carried out acts of torture on several occasions. The court indicated that, based on the IMT and the Canadian case of *Sivakumar*,[568] crimes against humanity are inhumane acts against a civilian population carried out in a systematic or widespread manner.

The second High Court decision, *X & Y v Refugee Status Appeals Authority*,[569] involved the exclusion of a person who was the chief engineer of a ship owned by the Liberation Tigers of Tamil Eelam (LTTE) and sunk during a confrontation with the Indian navy in January 1993. At the time, it was carrying several LTTE members and substantial quantities of arms and explosives. It had also been found by the Refugee Status Appeals Authority (RSAA) that the LTTE had committed crimes against humanity. The court examined several issues related to exclusion and upheld the RSAA decision.[570] The Court of Appeal overturned this decision on 20 October 2009.[571] While most of the judgment deals with the issue of complicity, one of the judges addressed the issue of whether war crimes could be committed in non-international armed conflicts.[572] He came to the conclusion that this was possible, having traced the historical developments in this area, including those at the ICTY, while also setting out the requirements for a situation reaching

565 Section 137(2) of the *Immigration Act 2009* sets out the exclusion provisions.

566 Before this date, it was the Refugee Status Appeals Authority (RSAA).

567 *Sequeiros Garate v Refugee Status Appeals Authority*, M826/97, High Court, 9 October 1997.

568 *Sivakumar v Canada (Minister of Employment and Immigration)*, [1994] 1 FC 433 [*Sivakumar*].

569 *X & Y v Refugee Status Appeals Authority*, CIV-2006-404-4213, High Court, 17 December 2007. This was the judicial review of RSAA Appeal Nos 74796 & 74797.

570 *Ibid* at para 110.

571 *X v Refugee Status Appeals Authority* [2009] NZCA 488.

572 *Ibid* at para 278 (Judge Baragwanath).

the threshold of a non-international conflict, based on the intensity of the conflict and the organization of the parties involved, again relying on ICTY jurisprudence.[573]

On appeal, the Supreme Court of New Zealand issued a decision on 27 August 2010,[574] limiting itself to an examination of crimes against humanity, concluding that the definition of crimes against humanity must be derived from international instruments, of which the Rome Statute was the most important.[575]

Most cases of relevance in New Zealand have dealt with crimes against humanity,[576] uniformly described as requiring a systematic or widespread attack.[577] More recently, this has expanded to include the four elements of this crime as described by the Canadian *Mugesera* case.[578] The underlying crimes discussed in the jurisprudence have been murder,[579] torture,[580] and persecution.[581] None of these crimes were further defined, with the exception of the crime of torture, where an early RSAA decision relied on the Convention against Torture to set out the parameters of the crime.[582]

---

573 *Ibid* at paras 210–23 and 228–34.

574 *The Attorney-General (Minister of Immigration) v Tamil X and the RSAA* [2010] NZSC 107 [*Tamil X*]; for a comment, see Ella Watt, "International Criminal Law and New Zealand Refugee Status Determinations: A Case Note on Attorney-General v Tamil X" (2012) 43 *Victoria University Wellington Law Review* 235–62.

575 *Tamil X*, above note 574 at paras 47–48.

576 RSAA Appeal No 1248/93, 31 July 1995, and RSAA Appeal Nos 74796 & 74797, 19 April 2006, refer in passing to violations of common art 3 of the 1949 Geneva Conventions and the 1977 Additional Protocol II.

577 RSAA Appeal No 1655/93, 23 November 1995; RSAA Appeal No 73823, 11 August 2003; RSAA Appeal No 74129, 29 July 2005; RSAA Appeal No 75896, 10 November 2006; RSAA Appeal No 74302, 26 June 2006; RSAA Appeal No 75634, 24 May 2006; and RSAA Appeal No 74796 & 74797, 19 April 2006; the one exception has been the case of RSAA Appeal No 72635, 6 September 2002, where the Canadian case of *Equizabal v Canada (Minister of Employment and Immigration)* (CA), [1994] 3 FC 514, was cited to say that the main element of the crime against humanity of torture is the additional component of barbaric cruelty; the *Equizabal* case had been following the 1994 Supreme Court of Canada decision in *Finta*, above note 129, on this point, which was overruled by *Mugesera*, above note 38.

578 RSAA Appeal No 74273, 10 May 2006, and RSAA Appeal Nos 74796 & 74797, 19 April 2006.

579 RSAA Appeal No 74302, 26 June 2006; RSAA Appeal No 75896, 10 November 2006; RSAA Appeal No 75896, 10 November 2006; and RSAA Appeal No 74273, 10 May 2006.

580 RSAA Appeal No 1655/93, 23 November 1995; RSAA Appeal No 75896, 10 November 2006; RSAA Appeal No 73343, 28 November 2002; and RSAA Appeal No 74273, 10 May 2006.

581 RSAA Appeal No 74302, 26 June 2006, and RSAA Appeal No 75896, 10 November 2006.

582 RSAA Appeal No 1655/93, 23 November 1995.

h) United Kingdom

Refugee decisions made by government agencies in the United Kingdom[583] can be appealed to the First-tier Tribunal (Immigration and Asylum Chamber), with a further appeal to the Upper Tribunal (Immigration and Asylum Chamber).[584] The decisions of the latter can be taken to the Court of Appeal and the Supreme Court. A Home Office manual[585] briefly describes the concepts of crimes against peace, war crimes, crimes against humanity, and genocide. These crimes have been interpreted at two court levels[586] as well as at the tribunal level.[587]

The *Gurung* case—involving a person who was a member of the Nepalese Communist Party between 1996 and 2000, attended meetings, and, on occasion, participated in protests against government land policies—addressed several issues regarding exclusion under article 1F(a). The tribunal noted, first of all, that the interpretation of article 1F(a) should have regard to the statutes of the ICTY, the ICTR, and the ICC as sources and to the jurisprudence decided pursuant to these instruments.[588]

---

583 Sections 1 and 2 of the *Asylum and Immigration Appeals Act* of 1993, which makes reference to the 1951 Refugee Convention. Section 55(1)(a) of the *Immigration, Asylum and Nationality Act 2006* also allows the secretary of state to issue a certificate during an appeal procedure to the effect that a person is not entitled to protection because 1F applies to this person; for a more detailed background, see Yakut-Bahtiyar, above note 541 at 187–203, while for a detailed overview of the exclusion process, see Singer, above note 12 at 200–39.

584 This is as of 15 February 2010; between 2004 and 2010, there was the Asylum and Immigration Tribunal (AIT) for the same purpose, while before 2004, there was an appeal tribunal called the Immigration Appeal Tribunal (IAT). See, in general, *AIDA Country Report: United Kingdom, Asylum Procedure, List of Authorities Intervening in Each State of the Procedure*, online: https://asylumineurope.org/reports/country/united-kingdom/asylum-procedure/general/list-authorities-intervening-each-stage-procedure/; see, also, Maria O'Sullivan, "The Intersection Between the International, the Regional and the Domestic: Seeking Asylum in the UK" in Susan Kneebone, ed, *Refugees, Asylum Seekers and the Rule of Law: Comparative Perspectives* (Cambridge: Cambridge University Press, 2009) 228 at 231–48.

585 Home Office, "Exclusion (Article 1F) and Article 33(2) of the Refugee Convention," above note 37 at 26–27.

586 *(Sri Lanka) v Secretary of State for the Home Department*, [2009] EWCA Civ 364, and *R (on the application of JS) (Sri Lanka) (Respondent) v Secretary of State for the Home Department* (Appellant), [2010] UKSC 15.

587 In 2004, the AIT mentioned in passing that for a person who kills soldiers in battle (in the Sri Lankan context), exclusion ground 1F(a) is not engaged as no war crimes were committed in such a situation; see *PK v Secretary of State for the Home Department*, [2004] UKIAT 00089.

588 *Gurung v Secretary of State for the Home Department*, [2002] UKIAT 04870 at para 34 [*Gurung*]; see, also, KM (exclusion; art 1F(a); art 1F(b)) Democratic Republic of Congo [2022] UKUT 00125 (IAC) at paras 19–26, which states that before 1 July 2002, the international sources for interpreting 1F(a) crimes were the jurisprudence of the IMT, ICTY, ICTR, and SCSL, while after this date, it was the ICC.

It also stated that "a crime against peace has been defined as including planning, preparation, initiation or waging of a war of aggression, or a war in violation of international treaties, agreements or assurances."[589] With respect to the latter concept, the Immigration Appeal Tribunal has made it clear that leaders of non-state organizations cannot commit crimes against peace.[590] These findings were consistent with international criminal law as it stood at the time of the decisions, although international criminal law has now broadened and clarified the definition of aggression used by the tribunals after the Second World War, which was the one applied in *Gurung*.

The concept of crimes against humanity was applied by the Upper Tribunal (Immigration and Asylum Chamber) to a situation in Zimbabwe where a female person had been involved in violent invasions of land owned by two white farmers and in the violent expulsion of their black farm workers from their houses and jobs on those farms.[591] The tribunal concluded that crimes against humanity applied because the attacks were "part of widespread systematic attacks against the civilian population of farmers and farm workers, carried out not just with the full knowledge of the regime but as a deliberate act of policy by it, with the intention of advancing its grip on power, suppressing opposition, and helping its supporters."[592] With respect to the underlying crimes, these invasions caused great physical and mental suffering as a result of the accompanying mob violence, with beatings administered to men and women, burnings, and lootings in a deliberately brutal and terrifying manner, as a result of which the crime against humanity of inhumane acts was engaged. Even though the tribunal did not rely upon the ICTY/ICTR jurisprudence regarding the crime against humanity of inhumane acts, and even though the international jurisprudence has not examined this situation in that context, the level of violence described in this case is consistent with the analysis and the elements described in the international jurisprudence and, as such, is a good example of applying existing international norms to a new fact pattern. On appeal, the court, while relying extensively on international

---

589 *Gurung*, above note 588 at para 2.2.1.

590 The Amberber case, referred to in Mark Symes, *Caselaw on the Refugee Convention: The United Kingdom's Interpretation in the Lights of the International Authorities* (London: Refugee Legal Centre, 2002) at 286–88.

591 *SK (Article 1F(a)—exclusion) Zimbabwe*, [2010] UKUT 327 (IAC).

592 *Ibid* at para 36.

criminal law precedents, agreed with the tribunal that the crime against humanity of inhumane acts had been committed.[593]

In a case dealing with a female detective on the Zimbabwean police force, who had been involved in a number of activities amounting to police abuses, such as attendance at two torture scenes, being part of the violent disruption of almost a dozen demonstrations, and a cover-up of a mass murder by burying bodies of persons killed by the police, an exclusion finding was upheld.[594] A UK tribunal had no difficulty coming to the conclusion that the police conduct in Zimbabwe during the time of her involvement fit the criteria of the chapeau element of the crime against humanity of having been carried out in a systematic or widespread manner. With respect to the underlying crimes, torture and inhumane acts were found to be the most relevant.[595] In this context of underlying crimes, the tribunal comes to the puzzling conclusion that it is somewhat bemused that the enumerated list of excludable acts in articles 7(1)(a)–(k) does not include crimes that have any obvious relationship to the "covering up" of a murder (e.g., conspiracy to pervert the course of justice, destruction of evidence, suppression of evidence, unlawful handling of bodies).[596] This conclusion is puzzling for two reasons: first, the assumption that this type of behaviour is seen as a substantive crime rather than a type of extended liability, accessory after the fact, and second, the observation that there is no international jurisprudence that has addressed this issue, which is incorrect.[597]

On the other hand, a low-ranking police officer, who had served for over ten years until 2011 in the Rapid Intervention Police in the Democratic Republic of the Congo, was found not to have been involved in crimes against humanity because, after extensive canvassing of the provisions of the Rome Statute,[598] the tribunal concluded that

---

593 *SK (Zimbabwe) v Secretary of State for the Home Department*, [2012] EWCA Civ 807; for a discussion of this case and the one following, see Kate Ogg, "Separating the Persecutors from the Persecuted: A Feminist and Comparative Examination of Exclusion from the Refugee Regime" (2014) 26:1 *International Journal of Refugee Law* 82 at 93–100.

594 *MT (article 1F (a) — aiding and abetting) Zimbabwe*, [2012] UKUT 00015 (IAC).

595 *Ibid* at paras 115–21, where substantial reliance is placed on the ICTY jurisprudence in this area even though the tribunal is incorrect in stating at para 121 that joint criminal enterprise requires a leadership role; for the application of the legal parameters to the facts in the case, see paras 127–31.

596 *Ibid* at para 122.

597 *Ibid* at para 124.

598 *KM (exclusion; art 1F(a); art 1F(b)) Democratic Republic of Congo*, [2022] UKUT 00125 (IAC) at paras 28–32.

the activities of the police unit he belonged to did not amount to crimes against humanity. The tribunal was of the view that

> although the evidence shows that human rights violations were widespread, when analysed, it also shows that many violations had nothing to do with the suppression of political dissent. Many of the reported violations were rooted in poor training, lack of effective command, corruption, and resulted from widespread impunity. Many of those who suffered human rights violations were ordinary citizens from whom members of the security forces sought to extort money or who were the subject of disproportionate force during arrest on suspicion of common crimes. It is possible to describe those violations as widespread and systematic, but a necessary element of the contextual elements of the chapeau of Article 7 is to link the operation or course of conduct to an "attack against the civilian population" which is "pursuant to or in furtherance of a State or organizational policy to commit such an attack."[599]

As well, some other areas of refugee law have provided indirect guidance to the meaning of the crimes contained in article 1F(a). The notion of internal armed conflict in article 15(c) of the Qualification Directive was given attention in three decisions by the Immigration Appeal Tribunal in 2008 and 2009:[600] *HH & others (Mogadishu: armed conflict: risk) Somalia v Secretary of State for the Home Department*;[601] *KH (Article 15(c) Qualification Directive) Iraq v Secretary of State for the Home Department*;[602] and *AM & AM (Armed Conflict: Risk Categories) Somalia v Secretary of State for the Home Department*.[603]

The first decision set out in great detail the history of the provisions in international law dealing with both international and internal armed conflicts, while it also canvassed academic literature, the jurisprudence of the International Court of Justice, and the ICTY, especially the *Tadić* case.[604]

599 *Ibid* at para 142, with more details in paras 143–47.

600 In a fourth decision, it was conceded by the government that the whole of Afghanistan amounted to such a conflict in the case of *GS (Existence of Internal Armed Conflict) Afghanistan v Secretary of State for the Home Department*, [2009] UKAIT 00010.

601 *HH & Others (Mogadishu: Armed Conflict: Risk) Somalia v Secretary of State for the Home Department*, [2008] AIT 00022 [*HH & Others*].

602 *KH (Article 15(c) Qualification Directive) Iraq v Secretary of State for the Home Department*, [2008] AIT 00023 [*KH*].

603 *AM & AM (Armed Conflict: Risk Categories) Somalia v Secretary of State for the Home Department*, [2008] AIT 00091 [*AM & AM*].

604 *HH & Others*, above note 601 at paras 255–70.

In applying the jurisprudence of the ICTY, the tribunal distilled two main propositions with respect to the notion of internal armed conflict: that it must amount to protracted armed violence between two parties, governmental or non-governmental, and that the conflict must be limited both in duration and location to only when and where two parties are engaged in such violence. Based on these two premises, it concluded that there was such a conflict in Somalia in the early 1990s, but only around Mogadishu.[605]

The second case built on the two general premises of the first, and after an in-depth examination of the ICTY caselaw and some jurisprudence of the SCSL and the ICC,[606] the tribunal came to the conclusion that the essential elements for a determination of an internal armed conflict are twofold: first, some degree in the organization of the parties to the conflict and an intensity of the conflict that goes beyond situations of internal disturbances and tensions, such as riots, isolated and sporadic acts of violence, or other acts of a similar nature, and second, further analyzing the element of intensity under four subheadings: the length or protracted nature of the conflict, the seriousness of and increase in armed clashes, the spread of clashes over the territory, and the increase in the number of forces.[607] Based on these parameters, it came to the conclusion that there was an internal armed conflict in the whole of Iraq.[608]

The third case again examined the situation in Somalia and applied the same jurisprudence as in the previous case. It took the view that given the lack of information available about the conditions in all of Somalia, it concluded that there was an internal armed conflict in central and southern Somalia and not just Mogadishu.[609]

The reliance on international humanitarian and criminal law by the Immigration Appeal Tribunal in the above decisions has been put into doubt by *QD & AH (Iraq) (Appellants) v Secretary of State for the Home Department (Respondent)*,[610] which states the following:

> International humanitarian law (IHL) is the name given to the body of law which seeks to protect both combatants and non-combatants

605 *Ibid* at paras 318–31.

606 *KH*, above note 602 at paras 71–80.

607 *Ibid* at paras 81–82.

608 *Ibid* at paras 147–57.

609 *AM & AM*, above note 603 at paras 128–49.

610 *QD & AH (Iraq) (Appellants) v Secretary of State for the Home Department (Respondent)*, [2009] EWCA Civ 620.

> from collateral harm in the course of armed conflicts. It thus has a specific area of operation. It also, however, has defined and limited purposes which do not include the grant of refuge to people who flee armed conflict.[611]

It added that "the phrase 'situations of international or internal armed conflict' in article 15(c) has an autonomous meaning broad enough to capture any situation of indiscriminate violence, whether caused by one or more armed factions or by a state."[612] As noted in the discussion with respect to Germany, this issue has been settled by the CJEU in favour of this interpretation.

i) United States

The United States has not ratified the Refugee Convention or the Rome Statute. As a result, a number of relevant terms have been decided in a more autonomous fashion than elsewhere, either legislatively or jurisprudentially. While the terms "genocide,"[613] "extrajudicial killing,"[614] "torture,"[615] and "child recruitment"[616] have been given meaning in the immigration portion of the *Immigration and Nationality Act* (*INA*), the

---

611 *Ibid* at para 16.

612 *Ibid* at para 35; see, also, HM and Others (Article 15(c)) Iraq CG [2010] UKUT 331 (IAC) at para 77; HK and others (minors — indiscriminate violence — forced recruitment by Taliban — contact with family members) Afghanistan CG [2010] UKUT 378 (IAC) at para 15.

613 *INA*, above note 47, s 212(a)(3)(E)(ii); this section refers for the definition of genocide to s 1091(a) of Chapter 50A of Title 18 of the US Code, where a description very similar to the one in arts I and II of the Genocide Convention can be found.

614 *Ibid*, s 212(a)(3)(E)(iii)(II); for the definition of extrajudicial killing, reference is made to s 3(a) of the *Torture Victim Protection Act* of 1991 (s 1350(3)(a) of Chapter 85 of Title 28 of the US Code), which says that this is a "deliberated killing not authorized by a previous judgment pronounced by a regularly constituted court affording all the judicial guarantees which are recognized as indispensable by civilized peoples. Such term, however, does not include any such killing that, under international law, is lawfully carried out under the authority of a foreign nation."

615 *INA*, above note 47, s 212(a)(3)(E)(iii)(I); this section refers for the definition of torture to s 2340(1) of Chapter 113C of Title 18 of the US Code, which is almost identical to the description of torture in art 7.2(e) of the Rome Statute rather than the more limited definition in art 1.1 of the Torture Convention (which has been replicated in s 1350(3)(b) of Chapter 85 of Title 28 of the US Code), while the United States has added its own definition in s 2340(2) for severe mental pain or suffering.

616 *INA*, above note 47, s 212(a)(3)(G). This was added on 3 October 2008 by virtue of the *Child Soldiers Accountability Act* of 2008; the definition of child recruitment, which can be found in the amended s 2442 of Chapter 118 of Title 18 of the US Code, is virtually identical to art 8.2(e)(vii) of the Rome Statute.

concept of persecution in the context of human rights violations has only been the subject of judicial interpretation.[617]

The United States regulates the granting of asylum in section 208 of the *INA*, which contains a number of exceptions (called mandatory bars to asylum).[618] None of them uses the words "genocide," "war crime,"[619] or "crimes against humanity"[620] or is based on the exclusion provision in the Refugee Convention dealing with such crimes. However, the exceptions used are of a type to ensure that claimants would not be granted asylum if involved in activities of that nature. The one used most frequently in dealing with human rights violators is the provision that disallows refugee protection for persons "ordering, inciting, assisting or otherwise participating in the persecution of any person on account of race, religion, nationality, membership in a particular social group, or political opinion."[621]

Refugee matters are decided by immigration judges and other decision makers under the *INA*. Appeals can be launched with an administrative tribunal called the Board of Immigration Appeals (BIA), the decisions of which are subject to judicial review by the US Courts of Appeals, with a further appeal to the US Supreme Court.[622]

---

617 The concept of crimes against humanity has been described in the jurisprudence (without any reference to international criminal law) as "crimes against humanity include murder, enslavement, deportation or forcible transfer, torture, rape or other inhumane acts, committed as part of a widespread [or] systematic attack directed against a civilian population" in the civil case of *The Presbyterian Church of Sudan v Talisman Energy, Inc*, No 07-0016-cv (2d Cir 2009).

618 *INA*, above note 47, s 208(b)(2)(A).

619 This term is used in a US immigration government document, the *Affirmative Asylum Procedures Manual* (*AAPM*), from the Refugee, Asylum, and International Operations Directorate, Asylum Division, US Citizenship and Immigration Services (May 2016), online (pdf): www.uscis.gov/sites/default/files/document/guides/AAPM-2016.pdf which states at 39: "Human rights abusers and modern-day war criminal cases, inquiries, or allegations, to include activity involving an individual suspected of having ordered or engaged in persecution of others, war crimes, genocide or torture." However, the notion of war crime is known in US law in general in § 2441 of Title 18 of the US Code, which provides a definition consistent with contemporary international criminal law, such as the statutes of the ICTY and the ICTR.

620 There have been calls to include this concept in US law; see, for instance, the testimony of Pamela Merchant, Executive Director, the Center for Justice & Accountability before the Subcommittee on Human Rights and the Law, US Senate Committee on the Judiciary, "From Nuremberg to Darfur: Accountability for Crimes Against Humanity," 24 June 2008.

621 *INA*, above note 47, s 208(b)(2)(A)(i).

622 Stephen H. Legomsky, "Refugees, Asylum and the Rule of Law in the USA" in Kneebone, above note 584 at 123–36; see, also, Kate Jastram, "Left Out of Exclusion: International Criminal Law and the 'Persecutor Bar' in US Refugee Law" (2014) 12:5 *Journal of International Criminal Justice* 1183 at 1183–96.

There is no difference in the US jurisprudence between the notions of persecution[623] as faced by victims when applying for asylum or when used to connote the harm inflicted by perpetrators of human rights violations. Sometimes the Court of Appeals clarified the meaning of aspects of this definition in cases dealing with perpetrators, while in other cases they have relied on victim-oriented cases to use the same parameters of persecution.[624] According to general persecution caselaw, the term "persecution" contemplates the infliction of suffering or harm, under government sanction, upon persons who differ from others in specified ways, namely, race, religion, national origin, or political opinion. Persecution comes in many forms, mental as well as physical; mental anguish, fear, and humiliation are all indicia of persecution.[625] The harm or suffering need not be physical but may take other forms, such as the deliberate imposition of severe economic disadvantage or the deprivation of liberty, food, housing, employment, or other essentials of life.[626] It also includes detention, arrest, interrogation, prosecution, imprisonment, illegal searches, confiscation of property, surveillance, beatings, or torture,[627] as well as arrest and detention for selling books containing disfavoured views.[628] However, not every harmful act is persecutory; acts do not rise to the level of persecution when they consist of only a few isolated incidents of verbal harassment or intimidation.[629]

The BIA in the *Rodriguez-Majano* case has indicated that engaging in acts of warfare in open combat taken in furtherance of political goals is not necessarily a persecutory act by saying that

> harm which may result incidentally from behavior directed at another goal, the overthrow of a government or, alternatively, the defense of

---

623 The United States uses a similar definition for persecution in s 101(a)(42) of the *INA* as contained in the Refugee Convention but specifically adds: "for purposes of determinations under this chapter, a person who has been forced to abort a pregnancy or to undergo involuntary sterilization, or who has been persecuted for failure or refusal to undergo such a procedure or for other resistance to a coercive population control program, shall be deemed to have been persecuted on account of political opinion, and a person who has a well-founded fear that he or she will be forced to undergo such a procedure or subject to persecution for such failure, refusal, or resistance shall be deemed to have a well-founded fear of persecution on account of political opinion."

624 For an example of the latter, see *Gao v US Attorney General*, 500 F3d 93 (2d Cir 2007).

625 *United States v Dailide*, 227 F3d 385 (6th Cir 2000).

626 *Abdel-Masieh v INS*, 73 F3d 579 (5th Cir 1996).

627 *Mansur v US Department of Homeland Security*, 494 F3d 281 (2d Cir 2007).

628 *Gao v US Attorney General*, 500 F3d 93 (2d Cir 2007).

629 *Sepulveda v Attorney Gen*, 401 F3d 1226 (11th Cir 2005).

> that government against an opponent, is not persecution. In analyzing a claim of persecution in the context of a civil war, one must examine the motivation of the group threatening harm.[630]

In this context, the board was of the view that reference to international laws governing warfare may be useful in determining whether actions taken in the context of warfare constitute persecution or are legitimate acts of war. However, if an act is done on one of the five protected grounds, it is persecution, even in wartime. It specified several aspects that it found not to be persecution but rather acts related to civil war, such as drafting of youths as soldiers, unofficial recruitment by force, disciplining members of rebel groups, prosecuting draft dodgers, engaging in military actions, attacking garrisons, and destruction of property.

This one case, which discussed the notion of war, was decided before the establishment of the ICTY and the ICTR, so it is understandable that the definition and reasoning of the tribunal in that case did not make any connection to international criminal law. However, it is hoped that with newer cases, this reliance on international law will become a more natural approach for tribunals and courts to take. Similarly, while the larger notion of crimes against humanity is not known in the US refugee legislation, the concept of persecution has largely taken its place, and while in international criminal law persecution is the only type of crimes against humanity, the US caselaw has been intuitively quite consistent in setting out the parameters of persecution in a matter consistent with the international jurisprudence regarding crimes against humanity in terms of the types of behaviour included in persecution.[631]

5) Observations

In order to determine whether exclusion law has been following international criminal law concepts in terms of the parameters of the chapeau elements of international crime and the specific crimes, it is first necessary to assess whether international criminal law itself has been able to provide a consistent approach in defining war crimes and

630 Matter of Rodriguez-Majano, BIA 19 I & N Dec 811 (BIA 1988).

631 Along the same lines, see Matter of Negusie, 27 I & N Dec 347 (BIA 2018), which also indicated that there was an intention by the legislator to have a consistent approach between the notion of persecution as a bar to asylum and the exclusion clause of the Refugee Convention, even where the language is not the same as is the case for 1F(a).

crimes against humanity. The crimes of aggression and genocide are less relevant in this context in that there has been no international guidance from international institutions for the crime of aggression, while genocide is not mentioned in article 1F(a). Given the direct reference in article 1F(a) to international instruments (which would include the statutes of the international tribunals and the ICC), one would expect that the national jurisprudence would have referred to those documents and their related jurisprudence.

The development of international criminal law as it pertains to war crimes and crimes against humanity, as well as to the elements of the underlying crimes, has been very consistent at the international level. This is not surprising given the fact that any differences of opinion between the trial chambers of the ICTY and the ICTR could be easily resolved by their joint Appeals Chamber. This was the case when the two theories surrounding the crime of rape were reconciled in the *Kunarac* judgment, in effect saying that the notions of coercive circumstances and consent are not alternatives but complementary. This approach can also be found in the Rome Statute. Similarly, in the context of the hate crime component of the crime against humanity of persecution, the ICTY was of the view that it did not constitute such a crime, and the ICTR reached the opposite view. The Appeals Chamber ruled that a hate crime could fall within the parameters of persecution, but on a narrower plane than had been advocated by the ICTR Trial Chamber, by requiring a link between hate speech and subsequent crimes, as well as requiring that the hate speech had to be violent.

As well, given the fact that the two internationalized tribunals (the result of agreements between the United Nations and national governments in Sierra Leone and Cambodia) had their statutes based primarily on the ICTY and ICTR statutes, it is not surprising that the jurisprudence of the SCSL and the ECCC has relied heavily on the ICTY and ICTR caselaw. On the other hand, the SCSL has not hesitated to break new ground when called upon to do so, as was the case when no other jurisprudence was available with regard to the war crime of child recruitment or forced marriage as a crime against humanity.

However, possibilities of divergence between the established jurisprudence of the ICTY and the ICTR and the Rome Statute, as negotiated in Rome in 1998, certainly existed. This would have had an effect at the national level because domestic authorities, in the criminal context and in civil cases, including exclusion, would have to apply different standards depending on when and where a particular crime had been defined. There are already some temporal elements to be considered even after the establishment of the first international institutions dispensing international criminal law, such as the fact that war crimes in non-international armed conflicts probably did not exist before 1990.

For the most part, such discrepancies have not materialized. As the Rome Statute was generally seen as the most comprehensive reflection of international criminal law in 1998, it has for the most part incorporated the ICTY and ICTR caselaw as it stood during the time of negotiations, with some notable exceptions (apart from providing more clarification for particular crimes, such as was done for the sexual violence crimes, which could have been brought under more general headings in the ICTY and ICTR statutes). One such variation pertains to the elements of the crime of torture, which have undergone a slight expansion when compared to the ICTY and ICTR caselaw. Of the three requirements of the Torture Convention—severe pain or suffering, for a particular purpose, inflicted by a state official—the ICTY/ICTR judges had already eliminated the latter while adding several other prohibited purposes. The Rome Statute has also deleted the purpose requirement, which is more a difference in style than substance, as the purpose element in the ICTY and ICTR caselaw had already become so broad as to be always present when this crime was committed.

Another example of divergence is that the crime against humanity of persecution has undergone an expansion from only three victim groups (political, religious, and racial) to seven named groups (political, racial, national, ethnic, cultural, religious, and gender). Furthermore, a formula has been adopted to include other groups if "universally recognized as impermissible under international law." Again, this does not represent a major difference with ICTY and ICTR caselaw as the crime of persecution as charged under the ICTY and ICTR jurisdictions never hinged on the victim group but rather on the activities carried out against such groups. The fact that the Rome Statute now requires that this crime must be connected to another crime is most likely a jurisdictional requirement and not part of substantive law.

The Rome Statute, while being the embodiment of international criminal law in 1998, is not as comprehensive as it may once have been in setting all the underlying crimes known in this area of international law. The ICTY has added the war crimes of causing terror, sniping, and shelling to the number of violations of international humanitarian law for which individual responsibility can be imposed.

At the national level, the discussion in refugee determination decisions with respect to war crimes has taken place primarily in the context of non-international conflicts. This happened at two levels: in interpreting the exclusion ground in article 1F(a) itself, and, in Europe, indirectly, by an examination of article 15(c) of the Qualification Directive. In the direct approach, ICTY jurisprudence was used to decide that war crimes could not be committed in such conflicts before 1990 (Canada and New Zealand), although in Belgium and the Netherlands, it was found to apply to situations in the late 1980s. Although the *Tadić* decision by the ICTY Appeals Chamber was factually related to an armed conflict situation in 1991, its more general reasoning and its reliance on customary international law, where some reference was made to national criminal decisions with findings of war crimes in non-international armed conflicts before that time, make it difficult to point to a precise date for the expansion for individual criminal liability from international armed conflicts to its non-international counterparts. As such, the Belgian and Dutch decisions cannot be said to be in error when putting them in the international criminal law context.

The examination of the Qualification Directive was based initially on international treaties regulating non-international armed conflicts such as common article 3 of the Geneva Conventions and Protocol II to determine whether an article 15(c) situation amounted to an internal armed conflict in countries such as Afghanistan (Germany), Iraq (France, Germany, Sweden, and United Kingdom), the Ivory Coast (Belgium), Burundi (Belgium), Somalia (United Kingdom), and Sudan (France), while a number of UK cases also incorporated the more detailed elaborations on this concept as developed in the ICTY jurisprudence. This reliance on international humanitarian law was put in doubt by a decision in the United Kingdom in 2009, which was of the view that the words "situations of international or internal armed conflict" in article 15(c) were broader than the threshold for non-international armed conflicts. The German Federal Administrative Court in 2010 adopted a different approach by saying that internal armed conflicts can occur outside the realm of international humanitarian law and then have an autonomous meaning, which was eventually adopted by the CJEU in 2014.

Crimes against humanity have received a great deal of treatment in all common law countries (except the United States), as well as in

Belgium, Germany, and the Netherlands. The courts in these countries agree with the main international element of this concept, a systematic or widespread attack against a civilian population with knowledge of the attack. These general aspects of crimes against humanity are consistent with international criminal law primarily because the national courts, in setting out these requirements, relied directly on international jurisprudence. In Australia, the FCAFC has provided more detail about one aspect of the definition by saying that police officers who are victimized are part of the civilian population, while in Canada, the same was said about people incarcerated in civilian prisons. The Netherlands came to the same conclusion for government officials such as village heads in Nepal. Again, these applications of the concept of crimes against humanity are consistent with international criminal law. This is directly the case with respect to police officers as the Australian court came to the same conclusion as the SCSL.[632]

With respect to the last international crime, aggression or crimes against peace, this is mentioned in general in both the UK Home Office manual and the Dutch *Aliens Manual* (the latter originally had a prescient reference to United Nations General Assembly Resolution 3314, which has now become part of the crime of aggression in the Rome Statute). In Canada, this crime was analyzed outside the confines of exclusion law as part of the issue of conscientious objectors, leading to the conclusion that it did not apply to regular soldiers, while in the United Kingdom, it was said that it could not be used in a situation involving non-government actors. Belgium applied this concept directly to a situation in Somalia in 1982 with respect to a high-level government official involved in the planning of an invasion in another country. While none of these national decision makers referred to the Rome Statute because their decisions preceded the 2010 Kampala Review Conference, it is remarkable that all the parameters for this crime were in accordance not only with international law at the time of the decisions but also with later understandings of the contours of this crime in international criminal law.

With regard to specific or underlying crimes, which are part of war crimes and crimes against humanity, in most cases such crimes were not discussed as it was clear that the organization under discussion had

---

632 *Sesay, Kallon and Gbao ("RUF")* (SCSL-04-15-T), Trial Chamber Judgment, 25 February 2009 at paras 87–88.

been involved in at least murder or torture (plus persecution in one early New Zealand tribunal decision, which also defined torture with reference to the Convention against Torture), both of which are mentioned as such crimes. However, the FCAFC discussed what type of control is required for the underlying crime of torture as defined by the Rome Statute and concluded that it has only to be factual, as opposed to legal, control and, as such, represents a useful contribution to international criminal law that has not made any finding on this specific point.

In the United Kingdom, the crime against humanity of inhumane acts was applied to a situation of violent invasions of land in Zimbabwe, as was the crime of forcible transfer by an Australian tribunal to a situation in Iraq where the southern marshes had been drained, resulting in people leaving that territory. In Belgium, a tribunal indicated that bombardment of civilians and the destruction of water wells amounted to war crimes, while the same was said in the Netherlands for the use of chemical weapons and human shields, where also, for the first time, an attack on a civilian object as a war crime was discussed. While there was no international jurisprudence with respect to the specific situations under consideration, the extrapolation from international jurisprudence and from the reasoning used at the national level was not at all at odds with the conclusion that the above atrocities amounted to war crimes or crimes against humanity. This is most likely the result of intuitively applying the same thinking at the national level to the very serious nature of the violations against civilians, although in the future a more direct examination of the international jurisprudence would be useful, along with a justification of why the fact situation before the national decision maker would fit within the parameters of the international framework. Similarly, in the Netherlands, the Council of State used the war crime of causing terror, based on the prohibition in Protocol II, to decide that this international humanitarian law prohibition also had an individual responsibility application, without making use of the ICTY jurisprudence, which had considered the same crime eight months earlier and had used the provisions of both Protocol I and Protocol II,[633] while in the same country, Geneva Convention IV, Protocol I, and the Rome Statute were invoked to determine the parameters of an attack on civilian objects.

633 *Galić* (IT-98-29-T), Trial Chamber Judgment, 5 December 2003 at paras 86–138, for a discussion of this crime, with paras 94–95 regarding Protocol II.

On the other hand, in Germany, the war crime of treacherous killing or wounding was addressed in detail without any benefit of recent international jurisprudence because there was none. The Federal Administrative Court was of the view that this crime, when carried out during an internal armed conflict, includes the elements of concealing a weapon and creating a false confidence in the opposite side of the conflict. This reasoning and conclusion by a national court could very well be of benefit, especially for the ICC, when called upon to interpret this crime as was already done by the prosecutor of that institution.

It can be concluded from the observations made above regarding the relationship between international and national jurisprudence with respect to international crimes that the exclusion jurisprudence has not strayed very much at all from the international jurisprudence and, as such, has taken the reference to international instruments in exclusion 1F(a) seriously and accurately. An exception to this general pattern is the United States.

With respect to US law and jurisprudence, the crime of persecution may result in deprivation of refugee status. The jurisprudence of the US Courts of Appeals does not distinguish between the notion of persecution from the perspective of the victims or as committed by the perpetrator. While international institutions have frowned on reliance on human rights instruments to define crimes against humanity because of the different purposes to be achieved in the two spheres of international law, namely, protection against a state for one and determining individual criminal responsibility for the other,[634] the difference of its application to the facts in specific cases seems to be more one of perception than reality.[635]

Similarly, while there is no direct cross-reference in the US legislation or jurisprudence to international criminal law, the definitions of genocide and torture in the *INA* are remarkably similar to the definitions of

634 See *Kupreškić et al* (IT-95-16), Trial Chamber Judgment, 14 January 2000 at paras 586–98.

635 In both US law and international criminal law, the persecution has to be committed on discriminatory grounds, which in US law is based on race, religion, nationality, membership in a social group, or political opinion, while the ICTY and ICTR statutes are narrower by only allowing this crime based on political, racial, and religious grounds, although the Rome Statute has actually expanded the groups that can be subject to persecution in any identifiable group as recognized in international law and as such is broader than US law. On the other hand, the ICTY/ICTR caselaw and the Rome Statute limit the parameters of these groups by saying that persecution has the same level of severity as the other crimes against humanity

the same crimes in the Rome Statute. Finally, while persecution is only one crime out of eleven possible crimes against humanity (although the equivalent of all the other crimes against humanity has been incorporated into persecution if a discriminatory intent was present), the US jurisprudence does not appear to be out of step in applying what would be, in theory, the narrower concept of persecution rather than using a larger number of crimes committed against a civilian population in a systematic or widespread fashion, the hallmarks of crimes against humanity. The situations in which persecution in the United States were held to be applicable were very similar to facts against which the other countries under consideration have used the concept of crimes against humanity in general as used in their legislation or jurisprudence. The one exception in the United States is declaring legislatively that the one-child policy in China, which includes abortion, amounts to persecution.

As a final observation, it can be said that when defining international crimes, there is a high degree of agreement internationally, while at the domestic level, the use of international instruments is widespread, with some attention being given to the most important jurisprudence coming out of the ICTY and the ICTR. Where there has not been such jurisprudence, the domestic courts have applied their own reasoning to the characterization of underlying crimes in a manner that cannot be faulted. However, since a trend can be detected in the national jurisprudence, where attention is being given to specific crimes less obvious than murder, torture, or rape, it will be necessary to go beyond the intuitive reasoning employed so far and utilize the international caselaw that has defined and circumscribed these crimes in great detail. Not only would the reasoning of the exclusion decision makers become more persuasive, it would also allow for a more consistent development of the overall national jurisprudence.

CHAPTER FOUR

Exclusion — 1F(a) Extended Liability, Defences, and Child Soldiers

A. EXTENDED LIABILITY

1) International Criminal Law

a) Introduction

Like domestic criminal law, international criminal law employs a number of concepts aimed at holding persons liable for the commission of international crimes in addition to having personally committed such crimes.[1] As a matter of fact, the majority of cases decided by international criminal institutions involved persons who had not personally committed these crimes.[2] The reason for that choice lies in the nature

1 For a historical overview of the various forms of extended liability in international criminal law, see Robert J. Currie & Joseph Rikhof, *International & Transnational Criminal Law*, 3d ed (Toronto: Irwin Law, 2020) at 710–11; this section regarding extended liability has relied heavily on the same book at 714–43. For an overview of forms of extended liability for the commission of international crimes at the domestic level, see Terje Einarsen & Joseph Rikhof, *A Theory of Punishable Participation in Universal Crimes* (Brussels: Torkel Opsahl Academic EPublisher, 2018) at 425–592.

2 "Personally" committing has been defined as follows: "The physical perpetration of a criminal act or the culpable omission of an act that was mandated by a rule of criminal law" (*Tadić* (IT-94-1-A), Appeals Chamber Judgment, 15 July 1999 at para 188; *Kaing Guek Eav alias Duch* (Case File 001/18-07-2007/ECCC/TC), Trial Chamber Judgment, 26 July 2010 at para 480 [*Duch*]) while the person "must have acted with the intent to commit the crime, or with an awareness of the substantial likelihood that the crime would occur as a consequence of his or her conduct," *Duch*, *ibid* at para 481; *Habré*, EAC, Trial Chamber Judgment, 30 May 2016 at para 1820; for the ICC context, see *Jean-Pierre Bemba Gombo, Aimé Kilolo Musamba, Jean-Jacques Mangenda Kabongo, Fidèle Babala Wandu and Narcisse Arido* (ICC-01/05-01/13), Trial Chamber Judgment, 19 October 2016 at para 58; *Ntaganda* (ICC-01/04-02/06), Trial Chamber Judgment, 8 July 2019 at para 735. Direct participation can also be found in a situation

of the international crimes, which, because of their scale and collective nature, call for an approach where the persons who are most culpable because of their leadership positions or directing minds usually do not interact with the victims of the crimes. A good example of this difference between national domestic law and international law is the attention given at the international level to legal concepts such as the liability of military commanders or senior persons within a civilian hierarchy who direct crimes from a distance or the concepts of joint criminal enterprise (JCE) or co-perpetration, where the criminal liability of a particular person within a larger group is difficult to pinpoint but where there is no doubt that the group as a whole was responsible for the commission of these crimes.[3]

However, while the jurisprudence with respect to the parameters of the international crimes of genocide, war crimes, and crimes against humanity has been quite consistent, the same cannot be said for extended liability. This is especially poignant when comparing the jurisprudence of the International Criminal Tribunal of the former Yugoslavia (ICTY) and the International Criminal Tribunal for Rwanda (ICTR) with that of the International Criminal Court (ICC). The ICTY and ICTR were instrumental in the development of the law in the area of JCE, which over the years extended its application from smaller groups involved in crimes to people administering entities such as camps where detainees were abused to, more recently, groups of people organizing and carrying out crimes over large territories. The ICC, on the other hand, has so far preferred a legal construct where the control over the international crimes by persons occupying high positions in governments

---

where the conduct of the accused was as much an integral part of the crimes as the crimes it enabled; see *Gacumbitsi* (ICTR-2001-64-A), Appeals Chamber Judgment, 7 July 2006 at para 161; *Ndindabahizi* (ICTR-01-71-A), Appeals Chamber Judgment, 16 January 2007 at para 123; *Kalimanzira* (ICTR-05-88-A), Appeals Chamber Judgment, 20 October 2010 at para 219; *Kanyarukiga* (ICTR-02-78), Trial Chamber Judgment, 1 November 2010 at para 622; *Munyakazi* (ICTR-97-36A-A), Appeals Chamber Judgment, 28 September 2011 at para 135; *Karemera et al* (ICTR-98-44-T), Trial Chamber Judgment, 2 February 2012 at para 1606.

3 For a general overview of the principles of liability in the Rome Statute, including the notion of hierarchy of blameworthiness, see *Katanga* (ICC-01/04-01/07), Trial Chamber Judgment, 7 March 2014 at paras 1383–87; for general comment regarding the relationship between the various modes of liability in the Rome Statute, see *Lubanga* (ICC-01/04-01/06), Trial Chamber Judgment, 14 March 2012 at para 999; *Gbagbo* (ICC-02/11-01/11), Pre-Trial Chamber, Decision of the Confirmation of Charges, 12 June 2014 at para 243; *Blé Goudé* (ICC-02/11-02/11), Pre-Trial Chamber, Decision of the Confirmation of Charges, 11 December 2014 at para 159; *Lubanga* (ICC-01/04-01/06 A5), Appeals Chamber Judgment, 1 December 2014 at para 462.

or non-governmental organizations was criminalized by utilizing the notion of co-perpetration. Neither approach is incompatible with the other, but there has been disagreement among international criminal institutions as to the proper basis of these legal concepts, which will be further explored later in this chapter. This chapter will discuss extended liability from both the perspective of forms of committing crimes by conduct before during, and after those crimes took place as well as criminal conduct, that has not resulted in crimes, the so-called inchoate offences of conspiracy, incitement, and attempt.

b) Ordering

Ordering[4] implies that a person in a position of authority uses that authority to convince another to commit an offence,[5] with the intent that a crime be committed in the realization of that act or omission or with the awareness of the substantial likelihood that a crime would be committed in the realization of that act or omission.[6]

---

4 For the distinctions between ordering, on the one hand, and soliciting, inducing (which are unique to the Rome Statute), and instigating (which is discussed below), on the other, see *Jean-Pierre Bemba Gombo, Aimé Kilolo Musamba, Jean-Jacques Mangenda Kabongo, Fidèle Babala Wandu and Narcisse Arido* (ICC-01/05-01/13), Trial Chamber Judgment, 19 October 2016 at paras 73–82; *Gbagbo and Blé Goudé* (ICC-02/11-01/15-1263-AnxC-Red), Trial Chamber, Reasons for oral decision of 15 January 2019 on the *Requête de la Défense de Laurent Gbagbo afin qu'un jugement d'acquittement portant sur toutes les charges soit prononcé en faveur de Laurent Gbagbo et que sa mise en liberté immédiate soit ordonnée*, and on the Blé Goudé Defence no case to answer motion, Public Redacted Version of Dissenting Opinion Judge Herrera Carbuccia, 16 July 2019 at paras 559–60.

5 *Nahimana, Barayagwiza and Ngeze ("Media")* (ICTR-99-52-A), Appeals Chamber Judgment, 28 November 2007 at para 481; *Kalimanzira* (ICTR-05-88-A), Appeals Chamber Judgment, 20 October 2010 at para 213; *Ndindiliyimana et al* (ICTR-00-56-A), Appeals Chamber Judgment, 11 February 2014 at para 365; *Nyiramasuhuko et al* (ICTR-98-42-A), Appeals Chamber Judgment, 14 December 2015 at paras 1911, 1915; *Case 002/02* (Case File No 002/19-09-2007/ECCC/TC), Trial Chamber Judgment, 16 November 2018 at para 3720; *Gbagbo and Blé Goudé* (ICC-02/11-01/15-1263-AnxB-Red), Trial Chamber, Reasons for oral decision of 15 January 2019 on the *Requête de la Défense de Laurent Gbagbo afin qu'un jugement d'acquittement portant sur toutes les charges soit prononcé en faveur de Laurent Gbagbo et que sa mise en liberté immédiate soit ordonnée*, and on the Blé Goudé Defence no case to answer motion, Public Redacted Version of Reasons of Judge Geoffrey Henderson, Trial Chamber, 16 July 2019 at para 1966; *Gbagbo and Blé Goudé* (ICC-02/11-01/15-1263-AnxC-Red), Trial Chamber, Reasons for oral decision of 15 January 2019 on the *Requête de la Défense de Laurent Gbagbo afin qu'un jugement d'acquittement portant sur toutes les charges soit prononcé en faveur de Laurent Gbagbo et que sa mise en liberté immédiate soit ordonnée*, and on the Blé Goudé Defence no case to answer motion, Public Redacted Version of Dissenting Opinion Judge Herrera Carbuccia, 16 July 2019 at para 559.

6 *Blaškić* (IT-95-14-A), Appeals Chamber Judgment, 29 July 2004, at paras 41–42; *Taylor* (SCSL-04-01-T), Appeals Chamber Judgment, 26 September 2013 at para 589; *Ntaganda*

For the person ordering the crime to be held responsible, it is required that the person who received the order actually proceeds to commit the offence.[7] As well, a causal link between the act of ordering and the physical perpetration of a crime needs to be demonstrated in that the order must have had a direct and substantial effect on the commission of the illegal act.[8] While ordering entails a superior-subordinate relationship between the person giving the order and the person carrying it out,[9] effective control will not have to be proven as it is not a necessary element of this mode of criminal participation, nor is a formal superior-subordinate relationship required for a finding of ordering, so long as the person possessed the authority to order, including de facto authority.[10] It is not necessary that an order be given in writing or in any particular form,[11] while the superior-subordinate relationship can be informal and of a temporary nature.[12] Presence at the scene of the crime is not required for this type of criminal responsibility.[13]

(ICC-01/04-02/06), Pre-Trial Chamber, Decision of the Confirmation of the Charges, 9 June 2014 at para 145; *Gbagbo* (ICC-02/11-01/11), Pre-Trial Chamber, 12 June 2014 at para 244; *Case 002/01* (Case File No 002/19-09-2007/ECCC/TC), Trial Chamber Judgment, 7 August 2014 at para 702; *Case 002/02* (Case File No 002/19-09-2007/ECCC/TC), Trial Chamber Judgment, 16 November 2018 at para 3720.

7 *Nahimana, Barayagwiza and Ngeze ("Media")* (ICTR-99-52-A), Appeals Chamber Judgment, 28 November 2007 at para 481; *Đorđević* (IT-05-87/1), Trial Chamber Judgment, 23 February 2011 at para 1871; *Tolimir* (IT-05-88/2-T), Trial Chamber Judgment, 12 December 2012 at para 906.

8 *Kamuhanda* (ICTR-99-54A-A), Appeals Chamber Judgment, 19 September 2005 at para 76; *Hategekimana* (ICTR-00-55B-A), Appeals Chamber Judgment, 8 May 2012 at para 67; *Ndindiliyimana et al* (ICTR-00-56-A), Appeals Chamber Judgment, 11 February 2014 at para 291; *Gbagbo* (ICC-02/11-01/11), Pre-Trial Chamber, Decision of the Confirmation of Charges, 12 June 2014 at para 244; *Nyiramasuhuko et al* (ICTR-98-42-A), Appeals Chamber Judgment, 14 December 2015 at para 1895.

9 *Semanza* (ICTR-97-20-A), Appeals Chamber Judgment, 20 May 2005 at para 360; *Haradinaj et al* (IT-04-84*bis*-T), Trial Chamber Judgment, 29 November 2012 at para 624; *Case 002/02* (Case File No 002/19-09-2007/ECCC/TC), Trial Chamber Judgment, 16 November 2018 at para 3720.

10 *Semanza* (ICTR-97-20-A), Appeals Chamber Judgment, 20 May 2005 at para 361; *Boškoski and Tarčulovski* (IT-04-82-A), Appeals Chamber Judgment, 19 May 2010 at para 164.

11 *Kamuhanda* (ICTR-99-54A-A), Appeals Chamber Judgment, 19 September 2005 at para 76; *Nyiramasuhuko et al* (ICTR-98-42-A), Appeals Chamber Judgment, 14 December 2015 at paras 1904, 1915; *Case 002/02* (Case File No 002/19-09-2007/ECCC/TC), Trial Chamber Judgment, 16 November 2018 at para 3720.

12 *Nizeyimana* (ICTR-2000-55C), Trial Chamber Judgment, 19 June 2012 at para 1464; *Ngirabatware* (ICTR-99-54-T), Trial Chamber Judgment, 20 December 2012 at para 1292.

13 *Boškoski and Tarčulovski* (IT-04-82-A), Appeals Chamber Judgment, 19 May 2010 at para 125.

c) Instigating

Instigating entails prompting another to commit an offence[14] with the intent that a crime be committed or prompting an act or omission with the awareness of the substantial likelihood that a crime would be committed in the realization of that act or omission.[15] A causal relationship between the instigation and the physical perpetration of the crime is required in the sense that the instigation contributed substantially to the conduct of the person committing the crime.[16] However, it will not be necessary to prove that the crime would not have been perpetrated

---

14 *Nahimana, Barayagwiza and Ngeze ("Media")* (ICTR-99-52-A), Appeals Chamber Judgment, 28 November 2007 at para 440; *Ngirabatware* (MICT-12-29-A), Appeals Chamber Judgment, 18 December 2014 at para 162; *Karadžić* (IT-95-5/18-T), Trial Chamber Judgment, 24 March 2016 at para 572; *Šešelj* (IT-03-67-T), Trial Chamber Judgment, 31 March 2016, at para 295; *Šešelj* (MICT-16-99-A), Appeals Chamber Judgment, 11 April 2018 at para 124; *Case 002/02* (Case File No 002/19-09-2007/ECCC/TC), Trial Chamber Judgment, 16 November 2018 at para 3719; *Gbagbo and Blé Goudé* (ICC-02/11-01/15-1263-AnxC-Red), Trial Chamber, Reasons for oral decision of 15 January 2019 on the *Requête de la Défense de Laurent Gbagbo afin qu'un jugement d'acquittement portant sur toutes les charges soit prononcé en faveur de Laurent Gbagbo et que sa mise en liberté immédiate soit ordonnée*, and on the Blé Goudé Defence no case to answer motion, Public Redacted Version of Dissenting Opinion Judge Herrera Carbuccia, 16 July 2019 at paras 561–62.

15 *Kordić and Čerkez* (IT-95-14/2-A), Appeals Chamber Judgment, 17 December 2004 at paras 27, 30; *Fofana and Kondewa ("CDF")* (SCSL-04-14-A), Appeals Chamber Judgment, 28 May 2008 at para 51; *Prlić et al* (IT-04-74), Trial Chamber Judgment, 29 May 2013 at para 226 (although this decision departs from previous Trial Chamber decisions in requiring a positive act at para 229); *Taylor* (SCSL-04-01-T), Appeals Chamber Judgment, 26 September 2013 at para 589; *Ntaganda* (ICC-01/04-02/06), Pre-Trial Chamber, Decision of the Confirmation of the Charges, 9 June 2014 at para 153; *Case 002/01* (Case File No 002/19-09-2007/ECCC/TC), Trial Chamber Judgment, 7 August 2014 at para 700; *Ngirabatware* (MICT-12-29-A), Appeals Chamber Judgment, 18 December 2014, at para 166; *Case 002/02* (Case File No 002/19-09-2007/ECCC/TC), Trial Chamber Judgment, 16 November 2018 at para 3720 (although it appears to divert from established ICTY/ICTR jurisprudence by saying that ordering cannot be carried out by omission).

16 *Nahimana, Barayagwiza and Ngeze ("Media")* (ICTR-99-52-A), Appeals Chamber Judgment, 28 November 2007 at para 678; *Munyakazi* (ICTR-97-36A-T), Trial Chamber Judgment, 5 July 2010 at para 428; *Đorđević* (IT-05-87/1), Trial Chamber Judgment, 23 February 2011 at para 1870; *Šešelj* (IT-03-67-T), Trial Chamber Judgment, 31 March 2016 at para 295 (which also adds the elements that the instigator used different forms of persuasion such as threats, enticement, or promises to the physical perpetrators of the crimes and that the incriminating statements must be clearly identifiable and their existence firmly established); *Gbagbo and Blé Goudé* (ICC-02/11-01/15-1263-AnxC-Red), Trial Chamber, Reasons for oral decision of 15 January 2019 on the *Requête de la Défense de Laurent Gbagbo afin qu'un jugement d'acquittement portant sur toutes les charges soit prononcé en faveur de Laurent Gbagbo et que sa mise en liberté immédiate soit ordonnée*, and on the Blé Goudé Defence no case to answer motion, Public Redacted Version of Dissenting Opinion Judge Herrera Carbuccia, 16 July 2019 at paras 563–64.

without the instigation.[17] Both express and implied conduct may constitute instigation.[18] Presence at the scene of the crime is not required for this type of criminal responsibility,[19] nor is any authority on behalf of the instigator.[20] Omission can also be a form of instigation if and when the instigator had a duty to prevent the crime from being brought about.[21]

d) Planning

Planning[22] requires that one or more persons plan or design the criminal conduct constituting one or more crimes that are later actually perpetrated with at least the awareness of the substantial likelihood that a crime will be committed in the execution of that plan.[23] Planning does

---

17 *Kordić and Čerkez* (IT-95-14/2-A), Appeals Chamber Judgment, 17 December 2004 at para 27; *Đorđević* (IT-05-87/1), Trial Chamber Judgment, 23 February 2011 at para 1870; *Šešelj* (IT-03-67-T), Trial Chamber Judgment, 31 March 2016 at para 295; *Gbagbo and Blé Goudé* (ICC-02/11-01/15-1263-AnxC-Red), Trial Chamber, Reasons for oral decision of 15 January 2019 on the *Requête de la Défense de Laurent Gbagbo afin qu'un jugement d'acquittement portant sur toutes les charges soit prononcé en faveur de Laurent Gbagbo et que sa mise en liberté immédiate soit ordonnée*, and on the Blé Goudé Defence no case to answer motion, Public Redacted Version of Dissenting Opinion Judge Herrera Carbuccia, 16 July 2019 at paras 563–64.

18 *Kamuhanda* (ICTR-99-54A-A), Appeals Chamber Judgment, 19 September 2005 at para 593; *Boškoski and Tarčulovski* (IT-04-82-A), Appeals Chamber Judgment, 19 May 2010 at para 157.

19 *Boškoski and Tarčulovski* (IT-04-82-A), Appeals Chamber Judgment, 19 May 2010 at para 125; *Haradinaj et al* (IT-04-84*bis*-T), Trial Chamber Judgment, 29 November 2012 at para 623; *Nyiramasuhuko et al* (ICTR-98-42-A), Appeals Chamber Judgment, 14 December 2015 at para 3327; *Gbagbo and Blé Goudé* (ICC-02/11-01/15-1263-AnxC-Red), Reasons for oral decision of 15 January 2019 on the *Requête de la Défense de Laurent Gbagbo afin qu'un jugement d'acquittement portant sur toutes les charges soit prononcé en faveur de Laurent Gbagbo et que sa mise en liberté immédiate soit ordonnée*, and on the Blé Goudé Defence no case to answer motion, Public Redacted Version of Dissenting Opinion Judge Herrera Carbuccia, 16 July 2019 at para 561.

20 *Stanišić and Župljanin* (IT-08-91-T), Trial Chamber Judgment, 27 March 2013 at para 96; *Gbagbo and Blé Goudé* (ICC-02/11-01/15-1263-AnxC-Red), Trial Chamber, Reasons for oral decision of 15 January 2019 on the *Requête de la Défense de Laurent Gbagbo afin qu'un jugement d'acquittement portant sur toutes les charges soit prononcé en faveur de Laurent Gbagbo et que sa mise en liberté immédiate soit ordonnée*, and on the Blé Goudé Defence no case to answer motion, Public Redacted Version of Dissenting Opinion Judge Herrera Carbuccia, 16 July 2019 at para 563.

21 *Ibid* at para 562.

22 Regarding the customary law character of planning, see *Ao An* (Case File No 004/02/07-09-2009-ECCC/OCIJ (PTC60)), Pre-Trial Chamber, Considerations on Appeals against Closing Orders, Opinion of Judges Baik and Bauvallet, 19 December 2019 at paras 583–88.

23 *Nahimana, Barayagwiza and Ngeze ("Media")* (ICTR-99-52-A), Appeals Chamber Judgment, 28 November 2007 at para 479; *Brima, Kamara and Kanu ("AFRC")* (SCSL-2004-16-A), Appeals Chamber Judgment, 22 February 2008 at para 301; *Kanyarukiga* (ICTR-02-78-A), Appeals Chamber Judgment, 8 May 2012 at para 258; *Taylor* (SCSL-04-01-T), Appeals

not require a finding of a position of authority.[24] It implies that one or several persons contemplated designing the commission of a crime at both the preparatory and execution phases.[25]

The level of participation in the planning of the accused must be substantial, such as actually formulating the criminal plan or endorsing a plan proposed by another.[26] The person who perpetrated the *actus reus* of the offence must have acted in furtherance of the plan.[27] In that respect, it will be sufficient to demonstrate that the planning was a factor substantially contributing to such criminal conduct.[28] Presence at the scene of the crime is not required for this type of criminal responsibility.[29]

e) Aiding and Abetting

While the terms "aiding" and "abetting"[30] are usually used conjunctively, the two notions within this concept are slightly different in that aiding refers to some form of physical assistance in the commission of a crime, while abetting connotes encouragement or another form of moral suasion. The *actus reus* of aiding and abetting consists of carrying out acts (specifically directed)[31] to provide practical assistance, encourage-

---

Chamber Judgment, 26 September 2013 at paras 491–94; *Mladić* (IT-09-92-T), Trial Chamber Judgment, 22 November 2017 at para 3564; *Case 002/02* (Case File No 002/19-09-2007/ECCC/TC), Trial Chamber Judgment, 16 November 2018 at para 3717.

24 *Kanyarukiga* (ICTR-02-78-A), Appeals Chamber Judgment, 8 May 2012 at para 258; *Haradinaj et al* (IT-04-84*bis*-T), Trial Chamber Judgment, 29 November 2012 at para 622; *Case 002/02* (Case File No 002/19-09-2007/ECCC/TC), Trial Chamber Judgment, 16 November 2018 at para 3719.

25 *Kordić and Čerkez* (IT-95-14/2-A), Appeals Chamber Judgment, 17 December 2004 at para 26.

26 *Seromba* (ICTR-2001-66-I), Trial Chamber Judgment, 13 December 2006 at para 303; *Brima, Kamara and Kanu ("AFRC")* (SCSL-2004-16-A), Appeals Chamber Judgment, 22 February 2008 at para 301; *Tolimir* (IT-05-88/2-T), Trial Chamber Judgment, 12 December 2012 at para 900.

27 *Galić* (IT-98-29-T), Trial Chamber Judgment, 5 December 2003 at para 168.

28 *Popović et al* (IT-05-88-T), Trial Chamber Judgment, 10 June 2010 at para 1006; *Kanyarukiga* (ICTR-02-78), Trial Chamber Judgment, 1 November 2010 at para 618.

29 *Boškoski and Tarčulovski* (IT-04-82-A), Appeals Chamber Judgment, 19 May 2010 at para 125.

30 For the notion of a hierarchy between soliciting and inducing, on the one hand, and aiding and abetting, on the other, see *Jean-Pierre Bemba Gombo, Aimé Kilolo Musamba, Jean-Jacques Mangenda Kabongo, Fidèle Babala Wandu and Narcisse Arido* (ICC-01/05-01/13), Trial Chamber Judgment, 19 October 2016 at para 85.

31 There was some uncertainty about this requirement, which appeared to have been laid to rest by *Perišić* (IT-04-81-A), Appeals Chamber Judgment, 28 February 2013 at paras 25–42 and 73; see, also, *Stanišić and Simatović* (IT-03-69-T), Trial Chamber Judgment, 30 May 2013 at para 1264; however, the Appeals Chamber of the Special Court for Sierra Leone (SCSL) took issue with this jurisprudence and was of the view that there is no such requirement; see *Taylor* (SCSL-04-01-T), Appeals Chamber Judgment, 26 September 2013 at paras 471–81

ment, or moral support, which has a substantial effect on the perpetration of an international crime.[32] Substantial has been defined as "if the criminal act most probably would not have occurred in the same way had not someone acted in the role that the suspect in fact assumed."[33] Either aiding or abetting alone is sufficient to render the perpetrator

---

and 486, which was confirmed by the ICTY Appeals Chamber itself in a comprehensive and detailed decision in *Šainović et al* (IT-05-87-A), Appeals Chamber Judgment, 23 January 2014 at paras 1617–51; see, also, *Case 002/01* (Case File No 002/19-09-2007/ECCC/TC), Trial Chamber Judgment, 7 August 2014 at para 710; *Popović et al* (IT-05-88-A), Appeals Chamber Judgment, 30 January 2015 at para 1764; *Stanišić and Simatović* (IT-03-69-A), Appeals Chamber Judgment, 9 December 2015 at paras 104–6; *Karadžić* (IT-95-5/18-T), Trial Chamber Judgment, 24 March 2016 at para 576; *Mladić* (IT-09-92-T), Trial Chamber Judgment, 22 November 2017 at para 3567.

32 *Nahimana, Barayagwiza and Ngeze ("Media")* (ICTR-99-52-A), Appeals Chamber Judgment, 28 November 2007 at para 482; Special Tribunal for Lebanon, Interlocutory Decision on the Applicable Law: Terrorism, Conspiracy, Homicide, Perpetration, Cumulative charging, STL-II-OI/I/AC/RI76bis, Appeals Chamber, 16 February 2011 at para 226; *Taylor* (SCSL-04-01-T), Appeals Chamber Judgment, 26 September 2013 at paras 362, 368–85, 390–92, and 401; *Case 002/01* (Case File No 002/19-09-2007/ECCC/TC), Trial Chamber Judgment, 7 August 2014 at para 704; *Popović et al* (IT-05-88-A), Appeals Chamber Judgment, 30 January 2015 at paras 1758 and 1812; *Mladić* (IT-09-92-T), Trial Chamber Judgment, 22 November 2017 at para 3567; *Case 002/02* (Case File No 002/19-09-2007/ECCC/TC), Trial Chamber Judgment, 16 November 2018 at para 3722. There had been disagreement at the Trial Chamber level as to whether the effect had to be "direct and substantial" (on the one hand, the cases of *Tadić* (IT-94-1), Trial Chamber Judgment, 7 May 1997 at paras 730, 738, and *Mucić et al (Čelebići Camp)* (IT-96-21), Trial Chamber Judgment, 16 November 1998 at paras 325–27; the requirement of "direct" had been added, while on the other, *Furundžija* (IT-95-17/1), Trial Chamber Judgment, 19 December 1998 at paras 225, 234; *Aleksovski* (IT-95-14/1), Trial Chamber Judgment, 25 June 1999 at para 61; *Rutaganda* (ICTR-96-3-T), Trial Chamber Judgment, 6 December 1999 at para 42; *Musema* (ICTR-96-13-T), Trial Chamber Judgment, 27 January 2000 at para 126; and *Blaškić* (IT-95-14), Trial Chamber Judgment, 3 March 2000 at paras 283–88 had not), but the directness requirement was eliminated in *Tadić* (IT-94-1-A), Appeals Chamber Judgment, 15 July 1999 at para 229; see, also, *Kayishema and Ruzindana* (ICTR-95-1-A), Appeals Chamber Judgment, 1 June 2001 at paras 191–94; *Karadžić* (IT-95-5/18-T), Trial Chamber Judgment, 24 March 2016 at para 575; *Šešelj* (IT-03-67-T), Trial Chamber Judgment, 31 March 2016 at para 353.

At the ICC, see *Ongwen* (ICC-02/04-01/15), Pre-Trial Chamber, Decision on the Confirmation of Charges, 23 March 2016 at para 43; *Al Mahdi* (ICC-01/12-01/15), Pre-Trial Chamber, Decision on the Confirmation of Charges, 24 March 2016 at para 26, which indicated that the contribution does not need to be substantial (as does the *Ongwen* decision); *Jean-Pierre Bemba Gombo, Aimé Kilolo Musamba, Jean-Jacques Mangenda Kabongo, Fidèle Babala Wandu and Narcisse Arido* (ICC-01/05-01/13), Trial Chamber Judgment, 19 October 2016 at paras 87–96, which goes further and indicates at para 93 that aiding and abetting "does not require the meeting of any specific threshold."

33 *Tadić* (IT-94-1), Appeals Chamber Judgment, 7 May 1997 at para 688.

criminally liable.[34] Aiding and abetting can be committed at a time and place removed from the actual crime.[35]

The *actus reus* of aiding and abetting may be perpetrated through an omission provided that this failure to act had a decisive effect on the commission of the crime. The *actus reus* and *mens rea* requirements for aiding and abetting by omission are the same as for aiding and abetting by a positive act. The critical issue to be determined is whether, on the particular facts of a given case, it is established that the failure to discharge a legal duty assisted, encouraged, or lent moral support to the perpetration of the crime and had a substantial effect on it.[36]

As well, the mere presence at the scene of a crime can be an example of an omission. While such presence of an individual in a position of superior authority does not suffice to conclude that they encouraged or supported the crime, the presence of a person with superior authority, such as a military commander, can be a probative indication for determining whether that person encouraged or supported the perpetrators of the crime.[37] Where the presence of a person bestows legitimacy on or provides encouragement to the actual perpetrator, that may be sufficient to constitute aiding and abetting.[38] Moreover, responsibility for having aided and abetted a crime by omission may arise, regardless of whether the person's presence at the crime scene provided encouragement to the perpetrators, if the person was under a duty to prevent the commission

34 *Vasiljević* (IT-98-32-A), Appeals Chamber Judgment, 25 February 2004 at para 102; *Haradinaj et al* (IT-04-84*bis*-T), Trial Chamber Judgment, 29 November 2012 at para 625; *Lukić* (IT-98-32/1-A), Appeals Chamber Judgment, 4 December 2012 at para 424.

35 *Fofana and Kondewa ("CDF")* (SCSL-04-14-A), Appeals Chamber Judgment, 28 May 2008 at para 72; *Perišić* (IT-04-81-T), Trial Chamber Judgment, 6 September 2011 at para 126; *Lukić* (IT-98-32/1-A), Appeals Chamber Judgment, 4 December 2012 at para 425; *Karadžić* (IT-95-5/18-T), Trial Chamber Judgment, 24 March 2016 at para 576.

36 *Orić* (IT-03-68-A), Appeals Chamber Judgment, 3 July 2008 at paras 42–46; *Mrkšić et al* (IT-95-13/1-A), Appeals Chamber Judgment, 5 May 2009 at paras 145–59; *Ndahimana* (ICTR-01-68-A), Appeals Chamber Judgment, 16 December 2013 at para 147; *Šainović et al* (IT-05-87-A), Appeals Chamber Judgment, 23 January 2014 at paras 1677–79; *Popović et al* (IT-05-88-A), Appeals Chamber Judgment, 30 January 2015 at paras 1740–41 and 1812; *Nyiramasuhuko et al* (ICTR-98-42-A), Appeals Chamber Judgment, 14 December 2015 at paras 2206, 2255; *Case 002/02* (Case File No 002/19-09-2007/ECCC/TC), Trial Chamber Judgment, 16 November 2018 at para 3724.

37 *Boškoski and Tarčulovski* (IT-04-82-T), Trial Chamber Judgment, 10 July 2008 at para 402; *Seromba* (ICTR-2001-66-I), Trial Chamber Judgment, 13 December 2006 at para 308; *Ngirabatware* (ICTR-99-54-T), Trial Chamber Judgment, 20 December 2012 at para 1295.

38 *Boškoski and Tarčulovski* (IT-04-82-T), Trial Chamber Judgment, 10 July 2008 at para 402; *Ngirabatware* (MICT-12-29-A), Appeals Chamber Judgment, 18 December 2014 at para 150.

of the crime but failed to act, provided that their failure to act had a substantial effect on the commission of the crime.[39] Aiding and abetting is also possible where a commander allows the use of resources under their control, including personnel, to facilitate the perpetration of a crime.[40]

The *mens rea* required for aiding and abetting is the knowledge or awareness of the substantial likelihood that the practical assistance, encouragement, or moral support assists or facilitates the commission of the offence, although the accused does not need to have the intent to commit the crime.[41] It is not necessary that the aider and abettor knows the precise crime that was intended and committed, but they must be aware of the essential elements of the crime committed by the principal offender, including the principal offender's state of mind.[42] However, the aider and abettor does not need to share the intent of the principal

39 *Mrkšić et al* (IT-95-13/1-A), Appeals Chamber Judgment, 5 May 2009 at para 49; *Karemera et al* (ICTR-98-44-T), Trial Chamber Judgment, 2 February 2012 at para 1431.

40 *Bagosora, Kabiligi, Ntabakuze and Nsengiyumva* (ICTR-98-41-T), Trial Chamber Judgment, 18 December 2008 at para 2009; *Ndindiliyimana et al* (ICTR-00-56-T), Trial Chamber Judgment, 17 May 2011 at para 1914; *Perišić* (IT-04-81-T), Trial Chamber Judgment, 6 September 2011 at para 128.

41 *Brđanin* (IT-99-36-A), Appeals Chamber Judgment, 3 April 2007 at para 484; *Taylor* (SCSL-04-01-T), Appeals Chamber Judgment, 26 September 2013 at paras 414–40 and 451; *Ndahimana* (ICTR-01-68-A), Appeals Chamber Judgment, 16 December 2013 at para 157; *Šainović et al* (IT-05-87-A), Appeals Chamber Judgment, 23 January 2014 at para 1172; *Ngirabatware* (MICT-12-29-A), Appeals Chamber Judgment, 18 December 2014 at para 155; *Karadžić* (IT-95-5/18-T), Trial Chamber Judgment, 24 March 2016 at para 577; *Šešelj* (IT-03-67-T), Trial Chamber Judgment, 31 March 2016 at para 353; *Mladić* (IT-09-92-T), Trial Chamber Judgment, 22 November 2017 at para 3576; *Case 002/02* (Case File No 002/19-09-2007/ECCC/TC), Trial Chamber Judgment, 16 November 2018 at para 3722. Article 25(3)(c) of the Rome Statute imposes a higher level of *mens rea* by adding the words "for the purpose of facilitating the commission"; see *Jean-Pierre Bemba Gombo, Aimé Kilolo Musamba, Jean-Jacques Mangenda Kabongo, Fidèle Babala Wandu and Narcisse Arido* (ICC-01/05-01/13), Trial Chamber Judgment, 19 October 2016 at paras 97–98, although *Chui* (ICC-01/04-02/12), Trial Chamber Judgment, Concurring Opinion of Judge Christine Van den Wyngaert, 18 December 2012 at para 25, seems to suggest that this additional wording might be jurisdictional rather than substantive.

42 *Nahimana, Barayagwiza and Ngeze ("Media")* (ICTR-99-52-A), Appeals Chamber Judgment, 28 November 2007 at para 482; *Brima, Kamara and Kanu ("AFRC")* (SCSL-2004-16-A), Appeals Chamber Judgment, 22 February 2008 at paras 242–43; *Fofana and Kondewa ("CDF")* (SCSL-04-14-A), Appeals Chamber Judgment, 28 May 2008 at para 367; Special Tribunal for Lebanon, Interlocutory Decision on the Applicable Law: Terrorism, Conspiracy, Homicide, Perpetration, Cumulative charging, STL-II-OI/I/AC/RI76bis, Appeals Chamber, 16 February 2011 at para 227; *Šainović et al* (IT-05-87-A), Appeals Chamber Judgment, 23 January 2014 at para 1773; *Popović et al* (IT-05-88-A), Appeals Chamber Judgment, 30 January 2015 at paras 1751, 1754, and 1794; *Mladić* (IT-09-92-T), Trial Chamber Judgment, 22 November 2017 at para 3567.

offender,[43] nor do they even need to know who is committing the crime.[44] With respect to aiding and abetting genocide, international tribunals have found that this form of commission is present if a person knowingly aided or abetted one or more persons in the commission of genocide while knowing that such a person or persons were committing genocide, even though the aider and abettor themself did not have the specific intent to destroy, in whole or in part, a national, ethnical, racial, or religious group as such.[45]

Aiding and abetting has been found present in the following circumstances: provision of arms and ammunition;[46] provision of military personnel;[47] provision of operational support, such as providing communications equipment and training, logistical support and safe havens in the form of a guest house, financial support, medical support, herbalists to bolster confidence of fighters, and security escorts for arms, ammunition, diamonds, drivers, messengers, and liaison personnel;[48] and provision of advice and direction in military strategy.[49]

f) Accessory After the Fact

Participation by aiding and abetting may occur before, during, or after the act is committed.[50] If the aiding and abetting occurs after the crime,

---

43 *Seromba* (ICTR-2001-66-I), Trial Chamber Judgment, 13 December 2006 at para 309; *Popović et al* (IT-05-88-A), Appeals Chamber Judgment, 30 January 2015 at para 1794; *Mladić* (IT-09-92-T), Trial Chamber Judgment, 22 November 2017 at para 3567; *Case 002/02* (Case File No 002/19-09-2007/ECCC/TC), Trial Chamber Judgment, 16 November 2018 at para 3722.

44 *Brđanin* (IT-99-36-A), Appeals Chamber Judgment, 3 April 2007 at paras 108 and 355; *Ngirabatware* (MICT-12-29-A), Appeals Chamber Judgment, 18 December 2014, at para 149.

45 *Akayesu* (ICTR-96-4-T), Trial Chamber Judgment, 2 September 1998 at para 545; *Krstić* (IT-98-33-A), Appeals Chamber Judgment, 19 April 2004 at para 140; *Rukundo* (ICTR-2001-70-A), Appeals Chamber Judgment, 20 October 2010 at paras 52, 61; *Kalimanzira* (ICTR-05-88-A), Appeals Chamber Judgment, 20 October 2010 at para 220; *Ngirabatware* (MICT-12-29-A), Appeals Chamber Judgment, 18 December 2014 at para 155; *Lukić* (IT-98-32/1-A), Appeals Chamber Judgment, 4 December 2012 at paras 458–59 regarding persecution; *Case 002/02* (Case File No 002/19-09-2007/ECCC/TC), Trial Chamber Judgment, 16 November 2018 at para 3722.

46 *Taylor* (SCSL-03-01-T), Trial Chamber Judgment, 18 May 2012 at para 6918.

47 *Ibid* at para 6927.

48 *Ibid* at paras 6937–43.

49 *Ibid* at para 6950; for other examples, see *Taylor* (SCSL-04-01-T), Appeals Chamber Judgment, 26 September 2013 at para 369.

50 *Nahimana, Barayagwiza and Ngeze ("Media")* (ICTR-99-52-A), Appeals Chamber Judgment, 28 November 2007 at para 482; *Fofana and Kondewa ("CDF")* (SCSL-04-14-A), Appeals Chamber Judgment, 28 May 2008 at para 71; *Lukić* (IT-98-32/1-A), Appeals Chamber Judgment, 4 December 2012 at para 425; *Jean-Pierre Bemba Gombo, Aimé Kilolo Musamba, Jean-Jacques*

it must be established that a prior agreement existed between the principal and the person who subsequently aided and abetted in the commission of the crime.[51]

g) Complicity

While the terms "complicity" and "aiding and abetting" appear to be similar,[52] they have been the subject of debate in the ICTY/ICTR jurisprudence. Since the ICTY and ICTR statutes contain a specific provision with respect to complicity in genocide,[53] while at the same time having a general provision of extended liability that includes aiding and abetting for genocide,[54] the question arose as to whether these two notions overlap. The answer given was that aiding and abetting is only one aspect of the larger notion of complicity and that for genocide, the *mens rea* for complicity that goes beyond aiding and abetting could possibly be the narrower, specific intent of genocide.[55] It has also been said that complicity in genocide requires a positive act, while aiding and abetting the same crime can be accomplished by failing to act or refraining from taking action.[56] The question remained unresolved at the ICTY and ICTR[57]

Mangenda Kabongo, Fidèle Babala Wandu and Narcisse Arido (ICC-01/05-01/13), Trial Chamber Judgment, 19 October 2016 at para 96; *Mladić* (IT-09-92-T), Trial Chamber Judgment, 22 November 2017 at para 3567; *Case 002/02* (Case File No 002/19-09-2007/ECCC/TC), Trial Chamber Judgment, 16 November 2018 at para 3723.

51 *Sesay, Kallon and Gbao ("RUF")*, (SCSL-04-15-T), Trial Chamber Judgment, 25 February 2009 at para 278; *Case 002/01* (Case File No 002/19-09-2007/ECCC/TC), Trial Chamber Judgment, 7 August 2014 at para 713; *Case 002/02* (Case File No 002/19-09-2007/ECCC/TC), Trial Chamber Judgment, 16 November 2018 at para 3722.

52 *Blagojević & Jokić* (IT-02-60-T), Trial Chamber Judgment, 17 January 2005 at para 777.

53 Articles 4(3)(e) and 2(3)(e), respectively.

54 Articles 7.1 and 6.1, respectively.

55 *Krstić* (IT-98-33-A), Appeals Chamber Judgment, 19 April 2004 at paras 137–39; *Ntakirutimana* (ICTR-96-10-A and ICTR-96-17-A), Appeals Chamber Judgment, 13 December 2004 at para 371; see, however, *Krstić* (IT-98-33-A), Appeals Chamber Judgment, Partial Dissenting Opinion of Judge Shahabuddeen, 19 April 2004 at paras 59–68; *Milošević* (IT-02-54-T), Trial Chamber, Decision on Motion for Judgment of Acquittal, 16 June 2004 at paras 290–97, and *Karemena, Ngirumpatse and Nzirorera* (ICTR-98-44-T), Trial Chamber, Decision on Defence Motions Challenging the Pleading of a Joint Criminal Enterprise in a Count of Complicity in Genocide in the Amended Indictment, 18 May 2006 at para 6; *Nyiramasuhuko et al* (ICTR-98-42-T), Trial Chamber Judgment, 24 June 2011 at para 5980.

56 *Akayesu* (ICTR-96-4-T), Trial Chamber Judgment, 2 September 1998 at paras 547–48; *Musema* (ICTR-96-13-T), Trial Chamber Judgment, 27 January 2000 at para 183.

57 *Krstić* (IT-98-33-A), Appeals Chamber Judgment, 19 April 2004 at para 142, n247; it would appear that from the *travaux préparatoires* of the Genocide Convention (see William A. Schabas, *Genocide in International Law: The Crime of Crimes*, 2d ed (Cambridge: Cambridge

but has been dealt with in the Rome Statute by separating the crime of genocide and the means of committing such a crime and by deleting the term "complicity."

h) Joint Criminal Enterprise

Before examining the legal parameters of JCE, an example given by a Trial Chamber as to the factual aspects of this notion might help elucidate when this notion is engaged. The *Kvočka* ruling had this to say:

> For instance, an accountant hired to work for a film company that produces child pornography may initially manage accounts without awareness of the criminal nature of the company. Eventually, however, he comes to know that the company produces child pornography, which he knows to be illegal. If the accountant continues to work for the company despite this knowledge, he could be said to aid or abet the criminal enterprise. Even if it was also shown that the accountant detested child pornography, criminal liability would still attach. At some point, moreover, if the accountant continues to work at the company long enough and performs his job in a competent and efficient manner with only an occasional protest regarding the despicable goals of the company, it would be reasonable to infer that he shares the criminal intent of the enterprise and thus becomes a co-perpetrator. The man who merely cleans the office after hours, however, and who sees the child photos and knows that the company is participating in criminal activity and who continues to clean the office, would not be considered a participant in the enterprise because his role is not deemed to be sufficiently significant in the enterprise.[58]

This same judgment also provided some insight into the factors that would be of significance in determining whether a person was part of a JCE:

University Press, 2009) at 339–41) and from the fact that one of the early international treaties employing universal jurisdiction as a ground for criminalization, the Torture Convention, uses the words "an act by any person which constitutes complicity or participation" (for background, see J. Hermann Burgers & Hans Danelius, *The United Nations Convention against Torture: A Handbook on the Convention against Torture and Other Cruel, Inhuman or Degrading Treatment or Punishment* (Dordrecht/Boston/London: Martinus Nijhoff, 1988) at 56–57) (as opposed to any of the other similar treaties, the counter-terrorism treaties), a persuasive argument can be made that the notion of complicity was an early reiteration of the aiding and abetting concept.

58 *Kvočka* (IT-98-30/1), Trial Chamber Judgment, 2 November 2001 at paras 285–86.

> The level of participation attributed to the accused and whether that participation is deemed significant will depend on a variety of factors, including the size of the criminal enterprise, the functions performed, the position of the accused, the amount of time spent participating after acquiring knowledge of the criminality of the system, efforts made to prevent criminal activity or to impede the efficient functioning of the system, the seriousness and scope of the crimes committed and the efficiency, zealousness or gratuitous cruelty exhibited in performing the actor's function. It would also be important to examine any direct evidence of a shared intent or agreement with the criminal endeavor, such as repeated, continuous, or extensive participation in the system, verbal expressions, or physical perpetration of a crime.[59]

With respect to the legal aspects of this concept, in general, the Appeals Chamber jurisprudence has distinguished three types of JCE.[60] In the first form of JCE, all of the co-perpetrators possess the same intent to effect the common purpose, the crime.[61] The second form of JCE, the "systemic" form, a variant of the first form, is characterized by the existence of an organized criminal system, in particular in the case of concentration or detention camps. This form of JCE requires personal knowledge of the organized system and intent to further the criminal purpose of that system. The third, "extended" form of JCE entails responsibility for crimes committed beyond the common purpose but that are nevertheless a natural and foreseeable consequence of the common purpose. The requisite *mens rea* for the extended form is twofold. First, the accused must have the intention to participate in and contribute to the common

---

59 *Ibid* at paras 285–86 and 311; see, also, *Mbarushimana* (ICC-01/04-01/10), Pre-Trial Chamber, Decision of the Confirmation of Charges, 16 December 2011 at para 284.

60 *Tadić* (IT-94-1-A), Appeals Chamber Judgment, 15 July 1999 at para 227; *Vasiljević* (IT-98-32-A), Appeals Chamber Judgment, 25 February 2004 at para 100; *Stakić* (IT-97-24-A), Appeals Chamber Judgment, 22 March 2006 at para 64. It is worth noting that in one of the first cases in which JCE was used, the *Tadić* case, the accused had been acquitted by the Trial Chamber since it could not be proven that he, as part of a larger group of five men, had played any part in the commission of murder. The Appeals Chamber found that there was criminal liability based on JCE even if there was no proof of the personal commission of any of the members in the JCE. For an subsequent detailed analysis that the *Tadić* case had correctly considered JCE to be part of customary international law, see *Đorđević* (IT-05-87/1-A), Appeals Chamber Judgment, 27 January 2014 at paras 32–58; *Popović et al* (IT-05-88-A), Appeals Chamber Judgment, 30 January 2015 at paras 1440 and 1672–74; *Tolimir* (IT-05-88/2-A), Appeals Chamber Judgment, 8 April 2015 at paras 280–84; *Prlić et al* (IT-04-74-A), Appeals Chamber Judgment, 29 November 2017 at paras 587–91.

61 *Haradinaj et al* (IT-04-84*bis*-T), Trial Chamber Judgment, 29 November 2012 at para 620.

criminal purpose. Second, in order to be held responsible for crimes that were not part of the common criminal purpose but that were nevertheless a natural and foreseeable consequence of it, the accused must also know that such a crime might be perpetrated by a member of the group and willingly take the risk that the crime might occur by joining or continuing to participate in the enterprise.[62]

The general requirements for this type of responsibility are as follows:

- a plurality of persons, who do not need to be organized in a military, a political, or an administrative structure.
- the existence of a common plan, design, or purpose that amounts to or involves the commission of a crime. There is no necessity for this plan, design, or purpose to have been previously arranged or formulated. The common plan or purpose may materialize extemporaneously and be inferred from the fact that a plurality of persons act in unison to put into effect a JCE.
- participation of the accused in the common design involving the perpetration of one of the international crimes. This participation need not involve commission of a specific crime under one of those provisions but may take the form of assistance in or contribution to the execution of the common plan or purpose; the participation in the enterprise must be significant, meaning an act or omission that makes an enterprise efficient or effective—for example, a participation that enables the system to run more smoothly or without disruption.[63]

More recently, some refinements and clarifications have been made to these general principles. In general, the doctrine of JCE can be used against high-level functionaries,[64] is not restricted to small-scale cases,

62 *Đorđević* (IT-05-87/1-A), Appeals Chamber Judgment, 27 January 2014 at paras 468 and 474; *Stanišić and Simatović* (IT-03-69-A), Appeals Chamber Judgment, 9 December 2015 at para 77; *Case 002/02* (Case File No 002/19-09-2007/ECCC/TC), Trial Chamber Judgment, 16 November 2018 at para 3606.

63 *Tadić* (IT-94-1-A), Appeals Chamber Judgment, 15 July 1999 at para 227; *Vasiljević* (IT-98-32-A), Appeals Chamber Judgment, 25 February 2004 at para 100; *Stakić* (IT-97-24-A), Appeals Chamber Judgment, 22 March 2006 at para 64; *Gatete* (ICTR-2000-61-A), Appeals Chamber Judgment, 9 October 2012 at paras 239, 241; *Šešelj* (MICT-16-99-A), Appeals Chamber Judgment, 11 April 2018 at paras 95–96; *Case 002/02* (Case File No 002/19-09-2007/ECCC/TC), Trial Chamber Judgment, 16 November 2018 at paras 3708–10.

64 *Krajišnik* (IT-00-39-A), Appeals Chamber Judgment, 17 March 2009 at para 194.

and can also apply to large criminal enterprises.[65] Conversely, where the common purpose includes crimes committed over a wide geographical area, a person may be found criminally responsible for their participation in the enterprise even if their contributions to the enterprise occurred only in a smaller geographical area.[66] With respect to the first two categories, it has been made clear that mere membership in the group having a common criminal purpose is not sufficient,[67] although an omission can amount to JCE participation for which it is not necessary to establish a duty to act.[68] However, it is not required that each member in the JCE is identified by name, but it can be sufficient to refer to categories or groups of persons.[69]

The requirement that the common plan, design, or purpose of a JCE is inherently criminal means that it must either have as its objective a crime or contemplate crimes as the means of achieving its objective.[70] The common criminal objective of the JCE may also evolve over time if the members agree on this expansion of means. It also means that the crimes that make up the common purpose may evolve and change over time, and as such, the JCE may have different participants at different times.[71]

---

65 *Brđanin* (IT-99-36-A), Appeals Chamber Judgment, 3 April 2007 at para 425.

66 *Tadić* (IT-94-1-A), Appeals Chamber Judgment, 15 July 1999 at para 199; *Popović et al* (IT-05-88-T), Trial Chamber Judgment, 10 June 2010 at para 1024.

67 *Brđanin* (IT-99-36), Trial Chamber Judgment, 1 September 2004 at para 263; *Karemera et al* (ICTR-98-44-T), Trial Chamber Judgment, 2 February 2012 at para 1437; *Case 002/02* (Case File No 002/19-09-2007/ECCC/TC), Trial Chamber Judgment, 16 November 2018 at para 3710.

68 *Stanišić and Župljanin* (IT-08-91-A), Appeals Chamber Judgment, 30 June 2016 at para 111; *Stanišić and Župljanin* (IT-08-91-A), Appeals Chamber Judgment, 30 June 2016 at paras 732–33; *Case 002/02* (Case File No 002/19-09-2007/ECCC/TC), Trial Chamber Judgment, 16 November 2018 at para 3710.

69 *Krajišnik* (IT-00-39-A), Appeals Chamber Judgment, 17 March 2009 at para 156; *Đorđević* (IT-05-87/1-A), Appeals Chamber Judgment, 27 January 2014 at paras 127–30; *Karemera* (ICTR-98-44-A), Appeals Chamber Judgment, 29 September 2014 at para 605; *Karadžić* (IT-95-5/18-T), Trial Chamber Judgment, 24 March 2016 at para 562.

70 *Brima, Kamara and Kanu ("AFRC")* (SCSL-2004-16-A), Appeals Chamber Judgment, 22 February 2008 at paras 76–80.

71 *Krajišnik* (IT-00-39-A), Appeals Chamber Judgment, 17 March 2009 at para 163; Special Tribunal for Lebanon, Interlocutory Decision on the Applicable Law: Terrorism, Conspiracy, Homicide, Perpetration, Cumulative charging, STL-II-OI/I/AC/RI76bis, Appeals Chamber, 16 February 2011 at paras 246–48; *Šainović et al* (IT-05-87-A), Appeals Chamber Judgment, 23 January 2014 at paras 609–11; *Karadžić* (IT-95-5/18-T), Trial Chamber Judgment, 24 March 2016 at para 563; *Mladić* (IT-09-92-T), Trial Chamber Judgment, 22 November 2017 at para 3561.

For persons in a criminal enterprise to be liable, it must be shown that they acted together, or in concert with each other, in the implementation of a common objective,[72] but it is not a legal requirement that they acted in unison.[73] It is not necessary that the persons carrying out the *actus reus* of the crime forming part of the common purpose have been participants in or members of the JCE. But if a JCE member used a non-member to commit a crime, that crime must be traced back to the member of the JCE.[74] Consequently, persons carrying out the crime need not share the intent of the crime with the participants in the common purpose, nor is the mental state of persons carrying out the crime a determinative factor in finding the requisite intent for the participants in a JCE. Knowledge of particular crimes, combined with continued participation in the execution of the common plan from which those crimes result, could be a basis to infer that they shared the requisite intent for the crimes in question.[75]

With respect to the contribution factor, the participation or contribution of an accused in the common purpose need not be substantive or criminal, but it should at least be a significant contribution to the crimes committed;[76] routine duties can amount to a contribution.[77] The fact that different persons might have different levels of involvement does not negate the existence of a JCE, and a different level of

72 *Popović et al* (IT-05-88-A), Appeals Chamber Judgment, 30 January 2015 at para 1050; *Mladić* (IT-09-92-T), Trial Chamber Judgment, 22 November 2017 at para 3561.

73 *Đorđević* (IT-05-87/1-A), Appeals Chamber Judgment, 27 January 2014 at paras 138–42.

74 *Krajišnik* (IT-00-39-A), Appeals Chamber Judgment, 17 March 2009 at paras 225–26; *Karadžić* (IT-95-5/18-AR98bis.1), Appeals Chamber Judgment (Rule 98bis), 11 July 2013 at para 79; *Đorđević* (IT-05-87/1-A), Appeals Chamber Judgment, 27 January 2014 at paras 165, 169, and 171; *Šainović et al* (IT-05-87-A), Appeals Chamber Judgment, 23 January 2014 at paras 1256–57; *Karemera* (ICTR-98-44-A), Appeals Chamber Judgment, 29 September 2014 at para 153; *Popović et al* (IT-05-88-A), Appeals Chamber Judgment, 30 January 2015 at paras 1050 and 1065; *Stanišić and Župljanin* (IT-08-91-A), Appeals Chamber Judgment, 30 June 2016 at paras 119 and 994–96; *Habré*, EAC, Trial Chamber Judgment, 30 May 2016 at paras 1905–8; *Mladić* (IT-09-92-T), Trial Chamber Judgment, 22 November 2017 at para 3561; *Case 002/02* (Case File No 002/19-09-2007/ECCC/TC), Trial Chamber Judgment, 16 November 2018 at para 3711.

75 *Karadžić* (MICT-13-55-A), Appeals Chamber Judgment, 20 March 2019 at paras 672 and 691–92.

76 *Krajišnik* (IT-00-39-A), Appeals Chamber Judgment, 17 March 2009 at para 215; *Šainović et al* (IT-05-87-A), Appeals Chamber Judgment, 23 January 2014 at paras 985 and 987. This implies a lesser level of contribution for JCE compared to aiding and abetting according to *Gotovina and Markač* (IT-06-90-A), Appeals Chamber Judgment, 16 November 2012 at paras 147 and 149.

77 *Stanišić and Župljanin* (IT-08-91-A), Appeals Chamber Judgment, 30 June 2016 at para 253.

involvement can be dealt with at the sentencing stage.[78] A person's position of authority and silent approval militate in favour of a finding that their participation was significant,[79] which includes a failure to ensure the investigation and punishment of crimes committed.[80]

With respect to the third category of JCE, a person

> can only be held responsible for a crime outside the common purpose, if under the circumstances of the case: (i) it was foreseeable that such a crime might be perpetrated by one or other members of the group and (ii) the accused willingly took that risk (*dolus eventualis*). The crime must be shown to have been foreseeable to the accused in particular.[81]

Willingly taking a risk means a decision to participate in a JCE with the awareness that crime was a possible (not probable) consequence of the implementation of that enterprise.[82] For third-category JCE liability, the accused does not need to be present at the scene of the crime,[83] nor do they need to possess the requisite intent for the crime falling

---

78 *Brđanin* (IT-99-36-A), Appeals Chamber Judgment, 3 April 2007 at para 432; *Đorđević* (IT-05-87/1), Trial Chamber Judgment, 23 February 2011 at para 1863; *Stanišić and Župljanin* (IT-08-91-A), Appeals Chamber Judgment, 30 June 2016 at para 121.

79 *Tolimir* (IT-05-88/2-T), Trial Chamber Judgment, 12 December 2012 at para 894; *Šainović et al* (IT-05-87-A), Appeals Chamber, 23 January 2014 at paras 1242 and 1368; *Popović et al* (IT-05-88-A), Appeals Chamber Judgment, 30 January 2015 at para 1385; *Stanišić and Župljanin* (IT-08-91-A), Appeals Chamber Judgment, 30 June 2016 at para 752.

80 *Đorđević* (IT-05-87/1-A), Appeals Chamber Judgment, 27 January 2014 at paras 454 and 460; *Šainović et al* (IT-05-87-A), Appeals Chamber Judgment, 23 January 2014 at paras 1233–34; *Stanišić and Župljanin* (IT-08-91-A), Appeals Chamber Judgment, 30 June 2016 at paras 121 and 734; *Mladić* (MICT-13-56-A), Appeals Chamber Judgment, 8 June 2021 at paras 193–94, 202, 229, 231, 236–37, 392–93, and 414–15.

81 *Brđanin* (IT-99-36-A), Appeals Chamber Judgment, 3 April 2007 at para 365; *Đorđević* (IT-05-87/1-A), Appeals Chamber Judgment, 27 January 2014 at para 906; *Šainović et al* (IT-05-87-A), Appeals Chamber Judgment, 23 January 2014 at paras 1281–82, 1525, 1538, and 1557; *Karemera* (ICTR-98-44-A), Appeals Chamber Judgment, 29 September 2014 at paras 623, 627, 630, and 634; *Popović et al* (IT-05-88-A), Appeals Chamber Judgment, 30 January 2015 at paras 1431–32 and 1701; *Stanišić and Župljanin* (IT-08-91-A), Appeals Chamber Judgment, 30 June 2016 at paras 614, 621, 958, and 967–76; *Prlić et al* (IT-04-74-A), Appeals Chamber Judgment, 29 November 2017 at paras 2836, 2891–93, 2896, and 3022–29.

82 *Brđanin* (IT-99-36-A), Appeals Chamber Judgment, 3 April 2007 at para 411; *Gotovina and Markač* (IT-06-90-A), Appeals Chamber Judgment, 16 November 2012 at paras 90 and 97; *Đorđević* (IT-05-87/1-A), Appeals Chamber Judgment, 27 January 2014 at paras 907, 911–13, and 926–27; *Tolimir* (IT-05-88/2-A), Appeals Chamber Judgment, 8 April 2015 at para 514; *Stanišić and Župljanin* (IT-08-91-A), Appeals Chamber Judgment, 30 June 2016 at para 1055; *Prlić et al* (IT-04-74-A), Appeals Chamber Judgment, 29 November 2017 at para 2836; *Karadžić* (MICT-13-55-A), Appeals Chamber Judgment, 20 March 2019 at paras 433–37.

83 *Tolimir* (IT-05-88/2-A), Appeals Chamber Judgment, 8 April 2015 at para 549.

outside the common purpose, nor is there an express time frame for the foreseeability criterion. The mental state of the person or persons carrying out the extended crime is not relevant for the finding of the mental state of the accused but is determinative to the finding of which extended crime was committed.[84] A JCE can also be a basis for liability in genocide and other special intent crimes, including the third category.[85]

The Appeals Chamber of the ICTY has provided a number of indicators to differentiate between aiding and abetting and JCE:

- Aiding and abetting generally involves a lesser degree of individual criminal responsibility than co-perpetration in a JCE.[86]
- The aider and abettor is always an accessory to a crime perpetrated by another person, the principal.
- In the case of aiding and abetting, no proof is required of the existence of a common concerted plan, let alone of the pre-existence of such a plan. No plan or agreement is required; indeed, the principal may not even know about the accomplice's contribution.[87]
- The aider and abettor carries out acts directed to assist, encourage, or lend moral support to the perpetration of a certain specific crime (murder, extermination, rape, torture, wanton destruction of civilian property, etc.), and this support has a substantial effect upon the perpetration of the crime. By contrast, in the case of acting in pursuance of a common purpose or design, it is sufficient for the participant to perform acts that in some way are directed

---

84 *Popović et al* (IT-05-88-A), Appeals Chamber Judgment, 30 January 2015 at para 1696; *Stanišić and Simatović* (IT-03-69-A), Appeals Chamber Judgment, 9 December 2015 at para 81.

85 *Brđanin* (IT-99-36-A), Appeals Chamber, Decision on Interlocutory Appeal, 19 March 2004 at paras 5–10; however, see Special Tribunal for Lebanon, Interlocutory Decision on the Applicable Law: Terrorism, Conspiracy, Homicide, Perpetration, Cumulative charging, STL-II-OI/I/AC/RI76bis, Appeals Chamber, 16 February 2011 at para 249 with respect to specific intent offences in general, as well as in this respect, *Đorđević* (IT-05-87/1-A), Appeals Chamber Judgment, 27 January 2014 at paras 77–84; *Popović et al* (IT-05-88-A), Appeals Chamber Judgment, 30 January 2015 at paras 1440 and 1708; *Stanišić and Župljanin* (IT-08-91-A), Appeals Chamber Judgment, 30 June 2016 at paras 595–600; *Mladić* (IT-09-92-T), Trial Chamber Judgment, 22 November 2017 at para 3435.

86 *Krnojelac* (IT-97-25-A), Appeals Chamber Judgment, 17 September 2003 at para 75; *Vasiljević* (IT-98-32-A), Appeals Chamber Judgment, 25 February 2004 at para 102; *Kvočka* (IT-98-30/1-A), Appeals Chamber Judgment, 28 February 2005 at para 92.

87 *Tadić* (IT-94-1-A), Appeals Chamber Judgment, 15 July 1999 at para 229.

to the furthering of the common plan or purpose, in at least a significant manner.[88]

- In the case of aiding and abetting, the requisite mental element is the knowledge that the acts performed by the aider and abettor assist the commission of a specific crime by the principal. By contrast, in the case of common purpose or design, more is required, namely, the intent to pursue a common purpose (which can be inferred from circumstantial evidence).[89]

JCE has been used outside the ICTY/ICTR context in the proceedings of the Special Court of Sierra Leone (SCSL),[90] as well as in the Extraordinary Chambers in the Courts of Cambodia (ECCC), although in the latter institution, it was decided that the third category was not part of customary international law, nor was it included in the law of Cambodia during the 1970s when the ECCC had jurisdiction.[91]

The Rome Statute has included a concept similar to JCE, common purpose,[92] the formulation of which was based on the 1997 International Convention for the Suppression of Terrorist Bombings and which is generally seen as encompassing JCE I and II but not the "outer

88 *Ibid* at para 229; *Krnojelac* (IT-97-25-A), Appeals Chamber Judgment, 17 September 2003 at paras 31–33; *Vasiljević* (IT-98-32-A), Appeals Chamber Judgment, 25 February 2004 at para 89; Special Tribunal for Lebanon, Interlocutory Decision on the Applicable Law: Terrorism, Conspiracy, Homicide, Perpetration, Cumulative charging, STL-II-OI/I/AC/RI76bis, Appeals Chamber, 16 February 2011 at para 227.

89 *Tadić* (IT-94-1-A), Appeals Chamber Judgment, 15 July 1999 at para 229; *Krnojelac* (IT-97-25-A), Appeals Chamber Judgment, 17 September 2003 at paras 31–33; *Vasiljević* (IT-98-32-A), Appeals Chamber Judgment, 25 February 2004 at para 102; *Kvočka* (IT-98-30/1-A), Appeals Chamber Judgment, 28 February 2005 at para 89; *Popović et al* (IT-05-88-A), Appeals Chamber Judgment, 30 January 2015 at para 1369; *Stanišić and Župljanin* (IT-08-91-A), Appeals Chamber Judgment, 30 June 2016 at paras 375, 480, 486, 915, and 917–22; *Case 002/02* (Case File No 002/19-09-2007/ECCC/TC), Trial Chamber Judgment, 16 November 2018 at paras 3712–16 (while also indicating that for JCE I, the standard of *mens rea* is *dolus directus* and not *dolus eventualis* as the latter is derived from JCE III and cannot be transposed to JCE I).

90 *Brima, Kamara and Kanu ("AFRC")* (SCSL-2004-16-A), Appeals Chamber Judgment, 22 February 2008 at paras 72–86, and *Sesay, Kallon and Gbao ("RUF")* (SCSL-04-14-A), Appeals Chamber Judgment, 26 October 2009 at paras 295–306 and 312–18.

91 *Case 002/01* (Case File No 002/19-09-2007-ECCC/SC), Supreme Court Chamber Judgment, 23 November 2016 at paras 773–810, 980–83 (regarding contribution), 986–87 (regarding contribution by omission), 1030–31 (examples of contribution), and 1053–55 (regarding intent); *Case 002/02* (Case File No 002/19-09-2007/ECCC/TC), Trial Chamber Judgment, 16 November 2018 at para 3707; *Ao An* (Case File No 004/02/07-09-2009-ECCC/OCIJ) (PTC60)), Pre-Trial Chamber, Considerations on Appeals against Closing Orders, Opinion of Judges Baik and Bauvallet, 19 December 2019 at paras 575–79.

92 Article 25.3(d).

limits" of JCE III.[93] This concept was first explored in 2011,[94] with the jurisprudence since that time providing the following parameters:

- Common purpose requires a common plan, the ingredients of which are the same as the common plan for perpetration.[95]
- The level of contribution should be significant,[96] which means a type of contribution that influences the commission of the crime as to its occurrence and way of commission, but the crime must not depend on the contribution or be conditioned by it.[97]
- Similar factors need to be applied, such as was done by the ICTY in the *Kvočka* case.[98]
- Contributions after the fact can also be part of this mode of liability.[99]

---

93 *Chui* (ICC-01/04-02/12), Trial Chamber Judgment, Concurring Opinion of Judge Christine Van den Wyngaert, 18 December 2012 at para 61, n77.

94 *Mbarushimana* (ICC-01/04-01/10), Pre-Trial Chamber, Decision of the Confirmation of Charges, 16 December 2011; for a general reference to this mode of liability, see *Ntaganda* (ICC-01/04-02/06), Pre-Trial Chamber, Decision of the Confirmation of the Charges, 9 June 2014 at para 158; *Gbagbo* (ICC-02/11-01/11), Pre-Trial Chamber, Decision of the Confirmation of Charges, 12 June 2014 at para 252.

95 *Mbarushimana* (ICC-01/04-01/10), Pre-Trial Chamber, Decision of the Confirmation of Charges, 16 December 2011 at para 271; *William Samoei Ruto, Henry Kiprono Kosgey and Joshua Arap Sang* (ICC-01/09-01/11), Pre-Trial Chamber, Decision on the Confirmation of Charges, 23 January 2012 at paras 353–54; *Katanga* (ICC-01/04-01/07), Trial Chamber Judgment, 7 March 2014 at paras 1620–42.

96 *Katanga* (ICC-01/04-01/07), Trial Chamber Judgment, 7 March 2014 at paras 1620–42; *Katanga* (ICC-01/04-01/07), Trial Chamber Judgment, Minority Opinion of Judge Christine Van den Wyngaert, 7 March 2014 at para 38, which also indicates at para 287 that there is no need to incorporate a specific direction requirement for contribution and in the same paragraph that both the *mens rea* and *actus rea* thresholds for this type of liability are "extremely low"; *Ongwen* (ICC-02/04-01/15), Pre-Trial Chamber, Decision on the Confirmation of Charges /15, Pre-Trial Chamber I, 24 March 2016 at para 27, which also said that the contribution does not need to be significant or reach a certain minimum degree (as was also the case in the *Ongwen* decision); *Gbagbo and Blé Goudé* (ICC-02/11-01/15-1263-AnxB-Red), Trial Chamber, Reasons for oral decision of 15 January 2019 on the *Requête de la Défense de Laurent Gbagbo afin qu'un jugement d'acquittement portant sur toutes les charges soit prononcé en faveur de Laurent Gbagbo et que sa mise en liberté immédiate soit ordonnée*, and on the Blé Goudé Defence no case to answer motion, Public Redacted Version of Reasons of Judge Geoffrey Henderson, Trial Chamber, 16 July 2019 at para 1960.

97 *Katanga* (ICC-01/04-01/07), Trial Chamber Judgment, 7 March 2014 at paras 1632–33.

98 *Mbarushimana* (ICC-01/04-01/10), Pre-Trial Chamber, Decision of the Confirmation of Charges, 16 December 2011 at para 284.

99 *Ibid* at paras 286–87; *William Samoei Ruto, Henry Kiprono Kosgey and Joshua Arap Sang* (ICC-01/09-01/11), Pre-Trial Chamber, Decision on the Confirmation of Charges, 23 January 2012 at paras 353–54.

- Whether or not a person is part of the group carrying out the agreed-upon crime is not an element for this mode of liability.[100]
- There is no need for a direct link between the contribution and the crime nor a spatial proximity.[101]
- The *mens rea* of this type of liability exists—that the person (i) means to engage in the relevant conduct that allegedly contributes to the crime and (ii) at least be aware that their conduct contributes to the activities of the group of persons for whose crimes they are alleged to bear responsibility.[102]
- Knowledge is sufficient to incur liability for contributing to a group of persons acting with a common purpose.[103]

i) Perpetration

As much as the ICTY and ICTR used JCE as their main tool to hold people responsible for the commission of international crimes, it appears that the ICC has become similarly enamoured by the concept of perpetration.[104]

---

100 *Katanga* (ICC-01/04-01/07), Trial Chamber Judgment, 7 March 2014 at para 1631; *Katanga*, (ICC-01/04-01/07), Trial Chamber Judgment, Minority Opinion of Judge Christine Van den Wyngaert, 7 March 2014 at para 286; with respect to the notion of group in this context, see the latter judgment at paras 191–93.

101 *Katanga* (ICC-01/04-01/07), Trial Chamber Judgment, 7 March 2014 at paras 1635–36.

102 *Mbarushimana* (ICC-01/04-01/10), Pre-Trial Chamber I, Decision of the Confirmation of Charges, 16 December 2011 at para 288; *William Samoei Ruto, Henry Kiprono Kosgey and Joshua Arap Sang* (ICC-01/09-01/11), Pre-Trial Chamber, Decision on the Confirmation of Charges, 23 January 2012 at paras 353–54; *Katanga*, (ICC-01/04-01/07), Trial Chamber Judgment, Minority Opinion of Judge Christine Van den Wyngaert, 7 March 2014 at para 24.

103 *Mbarushimana* (ICC-01/04-01/10), Pre-Trial Chamber, Decision of the Confirmation of Charges, 16 December 2011 at para 289; *William Samoei Ruto, Henry Kiprono Kosgey and Joshua Arap Sang* (ICC-01/09-01/11), Pre-Trial Chamber, Decision on the Confirmation of Charges, 23 January 2012 at paras 353–54; *Katanga*, (ICC-01/04-01/07), Trial Chamber Judgment, Minority Opinion of Judge Christine Van den Wyngaert, 7 March 2014 at para 288.

104 Section 25.3(a) of the Rome Statute, which allows for perpetration, joint perpetration (also called co-perpetration), and perpetration through another person, has been used in most of the warrants for arrest issued. Co-perpetration was rejected by a majority of judges of the Appeals Chamber of the ICTY/ICTR in *Stakić* (IT-97-24-A), Appeals Chamber Judgment, 22 March 2006 at paras 58–63; *Gacumbitsi* (ICTR-2001-64-A), Appeals Chamber Judgment, Separate Opinion of Judge Shahabuddeen, 7 July 2006 at paras 42–52; *Gacumbitsi* (ICTR-2001-64-A), Appeals Chamber Judgment, Separate Opinion of Judge Schomburg on the Criminal Responsibility of the Appellant for Committing Genocide, 7 July 2006 at paras 17–27; *Simić* (IT-95-9-A), Appeals Chamber Judgment, Dissenting Opinion of Judge Schomburg, 28 November 2006 at paras 11–21; *Prlić et al* (IT-04-74), Trial Chamber Judgment, 29 May 2013 at para 210; *Đorđević* (IT-05-87/1-A), Appeals Chamber Judgment, 27 January

There are three forms of committing a crime as a perpetrator, where a person

(a) physically carries out the objective elements of the offence (commission of the crime in person, or direct perpetration);
(b) has, along with others, control over the offence by reason of the essential tasks assigned to him or her (commission of the crime jointly with others, or co-perpetration); or
(c) controls the will of those who carry out the objective elements of the offence (commission of the crime through another person, or indirect perpetration).[105]

As well, the distinction between principals and accessories in a situation with a plurality of persons can also be made along a spectrum in which different aspects of the involvement are emphasized. If the objective manifestation of the crime (in that all the elements are carried out by the same person) is the focal point of investigation, this can be called an objective approach with a person liable as a principal. The subjective approach does not primarily examine the level of contribution but rather the shared intent to carry out a crime, which is done in the JCE or common purpose doctrine. Co-perpetration focuses on the degree of control held by a person who is removed from the scene of the crime but has control of or is the mastermind behind the commission of the offences.[106]

The *actus reus* of co-perpetration is twofold: the existence of an agreement or common plan,[107] which for a time had been possibly

---

2014 at paras 63–65; see, also, Special Tribunal for Lebanon, Interlocutory Decision on the Applicable Law: Terrorism, Conspiracy, Homicide, Perpetration, Cumulative charging, STL-II-OI/I/AC/RI76bis, Appeals Chamber, 16 February 2011 at para 256.

105 *Lubanga* (ICC-01/04-01/06), Pre-Trial Chamber, Decision on the Confirmation of Charges, 29 January 2007 at para 332; *Katanga and Chui* (ICC-01/04-01/07), Pre-Trial Chamber, Decision of the Confirmation of the Charges, 30 September 2008 at para 480; *Garda* (ICC-02/05-02/09), Pre-Trial Chamber, Decision of the Confirmation of the Charges, 8 February 2010 at para 153.

106 *Katanga* (ICC- ICC-01/04-01/07), Trial Chamber Judgment, 7 March 2014 at paras 1390–97; *Lubanga* (ICC-01/04-01/06 A5), Appeals Chamber Judgment, 1 December 2014 at paras 460–73; *Jean-Pierre Bemba Gombo, Aimé Kilolo Musamba, Jean-Jacques Mangenda Kabongo, Fidèle Babala Wandu and Narcisse Arido* (ICC-01/05-01/13), Trial Chamber Judgment, 19 October 2016 at para 62; *Ntaganda* (ICC-01/04-02/06), Trial Chamber Judgment, 8 July 2019 at para 780.

107 *Blé Goudé* (ICC-02/11-02/11), Pre-Trial Chamber, Decision of the Confirmation of Charges, 11 December 2014 at para 134; *Gbagbo and Blé Goudé* (ICC-02/11-01/15-1263-AnxB-Red),

replaced by the requirement of shared intent[108] between two or more persons, and the coordinated essential contribution[109] by each of these persons resulting in the commission of a crime. With respect to the first of these requirements, the agreement does not have to be explicit, nor does the plan have to be specifically directed at committing a crime, but only if its implementation embodies a sufficient risk that, in the ordinary course of events, a crime will be committed.[110] The agreement or common plan need not be specifically directed at the commission of offence(s) and may include non-criminal goals; however, it is necessary for the agreement or common plan to involve a critical element of criminality.[111]

As to essential contribution, there is no need to establish presence at the scene of the crime or that there was a direct and physical link between the contribution and the commission of the crime.[112] The essential contribution appeared to have been replaced by a different element, the direct contribution,[113] but the original approach was restored by the first appeal decision in this area, while also clarifying that this

---

Reasons for oral decision of 15 January 2019 on the *Requête de la Défense de Laurent Gbagbo afin qu'un jugement d'acquittement portant sur toutes les charges soit prononcé en faveur de Laurent Gbagbo et que sa mise en liberté immédiate soit ordonnée*, and on the Blé Goudé Defence no case to answer motion, Public Redacted Version of Reasons of Judge Geoffrey Henderson, Trial Chamber, 16 July 2019 at para 1907.

108 *Chui* (ICC-01/04-02/12), Trial Chamber Judgment, Concurring Opinion of Judge Christine Van den Wyngaert, 18 December 2012 at paras 32–35.

109 *Jean-Pierre Bemba Gombo, Aimé Kilolo Musamba, Jean-Jacques Mangenda Kabongo, Fidèle Babala Wandu and Narcisse Arido* (ICC-01/05-01/13), Trial Chamber Judgment, 19 October 2016 at para 65; *Ntaganda* (ICC-01/04-02/06), Trial Chamber Judgment, 8 July 2019 at para 774.

110 *Lubanga* (ICC-01/04-01/06), Trial Chamber Judgment, 14 March 2012 at paras 983–88; *Lubanga* (ICC-01/04-01/06 A5), Appeals Chamber Judgment, 1 December 2014 at paras 445–51; *Jean-Pierre Bemba Gombo, Aimé Kilolo Musamba, Jean-Jacques Mangenda Kabongo, Fidèle Babala Wandu and Narcisse Arido* (ICC-01/05-01/13), Trial Chamber Judgment, 19 October 2016 at para 66; *Ntaganda* (ICC-01/04-02/06), Trial Chamber Judgment, 8 July 2019 at para 775.

111 *Jean-Pierre Bemba Gombo, Aimé Kilolo Musamba, Jean-Jacques Mangenda Kabongo, Fidèle Babala Wandu and Narcisse Arido* (ICC-01/05-01/13), Trial Chamber Judgment, 19 October 2016 at para 67.

112 *Lubanga* (ICC-01/04-01/06), Trial Chamber Judgment, 14 March 2012 at paras 1004–5; *Lubanga* (ICC-01/04-01/06 A5), Appeals Chamber Judgment, 1 December 2014 at para 469; *Jean-Pierre Bemba Gombo, Aimé Kilolo Musamba, Jean-Jacques Mangenda Kabongo, Fidèle Babala Wandu and Narcisse Arido* (ICC-01/05-01/13), Trial Chamber Judgment, 19 October 2016 at para 69; *Ntaganda* (ICC-01/04-02/06), Trial Chamber Judgment, 8 July 2019 at para 776.

113 *Chui* (ICC-01/04-02/12), Trial Chamber Judgment, Concurring Opinion of Judge Christine Van den Wyngaert, 18 December 2012 at paras 40–48.

contribution is at a level where the co-perpetrator had the power to frustrate the commission of the crime.[114]

The *mens rea* of this type of liability has three aspects: the subjective element of the co-perpetrators with respect to underlying crime, the fact that the co-perpetrators are all mutually aware and mutually accept that implementing their common plan may result in the realization of the objective elements of the crime; and the fact that the persons are aware of the factual circumstances enabling them to jointly control the crime.[115]

The following table sets out the differences between aiding and abetting, JCE, and co-perpetration.

TABLE 4.1

	Actus reus	***Mens rea***
Aiding and abetting	• substantial contribution	• knowledge of commission of act
JCE (only basic and systemic forms)	• common plan • significant contribution	• intent to further common plan
Co-perpetration	• common plan • coordinated essential contribution	• mutual awareness and acceptance of plan resulting in a crime • awareness of the factual situation

Co-perpetration has two other permutations: co-perpetration through another person and indirect co-perpetration.

The difference of opinion with respect to the notion of essential contribution as an element of joint perpetration at the trial level at the ICC was repeated with respect to perpetration through another person. The issues of debate were whether committing a crime through a physical person, as article 25.3(a) appears to indicate, can also be expanded to the commission of the crime through an organization and whether article 25.3(a) would allow combining two of the specifically

114 *Lubanga* (ICC-01/04-01/06 A5), Appeals Chamber Judgment, 1 December 2014 at paras 469 and 473; *Al Mahdi* (ICC-01/12-01/15), Trial Chamber Judgment, 27 September 2016 at para 19; *Ntaganda* (ICC-01/04-02/06), Trial Chamber Judgment, 8 July 2019 at para 779.

115 *Lubanga* (ICC-01/04-01/06), Trial Chamber Judgment, 14 March 2012 at paras 1012–13; *Jean-Pierre Bemba Gombo, Aimé Kilolo Musamba, Jean-Jacques Mangenda Kabongo, Fidèle Babala Wandu and Narcisse Arido* (ICC-01/05-01/13), Trial Chamber Judgment, 19 October 2016 at para 70.

mentioned types of non-direct perpetration—joint perpetration and perpetration through another person—into a combined form of these two types and use the notion of indirect co-perpetration. In short, it seems that the majority of the judges, including the appeal judges, have favoured an approach that would allow the broadest forms of liability under this article.

With respect to perpetration through an organization, it has been acknowledged that the notion of the perpetrator behind the perpetrator or a device to capture leaders in an organization who utilize not only persons who cannot be held responsible for their crimes but also persons who were involved and responsible for execution of crimes themselves can be applied to the international sphere to certain types of organizations[116] provided that the following criteria are met:

- the leader must have control over the organization;
- the organization must consist of an organized and hierarchical apparatus of power; and
- the execution of crimes must be secured by an almost automatic compliance with the orders issued by the leader.[117]

These elements have been subject to some elaboration. With respect to the criteria that the organization must be based on hierarchical relations between superiors and subordinates, the organization must also be composed of sufficient subordinates to guarantee that superiors' orders will be carried out, if not by one subordinate then by another, meaning that the leader must use their control over the apparatus to execute crimes and that they, as the perpetrator behind the perpetrator, can mobilize the authority and power within the organization to secure compliance with their orders.[118]

---

116 *Lubanga* (ICC-01/04-01/06 A5), Appeals Chamber Judgment, 1 December 2014 at para 465; this approach has not found uniform agreement by the ICC judiciary; see *Chui* (ICC-01/04-02/12), Trial Chamber Judgment, Concurring Opinion of Judge Christine Van den Wyngaert, 18 December 2012 at paras 58–64; *Katanga*, (ICC-01/04-01/07), Trial Chamber Judgment, Minority Opinion of Judge Christine Van den Wyngaert, 7 March 2014 at paras 277–79; *Blé Goudé* (ICC-02/11-02/11-186-Anx), Pre-Trial Chamber, Decision of the Confirmation of Charges, Partially Dissenting Opinion of Judge Christine Van den Wyngaert, 11 December 2014 at para 5.

117 *Katanga* (ICC-01/04-01/07), Trial Chamber Judgment, 7 March 2014 at paras 1404–13; *Ntaganda* (ICC-01/04-02/06), Trial Chamber Judgment, 8 July 2019 at paras 777–78.

118 *Katanga* (ICC-01/04-01/07), Trial Chamber Judgment, 7 March 2014 at paras 1408–9; *Ongwen* (ICC-02/0401/15), Trial Chamber Judgment, 4 February 2021 at para 2784.

With respect to the notion of the execution of the crimes secured by almost automatic compliance with the orders, it has been said that the organization must be structured in a way that enables the leader to actually secure the commission of crimes, meaning that the leader's control over the apparatus allows them to utilize their subordinates as mere gears in a giant machine to produce the criminal result. It also means that the successful execution of the plan will not be compromised by a subordinate's failure to comply with an order. Any subordinate who does not comply can simply be replaced by another who will carry out such an order. Or they can put only those persons who effectively control at least part of an apparatus of power as the overseers of the criminal activity. This can be accomplished, for instance, through intensive, strict, and violent training regimens.[119] This form of control, where there is almost automatic compliance with the orders of the leaders, is different from the model of liability of ordering because the leader does not merely order the commission of a crime but essentially decides whether and how the crime will be committed.[120]

With respect to the *mens rea* of this type of liability, the indirect perpetrator must be aware of the ingredients fundamental to their exertion of control over the crime given that they depend on the form of indirect commission involved and that the indirect perpetrator was aware of the position they held within the organization and its essential features, which secured the functional automatism.[121]

The expansion of perpetration to certain organizations led to the development of the notion of indirect co-perpetration, which has been described as follows: "a new axis for the attribution of criminal responsibility: in addition to the horizontal axis (joint perpetration) and the vertical axis (perpetration through another person), a new diagonal axis (indirect co-perpetration) was created."[122] The elements of this form of liability are as follows:

---

119 *Katanga* (ICC-01/04-01/07), Trial Chamber Judgment, 7 March 2014 at paras 1411–12.

120 *Katanga and Chui* (ICC-01/04-01/07), Pre-Trial Chamber, Decision of the Confirmation of the Charges, 30 September 2008 at para 518.

121 *Katanga* (ICC-01/04-01/07), Trial Chamber Judgment, 7 March 2014 at paras 1414–15; *Ongwen* (ICC-02/0401/15), Trial Chamber Judgment, 4 February 2021 at para 2783.

122 *Chui* (ICC-01/04-02/12), Trial Chamber Judgment, Concurring Opinion of Judge Christine Van den Wyngaert, 18 December 2012 at para 59.

- the perpetrator must be part of a common plan or an agreement with one or more persons;
- the perpetrator and the other co-perpetrator(s) must carry out essential contributions in a coordinated manner that result in the fulfillment of the material elements of the crime;
- the perpetrator must have control over the organization;
- the organization must consist of an organized and hierarchical apparatus of power; and
- the execution of the crimes must be secured by almost automatic compliance with the orders issued by the perpetrator.[123]

These criteria have been further explained by saying that this form still rests on the notion of reciprocal imputation of coordinated actions performed by each co-perpetrator. The only difference with direct co-perpetration is that the objective elements of the crime are executed by other persons who are utilized by the co-perpetrators for the commission of the crime. This form of responsibility combines the commission of a crime jointly with another (in which each of a plurality of persons has the capacity to frustrate the commission of the crime by not performing their coordinated contributive acts within the framework of an agreement among them) with the commission of a crime through another person (in which a person commits the crime by subjugating another person's will rather than personally and directly executing the objective elements of the crime).[124]

---

123 *Ntaganda* (ICC-01/04-02/06), Trial Chamber Judgment, 8 July 2019 at para 773; *Gbagbo and Blé Goudé* (ICC-02/11-01/15-1263-AnxB-Red), Trial Chamber Judgment, Reasons for oral decision of 15 January 2019 on the *Requête de la Défense de Laurent Gbagbo afin qu'un jugement d'acquittement portant sur toutes les charges soit prononcé en faveur de Laurent Gbagbo et que sa mise en liberté immédiate soit ordonnée*, and on the Blé Goudé Defence no case to answer motion, Public Redacted Version of Reasons of Judge Geoffrey Henderson, Trial Chamber, 16 July 2019 at para 1922; *Ongwen* (ICC-02/0401/15), Trial Chamber Judgment, 4 February 2021 at paras 2787–88; the debate and disagreements with respect to this form of liability were laid to rest by the Appeals Chamber in the *Ntaganda* case, where a majority accepted indirect co-perpetration; see *Ntaganda* (ICC-01/04-02/06 A A2), Appeals Chamber Judgment, 30 March 2021 at paras 879–80, with an elaborate opinion in favour of the majority by Separate Opinion of Judge Luz Del Carmen Ibáñez Caranza on Mr. Ntaganda's appeal at paras 213–381, while a contrary view can be found in the Separate Opinion of Judge Howard Morrison on Mr. Ntaganda's appeal at paras 3–42, as well as in the Partly Concurring Opinion of Judge Chile Eboe-Osuji at paras 14–102.

124 *Ongwen* (ICC-02/04-01/15), Pre-Trial Chamber, Decision on the Confirmation of the Charges 23 March 2016 at para 39.

j) Command/Superior Responsibility[125]

A superior will be subject to individual criminal liability if the following elements exist: there was a superior-subordinate relationship; the superior knew or had reason to know that a criminal act was about to be, was being, or had been committed; and there was a failure to take necessary and reasonable measures to prevent or punish the conduct in question.[126]

A superior-subordinate relationship exists where a superior has effective command and control over a subordinate, meaning that the superior has the material ability to prevent or punish the subordinate's criminal conduct.[127] Superior responsibility can arise by virtue of the superior's de jure or de facto power over the relevant subordinate, either formal or informal and within a military or civilian hierarchy.[128] The

---

125 For a historical overview, see *Ao An* (Case File No 004/02/07-09-2009-ECCC/OCIJ) (PTC60)), Pre-Trial Chamber, Considerations on Appeals against Closing Orders, Opinion of Judges Baik and Bauvallet, 19 December 2019 at paras 592–94; regarding the various theories of command/superior responsibility, see *Bemba* (ICC-01/05-01/08A), Appeals Chamber Judgment, Concurring Separate Opinion of Judge Eboe-Osuji, 8 June 2018 at paras 187–269, including the difference between complicity and command/superior responsibility at paras 217–31.

126 *Orić* (IT-03-68-A), Appeals Chamber Judgment, 3 July 2008 at para 18; *Gotovina and Markač* (IT-06-90-A), Appeals Chamber Judgment, 16 November 2012 at para 128; *Case 002/02* (Case File No 002/19-09-2007/ECCC/TC), Trial Chamber Judgment, 16 November 2018 at para 3725; for a more detailed description, see article 28 of the Rome Statute and its interpretation in *Bemba* (ICC-01/05-01/08), Pre-Trial Chamber, Decision of the Confirmation of Charges, 15 June 2009 at paras 408–48, following closely the ICTY/ICTR jurisprudence; see, also, *Ntaganda* (ICC-01/04-02/06), Pre-Trial Chamber, Decision of the Confirmation of the Charges, 9 June 2014 at para 164; *Bemba* (ICC-01/05-01/08), Trial Chamber Judgment, 21 March 2016 at para 170 (with a discussion regarding the nature of this form of liability at paras 171–74); given that this form of liability is one of omission, the ICC judiciary has expressed some doubt as to whether it should be used if the evidence discloses that a person was involved in deliberate conduct that resulted in the commission of crimes; see *Ongwen* (ICC-02/04-01/15), Pre-Trial Chamber Judgment, Decision on the Confirmation of Charges, 23 March 2016 at para 147.

127 *Orić* (IT-03-68-A), Appeals Chamber Judgment, 3 July 2008 at para 20; *Bagosora and Sengiyumva* (ICTR-98-41-A), Appeals Chamber Judgment, 14 December 2011 at para 642; *Ndindiliyimana et al* (ICTR-00-56-A), Appeals Chamber Judgment, 29 September 2014 at para 378; *Nizeyimana* (ICTR-00-55C-A), Appeals Chamber Judgment, 29 September 2014 at para 342; *Karemera* (ICTR-98-44-A), Appeals Chamber Judgment, 29 September 2014 at paras 254, 258; *Popović et al* (IT-05-88-A), Appeals Chamber Judgment, 30 January 2015 at para 1857; *Nyiramasuhuko et al* (ICTR-98-42-A), Appeals Chamber Judgment, 14 December 2015 at para 995; *Bemba* (ICC-01/05-01/08), Trial Chamber Judgment, 21 March 2016 at paras 176, 178, 180–90.

128 *Mucić et al (Čelebići Camp)* (IT-96-21), Trial Chamber Judgment, 16 November 1998 at paras 195–97; *Ndahimana* (ICTR-01-68), Trial Chamber Judgment, 30 December 2011 at para 726; *Nizeyimana* (ICTR-2000-55C), Trial Chamber Judgment, 19 June 2012 at para 1476; *Taylor* (SCSL-03-01-T), Trial Chamber Judgment, 18 May 2012 at para 493; *Prlić et al* (IT-04-74), Trial Chamber Judgment, 29 May 2013 at para 242; *Karadžić* (IT-95-5/18-T), Trial Chamber Judgment, 24 March 2016 at para 580; *Mladić* (IT-09-92-T), Trial Chamber Judgment, 22 November 2017 at para 3569.

possession of de jure power may not suffice for the finding of superior responsibility if it does not manifest itself in effective control[129] or if it only amounts to influence.[130] A superior cannot incur responsibility for crimes committed by a subordinate before they assumed their position as superior.[131] The superior-subordinate relationship need not be of a permanent nature but instead could arise on an ad hoc or temporary basis,[132] such as when acting for another commander.[133] A superior may, however, incur superior responsibility no matter how far down the chain of authority the subordinate may be and even if the subordinate has participated in the crimes through intermediaries.[134] A superior does not necessarily need to know the exact identity of the subordinates who perpetrated the crimes in order to incur liability.[135]

With respect to the second requirement, this element is fulfilled if a superior knew or had reason to know that a subordinate's criminal act had been carried out, was taking place, or was about to happen.[136] In the case of specific intent crimes, such as genocide, they require proof that

---

129 *Halilović* (IT-01-48-A), Appeals Chamber Judgment, 16 October 2007 at para 204; *Bizimungu et al* (ICTR-99-50-T), Trial Chamber Judgment, 30 September 2011 at para 1873; *Stanišić and Župljanin* (IT-08-91-T), Trial Chamber Judgment, 27 March 2013 at paras 112–13.

130 *Bizimungu et al* (ICTR-99-50-T), Trial Chamber Judgment, 30 September 2011 at paras 1891–93; *Nizeyimana* (ICTR-2000-55C), Trial Chamber Judgment, 19 June 2012 at para 1476; *Taylor* (SCSL-03-01-T), Trial Chamber Judgment, 18 May 2012 at para 493.

131 *Hadžihasanović et al* (IT-01-47-AR72), Appeals Chamber, Decision on Interlocutory Appeal Challenging Jurisdiction in Relation to Command Responsibility, 16 July 2003 at paras 37–56; *Halilović* (IT-01-48-A), Appeals Chamber Judgment, 16 October 2007 at para 67; *Stanišić and Župljanin* (IT-08-91-T), Trial Chamber Judgment, 27 March 2013 at para 114; for the opposite view, see *Sesay, Kallon and Gbao ("RUF")* (SCSL-04-15-T), Trial Chamber Judgment, 2 March 2009 at paras 294–306, which was overruled on appeal in *Sesay, Kallon and Gbao ("RUF")*, SCSL-04-14-A, Appeals Chamber Judgment, 26 October 2009 at para 874.

132 *Nyiramasuhuko et al* (ICTR-98-42-T), Trial Chamber Judgment, 24 June 2011 at para 5648; *Perišić* (IT-04-81-T), Trial Chamber Judgment, 6 September 2011 at para 138; *Stanišić and Župljanin* (IT-08-91-T), Trial Chamber Judgment, 27 March 2013 at para 114.

133 *Bemba* (ICC-01/05-01/08), Trial Chamber Judgment, 21 March 2016 at para 177.

134 *Orić* (IT-03-68-A), Appeals Chamber Judgment, 3 July 2008 at para 20; *Popović et al* (IT-05-88-A), Appeals Chamber Judgment, 30 January 2015 at para 1892; *Bemba* (ICC-01/05-01/08), Trial Chamber Judgment, 21 March 2016 at para 179; *Bemba* (ICC-01/05-01/08A), Appeals Chamber Judgment, Separate Opinion of Judge Van den Wyngaert and Judge Morrison, 8 June 2018 at paras 33–36.

135 *Bizimungu* (ICTR-00-56B-A), Appeals Chamber Judgment, 30 June 2014 at para 79.

136 *Kordić and Čerkez* (IT-95-14/2-A), Appeals Chamber Judgment, 17 December 2004 at para 839; *Bagosora and Sengiyumva* (ICTR-98-41-A), Appeals Chamber Judgment, 14 December 2011 at para 642; *Ntabakuze* (ICTR-98-41A-A), Appeals Chamber Judgment, 8 May 2012 at para 248; *Karemera* (ICTR-98-44-A), Appeals Chamber Judgment, 29 September 2014 at para 307; *Bemba* (ICC-01/05-01/08A), Appeals Chamber Judgment, Separate Opinion of Judge Van den

the superior was aware of the criminal intent of the subordinate.[137] A superior had reason to know only if the information was available to them, which would have put them on notice of offences committed by subordinates.[138] The "reason to know standard" is met if the superior possessed information sufficiently alarming to justify further inquiry.[139]

With respect to the third requirement, necessary measures mean appropriate actions, which show that the superior genuinely tried to prevent the commission of acts by subordinates or punish such crimes after they had been committed,[140] while reasonable measures are those falling within the material powers of the superior.[141] A superior is not expected to perform the impossible but must use every means within their ability.[142] Such measures may include carrying out an investigation, transmitting information in a superior's possession to the proper administrative or prosecutorial authorities, issuing special orders aimed at bringing unlawful practices of subordinates in compliance with the

---

Wyngaert and Judge Morrison, 8 June 2018 at paras 38–47; *Case 002/02* (Case File No 002/19-09-2007/ECCC/TC), Trial Chamber Judgment, 16 November 2018 at para 3725.

137 *Karemera* (ICTR-98-44-A), Appeals Chamber Judgment, 29 September 2014 at para 307.

138 *Krnojelac* (IT-97-25-A), Appeals Chamber Judgment, 17 September 2003 at para 156; *Ndindiliyimana et al* (ICTR-00-56-A), Appeals Chamber Judgment, 11 February 2014 at paras 396–97; *Bemba* (ICC-01/05-01/08), Trial Chamber Judgment, 21 March 2016 at paras 191–96.

139 *Strugar* (IT- IT-01-42A), Appeals Chamber Judgment, 17 July 2008 at para 298; *Popović et al* (IT-05-88-A), Appeals Chamber Judgment, 30 January 2015 at para 1910; *Mladić* (IT-09-92-T), Trial Chamber Judgment, 22 November 2017 at para 3570.

140 *Ndahimana* (ICTR-01-68-A), Appeals Chamber Judgment, 16 December 2013 at para 79; *Gbagbo* (ICC-02/11-01/11), Pre-Trial Chamber, Decision of the Confirmation of Charges, 12 June 2014 at para 264; *Bizimungu* (ICTR-00-56B-A), Appeals Chamber Judgment, 30 June 2014 at para 133; *Case 002/01* (Case File No 002/19-09-2007/ECCC/TC), Trial Chamber Judgment, 7 August 2014 at para 716; *Popović et al* (IT-05-88-A), Appeals Chamber Judgment, 30 January 2015 at para 1927; *Bemba* (ICC-01/05-01/08), Trial Chamber Judgment, 21 March 2016 at paras 202–4; *Case 002/02* (Case File No 002/19-09-2007/ECCC/TC), Trial Chamber Judgment, 16 November 2018 at para 3726.

141 *Orić* (IT-03-68-A), Appeals Chamber Judgment, 3 July 2008 at para 177; *Popović et al* (IT-05-88-A), Appeals Chamber Judgment, 30 January 2015 at paras 1927–31; *Bemba* (ICC-01/05-01/08A), Appeals Chamber Judgment, 8 June 2018 at paras 167–70; *Bemba* (ICC-01/05-01/08A), Appeals Chamber Judgment, Separate Opinion of Judge Van den Wyngaert and Judge Morrison, 8 June 2018 at paras 51–56 (regarding causation); Judgment, *Bemba* (ICC-01/05-01/08A), Concurring Separate Opinion of Judge Eboe-Osuji, 8 June 2018 at paras 156–86 (regarding causation) and 270–82; *Case 002/02* (Case File No 002/19-09-2007/ECCC/TC), Trial Chamber Judgment, 16 November 2018 at para 3726.

142 *Popović et al* (IT-05-88-T), Trial Chamber Judgment, 10 June 2010 at para 1043; *Đorđević* (IT-05-87/1), Trial Chamber Judgment, 23 February 2011 at para 1887; *Perišić* (IT-04-81-T), Trial Chamber Judgment, 6 September 2011 at para 157; *Stanišić and Župljanin* (IT-08-91-T), Trial Chamber Judgment, 27 March 2013 at para 116.

rules of war, protesting against or criticizing criminal action, reporting the matter to the competent authorities, or insisting before a superior authority that immediate action be taken.[143]

k) Membership

Membership was a form of accessory liability and an inchoate offence after the Second World War.[144] The Statute of the International Military Tribunal (IMT) allowed it to declare any organization criminal, and four organizations were given this predicate: the Leadership Corps of the Nazi Party, the Gestapo, the SD, and the SS.[145] This concept was also applied to other organizations in national legislation and jurisprudence.[146] Under this system, a person was held liable if they belonged to a designated organization and had knowledge that the organization was used for criminal purposes or, as the IMT put it:

> A criminal organization is analogous to a criminal conspiracy in that the essence of both is co-operation for criminal purposes. There must be a group bound together and organized for a common purpose. The group must be formed or used in connection with the commission of the crimes denounced by the Charter. Since the declaration with the organizations and groups will, as has been pointed out, fix the criminality of its members, that definition should exclude persons who had no knowledge of the criminal purposes or acts of the organization and those who were drafted by the state for membership, unless they were personally implicated in the commission of acts declared criminal by

143 *Popović et al* (IT-05-88-A), Appeals Chamber Judgment, 30 January 2015 at paras 1932–33; *Bemba* (ICC-01/05-01/08), Trial Chamber Judgment, 21 March 2016 at paras 199–201 and 205–9; *Karadžić* (IT-95-5/18-T), Trial Chamber Judgment, 24 March 2016 at para 588; *Mladić* (IT-09-92-T), Trial Chamber Judgment, 22 November 2017 at para 3571.

144 For a detailed analysis, see Elies van Sliedregt, *Individual Criminal Responsibility in International Law* (Oxford: Oxford University Press, 2012) at 26–33, and Shane Darcy, *Collective Responsibility and Accountability Under International Law* (Leiden: Transnational Publishers, 2007) at 257–91.

145 *Trial of the Major War Criminals before the International Military Tribunal, Nuremberg, 14 November 1945–1 October 1946*, vol XXII at 505, 511, and 516–17, online: www.loc.gov/item/2011525338_NT_Vol-XXII; Darcy, above note 144 at 278.

146 Van Sliedregt, above note 144 at 26–33, and Darcy, above note 144 at 26–28, referring to legislation in Norway, France, and the Netherlands and decisions by Polish courts and US military courts in occupied Germany with respect to concentration camps as criminal organizations.

> Article 6 as members of the organization. Membership alone is not enough to come within the scope of these declarations.[147]

This concept has fallen into disuse since that time,[148] but the judicial reasoning for not applying this concept is unclear. The discussion of membership was part of developing the JCE approach, and in that context, it has been made clear that mere membership in a JCE without a further plan or activities is not sufficient to attract liability.[149]

There has been one unequivocal comment about the notion of membership in the ICTY, in the *Stakić* case:

> [T]he Trial Chamber emphasises that joint criminal enterprise can not be viewed as membership in an organisation because this would constitute a new crime not foreseen under the Statute and therefore amount to a flagrant infringement of the principle *nullum crimen sine lege*.[150]

This judgment refers to a decision by the Appeals Chamber, which came to the same conclusion but in doing so made mention of the explanatory report of the secretary-general establishing the ICTY, including this: "The Secretary General believes that this concept should not be *retained* in regard to the International Tribunal."[151]

This could be interpreted as an acknowledgement that membership in criminal organizations was part of international criminal law in 1993 but that for jurisdictional reasons it was deemed not desirable to include it in the Statute of the ICTY.[152] The *Stakić* decision does not refer to this part of the Appeals Chamber's decision and does not

---

147 *Trial of the Major War Criminals before the International Military Tribunal, Nuremberg*, above note 145 at 500.

148 There have been some musings about this type of liability in modern times in academic literature; see Darcy, above note 144 at 282–84.

149 *Kvočka* (IT-98-30/1), Trial Chamber Judgment, 2 November 2001 at para 281; *Simić* (IT-95-9-T), Trial Chamber Judgment, 17 October 2003 at para 158; *Brđanin* (IT-99-36), Trial Chamber Judgment, 1 September 2004 at para 263.

150 *Stakić* (IT-97-24), Trial Chamber Judgment, 31 July 2003 at para 433.

151 *Milutinović* (IT-99-37-AR72), Appeals Chamber, Decision on Dragoljub Ojdanić's Motion Challenging Jurisdiction — Joint Criminal Enterprise, 21 May 2003 at paras 24–26; the report referred to is UN Doc S/25704, *The Report of the Secretary General Pursuant to Paragraph 2 of Security Council Resolution 808* (3 May 1993), online (pdf): www.icty.org/x/file/Legal%20 Library/Statute/statute_re808_1993_en.pdf, which makes this comment at para 51.

152 *Milutinović* (IT-99-37-AR72), Appeals Chamber, Decision on Dragoljub Ojdanić's Motion Challenging Jurisdiction — Joint Criminal Enterprise, 21 May 2003 at para 26.

provide any further analysis of this statement, nor does it make any reference to the practice in this regard after the Second World War.[153]

During the negotiations for the Rome Statute, France made a proposal to include a provision dealing with criminal organizations as part of the debate to have legal persons fall within jurisdiction of the ICC, but there was not sufficient support to make either variation part of the Statute.[154]

l) Conspiracy

Conspiracy in international criminal law is only possible for genocide, and then only under the statutes of the ICTY, ICTR, and ECCC. Conspiracy to commit genocide is an agreement between two or more persons to commit the crime of genocide. The act of entering into an agreement to commit genocide constitutes the *actus reus* of conspiracy to commit genocide. The individuals involved in the conspiracy must possess the same *mens rea* as genocide, namely, the specific intent to destroy, in whole or in part, a national, ethnic, racial, or religious group. As an inchoate crime, it is the agreement itself that is punishable, regardless of whether genocide is committed as a result of the agreement.[155] Conspiracy is a continuing crime in the sense that individuals are capable of joining a conspiracy even after the initial agreement and may be held liable for such conspiracy as though they were an original conspirator.[156]

---

153 As well, the judgment is not clear as to whether membership is a crime or a mode of liability; although in the excerpt it speaks of membership as a crime, it also equates this notion with JCE, which is generally seen as a mode of liability. However, the Appeals Chamber of the SCSL is quite unequivocal that membership is not included in its Statute; see *Taylor* (SCSL-04-01-T), Appeals Chamber Judgment, 26 September 2013 at para 398.

154 Darcy, above note 144 at 283–84.

155 *Nahimana, Barayagwiza and Ngeze ("Media")* (ICTR-99-52-A), Appeals Chamber Judgment, 28 November 2007 at paras 894–98; *Seromba* (ICTR-2001-66-A), Appeals Chamber Judgment, 12 March 2008 at paras 218, 221; *Tolimir* (IT-05-88/2-T), Trial Chamber Judgment, 12 December 2012 at paras 785–86 (which also indicate that since this offence was based on a common law concept, common law principles can be used to define its parameters); *Karemera* (ICTR-98-44-A), Appeals Chamber Judgment, 29 September 2014 at para 643; *Popović et al* (IT-05-88-A), Appeals Chamber Judgment, 30 January 2015 at para 544; *Tolimir* (IT-05-88/2-A), Appeals Chamber Judgment, 8 April 2015 at para 582; *Nyiramasuhuko et al* (ICTR-98-42-A), Appeals Chamber Judgment, 14 December 2015 at paras 469, 473, 649.

156 *Popović et al* (IT-05-88-T), Trial Chamber Judgment, 10 June 2010 at paras 870–76; *Tolimir* (IT-05-88/2-T), Trial Chamber Judgment, 12 December 2012 at para 785.

m) Incitement

A person may be found guilty of direct and public incitement to commit genocide if they directly and publicly incited the commission of genocide (the *actus reus*) and had the intent to directly and publicly incite others to commit genocide (the *mens rea*). To be direct, the incitement must be a specific appeal to commit a genocidal act and must be more than a vague or an indirect suggestion. As an inchoate crime, direct and public incitement to commit genocide is punishable even if no act of genocide has resulted from the incitement or if the effects of the incitement are extended in time.[157] When assessing the public element of the incitement, factors such as the place where the incitement occurred and whether the attendance was selected or limited can be taken into account, but the number of persons present is not an essential factor in this assessment.[158]

The crime is completed as soon as the discourse in question is uttered or published even though the effects of the incitement may extend over time.[159] However, implicit language may be direct because incitement does not have to involve an explicit appeal to commit genocide. To determine whether a speech is direct, it should be viewed in light of its cultural and linguistic context, its audience and how the speech was understood by its intended audience, and the political and community affiliations of the inciter.[160]

The *mens rea* required for the crime of direct and public incitement to commit genocide presupposes a genocidal intent in that the person

---

157 *Nahimana, Barayagwiza and Ngeze ("Media")* (ICTR-99-52-A), Appeals Chamber Judgment, 28 November 2007 at paras 678, 692, 720; *Nyiramasuhuko et al* (ICTR-98-42-A), Appeals Chamber Judgment, 14 December 2015 at paras 2335, 2676–77, 2781, 3338, 3345.

158 *Nzabonimana* (ICTR-98-44D-A), Appeals Chamber Judgment, 29 September 2014 at para 231; *Ngirabatware* (MICT-12-29-A), Appeals Chamber Judgment, 18 December 2014 at para 52.

159 *Nahimana, Barayagwiza and Ngeze ("Media")* (ICTR-99-52-A), Appeals Chamber Judgment, 28 November 2007 at para 723; *Muvunyi* (ICTR-00-55A-T), Trial Chamber Judgment, 11 February 2010 at para 24; *Nzabonimana* (ICTR-98-44D-T), Trial Chamber Judgment, 31 May 2012 at para 1752; *Ngirabatware* (MICT-12-29-A), Appeals Chamber Judgment, 18 December 2014 at para 52.

160 *Kajelijeli* (ICTR-98-44A-T), Trial Chamber Judgment, 1 December 2003 at para 856; *Nahimana, Barayagwiza and Ngeze ("Media")* (ICTR-99-52-A), Appeals Chamber Judgment, 28 November 2007 at paras 698–701; *Bikindi* (ICTR-01-72-T), Trial Chamber Judgment, 2 December 2008 at paras 387–89 (including the possibility of songs amounting to incitement); *Muvunyi* (ICTR-00-55A-T), Trial Chamber Judgment, 11 February 2010 at para 251; *Nzabonimana* (ICTR-98-44D-T), Trial Chamber Judgment, 31 May 2012 at para 1753; *Nyiramasuhuko et al* (ICTR-98-42-A), Appeals Chamber Judgment, 14 December 2015 at para 2678.

who is inciting to commit genocide must have themselves the specific intent to commit genocide.[161]

n) Attempt

There has been no jurisprudence regarding the content of this crime at the ICTY/ICTR,[162] but the Rome Statute gives the following detailed description:

> Attempts to commit such a crime by taking action that commences its execution by means of a substantial step, but the crime does not occur because of circumstances independent of the person's intentions. However, a person who abandons the effort to commit the crime or otherwise prevents the completion of the crime shall not be liable for punishment under this Statute for the attempt to commit that crime if that person completely and voluntarily gave up the criminal purpose.[163]

---

161 *Rutaganda* (ICTR-96-3-A), Appeals Chamber Judgment, 26 May 2003 at para 524; *Muvunyi* (ICTR-00-55A-T), Trial Chamber Judgment, 11 February 2010 at para 28; *Nzabonimana* (ICTR-98-44D-T), Trial Chamber Judgment, 31 May 2012 at para 1751; *Ngirabatware* (MICT-12-29-A), Appeals Chamber Judgment, 18 December 2014 at para 58; *Nyiramasuhuko et al* (ICTR-98-42-A), Appeals Chamber Judgment, 14 December 2015 at para 3338.

162 Except to say that attempt is by definition an inchoate crime, inherent in the criminal conduct per se, and as such it is punishable as a separate crime irrespective of whether or not the intended crime is accomplished; see *Akayesu* (ICTR-96-4-A), Appeals Chamber Judgment, 1 June 2001 at para 473; *Rutaganda* (ICTR-96-3-T), Trial Chamber Judgment, 6 December 1999 at paras 34–35; *Musema* (ICTR-96-13-T), Trial Chamber Judgment, 27 January 2000 at paras 115–16; *Semanza* (ICTR-97-20-T), Trial Chamber Judgment, 15 May 2003 at para 378.

163 Article 25.3(f); this has been elaborated on by saying that attempt to commit a crime "is a crime in which the objective elements are incomplete, while the subjective elements are complete"; see *Katanga and Chui* (ICC-01/04-01/07), Pre-Trial Chamber, Decision of the Confirmation of the Charges, 30 September 2008 at paras 458–60; *Ntaganda* (ICC-01/04-02/06), Decision of the Confirmation of the Charges, 9 June 2014 at para 175; Decision of the Confirmation of Charges, *Gbagbo* (ICC-02/11-01/11), Pre-Trial Chamber, 12 June 2014 at para 201; *Blé Goudé* (ICC-02/11-02/11), Pre-Trial Chamber, Decision of the Confirmation of Charges, 11 December 2014 at para 121; *Gbagbo and Blé Goudé* (ICC-02/11-01/15-1263-AnxC-Red), Trial Chamber, Reasons for oral decision of 15 January 2019 on the *Requête de la Défense de Laurent Gbagbo afin qu'un jugement d'acquittement portant sur toutes les charges soit prononcé en faveur de Laurent Gbagbo et que sa mise en liberté immédiate soit ordonnée*, and on the Blé Goudé Defence no case to answer motion, Public Redacted Version of Dissenting Opinion Judge Herrera Carbuccia, 16 July 2019 at para 442.

2) The Views of the UNHCR

In general, the United Nations High Commissioner for Refugees (UNHCR) has stated that a person can be excluded if that person "committed, or made a substantial contribution to, the criminal act, in the knowledge that his or her act or omission would facilitate the criminal conduct."[164] With respect to 1F(a) liability, the 2003 *Background Note* refers to the Rome Statute and the jurisprudence of the ICTY to explore other aspects of extended liability, especially aiding and abetting, JCE, and command responsibility.[165] It goes on to say that there are special circumstances where the general rules of attributing liability can be relaxed somewhat in situations of very egregious commissions of human rights, such as in the case of "senior officials of repressive regimes" and "organisations which commit violent crimes or incite others to commit them."[166]

In the view of the UNHCR, senior officials of repressive regimes can be subject to exclusion in the sense that "a presumption of individual responsibility reversing the burden of proof may arise as a result of such a senior person's continued membership of a government (or part of it) clearly engaged in activities that fall within the scope of Article 1F."[167]

Similarly, with respect to violent groups, the *Background Note* indicates:

> Nevertheless, the purposes, activities and methods of some groups, sub-groups or organisations are of a particularly violent nature, for example where this involves indiscriminate killing or injury of the civilian population, or acts of torture. Where membership of such a group is voluntary, it raises a presumption that the individual concerned has somehow contributed significantly to the commission of violent crimes, even if this is simply by substantially assisting the organisation to continue to function effectively in pursuance of its aims. In such cases, burden of proof is reversed.[168]

164 UNHCR, *Background Note on the Application of the Exclusion Clauses: Article 1F of the 1951 Convention relating to the Status of Refugees* (4 September 2003) at 19, para 51, online: www.refworld.org/docid/3f5857d24.html [*Background Note*]; UNHCR, *Statement on Article 1F of the 1951 Convention* (July 2009) at 9, online: www.unhcr.org/protection/operations/4a5edac09/unhcr-statement-article-1f-1951-convention.html.

165 *Ibid* at 20–21, paras 51–56.

166 *Ibid* at 22, 23.

167 *Ibid* at 22, para 58.

168 *Ibid* at 23, para 60.

Even with a reverse burden, further caution is advised in the *Background Note*:

> [B]y ensuring before arriving at a decision to exclude that the activities of the group are scrutinized as well as the role of the individual in the group, including whether the person was associated with the group when it was violent. Lastly, attention is drawn to the complex situation of fragmentation of groups and the influence of factions within a larger group.[169]

3) National Refugee Jurisprudence

a) Australia

Five court decisions have provided guidance regarding the notion of complicity[170] in the refugee context,[171] three at the Federal Court of

169 *Ibid* at 23–24, para 61.

170 There have been exclusion findings based on personally carrying out killings, such as in *VZL and Minister for Immigration and Multicultural Affairs*, [2000] AATA 191 (killing civilians in Sri Lanka as a member of the Sri Lankan army), N95/08964 [1996] RRTA 691 (as a member of an army liquidation squad in the Philippines), N93/00914 [1994] RRTA 828 (as a member of a killing team in the Philippine police), and V94/02580, [1995] RRTA 1918 (as a commando leader in the Phalange/Lebanese Forces); bombings (*MD Shahidul and Minister for Immigration and Multicultural Affairs*, [1998] AATA 331 (in Bangladesh in 1995)); and acts of torture, such as in *N96/1441 and Minister for Immigration and Multicultural Affairs*, [1998] AATA 619 (as a member of the Lebanese Armed Forces between 1991 and 1993), and V94/01334 [1995] RRTA 1626 (as a member of the Turkish police between 1986 and 1989). Another case from Lebanon was decided on the concept of ordering killings during the massacre at the Sabra refugee camp in 1982, V95/03566, [1997] RRTA 334.

171 There have been some cases in the immigration context that shed further light on the notion of association. At the court level, both the Federal Court of Australia (FCA) and the Federal Court of Australia, Full Court (FCAFC), provided clarification on this issue in the *Haneef* case (*Haneef v Minister for Immigration and Citizenship*, [2007] FCA 1273, and *Minister for Immigration & Citizenship v Haneef*, [2007] FCAFC 203). This case involved Dr. Haneef, who had been arrested on 2 July 2007 by the Australian Federal Police and later charged with having intentionally provided resources, a SIM card, to a terrorist organization. The minister for citizenship and immigration cancelled his visa based on association with an individual, a group, or an organization suspected of having been, or being, involved in criminal conduct. Both levels of court were of the view that the minister's approach regarding association, that any type of association, even friendship or innocent association, was too wide and that association means "some sympathy with, or support for, or involvement in, the criminal conduct of the person, group or organisation. The association must be such as to have some bearing upon the person's character" (at para 130 of the FCAFC decision); the FCA decision at para 230 expresses the notion of association as follows: "an alliance or link or combination between the visa holder with the persons engaged in criminal activity." At the level of the Administrative Appeals Tribunal, the issue of association was discussed in

Australia level[172] and two at the appeals level.[173]

The *SHCB* case involved a person from Afghanistan who reported individuals to the security service, KhAD, with the knowledge that these individuals could become victims of war crimes or crimes against humanity. The Federal Court of Australia upheld the tribunal decision to exclude this person based on complicity by indicating that international crimes can be committed as accessories but that mere membership in KhAD was not sufficient. Accessory liability, according to the court, requires evidence of acting intentionally and with the knowledge of the group's intention to commit the crime. The court found, in addition to this factor, the applicant's rank in KhAD and his role in providing information sufficient to establish the element of joint purpose. On appeal, the Federal Court of Australia, Full Court (FCAFC) agreed with all aspects of the decision of the lower court below, especially the finding that it is not necessary that the appellant personally committed a war crime or a crime against humanity or that there be a finding with respect to a specific incident. In its view, what is required is evidence of many such incidents and a conclusion that the appellant took steps as an officer of KhAD knowing that such acts would be the consequence of his steps.[174]

In the *WAKN* case, the applicant was a former senior member of the Wahdat Army in Afghanistan charged with supervising a regiment. Senior members of this organization had been identified as those likely responsible for human rights violations in Afghanistan. Citing *SHCB*, the court found that more than membership in an organization was required but upheld the decision of complicity because the applicant had

---

the cases of *Hapugoda and Minister for Immigration and Multicultural and Indigenous Affairs*, [2002] AATA 330; *Grabovica and Minister for Immigration and Multicultural and Indigenous Affairs*, [2003] AATA 110; and *Lunja and Minister for Immigration and Multicultural and Indigenous Affairs*, [2004] AATA 563; the tribunal was of the view that association required an alliance or a link but not membership in an organization and also indicated that whether such a link constituted an association should be determined using such factors as the duration, nature, degree, and frequency of the association. This approach was confirmed in *Adekoya and Minister for Immigration and Border Protection (Migration)*, [2017] AATA 2028.

172 *SHCB and Minister for Immigration & Multicultural and Indigenous Affairs*, [2003] FCA 229 [*SHCB* FCA]; *WAKN v Minister for Immigration and Multicultural and Indigenous Affairs*, [2004] FCA 1245 [*WAKN*]; and *MRWF v Minister for Immigration & Border Protection*, [2018] FCA 504 [*MRWF*].

173 *SHCB v Minister for Immigration & Multicultural and Indigenous Affairs*, [2003] FCAFC 308 [*SHCB* FCAFC] and *SZCWP v Minister* for *Immigration & Multicultural & Indigenous Affairs*, [2006] FCAFC 9.

174 *SHCB* FCAFC, above note 173; this is the judicial review of *SAL and Minister for Immigration and Multicultural and Indigenous Affairs*, [2002] AATA 1164.

held a position of authority and would, therefore, have been expressly involved in decision making and security questions and had specific knowledge of the human rights violations that were being committed.[175]

In the *SZCWP* decision, involving a Nepalese citizen who had been associated with Maoist insurgents, the tribunal had used the Rome Statute definition of criminal liability and found that membership was not enough, citing the test for complicity from the *SHCB* case—aiding, abetting, or contributing to an intentional act and knowing the group's intent to commit a crime. The majority of judges on the FCAFC found that the tribunal had been correct in focusing on a common purpose, rather than on identifying specific acts in which the applicant had been involved, and upheld the exclusion of the applicant.[176]

In 2018, the Federal Court of Australia was called upon to assess the involvement of a person belonging to the Jandarma and Jandarma Istihbarat ve Terörle Mücadele (JITEM), the Turkish gendarmerie and the intelligence agency of the gendarmerie, respectively, both of which were heavily involved in the Turkish-PKK (Kurdistan Workers' Party) conflict in the 1990s and had been involved in human rights abuses and

---

175 *WAKN*, above note 172; this is the judicial review of *WBR and Minister for Immigration and Multicultural Affairs*, [2006] AATA 754 [*WBR*].

176 *SZCWP v Minister for Immigration and Multicultural and Indigenous Affairs*, [2006] FCAFC 9; this was the judicial review of *SRDDDD and Minister for Immigration and Multicultural and Indigenous Affairs*, [2004] AATA 150. The Administrative Appeals Tribunal of Australia (AAT) in earlier cases had relied quite heavily on Canadian jurisprudence to circumscribe the notion of complicity and had used the same wording as Canadian cases, such as the fact that membership in a brutal organization can amount to complicity (*WAV and Minister for Immigration and Multicultural Affairs*, [2002] AATA 463, and *"AXOIB" and Minister for Immigration and Multicultural Affairs*, [2002] AATA 365) [*"AXOIB"*]; or the terminology of knowing and personal participation (the cases of *N1998/532 and Minister for Immigration and Multicultural Affairs*, [1999] AATA 116; *W97/164 and Minister for Immigration and Multicultural Affairs*, [1998] AATA 618; *SAL and Minister for Immigration and Multicultural and Indigenous Affairs*, [2002] AATA 1164; *"AXOIB," ibid*; *SAH and Minister for Immigration and Multicultural and Indigenous Affairs*, [2002] AATA 26; *SROOOO and Minister for Immigration and Multicultural and Indigenous Affairs*, [2006] AATA 91; *WBR*, above note 175); or shared or common purpose (the cases of *N1998/532 and Minister for Immigration and Multicultural Affairs*, [1999] AATA 116; *W97/164 and Minister for Immigration and Multicultural Affairs*, [1998] AATA 618; *VAG and Minister for Immigration and Multicultural and Indigenous Affairs*, [2002] AATA 1332; *SAH and Minister for Immigration and Multicultural and Indigenous Affairs*, [2002] AATA 263; *SAL and Minister for Immigration and Multicultural and Indigenous Affairs*, [2002] AATA 1164; *SROOOO and Minister for Immigration and Multicultural and Indigenous Affairs*, [2006] AATA 91; *WBR*, above note 175). More recently, reference has been made to the accountability provision in the Rome Statute (as well as the Canadian jurisprudence but excluding membership following the FCAFC *SHCB* case) in *WBV and Minister for Immigration and Citizenship*, [2007] AATA 2046.

crimes against humanity.[177] The court started out by setting the overarching proposition of complicity as originally determined in the *SHCB* Full Court decision by saying:

> [I]n order to bear criminal responsibility for an act under the Rome Statute, a person need not have directly committed that act him or herself. He or she must, however, have aided, abetted or otherwise assisted in its commission or attempted commission or have contributed to its commission or attempted commission by persons acting with a common purpose. The person must act intentionally and must have knowledge of the intention of the group to commit the crime.[178]

Then it repeated the essential elements of such liability:

- the applicant need not actually have directly committed the act in question;
- there must be awareness of the act of participation and a conscious decision to participate in aiding, abetting or otherwise assisting in the commission of the crime. This includes planning, instigating, ordering or committing;
- there does not necessarily need to be a finding with respect to a specific incident. If there are many such incidents and the applicant took steps knowing that those actions would result in criminal activity that would suffice;
- there must be the "requisite intent" to assist in the act; mere knowledge is not sufficient;
- presence alone at the scene of a crime is not sufficient, but if presence is coupled with other circumstantial or other evidence then it may be used;
- membership of an organisation is usually insufficient by itself to establish complicity, depending on the principal aims of the organisation and the closeness of the applicant to the organisation's decision-making process; and
- rank may be an important factor. A high-ranking officer may be held responsible as they are closer to the decision-making process.[179]

---

177 *MRWF*, above note 172.

178 *Ibid* at para 59; for a detailed discussion of the concept of aiding and abetting and JCE in international criminal law, see *GZCK v Minister for Home Affairs*, [2021] FCA 1618 at paras 170–87 [*GZCK*].

179 *Ibid* at para 58.

Last, it made reference to the *Ezokola* decision of the Canadian Supreme Court[180] by repeating its crucial finding that "the requirement of a significant contribution is critical to prevent an unreasonable extension of the notion of criminal participation in international criminal law."[181]

At the tribunal level, the Administrative Appeals Tribunal of Australia (AAT) had to assess whether complicity was present in a situation where a member of the Burmese Navy participated in the shooting of fleeing student activists during the 1988 democracy movement. The claimant had said that he had not shot anybody; indeed, he tried not to do so but was aware that during this period at least ten to fifteen students were being killed each day in this manner in August and September 1988. In addition, female students were being brought into the Navy barracks and, under the pretext that they were prostitutes, raped and killed. He never participated in this. The tribunal, while being of the view that crimes against humanity were committed during this time, did not find the claimant excludable as he was a minor player during these events and did not share the common purpose of killing fleeing activists.[182]

An officer in the Sri Lankan army between 1978 and 1983 and 1989 and 1993, who had been involved personally in what he termed "low-level torture" and who then handed his victims over for more severe treatment if they did not cooperate, was found to have been involved in war crimes and crimes against humanity.[183]

The issue of responsibility in situations where information was gathered and passed on for repressive purposes has been the subject of discussion in several AAT decisions, as well as the above-mentioned *MRWF* case. In 1998, a person was excluded from refugee protection for carrying out surveillance activities on behalf of the Front Islamique du Salut (FIS) in Algeria between 1994 and 1997 that resulted in systematic assassination of police officers by that organization.[184] In another case, the claimant held the position of volunteer leader of a village protection unit in Sri Lanka for six years, from 1988 to 1994.

---

180 See below note 267.

181 *MRWF*, above note 172 at paras 63–64.

182 *W97/164 and Minister for Immigration and Multicultural Affairs*, [1998] AATA 618.

183 *SRNN and Department of Immigration and Multicultural Affairs*, [2000] AATA 983.

184 *W98/45 and Minister for Immigration and Multicultural Affairs*, [1998] AATA 948; see, also, *SRL and Minister for Immigration and Multicultural Affairs*, [2000] AATA 128, for a similar situation in Sri Lanka.

In this capacity, he led a group of up to thirty people who carried out patrols in local villages, seeking information to suppress anti-government violence and terrorism. He had also personally reported at least ten people to officials of the United National Party in the knowledge that such people would be tortured or killed by the Sri Lankan army or security forces. The claimant was excluded for complicity.[185] In a similar situation, this time involving a KhaD officer in Afghanistan who reported suspicious activities to his superiors, resulting in people being arrested by KhAD with dire consequences, the AAT made a finding of complicity in international crimes.[186]

In a different type of situation, complicity was found where a person was facilitating the travel of Black Tiger missions of the Liberation Tigers of Tamil Eelam (LTTE) in Sri Lanka into enemy-controlled areas in the knowledge that the LTTE intended to bomb civilian targets.[187] On the other hand, a person working in the coding department of KhAD, where he was responsible for transferring information, such as repairing of roads, building or repairing of mosques, or financial matters, such as the wages of employees, from non-military government departments, including KhAD, to other departments was found not to be complicit. In this context, the tribunal commented that mere membership in an organization was not sufficient to attract liability under article 1F.[188] An officer in the Iraqi army was found not to be complicit in the crimes against humanity committed by the army between 1986 and 2003 even though he admitted knowledge of the activities of the Iraqi army. The AAT indicated that knowledge, in and of itself, does not mean that he was a part of a common purpose or aided or abetted those activities.[189]

In another decision, a person was found not to be complicit even though the organization he belonged to, the Patriotic Union of Kurdistan (PUK), had committed war crimes and crimes against humanity according to the tribunal. The claimant was not complicit because he had only carried out political activities, such as persuading people that the PUK

---

185 *"AXOIB,"* above note 176; see, also, *MZYVM v Minister for Immigration and Citizenship*, [2013] FCA 79, and *GZCK*, above note 178, for similar fact situations.

186 *VAB and Minister for Immigration and Multicultural and Indigenous Affairs*, [2001] AATA 990.

187 *GZCK and Minister for Home Affairs (Migration)*, [2019] AATA 656, confirmed on appeal in *GZCK*, above note 178.

188 *SROOOO and Minister for Immigration and Multicultural and Indigenous Affairs*, [2006] AATA 91.

189 *SAH and Minister for Immigration and Multicultural and Indigenous Affairs*, [2002] AATA 263 at para 59.

supported their interests and was the party they should support. He also found food and accommodation for party members. The only activity going beyond this work was one occasion involving handing over prisoners who had been captured after a clash with an Islamic group. Subsequently, it was found that these prisoners had been killed, but the claimant had had no appreciation that this was going to happen.[190]

From the jurisprudence, which in 2018 provided a conceptual framework for complicity based on Canadian and UK precedents, at both the court and the tribunal level, it can be ascertained that most cases have dealt with the notion of aiding and abetting in which the specific aspects of handing over a person to maltreatment or providing information with the same result comprised most of the situations assessed. The cases where liability was found not to exist was because the link between the person concerned and the commission of the international crime was too tenuous, which could have been expressed in international criminal law language as a lack of a substantial contribution. However, the refugee decision makers have not relied (apart from one instance) on international criminal law but charted their own course in determining what amounted to extended liability without providing a detailed analytical framework but using ad hoc reasoning, which, in the circumstances, likely yielded the same result as utilizing an international criminal law approach. In this context, it is clear that the notion of membership has been rejected.

b) Belgium

The general principles with respect to indirect involvement have remained constant in Belgium,[191] based on the legislative text that arti-

---

190 *VAG and Minister for Immigration and Multicultural and Indigenous Affairs*, [2002] AATA 1332. For another case where a lack of knowledge of the purpose of information could have led to unfortunate consequences, see *"WAR" and Minister for Immigration and Multicultural Affairs*, [2001] AATA 475.

191 There have been a number of cases where persons were excluded for direct involvement in the crimes against humanity of torture (CCE No 13.733, 4 July 2008, for a member of a security service during the Saddam Hussein regime in Iraq; CCE No 16.991, 8 October 2008, in regards to a soldier of the Charles Taylor regime in Liberia; CCE No 18.233, 31 October 2008, involving a soldier in charge of a rebel group in the Ivory Coast in 2001–5; and CCE No 24.924, 24 March 2009, for a soldier of a border unit during the Saddam Hussein regime in Iraq), while more recently, persons who tortured prisoners in Syria (CCE No 149.555, 13 July 2015 and CCE No 206.069, 27 June 2018) and Afghanistan (CCE No 213.664, 10 December 2018) as well as a commando in the Afghani army who was personally involved in the killing

cle 1F also applies to persons who have intentionally incited or participated in article 1F activities,[192] although the wording to describe these principles has varied somewhat over the years.

The Council of State said in 2001 that to commit international crimes, it is sufficient that a person participates in the preparation or execution of acts, which amount to article 1F(a) activities.[193] In 2006, the same court said that the requirement was more akin to knowing participation and personal participation,[194] while in 2008 the court adjusted this language to say that an individual could be responsible for the commission of crimes, in addition to personally committing them, by making a substantial contribution with knowledge of the crime.[195] A later refinement was that it had to be a substantial personal contribution with knowledge and no defence.[196] The council has also indicated that in situations with a large number of killings and acts of torture there is no need to precisely describe to which acts a person has made the contribution.[197] At the tribunal level, the substantial contribution requirement set out by the Council of State has been repeated but with the addition of the notion of an immediate effect.[198] More recently, the tribunal also relied on article 25(3)(d) of the Rome Statute to articulate the requirements of a common purpose, that is, making an intentional contribution to the crimes for the purpose of furthering the commission of such crimes in the knowledge of the intention of the group to commit these crimes. This was regarding persons involved in training several security forces belonging to the Fatah organization in Gaza, which were involved in a power struggle with groups belonging to Hamas. Based on the responsibility of the person concerned with the training and the purpose and nature of the

---

of civilians during a non-international armed conflict (CCE No 228.260, 30 October 2019) were also excluded.

192 *Aliens Act*, s 55/2.

193 CE No 94.321, 27 March 2001 at para 2.4.2.

194 CE No 165.722, 8 December 2006 at para 1.2; while the judgment is in Dutch, these words are in English, which mirrors the language used in Canadian and Dutch jurisprudence.

195 CE No 184.647, 24 June 2008 at para 3.1.1 with reference to the Rome Statute.

196 CE No 186.913, 8 October 2008 at para 2.4 also with reference to the Rome Statute; this approach was also used in the case of CCE 14.567, 29 July 2008; a substantial contribution was defined, with reference to the ICTY jurisprudence, as a criminal act, which most probably would not have occurred in the same way had someone not acted in the role that the suspect in fact assumed; see CCE No 253.089, 20 April 2021.

197 CE No 165.722, 8 December 2006 at para 1.2.

198 CCE No 11.020, 8 May 2008, and CEE No 25.649, 3 April 2009 (which refers to art 25 of the Rome Statute).

training, the tribunal came to the conclusion that he was complicit.[199] It is interesting to note that in applying the common purpose of the Rome Statute, the tribunal did not pay attention to the requirement of a common plan, thereby conflating the concepts of aiding and abetting and common purpose, much along the same lines as the UK Supreme Court had done in 2010 in the *JS* case for the concept of JCE.[200]

These principles have been applied in a variety of situations, mostly in aiding and abetting– or association-type analyses, but also on occasion in situations where a person had a command function, in which capacity they gave orders for the killing and raping of civilians in Somalia during its civil war.[201] Membership as a heading for liability has usually been rejected.[202] Persons who facilitated international crimes with material assistance have been excluded,[203] as has a person who encouraged crimes against humanity during the 1994 Rwanda genocide.[204] With respect to the aiding and abetting–type cases, arresting persons and then handing them over has led to exclusion for persons involved in this activity in Afghanistan (members of military security who would conduct surveillance on other soldiers and would hand over persons suspected of anti-government activities to KhAD in the knowledge that death or torture would follow)[205] and Iraq (a member of the Fedayeen Saddam security service who was involved in arrests and handing people over to the other security services for severe interrogation;[206] a member of the Mudiriyat al-Amn al-Am security service with

199 CCE No 80.570, 2 May 2012.

200 See below note 667.

201 CCE No 49.298, 10 October 2010; this case concerned the second in command of the rebel group Somali Patriotic Movement (SPM) and its faction, the Somali Salvation Democratic Front (SSDF).

202 See Sibylle Kapferer, "Exclusion Clauses in Europe: A Comparative Overview of State Practice in France, Belgium and the United Kingdom" (supp, 2000) 12 *International Journal of Refugee Law* at 211, with respect to the FIS in Algeria, as well as CPRR No 99-0316/E430, 16 July 2001, and CPRR No 04-2088/E666, 22 February 2006, both with respect to members of KhAD in Afghanistan.

203 See Kapferer, above note 202 at 211, regarding Algerian and Rwandan situations; more recently, it was applied to a person who belonged to an elite unit of the LTTE in Sri Lanka that was involved in the forcible recruitment of civilians to carry out dangerous labour during the conflict with the Sri Lankan army; see CCE, No 259.686, 30 August 2021.

204 CCE No 5393, 21 December 2007; this case relied heavily on ICTR jurisprudence, both for legal concepts and factual information.

205 CPRR No 99-0540/W5789, 2 September 1999.

206 CCE No 30.244, 31 July 2009; for another case with a member of the Fedayeen Saddam, see CCE No 5855, 17 January 2008.

the same functions;[207] and a member of the military who was part of the massacre of Basra in 1999, where he handed over survivors to security services;[208] persons who had important functions in the Ba'ath Party in Iraq during the Saddam Hussein regime, in which capacity they carried out physical surveillance and arrested opponents of the party as well as deserters from the army in the knowledge that harm would befall them;[209] and a person who had a long career culminating in important functions in the internal security apparatus in Iraq during the same era, in which capacity he was either responsible for or oversaw others who carried out electronic surveillance of political opponents of the regime).[210] This type of complicity was used again against a soldier in Eritrea involved in arresting civilians,[211] a police officer doing the same in Iraq,[212] a member of Spetsnaz in Chechnya also arresting people,[213] and a person in the Ivory Coast arresting people at road blocks during a civil war.[214]

A more indirect application of this principle was the situation of a person who was a high-level functionary of Amal in Lebanon between 1981 and 1988 and who was aware of the commission of crimes against humanity by this organization. However, responsibility was primarily derived from his involvement in a prisoner exchange between Amal and Syria knowing full well that the prisoners who would be handed over to Syria would be tortured.[215] This approach can also be seen in a case of a judge in Afghanistan under the Najibullah regime who was involved in sham proceedings with a dearth of evidence and confessions obtained under torture, while also imposing disproportionately heavy sentences, including the death penalty, and was found to be complicit.[216]

---

207 CCE No 19.355, 27 November 2008; for other cases with members of the Mudiriyat al-Amn al-Am, see CCE No 364, 22 June 2007, and CEE No 19.355, 27 November 2008.

208 CCE No 11.020, 8 May 2008.

209 CCE No 67.169, 23 September 2011; CCE No 76.913, 9 March 2012; and CCE No 72.230, 20 December 2011; the latter case also indicates that it is not membership in the Ba'ath Party itself that is objectionable (following the decision of the Court of Justice of the European Union [CJEU] in *Bundesrepublik Deutschland v B and D*, C-57/09 and C-101/09, 9 November 2010) but the activities carried out in addition to being a member.

210 CCE No 79.794, 20 April 2012.

211 CCE No 218.412, 18 March 2019.

212 CCE No 226.560, 24 September 2019.

213 CCE No 160.633, 22 January 2016.

214 CCE No 108.962, 3 September 2013.

215 CCE No 37.011, 14 January 2010.

216 CCE No 216.093, 30 January 2019.

Most cases in this area have found excludable those who carried out spying or surveillance as part of their functions and would pass on adverse information to the security apparatus of their country, resulting in the torture and often killing of the people who were arrested as a result. The person excluded would have been aware of the fate that awaited the people about whom they provided the information.

A number of cases from claimants from Iraq who had performed such activities during the Saddam Hussein regime were considered in recent years. The Council of State found this behaviour objectionable when it was done by a member of the Ba'ath Party who passed on information to the Mukhabarat security service[217] and when a member of the JAK did the same in relation to other security departments.[218] At the tribunal level, Ba'ath members' activities amounting to passing information to security services were also found to be a nefarious form of participation,[219] as was the gathering of information about deserters by a member of the military[220] and by a PUK member about fellow associates.[221] The same result befell persons who had, while students in Ethiopia during the Red Terror period of the Mengistu regime, informed on fellow students whom they suspected of anti-governmental activities or tendencies,[222] as did a person involved in spying for KhAD.[223] An informer for the Islamic State in Iraq and Syria (ISIS) in Syria,[224] a member of the military in Iraq during Saddam Hussein's regime informing on other military personnel,[225] and persons writing reports for the Palestinian intelligence service resulting in arrests and then torture[226] were all found to be complicit.

A large group of cases made use of the exclusion ground in situations where no contribution or direct result of an activity could be discerned, but the association of the person in question with questionable organizations or crimes was close enough to attract liability.

---

217 CE No 186.913, 8 October 2008.

218 CE No 184.647, 24 June 2008.

219 CCE No 14.567, 29 July 2008, and CCE No 22.001, 26 January 2009.

220 CCE No 24.662, 17 March 2009.

221 CCE No 36.054, 16 December 2009.

222 CPRR No 94-1502/W1916, 9 August 1995, and CE No 93.579, 27 February 2001.

223 CPRR No 2779/W10, 12 January 2005.

224 CCE No 239.574, 11 August 2020.

225 CCE No 103.188, 22 May 2013.

226 CCE No 213.943, 13 December 2018, and CCE No 220.460, 29 April 2019.

A case in Rwanda involved a chief of staff of a minister in the cabinet responsible for the 1994 genocide. The tribunal was of the view that since this minister was one of the architects of the genocide, a close association with such a person involving participation in policy making would lead to exclusion.[227] A senior officer in the Iraqi Republican Guard, who had a long career in the army, had a high position as a commander of tank units of between 3,800 and 8,000 men was excluded, as these indicators pointed to a sufficient connection with the military and security apparatus that was involved in gross human rights violations.[228] Other persons with senior positions, such as a high official in the Ba'ath Party,[229] a unit head in the Mukhabarat, a security organization during the regime of Saddam Hussein,[230] an officer in the Eritrean army imposing harsh penalties on the soldiers for which he was responsible,[231] and a military advisor and senior member in the headquarters of the Syrian military, which worked closely with the Syrian security apparatus responsible for crimes against humanity,[232] were all found complicit. A person who was the head of a village in China and in that position was responsible for enforcing the one-child policy was excluded for the same reason,[233] as was a person involved in recruiting children for the LTTE in Sri Lanka.[234] An interesting case, again out of Iraq, involved a senior member of the Iraqi intelligence service who was found to be involved in crimes against humanity because of an attempt to murder prominent Kurdish opposition members as part of an unsuccessful convoy ambush.[235] While attempt is a form of liability in international criminal law,[236] it has never been used at that level.

In other situations, several factors were considered indicative of a close association and therefore responsibility.[237] Some factors con-

227 CPRR No 97-0017/W5049, 5 November 1998, which referred to Canadian jurisprudence; see, also, Kapferer, above note 202 at 213, for another similar situation in Rwanda.

228 CCE No 25.061, 26 March 2009.

229 CCE No 94.846, 10 January 2013.

230 CCE No 138.035, 6 February 2015.

231 CCE No 210.729, 9 October 2018.

232 CCE No 264.267, 25 November 2021; see, also, CCE No 250.390, 4 March 2021.

233 CCE No 253.089, 20 April 2021; the case relied on the Rome Statute dealing to conclude that forced abortions amounted to crimes against humanity.

234 CCE No 252.440, 9 April 2021.

235 CCE No 210.830, 11 October 2018.

236 See above in Section A(1)(m).

237 For some older cases, see Kapferer, above note 202 at 210–11, regarding involvement in the Turkish Dev-Sol terrorist organization and a member of a Zairean security organization

sidered for persons who had lower positions in organizations involved in crimes against humanity were the duration of the service with that organization, whether the person had joined voluntarily, and whether they had an opportunity to leave safely but had not availed themselves of that possibility.

This approach was used in a case involving an individual who served ten years as a guard for the Iraqi Olympic Committee, a notorious paramilitary organization headed by Uday Hussein.[238] It was also used against a person who had been a driver and personal assistant of the head of the Jash military command, a relatively small unit of about 1,500 soldiers that had been actively involved in the brutal Anfal campaign in northern Iraq.[239] A similar result was achieved in a case of a member of the Special Forces and then the Republican Guard of the Iraqi army, which had been involved in putting down the insurrection in Kerbala in 1991.[240] Involvement in other notorious organizations, such as special units in the Mobutu regime in Zaire for over two years without any disassociation or having a senior position with authority in a violent organization, such as FIS in Algeria, also drew negative attention.[241]

This willingness to find persons liable for an association with nefarious organizations does not extend to all entities. While persons who carried out specific activities that contributed to international crimes for KhAD in Afghanistan were excluded, this has not been the case for more senior members whose connection was less direct. Two cases in 2001 involving directors of sections within KhAD were not held responsible for the well-known crimes against humanity it committed. Both persons had long careers, had several promotions leading to senior positions, knew about the activities of KhAD, and could have left when they had an opportunity to do so. In both cases, the tribunal was of the view that not every high functionary or member in this organization should be painted with the same brush of exclusion as such an approach would ignore the principle of individual responsibility.[242] This lack of nexus to international crimes was an issue in the situation of a member of a secret

operating in youth and student circles.

238 CCE No 2055, 27 September 2007.

239 CCE No 25.001, 24 March 2009.

240 CCE No 25.649, 3 April 2009.

241 See Kapferer, above note 202 at 212–13.

242 CPRR No 99-0316/E430, 16 July 2001, and CPRR No 99-0992/E429, 16 July 2001.

policy organization in Iraq during the Saddam Hussein regime,[243] and, again in Iraq, a member of the special operations forces who worked with the American army was found not to have a connection with the detention/interrogation centres where torture occurred.[244]

The same outcome was arrived at with a person who had been the minister of state organs in Afghanistan between 1982 and 1989. The tribunal said that one should not equate a function within a government with the commission of human rights abuses by that government and that a person who has no influence on the policy related to such abuses should not suffer negative consequences from being in a particular function. In this case, the person's job duties were more of an administrative nature or amounted at best to ideological propaganda.[245] Other cases with an insufficient level of contribution involved operating liquor stores on behalf of the LTTE,[246] being a driver in the Syrian army during raids against the Muslim brotherhood,[247] and being a soldier in the Syrian army.[248] Complicity was also absent in the situation of a person who had been the *chef du cabinet* of the minister of health in Rwanda during the genocide; while he had been excluded originally, the tribunal found that as a result of new evidence submitted, primarily the fact that his former superior had been acquitted by the ICTR, it was no longer reasonable to maintain the exclusion even though an acquittal by the ICTR did not mean by itself that exclusion could not apply to this superior.[249] While these cases were rather clear-cut, one other case in Belgium can be seen as more controversial. A tribunal decided that a bodyguard of the police chief in Latakia, Syria, who had twice been involved in the at times violent arrests of smugglers and drug dealers (such as hitting persons with an electric baton and a gun, as well as on one occasion pouring hot water over an arrested person), was not complicit as his actions did not amount to a substantial contribution.[250]

Like in Australia, Belgium refugee tribunals have not relied on the international criminal law concepts related to extended liability but

243 CCE No 104.074, 31 May 2013.
244 CCE No 128.506, 2 September 2014.
245 CCE No 26.511, 27 April 2009.
246 CCE No 120.077, 4 March 2014.
247 CCE No 121.274, 21 March 2014; see, also, CCE No 145.401, 12 May 2015.
248 CCE No 122.130, 4 April 2014.
249 CCE No 76.004, 28 February 2012.
250 CCE No 122.812, 22 April 2014.

were willing to extend the parameters of this type of responsibility into peripheral areas if they felt the situations demanded it. Apart from the aiding and abetting type of complicity applied to activities of handing persons and information over to organizations, which would in most cases lead to torture for the victims, the refugee decision makers also applied this type of reasoning to situations where persons carried out support functions in notorious organizations, although they fell short of finding that membership in such organizations was sufficient. At times, factors such as the manner of joining an organization, the manner and reason for abandoning an organization, and a person's career path in an organization carried a great deal of weight in coming to a finding of liability. While no international criminal law was referred to in the decisions under consideration, the adding and abetting approach has a clear resemblance to ICTY/ICTR jurisprudence, and some of the factors mentioned to arrive at a conclusion of a common purpose can be detected in earlier ICTY caselaw.

c) Canada

Canadian courts[251] originally distinguished four types of complicity,[252] all derived from the word "committed" in article 1F(a) of the Refugee Convention and all based on the notion of personal and knowing participation: being present at the commission of an international crime if combined with authority; membership in a brutal, limited purpose organization; aiding and abetting in an international crime; and having a shared criminal purpose. The latter two were applicable to all types of organizations. The difference between the aiding and abetting and the shared purpose type of complicity appeared to lie in the proximity between the person being complicit and the organization they belong to. If the proximity was close and they were seen making a contribution to

---

251 The Department of Citizenship of Immigration Canada has issued a manual that addresses the issue of complicity for war crimes and crimes against humanity in the context of immigration, but the principles stated are directly derived from the exclusion jurisprudence in this area; see *Operations Manual, Enforcement 18 — War Crimes and Crimes against Humanity*, ch 8, online (pdf): www.canada.ca/content/dam/ircc/migration/ircc/english/resources/manuals/enf/enf18-eng.pdf.

252 There have also been two cases where a person was excluded because of direct involvement, *Sabadao v Canada (Citizenship and Immigration)*, 2014 FC 815, for a member of the armed forces in the Philippines, and *Nathaniel v Canada (Public Safety and Emergency Preparedness)*, 2020 FC 32, for a police officer in Nigeria (as well as, in part, in *Ghazala Asif Khan v Canada (Citizenship and Immigration)*, 2017 FC 269).

the organization, the aiding and abetting type of complicity is at play, while a more distant connection between such a person and the criminal activities of an organization suggested that the shared purpose analysis was the preferable approach.

The first case for complicity is the 1992 decision of *Ramirez* in the Federal Court of Appeal, which set out a number of guiding principles by saying:

> What degree of complicity, then, is required to be an accomplice or abettor? A first conclusion I come to is that mere membership in an organization, which from time to time commits international offences is not normally sufficient for exclusion from refugee status. It seems apparent, however, that where an organization is principally directed to a limited, brutal purpose, such as a secret police activity, mere membership may by necessity involve personal and knowing participation in persecutorial acts. Similarly, mere presence at the scene of an offence is not enough to qualify as personal and knowing participation though, again, presence coupled with additional facts may well lead to a conclusion of such involvement. At bottom, complicity rests in such cases, I believe, on the existence of a shared common purpose and the knowledge that all of the parties in question may have of it. Such a principle reflects domestic law (e.g., subsection 21(2) of the *Criminal Code*), and I believe is the best interpretation of international law.[253]

Three other Federal Court of Appeal cases added to this understanding in the nineties. *Moreno* repeated the general tenets of the *Ramirez*

253 *Ramirez v Canada (Minister of Employment and Immigration*, [1992] 2 FC 306 at 317 [*Ramirez*]. It goes on to say, "in my view, it is undesirable to go beyond the criterion of personal and knowing participation in persecutorial acts in establishing a general principle. The rest should be decided in relation to the particular facts" (at 318). The court relied on two US Federal Court of Appeals Second World War cases to come to this conclusion: *Laipenieks* (which in turn refers to the US seminal case on this issue, the *Fedorenko* case by the United States Supreme Court) and *Osidach*. It also relied on the *Charter* of the IMT, including the provision dealing with membership (albeit indirectly by referring to Atle Grahl-Madsen, *The Status of Refugee in International Law, Volume I, The Status of Refugees in International Law* (Leiden: AW Sijthoff, 1966) at 277). With respect to the interpretation of the exclusion clause, the court says, "[I]t would nevertheless appear that, in the aftermath of Second World War atrocities, the signatory states to this 1951 Convention intended to preserve for themselves a wide power of exclusion from refugee status where perpetrators of international crimes are concerned" (at 310) and "an international convention cannot be read in the light of only one of the world's legal systems" (at 312). Incidentally, s 21(2) of the *Criminal Code*, RSC 1985, c C-46, to which the court refers, is the section setting out the concept of common intention.

case by indicating that it was well settled that personal involvement in international offences must be established and that acts or omissions amounting to passive acquiescence or mere membership are not a sufficient basis for invoking the exclusion clause. An exception to this general rule arose where the organization is one whose very existence was premised on achieving political or social ends by any means deemed necessary. Membership in a secret police force was deemed sufficient grounds for invoking the exclusion clause. Membership in a military organization involved in armed conflict with guerrilla forces would come within the ambit of the general rule and not the exception.[254]

This was followed by the *Sivakumar* judgment, in which the court was of the view that association with a person or an organization responsible for international crimes might constitute complicity if there was personal and knowing participation or tolerance of the crimes. Mere membership in a group responsible for international crimes, unless it is an organization that has a limited, brutal purpose, was not enough. Moreover, the closer one is to a position of leadership or command within an organization, the easier it is to draw an inference of awareness of the crimes and participation in the plan to commit the crimes.[255]

Last, *Bazargan* set out general parameters of complicity by saying that active membership in an organization carrying out war crimes or crimes against humanity was not required but that a person is complicit if this person contributed, directly or indirectly, remotely or

---

254 *Moreno v Canada (Minister of Employment and Immigration*, [1994] 1 FC 298 [*Moreno*]. This case has been mentioned by the Appeals Chamber of the ICTY in *Kunarac et al* (IT-96-23/IT-96-23/1), Appeals Chamber Judgment, 12 June 2002 at para 98, n114.

255 See *Sivakumar v Canada (Minister of Employment and Immigration)*, [1994] 1 FC 433 at 448 [*Sivakumar*] (the *Sivakumar* case has also been mentioned by the Appeals Chamber of the ICTY in *Kunarac et al* (IT-96-23/IT-96-23/1), Appeals Chamber Judgment, 12 June 2002 at para 98, n114). This judgment, at 444, also came to the conclusion that non-governmental organizations can also commit crimes against humanity by relying on the *Charter of the International Military Tribunal*, post–Second World War jurisprudence, the decision of the International Court of Justice in the case of *Reservations to the Convention* on *Genocide, Advisory Opinion* (28 May 1951, ICJ Rep (1951) 15), and the work of the International Law Commission with its Draft Code of Crimes Against the Peace and Security of Mankind (UN Doc A/51/10, *Report of the International Law Commission on the Work of its Forty-eighth Session*, Official Records of the General Assembly, Fifty-first Session, Supplement No 10, Ch II). This proposition was confirmed in the cases of *Cardenas v Canada (Minister of Employment and Immigration)*, 93-A-171; *Baqri v Canada (Minister of Citizenship and Immigration)*, [2002] 2 FC 85; and *Thomas v Canada (Citizenship and Immigration)*, 2007 FC 838.

immediately, to this organization or made these activities possible while being aware of the activities of the organization.[256]

The general principles in respect to brutal, limited purpose organizations had been fleshed out in subsequent jurisprudence, both in terms of the parameters of such organizations and what the notion of membership entails. The Federal Court specifically stated that when dealing with membership in an organization, the first step is to look at the type of organization and whether the main purpose of the organization was achieved through crimes against humanity or war crimes.[257] If so, membership in an organization that has a limited, brutal purpose does not automatically result in exclusion; rather, it creates a rebuttable presumption of complicity.[258]

It became clear that the Federal Court was of the view that since mere membership and knowledge of the activities of a brutal, limited purpose organization were an almost foregone conclusion for the purposes of attracting liability, the characterization of an organization as brutal and limited would be subject to a high degree of scrutiny. This trend started with the *Hajialikhani* case in 1998[259] and was confirmed by the *Mukwaya* case in 2001.[260] The phrase used in both cases to express the level of scrutiny was that the initial decision maker had to be free from doubt that the organization was principally directed to a limited, brutal purpose; as well, membership in a brutal organization had to coincide in time with the period or periods that the organization was conducting activities that would attract the characterization of brutal, according to the *Hajialikhani*, *Yogo*,[261] and *Mukwaya* cases.

Not long before the decision of the Supreme Court of Canada in the *Ezokola* case, discussed below, it appeared that an inconsistent approach was already developing among Federal Court judges in three cases in

---

256 *Ministre de la Citoyenneté et de l'Immigration c Mohammad Hassan Bazargan*, A-400-95 [*Bazargan*].

257 *Pushpanathan v Canada (Minister of Citizenship and Immigration)*, 2002 FCT 867 [*Pushpanathan*]; *Thomas v Canada (Citizenship and Immigration)*, 2007 FC 838.

258 *Mendez-Leyva v Canada (Minister of Citizenship and Immigration)*, 2001 FCT 523; see, also, *Savundaranayaga v Canada (Citizenship and Immigration)*, 2009 FC 31, and at the appeal level, *Oberlander v Canada (Attorney General)*, 2009 FCA 330.

259 *Canada (Minister of Citizenship and Immigration) v Hajialikhani*, [1999] 1 FC 181. See, also, *Balta v Canada (Minister of Employment and Immigration)*, IMM-2459-94, and *Nagamany v Canada (Minister of Citizenship and Immigration)*, 2005 FC 1554.

260 *Mukwaya v Canada (Minister of Citizenship and Immigration)*, 2001 FCT 650 [*Mukwaya*].

261 *Yogo v Canada (Minister of Citizenship and Immigration)*, 2001 FC 390 [*Yogo*].

2011–12. In the first case, *Pourjamaliaghdam*,[262] the exclusion of a woman who passed on information to SAVAK between 1976 and 1979 by making audio recordings of telephone conversations critical of the shah while working in a military hospital was overruled. In deciding this case, the court was asked to declare that membership in a brutal organization was not a category of liability as this notion had been overtaken by recent judicial developments. Specifically, these refer to the 2010 decision by the supreme courts in the United Kingdom and New Zealand[263] and the Rome Statute. Examining these sources as well as the most pertinent Canadian jurisprudence, the court concluded that, for the most part, the Canadian jurisprudence was in line with both the new caselaw in other countries as well as article 25 of the Rome Statute. Where there might be some slight differences, such as with the issue of membership, there is no reason to abandon the long-standing tradition in Canadian courts in this respect and bring the Canadian jurisprudence in "perfect alignment" with the foreign one if there are differences. However, the court did provide caution in using the notion of membership on a number of levels: that it should be an unusual occurrence; that membership is a rebuttable presumption (meaning that "the presumption can be rebutted by evidence of a lack of knowledge of the organisation's purpose or an absence of direct or indirect involvement in the group's activities"); that the standard of proof for this type of liability is much higher than for other forms of liability; that the characterization as a brutal organization has to be free from doubt; that in most cases it would be better to use the normal type of complicity analysis unless it is "fairly clear that the presumption applies based on the evidence of the nature of the group";[264] and that the decision maker must take into account the remainder of the evidence and apply the six-factor approach to see if complicity results. The court also provided a reiteration of the notion of membership, the existence of an institutional link between the organization and the person, accompanied by a more than nominal commitment to the organization's activities. In the second case, *Thurairajah*,[265] the subject was a Sri Lankan of Tamil ethnicity who worked for the LTTE from December 1992 to October 1995. In the first year, he worked at the Archive Desk in the Tinnevelly camp. He then got a promotion and worked in the

262 *Pourjamaliaghdam v Canada (Citizenship and Immigration)*, 2011 FC 666 [*Pourjamaliaghdam*].

263 See below, sections A(3)(g & h).

264 *Pourjamaliaghdam*, above note 262 at para 53.

265 *Thurairajah v Canada (Citizenship and Immigration)*, 2011 FC 891 [*Thurairajah*].

Finance Department in the Chankanai camp, where he was charged with collecting taxes that were then used to pay, notably, the services of the LTTE fighters. The Federal Court found that the conclusion of the tribunal to exclude the subject was reasonable given the fact that membership in a brutal organization is sufficient to lead to complicity and therefore exclusion and, as such, was following the previous case.

However, in the third case regarding membership in a brutal organization, *Khan*,[266] the non-exclusion of a driver for KhAD was upheld by the court based on the fact that this person had fulfilled the requirements of the rebuttable presumption for membership in a brutal organization and the lack of knowledge of the purposes of KhAD (which did not go beyond common or "street" knowledge), especially in large organizations such as KhAD, where lower-level operatives in one particular section might not be aware of crimes against humanity committed in other sections. The court said that the tribunal "is obliged to consider the nature of the membership at issue and determine whether it gives rise to a sharing of the organization's common purpose of achieving its goals through brutality and violence against civilians" and "[w]here the organization is one directed to a limited brutal purpose, one's position in such an organization is a significant factor."[267] This reasoning, which was increasingly followed by other judges,[268] was already signalling the *Ezokola* approach two years later.

The approach with respect to complicity, including the notion of membership, changed because of a judgment of the Supreme Court of Canada in 2013. The case[269] concerned a person who began his career

---

266 *Canada (Citizenship and Immigration) v Khan*, 2011 FC 982.

267 *Ibid* at paras 72 and 75.

268 This approach was also followed in four more decisions in 2012, in the cases of the *Minister of Public Safety and Emergency Preparedness v Duroseau*, 2012 FC 342, involving a member of the Tontons Macoutes (or *Voluntaires de la sécurité national* or *VSN*) during the Duvalier regime in Haiti between 1968 and 1985; *Saintilus v Canada (Citizenship and Immigration)*, 2012 FC 1105, with respect to the Armed Forces of Haiti (FADH) between 1991 and 1994; *Seyoboka v Canada (Citizenship and Immigration)*, 2012 FC 1143, regarding the army (FAR) in Rwanda during the 1994 genocide; and *Mupenzi v Canada (Citizenship and Immigration)*, 2012 FC 1304, with respect to Radio Rwanda during the genocide.

269 *Ezokola v Canada (Citizenship and Immigration)*, 2013 SCC 40 [*Ezokola*]; for commentaries, see Livio Zilli, "*Ezokola v Canada*: The Correct Place of International Criminal Law in International Refugee Law-Making" (2014) 12:5 *Journal of International Criminal Justice* 1217–31; Zoë Egelman, "Punishment and Protection, Two Sides of the Same Sword: The Problem of International Criminal Law Under the Refugee Convention" (2018) 59:2 *Harvard International Law Journal* 461 at 484–86, and Nancy Weisman, "Recent Jurisprudential Trends in the Interpretation of Complicity in Article 1F(a) Crimes" in Idil Atak & James C. Simeon, eds, *The Criminalization of*

with the government of the Democratic Republic of the Congo (DRC) in January 1999. He was hired as a financial attaché at the Ministry of Finance and was assigned to the Ministry of Labour, Employment, and Social Welfare in Kinshasa. He later worked as a financial adviser to the Ministry of Human Rights and the Ministry of Foreign Affairs and International Cooperation. In 2004, he was assigned to the Permanent Mission of the DRC to the United Nations in New York. In his role as second counsellor of the embassy, he represented the DRC at international meetings and UN entities, including the UN Economic and Social Council. He also acted as a liaison between the Permanent Mission of the DRC and UN development agencies. In 2007, the appellant served as acting *chargé d'affaires*. In this capacity, he led the Permanent Mission of the DRC and spoke before the Security Council regarding natural resources and conflicts in the DRC. He worked at the Permanent Mission until January 2008, when he resigned and fled to Canada.[270]

He had been excluded due to his association with the government of the DRC, which, during the time of his employment, had been involved in crimes against humanity. This exclusion was overturned by the first-level court, the Federal Court, which was of the view that the existing jurisprudence required that there needed to be a nexus between a person and the crimes committed by an organization that was not present in this case.[271] On appeal, the decision of the Federal Court was overturned and the original exclusion decision restored while indicating that "a senior official may, by remaining in his or her position without protest and continuing to defend the interests of his or her government while being aware of the crimes committed by this government demonstrate 'personal and knowing participation' in these crimes and be complicit with the government in their commission."[272]

Migration, Context and Consequences (Montreal & Kingston: McGill-Queen's University Press, 2018) at 119–26; for a discussion of subsequent jurisprudence, see Camille Lefebvre & Fannie Lafontaine, "The Exclusion Clause in Canada: Prioritizing Practical Expediency" (2021) 33:3 *International Journal of Refugee Law* 405–35.

270 *Ezokola*, above note 269 at paras 11–13.

271 *Ezokola v Canada (Citizenship and Immigration)*, 2010 FC 662 at para 70; the court referred to arts 25, 28, and 30 of the Rome Statute (at paras 85–86) as well as the decision of the UK Supreme Court in *JS* (below note 272 at paras 78–82), although most of the analysis is based on Canadian jurisprudence.

272 *Canada (Citizenship and Immigration) v Ekanza Ezokola*, 2011 FCA 224 at para 72; the Court of Appeal also makes reference to the Rome Statute (at paras 64–67) and (at para 68) the UK case of *JS (Sri Lanka) v Secretary of State for the Home Department*, [2009] EWCA Civ 364

The analysis of the Supreme Court is very much based on international criminal law in the sense that the Court makes an inquiry as to which are the broadest forms of extended liability, both under the ICTY/ICTR statutes and the Rome Statute, on the understanding that Canadian exclusion law should not go beyond these forms of liability in international law.[273] As a result, the Court examines the concepts of common purpose[274] and JCE[275] and comes to the conclusion that, based on these forms of liability, a new overarching test of voluntary, significant, and knowing contribution to the organization's crime or criminal purpose[276] should replace the previous personal and knowing participation test as the latter had gone too far by also allowing the capture of individuals based on mere association or passive acquiescence.[277] The Court provided some clarification of each of these elements. With respect to voluntary contribution, the Court said that "to assess the voluntariness of a contribution, decision makers should, for example, consider the method of recruitment by the organization and any opportunity to leave the organization. The voluntariness requirement captures the defence of duress which is well recognized in customary international criminal law."[278] With respect to significant contribution, the Court was of the view that not only is contribution to specific iden-

---

(see below at note 657) and is of the view that the personal and knowing participation test is in accordance with art 25 of the Rome Statute (at para 68).

273 *Ezokola*, above note 269 at paras 42–46.

274 *Ibid* at paras 54–61, specifically utilizing the Decision of the Confirmation of Charges, *Mbarushimana* (ICC-01/04-01/10), Pre-Trial Chamber I, 16 December 2011.

275 *Ibid* at paras 62–67, relying specifically on *Tadić* (IT-94-1-A), Appeals Chamber Judgment, 15 July 1999, and *Brđanin* (IT-99-36-A), Appeals Chamber Judgment, 3 April 2007. It is interesting to see that when discussing the notion of aiding and abetting in comparison with JCE in this context at para 63, the Court is of the view that "[w]hile aiding and abetting likely requires a substantial contribution to a certain specific crime, joint criminal enterprise and common purpose liability can arise from a significant contribution to a criminal purpose. To the extent that the ICTY Trial Chamber may be seen to have applied a more exacting standard in *Prosecutor v Jovica Stanišić*, IT-03-69-T, Judgment, 30 May 2013 (ICTY, Trial Chamber I), it is not in accordance with prevailing appellate authority." Insofar as the Court is criticizing the specifically directed requirement for aiding and abetting, as set out at the ICTY Appeals Chamber level in *Perišić* (IT-04-81-A), Appeals Chamber Judgment, 28 February 2013, at paras 25–42 and 73, it foreshadows the same concerns as set out by the SCSL in *Taylor* (SCSL-04-01-T), Appeals Chamber Judgment, 26 September 2013, at paras 471–81 and 486, which were confirmed by the ICTY Appeals Chamber itself in a comprehensive and detailed decision in *Šainović et al* (IT-05-87-A), Appeals Chamber Judgment, 23 January 2014, at paras 1617–51.

276 *Ezokola*, above note 269 at para 84.

277 *Ibid* at para 85.

278 *Ibid* at para 86.

tifiable crimes necessary but also "wider concepts of common design, such as the accomplishment of an organisation's purpose by whatever means are necessary."[279] Last, with respect to knowing contribution, it is necessary that "the official must be aware of the government's crime or criminal purpose and aware that his or her *conduct* will assist in the furtherance of the crime or criminal purpose."[280]

Applying the overarching test, recourse can be had to a number of factors, for which the Court found inspiration in the *JS* decision of the UK Supreme Court,[281] as well as in previous Canadian jurisprudence,[282] that would guard "against a complicity analysis that would exclude individuals from refugee protection on the basis of mere membership or failure to dissociate from a multifaceted organization which is committing war crimes."[283] Insofar as this factor test would make exclusion possibly easier than a criminal conviction, this is justified as a result of the fact that refugee exclusion proceedings are of a different nature than criminal trials.[284] The Court also made it clear that this overarching test represents the outer limits of extended liability but that other forms of liability, such as aiding and abetting and command responsibility, can still play a role in an exclusion determination.[285]

The factors that can play a role are slightly less stringent than the ones set out in the *JS* case. This is not done by deleting its factor of the person's own personal involvement and role in the organization but instead by building on the seven-factor approach of the previous Canadian jurisprudence and adding one new, crucial factor: the person's duties and activities within the organization. The complete list of factors is

(i) the size and nature of the organization;
(ii) the part of the organization with which the refugee claimant was most directly concerned;
(iii) the refugee claimant's duties and activities within the organization;
(iv) the refugee claimant's position or rank in the organization;

279 *Ibid* at para 87 (relying directly on the *JS* case and indirectly on *Vasiljević* (IT-98-32-A), Appeals Chamber Judgment, 25 February 2004 at para 89, which uses similar language).
280 *Ibid* at para 89 (which is based on art 30 of the Rome Statute).
281 *Ibid* at paras 70–72 (see below at note 669).
282 *Ibid* at para 73.
283 *Ibid* at para 74.
284 *Ibid* at paras 37–40.
285 *Ibid* at paras 41, 50, and 97.

(v) the length of time the refugee claimant was in the organization, particularly after acquiring knowledge of the group's crime or criminal purpose; and
(vi) the method by which the refugee claimant was recruited and the refugee claimant's opportunity to leave the organization.[286]

While the Court has made it clear that membership in a brutal organization is no longer a form of liability for exclusion, the notion of a brutal, limited purpose organization has not been abandoned completely; it is now part of the first factor[287] in that it seems that belonging to such an organization could affect the importance and possibly the relevance of the other factors. The *mens rea* requirement is met if a person is aware of the crime or criminal purpose and is aware that their conduct will assist in the furtherance of the crime or criminal purpose.[288] Some of these aspects were clarified more recently by saying that the purpose of the organization does not have to be exclusively criminal and that it is easier to establish a link between the contribution and the criminal purpose if the group has a limited, brutal purpose; as well, the notion of voluntary, significant, and knowing contribution does not require a direct causal link between the conduct of the person concerned and the purpose of the organization, only that there is a contribution.[289]

In terms of assessing the decision in the context of international criminal law, the Court, like its counterparts in the United Kingdom and New Zealand, exhibits a good understanding of the international criminal law concepts of extended liability, especially JCE and common purpose. However, like the UK Supreme Court, when setting out the requirements for these forms of indirect involvement, it only discusses their *actus reus* aspects and again uses the *mens rea* of aiding and abetting and knowledge rather than the intent to pursue a common purpose, which are the hallmarks of both JCE and common purpose.[290] As such, while the analysis is very helpful to enunciate an overarching test for exclusion purposes, it would have been better from an international criminal law perspective to address all the elements of these two types of liability and then indicate that from a refugee perspective not all of

286 *Ibid* at para 94; the details of each factor are described at paras 94–99.

287 *Ibid* at para 95. While the second factor appears to be new as well, in actuality, this "drilling-down" approach had already been used by the Federal Court since 2006.

288 *Ezokola*, above note 269 at para 89.

289 *Al-Fahham v Canada (Citizenship and Immigration)*, 2022 FC 322.

290 See Currie & Rikhof, above note 1 at 723–28.

these elements are essential rather than ignore them completely. Such an approach would also have clarified why the Court was of the view that JCE and common purpose are the broadest forms of extended liability, which is not the case as they address different types of perpetrators rather than extending the circle of liability beyond, for instance, aiding and abetting. While the *Ezokola* decision has relegated the notion of membership in a brutal organization to one aspect of the factor approach rather than an independent heading of complicity, the past cases in this area still have some utility.

Most determinations that organizations are brutal pertain to governmental security and secret services entities. Examples of this are KhAD in Afghanistan;[291] the ShIK in Albania;[292] the Agence nationale de renseignements (ANR), Movement for the Liberation of Congo (MLC), and SNIP in the DRC;[293] the Bureau of National Investigations (BNI) in Ghana;[294] the Sahana or SAVAK in Iran;[295] the Mukhabarat in Iraq;[296] Securitate in Romania;[297] and the International Security Organisation (ISO) in Uganda.[298] Other governmental organizations have also been deemed to have a brutal and limited purpose, such as the National Security Courts in Somalia,[299] the Armed Forces Revolutionary Council (AFRC) in Sierra Leone,[300] and the political organization PUK in Iraq,[301] while specialized military units have also been given this predicate, such as the military courts in Somalia,[302] death squads such as Battalion 3-16

---

291 *Canada (Minister of Citizenship and Immigration) v Mohsen*, IMM-3246-99; *Rasuli v Canada (Minister of Citizenship and Immigration)*, IMM-3119-95; *Zadeh v Canada (Minister of Employment and Immigration)*, IMM-3077-94; and *Zazai v Canada (Minister of Citizenship and Immigration)* 2004 FC 1356.

292 *Lalaj v Canada (Minister of Citizenship and Immigration)*, IMM-4779-99.

293 *Diasonama v Canada (Minister of Citizenship and Immigration)*, 2005 FC 888; *Molebe v Canada (Citizenship and Immigration)*, 2007 FC 138; *Zoya v Canada (Minister of Citizenship and Immigration)*, IMM-5256-99.

294 *Kudjoe v Canada (Minister of Citizenship and Immigration)*, IMM-5129-97.

295 *Nejad v Canada (Minister of Citizenship and Immigration)*, IMM-4624-93, and *Shakarabi v Canada (Minister of Citizenship and Immigration)*, IMM-1371-97 [*Shakarabi*].

296 *Sumaida v Canada*, [2000] 3 FC 66 [*Sumaida*].

297 *Szekely v Canada (Minister of Citizenship and Immigration)*, IMM-6031-98.

298 *Mutumba v Canada (Citizenship and Immigration)*, 2009 FC 19.

299 *Demiye v Canada (Minister of Employment and Immigration)*, A-137-93.

300 *Thomas v Canada (Citizenship and Immigration)*, 2007 FC 838.

301 *Hovaiz v Canada (Minister of Citizenship and Immigration)*, IMM-2012-01.

302 *Mohamud v Canada (Minister of Employment and Immigration)* (1994), 83 FTR 267.

in Honduras,[303] and Guardia de Hacienda in Guatemala.[304] Non-governmental organizations are not immune to being characterized as brutal, as can be seen in the cases of the Lord's Resistance Army (LRA) in Uganda,[305] the Oodua Peoples Congress (OPC) in Nigeria,[306] and the LTTE in Sri Lanka.[307]

The caselaw of the Federal Court makes a number of observations regarding the parameters of membership in a brutal, limited purpose organization. To be a member of a brutal and limited purpose organization, formal membership coupled with active participation in unlawful acts is not required; simply belonging to such an organization is sufficient.[308] There is no need to be a formal member of the criminal group in question to be found complicit of its crimes by association. According to the Federal Court, an individual is a member of an organization if they devote themself full time or almost full time to the organization or if they are associated with members of the organization, especially for a lengthy period of time.[309] Belonging to an organization is assumed where people join voluntarily and remain in the group for the common purpose of actively adding their personal efforts to the group's cause.[310] The expression "membership in a particular group" implies the existence of an institutional link between the organization and an individual, accompanied by more than nominal involvement in the activities of the organization.[311] There is no need to identify the specific acts in which the individual has been involved because of the notoriety and singular purpose of the group.[312]

This low threshold for membership had not been met earlier in a case of a person who had been involved in the distribution of pamphlets for the MKO (Mujahedeen-e-Khalq), a terrorist organization, as well as

303 *Valle Lopes v Canada (Citizenship and Immigration)*, 2010 FC 403.

304 *Cordon v Canada (Minister of Citizenship and Immigration)*, IMM-1889-97 [*Cordon*].

305 *Obita v Canada (Minister of Citizenship and Immigration)*, 2006 FC 178.

306 *Kabir v Canada (Minister of Citizenship and Immigration)*, 2003 FCT 657.

307 *Pushpanathan*, above note 257, and *Nagamany v Canada (Minister of Citizenship and Immigration)*, 2005 FC 1554.

308 *Shakarabi*, above note 295, and *Canada (Minister of Citizenship and Immigration) v Mohsen*, IMM-3246-99.

309 *Canada (Minister of Citizenship and Immigration) v Owens*, IMM-5668-99, which also stated that membership goes beyond that of being a mere supporter or sympathizer.

310 *Saridag v Canada (Minister of Employment and Immigration)*, [1995] 1 FC null.

311 *Harb v Canada (Minister of Citizenship and Immigration)*, 2003 FCA 39 [*Harb*].

312 *Pushpanathan*, above note 257.

in the videotaping for international MKO broadcasts. The court felt that this did not amount to nominal involvement, nor did the person have knowledge that the MKO was involved in violent activities, but rather that it was only engaged in civil disobedience.[313] The same was said for a member of KhAD in Afghanistan who only performed administrative tasks far away from locations of torture and other crimes.[314]

According to the caselaw, to determine whether a hybrid organization, which not only has a brutal purpose but engages in other, legitimate activities (such as education or providing health and other charitable services), should be considered a brutal, limited purpose one, it is necessary to look at what the organization's *sine qua non* is—that is, would the organization only exist for its benign projects? Or, put differently, is there any evidence that political objectives can be separated from militaristic activities?[315] Being a member of a peaceful organization or section that has not severed its ties drastically with its violent sister organization, wing, or section will bring a person within the parameters of membership of the entire organization, which is then considered violent.[316]

The Canadian jurisprudence has indicated that non-brutal organizations are entities that have a legitimate purpose but have committed war crimes or crimes against humanity that were outside their main function or incidental to their mandate. The types of organizations considered have ranged from regular armed forces[317] and ministries of the interior, including prisons,[318] to other state organs that have the capacity to affect large numbers of people, such as other ministries, courts,[319] police forces,[320]

---

313 *Atabaki v Canada (Minister of Citizenship and Immigration)*, 2005 FC 969.

314 *Canada (Minister of Citizenship and Immigration) v Mohsen*, IMM-3246-99.

315 *Mehmoud v Canada (Minister of Citizenship and Immigration)*, IMM-1734-97 (with respect to the SSP (Sepah-e-Sahaba) in Pakistan); *Pushpanathan*, above note 257 (involving the LTTE in Sri Lanka); *Obita v Canada (Minister of Citizenship and Immigration)*, 2006 FC 178 (involving the LRA in Uganda); *Thomas v Canada (Citizenship and Immigration)*, 2007 FC 838 (in general).

316 *Cardenas v Canada (Minister of Employment and Immigration)*, 93-A-171.

317 *Ramirez*, above note 253; *Moreno*, above note 254; *Cordon*, above note 304.

318 *Gutierrez v Canada (Minister of Employment and Immigration)*, IMM-2170-93 [*Gutierrez*]; *Mohammad v Canada (Minister of Citizenship and Immigration)*, IMM-4227-94; *Alza v Canada (Minister of Citizenship and Immigration)*, IMM-3657-94.

319 *Aden v Canada (Minister of Citizenship and Immigration)*, IMM-2912-95; *Omar v Canada (Minister of Citizenship and Immigration)*, 2004 FC 861; *Kaburundi v Canada (Citizenship and Immigration)*, 2006 FC 361; *Han v Canada (Minister of Citizenship and Immigration)*, 2006 FC 432; *Al-Fahham v Canada (Citizenship and Immigration)*, 2022 FC 322.

320 *Randhawa v Canada (Minister of Employment and Immigration)*, IMM-5540-93; *Kiared v Canada (Minister of Citizenship and Immigration)*, IMM-3172-97; *Cabrera v Canada (Minister of Citizenship and Immigration)*, IMM-4657-97; *Ali v Canada (Public Safety and Emergency*

militias,[321] liberation movements, and political parties.[322] The notion of complicity in non-brutal organizations based on aiding and abetting has been applied in many different situations.

Complicity has been inferred in these organizations when a person handed people over to organizations involved in the commission of crimes against humanity with the knowledge that such people would come to harm. One example is when a member of the National Police Force of Ghana between 1980 and 1991 joined a special undercover unit and arrested people who were then handed over to the BNI for interrogations that regularly included beatings and other forms of torture.[323] Similarly, a soldier in the Uruguayan military[324] who transported prisoners to clandestine detention centres and a sergeant in the Angolan National Police (ANP) in Angola in 1997–98 who escorted prisoners to and from interrogations and trial where they knew torture was carried out were excluded.[325] As well, a member of the Algerian police who spent twenty-seven years in an anti-terrorism unit, where he participated in numerous actions, including arresting suspected terrorists whom he then handed over to a specialized unit in the knowledge that they would be tortured, was upheld.[326] Another case involved a sergeant in the Palestinian National Security Service (NSF) whose duties involved manning checkpoints in Gaza and the West Bank; he would stop suspicious cars for an inspection while at other times the checkpoints were given specific vehicles or individuals to watch out for; if one of these individuals was found at a checkpoint, it was the responsibility of the applicant and the other staff at the checkpoint to arrest that

---

Preparedness), 2021 FC 698; *Ukoniwe v Canada (Public Safety and Emergency Preparedness)*, 2021 FC 753.

321 *Srour v Canada (Solicitor General)*, IMM-1778-94; *Harb*, above note 311; *Harb v Canada (Minister of Citizenship and Immigration)*, 2002 FCT 512.

322 *Goncalves v Canada (Minister of Citizenship and Immigration)*, 2001 FCT 806; *Shrestha v Canada (Minister of Citizenship and Immigration)*, 2002 FCT 887; see, in general, Asha Kaushal & Catherine Dauvergne, "The Growing Culture of Exclusion: Trends in Canadian Refugee Exclusions" (2011) 23:1 *International Journal of Refugee Law* 54 at 89–91.

323 *Sulemana v Canada (Minister of Citizenship and Immigration)* (1995), 91 FTR 53.

324 *Gutierrez*, above note 318.

325 *Januario v Canada (Minister of Citizenship and Immigration)*, 2002 FCT 527; for similar situations, see, also, *Gracias-Luna v Canada (Minister of Citizenship and Immigration)*, [1995] FCJ No 812 [*Gracias-Luna*]; *Guardado v Canada (Minister of Citizenship and Immigration)*, IMM-2344-97; *Yang v Canada (Minister of Citizenship and Immigration)*, MM-1372-98.

326 *Mekhachef v Canada (Citizenship and Immigration)*, 2014 FC 142; see, also, for a similar situation in Nigeria, *Popoola v Canada (Public Safety and Emergency Preparedness)*, 2021 FC 305.

person until one of the other branches of the General Security Service could take custody of the detainee, resulting in torture.[327]

Another group with many cases involves situations where individuals provided information to organizations, resulting in possible harm to the subjects of this information. This has happened in Ethiopia (names disclosed to the Ethiopian security service);[328] Iran (liaison agent between regular police and SAVAK, the secret Iranian police);[329] Ecuador (liaison officer between two army groups);[330] Iraq (providing information regarding the opposition to the Mukharabat secret police,[331] as well as providing information to the PUK, resulting in assassinations by that group);[332] Albania (overseer of the information-gathering activities of ShIK, the secret police);[333] Angola (a member of a youth organization that had as its purpose the infiltration of UNITA, the National Union for the Total Independence of Angola);[334] Lebanon (providing information to the South Lebanese Army (SLA[335] or Syrian army[336]); Sri Lanka (identifying innocent people as LTTE members to the Sri Lankan army);[337] Congo (working in the CSE-Comité de Sécurité de l'Etat) in the late 1990s, in which capacity she would listen incognito to conversations of individuals in public places and report on their opinions to the CSE);[338] and Colombia (a soldier in the army whose task was to survey members of the Revolutionary Armed Forces of Colombia (FARC) and paramilitaries by listening to, taping, or intercepting communications;[339] and a policeman involved in intelligence gathering).[340]

A third group involved high officials who were found to be involved in international crimes, usually based on the factor approach set out in *Ezokola*, where the function of the person was given prominence. This

327 *Shalabi v Canada (Public Safety and Emergency Preparedness)*, 2016 FC 961.
328 *Bamlaku v Canada (Minister of Citizenship and Immigration)*, IMM-846-97 [*Bamlaku*].
329 *Bazargan*, above note 256; *Shakarabi*, above note 295.
330 *Albuja v Canada (Minister of Citizenship and Immigration)*, [2000] 2 FC 538.
331 *Sumaida*, above note 296.
332 *Hovaiz v Canada (Minister of Citizenship and Immigration)*, IMM-2012-01.
333 *Lalaj v Canada (Minister of Citizenship and Immigration)*, IMM-4779-99.
334 *Goncalves v Canada (Minister of Citizenship and Immigration)*, 2001 FCT 806.
335 *Harb*, above note 311; *Alwan v Canada (Minister of Citizenship and Immigration)*, 2004 FC 807; *Salami v Canada (Minister of Citizenship and Immigration)*, IMM-6023-02.
336 *Diab v Canada (Minister of Employment and Immigration)*, IMM-3162-93.
337 *Kathiravel v Canada (Minister of Citizenship and Immigration)*, 2003 FCT 680 [*Kathiravel*].
338 *Bukumba v Canada (Minister of Citizenship and Immigration)*, 2004 FC 93.
339 *Parra v Canada (Citizenship and Immigration)*, 2016 FC 364.
340 *Durango v Canada (Citizenship and Immigration)*, 2018 FC 146.

happened in countries as diverse as Ethiopia (with a senior official in the Relief and Rehabiliation Commission in the Mengistu regime during a time when this regime carried out a policy of starvation of the inhabitants of Eritrea);[341] Nepal (an inspector in the police department);[342] Pakistan (an assistant sub-inspector of police in the city of Hyderabad,[343] an inspector in the Sialkot District,[344] a lieutenant colonel and a member of the joint Pakistani military, and the police Field Interrogation Team in Karachi);[345] Albania (a high functionary in the interior department of the communist regime in Albania between 1961 and 1993);[346] Tunisia (a high functionary in the Tunisian police between 1988 and 2013);[347] India (a senior member of the Punjabi police force);[348] Rwanda (a lieutenant and acting battalion commander in the Rwandan army (FAR) between 1985 and 1994);[349] Burundi (the second-in-command of a battalion involved in a massacre in 2002);[350] and Iraq (with a member of the Ba'ath Party during Saddam Hussein's regime who also had senior positions in the Iraqi Ministry of Trade, where one of his duties was to indoctrinate new recruits into the party).[351]

A fourth category of cases involves persons who provided support functions. Examples include being a guard, which was the situation in the *Ramirez* case while more recently, the *Carrasco* case, involving a prison guard in Nicaragua;[352] and a driver and part-time bodyguard of the local militia leader and KhAD chief in Afghanistan.[353] This category also applied to a soldier of the Yugoslav People's Army peripherally involved in the killing of civilians;[354] a soldier of the Honduran armed forces involved in the torturing and killing of prisoners;[355] a soldier

---

341 *Gebremedhin v Canada (Citizenship and Immigration)*, 2013 FC 380.
342 *Sapkota v Canada (Citizenship and Immigration)*, 2013 FC 790.
343 *Talpur v Canada (Citizenship and Immigration)*, 2016 FC 822.
344 *Ali v Canada (Public Safety and Emergency Preparedness)*, 2021 FC 698.
345 *Ghazala Asif Khan v Canada (Citizenship and Immigration)*, 2017 FC 269.
346 *Bajraktari v Canada (Public Safety and Emergency Preparedness)*, 2016 FC 1136.
347 *Hadhiri v Canada (Citizenship and Immigration)*, 2016 FC 1284.
348 *Bedi v Canada (Public Safety and Emergency Preparedness)*, 2019 FC 1550.
349 *Musabyimana v Canada (Public Safety and Emergency Preparedness)*, 2018 FC 50.
350 *Budigoma v Canada (Citizenship and Immigration)*, 2022 FC 594
351 *Al-Fahham v Canada (Citizenship and Immigration)*, 2022 FC 322.
352 *Carrasco v Canada (Minister of Citizenship and Immigration)*, 2008 FC 436 [*Carrasco*].
353 *Zadeh v Canada (Minister of Employment and Immigration)*, IMM-3077-94.
354 *Cibaric v Canada (Minister of Citizenship and Immigration)*, IMM-1078-95.
355 *Fletes v Canada (Minister if Employment and Immigration)*, 83 FTR 49.

involved in counter-insurgency operations in El Salvador;[356] a civilian driver on a military base in El Salvador between 1988 and 1992 (in which capacity he would drive persons belonging to a death squad to and from the base, together with captives);[357] a person who transported weapons and ammunitions and who found safe meeting places for the commandants of the Farabundo Martí National Liberation Front (FMLN) in El Salvador;[358] and a member of the Venezuelan military involved in the suppression of riots.[359]

A fifth group of cases deals with increasing the efficiency of an organization, such as being an intelligence officer in a prison in Iran;[360] a policeman in charge of political prisoners in a military hospital in Uruguay;[361] a security guard at a hospital where forced abortions were carried out in China;[362] and a soldier providing maintenance and loading ordinance onto planes used to bomb civilians in Guatemala.[363] As well, financing of war crimes or crimes against humanity will also lead to imputation of liability,[364] such as serving for twenty-two years in the Palestine Martyrs' Families Foundation, which paid money to family members who committed terrorist acts.[365]

The factor approach enunciated by the Supreme Court in the *Ezokola* decision, which can be seen as the sixth category of cases, had its genesis in the concept of complicity based on a shared purpose, which was applied and given more substance already by the Federal Court in five 2005 cases.[366] This mode of liability was originally identified by the Federal Court of Appeal but had not been fleshed out and had been conflated with the notion of aiding and abetting. While the

---

356 *Penate v Canada (Minister if Employment and Immigration)*, [1994] FC 79 [*Penate*].

357 *Guardado v Canada (Minister of Citizenship and Immigration)*, IMM-2344-97.

358 *Aguilar v Canada (Minister of Citizenship and Immigration)*, IMM-4491-99.

359 *Rojas v Canada (Minister of Citizenship and Immigration)*, 2003 FCT 394.

360 *Torkchin v Canada (Minister of Employment and Immigration)*, A-159-92.

361 *Alza v Canada (Minister of Citizenship and Immigration)*, IMM-3657-94.

362 *Chen v Canada (Minister of Citizenship and Immigration)*, IMM-541-00.

363 *Ordonez v Canada (Minister of Citizenship and Immigration)*, IMM-2821-99; see, also, *Salgado v Canada (Minister of Citizenship and Immigration)*, IMM-2463-05, for a similar situation in El Salvador.

364 *Aguilar v Canada (Minister of Citizenship and Immigration)*, IMM-4491-99; *Chitrakar v Canada (Minister of Citizenship and Immigration)*, 2002 FCT 888; *Pushpanathan*, above note 259.

365 *Khudeish v Canada (Citizenship and Immigration)*, 2020 FC 1124.

366 *Fabela v Canada (Minister of Citizenship and Immigration)*, 2005 FC 1028; *Bedoya v Canada (Minister of Citizenship and Immigration)*, 2005 FC 1092; *Ali v Canada (Solicitor General)*, 2005 FC 1306; *Catal v Canada (Minister of Citizenship and Immigration)*, 2005 FC 1517; and *Ardila v Canada (Minister of Citizenship and Immigration)*, 2005 FC 1518.

Canadian jurisprudence in these five cases did not provide an in-depth analysis of the notion of shared purpose, it did provide an approach to determining whether a person should be considered excluded on this basis, based on six distinct factors: the nature of the organization; the method of recruitment; age; position and rank of the individual; knowledge of atrocities; the length of time in the organization; and whether there was an opportunity to dissociate from the organization. The 2006 cases of *Kasturiarachchi*[367] and *Torres Rubianes*[368] made it clear that not all six factors are of equal importance, and it seems that of the six, the age and method of recruitment factors might not figure as prominently as the other four. The case of *Justino*, decided in the same year, stands for the proposition that rank does not necessarily involve a leading position within an organization.[369]

The dissociation factor had received some attention in earlier cases as part of a more general discussion of complicity. The concept of dissociation as an element of complicity was first introduced as a separate concept by the *Penate*[370] decision and expanded by the case of *Gutierrez*[371] in situations involving the El Salvadoran army and the Uruguayan Ministry of the Interior, respectively. The court held in *Gutierrez* that, in addition to the two requirements of personal and knowing participation, there is an additional element, the failure to dissociate from the organization at the earliest safe opportunity. The court fleshed out this last requirement by dividing it among several factors:

- the period of time that the person was a member;
- the earliest possible date the person had an opportunity to leave the organization;
- the consequences that the person would have been exposed for speaking out against the commission of international offences, for failing to respond to orders, or for desertion; and
- the circumstances in which the person left the organization.

The factor regarding the consequences a person would face has been the subject of a number of cases in which an analysis took place comparing the penalty a person would face upon desertion with the

---

367 *Kasturiarachchi v Canada (Minister of Citizenship and Immigration)*, 2006 FC 295 [*Kasturiarachchi*].

368 *Torres Rubianes v Canada (Minister of Citizenship and Immigration)*, 2006 FC 1140 [*Torres Rubianes*].

369 *Justino v Canada (Minister of Citizenship and Immigration)*, 2006 FC 1138 [*Justino*].

370 *Penate*, above note 356.

371 *Gutierrez*, above note 318.

type of activities the person was involved in,[372] along the same lines as the proportionality requirement for the defence of duress. In all cases, the person had been found complicit based on their activities in the organization, and nothing turned on the notion of dissociation in the sense that the person was found not excluded as a result of a lack of early dissociation.[373] More recently, the notion of dissociation was used in a more independent fashion by making it part of the voluntariness factor as set out by the Supreme Court in the *Ezokola* decision.[374]

The six factors were applied in 2006 and 2007 when twelve out of fourteen persons applying for refugee protection were excluded on this basis. The diverse situations included organizations such as the Uzbekistan police;[375] the Sri Lankan police;[376] the Colombian army;[377] the Philippine army;[378] the Ministry of the Interior of Angola;[379] the Algerian terrorist group Islamic Salvation Front (FIS);[380] the Burundian government[381] and army;[382] the Peruvian Republican Guard;[383] the Russian Department of Criminal Investigation in Chechnya;[384] the Administrative Security Agency in Colombia;[385] the Zimbabwean police;[386] the Mauritanian army;[387] and the Haitian National Police.[388]

372 *Cibaric v Canada (Minister of Citizenship and Immigration)*, IMM-1078-95, and *Canada (Minister of Citizenship and Immigration) v Asghedom*, 2001 FCT 972 [*Asghedom*].

373 There could be one exception where an intimation was made that in spite of involvement in atrocities, a person is not complicit and can remain with the organization if desertion would result in greater risk than continuing involvement, the *Asghedom* case, *ibid*; however, it is not clear from the decision that being absolved from accountability is the result of the defence of duress in not obeying orders or from not deserting at the earliest safe opportunity.

374 For a detailed application, see *Rutayisire v Canada (Citizenship and Immigration)*, 2021 FC 970.

375 *Akramov v Canada (Minister of Citizenship and Immigration)*, 2006 FC 122.

376 *Kasturiarachchi*, above note 367.

377 *Torres Rubianes*, above note 368, although not in *Bonilla Vasquez v Canada (Minister of Citizenship and Immigration)*, 2006 FC 1302.

378 *Sabadao v Canada (Minister of Citizenship and Immigration)*, 2006 FC 292, although in an indirect fashion by not mentioning or analyzing the six factors but instead making inferences in that regard.

379 *Justino*, above note 369.

380 *Chougui v Canada (Citizenship and Immigration)*, 2006 FC 992, although in an indirect fashion by not mentioning or analyzing the six factors but instead referring to a common purpose.

381 *Ryivuze v Canada (Citizenship and Immigration)*, 2007 FC 134.

382 *Budigoma v Canada (Citizenship and Immigration)*, 2022 FC 594.

383 *Ponce Vivar v Canada (Public Safety and Emergency Preparedness)*, 2007 FC 286.

384 *Petrov v Canada (Citizenship and Immigration)*, 2007 FC 465.

385 *Rivaldo Escorcia v Canada (Citizenship and Immigration)*, 2007 FC 644.

386 *Dzimba v Canada (Citizenship and Immigration)*, 2007 FC 500.

387 *Sidna v Canada (Citizenship and Immigration)*, 2007 FC 1046.

388 *Merceron v Canada (Citizenship and Immigration)*, 2007 FC 265.

The reason for this success in 2006 and 2007 could be the fact that, unlike in 2005, when the tribunal applied this concept to either vast areas of a country or large organizations, in the latter two years the six-factor approach was acceptable when used in smaller but notorious parts of the country, such as the Emergency Zones in Peru in the 1980s;[389] the city of Grozny in Chechnya;[390] in specific regions of Colombia;[391] or with respect to persons with a very long service record in organizations with a notorious reputation.[392] More recently, it held that it is not always necessary to "drill down" to the smallest unit in an organization if there is also evidence that the larger organization was involved in nefarious activities.[393]

More recently, the jurisprudence continued this trend for persons working for the secret service of Cameroon;[394] for a member of the Algerian national police (Direction générale de la Sûreté nationale or DGSN) and the Algerian prison system;[395] a member of the Georgian police;[396] a member of the Colombian military operating in the Uraba region;[397] the head of a neighbourhood self-defence organization/security committee in Burundi;[398] a prefect during the genocide in Rwanda;[399] a member of the Mouvement de libération du Congo (MLC) in the DRC;[400] a person in the Congolese Armed Forces (FAC) who created and maintained a computer network to connect the chief of staff's office with the other units of the army throughout the country;[401] and a person guarding and escorting shipments of funds between the airport and the central bank and protecting the headquarters of the Congolese television station in

389 *Ponce Vivar v Canada (Public Safety and Emergency Preparedness)*, 2007 FC 286.

390 *Petrov v Canada (Citizenship and Immigration)*, 2007 FC 465.

391 *Rivaldo Escorcia v Canada (Citizenship and Immigration)*, 2007 FC 644.

392 *Dzimba v Canada (Citizenship and Immigration)*, 2007 FC 500, and *Sidna v Canada (Citizenship and Immigration)*, 2007 FC 1046, in the Zimbabwean police and Mauritanian army, respectively.

393 *Ali v Canada (Public Safety and Emergency Preparedness)*, 2021 FC 698.

394 *Tchoumbou v Canada (Citizenship and Immigration)*, 2008 FC 585.

395 *Bouasla v Canada (Citizenship and Immigration)*, 2008 FC 930.

396 *Liqokeli v Canada (Citizenship and Immigration)*, 2009 FC 530.

397 *Bonilla v Canada (Citizenship and Immigration)*, 2009 FC 881.

398 *Ndabambarire v Canada (Citizenship and Immigration)*, 2010 FC 1.

399 *Rutayisire v Canada (Citizenship and Immigration)*, 2010 FC 1168.

400 *Ishaku v Canada (Citizenship and Immigration)*, 2011 FC 44.

401 *Mata Mazima v Canada (Citizenship and Immigration)*, 2012 FC 698.

Brazzaville.[402] It was also applied to a person who had been trained as an electrical engineer, joined the Sri Lankan navy, and rose to the rank of commodore because of his work on equipment performance and technical matters, coupled with his senior position, his involvement in strategy meetings, and his knowledge of the violence Sri Lanka;[403] a recruiter for the Council for the Defense of Democracy/Forces for the Defense of Democracy in Burundi between 1998 and 2003 (while also reiterating that it was not necessary to identify specific crimes committed by organizations involved in crimes against humanity);[404] and in a case involving a soldier of the Indian army.[405] The factor approach was also applied in cases even more peripheral, such as a chemistry student providing acid to the Shining Path organization in Peru, which used the acid to make bombs to carry out attacks against civilians;[406] standing guard on a pedestrian bridge in Sarajevo during the war between Serbia and Croatia;[407] repairing vehicles belonging to ISIS in Syria;[408] and collecting and reporting intelligence on foreign journalists for purposes that may have included intimidation, threats, and violence in Venezuela.[409]

Some other connections between activities of individuals and organizations involved in international crimes have been too tenuous to qualify as complicity, such as the case of a pilot in the Peruvian air force without sufficient links between his employment and the security zones where crimes against humanity were committed;[410] an aircraft mechanic

---

402 *Nsika v Canada (Citizenship and Immigration)*, 2012 FC 1026; regarding the second element, the court remarked that "ensuring a regime's ability to broadcast its propaganda may well further its ability to commit international crimes and thus provide a basis for a finding of responsibility for crimes against humanity," while relying on *Nahimana, Barayagwiza and Ngeze ("Media")* (ICTR-99-52-A), Appeals Chamber Judgment, 28 November 2007.

403 *Kuruparan v Canada (Citizenship and Immigration)*, 2012 FC 745.

404 *MR MJS v Canada (Citizenship and Immigration)*, 2013 FC 293.

405 *Khasria v Canada (Public Safety and Emergency Preparedness)*, 2016 FC 773, where the court found the following factors of importance to reach this conclusion: he was a member of Charlie Company in the 18th Punjab Regiment; he admitted to taking part in at least one cordon-and-search operation, and the documentary evidence states that massive human rights violations were committed by the Indian army during such operations; and he was among a group of soldiers who received medals, two of which relate to counterinsurgency operations that had led to widespread and systematic human rights violations.

406 *Moya v Canada (Citizenship and Immigration)*, 2014 FC 996.

407 *Jelaca v Canada (Citizenship and Immigration)*, 2018 FC 887.

408 *Massroua v Canada (Citizenship and Immigration)*, 2019 FC 1542 [*Massroua*].

409 *Villegas v Canada (Citizenship and Immigration)*, 2020 FC 736.

410 *Zoeger la Hoz v Canada (Minister of Citizenship and Immigration)*, 2005 FC 762.

and flight engineer in the Nicaraguan/Sandinista air force whose rank was too low to attribute liability;[411] an executive member of the youth wing of the Awami League (AL) in Bangladesh without a sufficient link between the human rights abuses of the Bangladeshi police and members of the AL;[412] and an accounting assistant in the headquarters of the Mexican army who organized the material resources required for the operations in the Chiapas region where human rights abuses were carried out.[413] It was also rejected in the situation of a magistrate (for a short period of time) in the DRC who had no influence on any decisions of the government related to the commission of crimes against humanity in that country[414] and in regard to a person who was an infiltrator, as part of secret operations against drug traffickers, of the Mexican army's special operations services.[415] More recently, the same result was achieved in situations of a person who was only present at the University of Butare during the Rwandan genocide;[416] was being a guard at a barrack in Prijedor in Bosnia during an episode of ethnic cleansing; [417] was serving in a different department of the Egyptian National Police from where human rights abuses were carried out;[418] or was a high-ranking soldier in the Burundian army during a time when this organization had carried out a number of coups and to which he had not been connected.[419] In other cases, it was held that the person was not complicit because he had no knowledge of the commission of international crimes, as with a soldier in Bosnia between 1991 and 1996[420] and a sergeant in the Directorate of Security of the National Army of Afghanistan in 2009.[421] Last, at times, the contribution was deemed not significant enough to fulfill the requirement for complicity, as was the case for a public relations officer in the Nigerian army;[422] for someone managing information

411 *Murillo v Canada (Minister of Citizenship and Immigration)*, 2002 FCT 1240.
412 *Chowdhury v Canada (Minister of Citizenship and Immigration)*, 2003 FCT 744.
413 *Collins v Canada (Minister of Citizenship and Immigration)*, 2005 FC 732.
414 *Mankoto v Canada (Minister of Citizenship and Immigration)*, 2005 FC 294.
415 *Hermida Gonzalez v Canada (Citizenship and Immigration)*, 2008 FC 1286.
416 *Nikuze v Canada (Citizenship and Immigration)*, 2013 FC 33.
417 *Blazic v Canada (Citizenship and Immigration)*, 2016 FC 901.
418 *Gerges v Canada (Citizenship and Immigration)*, 2018 FC 106.
419 *Niyungeko v Canada (Citizenship and Immigration)*, 2019 FC 820.
420 *Velimirovic v Canada (Citizenship and Immigration)*, 2019 FC 1156.
421 *Sailab v Canada (Public Safety and Emergency Preparedness)*, 2020 FC 773.
422 *Canada (Citizenship and Immigration) v Hammed*, 2020 FC 130.

holdings and protecting information concerning political opponents in the DRC;[423] or for someone managing a barbershop in a prison in Iraq.[424]

More detail regarding *mens rea* for complicity than was set out in the *Ezokola* case can be found in older cases that say that the mental element is knowledge of war crimes or crimes against humanity. This also includes the fact that one must have known about the criminal activities committed by the organization to which one belonged[425] or was wilfully blind to those activities.[426] Knowledge may be factually implied, and professed ignorance may be found not to be credible in light of the position held by the person concerned, the scale of the violence, and the general historical and political environment in which the acts occurred.[427]

Canada has applied the notion of complicity to a large number of cases, over 300. While the earliest case in this area of law, the *Ramirez* case, sought a close link with international criminal law (as it existed in 1992 at the time of its decision) to develop the various computations of extended liability, aiding and abetting, membership, and common purpose, the jurisprudence since that time has built on the principles developed in that case rather than relying on more recent developments in international criminal law.[428] This changed at the conceptual level when the Supreme Court in 2013 in the *Ezokola* case did rely heavily on both the ICTY/ICTR and the Rome Statutes and their jurisprudence when developing a new but incremental approach with respect to complicity. However, since that time, the Federal Court has used the same methodology as before by utilizing the *Ezokola* case rather than examining more recent international criminal law cases.

---

423 *Canada (Citizenship and Immigration) v Katanda*, IMM-8371-13, 28 January 2015.

424 *Canada (Public Safety and Emergency Preparedness) v Mahmood*, 2021 FC 800.

425 *Bahamin v Canada (Minister of Employment and Immigration)*, 171 NR 329; *Cordon*, above note 304; *Mohammad v Canada (Minister of Citizenship and Immigration)*, IMM-4227-94; *Shakarabi*, above note 295; *Salazar v Canada (Minister of Citizenship and Immigration)*, IMM-977-98; *M v Canada (Minister of Citizenship and Immigration)*, 2002 FCT 833.

426 *Cordon*, above note 304; *Loayza v Canada (Minister of Citizenship and Immigration)*, 2006 FC 304; however, surprisingly, one court found that using the language of "knew or ought to have known" was too close to guilt by association; see *Aazamyar v Canada (Citizenship and Immigration)*, 2015 FC 99.

427 *Mugesera v Canada (Minister of Citizenship and Immigration)*, 2005 SCC 40; *Kasturiarachchi*, above note 367; *Torres Rubianes*, above note 368.

428 Although one case referred to the Rome Statute for the notion of command responsibility in passing; see *Ezokola v Canada (Minister of Citizenship and Immigration)*, 2010 FC 662.

d) France

In general, a person can be excluded from refugee protection in France if they have personally participated[429] or were directly involved in article 1F activities. Membership in a political or government organization associated with international crimes is not a concept that has been applied in France.[430]

This general principle has been applied in a number of cases,[431] primarily in situations arising out of the 1994 genocide in Rwanda, where there had been no evidence of direct involvement by individuals in international crimes.[432] It should be noted that in these cases the notion of dissociation was deemed to be of great importance in that when a person has an association with an undesirable group or a criminal event and has not severed their ties with that situation, this has been considered negatively in each of the cases below.[433]

The wife of President Habyarimana, whose death in April 1994 became an important impetus for the genocide in Rwanda, was excluded from refugee protection in France because she belonged to the premier inner circle or *akasu*, which planned the genocide, and because, within this group, she was instrumental in enunciating the policy surrounding the execution of that event.[434]

Remaining at the national level, the minister of justice, who served in the interim government in place during the genocide, was also found to have been complicit, not only because of his function in a government guilty of systematic massacres but also because, in the exercise of his

---

429 Nicole Michel, "Purpose and Principles of the United Nations: The Way in Which France Applies 1F(c)" in P.J. van Krieken, ed, *Refugee Law in Context: The Exclusion Clause* (The Hague: T.M.C. Asser, 1999) at 297; there was also a case regarding a member of an elite military unit during Macedonia's civil war in 2001–2 who was personally involved in killing and torturing civilian members of the Albanian minority as well as the destruction of their property (CNDA, 18 November 2014, 9018932, MK), as well as a person directly involved in an assassination on behalf of the LTTE in Sri Lanka (CNDA, 10 January 2014, 12007633) and a member of the police involved in torture in Afghanistan (CNDA, 15 February 2018, 14020621, MG).

430 CE, 25 March 1998, 170172, Mahboub; see, also, Michel, above note 429 at 297.

431 Principles of complicity have also been considered in 1F(b) and especially 1F(c), the latter of which has been used extensively to address crimes against humanity. The caselaw pertaining to these clauses will be discussed in Chapter 5.

432 There had been one early case of direct involvement where a Russian soldier had killed about thirty civilians during the Chechnyan conflict in 1995, in CRR, 5 May 1997, 307510, Galimow.

433 See, in general, on this trend, Michel, above note 429 at 298.

434 CRR, 15 February 2007, 564776, Mme K veuve H; this decision was upheld by the Council of State in 2010; see Correspondent's Report, France (2010) 13 *Yearbook of International Humanitarian Law* at 491–92.

function, he participated in a radio broadcast asking the population for solidarity with the government. The fact that he was also mentioned as a category 1 suspect on the government of Rwanda's list of genocide suspects (meaning that he was sought as a person involved in the planning of the genocide) played an important role for the article 1F determination.[435] The same was said for a high official in the Ministry of the Interior[436] and the military.[437]

A career major in the Rwandan army, who was the commander of a battalion west of the capital Kigali in an area notorious for the massacres carried out during the genocide, was also found to be complicit.[438] Likewise, a journalist who was in charge of broadcasting the extreme propaganda of the interim government, and thereby contributing indirectly to the genocide, was also excluded.[439]

The same result was achieved with powerful local functionaries, such as a *bourgmestre*,[440] who had facilitated and encouraged the local militia in the killing of Tutsis by his authoritative presence at road blocks; a *préfet*,[441] who had taken the job on a voluntary basis and presided over the prefectorial security council, which decided where to place roadblocks and in that manner contributed to the executions of Tutsis; and a *sous-préfet*,[442] who was excluded in more general terms for saying that during the genocide most persons with his and higher positions had been indispensable in making the genocide possible by tolerating and encouraging the acts accompanying it. Similarly, a local university teacher and doctor was also excluded because he had been part of several meetings to plan the genocide in his community.[443] And last, a person was found complicit by being present at barricades while

435 CRR, 12 October 2006, 558295, Mponampeka.

436 CRR, 8 October 1999, 301072, MH.

437 CNDA, 23 September 2021, 20030019, MN.

438 CRR, 21 March 2003, 352817, Ntilikina; see, also, CNDA, 15 October 2010, 8016600, M; see, also, CNDA, 23 September 2021, 20030019, MN.

439 CRR, 23 October 1997, 294336, Bicamumpaka.

440 CNDA, 15 July 2009, 549950/05024108, N alias N.

441 CRR, 25 March 2003, 383865, Bucyibaruta.

442 CRR, 13 April 2005, 375214, S; the tribunal also indicated that the fact that this person's name did not appear on any of the lists of *génocidaires* emanating from the government of Rwanda was irrelevant for serious reasons for considering that he was complicit in the genocide.

443 CRR, 16 December 2003, 420926, Rwamucyo.

having authority and, as such, giving encouragement to persons killing Tutsis in the 1994 Rwanda genocide.[444]

On the other hand, a bank manager at the national bank of Rwanda, who had no connection with any of the radical political parties and who had not expressed any extremist views in the exercise of her functions, fell outside the parameters of the exclusion provision.[445] This was also the case for a lieutenant colonel in the north of the country who had helped a number of students escape being killed;[446] for a person who sold beer to *génocidaires*;[447] and for a priest who had given refuge to Tutsis but then fled while leaving the keys to the buildings where these refugees were hiding.[448]

A captain in the Rwandan army who was stationed in the Kivu region in the DRC in 2001, during a time when the Rwandan army committed war crimes against the local population as well as crimes against humanity, was excluded because his troops had killed sixty civilians. Although he claimed that he had not participated or assisted in the massacre, the tribunal was of the view that because he oversaw burying the bodies of the murdered victims in an area notorious for atrocities carried out by the Rwandan army, this was sufficient to bring him within article 1F of the Refugee Convention. As well, heads of a battalion were also excluded.[449]

There have been a number of French exclusion cases not involving Rwanda, including a person involved in the recruitment and training of members of the militia group, the CNDP (Congrès national pour la Défense du peuple) in the DRC, who was considered complicit in the war crimes carried out by this group.[450] A member of the religious police of the Taliban in Afghanistan involved in the arrest of civilians was excluded,[451] as was a high-level member of the PKK in Turkey in charge

444 CNDA, 12 June 2013, 90117369, MM.

445 CRR, 3 January 2005, 434055, Mme N ép B; in this case, the fact that her name did not appear on any list was seen as another piece of exculpatory evidence.

446 CRR, 18 January 2000, 337421, Nzungize; the fact that his name does not appear on any lists is again seen as exculpatory.

447 CE, 14 June 2010, 320630, MA c/ OFPRA; CE 14 June 2010, 304816, OFPRA c/ M; see, also, Correspondent's Report, France, above note 434.

448 CE, 26 January 2011, 312833.

449 CNDA, 15 May 2018, 11013546, MN, and CNDA, 20 February 2019, 14033102, MG.

450 CNDA, 17 November 2010, 8015887, MT.

451 CNDA, 25 March 2014, 12023208, MA.

of logistics[452] and a battalion captain in the Syrian national army that had committed war crimes against civilians.[453]

France also used a methodology resembling a factor approach in other cases. It was used against a commander of the presidential guard of the head of state of the Central African Republic because he belonged to an organization known for numerous human rights violations, he had knowledge of these violations, and he did not dissociate himself from this organization.[454] The same factors were in play for a colonel and head of medical services in a Syrian hospital who visited prisons a couple of times a week where torture occurred; his length of service, no dissociation, his knowledge, and the fact that being present provided encouragement to the torturers were sufficient.[455] In another case from the Central African Republic, a person who trained child soldiers for a militia involved in human rights violations was found complicit because of his importance in the military hierarchy, the result of his role as trainer, his nationality, and his family's ties with one of the militia leaders.[456]

Four cases leading to complicity were the result of fundraising efforts in France for the LTTE; one person had been convicted for this activity in a criminal court; [457] the latter situation, exclusion after a criminal conviction for fundraising, also occurred where this was done on behalf of the ACSAP, a terrorist organization in Turkey.[458]

Exclusion did not follow in the case of two Serbian police officers stationed in Kosovo in 1999 during the armed conflict between Serbia and the KLA. While it was clear that Serbian forces, including the police, carried out war crimes and crimes against humanity in Kosovo during that time, there was no evidence that these two individuals had been involved.[459] A lack of nexus was also found in France when it was

452 CNDA, 23 June 2016, 12025076, MK.

453 CNDA, 22 November 2021, 20021427, MS.

454 CNDA, 7 October 2014, 13003572, MBG; see, also, for a person associated with the LTTE, CE, 3 December 2020, 433161, MS, and for a members of Gaddafi's female bodyguard in Libya, CNDA, 2 June 2020, 18031988, Mme M.

455 CNDA, 30 October 2015, 15000096, MA.

456 CNDA, 9 November 2018, 17009037, MI.

457 CNDA, 15 July 2014, 11016153, MS; CNDA, 4 July 2018, 16040253, MJ; CNDA, 14 December 2018, 17034992, MR; CNDA, 14 December 2018, 17030884, MM; the first case mentioned here is the one with the conviction, which was confirmed on appeal in CE, 13 March 2020, 423579, B; see, also, CE, 19 June 2020, 427471/419803, MM.

458 CNDA, 11 October 2018, 17014478, MB.

459 CRR, 18 May 2006, 548090, Kurta; CE, 6 December 2010, OFPRA c/ M R, 312305.

established that a person was gathering information on political opponents for the police in the DRC, but since there were no consequences for other people, it only amounted to counter-espionage, and no exclusion followed.[460] Last, being a soldier in Syria in a conflict zone, without evidence that the unit he belonged to had been involved in crimes against humanity, had the same result.[461]

The jurisprudence in France, like in Australia and Belgium, has relied little on international criminal law with respect to extended liability. In most cases, liability was found in the most egregious cases arising out of the Rwandan genocide and, as such, not in contradiction, with similar results as arrived at by the ICTR. The methodology used in France to conclude complicity was often a combination of finding that a person occupied a high position in the Rwandan government or the militia, while also giving a great deal of weight to the factor of dissociation from the organization involved in the genocide. An analysis along the lines of command responsibility would have been more in line with international criminal law but would have resulted in exclusion as well.

e) Germany

The *Asylum Act* states that 1F(a) also applies to persons "who have incited others to commit the crimes or acts listed there or otherwise been involved in such crimes or acts."[462] There has been one decision that has interpreted this provision, involving a Rwandan person who, while living in Germany, became president of the Forces Démocratiques de Libération du Rwanda (FDLR), a Hutu exile organization founded in 1999, which has armed combatant units in the eastern part of the DRC and has committed numerous war crimes and crimes against humanity in that area. As president, he directed the operations of the FDLR from Germany and for that reason had already become the subject of a criminal prosecution.[463]

The court was of the view that the activities of this person would fall within the parameters of command responsibility as set out in article 28 of the Rome Statute, specifically because "he exerts a significant

---

460 CNDA, 10 October 2013, 6014596, MB.

461 CE, 27 November 2020, 428703, MA; see, also, CE, 19 June 2020, 431731, OFPRA c MA.

462 Section 3(2), last sentence; this is a result of the implementation of the Qualification Directive, which employs the same language in art 12.3.

463 Bundesverwaltungsgericht (Federal Administrative Court), BverwG 10 C 2.10, 31 March 2011, at paras 2, 4, and 6.

influence over the organisation, and has unrestricted power of command and disposition within the FDLR," while at the same time he is "its supreme military commander ... and is consequently empowered both to issue commands for strategic missions and to suppress certain acts or methods of combat." Finally, he also "exercised a *de facto* power of command," so the commanders in the field were subordinate to this person and "had regularly sought close contact with the Complainant via satellite telephone, e-mail or conventional telephone connections, in order to take his orders or at least obtain his consent for certain military actions," while all the while being aware that this organization was committing serious war crimes and crimes against humanity.[464]

f) The Netherlands

The main parameters of indirect liability are set out in the *Aliens Manual*, which states that if a person had knowing and personal participation in international crimes, exclusion under article 1F can be applied against such a person.[465]

According to the manual, knowing participation is present when

a) the alien was employed by an organization that the IND[466] has shown has committed in a systematic or widespread manner crimes mentioned in article 1F of the Refugee Convention;
b) the alien belonged to an organization that the minister has designated as a group to which normally article 1F of the Refugee Convention applies; and
c) an alien has participated in activities that he knew or should have known were activities set out in article 1F of the Refugee Convention.

---

464 Bundesverwaltungsgericht (Federal Administrative Court), BverwG 10 C 2.10, 31 March 2011, at paras 30–33.

465 *Vreemdelingencirculaire* 2000 (C), art C2/7.10.2.4; while the manual is in Dutch, the words "knowing participation" and "personal participation" are set out in English, a parlance that is used in other official documents and the jurisprudence. This terminology stems originally from the Canadian caselaw, which is clear from the fact that the seminal Canadian case, *Ramirez*, is mentioned in this context in the Dutch case of Rb, The Hague, Awb 02/12057, 19 December 2002; see, also, Rb, The Hague, 04/51818, 28 June 2006; Letter from the State Secretary of Justice to the House of Commons, 1997–98 Session, 19 637, nr 295, 28 November 1997 at 7–8; Adviescommissie voor Vreemdelingenzaken, "Artikel 1F Vluchtelingenverdrag in het Nederlands vreemdelingenbeleid" (The Hague, Adviescommissie voor Vreemdelingenzaken, 2008) at 15, and Kamerstuk 19637, Vreemdelingenbeleid, Nr 1808, 4 April 2014 at 5.

466 Immigratie en Naturalisatiedienst or Immigration and Naturalisation Service.

With respect to categories (a) and (b), the IND will determine whether an exception applies to the rule that the alien had knowledge or should have had knowledge of the commission of the crimes; the IND calls this a "significant exception."

Personal participation is present in at least one of the following situations:

a) the alien has committed a crime as set out in article 1F of the Refugee Convention;
b) a crime as set out in article 1F has been committed under the order or responsibility of the alien;
c) the alien has facilitated a crime as set out in article 1F of the Refugee Convention; or
d) the alien belongs to a group that the minister has designated as a group to which normally article 1F of the Refugee Convention applies.

The category under (c) is further clarified by indicating that facilitating involves making a substantial contribution, which means a contribution that had an effect on the commission of the crime and would likely not have taken place if nobody had fulfilled the role of the person concerned or if the person concerned had taken the opportunity to prevent the crime, while regarding (d), it is said that the IND will determine whether there is a "significant exception" as described in the "knowing participation" section.[467]

The Council of State has approved this approach.[468] While there is no particular sequence that has to be followed in assessing personal and knowing participation,[469] both aspects of this test have to be addressed by the decision maker.[470] There is no need to provide concrete examples of the results of the personal and knowing participation of the asylum seeker as long as it can be shown that they were involved in acts that

467 *Vreemdelingencirculaire* 2000 (C), art C2/7.10.2.4; the Council of State has said that arts 25 and 27–33 of the Rome Statute provide a good interpretation tool for the personal and knowing participation test set out in the manual; see AbRS, 1 June 2011, nr 201005191/V1.

468 AbRS, 27 October 2003, nr 200305116/1, and AbRS, 13 April 2005, nr 200408522/1 at para 2.2.6.

469 Rb, The Hague, Awb 04/51818, 28 June 2006.

470 Rb, Roermond, Awb 01/48721, 4 February 2003.

increased the risk of death or torture of the victim and the asylum seeker was aware of that risk.[471]

The minister responsible for immigration and asylum[472] has designated[473] a number of categories within organizations where membership results in the rebuttable presumption set out above under both knowing and personal participation, such as non-commissioned officers and officers in KhAD and WAD, security organizations in Afghanistan between 1978 and 1992;[474] senior and general officers of the police

471 AbRS, 13 August 2004, nr 200402430/1; AbRS, 2 August 2005, nr 200401637/1; and AbRS, 31 August 2005, nr 200502650/1.

472 A generic indicator is used here as the specific titles for this minister have changed over the years.

473 A designation to declare senior persons undesirable has happened elsewhere. Canada, in the immigration context, has a provision in the *Immigration and Refugee Protection Act*, SC 2001, c 27, s 35(1)(b) that allows the minister of citizenship and immigration to designate a regime that has been involved in genocide, war crimes, crimes against humanity, and terrorist activities, the result of which senior officials (as set out in the *Immigration and Refugee Protection Regulations*, SOR/2002-227, s 16) are inadmissible, as part of a non-rebuttable presumption, to Canada, which has been interpreted in *Canada (Citizenship and Immigration) v Kassab*, 2020 FCA 10. In the refugee context a number of Federal Court decisions have found senior people in notorious regimes excludable using the same reasoning as in the immigration context, but this practice had been recently declared inappropriate as, among other reasons, the designation by a minister was missing (*Ezokola v Canada (Minister of Citizenship and Immigration)*, 2010 FC 662). In New Zealand, the connection between a notorious government and persons working for such a government results in visa refusal, which is set out in the following manner: "[A]pplicants are considered to pose a risk to New Zealand's international reputation if they have or have had an association with, membership of, or involvement with, any government, regime, group or agency that has advocated or committed war crimes, crimes against humanity and/or other gross human rights abuses" (ss A5.30 and A5.50 of the *Immigration New Zealand (INZ) Operational Manual* (1 December 2022), online: www.immigration.govt.nz/opsmanual/#35439.htm, which has been interpreted in *H v The Minister of Immigration*, [2019] NZHC 2870 at paras 62–63, 69–70, 74–75, and 79–80, and *AB v Chief Executive of the Department of Labour*, [2011] NZHC 1048 at paras 30–34).

474 Letter from the State Secretary of Justice to the House of Commons, 1999–2000 Session, 19 637, nr 520, 3 April 2000 at para 3.1. This decision was based on an extensive official report (Ambtsbericht) by the minister of foreign affairs earlier in the year regarding the security services in Afghanistan and their close connection to the human rights abuses carried out in Afghanistan during that time period, as well as the role played by the officer corps in those abuses. Such official reports are considered by the courts as expert reports, which are considered reliable and can be relied upon by the minister responsible for refugee matters, unless there are serious doubts about their accuracy (see Rb, The Hague, Awb 09/1989, 25 March 2011, and Rb, The Hague, Awb 09/24228, 28 June 2011). For a detailed background of the exclusion policy in respect to these groups, see Zarif Yakut-Bahtiyar, *Exclusion Clauses of the Refugee Convention in Relation to National Immigration Legislations, European Policy and Human Rights Instruments: Article 1F Versus the Non-refoulement Principle* (Nijmegen: Wolf Legal Publishers, 2016) at 169–78. This organization was called KhAD from 1978 until 1987, after which it was called the WAD; see, also, the *Aliens Manual*, 2000 (C), art C7/2.2.

(Sarandoy);[475] certain specific categories of persons belonging to the Hezb-i-Wahdat (or Islamic Unity Party of Afghanistan) of the same regime in Afghanistan;[476] certain senior officials in Iraq during the Ba'ath Party regime of Saddam Hussein;[477] and corporals and non-civilian leaders in the RUF during its terror campaigns between 1998 and 2001 in Sierra Leone.[478]

These designations and the evidence upon which they were based, have been the subject of judicial consideration. In general, the approach wherefrom a rebuttable presumption is introduced has received judicial approval.[479]

With respect to specific designations, the KhAD/WAD one has received the most attention. The Council of State determined that the minister responsible for immigration and asylum is entitled to rely on the official report of the minister of foreign affairs, including the conclusion that all non-commissioned officers were part of the more notorious section of KhAD/WAD and, as such, were personally involved in the interrogation, torture, and execution of suspects. From this it follows that there is a presumption of personal and knowing participation of persons employed in these named categories.[480]

---

475 Letter from the Minister of Immigration and Integration to the House of Commons, 2002–3 Session, 19 637, nr 695 (7 November 2002). The letter specifies in more detail which parts of the police services are covered for purposes of art 1F; three specific sections of the police are mentioned. The designation was again based on an official report by the minister of foreign affairs; see, also, the *Aliens Manual*, 2000 (C), art C7/2.2.

476 Letter from the Minister and State Secretary of Justice to the House of Commons, 2007–8 Session, 31 200 VI (9 June 2008), attaching Notitie betreffende de toepassing van artikel 1F Vluchtelingenverdrag at 12, n10; see, also, the *Vreemdelingencirculaire*, 2000 (C), art C7/2.2.

477 Officers in the Special Security Services and the heads of the General Security Services, the Military Intelligence Services, and the General Intelligence Service. Letter from the Minister of Immigration and Integration to the House of Commons, 2003–4 Session, 19 637, nr 811, 8 April 2004; the designation was again based on an official report by the minister of foreign affairs.

478 Letter from the Minister of Immigration and Integration to the House of Commons, 2003–4 Session, 19 637, nr 829, 23 June 2004, again based on a report from the Ministry of Foreign Affairs.

479 AbRS, 28 August 2003, nr 200302892/1. For a commentary on this approach, see Thomas Spijkerboer & B.P. Vermeulen, *Vluchtelingenrecht* (Nijmegen: Ars Aequi Libri, 2005) at 101–4.

480 AbRS, 28 August 2003, nr 200302892/1; AbRS, 30 November 2004, nr 200404008/1; and AbRS, 17 January 2005, nr 200406828/1. The information in the official report of the minister of foreign affairs was also found to be conclusive where the applicant provided different information about these organizations (AbRS, 13 April 2005, nr 200408522/1, and AbRS, 12 July 2004, nr 200401436/1); see, also, the Letter from the Minister of Foreign Affairs to the President of the House of Commons, Reference BZDOC-853412865-43, 22 May 2018.

The same court was of the view that the evidence brought forward by organizations such as Amnesty International, the UNHCR,[481] and others[482] to show that the evidence in the report from the minister of foreign affairs was flawed was not sufficient to cast doubt on the accuracy and comprehensiveness of that report.[483] With respect to the UNHCR report, it was of the view that although that organization should be given a great deal of deference, the fact remained that most of its submissions were based on sources that had already been rejected earlier by the council, and as such, the report was not conclusive to displace the conclusions in the foreign affairs report.[484] The Council of State was also of the view that the decision of the Court of Justice of the European Union,[485] which held that membership in a listed terrorist organization cannot automatically lead to exclusion but that an individual assessment of the role of that individual in that organization is required, was not incompatible with the designation approach taken in the Netherlands.[486]

481 UNHCR, *Note on the Structure and Operation of the KhAD/WAD in Afghanistan 1978–1992*, May 2008; see, also, Yakut-Bahtiyar, above note 474 at 170–81.

482 See, for instance, Adviescommissie voor Vreemdelingenzaken, above note 465 at 15 and 45–57.

483 AbRS, 24 September 2009, nr 200901907/1 (which also indicated that the difficulty in finding more substantial information given the situation in Afghanistan is no reason not to rely on the original official report), and AbRS, 17 March 2010, nr 200906595/1 (which even rejected a number of documents of the Afghan government in this respect); see, also, Rb, The Hague, Awb 08/14420, 14 March 2013; Rb, The Hague, Awb 09/39826, 10 June 2013; and Rb, The Hague, Awb, 17/9050, 11 December 2018.

484 AbRS, 24 September 2009, nr 200901907/1 (referring to AbRS, 30 November 2004, nr 200404008/1), as well as AbRS, 21 October 2011, nr 201006769/1, and AbRS, 13 April 2012, nr 201100658/1 (which refers to updated information by the UNHCR, dated 9 July 2009 and 4 October 2010 and which was the appeal of Rb, The Hague, Awb 10/17614, 1 June 2011, which had come to the conclusion that this new information had not been taken into proper consideration by the government as opposed to earlier courts at the same level, such as Rb, Amsterdam, Awb 06/24277, 22 February 2011, and Rb, The Hague, Awb 10/38907, 29 December 2011); see, also, at the District Court level on this issue, Rb, The Hague, Awb 05/55911, 20 November 2006; Rb, The Hague, Awb 07/1805, 2 February 2007; Rb, The Hague, Awb 09/2422, 17 December 2010; Rb, The Hague, Awb 06/24277, 22 February 2011; Rb, The Hague, Awb 09/24228, 28 June 2011; Rb, Haarlem, Awb 10-3494, 13 July 2012; and Rb, The Hague, Awb 09/39826, 10 June 2013, while at the Court of Appeal level, see Hof, The Hague, 200.232.293-01, 18 February 2019.

485 *Bundesrepublik Deutschland v B and D*, C-57/09 and C-101/09, 9 November 2010, at paras 94 and 98.

486 AbRS, 13 April 2012, nr 201100658/1; see, also, Rb, The Hague, Awb 09/1989, 25 March 2011; Rb, The Hague, Awb 09/24228, 28 June 2011; Rb, The Hague, Awb 10/38907, 29 December 2011; Rb, The Hague, Awb 08/9429, 14 August 2014 (which also indicated that the decision of the Supreme Court of Canada in the *Ezokola* case, above note 268, had no effect on this designation either); see, also, Rb, The Hague, Awb, 17/9050, 11 December 2018, and Hof,

With respect to the second designation, the police in Afghanistan belonging to sections that were specifically included in the letter from the minister responsible for immigration and asylum were found to be justifiably excluded based on their functions.[487] On the other hand, in situations where the persons had belonged to the police but in sections not mentioned in the report, it was incumbent on the decision maker to find personal and knowing participation by regular types of evidence.[488] The designation approach was also successfully used in Iraqi cases[489] and one Sierra Leonian case.[490]

The presumption of personal and knowing participation for designated categories can be rebutted if there was a significant exception to the policy applicable to the individual's particular situation. A short training period before taking up duties with a designated organization;[491] employment with the civilian (as opposed to the military) KhAD/WAD;[492] and documents from the Afghan government that the claimant has no criminal record[493] or that they were not listed as a human rights abuser were not deemed to be exceptional.[494] On the other hand, a letter issued by the consulate department of the Dutch Ministry of Foreign Affairs providing exculpatory evidence with respect to a specific individual by saying that he "has not committed any crime against humanity

---

200.232.293-01, 18 February 2019. The same conclusion was reached in AbRS, 29 February 2012, nr 201106216/1, with respect to the Hezb-i-Wahdat designation in Afghanistan, which was on appeal from the District Court, Rb, The Hague, Awb 09/29907, 4 May 2011, which had come to the opposite conclusion.

487 Rb, The Hague, Awb 05/12044, 6 February 2006, and Rb, The Hague, Awb 05/39711, 19 June 2007.

488 AbRS, 28 September 2007, nr 200705217/1.

489 Rb, The Hague, Awb 02/81866, 3 November 2004; AbRS, 26 June 2009, nr 200808309/1/V3; Rb, Maastricht, Awb 08/28430, 17 June 2009; Rb, Haarlem, Awb 08/34187, 1 June 2010.

490 Rb, The Hague, Awb 09/19929, 23 April 2010.

491 AbRS, 22 December 2009, nr 2009040231; a government document indicates that such an exception could also be applied in situations where the person had a short appointment or the person was not promoted; see Notitie betreffende de toepassing van artikel 1F Vluchtelingenverdrag, above note 476 at 14.

492 Rb, The Hague, Awb 09/8838, 13 April 2010; in another case, it was said that an officer for the National Guard, a part of KhAD/WAD, could be painted with the same brush as the officials mentioned in the official report (AbRS, 27 June 2005, nr 200410175/1).

493 AbRS, 29 October 2009, nr 200901921/1.

494 Rb, The Hague, Awb 06/37778, 17 April 2007; Rb, The Hague, Awb 07/27288, 30 October 2007; and Rb, The Hague, Awb 09/8838, 13 April 2010.

rights during his duty there" required the immigration decision maker to further investigate this claim.[495]

In situations outside the designation approach, persons have been held responsible for knowing and personal participation in a myriad of situations ranging from presence at the scene with authority to common purpose–type cases.[496]

Membership in an organization or a government does not lead necessarily to exclusion unless the person was responsible for or facilitated the commission of article 1F crimes and unless the person continued to be employed in a high function within a government involved in international crimes, knowing that such activities took place.[497] Mere presence at the scene was considered once but rejected as a sufficient basis in a situation where a member of the Sarandoy in Afghanistan was present during house searches that did not result in any arrests.[498]

Handing over persons to organizations where these persons would be subject to torture or killing with the knowledge that this would be the result has been found objectionable in a number of cases, including in Afghanistan, where involvement in house searches with arrests and handovers to KhAD was knowing and personal participation,[499] as was a prosecutor handing over a file to KhAD.[500] The same conclusion was reached in the case of a member of the Hezb-i-Wahdat who handed over thieves to the military operational section of the same organization.[501]

Personal and knowing participation was also present in handing over people in countries as diverse as Azerbaijan (member of the Ministry of National Security to another, notorious section of the same department);[502] Eritrea (member of the military police passing on people to his commanders);[503] Iraq (commander of a unit involved in combating Kurdish guerrillas, which were transferred after capture to

495 Rb, The Hague, Awb 08/14420, 14 May 2013.

496 For a situation where a person had personally been involved in crimes against humanity, see Rb, The Hague, NL 20.13885, 2 September 2021.

497 Rb, The Hague, Awb 00/77691, 5 December 2002.

498 AbRS, 12 December 2003, nr 200305099/1. For exclusion of a member of the local Sarandoy who was held responsible for handing over political prisoners, see Rb, The Hague, 02/6467, 9 November 2004.

499 AbRS, 7 August 2003, nr 200301812/1.

500 AbRS, 28 April 2004, nr 200307677/1.

501 AbRS, 13 August 2004, nr 200402430/1.

502 AbRS, 31 August 2005, nr 200502650/1.

503 Rb, The Hague, Awb 06/3863, 5 April 2007.

the Iraqi intelligence service,[504] and an informer for the Mukhabarat who was instrumental in capturing and handing over deserters to that security service);[505] Iran (member of the Islamic Revolutionary Guard handing over persons to other sections of the same organization,[506] as well as the same situation for a member of the Kurdish Democratic Party of Iran [KDPI]);[507] Gambia (inspector handing over persons to the National Intelligence Agency);[508] Lebanon (a member of the Amal militia who handed over Hezbollah fighters to the security service);[509] Palestine territories (a member of Fatah arresting people suspected of collaboration with Israel and then giving them over to a more violent section of the same organization;[510] as well as a person who was a communications officer for the Palestine Liberation Organization [PLO], in which capacity he had unmasked a spy whom he handed over to his brother, who killed the alleged spy);[511] Sierra Leone (an officer in the army who handed people over to a notorious prison);[512] and Sri Lanka (a police officer with a special task force of the Sri Lankan government arresting people and handing them over to a special camp, leading to their execution).[513] More recently, another nine judgments addressed this situation, one by the Council of State (applying exclusion to a policeman in Northern Iraq tasked with arresting persons involved in bombings of shops)[514] and eight by a district court (one with respect to a police officer and a sergeant in Turkey,[515] both of whom handed over people after arrest; a soldier in Nigeria who arrested persons and then handed them over to his superior;[516] one with respect to a member of the Republican Guard in Syria who carried out inspections and arrests at road blocks;[517] two with respect to persons in Syria assisting in police

504 Rb, The Hague, Awb 02/46550, 24 June 2004.
505 Rb, The Hague, Awb 03/46645, 21 February 2006.
506 Rb, The Hague, Awb 03/62793, 7 April 2005.
507 Rb, The Hague, Awb 05/25943, 28 April 2006.
508 Rb, The Hague, NL 17.4014, 21 November 2017.
509 Rb, The Hague, Awb 06/16164, 27 July 2006.
510 Rb, The Hague, Awb 03/30624, 7 July 2005.
511 Rb, The Hague, Awb 03/38436, 18 January 2007.
512 AbRS, 16 January 2006, nr 200506590/1.
513 Rb, The Hague, Awb 02/63919, 15 September 2005.
514 AbRS, 18 April 2013, nr 201109876/1.
515 Rb, Roermond, Awb 13/13175, 3 December 2013, and Rb, The Hague, Awb 14/3475, 3 March 2015, upheld on appeal in AbRS, 16 September 2015, nr 201502212/1.
516 Rb, The Hague, Awb 16/5323, 19 May 2016.
517 Rb, The Hague, Awb 15/12382, 14 June 2016.

raids and, in that capacity, arresting and handing over other persons;[518] one with respect to a police officer in Iraq;[519] one in regard to a police officer in Algeria;[520] and one in a situation where a person working in a notorious prison in Libya escorted persons to and from interrogation sessions).[521]

Another form of personal and knowing participation has, as in other countries, been used in the Netherlands: providing information to organizations that are known to inflict death or torture on their victims, with the result that the persons about whom information was provided came to harm. Five such cases were decided in the context of Afghanistan. A person who worked for KhAD as an analyst, who had as a function the gathering of anti-government sentiments from letters that had been opened and passing on this information to other sections of KhAD for further action, was excludable even if this information was screened first by another section. The Council of State was of the view that this person was responsible because his actions were the starting point of later human rights abuses.[522] It held the same view for an officer in the army who, as head of the communication division, transferred coded messages to Kabul with serious human rights consequences.[523] Excluded as well were a member of the political committee of the university informing on fellow students and teachers;[524] a political secretary of the Political Affairs section of the Sarandoy;[525] and another person from the Political Directorate of the Sarandoy who had discussions with village elders regarding views about the government, which were reflected in his reports for the Ministry of Internal Affairs.[526]

In the same vein, the courts excluded from refugee protection a courier for the HOS (Croatian Defence Forces) in Bosnia-Herzegovina who transported secret information, which contributed to the crimes

518 Rb, The Hague, Awb 13/13175, 26 April 2016, and Rb, The Hague, NL 19.10728, 17 December 2019; involvement in raids lead to the same result for soldiers in Eritrea; see Rb, The Hague, Awb 14/18073, 29 April 2015, and AbRS, 201506938/1, 25 November 2015.

519 Rb, The Hague, Awb 16/6954, 7 March 2017.

520 Rb, The Hague, NL 16.28, 12 January 2017.

521 Rb, The Hague, NL 20.17799, 18 May 2021.

522 AbRS, 2 August 2004, nr 200401637/1.

523 Rb, The Hague, Awb 02/3934, 25 September 2003.

524 AbRS, 11 July 2005, nr 200503613/1.

525 Rb, The Hague, Awb 03/66479, 4 February 2005; Rb, The Hague, Awb 03/59815, 6 April 2007.

526 Rb, The Hague, Awb 04/728, 10 March 2005.

committed by the HOS;[527] a member of the intelligence services AND and SNIP during the Mobutu regime in the DRC who maintained files and interrogated people who had been arrested;[528] a member of the Ba'ath Party in Iraq who kept tabs on fellow citizens in his neighbourhood;[529] a person who worked for the surveillance section of SAVAK in Iran whose reports would have been used for interrogation purposes, including torture;[530] and a member of the Eritrean Liberation Front (ELF) in Eritrea between 1963 and 1975 (at a time when this organization was engaged in a non-international armed conflict with Ethiopian government troops) for gathering information about fellow citizens that resulted in some of these persons being killed, tortured, or forcibly disappeared.[531] Along the same lines, a major in the Armenian National Security Service (ANV) who collected information himself about political opponents while also being responsible for others who carried out the same task, with the result that such opponents ended up being tortured or inhumanely treated by the police or other security organizations, was excluded; the court stated that there was no need to adduce evidence that the persons about whom information was gathered and passed were in fact tortured or treated inhumanely.[532] A person making lists of Tutsis to be killed and then passing them on to the Interhamwe during the 1994 genocide, while also provding information on other occasions, was also found to be complicit.[533] The same result occurred in other situations, such as the person of the Ba'ath Party in Iraq who reported people for not showing up at party meetings;[534] an informant for the intelligence service of the SLA, an Israeli proxy in Lebanon;[535] an informant for the intelligence service in Gambia;[536] a spy for the LTTE

527 Rb, The Hague, Awb 03/51827, 5 April 2005.

528 Rb, The Hague, Awb 05/41229, 18 April 2006; similarly, for a member of the DEMIAP, another intelligence agency, see Rb, The Hague, Awb 03/11376, 9 June 2005.

529 Rb, The Hague, Awb 03/63545, 19 June 2006.

530 Rb, Utrecht, Awb 09/3965, 27 October 2010; for a similar situation in Turkey, see Rb, The Hague, NL 20.8197, 2 August 2021, as well as in Syria, Rb, The Hague, Awb 20/258, 14 December 2021.

531 Rb, The Hague, Awb 10/28846, 23 June 2011.

532 Rb, Assen, Awb 10/42733, 17 January 2012.

533 Rb, The Hague, Awb 13/29482 and 13/29483, 25 March 2014.

534 AbRS, 28 March 2013, nr 201107951/1.

535 AbRS, 3 December 2013, nr 201211236/1.

536 Rb, The Hague, Awb 16/27787, 20 June 2017.

in Sri Lanka;[537] informants in Syria[538] and Guinea;[539] a guide and guard of the PKK providing information about opponents of this group;[540] an employee in northern Iraq who collected information about criminal and terrorists and put that information in reports that he then passed on to his superiors, who in turn directed an arrest team to apprehend the persons mentioned in the reports.[541] As well, a soldier in the Eritrean army, who was a trainer and guard in a military camp and who reported soldiers who were uncooperative when punished for desertion to superiors, was found to be complicit.[542]

Interestingly, Dutch courts have also excluded persons who occupied senior positions in their organization and, in that capacity, either themselves directly or through the work of their underlings, provided information or intelligence to other organizations; this was the case for majors in the Armenian National Security Service;[543] a major in Savak, the intelligence service of the Shah of Iran;[544] senior officers in the Iraqi intelligence service,[545] the Turkish intelligence service,[546] and the Basij in Iran.[547] Last, while virtually all cases regarding complicity deal with activities before a person came to a country of refuge, there is also one Dutch case where gathering information about a person living in a country of refuge was seen as objectionable: carrying out such activities about Syrians in Germany on behalf of the Syrian intelligence service.[548] Not all information gathering and sharing with repressive organizations will lead to exclusion. A member of the PUK in Kurdistan in Iraq who reported on activities of the Kurdistan Democratic Party was found not

537 Rb, The Hague, Awb 12/39207, 8 November 2019.

538 AbRS, 7 January 2016, nr 201505169/1.

539 Rb, The Hague, Awb 14/12940, 23 January 2015.

540 Rb, Den Bosch, Awb 11/19645, 31 March 2014.

541 Rb, Middelburg, Awb 12/11771, 31 July 2014.

542 Rb, The Hague, Awb 15/9196, 29 March 2016; see, also, Rb, The Hague, Awb 15/7085, 1 October 2015.

543 Rb, Assen, Awb 10/42733, 17 January 2012, and Rb, The Hague, Awb 10/42733 and 10/43122, 26 January 2012.

544 AbRS, 3 February 2016, nr 201503747/1.

545 Rb, Haarlem, Awb 12/26943 and 12/26950, 7 May 2013; see, also, Rb, The Hague, NL 19.14284, 7 January 2021.

546 Rb, The Hague, NL 20.8200, 24 November 2021; the court refers to the *Ezokola* judgment of the Canadian Supreme Court, above note 268.

547 Rb, Zwolle, Awb 12/38326, 8 April 2014; see, also, Rb, The Hague, NL 20.15081, NL 20.15083, and NL 20.15085, 26 March 2021 (confirmed on appeal in AbRS, 1 October 2021, nr 202102178/1).

548 Rb, The Hague, NL 19.6344, 26 August 2019.

to fall within article 1F because he thought that his reporting would at most lead to an oral warning.[549]

A third form of excludable behaviour can be generally described as carrying out support functions. This type of aiding and abetting has been the subject of discussion in many cases. A captain in the Afghani army who carried out interpreter and translation functions for the Soviet-occupying army facilitated the human rights abuses perpetrated by the Soviets,[550] as did a fighter pilot in the Afghani air force with the task of protecting bombers targeting civilians.[551] A soldier in the Iraqi army who provided target coordinates during the Iran-Iraq war and the Anfal campaign against Kurdish civilians was seen as having contributed to the commission of war crimes.[552] Likewise, a member of UNITA in Angola who shot at enemy columns, helped abduct young persons to fight for UNITA, and gathered food from villages was excluded,[553] as was a soldier in Abkhazia who assisted in the rape and murder of civilians and the plunder of their properties.[554]

Two cases dealing with persons who were employed in the military industrial complex in Iraq were excluded under article 1F. One person was the supervisor of a secret facility that produced airplane bombs with chemical or explosive charges. These bombs were later used as part of military actions.[555] The second person was responsible for part of the production of poison gas, which was used in the Iraq-Iran war.[556] Both were aware of the outcome of the weaponry they helped produce. The personal secretary of the director of the Shahid Nazaran prison in Tehran, who was responsible for the coordination of the work of the director and the distribution of director's instructions, made a substantial contribution to the crimes committed in that facility.[557]

---

549 AbRS, 16 January 2004, nr 200305320/1.

550 AbRS, 2 June 2004, nr 200308871/1; see, also, Rb, The Hague, Awb 15/1712, 8 December 2015, for the Syrian security service; however, the opposite conclusion was reached in the situation of an interpreter with the Iraqi security services, Rb, Assen, Awb 25 May 2010.

551 Rb, The Hague, Awb 03/53060, 5 August 2005.

552 AbRS, 14 December 2010, nr 200909884/1/V3; for another case where a person was excluded for support activities during the Anfal campaign, see Rb, Assen, Awb 09/18111, 9 September 2010.

553 Rb, The Hague, Awb 03/42888, 3 May 2005.

554 Rb, The Hague, NL 19.27863, 14 April 2021; this case refers to the *Ezokola* judgment of the Canadian Supreme Court, above note 268.

555 Rb, The Hague, Awb 02/83493, 12 December 2003.

556 Rb, The Hague, Awb 03/66472, 28 June 2005.

557 Rb, The Hague, Awb 03/40505, 10 January 2006.

At times, the link between the activities of an individual and the international crimes committed by a government was too tenuous to amount to knowing and personal participation. For instance, an Iraqi fighter pilot who was involved in bombardments during the Anfal campaign and during the war with Iran was found not to be excludable as there was not more precise evidence of his role in crimes committed against civilians in these events.[558] Also in relation to Iraq, an officer of the security service in charge of the maintenance of buildings was seen as too far removed to attract liability.[559] Similarly, a prison official in the Ghasr detention centre in Tehran, who only had responsibility for food quality, hygiene, and safety in the cell blocks but was not involved in decision making regarding interrogation or the fate of the prisoners, was found not to fall within the parameters of article 1F.[560] Along the same lines, with respect to a person working in an abortion clinic in China who administered injections and provided general treatment, it was not clear whether these duties contributed to the babies being aborted as part of the one-child policy.[561] A local functionary of the Ba'ath Party in Iraq who was responsible for carrying out edicts of the Revolutionary Command Council (RCC) was found not to be excluded as it was not clear that this work amounted to the facilitation of crimes committed in Iraq.[562]

The fourth and largest group of cases where personal and knowing participation was discussed in the jurisprudence was where the refugee claimant was not as closely associated with atrocities as those under the aiding and abetting–type approach. These cases with a more remote association usually involved people occupying very senior positions in organizations, with an overall responsibility for the implementation of

558 Rb, The Hague, Awb 06/60302, 14 September 2004; where the connection between the pilot's actions and the resulting crimes against humanity had been closer, exclusion followed; see Rb, Zwolle, Awb 01/55128, 6 February 2004, as well as Rb, Den Bosch, Awb 11/5965, 27 January 2012, regarding a pilot of the Ethiopian air force during the Mengistu regime when it was bombarding civilian targets and the civilian population during the 1987–88 civil war who was excluded for both war crimes and crimes against humanity.

559 Rb, Zwolle, Awb 09/40840, 28 April 2010; however, this was overturned on appeal in AbRS, 1 June 2011, nr 201005191/V1, because the court had overlooked the fact that this person also had access to files with respect to employees of that organization who were suspected of corruption; the person concerned passed on that information to other parts of the organization, resulting in the commission of crimes against humanity against these employees, such as torture and disappearances, and thereby facilitating these crimes.

560 Rb, The Hague, Awb 03/44162, 13 July 2004.

561 Rb, The Hague, Awb 09/513, 3 November 2009.

562 Rb, Haarlem, Awb 11/2239, 13 February 2012.

policies of human rights violations, or functionaries in senior ranks who were closer to the actual carrying out of war crimes or crimes against humanity.

Cases involving senior officials were situations with high-level members of the Ba'ath Party[563] and generals in the Iraqi army[564] and, because of their influence in military, political, and legislative policy, were found to be closely associated with this regime that carried out crimes against humanity. In Afghanistan, members of the Central Committee of the People's Democratic Party of Afghanistan (PDPA) and its Politburo[565] and a very senior member of the Hezb-i-Whadat, an organization well known for the use of torture of civilians, was excluded,[566] as were two ministers of the Ministry of Justice and the deputy minister of the Ministry of Tribes and Nationalities because their departments provided

563 Rb, Haarlem, Awb 08/34187, 1 June 2010; Rb, Zutphen, Awb 10/5445, 1 December 2010.

564 Rb, Den Bosch, Awb 08/22199, 1 March 2010; Rb, Zwolle, Awb 09/40819, 9 April 2010.

565 AbRS, 11 February 2004, nr 200306693/1; Rb, The Hague, Awb 03/38359, 31 December 2004; and Rb, The Hague, Awb 03/23265, 9 March 2005. Such an approach was not uniform, as can be seen from two cases where the policy function was not as clear-cut as in the preceding three judgments (Rb, The Hague, Awb 01/37861, 4 September 2003, and Rb, The Hague, Awb 04/28989, 8 September 2005) and exclusion was not applied, although the last case was overturned on appeal and reconsidered, resulting this time in exclusion, in Rb, The Hague, Awb 09/16643 and Awb 09/16646, 25 March 2011; this time, the District Court came to the conclusion that given the fact that they belonged to the highest executive organs of a repressive regime, the personal participation portion of the complicity was fulfilled in that such a regime could not function effectively without these types of apparatus. The knowing participation portion of complicity was arrived at by pointing to considerations such as the type of regime (with its absolute loyalty, unanimous decision making, hierarchical relationships, and the identification of the party with the state), the lengthy duration of the membership in these organs of the persons concerned, the fact that they never distanced themselves from the regime, and their knowledge of the commission of the crimes; they also took into consideration the same judgment of the CJEU as set out above and were of the view that the requirements of that case had been fulfilled because of the assessment of the personal circumstances of the individuals in question, while the argument that they should not be excluded because they had never been criminally charged was dismissed by saying that these two approaches are different with their own distinct criteria; this decision of the District Court was upheld by the Council of State nine months later in a very short judgment in AbRS, 9 December 2011, nr 201104671/1/V1. The result of non-exclusion was also achieved for regular members of the PDPA, many of whom had connections with KhAD but not always close enough to reach a finding of knowing and personal participation (Rb, The Hague, Awb 02/48953, 26 January 2004).

566 Rb, The Hague, Awb 00/7608, 1 March 2004.

logistical and personnel support to KhAD/WAD and as such played a crucial role in the work of that organization.[567]

The governor of the National Bank of Rwanda, who was responsible for the funds of the Rwandan government, used in part to purchase weapons to carry out the genocide, was found to have contributed, especially because he had not distanced himself from the regime even months after the genocide had started.[568]

A person in charge of fifty PKK fighters, who was also a member of the most important policy and executive organs of the PKK, was excluded as she had personally and knowingly participated in war crimes committed by this organization.[569] A colonel in the army of the Mobutu regime in the DRC who had leading functions in a government organization that carried out systematic and widespread human rights abuses must have known of these abuses and facilitated them.[570] Two senior officers in the Iraqi army who were heads of units (including the notorious Jash unit) during the Anfal campaign, which had been actively involved in war crimes and crimes against humanity, were also excluded.[571] A major in the Afghani police force in Kabul, in charge of a unit of ten police officers, which not only investigated crimes but also had the authority to carry out preventative arrests, substantially contributed to the crimes committed by this police force, considering his position and the tasks he was asked to carry out.[572] A lieutenant in charge of a commando unit in Afghanistan, regiment 466, consisting of sixty soldiers, which was notorious for human rights abuses, was also considered a personal and knowing participant,[573] as was the person in command of a local police station in Uganda.[574] At a lower level, a member of the Abu Nidal Organization, a terrorist entity in the Palestinian territories, who had voluntarily joined, stayed with the organization for ten years, and did not dissociate at an opportune and safe time, while also teaching young people the ideology of the organization,

567 Rb, The Hague, Awb 03/44039, 14 February 2006; Rb, The Hague Awb 01/20518, 29 April 2004; and AbRS, 11 February 2004, nr 200306693/1.

568 Rb, The Hague, Awb 10/4388, 23 December 2010.

569 AbRS, 23 July 2004, nr 200402639/1 and 200402651/1.

570 Rb, The Hague, Awb 03/19330, 9 November 2004.

571 AbRS, 28 June 2005, nr 200500478/1, and Rb, The Hague, Awb 03/53739, 16 February 2006.

572 AbRS, 12 November 2003, nr 200304459/1.

573 Rb, The Hague, Awb 01/17246, 13 November 2002.

574 Rb, The Hague, NL 20.13885, 2 September 2021; the court referred to the *Ezokola* decision by the Canadian Supreme Court, above note 268.

participated knowingly and personally.[575] It was also applied to a person who had been a member of the gendarmerie in the Ivory Coast, which had been loyal to the ex-president Laurent Gbagbo in a military camp in Abidjan during the 2010–11 election crisis, and who was also involved in the preparation and execution of attacks against civilians and UN peacekeepers was considered complicit.[576]

More recently, on two occasions a court sought a more direct connection to the principles of command/superior responsibility in the Rome Statute, and on one occasion the person was held not responsible. In the first case, a district court came to this conclusion as the only evidence was that the person had a high position during the genocide in Rwanda and it was not clear whether the requirements that the person had influence and the ability to punish the persons involved were fulfilled.[577] In the second case, the Council of State overruled a lower court decision, which had found that a person who had been a platoon commander in Syria was not responsible because the crimes were committed by his soldiers after he had handed them over to another commander under his command, which, according to the Council of State, was not relevant, while also saying that this person had not taken any measure to prevent these crimes from occurring by stopping his soldiers from leaving, although he knew they would commit international crimes.[578] In other cases, some aspects of the concepts of command/superior responsibility were mentioned without reference to international jurisprudence, as was the case of a senior official in the Basij in Iran, where people under his command mistreated civilians and he did not use measures within his power to prevent or mitigate such mistreatment.[579] This was also the case in a situation in Eritrea where a person had command over others who were involved in torture and he did nothing to prevent it.[580]

In other cases, complicity for high officials continued to be arrived at in a more general fashion rather than examining the specifics of command/superior responsibility. In three parallel cases, leaders of three different militia groups in the Ituri region of the DRC who decided to

575 Rb, The Hague, Awb 01/8334, 2 June 2003.

576 AbRS, 28 December 2014, nr 201302334/1.

577 Rb, The Hague, SGR 14-9106, 9 July 2015, relying on ICTR jurisprudence.

578 AbRS, 25 May 2015, nr 201506251/1, relying on ICTY and ICC jurisprudence.

579 Rb, Middelburg, Awb 12/20698, 1 August 2013.

580 AbRS, 6 November 2019, nr 201808972/1; interestingly, reference is made to the *Ezokola* case of the Supreme Court of Canada, above note 268.

cooperate and together attack civilians in that region were found complicit because of their leadership and their influence on the soldiers of these groups who had been involved in massive international crimes.[581] In another case, the leadership role was much more direct, such as when, during the Rwandan genocide, a person ordered militia to set up roadblocks and was being kept informed of the progress of the genocide while at the same time also playing an important role with the RTML radio station and the newspaper *Kangura*, both of which had been vehicles of hate propaganda in 1994.[582] This was also the result in the case of a senior official in a paramilitary unit in the Central African Republic.[583] Last, there are the cases of a person in a leadership position who was responsible for the coordination and logistics of the use of so-called hell canons in Aleppo in Syria[584] and the head of the logistics department in charge of providing large amounts of weapons and munition in Afghanistan[585] or, at a lower level, where a person had a coordinating role in ensuring safety in a neighbourhood in Baghdad,[586] while a brigadier general in Afghanistan in his function as the head of political affairs of various units in the army facilitated the security forces in carrying out their nefarious activities.[587]

Sometimes the line between participation as a result of close association and non-exclusion is finely drawn. At times, cases in the periphery did result in exclusion, such as involvement in the weapons-for-diamonds trade between RUF rebels in Sierra Leone and the Taylor government in Liberia;[588] transporting persons on suicide missions in Sri Lanka;[589] involvement in demonstrations in Syria, either by driving demonstrators toward security services[590] or using violence to prevent people from escaping;[591] being an interpreter for the Syrian security

581 AbRS, 23 June 2014, nr 201300768/1; AbRS, 27 June 2014, nr 201310225/1; and AbRS, 27 June 2014, nr 201310217/1; the reasoning in these cases is similar and resembles somewhat the analyis of co-perpetration mentioned in art 25(3)(a) of the Rome Statute, which also requires a leadership component according to ICC jurisprudence.

582 Rb, Oost-Brabant, SHE 18/2181, 14 February 2020.

583 Rb, The Hague, Awb 15/15956, 9 March 2016.

584 AbRS, 29 August 2018, nr 201803118/1.

585 AbRS, 10 December 2014, nr 201404725/1.

586 AbRS, 11 March 2014, nr 201210609/1.

587 Rb, The Hague, NL 16.838, 6 October 2016.

588 AbRS, 28 May 2014, nr 201303363/1.

589 Rb, Amsterdam, Awb 12/16421, 19 July 2013.

590 AbRS, 17 October 2018, nr 201802357/1.

591 Rb, The Hague, Awb 18/5312, 1 October 2019.

services;[592] being in charge of the budget for the division of the Centre d'Etudes et de Recherches Scientifiques (CERS) in Syria, which was responsible for the production and storage of chemical weapons;[593] being a soldier in Syria who participated in a 1982 attack on Hama as part of a tank battalion that had a crucial role in this attack;[594] being a member of the Republican Democratic Movement (MDR) in Rwanda during the genocide, in which capacity they carried out propaganda and information activities;[595] being an employee at a communication and operation centre in a Syrian security service, in which capacity he transmitted orders to field units;[596] being a radar operator for the Syrian air force when it was involved in attacking civilians;[597] and creating communication codes for Hezbollah fighters in Palestine and providing them with food, as well as participating in armed patrols.[598]

On the other hand, exclusion does not always follow in similar situations. A member of the powerful Loya Jirga was found not to have personally and knowingly participated since it was not clear from the evidence presented exactly how much influence this body had on the communist regime in Afghanistan.[599] Similarly, in two cases from Bosnia-Herzegovina, exclusion was not applied because of a lack of influence on the decision-making process leading to international crimes for a person in the Territorial Defence Force without an important position[600] or because the person was a civilian in the defence secretariat and did not have any power.[601] A soldier in the Yugoslav army in Kosovo was found not to be responsible for war crimes, although he belonged to a unit that was involved in forcibly removing Albanian Kosovars, on the ground that these activities were carried out by dozens of soldiers, including him, but it had not been shown that he had made a direct contribution or that his presence made a difference in the outcome of the events.[602] Similarly, a member of the LTTE who had been part

---

592 AbRS, 26 October 2016, nr 201509493/1.
593 AbRS, 29 June 2016, nr 201507522/1.
594 Rb, The Hague, NL 18.14281, 10 May 2019.
595 Rb, The Hague, Awb 13/29202, 13 March 2015.
596 Rb, The Hague, Awb 14/2126, 9 December 2015.
597 Rb, The Hague, Awb 15/11496, 8 December 2015.
598 Rb, The Hague, NL 18.10336, 7 November 2018.
599 AbRS, 17 December 2004, nr 200406525/1.
600 AbRS, 11 July 2007, nr 200702071/1.
601 Rb, The Hague, Awb 04/50120, 17 January 2006.
602 Rb, The Hague, Awb 05/377, 8 May 2007.

of the propaganda apparatus, a spy, and an administrative clerk and involved in a failed suicide mission was not sufficiently associated with this organization to be excluded.[603]

A person in Sri Lanka who assisted in the transport of satellite phones and medication to the LTTE was also absolved from involvement due to a lack of connection between this activity and possible crimes by the LTTE.[604] As well, an aircraft mechanic who serviced airplanes in the Sudanese air force was found not to be complicit as the planes he was assigned to were training planes and not fighter planes, which were used to carry out bombardments of the civilian population.[605] This was also the case for an internet administrator in Syria because the internet can be used for both beneficial and nefarious purposes, even in a country rife with human rights abuses.[606] A person who had worked for organizations that in turn carried out activities for the Central Intelligence Agency (CIA) in Afghanistan, which might have been involved in international crimes, was found not to be complicit as the organizations he worked for also worked for other American entities.[607] The same was said about an oil trader in Jordan during the international oil embargo against Iraq and the Oil-for-Food Programme who did not pass his profits on to Iraq while Iraqi people lacked food and medication as there was no causal connection.[608]

The Netherlands is unique among the countries examined in this study, as the legislator has set out in some detail what amounts to personal and knowing participation, while also in this context making provision for certain members of specifically designated organizations to have complicity raised against them as a rebuttable presumption. A great deal of the jurisprudence has examined the details of the designation, the evidence used to come to such a conclusion, and which members would fall under the designation.

Outside the designation approach, exclusion based on complicity bears more than a passing resemblance to the Canadian jurisprudence, in addition to having the largest number of exclusion decisions, in that three types of extended liability have been examined by the courts:

603 Rb, The Hague, Awb 03/6907, 1 June 2004.

604 Rb, The Hague, Awb 17/4891, 22 February 2018.

605 Rb, The Hague, Awb 15/19296, 10 May 2016.

606 Rb, The Hague, Awb 14/26349, 18 September 2015.

607 Rb, The Hague, NL 17.10150 VK, 26 February 2018.

608 Rb, Overijssel, Awb 15/2845, 17 July 2015.

presence at the scene of an international crime, aiding and abetting, and a form of common purpose, the latter two in most detail. Aiding and abetting has been applied the most to situations involving handing over people to harm or passing along information resulting in persons being subject to international crimes. The common purpose doctrine has not been analyzed as precisely as in Canada, where a framework and overarching approach, together with seven specific factors, has been set out within which a finding of complicity can emerge if a majority of these factors is present. In the Netherlands, common purpose is found more readily if two factors are present: a senior position in an organization and knowledge of the commission of international crimes by that organization. If the person was employed in such an organization at a lower level, more factors akin to the ones found in the Canadian jurisprudence, such as duration of involvement, dissociation, and the manner of joining the organization, are required to conclude personal and knowing participation. The Dutch courts developed this jurisprudence mostly without using international criminal law jurisprudence, but, as with the other countries discussed so far, little fault can be found in the lines drawn between exclusion and non-exclusion.

g) New Zealand

There have been two cases in New Zealand regarding exclusion and modes of criminal liability that have attracted judicial consideration. The first court decision,[609] the *Sequeiros Garate* case, was decided in 1997 and involved a policeman from Peru who was a member of an anti-terrorist squad in 1991–92 responsible for the capture and interrogation of members of the Shining Path, a terrorist organization according to the court. In that capacity, he had arrested between thirty and forty suspects and had personally carried out acts of torture on a number of occasions. While not necessary for determination for the case at hand, the court adopted the position set out in the Canadian jurisprudence that membership in a brutal, limited purpose organization could amount to liability for the purpose of exclusion under article 1F(a).[610]

609 *Sequeiros Garate v Refugee Status Appeals Authority*, M826/97, High Court, 9 October 1997 [*Sequeiros Garate*].

610 It referred to the cases of *Ramirez* and *Equizabal* (below note 781).

The second court decision, *X & Y v Refugee Status Appeals Authority*,[611] involved the exclusion of a person who was the chief engineer of a ship that was owned by the LTTE and was sunk during a confrontation with the Indian navy in January 1993. At the time, it was carrying several LTTE members and substantial quantities of arms and explosives, and the Refugee Status Appeals Authority (RSAA) had found that the LTTE had committed crimes against humanity. The notion of complicity was summarized, by again relying on the Canadian caselaw, as participating in, assisting, or contributing to the furtherance of a systematic and widespread attack against civilians knowing that the act will comprise part of the complicity or taking the risk that it will do so, without the need for a specific event to be linked to the accomplice's own acts.[612] The tribunal decision was upheld.[613]

The Court of Appeal overturned this decision in 2009.[614] With respect to complicity, one judge of the court, Hammond J, was of the view that, instead of the Canadian jurisprudence, the more recent caselaw of the UK Court of Appeal should be followed, resulting in a less generous acceptance of the notion of membership but instead a close linkage with international criminal law concepts of extended liability, such as set out in the Rome Statute or developed by international tribunals in respect to JCE.[615] Applying these principles, the court felt that the combination of the unquantifiable risk that the cargo on the ship would be used unlawfully and the person's presence on the ship (even in the face of the lack of credibility of the claimant) could not result in a finding of complicity based on JCE.[616] Another judge, Arnold J, was less equivocal regarding the lack of the importance of the Canadian jurisprudence in the area of complicity, and when examining this jurisprudence in detail,[617] together with the recent UK court of appeal jurisprudence,[618] he was of the view that membership could

611 *X & Y v Refugee Status Appeals Authority*, CIV-2006-404-4213, High Court, 17 December 2007; this was the judicial review of the RSAA Appeal Nos 74796 & 74797, 19 April 2006.

612 *Ibid at para* 81.

613 *Ibid at para* 110.

614 *X v Refugee Status Appeals Authority* [2009] NZCA 488.

615 *Ibid* at paras 95–107.

616 *Ibid* at paras 109–12.

617 *Ibid* at paras 152–55.

618 *Ibid* at paras 156–68.

still be used as a form of complicity. However, he agreed in the result with Hammond J.[619]

The Supreme Court of New Zealand issued a decision with respect to the same case on 27 August 2010 in which it made several relevant findings.[620] In terms of sources of extended liability, the Rome Statute was found to be the most authoritative instrument to provide the various modes of liability in international criminal law,[621] one of which is JCE, which was also the most appropriate one in this situation.[622] After canvassing in detail the concept of JCE and the Canadian and UK jurisprudence[623] in the area of extended liability, the court came to the following conclusion:

> Refugee status decision-makers should adopt the same approach to the application of joint enterprise liability principles when ascertaining if there are serious reasons to consider that a claimant seeking recognition of refugee status has committed a crime or an act within art 1F through being complicit in such crimes or acts perpetrated by others. That approach fully reflects the principle that those who contribute significantly to the commission of an international crime with the stipulated intention, although not direct perpetrators of it, are personally responsible for the crime. This principle is now expressed in arts 25 and 30 of the Rome Statute and was earlier well established in customary international law. Its application recognises the importance of domestic courts endeavouring to develop and maintain a common approach to the meaning of the language of an international instrument which is given effect as domestic law in numerous jurisdictions of state parties.[624]

---

619 *Ibid* at paras 169–71.

620 *The Attorney-General (Minister of Immigration) v Tamil X and the RSAA* [2010] NZSC 107 [*Tamil X and the RSAA*]; for a commentary, see Ella Watt, "International Criminal Law and New Zealand Refugee Status Determinations: A Case Note on *Attorney-General v Tamil X*" (2012) 43:2 *Victoria University Wellington Law Review* 235–62.

621 *Tamil X and the RSAA*, above note 620 at paras 51–53.

622 *Ibid* at paras 56 and 71, referring to JCE III.

623 *Ibid* at paras 51–69; the court indicates at paras 58–61 that the notion of shared purpose as used in the Canadian jurisprudence is, in effect, a reference to JCE, while at paras 66–69, the court discusses and agrees with the *JS* decision of the UK Supreme Court, which is discussed below.

624 *Ibid* at para 70.

Based on the facts of the case, the court concluded that the claimant should not be excluded. While it was clear that he supported the LTTE in general and had done so in the past, the past activities did not reach the threshold of complicity, while the activities underlying the case could not support an exclusionary finding as the weapons on the ship never reached the LTTE for a possible criminal purpose. In the view of the court, while the conditions for a JCE were fulfilled,[625] there could be no exclusion as JCE required a completed crime or, in the words of the court, "had it been shown that he participated in voyages where armaments were delivered to the Tamil Tigers in Sri Lanka and subsequently that organisation committed crimes against humanity, the position would be different."[626] In this context, the court finds that the words in article 25.3(d) of the Rome Statute, "in any other way contributes," still require the commission of an offence; conspiracy cannot be read into this provision.[627]

At the tribunal level, it is notable that in its jurisprudence the RSAA has relied heavily on the Canadian jurisprudence, in most cases by direct reference, but sometimes also by quoting New Zealand cases that had mentioned Canadian caselaw. The jurisprudence most used is the

---

625 *Ibid* at para 71, expressed by the court as follows: "At all times he knew the vessel was transporting its cargo of armaments and munitions for use by the Tamil Tigers. By applying his expertise in a pivotal role for the voyage he was making a significant contribution to the Tamil Tigers' activities. He knew of the crimes against humanity that were being committed by that organisation and must have foreseen the likelihood that the arms, if delivered, would be used by the Tamil Tigers to commit future offences. His assistance, albeit in advance of operations, would further that purpose. It matters not on a test based on joint criminal enterprise principles that the actual cargo for the voyage might equally have been used only for legitimate purposes in military operations. The respondent took the risk that the armaments would be used to commit a crime against humanity. The Authority was entitled to hold that all this established the necessary elements of the respondent's personal responsibility as part of a joint criminal enterprise under arts 25 and 30 of the Rome Statute."

626 *Ibid* at para 79. This approach whereby liability is not accepted in a situation where it is not clear that weapons did not reach the recipient or it is not clear that these weapons were used to commit international crimes is not unique. The same result was achieved in the criminal trial of Guus van Kouwenhoven in the Netherlands, who had been involved in shipping weapons to Charles Taylor in Liberia. The trial court did not find him guilty of aiding and abetting in war crimes but only of circumventing United Nations sanctions (see Rb, The Hague, Awb 09/750001-05, 28 July 2006; on appeal, he was acquitted of all charges by the Court of Appeal, or Gerechtshof, Hof, The Hague, 22-004337-06V, 10 March 2008, but the Supreme Court of the Netherlands, or Hoge Raad, overturned the decision of the Court of Appeal, HR, 08/01322, 4 April 2010).

627 *Ibid* at paras 71–76. There had already been agreement that the requirements of attempt as defined in the Rome Statute were not present on the fact of the case, at para 50.

early trilogy of the Federal Court of Appeal cases of *Ramirez*, *Moreno*, and *Sivukamar*[628] but also the more recent Supreme Court of Canada case of *Mugesera*.

The general tenets of the main types of complicity, as set out in *Ramirez*, shared common criminal purpose,[629] and aiding and abetting,[630] have found their way into the jurisprudence of the RSAA on a regular basis, in most cases as separate concepts but sometimes by mentioning them both.[631] Along the same lines, two cases, again referring to the Canadian Federal Court of Appeal jurisprudence, indicate that it is possible for a person to commit a war crime or a crime against humanity as an accomplice even though the individual has not personally committed the acts amounting to such a crime.[632]

Presence at the scene of international crimes was considered in the case of a Bedouin applicant from Kuwait who became stateless. The applicant had worked for the Kuwaiti minister of the interior. His role was primarily clerical, although he also escorted individuals to a prison and was present during torture. The tribunal concluded that the only role he had in the torture of detainees was his voluntary presence for no reason other than curiosity. It concluded that as the applicant had voluntarily placed himself at the scene of torture, he had shown a knowing and willing association with these extreme acts and that his presence had encouraged those engaged in those acts of torture. It also found that the evidence showed that he intended to give that encouragement.[633]

Membership in a brutal, limited purpose organization has also attracted liability in New Zealand,[634] and this notion has been examined in several cases: the Iraqi Republican Guard (IRG) in Iraq;[635]

628 It has also cited the Federal Court of Appeal cases of *Bazargan*, *Sumaida*, and *Harb*, but much less frequently, while at times reference has been made to some cases of the Federal Court.

629 RSAA Appeal No 74591, 23 June 2004; RSAA Appeal No 74646, 26 June 2003; RSAA Appeal No 74129, 29 July 2005; RSAA Appeal No 75130, 31 March 2005; and RSAA Appeal No 74273, 10 May 2006.

630 RSAA Appeal No 1248/93, 31 July 1995; RSAA Appeal No 75095, 20 December 2004; and RSAA Appeal No 75896, 10 November 2006.

631 RSAA Appeal Nos 74129 and 74302; in one case, *Ramirez* was also cited for the concept that mere presence at a crime is not sufficient to be considered complicit: RSAA Appeal No 72635.

632 RSAA Appeal No 74129, 29 July 2005, and RSAA Appeal No 75692, 3 March 2006.

633 RSAA Appeal No 72635, 6 September 2002.

634 However, "mere membership of a broad nationalist organisation that advocates and pursues armed struggle, in the course of which human rights abuses have occurred, is not sufficient for exclusion"; see RSAA Appeal No 73122-25/2001, 20 June 2002.

635 RSAA Appeal No 75900, 21 November 2006.

the Presidential Guard in Iraq;[636] KhAD in Afghanistan;[637] the FIS in Algeria;[638] and the LTTE in Sri Lanka.[639] In the first case, the RSAA was of the view that for an organization to be considered a brutal, limited purpose organization it needed to be shown that all or a sufficient number of the units of such an organization routinely engaged in human rights violations or breaches of the laws of war, which was not the case for the IRG. The other entities, except for the FIS, were found to be such organizations.

The application of the general principles of complicity based on aiding and abetting covers a wide spectrum of activities. Handing over a person to an organization that has committed war crimes or crimes against humanity was considered in a case involving a person who had voluntarily enlisted in the Sri Lankan army, in which capacity he participated in three or four raids on Tamil villages over a period of three years' service. He assisted in the roundups by preventing any people from escaping and forcing them into trucks, which took them to a Sri Lankan army camp. The appellant knew that those who were brought to the camp would not return to their villages but would probably be tortured or killed in the camp. He took no active part in the interrogation, torture, or killing of these civilians, but he guarded them in the camp, thus ensuring that they did not escape. He was excluded because he did not take active steps to dissociate himself from these crimes, which he clearly knew were taking place.[640]

Providing another type of assistance was deemed to be insufficient in the case of a man from Nepal despite the fact that he knowingly provided medical supplies to the militia of Maoist separatists. Although the appellant admitted to other activities and involvement with the Maoists, the RSAA decided that his political support was confined to the peaceful political platform of the CPN-Marxist and CPN-Marxist-Leninist parties, and at no stage did he belong to or support the aims, strategies, and actions of the Maoists.[641]

Providing intelligence leading to harm was considered to be complicity in several cases. In one case, an applicant from Afghanistan

636 RSAA Appeal No 76142, 4 December 2007.
637 RSAA Appeal No 71255, 21 October 1999.
638 RSAA Appeal No 74540, 1 August 2003.
639 RSAA Appeal No 1248/93, 31 July 1995.
640 RSAA Appeal No 73343, 28 November 2002.
641 RSAA Appeal No 75946, 2 March 2007.

informed to KhAD on fellow students who were affiliated or sympathized with the Mojahedin. There was evidence that at least one of the students was tortured and died as a result. The tribunal found that despite the applicant's allegations not to have known what the information he supplied was used for, he must have been aware of the policy of identifying and arresting anti-government individuals even if he did not know the specific plans for torturing those on whom he informed. Evidence was found to conclude that the appellant was aware that further investigation would come to those on whom he reported. He was aware that torture was a possibility that could result from his involvement and was, therefore, complicit.[642]

Another case involved an applicant from India who had been part of the Congress Party. He served as an informant in the Indian security forces in the Punjab in the early 1990s. He testified that a substantial number of those on whom he informed were later killed or tortured by security forces due to the information he supplied on them. He claimed to have been fighting against terrorism. He did not himself commit the acts of murder or torture, but they occurred as a direct result of his espionage. The RSAA found that because the applicant was a voluntary member of the forces, knew that the suspects he informed on were being killed or tortured, and chose not to disengage at the earliest opportunity despite his knowledge of these consequences, he shared the common purpose of suppressing the Sikh militancy, thus fulfilling the requirements for complicity.[643]

Other cases concluded that providing intelligence can amount to complicity, but the persons were not excluded. The first case involved an applicant from Lebanon who was involved with the SLA as an informer. He provided this information for money. The information was found by the RSAA to be "mundane" and to consist of information on stolen vehicle sightings and similar information. There was no evidence that any of the information he provided led to any crimes committed against anyone on whom he informed. As there was no evidence that the appellant directly participated in any acts, had a position

642 RSAA Appeal No 73823, 11 August 2003.

643 RSAA Appeal No 74273, 10 May 2006; see, also, RSAA Appeal No 71335, 12 September 2000, and RSAA Appeal No 74982, 7 May 2004 (the LTTE in Sri Lanka), as well as RSAA Appeal No 75634, 24 May 2006 (the National Security Service in Somalia).

of leadership, or provided information leading to actual mistreatment, the applicant was found not to be complicit.[644]

In another case, involving a man from Afghanistan who was a *turan* (similar to lieutenant) of the army, the decision was that although the appellant worked with KhAD by gathering information, he had no involvement with the imprisonment, torture, or execution of informants or civilians, regardless of the fact that he was aware that a division of KhAD did engage in torturing people. The appellant worked for a different military division, and the RSAA decided that his duties could not have amounted to personal and knowing participation in persecutory acts.[645]

Some other cases examined whether providing financial support to an organization involved in crimes against humanity could amount to complicity but concluded that while this would be possible in general, complicity was not established on the facts of these cases.[646]

Last, there are other decisions dealing with complicity based on a shared criminal purpose analysis. One case dealt with an applicant whose work with the LTTE involved heading a training camp, recruiting members, serving as a village military commander, forcibly collecting funds, and forcibly conscripting children. The RSAA, which did not engage in an analysis of whether the LTTE was a brutal organization (unlike in another LTTE case), found that if he was not personally responsible, there were serious reasons to find the applicant complicit in the crimes of the LTTE. He had been more than just a member; he had an important role in the organization, had been a long-time member, and had the opportunity to leave but did not. As a result, he was found to have shared the organization's purpose.[647]

On the other hand, this type of complicity was found not to be applicable in other cases, including a situation of an imam from Algeria who claimed to seek political change through democratic means. He had had some minor contact with a radical cleric in Syria who might

644 RSAA Appeal No 75130, 31 March 2005; see, also, RSAA Appeal No 2071, 14 July 1995 (the Komiteh in Iran); RSAA Appeal No 74646, 26 June 2003, and RSAA Appeal No 74982, 7 May 2004 (both for the Sri Lanka army).

645 RSAA Appeal No 71255, 21 October 1999.

646 RSAA Appeal No 73122, 20 June 2002 (the PKK in Turkey); RSAA Appeal No 74302, 26 June 2006 (the CPNM in Nepal); RSAA Appeal No 74951, 23 June 2004 (the Conservative Party in Colombia); and RSAA Appeal No 75896, 10 November 2006 (the UPF in Nepal).

647 RSAA Appeal No 1248/93, 31 July 1995; see, also, RSAA Appeal No 74129, 29 July 2005 (the RSS in India), and RSAA Appeal No 71398, 10 February 2000 (the Armed Forces of Liberia).

have been involved in crimes against humanity. The tribunal found that there was no basis for a link with any activities of the Syrian cleric.[648]

The same conclusion was reached in a case of a member of the Maoist Party in Nepal. The person had been a low-level member, involved solely in administrative assistance, who was interested in supporting humanitarian work rather than the violent aims of the party. Finally, as he did not hold a position of authority or have any input into their decisions, the applicant was found not to have a shared common purpose, despite the tribunal's finding that the applicant knew that the CPN was committing attacks and that country information indicated that the attacks were widespread.[649]

In conclusion, until 2009, the courts and tribunals in New Zealand had not sought a connection with international criminal law for extended liability. This has changed and will affect the analysis of future decisions of refugee decision makers, although not necessarily the result in every type of complicity. It is likely that the use of aiding and abetting as liability will remain largely unchanged since the language used to identify this concept was already similar to international criminal law, such as making a substantial contribution with knowledge of its impact on the crime, while at the same time little can be gained from applying international jurisprudence to specific fact situations given the paucity on the international level in this context.

However, two other areas of complicity law will likely undergo modifications in the application by refugee decision makers. While the Supreme Court did not explicitly abandon the notion of membership, this form of complicity might lose some of its currency if no direct connection to current international criminal law can be made. The situation with common purpose is slightly different in that this notion is known in international law, but the analysis coming to a finding of liability will become more complicated because the courts and tribunals in New Zealand, until 2009, almost intuitively would come to a conclusion of common purpose but will now be forced to apply a difficult legal

648 RSAA Appeal No 73673, 15 February 2005.

649 RSAA Appeal No 75095, 20 December 2004; see, also, for other examples of an insufficient link RSAA Appeal No 2516, 21 June 1996 (the PDPA in Afghanistan); RSAA Appeal No 74381, 15 December 2003 (the CPN [Unified Marxist-Leninist] in Nepal); RSAA Appeal No 72038, 30 November 2000 (the SJN in Nepal); and RSAA Appeal No 76060, 18 December 2007, and RSAA Appeal No 76505, 14 June 2010 (the Ba'ath Party during the Saddam Hussein regime in Iraq).

concept to situations that might not always provide the evidence available to conduct a JCE analysis. This is because a typical refugee decision is based on evidence provided by the refugee claimant in combination with general human rights reporting on the situation and organization with which this person is connected. It is not often that evidence in such proceedings allows for an assessment of the existence of a common plan.

h) United Kingdom

In general, the *Immigration Rules* indicate that 1F exclusion also applies if a person has instigated or otherwise participated in exclusion crimes.[650] The seminal case in the United Kingdom on exclusion had been the *Gurung* decision by the Immigration Appeal Tribunal.[651] This involved a person who, as a member of the Nepalese Communist Party between 1996 and 2000, attended meetings and on occasion participated in protests against government land policies. Recently, some high-level court decisions have provided more contemporary guidance toon the application of article 1F(a) of the Refugee Convention.

Gurung addressed the notion of complicity by reiterating that concepts found in the statutes of the international tribunals and the ICC, such as aiding, abetting, or otherwise assisting in the commission of international crimes, including providing the means for their commission, should play an important role in setting the parameters of exclusion in that regard.[652] As an example, the tribunal found that providing a safe house to members of the LTTE would not amount to aiding and abetting but that transporting explosives for that organization would.[653]

In the context of complicity, the tribunal held that, relying on the Canadian case of *Ramirez*, membership in an organization could lead to exclusion provided that the organization's principal or dominant purpose was the commission of international crimes and taking into account the specific role of the individual within that organization.[654]

650 Rule 339AA, second para.

651 *Gurung*, [2002] UKIAT 04870. There has been one case in the United Kingdom where a person was excluded for direct involvement, [2015] UKAITUR AA040782014, regarding a platoon commander of the Eritrean army.

652 *Gurung*, above note 651 at para 109.

653 *Ibid* at para 108.

654 *Ibid* at paras 105, 114, and 151.3; this was slightly expanded upon in the case of *MR v Secretary of State for the Home Department*, UKAIT AS/00192/2007, 21 July 2008, which suggests at para 31 that membership alone rather than the specific role of the individual would be sufficient, while in another Asylum and Immigration Tribunal case, *Sivanantharajan v SSHD*,

For example, the tribunal was of the view that an organization with significant support among the population and with aims and objectives covering political, social, economic, and cultural issues leading to a parliamentary, democratic mode of government and the safeguarding of basic human rights but that has, in a limited way or for a limited period, created an armed wing in response to atrocities committed by a dictatorial government would not be considered an organization with such a dominant purpose. On the other hand, an organization that has increasingly come to focus on terrorism as a modus operandi, and in its recruitment policy, structure, and strategy has become almost entirely devoted to the execution of terrorist acts that are seen as a way of winning the war against the enemy, even if the chosen targets are primarily military, would be seen as a problematic type of organization.[655]

The Court of Appeal had an opportunity to pronounce itself on the issue of complicity in the article 1F(a) context in the *JS* case.[656] This involved a member of the LTTE who, between 1997 and 2000, took part in various military operations against the Sri Lankan army. In 2000, he had been fighting as a platoon leader in charge of forty-five soldiers trying to protect the LTTE's supply lines to the coast when he was injured. He required medical treatment for six months. Upon his return, he became one of the chief security guards for the LTTE Intelligence Division's leader, while from 2004 to 2006 he served as second in command of the Intelligence Division's combat unit.[657]

Since the main issue in this case evolved around the notion of complicity, the court canvassed in detail international materials on this issue, such as the Rome Statute and the jurisprudence of the ICTY,[658] as well as the Canadian Federal Court of Appeal caselaw[659] and the jurisprudence of the Immigration Appeal Tribunal and UK courts in all areas of exclusion.[660] The court came to the conclusion that, as indicated in *Gurung*, there should be a close link between international law sources and exclusion under article 1F(a) and that priority should be given to

UKAIT AA/01049/2008, 4 December 2008, the view was held that membership in itself is not sufficient but that something more is required (at paras 36–38).

655 *Gurung*, above note 651 at paras 112–13.

656 *JS (Sri Lanka) and Secretary of State for the Home Department*, [2009] EWCA Civ 364.

657 *Ibid* at paras 8–14.

658 *Ibid* at paras 30–52.

659 *Ibid* at paras 53–58.

660 *Ibid* at paras 59–92.

all aspects of indirect liability as regulated by the Rome Statute, including its concepts of command/superior liability, aiding and abetting, and common purpose/JCE. Where such notions have not completely crystallized, regard could be shown to the ICTY jurisprudence, especially with respect to the development of JCE.[661]

With respect to membership in a brutal organization, the court agrees with *Gurung* in general by saying that "a person who becomes an active member of an organisation devoted exclusively to the perpetration of criminal acts may be regarded as a person who has conspired with others to commit such acts and will be criminally responsible for any acts performed in pursuance of the conspiracy."[662] The court goes on to state: "Active membership is considered to be present when there is the requisite proximity between the person and the crime or crimes in question which in the case of an active member of an organisation dedicated entirely to terrorist activities is unlikely to present any problem."[663]

The court makes it clear that in situations of hybrid organizations or an organization that pursues its political ends in part by acts of terrorism and in part by other means, the analysis has to be different. The court does not describe in detail how this analysis should be conducted but agrees in general with *Gurung* that there is a need to consider the extent to which an organization is fragmented but disagrees with the factors to be assessed in *Gurung* to determine the dominant purpose of an organization.[664]

In conclusion, with respect to the law to be applied, the court says the following with respect to JCE liability:

1. there has to have been a common design that amounted to or involved the commission of a crime provided for in the statute;
2. the defendant must have participated in the furtherance of the joint criminal purpose in a way that made a significant contribution to the crime's commission; and
3. the participation must have been with the intention of furthering the perpetration of one of the crimes provided for in the statute.[665]

---

661 *Ibid* at paras 115–22.

662 *Ibid* at para 107.

663 *Ibid*.

664 *Ibid* at paras 107 and 111–14.

665 *Ibid* at para 119. At para 120, referring to the common purpose article of the ICC Statute, the court says: "The clause which may need the most unpacking is article 23(3)(d), dealing with joint criminal enterprise liability. In particular, the clause says nothing about the degree

Indicating that the essence of complicity lies in "whether there are serious reasons to consider the asylum applicant to be guilty of an international crime or crimes applying those principles,"[666] the court was of the view that the tribunal had not properly applied these principles of joint criminal enterprise to this case.[667]

The Court of Appeal decision was appealed to the Supreme Court, which issued its unanimous judgment on 17 March 2010.[668] Like the Court of Appeal, the Supreme Court was of the view that the main issue in this case was the notion of extended liability and canvassed a wide range of sources in this area, including the Rome Statute; the ICTY jurisprudence, especially in regards to JCE; foreign jurisprudence (including Canadian, American, and German); and the views of the UNHCR to determine the desirable parameters of this concept.[669] Like the Court of Appeal, it was of the view that the starting point for assessing extended liability should be the Rome Statute.[670]

The court says *in obiter* that membership in a brutal organization by itself is not sufficient to result in complicity[671] but that the essential test for extended liability is "if there are serious reasons for considering him voluntarily to have contributed in a significant way to the organisation's ability to pursue its purpose of committing war crimes, aware that his assistance will in fact further that purpose."[672] The court makes positive mention of the six-factor, common purpose approach developed in the Canadian jurisprudence by saying the following:

> It is surely preferable to focus from the outset on what ultimately must prove to be the determining factors in any case, principally (in

---

of contribution required or about the third category of joint criminal enterprise liability recognized in *Tadic*, that is, where a crime was committed as a foreseeable way of effecting a shared criminal intent and the defendant knowingly took the risk of this happening."

666 *Ibid* at para 120.

667 *Ibid* at para 123.

668 *R (on the application of JS) (Sri Lanka) (Respondent) v Secretary of State for the Home Department* (Appellant), [2010] UKSC 15; for a discussion of this and subsequent cases, see Satvinder Singh Juss, "The Notion of Complicity in UK Refugee Law" (2014) 12:5 *Journal of International Criminal Justice* 1201–16.

669 Above note 668 at paras 9–24 (Lord Brown) and 42–43 (Lord Hope).

670 *Ibid* at para 47 (Lord Hope).

671 *Ibid* at para 2 (Lord Brown), indicating that this was a common ground among the parties, while at para 57, Lord Kerr says it was wise for the secretary of state not to rely on this aspect of the Canadian case of *Ramirez*; see, also, Lord Hope at para 49.

672 *Ibid* at paras 38 (Lord Brown) and 49 (Lord Hope), although the latter equates the term "significant" with "substantial" for the level of contribution.

> no particular order) (i) the nature and (potentially of some importance) the size of the organisation and particularly that part of it with which the asylum-seeker was himself most directly concerned, (ii) whether and, if so, by whom the organisation was proscribed, (iii) how the asylum-seeker came to be recruited, (iv) the length of time he remained in the organisation and what, if any, opportunities he had to leave it, (v) his position, rank, standing and influence in the organisation, (vi) his knowledge of the organisation's war crimes activities, and (vii) his own personal involvement and role in the organisation including particularly whatever contribution he made towards the commission of war crimes.[673]

In the final analysis, the Supreme Court was of the view that the *Gurung* approach was too broad for recognizing membership as a type of complicity,[674] while the path taken by the Court of Appeal was too narrow by using domestic notions of liability in requiring participation in international crimes.[675] The case was sent back for a redetermination of the asylum claim.[676]

In the first UK Upper Tribunal (Immigration and Asylum Chamber) (UKUT) case since the Supreme Court decision, these principles were applied in a situation in Zimbabwe where a woman had been involved in violent invasions of land owned by two white farmers and the violent expulsion of their black farm workers from their houses and jobs on those farms.[677] It was found with respect to the person's involvement that she was excludable on the basis of a joint enterprise in domestic law since she had been part of such mob violence, including meting out

673 *Ibid* at paras 30–31 (Lord Brown) and 54–55 (Lord Kerr), although the latter points out that these factors are not exhaustive.

674 *Ibid* at paras 44–46 (Lord Hope).

675 *Ibid* at paras 26 and 38 (Lord Brown) and 48 (Lord Hope); this seemed to be based on the analysis of JCE I of low-level participants (Lord Brown at paras 19–20, as well as para 37).

676 *Ibid* at para 40. This was done in September 2014 by the First-tier Tribunal (Immigration and Asylum Chamber) (FTT), which decided not to exclude the person as there was no nexus between the crimes of the LTTE and this person; this decision was upheld on appeal in September 2015 by the UKUT, whose decision in turn became subject to permission to appeal to the Court of Appeal, which was refused in March 2017; see *JS (Sri Lanka) v SSHD* (2017), [2017] EWCA Civ 303 at paras 11–18 and 44.

677 *SK (Article 1F(a)—exclusion) Zimbabwe*, [2010] UKUT 327 (IAC).

beatings.[678] Another case dealt with the complicity of a person who was a member of the Basij in Iran whose mission it was to maintain law and order and to enforce ideological and Islamic learnings; the person was complicit not because of his membership in this organization but because he handed individuals over to other units of the Basij knowing that they would be seriously ill-treated.[679] As well, a person with a senior leadership role within an organization called Hizb-i-Islami in Afghanistan in the 1990s, which was a group involved in the civil war in Afghanistan between 1992 and 1996, was also found to be complicit.[680] The same result was achieved when an appeal tribunal decided that the possible involvement of a member of the Ba'ath Party in 2001 to 2003 in Iraq, who had not been excluded by the first-level tribunal, should have been, based not only on the final rank and position he had occupied in those years but also on his role in possible war crimes in the early 1990s.[681] More recently, the UKUT found a woman who had had a senior role in a women's prison under the control of the Islamic Revolutionary Guard Corps in Iran in which political prisoners were detained and tortured complicit for crimes against humanity; on a regular basis over a period of years, she was directly responsible for removing those prisoners listed for interrogation and ensuring that they were transferred directly to the separate torture facility, in the full knowledge of what would befall them on being left there, while in later years she had a supervisory and controlling function in the prison.[682] While relying on the Rome Statute, the tribunal found that she was guilty of aiding and abetting, which was described as encompassing any assistance, physical or psychological, that has a substantial effect on the commission of the crime, for which it was not necessary to establish a common purpose.[683] On the other hand, it was held that a doctor involved in assisting torturers and victims of torture was found not to

---

678 *Ibid* at paras 42–43. The tribunal added, in the following paragraph, that if there was an additional legal requirement of a substantial contribution to this concept, then that element was also fulfilled on the evidence.

679 AA (Article 1F(a) — complicity — Arts 7 and 25 ICC Statute) Iran [2011] UKUT 00339 (IAC); this decision was upheld on appeal in *AA-R (Iran) v Secretary of State for the Home Department*, [2013] EWCA Civ 835.

680 *AN (Afghanistan) v Secretary of State for the Home* Department, [2015] EWCA Civ 684.

681 [2015] UKAITUR AA071322015.

682 AB (Article 1F(a) — defence — duress) Iran, [2016] UKUT 376 (IAC).

683 *Ibid.*

be complicit due to a lack of knowledge about which persons he treated would be subject to this treatment.[684]

In summarizing the UK jurisprudence, the same observation made in respect to New Zealand can also be made for the United Kingdom, with some additional comments more specific to the reasoning of the Supreme Court. The decision contains some puzzling aspects. One of them is the rejection of the Court of Appeal decision for confining "Article 1F liability essentially to just the same sort of joint criminal enterprises as would result in convictions under domestic law" since the analysis of the Court of Appeal took place completely within the realm of international law, with only one reference to British law, and not in the paragraph quoted by the Supreme Court as being problematic. Another methodological issue is the recognition of the six-factor approach as developed by Canadian courts to ascertain a shared or common purpose. The court finds this approach useful, although it would not restrict it to the six factors used by the Canadian Federal Court. But it also says that one of the factors could be the nature of the organization, thereby making it possible to engage in an assessment of whether an organization has a brutal, limited purpose, but only for the limited goal of establishing JCE or common purpose liability, an approach followed a couple of years later by the Supreme Court of Canada.

Last, in terms of methodology, the Supreme Court is of the view that the tripartite distinction of JCE is not useful, although it appears that the court meant only for the situation at hand, to which only a JCE I analysis was appropriate. However, it also says that the *Krajišnik* Appeals Chamber judgment is not relevant as it pertains to high-level operatives. This comment is odd as *Krajišnik* dealt specifically with JCE I rather than the case cited by the court, *Brđanin*. Also odd is the fact that when referring to the ICTY caselaw to set out the requirements for JCE, the court mentions only in passing the very aspect that makes JCE unique: the common design (which, incidentally, is mentioned by the Court of Appeal and quoted by the Supreme Court as part of the objectionable paragraph in the Court of Appeal decision).

The latter methodological issue probably explains why the Supreme Court concluded that the essence for liability for exclusion is "if there

684 *MAB (Iraq) v The Secretary of State for the Home Department*, [2019] EWCA Civ 1253, followed by AB (preserved FtT findings; Wisniewski principles) Iraq [2020] UKUT 268 (IAC).

are serious reasons for considering him voluntarily to have contributed in a significant way to the organization's ability to pursue its purpose of committing war crimes, aware that his assistance will in fact further that purpose." While the analysis is couched in JCE language, the test for complicity suggested by the court for not including as part of this test the common design aspect closely resembles the notion of aiding and abetting in international criminal law, especially since the court equates "significant" with "substantial." This means that either the court has provided an incomplete definition of JCE or has collapsed all aspects of complicity known in international criminal law into only one type, aiding and abetting, a comment that was also made when discussing the *Ezokola* judgment by the Supreme Court of Canada, above.

The result of the Supreme Court analysis in terms of the relationship between international criminal law and domestic criminal law for the purposes of refugee law, and in terms of laying down a test purporting to be, in general, a test of complicity but in reality only represents one type of extended liability, is that it might not have helped elucidate the parameters of complicity as much as it had hoped. This is clear from the first judgment at the tribunal level, which states that the claimant was excludable on a JCE basis, while the facts, beating people, would have allowed for a conclusion of aiding and abetting or even direct participation. This illustrates the problem of tribunals, when following the Supreme Court precedent, attempting to put the facts into the legal straitjacket of the difficult concept of JCE and ignoring other easier and more appropriate forms of extended liability. However, later cases appeared to be more interested in following the factor approach to come to an exclusion finding than attempting this JCE analysis.

i) United States

Extended liability of asylum seekers for serious criminal acts is addressed in the *Immigration and Nationality Act* (*INA*), which says that such a claimant is not entitled to protection in circumstances of "ordering, inciting, assisting or otherwise participating in the persecution of any person on account of race, religion, nationality, membership in a particular social group, or political opinion."[685]

---

685 8 USC, s 208(b)(2)(A)(i); this exception can also be found in s 101(a)(42) as part of the definitional portion of the statute. This is one of the mandatory bars to asylum, the persecutor bar.

These concepts[686] have been assessed in a number of cases, starting with the seminal decision of the US Supreme Court in the case of *Fedorenko*, of which the following *dictum* regarding assisting has been repeated in the modern-day context:

> Thus, an individual who did no more than cut the hair of female inmates before they were executed cannot be found to have assisted in the persecution of civilians. On the other hand, there can be no question that a guard who was issued a uniform and armed with a rifle and a pistol, who was paid a stipend and was regularly allowed to leave the concentration camp to visit a nearby village, and who admitted to shooting at escaping inmates on orders from the commandant of the camp, fits within the statutory language about persons who assisted in the persecution of civilians. Other cases may present more difficult line-drawing problems, but we need decide only this case.[687]

While personal culpability is required for a finding that an individual is responsible for persecution, personal involvement in killing or torture is not necessary to impose responsibility for assisting or participating in persecution.[688] Assistance in persecution is present when a person objectively furthers the persecution of others,[689] which has also been said to involve acts that are more than peripheral,[690] or by provid-

686 A number of the decisions mentioned here have come from denaturalization cases rather than asylum cases, but the concepts have been deemed to be the same; see *Naujalis v INS*, 240 F3d 642 (7th Cir 2001); *Hernandez v Reno*, 258 F3d 806 (8th Cir 2001) [*Hernandez*]; *Vukmirovic v Ashcroft*, 362 F3d 1247 (9th Cir 2004); *Singh v Gonzales*, 417 F3d 736 (7th Cir 2005) [*Singh*]; *Higuit v Gonzales*, 433 F3d 417 (4th Cir 2006) [*Higuit*]; *Xie v INS*, 434 F3d 136 (2d Cir 2006); and *Gao v US Attorney General*, 500 F3d 93 (2d Cir 2007) [*Gao*].

687 *Fedorenko v United States*, 499 US 490 (United States Supreme Court, 1981) [*Fedorenko*]. See, also, Lori K. Walls, "The Persecutor Bar in U.S. Immigration Law: Toward a More Nuanced Understanding of Modern 'Persecution' in the Case of Forced Abortion and Female Genital Cutting" (2007) 16:1 *Pacific Rim Law & Policy Journal* 227 at 229–35; Kathryn White, "A Chance for Redemption: Revising the 'Persecutor Bar' and 'Material Support Bar' in the Case of Child Soldiers" (2010) 43 *Vanderbilt Journal of Transnational Law* 191 at 195–200; Kate Jastram, "Left Out of Exclusion: International Criminal Law and the 'Persecutor Bar' in US Refugee Law" (2014) 12:5 *Journal of International Criminal Justice* 1183–99; Egelman, above note 268 at 492–98; and David Romanov, "Recalibrating the Scales: Balancing the Persecutor Bar" (2020) 61:1 *Boston College Law Review* 385–418.

688 *Ofusu v McElroy*, 98 F3d 694 (2d Cir 1996); see, also, *United States v Breyer*, 41 F3d 884 (3d Cir 1994), and *United States v Koreh*, 59 F3d 431 (3d Cir 1995).

689 *Higuit*, above note 686.

690 *Ghazaryan v Gonzales*, 172 Fed Appx 139 (9th Cir 2006).

ing purposeful, material assistance.[691] At the lowest level, the distinction lies "between genuine assistance in persecution and inconsequential association with persecutors"[692] or between active conduct with direct consequences for the victim and tangential to the acts of oppression and passive in nature.[693] In terms of methodology, a two-step process is recommended in coming to a complicity finding, which requires that there must have been some nexus between the perpetrator's actions and the persecution of others and, if such a nexus is shown, that the person must have acted with knowledge.[694]

However, mere acquiescence or membership in an organization that engages in persecution is not sufficient to bar an individual from a grant of asylum. The claim must be denied "only if the individual's action or inaction furthered the persecution in some way."[695]

In the jurisprudence involving Second World War cases, the following activities have been considered to be assisting in persecution:

- serving as a guard in a concentration camp;[696]
- serving as a guard who stood armed at the edge of a pit in which both live and dead people had been thrown since his presence forced the victims to remain in the pit waiting to be murdered;[697]
- being a member of the Death's Head Battalion who served as an armed uniformed guard at Sachsenhausen concentration camp patrolling outside camp gates and escorting prisoners to and from work sites with orders to shoot;[698]
- being a member of a force dedicated to the extermination of large numbers of civilians;[699]

---

691 *Miranda Alvarado v Gonzales*, 449 F3d 915 (9th Cir 2006).

692 *Singh*, above note 686; *Parlak v Holder*, 578 F3d 457 (6th Cir 2009) [*Parlak*].

693 *Balachova v Mukasey*, 547 F3d 374 (2d Cir 2008).

694 *Diaz-Zanatta v Holder*, 558 F3d 450 (6th Cir 2009) [*Diaz-Zanatta*]; *Parlak*, above note 692.

695 *Fedorenko*, above note 687; *Laipenieks v INS*, 750 F2d 1427 (9th Cir 1985); Matter of Rodriguez-Majano, 19 I&N Dec 811, 814–15 (BIA 1988); *United States v Sprogis*, 763 F2d 115 (2d Cir 1985); *Petkiewytsch v INS*, 945 F2d 871 (6th Cir 1991), although membership with seeming participation is sufficient according to *Kalejs v INS*, 10 F3d 441 (7th Cir 1993).

696 *Fedorenko*, above note 687; *United States v Kairys*, 782 F2d 1374 (7th Cir 1986); *Schellong v INS*, 805 F2d 655 (7th Cir 1986); *Titjung v Reno*, 199 F3d 393 (7th Cir 1999); *Kulle v INS*, 825 F2d 1188 (7th Cir 1987).

697 *United States v Reimer*, 356 F3d 456 (2d Cir 2004); *United States v Kumpf*, 438 F3d 785 (7th Cir 2006).

698 *United States v Schmidt*, 923 F2d 1253 (7th Cir 1991); see, also, *United States v Geiser*, 527 F3d 288 (3d Cir 2008).

699 *United States v Ciurinskas*, 148 F3d 729 (7th Cir 1998).

- being a guard at a vital railway facility;[700]
- being a writer for a Nazi propaganda newspaper; there was no showing of actual persecution resulting from such propaganda activities, a climate of opinion in which such persecution was acceptable;[701]
- as a Latvian police chief ordering arrests under the instructions from the Nazis.[702]

On the other hand, a person performing various ministerial tasks for the Nazis when they occupied Latvia was seen as passively accommodating the occupying authorities rather than assisting in persecution.[703]

The parameters of complicity have also been considered in some detail in several modern-day situations since 2003. They can be loosely grouped together in cases discussing presence at the scene of persecutorial activities, assisting in transferring persons or information resulting in harm to the victims, and providing support functions.[704] The issue of knowledge or "scienter" has also been given some attention in the jurisprudence. There have been two cases dealing with assistance while being present. The first one involved an army lieutenant assigned as an instructor at the military academy in San Salvador in 1989 who was ordered to be part of a mission to kill a Jesuit priest at the university in the same city. He prepared for the mission by donning battle fatigues, painting camouflage on his face, and fetching his rifle and ammunition. He then accompanied the thirty to forty members of the Atlacatl Battalion assigned to the mission. At the university, he walked around but did not give orders, fire his gun, seize anyone, or block anyone's attempted escape. But when he returned to the base, he assisted in destroying logbooks identifying the soldiers who had participated in the raid and killed eight persons. The court indicated "that mere, passive presence does not amount to assistance. The court concluded that if the person had been involved in the planning beforehand, he would have been

700 *Naujalis v INS*, 240 F3d 642 (7th Cir 2001).

701 *United States v Sokolov*, 814 F2d 864 (2d Cir 1987); *United States v Koreh*, above note 688.

702 *Maikovskis v INS*, 773 F2d 435 (2d Cir 1985).

703 *United States v Sprogis*, 763 F2d 115 (2d Cir 1985).

704 Direct participation in killing and torture is also included in assisting or participating; see *Mendoza-Lopez v Gonzales*, No 04-71182 (9th Cir 2006).

guilty in assisting but he was involved as an accessory after the fact, which is probably not enough to be a persecutor."[705]

The second case involved a long-time member (between 1983 and 1999) of the gendarmerie in Cameroon who was considered to be involved in persecution because of his participation in the quelling of a student uprising at the University of Yaounde. The gendarmerie had beaten the students and stood in line, driving the students back. As well, according to the court, "he furthered persecution simply by his participation in what appears to be a phalanx or show of force by the gendarmerie against the students. An alien's physical presence can provide assistance in persecution when that presence impedes the movement of those persecuted or otherwise subjects them to an increased risk of harm."[706]

A case that could be considered to fall in the same category of being present without assisting involved a military cadet in Armenia who participated in a search operation of a hoUnited Statese, together with two officers and other soldiers, after which two girls were taken to a car and raped. The cadet's involvement was that he reached out to take one of the girls to the car and was rebuffed, while refusing to participate in the rape. The act of reaching out to the girl was not sufficient to bring him within the persecutor bar, nor was his inaction to prevent the rape as he had been relieved of his weapon, handcuffed when the rape took place, and beaten afterward for refusing to participate.[707]

With respect to the handing over of persons or information, assisting in persecution includes arresting persons if the applicant believes these persons would be persecuted on account of a protected ground, while it may also include reporting dissident activities if the reporting leads to the persecution of others on account of a protected ground.[708] This result was also achieved when a member of the Salvadoran National Guard was found to be complicit after he investigated, arrested, and interrogated people because of their ties to leftist groups and then turned these individuals over to his superiors knowing that they would likely be tortured.[709]

In the *Singh* case, a member of the police force in the Punjab in India between 1969 and 1992 was involved in raids carried out by the police

705 *Doe v Gonzalez*, 484 F3d 445 (7th Cir 2007).
706 *Ntamack v Holder*, 372 Fed Appx 407 (4th Cir 2010).
707 *Balachova v Mukasey*, 547 F3d 374 (2d Cir 2008).
708 *Ofosu v McElroy*, 933 F Supp 237 (SDNY 1995).
709 *Criollo v Lynch*, 647 Fed Appx 731 (9th Cir 2016).

against militant Sikhs, which often resulted in systematic arrests, torture, and sometimes killing of detained persons. His role was to stand guard outside homes to prevent occupants from escaping, while his colleagues arrested and beat people inside those homes; he would also be present during torture sessions at the police station. The court was of the view that simply being a member of the Punjabi police force was not sufficient to meet the threshold of complicity, but the combination of participating in raids, preventing people from escaping, transporting detainees from those homes to the police station, and regularly being present at torture sessions at the police station would raise his participation to a level of assistance, especially given his lengthy employment with the police and his knowledge of the abuse by his colleagues. The court did expand on the notion that mere membership cannot result in assistance by saying that it came to this conclusion with respect to the Punjabi police because the police also served traditional, legitimate enforcement purposes and did not exclusively engage in the persecution of innocent Sikhs, unlike Nazi concentration camps, whose existence was premised upon such persecution.[710]

With respect to providing information resulting in persecution, in the *Higuit* case, an intelligence officer in the Philippine army during the Marcos regime provided information to his superiors about the leftist New People's Army (NPA) that would result in the arrest, torture, imprisonment, and death of members of that organization. This was deemed to be assistance in persecution in that he objectively furthered the persecution of others and had knowledge of the fate of the persons about whom he was providing information.[711] As well, the persecutor bar was applied in a situation where a member of the South Vietnamese Army sought out and interrogated communists and North Vietnamese sympathizers, whom he would beat in order to extract information, and if none was forthcoming, he would transfer them to another place for torture.[712] A soldier in Guatemala who provided information about suspected guerillas was also found to be complicit,[713] as was a surveillance

710 *Singh*, above note 686; regarding the issue that membership is not sufficient to be ineligible for asylum as a persecutor, see, also, *Kalubi v Ashcroft*, 364 F3d 1134 (9th Cir 2004).

711 *Higuit*, above note 686.

712 *Ngyuen v Holder*, 336 Fed Appx 680 (9th Cir 2009).

713 *Alvaradomayen v Lynch*, 637 Fed Appx 408 (9th Cir 2016).

agent for a law enforcement task force in the Philippines that frequently targeted rival political figures.[714]

On the other hand, the court distinguished the above cases in the *Diaz-Zanatta* decision. Diaz-Zanatta had begun working for Peruvian army intelligence in 1993 after graduating from military intelligence school. The Immigration Judge and Board of Immigration Appeals (BIA) found that she had assisted or otherwise participated in persecution and was therefore ineligible for asylum and withholding of removal. They based this finding on an interpretation of *Fedorenko*, standing for the proposition that her knowledge with respect to the persecutions was immaterial. However, the Court of Appeals found that there had been no consideration of whether the record established a nexus between the intelligence Diaz-Zanatta had gathered and the persecution of individuals at the hands of the Peruvian military or whether she had prior or contemporaneous knowledge of such persecutions. While Diaz-Zanatta assisted the Peruvian military intelligence community, that community, like the Punjabi police in *Singh*, engaged in traditional, legitimate exercises. Diaz-Zanatta's case was therefore dissimilar to *Fedorenko*, which dealt with concentration camps whose complete existence was premised on the persecution of innocent civilians. The Court of Appeal also distinguished *Higuit* in that Higuit, a military intelligence official during the Marcos regime in the Philippines, had admitted that individuals he investigated were imprisoned and killed.[715]

With respect to support functions, there have been a number of cases involving women who were involved in enforcing the one-child policy in China, which the United States considers persecution.[716] In the *Xie* case, it was decided that a person who was a driver between 1990 and 1992 for the Department of Health in Fujian Province in China, in which capacity he would transport pregnant women to hospitals where

714 *Aguilar v Lynch*, 621 Fed Appx 443 (9th Cir 2015).

715 *Diaz-Zanatta*, above note 694.

716 The United States uses a similar definition for persecution as contained in the Refugee Convention in s 101(a)(42) of the *INA* but specifically adds: "For purposes of determinations under this chapter, a person who has been forced to abort a pregnancy or to undergo involuntary sterilization, or who has been persecuted for failure or refusal to undergo such a procedure or for other resistance to a coercive population control program, shall be deemed to have been persecuted on account of political opinion, and a person who has a well founded fear that he or she will be forced to undergo such a procedure or subject to persecution for such failure, refusal, or resistance shall be deemed to have a well founded fear of persecution on account of political opinion." See, also, Walls, above note 687 at 245–47.

forced abortions were performed as part of the Chinese one-child policy, was assisting in persecution. After examining the post–Second World War jurisprudence in detail and concluding that the main tenet of complicity is actively assisting rather than passively accommodating, the court was of the view that Xie played an active and direct, albeit minor, role in persecution.[717] The same was said for a person who had been a guard at a birth control facility on an ongoing basis;[718] a person who had guarded ten women scheduled for abortions over a period of three months;[719] a person who for over twenty years reported the identities of women with unauthorized pregnancies;[720] and another who, as a family planning clerk, knew that reporting women who were in violation of the family planning policy to the director of his office would result in those women suffering forced abortions.[721]

However, another person, Weng, was found not to be involved in persecutorial acts by the Federal Court of Appeals. She was a nurse's assistant working at a public hospital in China in which forced abortions were performed pursuant to the country's family planning policy. Regarding the question of whether she was a persecutor, the court found that her involvement had not been "active with direct consequences for the victims," as had been the case in the *Xie* judgment. Her post-surgical care did not contribute to or facilitate the victim's forced abortions in any direct or active way. While she did guard patients once who were awaiting forced abortions, her conduct, taken as a whole, did not support a finding that the line had been crossed. It was only one time, she was unarmed, she only guarded the patients for ten minutes, and she helped one person escape, for which she later lost her job.[722]

In another case dealing with an abortion clinic worker, the same court that had decided the *Xie* and *Weng* cases was called upon to determine the contours of complicity in a situation involving a maternity nurse. Her duties included tending to pregnant women, assisting in the performance of ultrasound and other prenatal examinations, participating in live-birth deliveries, caring for newborns, and providing

717 *Xie v INS*, 434 F3d 136 (2d Cir 2006) [*Xie*].

718 *Guo Liang Lin v Keisler*, 251 Fed Appx 37 (2d Cir 2007); see, also, *Chen v US Attorney General*, 513 F3d 1255 (11th Cir 2008).

719 *Xiao Yun Dong v Holder*, No 09-1885-ag-NAC (2d Cir 2010).

720 *Suzhen Meng v Holder*, 770 F3d 1071 (2d Cir 2014).

721 *Li v Lynch*, 646 Fed Appx 113 (2d Cir 2016).

722 *Weng v Holder*, 562 F3d 510 (2d Cir 2009) [*Weng*].

recovery care to women who had undergone forced abortions. She did not participate in the abortion procedure itself, but the examinations in which she assisted were sometimes used to determine a fetus's position so that a forced abortion could be performed without threatening the life of the mother. The court was of the view that this situation was closer to the *Weng* case because the examinations in which she had assisted had not contributed to or facilitated the abortions in any direct or active way, nor was it more likely that abortions would occur as a result of her involvement.[723] This was also said in the case of a midwife who participated in multiple mandatory birth control procedures by handing equipment to doctors performing these procedures and was found not to be complicit.[724]

Another type of support function was explored in two detention situations. A female prison staffer in a detention facility in Armenia who was responsible for escorting prisoners to special cells where they would be severely beaten was found to be complicit on the ground that she was not a mere member of the staff but involved in acts that were more than peripheral to persecution. The court also said that the fact that she was under no compulsion to continue her employment plus the fact that she knew or was aware to a high probability that the prisoners she was escorting would be subject to abuse were factors to consider.[725]

The *Miranda Alvarado* decision touched on the outer limits of assistance in a situation of an interpreter at torture sessions of guerrilla members by the Peruvian Civil Guard. The court repeated the adage that complicity means providing purposeful material assistance or, put in other words, did the acts further the persecution, or were they tangential to it? With respect to this situation, it felt that "without the translation there would be no reason for the torture to occur as it did, as its point was to elicit information." As such, the acts in this case amounted to assistance as they were integral to the persecution.[726] Yet in the *Im* case, involving a prison guard in Cambodia in 1979 after the Vietnamese army had invaded the country and removed the Khmer Rouge government, a different conclusion was reached. Im's duties included distributing rice to the prisoners, taking them to bathe or

---

723 *Yan Yan Lin v Holder*, 584 F3d 75 (2d Cir 2009).

724 *Yaqin Chen v AG of the United States*, 622 Fed Appx 155 (3d Cir 2016).

725 *Ghazaryan v Gonzales*, above note 690.

726 *Miranda Alvarado v Gonzales*, 449 F3d 915 (9th Cir 2006) [*Miranda Alvarado*] (at para 50 in quoted material, above in text).

receive medical attention, overseeing their fitness and hygiene routines, and unlocking the prisoners' cells when scheduled for interrogation and handing them over to another guard, who would escort them to the interrogation room. Relying on the *Fedorenko* case and contrasting this situation with that of the *Miranda Alvarado* judgment, the court was of the view that this case "falls safely on the non-culpable side" since Im never beat any prisoner, did not decide who was imprisoned, and had no say in which prisoners would be interrogated.[727]

For other types of support functions, it was held that participating as a member of the Armenian police in raiding parties at the homes of Jehovah's Witnesses, where beatings would occur, amounted to assistance in persecution.[728]

The case of *Parlak* involved a leading member of the National Liberation Front of Kurdistan (ERNK), which had close ties to the PKK. Among several allegations, the BIA found that he had assisted with PKK fundraising and transported weapons into Turkey for use by the PKK, thus assisting in the persecution of others. The court distinguished the case of *Diaz-Zanatta* by saying that in this case, "Parlak's level of assistance is an order of magnitude greater than the harshest assessment one could possibly make about Diaz-Zanatta, and we find that a nexus exists between Parlak's actions and the persecution of others and that Parlak acted knowingly."[729]

On the other hand, the *Gao* case involved the chief officer of the Quingdao City Culture Management Bureau from 1997 until 2000 who was responsible for inspecting bookstores to determine whether they were selling any prohibited materials, including politically sensitive materials. He was found not to be assisting in persecution because while the violation of the laws he was enforcing could result in arrest, prosecution, or detention, there was no evidence that any person suffered this fate because of his inspections. The court contrasted this case with another Chinese case, the *Xie* decision, where there had been a direct connection between the person's activities and persecution. The court also followed the *Singh* case by saying that if the Culture Management Bureau had existed solely to persecute individuals for distributing politically disfavoured materials and not also enforcing copyright and

727 *Im v Gonzales*, 497 F3d 990 (9th Cir 2007) [*Im*].

728 *Shirvanyan v Gonzales*, 03-70308 (9th Cir 2003).

729 *Parlak*, above note 692; *certiorari* to the Supreme Court was denied on 14 June 2010 (see *Parlak v Holder*, 130 S Ct 3445 — Supreme Court, 2010).

pornography laws, culpability could have been found in membership in this organization.[730] The same conclusion as in *Parlak* was also reached in a situation of a sentry at an intelligence agency building who spoke to superiors about prisoner abuse in India but was not actively involved in persecution[731] and a soldier signing fuel receipts in Bosnia.[732]

The issue of knowledge of the acts committed by an organization in which a person had been involved was discussed in some detail in the case of *Castañeda-Castillo* in 2007. This person was a member of an anti-terrorist unit of the Peruvian military in 1985, which was carrying out operations against the Shining Path, described as a Maoist revolutionary organization in the judgment. During one such operation, the unit, consisting of four patrols, entered a village where a dozen innocent persons were shot and killed. Two patrols entered the village, while two other units, including the one to which Castañeda belonged, stayed outside the village to block escape routes. Castañeda claimed that he only found out about the massacre three weeks later and did not know beforehand that such an event would occur. The Immigration Judge and the BIA had found him not credible, while they also appeared to be of the view that the act of persecution does not require knowledge. The Court of Appeals disagreed and indicated that in order to assist in persecution, not only is an activity with a nexus to persecution required but also knowledge or wilful blindness, in the sense that the person must have had some level of prior or contemporaneous knowledge that persecution was being conducted.[733] The courts in *Gao*,[734] *Diaz-Zanatta*,[735] and *Parlak*[736] have followed the *Castañeda-Castillo* approach by saying that knowledge or wilful blindness is required to find that a person has assisted in persecution.

In conclusion, while the United States applies a different framework with respect to exclusion, including extended liability, than the other countries under consideration, the outcomes of the jurisprudence in drawing the circle of persons who should not be given the benefit of asylum due to involvement in international crimes are not that different

---

730 *Gao*, above note 686.

731 *Kumar v Holder*, 728 F3d 993 (9th Cir 2013).

732 *Krstic v Barr*, 804 Fed Appx 614 (9th Cir 2020).

733 *Castañeda-Castillo v Gonzales*, 488 F3d 17 (1st Cir 2007) [*Castañeda-Castillo*].

734 *Gao*, above note 686.

735 *Diaz-Zanatta*, above note 694.

736 *Parlak*, above note 692.

from those in these other countries. As a matter of fact, the jurisprudence is quite similar in that the courts have identified a number of concepts of extended liability, which have also been used in the other eight countries. Presence at the scene of a crime can give rise to liability, as can aiding and abetting. The latter form of complicity has been applied in the caselaw in the same manner as in the other countries, in situations of handing over people to become the subject of ill-treatment, providing information about a victim resulting in that person being maltreated, and involving support functions, often connected to detention facilities. Even the concept of membership, while said not to apply in earlier cases as a general principle, is mentioned with approval on some recent occasions.

Where the United States differs from the other countries is that there has been no jurisprudence providing guidance with respect to the notion of common purpose. This is not surprising, as the legislation on which the jurisprudence is based is narrower by referring to "participating," rather than "committing," as is the case in exclusion 1F(a). As a last comment, while it is likely that other countries will start relying on international criminal law, the United States will likely continue to develop its complicity principles independently.[737]

j) Observations

Until recently, the relationship between international criminal law and refugee law in extended liability was tenuous. Both areas of law developed their notions of who was indirectly culpable of committing international crimes independently from each other after a cautious foray into post–Second World War jurisprudence in some early refugee caselaw, which was not sustained in any meaningful and widespread manner after that. Since international criminal law has come to the attention of domestic courts in applying refugee law since 2009 in Canada, the United Kingdom, and New Zealand, this part of the chapter will first set out the development of extended liability in international criminal law followed by the application of that law in the domestic arena.

International criminal law as practised at the international level has been quite consistent in applying notions of indirect liability, except for

737 Although there has been a reference to the extended liability concepts set out in the Rome Statute in the civil liability case of *The Presbyterian Church of Sudan v Talisman Energy, Inc*, No 07-0016-cv (2d Cir 2009).

co-perpetratorship and JCE III. The ICTY/ICTR jurisprudence rejected co-perpetratorship (which in this context also includes other forms of perpetratorship) as a form of extended liability, but it has figured prominently in ICC jurisprudence, while the reverse is true of JCE, which has been used in most of the ICTY cases, but much less so at the ICC. To be sure, in both the ICC and ICTY contexts, alternative charges were also laid, together with either co-perpetration or JCE charges, but the jurisprudence at the ICC regarding extended liability has been concentrating on the contours of co-perpetrators, in the same manner in which the JCE caselaw dominated the judicial debate earlier at the ICTY/ICTR. The discussion of common purpose in article 25(3)(d) of the Rome Statute, the ICC equivalent of JCE (and in the ICC jurisprudence since 2011), has shown similarities with the ICTY caselaw, although it appears that the level of contribution is lower than for JCE, while the issue of whether JCE III is part of the common purpose notion (the subject of academic commentary) has not yet been answered by ICC judges.

This debate has had some effect on the interpretation of JCE at the domestic level, both in the criminal and the refugee context. In the criminal context, most common law countries have provisions in their criminal legislation for common intention, which is akin to JCE III and will raise the issue of whether these countries will apply their own national interpretation of extended liability or will yield to the ICC interpretation of its Statute, which they have ratified and implemented into their domestic legislation. It is likely that if situations arise where domestic jurisdictions can charge persons with broader forms of liability, they will likely do so. Countries such as Australia, Canada, New Zealand, and the United Kingdom did not make exceptional provisions to adjust their regular forms or liability or inchoate offences when implementing the Rome Statute. Conspiracy, incitement, and as common intention come to mind in this context. However, as it turns out, domestic courts have infused their reasoning, when applying domestic extended liability concepts, with references to international criminal law on a regular basis.[738]

Similarly, regarding refugee law, the question of which notions prevail in the event of disagreement between international institutions will need to be addressed now that all countries surveyed in this study have relied on international criminal law concepts as developed by the ICTY,

---

738 See Einarsen & Rikhof, above note 1 at 425–27, 504–15, and 588–91.

ICTR, and ICC. Again, the JCE III question comes to mind as the highest courts in Canada, New Zealand, and the United Kingdom, between 2010 and 2013, examined JCE based on international law but left the JCE III question either undecided, in that the situation before them did not require an analysis of that particular aspect of extended liability (Canada and the United Kingdom), or did not conduct an in-depth legal analysis of this concept (New Zealand). The interaction between international criminal law, domestic criminal law, and refugee law has been to some extent highlighted in the decision of the UK Supreme Court in the sense that it criticized the Court of Appeal for relying on UK criminal law as being too restrictive in the interpretation of the term "committed" in article 1F(a). It called upon refugee decision makers to apply the broader concepts embedded in international criminal law. On the other hand, the Supreme Court of Canada avoided this dilemma three years later by assessing the parameters of the broadest notions of extended liability in international criminal law as expressed by both the ICTY (for JCE) and the ICC (for common purpose), extracted the essence of these two concepts, and declared that extended liability in exclusion law could not be broader than the underlying common elements in these two concepts.

The jurisprudence on extended liability in exclusion law in these three countries can be summarized by noting that the original parameters of this concept, which originated from post–Second World War jurisprudence, was interpreted as personal and knowing participation and widely used at the national level, but it was then quickly replaced by a more independent approach to complicity. This trend repeated itself between 2010 and 2013, where the highest courts based their new approach on complicity on international criminal law concepts of extended liability with direct reference to jurisprudence from this area of law, but where in those same judgments an expansion of that jurisprudence was already noticeable. The more independent portion of these judgments became the touchstone for subsequent refugee tribunals in their jurisprudence where it was applied in a large number of diverse situations of extended liability. The same trend can be seen in civil law countries but in a more decentralized fashion.

As a result, it can be seen that in the area of complicity in exclusion law, international criminal law has played a very useful but temporary role, just long enough for refugee decision makers to incorporate the essential elements of international criminal law concepts into the relevant refugee notions but then to move on and use those crucial elements to develop a more independent course to deal with many more situations on the ground than international criminal law had dealt with due to the limited number of geographical instances discussed in its jurisprudence.

As explained above, when discussing the decision of the UK Supreme Court, the reasoning in that judgment is not without its methodological problems. The court concluded that the essence for liability for exclusion is "if there are serious reasons for considering him voluntarily to have contributed in a significant way to the organization's ability to pursue its purpose of committing war crimes, aware that his assistance will in fact further that purpose." While the analysis is couched in JCE language, the test for complicity suggested by the court by not including as part of this test the common design aspect closely resembles the notion of aiding and abetting in international criminal law, especially since the court equates "significant" with "substantial." This means that either the court has provided an incomplete definition of JCE or has collapsed all aspects of complicity known in international criminal law into only one type, aiding and abetting.[739] The result of the Supreme Court analysis in terms of the relationship between international criminal law and domestic criminal law for the purposes of refugee law, and in terms of laying down a test purporting to be a general test of complicity but in reality only representing one type of extended liability, is that it might not have helped elucidate the parameters of complicity as much as the Court had hoped.

The judgment of the Supreme Court of Canada also exhibits some suspect reasoning. Like the UK Supreme Court, when setting out the requirements for these forms of indirect involvement, it only discusses their *actus reus* aspects and again uses the *mens rea* of aiding and abetting, knowledge, rather than the intent to pursue a common purpose, which are the hallmarks of both JCE and common purpose. As such, while the analysis is very helpful to enunciate an overarching test for exclusion purposes, it would have been better from an international

739 The Supreme Court of New Zealand was clearer in describing JCE by including the common intention element and restricting the general definition given in the UK Supreme Court to the JCE concept. However, this judgment is not free from confusion either as the court had stated earlier in its judgment that the situation at hand pertained to a JCE III fact pattern but then used the UK judgment and adopted its general definition even though that definition pertained to JCE I.

criminal law perspective to address all the elements of these two types of liability and then indicate that, from a refugee perspective, not all of these elements are essential rather than ignore them completely. Such an approach would also have clarified why the Court was of the view that JCE and common purpose are the broadest forms of extended liability, which is not the case; they address different types of perpetrators rather than extending the circle of liability beyond, for instance, aiding and abetting.

One other aspect of complicity that was addressed in these two decisions was the notion of membership as an independent head of liability. While Canada, New Zealand, and the United Kingdom had originally accepted that membership in an organization dedicated to a limited, brutal purpose could amount to a rebuttable presumption for complicity, this changed as a result of these two Supreme Court judgments rejecting this notion. In general, membership as a form of complicity is in retreat. The Supreme Court of New Zealand did not address the issue of membership in its 2010 decision but followed the UK decision of the same year for all other aspects and might go in the same direction as its British counterpart when called upon directly, which was the case in Australia in 2018, where membership was rejected as part of its reliance on the UK and Canadian judgments. The courts in the United States are divided on this issue in that even though the statement that membership is not participation has been repeated in several cases, some courts are of the view that membership in an organization whose complete existence is premised upon persecution could amount to aiding and abetting.

On the European continent, Belgian and French jurisprudence have rejected this notion of membership, while in the Netherlands, a unique approach has been developed outside the judicial system. In the latter country, the minister in charge of immigration and asylum matters can designate certain categories of functionaries in specific regimes against whom personal and knowing participation can be levelled as a rebuttable presumption, which is similar to the judicial processes used to come to a similar conclusion regarding brutal organizations originally in Canada and New Zealand.

Other countries, including New Zealand until the pronouncement of the decision of its Supreme Court, have not used the JCE analysis to find liability on a common purpose basis. This category of complicity has been discussed in the jurisprudence of those countries as part of personal and knowing participation (Belgium and the Netherlands) or, even more generally, as part of complicity for crimes under article 1F(a) (France). In those countries, this notion has not been conceptually analyzed, but instead the courts have assessed a number of factors to determine whether they would result in complicity. It seems that the cases examined when using these factors to assess almost intuitively whether an association with a criminal group or organization amounted to culpable exclusion would have yielded a similar result as when using a formal JCE analysis. Taken with the comment made above about the conceptual difficulty of using JCE, together with the evidentiary difficulty of finding a common design in the often-cursory refugee proceedings, a factor approach might not be out of place when employing exclusion. The validity of this approach is also confirmed by the fact that the ICTY, in an earlier case, employed a number of these same factors at the same time as using a JCE analysis, thereby preserving a link with international criminal law.

In general, the factors examined in all the jurisprudence have been the manner in which a person joined an organization (Belgium, Canada, the Netherlands, New Zealand, United Kingdom); the nature of the organization (Belgium, Canada, France, the Netherlands, United Kingdom); the size of the organization (United Kingdom); whether the organization was proscribed and by whom (United Kingdom); the rank obtained in the organization (CJEU,[740] Australia, Belgium, Canada, France, New Zealand, the Netherlands, United Kingdom); the standing or influence in the organization (France, the Netherlands, United Kingdom); the time served (Belgium, Canada, New Zealand, United Kingdom); the person's age (Canada); and the manner in which a person dissociated themselves from the organization (CJEU,[741] Belgium, Canada, France, New Zealand, the Netherlands, United Kingdom). Not all factors are of the same significance (Canada), nor are they exhaustive (United Kingdom). The United States has not examined this notion in its courts, most likely because of the wording in its enabling statute.

The courts in all the countries have examined other aspects of complicity in a wide array of cases, thereby contributing to the development of international criminal law in these areas. These forms of liability,

---

740 *Bundesrepublik Deutschland v B and D*, C-57/09 and C101/09, 9 November 2010 at para 97, albeit in the context of exclusion 1F(b).

741 *Ibid.*

such as presence at the scene of a crime and, especially, aiding and abetting, have rarely been given a detailed factual treatment by international institutions due to their policies of only pursuing those most responsible for international crimes.[742]

The jurisprudence in Canada, the Netherlands, New Zealand, and the United States and a manual in the United Kingdom all reflect the view that presence at an international crime can amount to complicity if this presence was with authority (Canada, United Kingdom), with influence (the Netherlands), with circumstantial or other evidence (Australia), or of long duration and with a view to encouraging the perpetrators (New Zealand) or if such presence impedes the movement of those persecuted or otherwise subjects them to an increased risk of harm (United States). Acquiescence or inaction would not result in liability according to Canadian and US caselaw.

The last type of complicity is universally accepted under the headings of participation, furthering, personal and knowing participation, assisting, and being integral to or actively involved in an organization, all of which require a substantial contribution to international crimes with the knowledge that these crimes would occur.[743] Activities such as providing information or intelligence about a person resulting in harm have been considered complicity by the courts or tribunals in all countries, while activities such as financing (Canada, New Zealand, United States), arresting a person and handing the person over (Belgium,

742 Very few persons have been convicted at the ICTY and the ICTR for such indirect involvement; at the ICTR in *Nntawukulilyayo* (ICTR-2005-82), Trial Chamber Judgment, 3 August 2010, a conviction was entered for transporting ammunition, soldiers, and gendarmes, while in *Rutaganda* (ICTR-96-3-T), Trial Chamber Judgment, 6 December 1999, the same was done for distributing guns and other weapons but in conjunction with other, more serious, activities. Aiding and abetting was only given detailed attention by the Special Court of Sierra Leone in the case of Charles Taylor, see *Taylor* (SCSL-03-01-T), Trial Chamber Judgment, 18 May 2012 at para 6915 and *Taylor* (SCSL-03-01-A), Appeals Chamber Judgment, 26 September 2013 at para 369.

743 It has also been expressed as exercising "a decisive influence on the criminal acts" by the Swiss Asylum Commission; see UNHCR, *Statement on Article 1F of the 1951 Convention, issued in the context of the preliminary ruling references to the Court of Justice of the European Communities from the German Federal Administrative Court regarding the interpretation of Articles 12(2)(b) and (c) of the Qualification Directive*, July 2009 at 24.

Canada, France, the Netherlands, New Zealand, United Kingdom, United States), and providing support functions (Australia, Belgium, Canada, France, the Netherlands, New Zealand, United States) have also attracted negative attention from the courts.

With respect to other types of extended liability, in Australia, the Netherlands, and the United States, ordering was found to be part of knowing and personal participation, while the same was said in Belgium and France for providing encouragement to commit international crimes; the US legislation refers to incitement, as does the Australian jurisprudence, which also includes planning. Ordering, planning, and instigating are mentioned in the European Qualification Directive. On the other hand, the New Zealand Supreme Court was of the view that conspiracy cannot be read into the word "committed" and that this was not a form of liability known in the Rome Statute and, as such, was outside the 1F(a) parameters, while in the United States, doubt has been cast on whether accessory after the fact can be part of participation.

The concept of command or superior responsibility as defined in international criminal law has been used in the Netherlands (albeit not always successfully), while the Supreme Court of Canada has indicated that it can be part of the overarching concept of complicity. More often, senior officials have been excluded in countries such as Australia, Belgium, Canada, France, Germany, the Netherlands, and the United Kingdom in a more informal fashion and only using the factors of having a high position and knowledge of the international crimes rather than utilizing the more onerous analysis inherent in the concept of command or superior responsibility. Knowledge has always been a requirement for complicity, while lesser forms of actual knowledge, such as awareness (Australia, New Zealand) and wilful blindness (Canada, the Netherlands, United States), have been included in the *mens rea* to commit crimes.

The jurisprudence examined in detail in these nine countries with respect to extended liability is remarkably consistent in utilizing the various forms of liability, such as presence at the scene of a crime, the aiding and abetting type of complicity, and the common purpose approach. So too is the fact that within the aiding and abetting category, all countries found that handing over people or information with the knowledge of harm amounted to complicity. Since the factual situations underlying such a legal determination lie along a wide spectrum, variations in results can be observed, especially in the outer reaches of complicity. Even so, it is striking to see that, for instance, interpreters carrying out work for people involved in human rights abuses were excluded both in the Netherlands and the United States.[744]

There are, however, interesting trends with two organizations, KhAD and the LTTE, that have been the subject of exclusion decisions in several countries. The approach to KhAD has not been the same in all countries. Canada occupied originally one extreme of the spectrum by finding that all members of KhAD were excludable by virtue of membership in that group (except if the contribution does not reach the threshold of nominal involvement), compared to a more central position in the Netherlands, where officers have been made subject to the rebuttable presumption of personal and knowing participation, while others were excluded using regular complicity principles. The other side of this spectrum is occupied by Australia, where some members were excluded for aiding and abetting activities, and by Belgium, which in some cases decided the same way as Australia but in other instances refused to exclude senior officials on the grounds that a particular function bore no resemblance to excludable behaviour. The situation with the LTTE is slightly different in that in Canada this organization was seen as a brutal organization, while in Australia, France, the Netherlands, New Zealand, and the United Kingdom, an appreciation is required of whether the contribution given to this organization leads to the commission of war crimes or crimes against humanity or whether the assistance was for legitimate conduct of warfare.

When comparing the complicity jurisprudence of the countries in this study, it can be said that the nine countries with dissimilar legislative frameworks have been very similar in their approach to war criminals, while their courts have, in general, been supportive of this approach and, in doing so, have utilized the basic concepts of international criminal law in a similar fashion even though, until recently, there had been no reliance on international jurisprudence. However, in the context of this study, two questions need to be asked: whether the developments at the national level have been consistent with international criminal law and whether this consistency or possible lack thereof is desirable.

In general, it would appear that the concepts developed by the national courts bear a high level of resemblance to the same concepts

744 See, also, for instance, Maarten Bolhuis, Tara Ditzel & Joris van Wijk, "Vergelijking van 1F-uitsluitingen van Syrische asielzoekers in Nederland en België" (2020) 8 *A&MR, Tijdschrift voor Asiel & Migrantenrecht* 385–90, indicating that the concepts of complicity are broader in the Netherlands than in Belgium.

under consideration by the international courts, although the analysis has rarely been as detailed as that employed by the international institutions, most likely because the courts at the national level are not specialized in international criminal law, nor do they provide lengthy deliberations, generally, for any issues related to refugee matters, especially in civil law countries. As well, several of the countries under consideration, such as Belgium, Canada, France, and New Zealand, were called upon to circumscribe the parameters of complicity before there was any international criminal law, apart from the post–Second World War jurisprudence. While in some instances post–Second World War cases were initially relied upon, as in Canada, it is understandable that the national courts and tribunals felt obliged to follow their own path after a precedent had been set in establishing the principles gleaned from this jurisprudence. It is remarkable that in continuing their own developments in the absence of any crossover from international criminal law, the national jurisprudence in extended liability is so consistent with the concepts of extended liability as expressed by their international counterparts.

For instance, the concept of aiding and abetting and its essential criterion of substantial contribution with knowledge at the national level are the same as the parameters given at the international level. The national decision makers have applied these general tenets of aiding and abetting to many more factual situations than the international institutions, both in a positive and a negative manner, thereby providing guidance in drawing a line between culpable behaviour leading to exclusion and acts that fall outside the periphery of extended liability. Since international jurisprudence typically deals with the persons most responsible, the notion of aiding and abetting has not been applied to factual situations as much as at the national level, and international institutions could well benefit from paying more attention to their national counterparts in this area of the law.

The situation is different with other aspects of extended liability, where the international jurisprudence has not only developed the analytical framework for these forms of liability but has applied them to many situations. The examples of command responsibility and JCE come to mind, with the new notions of perpetration and common purpose in the Rome Statute as examples. As seen above, these types of liability have been used directly by the highest courts of common law countries, except the United States, although it was to develop a *sui generis* approach regarding complicity. Such direct references to international criminal law have not occurred in any meaningful manner in civil law countries.

This is desirable up to a point. When adopting international criminal concepts for refugee purposes, several considerations should be kept in mind, some of which have been mentioned above in the discussion regarding membership but are worthwhile repeating in a general sense. One such consideration is the criminal law of the countries in question as they inform the sense of culpability in that particular country. The criminal laws of the countries under consideration differ from each other, with the most obvious examples in extended liability being conspiracy and common intention (except the United States) in common law countries and forms of perpetration in civil law countries (although only in Germany).

Another consideration is the nature of refugee proceedings compared to criminal proceedings. Because of the lower standard of proof, the relaxed rules of evidence, and the need to keep asylum procedures short in order to accommodate the large number of asylum seekers, the evidence in asylum proceedings is typically of a different magnitude than in criminal trials, both nationally and internationally.[745] Most asylum hearings consist of the testimony of an asylum applicant, often accompanied by a written statement given earlier, in combination with reputable human rights reporting, which generally sets out the country situations and the activities of specific organizations with a connection to the applicant.

With respect to the first consideration, it will be tempting for national refugee decision makers to infuse their reasoning with reference to national laws where those national laws provide a possibility of extended liability and international criminal law does not. However, if those decision makers profess to apply exclusion 1F(a) and intend to have the reference to international instruments in that article apply to both the international crimes and the modes of liability, a

745 See, in Canada, *Ezokola*, above note 268 at paras 37–40, while in the Netherlands in general between the differences between these two proceedings, Rb, The Hague, Awb 09/16643 and Awb 09/16646, 25 March 2011, at para 2.33, as well as an official document of the Dutch parliament, "Kamerstuk 19637, Vreemdelingenbeleid, Nr 1808," 4 April 2014 under "1. Het 1F Beleid," "Verschil vreemdelingenrecht en strafrecht"; see, also, Jennifer Bond, "Principled Exclusions: A Revised Approach to Article 1(F)(A) of the Refugee Convention" (2013) 35:1 *Michigan Journal of International Law* 34–42.

reference to national variations of liability is less desirable than seeking a connection with international criminal law. The question can then be raised as to whether international criminal law should be applied in all circumstances even when these international legal concepts have been introduced from specific national systems such as JCE III and co-perpetration. The answer to that question lies in the transfer of national concepts to the international plane where these concepts were further developed in situations not anticipated by national legislators and courts, thereby reaching the status of a *sui generis* body of law. In that sense, the concepts related to extended liability have achieved their own meaning in international criminal law and should be applied in their own independent manner by refugee decision makers.

The second consideration, which deals with the nature of refugee procedures, is more practical than principal in nature but still no less of a concern. This would call for an approach where the fundamental reasons for having chosen a less formal type of process are not violated while at the same time applying as much as possible the concepts of liability set out in international criminal law. Based on this reasoning, the notion of command responsibility could be utilized at the national level in situations involving high officials in military or civilian organizations. General human rights reporting, combined with the narrative of the person concerned, will allow a finding of the requirements of control and knowledge. Having come to the point where these two requirements are found to exist, it is in most cases not a stretch to include a deliberation of the third requirement, the lack of prevention or punishment, since these factors can be easily deduced from the same sources of information used in refugee procedures. Only the analysis of the facts requires an adjustment to bring the reasoning in line with international criminal law.

Finally, there is much to support incorporating international concepts into the practice of national refugee decision makers as long as these concepts are developed in a coherent and easy-to-apply framework in refugee law, which has largely been the case.

A final comment related to the relationship between international criminal law and exclusion 1F(a) is the observation made that exclusion 1F(a) should allow for a more granular approach regarding the seriousness of the crimes committed and the personal circumstances of the perpetrator when committing those crimes, which would be akin to the two-step process of conviction and sentencing in criminal law.[746] Apart from the general observations made above regarding the difference between criminal trials and refugee proceedings, which have been emphasized by both Canadian and Dutch jurisprudence,[747] it can also be said that the factors taken into consideration for complicity because of the jurisprudence by the highest courts in common law countries include some more personal and contextual elements, such as the person's duties and activities within the organization, the length of time spent in the organization, the method by which the person was recruited and the opportunity to leave the organization,[748] and the requirement that a contribution to the organization must be made voluntarily. This goes beyond the defence of duress[749] and includes a situation where a person "had no realistic choice but to participate in the crime."[750] In addition, as in criminal law, where conviction and sentencing are separated, the process of determining the excluded person's status and a balancing between the seriousness of the offence and the level of persecution a person faces upon return, during the *refoulement* stage is also a bifurcated process.[751] Even more personal circumstances, such as health issues, parenthood, and establishment in the country of refuge, are taken into consideration at another stage of possible removal of persons who have been involved in serious crimes and do not face *refoulement*, the so-called humanitarian and compassionate stage of removal from a country of refuge.[752] All countries under considera-

---

746 See Jennifer Bond, "Excluding Justice: The Dangerous Intersection Between Refugee Claims, Criminal Law, and 'Guilty' Asylum Seekers" (2012) 24:1 *International Journal of Refugee Law* 37 at 47–48 and 55–59; Magali Maystre, "The Interaction Between International Refugee Law and International Criminal Law with Respect to Child Soldiers" (2014) 12:5 *Journal of International Criminal Justice* 975 at 995–96; Kate Ogg, "Separating the Persecutors from the Persecuted: A Feminist and Comparative Examination of Exclusion from the Refugee Regime" (2014) 26:1 *International Journal of Refugee Law* 82 at 102–11; Elies van Sliedregt, "International Outlaws" (2020) 33:3 *Leiden Journal of International Law* 535 at 537–38, and Lefebvre & Lafontaine, above note 269 at 418–25.

747 See, also, European Asylum Support Office (EASO), *Exclusion: Articles 12 and 17 Qualification Directive*, 2d ed (2020) at 52–53, online: https://euaa.europa.eu/sites/default/files/EASO_Exclusion_second_edition_JA_EN.pdf.

748 See *Ezokola*, above note 269 at para 91.

749 See Section B, below, for defences, including duress; this contextual approach with respect to criminal involvement can also be found in the discussion by the courts in the modern approach taken in the context of serious crime in 1F(b), which emphasizes, among other factors, the personal circumstances of the person concerned; see Chapter 5, Section A(4).

750 *Ezokola*, above note 269 at para 86.

751 See Chapter 6 for a detailed discussion of all aspects of *refoulement*.

752 See Chapter 7 for a detailed discussion of this process.

tion that apply exclusion also have *refoulement* and humanitarian and compassionate processes in place, which, taken together, cover virtually all personal and contextual considerations usually found during the sentencing phase of a criminal trial.

B. DEFENCES

1) International Criminal Law

The Rome Statute contains the most comprehensive enumeration of defences available in international criminal law.[753] The most common defences used in the refugee context are the defence of superior orders and the defence of duress. Both are now defined with some specificity in the Rome Statute, as follows:[754]

> 1. The fact that a crime within the jurisdiction of the Court has been committed by a person pursuant to an order of a Government or of a superior, whether military or civilian, shall not relieve that person of criminal responsibility unless:
>   (a) the person was under a legal obligation to obey orders of the Government or the superior in question;
>   (b) the person did not know that the order was unlawful; and
>   (c) the order was not manifestly unlawful.
>
> 2. For the purposes of this article, orders to commit genocide or crimes against humanity are manifestly unlawful.
>
> . . .
>
>   (d) The conduct which is alleged to constitute a crime within the jurisdiction of the Court has been caused by duress resulting from a threat of imminent death or of continuing or imminent serious bodily harm against that person or another person, and the person acts necessarily and reasonably to avoid this threat, provided that the person does not intend to cause

753 Rome Statute, arts 31–33. There is no distinction made in the Statute between justifications and excuses (as in civil law) in which justifications connote that the conduct was acceptable and therefore lawful (such as self-defence), whereas with excuses the unlawfulness of the conduct is conceded, but the person should not be blamed in the circumstances, such as mistake of fact.

754 *Ibid*, arts 31.1(d) and 33.

a greater harm than the one sought to be avoided. Such a threat may either be:

(i) Made by other persons; or

(ii) Constituted by other circumstances beyond that person's control.[755]

Some comments can be made about these two defences. The first one is that they are closely related. With the defence of superior orders a person follows commands given by persons higher in the hierarchy than themself for the simple reason that, especially in the military context, organizations cannot function unless orders are obeyed. Duress will also occur in a situation where a person is ordered to follow a certain cause of action, a crime, but in this context these orders are accompanied by a threat. The result is that a person follows orders in the latter situation, not because they feel an obligation as a matter of discipline within an organization but because they now have to make a moral choice: whether to give priority to their own well-being or that of their victim.

The difference in the context in which the two defences operate is also reflected in the result if the requirements for the defences have been accepted. If the duress is acknowledged as having been present during the commission of the crimes, a person is fully absolved from criminal liability and will be acquitted. The defence of superior orders, on the other hand, even if accepted, will only result in a mitigation of sentence and, as such, is a limited defence.[756] This also means in the refugee area that if a defence of superior orders is raised in isolation (although often the two defences are intertwined in specific fact situations and difficult to separate), it has no place in exclusion as it is not possible to have a less than full exclusion.

This last point should be tempered with the realization that the limited availability as a defence has changed with the advent of the Rome Statute. This situation is still the same for the crimes of genocide

755 For a discussion of the other defences in the Rome Statute, such as mental incapacity, intoxication, self-defence, and mistake of fact and law, see van Sliedregt, above note 144 at 224–42 and 269–86; for a discussion of the defence of mistake of fact, see *Ali Muhammad Ali Abd-Al-Rahman* ("Ali Kushayb"), (ICC-02/05-01/20), Pre-Trial Chamber, Decision on the Confirmation of Charges, 9 July 2021 at paras 74–84.

756 This was the approach in the statutes of the IMT (art 8), ICTY (art 7(4)), ICTR (art 6(4)), and SCSL (art 6(4)).

and crimes against humanity but not for war crimes where the superior orders defence has, since 2002, been given the status of a full defence.

There has been little jurisprudence from international criminal institutions in recent years related to these two defences.[757]

The defence of superior order was addressed in the first ECCC judgment, which recognizes the change in position in international law by indicating that the IMT Statute did not allow such a full defence for war crimes but that the Rome Statute does, and comes to the conclusion that the defence is not available in any event, as the crimes committed by the accused were unlawful, of which he was aware.[758]

---

757 For jurisprudence of defences after the Second World War, see *United Nations War Crimes Commission, Law Reports of Trials of War Criminals, Vol XV, Digest of Laws and Cases* (London: His Majesty's Stationary Office, 1949) at 157–88. The ICTY has discussed three defences apart from the defence of duress: the *tu quoque* defence, reprisals, and self-defence (with a brief reference but no discussion regarding necessity in *Aleksovski* (IT-95-14/1-A), Appeals Chamber Judgment, 24 March 2000 at paras 52 and 54). The *tu quoque* defence, which stands for the proposition that if one party commits atrocities, the other party should be justified in doing the same was rejected in a number of decisions, such as *Kupreškić et al* (IT-95-16), Trial Chamber, Decision on Evidence of the Good Character of the Accused and The Defence of Tu Quoque," 17 February 1999; *Kupreškić et al* (IT-95-16), Trial Chamber Judgment, 14 January 2000 at paras 511, 515–20, and 765; *Kunarac et al* (IT-96-23/IT-96-23/1), Appeals Chamber Judgment, 12 June 2002 at para 87; *Limaj et al* (IT-03-66-T), Trial Chamber Judgment, 30 November 2005 at para 193; *Stanišić and Župljanin* (IT-08-91-T), Trial Chamber Judgment, 27 March 2013 at para 16. The defence of reprisals was examined in *Kupreškić et al* (IT-95-16), Trial Chamber Judgment, 14 January 2000 at paras 527–36, and *Martić* (IT-95-11-T), Trial Chamber Judgment, 12 June 2007 at paras 464–68, while self-defence was discussed in *Kordić and Čerkez* (IT-95-14/2), Trial Chamber Judgment, 26 February 2001 at paras 448–52 (which was accepted as long as it is raised on a personal level rather than as an issue of military self-defence); *Situation on Registered Vessels of Comoros, Greece and Cambodia, Article 53(1) Report*, ICC OTP, 6 November 2014 at paras 56–61; *Bagosora, Kabiligi, Ntabakuze and Nsengiyumva* (ICTR-98-41-T), Trial Chamber Judgment, 18 December 2008 at para 1999; *Boškoski and Tarčulovski* (IT-04-82-A), Appeals Chamber Judgment, 19 May 2010 at paras 31–36, 45–46, 51 (although the latter discussed the issue of self-defence at the state level against terrorist attacks). At the SCSL, the minority of a trial chamber raised the prospect of the defence of state necessity (*Fofana and Kondewa ("CDF")* (SCSL-04-14-T), Trial Chamber, Separate Concurring and Partially Dissenting Judgment of Justice Bankole Thompson, Judgment, 2 August 2007 at paras 68–92), but this was rejected on appeal (*Fofana and Kondewa ("CDF")* (SCSL-04-14-A), Appeals Chamber Judgment, 28 May 2008 at para 247; the defence of mental disease or defect was discussed in great factual detail in *Ongwen* (ICC-02/0401/15), Trial Chamber Judgment, 4 February 2021 at paras 2450–580.

758 *Kaing Guek Eav alias Duch* (Case File 001/18-07-2007/ECCC/TC), Trial Chamber Judgment, 26 July 2010 at paras 551–52 (during the appeal, duress was only discussed in the context of mitigation of sentence; see *Kaing Guek Eav alias Duch* (Case File 001/18-07-2007-ECCC/SC), Supreme Court Chamber Judgment, 3 February 2012 at para 364).

Both the ECCC and the ICTY[759] have examined the defence of duress, while it was also discussed by the ICC.[760] The ECCC and the ICTY dealt with the unusual situation of duress where the threat against the accused is the same as the crime they were asked to carry out, to kill or be killed. Both tribunals concluded that duress in those circumstances is not a full defence but can only be used in mitigation of a sentence. This was expressed by the majority of the Appeals Chamber of the ICTY in the following manner: "We take the view that duress cannot afford a complete defence to a soldier charged with crimes against humanity or war crimes in international law involving the taking of innocent lives."[761] The ECCC Trial Chamber said it this way: "Duress cannot however be invoked when the perceived threat results from the implementation of a policy of terror in which he himself has willingly and actively participated."[762] The ICC discussed duress both at the pre-trial and trial stages in the same case.[763] After repeating the requirements of duress in article 31(1)(d) of the Rome Statute, the Trial Chamber explained that

> the words "imminent" and "continuing" refer to the nature of the threatened harm, and not the threat itself. It is not an "imminent threat" of death or a "continuing or imminent threat" of serious bodily harm—the Statute does not contain such terms. Rather, the threatened harm in question must be either to be killed immediately ("imminent death"), or to suffer serious bodily harm immediately or in an ongoing manner ("continuing or imminent serious bodily harm"). On this understanding, duress is unavailable if the accused is threatened with serious bodily harm that is not going to materialise sufficiently soon. A merely abstract danger or simply an elevated

---

759 The ICTR has addressed the defence of duress as well only to reject it due to a lack of credibility and without discussing its elements; see *Kamuhanda* (ICTR-99-54), Trial Chamber Judgment, 22 January 2004 at paras 78–80.

760 *Ongwen* (ICC-02/04-01/15), Pre-Trial Chamber, Decision on the Confirmation of Charges, 23 March 2016 at paras 150–56.

761 *Erdemović* (IT-96-22), Appeals Chamber Judgment, Joint Separate Opinion of Judge McDonald and Judge Vohrah, 7 October 1997 at para 88, which was accepted by the majority of the Chamber in *Erdemović* (IT-96-22), Appeals Chamber Judgment, 7 October 1997 at para 19.

762 *Kaing Guek Eav alias Duch* (Case File 001/18-07-2007/ECCC/TC), Trial Chamber Judgment, 26 July 2010 at para 557.

763 *Ongwen* (ICC-02/04-01/15), Pre-Trial Chamber, Decision on the Confirmation of Charges, 23 March 2016 at paras 150–56 during the pre-trial stage and at trial in *Ongwen* (ICC-02/0401/15), Trial Chamber Judgment, 4 February 2021 at paras 2581–88 and 2668–72.

probability that a dangerous situation might occur—even if continuously present—does not suffice.[764]

While amnesties and immunities are, strictly speaking, not defences, a general amnesty is sometimes raised as an impediment against initiating procedures against persons who have committed genocide, war crimes, and crimes against humanity. The SCSL,[765] the ECCC,[766] and the ICC[767] have made it clear that amnesties cannot be invoked against such serious crimes.[768] On the other hand, while international tribunals are allowed to prosecute sitting heads of state,[769] this is generally not the case for national institutions.[770]

2) The Views of the UNHCR

The 2003 UNHCR's *Background Note on the Application of the Exclusion Clauses* discusses three defences: superior orders, duress, and

764 *Ongwen* (ICC-02/0401/15), Trial Chamber Judgment, 4 February 2021 at para 2582; the court was of the view that in the circumstances of the case at hand, only this first legal question was relevant, not the other two requirements; see paras 2583–85 and 2669–70; with respect to that one requirement, that court found at para 2668 that "[t]he evidence indicates that in the period of the charges, Dominic Ongwen did not face any prospective punishment by death or serious bodily harm when he disobeyed Joseph Kony. Dominic Ongwen also had a realistic possibility of leaving the LRA, which he did not pursue. Rather, he rose in rank and position, including during the period of the charges. Finally, he committed some of the charged crimes in private, in circumstances where any threats otherwise made to him could have no effect." The argument that Ongwen had been a victim himself was dismissed at para 2672.

765 *Kallon and Kamara*, SCSL-2004-15-AR72(E) and SCSL-2004-16-AR72(E), Decision on Challenge to Jurisdiction: Lomé Accord Amnesty, 13 March 2004 at para 82.

766 *Ieng* (Case File 002/19-09-2007-ECCC/OCIJ) (PTC03), Pre-Trial Chamber, Decision on Appeal against Provisional Detention Order, 17 October 2008 at para 61.

767 *Gadafi* (ICC-01/11-01/11), Pre-Trial Chamber, Decision on the Admissibility Challenge by Dr. Saif Al-Islam Gadafi pursuant to arts 17(1)(c), 19, and 20(3) of the Rome Statute, 5 April 2019 at paras 61–78.

768 See, also, the decision of the European Court of Human Rights in the case of *Margus v Croatia*, Application No 4455/10, 27 May 2014.

769 Statute of the ICTY (art 7(2), ICTR (art 6(2), SCSL (art 6(2), and ICC (art 27). The SCSL is an international court for this purpose even though it was created by an agreement between the United Nations and Sierra Leone; see *Taylor* (SLSC-2003-0101), Decision on Immunity from Jurisdiction, 31 May 2004 at paras 51–53.

770 *Arrest Warrant of 11 April 2000 (Democratic Republic of the Congo v Belgium)*, International Court of Justice, 14 February 2002, ICJ Rep (2002) ICJ General List 121, at paras 54–61; regarding immunities in general, see, also, Currie & Rikhof, above note 1 at 641–704.

self-defence.[771] For all three, reference is made to the relevant provisions of the Rome Statute, while for the defence of superior orders, the provisions of the Charter of the International Military Tribunal and the Statute of the ICTY are mentioned. With respect to duress, the *Background Note* adds:

> Where duress is pleaded by an individual who acted on the command of other persons in an organisation, consideration should be given as to whether the individual could reasonably have been expected simply to renounce his or her membership, and indeed whether he or she should have done so earlier if it was clear that the situation in question would arise. Each case should be considered on its own facts. The consequences of desertion plus the foreseeability of being put under pressure to commit certain acts are relevant factors.[772]

3) National Refugee Jurisprudence

a) Australia

Four judgments by the Federal Court have made comments on defences in the exclusion context:[773] the Federal Court of Australia in the *SHCB* and *GZCK* cases and the Federal Court of Australia, Full Court, in the *SHCB* and *SRYYY* decisions. In the *SHCB* case, the court found that the defence of duress could be used against allegations of war crimes and crimes against humanity but that it did not apply in this situation, due to the applicant's claims not to have known about the activities of KhAD. The Full Court endorsed this position. A similar result was arrived at in the *GZCK* case,[774] where duress was allowed for one inci-

771 UNHCR, *Background Note*, above note 164 at 25–26, paras 66–71.

772 *Ibid* at 26, para 70; for a general overview of defences and their applicability to 1F(a), see Bond, above note 746 at 47–56 and 67–70.

773 *SHCB* FCA, above note 172; *SHCB* FCAFC, above note 173; *SRYYY v Minister for Immigration and Multicultural and Indigenous Affairs*, [2005] FCAFC 42, and *GZCK*, above note 178.The Refugee Review Tribunal examined the defence of duress in the cases of V94/01334 [1995] RRTA 162; N96/12101 [1996] RRTA 3349; V96/04174, [1997] RRTA 2507; and N96/12254 [1997] RRTA 492. The AAT has discussed the defence of duress in cases of *N1998/532 and Minister for Immigration and Multicultural Affairs*, [1999] AATA 116, and *W97/164 and Minister for Immigration and Multicultural Affairs*, [1998] AATA 618, and the defence of superior orders in the cases of *W97/164 and Minister for Immigration and Multicultural Affairs*, [1998] AATA 618, and *SRYYY and Minister for Immigration and Multicultural Affairs*, [2006] AATA 320.

774 *GZCK*, above note 178 at paras 245–53.

dent but not another, based on the requirement of facing imminent death or serious bodily harm as well as proportionality.

In the *SRYY* judgment, the defence of superior orders was examined. The court found that the Rome Statute provides for a defence of superior orders and a defence of duress, which are distinct. The court cited two opposing views of the defence of superior orders. On the one hand, some argue that superior orders is only a mitigating factor, which can support a defence of duress but is not on its own a complete defence. On the other hand, some argue that superior orders, if reasonably perceived to be lawful, can be a full defence. The court was of the view that the Rome Statute was a compromise between these positions and that it is difficult to discern a clear rule of international customary law.

The court concluded, for the same reasons, that the Rome Statute was an appropriate instrument to define 1F(a) crimes and that this defence should have been examined to see if the applicant's acts came within it. It rejected the argument that because article 1F did not deal with criminal law, defences were not available to applicants being examined under the exclusion clauses. The court also indicated that the defence of superior orders applies only to orders that the applicant does not know are unlawful and that are not manifestly unlawful. It is not the applicant's act but the superior's orders that need to be assessed as manifestly unlawful. To determine whether the orders were manifestly unlawful, it is necessary to assess the conduct of the war crime and the nature of the superior orders.

b) Belgium

Both the defences of superior orders and duress have been raised on several occasions in crimes arising out of situations in Lebanon, Zaire, and Ethiopia but were rejected each time due to a lack of credibility[775] or because the legal requirements were not met: for superior orders, the order was manifestly unlawful, which was known to the claimant, and for duress, there was no evidence of coercion.[776]

In another case, the defence of duress was accepted in a situation of a woman who was a member of the PKK and, in that capacity, took part in armed combat against the Turkish army while also providing information about Turkish collaborators. Her argument that she

---

775 See Kapferer, above note 202 at 214.

776 CCE No 214.472, 20 December 2018, and CCE No 253.089, 20 April 2021, with reference to the Rome Statute for the defence of superior orders.

had been forcibly recruited into the PKK and that desertion was not an option because of threats of being killed, raped, or tortured was accepted.[777] On one occasion, an exclusion decision was overturned because the decision maker had not sufficiently considered the defence of duress when it was raised.[778]

c) Canada[779]

The defence[780] of superior orders was considered by the Federal Court of Appeal in the *Equizabal*[781] case, involving a soldier from Guatemala, but not accepted on the facts of the case as the order to torture people was a manifestly unlawful order in the sense that it offended the conscience of every reasonable, right-thinking person and was an order that was obviously and flagrantly wrong.[782] Following orders to murder a person was considered manifestly unlawful in the *Carrasco* case in 2008.[783] More recently, the Federal Court was of the view that this defence was not possible in situations of crimes against humanity in the DRC, taking into account the most recent developments in international criminal law, specifically the Rome Statute.[784]

The defence of duress was addressed in two early Federal Court of Appeal decisions, *Ramirez* and again *Equizabal*, which together found that the defence is present if there is an imminent, real, and inevitable threat and the risk of harm to the perpetrator is disproportionate to the harm they are asked to carry out on the victim. The defence was rejected in both instances. It was also addressed by the same court in the Second World War case of *Oberlander* in 2009, setting out the same

777 CPRR No 97-2573/E356, 7 September 1999.

778 CCE No 119.929, 28 February 2014.

779 For a general overview, see Jennifer Bond, "The Defence of Duress in Canadian Refugee Law" (2016) 41:2 *Queen's Law Journal* 409–54; Joseph Rikhof, "Update on Exclusion and Inadmissibility Jurisprudence: New Developments Since the Decisions of the Supreme Court of Canada in *Ezokola* and *Febles*," Canadian Association for Refugee and Forced Migration Studies (CARFMS/ACERMF) Working Paper No 2017/2 (April 2017) at 17–28, online (pdf): https://carfms.org/wp-content/uploads/2017/04/CARFMS-WPS-No10-Joseph-Rikhof.pdf, and Lefebvre & Lafontaine, above note 269.

780 Motivation to commit an offence is not a defence; see *Bamlaku*, above note 328; *Shakarabi*, above note 295; *Sumaida*, above note 296.

781 *Equizabal v Canada (Minister of Employment and Immigration)* (CA), [1994] 3 FC 514 [*Equizabal*].

782 The defence is also briefly considered in the case of *Canada (Minister of Citizenship and Immigration) v Asghedom*, 2001 FCT 972, where it was subsumed in the defence of duress.

783 *Carrasco*, above note 352.

784 *Betoukoumesou v Canada (Citizenship and Immigration)*, 2014 FC 591.

requirements but also suggesting that conscription in a brutal organization combined with severe sanctions for desertion should be assessed as part of the defence of duress.[785]

One Federal Court judgment discussed the defence of duress in a different context the *Valle Lopes* case,[786] involving a person who had joined the Directorate of Special National Investigations for Honduras (also referred to as Battalion 3-16) and participated in acts of kidnapping and torture against a civilian. The issue of duress was raised in the context that he would face being killed if he deserted this unit, which was rejected by the court since he could have escaped earlier without danger of imminent harm.

This defence was addressed another six times at the Federal Court level. In the case of *Asghedom* in 2001, it was accepted in a situation involving the Ethiopian army during the Mengistu regime.[787] In *Kathiravel* in 2003, involving a person captured by the Sri Lankan army, the court rejected the defence due to a lack of proportionality.[788] The same result was achieved for the same reason in the 2008 *Carrasco* decision,[789] while in the *Massroua* case, in a situation involving ISIS in Syria, the court said that the person was never physically harmed or subjected to threats.[790] In another case, involving an imam in the United Arab Emirates who provided information to the security organizations of that country under the threat that he and his family might be deported to Iraq, where their lives would be at risk, the court overruled the original negative decision by saying that the defence of duress had not been properly assessed.[791]

The Federal Court of Appeal in the *Ramirez* case also concluded that remorse does not constitute a defence. Last, the fact that a person had been the subject of a domestic amnesty was not considered a relevant factor for an allegation of crimes against humanity in the *Carrasco* case.[792]

---

785 *Oberlander v Canada (Attorney General)*, 2009 FCA 330.

786 *Valle Lopes v Canada (Citizenship and Immigration)*, 2010 FC 403 [*Valle Lopes*].

787 *Canada (Minister of Citizenship and Immigration) v Asghedom*, 2001 FCT 972 [*Ashgedom*], the same conclusion was reached in *Canada (Citizenship and Immigration) v Hammed*, 2020 FC 130 for a situation in Nigeria.

788 *Kathiravel*, above note 337.

789 *Carrasco*, above note 352.

790 *Massroua*, above note 408.

791 *Al Khayyat v Canada (Citizenship and Immigration)*, 2017 FC 175.

792 *Carrasco*, above note 352.

d) France

The defence of duress was raised in France a couple of times but not always accepted because of a lack of credibility or because the legal requirements were not met: in one situation involving a member of the military intelligence in Iraq who said that he had been forced to participate in special operations, which included the arrest, interrogation, and torture of civilians; and another for a person who had been forcibly recruited into the Tontons Macoute in Haiti.[793] This defence was also rejected in a situation where a person belonging to a secret society in Nigeria had indicated that he could not leave the organization because of psychological pressure.[794] The same was said in a 1F(b) situation where a person had assisted her mother in performing female genital mutilation (FGM) for twenty years, and the tribunal was of the view that the authority of her mother or the pressure of the community was not sufficient to amount to a threat of death or continuous or imminent serious injury.[795]

On the other hand, the refugee tribunal has said that the decision maker should have considered the same defence in the case of a collaborator with the security service in Iraq because of the extremely coercive and violent character of the Saddam Hussein regime.[796] The same result was achieved in the context of 1F(b) in a situation in the DRC where a minor was recruited by a criminal gang and committed serious crime due to the person's vulnerability and duress.[797]

A domestic amnesty was rejected as a defence in a situation where a person had committed murder during a civil war in Lebanon.[798]

e) The Netherlands

The *Aliens Manual* sets out in some detail the parameters of the defences of superior orders, duress, and self-defence. While the text of the superior order defence refers to the language of article 33 of the Rome Statute, the other defences are given a broader application by saying for duress:

793 Kapferer, above note 202 at 213–14.

794 CRR, 3 July 2007, 566454, E.

795 CNDA, 12 November 2019, 19007358, Mme T.

796 CRR, 5 July 2007, 469930, M.

797 CNDA, 18 October 2016, 15031596 C.

798 Frédéric Tiberghien, *La protection des réefugiés en France* (Aix-en Provence: Presses Universitaires D'Aix-Marseille, 1988) at 469, and CRR, 22 December 2000, 346184, Hatem, which was a 1F(b) case.

> [I]f one of the following situations is present duress will not lead to exculpation the responsibility of the alien:
> - if the claim of duress is not credible;
> - if the person concerned had the possibility to dissociate himself from the crime;
> - if the person concerned was employed for a considerable time in an organization when the foreseeable was applied;
> - if the degree of duress is not proportional to the seriousness of the crime committed by the person concerned.

Similarly, this is said for self-defence:

> [If] one of the following situations is present the claim of self-defence will not lead to exculpation of the responsibility of the alien:
> - the threat to the person alien is not credible;
> - the threat against which alien defended himself is not proportional to the seriousness of the crime committed by alien;
> - if it must have been clear to the alien that the crime committed by him would not have avoided the threat;
> - if alien did commit not just one crime but a number of crimes over a longer period of time.[799]

The provisions of this manual have been subject to interpretation.[800] The Council of State has said that the defence of superior orders is usually not available in principle,[801] nor is it compatible with the career of a person involving several promotions. It has also indicated that remorse is not a defence.[802] The same was said for a person who continued to be involved with an organization even though he could have foreseen that he was going to be ordered to engage in international crimes.[803] In applying the test of superior orders, a district court indicated that the killing of civilians in a non-armed conflict situation as a

799 *Vreemdelingencirculaire* 2000 (C), art C2/7.10.2.5.

800 On one occasion, the defence of diminished mental capacity was raised where the person became involved in international crimes for UNITA in Angola after his parents had been violently killed, but this was rejected (Rb, The Hague, Awb 03/25104, 23 March 2004).

801 The Hague, Awb 04/20046, 24 February 2005, for a soldier in the Ugandan army (relying on the Charter of the IMT as well as the Rome Statute); see, also, Rb, The Hague, Awb 16/28180, 17 March 2017, involving a soldier in Iraq, and Rb, The Hague, NL 18.14281, 10 May 2019, involving a soldier in the Syrian army, relying exclusively on the Rome Statute.

802 AbRS, R02.90.4725, 7 November 1995.

803 Rb, The Hague, Awb 02/93493, 28 October 2004, for a member of a Maoist group in Nepal.

member of the Ugandan People's Defence Force was manifestly unlawful, referring to the *Charter* of the IMT and the Rome Statute.[804]

The defence of duress has been raised on several occasions. It was not accepted in situations where the claim was not credible,[805] where there was no compulsion,[806] where a person could have left the organization in a safe manner at an earlier time,[807] or where a person occupied a senior position from which it was difficult to deduce if he could have been subject to threats.[808] The defence was accepted where the threats against the person were so severe as part of forcible recruitment that it could not reasonably demand that he refused to enter the organization,[809] while more recently, in a case of a member of the Garde Civil in the DRC, the threats against him for possible desertion were credible as members of his family had been severely mistreated after he had left on an earlier occasion,[810] just as the threats against a person's sisters were credible after he had been mistreated himself.[811]

Last, remorse is not a defence.[812]

f) New Zealand

The defence of duress has been examined in a few cases. The defence was accepted in 2003 in the situation of the person who had informed on members of the LTTE to the Sri Lankan army. The RSAA concluded that during his abduction by the LTTE, he had not been involved in fighting but had, due to threats of death to himself and his family, provided shelter to LTTE members. The tribunal indicated that duress/

---

804 Rb, The Hague, Awb 08/18867, 4 May 2009.

805 Rb, The Hague, Awb 03/22067, 4 February 2005, for a person involved in the one-child policy in China.

806 Rb, The Hague, Awb 13/13175, 26 April 2016.

807 In general, see AbRS, 3 March 2006, nr 200506835/1, and AbRS, 6 August 2004, nr 200402337/1; regarding specific situations, Rb, The Hague, Awb 04/13902, 28 April 2005, for a soldier of the Serbian army in Kosovo; Awb 03/52476, 24 February 2005, regarding a soldier in the Russian army deployed in Chechnya; Rb, The Hague, Awb 13/13175, 26 April 2016, involving a soldier in the Syrian air force; Rb, The Hague, Awb 16/28180, 17 March 2017, regarding a soldier in Iraq (while also indicating that the proportionality requirement had not been met either); Rb, The Hague, NL 18.14281, 10 May 2019, as well as Rb, The Hague, NL 18.19332, 25 July 2019, both involving soldiers in the Syrian army.

808 AbRS, 4 October 2005, nr 200503774/1, for a member of the RUF in Sierra Leone.

809 Rb, The Hague, Awb 96/10536, 2 April 1997.

810 Rb, The Hague, Awb 03/17838, 2 October 2003.

811 Rb, The Hague, Awb 15/1712, 8 December 2015.

812 AbRS, R02.90.4725, 7 November 1995.

coercion is marked by the absence of the intent of the applicant. To meet this requirement, it is necessary to show that the act was done to avoid imminent and grave peril, that the act must be reasonable, that the situation must deprive the individual of the ability to choose, and that the harm caused must be proportionate to the harm avoided. It concluded that as the applicant was never voluntarily involved with either the LTTE or the Sri Lankan army and did face grave and imminent peril if he did not cooperate, the defence applied in his case.[813]

In 2006, the defence of duress/coercion was denied in a case involving a Somali man who claimed that his access to sensitive information prevented him from attempting to leave his work with the National Security Service. The RSAA decided that a claim of duress and/or coercion can only be applied in situations where there is a threat of imminent death or of continuing or imminent bodily harm against that person or another person—a threat that they concluded was not present in the appellant's situation based on evidence that suggested he kept the job simply out of a need for employment.[814]

g) United Kingdom

At the policy level, a Home Office manual indicates that superior orders, duress, self-defence, and defence of others can be invoked as defences as part of an exclusion analysis; as in the Netherlands, the details are inspired by the Rome Statute without mentioning it,[815] while also going beyond some of the requirements set out in international criminal law by saying:

> Where duress is pleaded by an individual, consideration must be given as to whether they could have reasonably chosen to leave the organisation, and why they did not do so earlier if it was clear the situation in question would arise. Each case must be considered on its own facts

813 RSAA Appeal No 74646, 26 June 2003.

814 RSAA Appeal No 75634, 24 May 2006; the defence was found to be present in RSAA Appeal No 75946, 2 March 2007 (the Samyukta Jana Morcha [SJN] in Nepal), and RSAA Appeal No 75675, 19 December 2005 (an informer for the local intelligence service in Iraq), but not in RSAA Appeal No 1655/93, 23 November 1995 (the Directorate General of Forces Intelligence [DGFI] in Bangladesh).

815 Home Office, "Exclusion (Article 1F) and Article 33(2) of the Refugee Convention" (28 June 2022), online: www.gov.uk/government/publications/asylum-instruction-exclusion-article-1f-of-the-refugee-convention/exclusion-article-1f-and-article-332-of-the-refugee-convention-accessible-version.

and the onus is on the claimant to prove that duress applies. The consequences of desertion plus being able to foresee being put under pressure to commit certain acts are relevant factors to take into account.[816]

The defence of duress was discussed in detail in one tribunal case.[817] The tribunal considered three issues: whether the defence of duress exists in all circumstances in international criminal law given the doubt placed on this general statement by the ICTY Appeals Chamber in the *Erdemović* case,[818] the burden and standard of proof when raising this defence, and the requirements applicable to the defence. With respect to the first issue, the tribunal was of the view that the dicta of the majority of the ICTY Appeals Chamber have been superseded by the more recent parameters of duress in the Rome Statute and that the defence of duress is generally applicable in 1F(a) situations.[819] Regarding the second issue, the tribunal states:

> We propose to proceed upon the view that an evidential burden is imposed on the appellant to raise the existence of circumstances such as would permit the defence to be given effect to, and that if that burden is met a persuasive onus shifts to the Secretary of State to establish that there are serious reasons for considering that the appellant did not act under duress.[820]

For the specific requirements of the defence, the tribunal repeats the five elements of article 31 of the Rome Statute.[821] Based on these

---

816 *Ibid* at 16.

817 AB (Article 1F(a) — defence — duress) Iran, above note 682; the details of the case are discussed in above note 684.

818 See above note 761.

819 AB (Article 1F(a) — defence — duress) Iran, above note 682 at paras 39–54.

820 *Ibid* at para 62; the court discusses the Canadian jurisprudence on this issue as set out in the *Oberlander* case but does not find it helpful for the specific question at hand at paras 60–61.

821 *Ibid* at para 63 (with more details at paras 71 and 73); the five cumulative elements are:

i. There must be a threat of imminent death or of continuing or imminent serious bodily harm;
ii. Such threat requires it to be made by other persons or constituted by other circumstances beyond the control of the person claiming the defence;
iii. The threat must be directed against the person claiming the defence or some other person;
iv. The person claiming the defence must act necessarily and reasonably to avoid this threat;
v. In so acting the person claiming the defence does not intend to cause a greater harm than the one sought to be avoided.

requirements, the tribunal concluded that the defence was not applicable in this case because the person concerned for many years "took no steps whatsoever to avoid compliance with her duties in the prison, despite her knowledge of the consequence for those taken to the torture facility."[822] In another case, the requirements of duress in the Rome Statute were set out while indicating that on the facts presented, the person had not faced imminent harm.[823]

h) United States

With respect to defences, personal motivation is not an excuse. A person need not act out of personal motivation or beliefs to be a persecutor; cooperation or support of an organization that is acting to persecute others is sufficient to qualify an individual as a persecutor.[824]

It has been said in a situation where a Bosnian-Serb in Bosnia-Herzegovina helped resist attacks from Serbian Croats on his village in 1990 that self-defence can be a defence when committing acts of persecution.[825]

There was a serious disagreement among several circuits of the Court of Appeals as to whether a defence of duress existed in immigration and refugee law. One view was that once it has been determined that a person ordered, incited, assisted, or otherwise participated in persecution on account of one of the five grounds, that person was barred from asylum. The law does not inquire further into the voluntariness of the person's action, nor is there an excuse once someone is found to be a persecutor. In other words, there is not a defence of duress in acts of persecution. This was the preferred view in the Fifth and Seventh Circuits.[826]

---

822 *Ibid* at para 78.

823 *AS (s 55 "exclusion" certificate — process) Sri Lanka*, [2013] UKUT 00571 (IAC) at paras 41–42 and 93–96.

824 *Maikovskis v INS*, 773 F2d 435 (2d Cir 1985); *Bah v Ashcroft*, 341 F3d 348, 351 (5th Cir 2003); *Singh*, above note 636.

825 *Vukmirovic v Ashcroft*, 362 F3d 1247 (9th Cir 2004).

826 See in the Fifth Circuit the case of *Bah v Ashcroft*, 341 F3d 348, 351 (5th Cir 2003), for a Sierra Leonian child soldier, while the Seventh Circuit followed Bah in the case of *Singh*, above note 686, involving a policeman in the Punjab in India, although the latter appears to be more a case of a combination of the defence of superior orders and duress; see, for more detail, Nicole Lerescu, "Barring Too Much: An Argument in Favor of Interpreting the Immigration and Nationality Act, Section 101(a)(42), to Include a Duress Exception" in (2007) 60 *Vanderbilt Law Review* 1875–907; see, also, Melissa James, "Fleeing the Maras: Child Gang Members Seeking Refugee Status in the United States" (2005) 25:3 *Children's Legal Rights Journal* 1 at 16.

The Eighth and Ninth Circuits[827] took the opposite view by allowing such a defence. When considering the defence, these courts were of the view that there were two requirements to establish the culpability of the applicant: personal involvement and purposeful assistance. The second requirement, purposeful assistance, factors in the totality of the surrounding circumstances, including the voluntariness of the applicant's acts.[828] As well, a number of factors with respect to assisting persecution needed to be taken into account to establish liability, such as whether the involvement was involuntary and compelled by threats of death, whether the person shared the persecutory motives of the group carrying out the crimes, whether the person expressed disagreement with actions of the group, and whether the person left the group at the first available opportunity and in doing so risked his life.[829]

The Supreme Court of the United States rendered a decision on this issue in March 2009[830] but did not provide a clear answer to the question of whether the defence should be considered in immigration and refugee law. The majority was of the view that the BIA, which had denied the defence, had done so for the wrong reasons but decided to have the board reconsider the case without providing a clear instruction as to which direction it should take; two of nine judges indicated explicitly that they were of the view that the defence should apply,[831] while three others explicitly took the opposite view.[832] For a while there had been no new cases applying these instructions, as a result of which the approach regarding defences remained uncertain.[833]

---

827 See the case of *Hernandez*, above note 686), dealing with a situation in Guatemala, while the Ninth Circuit took this position in the case of *Miranda Alvarado v Gonzales*, 449 F3d 915, 926 (9th Cir 2006), a case from Peru. The Second Circuit, in the case of *Xie v INS*, 434 F3d 136 (2d Cir 2006) from China, appears to be searching for a middle ground; see Lerescu, above note 826, for more details.

828 *Miranda Alvarado v Gonzales*, 449 F3d 915 (9th Cir 2006).

829 *Hernandez*, above note 686.

830 *Negusie v Holder*, 129 S Ct 1159 (2009).

831 Justices Stevens and Beyer.

832 Justices Scalia, Alito, and Thomas.

833 This has resulted in a number of commentators exhorting refugee decision makers to allow the use of defences, especially in the case of child soldiers; see White, above note 688 at 191–222; Frank M. Walsh, "Navigating the Series of Rocks: Applying the Lessons from the Material Support Bar, De Minimis, and Age of Consent Exceptions to the Persecutor Bar" (2010) 22:2 *Florida Journal of International Law* 227–50; Karl Goodman, "*Negusie v Holder*: The End of the Strict Liability Persecutor Bar" (2009) 13:1 *New York City Law Review* 143–70; David A. Karp, "Setting the Persecutor Bar for Political Asylum After *Negusie*" (2009) 61 *Florida Law Review* 933–44; Melanie Johns, "Adjusting the Asylum Bar: *Negusie v Holder* and the Need to

The BIA attempted to resolve this issue in 2018 as part of the remand in the case of *Negusie*.[834] The BIA, when discussing the defence of duress, first established that the unavailability of withholding the deportation provision for aliens who engage in persecution bears a more than passing similarity to the exclusion provision of the Refugee Convention, and that even where the language is different, it had been the intention of the drafters of the US section of that provision to be consistent with the international language, including 1F(a) of the convention. Having established this connection between US and international refugee law, the BIA then indicated that since international criminal law, the UNHCR, and the jurisprudence of other common law countries all recognize the defence of duress, the same should apply in the United States. Next, the tribunal went on to determine the parameters of this defence and was of the view that while relying on US criminal law and international criminal law, specifically the Rome Statute, as well as other common law jurisprudence, the following are the requirements for the defence:

> [A]t a minimum the applicant must establish by a preponderance of the evidence that he (1) acted under an imminent threat of death or serious bodily injury to himself or others; (2) reasonably believed that the threatened harm would be carried out unless he acted or refrained from acting; (3) had no reasonable opportunity to escape or otherwise frustrate the threat; (4) did not place himself in a situation in which he knew or reasonably should have known that he would likely be forced to act or refrain from acting; and (5) knew or reasonably should have known that the harm he inflicted was not greater than the threatened harm to himself or others. Only if the applicant establishes each

---

Incorporate a Defence of Duress into the Persecutor Bar" (2010) 40:2 *Golden Gate University Law Review* 235–62; Leah Durland, "Overcoming the Persecutor Bar: Applying a Purposeful Mens Rea Requirement to 8 USC at para 1101(1)(42)" (2010) 32 *Hamline Law Review* 571– 608; Jennifer C. Everett, "The Battle Continues: Fighting for a More Child-Sensitive Approach to Asylum for Child Soldiers" (2009) 21:2 *Florida Journal of International Law* 286–356; Joshua Dankoff, "Advocating Duress and Infancy Exceptions to the Persecutor Bar to Asylum for Former Child Soldiers" (2011) 31:1 *Children's Legal Rights Journal* 43 at 50; and Elisabeth A. Rossi, "A Special Track for Former Child Soldiers: Enacting a Child Soldier Visa as an Alternative to Asylum Protection" (2013) 31:2 *Berkeley Journal of International Law* 392 at 438–45.

834 Matter of *Negusie*, 27 I & N Dec 347 (BIA 2018), online: www.justice.gov/eoir/page/file/1075801/download [*Negusie*]; see, also, indirectly, *Hernandez-Hernandez v Barr*, 789 Fed Appx 898 (2nd Cir 2019).

> element by a preponderance of the evidence would it be appropriate to consider whether the duress defense applies.[835]

The BIA then provided more detail on each of those elements by relying on US criminal law and Canadian exclusion law. Last, the BIA said the following about the burden and standard of proof for this defence:

> Once the DHS has met … its initial burden, the burden shifts to the alien to show by a preponderance of the evidence that the persecutor bar does not apply, either because he did not engage in persecution or because he acted under duress. An applicant must satisfy each element of the 5-part duress standard by a preponderance of the evidence. Only then will the adjudicator consider whether a duress defense to the persecutor bar is warranted.[836]

Based on these considerations, the applicant, Negusie, had not met the requirements for the defence as he received only verbal reprimands for not following orders, and he had not faced an imminent threat of death or serious bodily injury. It was also clear that he had had a reasonable opportunity to escape or otherwise avoid guarding the prisoners who were subjected to harm and torture.

However, this ruling was vacated by the attorney general on 5 November 2020;[837] this decision is under appeal at the Fifth Circuit Court of Appeals, which had originally rejected this defence twenty years ago.[838]

i) Observations

A number of defences have been examined in the countries under consideration. Personal motivation was considered not to be a defence in Canada, the United Kingdom, and the United States, while the same was said in Canada and France for a national amnesty and in Canada,

---

835 *Negusie, ibid.*

836 *Ibid.*

837 Matter of *Negusie*, 28 I&N Dec 120 (AG 2020), Interim Decision No 3999; the power to vacate a BIA decision is set out in 8 CFR at para 10003.1(d)(7)(i) in conjunction with 1003.1(h)(1)(i); see, also, s 1.4(f) of the policy manual of the Executive Office for Immigration Review (EOIR), US Department of Justice, Immigration Court Practice Manual (14 November 2022), online (pdf): www.justice.gov/eoir/book/file/1528921/download .

838 See UNHCR, Brief of United Nations High Commissioner for Refugees as Amicus Curiae Supporting Petitioner in the case of *Daniel Girmai Negusie v Merrick Garland*, US Attorney General, No 21-60314, 4 August 2021.

the Netherlands, and the United Kingdom for remorse. Self-defence was considered and accepted in the United Kingdom and the United States.

The defence of superior orders was considered by the courts in Australia, Belgium, Canada, and the Netherlands and in the manual in the United Kingdom and rejected in all cases in the United Kingdom and the Netherlands on a principal basis, and in Australia, Belgium, Canada, and the Netherlands in some cases because the main requirement, the manifestly lawful order, was not considered present in the circumstances.

The defence of duress has been considered in all countries under consideration except Germany, with the Rome Statute definition as a starting point in Australia, Canada, the Netherlands, the United Kingdom, and the United States.

Both at the international level and the domestic level, there is a dichotomy in the application of this defence in that it has been applied to two different conceptual situations. The ICTY applied the defence to a situation where it was raised in a context where a person faced the threat of immediate execution if they did not carry out orders to kill other people. This can be contrasted with the situation examined in the ECCC, where a person had been a member of a government agency for a long time but felt he would be killed if he left that organization. In the latter case, there is no immediate or possibly ongoing threat to carrying out international crimes, but the threat is present at a different level. The ICC has applied this defence in a more regular situation, involving a situation of lesser severity between the harm against the person and the harm threatened.

In most countries, the more detailed elements of the defence have been developed as an amalgam of the criteria set out in the Rome Statute and the requirements of their own domestic criminal law, and the results have been remarkably consistent. Most countries refer to the five requirements mentioned in some detail above in the US jurisprudence, while the two requirements with the most ambiguity, the notion of imminency and the level of reasonableness with respect to the harm caused, were already resolved before the ICC case of *Ongwen* conclusively addressed them in 2021. Imminency was found to also include future threats, which would not occur immediately but were slightly further removed in time, while the reasonableness was set at the level of the modified objective standard, meaning the standard of a reasonable person similarly situated. The national jurisprudence has also agreed that the burden of proof is on the person claiming the defence, and that all requirements were made after the government had proven the excludable acts in question, while the standard to prove these acts and the defence is the same, namely, serious grounds for considering.

While on its face, the duress test as enunciated in international criminal law would have less application in an organizational setting due to the lack of immediacy to the commission of specific crimes, this approach in relation to duress is not new. It was already applied after the Second World War in the *Einsatzgruppen* case, where it was said that "one who embarks on a criminal enterprise of obvious magnitude is expected to anticipate what the enterprise will logically lead to" and "the failure to attempt disengagement from so catastrophic an assignment might well spell the conclusion that the defendant involved had no deep-seated desire to be released."[839] It would appear that from both the ECCC and the domestic jurisprudence, persons who got themselves involved in notorious organizations will get less sympathy than in the more immediate situations of duress, when they want to leave, as they were responsible for getting themselves in this predicament in the first place, with their eyes open to the nature of the organization.

Relying on defences has not been a very good proposition for persons who initially were found to be excluded. The defence of duress, which was raised the most in thirty-three cases in the countries under consideration, was rejected twenty-six times and referred back to another decision maker once; superior order was raised nine times, denied seven times, and sent back for reconsideration twice; the defence of diminished capacity was raised once and rejected, while the opposite was the case for self-defence; the quasi-defences of remorse (raised once) and amnesties (raised four times) were all unsuccessful. This means that the chance of being successful in raising a defence is just under 15 percent (seven times out of forty-seven), in most cases because the person was found not to be credible, while often in the other situations, the legal requirements were not met.

C. CHILD SOLDIERS

1) Introduction

Children who have been involved in armed conflict will not necessarily remain in their own countries. They often will leave in search of a better

839 The *Einsatzgruppen case, Trial of Otto Ohlendorf, et al*, United States Military Tribunal, Nuremberg, *Trials of War Criminals Before the Nueremberg Military Tribunals*, vol 4, (1947) at 481 & 482.

life, either by themselves or accompanied by their families. While most of the children have travelled to a neighbouring country or a country in the same region, it is certainly not uncommon to see these children take lengthy and perilous journeys, overland or by sea, to reach countries in Europe, North America, Australia, and New Zealand. This phenomenon is not new. Throughout history, every time there has been a mass migration movement, children constituted a major part of these exoduses. From such upheavals after the First and the Second World War, primarily within and from Europe, to similar events after the uprisings in Hungary in the 1950s and Czechoslovakia in the 1960s, to the refugees coming from Chile and southeast Asia in the 1970s, to the more recent events involving the large-scale Mediterranean sea and overland voyages into Europe still ongoing, and to the very recent plight of the Rohingya people arriving in Bangladesh, children have been the most visible representation of these terrible events.

The situation of children in general should also be placed in the larger context of global asylum movements. The global asylum situation is grim. According to the UNHCR, as of mid-2022 there were 103 million people displaced in the world, of whom 36.5 million were children; 53.2 million were internally displaced, while 32.5 million were refugees, and 4.9 million were asylum seekers.[840] Most of these people are living in refugee camps administered by the UNHCR in conjunction with the states to which they fled. Of these child refugees, over 300,000 were unaccompanied or separated from their families in 2015–16, which is a five-fold increase from 2010–11.[841] Almost all of these instances occurred at the US-Mexican border or in Europe.[842]

Various areas of law have been involved in addressing the unique situation of the responsibility of child soldiers for international crimes, including international law and refugee law.[843]

---

840 UNHCR, *Refugee Data Finder, Key Indicators*, 2022, online: www.unhcr.org/refugee-statistics.

841 UNICEF, *A Child Is a Child: Protecting Children on the Move from Violence, Abuse and Exploitation*, Executive Summary (New York: UNICEF, May 2017) at 4.

842 *Ibid*; See, also, UNICEF, Ad Hoc Committee on Refugees and Stateless Persons, *A Deadly Journey for Children: The Central Mediterranean Migration Route* (February 2017), online (pdf): www.unicef.org/sites/default/files/press-releases/glo-media-UN053732.pdf, and UN Human Rights Council Advisory Committee, *Global Issue of Unaccompanied Migrant Children and Human Rights*, UN Doc A/HRC/36/51 (24 July 2017) at 6–10.

843 For general discussions of the phenomenon of child soldiers, see Mark Drumbl & Jastene Barrett, eds, *Research Handbook on Child Soldiers* (Cheltenham, UK & Northampton, US: Elgar, 2019), chs 1–12; for responsibility of child soldiers, *ibid*, chs 13–18; for the treatment of

2) International Law

Although the opposite has been argued,[844] the criminal responsibility of children is not by itself considered objectionable in the international law dealing with war situations. As early as post–Second World War jurisprudence, some examples can be found where children were tried and convicted for war crimes while taking into account the special circumstances of their young age. The *Bommer* case[845] determined that two girls between the ages of sixteen and eighteen should receive reduced sentences because of extenuating circumstances, while a third girl under the age of sixteen should be "freed from responsibility on account of her age." All three had been accused and stood trial for the war crime of theft and receiving stolen goods.

In international humanitarian law, this same dual approach, albeit implicitly, can be found in article 77 of Protocol I and article 6.4 of Protocol II, reflected as follows:

> 1. If arrested, detained or interned for reasons related to the armed conflict, children shall be held in quarters separate from the quarters of adults, except where families are accommodated as family units as provided in Article 75, paragraph 5.
> 2. The death penalty for an offence related to armed conflict shall not be executed on persons who had not attained the age of eighteen years at the time the offence was committed.

International human rights law, in the form of the Convention of the Rights of the Child, recognizes implicitly the fact that children can be tried for war crimes by saying that "no child shall be alleged as, be accused of, or recognized as having infringed the penal law by reason of

---

child soldiers for inclusion for asylum, see Joseph Rikhof, "Child Soldiers and Asylum — Duality or Dilemma," *ibid* at 397–400; for a detailed discussion of the applicability of defences to the specific situation of child soldiers, see Windell Nortje & Noelle Quenivet, *Child Soldiers and the Defence of Duress Under International Criminal Law* (London: Palgrave Macmillan, 2020).

844 Sonja Grover, "'Child Soldiers' as 'Non-Combatants': The Inapplicability of the Refugee Convention Exclusion Clause" (2008) 12:1 *International Journal of Human Rights* 53 at 53; Nienke Grossman, "Rehabilitation or Revenge: Prosecuting Child Soldiers for Human Rights Violations" (2007) 38 *Georgetown Journal of International Law* 323 at 346–52.

845 "Case No. 50: Trial of Alois and Anna Bommer and Their Daughters," French Permanent Military Tribunal, *Law Reports of Trials of War Criminals*, vol IX (London, 1949) 62, online (pdf): https://tile.loc.gov/storage-services/service/ll/llmlp/Law-Reports_Vol-9/Law-Reports_Vol-9.pdf.

acts or omissions that were not prohibited by national or international law at the time they were committed."[846]

This principle of accountability has been further developed in the Paris Commitments and the Paris Principles,[847] the former of which states:

> To ensure that children under 18 years of age who are or who have been unlawfully recruited or used by armed forces or groups and are accused of crimes against international law are considered primarily as victims of violations against international law and not only as alleged perpetrators. They should be treated in accordance with international standards for juvenile justice, such as in a framework of restorative justice and social rehabilitation.[848]

At the international criminal law level, the ICC has no jurisdiction to try any person under the age of eighteen. The 1996 Report of the Preparatory Commission on the Establishment of an International Criminal Court indicated that "the need for including a provision setting an age limit at which an individual could be regarded as not having the requisite *mens rea* was widely supported. The question of what that age should be, however, would require common agreement."[849]

Two years later, this concept of a minimum age for criminal responsibility was still retained in the final Report of the Preparatory Committee on the Establishment of an International Criminal Court, which was the basis for the Rome Conference,[850] but no agreement on the exact age was set out in this document (it varied from twelve to eighteen years old). Finally, it was decided that the court does not have jurisdiction over any person who was under eighteen at the time of the

---

846 Article 40.2(a).

847 During a high-profile conference in 2007 in Paris regarding child soldiers, a number of commitments (officially called "The Paris Commitments to Protect Children from Unlawful Recruitment or Use by Armed Forces or Armed Groups" and "The Principles and Guidelines on Children Associated with Armed Forces or Armed Groups") in this area were made by state representatives, which can be considered influential although not reaching the level of a binding treaty. The Paris Commitments call upon states to prohibit the recruitment or use of children under the age of eighteen while also ensuring that persons who have been involved in such practices be investigated and prosecuted, while the Paris Principles provide further elaboration of the Commitments.

848 Commitment 11. Principles 3.6–3.7, 7.6, and 8.7–8.11 provide more detail.

849 UN Doc A/51/22 at 45, para 201.

850 A/CONF.183/2/Add.1, 14 April 1998, Addendum, Part One, Draft Statute for the International Criminal Court, art 26, "Age of Responsibility."

alleged commission of the crime, thereby avoiding setting an age limit for criminal responsibility for minors.[851]

Neither the ICTY nor the ICTR has a specific prohibition to deal with young offenders, but on the other hand, neither has special provisions related to the trials of juveniles except for the sentencing provisions, which require the tribunals to take the individual circumstances of the convicted person into account. The report of the secretary-general to the United Nations Security Council regarding the establishment of the ICTY did mention age as a possible defence.[852] No person under the age of eighteen years has been indicted by either of the two international tribunals, although in one ICTY case, the following statement was made:

> In its Final Brief, the Defence submits that even if the beating by the youth was considered to have caused Milisav Milovanovic's death, there can be no criminal liability for a war crime committed by an individual below the age of 18. The Trial Chamber considers this submission as completely unfounded in law, as no such rule exists in conventional or customary international law. What is relevant for this case is not the age of the perpetrator, but the alleged acts or omissions of the Srebrenica military police to prevent this incident.[853]

The SCSL has a number of provisions dealing with children because of the many child soldiers who have been involved in the conflict for which the SCSL has jurisdiction. The age of criminal responsibility to be included in its statute was the cause of a debate that moved across the spectrum of holding children as young as seven responsible to an approach whereby all children should be considered victims.[854] A com-

---

851 *Ibid*; see, also, Roy S. Lee, *The International Criminal Court: The Making of the Rome Statute — Issues, Negotiations, Results* (The Hague: Kluwer Law International, 1999) at 201 and 327; and Roger S. Clark & Otto Trifferer, "Article 26: Exclusion of Jurisdiction over Persons Under Eighteen" in Otto Triffterer, ed, *Commentary on the Rome Statute of the International Criminal Court: Observers' Notes, Article by Article* (Baden-Baden: Nomos, 1999) at 499.

852 UN Doc S/25704, above note 151 at 58.

853 *Orić* (IT-03-68-T), Trial Chamber Judgment, 30 June 2006 at para 400.

854 Rodney Dixon & Kharim A.A. Khan, eds, *Archbold International Criminal Courts: Practice, Procedure and Evidence*, 2d ed (London: Sweet & Maxwell, 2005) at 460; William A. Schabas, *The UN International Criminal Tribunals: The Former Yugoslavia, Rwanda and Sierra Leone* (Cambridge: Cambridge University Press, 2006) at 141; Joshua A. Romero, "The Special Court for Sierra Leone and the Juvenile Soldier Dilemma" (2004) 2:1 *Northwestern Journal of International Human Rights* 8; Michael Custer, "Punishing Child Soldiers: The Special Court for Sierra Leone and the Lessons to Be Learned from the United States' Juvenile Justice System" (2005) 19 *Temple International & Comparative Law Journal* 449.

promise was reached in article 7.1, whereby the SCSL has jurisdiction over juvenile offenders who were between fifteen and eighteen years of age at the time of the commission of the offence, while at the same time, measures were put in place to ensure that the trial process is in accordance with internationally accepted standards.

The other internationalized criminal tribunal, the ECCC, has no provisions regarding juveniles even though it was negotiated after the SCSL. The reason is most likely because the ECCC has only tried senior leaders and those most responsible. The regulation regarding the criminal procedure for the East Timor Special Panels for Serious Crimes provided for a minimum age of twelve years for criminal responsibility and has incorporated special rules for pre-trial detention, trial proceedings, and sentencing for persons between twelve and sixteen years old. The *Criminal Code of Bosnia and Herzegovina*, which deals with the most serious offences in its territory, only holds children over fourteen years responsible for such crimes, while it contains many provisions setting special measures for the sentencing of persons between fourteen and eighteen years of age.

3) Refugee Law[855]

In the refugee context, the UNHCR addressed the issue of exclusion and children in a guideline issued in 2009:

> When determining individual responsibility for excludable acts, the issue of whether or not a child has the necessary mental state (or *mens rea*), that is, whether or not the child acted with the requisite intent and knowledge to be held individually responsible for an excludable act, is a central factor in the exclusion analysis. This assessment needs to consider elements such as the child's emotional, mental and intellectual development. It is important to determine whether the child was sufficiently mature to understand the nature and consequences of his/her conduct and, thus, to commit, or participate in, the commission of the crime. Grounds for the absence of the *mens rea* include, for example, severe mental disabilities, involuntary intoxication, or immaturity.

855 For views of commentators, see Maystre, above note 746 at 975–96; Jennifer Bond & Michelle Krech, "Excluding the Most Vulnerable: Application of Article 1F(a) of the Refugee Convention to Child Solders" (2016) 20:4 *International Journal of Human Rights* 567–88, both of which argue for the non-application of the exclusion clauses in the situation of child soldiers.

> If mental capacity is established, other grounds for rejecting individual responsibility need to be examined, notably whether the child acted under duress, coercion, or in defence of self or others. Such factors are of particular relevance when assessing claims made by former child soldiers. Additional factors to consider may include: the age at which the child became involved in the armed forces or group; the reasons for which s/he joined and left the armed forces or group; the length of time s/he was a member; the consequences of refusal to join the group; any forced use of drugs, alcohol or medication; the level of education and understanding of the events in question; and the trauma, abuse or ill-treatment suffered.[856]

The Netherlands has provided guidance regarding the issue of child soldiers since 2003 in its *Aliens Manual*, which instructs decision makers not to consider exclusion for child soldiers under the age of fifteen years.

For child soldiers between fifteen and eighteen years of age, each case has to be considered on its own facts, but a number of factors need to be taken into consideration, such as the age at the moment of joining an organization; whether the child entered the organization under force or voluntarily; the consequences of refusing to join; events affecting the free will upon joining; the duration of employment as a child soldier; the possibility of early dissociation from the organization and/or from personal participation in crimes; the forced use of drugs and/or medication; and promotions for "good results." With respect to the factor of refusing to become a child soldier, the manual makes it clear to take into account whether the minor could reasonably be expected to resist the pressure placed upon them, while events affecting the will are related to traumatic events.[857]

There has been some interpretation of these guidelines. In a case involving a person who worked for UNITA in Angola from the age of fifteen to seventeen, the person was excluded on the basis that, as head of logistics, he was sufficiently connected to the crimes committed by

856 UNHCR, *Guidelines on International Protection: Child Asylum Claims Under Articles 1(A)2 and 1(F) of the 1951 Convention and/or 1967 Protocol relating to the Status of Refugees*, HCR/GIP/09/08 (22 December 2009) at 24, para 64. See, also, UNHCR, *Advisory Opinion from the Office of the United Nations High Commissioner for Refugees (UNHCR) Regarding the International Standards for Exclusion from Refugee Status as Applied to Child Soldiers* (12 September 2005) at 8–11; see, also, James Hathaway & Michelle Foster, *The Law of Refugee Status*, 2d ed (Cambridge: Cambridge University Press, 2014) at 528.

857 *Vreemdelingencirculaire* 2000 (C), art C2/7.10.2.4.

this organization to fall within the parameters of complicity.[858] In two other cases — one person who worked for the RUF in Sierra Leone and another for UNITA — the defences of duress and being under the influence of drugs were raised but rejected as the criteria for these defences were not made out. In the RUF case, it was also said that it was not credible that the person could not have refused to engage in rapes and arson, while it was also not credible that he could not have left the camp where he had been stationed given the lax security there.[859] A lack of credibility also led to a finding of exclusion in the UNITA case.[860] In a third case, a soldier who had been working for the Ugandan army from a young age was also excluded, although his involvement was only assessed from the age of fifteen. It was said that since that age, he had had the choice of extracting himself from the army but had not done so.[861] A similar result was reached in relation to a person who had belonged to the PKK in Turkey, had become a member voluntarily at the age of fifteen, was complicit in terrorist activities, and stayed on for another ten years.[862] On the other hand, four district courts overruled the assessments of the decision makers with respect to child soldiers because it was not apparent that the age of the claimants had been taken into consideration.[863] In another case, an exclusion finding by the decision maker was rejected on appeal with respect to a person who had been a member of the RUF and, in that capacity, had carried out a number of serious criminal acts. The considerations in this case included the fact that the person had been voluntarily recruited when fifteen years old, an age close to the legislative prohibition; the fact that the decision maker had interpreted the factor of "events affecting the free will upon joining" too narrowly by requiring a lack of *mens rea* while the legislative intent was to take into account severe traumatization as a result of recruitment with very serious violence; and the fact that the person had been under constant threat to carry out such

858 AbRS (Raad van State, Afdeling Bestuursrechtspraak, or Council of State, Administrative Jurisdiction Division, for appeals from the district courts), May 2006, 200601236/1.

859 Rb, The Hague, Awb 02/3824, 7 October 2003.

860 Rb, The Hague, Awb 03/52062, 22 December 2004.

861 Rb, The Hague, Awb 04/20056, 24 February 2005.

862 Rb, The Hague, Awb 12/39626, 25 April 2014.

863 Rb (Rechtbank), The Hague, Awb 02/50465, 4 December 2003 for Sierra Leone; Rb, The Hague, Awb 02/89347, 13 February 2004 for Turkey; Rb, The Hague, Awb 05/51473, 25 January 2007 for Afghanistan; Rb, The Hague, AWB 04/23019, 17 February 2005 for Sri Lanka.

criminal acts and that refusing to do so had resulted in the killing or mistreatment of others in the same position.[864]

In Canada, there has been some jurisprudence regarding the liability of children for international offences. In the *Saridag* case, the court decided that a person who was a member of a terrorist organization in Turkey while between eleven and thirteen years old could be denied asylum as long as it could be established that the person "had knowledge of some of the acts of violence."[865] The *Ramirez* case dealt with a member of the Salvadoran army who had enlisted voluntarily for a period of two years at the age of fifteen out of revenge for atrocities committed against close members of his family by insurgents. As a member of the army, he participated in excess of 100 engagements and was present during the tortures and killings of many prisoners; he was excluded on that basis, while his defence of duress was rejected as the requirement of proportionality was not met.[866] Another person, Penate, who joined the Salvadoran army in 1978 when he was thirteen years old, was also excluded based on the fact that he remained in the army until 1988 and gradually rose to the rank of sergeant and that he continued to participate in combat missions, planning and carrying out the attacks.[867] This also happened in the *Gracias-Luna* case, involving a person who was forcibly recruited into the Salvadoran army at age fifteen; was appointed after five months' training to be the interrogator for his army unit; and conducted eight interrogations in four months and, after the initial interrogation, would pass the guerrilla suspects to a specialized army unit called S2 for further interrogation and torture.[868] Additionally, a number of other decisions indicated that young persons under the age of eighteen who had been forcibly recruited into the armed forces and were involved indirectly in the commission of international crimes should be excluded.

While the above cases in Canada mention age in passing to conclude that a young person can be held responsible for international offences, this issue was only analyzed in some detail by the Federal Court of Appeal in Canada in the case of *Poshteh*. This case involved a person involved in distributing propaganda on behalf of the Mujahedin-e-Khalq (MEK) in Iran for a two-year period, for which he was given a deportation

---

864 Rb, The Hague, Awb 04/22429, 4 April 2005.

865 *Saridag v Canada (Minister of Employment and Immigration)*, IMM-5691-93 [*Saridag*].

866 *Ramirez*, above note 253.

867 *Penate*, above note 356.

868 *Gracias-Luna*, above note 325.

order under Canadian immigration law for being a member of a terrorist organization. He was between sixteen and eighteen years old at the time. The court made this comment regarding age and responsibility:

> While a finding of membership in a terrorist organization may be possible for a minor of any age, it would be highly unusual for there to be a finding of membership in the case of a young child, say, under the age of twelve. . . . [M]atters such as knowledge or mental capacity are the types of considerations to be taken into account in deciding whether a determination of membership in a terrorist organization in the case of a minor is to be different than in the case of an adult.[869]

There have been two early decisions by tribunals in Australia with respect to child soldiers who were members of the RUF in Sierra Leone. Both had personally killed and tortured civilians, and both claimed that it had been the result of duress as well as forced drug ingestion. In the first case, the narrative of the claimant was not found to be credible with respect to these defences.[870] In the second case, the elements of duress were found not to be present because the claimant had not received specific orders to kill or abuse people, while at the same time he had the choice not to carry out these crimes without necessarily attracting censure.[871]

In France, the refugee tribunal has recognized in general that child soldiers should be given special considerations because of their age. For instance, a young person who had been forcibly recruited by the FARC in Colombia, in a situation of particular vulnerability, was only marginally involved in carrying out surveillance of his neighbourhood on behalf of the FARC and had dissociated himself from the organization whose methods he did not support should not be punished by being excluded from the refugee process.[872] The same reasoning was used for a child soldier in Liberia.[873]

In another case, a child soldier who had been forcibly recruited by the RUF in Sierra Leone after several members of his family were killed by this rebel force, who had pillaged and participated under threats against his life in attacks against civilians and who had left the RUF two

869 *Poshteh v Canada (Minister of Citizenship and Immigration)*, 2005 FCA 85 at paras 48 and 53.

870 N96/12254, [1997] RRTA 492.

871 *N1998/532 and Minister for Immigration and Multicultural Affairs*, [1999] AATA 116.

872 CRR, 26 May 2005, 459358, V.

873 CNDA, 4 October 2021, 21019250, MC.

months after joining, was found not to be excludable.[874] The same conclusion was reached in a similar situation for a member of the National Congress for the Defence of the People (CNDP) in the DRC.[875]

In Belgium, a minor who had been forcibly recruited by the LTTE in Sri Lanka at the age of thirteen and stayed with this organization for seven years, during which time he became the bodyguard for a senior officer involved in reconnaissance missions against the Sri Lankan army, was found to face persecution if returned to Sri Lanka and also found not to be excludable. The latter finding was based on a combination of his recruitment at a young age, the limited duration of his involvement as an adult, and the fact that his involvement did not amount to war crimes (as it was allowed under international humanitarian law) and was not significant enough to be considered complicity.[876] The opposite result was reached in a situation of a person who became an informer for ISIS at the age of fifteen because of his maturity and independence at that age, which negated a lack of *mens rea* required to find him not excluded.[877]

In the United Kingdom, the issue of child soldiers is discussed in a government manual, which states:

> The application of exclusion clauses to asylum claims from children will be rare and must always be exercised with great caution, given the particular circumstances and vulnerabilities of children. Exclusion on grounds of crimes or acts committed by children must always involve an assessment of their ability to understand acts that they may have been ordered to undertake and how far they can be held criminally responsible for them. If there are serious reasons for believing that a claimant (whether a child or an adult at the time of the claim) committed acts or crimes contrary to Article 1F whilst they were a child, for example, while being compelled to serve with armed forces or an armed group, the individual is more likely to have been a victim of offences against international law than a perpetrator.[878]

In the United States, a child soldier was found to be involved in persecution in Sierra Leone and not entitled to asylum status primarily

874 CRR, 28 January 2005, 448119, C.
875 CNDA, 20 December 2010, 10004872, Mr. N.
876 CCE 115.005, 3 December 2013.
877 CCE 239.574, 11 August 2020.
878 "Exclusion (Article 1F) and Article 33(2) of the Refugee Convention," above note 815 at 7–8.

because the defence of duress upon which he relied was rejected on principle.[879]

A tribunal in Luxembourg applied the exclusion clause to a child soldier who had committed war crimes in Liberia, and in Denmark, an LTTE soldier was not excluded because of his age, rank, and lack of knowledge with respect to the attack on the target.[880]

4) Observations

Before examining trends in the jurisprudence with respect to child soldiers in the asylum context, it would be useful to point out that government manuals in both the Netherlands and the United Kingdom urge decision makers to use caution when applying exclusion to children given their often vulnerable situations and possible recourse to defences. The Netherlands has gone as far as to not use exclusion for children who were fifteen or younger at the time they committed offences. The Dutch approach is not used in the UK manual or the jurisprudence of the courts of the other countries.

With respect to all countries that have used exclusion on children, some statistical background will help. Twenty-five situations have been discussed in national jurisprudence in a dozen countries on four continents: Europe (Turkey), Latin America (Colombia and El Salvador), Asia (Afghanistan, Iran, Nepal, and Sri Lanka), and Africa (Angola, DRC, Liberia, Sierra Leone, and Uganda). In the nine countries of interest, six assessed these claims: the Netherlands (with ten exclusion cases), Canada (with five exclusion judgments), France (with four decisions), the United States (with one exclusion judgment), Australia (with two cases), and Belgium (with one situation). It can be expected that this number will rise, especially in countries such as Germany, the Netherlands, and Sweden, which have had a large influx of asylum seekers recently and have put in place rigorous processes to assess both legitimate refugee claims and persons who might have been involved in criminal activities before arriving in Europe.

---

879 *Bah v Ashcroft*, 341 F3d 348, 351 (5th Cir 2003).

880 European Legal Network on Asylum (ELENA), "International Course on the Application of Article 1C and Article 1F of the 1951 Convention Relating to the Status of Refugees" (17–19 January 2003) at 34, online (pdf): https://ecre.org/wp-content/uploads/2016/07/ELENA-Background-Paper-for-the-International-Course-on-Article-1C-and-Article-1F-of-the-Refugee-Convention_January-2003.pdf.

With respect to exclusion, apart from the issue of credibility, age has played an important role in countries such as the Netherlands, France, Denmark, and Belgium. In the Netherlands, legislation makes it clear that children who were under the age of fifteen should not be excluded, while in France, young age was relevant in a case involving a child soldier from Colombia. In Belgium, a person from Sri Lanka was found not to be excluded because of his age, the short duration in the armed group, and his nominal involvement in criminal acts. These three factors led to the same result in France for child soldiers from Colombia and the DRC, in Denmark for a person from Liberia, and in the Netherlands for a person from Sierra Leone. In this last case, having post-traumatic stress disorder (PTSD) and being under constant threat were seen as factors to be considered as well. However, if a person had been able to leave the organization easily, as was found in the Netherlands in respect to a person from Uganda, or if the person continued to work for the organization for a long time after the age of fifteen, as was the case again in the Netherlands for a person from Turkey, exclusion will follow.

Common law countries such as Australia, Canada, and the United States will determine each case on its own merits, regardless of any age, as was done for situations in Sierra Leone, El Salvador, Iran, and Turkey. Given the fact that child soldiers in exclusion proceedings often were directly involved in criminal acts (unlike many cases involving adults, where the allegations are based on indirect involvement) but were also often under the influence of drugs or alcohol or were acting under duress, these defences, especially that of duress, have played an important role in exclusion proceedings. The results have been mixed. In Australia, the duress argument was found not to be credible for a case originating in Sierra Leone. This was the case in the Netherlands regarding the same country, as well as for Angola, while in the United States, duress was rejected on principle in respect to a child soldier from Sierra Leone and in Canada for a child soldier from El Salvador.

In conclusion, unless a child soldier is under or close to fifteen years old, left the armed unit fairly quickly, or can raise the defence of duress with credibility, the chances of being excluded are fairly high (sixteen out of twenty-five cases or 64 percent). However, when raising a credible defence in such situations and comparing the outcome of defences between adults and children, it becomes clear that the latter, due to their unique situation, will be twice as successful as adults (three out of eleven cases or 27 percent compared to 15 percent).

CHAPTER FIVE

Exclusion — 1F(b) and 1F(c)

A. EXCLUSION 1F(B)

1) Introduction

Article 1F(b) reads as follows: "He has committed a serious non-political crime outside the country of refuge prior to his admission to that country as a refugee."

The most important issues, which have been the subject of academic debate and jurisprudence, are the concept of what constitutes a serious crime and the parameters of the notion of political crime. The latter issue has also been raised in the context of the development of the legal proscriptions of terrorism. As well, the connection between refugee law and extradition law[1] has been considered both in the areas of exclusion and *refoulement*. The concern with extradition and *refoulement* is that a person can have claimed or even been granted asylum but is also the subject of an extradition request by the country against which they have claimed a fear of persecution, raising the prospect of a possible hierarchy between asylum and extradition. This problem will be addressed

---

1 The difference between expulsion and extradition is generally described as follows: "[E]xpulsion of an alien is a unilateral act undertaken by a State to remove an alien whose continuing presence in its territory is contrary to the public interests of the territorial State. In contrast, the extradition of an alien requires the consensual cooperation of two States and is usually undertaken by the territorial State pursuant to a bilateral or other treaty in the interest of the requesting State in order to facilitate the enforcement of its national criminal law." (UN Doc A/CN.4/565, *Expulsion of Aliens, Memorandum by the Secretariat*, International Law Commission, Fifty-eighth Session, Geneva, 1 May–9 June and 3 July–11 August 2006, 10 July 2006 at 71–72, para 83.)

in Chapter 6. In this chapter, the relationship between extradition and exclusion will be examined.

a) Extradition

As we saw in Chapter 2, extradition and asylum figured in the debates leading up to the Refugee Convention but not prominently and again primarily in conjunction with the issue of *refoulement*. The main reason this issue had surfaced at the negotiations of the convention was that the United Nations High Commissioner for Refugees (UNHCR) Statute excluded persons who had "committed a crime covered by the provisions of treaties of extradition,"[2] while the comparable provision of the convention was drafted in broader language similar to the final text set out above. Most commentators believe that because of this difference in language, an automatic transfer of extradition principles to the exclusion context was not intended and is therefore not justified,[3] which has also been the view in the jurisprudence.[4] Two aspects of extradition law that might find some resonance in exclusion law are the double criminality requirement and the concept of political offender.

The double criminality requirement means that the conduct of the person whose extradition is requested is a crime in both the country that made the request as well as the country to which the request is

2 Article 7(d).

3 Geoff Gilbert, "Current Issues in the Application of Exclusion Clauses" in Erika Feller, Volker Türk & Frances Nicholson, eds, *Refugee Protection in International Law: UNHCR's Global Consultations on International Protection* (Cambridge: Cambridge University Press, 2003) at 446–48; Atle Grahl-Madsen, *The Status of Refugee in International Law*, vol I (Leiden: AW Sijthoff, 1966) at 290–91; Satvinder Singh, "Will Acceptance of a Universally Approved Definition of Terrorism Make Article 1F of the 1951 Refugee Convention More Effective in Excluding Terrorists?" (2006) 2:3 *Journal of Migration and Refugee Issues* at 113; James Hathaway & Michelle Foster, *The Law of Refugee Status*, 2d ed (Cambridge: Cambridge University Press, 2014) at 549; Yao Li, *Exclusion from Protection as Refugee: An Approach to a Harmonizing Interpretation in International Law* (Leiden & Boston: Brill Nijhoff, 2017) at 103–9; Sibylle Kapferer, *The Interface Between Extradition and Asylum* (November 2003) UNHCR Legal and Protection Policy Research Series PPLA/2003/05 at 102–3, paras 318–21, online (pdf): www.unhcr.org/3fe84fad4.pdf.

4 See in Australia, *Minister for Immigration and Multicultural Affairs v Singh*, [2002] HCA 7 at para 105 [*Singh*]; in Canada, *Gil v Canada (Minister of Employment and Immigration)* (CA), [1995] 1 FC 508 [*Gil*]; *Zrig v Canada (Minister of Citizenship and Immigration)*, 2003 FCA 178 at para 67 [*Zrig*, 2003]; and, indirectly, *Febles v Canada (Citizenship and Immigration)*, 2014 SCC 68 at paras 44–49 [*Febles*]; in New Zealand, *The Attorney-General (Minister of Immigration) v Tamil X and the RSAA*, [2010] NZSC 107 at paras 86–88 [*Tamil X*]; in the United Kingdom, *T and Immigration Officer*, [1996] AC 742, Lord Mustill [*Immigration Officer*]; and in the United States, *McMullen v INS*, 788 F2d 591 (9th Cir 1986).

directed. While this does not appear to be a difficult condition to adhere to, there are three different ways to interpret this requirement. There is the objective method, in which the label of the offence has to be the same in both countries. There is the subjective methodology, whereby an inquiry is made as to whether the essential elements of the offence charged in one country correspond to the elements of an offence in the other country, no matter what the offences are called in either country. And third, double criminality can be accomplished by assessing whether the conduct of the accused is criminal in both countries, in what has been termed the "subjective, abstract approach." The first method was never applied, while the comparing of elements was popular until recently, when the abstract approach gained more currency.[5]

Related to the issue of double criminality is the definition of extraditable crimes. Two approaches are employed: either setting out an enumeration of all extraditable offences in the extradition treaties between two countries or indicating in the treaty that all offences with a minimum penalty amount to an extraditable offence. The latter approach is used more often nowadays.[6] In this context, it is useful to

---

5 Geoff Gilbert, *Responding to International Crime* (Leiden/Boston: Martinus Nijhoff, 2006) at 101–9; Yao Li, *Exclusion from Protection as Refugee: An Approach to a Harmonizing Interpretation in International Law* (Leiden & Boston: Brill Nijhoff, 2017) at 95; Robert J. Currie & Joseph Rikhof, *International & Transnational Criminal Law*, 3d ed (Toronto: Irwin Law, 2020) at 534–35. Gilbert notes at 73 that double criminality is not always necessary and gives as an example the UK *Extradition Act 2003*, where, for serious, enumerated offences, no double criminality is required; see, also, Kapferer, *Interface*, above note 3 at 64–68. The correspondence of essential elements approach is used in Canadian immigration law, where s 36(1)(b) & (c) of the *Immigration and Refugee Protection Act*, SC 2001, c 27 [*IRPA*], makes a person inadmissible who has been convicted or has committed an offence outside Canada; see *Li v Canada (Minister of Citizenship and Immigration)*, [1997] 1 FC 235.

6 Gilbert, above note 5 at 71–74, who indicates that the minimum punishment in the European system is either one year within the European Convention on Extradition approach or three years as part of the European arrest warrant framework. In Australia, the minimum penalty is one year (art 5 of the *Extradition Act 1988*); in Canada, it is two years (art 3(1) of the *Extradition Act*, SC 1999, c 18); New Zealand has the same minimum as Australia (art 4 of the *Extradition Act 1999*), while the United States does not state a minimum but refers to acts of violence as extraditable offences (*United States Code*, ch 18, s 3181(b)); see, also, UNHCR, Guidelines on International Protection: Application of the Exclusion Clauses: Article 1F of the 1951 Convention relating to the Status of Refugees, HCR/GIP/03/05 (4 September 2003), online: www.unhcr.org/publications/legal/3f7d48514/guidelines-international-protection-5-application-exclusion-clauses-article.html [*Exclusion Guidelines*]; Kapferer, *Interface*, above note 3 at 59–63. Interesting in this context is the observation by the Supreme Court of Canada that a connection can be made between an extradition offence and exclusion 1F(b), *Gavrila v Canada (Justice)*, 2010 SCC 57 at para 12, while s 105(3) of the *IRPA* states that a

know that in an international law instrument, the notion of serious crimes in organized crime has been set at four years.[7]

The political offender concept in extradition law has been controversial as this doctrine attempts to justify the commission of crimes in extraordinary circumstances, such as resistance against dictatorships, violent regimes or as an exercise of the right of self-determination.[8] Extradition law has developed mechanisms to ensure that persons involved in what would otherwise be common crimes would not be subject to extradition if the offence had been committed for a political purpose. Several theories, which have been developed to circumscribe the circumstances amounting to such a political purpose, are now reflected in two main types of political offences. The first category is the absolute or purely political offences, which are direct attacks on the integrity of the state, such as treason, espionage, subversive propaganda, or membership in a prohibited political party. Second, there are the relative political offences, which are regular offences but with the political motivation to bring about a change within a state. A combination of these two types of offences is also possible, such as with compound political offences with elements of both absolute and relative offences, while a sequential commission of first a common offence and then a political offence is called connected political offences.[9]

The second category of offences has been the subject of extensive national jurisprudence, and from this jurisprudence the most satisfactory approach has come out of the Swiss judiciary, which developed the predominance and proportionality test. This test entails an assessment of the political motivation, and if the reason for engaging in common crimes is predominantly political, in the sense of there being a direct relationship between the offence and the political goal sought, one part of the test

---

surrender order under the *Extradition Act* is deemed to be rejection of a refugee claim based on exclusion ground 1F(b).

7 International Convention against Transnational Organized Crime, GA Res 55/25, 15 November 2000, art 2(b)

8 Currie & Rikhof, above note 5 at 538–39.

9 Gilbert, above note 5 at 200–5; Nadia Yakoob, "Political Offender or Serious Criminal? Challenging the Interpretation of 'Serious, Non-political Crimes' in *INS v Aquirre-Aguirre*" (2000) 14 *Georgetown Immigration Law Journal* 545 at 552–63; Nicholas Blake, "Exclusion from Refugee Protection: Serious Non Political Crimes After 9/11" (2003) 4 *European Journal of Migration and Law* 425 at 428–34; Currie & Rikhof, above note 5 at 539–40; Kapferer, *Interface*, above note 3 at paras 75–81; Li, *Exclusion from Protection*, above note 5 at 96–97; for a suggestion to expand the notion of political crime, see Amar Khoday, "Resisting Criminal Organizations: Reconceptualizing the 'Political' in International Refugee Law" (2016) 60:3 *McGill Law Journal* 461 at 482–87.

is fulfilled. Connected to this part of the test is the context in which the crimes are carried out in that the more oppressive a state apparatus is or if the crime is carried out during a civil war, the more likely that this leg of the test can be accepted. Conversely, resort to violent means in a democratic society with a fully independent court system will rarely be considered a political offence as there are other means in such a society to accomplish political objectives. Furthermore, the requirement of proportionality must be fulfilled, which means that the violence of the criminal act or the damage caused by it needs to be weighed against the purpose to be achieved. If the result of the crimes causes unpredictable damage or a large number of victims who have no connection to the object of the attack, this part of the test has not been met.[10]

Not only has the methodology whereby a person can rely on a political offender exemption been clarified and narrowed over the years, in some circumstances international treaties regulating state responses to certain criminal behaviours have simply excluded the offences set out in these treaties from being subject to this exemption at all. This has especially been the case with treaties in the counter-terrorism area.[11]

b) Terrorism

At the international level, defining "terrorism"[12] has been elusive.[13] Even if it had been possible to define terrorism before the Second World War as "criminal acts directed against the State and intended to create a

---

10 Gilbert, above note 5 at 205–28; For a recent discussion of the notion of political crimes, see *Gavrić v Refugee Status Determination Officer, Cape Town and Others*, [2018] ZACC 38 at paras 92–106.

11 Gilbert, above note 5 at 259–76; Currie & Rikhof, above note 5 at 540–41. Outside the counter-terrorism area, this provision can also be found in the International Convention for the Protection of All Persons from Enforced Disappearance, which came into force on 23 December 2010 (art 13.1), while in the European Union, two directives have added the following provision to the equivalent of exclusion 1F(b): "Particularly cruel actions, even if committed with an allegedly political objective, may be classified as serious non-political crimes" (art 28.1(a)(ii) of Council Directive 2001/55/EC of 20 July 2001 regarding temporary protection and art 12.2(b) of Directive 2011/95/EU of the European Parliament and of the Council of 13 December 2011 (recast) [the Qualification Directive]).

12 For a detailed overview of the concepts of terrorism and legal responses to it, see the following recent books: Erica Chenoweth et al, eds, *The Oxford Handbook of Terrorism* (Oxford: Oxford University Press, 2019), and Ben Saul, ed, *Research Handbook on International Law and Terrorism*, 2d ed (Cheltenham, UK & Northampton, US: Elgar, 2020); see, also, Li, above note 5 at 299–306.

13 Currie & Rikhof, above note 5 at 355–61; see, also, Marcello Di Filippo, "The Definition(s) of Terrorism in International Law" in Saul, above note 12 at 2–15.

state of terror in the mind of particular persons, or a group of persons or the general public,"[14] such a definitional consensus has proved more difficult over time.

An attempt to conclude a comprehensive counter-terrorism treaty has not been successful so far, primarily because of the difficulty in finding an all-encompassing definition and the related issue of whether such a definition should apply to both states and national liberation movements.[15] However, the negotiations on the Comprehensive Convention on International Terrorism resulted in the following draft definition of terrorism in 2005:

> 1. Any person commits an offence within the meaning of the present Convention if that person, by any means, unlawfully and intentionally, causes:
>   (a) Death or serious bodily injury to any person; or
>   (b) Serious damage to public or private property, including a place of public use, a State or government facility, a public transportation system, an infrastructure facility or to the environment; or
>   (c) Damage to property, places, facilities or systems referred to in paragraph 1 (b) of the present article resulting or likely to result in major economic loss; when the purpose of the conduct, by its nature or context, is to intimidate a population, or to compel a government or an international organization to do or to abstain from doing any act.[16]

While a binding definition at the international level has not been accomplished, certain manifestations of terrorism have been the subject

14 The Convention for the Prevention and Punishment of Terrorism (16 November 1937), 19 (1938) 23 *League of Nations Official Journal* art 1.2; art 2 sets out which types of serious criminal acts are included in the definition of terrorism, such as very serious offences against the person, as well as serious damage to property. The convention never came into force.

15 Currie & Rikhof, above note 5 at 359–60.

16 UN Doc A/C.6/65/L.10, 3 November 2010, Appendix I; the Sixth Committee of the United Nations, which has been tasked with developing this treaty, recommended in its latest report in 2021 to "establish a working group with a view to finalizing the process on the draft Comprehensive Convention on International Terrorism as well as discussions on the item included in its agenda by Assembly resolution 54/110 concerning the question of convening a high-level conference under the auspices of the United Nations." (UN Doc A/75/437, 20 November 2020, para 25); see, also, Amrith Rohan Perera, "The Draft United Nations Comprehensive Convention on International Terrorism" in Saul, above note 12 at 120–28; see, also, at the national level, Bundesverwaltungsgericht (Federal Administrative Court), BverwG 1A 3.17, 22 August 2017 at para 22.

of eleven specialized treaties,[17] which prohibit criminal acts against aviation,[18] maritime terrorism,[19] hostage taking,[20] and acts against internationally protected persons,[21] as well as, more recently, treaties addressing broader issues related to terrorism, such as terrorist bombings,[22] financing of terrorism,[23] and nuclear terrorism.[24] Because of the description

17 See, for a background, Currie & Rikhof, above note 5 at 408–34; sometimes included in such a listing as well is the Convention on the Marking of Plastic Explosives for the Purpose of Detection and the Convention on the Physical Protection of Nuclear Material (see United Nations Treaty Collection, "Text and Status of the United Nations Conventions on Terrorism," online: https://treaties.un.org/Pages/DB.aspx?path=DB/studies/page2_en.xml).

18 Convention on Offences and Certain Other Acts Committed on Board Aircraft, signed at Tokyo on 14 September 1963 (704 UNTS 219); Convention for the Suppression of Unlawful Seizure of Aircraft, signed at the Hague on 16 December 1970 (860 UNTS 105); and Protocol on the Suppression of Unlawful Acts of Violence at Airports Serving International Civil Aviation, supplementary to the Convention for the Suppression of Unlawful Acts against the Safety of Civil Aviation, signed at Montreal on 24 February 1988 (974 UNTS 177); see, for more detail, Julie Atwell, "Aviation and International Terrorism" in Saul, above note 12 at 47–59.

19 Convention for the Suppression of Unlawful Acts against the Safety of Maritime Navigation, concluded at Rome on 10 March 1988 (1678 UNTS 221), and Protocol for the Suppression of Unlawful Acts against the Safety of Fixed Platforms Located on the Continental Shelf, done at Rome on 10 March 1988 (1678 UNTS 304); for more detail, see Efthymios Papastavridis, "Maritime Terrorism in International Law" in Saul, above note 12 at 60–79.

20 International Convention against the Taking of Hostages, adopted by the General Assembly of the United Nations on 17 December 1979 (1316 UNTS 205).

21 Convention on the Prevention and Punishment of Crimes against Internationally Protected Persons, including Diplomatic Agents, adopted by the General Assembly of the United Nations on 14 December 1973 (1035 UNTS 167), as well as the Convention on the Safety of United Nations and Associated Personnel, concluded on 9 December 1994 (2051 UNTS 391).

22 International Convention for the Suppression of Terrorist Bombings, adopted by the General Assembly of the United Nations on 15 December 1997 [Terrorist Bombings Convention]. This instrument criminalizes activities where "a person unlawfully and intentionally delivers, places, discharges or detonates an explosive or other lethal device in, into or against a place of public use, a State or government facility, a public transportation system or an infrastructure facility: (a) with the intent to cause death or serious bodily injury; or (b) with the intent to cause extensive destruction of such a place, facility or system, where such destruction results in or is likely to result in major economic loss" (art 2.1); for more detail, see Samuel Witten, "The International Convention for the Suppression of Terrorist Bombings," in Saul, above note 12 at 109–19.

23 International Convention for the Suppression of the Financing of Terrorism, adopted by the General Assembly of the United Nations on 9 December 1999 [Terrorist Financing Convention]. This convention asks states to criminalize these activities: "any other act intended to cause death or serious bodily injury to a civilian, or to any other person not taking an active part in the hostilities in a situation of armed conflict, when the purpose of such act, by its nature or context, is to intimidate a population, or to compel a government or an international organization to do or to abstain from doing any act" (art 2.1(b), while art 2.1(a) criminalizes acts already prohibited by the earlier UN counter-terrorism treaties); for more details, see Ilias Bantekas, "The International Law on Terrorist Financing" in Saul, above note 12 at 97–108.

24 International Convention for the Suppression of Acts of Nuclear Terrorism, New York, adopted by the General Assembly of the United Nations on 13 April 2005. This treaty makes

in the last three treaties, a general definition of terrorism is emerging that is very similar to the one set out above as part of the draft Comprehensive Convention on International Terrorism.[25] Only the first and the last three of the above treaties have excluded the political offence exception.[26]

One international declaration has had an impact on the interpretation of the relationship between terrorism and exclusion, Security Council Resolution 1373, which says:

> 3(f) Take appropriate measures in conformity with the relevant provisions of national and international law, including international standards of human rights, before granting refugee status, for the purpose of ensuring that the asylum-seeker has not planned, facilitated or participated in the commission of terrorist acts;
>
> (g) Ensure, in conformity with international law, that refugee status is not abused by the perpetrators, organizers or facilitators of terrorist acts, and that claims of political motivation are not recognized as grounds for refusing requests for the extradition of alleged terrorists . . .
>
> 5 *Declares* that acts, methods, and practices of terrorism are contrary to the purposes and principles of the United Nations and that knowingly financing, planning and inciting terrorist acts are also contrary to the purposes and principles of the United Nations.[27]

---

a number of activities related to nuclear materials criminal, all of which have to be carried out with the additional elements of "(i) with the intent to cause death or serious bodily injury; or (ii) with the intent to cause substantial damage to property or to the environment" (arts 2.1 & 2.2); for more details, see David Fidler, "Nuclear, Chemical and Biological Terrorism in International Law" in Saul, above note 12 at 80–96.

25 Resolution 1566 of the Security Council (UN Doc S/RES/1566 (2004), at para 3, already contained a combination of a reference to the international counter-terrorism conventions in combination with the added mental element of the intention to intimidate a population or compel government; see, also, Special Tribunal for Lebanon, Interlocutory Decision on the Applicable Law: Terrorism, Conspiracy, Homicide, Perpetration, Cumulative Charging, STL-II-OI/I/AC/RI76bis, Appeals Chamber, 16 February 2011, at paras 85–113; for more details, see Guénaël Mettraux, "The United Nations Special Tribunal for Lebanon: Prosecuting Terrorism" in Saul, above note 12 at 588–99.

26 For a discussion of forms of liability in these treaties, see Terje Einarsen & Joseph Rikhof, *A Theory of Punishable Participation in Universal Crimes* (Brussels: Torkel Opsahl Academic EPublisher, 2018) at 272–76.

27 UN Doc S/RES/1373 (2001); for more details, see Luis Miguel Hinojosa-Martínez, "A Critical Assessment of United Nations Security Council Resolution 1373" in Saul, above note 12 at 564–87. The connection between terrorism and exclusion has been confirmed in other resolutions

There are also regional counter-terrorism treaties in Europe,[28] the

of the Security Council, such as UN Doc S/RES/1377 (2001), UN Doc S/RES/1624 (2005), and UN Doc S/RES/2178 (2014), the latter of which refers to "perpetration, planning, or preparation of, or participation in, terrorist acts or the providing or receiving of terrorist training, including in connection with armed conflict." There had been an earlier resolution (UN Doc S/RES/1269 (1999)), which stated in more general terms: "deny those who plan, finance or commit terrorist acts safe havens by ensuring their apprehension and prosecution or extradition and take appropriate measures in conformity with the relevant provisions of national and international law, including international standards of human rights, before granting refugee status, for the purpose of ensuring that the asylum-seeker has not participated in terrorist acts." This connection between acts contrary to the purposes and the principles of the United Nations and terrorism can also be found at preambular para 31 of the EU Qualification Directive, above note 11. See, also, European Asylum Support Office (EASO), *Exclusion: Articles 12 and 17 Qualification Directive, Judicial Analysis*, 2d ed (2020) at 46–52, online (pdf): https://euaa.europa.eu/sites/default/files/EASO_Exclusion_second_edition_JA_EN.pdf [Exclusion].

28 Council of Europe Convention on the Suppression of Terrorism, concluded at Strasbourg on 27 January 1977. There is also the Council of Europe Convention on the Prevention of Terrorism, concluded at Warsaw on 16 May 2005, which does not contain a definition of terrorism but criminalizes extended liability, such as recruitment and training. The source for these two instruments was the Council of Europe. However, in the context of the European Union, the Council Common Position of 27 December 2001 (which was repeated a year later in the 2002 Council Framework Decision 002/475/JHA of 13 June 2002 on combating terrorism, which was replaced by Directive (EU) 2017/541 of the European Parliament and of the Council of 15 March 2017) on the application of specific measures to combat terrorism provides a more detailed definition, which was expanded in the latter instrument, which says in art 3:

> 1. Member States shall take the necessary measures to ensure that the following intentional acts, as defined as offences under national law, which, given their nature or context, may seriously damage a country or an international organisation, are defined as terrorist offences where committed with one of the aims listed in paragraph 2:
>   (a) attacks upon a person's life which may cause death;
>   (b) attacks upon the physical integrity of a person;
>   (c) kidnapping or hostage-taking;
>   (d) causing extensive destruction to a government or public facility, a transport system, an infrastructure facility, including an information system, a fixed platform located on the continental shelf, a public place or private property likely to endanger human life or result in major economic loss;
>   (e) seizure of aircraft, ships or other means of public or goods transport;
>   (f) manufacture, possession, acquisition, transport, supply or use of explosives or weapons, including chemical, biological, radiological or nuclear weapons, as well as research into, and development of, chemical, biological, radiological or nuclear weapons;
>   (g) release of dangerous substances, or causing fires, floods or explosions, the effect of which is to endanger human life;
>   (h) interfering with or disrupting the supply of water, power or any other fundamental natural resource, the effect of which is to endanger human life;
>   (i) illegal system interference, as referred to in Article 4 of Directive 2013/40/EU of the European Parliament and of the Council (1) in cases where Article

Americas,[29] the Arab world,[30] Africa,[31] and Asia.[32] Their approach to defining terrorism varies, although none of them recognizes the political offences exception.

Most of the treaties criminalize conduct that had already been mentioned in the international treaties dealing with the various aspects of terrorism and were in force at the time of the conclusion of the regional instrument, with the exception of the Organization of American States (OAS) treaty, which limited itself to the narrow issue of its title, and with the exception of the Organization of African Unity (OAU) treaty, which

---

9(3) or point (b) or (c) of Article 9(4) of that Directive applies, and illegal data interference, as referred to in Article 5 of that Directive in cases where point (c) of Article 9(4) of that Directive applies;

(j) threatening to commit any of the acts listed in points (a) to (i).

2. The aims referred to in paragraph 1 are:
   (a) seriously intimidating a population;
   (b) unduly compelling a government or an international organisation to perform or abstain from performing any act;
   (c) seriously destabilising or destroying the fundamental political, constitutional, economic or social structures of a country or an international organisation.

Article 4 refers to offences related to a terrorist group, while arts 5–13 provide detailed descriptions of offences related to terrorist activities. Article 14 requires that members of the European Union include the modes of liability of aiding and abetting, incitement, and attempt within their legislation; for a discussion of extended forms of liability for terrorist offences, see Joseph Rikhof, "Complicity in Exclusion for Terrorist Crimes" in James C. Simeon, ed, *Terrorism and Asylum* (Leiden & Boston: Brill Nijhoff, 2020) at 156–71; for a more general discussion regarding the regulation of terrorism offences in Europe, see Cian C. Murphy, "The Legal Response to Terrorism of the European Union and Council of Europe" in Saul, above note 12 at 614–25.

29 Organization of American States (OAS) Convention to Prevent and Punish Acts of Terrorism Taking the Form of Crimes against Persons and Related Extortion that are of International Significance, concluded at Washington, DC, on 2 February 1971, and the Inter-American Convention against Terrorism, 3 June 2002; see, also, Mirko Sossai, "The Legal Response of the Organisation of American States in Combating Terrorism" in Saul, above note 12 at 626–38.

30 Arab Convention for the Suppression of Terrorism, signed at a meeting held at the General Secretariat of the League of Arab States in Cairo on 22 April 1998, and Convention of the Organisation of the Islamic Conference on Combating International Terrorism, adopted at Ouagadougou on 1 July 1999; for more details, see Katja Samuel, "The Legal Response to Terrorism of the Organization of Islamic Cooperation" in Saul, above note 12 at 639–53.

31 Organization of African Unity (OAU) Convention on the Prevention and Combating of Terrorism, adopted at Algiers on 14 July 1999; see, also, Martin Ewi & Anton Du Plessis, "Counterterrorism and Pan-Africanism: From Non-action to Non-indifference" in Saul, above note 12 at 654–68.

32 South Asian Association for Regional Cooperation (SAARC) Regional Convention on Suppression of Terrorism, signed at Kathmandu on 4 November 1987, and the ASEAN Convention on Counter Terrorism, signed at Cebu, Phillipines, on 13 January 2007; for more details, see Rohan Gunaratna & Gloria Cheung, "Regional Legal Responses to Terrorism in Asia and the Pacific" in Saul, above note 12 at 669–87.

defines terrorism by combining the general descriptions of both the Terrorist Bombings and the Terrorist Financing conventions. Some of the regional treaties, in addition to the reiteration of the international treaty offences, added other components to the definition, such as the use of bombs or other weapons, which could endanger the public (the Council of Europe convention); damage to the environment and natural resources; engaging in a general insurrection (the OAU convention); murder and serious attacks against the physical integrity of persons; the use of weapons to carry out indiscriminate violence (the South Asian Association for Regional Cooperation [SAARC] convention); and activities that cause panic among people by harming them or causing damage to property or the environment (the League of Arab States convention and the Islamic Conference on Combating International Terrorism instrument).

The two treaties pertaining to the Americas also have a reference to asylum, the older one indicating that nothing in the convention "shall impair the right of asylum,"[33] while the more recent instrument takes the opposite approach by saying that

> each state party shall take appropriate measures, consistent with the relevant provisions of national and international law, for the purpose of ensuring that refugee status is not granted to any person in respect of whom there are serious reasons for considering that he or she has committed an offense established in the international instruments listed in Article 2 of this Convention.[34]

On the national level, recent anti-terrorism criminal legislation follows a variation of the pattern set out in the Draft Comprehensive Treaty by having similar types of offences related to serious crimes against persons or property combined with the added mental element of the intention to intimidate a population or compel a government, often accompanied by a reiteration of the crimes contained in the ten international conventions in this area. For the countries under consideration in this study,[35] Table 5.1 sets out the various elements of the terrorism offences in their criminal statutes.

---

33 Convention to Prevent and Punish Acts of Terrorism Taking the Form of Crimes against Persons and Related Extortion that are of International Significance, above note 29, art 6.

34 *Ibid*, art 12; art 13 has the same wording but in relation to asylum.

35 For other countries, see Legislationline.org under "Counter-Terrorism"; see, also, James C. Simeon, "The Evolving Common Law Jurisprudence Combatting the Threat of Terrorism in the United Kingdom, United States, and Canada" (2019) 8:1 *Laws* 5 at 2–13 online: www.semanticscholar.org/paper/The-Evolving-Common-Law-Jurisprudence-Combatting-wof-Simeon/66c6af88568a985675f5b2e911842398444a4c1a4.

TABLE 5.1

	Intimidation or Compel Element	Underlying Crimes from International Conventions	Additional Mental Element
Australia[36]	Yes	Yes	Yes; acts carried out for an ideological, a political, or a religious purpose
Belgium[37]	Yes	In part	No
Canada[38]	Yes	Yes	Yes; acts carried out for an ideological, a political, or a religious purpose
France[39]	Only reference to intimidation or terror in general	In part	No
Germany[40]	Yes, while adding "significantly impair or destroy the fundamental political, economic, or social structures of a state or an international organization"	Yes	No

36 *Criminal Code Act 1995*, s 100.1(1) under "terrorist act."

37 *Criminal Code*, s 137.

38 *Criminal Code*, RSC 1985, c C-46, s 83.01; the additional mental element had been declared unconstitutional in the first criminal case under this legislation on 24 October 2006 by a trial judge (*R v Khawaja* (2006), 214 CCC (3d) 399), but this decision was overruled, and this element was restored on appeal on 17 December 2010 by the Ontario Court of Appeal in *R v Khawaja*, 2010 ONCA 862.

39 *Criminal Code*, s 421-1.

40 *Criminal Code*, s 129(a)(2).

	Intimidation or Compel Element	**Underlying Crimes from International Conventions**	**Additional Mental Element**
Netherlands[41]	Yes, while adding "seriously disrupting or destroying the fundamental political, constitutional, economic, or social structures of a country or an international organisation"	In part	No
New Zealand[42]	Yes, plus introduction or release of a disease-bearing organism	Yes	Yes; acts carried out for an ideological, a political, or a religious purpose
United Kingdom[43]	Yes	Yes	Yes
United States[44]	Yes, plus "to affect the conduct of a government by mass destruction, assassination, or kidnapping"	Yes	No

41 *Criminal Code*, ss 83–83a.

42 *Terrorism Suppression Act 2002*, s 5.

43 *Terrorism Act 2000*, s 1, as amended by *Terrorism Act 2006* (s 20); for a discussion, see *R v Gul*, [2013] UKSC 64.

44 *United States Code*, Title 18, s 2331.

One recent aspect in dealing with international terrorism has been the listing of organizations or individuals involved in terrorist activities. The practice of listing serves two purposes. At the international level, the listing of organizations and purposes has as its main purpose to have the assets of these persons frozen and forfeited, while at the national level, a designation of an organization as a terrorist entity would result in ameliorating the burden of proving that such an entity fits within all the requirements of the definition of terrorism.

The international practice of issuing sanctions by the United Nations Security Council expanded in 1999 from purely economic sanctions to include freezing the assets of organizations and individuals and the use of travel bans against individuals, both government functionaries and private individuals, set out in a list attached to the resolution.[45] Several other Security Council resolutions have followed, adding names to the original list. Resolution 1373 has become a landmark in this area as it was issued very soon after the 9/11 terrorist attacks and added new forms of freezing assets.[46]

The implementation of these resolutions at the national level is done in the European Union through regulations issued by the Council of the European Union.[47] In other countries, these resolutions are implemented directly by specific legislation and updated when necessary.[48]

---

45 UN Doc S/RES/1267 (1999). This was the result of the 1999 bombings in Kenya and Tanzania.

46 See, for details, Lisa Ginsborg, "The United Nations Security Council's Counter-terrorism ISIL (Da'esh) and Al-Qaida Sanctions Regime" in Saul, above note 12 at 550–63; for an overview, see UN Doc, "Security Council Committee pursuant to resolutions 1267 (1999) 1989 (2011) and 2253 (2015) concerning Islamic State in Iraq and the Levant (Da'esh), Al-Qaida and associated individuals, groups, undertakings and entities."

47 For instance, European Council Common Position of 27 December 2001 on the application of specific measures to combat terrorism (2001/931/CFSP) and European Council Regulation (EC) No 2580/2001 of 27 December 2001 on specific restrictive measures directed against certain persons and entities with a view to combating terrorism both implement UN Security Council Resolution 1373, but other regulations have been issued before as well as after each time the Security Council issued a new or amended listing and most recently as a result of Council Decision (CFSP) 2016/1693 of 20 September 2016 concerning restrictive measures against ISIL (Da'esh) and Al-Qaeda and persons, groups, undertakings and entities associated with them and Council Regulation (EU) 2016/1686 of 20 September 2016 imposing additional restrictive measures directed against ISIL (Da'esh) and Al-Qaeda, and natural and legal persons, entities, or bodies associated with them can apply sanctions autonomously in regards to those groups; see, also, Murphy, above note 28.

48 This is done by regulations under unique legislation: the *Charter of the United Nations Act 1945* in Australia; *the United Nations Act*, RSC 1985, c U-2, in Canada; the *United Nations Act 1946* in New Zealand; and the *United Nations Act 1945* in the United Kingdom. In the United States, there is no overarching legislation, and each resolution is implemented by a specific legislative act.

The listing and delisting of persons by the Security Council have been criticized because of the lack of transparency and judicial oversight, the result being that some of its implementation has been more closely scrutinized in recent years.[49]

A relatively new development in the European Union has been the use of the European Council regulations in areas other than the freezing of assets. In 2010, the European Court of Justice examined two of these practices in cases stemming from Germany. In the first case, German prosecutors had charged two members of a listed organization with the criminal offence of being a member of a terrorist organization without adducing further evidence of the purposes of that organization. While the court felt that, in this specific case, the reliance on the regulation was unwarranted as the membership preceded the listing, the court appears to have had no objections to using the listed entities for purposes other than originally anticipated.[50]

The second case examined the use of listing in the context of an exclusion 1F(b) and (c) situation, and it concluded that a listing is conclusive for the determination with respect to the terrorist organization but not for the individual liability of a member of that organization, or in the words of the court:

> First, it is clear that terrorist acts, which are characterised by their violence towards civilian populations, even if committed with a purportedly political objective, fall to be regarded as serious non-political crimes. It is clear that the Security Council takes as its starting point the principle that international terrorist acts are, generally speaking and irrespective of any State participation, contrary to the purposes and principles of the United Nations.

---

49 The Security Council of the United Nations has attempted to address some of these problems by appointing an ombudsperson to assist the Al-Qaida and Taliban Sanctions Committee in its consideration of delisting requests received from individuals and entities subject to the Security Council's relevant sanctions measures against al Qaeda and the Taliban, which seek removal from the committee's consolidated list (UN Doc S/RES1904 (2009)); for more details, see Ginsborg, above note 46 at 550–63, as well as UN Doc, "Ombudsperson to the ISIL (Da'esh) and Al-Qaida Sanctions Committee."

50 *Generalbundesanwalt beim Bundesgerichtshof v E and F*, Case C-550/09, European Court of Justice, 29 June 2010, at paras 61–62; as a matter of fact, a listing of an organization is "a strong indication that it either is a terrorist organisation or is suspected to be such an organisation. Such a circumstance must thus necessarily be taken into account by the competent national authorities when they must, as a first step, determine whether the organisation in question has committed terrorist acts." (See *H T v Land Baden-Württemberg*, C373/13, 24 June 2015 at para 83.)

> ... It follows that—as is argued in their written observations by all the Governments which submitted such observations to the Court, and by the European Commission—the competent authorities of the Member States can also apply Article 12(2)(c) of Directive 2004/83 to a person who, in the course of his membership of an organisation which is on the list forming the Annex to Common Position 2001/931, has been involved in terrorist acts with an international dimension.
>
> It is clear from the wording of those provisions of Directive 2004/83 that the competent authority of the Member State concerned cannot apply them until it has undertaken, for each individual case, an assessment of the specific facts within its knowledge, with a view to determining whether there are serious reasons for considering that the acts committed by the person in question, who otherwise satisfies the conditions for refugee status, are covered by one of those exclusion clauses.
>
> As a consequence, first, even if the acts committed by an organisation on the list forming the Annex to Common Position 2001/931 because of its involvement in terrorist acts fall within each of the grounds for exclusion laid down in Article 12(2)(b) and (c) of Directive 2004/83, the mere fact that the person concerned was a member of such an organisation cannot automatically mean that that person must be excluded from refugee status pursuant to those provisions.[51]

Common law countries, in addition to using listing for freezing purposes, have provisions in their criminal legislation that allow the executive at the ministerial level to designate an entity as a terrorist

51 *Bundesrepublik Deutschland v B and D*, C-57/09 and C-101/09, European Court of Justice, 9 November 2010, at paras 81, 84, 87, & 88 [*B and D*]; see, also, *Commissaire général aux réfugiés et aux apatrides v Mostafa Lounani*, Case C573/14, 31 January 2017 at para 72 [*Lounani*], and *Shajin Ahmed v Bevándorlási és Menekültügyi Hivatal*, Case C369/17, 13 September 2018 at para 48; for a discussion of the first two cases, see Zarif Yakut-Bahtiyar, *Exclusion Clauses of the Refugee Convention in Relation to National Immigration Legislations, European Policy and Human Rights Instruments; Article 1F Versus the Non-refoulement Principle* (Nijmegen: Wolf Legal Publishers, 2016) at 99–108; Anna Magdalena Kosińska, "The Problem of Exclusion from Refugee Status on the Grounds of Being Guilty of Terrorist Acts in the CJEU Case-law" (2017) 19:4 *European Journal of Migration and Law* 425–46; Olga Łachacz, "The Application and the Scope of the Refugee Status Exclusion Clause in the Court of Justice of the EU Judgment in the 'Lounani' Case" (2017) 1 *European Journal of Public Matters* 97–106; Sarah Singer, "The War on Terror and Refugee Law" in Satvinder Singh Juss, ed, *Research Handbook on International Refugee Law* (Cheltenham, UK & Northampton, US: Elgar, 2019) at 386–88 [Singer, "War"]; and Janja Simentić, "To Exclude or Not to Exclude, That Is the Question: Developments Regarding Bases for Exclusion from Refugee Status in the EU" (2019) 20 *German Law Journal* 111–24.

organization.[52] This designation is done on the standard of reasonable grounds or similar language,[53] which would give rise to an argument that since the level of designation is at a similar evidentiary level as a finding of exclusion in the refugee context, a designation with respect to an organization would be very persuasive for refugee decision makers, especially given the involvement of the highest executive functionaries. The second decision of the European Court of Justice would support such an approach.

Last, with respect to terrorism and refugee law, most of the discussion and jurisprudence in this area has taken place as part of exclusion 1F(b), although terrorism has also been considered as part of 1F(c) and will also be examined under that heading.

2) The Views of the UNHCR

The most comprehensive views of the UNHCR with respect to exclusion 1F(b) are contained in the 2003 *Background Note* regarding exclusion[54] and the 2009 *Statement* regarding 1F.[55] The *Background Note* under 1F(b) discusses three areas: the meaning of serious crime, the parameters of non-political crime, and being outside the country of refuge,[56]

---

52 In Australia, this is regulated in s 102.1(2) of the *Criminal Code Act 1995*; in Canada, in s 83.05 of the *Criminal Code*; in New Zealand, in s 20 (for interim designations) and s 22 (for final designations) of the *Terrorism Suppression Act 2002*; and in the United Kingdom, in s 3 of the *Terrorist Act 2000*. In the United States, the approach is slightly different in that while it is also at the highest executive level (the secretary), the standard of proof is not framed as reasonable grounds but as "finds"; also, the designation is not made in the context of a criminal statute but in the context of immigration, namely, by virtue of s 219 of the *Immigration and Nationality Act* [*INA*], to which the criminal statute, s 2339B of the *United States Code*, Title 18, refers.

53 "Has cause" in New Zealand for interim designations and "believes" in the United Kingdom.

54 UNHCR, *Background Note on the Application of the Exclusion Clauses: Article 1F of the 1951 Convention to the Status of Refugees*, 4 September 2003, online: www.refworld.org/docid/3f5857d24.html [*Background Note*].

55 UNHCR, *Statement on Article 1F of the 1951 Convention* (July 2009), online: www.unhcr.org/protection/operations/4a5edac09/unhcr-statement-article-1f-1951-convention.html [*Statement*], issued in the Context of the Preliminary Ruling References to the Court of Justice of the European Communities from the German Federal Adminitrative Court Regarding the Interpretation of Articles 12(2)(b) and (c) of the Qualification Directice, July 2009, online: www.unhcr.org/protection/operations/4a5edac09/unhcr-statement-article-1f-1951-convention.html.

56 *Ibid* at 14–16, paras 38–45; see, also, European Asylum Support Office (EASO), *Practical Guide on Exclusion for Serious (Non-political) Crimes* (December 2021) at 20, online (pdf): https://euaa.europa.eu/sites/default/files/publications/Practical_Guide_on_Exclusion_for_Serious_NonPolitical_Crimes.pdf [*Practical Guide*].

while it also addresses the issue of terrorism.[57] The 2009 *Statement* addresses in general the same issues[58] while also examining the limits of liability for 1F(b) crimes.[59]

With respect to serious crimes,[60] the *Background Note* makes a number of comments, such as that the gravity of the crimes should be based on international standards and not those of either the country of origin or the country of refuge. A serious crime refers to a "capital crime or a very grave punishable act, such as murder, rape, arson and armed robbery or accompanied by the use of deadly weapons, involve[s] serious injury to persons, or there is evidence of serious habitual criminal conduct and other similar factors."[61] The *Background Note* does not provide a numerical indication as to maximum penalties[62] but instead gives some factors to assess the seriousness of the crime, such as the nature of the act, the actual harm inflicted, the form of procedure used to prosecute the crime, the nature of the penalty for such a crime, and whether most jurisdictions would consider the act in question a serious crime.[63]

---

57 UNHCR, *Statement*, above note 55 at 28–33, paras 79–86.

58 The notion of "non-political" is given attention at 12, s 2.3.1, while the seriousness of the crime is discussed at 19–21, s 4.1.1.1.

59 *Ibid* at 20–22, s 4.1.1.1, as well as 24–25, s 4.1.1.3.

60 For academic writing regarding this issue, see Grahl-Madsen, above note 3 at 294–97, mentioning murder, arson, and armed robbery as examples of serious crimes; Gilbert, above note 3 at 449–50, referring to a very grave act; Akbar Rusalov, "Criminals as Refugees: The 'Balancing Exercise' and Article 1F(B) of the Refugee Convention" (2002) 16 *Georgetown Immigration Law Journal* 815 at 819, referring to various factors and not just a maximum penalty; Martin Gottwald, "Asylum Claims and Drug Offences: The Seriousness Threshold of Article 1F(b) of the 1951 Convention Relating to the Status of Refugees and the UN Drug Conventions" (2006) 10 *International Journal of Refugee Law* 81 at 90–92 and 99–104, using the various factors of the *Background Note* for application to drug offences; James Hathaway & Michelle Foster, *The Law of Refugee Status*, 2d ed (Cambridge: Cambridge University Press, 2014) at 546–554, seeking a connection with extraditable crimes; and Anne Aagten, "Migrant Smuggling in the Mediterranean: An Excludable Act Under Article 1F(b) Refugee Convention?" (2018) 2 *Crimmigratie & Recht* 59–75; see, also, EASO, *Practical Guide*, above note 56 at 13–18.

61 *Background Note*, above note 54 at para 40.

62 The Statement indicates that penalties should be considered part of an assessment of all the circumstances of the crime, above note 55 at 20.

63 *Background Note*, above note 54 at 14, paras 37–39; this is also reflected in the *Statement*, at 12 and 19–20. In this context, see, also, Council of Europe, Committee of Ministers, Recommendation Rec(2005)6 of the Committee of Ministers to member states on exclusion from refugee status in the context of art 1F of the Convention relating to the Status of Refugees of 28 July 1951, 23 March 2005 at para 1e, which says: "[W]hile examining the 'seriousness' of a non-political crime in the context of Article 1.F.*b* the nature of the crime and the harm inflicted are relevant factors. Other relevant factors could be whether most jurisdictions of the member states of the Council of Europe would consider the act in question as a serious

Support for a terrorist organization, according to the *Statement*, can lead to a conclusion of serious crime, but any affiliation with such a group should not automatically lead to the application of the exclusion clauses.[64] The same is said about financial support for a terrorist organization in that the amounts of money donated should be taken into consideration.[65]

Regarding the non-political issue,[66] the UNHCR *Background Note* favours the Swiss test as enunciated in the extradition context, with its emphasis on the predominance and proportionality aspects of the assessment.[67] It also states with respect to terrorism-related activities that it is likely in most cases that these tests will not be met,[68] although "it is not

---

crime, the form of procedure used to prosecute the crime, and the severity of punishment in case of a conviction." Along the same lines, by suggesting a contextual approach, see Ned Djordjevic, "Exclusion Under Article 1F(b) of the Refugee Convention: The Uncertain Concept of Internationally Serious Common Crimes" (2014) 12:5 *Journal of International Criminal Justice* 1057 at 1064–74, and Li, above note 5 at 322–25.

64 UNHCR, *Statement*, above note 55 at 21–22 and 24–25; see, also, UNHCR, *Addressing Security Concerns Without Undermining Refugee Protection — UNHCR's Perspective* (17 December 2015) at 4, para 18, online: https://www.refworld.org/docid/5672aed34.html; European Council on Refugees and Exiles (ECRE), "Position on Exclusion from Refugee Status, PP1/03/2004/Ext/CA, March 2004" (2004) 16:2 *International Journal Refugee Law* at 259 and 271–72.

65 UNHCR, *Statement*, above note 55 at 29, para 82.

66 For academic writings, see Grahl-Madsen, above note 3 at 298–99; Rusalov, above note 60 at 820–21; Gilbert, above note 3 at 448–49; Hathaway & Foster, above note 60 at 554–58; and Guy S. Goodwin-Gill & Jane McAdam, *The Refugee in International Law,* 4th ed (Oxford: Oxford University Press, 2021) at 212–13; all agree with the UNHCR approach; see, also, EASO, *Practical Guide*, above note 56 at 18–19.

67 UNHCR, *Background Note*, above note 54 at 31, para 81. See, also, Council of Europe, Recommendation Rec(2005)6, above note 63 at para 1d, which says: "'[W]ith respect to Article 1.F.*b*, a crime should be considered 'non-political' if it was committed for personal reasons or gain rather than for political reasons, if there is no clear link between the crime and the political goal pursued or if the act was disproportionate to the political objective. Egregious acts of violence, including for example acts that involve random killing and other physical assaults carried out indiscriminately on the population, should also be considered to be non-political. For a crime to be regarded as political in nature, the political objectives should be consistent with human rights principles. International anti-terrorism instruments adopted within the framework of the United Nations and the Council of Europe which specify certain crimes as non-political should provide guidance for determining the political element of a crime." See, also, Li, above note 5 at 325–31.

68 UNHCR, *Background Note*, above note 54 at 31, para 81; see, also, Hathaway & Foster, above note 60 at 558–62; Sarah Singer, *Terrorism and Exclusion from Refugee Status in the UK: Asylum Seekers Suspected of Serious Criminality* (Leiden & Boston: Brill Nijhoff, 2015) at 69–83 [Singer, *Exclusion*]; Singer, "War," above note 51 at 378–80.

the 'terrorist' label attached to such acts which prompts the application of the exclusion clauses, but the nature and seriousness of the crimes."[69]

With respect to the removal of the political offence, in several treaties it is said that "such a designation is significant in determining the political element of a crime in the Article 1F context but should nevertheless be considered in light of all relevant factors."[70] The *Statement* also indicates that the deletion of the term "political" for "particularly cruel actions" in the Qualification Directive[71] is problematic as these words are vague and no meaning has been given to this phrase in international law, only in the legislation of a few European countries.[72]

"Outside the country" of refuge means, according to the UNHCR, before coming to the country of refuge, either from the country of origin or a third country. "Outside the country" connotes a lack of physical presence rather than a legal one, meaning that if an asylum seeker commits a crime inside the country of refuge before being recognized as a refugee, they would not be subject to 1F(b).[73]

The *Background Note* also addresses the issue of expiation, in the sense of whether the serving of a sentence for a criminal conviction or obtaining an amnesty or a pardon has the effect of extinguishing a 1F(b) exclusion finding. With respect to serving time for a criminal offence, the *Background Note* is equivocal by saying that, in most cases, exclusion should not apply, but there could be circumstances, such as "passage of time since the commission of the offence, the seriousness of the offence, the age at which the crime was committed, the conduct of the individual since then, and whether the individual has expressed regret or renounced criminal activities," where the person was still undeserving of protection

---

69 UNHCR, *Statement*, above note 55 at 21.

70 UNHCR, *Background Note*, above note 54 at 15, paras 41–42, 29–30, and 80–82, which is also the position in the *Statement*, above note 54 at 23.

71 Qualification Directive, above note 11, art 12(2)(b).

72 UNHCR, *Statement*, above note 55 at 23.

73 UNHCR, *Background Note*, above note 54 at 16, paras 44–45; see, also, UNHCR, *Luis Alberto Hernandez Febles v Minister of Citizenship and Immigration: Factum of the Intervener* (11 March 2014) at paras 18–19 [*Febles*, Factum]. Along the same lines, see Grahl-Madsen, above note 3 at 299–304, and Hathaway & Foster, above note 60 at 544–46; see, also, Sharelle Aitchison & Martin Treadwell, "Staged Interpretation of Article 1F(b): 'Serious non-political crime outside the country of refuge prior to [his or her] admission to that country as a refugee'; A Periaktos, Scene Setting Problem?" in James C. Simeon, ed, *Serious International Crimes, Human Rights and Forced Migration* (London: Routledge, 2022) at 280–307 [*Serious International Crimes*].

and exclusion could still be used.[74] A similar approach is taken with amnesties and pardons, where questions such as the seriousness of the crime and the expression of the democratic will of the country issuing an amnesty are issues to be considered, in addition to whether the person had been held accountable in other ways.[75]

3) CJEU Jurisprudence

There have been two exclusion cases decided by the Court of Justice of the European Union (CJEU), all in the context of the EU equivalent of exclusion grounds 1F(b), articles 12(2)(b) and 17(1)(b) of the Qualification Directive.[76]

The first case, mentioned earlier with respect to the practice of listing of terrorist organizations,[77] pertained to both exclusion grounds 1F(b) and (c).[78] The case originated in Germany and dealt with two persons. The first one, B, had been a sympathizer of Dev-Sol in Turkey during his youth and had supported armed guerrilla warfare in the mountains for a time. He got arrested in 1995 and was sentenced to life imprisonment.

---

74 UNHCR, *Background Note*, above note 54 at 27, para 73; UNHCR, *Febles*, Factum, above note 73 at para 20, which goes on to say that this applies to 1F(a) or 1F(c) crimes, or at para 24, when the person poses a threat to the community or the security of the receiving State; see, also, the UNHCR *Handbook on Procedures and Criteria for Determining Refugee Status and Guidelines on International Protection Under the 1951 Convention and the 1967 Protocol relating to the Status of Refugees*, HCR/1P/4/Eng/Rev.4 (February 2019) at para 157 , online (pdf): www.refworld.org/docid/5cb474b27.html [*Handbook*], which states this proposition as "unless it can be shown that, despite the pardon or amnesty, the applicant's criminal character still predominates." See, also, Hathaway & Foster, above note 60 at 543–44 and Goodwin-Gill & McAdam, above note 66 at 216–19.

75 UNHCR, *Background Note*, above note 54 at 27, para 75.

76 *Shajin Ahmed v Bevándorlási és Menekültügyi Hivatal*, Case C369/17, 13 September 2018, at para 44, which says: "The content and structure of Article 17(1)(a) to (c) of Directive 2011/95, concerning exclusion from eligibility for subsidiary protection, bear similarities to Article 12(2)(a) to (c) of that directive, relating to exclusion from refugee status, which itself reproduces, in essence, the content of Article 1(F)(a) to (c) of the Geneva Convention." This case dealt with exclusion from subsidiary protection as set out in art 17(1), but, as can be seen, the court is of the view that the same principles should apply as those set out in art 12(2) dealing with refugee protection, which is further expressed as follows at para 45: "It is clear, furthermore, from the preparatory documents relating to Directive 2011/95 . . . that Article 17(1)(a) to (c) of Directive 2011/95 follows from the EU legislature's intention to introduce grounds for exclusion from subsidiary protection similar to those applicable to refugees." For a discussion of the case, see EASO, *Practical Guide*, above note 56 at 13–14 and 17–18.

77 See Section A(1)(b), above in this chapter.

78 *B and D*, above note 51.

In 2001, he was given another life sentence for killing a fellow prisoner, an offence to which he confessed. During a six-month conditional release for health problems, B fled to Germany at the end of 2002 and applied for asylum and recognition of refugee status. His application for asylum was rejected as unfounded based on the grounds that he had committed serious non-political crimes.[79] The second person, D, had been a guerrilla fighter and senior official of the Kurdistan Workers' Party (PKK). Due to political differences with its leadership, he left the PKK in 2000 and since then had been under threat. In 2001, he applied for asylum in Germany, where he was recognized as a refugee on the basis of the national law in force at that time. In 2002, D's refugee status was revoked; according to the Bundesambt, there were serious reasons for believing that D had committed a serious non-political crime outside Germany before his admission as a refugee and that he was guilty of acts contrary to the purposes and principles of the United Nations.[80]

The pertinent questions regarding exclusion before the CJEU were as follows:

1) Is membership of an organisation which is on an EU list of terrorist persons, groups and entities in relation to a person who has actively supported the armed struggle waged by that organisation and perhaps had a prominent position within that organisation a cause of serious non-political crime or acts contrary to the purposes and principles of the United Nations within the meaning of Article 12 (2) (b) or (c) of the Qualification Directive?
2) If so, does exclusion from refugee status pursuant to Article 12 (2) (b) or (c) of the Qualification Directive require that the person concerned continues to represent a danger for the host Member State?
3) If question 2 is to be answered in the negative: Is it conditional upon a proportionality test being undertaken in relation to the particular case?
4) If a proportionality test applies, must it be taken into consideration that the person is protected against deportation under Article 3 of the ECHR and is exclusion disproportionate only in exceptional cases having particular characteristics?[81]

79 *Ibid* at paras 43–56.
80 *Ibid* at paras 57–63.
81 *Ibid* at para 67.

With respect to the first question, the court first addressed the point of whether terrorism can fall within exclusion 1F(b) and (c) and indicated that "it is clear that terrorist acts, which are characterised by their violence towards civilian populations, even if committed with a purportedly political objective, fail to be regarded as serious non-political crimes,"[82] while for 1F(c), the court says with reference to UN documents, specifically UN Security Council resolutions 1373 and 1377, "that international terrorist acts are, generally speaking and irrespective of any State participation, contrary to the purposes and principles of the United Nations."[83] The court goes on to discuss the relationship between membership in a listed organization and involvement in terrorist acts, for which it says that mere membership in such an organization is not sufficient for finding a person excluded but that an individual assessment of the person's involvement needs to be undertaken.[84] However, a listing of an organization involved in terrorist acts with an international dimension can be used to assess the terrorist nature of the organization to which the person belonged.[85] To determine whether a person has been involved in terrorist activities, both objective and subjective criteria need to be examined, specifically "the true role played by the person concerned in the perpetration of the acts in question; his position within the organisation; the extent of the knowledge he had, or was deemed to have, of its activities; any pressure to which he was exposed; or other factors likely to have influenced his conduct."[86] Occupying a prominent position in a terrorist organization is also an important consideration.[87]

Regarding the second question, the court was of the view that danger to security is not a factor in an exclusion determination, saying:

> In that regard it should be pointed out that the grounds for exclusion at issue were introduced with the aim of excluding from refugee status persons who are deemed to be undeserving of the protection which that status entails and of preventing that status from enabling those who have committed certain serious crimes to escape criminal liability. Accordingly, it would not be consistent with that dual objective to

82 *Ibid* at para 81.

83 *Ibid* at para 83.

84 *Ibid* at paras 88–94; see, also, Chapter 3, Section A(2(b)).

85 *Ibid* at para 90.

86 *Ibid* at para 97.

87 *Ibid* at para 98.

> make exclusion from refugee status conditional upon the existence of a present danger to the host Member State.[88]

According to the court, there is no need for a proportionality assessment because "[e]xclusion from refugee status on one of the grounds laid down in Article 12(2)(b) or (c) of Directive 2004/83, as stated in respect of the answer to the first question, is linked to the seriousness of the acts committed, which must be of such a degree that the person concerned cannot legitimately claim the protection attaching to refugee status under Article 2(d) of that directive"[89] as that would require a "fresh assessment of the level of seriousness of the acts committed."[90]

The second case[91] involved a person who had obtained refugee status because of the risk of persecution that he faced in his country of origin as his father was a high-ranking officer in the Najibullah regime.[92] Criminal proceedings were subsequently brought in Hungary against him, and he received a sentence of two years and loss of civic rights for four years for attempted murder and a separate sentence of four years and loss of civic rights for three years for attempted blackmail.[93]

The question referred to the court was

> Does it follow from the expression "he or she has committed a serious crime" used in Article 17(1)(b) of [Directive 2011/95] that the penalty provided for a specific crime under the law of the particular Member State may constitute the sole criterion to determine whether the person claiming subsidiary protection may be excluded from it?[94]

The court's answer was in the negative:

> [T]he answer to the question referred is that Article 17(1)(b) of Directive 2011/95 must be interpreted as precluding legislation of a Member State pursuant to which the applicant for subsidiary protection is deemed to have "committed a serious crime" within the meaning of that provision, which may exclude him from that protection, on the basis of the sole criterion of the penalty provided for a specific

88 *Ibid* at para 104; see, also, Joined cases C-331/16 and C-366/16, *K v Staatssecretaris van Veiligheid en Justitie* and *HF v Belgische Staat*, 2 May 2018 at para 50.

89 *B and D*, above note 51 at para 108.

90 *Ibid* at para 109.

91 *Shajin Ahmed v Bevándorlási és Menekültügyi Hivatal*, Case C369/17, 13 September 2018.

92 *Ibid* at para 15.

93 *Ibid* at para 18.

94 *Ibid* at para 31.

> crime under the law of that Member State. It is for the authority or competent national court ruling on the application for subsidiary protection to assess the seriousness of the crime at issue, by carrying out a full investigation into all the circumstances of the individual case concerned.[95]

The court relied on this interpretation on the dicta in the previous case that an individual assessment needs to be carried out in each case,[96] as well as on the jurisprudence of some of the highest courts in the European Union[97] and in the UNHCR *Handbook*.[98] For this individual assessment, the penalty provided in the national criminal code is particularly important,[99] but other factors should be considered as well, "such as, inter alia, the nature of the act at issue, the consequences of that act, the form of procedure used to prosecute the crime, the nature of the penalty provided and the taking into account of whether most jurisdictions also classify the act at issue as a serious crime."[100]

4) National Refugee Jurisprudence

a) Australia

All aspects of article 1F(b) have been examined in Australian jurisprudence relating to refugee determinations, both at the court and the tribunal levels. In terms of interpretation, the Federal Court of Australia was of the view that while the Refugee Convention should not be interpreted narrowly, for exclusion under article 1F(b), it should be borne in mind that in addition to addressing the issue of a fugitive offender, the clause also operates to protect the order and safety of the receiving state.[101] This led to the conclusion in those cases that a broad interpretation was called for, but, more recently, the High Court of Australia expressed that 1F(b) should be interpreted "restrictively and applied with caution

---

95 *Ibid* at para 58.

96 *Ibid* at para 55.

97 *Ibid* at para 56, which is derived from the 2016 version of the EASO, *Exclusion*, above note 27.

98 *Ibid* at para 57.

99 *Ibid* at para 55.

100 *Ibid* at para 56.

101 *Dhayakpa v Minister for Immigration and Ethnic Affairs* (1995), 62 FCR 556 [*Dhayakpa*], approved by the Federal Court of Australia; by the Full Court in *Ovcharuk v Minister for Immigration and Multicultural Affairs*, [1998] FCA 1314 [*Ovcharuk*]; and by the High Court in *Singh*, above note 4; see, also, *FTZK v MIBP*, [2014] HCA 26 at paras 69–70 [*FTZK*], although the Court emphasized the notion of state sovereignty.

because of the serious consequences of excluding from protection under the Convention a person who has a well-founded fear of persecution."[102]

With respect to the concept of crimes, the term "committed" in article 1F(b) does not require a conviction or even a criminal charge to be applicable.[103] However, if a person has been convicted and sentenced in a foreign country, these convictions are binding upon the decision maker if article 1F(b) is applied to the same underlying facts. If the facts regarding the article 1F(b) crimes are not related to the facts of the conviction, the conviction and sentencing can be used as evidence but are not binding.[104] When determining what amounts to a crime, there is no "requirement that every element of an identified offence must be able to be identified and particularised before the article may be relied upon."[105]

What constitutes a crime is not to be determined by the law of the country of origin but rather by the laws of the country of refuge, even if the conduct took place outside that country.[106] The law applicable is the law at the time the acts were committed rather than when the person came to Australia.[107] If a person commits a crime, such as drug trafficking, which begins outside Australia but continues in Australia, article 1F(b) is still engaged as it is a continuing crime.[108]

Originally, the Australian courts considered that the concept of a serious crime should be applied to grave crimes,[109] but, more recently, a new approach was developed by the High Court of Australia, using a more contextual approach by saying, "Recognition that a crime is a 'common crime' may be premised on the character and nature of the crime, the

102 *FTZK, ibid* at para 75.

103 *YYMT and Anor and FRFJ and Anor*, [2010] AATA 447 at para 22 [*YYMT and Anor*].

104 *Ibid* at para 120; this also applies to conviction in absentia in a foreign country; see *ZYVZ v Minister for Immigration, Citizenship, Migrant Services and Multicultural Affairs*, [2020] FCA 28 [*ZYVZ*].

105 *Ovcharuk*, above note 101.

106 *Ibid.*

107 *"WAT" and Minister for Immigration and Multicultural and Indigenous Affairs*, [2002] AATA 1150 [*"WAT"*], and *YYMT and Anor*, above note 103 at para 29.

108 *Dhayakpa*, above note 101, and *Ovcharuk*, above note 101; this approach continued with Australian decision makers finding drug trafficking into Australia to be within the parameters of 1F(b) (see *NADB v Minister for Immigration and Multicultural Affairs*, [2002] FCA 200 [*NADB*]; *"WAT,"* above note 107; the same was said for people smuggling in *JSDW and Minister for Immigration and Border Protection (Migration)*, [2017] AATA 2420 [*JSDW*].

109 *Singh*, above note 4; *SZJRI v Minister for Immigration & Citizenship*, [2008] FCA 1090 [*SZJRI*]; *Ballibay and Minister for Immigration and Multicultural Affairs*, [2000] AATA 1147 [*Ballibay*]; *SRLLL and Minister for Immigration Multicultural and Indigenous Affairs*, [2002] AATA 795 [*SRLLL*].

modes of prosecution and the penalties which can be imposed."[110] The following crimes have been considered to be serious crimes: murder,[111] abduction and rape,[112] drug trafficking,[113] people smuggling,[114] extortion,[115] and arson and malicious damage to property.[116]

The issue of political crimes has been considered in a number of cases, including at the High Court of Australia.[117] The case before the High Court was about a person from India who had knowingly and actively participated in the unlawful killing of a police officer and other targets by providing information and intelligence about their whereabouts and movements, as well as providing weapons to other members of the Khalistan Liberation Force (KLF) for the purpose of killing them. The tribunal had also found that "despite the assertions by the applicant that his involvement with the KLF were directed solely at achieving the creation of the independent Sikh state of Khalistan, one particular crime was carried out as an act of revenge or retribution against a particular police officer for the alleged torture of a KLF member."[118]

---

110 *FTZK*, above note 101 at para 78; see, also, *JSDW*, above note 108, considering the central role of the person played in the crime as well as the three-and-a-half-year sentence imposed by the criminal court (at para 64).

111 *Singh*, above note 4; *SZJRI*, above note 109; *Ballibay*, above note 109; *SRLLL*, above note 109. Some cases applied 1F(b) in combination with 1F(a) to conclude that killing of civilians amounted to serious crimes as well as crimes against humanity; see, e.g., *VZL and Minister for Immigration and Multicultural Affairs*, [2000] AATA 191; V94/02580, [1995] RRTA 1918; V95/03373, [1996] RRTA 2452; and N96/12101 [1996] RRTA 3349.

112 *ZYVZ*, above note 104.

113 *Dhayakpa*, above note 101; *Ovcharuk*, above note 101; *NADB*, above note 108; and *"WAT,"* above note 107, for drug trafficking into Australia; while *W275/01A v Minister for Immigration and Multicultural Affairs*, [2002] FCA 773 [*W275/01A*]; *"WAR" and Minister for Immigration and Multicultural Affairs*, [2001] AATA 475; and *"SRIII" and Minister for Immigration and Multicultural Affairs*, [2001] AATA 945 dealt with drug trafficking without any connection to Australia.

114 *"SRBBBB" and Minister for Immigration and Multicultural and Indigenous Affairs*, [2003] AATA 1066 [*"SRBBBB"*]; *SRCCCC and Minister for Immigration and Multicultural and Indigenous Affairs*, [2004] AATA 315 [*SRCCCC*]; *JSDW*, above note 108; and *DHKW and Minister for Home Affairs (Migration)*, [2019] AATA 4393.

115 *SRL and Minister for Immigration and Multicultural Affairs*, [2000] AATA 128.

116 *"WBA" and Minister for Immigration and Multicultural and Indigenous Affairs*, [2003] AATA 1250 [*"WBA"*].

117 *Singh*, above note 4; for a discussion, see Peter Billings & Rebecca Ananian-Welsh, "Counterterrorism and the Exclusion of Refugees and Refugee-Citizens from Australia" in Simeon, *Terrorism and Asylum*, above note 28 at 196–98, as well as Administrative Appeals Tribunal (AAT), "Guide to Refugee Law in Australia" at 7.45–7.47, online: www.aat.gov.au/guide-to-refugee-law-in-australia.

118 *Singh*, above note 4 at paras 11–12.

According to the court, for a crime to be political, two requirements must be fulfilled: the existence of a political purpose and proportionality. For the former, it was said that "the first is the requirement that political purpose be the only purpose of the crime in question. In the absence of anything in the text of the Convention to suggest otherwise, there is no reason why the political purpose should be the sole or, even, the dominant purpose of the crime, so long as it is a significant purpose."[119] With respect to the latter requirement, the same judge indicated:

> A crime is unlikely to have a political purpose if it has no relevant connection with the political aims of those involved in its commission. So, too, as has been explained in other legal contexts, "proportionality" is a useful indicator of purpose. The true purpose of actions which are unnecessary or disproportionate to the end which is said to justify those actions is unlikely to be the achieving of that end but is likely to be the satisfaction of some other and different purpose. Actions which are either unnecessary or disproportionate to the political objectives which are said to justify them are, perhaps, usefully described as "terrorist" activities. But for the purposes of Art 1F(b), that description is not, of itself, determinative. The issue is whether the actions in question were undertaken for a political purpose, in the sense that that purpose was a significant purpose.[120]

In applying the decision of the High Court, the Federal Court of Australia found that these requirements for political offences were not made out in a case of drug trafficking, even though this smuggling was carried out as part of a political struggle against a government. The Court found that an incidental connection to a political goal is not sufficient to make this type of activity a political crime.[121]

The High Court decision was rendered in March 2002. Five months earlier, the *Migration Act 1958* had been amended by including a description of political offences.[122] This new provision read as follows:

---

119 *Ibid* at para 44, Gaudron J.

120 *Ibid* at paras 46–47, Gaudron J; along the same lines, Gleeson CJ at paras 20–22 (a passage with which Blake, above note 9 at 441, agrees), as well as Kirby J at paras 120–28, who also points to the difference between extradition law and refugee law (at para 105) and to the fact that political crimes should not be judged in the context of political processes in countries such as Australia (at para 106).

121 *W275/01A*, above note 113.

122 See *YYMT and Anor*, above note 103 at para 14.

(1) for the purposes of the application of this Act and the regulations to a particular person, Article 1F of the Refugees Convention as amended by the Refugees Protocol has effect as if the reference in that Article to a non-political crime were a reference to a crime where the person's motives for committing the crime were wholly or mainly non-political in nature.

(2) subsection (1) has effect subject to subsection (3).

(3) for the purposes of the application of this Act and the regulations to a particular person, Article 1F of the Refugees Convention as amended by the Refugees Protocol has effect as if the reference in that Article to a non-political crime included a reference to an offence that, under paragraph (a), (b), (c) or (d) of the definition of political offence in section 5 of the *Extradition Act 1988*, is not a political offence in relation to a country for the purposes of that Act.[123]

This provision was analyzed in some detail in a tribunal decision.[124] The term "motives" in the amendment was viewed as being different

123 Section 91T; this section was subsequently revoked and replaced by s 5, which under "non-political crime" maintains the same language. The portion of s 5 of the *Extradition Act 1988* referred to in s 5 of the *Migration Act 1958* is called "political offence," meaning "an offence against the law of the country that is of a political character (whether because of the circumstances in which it is committed or otherwise and whether or not there are competing political parties in the country), but does not include:

(a) an offence that involves an act of violence against a person's life or liberty; or
(b) an offence prescribed by regulations for the purposes of this paragraph to be an extraditable offence in relation to the country or all countries; or
(c) an offence prescribed by regulations for the purposes of this paragraph not to be a political offence in relation to the country or all countries."

The regulation in question is Extradition Regulations 1988, which in s 2B excludes a large number of activities from being political, including the ones contained in nine international counter-terrorism conventions as well as the Torture Convention and the Genocide Convention and in addition the following acts:

(a) the offence is constituted by taking or endangering, attempting to take or endanger, or participating in the taking or endangering of, the life of a person; and
(b) the offence is committed in circumstances in which the conduct mentioned in paragraph (a) creates a collective danger, whether direct or indirect, to the lives of other persons.

124 *YYMT and Anor*, above note 103; the tribunal also indicated that the new provision could only apply after an asylum seeker had made an application since the coming of force of this section (at paras 209–10). The new section had been mentioned in two other cases but not applied to the situations at hand; see *SRLLL*, above note 109, and *"WBA,"* above note 116.

from intention but referring to the reason for carrying out an act.[125] The decision also makes it clear that the political exception has been narrowed compared to the High Court decision by virtue of the words "wholly or mainly" political rather than significant.[126]

As is the case under article 1F(a), it is not only persons who personally commit article 1F(b) crimes that can be excluded from the protections of the Refugee Convention but also those who are indirectly involved.[127] That said, the jurisprudence has, for the most part, examined situations where claimants carried out the crimes themselves. Two tribunal decisions found that persons could not be excluded because their activities were too far in the periphery of knowing and personal participation to hold their involvement against them. Both cases involved crew members of ships that were used for people-smuggling purposes. A mechanic who occasionally carried out repairs on the ship's engine[128] and a person who caught fish and cooked meals for the crew a couple of times during a three-month voyage were found not to fall within the parameters of article 1F(b).[129] Last, the concept of expiation is not accepted in Australia.[130]

In analyzing the developments in Australia regarding exclusion 1F(b), two aspects stand out. The first one is that in the political offence exception, the Swiss approach from the area of extradition law has found resonance also in refugee law by emphasizing the dominant and proportionality approach, even though neither extradition law nor the Swiss approach is specifically mentioned. Second, in the same area of political crime, there has been some conflict as to the exact manner of expressing the test to be applied between the legislator and the courts. Clearly, the legislator felt that the High Court had watered down this test too much by changing one part of this test from "dominant purpose" to "significant purpose" and reacted by imposing an even higher test that read as "wholly or mainly non-political." As well, the legislator limited the judicial discretion even further by specifically listing what crimes could not fall within the notion of political crime. This is a long list and includes most activities considered terrorist in international

125 *YYMT and Anor*, above note 103 at paras 215–16.
126 *Ibid* at para 223.
127 *Singh*, above note 4, where the indirect involvement was never raised as an issue of concern.
128 *"SRBBBB,"* above note 114.
129 *SRCCCC*, above note 114.
130 AAT, "Guide to Refugee Law," above note 117 at 7.48.

treaties, even though those treaties themselves have not always excluded the political offence exception. The fact that this hardened approach took place soon after the 9/11 attacks is probably not a coincidence.

b) Belgium

There have been a number of cases involving 1F(b). With respect to a foreign conviction, one case indicated that deference should be given to foreign convictions if the article 1F(b) assessment is made on the same facts, while it would be part of the evidence to be considered if the article 1F(b) examination is used for a different fact pattern.[131]

What constitutes a serious crime involved the consideration of a number of factors, such as

- the nature of the act, which involves a consideration of the level of violence, the modus operandi, the use of deadly weapon;
- the penalty, which can be a reference to a maximum penalty in the legislation or length of the imposed penalty;
- the actual damage inflicted upon a person or property; and
- the rules of procedure surrounding the crime, which means for instance whether the crime is considered a serious or less serious crime in the legislation.[132]

Based on these criteria, a person who had entered an arranged marriage in Syria as a minor with another minor had not committed a 1F(b) crime, even though such a marriage is not allowed under Belgian criminal law.[133]

Some older cases addressed the issue of political crimes and came to the conclusion, without further analysis, that the revenge acts by the Turkish Dev-Sol organization against civilian targets were always non-political crimes and that participation in a bomb attack against a textile factory and against the police was of a non-political character, even though they might have been politically inspired. Similarly, a

131 CCE No 163.448, 3 March 2016.

132 CCE No 239.570, 11 August 2020 at para 2.7; it is interesting to note that these criteria appear to be inspired by the CJEU decision of *Shajin*, above, without referring to it but instead to a supporting document used by the CJEU, the 2016 EASO, *Exclusion*, above note 27; another case, decided on the same day by the same decision maker, makes it clear that these criteria are actually from the UNHCR *Background Note*, above note 54; see CCE No 239.574, 11 August 2020; see, also, CCE No 253.089, 20 April 2021, with a reference to the UNHCR document.

133 CCE No 260.333, 7 September 2021.

deliberate failure of a Liberation Tigers of Tamil Eelam (LTTE) member, who worked as a security officer for a bank in Sri Lanka, to give warning of an LTTE attack against that bank and his participation in an attack on a train carrying soldiers were deemed to be 1F(b) activities.[134] As well, a member of the Radical Students Union in India, which was a clandestine front organization of the People's War Group (PWG) or Naxalites, who was at first indirectly but then directly involved in murder, bomb attacks, kidnapping, torture, mutilation (female genital mutilation [FGM]), and summary executions, was excluded even though the PWG ostensibly carried out these activities for a political purpose. The fact that this person felt he could not leave, after serving in the organization for four years, because of duress considerations as set out in article 31 of the International Criminal Court (ICC) Statute was also irrelevant as he knew what to expect when he joined this organization.[135]

A member of the Muttahida Qaumi Movement (MQM) in Pakistan, during a time when it was known to have been involved in a large number of violent activities, such as murder, while also operating torture chambers, who had moved up in the local hierarchy of this organization until he carried out important functions, such as working in the president's office and being the president's body guard at a particularly violent time in Karachi, combined with the fact that he had joined the MQM voluntarily and aware of its strategies, was excluded even though he had not personally committed violent acts.[136] This application of 1F(b) to persons indirectly involved in serious crimes was confirmed in other cases and, as in 1F(a), involves a substantial contribution with an immediate effect on the crime along with the intention of committing this crime; this was not the case for a person working for the Afghani security service in 1993–95 who actively tried to avoid handing over persons he had arrested for regular crimes to an investigative prosecutor with a reputation for inflicting torture.[137]

---

134 Sibylle Kapferer, "Exclusion Clauses in Europe — A Comparative Overview of State Practice in France, Belgium and the United Kingdom" (supp, 2000) 12 *International Journal of Refugee Law* 195 at 201.

135 CCE No 33.720, 3 November 2009; torture as a serious crime has been confirmed on a number of occasions, most recently in CCE No 217.299, 22 February 2019; CCE No 230.683, 20 December 2019; and CCE No 239.574, 11 August 2020; the analysis is based on references to both international and Belgian criminal law.

136 CPPR No 99-0164/W5686, 17 September 1999.

137 CCE No 230.683, 20 December 2019; see, on the other hand, CCE No 239.574, 11 August 2020, where exclusion was applied, as was the case of a person who had worked for a

With respect to expiation, there was a 2008 case involving a Kosovar refugee in Germany, who had raped his twelve-year-old niece and was sentenced by the German criminal court to three years' incarceration but who had obtained early release on the condition that he would go back to Kosovo, who came to Belgium as an asylum seeker. The refugee tribunal was of the view that since rape was a serious crime in the Belgian criminal code and a partial sentence serving might be a mitigating circumstance but did not affect the application of 1F(b), this person should be excluded.[138] However, the position in the jurisprudence regarding expiation became more nuanced more recently by saying that this is not conclusive in itself and other factors, as set out in the UNHCR Handbook, should be considered as well.[139]

c) Canada

The Supreme Court of Canada has said of the purposes of exclusion 1F(b):

> Excluding people who have committed serious crimes may support a number of subsidiary rationales—it may prevent people fleeing from justice; it may prevent dangerous and particularly undeserving people from entering the host country. However, Article 1F(*b*) cannot be confined to any of these subsidiary purposes. Excluding people who have committed crimes in other countries prior to seeking refugee protection may serve other state interests. It may help preserve the integrity and legitimacy of the refugee protection system, and, hence, the necessary public support for its viability. It may deter states from exporting criminals by pardoning them or imposing disproportionately lenient sentences while supporting their departure elsewhere as refugees. Finally, it may allow states to reduce the danger to their society from all serious criminality cases taken together, given the

number of security services of the Kurdish Democratic Party, in which capacity he handed people over to interrogators of these services, resulting in torture, while on occasion he was also personally involved in such practices, as well as CCE No 226.910, 30 September 2019, regarding a person working for the Afghani security services in a similar capacity; it was also applied in a situation of a person who wrote reports for the Palestinian intelligence service resulting in arrests and then torture of the subject of those reports; see CCE No 213.943, 13 December 2018; see, also, CCE No 253.089, 20 April 2021, for involvement in the enforcement of China's one-child policy, which resulted in forcible abortions.

138 CCE No 16.779, 30 September 2008.

139 CCE No 27.479, 18 May 2009; CCE No 63.606, 21 June 2011; CCE No 69.656, 8 November 2011; and CCE No 118.284, 31 January 2014.

> difficult task and potential for error when attempting to determine whether criminals from abroad (on whom they have more limited sources of information than on domestic criminals) are no longer dangerous. Whatever rationales for Article 1F(*b*) may or may not exist, its purpose is clear in excluding persons from protection who previously committed serious crimes abroad.[140]

According to the jurisprudence, the phrase "outside the country of refuge prior to his admission" in article 1F(b) literally means that only persons who entered Canada after having their claim to refugee status recognized by a visa officer overseas, or persons who made their claim for refugee status at a port of entry and were admitted to Canada pending a determination of their claim for refugee protection, could be excluded. It is not necessary to take the phrase literally because the objective of the convention is furthered by the application of the exclusion at the time of making an application for Refugee Convention status, whenever that application is made.[141]

For the notion of what is a crime for the purposes of this provision, the criminal law of the country of refuge should be the determining factor, although at times some lip service has been paid to the fact that a crime has also been addressed at the international level, such as corruption or drug trafficking, which is seen as bolstering the reliance on national law in Canada.[142]

---

140 *Febles*, above note 4 at para 36, while referring to other judgments in countries such as Australia, Belgium, France, Germany, New Zealand, and the United Kingdom, as well as the CJEU at paras 49–57; the purposes of exclusion in general were described at para 29 as follows: "The *Refugee Convention* is not itself an abstract principle, but an agreement among sovereign states in certain specified terms, negotiated by them in consideration of the entirety of their interests. In *R (European Roma Rights Centre) v Immigration Officer at Prague Airport*, [2004] UKHL 55, [2005] 2 AC 1 at para 15, the UK House of Lords stated (at para 14) that the Refugee Convention to represent a compromise between competing interests, in this case between the need to ensure humane treatment of the victims of oppression on the one hand and the wish of sovereign states to maintain control over those seeking entry to their territory on the other."

141 *Canada (Citizenship and Immigration) v Li*, 2010 FCA 75.

142 *Kovacs v Canada*, 2005 FC 1473 [*Kovacs*]; *Jayasekara v Canada (Citizenship and Immigration)*, 2008 FCA 404 at para 43 [*Jayasekara*]; *Notario v Canada (Citizenship and Immigration)*, 2014 FC 1159 [*Notario*], although this last case is slightly more circumspect by saying at para 40 that "there is no hard and fast rule that the conduct must be criminal in the potential country of refuge" and that "the gravity of a crime must be judged against international standards." More recently, the court was of the view in *Ma v Canada (Citizenship and Immigration)*, 2018 FC 252 [*Ma*], at para 35, that it was "reasonable in deciding not to conduct an equivalency analysis. The jurisprudence suggests that the equivalency analysis is geared to

For a crime to be considered serious in Canada for the purpose of article 1F(b), it must be a capital crime or a very grave punishable act. There is a strong presumption that any crime or its equivalent that carries a maximum penalty of more than ten years in Canadian criminal law is a serious crime even though the actual sentence imposed abroad might be much less than the maximum penalty. Factors such as the elements of the crime, the mode of prosecution, the penalty prescribed, the facts, and the mitigating and aggravating circumstances underlying the conviction should be considered in that context and could rebut the above presumption, while being balanced in a meaningful manner.[143] For instance, "constraint short of duress may be a relevant mitigating factor in assessing the seriousness of the crime committed, while the harm caused to the victim or society, the use of a weapon, the fact that the crime is committed by an organized criminal group could also be relevant factors to be considered."[144] This approach was approved and clarified by the Supreme Court of Canada in the *Febles* case:

> The Federal Court of Appeal in Chan v. Canada (Minister of Citizenship and Immigration), [2000] 4 F.C. 390 (C.A.), and Jayasekara has taken the view that where a maximum sentence of ten years or more could have been imposed had the crime been committed in Canada, the crime will generally be considered serious. I agree. However, this generalization should not be understood as a rigid presumption that is impossible to rebut. Where a provision of the Canadian Criminal Code, R.S.C. 1985, c. C-46, has a large sentencing range, the upper end being ten years or more and the lower end being quite low, a claimant whose crime would fall at the less serious end of the range

---

inadmissibility for criminality. . . . It is advisable to not mix the tests for issues of criminal inadmissibility with issues of exclusion under Article 1F(b)"; see, also, *Okolo v Canada (Citizenship and Immigration)*, 2021 FC 1100, which was not willing to accept a finding of two immigration tribunals as conclusive for an exclusion finding for the same reason. On the other hand, the judges in *Hasani v Canada (Citizenship and Immigration)*, 2020 FC 125 [*Hasani*], and *Brown v Canada (Citizenship and Immigration)*, 2022 FC 736 [*Brown*], appeared to carry out such an equivalency examination.

143 *Chan v Canada (Citizenship and Immigration)*, A-294-99; *Jayasekara*, above note 142 at para 44 (relying on the UNHCR *Exclusion Guidelines*, above note 6 at para 38 as well as jurisprudence in New Zealand, the United Kingdom, and United States at para 44); *Noha v Canada (Citizenship and Immigration)*, 2009 FC 683 [*Noha*]; *Benitez Hidrovo v Canada (Citizenship and Immigration*, 2010 FC 111; *Nava Flores v Canada (Citizenship and Immigration)*, 2010 FC 1147 [*Nava Flores*]; *Németh v Canada (Justice)*, 2010 SCC 56 at para 45.

144 *Jayasekara*, above note 142 at para 45.

> in Canada should not be presumptively excluded. Article 1F(b) is designed to exclude only those whose crimes . . . are serious. . . . However, as indicated, the presumption may be rebutted in a particular case. While consideration of whether a maximum sentence of ten years or more could have been imposed had the crime been committed in Canada is a useful guideline, and crimes attracting a maximum sentence of ten years or more in Canada will generally be sufficiently serious to warrant exclusion, the ten-year rule should not be applied in a mechanistic, decontextualized, or unjust manner.[145]

The new factor related to the sentencing range has been explored in Federal Court jurisprudence to the effect that potential Canadian sentences should be assessed in this context, for which actual foreign sentences imposed can be an important consideration.[146]

With respect to the penalty described, a decision maker should not take into account the cumulative effect of the penalties that could be imposed for all the offences committed by a person.[147] On the other hand, a decision maker should not confuse maximum penalties that can be imposed for the commission of an offence with a mandatory minimum sentence in that the latter has no role to play in the assessment of

---

145 *Febles*, above note 4 at para 62. For commentaries on this case, see James Billingsley, "No Second Chances: The Default Exclusion of Refugee Claimants on Grounds of Serious Criminality: A Case Comment on *Febles v Canada*" (2015) 20 *Appeal: Review of Current Law and Law Reform* 99 at 100–19; Joseph Rikhof, *Update on Exclusion and Inadmissibility Jurisprudence: New Developments Since the Decisions of the Supreme Court of Canada in* Ezokola *and* Febles (April 2017), Canadian Association for Refugee and Forced Migration Studies (CARFMS/ACERMF) Working Paper No 2017/2 at 14–17, online (pdf): https://carfms.org/wp-content/uploads/2017/04/CARFMS-WPS-No10-Joseph-Rikhof.pdf; and Molly Joeck, "Canadian Exclusion Jurisprudence Post-Febles" (2021) 33:1 *International Journal of Refugee Law* 54–88.

146 *Profitt v Canada (Citizenship and Immigration)*, IMM-3193-83 [*Profitt*]; *Jung v Canada*, 2015 FC 464 [*Jung*]; *Tabagua v Canada (Citizenship and Immigration)*, 2015 FC 709 [*Tabagua*]; *Mohamed v Canada (Citizenship and Immigration)*, 2015 FC 1006 [*Mohamed*]; *AB v Canada (Citizenship and Immigration)*, 2016 FC 1385; *Notario*, above note 142; *Narkaj v Canada (Citizenship and Immigration)*, 2015 FC 26 [*Narkaj*]; *Hersy v Canada (Citizenship and Immigration)*, 2016 FC 190; *Mustafa v Canada (Citizenship and Immigration)*, 2016 FC 116 [*Mustafa*]; *Omar v Canada (Citizenship and Immigration)*, 2016 FC 602 [*Omar*]; *Sajid v Canada (Citizenship and Immigration)*, 2016 FC 981 [*Sajid*]; *Nwobi v Canada (Citizenship and Immigration)*, 2018 FC 317 [*Nwobi*, 2018]; *Magoya v Canada (Citizenship and Immigration)*, 2019 FC 1353; *Hashi v Canada (Citizenship and Immigration)*, 2020 FC 309 [*Hashi*]; *Lin v Canada (Citizenship and Immigration)*, 2021 FC 1329 [*Lin*]; *Ayorinde v Canada (Citizenship and Immigration)*, 2022 FC 20 [*Ayorinde*]; *Ahmad v Canada (Citizenship and Immigration)*, 2022 FC 455 [*Ahmad*].

147 *Vucaj v Canada (Citizenship and Immigration)*, 2013 FC 381 [*Vucaj*].

what constitutes a serious crime.[148] The Federal Court has held that the mode of prosecution referred to above relates to the choice made by a foreign prosecutor in deciding to proceed in the case of hybrid offences. This choice could be proceeding with either the more serious variation of the offence in question by way of indictment or with the less serious manner of laying a charge by using a summary or misdemeanour offence. The implication of a preference in which a prosecutor went ahead with the less serious charge is a factor in favour of the asylum seeker.[149] A foreign prosecutor dismissing or withdrawing charges does not in itself undermine the applicability of an exclusion finding.[150]

On the other hand, if an offence is committed outside Canada but the behaviour amounts to a hybrid offence in Canada, of which the summary variation has a maximum penalty much higher than other summary offences in Canada (such as the offence of sexual interference), a person can be excluded.[151] The courts have indicated that the seriousness of an offence is measured by the criminal law in Canada at the time of the refugee determination[152] rather than at the time of commission.[153] A lenient sentence does not diminish the seriousness of the crime.[154] Aggravating factors can include habitual criminal conduct as well as possible psychological harm to victims;[155] absconding from the jurisdiction where the crime was committed;[156] and committing crimes after being given protection in another country.[157] Mitigating

---

148 *Canada (Citizenship and Immigration) v Nwobi*, 2014 FC 520 [*Nwobi*, 2014].

149 *Canada (Citizenship and Immigration) v Lopez Velasco*, 2011 FC 627 [*Lopez Velasco*]; and *Canada (Citizenship and Immigration) v Ammar*, 2011 FC 1094 [*Ammar*]. In the same vein, see *Vucaj*, above note 147, and *Narkaj*, above note 146. For examples where exclusion was upheld, see *Hernandez Gomez v Canada (Citizenship and Immigration)*, 2014 FC 271 [*Hernandez Gomez*]; *Reyes v Canada (Citizenship and Immigration)*, 2015 FC 1015 [*Reyes*]; and *Ma*, above note 142.

150 *Hashi*, above note 146.

151 *Canada (Citizenship and Immigration) v Raina*, 2012 FC 618 [*Raina*].

152 *Guerra Diaz v Canada (Citizenship and Immigration)*, 2013 FC 88 [*Guerra Diaz*]; *Gamboa Micolta v Canada (Citizenship and Immigration)*, 2013 FC 367 [*Gamboa Micolta*]; and *Notario v Canada (Citizenship and Immigration)*, 2014 FC 1159.

153 *Sanchez v Canada (Citizenship and Immigration*, 2013 FC 913 [*Sanchez*, 2013] (upheld on appeal in *Sanchez v Canada (Citizenship and Immigration)*, 2014 FCA 157 [*Sanchez*, 2014]).

154 *Sanchez*, 2013, above note 153; *Ma*, above note 142.

155 *Poggio Guerrero v Canada*, 2010 FC 384; *Raina*, above note 151; *Gamboa Micolta*, above note 152; *Gudima v Canada (Citizenship and Immigration)*, 2013 FC 382 [*Gudima*]; and *Canada (Citizenship and Immigration) v Pierre*, 2013 FC 810 [*Pierre*].

156 *Gamboa Micolta*, above note 152; *Unachukwu v Canada (Citizenship and Immigration)*, 2014 FC 199 [*Unachukwu*].

157 *Narkaj*, above note 146.

circumstances can include admission of guilt by the claimant; a favourable plea bargain; a troubled childhood;[158] the claimant's age;[159] a lack of previous convictions; a limited amount of drugs; the fact that the substance contained methamphetamine as opposed to pure methamphetamine;[160] the claimant's refugee status and life in a marginalized neighbourhood;[161] and the claimant's addiction to painkillers resulting from an injury incurred during a criminal gang fight; their cooperation with authorities and their role as an instrumental key witness for the Crown; and the lack of weapons in the drug trafficking offence and the absence of serious injury resulting from the offence.[162] Although mitigating circumstances are part of the considerations of the decision maker, these circumstances are only relevant if they relate to the commission of the offence at that time and not to issues with respect to the character of the refugee claimant after the event in question (which brings up the question of expiation, discussed below in the text associated with footnotes 218–30). As such, post-conviction conduct that sheds light on the factors highlighted in *Jayasekara*, such as probation and parole violations related to the offence in question, is relevant for article 1F(b).[163] However, a full defence such as duress goes beyond being a mitigating factor and instead negates liability under article 1F(b) if accepted.[164]

---

158 *Gudima*, above note 155; *Narkaj*, above note 146.

159 Exclusion can still be applied even if the person was a minor when they committed an offence; see *Gardijan v Canada (Citizenship and Immigration)*, 2022 FC 421 [*Gardijan*].

160 *Shire v Canada (Citizenship and Immigration)*, 2012 FC 97.

161 *Ibid*.

162 *Vucaj*, above note 147.

163 *Jayasekara*, above note 142; *Chernikov v Canada (Citizenship and Immigration)*, 2013 FC 649 [*Chernikov*]. However, see *Profitt*, above note 146 where it is said that "evidence of unflattering post-conviction noncriminal behaviour (e.g., failure to accept full responsibility for one's past) is also irrelevant," while in *Ma*, above note 142 at para 43, Favel J said, "I do not see the fact that the Applicant continued working with the village council after completing his sentence as extraneous to the offence."

164 *Guerra Diaz*, above note 152; and *Villalobos v Canada (Citizenship and Immigration)*, 2015 FC 60 [*Villalobos*]. In *Jimenez v Canada (Citizenship and Immigration)*, 2012 FC 1231, the claim regarding duress was rejected because the applicant, who had the onus to prove this claim, did not provide any evidence in support.

The following have all been held to be serious crimes for the purposes of article 1F(b) in Canada: murder,[165] manslaughter,[166] drug trafficking,[167] human trafficking and pimping,[168] aggravated assault,[169] assault,[170] assault with a deadly weapon,[171] sexual assault,[172] spousal assault,[173] drunk driving causing bodily harm,[174] bombing,[175] *coup d'états* (including activities such as delivering weapons and seizing radio and

---

165 *AC v Canada (Minister of Citizenship and Immigration)*, 2003 FC 1500 [*AC*]; *Feimi v Canada (Citizenship and Immigration)*, 2012 FC 262 (upheld on appeal in *Feimi v Canada (Citizenship and Immigration)*, 2012 FCA 325); *Tincul v Canada (Citizenship and Immigration)*, 2013 FC 628; and *Nwobi*, 2014, above note 148.

166 *Abu Ganem v Canada (Citizenship and Immigration)*, 2011 FC 1147 [*Abu Ganem*].

167 *Malouf v Canada (Minister of Citizenship and Immigration)*, A-19-95; *Chan v Canada (Citizenship and Immigration)*, A-294-99; *Canada (Minister of Citizenship and Immigration) v Maan*, 2005 FC 1682; *Garcia Médina v Canada (Minister of Citizenship and Immigration)*, 2006 FC 62; *Canada (Minister of Citizenship and Immigration) v Jan*, 2006 FC 40; *Garcia Rodriguez v Canada (Citizenship and Immigration)*, 2007 FC 462 [*Garcia Rodriguez*]; *Jayasekara*, above note 142; *Chawah v Canada (Citizenship and Immigration)*, 2009 FC 324; *Betancour v Canada (Citizenship and Immigration)*, 2009 FC 767; *Roberts v Canada (Citizenship and Immigration)*, 2011 FC 632; *Rojas Camacho v Canada (Citizenship and Immigration)*, 2011 FC 789 [*Rojas Camacho*]; *Poggio Guerrero v Canada (Citizenship and Immigration)*, 2012 FC 937; *Martinez Cuero v Canada (Citizenship and Immigration)*, 2012 FC 191; *Vucaj*, above note 147; *Sanchez*, 2013, above note 153 (upheld on appeal in *Sanchez*, 2014, above note 153; *Nwobi*, 2014, above note 148; *Villalobos*, above note 164; *Skoro v Canada (Citizenship and Immigration)*, 2015 FC 139; *Nwobi*, 2018, above note 146; *Rodrigues Candelario v Canada (Citizenship and Immigration)*, 2018 FC 864; and *Brown*, above note 142.

168 *Abbas v Canada (Citizenship and Immigration)*, 2019 FC 12.

169 *Omar*, above note 146.

170 *Canada (Minister of Citizenship and Immigration) v Nyari*, 2002 FCT 979 [*Nyari*]; *Nava Flores*, above note 143; *Reyes*, above note 149.

171 *Hernandez Febles v Canada (Citizenship and Immigration)*, 2011 FC 1103 (upheld on appeal in *Hernandez Febles v Canada (Citizenship and Immigration)*, 2012 FCA 324, and in *Febles*, above note 4.

172 *Shamlou v Canada (Minister of Citizenship and Immigration)*, IMM-4967-94; the same was decided about other sexual offences in *Raina v Canada (Minister of Citizenship and Immigration)*, 2011 FC 19, and *Arevalo Pineda v Canada (Citizenship and Immigration)*, 2010 FC 454, but minor sexual offences do not result in exclusion according to *Lopez Velasco*, above note 149, and *Ammar*, above note 149.

173 *Radi v Canada (Citizenship and Immigration)*, 2012 FC 16 [*Radi*]; *Unachukwu*, above note 156; *Ahmad* , above note 146.

174 *Chernikov*, above note 163.

175 *Gil*, above note 4.

TV stations),[176] kidnapping,[177] sabotage,[178] armed robbery,[179] arson,[180] terrorist acts,[181] serious crimes as an organized crime gang member,[182] child abduction,[183] and producing child pornography.[184] In addition, economic crimes such as embezzlement,[185] smuggling,[186] tax evasion,[187] money laundering,[188]customs smuggling,[189] illegal arms exports,[190] weapons offences,[191] taking bribes,[192] offering bribes,[193] usury,[194] fraud,[195] burglary,[196] evading arrest,[197] use of a forged document,[198] forgery of a passport,[199] forgery and identity fraud,[200] and theft involving large amounts of money[201] have all been found to be excludable

176 *Gregorio v Canada (Minister of Citizenship and Immigration)*, IMM-1447-98 [*Gregorio*].

177 *Taleb v Canada (Minister of Citizenship and Immigration)*, IMM-1449-98.

178 *Vergara v Canada (Minister of Citizenship and Immigration)*, 2001 FCT 474 [*Vergara*].

179 *Ibid*; *Sharma v Canada (Minister of Citizenship and Immigration)*, 2003 FCT 289 [*Sharma*]; and *Valdespino Partida v Canada (Citizenship and Immigration)*, 2013 FC 359 [*Valdespino Partida*].

180 *Zrig v Canada (Minister of Citizenship and Immigration)*, 2001 FCT 1043 [*Zrig*, 2001].

181 *Zrig*, 2003, above note 4; *Mohamed*, above note 146.

182 *Cho v Canada (Citizenship and Immigration)*, 2013 FC 45.

183 *Kovacs*, above note 142; *Paris Montoya v Canada (Minister of Citizenship and Immigration)*, 2005 FC 1674.

184 *Gardijan*, above note 159.

185 *Xie v Canada (Minister of Citizenship and Immigration)*, 2004 FCA 250; *Ma*, above note 142.

186 *Lai v Canada (Minister of Citizenship and Immigration)*, 2005 FCA 125 [*Lai*].

187 *Ibid*; *Simkovic v Canada (Citizenship and Immigration)*, 2014 FC 113.

188 *Naranjo v Canada (Citizenship and Immigration)*, 2011 FC 1127; *Talanov v Canada (Citizenship and Immigration)*, 2020 FC 484.

189 *Florea v Canada (Minister of Citizenship and Immigration)*, 2005 FC 1472.

190 *Sajid*, above note 146.

191 *Hernandez Gomez*, above note 149.

192 *Vlad v Canada (Citizenship and Immigration)*, 2007 FC 172.

193 *Lai*, above note 186.

194 *Rudyak v Canada (Minister of Citizenship and Immigration)* 2006 FC 1141 [*Rudyak*].

195 *Iliev v Canada (Minister of Citizenship and Immigration)*, 2005 FC 395; *Lai*, above note 186; *Hany Zeng v Canada (Citizenship and Immigration)*, 2008 FC 956; *Xu v Canada (Minister of Citizenship and Immigration)*, 2005 FC 970; *Codas Martin v Canada (Citizenship and Immigration)*, 2007 FC 994; *Noha*, above note 143; *Jung*, above note 146; *Notario*, above note 142; *Santha v Canada (Citizenship and Immigration)*, 2021 FC 1353; *Ayorinde*, above note 146.

196 *Pierre*, above note 155; *Gamboa Micolta*, above note 152; in two other cases, breaking and entering was not considered to be a serious crime: in *Vucaj*, above note 147 and *Narkaj*, above note 146.

197 *Gamboa Micolta*, above note 152.

198 *Durango v Canada (Citizenship and Immigration)*, 2018 FC 146.

199 *Hasani*, above note 142; *AB v Canada (Citizenship and Immigration)*, 2022 FC 711.

200 *Tabagua*, above note 146; *Mustafa*, above note 146.

201 *Ivanov v Canada (Minister of Citizenship and Immigration)*, 2004 FC 1210; *Farkas v Canada (Citizenship and Immigration)*, 2007 FC 277; and *Valdespino Partida*, above note 179, although in one case an exclusion involving robbery and theft by the tribunal was overruled by the

crimes. This is because exclusion under article 1F(b) refers to serious crimes in general, without making a distinction between violent crime and purely economic crime.[202] However, shoplifting, even when committed in a habitual fashion, is not a serious crime,[203] nor is writing a false cheque,[204] simple drug possession,[205] or providing money and untraceable phones to a drug cartel in Mexico.[206] A conviction for causing death by dangerous driving was also found not to be excludable on the specific facts of the case.[207]

A foreign conviction can be relied upon as long as the foreign laws are not so unjust as to be intolerable[208] and there is no challenge to the integrity of the applicant's conviction or the judicial system of the foreign country.[209] However, if the judicial system is allegedly corrupt, a decision maker can go behind the record of conviction.[210] The fact that charges were dismissed in a foreign jurisdiction does not, by itself, mean that a serious crime was not committed, and the decision maker can rely on other evidence, including the evidence adduced in the criminal trial that did not result in a conviction, to assess whether exclusion under article 1F(b) should be applied. Factors with respect to the use of the evidence that led to the dismissal of charges include whether the dismissal was for technical or legal reasons, as well as in which country the dismissal took place.[211]

Since both articles 1F(a) and 1F(b) use the term "committed," it means that not only persons who personally committed serious, non-political crimes are captured by article 1F(b) but also persons who

---

Federal Court without further reasons, in the case of *Canada (Citizenship and Immigration) v Pulido Diaz*, 2011 FC 738.

202 *Xie v Canada (Minister of Citizenship and Immigration)*, 2003 FC 1023.

203 *Brzezinski v Canada (Minister of Citizenship and Immigration)*, [1998] 4 FC 525.

204 *Canada (Citizenship and Immigration) v Toktok*, 2013 FC 1150 [*Toktok*].

205 *Mohamad Jawad v Canada (Citizenship and Immigration)*, 2012 FC 232.

206 *Notario*, above note 142.

207 *Okolo v Canada (Citizenship and Immigration)*, 2021 FC 1100; see, also, *Lin*, above note 146.

208 *Notario*, above note 142.

209 *Abu Ganem*, above note 166; *Mansouri v Canada (Citizenship and Immigration)*, 2018 FC 144; *Karicka v Canada (Citizenship and Immigration)*, 2021 FC 1005.

210 *Altun v Canada (Citizenship and Immigration)*, 2012 FC 1034; *Toktok*, above note 204; *Ma*, above note 142; *Gurbuz v Canada (Citizenship and Immigration)*, 2018 FC 684.

211 *Jawad v Canada (Citizenship and Immigration)*, 2012 FC 232.

were complicit in committing such activities.[212] This includes the notion of being a member of an organization with a limited, brutal purpose.[213]

With respect to political crimes, the Federal Court of Appeal upheld a tribunal decision to exclude an individual who had placed many Molotov cocktails in crowded business premises owned by wealthy supporters of the Khomeini government in Iran and by members of local revolutionary committees. The court stated that while the political offence exception occurs in both extradition and refugee law, there are substantial differences between the two systems; therefore, "these considerations would seem to . . . point to a need for even greater caution in characterizing a crime as political for the purposes of applying article 1F(b) than for the purpose of denying extradition."[214] After considering in detail the extradition law of other countries, the court decided that the incidence test from extradition law was also the most appropriate to assess the political offence exception in refugee law. In applying this test to the facts of the case, the court was of the view that there was no objective, rational connection between injuring the commercial interests of certain wealthy supporters of the regime and any realistic goal of forcing the regime itself to fall or change its ways or politics. This nexus was too tenuous to justify the kind of indiscriminate violence admitted to by the refugee claimant.[215] Furthermore, the means employed by the person would deny them from any claim of being political in nature,

---

212 *Gregorio*, above note 176; *Zrig*, 2003, above note 4 (relying on Australian jurisprudence); *Jaouadi v Canada (Minister of Citizenship and Immigration)*, 2005 FC 1256; and *Rudyak*, above note 194.

213 *Chong v Canada (Minister of Citizenship and Immigration)*, 2001 FCT 1335, which stands for the proposition that Hong Kong triads have a single, brutal purpose, that being the commission of crime for financial gain, while *Zrig*, 2003, above note 4, says the same about membership in a terrorist organization.

214 *Gil*, above note 4. For a comment, see James C. Hathaway & Colin J. Harvey, "Framing Refugee Protection in the New World Disorder" (2001) 34:2 *Cornell International Law Journal* 257 at 299.

215 *Gil*, above note 4. No claimant has been able to convince a court so far that their criminal activities fit the political offence exception, primarily by already failing this first part of the test, which was said not to apply in *Gregorio*, above note 176, during a *coup d'etat* in Venezuela, nor in the kidnapping of a terrorist for the FBI in exchange for $2 million and US citizenship (*Taleb v Canada (Minister of Citizenship and Immigration)*, IMM-1449-98), nor armed robbery and acts of sabotage against the Chilean government as a member of the communist party (*Vergara*, above note 178). The same conclusion was reached in a situation where a person had been involved in armed robberies in Nepal as a member of the Communist party (*Sharma*, above note 179); where a person had committed arson as part of the political goal of establishing a fundamentalist government in Tunisia (*Zrig*, 2001, above

not because innocent bystanders were killed but because the attacks were not carried out against armed adversaries and were bound to injure the innocent. "Violence of a sort where deadly force is directed against unarmed civilian commercial targets in circumstances where serious or death to innocent bystanders is simply inevitable, is wholly disproportionate to any legitimate objective, even if such bystanders are the family of the president of a repressive regime."[216] Whenever the notion of political crimes was raised as an argument, it was rejected each time.[217]

With respect to expiation, the Supreme Court of Canada had stated *in obiter* that exclusion under article 1F(b) would not apply in a situation where a person has already been convicted of the crimes and served their sentence.[218] This statement became eroded over time[219] until the Federal Court of Appeal explicitly came to a different conclusion than the Supreme Court.

Based on the purposes of article 1F(b) and the factors to be considered in deciding whether a crime is serious, as discussed above, the court came to the conclusion that a conviction and sentence served is one of the factors to be considered and that such an event does not bar

---

note 180); and where a person had committed economic crimes such as fraud, smuggling, and tax evasion in China (*Lai*, above note 186).

216 *Gil*, above note 4; *Gregorio*, above note 176; and *AC*, above note 165; in the last case, which involved the killing of the president of Bangladesh in the early 1970s as part of an attempt to overthrow the government but also the killing of his family and entourage, the political defence exemption was found not to be applicable, but the reasoning is not clear as to whether it was based on only the lack of proportionality or also the lack of nexus.

217 *Gregorio*, above note 176; *Vergara*, above note 178; *Sharma*, above note 179; and *Durango v Canada (Citizenship and Immigration)*, 2012 FC 1081.

218 *Canada (Attorney General) v Ward*, [1993] 2 SCR 689, followed by *Chan v Canada (Citizenship and Immigration)*, A-294-99; *Vergara*, above note 178 (which did apply the exclusion clause for crimes the claimant had not been convicted of); *Nyari*, above note 170 (where exclusion was applied because the claimant had escaped from prison and had not served his complete sentence); *Garcia Médina v Canada (Minister of Citizenship and Immigration)*, 2006 FC 62; *Al Husin v Canada (Minister of Citizenship and Immigration)*, 2006 FC 1451; and *Garcia Rodriguez*, above note 167 (where the person had not served his sentence because he breached his probation upon release).

219 *Zrig*, 2003, above note 4 at para 129, *in obiter* indicating that "it follows that under Article 1F(*b*) it is possible to exclude both the perpetrators of serious non-political crimes seeking to use the Convention to elude local justice and the perpetrators of serious non-political crimes that a State feels should not be allowed to enter its territory, whether or not they are fleeing local justice, whether or not they have been prosecuted for their crimes, whether or not they have been convicted of those crimes and whether or not they have served the sentences imposed on them in respect of those crimes."

the application of exclusion under article 1F(b).[220] This approach was followed at the tribunal and Federal Court levels.[221]

This issue of expiation was laid to rest by the Supreme Court in 2014 in the *Febles* case, although the Court was divided.[222] The majority relied on the various means of treaty interpretation provided by article 31(1) of the Vienna Convention on the Law of Treaties (the ordinary meaning of the text of article 1F(b); its context; the object and purpose of the Refugee Convention as a whole and article 1F(b); the *travaux préparatoires*; and 1F(b) jurisprudence) to set the following propositions regarding expiation for 1F(b):

- The meaning of the words used in 1F(b) only refers to circumstances during the commission of the crime and not subsequent to it.[223]
- Article 1F(b) does not only apply to fugitives from justice because exclusion 1F(a) and (b) both use the term "committed," and there was no suggestion that 1F(a) should only be applied to fugitives.[224]
- With respect to reliance on the *travaux préparatoires*, there is no reason to rely on them as that would only be necessary if the meaning of 1F(b) was ambiguous or obscure, which it is not; additionally, "the aim of the drafters was to protect the dignity of refugee status by excluding serious criminals from such status."[225]
- After canvassing earlier Canadian jurisprudence as well as the caselaw of the CJEU, Australia, Belgium, France, New Zealand, and the United Kingdom, it concludes that "the dominant tide of the jurisprudence is inconsistent with the conclusion that Article 1F(*b*) operates so as to exclude only fugitives, as well as with the

220 *Ibid* at paras 27, 41, and 57.

221 *Noha*, above note 143; *Nava Flores*, above note 143; *Rojas Camacho*, above note 167; *Abu Ganem*, above note 166; *Martinez Cuero v Canada (Citizenship and Immigration)*, 2012 FC 191; *Poggio Guerrero v Canada*, 2012 FC 384; *Cho v Canada (Citizenship and Immigration)*, 2013 FC 45; *Ospina Velasquez v Canada (Citizenship and Immigration)*, 2013 FC 273; *Valdespino Partida*, above note 179; *Sanchez*, 2013, above note 153; and *Radi*, above note 173.

222 *Febles*, above note 4.

223 *Ibid* at paras 17–18.

224 *Ibid* at paras 21–22.

225 *Ibid* at paras 38–40; the majority relied at para 40 on the *B and D* case of the CJEU for this conclusion; see above note 51.

proposition that post-crime conduct must be balanced against the crime's seriousness."[226]

- The Refugee Convention has two purposes that need to be balanced: the humane treatment of victims of oppression and the needs of signatory countries to control who enters their territories.[227]
- Article 1F(b) serves one purpose: to exclude all persons who have committed a serious crime and not only a subset of fugitives of justice or serious criminals who are undeserving at the time of the refugee application.[228]

The minority in the *Febles* case, after canvassing the *travaux préparatoires* in some detail and examining the (largely the same) jurisprudence of the CJEU, Australia, Belgium, France, New Zealand, and the United Kingdom,[229] reached the following conclusions:

> Two related observations emerge from this review. The first is that, like the international agreements relating to refugees which were consolidated and revised by the *Refugee Convention*, Article 1F(*b*) was originally intended to maintain the integrity of the status of refugee by excluding fugitives. The *travaux préparatoires* confirm that the exclusion of those who have committed serious and unpunished crimes was not only a practical concern; it was a moral one for the integrity of the international system of refugee protection. But as the recent international jurisprudence shows, it remains far from clear that the signatories to the *Refugee Convention* intended to exclude all individuals who were believed to have committed serious non-political crimes, without regard for whether they had been rehabilitated. In my view, this leaves it open to this Court to reach its own conclusion as to how to interpret the scope of 1F(*b*). The requisite good faith interpretive approach mandates not divorcing the text of Article 1F(*b*) from its human rights purpose.... There is little or no authority for the proposition that *everyone* who has committed a serious non-political crime outside the country of refuge remains permanently undeserving of the *Refugee Convention*'s protection regardless of their supervening personal circumstances. Such a relentlessly exclusionary—and

226 *Ibid* at paras 43–59, while the quotation is at para 59.

227 *Ibid* at paras 29–30.

228 *Ibid* at paras 35–36.

229 *Ibid* at 103–26.

> literal—approach would contradict both the "good faith" approach to interpretation required by the *Vienna Convention* as well as the *Refugee Convention*'s human rights purpose. In my view, depending on the seriousness of the crime, if an individual is believed to have committed a serious non-political crime, the purpose of Article 1F(*b*) can be met where the individual's circumstances reflect a sufficient degree of rehabilitation or expiation that the claimant ought not to be disqualified from the humanitarian protection of the *Refugee Convention*. The completion of a sentence, along with factors such as the passage of time since the commission of the offence, the age at which the crime was committed, and the individual's rehabilitative conduct, will all be relevant. On the other hand, individuals who have committed such serious crimes that they must be considered undeserving of the status of being a refugee would be excluded.[230]

The *Febles* decision regarding expiation has been applied only once since 2014.[231]

Some final comments regarding the Canadian jurisprudence regarding 1F(b) might be helpful at this point. In comparing international law with national refugee law, the Federal Court of Appeal, while pointing out that refugee law has different purposes than extradition law, still undertook a detailed comparative analysis of the extradition law as applied in a number of other countries in the area of the political exception and came to the conclusion that the combination of a dominance and proportionality assessment as used in international extradition law was also the most appropriate in exclusion law. The jurisprudence has taken the view that all aspects of complicity as used for exclusion 1F(a) purposes can also be applied to exclusion 1F(b), including the notion of membership, although it is likely that the latter concept will be less utilized now that the notion of membership in 1F(a) has been severely circumscribed due to the *Ezokola* decision by the Supreme Court (below note 355), and keeping in mind that the vast majority of cases in 1F(b) have been in the context of personal conduct rather than as part of a larger group of perpetrators. Last, while in most instances the jurisprudence to determine the parameters of criminality has relied on Canadian law, there have been a couple of occasions where inspiration was sought from international instruments.

---

230 *Ibid* at paras 128–32.

231 *Skoro v Canada (Citizenship and Immigration)*, 2015 FC 139.

d) France

The purpose of 1F(b) was seen in France as both the protection of society and the exclusion of criminals.[232] Traditionally, the notion of serious crime had not been connected to specific crimes as set out in the French *Criminal Code*, but the *Code* was used as a source to exclude a person for a crime that had a lengthy maximum attached to it. More recently, even this connection to the legislation has been abandoned in favour of setting out an abstract notion, by referring to a grave crime to determine what conduct amounts to a serious crime,[233] although at times a factor approach of mitigating and aggravating circumstances to rebut such a presumption of grave crimes (as used in the countries discussed above) has also been used.[234] Foreign convictions from other countries have been accepted as evidence in French proceedings.[235]

The majority of French jurisprudence since 1950 deals with the determination of factual situations that can demonstrate the commission of serious crimes. A wide variety of criminal behaviour has been brought within this notion of serious crime, including collective crimes committed during armed conflicts, offences by terrorist organizations, and single crimes carried out by individuals in isolated instances.

Killing or attempted killing connected to inter-ethnic violence or as part of armed conflicts,[236] such as in Senegal as committed by the Mouvement des Forces démocratique de la Casamance (MFDC);[237] in the Ivory Coast by the Mouvement patriotique de Côte d'Ivoire (MPCI) (later Forces nouvelles);[238] in Togo by the Régiment commando de la garde présidentielle (RCGP);[239] and by Charles Taylor's forces

---

232 CE, 4 May 2011, 320910, OFPRA c/ MA.

233 Frédéric Tiberghien, *La protection des refugies en France* (Aix-en Provence: Presses Universitaires D'Aix-Marseille, 1988) at 103–4 and 468–69; CNDA, 27 October 2014, 14016605, ME, and CNDA, 3 November 2015, 10013998, MB.

234 CRR, 26 May 2005, 459358, V; CRR, 28 January 2005, 448119, C; CRR, 4 April 2005, 487639, N; CNDA, 15 January 2009, 594649, R; CNDA, 22 July 2013, 9015396, MM.

235 CNDA, 22 July 2013, 9015396, MM, for a conviction in Germany, and CNDA, 2 March 2017, 140036180, MM, for a conviction in Bangladesh, even though it was recognized that courts in that country at times engage in political proceedings, but that was not the case in the situation at hand; in another case, the contents of an extradition request from Turkey were deemed insufficient to reach the threshold for exclusion; see CE, 28 November 2016, 389733, as well as CNDA, 28 September 2018, 13024407, MB.

236 Tiberghien, above note 233 at 469, and Kapferer, above note 134 at 199–200.

237 CRR, 18 April 1997, 291084, Danso.

238 CNDA, 12 February 2009, 598383, K.

239 CNDA, 11 January 2011, 10004142, MK.

in Liberia;[240] as well as guerrilla operations carried out by the Front patriotique Rolingya (RPF) and the Organization de solidarité Rolingya (RSO) in Burma,[241] have all fallen within the framework of article 1F(b) of the convention. The same result was reached in killings of Albanians by Serb police forces;[242] murder, kidnapping, and theft by the Georgian army during the civil war in Abkhazia;[243] during the civil war in Chechnya;[244] in Colombia in connection with torture;[245] by armed militia killings in Haiti;[246] and child recruitment by the LTTE in Sri Lanka[247] and Chad.[248]

Along the same lines, torture and extortion carried out between 1979 and 1996 on behalf of the Lebanese Forces during the civil war in Lebanon were considered to be serious crimes,[249] as was pillage of the civilian population by government armed forces (Service d'action et de renseignements militaire [SARM] and La division spéciale présidentielle [DSP]) under the Mobutu regime in the Democratic Republic of the Congo.[250] Pillage, rape, and killing of civilians by rebel groups (the Movement for the Liberation of Congo [MLC], Rassemblement congolais pour la democratie [RCD],[251] and the Lendu[252]) at a later time in the Democratic Republic of the Congo; acts of sabotage against public infrastructure institutions by the Mouvement congolais pour de démocratie et le développement intégral (MCDDI), and the Ninja Militia, again in the Democratic Republic of the Congo;[253] and acts of

240 CRR, 8 December 1997, 316623, Brown.

241 CRR, 7 July 1997, 272114, Hamid Husain; this case was considered on appeal by the Council of State in 2000 and sent back for redetermination because the decision maker had failed to address the exclusion question; see CE, 15 May 2000, 190059, Hamid.

242 CRR, 18 May 2006, 548090, Kurta.

243 CRR, 20 October 2005, 537046, T.

244 CNDA, 15 December 2009, 637456/08017677, S.

245 CNDA, 15 January 2009, 594649, R.

246 CRR, 3 May 2007, 586579, J.

247 CNDA, 28 July 2016, 16011229, MS; CNDA, 20 April 2017, 12033163, MK; CNDA, 27 January 2021, 19030210, MM.

248 CNDA, 1 February 2017, 16027532, MT.

249 CRR, 22 December 2000, 346184, Hatem.

250 CRR, 14 December 2000, 336795, Bolinga.

251 CRR, 20 June 2003, 412882, Mabika Konde.

252 CRR, 4 April 2005, 487639, N.

253 CRR, 2 October 2003, 417790, Matongo Valenes; see, also, CRR, 10 November 2005, 549184, M, and CNDA, 13 December 2007, 581575, D.

violence and pillage in Kosovo by local Serb militias[254] or Serb police[255] were given the same treatment.

A *coup d'état* attempt resulting in numerous deaths in Azerbaijan[256] and murder as part of another *coup d'état* in the Comores[257] also led to exclusion from refugee protection. An assassination attempt in Pakistan by the Ismanai Student Organization (OSI) against the leader of a political movement;[258] a bomb attack against the headquarters of the militia in Georgia;[259] an attempt to carry out an attack by the Peruvian terrorist organization Movimiento Revolucionario Túpac Amaru (MRTA);[260] the killing of civilians and police officers in Nigeria by the Oodua Peoples Congress (OPC);[261] using terrorist methods such as attacks against the civilian population in Turkey and other countries by the PKK;[262] attacks on banks and assassinations by the Communist Party of Turkey/Marxist-Leninist–Liberation Army of the Workers and Peasants of Turkey (TKP/ML-TIKKO), also in Turkey;[263] and terrorist attacks in Algeria by the Islamic Salvation Front (FIS)[264] and the Groupe islamique armé (GIA)[265] and in Morocco by the Groupe islamique combattant marocain (GICM)[266] were also viewed as article 1F(b) crimes.

Regular crimes such as murder,[267] attempted murder, aggravated theft and assault,[268] robbery and extortion,[269] drug trafficking,[270]

---

254 CRR, 16 November 2006, 521885, Vesic.

255 CRR, 2 April 2007, 547636, C.

256 CRR, 25 July 2006, 538535, Tagiyev.

257 CRR, 15 March 2007, 545096, M.

258 CRR, 22 October 1996, 302813, Ahsan Mehmood; see, also, Tiberghien, above note 233 at 469.

259 CRR, 31 January 1997, 302492, Bordzikidze.

260 CRR, 22 October 1997, 315086, Mendoza Martinez.

261 CRR, 9 January 2003, 406014, Awobajo; see, also, CRR, 23 July 2003, 432671, Omoregie Daniels, who had participated in lynchings with a radical branch of the OPC, the Adams group.

262 CE, 9 November 2005, 254882, A; see, also, CRR, 11 May 2006, 523285, Ucar; and CNDA, 18 December 2009, 606915/07010052, A.

263 CNDA, 31 January 2008, 536076, C.

264 CE, 15 May 1996, 153491, MR.

265 CRR, 26 October 2005, 399706, K.

266 CNDA, 15 February 2013, 10005048, MB.

267 CNDA, 3 November 2015, 10013998, MB; CNDA, 27 February 2015, 14017954, MB; CNDA, 8 November 2016, 13005613, MK; CNDA, 21 December 2017, 16036205, MA (this case also made clear that a causal connection is required between the action of a person and a subsequent crime); CNDA, 2 March 2017, 140036180, MM.

268 CNDA, 22 July 2013, 9015396, MM.

269 CNDA, 18 October 2016, 15031596, MV.

270 CE, 13 November 2020, 428582.

torture,[271] and procuring have also been held to be serious crimes.[272] So too have embezzlement,[273] burglary,[274] FGM,[275] organized crime,[276] and the commission of violent acts by street gangs in Haiti.[277] Aggressive behaviour during a public discourse is not a serious crime even if the person had received a conviction for these acts in the country of origin.[278]

With respect to the notion of political crimes, the Council of State has made it clear that the political objectives of the persons carrying out serious crimes must be balanced against the degree of legitimacy of the violence employed.[279] Applying this standard, it has been said that terrorist methods, such as attacks against a civilian population in furtherance of a political goal, as used by the PKK, do not bring a criminal act within the rubric of a political crime.[280] The same result was achieved in a situation where a person was involved in a *coup d'état* in Azerbaijan to obtain democracy that caused a large number of fatalities.[281]

On the other hand, this balance was achieved in a situation where a person had joined a unit of combatants in Chechnya after his village was destroyed by Russian bombardments during the first civil war. He participated in actions against Russian armed forces in defence of the Chechnyan people and his own family but did not violate the rules of war while engaged in such actions.[282]

Complicity for the purposes of article 1F(b) is present when people participate directly or indirectly in the planning, preparation, and commission of serious non-political crimes. Direct participation has

---

271 CE, 7 June 2017, 396261.

272 Kapferer, above note 134 at 199.

273 CE, 8 December 2021, 447044, OFPRA c MA.

274 CRR, 21 July 2006, 509322, Toskic.

275 CNDA, 12 November 2019, 19007358, Mme T; in this case, the defence of duress was rejected as the person concerned had assisted her mother for twenty years and the authority of her mother or the pressure of the community is not sufficient to amount to a threat of death or continuous or imminent serious injury.

276 CNDA, 3 November 2015, 10013998, M B.

277 CRR, 2 April 2007, 587983, C.

278 Tiberghien, above note 233 at 469.

279 CE, 28 February 2001, 195356, S. For cases before 2001, see Kapferer, above note 134 at 199–200, indicating that art 1F(b) was applied to the crimes of murder and attempted murder regardless of the political motive, especially in situations involving armed opposition movements.

280 CRR, 9 January 2003, 362645, Altun; see, also, CRR, 11 May 2006, 523285, Ucar.

281 CRR, 25 July 2006, 538535, Tagiyev.

282 CRR, 25 January 2007, 552944, S.

been found in acts of violence against civilian targets and in armed attacks against the military forces of a country, such as in combat and the transport of weapons for the LTTE.[283] A combination of being an instructor in a rebel group in Senegal and direct participation in armed confrontations against government forces, resulting in dozens of deaths, constitutes excludable behaviour,[284] as does being a political instructor for PKK combatants.[285] Organizing and financing a bomb attack against the headquarters of the Georgian militia[286] was also found to amount to complicity.

Indirect participation may lead to exclusion if a person is an instigator or accomplice in serious crimes,[287] hostage taking to extract money for the LTTE, stealing ammunition and grenades from an army depot for the FIS in Algeria, attempting to extort funds for the PKK in Turkey,[288] or providing financial logistical support for the OPC in Nigeria.[289] Being a watchman during an assassination by the TKP/ML-TIKKO in Turkey,[290] providing information to Russian security forces, resulting in the deaths of several Chechnyan independence fighters,[291] and transporting prisoners and dead bodies for Serb police forces during the ethnic cleansing of Kosovo[292] also fall within the parameters of this type of participation.

However, providing food and medicine for armed movements falls below the complicity threshold.[293] A person in a vulnerable situation who was pressed into becoming a member of the LTTE and participating in an action against the Sri Lankan army, who then left the LTTE while on leave (after asking to be dismissed on several occasions), cannot be considered to have committed 1F(b) activities.[294] The same was said for a young person who was pressured to be part of an honour

283 Kapferer, above note 134 at 200.
284 CRR, 18 April 1997, 291084, Danso.
285 CRR, 11 May 2006, 523285, Ucar.
286 CRR, 31 January 1997, 302492, Bordzikidze.
287 CNDA, 2 March 2017, 14003618o, MM.
288 Kapferer, above note 134 at 200.
289 CRR, 9 January 2003, 406014, Awobajo.
290 CNDA, 31 January 2008, 536076, C.
291 CNDA, 15 December 2009, 637456/08017677, S; the tribunal states this proposition in general but is of the view that the facts in this specific case would not lead to exclusion.
292 CRR, 2 April 2007, 547636, C.
293 Kapferer, above note 134 at 200.
294 CRR, 13 September 2005, 509227, Mlle T.

killing but only brought a weapon and witnessed the killing[295] and another vulnerable and isolated young person who had been forcibly recruited into a gang in the DRC and remained in that gang due to physical and psychological pressure that prevented him from distancing himself from them.[296]

A combination of being forcibly recruited by the Revolutionary Armed Forces of Colombia (FARC) at a young age, being in a situation of particular vulnerability, being only marginally involved by carrying out surveillance of his neighbourhood on behalf of the FARC, and dissociating himself from the organization whose methods he did not support by fleeing to France was sufficient to excuse a person from complicity in serious crimes.[297] A child soldier who had been forcibly recruited by the Revolutionary United Front (RUF) in Sierra Leone after several members of his family had been killed by them, had participated under threat in attacks against civilians and pillaging, and had left the RUF two months after enrolling was also found not to be excludable.[298]

On the other hand, mitigating circumstances did not absolve an adult who had been forcibly recruited by the rebel group Lendus in the Democratic Republic of the Congo and had personally participated in murder, attacks on civilians, and pillaging under the orders of his superiors while under the influence of alcohol and drugs and was found to be complicit in article 1F(b) crimes.[299] Similarly, a young person in Colombia who joined a paramilitary group voluntarily to avenge the killing of his entire family by criminal gangs and had personally murdered and tortured members of the FARC and the gang members responsible for the killing of his family was excluded in spite of his young age and traumatic experiences.[300]

Mere membership in an organization that carries out excludable offences is not sufficient to invoke article 1F(b).[301]

---

295 CE, 7 April 2010, 319840, MH et 327959, OFPRA c/ MH.

296 CNDA, 18 October 2016, 15031596 MV.

297 CRR, 26 May 2005, 459358, V.

298 CRR, 28 January 2005, 448119, C. The same result was achieved in a similar situation in the case of CNDA, 20 December 2010, 10004872, Mr. N, for a member of the National Congress for the Defense of the People (Congrès national pour la défense du people [CNDP]) in the Democratic Republic of the Congo.

299 CRR, 4 April 2005, 487639, N.

300 CNDA, 15 January 2009, 594649, R.

301 CNDA, 21 December 2017, 16036205, MA.

The jurisprudence with respect to the meaning of "outside the country of refuge" has fluctuated; at times, the commission of an offence in France was not seen as an impediment to applying article 1F(b).[302] It appeared that this issue was laid to rest by the Council of State in 1998 when it stated that offences committed in the country of refuge could be used to apply the *refoulement* provision of the Refugee Convention but not exclusion under article 1F(b).[303] However, in a more recent decision, article 1F(b) was applied to a member of the FIS and GIA, considered terrorist organizations in Algeria, who had been convicted by a French criminal court of a number of offences in France, such as transporting weapons, vehicles, and forged documents, as well as supporting terrorism.[304] It would appear that the distinction was found (as it had been in the past when article 1F(b) was applied to offences committed in France)[305] that the provision was not applicable for regular offences wholly committed in French territory but that it could be used if its parameters included support functions for terrorist organizations that operated primarily outside France.

Last, expiation has not found any traction in the tribunal jurisprudence where convictions in foreign countries, or even in France, have not prevented the application of article 1F(b).[306] On the other hand, one decision by the Council of State held that expiation for a 1F(b) crime does not necessarily mean that exclusion can be applied. In this case, the refugee tribunal was of the view that since the punishment, to which the applicant had been sentenced in Italy, had been fully served, it should result in the inapplicability of the exclusion clause. The Council of State found that the tribunal should have inquired as to whether the circumstances could have resulted in the application of 1F(b), because of the serious non-political crimes committed in the past, and whether the applicant's presence in France could be considered a danger or a risk to the population.[307]

---

302 Tiberghien, above note 233 at 103 and 468–69, and CRR, 14 November 1997, 290466, Can.

303 CE, 25 September 1998, 165525, Rajkumar (see, also, implicitly, CRR, 22 January 1999, 322914, Tat). Hathaway & Foster, above note 60 at 300, take umbrage with the position of the CRR but do not seem to be aware of the fact that the Council of State overturned the tribunal decision.

304 CRR, 26 October 2005, 399706, K.

305 Tiberghien, above note 233 at 468; CRR, 14 November 1997, 290466, Can.

306 Tiberghien, above note 233 at 468–69; CRR, 14 November 1997, 290466, Can; CRR, 22 January 1999, 322914, Tat; CRR, 26 October 2005, 399706, K; and CRR, 21 July 2006, 509322, Toskic.

307 CE, 4 May 2011, 320910, OFPRA c/ MA.

In assessing the jurisprudence of the French tribunals in relation to international law, two aspects need to be considered: the fact that in France, article 1F(b) has been used to primarily address war crimes in non-international armed conflicts and that, more recently, terrorist activities have been brought within its parameters. Complicity principles have been applied to both types of activities. No reference to international criminal law jurisprudence has been used to explain the conclusions reached in respect to civil war or specific war crimes, such as murder, torture, or pillage. The same comment can be made in respect to extended liability for the use of article 1F(b) for war crimes or acts of terrorism, although the French caselaw is consistent on this point with the notions of extended liability in exclusion 1F(a) by the same tribunals. However, even though such references are missing, the instances where civil war, terrorism, and complicity in these activities were virtually always of such a nature that an application of the principles, set out in either international criminal law (ICL) or the international terrorist conventions, would have resulted in the same outcomes.

This also holds true for the use of international extradition law when providing the contours of the political offence exception; like in other countries, the dominant and proportionality principles have been given due attention in the exclusion 1F(b) context. Given the use of this provision for war crimes in non-international armed conflicts, France found itself in the unique position of examining political offence exception claims but had no difficulty determining whether proportionality was present on these occasions, although this approach has the possibility of widening the scope of excludable behaviour compared to the use of 1F(a) insofar as it relates to war crimes and the issue of collateral damage.

e) Germany

In Germany, the main purpose of exclusion 1F(b) was seen as "protect refugee status from abuse, by keeping it from being granted to undeserving applicants," and to "prevent refugee status from being discredited by including criminals in the group of recognised refugees."[308]

The notion of serious crime was originally given a broad meaning by making any offence in Germany with a penalty of at least one year

308 Bundesverwaltungsgericht (Federal Administrative Court), BverwG 10 C 48.07, 14 October 2008 at paras 29–30.

serious.[309] This approach has been modified by the highest administrative court, which held that the crime "must be a capital crime or a punishable act that is categorised as especially grave in most legal systems and prosecuted accordingly in criminal law."[310]

This court has also indicated that a crime is non-political if it is committed predominantly for other motives (such as personal reasons or gain). Where no clear link exists between the crime and its alleged political objective or when the act in question is disproportionate to the alleged political objective, non-political motives are predominant.[311] A person in Chechnya who killed two soldiers and took another hostage in order to free his brother from Russian captivity was not engaged in a political crime, even though he was a resistance fighter, since this act was carried out for a personal motive.[312] In this context, particularly cruel actions may be classified as serious non-political crimes according to the Qualification Directive, which is apt in the terrorism context, according to the jurisprudence.[313]

While there is no international definition for terrorism, some indicia to give this rather vague concept useful parameters can be found in several sources, such as the Council of the European Union's Common Position of 27 December 2001 on the Application of Specific Measures to Combat Terrorism. This position makes it clear that

---

309 UNHCR, *Asylum in the European Union: A Study of the Implementation of the Qualification Directive* (November 2007) at 98–99, online: www.unhcr.org/protection/operations/47302b6c2/asylum-european-union-study-implementation-qualification-directive-2007.html.

310 Bundesverwaltungsgericht (Federal Administrative Court), BverwG 10 C 7.09, 10 February 2010 at para 47; see, also, Bundesverwaltungsgericht (Federal Administrative Court), BverwG 10 C 24.08, 24 November 2009 at para 41, and Bundesverwaltungsgericht (Federal Administrative Court), BverwG 10 C 48.07, 14 October 2008 at para 19 (which refers to the UNHCR 2003 *Exclusion Guidelines*, above note 6, rather than the UNHCR Handbook); these decisions also indicated at the same paras, again following UNHCR views, that the notion of crimes had to be determined by international standards and not national ones.

311 Bundesverwaltungsgericht (Federal Administrative Court), BverwG 10 C 48.07, 14 October 2008 at para 20; Bundesverwaltungsgericht (Federal Administrative Court), BverwG 10 C 7.09, 10 February 2010 at para 48; Bundesverwaltungsgericht (Federal Administrative Court), BverwG 10 C 24.08, 24 November 2009 at para 42. This is also based on the UNHCR Handbook and 2003 *Exclusion Guidelines*, above note 6.

312 Bundesverwaltungsgericht (Federal Administrative Court), BverwG 10 C 7.09, 10 February 2010 at para 49.

313 Bundesverwaltungsgericht (Federal Administrative Court), BverwG 10 C 48.07, 14 October 2008 at para 20.

> certain intentional acts (such as attacks on a person's life or physical integrity) become "terrorist acts" if—first—given their nature or context, they may seriously damage a country or an international organisation, and are defined as an offence under national law, and if—second—they are committed with the aim of seriously intimidating a population, or unduly compelling a government or an international organisation to perform or abstain from performing any act, or of seriously destabilising or destroying the fundamental political, constitutional, economic or social structures of a country or international organisation.[314]

In addition, according to German caselaw, the use of weapons dangerous to public safety and attacks on the lives of non-participants in an armed conflict to achieve political goals are be considered terrorist acts.[315]

The jurisprudence from Germany has addressed the issue of complicity in respect to article 1F(b), specifically in relation to terrorist organizations. It has said that a person making a substantial contribution to criminal acts, in the knowledge that their act or omission would facilitate the criminal conduct, would be responsible for an article 1F(b) crime. This would include persons who perform advance acts in support of terrorist activities[316] or who actively support the armed struggle of a terrorist organization.[317] The fact that an organization, such as the Dev-Sol in Turkey, has been placed on a prohibited list does not absolve the government from the obligation to show that a member supported this organization, implying that membership alone is not sufficient to attract

314 *Ibid.*

315 *Ibid*; see, also, Bundesverwaltungsgericht (Federal Administrative Court), BverwG 10 C 46.07, 25 November 2008 at para 23.

316 Bundesverwaltungsgericht (Federal Administrative Court), BverwG 10 C 48.07, 14 October 2008 at para 21; along the same lines, in the context of immigration, Bundesverwaltungsgericht (Federal Administrative Court), BverwG 1 C 19.09, 26 October 2010 at para 23.

317 Bundesverwaltungsgericht (Federal Administrative Court), BverwG 10 C 48.07, 14 October 2008 at para 22. In an earlier case, this court expressed this as involvement going beyond membership but that it needed to involve participation in the activities of the organization or financial support. It also indicated that objectionable involvement in a terrorist organization could depend on factors such as the violent nature of the organization and whether any supported activities of the person resulted in a danger to the security of the country; see Bundesverwaltungsgericht (Federal Administrative Court), BverwG 9 C 31.98, 30 March 1999 at 13–14.

article 1F(b) liability.[318] In another case, it said that the principles of complicity are derived from criminal law, such as instigation and aiding and abetting.[319] There is no requirement in article 1F(b) that the person continues to be a danger to the country where they are residing. This is a requirement for the application of the exception to the *refoulement* provision of the Refugee Convention but not for exclusion.[320]

German court decisions have shed some light on aspects of the relationship between international law and refugee law. In defining terrorism, reliance was placed on a December 2001 European document, which had a description of terrorism that was similar to the later definition in the draft Comprehensive Convention on International Terrorism, while the notion of political crime also echoed the dominance theory from extradition law. Like in France, German courts had no difficulty in applying the test for political offences to armed conflict situations. Last, the description of the term "committed" in exclusion 1F(b) was defined along the same lines as in exclusion 1F(a) for one aspect of extended liability, aiding and abetting, where the substantial contribution with knowledge was seen as an essential element for this form of complicity. These are the same parameters as are set out in international criminal law.

---

318 Bundesverwaltungsgericht (Federal Administrative Court), BverwG 10 C 48.07, 14 October 2008 at paras 17–18. This part of the decision was upheld by the European Court of Justice, from which a preliminary ruling had been requested by the Federal Administrative Court in the case of *B and D*, above note 51 at paras 87–99. The decision of the Federal Administrative Court overruled government practice and lower court decisions, which had allowed this broader form of exclusion; see UNHCR, *Asylum in the European Union*, above note 309 at 15–16.

319 Bundesverwaltungsgericht (Federal Administrative Court), BverwG 10 C 26.10, July 7, 2011 at para 38 (in which the court indicates that the reference to the terms "instigate" and "otherwise instigate" in arts 12 and 17 of the Qualification Directive, above note 11, are not intended to expand on the parameters of exclusion 1F in the Refugee Convention "but only to make it more specific with regard to the difference in the understanding of perpetration, instigation and other forms of participation in the criminal codes of the Member States"); Bundesverwaltungsgericht (Federal Administrative Court), BverwG 10 C 13.11, 4 September 2012 at para 24.

320 Bundesverwaltungsgericht (Federal Administrative Court), BverwG 10 C 48.07, 14 October 2008 at paras 27–30. This was also upheld by the European Court of Justice in the case of *B and D*, above note 51 at paras 100–5.

f) The Netherlands[321]

The Dutch *Aliens Manual* only provides in detail the parameters of the notion of non-political crime.[322] The starting point for assessing whether a crime is political is the application of the dominance test for whether crimes such as assault, drug trafficking, armed robberies, and arson are subsidiary and proportional to the political purpose. Such relative political crimes can be considered to fall within the political exception if

- there is a direct connection between the crime and the political purpose;
- the crime is an effective means to accomplish the political purpose;
- there was no peaceful means available; and
- there is a reasonable connection between the crime and the political purpose.

The manual goes on to say that certain crimes are by definition non-political:

- murder, killing, and rape;
- war crimes as defined by article 8 of the Rome Statute;
- crimes against humanity as defined by article 7 of the Rome Statute;
- genocide as defined by article 6 of the Rome Statute;
- torture;
- slavery and slave trade; or
- crimes as defined by a binding international instrument which indicates that the crime described in that instrument does not amount to a political crime or does not lead to refugee status.

According to the manual, there are also the purely political offences that are directed at the state. Such offences do not require a dominant purpose assessment and will not lead to exclusion. Examples of such offences are high treason and interference with elections.[323]

---

321 For an overview of the practice in the Netherlands between 2000 and 2010, see Maarten P. Bolhuis & Joris van Wijk, "Alleged Terrorists and Other Perpetrators of Serious Non-political Crimes: The Application of Article 1F(b) of the Refugee Convention in the Netherlands" (2016) 29:1 *Journal of Refugee Studies* 19–38, which comes to the following conclusion: "This study suggests that the Netherlands tends to exclude anyone who has ever committed a serious non-political crime outside the Netherlands and that factors such as dangerousness, rehabilitation and expiation are irrelevant in determining whether the crime is serious" (at 33).

322 *Vreemdelingencirculaire* 2000 (C), art 7.10.2.2 [*Aliens Manual*].

323 The manual also gives as examples some offences set out in the Dutch *Criminal Code*.

In applying the above principles regarding political offences, a district court overruled a decision of the minister responsible for immigration to exclude a person from Iraq who belonged to the Al Da'wa Party, which had as its purpose the overthrow of the Saddam Hussein regime. The asylum seeker gathered information about the members of the Mukhabarat, one of the secret services in Iraq, and the members of the Ba'ath Party. This information resulted in the killing of two men. The court was of the view that in this situation the requirement of a direct connection between the crime and the political purpose was met, as was the fact that providing information was an effective manner of accomplishing change. There was also no doubt that since peaceful means could not be used in Iraq at that time, given the repressive character of the Saddam Hussein regime, the crime was also proportional.[324] The opposite conclusion was reached with respect to a person who had carried out activities for the Dev-Sol organization in Turkey;[325] a person who, as a member of a Maoist group in Nepal, had participated in attacks on police stations and banks;[326] and a person involved in violence during an election in Nigeria[327] because there were more peaceful means available in Turkey, Nepal, and Nigeria to effect change.

Exclusion under article 1F(b) is also applicable in situations where a person was involved in activities deemed to be non-political by international instruments, such as terrorist activities, as set out in the European Convention, carried out by the Popular Front for the Liberation of Palestine (PFLP) in Lebanon[328] and the Abu Nidal Organization in the Palestinian territories.[329]

Reliance on an international instrument to determine if a crime falls within the parameters of 1F(b) was also used for torture, as defined by the

---

324 Rb, The Hague, Awb 02/60920, 19 July 2004.

325 Rb, The Hague, Awb 04/40384, 24 May 2005. In the context of extradition, the Supreme Court of the Netherlands was of the view that the attacks carried out in Turkey by the PKK did not fall within the parameters of a political offence; see HR, 02853/02U, 7 May 2004 at 3.4.12; this case has been mentioned by the International Criminal Tribunal for the former Yugoslavia (ICTY) in the context of internal armed conflict in Judgment, *Brđanin* (IT-99-36), Trial Chamber, 1 September 2004 at para 179.

326 Rb, The Hague, Awb 03/26897, 2 July 2004.

327 Rb, Zwolle, Awb 13/24563, 15 July 2014.

328 Rb, The Hague, Awb 04/51818, 28 June 2006.

329 Rb, The Hague, Awb 01/8334, 2 June 2003, which also added the two UN resolutions mentioned in the manual.

Torture Convention, in the case of a member of the Armenian police,[330] although if acts amounting to severe pain and suffering are inflicted by a person not acting in an official capacity, they are not torture.[331] With respect to serious economic crimes, embezzlement and accepting bribes were found to fall within the parameters of article 1F(b); this was especially the case since the crimes were carried out over a lengthy period of time and involved very large amounts of money, and corruption is viewed internationally as a serious crime.[332] The same reasoning was used to determine that drug smuggling is seen internationally as a threat to the community when the court referenced United Nations conventions for the suppression of this crime.[333] This reasoning has also been rejected in a situation of FGM; initially, the court found that this was a serious crime, but the exclusion of a woman who had assisted her mother in Sierra Leone with FGM was overruled because it could not be said that the requirement of knowing participation had been fulfilled, in the sense that she knew or could have known that these acts were criminal; in reaching this conclusion, the court relied on the fact that FGM was not prohibited by law in Sierra Leone, that it is widely practised in the area of Sierra Leone where she lived and in the ethnic group she belonged to, and that it was not clear whether the messages of anti-FGM groups in Sierra Leone had reached the village where she lived.[334] On appeal, it was said that FGM does not amount to a serious crime for several reasons but primarily because there is not yet international consensus that it is a crime (even though both the Convention on the Rights of the Child, article 24(3), and article 5 of the Maputo Protocol refer to harmful practices of children and women). There is no international treaty to combat this practice, and even though the Dutch *Criminal Code* makes this a crime, this is not so in Sierra Leone or countries surrounding the Netherlands.[335]

In general, what constitutes a crime should be determined by the law of the country of refuge rather than the country of origin, although this can be bolstered by reference to international instruments; this was,

330 Rb, The Hague, Awb 02/88995, 28 October 2004.

331 Rb, The Hague, NL 19/4708, 19 December 2019.

332 AbRS, 30 December 2009, nr 200902983/1.

333 AbRS, 27 September 2013, nr 201202758/1; however, not every type of drug smuggling amounts to a serious crime according to AbRS, 14 September 2015, nr 201407968/1.

334 Rb, Assen, Awb 11/20054, 14 August 2012.

335 AbRS, 10 February 2014, nr 201208875/1.

for the most part, an implicit assumption when setting what activities amounted to serious crime, but it has also been said explicitly.[336]

The exclusion of a person convicted in absentia in Lebanon to life imprisonment for drug trafficking was overruled by the court because the evidence for this crime was not considered persuasive, nor was the basis for the sentencing clear from the evidence; it was also unclear whether a Dutch court would have agreed in such circumstances.[337] However, in another case, a conviction in Serbia was accepted as it could not be said that the court system in that country was so suspect that their decision could not be utilized; similarly, it could not be said that the allegation of corruption in the Serbian judicial system had had an effect on this case; as a result, the court in the Netherlands could not go behind the conviction in Serbia even if the person concerned raised the issue of self-defence for the first time during the exclusion proceeding.[338]

With respect to the notion of "serious," it has been said that the nature of the acts and the magnitude of their consequences are factors that play a role in making such a determination.[339]

The following are also considered serious crimes: murder;[340] attempted manslaughter;[341] torture;[342] piracy;[343] assault causing death;[344]

---

336 Rb, The Hague, Awb 11/6120, 11 July 2012.

337 Rb, Roermond, Awb 11/11895, and Awb 11/12411, 17 February 2012.

338 Rb, Roermond, Awb 13/16907, 3 December 2013; see, also, indirectly, for a conviction in Turkey, Rb, The Hague, Awb 12/39765, 20 February 2014, and Rb, Middelburg, Awb 13/254, 27 February 2014, as well as for a conviction in Germany in AbRS, 14 September 2015, nr 201407968/1, and Ghana in AbRS, 8 December 2014, nr 201403749/1.

339 Rb, The Hague, Awb 12/39765, 20 February 2014; the court relied on an older version of the manual for this proposition; the present manual does not have a specific entry of this notion in the context of art 1F(b), but there is some reference to the concept of a (particular) serious offence in the discussion of public order as part of *refoulement*, which refers to the nature and seriousness of the crime as well as the time that has elapsed since its commission; see *Aliens Manual*, above note 322 at art 7.10.1.

340 Rb, The Hague, Awb 11/6120, 11 July 2012; Rb, Rotterdam, Awb 11/21834, 21 March 2013; Rb, The Hague, Awb 13/16907, 25 April 2013; Rb, Roermond, Awb 13/16907, 3 December 2013; Rb, The Hague, Awb 16/18594, 7 March 2017; Rb, The Hague, NL 20.19271, 23 July 2021; Rb, The Hague, NL 21.16506, 7 March 2022.

341 Rb, Middelburg, Awb 13/254, 27 February 2014.

342 Rb, Awb 10/42733 and 10/43122, 26 January 2012.

343 Rb, Zwolle, Awb 14/9363, 1 July 2014; Rb, Utrecht, Awb 14/12579, 10 July 2014; Rb, Utrecht, Awb 14/12581, 10 July 2014; Rb, Utrecht, Awb 14/12590, 10 July 2014; Rb, Utrecht, 10/07/14; Awb 14/12595, 10 July 2014.

344 Rb, Groningen, Awb 13/30281, 15 July 2014.

aggravated assault;[345] rape;[346] terrorism;[347] abduction;[348] people smuggling;[349] hostage taking;[350] and theft with violence.[351] Accepting bribes by an Afghani judge was seen as a form of corruption and, as such, could be considered a serious crime unless it occurred on only one occasion, which was not the case here.[352]

Complicity in 1F(b) crimes has the same elements as in 1F(a), knowing and personal participation.[353] A person who was the president of the political wing of the Al-Jihad al-Islami in the Palestinian territories, at a time when the military wing carried out attacks against military and civilian targets in Israel, was excluded for complicity under article 1F(b).[354] A person guarding migrants smuggled from Libya to Italy who were confined to barracks without allowing them to leave was making a substantial contribution to the crime of hostage taking. However, the court did not find this person complicit because the second aspect of this requirement, knowing participation, was not met; at the time of his involvement, he had been a minor; he had been seriously traumatized by the death of his mother at an early age; he had been abused by his father; the civil war in Libya was violent; and there was a lack of trust in adults in positions of authority; these all put into serious doubt whether he was in a position of independent decision making. Last, and connected to the vulnerability just discussed, his defence of duress was accepted; he had no reasonable avenue of escape, had been severely punished when not following orders, and could expect the same treatment in the future.[355] A similar result was achieved when a person who was a member of a street gang in El Salvador, had stood guard for this organization, and bought and transported weapons for it was found not to be responsible

345 Rb, Zwolle, Awb 13/24563, 15 July 2014; Rb, Groningen, Awb 13/30281, 15 July 2014; Rb, The Hague, Awb 16/18594, 7 March 2017; Rb, The Hague, NL 19/12970, 20 May 2020; Rb, The Hague, NL 19/5360, 8 November 2019.

346 AbRS, 27 January 2015, nr 201309401/1; Rb, The Hague, NL 17/94301, 25 May 2017; Rb, The Hague, NL 19/22049, 16 December 2020.

347 Rb, The Hague, Awb 12/39207 and 12/39209, 8 November 2019; Rb, The Hague, NL 20.19271, 23 July 2021 (involving a person who had already been convicted for this crime as well as murder in the criminal courts).

348 Rb, The Hague, Awb 12/39765, 20 February 2014.

349 Rb, The Hague, Awb 17/2027, 15 August 2017, and Rb, The Hague, NL 19/4708, 19 December 2019.

350 Rb, The Hague, NL 19/4708, 19 December 2019.

351 AbRS, 8 December 2014, nr 201403749/1.

352 Rb, The Hague, Awb 12/7444, 2 October 2012; the person was also excluded under art 1F(c).

353 Rb, The Hague, NL 21.16506, 7 March 2022.

354 Rb, The Hague, Awb 02/71646, 2 November 2004.

355 Rb, The Hague, NL 19/4708, 19 December 2019.

for the crimes alleged, complicity in murder and manslaughter, because her activities were not causally connected to those specific crimes. The defence of duress, based on her being threatened with sexual abuse and death if she refused to participate in the actions of a gang well known for its cruelty, was not properly addressed by the government.[356]

Other instances where defences were raised in the 1F(b) context were rejected on factual grounds. One example is of a member of a subclan in Somalia who killed a person from another subclan because his brother had been killed earlier by a member of the other subclan. The defence of duress was rejected because he had had a safe avenue of escape and had not killed out of fear of imminent death. The defence of superior orders was also rejected because the element of the need to obey orders of a government or superior, as set out in article 33 of the Rome Statute, was not made out in this case; he had no such obligation.[357] Similarly, a person who had been a member of the Peoples Democratic Party in Nigeria, committed assault during election violence, and alleged he had been forced to carry out these crimes, this defense was rejected, as he had had a safe avenue of escape and had voluntarily joined the group knowing what would be expected of him.[358]

The notion of expiation has not been directly analyzed in the jurisprudence, but by relying on foreign convictions where the people had fully served the foreign sentence, this part of expiation has not found any traction in the jurisprudence.[359]

As in Australia, the legislator in the Netherlands decided to provide guidance to the courts in determining what amounts to a political crime. In the Netherlands, however, it appears to be less a reaction to an undesirable development in the jurisprudence than a more general approach to setting out the government's understanding of various principles in the three exclusion clauses and even in refugee law

356 Rb, The Hague, NL 21.16506, 7 March 2022; of interest is that the court makes it clear that mere membership in this gang is not sufficient reason for exclusion, while in addressing the parameters of complicity, it refers to the judgment of the Supreme Court of Canada in *Ezokola v Canada (Citizenship and Immigration)*, 2013 SCC 40 [*Ezokola*]. See also below note 682.

357 Rb, The Hague, Awb 11/6120, 11 July 2012.

358 Rb, Zwolle, Awb 13/24563, 15 July 2014.

359 Other parts of expiation were not recognized by first-instance decision makers; see Bolhuis & Van Wijk, above note 321. Another issue that was briefly addressed in the Dutch jurisprudence is the notion of continuous crimes, which had started outside the Netherlands but were completed inside the country, such as drug or people smuggling; one older case was of the view that such case would not violate the notion of "outside the country of refuge," but this proposition was rejected in Rb, The Hague, Awb 06/62883, 4 July 2007.

as a whole. The Dutch *Aliens Manual* circumscribes the tenets of the political offence exception in terms of accordance with international extradition law, the predominance and proportionality test, and then goes on to provide a listing of specific crimes that, by definition, are not political. Unlike in Australia, this listing is connected to international conventions in general, which makes the application broader than in Australia. Subsequent jurisprudence has provided an interpretation of the terms used in the manual as well as other aspects of 1F(b), such as what constitutes a crime, what is a serious crime, the effect of foreign convictions on a finding of criminality, and the influence of international instruments regarding the understanding of what constitutes a serious crime. Regarding the latter aspect, the Dutch jurisprudence is unusual in that, although in most cases this reliance on international instruments was either used as a point of clarification, as was the case with torture, or as a supporting argument for a crime that existed in the Netherlands, as was the case for drug smuggling and corruption, this argument was taken to an unfortunate extreme by refusing to accept a crime as serious that was criminalized in the Netherlands but not yet at the international level, as was the case with FGM.

g) New Zealand

The purpose of 1F(b) is to prevent fugitives from avoiding punishment for their crimes and to protect the security of states.[360] The New Zealand Court of Appeal has stated that the notion of crime should take the criminal law of the country of refuge as a starting point, in which both the maximum penalty set out by law and the likely sentence to be imposed in the circumstances of the case are important, or, in the words of the court:

> [T]o classify any crime as serious requires an evaluation not only of the elements which form the crime, but also of its facts and circumstances, as well as the circumstances of the offender which are relevant for the purposes of the criminal law. The level of penalty inflicted or likely to be inflicted in those circumstances by the contracting state and probably by the state in which the crime was committed are relevant factors.[361]

360 *Tamil X*, above note 4 at para 82.

361 *S v Refugee Status Appeals Authority*, [1998] 2 NZLR 291 at para 2.

It went on to say, "[E]xclusion is directed to offending in the upper end of the scale, which is likely to attract a severe penalty, at least in the nature of imprisonment for an appreciable period of years."[362] This latter approach resulted in a decision where crimes, such as wounding, assault with a weapon, or conspiracy to commit serious crimes, were found to be within the range of the maximum penalty imposed, but because of the personal factors related to the asylum claimant, it was found that the person would not receive more than between eighteen months and two years in prison. This was considered not to be at the upper end of the scale leading to imprisonment for an appreciable period of years and, as such, would not be considered a serious crime.[363] The same result was reached for attempted rape in the United Kingdom, where a court imposed a two-year sentence.[364]

This approach was modified in 2017 when the immigration tribunal started using the following non-exhaustive factors to determine seriousness:

(a) the elements that form the crime;
(b) the facts and circumstances of the crime (including, in cases of financial crime, the quantum concerned and the consequences);
(c) the circumstances of the offender that are relevant for the purposes of the criminal law, and any other aggravating or mitigating features;
(d) the level of penalty likely to be inflicted in those circumstances (in particular, would it be likely to attract a sentence of imprisonment for an appreciable number of years);
(e) other indicators that the state in which the crime was committed considers the crime to be serious;
(f) other indicators that New Zealand and other contracting states consider the crime to be serious;
(g) other recognition by the international community of the severity of the crime.[365]

---

362 *Ibid* at para 3.

363 RSAA Appeal No 76157, 26 June 2008 at paras 196–200.

364 EC (Sri Lanka), [2017] NZIPT 801021, 12 April 2017.

365 AF (Mexico), [2018] NZIPT 801315, 28 September 2018 at para 100, referring to CK (China), [2017] NZIPT 800775-776; with respect to the last factor, the tribunal mentioned the fact that art 2(b) of the Convention against Transnational Organized Crime defines a serious crime as conduct for which a penalty of at least four years can be imposed, indicating that "while this refers to an international convention separate from the international refugee law

Murder,[366] torture,[367] cannibalism,[368] extortion,[369] aggravated robbery,[370] bribery, transnational drug smuggling,[371] and the scuttling of a vessel[372] have all been considered serious crimes but only if committed outside New Zealand due to the wording of 1F(b).[373] On the other hand, one tribunal found that being convicted for a number of violence-related offences, such as threatening with violence or affray in the United Kingdom and assault with a weapon, assault, and threatening bodily harm in Canada (none of which individually resulted in a sentence of over two years), did not amount to serious crimes. Nor did convictions of driving without a driver's licence in the United Kingdom or immigration fraud in Poland and Canada by saying that "his offences, and particularly those involving violence, while reprehensible, are not of such a serious nature that the appellant should be excluded from the protection of the Refugee Convention."[374] Using the same terminology, a serious assault on a victim who was hospitalized was not considered a serious offence,[375] nor was vandalism.[376] This result was reached for a person with convictions for robberies and assault, this time primarily because of "the circumstances of the appellant's gang recruitment, his maturity and the gang pressure he was subject to, as well as the fact no charges were laid for assault, and the juvenile detention school sentence was for the purpose of rehabilitation."[377] However, the assessment was different when he was involved in the same activities for the same gang

---

regime, it does reflect representative state consensus on serious crime and demonstrates political will to address global issues of serious crime" (at para 98); see, also, AY (Malaysia), [2019] NZIPT 801143, 27 May 2019 at para 195.

366 RSAA Appeal No 70447, 30 June 1997; RSAA Appeal No 70432, 7 May 1998; RSAA Appeal No 71398, 10 February 2000; RSAA Appeal No 74273, 10 May 2006.

367 RSAA Appeal No 74273, 10 May 2006.

368 RSAA Appeal No 70432, 7 May 1998.

369 RSAA Appeal No 71398, 10 February 2000.

370 RSAA Appeal No 71398, 10 February 2000; RSAA Appeal No 70001, 30 April 1997; see, also, AF (Mexico), [2018] NZIPT 801315, 28 September 2018 at para 140.

371 AH (Mexico), [2020] NZIPT 801631, 11 June 2020.

372 *Tamil X*, above note 4 at paras 81, 84; this decision has already been discussed in the previous chapter in respect to art 1F(a).

373 AP (Iran), [2011] NZIPT 800012, 29 September 2011, and BS (Fiji), [2012] NZIPT 800041, 3 August 2012.

374 EC (Sri Lanka), [2017] NZIPT 801021, 12 April 2017 at para 126.

375 AF (Mexico), [2018] NZIPT 801315, 28 September 2018 at para 115.

376 *Ibid* at para 118.

377 AY (Malaysia), [2019] NZIPT 801143, 27 May 2019 at paras 234.

by the time he was nineteen, where the balance of mitigating and aggravating circumstances led the tribunal to say:

> The Tribunal acknowledges the mitigating factors relevant in this case: the appellant's mental and psychological make-up after having been forced into gang membership at age 13; his forced exposure to violence and coercion to commit acts of violence as a 13 and 14-year-old, including through the threats of serious physical violence from gang members; and the threats to his physical safety and of violent attacks due to his refusal to re-join the gang. However, it also has considered the fact that he was not under any immediate threat to his safety at the time of the attack; he sought out and drove into the gang members unprovoked; he was of the age of criminal responsibility; and in both Malaysia and New Zealand he would be facing imprisonment for an appreciable number of years.[378]

The Supreme Court of New Zealand discussed the concept of political crimes in a case of a ship's chief engineer involved in transporting weapons to support the LTTE in its conflict against the Sri Lankan government. Before discussing the parameters of this notion, the court considered the purpose of exclusion to be twofold: (1) "to ensure those who commit serious non-political crimes do not avoid legitimate prosecution by availing themselves of Convention protection" and (2) "to protect the security of states in which refuge is sought by providing an exception from Convention obligations in respect of those with a propensity to commit serious non-political crimes."[379] It then enunciated the predominance test, relying on academic writing and an important case of the UK House of Lords, as the appropriate vehicle to determine whether a crime was political, taking into account the situation of the country of origin.[380] The person's motivation was seen as clearly political because he used his skills as an engineer to support the political purposes of the LTTE.[381]

At the tribunal level, the political exception has often been applied, using the same predominance test even before the decision of the Supreme Court. On that basis, it was felt that the torture and killing of Sikh militants by Indian government security forces were deemed to be

378 *Ibid* at para 235.

379 *Tamil X*, above note 4 at para 82

380 *Ibid* at paras 88–91.

381 *Ibid* at paras 95–96.

"wholly disproportionate" to any legitimate political objective of combating terrorists who wanted to overthrow a democratically elected government.[382] The same conclusion was reached for a member of the LTTE as this organization was involved in a "full-scale war accompanied by gross human rights abuses aimed at innocent civilians and wide-scale terrorist activities."[383] Again, a South African person who participated in an attack against African National Congress (ANC) supporters out of revenge for the murder of his father by the ANC was seen as devoid of any political motives.[384]

Exclusion was also the result for a soldier of the Armed Forced of Liberia, which was engaged in an armed conflict with the National Patriotic Front of Liberia (NPFL) of Charles Taylor. The claim that he was part of an armed force defending the structure of the state was rejected as there was no meaningful causal link between that purpose and the killing of civilians and acts of cannibalism. Furthermore, these actions had no effect on the conflict in Liberia.[385] A member of the Janatha Vimukthi Peramuna (JVP) in Sri Lanka, who was involved under threat of violence in a large number of robberies of shopkeepers and who used the proceeds of those crimes for personal use, such as buying drugs, was found not to fall within the parameters of the political exception even though the JVP had a political purpose.[386] A person connected to the All India Sikh Students Federation (AISSF), whose political objective was the establishment of an independent Khalistan, was excluded as there was no causal link between the killing of Hindu traders and the political goal; in addition, such means employed in a democratic society such as India were disproportionate to that goal.[387]

On the other hand, the political defence was accepted for a member of the Oromo Liberation Front (OLF) in Ethiopia, which strived for independence for the Oromo people. As a member of this organization, he had been involved in the transporting of small boxes, which he suspected contained small arms. The tribunal was of the view that even if such activities amounted to serious crimes, they would have been

382 RSAA Appeal No 74273, 10 May 2006 at para 69.
383 RSAA Appeal No 71335, 12 September 2000 at paras 24, 29.
384 RSAA Appeal No 70447, 30 June 1997.
385 RSAA Appeal No 71398, 10 February 2000.
386 RSAA Appeal No 70001, 30 April 1997.
387 RSAA Appeal No 70432, 7 May 1998; see, also, RSAA Appeal No 29/91, 17 February 1992.

proportional to the political purpose of the OLF.[388] The same result was achieved for a person who smuggled people out of North Korea because his motivation arose out of a particular political context and his methods were proportionate to the political end that he embraced.[389]

Exclusion under article 1F(b) has also been applied to persons who not only committed the serious political crime themselves but also were complicit. The parameters of complicity for this exclusion ground are the same as for article 1F(a) in New Zealand, and in cases where this notion was applied, it usually involved aiding and abetting,[390] although one category of persons is excluded by law: any member of a terrorist entity designated under the *Terrorism Suppression Act 2002*.[391]

Defences have been raised sporadically in the context of exclusion 1F(b). In one case, duress was raised by a person who had committed robberies and assault, but it was found not to apply because the New Zealand *Criminal Code* states specifically that this defence cannot be raised as a full defence for a number of serious offences, including robbery and injuring with intent to cause grievous bodily harm. However, it is one of the factors in play when determining whether a 1F(b) crime is serious.[392] In another case, the same defence was raised for bribery and transnational drug smuggling, and here the tribunal assessed the facts based on the elements of this defence as contained in article 31(1)(d) of the Rome Statute; they rejected the defence because the person had a reasonable avenue of escape.[393]

The lack of expiation, in the sense that "factors extraneous to the offending, such as propensity to commit crime, any present or future danger to the host society, or post-crime rehabilitation and expiation, are excluded from the inquiry,"[394] has been applied at both the court and tribunal level when saying that the seriousness of a crime bears no relation to matters extraneous to the offending, and there is nothing in

388 RSAA Appeal No 71150, 4 March 1999.

389 AC (North Korea), [2019] NZIPT 801589, 18 November 2019 at paras 118–23.

390 RSAA Appeal No 74273, 10 May 2006, providing information resulting in the killing of people in India; RSAA Appeal No 71335, 12 September 2000, compiling a list of political opponents resulting in assassinations in Sri Lanka; RSAA Appeal No 71398, 10 February 2000, restraining victims while they were being killed in Liberia; RSAA Appeal No 70001, 30 April 1997, being part of a group carrying out robberies in Sri Lanka.

391 *Immigration Act 2009*, s 16(1)(b).

392 AY (Malaysia), [2019] NZIPT 801143, 27 May 2019.

393 AH (Mexico), [2020] NZIPT 801631, 11 June 2020.

394 AF (Mexico), [2018] NZIPT 801315, 28 September 2018 at para 95

article 1F(b) to justify reading into its provisions restrictive or qualifying words.[395]

An interesting aspect in the New Zealand jurisprudence has been the evolution of the concept of what constitutes a serious crime by starting with a number of factors and then emphasizing one of them, the possible sentence a person could receive in New Zealand, followed by using a larger number of factors, which examine both aggravating and mitigating circumstances. The concept of political crime has been the subject of several cases in New Zealand, and as in other countries in this study, the extradition test of predominance and proportionality was the one chosen as the most appropriate for refugee purposes, including in armed conflicts. Another indirect link to international law can be found in the fact that extended liability and the defence of duress were seen as having the same parameters in exclusion grounds 1F(a) and 1F(b).

h) United Kingdom

It was already said in 1996 by the House of Lords that the most important underlying purpose of 1F(b) is that there are those "whose criminal habits make it unreasonable for them to be forced on to a host nation against its will."[396] More recently, this was expanded by pointing to the dual purpose of 1F(b), striking a balance between humane treatment of victims of oppression and the other interests of signatory countries,[397] as well as saying that "the objective is that the refugee framework should not stand in the way of serious criminals facing justice. The exclusion clauses should be applied scrupulously to protect the Convention's integrity and to prevent abuse."[398]

More specifically, the government's manual, "Exclusion (Article 1F) and Article 33(2) of the Refugee Convention" has a few observations

---

395 *S v Refugee Status Appeals Authority*, [1998] 2 NZLR 291; EC (Sri Lanka), [2017] NZIPT 801021, 12 April 2017 at paras 108–10; AF (Mexico), [2018] NZIPT 801315, 28 September 2018; AH (Mexico), [2020] NZIPT 801631, 11 June 2020, in which the last three decisions relied on Canadian and UK jurisprudence in support of this proposition.

396 *Immigration Officer*, above note 4 at 875.

397 *AH (Algeria) v Secretary of State for the Home Department*, [2015] EWCA Civ 1003 at paras 29–30 [*AH*, 2015], relying on the *Febles* case of the Supreme Court of Canada, above note 4.

398 *AH*, 2015, *ibid*; see, also, KM (exclusion; article 1F(a); article 1F(b)) Democratic Republic of Congo [2022] UKUT 00125 (IAC), which adds at para 51: "Another intention is to exclude those who have committed serious common crimes because they pose a risk to the integrity of the system of international protection as well as to mitigate the potential risk to the host state."

in respect to exclusion under article 1F(b). It considers a serious crime "any particularly cruel action."[399] Furthermore, the manual states that the length of a prison sentence alone is not determinative of whether the claimant should be excluded under article 1F(b).[400]

> More important than the sentence is the nature and context of the crime, the harm inflicted, the part played by the claimant, and whether most jurisdictions would consider it a serious crime. Examples include murder, rape, arson, and armed robbery. Other offences that may be regarded as serious include those that are accompanied by the use of deadly weapons or involve serious injury to persons or if there is evidence of serious habitual criminal conduct. Other crimes, though not accompanied by violence, such as large-scale fraud, may also be regarded as serious for the purposes of Article 1F(b).[401]

---

399 UK Home Office, "Exclusion (Article 1F) and Article 33(2) of the Refugee Convention" (28 June 2022) at page 28, online: www.gov.uk/government/publications/asylum-instruction-exclusion-article-1f-of-the-refugee-convention/exclusion-article-1f-and-article-332-of-the-refugee-convention-accessible-version; in an earlier version of the manual, this assessment was based on a comparison with the notion of a particularly serious crime, which is defined in s 72 of the *Nationality, Immigration and Asylum Act 2002* as amended by the *Nationality and Borders Act, 2022*, s 38, and which considers such a crime for the purposes of art 33.2 of the Refugee Convention any conviction for which a sentence of at least twelve months has been imposed; however, doubt was placed on equating these two concepts in *AH*, 2015, above note 397 at paras 35–36.

400 UK Home Office, above note 399 at pages 28–29; for this proposition, it relied on *AH (Algeria) v Secretary of State for the Home Department*, [2012] EWCA Civ 395 [*AH*, 2012], which at para 54 said: "Sentence is, of course, a material factor but it is not a benchmark. In deciding whether the crime is serious enough to justify his loss of protection, the Tribunal must take all facts and matters into account, with regard to the nature of the crime, the part played by the accused in its commission, any mitigating or aggravating features and the eventual penalty imposed." This approach was already foreshadowed in an earlier decision by the High Court involving possession of a pistol with ammunition; while the court declined to determine whether this activity was serious in the sense that the legislative presumption should apply wherever a person has committed an offence where the maximum punishment for the particular offence is two years or rather where two years or more is the likely actual punishment for the crime in question, *in obiter* it cast some doubt on the crime in question by saying that with this presumption, "there is the prospect of offences such as burglary or causing death by careless driving falling with Article 1F(b)"; see *Polat, R (On the Application Of) v The Secretary of State for the Home Department*, [2011] EWHC 3445 (Admin) at para 73.

401 UK Home Office, above note 399 at pages 28–29; an earlier manual used to say that "irrespective of the actual length of sentence, or the length of sentence, which might be expected if the crime were tried in the United Kingdom" and that a serious crime is also a crime if it is mentioned in a regulation under the *Nationality, Immigration and Asylum Act 2002*, namely, the *Nationality, Immigration and Asylum Act 2002 (Specification of Particularly*

With respect to foreign convictions, the manual states:

> Whichever clauses of Article 1F apply, the person does not have to have been prosecuted or convicted of any offence in any country. Equally, evidence of the acquittal of a person accused of a crime or a pardon following conviction, does not necessarily mean that exclusion cannot or should not be applied. Each case must be considered on its individual merits. Evidence of a conviction will usually provide serious reasons for considering that they have committed the crime and decision makers will not normally need to examine at length the evidential basis for the conviction. Decision makers must keep in mind the possibility that an asylum claimant who was a known opponent of their country's authorities may be the victim of false charges and that a criminal prosecution or conviction in their country of origin may in fact constitute evidence of persecution, especially in countries where standards of judicial fairness fall well short of internationally accepted standards.[402]

A political crime is defined in the manual, by a reference to the seminal House of Lords' case in this area, as follows:

> (1) it is committed for a political purpose, that is to say with the object of overthrowing or subverting or changing the government of a state or inducing it to change its policy; and
> (2) there is a sufficiently close and direct link between the crime and the alleged political purpose.[403]

In determining whether such a link exists, the court will bear in mind the means used to achieve the political end and will have particular regard to whether the crime was aimed at a military or governmental

---

Serious Crimes) Order 2004, which contained primarily terrorist offences, proceeds of crime offences, and serious drug offences; however, this regulation was declared ultra vires by the Court of Appeal in *EN (Serbia) & KC (South Africa) v Home Secretary*, [2009] EWCA Civ 630 at para 83.

402 UK Home Office, above note 399 at page 14; this excerpt was also referred to in *Gavrić v Refugee Status Determination Officer, Cape Town and Others*, [2018] ZACC 38 at paras 90 and 107.

403 UK Home Office, above note 399 at page 29; the reference is from *Immigration Officer*, above note 4 at 786–87, which also refers to the Canadian case of *Gil*, above note 4; see, also, Singer, *Exclusion*, above note 68 at 69–83, while KM (exclusion; article 1F(a); article 1F(b)) Democratic Republic of Congo [2022] UKUT 00125 (IAC) at paras 53 and 161, said that this exception cannot apply to state agents.

target, on the one hand, or a civilian target, on the other, and in either event whether it was likely to involve the indiscriminate killing or injuring of members of the public.[404] The document adds that crimes such as "murder, rape and serious assault, or other violent acts which result in indiscriminate harm or death to the public, will usually fail to establish a sufficient link to the achievement to a political objective."[405]

With respect to the crime being committed outside the country of refuge prior to admission as a refugee, the manual states that this means up to "the time of issuing a residence permit following a grant of refugee status. As such, crimes committed in the UK before an individual is granted refugee status (and issued a residence permit . . . fall within the scope of Article 1F(b)." It adds: "[A] crime such as conspiracy to import drugs may have both an international and domestic dimension—that is committed both overseas, before the asylum seeker came to the UK, and continued in the UK after arrival. Continuous crimes such as this can also be considered as being committed outside the country of refuge."[406] Last, the manual indicates that having been punished or having received a pardon or amnesty does not prevent the application of the exclusion clause, nor does expiation or the passage of time.[407]

Consistent with the factor approach for the notion of serious crime, a court had already said in 2011, about a fourteen-year-old boy who killed his half-brother in Afghanistan, that an assessment of this issue

> requires the minister to look at all the circumstances of the case; not just the nomenclature of the crime and the basic scenario. Because a serious crime is the trigger of the exclusion, the whole factual and legal matrix must be evaluated with care and some precision. A starting point must be a correct analysis of the law in this country and the country where the crime is said to have occurred. The individual factual matrix of the alleged crime must be examined with care; which

404 UK Home Office, above note 399 at page 29.

405 *Ibid.*

406 *Ibid* at page 30.

407 *Ibid* at page 19; see, along the same lines, AA (Exclusion clause) Palestine, [2005] UKIAT 00104, at para 40; *AH*, 2015, above note 397 at para 32; and *AAS and Others v Secretary of State for the Home Department*, UKUT, AA/08375/2011, 14 May 2019 at para 52 [*AAS*], the latter relying on the *Febles* case of the Supreme Court of Canada: see above note 4; also, with respect to the non-applicability of a foreign immunity from prosecution for exclusion 1F(b), see the decision by the High Court of Ireland in *HO v Refugee Appeals Tribunal & Anor*, [2014] IEHC 494 at paras 65–69, while relying for this proposition on the CJEU decision in *B and D*, above note 51.

must include any points advanced as providing a potential defence (both legal and factual). The age and circumstances of the alleged offender are also important. The likely punishment, if found guilty, is also to be considered. I also regard it as being important that the minister keeps a sense of proportion and balance about the case. It is only when the matter has been examined in this way may the decision be regarded as lawful. It must be a serious crime—that goes, almost, without saying—but the whole circumstances must be evaluated, as I have described, before concluding there is a serious belief that the individual in question has committed a serious crime. The nomenclature of the crime is of less importance than the circumstances of the crime properly evaluated as I have heretofore set out. An acute sense of the reality is a useful lodestar when considering this broad tapestry of factors. Some cases will be able to be analysed in a very straightforward way—others less so.[408]

Other jurisprudence of the courts and tribunals have indicated that crimes such as attacks on military barracks and bomb attacks;[409] threat of serious violence;[410] indiscriminate killing and injury of members of the public;[411] smuggling guns, undertaking armed attack missions, and preparing for a suicide mission;[412] malicious wounding;[413] torture;[414]

408 *R (ABC a minor) v Home Secretary*, [2011] EWHC 2937 (Admin) at para 32; furthermore, apart from departing from the legislative intent as set out in the first case above, the court came to the interesting conclusion that "it is too simplistic . . . to say that all allegations of crimes involving the death of an individual are a serious crime" (at para 35) and then overruling the exclusion decision as there had been no analysis of culpability, which is a different analysis for children than for adults, nor had there been sufficient attention given to a possible defence in this case as the boy killed his half-brother when this other boy was assaulting him (at paras 42–44 and 48).

409 *Immigration Officer*, above note 4 at 777.

410 *Gurung v Secretary of State for the Home Department*, [2002] UKIAT 04870 at para 135 [*Gurung*].

411 *B, Re*, [1997] EWCA Civ 802.

412 AA (Exclusion clause) Palestine [2005] UKIAT 00104, at para 46, which adds at para 66 that in the UNHCR *Handbook*, "para 155 elevates the gravity of a "serious non-political crime" to "a capital crime or a very grave punishable act," which is an unwarranted gloss on "serious."

413 *Boroumand, R (on the application of) v Secretary of State for the Home Department*, [2010] EWHC 225 (Admin) at paras 56–57.

414 *A (Iraq) v Secretary of State for the Home Department*, [2005] EWCA Civ 1438, at paras 11–12; KM (exclusion; article 1F(a); article 1F(b)) Democratic Republic of Congo [2022] UKUT 00125 (IAC) at para 160.

and hijacking of a plane[415] are article 1F(b) crimes; so too are economic crimes such as massive fraud.[416]

With respect to terrorism as a crime, it was said at the tribunal level that

> it remains crucial not to equate Art 1F with a simple anti-terrorism clause. Regular use of the concept of terrorism as a tool for identifying crimes contrary to Art 1F must await definitive codification by the international community.... At the same time, it may be obvious in a particular case that active involvement in crimes which have been or can properly be described as acts of terrorism will be serious enough to fall within Art 1F(b).[417]

This stands in some contrast to the views of the House of Lords six years earlier to the effect that

> once it is made clear that terrorism is not simply a label for violent conduct of which the speaker deeply disapproves, the term is capable of definition and objective application. I quote again from the League of Nations Convention of 1937: "'Acts' of terrorism mean criminal acts directed against a State and intended or calculated to create a state of terror in the minds of particular persons, or a group of persons or general public." The Convention never came into force, but the definition is serviceable, and I am content to adopt it.[418]

Indirect participation can also lead to exclusion. Knowing and abetting torture by handing over persons who had been arrested by the person concerned was one example of such involvement.[419] In this context, the saga of the *AH* case is illustrative. This involved a stateless person, formerly of Algerian nationality, who in 1993 was convicted

---

415 *AAS*, above note 407 at para 122.

416 *XY v the Secretary of State for the Home Department*, [2017] UKAITUR AA099192014 at paras 43–44.

417 *Gurung*, above note 410 at paras 100–1.

418 *Immigration Officer*, above note 4, Lord Mustill at 758; see, also, David Bonner & Ryszard Cholewinski, "The Response of the UK Legal and Constitutional Orders to the 1991 Gulf War and Post-9/11 'War' on Terrorism" in Anneliese Baldaccini & Elspeth Guild, eds, *Terrorism and the Foreigner: A Decade of Tension Around the Rule of Law in Europe* (Leiden/Boston: Martinus Nijhoff, 2007) at 139–40.

419 KM (exclusion; Article 1F(a); Article 1F(b)) Democratic Republic of Congo [2022] UKUT 00125 (IAC) at paras 151–53, 160, and 164, although the tribunal makes a connection between indirect liability and the seriousness of the crime at para 160.

of and sentenced to death in absentia in Algeria for involvement in a bombing at the Algiers Airport. At the time of that trial, he was in France. In 1999, he was convicted in France of being a member of an association created specifically for the preparation of acts of terrorism (namely, possession of false identity documents), sentenced to two years' imprisonment, and made subject to a deportation order.[420] The court said that while a foreign conviction should be given credence, it was not clear from the tribunal's reasoning "whether the type of crime of which the person was convicted in France could have been concluded on the basis of the very limited findings of the French Appeal Court that the particular offence of which this Appellant was convicted crossed the threshold of seriousness for the purpose of Article 1F(b)."[421] The case was sent back to an immigration tribunal, which issued a judgment a year later, saying that, with the benefit of more detailed information on the French procedures, reliance on these French court documents was proper in this case,[422] while with respect to the substance, it found that the person had committed serious crimes; the latter was based on the fact that the person's involvement within the criminal conspiracy was more than peripheral and that his participation was not limited to the possession of these documents but also using these documents to move within and outside France in support of other senior members of this association, some of whom were planning and executing terrorist acts of which he had knowledge.[423] This finding was upheld on appeal, saying that the person "was giving succour to a terrorist cause, and doing so as a senior conspirator; and as such had plainly committed a 'serious non-political crime' within the meaning of Article 1F(b)."[424]

In applying the political offence test, the House of Lords was of the view that a member of the FIS in Algeria had not fit the requirements of its test when involved in bomb attacks and attacks on military

420 *AH*, 2012, above note 400 at para 47.

421 *Ibid* at para 16, where the judge says: "I readily accept that the fact of a conviction by a court may well make the task of assessing whether a person falls within Article 1F much easier, but it will do so only if the nature of the offence of which the person has been convicted and/or the findings made by the court are sufficient to enable the Tribunal to reach a conclusion as to the individual's 'own personal involvement and role in the organisation,' or the 'true role' played by the individual in the acts perpetrated by the organisation."

422 *AH (Article 1F(b) — 'serious') Algeria*, [2013] UKUT 00382 (IAC) at para 94.

423 *Ibid* at paras 98–102.

424 *AH*, 2015, above note 397 at para 45.

barracks,[425] while an Islamic Jihad armed militant in Gaza was considered to be falling within the parameters of article 1F(b), in which one factor was that this organization was on a UK terrorist organization list.[426] A senior commander of the PKK was excluded as the activities of his organization involved the indiscriminate killing of civilians, thereby nullifying the political purpose. The same happened to a number of persons who hijacked a plane in Afghanistan to effect an escape from political oppression of the Taliban, which had threatened harm, because there was no sufficiently close and direct link between the hijacking and its political purpose of escaping persecution.[427] On the other hand, a political purpose was found to be present and the means not disproportionate in attacks against military personnel by the LTTE and the attempted poisoning of the wife of former Zairean president Mobutu.[428]

The defence of duress was raised in one 1F(b) case, but it was rejected because the element of threat of serious and imminent harm was not met, and there had also been alternative means of escape to avert the harm.[429]

i) United States

While the text of article 1F(b) has been incorporated into the *Immigration and Nationality Act (INA)*,[430] this legislation has four other criminal bars to asylum, in addition to this exclusionary provision, of which the terrorism bar will also be the subject of this section.[431]

---

425 *Immigration Officer*, above note 4.

426 *AA (Exclusion clause) Palestine*, [2005] UKIAT 00104 at 49; the listing instrument mentioned is the *Terrorism Act 2000 (Proscribed Organisations) (Amendment) Order 2000*.

427 *AAS*, above note 407 at paras 118–22, while relying at para 85 on the case of *MT (Article 1F (a) — aiding and abetting) Zimbabwe*, [2012] UKUT 00015, which had examined this defence in the context of 1F(a).

428 See Kapferer, above note 134 at 204.

429 *AAS*, above note 407 at paras 103–4,

430 Section 208(b)(2)(A)(iii).

431 Section 208(b)(2)(A) contains the following six bars:

(i) the alien ordered, incited, assisted, or otherwise participated in the persecution of any person on account of race, religion, nationality, membership in a particular social group, or political opinion;

(ii) the alien, having been convicted by a final judgment of a particularly serious crime, constitutes a danger to the community of the United States;

(iii) there are serious reasons for believing that the alien has committed a serious nonpolitical crime outside the United States prior to the arrival of the alien in the United States;

With respect to the concept of serious non-political crimes, the methodology employed in general to determine whether a crime is serious depends on such factors as the nature of the crime according to US precedents, the value of any property involved, the length of sentence imposed and served, and the usual punishments imposed for comparable offences in the United States.[432] Murder;[433] attempted manslaughter;[434] kidnapping;[435] arson, armed robbery, and random acts of violence against civilians;[436] assault;[437] drug trafficking;[438] possession with intent

---

(iv) there are reasonable grounds for regarding the alien as a danger to the security of the United States;

(v) the alien is described in subclause (I), (II), (III), (IV), or (VI) of s 212(a)(3)(B)(i) or s 237(a)(4)(B) (relating to terrorist activity), unless, in the case only of an alien described in subclause (IV) of s 212(a)(3)(B)(i), the Attorney General determines, in the Attorney General's discretion, that there are not reasonable grounds for regarding the alien as a danger to the security of the United States; or

(vi) the alien was firmly resettled in another country prior to arriving in the United States.

The last one is not criminal and will not be discussed; the first one has been examined in Chapter 4, while categories (ii) and (iv) are related to *refoulement* as the wording is the same as in s 33.2 of the Refugee Convention and as such will be discussed in Chapter 6 (although it has been said that the legislative enumerations of particularly serious crimes are by definition also serious crimes for the purposes of exclusion in category (iii); see *Go v Holder*, 640 F3d 1047 (9th Cir 2011)). For the interplay of these provisions and the view of the court that category (v) is not in violation of the Refugee Convention and Protocol, see *Khan v Holder*, 584 F3d 773 (9th Cir 2009) [*Khan*].

432 James Sloan, "The Application of Article 1F of the 1951 Convention in Canada and the United States" (supp, 2000) 12 *International Journal of Refugee Law* 222 at 243; see, also, *Mahini v INS*, 779 F2d 1419 (9th Cir 1986) [*Mahini*].

433 *McMullen v INS*, 788 F2d 591 (9th Cir 1986) [*McMullen*]; *Khouzam v Ashcroft*, 361 F3d 161 (2d Cir 2004); *Belov v Holder*, 385 Fed Appx 624 (9th Cir 2010) (relying on witnesses in addition to a Russian indictment and arrest warrant, although an Interpol Red Notice issued at the request of Russia was deemed to be insufficient evidence as such notices were deemed unreliable in *Tatintsyan v Barr*, 799 Fed Appx 965 (9th Cir 2019); *Silva-Pereira v Lynch*, 827 F3d 1176 (9th Cir 2016); *Contreras-Gonzalez v Barr*, 839 Fed Appx 611 (2d Cir 2020); the latter case also indicated that an Interpol Red Notice based on an arrest warrant issued by a judge in the Dominican Republic outweighs contrary testimony during an immigration hearing by the person concerned.

434 *Marroquin-Retana v AG United States*, 675 Fed Appx 216 (3d Cir 2017).

435 *Saldana v United States AG*, 431 Fed Appx 801 (11th Cir 2011).

436 *McMullen*, above note 433.

437 *Zheng v Holder*, 698 F3d 710 (8th Cir 2012).

438 *Go v Holder*, above note 431; *Qamar v Lynch*, 664 Fed Appx 90 (2d Cir 2016).

to distribute heroin[439] or marijuana;[440] embezzlement;[441] selling organs for profit on the black market;[442] and theft for which a sentence of fifteen years was imposed[443] are serious crimes, while participation in resistance activities and supporting a coup against a military government were found not to be serious non-political crimes.[444]

Both the Federal Court of Appeals and the Supreme Court have considered the notion of political crimes. The Federal Court in the *McMullen* case, involving a member of the Provisional Irish Republican Army (PIRA), which was involved in terrorist attacks against civilians, said the following about such crimes:

> A balancing approach including consideration of the offense's "proportionality" to its objective and its degree of atrocity makes good sense.... Moreover, this approach better recognizes the type of crime involved in this and most such cases. There is a distinction between "pure" political crimes, such as sedition, treason, and espionage, and "relative" political crimes, crimes that have both common law criminal aspects and political aspects.... An approach that considers the proportionality and atrocity of a particular course of conduct is better suited to the analysis of "relative" political offenses under the Convention and Protocol.[445]

It was also of the view that "motivation is not itself determinative of the political character of any given act," but that the critical issue is "whether there is a close and direct causal link between the crime committed and its alleged political purpose and object."[446] As a result, not every criminal act that in some sense contributes to the political goal amounts to a political offence. The terrorist methods of the PIRA, "indiscriminate bombing campaigns, murder, torture, and maiming of innocent civilians who disagreed with the PIRA," were not justified by its political goal of establishing an independent Ireland.[447]

---

439 *Mahini*, above note 432.

440 *Arauz v Rivkind*, 834 F2d 979 (11th Cir 1987).

441 *Kenyeres v Ashcroft*, 538 US 1301 (2003); *Guo Wang v Eric Holder*, Docket No 07-5369-ag (2d Cir 2009) [*Guo Wang*]; and *Jiang Guan v Barr*, 925 F3d 1022 (9th Cir 2019).

442 *Guo Wang*, above note 441.

443 Regina Germain, *AILA Asylum Primer: A Practical Guide to U.S. Asylum Law and Procedure* (Washington, DC: American Immigration Lawyers Association, 2007) at 110.

444 *Ibid* at 110.

445 *McMullen*, above note 433.

446 *Ibid* at 597.

447 *Ibid*.

The Supreme Court confirmed the ruling of the Federal Court of Appeals in *McMullen* but clarified some aspects of the predominance theory by saying:

> Our decision takes into account that the [Board of Immigration Appeals'] test identifies a general standard (whether the political aspect of an offense outweighs its common-law character) and then provides two more specific inquiries that may be used in applying the rule: whether there is a gross disproportion between means and ends, and whether atrocious acts are involved.[448]

The situation in question involved a student in Guatemala who protested with fellow students against various government policies and actions by burning buses, assaulting passengers who refused to leave those buses, and vandalizing and destroying private property, which the tribunal had found to be a serious political crime. This had been overruled by the Federal Court of Appeals, which was of the view that the *McMullen* test for political crimes had been met in this case. The Supreme Court disagreed with the reasoning of the lower court.

This test was applied where a person had been part of a demonstration in Nigeria against the military government, which refused to install the legally elected president. During this demonstration, police beat participants including the claimant, who then left the demonstration to get a knife, with which he killed a police officer. The court felt that this was not a political crime as the killing was disproportionate to the objective of the demonstration. The self-defence argument was also rejected as he had not been in any immediate danger.[449] Similarly, criminal acts of burning buses, breaking windows, and fighting with the police outweighed the political motive of protesting important political and social issues.[450] The supervision of the beating of eleven prisoners of war (POWs) by an officer of the Indian army had no political nature or objective; the beatings were carried out of anger and in retaliation for suspected atrocities by the POWs, not to achieve any strategic or tactical military objective; as well, his participation in the capture and beating of thirty to forty random Bangladeshi civilians was disproportionate

448 *INS v Aguirre-Aguirre*, 526 US 415 (1999).

449 *Efe v Ashcroft*, 293 F3d 899 (5th Cir 2002). It was also applied and rejected in the context of terrorist activities carried out in Northern Ireland in the case of *McAllister v AG of the United States*, 444 F3d 178 (3d Cir 2006) [*McAllister*].

450 *Chay-Velasquez v Ashcroft*, 367 F3d 751 (8th Cir 2004).

to the stated political objective; he did not explain whether alternative means of gathering intelligence about Pakistan's border defenses were available, from the civilians or otherwise, and the argument that the crimes were political in nature because they occurred in the context of a military conflict was unconvincing.[451]

In contrast, a case where a person who had thrown rocks during political rallies in Ethiopia and had been excluded for a non-political crime but had also claimed that these acts were never directed at civilians but were done in self-defence against the violence of the police was sent back to the tribunal to reconsider this defence.[452] A foreign conviction for a serious crime is not to be taken at face value because at times a criminal prosecution can be commenced for political reasons, as was the case for a Ukrainian claimant who was subjected to a groundless prosecution for rape because of his outspoken political beliefs.[453]

The other exclusionary portion in article 208 of the *INA*, which bears similarities to serious non-political crimes and was given legislative treatment, deals with terrorist activities.[454] While the notion of terrorism was certainly known in the United States before the attacks of 11 September 2001, and while persons involved in terrorist activities had already been excluded for such activities by virtue of article 1F(b), both criminal and immigration legislation has been substantially altered since that date, primarily by the *USA Patriot Act* of 2001[455] and the *REAL ID Act* of 2005.[456] As a result of the amendments introduced by these two Acts, the *INA* has expanded its definitions for concepts related to terrorism, including the meaning of terrorist activity, as well as having bars for asylum seekers who have engaged or are likely to engage in terrorist activities, have incited terrorist activity with the intention to cause death or serious bodily harm, are a representative of a foreign terrorist organization or a political or social group that

---

451 *Singh v Holder*, 533 Fed Appx 712 (9th Cir 2013).

452 *Berhane v Holder*, Docket No 09-3153 (6th Cir 2010).

453 *Abramov v Ashcroft*, Docket No 03-71856 (9th Cir 2004).

454 *INA*, s 208(b)(2)(A)(v).

455 The official name is the *Uniting and Strengthening America by Providing Appropriate Tools Required to Intercept and Obstruct Terrorism Act of 2001 (USA PATRIOT)*.

456 See Germain, above note 443 at 113, and Michael John Garcia & Ruth Ellen Wasem, *Immigration: Terrorist Grounds for Exclusion and Removal of Aliens*, Congressional Research Service Report for Congress (12 January 2010) at 3–6 , online (pdf): https://sgp.fas.org/crs/homesec/RL32564.pdf.

endorses or espouses terrorist activity, or are a member of a terrorist organization.[457]

The definition of terrorist activity includes

(i) the hijacking or sabotage of any conveyance, including an aircraft, vessel, or vehicle;
(ii) the seizing or detaining, and threatening to kill, injure, or continue to detain, another individual in order to compel a third person, including a governmental organization to do or abstain from doing any act as an explicit or implicit condition for the release of the individual seized or detained;
(iii) a violent attack upon an internationally protected or upon the liberty of such a person;
(iv) an assassination;
(v) the use of any
   a. biological agent, chemical agent, or nuclear weapon or device, or
   b. explosive, firearm, or other weapon or dangerous device, other than for mere personal monetary gain,

   with intent to endanger, directly or indirectly, the safety of one or more individuals or to cause substantial damage to property;
(vi) or the threat, attempt, or conspiracy to do any of the foregoing.[458]

Engaging in terrorist activity in an individual capacity or as a member of an organization has been defined in detail, including concepts such as committing, preparing, gathering information, soliciting funds or individuals, and providing material support for terrorist activity.[459]

---

457 *INA*, s 212(a)(3)(B)(i)(I), (II), (III), (IV), and (VI) as a result of the reference in s 208(b)(2)(A)(v).

458 *Ibid*, s 212(a)(3)(B)(iii) as a result of the reference in s 208(b)(2)(A)(v). This definition is broader than the criminal definition contained in s 2331 of the US Code, Title 18, in that the element of compelling a person or an organization to do or refrain from doing something is a general one in the criminal context but only applies to one aspect of the immigration definition. In addition to these described activities, the courts have held that an armed attack by dissidents on the military of a country, including attacking the military's convoy, constitutes terrorist activity (*Khan*, above note 431, in the Kashmir region in India), as does the attempt to carry out a coup in the Philippines (*Zumel v Lynch*, 803 F3d 463 (9th Cir 2015).

459 *Ibid*, s 212(a)(3)(B)(iv). The criminal statute contains prohibitions for harbouring or concealing a terrorist (Title 18, c 113B of the *United States Code*, s 2339), providing material support to terrorists (s 2339A) or to terrorist organizations (s 2339B), in respect to terrorism financing (s 2339C), and receiving military type training from a foreign terrorist organization (s 2339D). Section 2339B was deemed to be constitutional by the Supreme Court in the case of *Holder v Humanitarian Law Project*, 130 S Ct 2705 (2010) (for a commentary, see "Correspondent's Report, United States" (2010) 13 *Yearbook of International Humanitarian Law* at 644–46).

The secretary of state can designate an organization as a terrorist organization if such an entity has engaged in terrorist activities,[460] although a group can also be considered to be engaged in terrorist activities without such a designation if such a group has "two or more individuals, whether organized or not, [and] engages in, or has a subgroup which engages in, terrorist activities."[461] "Group" in this context can also include state actors.[462]

Because of the broad application of the terrorist organization provisions, the *INA* contains a waiver provision that allows the secretaries of

---

460 *Ibid*, s 212(a)(3)(B)(vi)(I) & (II). There are two tiers of designation. The most cumbersome is set out at subpara I and refers to the procedure set out in s 219 of the *INA*, which is based on the factors that the entity is a foreign organization, is involved in terrorist activity, and threatens the security of US nationals or the national security of the United States and includes the fact that the designation stays in effect until revoked (these are called foreign terrorist organizations or FTOs). As of 20 May 2022, there were seventy-six entities listed as Tier I terrorist organizations (with nineteen removed) according to the FTO list of the Bureau of Counterterrorism of the Department of State. Second-tier designations, set out at subpara II, can be effected by the secretary of state in consultation with or upon the request of the attorney general or the secretary of homeland security after a finding that any organization engages in terrorist activity; there are fifty-five Tier II entities (with three delisted) according to the Terrorism Exclusion List (TEL) of the Bureau of Counterterrorism. The result of these designations is that a person who provides material support to a Tier I or Tier II organization is inadmissible automatically, while for a Tier III (non-designated) terrorist organization, the person is not inadmissible if they can show, by clear and convincing evidence, that they did not know and could not reasonably have known that the organization was a terrorist organization (s 212(a)(3)(B)(iv)(VI)(dd). Some earlier judicial challenges to the designation process were unsuccessful; see *People's Mojahedin Organization of Iran v Albright*, 182 F3d 17 (DC Cir 1999); see, also, Maryellen Fullerton, "Terrorism, Torture, and Refugee Protection in the United States" (2011) 29:4 *Refugee Survey Quarterly* 4 at 11–14.

461 *INA*, s 212(a)(3)(B)(vi)(III); this is the Tier III terrorist organization. The Federal Court of Appeals in the cases of *Singh-Kaur v Ashcroft*, 385 F3d 293 (3d Cir 2004) [*Singh-Kaur*], and *McAllister*, above note 449 has indicated that the lack of designation of a particular organization is not conclusive for exclusion purposes as a person can fall within the parameters of the terrorist bar when involved in either a terrorist activity or a terrorist organization; in 2010, the *Refugee Protection Act* was introduced to eliminate the Tier III designation, but this never became law (S 3113, 111th Congress (2010), s 4(4)(c)). On the other hand, an entire organization does not automatically become a terrorist organization just because some members of the group commit terrorist acts (*Khan v Holder*, 766 F3d 689 (7th Cir 2014)), while an organization is not a terrorist one if only one of its members commits an act of armed violence without direct or indirect authorization (*Hussain v Mukasey*, 518 F3d 534 (7th Cir 2008)), which was emphasized in *Uddin v AG of the United States*, Docket No 17-1056, 6 September 2017 (3d Cir), in saying "absent such a finding regarding authorization by a group's leaders, Tier III status cannot be assigned to a group."

462 *AA v AG of the United States*, 973 F3d 171 (3d Cir 2020) [*AA*], which applied it to militia that were part of the Syrian government.

state and homeland security, in consultation with the attorney general, to exempt certain groups of the application of the latter, undesignated category. Those secretaries have applied this exemption on twenty-four occasions.[463] As well, according to this provision, the same functionaries can provide additional situational exemptions for persons providing support to undesignated terrorist organizations, which apply to the following categories, each of which are set out in specific memoranda with detailed requirements:

- material support under duress
- solicitation under duress
- military-type training under duress
- voluntary medical care
- certain applicants with existing immigration benefits
- Iraqi uprisings
- Afghan allies
- Afghan civil servants
- certain limited material support
- insignificant material support[464]

The assessment to determine that this exclusion would not apply to individuals who were under duress under the first three categories depends on the degree of duress and, if warranted, by the totality of

---

463 This waiver is set out in s 212(d)(3)(B)(i) of the *INA*, which was the result of an amendment in the *Consolidated Appropriations Act*, 2008, Public Law 110-161, Div J, s 691(a). Section 691(b) of this Act names the following ten groups: Karen National Union/Karen Liberation Army (KNU/KNLA); Chin National Front/Chin National Army (CNF/CNA); Chin National League for Democracy (CNLD); Kayan New Land Party (KNLP); Arakan Liberation Party (ALP); Tibetan Mustangs; Cuban Alzados; Karenni National Progressive Party (KNPP); appropriate groups affiliated with the Hmong; and appropriate groups affiliated with the Montagnards. On 1 July 2008, the *Consolidated Appropriations Act, 2008*, was amended by Public Law 110-257, which added the ANC to this list. Since that time, there have been fourteen more such waivers involving groups in eight counties; see US Citizenship and Immigration Services (USCIS), "Terrorism-Related Inadmissibility Grounds (TRIG) — Group-Based Exemptions" (19 November 2019), online: www.uscis.gov/laws-and-policy/other-resources/terrorism-related-inadmissibility-grounds-trig/terrorism-related-inadmissibility-grounds-trig-group-based-exemptions.

464 USCIS, "Terrorism-Related Inadmissibility Grounds (TRIG) — Situational Exemptions" (29 August 2020), online: www.uscis.gov/laws-and-policy/other-resources/terrorism-related-inadmissibility-grounds-trig/terrorism-related-inadmissibility-grounds-trig-situational-exemptions; for a historical overview, see *Sesay v Attorney General of the US*, 787 F3d 215 (3d Cir 2015) [*Sesay*].

the circumstances.[465] Factors considered in relation to whether duress was present in the first three categories include whether the claimant "reasonably could have avoided, or took steps to avoid, providing material support, the severity and type of harm inflicted or threatened, to whom the harm was directed, the perceived imminence of the harm threatened and the perceived likelihood that the harm would be inflicted and any other relevant factor regarding the circumstance under which the applicant felt compelled to provide the material support," while the totality of the circumstances includes "the amount, type of material support provided, the frequency of material support provided, the nature of the activities committed by the terrorist organization, the alien's awareness of those activities, the length of time since material support was provided, the alien's conduct since that time, and any other relevant factor."[466] The second last category, certain limited material support, includes certain routine commercial transactions, certain routine social transactions, certain humanitarian assistance, and material support provided under substantial pressure that does not rise to the level of duress ("sub-duress pressure").[467] The category of insignificant material support includes a lack of *mens rea* of knowledge, in the sense that a person did not know and reasonably should not have known that the support they provided could be directly used to engage in violent or terrorist activity, while the person also needed to show a lack of intent in furthering an organization's violent or terrorist activities. Activities constituting insignificant material support are present if the support is of a minimal amount and the person reasonably believed that it would be inconsequential in effect.[468]

---

465 USCIS, Jonathan Scharfen, Deputy Director, Interoffice Memorandum, "Processing the Discretionary Exemption to the Inadmissibility Ground for Providing Material Support to Certain Terrorist Organizations" (24 May 2007), online (pdf): www.aclusocal.org/sites/default/files/wp-content/uploads/2014/07/Processing-the-Discretionary-Exemption-to-the-Material-Support-Inadmissibility-Ground-May-24-2007.pdf.

466 *Ibid* at 5; these details are repeated by reference to this memorandum in footnotes in the other two subsequent policy memoranda dealing with duress, both issued on 23 February 2011; for a discussion, see *AA*, above note 462.

467 See USCIS, Policy Memorandum PM-602-0112, "Implementation of the Discretionary Exemption Authority Under s 212(d)(3)(B)(i) of the Immigration and Nationality Act for the Provision of Certain Limited Material Support" (8 May 2015).

468 See USCIS, Policy Memorandum PM-602-0113, "Implementation of the Discretionary Exemption Authority Under s 212(d)(3)(B)(i) of the Immigration and Nationality Act for the Provision of Insignificant Material Support" (8 May 2015).

With respect to the application of the legislation at the individual level, the term "representative of a terrorist organization" includes "an officer, official, or spokesman of an organization, and any person, who directs, counsels, commands, or induces an organization or its members to engage in terrorist activity."[469] The attorney general can waive the finding of being barred from asylum for this category if there are no reasonable grounds for regarding the person as a danger to the security of the United States.[470] Membership in a terrorist organization can lead to exclusion but only in the case of a non-designated organization and only when the claimant knew, or should reasonably have known, that the organization was a terrorist organization.[471]

Most of the US jurisprudence has dealt with the parameters of material support as part of the definition of engaging in a terrorist activity, but a 2005 decision by the Court of Appeals discussed other issues as well. This decision was of the view that the definition of terrorist activity as set out in the *INA* was not so vague as to be found unconstitutional, while it was also of the opinion that a distinction between combatants and non-combatants for a situation that had risen to an armed conflict in the international humanitarian law sense was not sustainable as this distinction is not set out in the legislation.[472] The list of examples in the material support definition is not exhaustive since other activities, such as are set out in the longer list in the criminal material support provision, can be included as well. The legislator's intention was to enact a broad concept of material support in the immigration context.[473]

The Court of Appeals was of the view that the Eritrean Liberation Front (ELF) was a terrorist organization, even though it fought for Eritrea's independence from Ethiopia, because it used violence, including kidnappings, hijackings of aircraft, shootings, and car bombings, and

469 *INA*, s 212(a)(3)(B)(v).

470 *INA*, s 208(b)(2)(A)(v).

471 *INA*, s 212(a)(3)(B)(vi) in conjunction with s 208(b)(2)(A)(v).

472 *McAllister*, above note 449; the situation in question was Northern Ireland during the time of the Troubles, while McAllister was a member of the Irish National Liberation Army (INLA); these points were confirmed in the case of *Khan*, above note 431, although the judges expressed some discomfort with such an outcome by saying, "[T]he INA does not provide an exception for armed resistance against military targets that is permitted under the international law of armed conflict." See, also, *Annachamy v Holder*, 686 F3d 729 (9th Cir 3 July 2012) [*Annachamy*].

473 *Singh-Kaur*, above note 461.

employed weapons in the fight for independence and for the forcible overthrow of the Ethiopian government. The judges also indicated that the activities of the person concerned, including collecting funds for the ELF; supplying the ELF with provisions such as sugar, shoes, and cigarettes; and passing along secret documents, amounted in the aggregate to material support. In addition to providing material support, she also fell within other provisions concerned with engaging in terrorist activities, such as collecting and passing on information that would be used by the ELF against the enemy, the government of Ethiopia; collecting funds for the ELF; organizing and recruiting members; and membership in a terrorist organization.[474] Interestingly, almost three years after this decision, certain support activities for the ELF became the subject of a group-based exemption, specifically, solicitation of funds or other things of value, solicitation of any individuals for membership, provision of material support, or receipt of military-type training from, or on behalf of, the ELF.[475]

Participation in military activities for the LTTE amounts to material support,[476] as does making annual payments of $300 in Colombia to the United Self-Defence Forces of Colombia (AUC);[477] paying dues and hanging posters for the Front for the Liberation of the Enclave of Cabinda (FLEC) in Angola;[478] carrying weapons, ammunition, food, and water for the RUF in Sierra Leone;[479] repairing weapons or allowing them to be repaired in the person's workshop in India;[480] passing out flyers, writing articles, and training people on the use of guns for the People's Mojahedin Organization (MEK) in Iran;[481] allowing the Farabundo Martí National Liberation Front (FMLN) in El Salvador the use of the person's kitchen and house overnight and giving directions through the jungle;[482] working for a newspaper under the control of the LTTE;[483]

474 *Haile v Holder*, 658 F3d 1122 (9th Cir 26 September 2011).

475 USCIS, Policy Memorandum, PM-602-0099, "Implementation of New Discretionary Exemption Under INA Section 212(d)(3)(B)(i) for Activities and Associations Relating to the Eritrean Liberation Front (ELF)" (15 June 2014).

476 *Perinpanathan v INS*, 310 F3d 594 (8th Cir 2002).

477 *Alturo v United States Attorney General*, 716 F3d 1310 (11th Cir 2013).

478 *Viegas v Holder*, 699 F3d 798 (4th Cir 2012).

479 *Sesay*, above note 464.

480 *Pathak v Gonzales*, 203 Fed Appx 829 (9th Cir 2006).

481 *Bojnoordi v Holder*, 757 F3d 1075 (9th Cir 2014).

482 *Barahona v Holder*, 691 F3d 349 (4th Cir 2012).

483 *Raghunathan v Holder*, Docket No 08-2475, 08-3147 (2d Cir 2010).

providing food and shelter to militant Sikh organizations, such as the Babbar Khalsa, the International Sikh Youth Federation, and the Khalistan Commando Force, combined with membership in these organizations;[484] and soliciting funds for the Jammu Kashmir Liberation Front (JKLF), even though these funds were for the non-violent, political wing, "because money donated to an organization's political wing is considered to be support for the militant wing as well."[485] It has also been held that there is no exception for individuals who provide material support to terrorist organizations when such organizations are engaged in legitimate political violence or when providing such support under duress. The case involved a person who had carried out activities for the LTTE in circumstances where LTTE operatives forced him to cook, dig trenches, fill sandbags, and help build fences; each time he was taken to perform these activities, he was kept under strict watch, there was no possibility of escape, and he believed that he would have been killed if he tried to escape or seek help from the police. Both arguments were rejected because the plain language of the Statute does not allow for the defence of duress. Regarding duress, the court pointed out that the legislation itself had set out under which circumstances the defence of duress could be raised in relation to material support, resulting in the finding that the judiciary could not expand on this legislative intent. It distinguished the Supreme Court decision of *Negusie*[486] as the decision was rendered in the different context of human rights violations, where the legislator had not occupied this area of law, while in addition, the Supreme Court had not been clear in its view as to the applicability of that defence.[487] It is likely that the result would have been different if the LTTE had not been on the Tier I listing of terrorist organizations.[488]

---

484 *Singh-Kaur*, above note 461.

485 *Khan*, above note 431 (confirming the same position as accepted in the case of *Humanitarian Law Project v Reno*, 205 F3d 1130 (9th Cir 2000)); see, also, *Khan v Holder*, 766 F3d 689 (7th Cir 2014), and *Abdu v Holder*, 345 Fed Appx 295 (9th Cir 2009), regarding the OLF in Ethiopia, although this activity for this organization was exempted in 2013 (see USCIS, Policy Memorandum PM-602-0096, "Implementation of New Discretionary Exemption Under INA Section 212(d)(3)(B)(i) for Activities and Associations Relating to the Oromo Liberation Front (OLF)" (31 December 2013)).

486 See Chapter 4, Section B.

487 *Annachamy*, above note 472.

488 The same conclusion was reached in *Alturo v States Attorney General*, 716 F3d 1310 (11th Cir 2013), in this case with respect to the AUC, another Tier I organization, as well as in *Benitez v US Attorney General*, 543 Fed Appx 913 (11th Cir 2013), regarding the FARC in Colombia, and *Sesay*, above note 464, regarding the RUF in Sierra Leone.

In summarizing the legislation and jurisprudence, the United States has the strictest use of article 1F(b) of all countries under consideration, especially for terrorism. The US legislation has defined what amounts to terrorism, which includes the emerging international description of this crime but goes further in setting out other activities amounting to terrorism. The law has also provided a broad spectrum for the meaning of being engaged in terrorist activities, including membership (to some discomfort of the courts), and has given the executive wide powers to designate organizations as terrorist. The notion of giving material support to a terrorist organization has also received a wide interpretation by the courts, wider than the parameters of complicity given in other countries for exclusion 1F(b) and wider than the notion of participation in the equivalent of exclusion 1F(a) in the US jurisprudence. In contrast to other countries, where defences are seen in the same manner as in 1F(a), namely, absolving a person from the exclusionary provision if the defences are made out, the United States, again as in 1F(a), has a very strict approach with respect to defences, especially duress. This defence is not available to persons connected to the 131 designated terrorist entities (with twenty-two delisted), while also being severely circumscribed for undesignated entities in only three broad categories of support to these entities, and then only with an approach that combines the requirements of duress, as set out in the other countries, with an analysis reminiscent of the criteria for complicity in other common law countries.

On the other hand, like in the other countries, the concept of serious crimes is approached in a contextual manner by examining a number of factors, while the notion of political crime has been defined in the United States by examining the predominant aspect of a political purpose in relation to the criminal activity carried out to achieve that purpose, while also engaging in a proportionality exercise to determine whether the means used to obtain the political purpose outweigh the negative consequences of the criminal activity.

j) Observations

A comparative analysis of the different aspects of the elements of exclusion under article 1F(b) allows for an assessment of how far the countries in this study have complied with the international norms pertaining to this exclusion provision. Attention will be given to international law, which has had an impact on the notion of terrorism and on the concept of political crime, which had its genesis in extradition law. Since complicity liability in articles 1F(a) and 1F(b) is described in the same manner as "committed," the national jurisprudence in relation to concepts of extended liability will also be examined, especially in relation to a possible connection to international criminal law.

However, before discussing these specific aspects of 1F(b), it would be useful to assess what the national jurisprudence has said about the purposes of 1F(b). Courts in several countries, such as Australia, France, and New Zealand, have pointed to the dual purpose of this provision, one of which is related to the undesirable behaviour of the individual, while the other is the protection and safety of the country of refuge; courts in other countries, such as Germany and the United Kingdom, also point to the fact that the refugee system would be discredited if persons with a criminal background were allowed to obtain refugee status. The Supreme Court of Canada has provided the most detailed description of the purpose of 1F(b) by synthesizing the above-mentioned purposes and adding that the integrity of a refugee system serves the public support for refugees in general, while also deterring other countries from encouraging criminals to go elsewhere to claim refugee status. Related to the purpose of this provision, courts in Australia, Canada, and the United Kingdom have indicated that exclusion 1F(b) should be interpreted restrictively and with caution.

As to a comparative analysis, while the jurisprudence in the nine countries under consideration exhibits a fairly high level of consistency in the use of article 1F(b) in the abstract, some variations occur in the concrete application of the clause. The judiciaries of Australia, Canada, the Netherlands, New Zealand, and the United Kingdom (and indirectly the CJEU) were of the view that when considering what constitutes a crime for the purposes of this provision, the criminal law of the country of refuge should be the determinative factor. At times, some lip service has been paid to the fact that a crime has also been addressed at the international level, such as corruption (Canada), drug trafficking (Canada and the Netherlands), and torture (the Netherlands), which is seen as bolstering the reliance on the national law in the country of refuge. However, in the Netherlands, an opposite and peculiar reasoning was used to say that a crime cannot be serious if there is not sufficient support for it in the international sphere, as was said in the case of FGM. Given the absence of any specific reference to international instruments in exclusion 1F(b), as opposed to exclusion 1F(a), this emphasis on the domestic law of the country of refuge is reasonable, especially since the methodology used to arrive at a conclusion of what constitutes a crime has not given rise to divergent results in any of the nine countries (except in the one case in the Netherlands, which is especially interesting as a French tribunal thought that FGM is a serious crime without reference to international instruments). In this context, an Australian case made it clear that the crime had to be in existence in the country of refuge at the time of its commission rather than at the time of the hearing.

Related to this concept is the role of a foreign conviction in determining whether a crime has been committed. An Australian tribunal would give a great deal of deference to a foreign conviction if the article 1F(b) assessment was made on the same facts; but it would only be part of the evidence to be considered if the article 1F(b) examination was used for a different fact pattern. Canadian courts have advised caution when using foreign convictions but would accept them if there was no question about the integrity of the foreign criminal law system. In the United States, it was said in one case that such a conviction should not be taken at face value. In France, foreign convictions have generally been accepted, but a tribunal refused to exclude a person who had been convicted in his country of origin of aggressive behaviour during public discourse, while in Belgium, the Netherlands, and the United Kingdom, convictions have been used in the same circumstances and with the same caveats as in Canada. The difference in opinion could very well have been the result of the origin of the country where the conviction was imposed in that more deference would be given to legal systems that operate in democracies with a strong and independent judiciary applying rules that are similar to the ones used in the country of refuge.

The concept of serious crime raises other issues. All countries have considered serious common crimes that affect the integrity of a person directly, such as killing, torture, kidnapping, assault, rape, or bombing, or indirectly, such as people smuggling, drug trafficking, or terrorist activities, to fall within the parameters of article 1F(b), while all countries, except Germany, have also specifically indicated that economic crimes such as property damage, arson, burglary, robbery, bribery, embezzlement, and large-scale theft or fraud are also serious crimes.

The reasoning used to conclude that a crime should be considered serious has been different in the nine countries. Some countries have stated in the past (Australia and France) or still do (Germany) that article 1F(b) applies to capital or grave crimes without utilizing a more detailed methodology, while other countries examined the maximum penalty that could be imposed for a particular crime in the criminal legislation (older Canadian and French cases)[489] or what penalty would likely be imposed if a person was tried criminally (in New Zealand, where a tribunal concluded that this sentence should be, at a minimum, between eighteen months and two years, and in the United Kingdom, where a twelve-month minimum is set out in the legislation). A third approach has been a more contextual method,[490] whereby a number of factors are used to determine whether a crime is serious, such as whether a penalty is indicated in the criminal legislation and the possible sentence, as well as possible mitigating and aggravating circumstances, which could affect the presumption regarding penalties. This was originally used in Canada and the United States but now has found more general acceptance, although the number and type of factors considered vary, as does the methodology, which in a number of instances was inspired by the UNHCR *Background Note* regarding exclusion, which refers to factors such as the nature of the act, the actual harm inflicted, the form of procedure used to prosecute the crime, the nature of the penalty for such a crime, and whether most jurisdictions would consider the act in question to be a serious crime.

The CJEU, in the context of determining whether a person had been involved in terrorist activities, referred to factors such as the person's position within the organization; the extent of the knowledge they had, or were deemed to have, of its activities; any pressure to which they were exposed; or other factors likely to have influenced their conduct. In the Netherlands, the nature of the act and the magnitude of its consequences are factors that play a role in determining seriousness. An Australian court recently referred to factors such as character and the nature of the crime, the modes of prosecution, and the penalties that can be imposed, while in Belgium, similar criteria were used while specifically considering whether violence was used during the commission of the crime or damage to property. As in Australia, New Zealand recently started to use a factor approach, while still utilizing the earlier approach, by examining indicia such as the elements of the crime; the

489 South Africa makes any crime punishable by imprisonment a serious crime; see s 4(1)(b) of the *Refugees Act 1998*.

490 The objective approach could be described by asking the question, "How serious is the crime?" while the contextual or subjective approach to the underlying question instead is "How serious is the crime committed by this particular person in this particular situation?"

facts and circumstances of the crime; the circumstances of the offender, which are relevant for the purposes of the criminal law, and any other aggravating or mitigating features; the level of penalty likely to be inflicted in those circumstances; other indicators that the state in which the crime was committed considers to be serious; and other recognition by the international community of the severity of the crime.[491] The United Kingdom follows an abbreviated form of the same approach as New Zealand, as does the United States. In France, tribunals are using a general approach by referring to a grave crime or applying a factor approach by using mitigating and aggravating circumstances to rebut such a presumption of grave crimes.

Canadian courts have been using a methodology similar to France's in that the starting point is a presumption of what amounts to a serious crime (in Canada's case, imprisonment for an offence in its *Criminal Code* of ten years or more) and then the application of mitigating or aggravating circumstances to determine whether behaviour for a crime that would attract less than the presumptive legislative maximum of imprisonment with aggravating circumstances in play would still be serious for 1F(b) purposes, and the opposite reasoning for crimes with a higher maximum with mitigating circumstances. A great deal of jurisprudence in the last ten years has wrestled with the details of this approach due to a decision by the Federal Court of Appeal, which held that factors such as the elements of the crime, the mode of prosecution, the penalty prescribed, and the facts and the mitigating and aggravating circumstances underlying the conviction should be considered in that context and could rebut the above presumption while being balanced in a meaningful manner. It went on to say that constraint short of duress may be a relevant mitigating factor in assessing the seriousness of the crime committed, while the harm caused to the victim or society, the use of a weapon, and the fact that the crime is committed by an organized criminal group could also be relevant factors. The Supreme Court

491 With respect to the last factor, the tribunal mentioned the fact that art 2(b) of the Convention against Transnational Organized Crime defines a serious crime as conduct for which a penalty of at least four years can be imposed. Another international instrument that could be considered in this context is art 2(c) of the 1961 Convention on the Reduction of Statelessness, which states: "A Contracting State may make the grant of its nationality in accordance with sub-paragraph (b) of paragraph 1 of this Article subject to one or more of the following conditions: . . . (c) that the person concerned has neither been convicted of an offence against national security nor has been sentenced to imprisonment for a term of five years or more on a criminal charge."

of Canada later approved of this approach by providing a clarification on the issue of the ten-year presumption, saying that it should not be applied in a mechanistic, decontextualized, or unjust manner, especially when a particular provision has a large sentencing range.

It would appear that while the type of factors and their application are rather similar across the board in both civil and common law jurisdictions, the conceptual starting point has been different in most countries, as well as in the CJEU, by assessing such factors in an independent manner by using them as indicators of seriousness in and of themselves, while Canada and France use as a starting point a presumption of seriousness and then apply such factors for rebuttal purposes. It does not appear that the end result of either methodology has made much difference in determining whether specific crimes are serious (apart from the fact that the first approach places some importance on a comparative approach with other jurisdictions) because there is a consensus as to the types of crimes that deserve this designation.

Apart from the methodology and general category of serious crimes set out above, it is worth mentioning some specific applications of article 1F(b) to criminal behaviour: the prohibition of people trafficking in some Australian and Dutch cases; *coup d'états* in Canada and France; the selling of human organs in the United States; cannibalism and the scuttling of a ship in New Zealand; preparing for a suicide mission in the United Kingdom; and child abduction in Canada. In France, article 1F(b) has often been used to exclude persons who were involved in the commission of war crimes in civil wars. None of the methodologies used above would have come to a different conclusion for these examples of serious crimes as in general these activities would occupy the higher range of seriousness in any approach taken to protect the physical integrity of persons, a hallmark for setting high penalties in criminal legislation.

One other aspect of article 1F(b), the fact that the activities set out in this exclusion clause must be committed outside the country of refuge, has been given some consideration in Australia, France, and the United Kingdom. In Australia and the United Kingdom (and very briefly in the Netherlands), there was no problem applying article 1F(b) to crimes that started outside its borders but continued inside those countries, specifically drug trafficking. In France, this provision has been applied by the tribunal to situations where the conduct occurred in France but was carried out in support of organizations that committed crimes outside

France, even though the highest administrative court had made it clear that 1F(b) only applied to acts outside the country of refuge.

The notion of expiation by reason of serving a sentence or receiving a pardon or amnesty has been rejected out of hand in Australia, Canada, New Zealand, and the United Kingdom, with the most detailed reasoning in the majority judgment of the Supreme Court of Canada in the *Febles* case. The same result was achieved indirectly in the Netherlands, while Belgium and France had a more nuanced approach by considering other factors, which mirrors the reasoning of the minority judgment of the Supreme Court of Canada in the *Febles* case.

With respect to serious crimes and another aspect of international law, all countries have used article 1F(b) to exclude persons who have been involved in terrorist activities. While the issue of terrorism became more prevalent after the 9/11 attacks, this exclusion clause had been used regularly in most countries before then, and there was little difficulty applying article 1F(b) to this type of behaviour even though the courts and tribunals could not rely on an internationally accepted definition. In most cases, the approach adopted was that a very serious crime with a political purpose was called terrorism, without any further analysis, while in other instances, the label of terrorism was predicated on a particular activity that had been prohibited in specific international or regional terrorism instruments, such as hijacking, hostage taking, or bombing. At times, reference was made to such an instrument, but at other times the connection between a named activity and such an instrument was obscure or absent.

It can be expected that with the most recent developments in international law there will be less of an ad hoc approach to activities deemed to be terrorism. There appears to be an emerging trend in regard to the elements of terrorism. Where the House of Lords felt obliged in 1996 to go back to a pre–Second World War draft convention for a definition of terrorism, more recently there have been signs of a consensus in the description of this phenomenon. At the United Nations, the draft Comprehensive Convention on International Terrorism provides a definition of terrorism, as do some EU documents, while at the national level, several countries have passed criminal legislation to combat terrorism, which invariably includes a definition. In this context, it is also worth mentioning that the Special Tribunal for Lebanon has recently provided a definition of terrorism, which found its basis in both conventional and customary international law. All of these sources set out two essential elements for a working definition of terrorism the commission of a very serious crime that affects the integrity of persons or property, including infrastructure, carried out to intimidate a population or force a government or an international organization to do something or refrain from doing something.

The approach taken by refugee decision makers, whereby either the specific international terrorism conventions are utilized or when an act cannot be brought within the confines of these instruments, is that the emerging comprehensive description it brought to bear will provide consistency in proceedings, while also ensuring that there is a diminished risk of describing activities from a particular political perspective. Countries where legislation or jurisprudence has gone beyond the parameters of this developing norm might need to reconsider their terrorism definition in this light.

Often using article 1F(b) for terrorism activities brought into play the issue of political crimes. All countries examined have applied the predominance and proportionality test. This test was already enunciated by the House of Lords in 1996, and this decision has been used by the highest courts in Australia (although the legislator clarified that the first part of the test would apply only to dominant purposes of the crimes carried out, while the High Court had required a lower standard in this regard, a significant purpose), Canada, New Zealand, and the United States, while in Belgium, France, and Germany, the same test was set out in tribunal and court decisions, with the Netherlands providing a detailed description of this test, including setting out which crimes are by definition not political (beyond the ones carrying this stigma in international terrorism conventions). This test is very similar to the test developed in international extradition law, and some courts have relied on extradition law to apply this approach to refugee law, while noting that the refugee context is slightly different.[492] In the United Kingdom, it has been said that this exception cannot be applied to state agents.

While the abstract test was the same in all countries, its application to the cases at hand has differed. For instance, when the political purpose for the commission of crimes was raised by an asylum seeker, this argument was rejected in Belgium, Canada, Germany, and the United States. It was rejected in most cases in the other five countries but was accepted on some occasions in slightly different situations. In Australia,

---

492 See, also, EASO, *Exclusion*, above note 27 at 82–85.

the High Court thought that the political views of a person who committed very serious crimes, including murder, for the independence of Khalistan in India were not sufficiently considered and sent the case back for a rehearing. In France, the political purpose was accepted for a Chechnyan freedom fighter in the civil war against Russia because he carried out his activities within the confines of the rules of war while defending his country and family. Similarly, in the United Kingdom, the political defence was accepted in the poisoning of the wife of President Mobutu of Zaire and for persons involved in attacks on behalf of the LTTE against military targets, while in New Zealand, the same result was achieved where a person was fighting for the liberation of Oromo in Ethiopia, for a ship's engineer involved in the transportation of arms on behalf of the LTTE in Sri Lanka, and for a person smuggling people out of North Korea. In the Netherlands, a person who provided information to a party opposed to the Saddam Hussein regime, resulting in the murder of two members of the security apparatus, was found to have acted for a political purpose while adhering to the proportionality principle.

While in most cases, except in France, article 1F(b) was applied to persons directly involved in serious crimes, the judiciary has not hesitated to extend the reach of this clause to persons who carried out such activities in an indirect fashion. The contours of complicity were specifically addressed in Australia, Belgium, Canada, the Netherlands, New Zealand, the United Kingdom, and the United States, in some instances by stating that the same principles that apply to article 1F(a) should also be used for article 1F(b). Germany employed the words "substantial contribution" to describe the level of involvement required for article 1F(b) activities, and a tribunal in France in some cases relied on factors such as duration, the intensity of the association with a nefarious group, and the manner of dissociation from it to determine complicity. At the lower end of indirect involvement, providing food and shelter to armed groups such as the LTTE was seen as complicity in the United States (even though it uses policy memoranda setting out the meaning of limited and insignificant material support for terrorist organizations) but not in France. In Australia, peripheral support functions by crews of ships involved in people smuggling were found not to amount to complicity. An association with a hybrid organization with both a peaceful and a militant faction was considered close enough to lead to exclusion in the Netherlands and the United States even though in both situations the association was with the peaceful element of the organization.

In this context, the issue of whether membership can be a form of complicity was resolved positively in Canada (although the issue has not been addressed in the jurisprudence since the Supreme Court of Canada had determined in the 1F(a) context that this could no longer be an independent form of complicity, which would have an effect on 1F(b) as well, a situation also applicable in the United Kingdom) and generally in the negative by the CJEU, in France, and Germany, while in New Zealand and the United States, membership in terrorist organizations is prohibited by legislation (in the United States in general and in New Zealand if these organizations have been designated).

This interplay between articles 1F(a) and 1F(b) regarding extended liability poses a conceptual dilemma. On the one hand, the same word is used in both provisions, but on the other hand, exclusion 1F(a) has a specific reference to international instruments, which now means international criminal law. Added to this dilemma is the fact that in other areas of exclusion 1F(b), a number of countries apply domestic criminal law, which invariably has a concept of indirect liability, often expressed by the term "committed." In general terms, there does not seem to have been much reluctance to equating the complicity principles developed by the national courts and tribunals for exclusion 1F(a) with the ones applicable to 1F(b). However, this was usually applied to one form of extended liability, aiding and abetting, and applied in virtually all cases before the decisions at the highest level in the United Kingdom and New Zealand in 2010 and Canada in 2013, where a closer connection with international criminal law was sought.

In Chapter 4, we saw that several international criminal law concepts find their origins in national criminal law. Aiding and abetting is universally known in domestic criminal law, while extended liability concepts, such as common intention, are used on a regular basis in common law countries and co-perpetration is used in civil law countries. In that sense, seeking a connection between domestic criminal law and refugee law for article 1F(b) would not be a problem, apart from the inconsistency that could ensue if decision makers venture outside the familiar territory of aiding and abetting. However, concern will arise when international criminal law has taken national criminal concepts and provided a new interpretation to make them more useful for the cases international institutions are called upon to adjudicate for perpetrators of collective crimes. Joint criminal enterprise comes to mind in this context. Last, there is a form of extended liability that was not known in international criminal law until recently[493]: command responsibility.

Because article 1F(b) fulfills a different role than 1F(a), in that it is primarily concerned with individual crimes for which traditional forms of extended liability were envisaged, which is apparent from the lack of reference to international instruments, caution should be exercised in applying forms of liability developed in international criminal law. A better source for forms of liability lies with transnational criminal law, especially the most recent terrorism conventions, such as the International Convention for the Suppression of Terrorist Bombings and the International Convention for the Suppression of the Financing of Terrorism, and the International Convention against Transnational Organized Crime. These conventions have many ratifications and represent the consensus of many states when negotiating the extended liability concepts set out in these treaties. For instance, the most recent treaty—namely, the one dealing with organized crime—has the following types of liability: organizing, directing, aiding, abetting, facilitating, counselling, and common purpose.[494]

While some of these modes of liability are known in international criminal law and guidance can be derived from the international jurisprudence, it is more likely that transnational criminal legal concepts will be interpreted by national criminal courts since the provisions of transnational treaties are typically implemented in national legislation. Where a concept, such as common purpose, which found its genesis in the International Convention for the Suppression of Terrorist Bombings and was then adopted for international criminal law purposes in the Rome Statute, will be given an authoritative interpretation by an international institution, it will have an effect at the national level, including on national decision makers, but this will be an exceptional case.

From this general perspective, some of which also pertains to 1F(a),[495] it would be useful to find a demarcation line between the parameters of

493 Article 6.1(b) of International Convention for the Protection of All Persons from Enforced Disappearance, which only came into force in December 2010, for the first time extends this concept outside the realm of international humanitarian and criminal law.

494 International Convention againt Transnational Organized Crime, art 5.1.

495 While, in general, it can be said that the overarching objective of 1F(a) is different because it reflects the international approach to find forms of liability to hold collectivities responsible, while 1F(b) is related to individual actions, this line has been blurred in the case of terrorist activities, which are often carried out by larger groups of individuals against larger groups of victims akin to 1F(a).

1F(a) and 1F(b), especially as the same word to connote complicity is used in both provisions: "committed." Given the fact that 1F(a) contains the inherent limitation that committed must relate to international criminal law, a limitation not found in 1F(b), two conceptual conclusions can be drawn from this juxtaposition. The first one is that "committed" in 1F(b) has the capacity to be broader than the same term used in 1F(a), and the second is that any distinction in terms of meaning should be kept to a minimum given the use of the same word. A solution to this possible dilemma could be that all forms of extended liability applicable to 1F(a) are also applicable to 1F(b) but that 1F(b), in addition, can also contain other forms of liability if there is a credible source for such forms of liability. This would mean that the entire body of international criminal law in terms of present forms of liability can be imported into 1F(b). In terms of credible sources of extended liability for 1F(b), transnational criminal law would be a very good candidate. Based on these observations, it would mean that 1F(b) would contain forms of international criminal law that are not used in transnational criminal law, or used sparingly, such as superior responsibility, but also that transnational criminal law forms of liability, which do not exist in international criminal law, are possible; threats come to mind. It bears noting at this juncture that neither international criminal law (at present) nor transnational criminal law allows for membership as an independent form of liability.[496]

While not used as much as in 1F(a), defences have played a role in 1F(b), with at times different results, even though in most cases the source for the parameters of the defence most used—duress—was the same as was used in 1F(a), article 31 of the Rome Statute. In most cases, duress was rejected on the basis that the person had a reasonable avenue of escape (the Netherlands, New Zealand, and the United Kingdom), because there was no fear of immediate harm (the Netherlands), because the person should have expected the type of pressure commonly associated with duress given the nature of the organization the person joined (Belgium, the Netherlands), or because this defence was specifically prohibited for the offence in question in the country's criminal law (New Zealand). In the United States, the application of duress is prohibited if a person belongs to the many designated terrorist organizations, while

496 Joseph Rikhof, "Complicity in Exclusion for Terrorist Crimes" in Simeon, above note 28 at 171–72; for a discussion of the possible influence of the provisions dealing with extended liability in domestic criminal law on the interpretation of 1F(b) complicity, see at 156–70 and 173.

for other such organizations, it is severely circumscribed as it combines the regular requirements of duress plus additional ones, which resemble complicity factors. The defence has been accepted in a case in the Netherlands where a person had no reasonable avenue of escape.

Self-defence was raised twice in the United States but rejected once because the person was not in immediate danger, while the court sent the case back to the tribunal to properly address this defence. The defence of superior orders was rejected in the Netherlands because the element of following a legal obligation to obey orders of a government or superior, as set out in article 33 of the Rome Statute, was not made out in this case as they had no such obligation. Constraint short of duress has been discussed in Canada as a mitigating circumstance in the determination of whether a crime is serious but does not serve to absolve a person completely from being excluded. In France, however, a person who was pressed into becoming a member of the LTTE while in a vulnerable situation, who participated in an action against the Sri Lankan army, and who left the LTTE while on leave, after having requested to be dismissed on several occasions, could not be considered to have committed 1F(b) activities.

Children have been given special attention in 1F(b) as they have been under 1F(a) even if they were not child soldiers. In France, a young person who had been pressured to be part of an honour killing but only brought a weapon and witnessed the killing was found not to fall within 1F(b), as well as another young person who had been forcibly recruited into a gang in the Democratic Republic of the Congo while vulnerable and isolated and had remained in that gang due to physical and psychological pressure that prevented him from distancing himself from the group. In the Netherlands, the same result was achieved for a young person who had guarded victims of people smuggling; there was no situation of knowing participation at the time of his involvement; he had been a minor; he had been seriously traumatized by the early death of his mother and abuse by his father; there were violent circumstances in the Libyan civil war; and he lacked trust in adults in positions of authority; overall, this put into serious doubt whether he was in a position of independent decision making. In New Zealand, the factors regarding the seriousness of the crimes of robbery and assault as a gang member in Malaysia were resolved in favour of a person who was under the age of nineteen as part of mitigating circumstances; this was also the case in the United Kingdom for a fourteen-year-old boy who had killed his half-brother in Afghanistan. On the other hand, a young person in Colombia who voluntarily joined a paramilitary group in order to avenge the killings of his entire family by criminal gangs and personally murdered and tortured members of the FARC and the members of the gang responsible for the killing of his family was excluded in spite of his young age and his traumatic experiences.

B. EXCLUSION 1F(C)

Article 1F(c) has been the most difficult article to infuse with independent meaning. While it has the oldest pedigree, in that its almost exact formulation as an exclusionary clause was already set out in the Universal Declaration of Human Rights, the drafters of the 1951 Refugee Convention were not able to provide a great deal of specific content to the words contained in this article, apart from some general and vague examples, such as a reference to subversion, which would provide guidance as to which activities could conceivably fall within its parameters.

While the jurisprudence in respect to articles 1F(a) and 1F(b) shows that courts have not found it difficult to make a connection to either international or domestic criminal law concepts for the substantive crimes or the modes of liability, the search for an approach in regard to article 1F(c) that would set it apart from the parameters of the other two articles has been problematic in the national jurisprudence, especially because of the lack of connection to a discernible body of international or domestic law. This is likely why there is no caselaw on this article in New Zealand or the United States, while the Netherlands has only recently begun exploring the provision, after they initially showed no indications of having any interest in using it.

1) The Views of the UNHCR

The question of the parameters of the phrase "guilty of acts contrary to the purposes and principles of the United Nations" has been addressed in the most detail in the 2009 *Statement on Article 1F*.[497] This statement

497 UNHCR, *Statement*, above note 55 at 13–15; specific comments with respect to terrorism and crimes against peacekeepers can be found in the UNHCR intervention before the Supreme Court of the United Kingdom in the cases of *Yasser al-Sirri (Appellant) v Secretary of State for the Home Department (Respondent)* and *DD (Afghanistan) (Appellant) v Secretary of State for the Home Department (Respondent)*, 23 March 2012.

indicates that 1F(c) should be interpreted "restrictively, narrowly and with caution"] because of "the vagueness of its terms, the lack of coherent State practice and the danger of being open to abuse."[498]

In terms of the types of activities that could fall within exclusion 1F(c), the document states that "crimes which are capable of affecting international peace and security, and peaceful relations between States would fall within this clause, as would serious and sustained violations of human rights."[499]

Terrorism can be an act contrary to the purposes and principles of the United Nations, but the document cautions that the fact that the UN, through General Assembly and Security Council resolutions, has declared that terrorism is within the realm of 1F(c) should not lead to an automatic application of this clause to all refugee claimants; an "individual assessment in each case should be undertaken to determine whether the acts in question meet the threshold required, in terms of their gravity, international impact, and implications for the maintenance of international peace and security."[500]

It is said that "in addition to persons in positions of State authority, individuals acting in a personal capacity, including as leaders of a group responsible for 'acts of terrorism' which are contrary to the

---

498 UNHCR, *Statement*, above note 55 at 13–14 and 26. This exhortation is also expressed by a number of commentators; see Grahl-Madsen, above note 3 at 286; Hathaway & Foster, above note 60 at 596; Penelope Mathew, "Resolution 1373—A Call to Pre-empt Asylum Seekers? (or 'Osama, the Asylum Seeker')" in Jane McAdam, ed, *Forced Migration, Human Rights and Security* (Oxford & Portland, OR: Hart, 2008) 19–62 at 37; Michael Kingsley Nyinah, "Exclusion Under Article 1F: Some Reflections on Context, Principles and Practice" (supp, 2000) 12 *International Journal of Refugee Law* 295 at 309; Edward Kwakwa, "Article 1F(c): Purposes and Principles of the United Nations" (supp, 2000) 12 *International Journal of Refugee Law* 79 at 86; Gilbert, "Current Issues in the Application of Exclusion Clauses," above note 3 at 457. Along the same lines, see ECRE, "Position on Exclusion from Refugee Status," above note 63 at 271; more circumspect is David McKeever, "Evolving Interpretation of Multilateral Treaties: Acts Contrary to the Purposes and Principles of the United Nations in the Refugee Convention" (2015) 64:2 *International and Comparative Law Quarterly* 405 at 414 and 421–42.

499 UNHCR, *Statement*, above note 55 at 14. It has been difficult to provide specificity for the parameters of this exclusion clause; see Grahl-Madsen, above note 3 at 284–85; Peter J. van Krieken, "Introduction" in Peter J. van Krieken, ed, *Refugee Law in Context: The Exclusion Clause* (The Hague: T.M.C. Asser, 1999) at 8; Nico Schrijver, "Interpreting the Principles and Purposes of the United Nations" in van Krieken, *ibid* at 238–46; Kwakwa, above note 498 at 91; Nyinah, above note 498 at 309–10; Gilbert, above note 3 at 455–56; Li, above note 5 at 334–38; Hathaway & Foster, above note 60 at 589–98; Goodwin-Gill & McAdam, above note 65 at 220–21; ECRE, "Position on Exclusion from Refugee Status," above note 63 at 270–71.

500 UNHCR, *Statement*, above note 55 at 13–14; see, also, Goodwin-Gill & McAdam, above note 60 at 225–31.

principles and purpose of the United Nations, could also be capable of falling under Article 1F(c),"[501] although membership alone in a terrorist organization should not lead to exclusion.[502] The term "guilty" refers to individual responsibility.[503]

2) CJEU Jurisprudence

There has been one case that exclusively addressed issues related to 1F(c).[504] This case involved a person who was convicted by the Criminal Court of Brussels of participation in the activities of a terrorist group, the Belgian cell of the Groupe islamique des combattants marocains (the Moroccan Islamic Combatant Group, [MICG]), for being a member of its leadership, criminal conspiracy, use of forged documents, and illegal residence; he was sentenced to six years in prison.[505] After he claimed refugee status, he was excluded for activities under 1F(c) at the first instance, and after a number of judicial interventions, including the highest Belgian administrative court, a refugee tribunal decided that exclusion did not apply because it had found him

> to be guilty of belonging to a terrorist group, but had not convicted him of committing or participating in a terrorist act. . . . According to the *Conseil du contentieux des étrangers* (CCE), no specific act by the

---

501 At 29–30; the 2003 UNHCR *Exclusion Guidelines*, above note 6, had in this context specifically indicated that it was of the view that this clause should only apply to persons in positions of power in states or state-like entities (at 6, para 17), but this has not been repeated in the 2009 *Statement*, as a result of state practice to the contrary. Academic literature is divided on this point in that some writers (Grahl-Madsen, above note 3 at 286; Gilbert, above note 3 at 457; Nyinah, above note 498 at 309; Penelope Mathew, "Resolution 1373," above note 496 at 29–30) have advocated that 1F(c) should only apply to high-level state or organizational functionaries, while others were of the opposite view (Kwakwa, above note 498 at 85; Hathaway & Foster, above note 60 at 587–89; Li, above note 5 at 338–40; McKeever, above note 498 at 431; and Goodwin-Gill & McAdam, above note 65 at 221–25).

502 At 15 and 27–28. The fact that terrorism can be included within the notion of 1F(c) has been acknowledged in the literature; see Gilbert, above note 3 at 455–56; Nyinah, above note 498 at 312–13; Goodwin-Gill & McAdam, above note 65 at 197; Mathew, above note 498 at 58–59; as well as by the ECRE, above note 63 at 272.

503 At 15. There is no explanation whether "guilty" in 1F(c) is a different type of responsibility than "committed," which is the term used in 1F(a) and 1F(b); Kwakwa, above note 498 at 84, suggests that this phrase requires "a higher threshold to establish culpability and would need an actual pronouncement of guilt by a competent body," but for a contrary view, see Li, above note 5 at 334.

504 *Lounani*, above note 51.

505 *Ibid* at para 29.

MICG, even in inchoate form, falling within the scope of that type of offence, had been established, nor had the fact of any personal conduct on the part of Mr Lounani giving rise to his individual liability for the performance of such an act, been established.[506]

These relevant questions were considered by the CJEU:

(1) Is Article 12(2)(c) of Directive 2004/83 to be interpreted as necessarily implying that, for the exclusion clause provided for therein to be applied, the asylum seeker must have been convicted of one of the terrorist offences referred to in Article 1(1) of Framework Decision 2002/475?

(2) If the first question is answered in the negative, can acts such as those ... of which Mr Lounani was found guilty by the Tribunal correctionnel de Bruxelles (Criminal Court, Brussels) on 16 February 2006 and of which he was convicted with respect to his participation in a terrorist organisation, be considered to be acts contrary to the purposes and principles of the United Nations within the meaning of Article 12(2)(c) of Directive 2004/83?

(3) For the purposes of considering the exclusion, on the grounds of his participation in a terrorist organisation, of a person seeking international protection, is the judgment convicting him of being a member of the leadership of a terrorist organisation, which finds that the person seeking international protection has not committed, attempted to commit or threatened to commit a terrorist act, sufficient for a finding of the existence of an act of participation or instigation within the meaning of Article 12(3) of Directive 2004/83 imputable to that person, or is it necessary for an individual examination of the facts of the case to be made and participation demonstrated in the commission of a terrorist offence or instigation of a terrorist offence as defined in Article 1 of Framework Decision 2002/475?[507]

With respect to the first question, the court makes two important observations: that while the UN Security Council has issued a number of resolutions in the area of terrorism, "the concept of 'acts contrary to the purposes and principles of the United Nations,' to be found in Article 1F(c) of the Geneva Convention and in Article 12(2)(c) of Directive

506 *Ibid* at para 36.

507 *Ibid* at para 39.

2004/83, cannot be interpreted as being confined to the commission of terrorist acts as specified in the Security Council Resolutions,"[508] and in addition, "that it is not a prerequisite for the ground for exclusion of refugee status specified in that provision to be held to be established that an applicant for international protection should have been convicted of one of the terrorist offences referred to in Article 1(1) of Framework Decision 2002/475."[509]

The court said the following about the second and third questions:

> In the light of all the foregoing, the answer to the second and third questions is that Article 12(2)(c) and Article 12(3) of Directive 2004/83 must be interpreted as meaning that acts constituting participation in the activities of a terrorist group, such as those of which the defendant in the main proceedings was convicted, may justify exclusion of refugee status, even though it is not established that the person concerned committed, attempted to commit or threatened to commit a terrorist act. For the purposes of the individual assessment of the facts that may be grounds for a finding that there are serious reasons for considering that a person has been guilty of acts contrary to the purposes and principles of the United Nations, has instigated such acts or has otherwise participated in such acts, the fact that that person was convicted by the courts of a Member State on a charge of participation in the activities of a terrorist group is of particular importance, as is a finding that that person was a member of the leadership of that group, and there is no need to establish that that person himself or herself instigated a terrorist act or otherwise participated in it.[510]

3) National Refugee Jurisprudence

a) Australia

There have only been three cases in Australia, all at the tribunal level, that have discussed article 1F(c), two of which addressed the issue of this exclusion ground in conjunction with the two other clauses in article 1F of the Refugee Convention. In an early tribunal case, the killing of civilians by a soldier of the NPFL, a rebel group operating in Liberia during a civil war, was considered a crime against humanity, a serious

508 *Ibid* at para 48.
509 *Ibid* at para 54.
510 *Ibid* at para 79.

non-political crime, and an act contrary to the purposes and principles of the United Nations. The latter concept was seen as including human rights violations.[511] In another case, a person was excluded on all three grounds, with article 1F(c) used to cover involvement in terrorist activities as a member of the Bhindrawale Tiger Force (BTF) in the Punjab in India. The tribunal relied on Security Council Resolution 1373, which had made the connection between terrorism and article 1F(c).[512] The third case, dealing with a person who had been involved in the hostage taking of US embassy personnel in Tehran, was also found to fall within the parameters of article 1F(c) by the tribunal.[513]

b) Belgium

Originally, a refugee tribunal in Belgium had indicated that article 1F(c) did not add a new element to its parameters, compared to article 1F(a), and exclusion based on article 1F(c) could only be used in conjunction with the two other clauses. Genocide had been held to fall within both articles 1F(a) and (c), while large-scale attacks and abuses by the FIS and other violent organizations in Algeria were covered by all three clauses.[514]

Article 1F(c) was used as a separate ground of exclusion where a person was involved with the religious police of the Taliban in Afghanistan as well as employed in a training camp of al Qaeda, based on the fact that support functions for terrorism have been declared as article 1F(c) activities by the United Nations.[515] This was the same reasoning applied to a high-ranking member who had contributed substantially to terrorist activities of the MICG and who had been sentenced to eight years in prison by a Belgian court. The fact that this group was not on any terrorist listing was irrelevant as the group had carried out

---

511 N96/12101 [1996] RRTA 3349.

512 *SRLLL*, above note 109; for a discussion, see Peter Billings & Ananian-Welsh, above note 117 at 200–1; see, also, AAT, "Guide to Refugee Law in Australia," above note 117 at 7.48–7.51.

513 Guy S. Goodwin-Gill & Jane McAdam, *The Refugee in International Law*, 3d ed (Oxford: Oxford University Press, 2007) at 188.

514 Kapferer, above note 134 at 198–99 and 205; see, also, CE No 39.015 (*Bennai c Etat Belge*), 17 March 1992 and CPPR No 95/1917/F390, 28 March 1995. The UNHCR has stated that the jurisprudence in Belgium in the case of "*XXX v Commissaire général aux réfugiés et aux apatrides*, CCE, N. 24.173 (4 March 2009) . . . required a leadership role in order to trigger the application of the exclusion clause of Article 1F(c). The court did not elaborate on the nature or seniority of the required leadership role." (UNHCR, *Statement*, above note 55 at n146).

515 CPRR No 03-3331/W10302, 5 December 2005.

activities set out as terrorist offences internationally and domestically.[516] In a second decision[517] involving the same person, the tribunal was of the view that while a criminal conviction plays an important role in an exclusion determination, a decision maker in the refugee context still needs to address the underlying facts of that conviction and ensure that these facts fit within the 1F(c) parameters. It said that, in this situation, this was not the case, even though another tribunal had upheld exclusion for a person earlier for participation in the same organization. The reasoning for this conclusion was twofold: based on the UNHCR 2003 *Exclusion Guidelines* and the 2010 European Court of Justice judgment in *B and D*, this exclusion ground should be interpreted narrowly in the sense that 1F(c) only applied to acts that constitute a threat to international peace and security, with the purpose of seriously intimidating a population or seriously destabilizing or destroying the fundamental political, constitutional, economic, or social structures of a country or an international organization, and from that premise it followed, according to the tribunal, that the activities of this person with the MICG, which in Europe did not go beyond membership, were insufficient to lead to exclusion. The tribunal also felt that being involved in an organization that facilitated two volunteers to fight American forces in Iraq did not meet the high threshold for 1F(c).

A person who participated in a PKK terrorist training camp in Turkey was excluded under article 1F(c), with the source of this connection between article 1F(c) and terrorism this time being the EU Qualification Directive.[518] The same reasoning was used for a person from a Tunisian background who had been involved in planning very serious terrorist attacks in Belgium on behalf of al Qaeda, for which he had been convicted by a Belgian criminal court and sentenced to ten years' imprisonment.[519] However, membership in a terrorist organization is not in itself a sufficient ground for exclusion from refugee status.[520] As a result of these decisions, article 1F(c) has been employed primarily to exclude persons involved in terrorist activities.

516 CCE No 18.307, 3 November 2008.

517 CCE No 64.356, 1 July 2011.

518 Qualification Directive, above note 11, preambular at para 22; CPRR No 02-2607/F2192, 19 October 2005.

519 CCE No 27.479, 18 May 2009.

520 CCE No 54.335, 13 January 2011.

c) Canada

Before 1998, this exclusion ground was primarily used to exclude persons who had been convicted of drug trafficking offences after being admitted to Canada. The judgments became progressively more sophisticated concerning the type of drug trafficking that should result in exclusion and in respect to the justification of why drug trafficking should be part of 1F(c).

In the *Pushpanathan* case, a Federal Court judge upheld the decision of the Refugee Convention Determination Division of the Immigration and Refugee Board in a very short judgment, saying merely that there was no reason to limit the application of this clause to persons in power,[521] while in the *Thamotharampillai* decision, the court relied on jurisprudence from the Federal Court of Appeal in the 1F(a) area to give exclusion ground 1F(c) a liberal interpretation;[522] it found that Thamotharampillai should be excluded because his offence had significant international implications in that it constituted an element of international criminal activity against which the United Nations has initiated, coordinated, and undertaken significant initiatives within its purposes and principles.

In the case of *Safi*, the tribunal had excluded from refugee protection an Afghani national who had been convicted of drug trafficking in Great Britain while a Canadian permanent resident and who had then been deported to Canada after having served his sentence. The judge upheld the decision on the following factors: the previous caselaw in this regard, the gravity of the offence, the nature of the drug (heroin), the quantity of the drug (two kilograms and a value of $2 million), international conventions dealing with drugs, and the documentary evidence before the tribunal.[523] In the *Kabirian* case, the court again upheld a tribunal decision excluding a refugee claimant, this time from Iran, who had been sentenced in Canada to three years' imprisonment for drug trafficking.[524] The court relied on *Thamotharampillai* for this result but also added that international conventions and protocols dealing with drug trafficking are relevant for the determination of the

---

521 *Pushpanathan v Canada (Minister of Employment and Immigration)*, IMM-240-93; the facts of the case were that Mr. Pushpanathan had been convicted of conspiracy to traffic in a narcotic, namely, heroin, with a street value of some $10 million.

522 *Thamotharampillai v Canada (Minister of Employment and Immigration)*, [1994] 3 FC 99 [*Thamotharampillai*].

523 *Safi v Canada (Minister of Citizenship and Immigration)*, 88 FTR 109 [*Safi*].

524 *Kabirian v Canada (Solicitor General)*, IMM-82-94 [*Kabirian*].

parameters of article 3 of the *Charter of the United Nations* and that 1F(c) could apply to both international and domestic drug trafficking.

In the *Atef* case,[525] a convicted heroin trafficker who had been sentenced to fifty-five months in prison was excluded from the refugee determination process. The court found that

> 1F(c) did not apply to all United Nations initiatives, only to those acts, which are criminal in nature; that F(c) could apply to acts committed both in the country of origin and the country of refuge; that F(c) could apply to persons who are not in a position of authority; that the courts had relied on other court cases in this area involving drug trafficking and that article 25 of the Draft Code of Crimes against the Peace and Security of Mankind of the International Law Commission,[526] which could be seen as, even in an uncompleted state, a clear intention by the United Nations to control the illicit drug trade.

In *Yasin*,[527] the tribunal decision to exclude a Turkish claimant who had been convicted and sentenced to ten months' imprisonment for trafficking in a small amount of heroin ($100 street value) was upheld. The judge relied on all previous jurisprudence in this area, but especially on the *Atef* case. The judge concluded that since 1F(c) prohibits acts that are against the purposes and principles of the United Nations, the amount of the drug trafficking was irrelevant, as were the circumstances surrounding the offence. In *Goyal*, the Federal Court overruled the tribunal decision to exclude a person from India who was convicted of possession for the purposes of trafficking for which he was sentenced to a three-month suspended sentence and given a $1,000 fine since minor offenders are not part of 1F(c). Not only did the judge set out some criteria for the concept of minor offences, such as the type of conviction, the nature of the narcotic, the amount of narcotic involved, and the sentence imposed by the judge, he also discussed the fact that it is not the maximum penalty that is relevant in determining minor or major offences but the actual sentence imposed.[528] Last, in the *Er* case, the decision to exclude a person who had been convicted for heroin trafficking with a value of $1.4 million was upheld.[529]

---

525 *Atef v Canada (Minister of Citizenship and Immigration)*, [1995] 3 FC 86 [*Atef*].

526 UN Doc Report of the International Law Commission on the Work of its Forty-eighth Session, Official Records of the General Assembly, Fifty-first Session, Supplement No 10, Chapter II.

527 *Yasin v Canada (Minister of Citizenship and Immigration)*, IMM-2887-94 [*Yasin*].

528 *Goyal v Canada (Minister of Citizenship and Immigration)*, 112 FTR 137 [*Goyal*].

529 *Er v Canada (Minister of Citizenship and Immigration)*, 113 FTR 312 [*Er*].

This approach changed with the Supreme Court decision in *Pushpanathan.*[530] After conducting an examination of the *travaux préparatoires* of the Refugee Convention and paying particular attention to the statements made by the French and Canadian delegates during the Social Committee debates in 1950, the majority of the Court came to the conclusion that the drafters felt that 1F(c) acts were residual to 1F(a) and (b) activities[531] and amounted to non-war-related crimes against humanity.[532] This in turn led to the conclusion that

> [i]n the light of the general purposes of the Convention ... and the indications in the *travaux préparatoires* as to the relative ambit of Article 1F(a) and F(c), the purpose of Article 1F(c) can be characterised in the following terms: to exclude those individuals responsible for serious, sustained or systematic violations of fundamental human rights which amount to persecution in a non-war setting.[533]

The Court declined to provide an exhaustive list of activities that could be part of 1F(c) but instead set out as the general principle for such activities "that where there is consensus in international law that particular acts constitute sufficiently serious and sustained violations of fundamental human rights as to amount to persecution, or are explicitly recognized as contrary to the purposes and principles of the United Nations, then article 1F(c) will be applicable."[534]

It goes on to identify two categories within this general principle. The first category is where a widely accepted international agreement or a United Nations resolution explicitly declares that the commission of certain acts is contrary to the purposes and the principles of the United Nations, or where other sources of international law, such as the International Court of Justice, have made such a determination, then there is

---

530 *Pushpanathan v Canada (Minister of Citizenship and Immigration)*, [1998] 1 SCR 982 [*Pushpanathan*].

531 *Ibid* at para 62.

532 *Ibid* at para 60.

533 *Ibid* at para 64; this was preceded by a statement of the Court as to the purpose of 1F(c) by saying at para 63: "when the tables are turned on persecutors, who suddenly become the persecuted, they cannot claim refugee status."

534 *Ibid* at para 65; this approach has been followed in other countries, such as the United Kingdom (see below) and the Czech Republic, where it was applied in a situation of collaborating with Cuban security forces and providing them with information on activities of other Cuban nationals living abroad, especially about their contacts with persons coming from Western countries or about their intentions to travel (or emigrate) to the West; see EASO, *Exclusion*, above note 27 at 93.

a strong indication that those acts will fall within article 1F(c). Forced disappearance, torture, terrorist acts, hostage taking, and apartheid would fall into this category.[535]

The second category is those acts that a court can determine for itself are serious, sustained, and systematic violations of human rights constituting persecution. According to the Court,

> This analysis involves a factual and a legal component. The court must assess the status of the rule which has been violated. Where the rule which has been violated is very near the core of the most valued principles of human rights and is recognized as immediately subject to international condemnation and punishment, then even an isolated violation could lead to an exclusion under Article 1F(c). The status of a violated rule as a universal jurisdiction offence would be a compelling indication that even an isolated violation constitutes persecution. To that end, if the international community were ever to adopt the Draft Statute for an International Criminal Court, . . . which currently includes trafficking in narcotics within its jurisdiction, along with war crimes, torture and genocide, then there would be a much greater likelihood of a court being able to find a serious violation of human rights by virtue of these activities.
>
> A serious and sustained violation of human rights amounting to persecution may also arise from a particularly egregious factual situation, including the extent of the complicity of the applicant. Assessing the factual circumstances of a human rights violation as well as the nature of the right violated would allow a domestic court, for example, to determine on its own that the events in the Tehran hostage-taking warrant exclusion under Article 1F(c).[536]

The majority concluded that drug trafficking does not fall within either of these categories, and until the international community makes it clear that such activities amount to a serious violation of fundamental rights amounting to persecution, there is no reason to bring it within the confines of 1F(c).[537] Reliance on the concept of crimes of international concern was rejected as setting the bar too low.[538]

---

535 *Pushpanathan*, above note 530 at paras 66–67.

536 *Ibid* at paras 70–71.

537 *Ibid* at paras 69, 72, and 74.

538 *Ibid* at para 72. The Canadian government had sought to connect the purposes and principles of the United Nations as set out in its *Charter*, which is addressed to states and not

The Court did not specifically address the question of acts committed in the country of refuge or the relevance of a conviction. The following quotation could provide an answer to the first issue:

> The parties sought to ensure that common criminals should not be able to avoid extradition and prosecution by claiming refugee status. Given the precisely drawn scope of Article 1F(b), limited as it is to "serious" "non-political crimes" committed outside the country of refuge, the unavoidable inference is that serious non-political crimes are not included in the general, unqualified language of Article 1F(c).[539]

With respect to the second issue, the reference by the majority to the Declaration to Supplement the 1994 Declaration on Measures to Eliminate International Terrorism,[540] which contains a specific reference to conviction in its article 3, would appear to support the notion that convictions are not a bar to using 1F(c) to exclude persons.[541]

The majority is less equivocal in answering the question of whether 1F(c) only applies to persons in authority or to private individuals as well by saying that "[a]lthough it may be more difficult for a non-state

---

to individuals, to activities that have been committed by individuals and been deemed by the international community so reprehensible that steps had been undertaken by the United Nations to curtail such activities. This connection was found by linking 1F(c) with that portion of international criminal law originating in the United Nations. A distinction was made, based on the work of the International Law Commission in regards to its Draft Code of Crimes against the Peace and Security of Mankind, between two types of crimes, namely, crimes under international law and crimes of international concern, and it was asserted that both types of crimes, insofar as they had not been subsumed within exclusion ground 1F(a), were contrary to the purposes and principles of the United Nations. Crimes under international law (or true international crimes) were crimes that had been declared criminal under international law and were subject to universal jurisdiction, such as piracy, war crimes, crimes against humanity, crimes against peace, and genocide, while crimes of international concern were crimes that have an international aspect, are regulated by multinational conventions by which states have undertaken to take action to combat such crimes by criminalizing the conduct in question, by prosecuting, or by extraditing an offender of such conduct. Ten types of crimes were identified to fall within the latter category: the unlawful use of chemical weapons; incitement of hate based on racial discrimination; slavery; torture; terrorism; drug trafficking on a large scale or with an international dimension; severe pollution of coastlines; interference with submarine cables; mercenaryism; and acts against the safety of United Nations associated personnel (Appellant factum, filed on 3 March 1997). The Court dismissed this argument at para 73, primarily because it found that some of these crimes were not serious enough for 1F(c) purposes.

539 *Ibid* at para 73.

540 UN Doc A/RES/51/120 (1996).

541 *Pushpanathan*, above note 530 at para 66.

actor to perpetrate human rights violations on a scale amounting to persecution without the state thereby implicitly adopting those acts, the possibility should not be excluded *a priori*."[542]

Since the decision of the Supreme Court, 1F(c) has been used in only one Canadian province, Quebec, in conjunction with 1F(a), to exclude persons involved in crimes against humanity, while as a separate heading more sparingly, but both in relation to allegations of terrorism and human rights violations.

At the Federal Court of Appeal level, 1F(c) issues have been addressed on two occasions, both in combination with another exclusion ground, 1F(a) in the *Harb* case[543] and 1F(b) in the *Zrig* case.[544] In the latter case, the court ruled that a person who participated in terrorist activities in an important capacity in the Islamic Tendency Movement (MTI)/Ennahda group in Tunisia would fall within the parameters of 1F(c) even though most of his activities had occurred before 1997, the date of the United Nations General Assembly resolution regarding the Declaration Measures to Eliminate International Terrorism,[545] used by the tribunal as the pivotal point when the United Nations became serious about terrorism. According to the court:

> On the question of terrorism, Bassiouni makes the following observation in *International Criminal Law*, at p. 766: The United Nations bodies and agencies have produced, between 1963–1999, fourteen international conventions, six draft conventions, thirty-four resolutions, forty-six reports, seven studies by the *Ad Hoc* Committee on International Terrorism, five Notes by the Secretary-General and eighteen miscellaneous documents pertaining to "terrorism," totalling 112 instruments and documents on the subject. It is thus not impossible that there was an international consensus on certain forms of terrorism . . . before January 1997.[546]

In *Harb*, the court was of the view that there is no difference between the concepts of complicity as developed in 1F(a) and the parameters of personal liability for 1F(c).[547]

---

542 *Ibid* at para 68.

543 *Harb v Canada (Minister of Citizenship and Immigration)*, 2003 FCA 39 [*Harb*].

544 *Zrig*, 2003, above note 4.

545 UN Doc A/RES/50/186 (1997).

546 *Zrig*, 2003, above note 4 at paras 179–80.

547 *Harb*, above note 543 at para 17.

The Federal Court repeated this latter proposition with specific reference to the six-factor approach with a person who was involved with the Awami League in Bangladesh, which had engaged in serious human rights violations.[548] Similarly, a claimant who had been a member of the Kataeb or the Phalangist militia within the Lebanese Forces, which had carried out "inhumane acts," was excluded on this ground, while the court relied on the complicity jurisprudence developed in the 1F(a) context.[549] In applying these complicity concepts, another Federal Court judge held that distributing leaflets and writing slogans over a period of eighteen months for the MEK in Iran did not meet the threshold of excludable behaviour for this clause.[550]

More recently, it was held that domestic violence was not part of 1F(c) as it was not specifically condemned as such an activity by the international community, as required by *Pushpanathan*, and did not fit the requirements set out in the same case of being a serious, sustained, and systemic violation of human rights.[551] While it could be argued that the first two elements were present with a person who had assaulted two women, resulting in injuries, the aspect of systemic was not borne out. In this context, "systemic" was defined as follows:

> [T]he word "systemic" as required by the Supreme Court to trigger the exclusion under Article 1F(c) refers to those acts which, by virtue of their impact on a system or which are done through an organized method according to a system, and not only by virtue of their being reflective of a broader social context of systemic or structural inequality, would come very near to violating "the core of the most valued principles of human rights."
>
> While gender-based violence as an issue is systemic because it is emblematic of a broader social issue of gender inequality, the act of an individual perpetrator in any given case is not necessarily so.[552]

---

548 *Islam v Canada (Citizenship and Immigration)*, 2010 FC 71.

549 *El Hayek v Canada (Citizenship and Immigration)*, 2005 FC 835.

550 *Bitaraf v Canada (Minister of Citizenship and Immigration)*, 2004 FC 898.

551 *Canada (Citizenship and Immigration) v Algazal*, 2021 FC 1212 at paras 28–58.

552 *Ibid* at paras 52–53; the court's definition of "systemic" is broader than what was proposed by the tribunal, which limited systemic situations to those where a person was involved in a larger organization or activities such as human trafficking (at paras 55 and 39).

d) France

Article 1F(c) has traditionally been applied in France to violations of human rights within the territory of a country not reaching the threshold of a civil war or, as expressed by the Council of State, "[A]cts contrary to the purposes and principles of the United Nations are those which are likely to affect international peace and security, peaceful relations between States and serious violations of human rights."[553]

Originally, only high government functionaries, such as heads of state or other senior officials, who committed, tried to cover up, tolerated, or encouraged such activities were excluded under this heading.[554] That said, the parameters of this ground for exclusion would not reach as far as to be applicable to the wife of a senior official of the Afghani government, which had been involved in human rights abuses,[555] or to an important functionary of this government without inquiring whether this person, an ambassador, had been personally guilty of acts contrary to the purposes and principles of the United Nations.[556]

However, the jurisprudence gradually expanded the scope of its application to lower-ranking persons without positions of power but who had committed such crimes in a personal capacity under orders from superiors. Examples of such cases involve a person working for an Algerian anti-terrorist unit, the secret service of the Iraqi military, the Hutu militia during the Rwandan genocide,[557] and a member of the Punjabi police.[558] This was followed by a trend in the late 1990s where the link between article 1F(c) and state involvement in crimes was severed by applying the clause to a member of an Islamist youth movement in Morocco who had been involved in a coup attempt and a participant in a failed coup attempt in Georgia.[559]

Cases since 2000 have continued these trends. The exclusion of high officials involved in human rights abuses was applied to a person who was the second in command of the security detail of President Mobutu

553 CE, 11 April 2018, 410897.

554 Tiberghien, above note 233 at 108; Nicole Michel, "Purpose and Principles of the United Nations: The Way in Which France Applies 1F(c)" in van Krieken, above note 499 at 297.

555 CRR, 20 February 1998, 3000572, Delshad.

556 CE, 25 March 1998, 170172, Mahboub.

557 Kwakwa, above note 498.

558 CRR, 21 February 1996, 293625, Singh.

559 Kwakwa, above note 498 at 90; see, also, Tiberghien, above note 233 at 104–8 and 470; Michel, above note 554 at 295–96; Kapferer, above note 134 at 205.

in Zaire,[560] to a senior officer in the army responsible for political education,[561] and to a battalion commander in the Civil Guard in the same regime.[562] A senior provincial official of a repressive government in Madagascar[563] was excluded on this basis, as was a senior officer in the Iraqi security services during Saddam Hussein's regime.[564] A director of administrative affairs of the Office of Special Operations in Syria, who had organized and attended a meeting of his military deputies, at the end of which it was decided to ambush demonstrators, a large number of whom died, was also excluded.[565]

Several persons who occupied senior positions during the time of political repression following a *coup d'état* on the island of Anjouan in the Comores were also excluded from refugee protection. Among those were its president[566] and the head of airport security,[567] while persons with lower-level positions who were still essential to the security of the president and his regime met the same fate, such as a member of the presidential security guard[568] and a police officer involved in the arrest of the president's political opponents.[569] A self-proclaimed mayor of Gonaives in Haiti in 2003–4 and the spokesperson and leader of three violent paramilitary groups, the Cannibal Army, the Raboteau Resistance Front, and the Arbonite Resistance Front, was excluded for acts against the purposes and principles of the United Nations because of his involvement in the commission of atrocities by these groups, including murders, extortion, looting and damage to property, and the use of firearms against civilians. The tribunal made it clear that he was not excluded because of his membership in these groups but because of his leadership functions in Gonaives and in the groups, including personally speaking on the radio on behalf of them while reporting and justifying the violent events they carried out, as well as in preparing a

560 CRR, 5 June 2000, 338011, Dembe Nyobanga, upheld by CE, 24 October 2001, 211309.
561 CRR, 2 November 2000, 336285, Matumba.
562 CRR, 23 June 2003, 418091, Ndebo, and CRR, 21 November 2003, 432770, Voungbo Ndebo.
563 CRR, 18 December 2006, 540733, Mme Soaline.
564 CRR, 23 May 2007, 577110, A; however, see CE, 17 January 2011, 316678.
565 CE, 11 April 2018, 410897.
566 CNDA, 3 December 2008, 629222, B.
567 CNDA, 13 February 2009, 629208, A.
568 CNDA, 13 February 2009, 629207, C.
569 CNDA, 7 July 2009, 643451/09002255, D.

list to eliminate opponents. In addition, he did not dissociate himself from the groups until it became too dangerous even for him.[570]

While membership by itself will not lead to exclusion,[571] other complicity principles were applied to lower-level operatives in governments involved in human rights violations, primarily in a number of cases where providing information led to the arrest and subsequent torture or imprisonment of political opponents in the Democratic Republic of the Congo,[572] Cameroon,[573] Iraq,[574] and Turkey.[575] The trend to hold responsible people who were not connected to a state under this heading of exclusion was also further developed in relation to both organizations with some state-like trappings and other groups, including terrorist organizations.

With respect to the first type of entities, the rebel group RUF, which operated in Sierra Leone, was considered to be worthy of attention for article 1F(c) purposes, resulting in the exclusion of a soldier who had voluntarily joined RUF, which was known for its particularly cruel methods, and carried out logistical tasks.[576] A person who assassinated suspected collaborators with Israel on behalf of the Fatah organization in the Palestinian territories in 1991 was excluded.[577] This provision was also applied to a member of a neo-Nazi paramilitary movement who carried out criminal activities in Russia[578] and to a member of an opposition party involved in deadly violence in Haiti.[579]

The tribunals have applied article 1F(c) to terrorist activities, usually relying on Security Council Resolution 1373 for that purpose and limiting such activities, only if they are of an international scope, in terms of gravity, international impact, and implications for international peace

570 CNDA, 6 September 2011, 10005808, ME.

571 CRR, 14 December 2000, 336795, Bolinga for membership in the SARM and DSP in the Democratic Republic of the Congo.

572 CRR, 22 July 1994, 237952, Cyprien; CRR, 8 December 2000, 348026, Mme Mosengana ép Okenge; CRR, 1 December 2000, 353968, Mme Kabaka Musampa ép Kufusura; CRR, 11 July 2003, 409666, M'Feret Mongo.

573 CRR, 11 September 2000, 345978, Ouba.

574 CRR, 17 October 2005, 482761, Z.

575 CRR, 29 April 2005, 511158, C.

576 CRR, 18 October 2000, 360046, Faye Bach; see, also, CRR, 24 October 2003, 410614, Dansocko.

577 CNDA, 4 December 2007, 443995, A; see, also, CNDA, 31 July 2009, 630580, MD.

578 CRR, 13 October 2000, 360574, Sapoval.

579 CRR, 9 January 2006, 548153, Lacoste.

and security;[580] no actual danger to the state is required.[581] As a result, a person was excluded from refugee protection for giving logistical support, such as providing false papers and visas in Tunisia to persons involved in the assassination of Commander Massoud in Afghanistan in September 2001[582] or performing other preparatory activities on behalf of the PKK.[583] A person of Algerian background was also excluded because he had participated in preparatory terrorist acts in France on behalf of al Qaeda, for which he had already been sentenced to six years' imprisonment.[584] The same fate befell a person who carried out logistical support functions for the Taliban in Pakistan, such as translating documents containing information about attacks against international and national armed forces in Afghanistan and indoctrinating youths in madrassas in the principles of jihad; he continued to be involved in such knowing and personal participation even though he could have dissociated himself earlier from this organization. With respect to the Taliban, the tribunal felt that because the organization is characterized by violent and massive attacks against both the civilian population and international and national armed forces and their methods, some of which are obviously terrorist in nature, are not isolated or due to rogue elements but are part of an overall strategy, this should result in a finding that these terrorist acts cannot find legitimacy in the political goal sought and can therefore be described as acts contrary to the purposes and principles of the United Nations.[585] A person who had been associated with a criminal group, which was preparing acts of terrorism in France, Turkey, and Russia, was also excluded.

A naval engineer for the Sea Tigers of the LTTE was found to be complicit, and although it was difficult to precisely point to a specific contribution, it was based on a number of factors, such as the duration of his involvement, the intensity of his involvement in an elite unit of the military branch of the LTTE, the nature of his involvement in logistics, his apparent agreement with the methods employed by this unit, and

580 CE, 11 April 2018, 402242; CE, 29 July 2020, 430891; and CE, 9 November 2021, 439891, MI; see, also, CNDA, 19 April 2019, 16040612, MS.

581 CNDA, 26 September 2017, 16029802, RMK.

582 CRR, 7 October 2006, 585731, Tebourski.

583 CNDA, 23 June 2016, 12025076, MK.

584 CNDA, 27 June 2008, 611731, M.

585 CNDA, 17 October 2011, 10005838, MA.

the lack of dissociation.[586] A high-level member of the PKK in charge of logistics was also excluded.[587] A person who recruited people for the LTTE and organized propaganda meetings for this organization during which he showed weapons to be used for attacks against Sri Lankan targets was found to fall within the parameters of 1F(c) as set out in the 2010 CJEU judgment.[588] Similarly, a person who supported the Islamic State in Iraq and Syria (ISIS) in Syria[589] and a person who participated in jihadist forums and the administration of an Islamist website used by Al-Qaeda in the Islamic Maghreb (AQIM) as a tool to recruit fighters for that organization were also excluded for 1F(c) terrorist activities.[590] Financing of terrorism was also considered a 1F(c) activity,[591] as was planning, financing, and participating in terrorism activities in Chechnya while living in France.[592] However, a person from Russia who had been convicted of numerous offences in France and who, during his detention, started to issue statements of apology and propaganda for terrorist groups was found not to be captured by this exclusion clause, especially since he had already been recognized as a refugee.[593]

Other types of criminal activities have also been brought within the parameters of 1F(c), such as forcible recruitment of minors into the LTTE, [594] torture of a kidnapped UN official,[595] and bribery of witnesses before the ICC[596] but not pimping[597] or rape and torture of a minor.[598]

France has made a connection between article 1F(c) and international human rights law in the sense that serious human rights violations without a connection to an armed conflict would fall within the parameters of this exclusion provision. This approach has continued

586 CNDA, 27 June 2008, 611731, M.
587 CNDA, 15 December 2016, MK.
588 CNDA, 30 November 2011, 11005411, MS.
589 CE, 10 May 2021, 430994, MA.
590 CNDA, 21 April 2011, 10014066, MR, alias H.
591 CNDA, 13 May 2013, 8007368, MK.
592 CNDA, 19 April 2019, 16040612, MS, with references to the CJEU cases of *B and D*, above note 51, and *Lounani*, above note 51.
593 CNDA, 31 December 2018, 17013391, MO.
594 CNDA, 17 May 2010, 9009414, MT; this was confirmed at a higher level in CNDA, 20 April 2017, 12033163, MK.
595 CE, 7 June 2017, 396261.
596 CNDA, 28 March 2020, 18035545, MA; the person had been convicted by the ICC for this offence.
597 CNDA, 25 June 2019, 180287385, Mme I; CNDA, 30 August 2019, 18052314, MA; CE, 14 October 2020, 428361.
598 CNDA, 12 March 2019, 17028590, Mme B.

even though the jurisprudence developed in international criminal law has expanded the reach of crimes against humanity to times of peace, thereby placing these types of activities within the framework of exclusion 1F(a). However, because of the traditional approach used by the French tribunals to article 1F(c), and possibly a lack of knowledge of recent developments in international criminal law, the tribunals continue to use article 1F(c) for the same type of activities, although more recently they have been augmented by also finding persons connected to terrorism excludable under this heading.

e) Germany

German courts have applied this exclusion clause to terrorist acts[599] but only if they have an international dimension,[600] and on one occasion to a situation where abuses were committed by a militia during an armed conflict in the Democratic Republic of the Congo because the UN Security Council deemed that that armed conflict is a threat to international peace.[601]

The position with respect to whether article 1F(c) activities can only be committed by persons connected to a state has fluctuated. Up until 1975, judicial authorities were of the view that since terrorist attacks fell within the parameters of this clause, and since individuals commit most terrorist attacks without being part of state entities, any individual can be involved in such activities. This was held in a 1972 case dealing with bomb and terrorist attacks, as well as in a decision a year later related to terrorist and sabotage attacks on Israel from Lebanese territory.[602] However, since 1975, the courts have been of the view that since articles 1 and 2 of the *Charter of the United Nations* were concerned with

599 Bundesverwaltungsgericht (Federal Administrative Court), BverwG 10 C 48.07, 14 October 2008 at para 26, as well as Bundesverwaltungsgericht (Federal Administrative Court), BverwG 10 C 26.10, 7 July 2011 at paras 28 and 39; and Bundesverwaltungsgericht (Federal Administrative Court), BverwG 10 C 26.12, 19 November 2013 at para 12, referring to resolutions 1969, 1373, and 1377 of the United Nations Security Council. Terrorism has been defined with reference to the Council Common Position of 27 December 2001 (see above note 27) in Bundesverwaltungsgericht (Federal Administrative Court), BverwG 1 C 13.10, 25 October 2011 at para 19.

600 Bundesverwaltungsgericht (Federal Administrative Court), BverwG 10 C 26.12, 19 November 2013 at para 12.

601 Bundesverwaltungsgericht (Federal Administrative Court), BverwG 10 C 2.10, 31 March 2011 at para 35; the resolution in question was Resolution 1493 (2003).

602 Goodwin-Gill & McAdam, above note 65 at 221.

international and not individual relations, this provision could only be used in situations between states.[603]

This changed again in a 2008 decision of the highest administrative court in Germany, which made it clear that German law should follow international and European consensus on this point, namely, Security Council Resolution 1373 and Recital 22 of the Preamble to the Qualification Directive. Neither of these makes a distinction between government representatives and other individuals when linking terrorist activities and the purposes and the principles of the United Nations.[604] The CJEU, to which the October 2008 decision of the Federal Administrative Court was referred for a preliminary ruling, confirmed this position on the same reasoning in 2010.[605]

In terms of activities that could fall within the parameters of 1F(c), apart from terrorism, the Federal Administrative Court addressed this issue in the case of the president of the Forces démocratiques de libération du Rwanda (FDLR), which was already mentioned in Chapter 4 when discussing 1F(a). The court concluded that since the Security Council of the United Nations had condemned the acts of violence systematically perpetrated against civilians, including the massacres, as well as other atrocities and violations of international humanitarian law and human rights, in particular, sexual violence against women and girls, had stressed the need to bring to justice those responsible, including those at the command level, and had imposed an arms embargo to prevent the further importation of arms and related materiel into the Democratic Republic of the Congo, the armed conflicts in this country amounted to a breach of international peace and, as such, contravened the aims and principles of the United Nations.[606]

The same court has also laid out some principles regarding complicity for 1F(c). Following the CJEU decision, it indicated that membership

603 *Ibid* at 221–22.

604 Bundesverwaltungsgericht (Federal Administrative Court), BverwG 10 C 48.07, 14 October 2008 at para 26; see, also, Bundesverwaltungsgericht (Federal Administrative Court), BverwG 10 C 46.07, 25 November 2008 at para 23; Bundesverwaltungsgericht (Federal Administrative Court), BverwG 10 C 2.10, 31 March 2011 at paras 37–42 and Bundesverwaltungsgericht (Federal Administrative Court), BverwG 10 C 26.10, 7 July 2011 at para 39.

605 *B and D*, above note 51 at paras 82–83; this approach was followed in Bundesverwaltungsgericht (Federal Administrative Court), BverwG 10 C 26.12, 19 November 2013 at para 12.

606 Bundesverwaltungsgericht (Federal Administrative Court), BverwG 10 C 2.10, 31 March 2011 at paras 35–36; Bundesverwaltungsgericht (Federal Administrative Court), BverwG 10 C 26.10, 7 July 2011 at para 36.

in a terrorist organization is not sufficient to invoke the exclusion clause but that a nexus is needed between the terrorist activities of the organization the supported acts of the person concerned in terms of both place and time.[607] However, because the standard of attribution for 1F(c) is lower than 1F(b) (which requires a criminal-type connection),[608] there is no need to show that the person actually influenced the activities of the terrorist organization or that there is a "spatial-organisational proximity" in the sense of a specific connection.[609] As such, "even purely logistical acts of support in advance, if they are of sufficient importance" or "serious ideological and propagandistic activities in favour of a terrorist organisation," are sufficient for complicity, although "merely spouting slogans of the organisation or distributing flyers" would be setting the bar too low,[610] as long as the activities were carried out during the same time period as the organization was involved in terrorist activities.[611] In this case, the lower court had held that the case of a head of cultural activities for the PKK in Turkey who also provided propaganda for the same organization would amount to complicity, but the Federal Administrative Court felt that more facts were needed to make this assessment and referred the case back for a new hearing.[612]

f) The Netherlands

In the Netherlands, exclusion under article 1F(c) was not applied as an independent ground until 2006[613] and has only been used on a few occasions. The *Aliens Manual* indicates that acts against the purposes

---

607 Bundesverwaltungsgericht (Federal Administrative Court), BverwG 10 C 26.12, 19 November 2013 at para 13.

608 Bundesverwaltungsgericht (Federal Administrative Court), BverwG 10 C 26.10, 7 July 2011 at para 39; Bundesverwaltungsgericht (Federal Administrative Court), BverwG 10 C 26.12, 19 November 2013 at para 16.

609 *Ibid.*

610 *Ibid* at para 15; the reference to support in advance was already made in Bundesverwaltungsgericht (Federal Administrative Court), BverwG 10 C 26.10, 7 July 2011 at para 39.

611 *Ibid* at para 16.

612 *Ibid* at para 17.

613 See the Netherlands' State Secretary of Justice, "Note on Article 1F to Parliament, November 1997" in van Krieken, above note 499 at 308. In 2006, a district court was of the view that the government could not proceed with a case based on both 1F(b) and 1F(c) after the 1F(b) allegation had been impossible to prove, based on this policy; Rb, The Hague, Awb 04/58340, 10 April 2006. There had been one case in 2003 where a person who had been employed in the weapon industry in Iraq under Saddam Hussein had been excluded for 1F(c) together with 1F(a) and 1F(b) grounds.

and principles of the United Nations are activities named as such by the United Nations Security Council or General Assembly and the International Court of Justice for crimes mentioned in the Rome Statute. The manual also explains that article 1F(c) should be used for persons at a level where they were aware of the position their state occupied within the international community and that their personal background was such that they were aware or must have been aware of the purposes and principles of the United Nations.[614]

In an early case, a district court concluded that since articles 1 and 2 of the UN Charter, containing the purposes and principles of the United Nations, are addressed to states, the government needs to point to concrete activities by the claimant to invoke this exclusion ground rather than relying on generally worded accusations.[615] In a decision in the same year, for a person who violated the rules relating to the Oil-for-Food Programme, established by the United Nations for Iraq, they concluded that he could not be excluded under article 1F(c) because this program was addressed to states and not individuals. In addition, this person carried out this violation as an owner of an import and export business and as such was not a state functionary as stipulated by the *Aliens Manual*.[616] Along the same lines, it has been said that 1F(c) only applies to persons occupying high positions in government organizations.[617]

On the other hand, the Libyan ambassador to Malta, during a time that the United Nations Security Council had imposed a weapons and aircraft maintenance embargo on Libya[618] for a lack of cooperation in relation to the downing of a plane in Lockerbie, Scotland, in 1988, including not extraditing two Libyan suspects,[619] was excluded from 1F(c); this was because both resolutions were connected to United Nations anti-terrorism efforts; because illegal weapon transports had taken place from Yugoslavia to Libya via Malta during the time she was the ambassador in Malta, the highest representative of Libya in Malta (following the CJEU case of *B and D* for this proposition); and because

614 *Vreemdelingencirculaire* 2000 (C), art 7.10.2.3.

615 Rb, The Hague, Awb 04/36169, 30 June 2006.

616 Rb, The Hague, Awb 03/46645, 21 February 2006.

617 Rb, The Hague, Awb 15/1712, 8 December 2015; in this case, all three exclusion grounds were utilized.

618 UN Doc S/RES/748 (1992).

619 UN Doc S/RES/731 (1992).

she was aware of these transports, all of which resulted in her knowing and personal participation in the facilitation of these transports.[620] A person who had belonged to the terrorist organization Al-Nusra in Syria between 2013 and 2015, and in which capacity had killed fourteen people, was also excluded.[621]

g) United Kingdom

Generally speaking, article 1F(c) should be interpreted restrictively and applied with caution.[622] It has been described in UK legislation as "acts of committing, preparing or instigating terrorism (whether or not the acts amount to an actual or inchoate offence), and acts of encouraging or inducing others to commit, prepare or instigate terrorism (whether or not the acts amount to an actual or inchoate offence)."[623] Terrorism is defined by reference to the *Terrorism Act 2000*.[624]

---

620 Rb, Arnhem, Awb 13/7809, 7 February 2014.

621 Rb, The Hague, NL 20.19271, 23 July 2021; this person had already been convicted in the criminal courts.

622 *Al-Sirri (FC) (Appellant) v Secretary of State for the Home Department (Respondent)*, [2012] UKSC 54 at para 16 [*Al-Sirri*, 2012]; it goes on to say in the same paragraph: "There should be a high threshold defined in terms of the gravity of the act in question, the manner in which the act is organised, its international impact and long-term objectives, and the implications for international peace and security."

623 *Immigration, Asylum and Nationality Act 2006*, s 54(1).

624 *Ibid*, s 54(2); the reference to the *Terrorism Act 2000* is to s 1, which in turn says:

> (1) In this Act "terrorism" means the use or threat of action where —
> (a) the action falls within subsection (2),
> (b) the use or threat is designed to influence the government or an international governmental organization or to intimidate the public or a section of the public, and
> (c) the use or threat is made for the purpose of advancing a political, religious, racial or ideological cause.
>
> (2) Action falls within this subsection if it —
> (a) involves serious violence against a person,
> (b) involves serious damage to property,
> (c) endangers a person's life, other than that of the person committing the action,
> (d) creates a serious risk to the health or safety of the public or a section of the public, or
> (e) is designed seriously to interfere with or seriously to disrupt an electronic system.
>
> (3) The use or threat of action falling within subsection (2) which involves the use of firearms or explosives is terrorism whether or not subsection (1)(b) is satisfied.
>
> (4) In this section —
> (a) "action" includes action outside the United Kingdom,

As with the other exclusion clauses, the rule in article 1F(c) has been given guidance in the UK Home Office manual "Exclusion (Article 1F) and Article 33(2) of the Refugee Convention."[625] This manual indicates that terrorism falls within the confines of this provision due to resolutions 1373, 1377, 1566, and 1624 of the Security Council of the United Nations[626] but must be on an international scale.[627] Both state and non-state actors can be the subject of this provision.[628] With respect to membership in a terrorist organization, the manual says:

> The fact that an individual may be on a list of terrorist suspects or be a member of a terrorist organisation does not mean that exclusion is automatically assumed to apply but may be evidence of such involvement. The question is: has the individual voluntarily contributed in a significant way to the organisation's ability to pursue its aim of committing acts of terrorism or serious crimes, aware that the assistance will in fact further that purpose?[629]

While it has been recognized in the jurisprudence that article 1F(c) can apply to both human rights violations and specific areas recognized by the United Nations to be contrary to its purposes and principles,[630] this exclusion clause has been almost exclusively utilized in connection to persons

---

(b) a reference to any person or to property is a reference to any person, or to property, wherever situated,

(c) a reference to the public includes a reference to the public of a country other than the United Kingdom, and

(d) "the government" means the government of the United Kingdom, of a Part of the United Kingdom or of a country other than the United Kingdom.

(5) In this Act a reference to action taken for the purposes of terrorism includes a reference to action taken for the benefit of a proscribed organisation.

625 UK Home Office, above note 399.

626 *Ibid* at 31.

627 *Ibid* at 32.

628 *Ibid*; the manual on the same page also briefly sets out the highlights of the *Al-Sirri*, 2012, above note 622, which will be discussed below.

629 *Ibid* at 33.

630 *KK (Article 1F(c), Turkey)*, [2004] UKIAT 00101 at para 76, basing this conclusion on the Canadian case of *Pushpanathan* and indicating that "the fact that an act does not fall within the first category does not prevent it from falling within the second"; see, also, *Y v Secretary of State for the Home Department*, [2006] UKSIAC 36/2004 at para 147, for the proposition that terrorism falls within the parameters of 1F(c); this approach was reiterated by the UK Supreme Court in *Al-Sirri*, 2012, above note 622 at para 13, while also relying on the *Pushpanathan* case in saying that "not every act which is condemned by the United Nations is for that reason alone to be deemed contrary to its purposes and principles" at para 14.

involved in terrorism. With respect to terrorism, a court of appeal defined terrorism as "the use for political ends of fear induced by violence"[631] but with an international dimension attached to it.[632] The Supreme Court, while relying on the definition of the Draft Comprehensive Convention on International Terrorism, the UNHCR *Exclusion Guidelines*, and the CJEU *B and D* judgment, agreed that this international dimension is part of 1F(c) while also saying that the "essence of terrorism is the commission, organisation, incitement or threat of serious acts of violence against persons or property for the purpose of intimidating a population or compelling a government or international organisation to act or not to act in a particular way."[633]

However, in one important case it was held that

> fighting against UN mandated forces would appear to be a clear example of action contrary to purposes and principles of the United Nations, acting in accordance with its Charter. Military actions mandated by decision of the UN Security Council are conducted on behalf of the entire international community. The expressed purpose of the UN is to establish peace and security in the areas in which ISAF forces

---

631 *Al-Sirri v Secretary of State for the Home Department*, [2009] EWCA Civ 222 at para 31 [*Al-Sirri*, 2009], while relying for this proposition on a resolution of the United Nations Security Council (UN Doc S/RES/1566) (2004), which states that terrorist acts are "acts . . . committed with the purpose to provoke a state of terror in the general public or in a group of persons or particular persons, intimidate a population or compel a government or an international organisation to do or abstain from doing any act."

632 *Al-Sirri*, 2009, above note 631 at para 32; see, also, *KJ (Sri Lanka), (Appellant) and The Secretary of State for the Home Department*, [2009] EWCA Civ 292 at para 36 [*KJ*]; and *SS v SSHD* (SC/56/2009, 30 July 2010)(SIAC), the latter of which specifically disagrees with the international dimension aspect at para 21 and which was approved on appeal in *SS (Libya) v Secretary of State for the Home Department*, [2011] EWCA Civ 1547 at para 27.

633 *Al-Sirri*, 2012, above note 622 at paras 37–39 while indicating at para 40 that plotting in one country to destabilize conditions in another could very well fall within these parameters; for a commentary, see Singer, *Exclusion*, above note 68 at 104–14 and 121; Sarah Singer, "Terrorism and Article 1F(c) of the Refugee Convention: Exclusion from Refugee Status in the United Kingdom" (2014) 12:5 *Journal of International Criminal Justice* 1075 at 1084–87. The case was remitted to the first-tier tribunal, which found that Al-Sirri should not be excluded, which was upheld on appeal; see *Al-Sirri (Asylum — Exclusion — Article 1F(c))*, [2016] UKUT 00448 (IAC) at paras 11 and 34. It has also been said that 1F(c) can include "a person who sets out to encourage terrorism and does so by circulating encouraging and destructive material over the internet many times a day for the best part of a year," which finding does not appeared to have been overruled on appeal; see *AE (Iraq) v Secretary of State for the Home Department*, [2021] EWCA Civ at paras 42–52.

> are mandated to operate, in order to achieve the goals set for UN involvement in Afghanistan.[634]

This decision was upheld on appeal by the Supreme Court.[635] The main issue of contention was the nature of the International Security Assistance Force (ISAF) as compared to another peacekeeping force, the United Nations Assistance Mission in Afghanistan (UNAMA), and whether their respective mandates would make a difference for the application of article 1F(c). The difference is that UNAMA was a traditional United Nations peacekeeping operation as an assistance mission under United Nations control, while ISAF was never under United Nations command but initially under the command of one nation and then NATO.[636] There was no doubt that attacks against USAMA would violate the 1994 Convention on the Safety of United Nations and Associated Personnel and would be a war crime under international criminal law and an act against the principles and purposes of the United Nations,[637] but it was argued that attacks against ISAF, as only a UN-mandated force (and as such would amount to armed opposition in a non-international armed conflict) as opposed to UN-controlled force, could only be a 1F(c) crime,

> where (i) the act or acts in question constitute a crime in international law; or (ii) the act or acts, which must be of sufficient gravity to have a negative impact on international peace and security, have been specifically identified as contrary to the purposes and principles of the United Nations, either by clear decision of the Security Council acting within its competence, or by way of agreement or consensus among states at large.[638]

---

634 *Secretary of State for the Home Department Appellant and DD (Afghanistan)*, [2010] EWCA Civ 1407, at para 65; the Security Council resolution in question was issued under Chapter VII of the UN Charter, entitled "Action with respect to Threats to the Peace, Breaches of the Peace, and Acts of Aggression." The same conclusion was reached in an Irish case a year later; see *AB v Refugee Appeals Tribunal and others*, [2011] IEHC 198 at para 56 (for a discussion, see Hillka Becker, "The Application of Article 1F UNCSR in International Protection Decision Making in Ireland in the Context of EU and International Law" in Simeon, *Serious International Crimes*, above note 72 at 222–25).

635 *Al-Sirri*, 2012, above note 622.

636 *Ibid* at para 58, with a background to both operations at paras 49–57; see, also, Goodwin-Gill & McAdam, above note 65 at 231–35.

637 *Al-Sirri*, 2012, above note 622 at paras 60–61 and 64; see also Chapter 3, Section B(1)(g)(ix).

638 *Ibid* at para 62.

This argument was rejected by the Supreme Court, which said that, while recognizing it was going beyond the *Pushpanathan* framework it had used as a basis to set out the parameters of 1F(c) earlier in its decision when discussing terrorism,

> in Pushpanathan, the court did not have to consider whether an attack on a United Nations body or a United Nations-mandated body constitutes acts contrary to the purposes and principles of the United Nations. We conclude that there is no basis for the view that such an attack can only be regarded as an act contrary to the purposes and principles of the United Nations in circumstances where (i) it is by consensus in international law explicitly recognised as being contrary to these purposes and principles, or (ii) it amounts to a serious and sustained violation of fundamental human rights. . . . In short, an attack on ISAF is in principle capable of being an act contrary to the purposes and principles of the United Nations. The fundamental aims and objectives of ISAF accord with the first purpose stated in article 1 of the United Nations Charter. By attacking ISAF, the appellant was seeking to frustrate that purpose. To hold that his acts are in principle capable of being acts contrary to the purposes and principles of the United Nations accords with common sense and is correct in law.[639]

As to the other aspects of article 1F(c), it is not required that the activities considered as contrary to the purposes and principles of the United Nations must be carried out by state authorities.[640]

As to the word "guilty" in the provision, originally it was said that this word does not incorporate a criminal standard of proof but merely means "responsible for,"[641] although this was changed later by

---

639 *Ibid* at paras 67–68; the conclusion was bolstered at para 58 by the observation of the court that the objectives of both missions were essentially the same, while the United Nations itself made a link between the two organizations. This conclusion has been criticized by Sandesh Sivakumaran, "Exclusion from Refugee Status: The Purposes and Principles of the United Nations and Article 1F(c) of the Refugee Convention" (2015) 26:3 *International Journal of Refugee Law* 350 at 366–70, and Goodwin-Gill & McAdam, above note 65 at 237–38.

640 *Al-Sirri*, 2009, above note 631 at para 39, relying on the *Pushpanathan* judgment as well as *El-Sayed El-Sebai Youssef v Secretary of State for the Home Department*, [2018] EWCA Civ 933 at para 61 [*El-Sayed El-Sebai Youssef*]. This had already been said at the tribunal level in the cases of *KK (Article 1F(c), Turkey)*, [2004] UKIAT 00101; *AA (Exclusion clause) Palestine*, [2005] UKIAT 00104; and *BE (Disobedience to orders, landmines) Iran*, [2007] UKAIT 00035 (12 March 2007).

641 *Al-Sirri*, 2009, above note 631 at para 35.

the Supreme Court, concluding that a person must have individual responsibility, which requires in turn

> an individualised consideration of the facts of the case, which will include an assessment of the person's involvement in the act concerned, his mental state and possible grounds for rejecting individual responsibility. As a general proposition, individual responsibility arises where the individual committed an act within the scope of article 1F(c), or participated in its commission in a manner that gives rise to individual responsibility, for example through planning, instigating or ordering the act in question, or by making a significant contribution to the commission of the relevant act, in the knowledge that his act or omission would facilitate the act.[642]

This was expanded upon by a subsequent Court of Appeal decision, which indicated that 1F(c) forms of extended liability are different and broader than the ones set out in 1F(a)[643] and would allow incitement to commit terrorist acts as a form of liability in the former,[644] although the court issued this note of caution:

> It may be helpful to consider separately the quality of the acts in question, and their gravity or severity. To adopt an illustration which arose in argument, it is easy to conceive of an immature 18 year old going on-line from his suburban bedroom, and using the most lurid terms in calling for international jihad. The nature or quality of this would, it seems to me, satisfy the requirements of Article 1F(c). It would represent active encouragement or incitement of international terror. However, it would be unlikely, without more, to be grave enough in its impact to satisfy the approach laid down in *Al-Sirri*. That might well require more: evidence of wide international readership, of large-scale

---

642 *Al-Sirri*, 2012, above note 622 at para 15; it goes on to say that, following the CJEU judgment in *B and D*, membership alone is not sufficient for personal liability; a similar approach had already been proposed almost a year earlier but based on the *JS* case of the UK Supreme Court by the High Court in *Polat, R (On the Application Of) v The Secretary of State for the Home Department*, [2011] EWHC 3445 (Admin) at paras 17 and 21. This was the same approach in Ireland as set out by the cases of *AB v Refugee Appeals Tribunal and others*, [2011] IEHC 198, and *IH (Afghanistan) v Refugee Appeals Tribunal and the Minister for Justice and Equality*, [2016] IEHC 14 (for a discussion, see Becker, above note 634 at 220–21).

643 *El-Sayed El-Sebai Youssef*, above note 640 at paras 74–75.

644 *Ibid* at para 84.

repetition or re-tweeting, or citation by those who were moved to join an armed struggle, for example.[645]

Forms of complicity that can be used for article 1F(c) include persons "who knowingly participate in the planning or financing of a specified crime or act or is otherwise a party to it, as a conspirator or an aider or abettor" but not a mere member of an organization involved in article 1F(c) activities.[646] Also excluded is a person in a hybrid organization such as the LTTE, which has carried out its political objectives with both military actions as well as terrorist activities, such as a "foot soldier in such an organisation, who has not participated in acts of terrorism, and in particular has not participated in the murder or attempted murder of civilians."[647] However, being in possession of extremist material, having a terrorist mindset, and an association with extremists are not sufficient to meet this high threshold.[648]

According to tribunal caselaw, the doctrine of expiation, either by serving a criminal sentence or obtaining a pardon or amnesty, has no role to play in the application of article 1F(c),[649] nor does remorse or a change of heart.[650]

Like in other countries, the United Kingdom applies exclusion 1F(c) mostly to terrorist activities, while it has been recognized that serious human rights violations could also result within its parameters. Unlike other countries, there has been an attempt to expand the reach of this article to other activities that have a connection to the purposes and principles of the United Nations, such as attacks against peacekeeping missions. The notion of extended liability has been given the most expansive treatment compared to other countries, both in terms of parameters of complicity and in referring to the inchoate offences of both conspiracy and incitement.

645 *Ibid* at para 85.

646 *KJ*, above note 632 at para 35; see, also, *SS v SSHD* (SC/56/2009, 30 July 2010) (SIAC) at para 20, mentioning financing, planning, and inciting terrorist acts as forms of complicity in addition to the ones set out in the legislation mentioned above.

647 *Ibid* at para 38.

648 *Secretary of State for the Home Department v NF*, [2021] EWCA Civ 17 at paras 34–38.

649 *KK (Article 1F(c), Turkey)*, [2004] UKIAT 00101, and *AA (Exclusion clause) Palestine*, [2005] UKIAT 00104.

650 *AA (Exclusion clause) Palestine*, [2005] UKIAT 00104.

h) Observations

In the nine countries under consideration, New Zealand and the United States have not used article 1F(c) in any refugee determinations, while the Netherlands only began to do so in 2006. All countries that applied this exclusion clause have utilized it sparingly (except France) and primarily in relation to two types of crimes: human rights violations and terrorist activities.

Australia, Belgium (specifically mentioning genocide), France, Germany, and the United Kingdom have used this provision in cases before both the tribunals and the courts. In Canada, the Supreme Court provided a detailed reasoning setting out in which circumstances article 1F(c) could apply; this was applied in other countries and, specifically, by the UK Supreme Court.

The connection between terrorism with an international dimension and article 1F(c) was made for the first time in Resolution 1373 of the UN Security Council in 2001, and this instrument provided the major impetus to bring terrorism activities under article 1F(c), in addition to using article 1F(b) for this purpose. All the jurisprudence in the seven countries that use 1F(c) to exclude persons for terrorism activities refers to this resolution, while in Belgium and Germany, the judiciary also mention European instruments making the same connection, such as the Qualification Directive.

There have been attempts to bring other crimes within the realm of this exclusion clause. The Dutch manual indicates that crime activities, which are specifically named as such by the United Nations Security Council or General Assembly, by the International Court of Justice, and in the Rome Statute, are 1F(c) crimes, while the Supreme Court of Canada has mentioned torture, hostage taking, apartheid, and forced disappearance. In the United Kingdom, attacks on United Nations personnel were also within the parameters of this exclusion ground, as was the torture of a UN official and contempt for the ICC in France. On the other hand, judges have rebuffed attempts to broaden the range of crimes, for drug trafficking and domestic violence in Canada, for violations of United Nations sanctions in the Netherlands, and for pimping in France.

As we saw in Chapter 2, article 1F(c) was intended by the drafters of the Refugee Convention to be a residual clause in relation to the other two exclusion clauses.[651] While such a role could have been usefully

---

651 Chapter 2, Section I(2).

fulfilled in the past, it would appear that with the strong development of international criminal law in the last few decades and its effect on article 1F(a), fewer activities identified in the past that exclusively fall within article 1F(c) still maintain this status. For instance, of the four specific activities (apart from terrorism) mentioned by the Canadian Supreme Court and alluded to in the Dutch manual, torture, apartheid, forced disappearance, and hostage taking, three are now included in the Rome Statute as crimes against humanity, while the fourth, hostage taking, is a war crime in the same instrument and would likely also fall under the crime against humanity of inhumane acts.

Similarly, the human rights violations carried out in a non–war crimes context in a serious, sustained, and systemic manner, as alluded to in the same Canadian judgment, while also underlying most of the body of jurisprudence in France, can now be seen as crimes against humanity since a connection to an armed conflict is no longer a requirement in international criminal law. When a Canadian court recently attempted to define the term "systemic" as used by the Supreme Court in an independent manner, its description was close to the notion of systematic for crimes against humanity. The same can be said for the decision of the UK Supreme Court, which finds attacks against United Nations personnel to be an article 1F(c) activity since such activities are included in the Rome Statute as war crimes applicable in both international and non-international armed conflicts,[652] as well as in the Convention on the Safety of United Nations and Associated Personnel. In Germany, the finding that armed conflicts constitute a breach of international peace was very much connected to the commission of war crimes and crimes against humanity. This connection between international criminal law and article 1F(c) is even stronger in the category of crimes under the Rome Statute as set out in the Dutch manual.

In addition to the possibility of subsuming article 1F(c) crimes under article 1F(a), all the crimes mentioned could also be article 1F(b) crimes as they all meet the seriousness of crime threshold.

In order to carve out activities under 1F(c), which are not part of the other two exclusion grounds, it would be useful first to set out a conceptual framework of 1F(c). At the highest level, it was already clear

652 Articles 8.2(b)(iii) and 8.2(e)(ii); given the broad wording of these articles, it is likely that both the UN-controlled and UN-mandated peacekeeping missions as set out in the UK Supreme Court judgment of *Al-Sirri* would be captured by these provisions in light of the ICC jurisprudence on this point so far; see also Chapter 3, Section B(1)(g)(ix).

from the negotiations in 1951 that the drafters were of the view that two main parameters should apply to 1F(c): that they were residual and they need to be criminal in nature.[653] To these two requirements some others have been added: that 1F(c) acts need to have a high threshold in terms of gravity[654] and need to have an international impact and long-term objectives, as well as implications for international peace and security.[655] Based on this general framework, it has been suggested that conduct amounting to serious or sustained human rights violations, such that would constitute persecution as defined in the Refugee Convention, should be included within 1F(c); that transnational criminal law could be a good source for the identification of 1F(c) crimes as long as the crimes set out in the suppression treaties fulfill the gravity requirement;[656] and that ethnic cleansing as a distinct crime should be included within 1F(c).[657]

If it is unlikely that new categories of crimes can be found for article 1F(c), with the possible exception of undermining actions taken pursuant to United Nations Security Council resolutions under its authority in Chapter VII of the UN Charter,[658] it seems that the main function of the provision could very well be to use this provision where the limitations of the other two clauses would make it impossible to bring crimes within their purview. For instance, it might be difficult for the purpose of article 1F(a) to prove the international elements of war crimes or crimes against humanity, such as the presence of an armed conflict or the existence of

---

653 See above Chapter 2, Section I(2); see, also, Li, above note 5 at 332–34; EASO, *Exclusion*, above note 27 at 89; Sivakumaran, above note 639 at 372–74; however, it has been said on one occasion in the jurisprudence that an 1F(c) act does not have to be criminal; see *El-Sayed El-Sebai Youssef*, above note 640 at para 75. "Criminal" in this context means individual criminal responsibility as set out in an international legal instrument.

654 *Al-Sirri*, 2012, above note 622 at para 16; see, also, Sivakumaran, above note 639 at 377–79, who adds that the severity of 1F(c) should at least be equivalent to the crimes set out in 1F(a).

655 *Al-Sirri*, 2012, above note 622 at para 16; see, also, Sivakumaran, above note 639 at 379.

656 *Ibid* at 375–77; this point was already made by the Canadian government in its submission to the Supreme Court in the *Pushpanathan* case, referring to what was at that time the emerging area of transnational criminal law, above note 530 at 536 but that was rejected by the majority of the Court. For the types of crimes that are regulated by transnational criminal law, see Currie & Rikhof, above note 5 at 364–476; examples are people smuggling and trafficking, drug trafficking, illicit manufacturing and trading in firearms, corruption, proceeds of crime and money laundering, child sex tourism, and cybercrime.

657 Joseph Rikhof, "Ethnic Cleansing and Exclusion" in Simeon, *Serious International Crimes*, above note 72 at 273–78.

658 See, also, Sivakumaran, above note 639 at 377.

systematic or widespread attacks on a civilian population but where violations of human rights were egregious. In such cases, article 1F(c) could be of assistance. Along the same lines, it would be possible to conceive of criminal behaviour, which has not yet found its way into international criminal law as underlying crimes (such as human rights violations amounting to crimes against humanity), or is lower on the spectrum than so far recognized by international criminal institutions such as the International Criminal Tribunal for the former Yugoslavia (ICTY), International Criminal Tribunal for Rwanda (ICTR), or ICC, such as hate crimes or crimes against property. Such human rights violations would need to be shown to be of grave concern to the United Nations.

Similarly, if a serious crime was committed on the territory of the country of refuge, article 1F(c) could be utilized instead of article 1F(b). However, this distinction appears to be narrowing in some cases as 1F(c) requires an international dimension for terrorist crimes, while in France, the territorial requirement in 1F(b) was circumvented in a situation where terrorist activities took place both in France and elsewhere—in other words, when there was an international dimension. In the same context, the jurisprudence in Australia and the United Kingdom have applied 1F(b) to drug smuggling when this was a continuous operation from international waters into national territory, again raising the spectre of an international dimension, although continuous is only one aspect of an international dimension. On the other hand, governments could see an advantage in using article 1F(c) over article 1F(b) as the political exception has no role for terrorist activities when using the former. Even though the political exception has been severely circumscribed for specific terrorist activities and is therefore outside the scope of article 1F(b), there is currently no general political exception prohibition for terrorism. The result is that this argument can be raised in the context of article 1F(b). It is possible that the popularity of article 1F(c) for terrorist activities since 2001 is due to this factor, especially in Belgium, Germany, and the United Kingdom.[659]

The limited scope of the crimes, which have been mentioned at the international level as being contrary to the purposes and principles of the United Nations, also has an impact on the scope of extended liability. As the five activities mentioned in this context—hostage taking,

659 Regarding overlap between 1F(c), on the one hand, and 1F(a) and 1F(b), on the other, see McKeever, above note 498 at 443.

torture, apartheid, forced disappearance, and terrorism—have been regulated in the transnational sphere, the types of extended liability need to be found in the same source. The forms of liability used in the treaties of interest are complicity;[660] commit, participate, abet, encourage, or cooperate;[661] participate as an accomplice;[662] committing, participating as an accomplice, or organizing or directing or participating in a common purpose;[663] and commits, orders, solicits, or induces the commission of an accomplice to participate or had command/superior responsibility.[664] Attacks against peacekeepers are regulated in the Convention on the Safety of United Nations and Associated Personnel, which uses the following forms of extended liability: participation as an accomplice,[665] a threat,[666] or an attempt[667] to commit. These are forms of liability are known for either 1F(a) or 1F(b) exclusion and, as such, are a consistent application of complicity methodology, even when using unfamiliar terminology such as organizing or ordering. The only exception is the reference to attempt to attack peacekeepers. The forms of liability mentioned in these six treaties are representative of all other transnational criminal law treaties[668] and, as such, could be used for other possible crimes within the confines of 1F(c).

Although the wording in article 1F(c) with respect to responsibility differs from articles 1F(a) and 1F(b) in that it refers to "guilty" rather than "committed," this initially had no discernible impact on the application of this clause in the jurisprudence as all countries applied it to persons who had indirect involvement in 1F(c) activities and usually in the same manner as had been done for 1F(a) and 1F(b). This is made clear in the CJEU *Lounani* case and in the caselaw in Belgium, Canada,

660 Article 4 in the Convention against Torture and Other Cruel, Inhuman or Degrading Treatment or Punishment.

661 Article III of the International Convention on the Suppression and Punishment of the Crime of Apartheid.

662 Article 1.2 of the International Convention against the Taking of Hostages.

663 Article 5 of the International Convention for the Suppression of the Financing of Terrorism, the most recent international terrorism treaty.

664 Article 6 of the International Convention for the Protection of All Persons from Enforced Disappearance.

665 Article 9(1)(e); if attacks against peacekeepers is considered a war crime under 1F(a), the Rome Statute, art 25(3) comes into play.

666 Article 9(1)(c).

667 Article 9(1)(d).

668 See Einarsen & Rikhof, above note 26 at 272–86.

France, Germany, the Netherlands, and the United Kingdom (in the latter through legislation as well).

However, given the wording in Resolution 1373 of the UN Security Council[669] and the interpretation of articles 12(3) and 17(2) of the Qualification Directive by the CJEU, it is possible that, unlike for 1F(a) and 1F(b), inchoate offences, such as incitement, attempt,[670] and conspiracy,[671] could be included within the parameters of the word "guilty" as it would appear that this notion could be broader than the notion of "committed" in 1F(a) and (b).[672] This development in terrorism is not entirely surprising as at both the international and domestic levels, it is recognized that to effectively prevent acts of terrorism, it is not only necessary to prohibit forms of extended liability carried out during or after the commission of such acts but, even more importantly, to also address preparatory activities. The result is that in the last decade the type and number of preparatory acts that have been criminalized

---

669 Recital 5 states: "Declares that acts, methods, and practices of terrorism are contrary to the purposes and principles of the United Nations and that knowingly financing, planning and inciting terrorist acts are also contrary to the purposes and principles of the United Nations."

670 See *Lounani*, above note 51 at para 81, which says: "Consequently, the fact, were it to be established as such, that the group of which Mr Lounani was one of the leaders may not have perpetrated any terrorist acts or that the volunteers who wanted to travel to Iraq and were helped by that group may not ultimately have committed such acts, is not, in any event, such as to preclude the conduct of Mr Lounani from failing to be regarded as contrary to the purposes and principles of the United Nations. The same is true, in the light of what is stated in paragraphs 41 to 54 and 66 to 70 of the present judgment, of the fact, mentioned by the referring court in its third question, that Mr Lounani has not committed, nor attempted to commit, nor threatened to commit terrorist offences, within the meaning of Article 1(1) of Framework Decision 2002/475." Article 1(1) of the Framework Decision mentioned in this decision has been replaced with *Directive (EU) 2017/541 of the European Parliament and of the Council of 15 March 2017*, which states in art 14(3): "Member States shall take the necessary measures to ensure that attempting to commit an offence referred ... is punishable." Attempt is also already mentioned on the previous page.

671 Conspiracy has been discussed for 1F(c) in the United Kingdom in *KJ*, above note 632 at para 35, and incitement was discussed in *El-Sayed El-Sebai Youssef*, above note 640 at paras 74–75, while inchoate offences are mentioned more generally in the *Immigration, Asylum and Nationality Act 2006*, s 54(1). There have been some passing references to conspiracy in the jurisprudence regarding 1F(b) in New Zealand and the United Kingdom, but they were not conclusive for the matter at hand; in the United States, there is a reference to inchoate offences in the definition of terrorism, which can be utilized in exclusion matters but which has not been the case so far.

672 Both in international criminal law and in national legislation, the word "committed" does not include inchoate offences, which are typically set out and defined separately; see, for instance, at the international criminal law level, the Rome Statute, art 25(3)(e) for incitement and art 25(3)(f) for attempt.

have expanded dramatically.[673] From this acknowledgement of the importance of addressing preparatory activities in criminal law, it is a small step to do the same in the exclusion area and include the ultimate forms of preparatory activities, the inchoate crimes of conspiracy, incitement, and attempt, within both criminal law and exclusion law. If this development continues in terrorism for 1F(c), it would only be logical to allow such forms of preparatory liability for all 1F(c) crimes.

In terms of the personal application of 1F(c), the approach that article 1F(c) crimes could only be committed by high-level state functionaries, as advocated by the UNHCR, has been abandoned in the CJEU judgment of *Lounani* and in the jurisprudence in Belgium, Canada, France, Germany, and the United Kingdom, and while this position was maintained in the Dutch jurisprudence as recently as 2015, it is likely that it will become less rigid as a result of the *Lounani* case and is already partially reflected in the most recent version of its government manual.

Previous convictions have not been a barrier to the use of this exclusion clause, whether domestic, as implicitly indicated by the CJEU and decided in Belgium, Canada, and the United Kingdom, or international, as in France, while it has also been applied to crimes committed within the country of refuge in Belgium, Canada, France, and the United Kingdom.

In conclusion, while 1F(c) is residual, it has some unique features. In terms of the general scope, like 1F(a), it can apply to activities in the country of refuge, and compared to 1F(b), there is no need for a criminal activity to have a political purpose. In terms of personal scope, it has a broader range of extended liability than either 1F(a) or (b), by including not only complicity but also inchoate offences, while the distinction between 1F(a) and 1F(b), that 1F(c) could only apply to persons of authority, has largely disappeared. On the other hand, there is still a need for an application of a conceptual framework, especially as set out by the Supreme Court in the United Kingdom, in which the development of future crimes can take place as at the moment there is a void in that area. Using transnational criminal law, with the caveat that the crimes identified in a particular case have the same international dimension as identified for terrorism, would be a good starting point, as would the

673 See Rikhof, "Complicity in Exclusion for Terrorist Crimes," above note 496 at 159–71; in this context, the observation by a German court in 2011 that it is possible for 1F(c) to also have non-criminal types of complicity when discussing preparatory acts seems to have been overtaken by legal developments in this area since that time.

possibility of other activities with implications for international peace and security, especially if identified as such by the United Nations Security Council. Ethnic cleansing would be a good candidate, as would crimes that are outside the transnational crime framework but were identified as crimes of similar gravity in the Malabo Protocol,[674] such as mercenaryism,[675] trafficking in hazardous wastes,[676] and the illicit exploitation of natural resources,[677] while the same can be said for the crime of ecocide before it becomes an international crime under 1F(a),[678] as long as they also have an international dimension.[679]

C. GENERAL CONCLUSION REGARDING EXCLUSION

This section of the chapter will examine whether exclusion law, as it has developed over the last seventy years, has been true to the aspirations of the drafters of the Refugee Convention, or whether the original intent behind the exclusion clauses has been overtaken by subsequent events, resulting in different interpretations of the meaning ascribed to terms introduced in these provisions in 1951. As well, this section will address how far the interpretation of the exclusion clause has been influenced by other areas of international law, such as international humanitarian law, international criminal law, and international human rights law, from their inception and in recent times. Last, an assessment will be made as to whether such concepts derived from these other fields of

---

674 Protocol on Amendments to the Protocol on the Statute of the African Court of Justice and Human Rights, art 28A(1); this treaty is not in force yet but provides an important direction by the international community as it was negotiated under the auspices of the African Union.

675 Article 28H.

676 Article 28L.

677 Article 28L *Bis*.

678 In this context, see the Independent Expert Panel for the Legal Definition of Ecocide, *Commentary and Core Text* (June 2021), online (pdf): https://static1.squarespace.com/static/5ca2608ab914493c64ef1f6d/t/60d1e6e604fae2201d03407f/1624368879048/SE+Foundation+Commentary+and+core+text+rev+6.pdf.

679 There is crime in the Rome Statute with an environmental aspect to it, in art 8(2)(b)(iv), which says that the following is a war crime: "intentionally launching an attack in the knowledge that such attack will cause incidental loss of life or injury to civilians or damage to civilian objects or widespread, long-term and severe damage to the natural environment which would be clearly excessive in relation to the concrete and direct overall military advantage anticipated." However, due to the very high threshold and the fact that it only applies in international armed conflict, any overlap between the crimes just mentioned and 1F(a) would be minimal.

international law should continue to play a role in the application of the exclusion clause. Before addressing these questions, a more general assessment of the role of the exclusion clauses will be provided, together with a comparative analysis of some overarching issues in the three exclusion provisions by the nine countries under consideration.

Exclusion represents a small (the number of exclusion cases compared with the overall refugee flow is most likely less than half of 1 percent in the countries under consideration)[680] but important aspect of the international refugee law regime in that if persons who do not deserve

680 There is no conclusive empirical evidence of this number, but it is estimated to be around 0.2 percent in Belgium (see the *2012 Annual Report* of the Office of the Commissioner General for Refugees and Stateless Persons (June 2013) at, 8, online (pdf): www.cgrs.be/sites/default/files/jaaverslagen/annual-report_cgrs_2012.pdf); around 0.25 percent in France (see Claire Saas, "The Changes to Laws and Immigration and Asylum in France" in Baldaccini & Guild, above note 418 at 258, n90); about 0.2 percent in Canada (extrapolating an average of 30,000 refugee claimants a year as set out in Intergovernmental Consultations on Migration, Asylum and Refugees, *Asylum Procedures: Report on Policies and Practices in IGC Participating States* (Geneva, December 2015) at 98, and almost 600 exclusion cases between 1998 and 2007 according to *Canada's Program on Crimes Against Humanity and War Crimes, Tenth Annual Report, 2006–2007*, Appendix 3, with 74 between 2008 and 2011 according to *Canada's Program on Crimes Against Humanity and War Crimes, 12th Report, 2008–2011* at 7, and 84 excluded between 2011 and 2015 according to the *Canada's Program on Crimes Against Humanity and War Crimes, 13th Report, 2011–2015*, under "Exclusion Statistics," compared to 83,655 asylum seekers in the same time period according to the Government of Canada, "Asylum Claims by Year — 2011–2016," online: www.canada.ca/en/immigration-refugees-citizenship/services/refugees/asylum-claims/processed-claims.html, resulting in 0.1 percent); and an average of 0.1 percent between 2008 and 2013 in the United Kingdom according to Singer, *Exclusion*, above note 68 at 173. The Netherlands has the most comprehensive statistics as the government reports on a regular basis to parliament and the number between 2000 and 2020 is around 0.4 percent; this is calculated based on three different reporting approaches, of which the first is extrapolation from the Letter from the Minister and State Secretary of Justice to the House of Commons, 2007–8 Session, 31 200 VI, Nr 160, 9 June 2008, attaching Notitie betreffende de toepassing van artikel 1F Vluchtelingenverdrag at 7, which gives the number of 700 exclusion cases between 2000 and 2008 with the Intergovernmental Consultations on Migration, Asylum and Refugees, *Asylum Procedures: Report on Policies and Practices in IGC Participating States* (Geneva, May 2009) at 235, online (pdf): https://publications.iom.int/system/files/pdf/igc_asylumprocedures_2009_bluebook.pdf, which provides the number of about 150,000 refugee claimants in the same time period, while the second is for the time period between 2008 and 2013, where the same number can be found by comparing the average number of exclusion cases (30, which is from "Kamerstuk 19637, Vreemdelingenbeleid, Nr 1808" (4 April 2014) Table 1) with the number of asylum seekers (around 70,000, which is from The World Bank, "Refugee Population by Country of Territory of Asylum — Netherlands," online: https://data.worldbank.org/indicator/SM.POP.REFG?locations=NL); the last approach is to examine the annual reports for the period between 2014 and 2021, which, after a decrease of one in 2015, shows a steady increase to ten in 2015 and then twenty between 2016

refugee protection are allowed to benefit from perceived loopholes in the refugee system, the integrity of the entire system will be questioned, more than if persons are denied asylum in error. Because of the high profile of exclusion cases and the concerns raised when persons who should have been the subject of article 1F(a) treatment have been able to live in their countries of refuge for years, several countries have established specialized war crimes units within their immigration departments.[681]

From a legal perspective, it has been said in the jurisprudence that exclusion fulfills several perspectives:

> Excluding people who have committed serious crimes may support a number of subsidiary rationales—it may prevent people fleeing from justice; it may prevent dangerous and particularly undeserving people from entering the host country. However, Article 1F(*b*) cannot be confined to any of these subsidiary purposes. Excluding people who have committed crimes in other countries prior to seeking refugee protection may serve other state interests. It may help preserve the integrity and legitimacy of the refugee protection system, and, hence, the necessary public support for its viability. It may deter states from exporting criminals by pardoning them or imposing disproportionately lenient sentences while supporting their departure elsewhere as

---

and 2020, for a total of about 110 in seven years; the sources for this last period are the "Rapportagebrief for International Misdrijven."

681 This was done in Canada in 1998 (see *Canada's Program on Crimes Against Humanity and War Crimes, Tenth Annual Report, 2006–2007*, "Introduction" (2008)); in the Netherlands in 1997 (see Letter from the State Secretary of Justice to the House of Commons, 1997–98 Session, 19 637, nr 295, 28 November 1997 at 2; REDRESS/FIDH, *Strategies for the Effective Investigation and Prosecution of Serious International Crimes: The Practice of Specialised War Crimes Units* (December 2010) at 14–15, online (pdf): www.eurojust.europa.eu/sites/default/files/assets/2010-redress-fidh-strategies-investigation-prosecution-international-crimes-en.pdf; and Hinde Chergui & Helen Oosterom-Staples, "The Impact on Immigration and Asylum Law in the Netherlands" in Baldaccini & Guild, above note 418 at 288–89); in Australia in 2002 (see Department of Immigration and Citizenship, *Annual Report 2006–2007* (2007), Chapter 1.3.2 "Preventing Unlawful Entry," "War Crimes Screening," online (pdf): www.homeaffairs.gov.au/reports-and-pubs/Annualreports/diac-annual-report-2006-07.pdf); in the United States in 2003 (see the Department of Homeland Security, Immigration and Customs Enforcement, "Human Rights Violations and War Crimes" (17 January 2023), online: www.ice.gov/features/human-rights-violators-and-war-crimes#event-human-rights-violators-and-war-crimes-timeline); in the United Kingdom in 2004 (see Asylum Policy Instructions on Exceptional Leave to Remain: Suspected War Criminals and Perpetrators of Crimes against Humanity and Genocide, at para 1; REDRESS/FIDH, *ibid* at 13–14); and in New Zealand in 2005 (see New Zealand Parliament, Parliamentary Debates (Hansard), 3 August 2006, Question 7).

refugees. Finally, it may allow states to reduce the danger to their society from all serious criminality cases taken together, given the difficult task and potential for error when attempting to determine whether criminals from abroad (on whom they have more limited sources of information than on domestic criminals) are no longer dangerous. Whatever rationales for Article 1F(*b*) may or may not exist, its purpose is clear in excluding persons from protection who previously committed serious crimes abroad.[682]

This balance between the individual right to flee persecution from the country of origin and the collective right of the country of refuge to prevent persons with a criminal background from taking advantage of the benefits associated with refugee status has played out against the background of larger international issues confronting countries processing asylum claimants. The flow of refugee seekers cannot be separated from turmoil taking place in other parts of the world or from new forms of crime affecting the refugee population. The fact that civil wars resulting in the commission of war crimes are still a regular occurrence; that the number of repressive governments causing crimes against humanity is not substantially decreasing; that people smuggling, organized crime, or other regular criminal activity in most countries has not abated; and that

682 *Febles*, above note 4 at para 36; in Canada, the purpose of 1F(a) was said to be that "those who create refugees cannot be refugees themselves" (in *Ezokola*, above note 356 at para 34) while similarly for 1F(c), the same court had indicated "when the tables are turned on persecutors, who suddenly become the persecuted, they cannot claim refugee status" (in *Pushpanathan*, above note 530 at para 63). In Australia, the *Febles* case was echoed in the following words with respect to 1F(b): "[I]n addition to address the issue of fugitive offender, the exclusion also operates on another level, namely to protect the order and safety of the receiving state" (in *Ovcharuk*, above note 101, and, also, *FTZK*, above note 101 at paras 69–70), while the Supreme Court of New Zealand emphasized maintaining the integrity of the refugee system in *Tamil X*, above note 4 at para 33. In the United Kingdom, it was said that the dual purpose of 1F(b) was striking a balance between humane treatment of victims of oppression and the other interests of signatory countries, as well as that "the objective is that the refugee framework should not stand in the way of serious criminals facing justice. The exclusion clauses should be applied scrupulously to protect the Convention's integrity and to prevent abuse" (*AH*, 2015, above note 397 at paras 29–30). In France, it was said that the purpose of 1F(b) was seen as both the protection of society and the exclusion of criminals (CE, 4 May 2011, 320910, OFPRA c/ MA), while in Germany, the dominant purpose of exclusion 1F(b) was seen as "protect refugee status from abuse, by keeping it from being granted to undeserving applicants" and to "prevent refugee status from being discredited by including criminals in the group of recognised refugees." (Bundesverwaltungsgericht (Federal Administrative Court), BverwG 10 C 48.07, 14 October 2008 at paras 29–30.)

politically motivated groups will still resort to violence in order to achieve their goals all have a direct impact on people fleeing those types of situations but will also result in the perpetrators of such crimes being able to ride the refugee wave, either at the same time or, more often, later, when it has become more advantageous to avoid justice in their country of origin.

While the vicissitudes of international events influence refugee movements, they also leave a mark on the appreciation of legal developments. It is a truism that new legal concepts or even entire new legal fields find their inspiration in important political or social events. The continuing development of international instruments dealing with issues such as genocide, war crimes, crimes against humanity, organized crime, and terrorism, as well as refinements in these areas of law, can all be connected to traumatic events preceding calls to adjust the legal means to address such criminal behaviour. This is true in international and domestic areas of criminal law, and it is no less true for exclusion in the area of refugee law, which has a close connection to criminal law.

As overarching comments with respect to exclusion, two things can be said. First, the various concepts in exclusion, including the conceptual definitions of the crimes set out in article 1F(a), the ancillary notions of complicity in all three clauses, the notion of political crimes in article 1F(b), and the residual function of article 1F(c), can be traced to parallel legal movements in other areas of law, such as international criminal law, extradition law, and domestic criminal law.

Second, in keeping pace with such developments, the judiciaries in the countries under consideration have recognized the need to stay connected with these areas of law while not shying away from providing their own interpretations regarding emerging legal concepts when necessary. In this context, it is also of interest to note that judges do not always appear to exhibit a great deal of sympathy with refugee claimants with a criminal background judging from the majority of decisions where the courts or tribunals agreed with the government representatives arguing exclusion cases.

This is not to say that exclusion was a guaranteed outcome when such an allegation was made as the judiciary has clearly followed an independent course if it thought that the government had overstepped its boundaries; this can be seen especially in the application of the outer parameters of complicity and the political offence approach. As a matter of fact, it could be concluded that, at times, governments felt it opportune to ensure that a particular interpretation of an aspect of the exclusion clauses could be taken out of the hands of the judiciary by providing a legislative gloss on such aspects. This can be seen with the definition of political crime in Australia, the parameters of serious crimes for the purposes of article 1F(b) and complicity for the purposes of article 1F(c) in the United Kingdom, declaring that members of designated terrorist organizations fall within article 1F(b) in New Zealand, and a number of terrorism-related concepts in the United States.

While the three exclusion clauses are supposed to serve different criminal activities, it is clear—from the language employed, the discussions during the *travaux préparatoires*, and the application by the national refugee tribunals and courts—that overlap among them is possible. For instance, serious crimes as a category are to be considered under article 1F(b), but when these activities exceed a particular threshold as established in international criminal law, they can also become article 1F(a) activities. Similarly, terrorist activities were traditionally dealt with under article 1F(b) until 2001, when the United Nations decided that they could also be brought under article 1F(c), a position adopted at the national level soon after. On the other hand, there will be some activities that will not amount to excludable acts in terms of the general scope of the three exclusion clauses, activities that were carried out by an asylum seeker entirely in the country of refuge. Article 1F(b) is not possible as it only applies to activities outside the country of refuge, while 1F(c) requires an international dimension for its criminal acts. Article 1F(a) could be invoked, but only if there is an armed conflict in the country of refuge or if the criminal activities are systematic or widespread, neither of which is likely.

With respect to 1F(a), the interaction between exclusion law and international criminal law has followed a different course in crimes compared to that of extended liability, and it is unlikely that this will change in the future. National exclusion decision makers have followed international criminal law quite closely when setting out the overarching elements for war crimes and crimes against humanity. This connection was originally based on the language of the statutes of the two international tribunals and the ICC, followed by a more sophisticated reliance on the jurisprudence of these institutions, especially that of the ICTY. For instance, the connection between crimes against humanity and armed conflict was abandoned, while it also became possible for war crimes to be committed during civil wars. This development was also followed in national refugee caselaw, where article 1F(a) was applied to more situations than before. This distinction is still being used in France, where the tribunals had been using a "division of labour" to avoid the older legal pitfalls in which article 1F(a) was used primarily for genocide; article 1F(b) also included war crimes committed during civil wars; and article 1F(c) was applied to crimes against humanity without an armed conflict nexus. This was most likely the result of the French position during the debates leading up to the Refugee Convention and the use of exclusion very shortly after its adoption.

The use of these international instruments and jurisprudence presents an alternative picture in terms of the underlying crimes, where originally exclusion was in most cases based on allegations of murder or torture. As the national decision makers became more familiar with international criminal law, they started to pay attention to other international crimes and were quite willing to rely on international precedents. However, where such international jurisprudence was not readily available, they were equally willing to develop their own parameters for these crimes. It can be expected that these tribunals and decision makers will now utilize less well-known underlying crimes as their familiarity with and confidence in international criminal law grow.

Most of the notions that form the elements of 1F(b), such as what is a crime; what is a serious crime; what law should apply for determining what a crime is; the meaning of "outside the country"; the concept of political crime; and the issue of expiation, were all in a considerable amount of flux at the international level. Only the parameters of political crimes had been resolved in a consistent and satisfactory manner, while the notion of what constitutes a crime had been, for the most part, determined in the jurisprudence by reference to domestic criminal codes, although there had been some reference to international instruments, mostly to bolster the designation of the domestic crime as an exclusion crime. There is a trend toward harmonization in the area of seriousness of the crime and expiation, the former choosing a subjective and contextual approach, away from the objective approach of looking at only the terms of imprisonment imposed on a particular crime in the domestic context, while expiation has for the most part been rejected by the judiciary. These are the issues that could still use some guidance from the highest national courts and international institutions, to avoid fragmentation of this important area of refugee law in the future, although it appears that, in Europe at least, the CJEU has undertaken this task in some areas.

The issue with 1F(c) is not that there has been disagreement among the various judicial decision makers as they all agree that acts of terrorism and human rights violations should fall within its description; this is universally acknowledged, as is, to some extent, that attacks against peacekeepers can be part of 1F(c). The more problematic question is whether there is an independent meaning of 1F(c) (which should generally be applied with restraint due to its broadness and lack of precision) as all forms of criminality used under this heading also fall easily within the parameters of 1F(a) and 1F(b). Based on the conceptual approach set out by the UK Supreme Court, it would be possible to include crimes such as ethnic cleansing and crimes affecting the environment within the 1F(c) framework.

When comparing the approach taken in the domestic context with the three exclusion clauses, one can detect many similarities in several of the concepts included in these provisions. The notions of war crimes and crimes against humanity in article 1F(a), both the international aspects and the elements of the underlying crimes, have been given very similar treatment, primarily because of the reliance on the decisions of the international criminal law institutions. The delineations of the seriousness of crimes and the acceptance of the predominance and proportionality theories to determine what amounts to a political crime in 1F(b), and the conceptual frameworks for 1F(c), plus the fact that 1F(c) activities can be carried out by both state and non-state agents, have not seen much difference in the views of the countries reviewed.

On the other hand, extended liability concepts have been approached differently by the judiciaries in these countries. With respect to notions of complicity, we have noted, when discussing article 1F(a), that the aiding and abetting type of complicity has not caused any difficulties in interpretation. These observations can be extended to the other two exclusion clauses, where it has been said that because of the word "committed" in articles 1F(a) and 1F(b), the same principles of complicity should apply, and where Germany has used the terminology of contribution to connote aiding and abetting for serious non-political crimes. As well, there is a recognition that a common purpose concept for associations, which are more remote than the aiding and abetting type of complicity, is also useful for extended liability outside article 1F(a). This can be seen especially in Canada for article 1F(b) and in France for article 1F(c), where both countries apply variations of the factor approach.

This brings another issue into focus with respect to extended liability, that such accountability is framed differently in the three exclusion clauses. Under article 1F(a), extended liability has been developed in step with the jurisprudence at the international level, primarily based on the use of the word "committed" in conjunction with the reference to international instruments. Forms of liability were initially based on a combination of post–Second World War precedents, domestic criminal law, and foreign refugee jurisprudence, which then developed into a *sui generis* approach, based in most countries on the unique personal and knowing participation test. Only in the last few years has international criminal law become a source of inspiration, giving the notion of accountability an international flavour as exhibited by judgments at the highest level in the United Kingdom, New Zealand, and Canada. Relying on international jurisprudence, the courts in the United Kingdom and Canada developed the new test of voluntary, personal, and significant contribution, accompanied by a factor approach. Because lower-level decision makers in these countries have already started using either the overarching test or the factor approach, this brief foray into international criminal law will likely end, and they will utilize this new *sui generis* approach without delving further into international jurisprudence in this area.

In article 1F(b), there is no reference to a source for extended liability, and the liability provision in article 1F(c) is couched in a different word, "guilty." However, for both 1F(b) and 1F(c), another area of international law, transnational criminal law, can be helpful. For 1F(b), it is possible to find forms of complicity not available in international criminal law as there is no limitation on international instruments there for 1F(b), such as threats, and for 1F(c), both for the forms of complicity entertained for 1F(a) and 1F(b) and for the inchoate offences of attempt, incitement, and conspiracy, based on recent developments on the international plane.

One aspect of extended liability needs special mention: membership in a criminal organization. As with article 1F(a), membership in an organization involved in article 1F(b) or 1F(c) activities yields different results in the countries examined in this study. Canada has used this type of liability for article 1F(b) crimes once, before the Supreme Court determined that this form of liability could not be used for 1F(a). In New Zealand, membership cases have not been discussed by the judiciary outside of article 1F(a), but the legislator has mandated that members of designated terrorist groups fall within the parameters of article 1F(b), while the United States has gone a step further by allowing membership for both designated and non-designated terrorist groups.

In comparing the jurisprudence of the countries examined, it can be said that exclusion 1F has met the challenges posed by changes in the political and legal frameworks remarkably well, even though the solutions offered were the result of a still largely decentralized legal structure. We can also see that in spite of some differences among jurisprudence regarding specific exclusion issues, the general trends are moving in the same direction, and it is hoped that domestic courts and tribunals will continue to use exclusion as a powerful means to ensure that all objectives of the Refugee Convention are met, while at the same time developing exclusion concepts with an even keener eye to the jurisprudence of their counterparts in other countries than has already happened recently in a few instances.

A helpful tool in achieving this national consistency would be placing more reliance on international law concepts than has been done so far. As discussed in previous chapters, the picture that emerges when examining the use of international law by refugee decision makers is blurry. In some instances, international law has been utilized as inspiration for the interpretation of exclusion concepts, while in other areas, this approach is still in its infancy. This is not always because of a lack of interest on the part of the courts and tribunals in the various countries but also because, at times, international law has not been helpful in providing guidance.

The above observation as to which norms of other areas of international law should be utilized for the interpretation of the exclusion clause is consistent with the theoretical legal framework developed in respect to the fragmentation of international law by the International Law Commission.[683] This framework is contained in a report containing forty-two conclusions, and the ones dealing with the interpretation of norms for special, self-contained regimes are the most apposite. Self-contained regimes are defined as follows: "[A] group of rules and principles

683 UN Doc A/CN.4/L.682/Add.1, International Law Commission, Fifty-eighth Session, 1 May to 9 June and 3 July to 11 August 2006, *Conclusions of the Work of the Study Group on the Fragmentation of International Law: Difficulties Arising from the Diversification and Expansion of International Law.* The United Nations General Assembly took note of the report in UN Doc A/RES 61/34 (2006).

concerned with a particular subject matter may form a special regime and be applicable as *lex specialis*." Such special regimes often have their own institutions to administer the relevant rules.[684] International refugee law and exclusion law within refugee law can be considered special regimes.[685] A special regime has its own unified object and purpose, with the consequence that their interpretation should reflect that object and purpose.[686] Other areas of law can be used for interpretation purposes where the special regime has not regulated a matter within its scope,[687] but, in general, specialized regimes should be treated as *lex specialis*,[688] which has priority over general law.[689]

Applying this framework, exclusion law would be the *lex specialis*, and the other areas of international law would be the general laws. The other areas of law can be used to provide an interpretation where there is doubt as to the meaning of certain principles in exclusion, keeping in mind its purpose and object. For the most part, the areas of law discussed above, such as the meaning of the various crimes as set out in international and transnational criminal law, will be helpful in furthering the purpose and object of the exclusion clauses, but this cannot be said for the complete transformation of the principles of international criminal law in extended liability. This same approach should also be used when new developments in international law are called upon to provide a novel interpretation of aspects of the exclusion clauses.

684 Rule 11.

685 According to the report, Rule 12: "[S]ometimes all the rules and principles that regulate a certain problem area are collected together so as to express a 'special regime.' Expressions such as 'law of the sea,' 'humanitarian law,' 'human rights law,' 'environmental law,' and 'trade law,' etc., give expression to some such regimes."

686 Rule 13.

687 Rule 15.

688 Rule 14.

689 Rule 5.

CHAPTER SIX

Refoulement

A. INTRODUCTION

The principle of *non-refoulement* prohibits the direct or indirect removal of refugees to a territory where they run the risk of being subjected to human rights violations.[1] This general principle has several permutations. While on the face of it, the obligation would apply to persons who are in the territory of a country of refuge, it has been stipulated that the prohibition of removal also applies to admission and entry at the border of a state.[2] As well, it has been said that the status of the person entering a country of refuge to attain this protection is irrelevant in that it applies to persons who are in the country legally or illegally.[3]

The notion of territory of a state has given rise to some difficult questions. For instance, when immigration officers fulfill preclearing duties at foreign airports to determine whether persons, including asylum seekers, can board a plane, are they exercising their duties on the territory of their own state, and, therefore, would a refusal amount to

1 *Németh v Canada (Justice)*, 2010 SCC 56 at para 19.

2 Guy S. Goodwin-Gill & Jane McAdam, *The Refugee in International Law*, 4th ed (Oxford: Oxford University Press, 2021) at 246.

3 *Ibid* at 247–48 and 310–11; James Hathaway, *The Rights of Refugees Under International Law*, 2d ed (Cambridge: Cambridge University Press, 2021) at 339; for the notion of constructive *refoulement* whereby states make lives for refugees so difficult that they "voluntarily" leave the country of refuge, see Penelope Mathew, "Constructive Refoulement" in Satvinder Singh Juss, ed, *Research Handbook on International Refugee Law* (Cheltenham, UK and Northampton, US: Elgar, 2019) at 207–23, and Penelope Mathew, "Refoulement" in Cathryn Costello, Michelle Foster & Jane McAdam, eds, *The Oxford Handbook of International Refugee Law* (Oxford: Oxford University Press, 2021) at 913–15.

refoulement in the case of an asylum seeker? The UK House of Lords concluded that such persons were not refugees in the sense of the 1951 Refugee Convention since they had not left their country of origin, or in the words of the court: "The conclusion must be that steps which are taken to control the movements of such people who have not yet reached the state's frontier are not incompatible with the acceptance of the obligations which arise when refugees have arrived in its territory."[4]

This question of whether the *non-refoulement* obligation has extraterritorial application comes into even starker focus when it involves persons on their way to a country of refuge in ships. While most commentators[5] and the United Nations High Commissioner for Refugees (UNHCR)[6] believe that there is such an extraterritorial application, the response to this question by the courts in certain countries has been considerably more muted. In 1991 when the US government intercepted Haitian refugees on the high seas, with the result that they ended up back in the country they were fleeing, the US Supreme Court concluded that this did not violate US law by saying:

> [B]oth the text and the negotiating history of Article 33 of the Convention indicate that it was not intended to have any extraterritorial effect. . . . This case presents a painfully common situation in which desperate people, convinced that they can no longer remain in their homeland,

---

4 *R v Immigration Officer at Prague Airport; ex parte European Roma Rights Centre*, [2004] UKHL 55 at para 64; for a commentary, see Hathaway, above note 3 at 347–49 (with a discussion of other forms of refusal of entry to asylum seekers at 314–37); Goodwin-Gill & McAdam, above note 2 at 425–27.

5 Hathaway, above note 3 at 308–29 (while at 329–49 for a commentary on the interaction of the law of the sea and the *non-refoulement* obligation, which is also discussed in Azadeh Dastyari & Daniel Ghezelbash, "Asylum at Sea: The Legality of Shipboard Refugee Status Determination Procedures" (2020) 32 *International Journal of Refugee Law* 1–27, and Violeta Moreno-Lax, "Protection at Sea and the Denial of Asylum" in Costello, Foster & McAdam, eds, *The Oxford Handbook of International Refugee Law*, above note 3 at 483–501, as well as Mathew, "Refoulement," above note 3 at 907–11.

6 UNHCR, *Note on the Principle of Non-refoulement* (November 1997), under heading E, "Territorial Application"; UNHCR, *Advisory Opinion on the Extraterritorial Application of Non-refoulement Obligations Under the 1951 Convention relating to the Status of Refugees and its 1967 Protocol* (26 January 2007) at 12 and 19, paras 24 and 43; UNHCR, *Maritime Interception Operations and the Processing of International Protection Claims: Legal Standards and Policy Considerations with Respect to Extraterritorial Processing* (November 2010) at 4, paras 12–13; UNHCR, *Submission by the Office of the United Nations High Commissioner for Refugees in the Case of* SS and Others v Italy *(Appl No 21660/18) before the European Court of Human Rights* (14 November 2019).

take desperate measures to escape. Although the human crisis is compelling, there is no solution to be found in a judicial remedy.[7]

Similarly, in Australia the judiciary ruled that a country of refuge can take steps to prevent the landing of persons who have been rescued from a sinking ship within the territorial waters of Australia and transfer them to a third country, again confirming the limitation of the obligation not to *refoule* people in the following words:

> [I]t should be added that this is a municipal, and not an international, court. Even if it were, whilst customary international law imposes an obligation upon a coastal state to provide humanitarian assistance to vessels in distress, international law imposes no obligation upon the coastal state to resettle those rescued in the coastal state's territory. This accords with the principles of the Refugee Convention. By Art 33, a person who has established refugee status may not be expelled to a territory where his life and freedom would be threatened for a Convention reason. Again, there is no obligation on the coastal state to resettle in its own territory.[8]

Another issue, which was already discussed during the *travaux préparatoires*, was the interplay between extradition and *refoulement*, which can be broken into two main questions. The first one is whether extradition and deportation proceedings can be carried out at the same time given the fact that their purposes are different. Second, does an extradition request for a refugee prevail over the obligation of *non-refoulement*? With respect to the first issue, the problem of disguised extradition comes into play. The difference between the two procedures, deportation and extradition, has been described as follows:

> [E]xpulsion of an alien is a unilateral act undertaken by a State to remove an alien whose continuing presence in its territory is contrary

7 *Sale v Haitian Centers Council*, 113 S Ct 2549 (1993); while this decision was criticized by the Inter-American Commission on Human Rights in the case of the *Haitian Centre for Human Rights et al v United States*, Case 10.675, Report No 51/96 at para 171, the House of Lords agreed with it in *R v Immigration Officer at Prague Airport; ex parte European Roma Rights Centre*, [2004] UKHL 55 at paras 17 and 68–71, although it retreated from this position in *R(ST) v Secretary of State for the Hoe Department*, [2012] UKSC 12 at para 21; for commentaries, see Goodwin-Gill & McAdam, above note 2 at 311–12, and Hathaway, above note 3 at 383–87.

8 *Ruddock v Vadarlis*, [2001] FCA 1329 at para 126, as well as *CPCF v Minister for Immigration and Border Protection*, [2015] HCA 1 at paras 483–89; for a commentary, see Peter Billings, "Operation Sovereign Borders and Interdiction at Sea: CPCF v Minister for Immigration and Border Protection" (2016) 23:2 *Australian Journal of Administrative Law* at 76–101.

> to the public interests of the territorial State. In contrast, the extradition of an alien requires the consensual cooperation of two States and is usually undertaken by the territorial State pursuant to a bilateral or other treaty in the interest of the requesting State in order to facilitate the enforcement of its national criminal law.[9]

This means that if deportation proceedings are used to circumvent the requirements of extradition law, even if an extradition request is outstanding, such proceedings might very well amount to an abuse of process.[10] It has also been said in this context that disguised extradition could occur if the deportation proceedings are a "sham or not bona fide," which would require a demonstration of "bad faith or improper purpose" that is difficult to prove.[11]

---

9 UN Doc A/CN.4/565, *Expulsion of Aliens, Memorandum by the Secretariat,* International Law Commission, Fifty-eighth Session, Geneva, 1 May–9 June and 3 July–11 August 2006 (10 July 2006) at 71–72, para 83. This has been further explained as "extradition involves basically three elements: acts of sovereignty on the part of two states; a request by one state to another state for the delivery to it of an alleged criminal; and the delivery of the person requested for the purposes of trial or sentence in the territory of the requesting state. Deportation is essentially a unilateral act of the deporting state in order to get rid of an undesired alien. The purpose of deportation is achieved when such alien leaves the deporting state's territory; the destination of the deportee is irrelevant to the purpose of deportation. One of the important distinguishing features between extradition and deportation is therefore the purpose of the state delivery act in question" (*Mohamed and Another v President of the Republic of South Africa and Others*, [2001] ZACC 18 at para 29); see, also, M. Cherif Bassiouni, *International Extradition: United States Law and Practice*, 6th ed (Oxford: Oxford University Press, 2014) at 213–23.

10 Sibylle Kapferer, *The Interface Between Extradition and Asylum* (November 2003) UNHCR Legal and Protection Policy Research Series PPLA/2003/05 at 61, para 168, online (pdf): www.unhcr.org/3fe84fad4.pdf; see, also, *QJ v Secretary of State for the Home Department*, SC/84/2009 (SIAC) at para 35, and *Canada (Minister of Citizenship and Immigration) v Seifert*, 2007 FC 1165 at paras 203–5.

11 *Branigan v Canada (Citizenship and Immigration)*, 2004 FC 245 at paras 19–23; *Rebmann v Canada (Solicitor General)*, [2005] 3 FC 285 at paras 9–10; *Froom v Canada (Minister of Citizenship and Immigration)*, 2003 FC 1127 at paras 28–30. In Germany, such a conflict is avoided in the legislation where s 60(4) of the *Residence Act* stipulates that "if a formal request for extradition or a request for arrest combined with a notification of intent to file a request for extradition has been received from another state, deportation of the foreigner to this state shall be permissible only with the approval of the authority which is responsible for approving extradition pursuant to Section 74 of the Act on International Mutual Assistance in Criminal Matters." See, also, UN Doc A/CN.4/625, International Law Commission, Sixty-second Session, Geneva, 3 May–4 June and 5 July–6 August 2007, *Sixth Report on the Expulsion of Aliens*, Maurice Kamto, Special Rapporteur (19 March 2010) at 13–26, paras 44–72, as well as Jeffrey G. Johnston, "Removing the Mask: Disguised Extradition Through Deportation as an Abuse of Process" in Robert J. Currie, ed, *Transnational and Cross-Border Criminal Law: Canadian Perspectives* (Toronto: Irwin Law, 2023) at 448–71.

With respect to the second issue, it is recognized that *refoulement* principles apply to both asylum claimants and to persons subject to extradition requests given the broad wording of article 33.1 of the 1951 Refugee Convention, which states that "no Contracting State shall expel or return (*refouler*) a refugee in any manner."[12] This is confirmed by the *non-refoulement* provisions in regional human rights and extradition treaties,[13] which prohibit extradition on similar grounds to the Refugee Convention, as well as by state practice.[14] In addition, human rights law, which goes beyond the Refugee Convention and does not allow *refoulement* to torture or cruel, inhuman, or degrading treatment or punishment, would also apply to extradition.[15]

However, the interplay or extradition and *refoulement* of refugees is also present on a different level, when a person who is seeking refugee status or who has obtained such status can also be subject to extradition proceedings in the first place. State practice is mixed in respect to persons who have obtained refugee status in that in some countries a person with refugee status cannot be extradited unless this status has been revoked, while in other countries the refugee status does not provide a bar to extradition.[16]

---

12 *Németh v Canada (Justice)*, 2010 SCC 56 at paras 32–34; *MJELR v Pollak*, [2010] IEHC 209; Goodwin-Gill & McAdam, above note 2 at 279–84; UNHCR, *Guidance Note on Extradition and International Refugee Protection* (April 2008) at 12, para 24.

13 Article 22(8) of the American Convention on Human Rights; art 13(4) of the Inter-American Convention to Prevent and Punish Torture; art 4(5) of the Inter-American Convention on Extradition; art 3.2 of the European Convention on Extradition; art 5 of the European Convention on the Suppression of Terrorism; art 19(2) of the *Charter of Fundamental Rights of the European Union*, and, indirectly, art 15 of the Inter-American Convention against Terrorism.

14 Goodwin-Gill & McAdam, above note 2 at 279–81; UNHCR, *The Interface Between Extradition and Asylum*, above note 10 at 77–79, paras 226–28; UNHCR, *Conclusions Adopted by the Executive Committee on the International Protection of Refugees No 17* (XXXI) Problems of Extradition Affecting Refugees 1980, at paras (d) & (e), and No 55 (XL) 1989, at para (k), online: www.unhcr.org/en-my/578371524.pdf.

15 UNHCR, *Guidance Note on Extradition and International Refugee Protection* (April 2008) at 16, paras 38–39; UNHCR, *The Interface Between Extradition and Asylum*, above note 10 at 45–48, paras 127–31, as a result of the interpretation by international monitoring bodies and at 48–49, paras 132–33, as a result of national jurisprudence.

16 UNHCR, *Guidance Note on Extradition and International Refugee Protection*, above note 15 at 21, para 49 and at 22–23, para 53, regarding the issue that in some countries the extradition authorities do not recognize a refugee determination by their refugee decision makers, especially in cases where the extradition request has been received from a third country; UNHCR, *The Interface Between Extradition and Asylum*, above note 10 at 89–90, paras 265–69; Goodwin-Gill & McAdam, above note 2 at 282–83. In the United Kingdom, the Home Office manual "Exclusion (Article 1F) and Article 33(2) of the Refugee Convention" (28 June 2022), online: www.gov.uk/government/publications/asylum-instruction-exclusion-article-1f-of-the-refugee-convention/exclusion-article-1f-and-article-332-of-the-refugee-convention-accessible-

However, there is more consensus that an extradition request for a person who is seeking refugee status should be suspended until a determination of the asylum claim has finally been decided.[17]

B. *REFOULEMENT* IN THE REFUGEE CONVENTION

1) Introduction

The Refugee Convention contains two provisions that allow for the removal of refugees with a criminal background, articles 32.1 and 33.2. The first provision reads: "The Contracting States shall not expel a refugee lawfully in their territory save on grounds of national security or public order." The second indicates that the prohibition against *refoulement* can be overcome where "a refugee whom there are reasonable grounds for regarding as a danger to the security of the country in which he is, or who, having been convicted by a final judgement of a particularly serious crime, constitutes a danger to the community of that country."[18]

Unlike article 1F(b), which can only be applied against refugee claimants who have committed their crimes outside the country of refuge, these provisions can be used against persons who have obtained refugee status and who later have become undesirable because of criminal conduct in their country of refuge.[19] This provision does not apply

version, indicates that a person who has refugee status or is to be granted such status should not be extradited, while in a 2010 decision by the Supreme Court of Canada, it was held that having refugee status does not prevent extradition, *Németh v Canada (Justice)*, 2010 SCC 56 at para 55, which was confirmed by *Gavrila v Canada (Justice)*, 2010 SCC 57 (for a commentary on these two cases, see Catherine Dauvergne, "The Troublesome Intersections of Refugee Law and Criminal Law" in Katja Franko Aas & Mary Bosworth, eds, *The Borders of Punishment: Migration, Citizenship, and Social Exclusion* (Oxford: Oxford University Press, 2013) at 84–89).

17 UNHCR, *The Interface Between Extradition and Asylum*, above note 10 at 94–96, paras 284–88; Goodwin-Gill & McAdam, above note 2 at 282; see, also, in the United Kingdom, the manual "Exclusion (Article 1F) and Article 33(2) of the Refugee Convention," above note 16 at 18–19. However, in Canada, the process is reversed in that no refugee claim will be processed until an extradition proceeding has been finalized; see s 105 of the *Immigration and Refugee Protection Act*, SC 2001, c 27 [*IRPA*].

18 This is repeated at the regional level in the 2004 European Qualification Directive (recast in 2011), art 21.2.

19 *T v Immigration Officer*, [1996] AC 742 at 771; *Pushpanathan v Canada (Minister of Citizenship and Immigration)*, [1998] 1 SCR 982 at para 58; *Attorney-General v Zaoui & Ors*, [2005] NZSC 38 at para 166 [*Zaoui & Ors*]; *Febles v Canada (Citizenship and Immigration)*, 2014 SCC 68 at paras 24–26; see, also, Geoff Gilbert, "Exclusion Under Article 1F Since 2001: Two Steps Backwards, One Step Forward" in Chetail & Bauloz, *Research Handbook on International Law and Migration*, above note 3 at 521–23; James Hathaway & Michelle Foster, *The Law of Refugee Status*, 2nd ed (Cambridge: Cambridge University Press, 2014) at 538–40; James C.

to excluded persons as they are not entitled to any benefits of the convention, including the protection against *refoulement*. They are removable unless they can rely on another human rights prohibition against *refoulement*; however, if exclusion was found to be applicable by a court, then it is an abuse of process by a government to use the same evidence to argue that the person is captured by article 33.2.[20]

Before examining the practice of the countries under consideration, some preliminary remarks are in order. While this book has distinguished the concepts of exclusion and *refoulement* as if they are considered at different times while a refugee claimant is in the country of refuge—exclusion when applying for refugee status and *refoulement* considerations at the time of removal—in practice these two concepts are intertwined, both from a legal and a temporal perspective.[21]

In the European Union, the Qualification Directive indicates that a person can not only be excluded from subsidiary protection on the 1F grounds of the Refugee Convention, but also if "he or she constitutes a danger to the community or to the security of the Member State in which he or she is present."[22] Similarly, in the United States, the grounds for exclusion (called the bar to asylum)[23] largely mirror the grounds for *refoulement* (called the bar for withholding of removal)[24] and are often considered at the same time as the initial asylum hearing, as is the case in France, Belgium, the Netherlands, and New Zealand. In Canada, a refugee claim can be held ineligible for a refugee determination hearing and can be determined in a deportation hearing instead based on the equivalent of exclusion and *refoulement* grounds.[25]

Simeon, "What Is the Future of *Non-refoulement* in International Refugee Law?" in Singh Juss, *Research Handbook on International Refugee Law*, above note 3 at 189–93 and 185–87, and Hathaway, above note 3 at 399–406.

20 See *R (on the application of Al-Siri) v Secretary of State for the Home Department*, [2021] EWCA Civ 113.

21 Hathaway, above note 3 at 399–406.

22 Qualification Directive, art 17.1(d), above note 18. This directive also allows *refoulement* for danger to the security in art 21.2(a).

23 Section 208(b)(2)(A) of the *Immigration and Nationality Act*, 8 USC, which has the equivalent of exclusion clauses 1F(a) and 1F(b) at subparas (i) and (iii) and the *refoulement* provisions at subparas (ii) and (iv).

24 *Ibid*, s 241(b)(3)(B), which has the exact language as the section just mentioned. The only difference lies in the standard of proof, which is higher for the *refoulement* stage—namely, a clear probability standard requires showing that it is more likely than not that persecution would be suffered; see *Alvarez-Flores v INS*, 909 F2d 1 (1st Cir 1990), and *Velasquez v Ashcroft*, 305 F3d 62 (1st Cir 2002).

25 *IRPA*, above note 17, s 101(1)(f).

The terms "national security," "danger to the community," and "public order" have been interpreted by the UNHCR[26] and in national legislation and jurisprudence,[27] while at the regional level, the Qualification Directive has provided some clarification with respect to "public order" and "national security" by saying that "the notion of national security and public order also covers cases in which a third country national belongs to an association which supports international terrorism or supports such an association."[28]

Regarding interpretation of these terms, the European Court of Human Rights has given general guidance with respect to the concept of national security:

> [I]t considers that the requirement of "foreseeability" of the law does not go so far as to compel States to enact legal provisions listing in detail all conduct that may prompt a decision to deport an individual on national security grounds. By the nature of things, threats to national security may vary in character and may be unanticipated or difficult to define in advance.[29]

and

> [I]t is true that the notion of "national security" is not capable of being comprehensively defined .... It may, indeed, be a very wide one, with a large margin of appreciation left to the executive to determine what is in the interests of that security. However, that does not mean that its limits may be stretched beyond its natural meaning.[30]

---

26 See below in sections B(2)(a) and B(3)(a).

27 As has the term "reasonable grounds," which was examined in Chapter 3, Section A(2)(a). The interpretation of these terms are often developed in immigration law rather than refugee law.

28 Qualification Directive, above note 18, perambular at para 37.

29 *Al-Nashif v Bulgaria*, 20 June 2002, Appl no 50963/99 at para 121.

30 *CG and Others v Bulgaria*, 24 April 2008, Appl no 1365/07 at para 43; this decision was in the context of art 8 of the European Convention on Human Rights, which states: "There shall be no interference by a public authority with the exercise of this right except such as is in accordance with the law and is necessary in a democratic society in the interests of national security, public safety or the economic well-being of the country, for the prevention of disorder or crime, for the protection of health or morals, or for the protection of the rights and freedoms of others."

General drug trafficking was not found to come within the parameters of this concept,[31] nor was human trafficking.[32] On the other hand, participation in extremist groups can be included in this notion.[33]

In Europe, an earlier EU directive, also outside the refugee context, had provided some parameters for the application of the concepts of public order and public security by saying, "[M]easures taken on grounds of public policy or of public security shall be based exclusively on the personal conduct of the individual concerned; previous criminal convictions shall not in themselves constitute grounds for the taking of such measures."[34] This directive was repealed in 2004 and its words replaced by the following:

1. Subject to the provisions of this Chapter, Member States may restrict the freedom of movement and residence of Union citizens and their family members, irrespective of nationality, on grounds of public policy, public security or public health. These grounds shall not be invoked to serve economic ends.
2. Measures taken on grounds of public policy or public security shall comply with the principle of proportionality and shall be based exclusively on the personal conduct of the individual concerned. Previous criminal convictions shall not in themselves constitute grounds for taking such measures. The personal conduct of the individual concerned must represent a genuine, present and sufficiently serious threat affecting one of the fundamental interests of society. Justifications that are isolated from the particulars of the case or that rely on considerations of general prevention shall not be accepted.[35]

---

31 *Ibid.*

32 *Raza v Bulgaria*, 11 February 2010, Appl no 31465/08 at para 53.

33 *Kaushal and Others v Bulgaria*, 2 September 2010, Appl no 1537/08 at para 28.

34 Council of the European Economic Community, Directive 64/221/EEC of 25 February 1964, art 3.

35 EC, Directive 2004/38/EC of 29 April 2004 on the right of citizens of the Union and their family members to move and reside freely within the territory of the Member States, art 27, online: https://eur-lex.europa.eu/legal-content/EN/TXT/?uri=CELEX%3A32004L0038; these provisions were in part based on the interpretation of an earlier decision by the Court of Justice of the European Union (CJEU), which was of the view that "for the purposes of deciding whether a national of another Member State may be expelled under the exception based on reasons of public policy, the competent national authorities must assess, on a case-by-case basis, whether the measure or the circumstances which gave rise to that expulsion order prove the existence of personal conduct constituting a present threat to the requirements of public policy"; see *Georgios Orfanopoulos and Others v Land Baden-Württemberg and*

3. Before taking an expulsion decision on grounds of public policy or public security, the host Member State shall take account of considerations such as how long the individual concerned has resided on its territory, his/her age, state of health, family and economic situation, social and cultural integration into the host Member State and the extent of his/her links with the country of origin.[36]
4. The host Member State may not take an expulsion decision against Union citizens or their family members, irrespective of nationality, who have the right of permanent residence on its territory, except on serious grounds of public policy or public security.[37]
5. An expulsion decision may not be taken against Union citizens, except if the decision is based on imperative grounds of public security, as defined by Member States.[38]

These provisions were interpreted by the Court of Justice of the European Union (CJEU),[39] which has set out the following propositions:

Between Raffaele Oliveri and Land Baden-Württemberg, C-482/01 and C-493/01, 29 April 2004 at para 77; see, also, the European Court of Justice in the case of *Ministerul Administrației şi Internelor — Direcția Generală de Paşapoarte Bucureşti v Gheorghe Jipa*, C-33/07, 10 July 2008, which stated at para 23 that "the concept of public policy presupposes, in any event, the existence, in addition to the perturbation of the social order which any infringement of the law involves, of a genuine, present and sufficiently serious threat to one of the fundamental interests of society," which was repeated by the same court in the case of *Ilonka Sayn-Wittgenstein v Landeshauptmann von Wien*, C-208/09, 22 December 2010 at para 86. Older cases had addressed other aspects of public policy set out in the directive, such as that general prevention is not a sufficient justification in the case of *Carmelo Angeleo Bonsignore v Oberstadtdirektor der Stadt Köln*, C 67-74, 26 February 1975 at "Operative Part," such as that circumstances not related to the case are irrelevant in the case of *Rezguia Adoui v Belgian State and City of Liège; Dominique Cornuaille v Belgian State*, C-115/81 and C-116/81, 18 May 1982, at "Operative Part," at para 2, and such as ensuring a balancing between the personal conduct and the public order in the case of *Arios Pagos (Greece) v Donatella Calfa*, C-348/96, 19 January 1999 at para 28. For a commentary on the provisions in this Citizenship Directive, including the relationship with the exclusion clauses, see Annelieke Beversluis et al, "Once a Criminal, Always a Threat? Investigating Whether the Dutch Practice of Applying Article 1F Refugee Convention Criteria to Article 27 Citizenship Directive Conforms with EU Law" (Migration Law Clinic, University of Amsterdam, July 2016), online (pdf): https://migrationlawclinic.files.wordpress.com/2016/07/migration-law-clinic_once-a-criminal-always-a-threat_july-2016-final-version.pdf. For the notions of public order in other countries, see UN Doc A/CN.4/565, *Expulsion of Aliens*, above note 9 at 236–40, paras 359–62, while for the concepts of national security, see at 242–47, paras 369–76.

36 Council of the European Union Directive 2004/38/EC, above note 35, art 28(1).

37 *Ibid*, art 28(2).

38 *Ibid*, art 28(3).

39 *Land Baden-Württemberg v Panagiotis Tsakouridis*, C-145/09, 23 November 2010 [*Land Baden Württemberg*].

- Imperative grounds of public security is a concept that is considerably stricter than serious grounds within the meaning of article 28(2) and should be limited to exceptional circumstances.[40]
- The concept of imperative grounds of public security presupposes not only the existence of a threat to public security but also that such a threat is of a particularly high degree of seriousness.[41]
- A state's internal and external security are included in the term "public security."[42]
- A threat to the functioning of the institutions and essential public services and the survival of the population, as well as the risk of a serious disturbance to foreign relations or to peaceful coexistence of nations, or a risk to military interests, may affect public security.[43]
- Trafficking in narcotics as part of an organized group could reach a level of intensity that might directly threaten the calm and physical security of the population as a whole or a large part of it.[44]
- An expulsion measure must be based on an individual examination of the specific case and can be justified on imperative grounds of public security only if, having regard to the exceptional seriousness of the threat, such a measure is necessary for the protection of the interests it aims to secure, provided that this objective cannot be attained by less strict means.[45]
- A balance must be struck more particularly between the exceptional nature of the threat to public security as a result of the personal conduct of the person concerned, assessed if necessary at the time when the expulsion decision is to be made, by reference in particular to the possible penalties and the sentences imposed, the degree of involvement in the criminal activity, and, if appropriate,

---

40 *Ibid* at para 40.

41 *Ibid* at para 41.

42 *Ibid* at para 43.

43 *Ibid* at para 44; see, also, *Joined cases C-331/16 and C-366/16, K v Staatssecretaris van Veiligheid en Justitie and HF v Belgische Staat*, 2 May 2018 at para 42 [*K and HF*].

44 *Land Baden-Württemberg*, above note 39 at para 47.

45 *Ibid* at para 49; in *K and HF*, above note 43 at para 52, the court stated that it must be "shown that the personal conduct of the individual concerned currently constitutes a genuine and sufficiently serious threat to a fundamental interest of society." While this "implies the existence in the individual concerned of a propensity to repeat the conduct constituting such a threat in the future, it is also possible that past conduct alone may constitute such a threat to the requirements of public policy" (at para 56, which is further elaborated on at paras 57–60).

the risk of reoffending, on the one hand, and, on the other, the risk of compromising the social rehabilitation of the person.[46]

More specifically, with respect to refugees, the CJEU has also made some statements in the context of the Qualification Directive. In one case,[47] the concepts of national security and public order were examined in the context of article 24(1) of that document, which says: "As soon as possible after their status has been granted, Member States shall issue to beneficiaries of refugee status a residence permit which must be valid for at least three years and renewable unless compelling reasons of national security or public order otherwise require." For the notion of national security, the court applied the same test it had used for the Citizenship Directive, discussed above,[48] "a threat to the functioning of the institutions and essential public services and the survival of the population, as well as the risk of a serious disturbance to foreign relations or to peaceful coexistence of nations, or a risk to military interests," with a particularly high degree of seriousness.[49] Public order was explained as follows: "[R]ecourse to that concept presupposes, in any event, the existence, in addition to the perturbation of the social order, which any infringement of the law involves, of a genuine, present and sufficiently serious threat affecting one of the fundamental interests of society."[50] While international terrorism would fall within this description,[51] an individual assessment of a person who supports an organization on a terrorist listing still needs to be carried out, taking into account the degree of seriousness of danger to national security or public order of the acts committed by this person.[52] A criminal conviction by itself is not sufficient to justify a finding of danger to the public, although the commission of a

---

46 *Land Baden-Württemberg*, above note 39 at para 50; see, also, *K and HF*, above note 43 at paras 62–63, 66–67, and 76, which also indicated that a finding of exclusion can play a role in this assessment but is not conclusive on its own (at paras 51 and 65).

47 *H T v Land Baden-Württemberg*, C373/13, 24 June 2015 [*H T*].

48 See above note 37.

49 *H T*, above note 47 at para 78.

50 *Ibid* at para 79.

51 *Ibid* at para 80.

52 *Ibid* at para 92; see, also, *K and HF*, above note 43, which stated at para 54: "That assessment must take into account the findings of fact made in the decision of exclusion from refugee status taken with respect to the individual concerned and the factors on which that decision was based, in particular the nature and gravity of the crimes or acts that that individual is alleged to have committed, the degree of his individual involvement in them and the possible existence of grounds for excluding criminal liability such as duress or self-defence."

criminal act together with other circumstances related to the situation of the person could result in such an assessment.[53] The court also indicated:

> [I]n the case of a third-country national who is staying illegally within the territory of a Member State and is suspected, or has been criminally convicted, of an act punishable as a criminal offence under national law, other factors, such as the nature and seriousness of that act, the time which has elapsed since it was committed and the fact that that national was in the process of leaving the territory of that Member State when he was detained by the national authorities, may be relevant in the assessment of whether he poses a risk to public policy within the meaning of that provision. Any matter which relates to the credibility of the suspicion that the third-country national concerned committed the alleged criminal offence is also relevant to that assessment.[54]

2) Danger to the Security

a) The Views of the UNHCR

The UNHCR has set out a few propositions with respect to the notion of danger to the security. First of all, it believes that in order to apply this exception a high threshold needs to be met, amounting to a "very serious danger rather than danger of some lesser order."[55] Then there must be an

---

53 *Z Zh and O v Staatssecretaris van Veiligheid en Justitie*, C-554/13, 11 June 2015, at para 51 [*Z Zh and O*]; this decision was made in the context of a different directive, Directive 2008/115/EC of the European Parliament and of the Council of 16 December 2008 on common standards and procedures in Member States for returning illegally staying third-country nationals.

54 *Z Zh and O*, above note 53 at para 65.

55 UNHCR, *Guidance Note on Extradition and International Refugee Protection* (April 2008) at para 14; UNHCR, *Advisory Opinion from the Office of the United Nations High Commissioner for Refugees (UNHCR) on the Scope of the National Security Exception Under Article 33(2) of the 1951 Convention Relating to the Status of Refugees*, 6 January 2006 at 5; UNHCR, *The Nationality, Immigration and Asylum Act 2002 (Specification of Particularly Serious Crimes) Order 2004, UNHCR Comments* (November 2004) at 2; UNHCR, *Note on Diplomatic Assurances and International Refugee Protection* (August 2006) at para 12; UNHCR, *Factum of the Intervenor, UNHCR, Suresh v the Minister of Citizenship and Immigration; the Attorney General of Canada, SCC No 27790*, 8 March 2001 at paras 15–16, 66 and 70; UNHCR, *Intervention by the Office of the United Nations High Commissioner for Refugees in the case of The Minister of Public Safety and Emergency Preparedness v Medhanie Aregawi Weldemariam*, 27 April 2021 at para 20; Eli Lauterpacht & Daniel Bethlehem, "Non-refoulement (Article 33 of the 1951 Convention)" in Erika Feller, Volker Türk & Frances Nicholson, eds, *Refugee Protection in International Law: UNHCR's Global Consultations on International Protection* (Cambridge: Cambridge University Press, 2003) at 136; Goodwin-Gill & McAdam, above note 2 at 269–71; Hathaway, above note 3 at 408–10, who is of the view that danger to the security applies to

individualized finding that the refugee poses a current or future danger to the host country.[56] As well, danger to the security only applies to the security of the country in which the person has been given refugee status.[57]

Another requirement suggested by the UNHCR is that *refoulement* must be proportionate to the present and future danger presented by the refugee. This requirement of proportionality has been broken down further into three other criteria: that there is a rational connection between the removal of the refugee and the elimination of the danger, that *refoulement* has been the last possible resort to eliminate the danger, and that the danger to the country of refuge must outweigh the risk[58] to the refugee upon *refoulement*.[59]

---

situations where "a refugee's presence or actions give rise to an objectively reasonable, real possibility of directly or indirectly inflicted substantial harm to the host's most basic interests, including the risk of an armed attack on its territory or its citizens, or the destruction of its democratic institutions." He goes on to say that danger to the security is not present "because property or economic interests might be adversely affected" or "in order to discourage the departure of other persons." For a discussion of danger to the public, see at 413–18. The European Asylum Support Office (EASO), *Ending International Protection: Articles 11, 14, 16 and 19 Qualification Directive (2011/95/EU): A Judicial Analysis* (December 2016) at 47, online (pdf): https://euaa.europa.eu/sites/default/files/Ending%20International%20Protection_Articles%2011_14_16%20and%2019%20QD%20EASO%20Judicial%20Analysis%20FINAL.pdf, makes mention of some inconclusive jurisprudence in Austria regarding the possibility of the trafficking of people on a large scale being a danger to the security.

56 UNHCR, *Note on Diplomatic Assurances and International Refugee Protection* (August 2006) at para 12; UNHCR, *Intervention by the Office of the United Nations High Commissioner for Refugees in the case of The Minister of Public Safety and Emergency Preparedness v Medhanie Aregawi Weldemariam*, 27 April 2021 at para 19; see, also, a decision of the Kenyan High Court in the case of *Kenya National Commission on Human Rights & another v Attorney General & 3 others*, 9 February 2017 at 12.

57 UNHCR, *Guidance Note on Extradition and International Refugee Protection* (April 2008) at para 14; UNHCR, *Advisory Opinion from the Office of the United Nations High Commissioner for Refugees (UNHCR) on the Scope of the National Security Exception Under Article 33(2) of the 1951 Convention Relating to the Status of Refugees* (6 January 2006) at 6; UNHCR, *Factum of the Intervenor, UNHCR, Suresh v the Minister of Citizenship and Immigration; the Attorney General of Canada, SCC No 27790* (8 March 2001) at para 67; UNHCR, *Intervention by the Office of the United Nations High Commissioner for Refugees in the case of The Minister of Public Safety and Emergency Preparedness v Medhanie Aregawi Weldemariam* (27 April 2021) at para 19; Lauterpacht & Bethlehem, above note 55 at 135; Goodwin-Gill & McAdam, above note 2 at 269; Hathaway, above note 3 at 411.

58 Risk in this context refers to the parameters of the protection contained in the Refugee Convention, that is, persecution. It does not refer to the human rights risks of torture and other cruel, inhuman, or degrading treatment or punishment as there is an absolute prohibition to remove persons to those situations.

59 UNHCR, *Advisory Opinion from the Office of the United Nations High Commissioner for Refugees (UNHCR) on the Scope of the National Security Exception Under Article 33(2) of the 1951 Convention Relating to the Status of Refugees* (6 January 2006) at 6–7; UNHCR, *The Nationality,*

b) National Refugee Jurisprudence

i) Australia

The *Migration Act 1958* has incorporated the *refoulement* provisions of article 33.2 of the Refugee Convention by saying that a person is not entitled to a protection visa if that person is considered by the minister on reasonable grounds "a danger to Australia's security" or, "having been convicted by a final judgment of a particularly serious crime, is a danger to the Australian community."[60] There has been no recent jurisprudence interpreting the danger to security aspect of this section except for saying that danger means actual danger as opposed to a risk of danger.[61] It has been suggested that a connection could be made to the notion of security offences in Australian criminal law, and as such, a number of activities related to terrorism could be considered as being a danger to the security of Australia.[62] It has also been suggested that for

---

Immigration and Asylum Act 2002 (Specification of Particularly Serious Crimes) Order 2004, UNHCR Comments (November 2004) at 2; UNHCR, *Factum of the Intervenor, UNHCR, Suresh v the Minister of Citizenship and Immigration; the Attorney General of Canada, SCC No 27790* (8 March 2001) at para 74–84; UNHCR, *Intervention by the Office of the United Nations High Commissioner for Refugees in the case of The Minister of Public Safety and Emergency Preparedness v Medhanie Aregawi Weldemariam* (27 April 2021) at para 21; Geoff Gilbert, "Current Issues in the Application of Exclusion Clauses" in Feller, Türk & Nicholson, above note 55 at 462–63; Goodwin-Gill & McAdam, above note 2 at 271–74; Lauterpacht & Bethlehem, above note 55 at 137–38 (they are of the view that the following factors should be considered in the balancing exercise: (a) the seriousness of the danger posed to the security of the country; (b) the likelihood of that danger being realized and its imminence; (c) whether the danger to the security of the country would be eliminated or significantly alleviated by the removal of the individual concerned; (d) the nature and seriousness of the risk to the individual from *refoulement*; (e) whether other avenues consistent with the prohibition of *refoulement* are available and could be followed, whether in the country of refuge or by the removal of the individual concerned to a safe third country); Hathaway, above note 3 at 418–23 (who is of the view that no balancing is required between a danger and the risk a refugee might face upon removal).

60 Section 36(1C).

61 *DOB18 v Minister for Home Affairs*, [2019] FCAFC 63 at paras 72–74 [*DOB18*].

62 Peter Billings & Rebecca Ananian-Welsh, "Counterterrorism and the Exclusion of Refugees and Refugee-Citizens from Australia" in James C. Simeon, ed, *Terrorism and Asylum* (Leiden & Boston: Brill Nijhoff, 2020) at 192–93, who refer to the *Criminal Code Act 1995*, Division 101 (Terrorism) and 102 (Terrorist Organizations). In addition, s 202 of the *Migration Act 1958* allows deportation for security reasons, and in that section, there is a reference regarding the meaning of security to s 4 of the *Australian Security Intelligence Organization Act 1979* (see, also, on this point, Administrative Appeals Tribunal (AAT), *Guide to Refugee Law in Australia* (2023) at 7.54, online: www.aat.gov.au/guide-to-refugee-law-in-australia, referring to *ENT19 v Minister of Home Affairs*, [2021] FCAFC 217 at para 122). As well, according to s 502 of the *Migration Act 1958*, the minister responsible for immigration and refugee matters can issue a certificate declaring that in the national interest of Australia a person

the interpretation of the concept of danger to the security of Australia, the jurisprudence of the highest court in New Zealand would be useful.[63]

ii) Belgium

The legislation protects a person from *refoulement* unless this person is a danger to the security or community of Belgium.[64] This general requirement is tempered by two other provisions that echo the CJEU jurisprudence and make it clear that the proportionality principle should play a role in determinations regarding public order or national security by saying that such a decision can only be based on the personal behaviour of the person concerned and cannot be based on economic grounds. In addition, criminal convictions by themselves are not conclusive, but the behaviour of the person concerned must amount to a genuine, actual, and sufficiently serious threat affecting one of the fundamental interests of society, while any reasoning based on preventative measures is not allowed.[65] As well, other factors, such as the seriousness or the nature of the breach of public order or national security, the danger emanating from the person concerned, the duration of their stay in Belgium, the links with the person's country of origin, their age, and the consequences for them and their family members, have to be taken into account.[66]

These provisions were applied in a situation pertaining to the security of Belgium where a member of the fundamentalist Islamic group Khatme Nubuwwat, which was known as radical and violent in Pakistan, was seen as a danger to the public order and security of Belgium by the Belgian security service even though there was no evidence that this group was active in Belgium. The Council of State upheld this assessment.[67] A danger to the national security was also found in a situation where a female imam was engaged in the spreading of an extreme version of

---

falls within the parameters of arts 1F, 32, and 33(2) of the Refugee Convention, which can affect both admission and removal according to s 503 of the same Act (see Billings & Ananian-Welsh, *ibid* at 188). For a discussion of the notion of danger to security and the issuance of a security certificate in respect to a supporter of ISIS in a different context, see *WWKJ and Minister for Foreign Affairs*, [2018] AATA 3894.

63 AAT, *Guide to Refugee Law in Australia*, above note 62 at 7.54, n292; see, also, *SZOQQ v Minister for Immigration and Citizenship*, [2012] FCAFC 40 at para 21 [*SZOQQ*]; for this New Zealand case, see Section B(2)(b)(vii) below in this chapter.

64 *Aliens Act (Law Regarding the Entry, Residence, Settlement and Removal of Aliens)*, 15 December 1980, arts 21, 22, and especially 55/3/1 and 55/4.

65 *Ibid*, art 23(1).

66 *Ibid*, art 23(2).

67 CE No 162.676, 25 September 2006.

Islam.[68] However, just being radical and having rigorous religious beliefs are not sufficient to come within the parameters of this concept.[69]

iii) Canada

The danger to the security provision of the Refugee Convention has been incorporated into Canadian law as follows with respect to a person "who is inadmissible on grounds of security, violating human or international rights or organized criminality if, in the opinion of the Minister, the person should not be allowed to remain in Canada on the basis of the nature and severity of acts committed or of danger to the security of Canada."[70] The second ground of *refoulement* applies to a person who "is inadmissible on grounds of serious criminality and who constitutes, in the opinion of the Minister, a danger to the public in Canada."[71]

Danger to the security is not defined in the legislation but has been given meaning in the jurisprudence, starting with the Supreme Court in the *Suresh* case, describing this concept as

> a serious threat to the security of Canada, whether direct or indirect, and bearing in mind the fact that the security of one country is often dependent on the security of other nations. The threat must be "serious," in the sense that it must be grounded on objectively reasonable suspicion based on evidence and in the sense that the threatened harm must be substantial rather than negligible.[72]

This has been expanded upon by a lower court, which indicated that terrorism can be a threat to security since the danger of security concept

68 CCE No 265.735, 16 December 2021.

69 CCE No 229.068, 20 November 2019; the judgment refers to the fact that the legislator had indicated that violent radicalization and suppression of freedom would be included within the notion of danger to the security.

70 *IRPA*, above note 17, s 115(2)(b); the security grounds are contained in s 34(1) and include activities such as subversion, espionage, terrorism, and acts of violence; the violations of human and international rights are contained in s 35(1)(a) and include war crimes, crimes against humanity, and genocide; the organized crime inadmissibility is set out in s 37(1)(a); for the proposition that this section is the "embodiment of Article 33(2) of the Refugee Convention into Canadian law," see *Ramanathan v Canada (Immigration, Refugees and Citizenship)*, 2017 FC 834 at para 43 [*Ramanathan*]. The concepts of "security" and "national security" contained in this section are of a different nature; see *Canada (Citizenship and Immigration) v Mason*, 2021 FCA 156.

71 *IRPA*, above note 17, s 115(2)(a).

72 *Suresh v Canada (Minister of Citizenship and Immigration)*, 2002 SCC 1 at para 90 [*Suresh*]; the Court also suggested a broad and flexible approach to national security at para 85. This definition was applied in *Re Almrei*, 2009 FC 1263 at para 81, and *Re Harkat* 2010 FC 1241 at paras 82–84.

"cannot be limited to instances where the personal safety of Canadians is concerned. It should logically extend to instances where the integrity of Canada's international relations and obligations [is] affected. It must be acknowledged that only through the collective efforts of nations will the threat of terrorism be diminished."[73] On the other hand, this concept is distinct from danger to the public, the latter encompassing threats of violence against the general population, although overlap is possible.[74]

This approach was applied to an operative for the Iranian Ministry of Intelligence Security who had received specialized training that qualified him as an assassin,[75] to an explosives expert and assassin for Babbar Khalsa International,[76] and to a member of the Egyptian Al-Jihad.[77] Involvement in the development of weapons of mass destruction in Iran[78] has also been considered a danger to the security of Canada, as has the development of chemical weapons in Syria.[79]

In a different context, danger to the security was found to be present in a situation where a person

> associated, supported and directed members of the Movement who in one fashion or another have sought to propagate violent messages of hate and have advocated the destruction of governments and multicultural societies. Mr. Zündel's activities are not only a threat to Canada's national security but also a threat to the international community of nations. Mr. Zündel can channel the energy of members of the White Supremacist Movement from around the world, providing funding to them, bringing them together and providing them advice and direction.[80]

The notion of the nature and severity of acts, which is contained in the same section as danger to the security, has the threshold of substantial gravity; it can apply to persons who have been directly or indirectly

---

73 *Re Zündel*, 2005 FC 295 at para 21 [*Zündel*].

74 *SR v Canada (Public Safety and Emergency Preparedness)*, 2019 FC 1118 at para 54 [*SR*].

75 *Ahani v Canada (Minister of Citizenship and Immigration)*, 2002 SCC 2.

76 *Sogi v Canada (Minister of Citizenship and Immigration)*, 2005 FC 262.

77 *Re Jaballah*, 2006 FC 346.

78 *SN v Canada (Citizenship and Immigration)*, 2016 FC 821; *Hadian v Canada (Citizenship and Immigration)*, 2016 FC 1182; *Moghaddam v Canada (Citizenship and Immigration)*, 2018 FC 1063; *Amiri v Canada (Citizenship and Immigration)*, 2019 FC 205.

79 *Alyafi v Canada (Citizenship and Immigration)*, 2021 FC 89.

80 *Zündel*, above note 73 at para 112; in another case, it was said that involvement in global terrorism could pose a danger to Canadian security; see *Re Jaballah*, 2016 FC 586 at para 157; this promotion of hatred messages has been extended to online versions as well; see *SR*, above note 74 at paras 64–65.

involved in serious criminal activities, such as organized crime, but there needs to be a link between the person and the organization as well as their role and responsibilities within that organization.[81] It was successfully used in the case of a leader of a Tamil organized crime gang operating in Canada,[82] while the test of substantial gravity was also met by a member of another street gang who had committed violent acts against rival gang members.[83]

In using this *refoulement* provision, the jurisprudence has indicated that a balancing exercise needs to take place between the danger a person represents and the risk this person would face upon removal, keeping in mind the high threshold of *refoulement*.[84] This balancing takes several steps. The first step is to determine whether the person is excludable or inadmissible. If that is established, an assessment is made whether such inadmissibility results in the additional element of present and future danger. Having completed the danger portion of the equation, there is a need to determine whether the person would personally face a risk to life, security, or liberty, taking into account that this has to be carried out contemporaneously and not based on the original finding of refugee status. The last step of the exercise involves determining how much of a danger there is in the continuing presence in Canada against the degree of risk, as well as against any other humanitarian and compassionate considerations.[85]

iv) France

According to the legislation in France, a person can be *refouled* if they are a serious danger to the public order, the public safety, or the security of the state, expressed as follows:

---

81 *Nagalingam v Canada (Minister of Citizenship and Immigration)*, 2008 FCA 153 at paras 75–76 [*Nagalingam*, 2008]; Immigration, Refugees and Citizenship Canada, *Operations Manual, Enforcement 28: Ministerial Opinions on Danger to the Public, Nature and Severity of the Acts Committed and Danger to the Security of Canada* (21 November 2017) at 16, online (pdf): www.canada.ca/content/dam/ircc/migration/ircc/english/resources/manuals/enf/enf28-eng.pdf.

82 *Sittampalam v Canada (Minister of Citizenship and Immigration)*, 2007 FC 687.

83 *Nagalingam v Canada (Citizenship and Immigration)*, 2012 FC 176 at para 157 [*Nagalingam*, 2012].

84 *Suresh*, above note 72 at paras 76–79 and 165.

85 *Ragupathy v Canada (Minister of Citizenship and Immigration)*, 2006 FCA 151 at para 18; *Nagalingam*, 2008, above note 81 at para 44; *Kanagasingam v Canada (Citizenship and Immigration)* 2009 FC 90 at paras 15–17and 23; *Nagalingam*, 2012, above note 83 at paras 148–50.

Refugee status is refused or terminated in the following situations:

1. There are serious reasons for considering that the presence in France of the person concerned constitutes a serious threat to the security of the State;
2. The person concerned has been sentenced as a last resort in France, in a Member State of the European Union or in a third State appearing on the list, fixed by decree in Council of State, of States whose legislation France recognizes and criminal courts in view of the application of the law within the framework of a democratic regime and the general political circumstances either for a crime or for an offense constituting an act of terrorism or a public apology for an act of terrorism or punished to ten years' imprisonment, and his presence poses a serious threat to French society.[86]

As in Belgium, the legislation incorporates the jurisprudence of the CJEU in setting out that personal circumstances need to be considered when making a decision regarding a danger to the security or public order, which has the following components:

> The travel ban on French territory can only accompany the surrender decision ... when the foreigner's stay in France constitutes an abuse of rights or if the personal behavior of the foreigner represents, with regard to public order or public security, a real, current and sufficiently serious threat against a fundamental interest of society.
>
> The enactment and duration of the travel ban ... are decided by the administrative authority taking into account the duration of the foreigner's presence on French territory, the nature and length of his ties with France, whether or not he has already been the subject of a deportation measure and the threat to public order represented by his presence in French territory.[87]

In seven cases, persons were found to be a danger to the security of France. The first case involved a person who was sentenced to five years' imprisonment for participation in a criminal association with a view of the preparation of a terrorist act.[88] The second case involved a

86 Article 511-7 of the *Code for Entry and Residence of Foreigners and Right of Asylum* (*CESEDA*); for an interpretation of this provision, see CE, 19 June 2020, 416032/416121, MK c OPPRA, and CE, 19 June 2020, 425231.

87 *CESEDA*, above note 86, arts 622-2 & 622-3.

88 CNDA, 15 February 2013, 10005048, MB; this person was also found to be a danger to the public.

person who, after being convicted of over seventy offences in a three-year period, including the use of weapons and violence against persons, continued his ideological support for the Islamic State in Iraq and Syria (ISIS) while incarcerated, which manifested in verbal and physical threats against fellow inmates and prison authorities. It was found that the combination of "a dangerousness and behavioral instability directed in particular against all forms of authority and a clear and manifest allegiance to an organization terrorist, which currently operates on French territory and which advocates in particular direct action against state officials," justified a finding of a current, real, and sufficiently serious threat to the security of France.[89] A leader in a Bangladeshi mosque who approved of Islamic radicalism but who hid his real convictions and activities was also found to be a danger to the security,[90] as was a person who had been seriously radicalized and close to al Qaeda.[91] A person suspected by the intelligence services of taking part in the second war of South Ossetia and, after arriving in France, was in contact with a number of persons involved in the jihadi movement and suspected of enlisting combatants and financing a terrorist organization was also found to be a danger.[92] The same result was reached in a situation where a person had recently been convicted of an act of terrorism combined with continuous and serious links to jihadi movements.[93] Involvement in a jihadi movement outside France could also amount to a threat to the security of France.[94]

In another case where a person had expressed, on the internet, sympathy with armed groups opposed to the Syrian regime, this threshold was not met,[95] nor was it where a person had participated in an intrusion of the Chad embassy in Paris to denounce the authoritarian regime of the president of that country, but where there had been no harm to persons, only damage to property.[96]

---

89 CNDA, 31 December 2018, 17013391, MO.

90 CNDA, 28 September 2018, 17021629, MK, upheld on appeal by the CE, 19 June 2020, 425231.

91 CNDA, 11 April 2019, 16037707.

92 CE, 29 December 2021, 448330, MM.

93 CE, 18 November 2021, 444991, OFPRA c MO.

94 CNDA, 14 June 2021, 21006354, MS.

95 CE, 2 March 2020, 426104, OFPRA c MR; see, also, CE, 12 February 2020, 426283, OPFRA c Mme E.

96 CNDA, 12 January 2021, 19048155, MM.

v) Germany

In Germany, the legislation has regulated the deportation of persons who are a threat to the security of Germany or its public order in two sections. The first one states that a deportation order can be given "in order to avert a special danger to the security of the Federal Republic of Germany or a terrorist threat."[97] The provision with respect to danger to the public is more detailed:

> [T]he same shall apply if the foreigner meets the conditions stipulated in section 3(2) of the Asylum Act. Application of subsection 1 may

97 Section 58(a)(1) of the *Act on the Residence, Economic Activity and Integration of Foreigners in the Federal Territory* (*Residence Act*); s 60(8), first sentence, of the same Act, incorporates the wording of the Refugee Convention by saying that refugee status can be ignored "if, for serious reasons, the foreigner is to be regarded as a threat to the security of the Federal Republic of Germany or constitutes a threat to the general public because he has been incontestably sentenced to a prison term of at least three years for a crime or a particularly serious offence." The notion of danger to the security is further elucidated in s 54(1) of the *Residence Act*, which states when explaining the notion of particularly serious public interest in expelling a foreigner that this public interest is present where a person

2. threatens the free democratic basic order or the security of the Federal Republic of Germany; this shall be assumed to be the case if there is reason to believe that the foreigner is or has been a member of an organisation which supports terrorism or he supports or has supported such an organisation or he is, in accordance with Section 89a (2) of the Criminal Code, preparing or has prepared a serious violent offence endangering the state described in Section 89a (1) of the Criminal Code, unless the foreigner recognisably and credibly distances himself from the activity which endangers the state,
3. was one of the leaders of an organisation which was incontestably banned because its purposes or its activity contravenes criminal law or it is directed against the constitutional order or the concept of international understanding,
4. is involved in violent activities in the pursuit of political or religious objectives or calls publicly for the use of violence or threatens the use of violence or
5. incites others to hatred against segments of the population; this shall be assumed to be the case where he exerts a targeted and permanent influence on other persons in order to incite or increase hatred against members of certain ethnic groups or religions, or he publicly, in a meeting or by disseminating writings in a manner which is suited to disturbing public safety and law and order,
   a) incites others to undertake arbitrary measures against segments of the population,
   b) maliciously disparages segments of the population and thus attacks the human dignity of others or
   c) endorses or promotes crimes against peace, against humanity, war crimes or acts of terrorism of comparable severity,

   unless the foreigner recognisably and credibly distances himself from his actions.

Article 54(2) sets out instances of a less severe level of concern, namely, a serious interest in expelling a foreigner.

> be waived if the foreigner represents a danger to the general public because he has been incontestably sentenced to a prison term or a term of youth custody of at least one year for one or more intentionally committed offences against life, physical integrity, sexual self-determination or property or for resisting enforcement officers if the criminal offence was committed using violence, using a threat of danger to life or limb, or with guile, or if it constitutes an offence pursuant to Section 177 of the Criminal Code.[98]

As in Belgium and France, and with similar language, the legislation incorporates the CJEU jurisprudence in setting out the requirement of considering the personal circumstances of a person subject to a danger assessment to balance them with the seriousness of the danger.[99]

There have been a few older cases where individuals in high positions in terrorist organizations have been found to constitute a danger to the security of Germany.[100] More recently, jurisprudence in this context has made it clear that support for terrorism must be a goal of an organization or of its activities and that the concept of support for a terrorist organization does not include merely expressing sympathy for terrorist activities.[101] While general support for or affiliation with an organization might not be sufficient to find somebody to be a danger to the security, it will be if this support manifests itself by being a leader or making contributions to violence or other forms of structural integration of a terrorist organization.[102] Another recent case[103] reiterated from previous jurisprudence some general propositions regarding the concept of danger to the security by saying that

98 *Ibid*, s 60(8), last two sentences of the *Residence Act* (s 3(2) of the *Asylum Act* is the section based on art 12.2 of the Qualification Directive, which in turn sets out exclusion 1F of the Refugee Convention, while art 177 of the *Criminal Code* refers to sexual assault offences).

99 *Ibid*, s 53.

100 See Gilbert, above note 19 at 458; European Council on Refugees and Exiles (ECRE), *The Impact of the EU Qualification Directive on International Protection* (October 2008) at 180, online (pdf): https://ecre.org/wp-content/uploads/2016/07/ECRE-The-Impact-of-the-EU-Qualification-Directive-on-International-Protection_October-2008.pdf.

101 Bundesverwaltungsgericht (Federal Administrative Court), BverwG 1 C 13.10, 25 October 2011 at paras 22–23; this was said in regard to the Tablighi Jamaat organization, which was further explained by saying at para 26 that its doctrine is directed at non-violence and has not given instructions to its members to use violence.

102 Bundesverwaltungsgericht (Federal Administrative Court), BverwG 1 C 8.11, 22 May 2012 at para 26; it would appear that the legislation set out at above note 91, which came into effect in 2017, has in some respect superseded this judgment.

103 Bundesverwaltungsgericht (Federal Administrative Court), BverwG 1 A 3.17, 22 August 2017.

> the term "security of the Federal Republic of Germany" ... must be interpreted more strictly than the term of "public security" within the meaning of general police law. The security of the Federal Republic of Germany comprises internal and external security and protects, from an internal perspective, the continued existence and functioning of the state and its institutions. That includes protection against the effects of violence and threats thereof on the carrying out of state function.... In this sense, acts of violence committed against bystanders aimed at propagating general insecurity are also targeted against the internal security of the state.[104]

The court went on to say that a particular threat is related to the risk that a person will carry out a threat but not the "the probability of occurrence at a specific time," while it is also not necessary that the preparation and execution of such threats coincide with any official action, such as the opening of a criminal investigation,[105] or that the threat exceeds the threshold of a specific threat.[106] This framework was applied to a person who sympathized with ISIS and "their ideology of martyrdom and had long been preoccupied with a plan to commit a serious act of violence in Germany using weapons that constitute a public danger."[107] His personal circumstances, such as his roots in and close connections to Germany, did not outweigh the danger of security to Germany, especially since he would be able to integrate into this country of citizenship.[108]

vi) The Netherlands

In the Netherlands, the concept of danger to the public order or national security is used in the *Aliens Act* to refuse resident status to a refugee claimant or to make them subject to removal proceedings.[109] Unlike

---

104 *Ibid* at para 21.

105 *Ibid* at para 23.

106 *Ibid* at para 25; for more details, see paras 26–29.

107 *Ibid* at para 30; for more details, see paras 31–33.

108 *Ibid* at para 41; see, also, for a case involving danger to the security and radical jihad, a case by the Austrian Supreme Administrative Court, Ro 2018/01/0014, 4 April 2019.

109 *Aliens Act 2000*, (Vw 2000), 1 April 2001, arts 3.1(b), 21(1)(c) & (d), 22(1)(c) & (d), 30b(1)(j) & (k), 35(1)(b) and (d), 66a(4), 66a(7)(b), and 67(1)(c); only the first one and the last three (which deal with deportation) refer to danger to security and public order (and on one occasion, the last one, also public safety), while the other ones, which deal with granting status, only refer to danger to the security or having received a final criminal conviction for offences with more than three years' imprisonment. The *Aliens Manual, Vreemdelingencirculaire* 2000 (B), art B1/4.4, indicates that no policy direction regarding the notion of national security has

Belgium, France, and Germany, the legislation in the Netherlands does not have a provision related to personal circumstances as related to the danger to the security or public order but instead has a general provision saying that when an application for resident status is made, circumstances such as the person's background, gender, and age must be considered.[110] There has been no jurisprudence setting out further details regarding the notion of danger to the security.

vii) New Zealand

New Zealand's immigration legislation has a reference to articles 32.1 and 33 of the Refugee Convention as an exception to the general rule of *non-refoulement*.[111] Deportation on the ground of being a threat or risk to security can only be carried out if the minister of immigration certifies that this is the case.[112] There is no provision with respect to the danger to the public.

Security has been defined in this legislation as

> (a) (i) the defence of New Zealand:
>
> (ii) the protection of New Zealand from acts of espionage, sabotage, and subversion, whether or not they are directed from or intended to be committed in New Zealand: the identification of foreign capabilities, intentions, or activities in or relating to New Zealand that affect adversely New Zealand's international well-being, reputation, or economic well-being:
>
> (iii) the protection of New Zealand from activities in or relating to New Zealand that—
>
> (A) are influenced by any foreign organization or any foreign person; and
>
> (B) are clandestine or deceptive, or threaten the safety of any person; and
>
> (C) affect adversely New Zealand's international well-being, reputation, or economic well-being:

---

been issued but that a criminal conviction is not a requirement in order to apply this concept, although specific indicators are needed to have an individual fall within its parameters and that a conviction for a terrorist offence in the Netherlands or abroad is such an indicator, as are very serious activities with a terrorist purpose.

110 *Aliens Act*, above note 109, art 31, with these specific personal circumstances mentioned in art 31(4)(c).

111 *Immigration Act 2009* (NZ), Public Act 2009 No 51, s 164(3).

112 *Ibid*, s 163(1).

(iv) the prevention of any terrorist act and of any activity relating to the carrying out or facilitating of any terrorist act;
(v) the prevention, investigation, and detection of organized crime, including transnational organized crime; and
(b) in an international security context, also includes the safety and stability of the international community, through co-operative measures such as international conventions and other arrangements or agreements between countries.[113]

The concept of danger to the security in the immigration context was given judicial attention earlier by the Supreme Court of New Zealand, which had defined this concept, while following the decision of the Supreme Court of Canada in *Suresh*, as "to come within article 33.2, the person in question must be thought on reasonable grounds to pose a serious threat to the security of New Zealand; the threat must be based on objectively reasonable grounds and the threatened harm must be substantial."[114]

The court was also of the view that article 33 of the Refugee Convention does not contain a requirement to balance the danger in article 33.2 with the risk in article 33.1, and as such, a proportionality assessment is not necessary.[115]

viii) United Kingdom

The implementation of article 33.2 finds form in several provisions. The *Immigration Rules* repeat the language of article 33.2 to indicate that persons falling into those categories will not be granted asylum[116] or persons whose asylum status can be revoked or not renewed.[117] Another legislative provision allows the secretary of state to issue a certificate during an appeal procedure to the effect that a person is not entitled to protection on the ground of national security,[118] while balancing is also not required, according to yet another piece of legislation.[119]

---

113 *Ibid*, s 4, under "Security."
114 *Zaoui & Ors*, above note 19 at paras 45 and 52.
115 *Ibid* at para 42.
116 *Immigration Rules*, ss 334(iii) and (iv), online: www.gov.uk/guidance/immigration-rules; see, also, "Exclusion (Article 1F) and Article 33(2) of the Refugee Convention," above note 16 at 34–35.
117 *Immigration Rules*, s 339B.
118 Section 55(1)(b) of the *Immigration, Asylum and Nationality Act 2006*.
119 Section 34(1)(b) of the *Anti-terrorism, Crime and Security Act 2001*; *Y v Secretary of State for the Home Department*, [2006] UKSIAC 36/2004 at para 153.

The contours of the concept of danger to the security were addressed by the House of Lords in the *Rehman* case, where the notion of a direct threat only to the United Kingdom was rejected in the following terms:

> [T]o require the matters in question to be capable of resulting "directly" in a threat to national security limits too tightly the discretion of the executive in deciding how the interests of the state, including not merely military defence but democracy, the legal and constitutional systems of the state need to be protected. I accept that there must be a real possibility of an adverse effect on the United Kingdom for what is done by the individual under inquiry but I do not accept that it has to be direct or immediate.[120]

ix) United States

The *refoulement* principle is set out in the United States using the language of article 33.2 of the Refugee Convention by saying that "the alien, having been convicted by a final judgment of a particularly serious crime, constitutes a danger to the community of the United States" and "there are reasonable grounds for regarding the alien as a danger to the security of the United States."[121] The legislation deems somebody who has been involved in terrorist activities (as defined elsewhere in the Act) to be "a danger to the security of the United States."[122] It says with respect to danger to the public:

120 *Secretary of State for the Home Department v Rehman*, [2001] UKHL 47 at para 16 [*Rehman*]; this issue is also addressed in the manual "Exclusion (Article 1F) and Article 33(2) of the Refugee Convention," above note 16, which states at 38: "Those considered to represent a danger to the security of the UK on grounds of extremism may include: those whose presence in the UK is deemed not conducive to the public good, on national security grounds, due to their character, conduct or associations; those who engage in unacceptable behaviours, in the UK or abroad, including undertaking, proposing to undertake or espousing extremist views which foment, justify or glorify terrorist violence to further particular beliefs or provoke others to commit terrorist acts; foment other serious criminal activity or seek to provoke others to such acts or foster hatred which may lead to inter-community violence; spread, incite, promote or seek to justify hatred on grounds of disability, gender, race, religion, sexual orientation, gender identity or for purposes of overthrowing democracy. This list is indicative, not exhaustive, and includes the use of any medium to promote extremist behaviour, including: writing, producing, publishing or distributing material; public speaking, including preaching, running a website or social media; using a position of responsibility, for example, teacher, community or youth leader to express extremist views."

121 *Immigration and Nationality Act*, above note 23, ss 208(b)(2)(A)(ii) and (iv), as well as s 241(b)(3)(B)(ii) and (iv).

122 *Ibid*, s 208(b)(2)(A)(v) and s 241(b)(3)(B)(iv), which refers to s 237(a)(4)(B), which deals with deportation but refers back for the definition of terrorist activities in s 212(a)(3). This

> [A]n alien who has been convicted of an aggravated felony (or felonies) for which the alien has been sentenced to an aggregate term of imprisonment of at least 5 years shall be considered to have committed a particularly serious crime. The previous sentence shall not preclude the Attorney General from determining that, notwithstanding the length of sentence imposed, an alien has been convicted of a particularly serious crime.[123]

The deeming provision regarding danger to the security does not apply to activities that do not threaten the security of the United States. In such situations, a two-prong test applies: first, to determine whether the activities carried out by an individual are terrorist in nature, and second, if so, whether such conduct then affects the security of the United States.[124]

Danger to the security has been described as "(1) endangers the lives, property, or welfare of United States citizens; (2) compromises the national defense of the United States; or (3) materially damages the foreign relations or economic interests of the United States."[125]

The phrase "is a danger to the security" should only apply to persons who actually pose a danger to the security of the United States rather than individuals who conceivably could be a danger or who have the ability to pose such a danger. As well, the danger envisaged in these words connotes a serious danger in the sense of any non-trivial level of danger to US security.[126]

---

expansion regarding the concept of danger to the security was added twice in 1996, first by the *Illegal Immigration Reform and Immigrant Responsibility Act of 1996* (*IIRIRA*), which states that an alien is ineligible for asylum if the attorney general decides that there are reasonable grounds for regarding the alien as a danger to the security of the United States *or* that the alien is inadmissible or removable for terrorist activity, and then by the US *Antiterrorism and Effective Death Penalty Act of 1996* (*AEDPA*), 104th Cong (1996), which amended the withholding of removal provision to specifically provide that an alien who engages in terrorist activity shall be considered to be an alien for whom there are reasonable grounds for regarding as a danger to the security of the United States; see, also, *Bellout v Ashcroft*, 363 F3d 975 (9th Cir 2004).

123 *Immigration and Nationality Act*, above note 23, s 241(b)(3)(B)(ii).

124 *Cheema v Ashcroft*, 350 F3d 1035 (9th Cir 2003) [*Cheema*], indicating that the activities carried out in the United States — fundraising and recruiting for terrorist activities in India — would affect the security of that country but not the security of the United States (see, regarding this case, Mary-Ellen Fullerton, "Terrorism, Torture, and Refugee Protection in the United States" (2011) 29:4 *Refugee Survey Quarterly* 4 at 24–25), and *Hosseini v Gonzales*, 464 F3d 1018 (9th Cir 2006) with the same result for Iran.

125 *Cheema*, above note 124.

126 *Yusupov v Attorney General of the US*, 518 F3d 185 (3d Cir 2008).

The danger to the security concept was applied to a member of the Palestinian designated terrorist group the Popular Front for the Liberation of Palestine (PFLP) who had undergone military training and had carried out spying duties for Syria and Turkey[127] and for a person with connections to al Qaeda.[128] More recently, the determination of what constitutes a danger to the security of the United States was incorporated into the process to designate Tier I terrorist organizations.[129]

3) Danger to the Community/Public Order

a) The Views of the UNHCR

The UNHCR has stated that the fact that a person has been convicted of a particularly serious crime does not in itself mean that they also meet the danger to the community requirement. This would depend on the nature and circumstances of the crime and other relevant factors, such as the likelihood of recidivism.[130]

The UNHCR is of the view that the gravity of the crimes should be judged against international standards, not simply by its categorization in the host state or the nature of the penalty. Serious crimes include murder, rape, arson, and armed robbery, while certain other offences could be considered serious if they are accompanied by the use of deadly weapons or involve serious injury to persons or there is evidence of serious habitual criminal conduct. In addition, factors to be considered include the nature of the act, the actual harm inflicted, the form of procedure used to prosecute the crime, and whether most jurisdictions would consider the act in question to be a serious crime. On the other hand, offences such as theft or the possession for personal use of illicit narcotic substances would not meet the threshold of seriousness. For a crime to meet the threshold of particularly serious means that only crimes that are particularly serious in nature should be considered to fall within the *refoulement* principle.[131]

---

127 *Mortagy v Ashcroft*, Docket No 02-60544 (5th Cir 2003).

128 *Malkandi v Mukasey*, 544 F3d 1029 (9th Cir 2008).

129 See Chapter 5, n460.

130 UNHCR, *Note on Diplomatic Assurances and International Refugee Protection*, above note 56 at 5, para 12; see, also, Goodwin-Gill & McAdam, above note 2 at 270, and Hathaway, above note 3 at 415.

131 UNHCR, *The Nationality, Immigration and Asylum Act 2002 (Specification of Particularly Serious Crimes) Order 2004, UNHCR Comments* (November 2004) at 2 and 4; see, also, Goodwin-Gill & McAdam, above note 2 at 270–71, and Hathaway, above note 3 at 413–15.

With respect to the second aspect, the danger to the community, it is essential to look not only at the commission of past crimes but also at the present and future danger, or in the words of the UNHCR:

> The burden of proof is on the State to prove that one or several convictions are symptomatic of the criminal, incorrigible nature of the person and that he is likely to do it again. As Article 33(2) is concerned with the present and future more than with the past, it seems that the authorities ought to give a refugee fair warning and a chance to mend his ways, before expulsion to a country of persecution is seriously considered.[132]

The UNHCR has advocated for a balancing approach to both aspects of article 33.2 of the Refugee Convention and has expressed concern about the automatic classification of certain crimes in legislation as particularly serious, in which case, it suggested that the other requirement of article 33.2, the danger to the community, should also be set out with some precision in the same legislation.[133]

b) National Jurisprudence

i) Introduction

Public order is mentioned as an exception to the principle of *non-refoulement* in article 32.1 of the Refugee Convention, and danger to the community, combined with a conviction by a final judgment of a particularly serious crime, can be found in article 33.2. In Europe, some clarification is given in the Asylum Procedures Directive (recast), which says that "the notion of public order may, inter alia, cover a conviction for committing a serious crime."[134]

The public order concept is retained in the legislation of Belgium, Germany, and the Netherlands (with one exception in the Netherlands where public order and public safety are used in the same provision[135]),

---

132 UNHCR, *The Nationality, Immigration and Asylum Act 2002 (Specification of Particularly Serious Crimes) Order 2004*, above note 131 at 2–3; UNHCR, *Note on Diplomatic Assurances and International Refugee Protection*, above note 56 at 5, para 12; see, also, Goodwin-Gill & McAdam, above note 2 at 270, and Hathaway, above note 3 at 416–18.

133 This was said in the particular situation of Australia; see Savitra Taylor, "Exclusion from Protection of Persons of 'Bad Character': Is Australia Fulfilling Its Treaty-Based Non-Refoulement Obligations?" (2001) 8:1 *Australian Journal of Human Rights* 83 at 88.

134 EC, Directive 2013/32 of 26 June 2013 on common procedures for granting and withdrawing international protection (recast), perambular at para 24, online: https://eur-lex.europa.eu/legal-content/en/TXT/?uri=celex%3A32013L0032.

135 *Aliens Act*, above note 109, art 67(1)(c).

while France uses the notions of both public order and public safety. The common law countries employ the concept of danger to the community (except Canada, which uses the term "danger to the public"), as does the Qualification Directive.[136] New Zealand will not be discussed as it has no specific legislation dealing with the notion of danger to the public or any jurisprudence in that regard.[137]

ii) Australia

The legislation has spelled out with some precision what is to be considered a particularly serious crime by referring to

> (a) a serious Australian offence; or
> (b) a serious foreign offence.[138]
>
> *serious Australian offence* means an offence against a law in force in Australia, where:
> (a) the offence:
> (i) involves violence against a person; or
> (ii) is a serious drug offence; or
> (iii) involves serious damage to property; or
> (iv) is an offence against section 197A or 197B (offences relating to immigration detention); and
> (b) the offence is punishable by:
> (i) imprisonment for life; or
> (ii) imprisonment for a fixed term of not less than 3 years; or
> (iii) imprisonment for a maximum term of not less than 3 years.
>
> *a serious foreign offence* means an offence against a law in force in a foreign country, where:
> (a) the offence:
> (i) involves violence against a person; or

136 Qualification Directive, above note 18, art 21.2(b).

137 The *Immigration Act 2009*, above note 111, s 161(1), contains a general provision dealing with deportation based on convictions for criminal offences; for jurisprudence in Austria, see EASO, *Ending International Protection*, above note 55 at 48, as well as the decision by its Supreme Administrative Court, Ra 2018/19/0522, 29 August 2019, which calls for a balancing approach and gives the following examples of particular serious crimes: murder, rape, child abuse, drug trafficking, and armed robbery. There also have been cases regarding this concept in the Czech Republic and Greece; see EASO, *Ending International Protection: Compilation of Jurisprudence*, 2d ed (2021) at 55–56 and 88, online (pdf): https://euaa.europa.eu/sites/default/files/publications/Ending-international-protection-2nd-edn-CJ.pdf.

138 Section 5M of the *Migration Act 1958*.

(ii) is a serious drug offence; or
(iii) involves serious damage to property; and

(b) if it were assumed that the act or omission constituting the offence had taken place in the Australian Capital Territory, the act or omission would have constituted an offence (the Territory offence) against a law in force in that Territory, and the Territory offence would have been punishable by:
(i) imprisonment for life; or
(ii) imprisonment for a fixed term of not less than 3 years; or
(iii) imprisonment for a maximum term of not less than 3 years.[139]

This 2001 change in legislation is believed to be the result of a number of decisions of the Federal Court of Australia,[140] which indicated that it was not possible to determine what amounted to a particularly serious crime by assessing only the nature of the crime without the circumstances of its commission.[141]

The jurisprudence has established that *refoulement* can only follow if the requirements of both being convicted of a particularly serious crime and being a danger to the community are fulfilled.[142] Danger means more than being a risk of danger and refers to actual danger,[143] but the standard is not as high as a very serious danger.[144]

In general, the concept of particularly serious crime "directs attention to all of the circumstances of the offence, rather than just to the maximum penalty fixed by statute, unless the case is one to which the deeming provisions of s 5M are applicable."[145] Drug trafficking has

---

139 *Ibid*, s 5(1); this provision has been criticized as too broad; see Chantal Bostock & Jason Cabarrús, "Short Shrift to International Non-refoulement Obligations? Australia's Approach to Criminal Deportation" (2020) 32:4 *International Journal of Refugee Law* 597 at 606; for an application of the seriousness of foreign offences, see *LCNB and Minister for Immigration and Border Protection*, [2015] AATA 463 at paras 9–18 and 117.

140 Taylor, above note 133 at 87.

141 *Betkhoshabeh v Minister for Immigration & Multicultural Affairs*, [1998] FCA 934; *Betkhoshabeh v Minister for Immigration & Multicultural Affairs*, [1999] FCA 16; and *A v Minister for Immigration & Multicultural Affairs*, [1999] FCA 227.

142 *Van Cuong Nguyen v Minister for Immigration & Multicultural Affairs [No 2]*, [2000] FCA 225 [*Van Cuong Nguyen*]; *SZOQQ*, above note 63 at para 52; *DOB18*, above note 61 at para 49.

143 *DOB18*, *ibid* at paras 72–73; this is also expressed later at para 83 as a present and serious risk; see, also, AAT, *Guide to Refugee Law in Australia*, above note 62 at 7.56–7.57.

144 *LKQD v Minister for Immigration, Citizenship, Migrant Services and Multicultural Affairs*, [2019] FCA 1591 at para 62.

145 *Re JRJZ and Minister for Home Affairs*, [2018] AATA 3687 at para 13.

been held to be a particularly serious crime,[146] as has manslaughter;[147] serious assaults on women;[148] a combination of "affray, recklessly causing injury and riot";[149] a combination of "numerous property offences such as burglary, theft and handling stolen goods; and numerous offences concerning the possession and trafficking of illicit drugs, in particular, heroin, and a number of offences involving or suggestive of violence or a preparedness to commit acts of violence, such as assault, assault with a weapon and possession of a weapon."[150]

The danger to the community provision is designed to protect one or more members of the Australian community from both immediate harm and harm in the reasonably foreseeable future and involves the consideration of many factors, such as

> the seriousness and nature of the crimes committed, the length of the sentence imposed, and any mitigating or aggravating circumstances. The extent of the criminal history is relevant as is the nature of the prior crimes, together with the period over which they took place. The risk of re-offending and recidivism and the likelihood of relapsing into crime is a primary consideration. The criminal record must be looked at as a whole and prospects of rehabilitation assessed. The assessment to be made goes to the future conduct of the person and this involves a consideration of character and the possibility or probability of any threat, which could be posed to a member or members of the Australian community.[151]

---

146 *Van Cuong Nguyen*, above note 142; *Te and Minister for Immigration and Multicultural Affairs*, [2000] AATA 848.

147 *WKCG and Minister for Immigration and Citizenship*, [2009] AATA 512 [*WKCG*]; *BHYK and Minister for Immigration and Citizenship*, [2010] AATA 662 [*BHYK*].

148 *Feliciano Tamayo and Department of Immigration*, [1994] AATA 384.

149 *HSCK and Minister for Home Affairs (Migration)*, [2019] AATA 4392 at para 94 [*HSCK*].

150 *WGKS and Minister for Immigration, Citizenship, Migrant Services and Multicultural Affairs*, [2020] AATA 38 at para 86 [*WGKS*], with a further explanation for why these offences are harmful to the community in paras 88–92.

151 *WKCG*, above note 147 at para 26; *BHYK*, above note 147; see, also, *SZOQQ*, above note 63 at para 52 (overturned on appeal on other grounds in *SZOQQ v Minister for Immigration and Citizenship*, [2013] HCA 12); this statement was clarified in *DOB18*, above note 61 at paras 83 when it says that the court agreed with the *WKCG* case if it meant that danger has the narrow meaning of present and serious risk; see, also, *HSCK*, above note 149 at para 105; *WGKS*, above note 150 at paras 39–40 and 46–54; *EWG17 v Minister for Immigration and Border Protection*, [2018] FCA 1536 at para 52; and AAT, *Guide to Refugee Law in Australia*, above note 62 at 7.55. For an application of these factors, see *Re JRJZ and Minister for Home Affairs*, [2018]

However, no balancing between danger to the community and the harm a person might face if returned is required in Australian jurisprudence.[152]

iii) Belgium

For a determination of danger to the public order, criminal convictions by themselves are not conclusive, but the behaviour of the person concerned must amount to an actual, real, and sufficiently serious threat to a fundamental interest of society.[153] It is the nature and seriousness of the criminal act that inform the notion of a particularly serious crime, not only the characterization of this conduct in the Belgian *Criminal Code*.[154] With respect to the notion of danger to the public, it is necessary to ascertain the nature and circumstances of the crime, while there also needs to be a link between the seriousness of the crime and the danger to the public.[155]

Initially, convictions for immigration offences, such as entering marriages to obtain immigration status[156] or other immigration document fraud,[157] were taken very seriously by Belgian administrative tribunals and invariably resulted in a finding of danger to the public order. Some cases have specifically taken into account the legislative requirements. In one case, both the personal involvement in the importing of drugs, for which the person had received twelve months' incarceration, as well as the actual danger this person represented resulted in a finding of danger to the public order.[158] On the other hand, in a 2010 case, a person who had received two convictions, one for forgery with a suspended

---

AATA 3687 at paras 33–48; *HSCK*, above note 149 at paras 107–40, and *WGKS*, above note 150 at paras 96–169.

152 *SZOQQ*, above note 63 at para 27; *LKQD v Minister for Immigration, Citizenship, Migrant Services and Multicultural Affairs*, [2019] FCA 1591 at para 63; *DOB18*, above note 61 at paras 51–52 and 63–64; *HSCK*, above note 149 at paras 104 and 148–50; *WGKS*, above note 150 at paras 62–66; see, also, AAT, *Guide to Refugee Law in Australia*, above note 62 at 7.57.

153 See above Section B(2)(b)(ii) for the text; see, also, CCE No 244.700, 5 June 2019; CCE No 242.852, 23 October 2020.

154 CCE No 177.066, 27 October 2016; CCE No 229.692, 2 December 2019; see, also, CCE No 229.921, 6 December 2019; CCE No 229.979, 9 December 2019; CCE No 240.702, 10 September 2020.

155 *Ibid* to all cases listed in note 154.

156 CCE No 1612-11083, 9 September 2007; CCE No 3108, 25 October 2007; CCE No 4958, 14 December 2007; CCE No 14.112, 7 July 2008; CCE No 20.094, 9 December 2008; CCE No 21.269, 9 January 2009; CCE No 26.508, 27 April 2009; CCE No 29.763, 9 July 2009.

157 CCE No 26.843, 30 April 2009.

158 CCE No 12.091, 30 May 2008.

sentence and one for international visa fraud resulting in imprisonment for fifteen months, was found not to be a danger to the public order as the crimes had occurred in 2002–4 and there was no evidence of recidivism.[159] The same result was achieved, again in 2010, for a person who had been convicted of participation in a criminal organization and was sentenced to three years since there was no indication of actual danger to the public order.[160] In 2019, a person convicted of the serious offences of kidnapping and attempted blackmail who received a suspended sentence of two years with probation was considered not to be a danger as he had fulfilled all the conditions of his probation.[161]

However, in most cases, a finding of danger to the public order is followed almost automatically as a result of a conviction for a serious crime, especially if the criminal conduct has been escalating over a number of years.[162] This occurred in situations of drug trafficking,[163] people smuggling,[164] illegal possession of weapons, attempted manslaughter,[165] breaking and entering,[166] and theft accompanied by violence.[167] Involvement in weapons' offences and forgery[168] also yielded this result, as did a finding of being a war criminal in another country.[169] While an earlier finding of exclusion will not necessarily result in a determination of a

159 CCE No 49.687, 18 October 2010; see, also, CCE No 240.702, 10 September 2020, for a situation of serious theft on three occasions between 2012 and 2014 but without further criminal conduct since that time.

160 CCE No 50.455, 20 October 2010.

161 CCE No 229.692, 2 December 2019.

162 CCE No 240.702, 10 September 2020; in this case, the person had nine convictions over nine years, starting with being in possession of illegal weapons and ending with assault.

163 CCE No 22.652, 3 February 2009, involving two convictions, four and five years, in a time span of ten years; CCE No 50.261, 27 October 2010, with a sentence of two years.

164 CCE No 229.921, 6 December 2019, with a sentence of six years; the likelihood of recidivism weighed heavily in discussing personal circumstances.

165 CCE No 229.979, 9 December 2019, with a conviction of seven years, while the danger determination was based on the fact that there had been previous criminal convictions in Italy, and the situation resulting in the conviction in Belgium was the result of a domestic dispute where there had been a gross disproportion between the reasons for the dispute and the extreme violence utilized to address it.

166 CCE No 32.630, 13 October 2009, found to be a danger against the public order even though there had been no conviction; CCE No 39.924, 9 March 2010, imprisonment of two months.

167 CCE No 49.839, 20 October 2010, with seven convictions in eight years with penalties between two months and two years; CCE No 40.555, 22 March 2010, with a non-custodial sentence.

168 CCE No 40.614, 23 March 2010.

169 CCE No 51.727, 26 November 2010; the country in question was the Netherlands.

danger to the public,[170] but if the exclusion in Belgium was based on substantial involvement in crimes against humanity with many victims, and there was little evidence of the person's integration into Belgian society, then a conclusion of danger is justified.[171]

The fact that a person was a minor at the time of the commission of the offence[172] or a long-term resident[173] or the conviction had been appealed[174] was found to be irrelevant for an assessment regarding the public order.

Where a person was held to be a danger to the community, decision makers then had to assess whether a person would be at risk if removed to the country of origin, and on several occasions, it was held that such a removal was not possible in view of likely human rights violations upon return.[175]

iv) Canada

The legislation stipulates that a person can be subject to *refoulement* if this person "is inadmissible on grounds of serious criminality and who constitutes, in the opinion of the Minister, a danger to the public in Canada."[176] Inadmissibility on grounds of serious criminality is defined as

> (a) having been convicted in Canada of an offence under an Act of Parliament punishable by a maximum term of imprisonment of at least 10 years, or of an offence under an Act of Parliament for which a term of imprisonment of more than six months has been imposed;
>
> (b) having been convicted of an offence outside Canada that, if committed in Canada, would constitute an offence under an Act of

---

170 CCE No 206.583, 5 July 2018; CCE No 213.486, 5 December 2018; and CCE No 213.667, 19 December 2018, involving persons who had been excluded in the Netherlands for involvement in KhAD in Afghanistan; the same conclusion was reached for a person in crimes against humanity in Chechnya in CCE No 200.572, 1 March 2018.

171 CCE No 193.338, 9 October 2017; the exclusion pertained to involvement in the general security service of the regime of Saddam Hussein in Iraq; see, also, CCE No 221.222, 18 October 2018, involving a person who had assisted the Taliban in Afghanistan but who had not been formally excluded but where his contribution to crimes against humanity was seen to be so serious as to outweigh any personal circumstances.

172 CCE No 32.630, 13 October 2009.

173 CCE No 22.652, 3 February 2009.

174 CCE No 40.614, 23 March 2010.

175 See, for instance, CCE No 193.338, 9 October 2017 (for Iraq), and CCE No 221.222, 18 October 2018 (for Afghanistan).

176 *IRPA*, above note 17, s 115(2)(a).

Parliament punishable by a maximum term of imprisonment of at least 10 years; or

(c) committing an act outside Canada that is an offence in the place where it was committed and that, if committed in Canada, would constitute an offence under an Act of Parliament punishable by a maximum term of imprisonment of at least 10 years.[177]

A government manual[178] has provided several factors to be considered by a decision maker when assessing danger to the public:

- criminal history and established patterns of violent criminal behaviour or threats of violent behaviour that suggest present and future danger to the public and evidence to support the person's pattern of behaviour;
- convictions for serious offences involving but not limited to violence, weapons, drug trafficking, human smuggling and trafficking, sexual offences, and economic crimes;
- documents illustrating an escalation of violence or of gravity in the convictions;
- convictions for actions by the person that caused or might reasonably be expected to have caused death, serious physical or psychological harm, or significant property damage;
- evidence to substantiate the link between the criminal conviction, the likelihood that the person will reoffend, and a pattern of increasingly serious criminal activity;

177 *Ibid*, s 36(1); s 36(1)(c) is broader than envisaged by art 33.2 of the Refugee Convention, which is interesting as the definition of "serious criminality" for the purposes of preventing a refugee claimant to have the claim heard by the administrative tribunal in s 101(2) is framed as follows: "A claim is not ineligible by reason of serious criminality under paragraph (1)(*f*) unless (*a*) in the case of inadmissibility by reason of a conviction in Canada, the conviction is for an offence under an Act of Parliament punishable by a maximum term of imprisonment of at least 10 years and for which a sentence of at least two years was imposed; or (*b*) in the case of inadmissibility by reason of a conviction outside Canada, the Minister is of the opinion that the person is a danger to the public in Canada and the conviction is for an offence that, if committed in Canada, would constitute an offence under an Act of Parliament that is punishable by a maximum term of imprisonment of at least 10 years." It has been said that not every offence with a penalty of more than ten years automatically results in being a serious criminal offence but that the essential factor is "whether the acts committed are of substantial gravity"; see *Nagalingam*, 2008, above note 81 at para 73, and *Makomena v Canada (Citizenship and Immigration)*, 2019 FC 894 at para 42 [*Makomena*].

178 Immigration, Refugees and Citizenship Canada, *Operations Manual, Enforcement 28*, above note 81 at 15–16.

- police, correctional services, or other credible source of information indicating that the person continues to pose a danger to the public;
- the circumstances of the offence(s) in order to provide insight into the level of risk the person may present to the public, evidence of rehabilitation on the part of the individual (education or training certificates, psychological reports, reports from the parole officer, evidence of employment, etc);
- multiple convictions, including serious offences, that could form the basis for a danger opinion; or
- a single conviction that may sustain a finding of danger to the public if it is clearly demonstrated that the person poses a present or future risk of danger to the public, as evidenced by the nature and circumstances of the offence. The jurisprudence indicates that it is possible to base a danger opinion on a single serious conviction when sufficient evidence exists.

The Supreme Court has set out the differences between danger to the security and danger to the public by stating:

> [W]e recognize that the two phrases may overlap. The latter phrase clearly is intended to address threats to individuals in Canada, but its application is restricted by requiring that any individual who is declared to be a "danger to the public" have been convicted of a serious offence.[179] . . .
>
> [T]he "danger to the public" provision allows the government to deport those who pose no danger to the security of the country *per se*—those who pose a danger to Canadians, as opposed to a danger to Canada—provided they have committed a serious crime.[180]

The danger to the public assessment involves the same general approach as danger to the security, including a balancing exercise.[181] The burden to prove the danger is on the government,[182] but the burden

179 *Suresh*, above note 72 at para 84.

180 *Ibid* at para 91.

181 *Hasan v Canada (Minister of Citizenship and Immigration)*, 2008 FC 1069 at para 28 [*Hasan*]; *Maio v Canada (Minister of Citizenship and Immigration)*, 2010 FC 354 at para 8 [*Maio*].

182 *Hasan*, above note 181 at para 13.

of proving risk is on the person to be removed.[183] This balancing is to be carried out with a view

> to determin[ing] whether the risk that the Applicant poses to the Canadian public outweighs the risks he faces if returned and "other humanitarian and compassionate circumstances." The risk to the Applicant is addressed separately in the weighing process and "other humanitarian and compassionate factors" cannot . . . mean anything other than humanitarian and compassionate factors "other" than risk.[184]

With respect to what amounts to a danger to the public, the court has said that

> the meaning of "public danger" is not a mystery: it must refer to the possibility that a person who has committed a serious crime in the past may seriously be thought to be a potential re-offender. It need not be proven—indeed it cannot be proven—that the person will reoffend. What . . . the subsection adequately focusses the Minister's mind on is consideration of whether, given what she knows about the individual and what that individual has had to say in his own behalf, she can form an opinion in good faith that he is a possible re-offender whose presence in Canada creates an unacceptable risk to the public.[185]

When assessing the danger portion of this type of *refoulement*, danger means present and future danger,[186] while it is also necessary to examine the actual circumstances of the case[187] and whether other considerations, such as rehabilitation[188] and the risk of reoffending,[189] are present. Hav-

---

183 *Ibid* at para 21; *Jama v Canada (Minister of Citizenship and Immigration)*, 2009 FC 781 at para 85 [*Jama*]; *Maio*, above note 181 at para 9.

184 *Jama*, above note 183 at para 91; *Maio*, above note 181 at para 9; such factors can include the presence of family in Canada, the degree of establishment in Canada, and the person's health; see *Baladie v Canada (Citizenship and Immigration)*, 2018 FC 706; *Nkouka v Canada (Citizenship and Immigration)*, 2018 FC 862 [*Nkouka*]; health can also include the examination of post-traumatic stress disorder (PTSD) issues; see *Recinos v Canada (Citizenship and Immigration)*, 2022 FC 518 [*Recinos*].

185 *Williams v Canada (Minister of Citizenship and Immigration)*, [1997] 2 FC 646

186 *Ibid*; *Mworosha v Canada (Citizenship and Immigration)*, 2017 FC 983.

187 *Galvez Padilla v Canada (Citizenship and Immigration)*, 2013 FC 247; *Ramanathan*, above note 70.

188 *Ghorvei v Canada (Minister of Citizenship and Immigration)*, 1997 138 FTR 149; *Villanueva v Canada (Minister of Citizenship and Immigration)*, 2008 FC 1341; *Nkouka*, above note 184; *Recinos*, above note 184.

189 *Cheikh v Canada (Citizenship and Immigration)*, 2017 FC 896; *Makomena*, above note 177; *JBL v Canada (Citizenship and Immigration)*, 2021 FC 487; *Mendez Caballero v Canada (Citizenship*

ing been released from immigration detention does not necessarily mean that a person cannot still be a danger to the public.[190]

Serious crimes for the purposes of *refoulement* include aggravated assault,[191] assault,[192] uttering threats and sexual interference with a minor,[193] sexual assault,[194] armed robbery,[195] and drug trafficking.[196] Economic crimes, such as fraud or forgery, can also be crimes for this purpose.[197] Usually, in order to find danger, a number of offences need to have resulted in convictions rather than just criminal charges,[198] but it is possible to arrive at such a conclusion based on only one violent criminal act.[199]

The assessment of the risk a person would face upon return when removed, after it was found that they were a danger to the public, was found not to be sufficient to reach the threshold of human rights violations in most cases, for the most part because of the lapse of time between the person becoming a refugee in Canada and the assessment regarding danger since in those cases the situation had changed in the country of origin.[200]

---

and Immigration), 2021 FC 856 [*Mendez Caballero*], in which case a criminal history of more than forty offences between 1991 and 2017 showed a clear propensity to commit further offences in the future.

190 *Recinos*, above note 184.

191 *Nguyen v Canada (Minister of Employment and Immigration)*, [1994] 1 FC 232; *Jama*, above note 183.

192 *Hoang v Canada (Minister of Employment and Immigration)* (1990), 120 NR 193; *Camara v Canada (Minister of Citizenship and Immigration)*, 2006 FC 168; *Hasan*, above note 181; however, in *Galvez Padilla v Canada (Citizenship and Immigration)*, 2013 FC 247, an assault resulting in minor injuries was considered not to meet the threshold for particularly serious crime at paras 37–46.

193 *Hasan*, above note 181.

194 *Barrera v Canada (Minister of Employment and Immigration)*, [1993] 2 FC 3.

195 *Mohamed v Canada (Minister of Citizenship and Immigration)*, 2008 FC 315; *Maio*, above note 181.

196 *Tran v Canada (Minister of Citizenship and Immigration)* (1997), 132 FTR 163; *Farshid-Ghazi v Canada (Minister of Citizenship and Immigration)* (1998), 142 FTR 117.

197 *Ramanathan*, above note 70 at paras 45–49; *Makomena*, above note 177.

198 *Bakchiev v Canada (Minister of Citizenship and Immigration)* (2000), 196 FTR 306, although contrary in the case of a member of a criminal gang; see *Thuraisingam v Canada (Solicitor General of Canada)*, IMM-4506-03.

199 *Veluppilai v Canada (Minister of Citizenship and Immigration)* (1999), 180 FTR 88.

200 See, for instance, *Mworosha v Canada (Citizenship and Immigration)*, 2017 FC 983 (for the Democratic Republic of the Congo), and *Mendez Caballero*, above note 189 (for Chile).

v) *France*[201]

In older jurisprudence, several principles with respect to danger to the public order were developed, such as that there should be a consideration of both the criminal activity and humanitarian needs. On that basis, a person who was convicted of serious crimes but who had lived in France for thirty-five years while being gainfully employed should not face deportation, nor should a person who was convicted of theft but had faced racial persecution during the occupation of France in the Second Word War, and nor should a person who was advanced in age.[202] Similarly, a person who was sentenced to twenty months' imprisonment but had a stable family life and a professional career and a person who had served with distinction in the Foreign Legion were not considered to be a danger to the public order.[203]

Criminal activity that has not resulted in a criminal conviction does not justify a public order stigma unless such activity is related to violent and militant groups with a political agenda, such as the independence of a Basque country or the hijacking of a plane,[204] and this activity is carried out on French soil.[205]

Lengthy sentences for serious crimes, such as drug trafficking, or for less serious but repeat crimes, such as theft, could lead to an adverse public order finding[206] but not minimal penalties for offences such as desertion from the Foreign Legion or vagrancy.[207]

More recently, it has happened that a decision regarding the danger to the public order has been made separately from and in addition to a conviction; such a decision regarding danger must take into account the nature of the offences committed, a risk of recidivism, and the person's general good behaviour upon release from prison.[208] This provision was not applied to a person who was sentenced to twelve months' imprisonment for participation in a prostitution ring[209] or to a per-

201 For the legislative provisions regarding danger to the public, see above Section B(2)(b)(iv).

202 Frédéric Tiberghien, *La protection des refugies en France* (Aix-en-Provence: Presses Universitaires D'Aix-Marseille, 1988) at 495.

203 *Ibid* at 491 and 494.

204 *Ibid* at 491–92 and 494.

205 *Ibid* at 495.

206 *Ibid* at 491–92.

207 *Ibid* at 493.

208 See, recently, CE, 10 June 2021, 440383, OFPRA c MA; CE, 18 November 2021, 441397, OFPRA c MA.

209 CRR, 1 February 2006, 533907, Mlle O, alias Mlle I.

son who was sentenced to ten years' imprisonment for the attempted assassination of his brother-in-law but who had received several reductions in his sentence because of good behaviour.[210] Even with a person who was sentenced in 2012 to eight years' imprisonment for two rapes and again to another three years in 2015 for another rape, it was decided that he was no longer a threat to society because he had made efforts to integrate himself into French society and undergone counselling in order to ensure that his threat to society was diminished.[211]

This stands in rather stark contrast to similar situations where two sentences of three years for sexual assault were deemed to be sufficient to constitute a danger to the public,[212] while the same was said for a sentence of five years for rape, combined with a lack of awareness of the seriousness of these crimes.[213] This was also the case for a sentence of twelve years for torturing and raping a minor;[214] a conviction for drug trafficking after a number of other convictions for lesser crimes both in France and Switzerland;[215] a sentence of four years for involvement in the illegal movement of foreigners into France, with a clear risk of recidivism;[216] and a sentence of eighteen years in 2010 for criminal association and fifteen years for three murders, showing an escalation of criminal behaviour.[217] A similar pattern of criminal behaviour involving the use of narcotics, issuing death threats, rebellion, and contempt, resulting in convictions in 2011 and 2016, while continuing to make death threats after release, also resulted in a danger finding even though the person had argued that he had turned his life around with stable employment and family life.[218] Being exposed to jihad and recruiting prisoners for that cause while continuing relationships with persons belonging to jihadi groups showed a risk of danger to the community even though the person had consulted a psychiatrist and had started compensating victims because these acts were part of his post-release

210 CE, 19 June 2020, 422740; see, also, with similar reasoning, CE, 10 June 2021, 440383, OFPRA c MA.

211 CE, 19 June 2020, 428140.

212 CRR, 25 July 2006, 507465, B.

213 CE, 17 June 2021, 437038, MD.

214 CNDA, 12 March 2019, 17028590, Mme B; see, also, CE, 23 April 2021, 438766, MK for a similar situation of rape.

215 CNDA, 6 April 2009, 634810, I.

216 CE, 10 June 2021, 440383, OFPRA c MA.

217 CE, 10 December 2020, 425040, MK.

218 CE, 29 July 2020, 433645, OFPRA c MH.

obligations.[219] Even a number of short convictions can lead to a finding of danger if these convictions occurred within a short period of time and show an increase in violent tendencies.[220]

vi) Germany[221]

Murder, manslaughter, kidnapping, serious cases of rape, hostage taking, malicious arson, and other serious crimes have been cited in the German jurisprudence as falling within the parameters of the legislation.[222] More recently, a man who had raped his wife and sexually abused his oldest daughter, for which he had been sentenced to forty-four months' incarceration, was considered to have committed a serious crime.[223]

With respect to the danger to the community aspect, it must be current and persisting, which means that there must be a risk of repetition or a continuation of the activities from which the danger emanates.[224] Other personal circumstances, such as the integration into German society, the length of stay in the country, and a stable family, are also factors to be considered.[225]

vii) The Netherlands[226]

According to the *Aliens Regulation*, the notion of danger to the public order includes persons for whom there are serious reasons for considering that they have committed a 1F crime, as well as persons who have been given a final sentence, including foreign convictions.[227] The same

---

219 CE, 18 November 2021, 441397, OFPRA c MA.

220 CNDA, 26 February 2021, 20035833, MA.

221 For the text of the danger to the public section, see above Section B(2)(b)(v).

222 ECRE, *The Impact of the EU Qualification Directive on International Protection*, above note 100 at 180; see, also, *EN (Serbia) & KC (South Africa) v Home Secretary*, [2009] EWCA Civ 630 at para 49 [*EN & KC*].

223 Bundesverwaltungsgericht (Federal Administrative Court), BverwG 1 C 19.11, 10 July 2012 at paras 3 and 43.

224 ECRE, *The Impact of the EU Qualification Directive on International Protection*, above note 100 at 181; see, also, Bundesverwaltungsgericht (Federal Administrative Court), BverwG 1 C 19.11, 10 July 2012 at paras 17 and 43.

225 *Ibid* at paras 21 and 42, although in this case the consideration of a stable family was nullified by the sexual violence the person had inflicted on his family; given all the circumstances, the person was given a temporary deportation order for seven years, a possibility envisaged in s 11 of the *Residence Act*.

226 For the legislative text, see above Section B(2)(b)(vi).

227 Sections 3.77.1(a)–(c) and 3.77.2 of the *Aliens Regulation 2000* (with more details in the *Vreemdelingencirculaire* 2000 (B), art B1/4.4.); the *Vreemdelingencirculaire* 2000 (C), s 7.10.1,

regulation follows the CJEU jurisprudence by ensuring that a number of personal circumstances are taken into account when assessing the seriousness of the crime, such as the duration of the person's time in the Netherlands, their family ties, and their cultural and social connections to their country of origin.[228] Regarding the danger to the public order, the person's behaviour must indicate that they are a real and serious threat to society.[229]

The jurisprudence has set out indicators for when a danger to the public assessment should be applied. Being a party to a murder for which a prison term of eight years was imposed would fit the requirement of a serious crime, as would a lengthy term of incarceration for manslaughter. This means that it is not the maximum penalty that can be imposed in the legislation but the actual penalty given by a criminal court, either a Dutch court or a foreign court, which is determinative of the application of the public order principle.[230] As well, a conviction for involvement in murder or manslaughter raises the spectre of danger to the public order[231] but not personal drug use[232] or visa fraud.[233] The second part of the danger to the public order equation cannot stand by

---

indicates that a conviction for a particular serious crime means a final conviction with a term of imprisonment of at least ten months.

228 Section 3.77.4 of the *Aliens Regulation 2000* with further details in the subsequent sections; these considerations do not apply to persons who have committed 1F crimes.

229 Section 8.22(1) of the *Aliens Regulation 2000* (with more details as to the types of danger to the public order, see the *Vreemdelingencirculaire* 2000 (B), art B1/4.4); this section in *the Aliens Regulation 2000* also refers to personal circumstances such as the duration of the stay in the Netherlands, the person's age, their state of health, their family, their social and cultural integration, as well as their ties with the country of origin; the *Vreemdelingen-circulaire* 2000 (C), s 7.10.1, says with respect to danger to the public order that there are a number of aspects to be considered:

- the danger is assessed on an individual basis;
- the type of crimes and the penalty imposed is taken into consideration;
- there is a presumption that the following crimes are considered a danger to the community: drug crimes, sexual crimes, violent crimes, arson, human trafficking, illegal trafficking in weapons, and illegal trafficking in human organs; and
- if crimes committed abroad seriously shock the public legal order and are considered serious crimes in the Netherlands.

230 Thomas Spijkerboer & B.P. Vermeulen, *Vluchtelingenrecht* (Nijmegen: Ars Aequi Libri, 2005) at 105.

231 AbRS, 20 December 2010, nr 201001418/1.

232 Rb, The Hague, Awb 06/40758, 29 March 2007.

233 Rb, The Hague, Awb 07/13096, 20 December 2007.

itself in that an assessment on this ground can only be followed by a criminal offence[234] but not necessarily a criminal conviction.[235]

The courts have repeated the legislative requirement that danger to the public order needs to be a genuine, present, and sufficiently serious threat affecting one of the fundamental interests of society, while adding that the element of recidivism should be considered in this context. The character of the offence can inform whether a threat is still present and terrorism is a crime, the effects of which can continue for a long time, as can the characterization of a present threat;[236] this also applies to the crime of torture.[237] All of these elements were accepted where a person had been sentenced to forty-five months' imprisonment for theft with violence, together with a high risk of repeating similar crimes.[238] The same result was achieved for a person who had been sentenced to short periods of incarceration four times in four years.[239] However, the lack of recidivism combined with a considerable amount of time since the last conviction can lead to an assumption that the person in question is not a danger to the public.[240] Similarly, if the person was convicted of one offence, the government needs to show why a danger of recidivism would follow from that fact.[241]

There have been several cases exploring the connection between exclusion and danger to the public order. In general, recidivism cannot be assumed if a person was excluded earlier for a 1F crime,[242] but it needs to be shown that the person still exhibited similar personal traits after a finding of exclusion.[243] The recent commission and seriousness of the exclusion crimes, in this case torture, and the fact that those crimes

---

234 Rb, The Hague, Awb 08/10523, 6 May 2008; Rb, The Hague, Awb 09/20930, 22 January 2010.

235 AbRS, 13 March 2013, nr 201208487/1; Rb, The Hague, Awb 19/8402 and Awb 20/1174, 17 July 2020.

236 AbRS, 12 September 2008, nr 200704924/1.

237 AbRS, 13 March 2013, nr 201208487/1.

238 AbRS, 8 December 2008, nr 200803064/1; see, also, Rb, The Hague, Awb 07/21380, 17 September 2008. In a different context, it was said that being merely suspected of having committed a crime is not sufficient to invoke the notion of public order; see Rb, The Hague, Awb 10/44468, 11 January 2011.

239 Rb, The Hague, Awb 08/5152, 20 August 2008.

240 Spijkerboer & Vermeulen, above note 230 at 105.

241 Rb, The Hague, Awb 07/30322, 2 April 2008; Rb, The Hague, Awb 10/16198, 29 November 2010.

242 AbRS, 16 June 2015, nr 201401560/1; Rb, The Hague, NL 20.13885, 2 September 2021.

243 Rb, The Hague, Awb 19/4682, 16 April 2020; see also AbRS, 16 December 2020, nr 201907281/1; Rb, The Hague, NL 21.3223, 1 April 2021; Rb, The Hague, Awb 20/127, 12 October 2021; these courts relied heavily on the CJEU case of *K and HF* (see above note 43).

were committed repeatedly over a seven-year period, warrant a finding of danger to the public order.[244] A combination of personal involvement in exclusion crimes, showing no remorse, the fact that the crimes had occurred recently, and that the person had committed other crimes in the Netherlands after the exclusion decision results in the same conclusion.[245] A lengthy time period between an exclusion finding and a danger assessment should generally be resolved in favour of the person concerned.[246] However, in recent decisions, courts have been of the view that such a long period between these decisions is not fatal for a danger assessment.[247] One court found that a person who had occupied an important and powerful position in Afghanistan in the 1980s, resulting in numerous crimes against humanity, who had been excluded in 2005 and, during that proceeding and other proceedings over the years, had consistently minimized his role in these crimes, could still be considered a danger to the public order, not because of the risk of recidivism but because he disturbed the peace of mind of society. This was the case because the Netherlands had a policy of no safe haven for war criminals and because of the risk that victims of the Afghani regime in which this person had operated could run into this person.[248] However, if there are serious humanitarian reasons at play, they can offset an earlier finding of exclusion.[249]

viii) United Kingdom

The interpretation of the meaning of a particularly serious crime and danger to the community[250] has been regulated by legislation, which says:

---

244 Rb, The Hague, Awb 16/6954, 7 March 2017; see, also, Rb, The Hague, NL 18.19332, 25 July 2019 and Rb, The Hague, NL 27863, 15 April 2021.

245 Rb, The Hague, NL 19.5360, 8 November 2019; see, also, Rb, The Hague, NL 20.13885, 2 September 2021, with respect to the lack of remorse for a situation of a person from Uganda.

246 Rb, The Hague, Awb 19/4682, 16 April 2020, which involved a period of eighteen years for a person who had served with special units in the Bosnian army between 1992 and 1994.

247 See, in general, Rb, The Hague, NL 20.13885, 2 September 2021.

248 Rb, The Hague, Awb 19/8402 and Awb 20/1174, 17 July 2020; see, also, with similar reasoning, Rb, The Hague, NL 19.13235, 29 September 2020 (also for Afghanistan); Rb, The Hague, Awb 19/9284, 28 June 2021 (for Iraq); and Rb, The Hague, NL 20.8197, 2 August 2021 (for Turkey); these cases were preceded by a decision involvng a person active in Afghanistan in the same time period, namely, Rb, The Hague, Awb 19/111, 8 January 2020.

249 Rb, The Hague, Awb 18/417 and Awb 19/1691, 14 November 2019, regarding a person from Afghanistan.

250 See s 339(AC)(ii) of the *Immigration Rules*.

(2) A person is convicted by a final judgment of a particularly serious crime if he is—

(a) convicted in the United Kingdom of an offence, and

(b) sentenced to a period of imprisonment of at least two years.

(3) A person is convicted by a final judgment of a particularly serious crime if—

(a) he is convicted outside the United Kingdom of an offence,

(b) he is sentenced to a period of imprisonment of at least 12 months, and

(c) he could have been sentenced to a period of imprisonment of at least 12 months had his conviction been a conviction in the United Kingdom of a similar offence.

(4) A person is convicted by a final judgment of a particularly serious crime and to constitute a danger to the community of the United Kingdom if—

(a) he is convicted of an offence specified by order of the Secretary of State, or

(b) he is convicted outside the United Kingdom of an offence and the Secretary of State certifies that in his opinion the offence is similar to an offence specified by order under paragraph (a).[251]

The secretary of state has issued an order pursuant to subsection 4(a) above, setting out that 127 offences in criminal statutes would be subject to the presumption of a particularly serious crime and danger to the community, primarily in anti-terrorism and drug and human trafficking.[252] These broad provisions have been scrutinized by the Court of Appeal and were found wanting. According to the court, the presumption in the legislation should apply to both the crime and the danger portion, not

251 Section 72 of the *Nationality, Immigration and Asylum Act 2002* as amended by the *Nationality and Borders Act 2022*, s 38; see also the Manual "Exclusion (Article 1F) and Article 33(2) of the Refugee Convention" at 35–37; s 72 goes on to say that the danger to the community portion presumption is rebuttable (s 6), that the presumption does not apply when the conviction has been appealed (s 7), and that the prohibition against balancing (as set out in s 34(1)(b) of the *Anti- terrorism, Crime and Security Act 2001*) applies when considering the presumption (s 8, which was accepted in *SB (cessation and exclusion) Haiti*, [2005] UKIAT 00036 at para 81). The legislation also indicates that the twelve-month period refers to the actual sentence imposed, not the maximum penalty that could be imposed, and also refers to the fact that suspended sentences are not included in the wording of this section (s 11).

252 *Nationality, Immigration and Asylum Act 2002 (Specification of Particularly Serious Crimes) Order 2004*.

only the danger portion, as indicated in the section. Second, it found that the order by the secretary of state was ultra vires, as some of the crimes in the order were *prima facie* not particularly serious and the court did not want to parse which crimes would fall into that category and which would not.[253] As a result, there still needs to be an investigation into a person's actual criminality and the risk posed to the United Kingdom.[254] Foreign convictions need to be proven by appropriate evidence, not just the person's own statement.[255]

The jurisprudence has provided guidance with respect to several of the other concepts contained within the phrases "particularly serious crimes" and "danger to the community." First, in order to *refoule* a person, both the requirement of the conviction being for a particularly serious crime as well as being a danger to the community have to be fulfilled,[256] although it is possible to take into account all of the offences committed, even if they were individually not particularly serious, for an assessment of danger.[257]

With respect to the notion of particularly serious crime, it has been said:

> I do not think that the crimes that are particularly serious are a constant, not varying from member state and not varying in time. Rather, the expression "particularly serious crime" must be applied to what is a crime under the domestic law of the member state when the question of refoulement arises.[258]

As well, particularly serious crimes are not restricted to offences against the person since offences such as theft, fraud, and offences against property can also be particularly serious crimes, as can drug offences, while "matters such as frequent repetition or a sophisticated

---

253 *EN & KC*, above note 222 at paras 80–83; see, also, earlier, to the contrary, *IH (s 72; "Particularly Serious Crime") Eritrea*, [2009] UKAIT 00012 at para 112.

254 *HAA (s 72: overseas conviction) Somalia*, [2012] UKUT 00366 (IAC) at para 15.

255 *Ibid* at para 22.

256 *EN & KC*, above note 222 at para 39; see, also, *Secretary of State for the Home Department v TB (Jamaica)*, [2008] EWCA Civ 977 at para 38; *AQ (Somalia) v Secretary of State for the Home Department*, [2011] EWCA Civ 695 at para 24; and *Secretary of State for the Home Department v MS (Somalia)*, [2019] EWCA Civ 1345 at paras 63–70.

257 *SB (cessation and exclusion) Haiti*, [2005] UKIAT 00036 at para 71.

258 *EN & KC*, above note 222 at para 40; see, also, *IH (s 72; "Particularly Serious Crime") Eritrea*, [2009] UKAIT 00012 at paras 31 and 72–73.

system or the participation of a number of offenders may aggravate the seriousness of an offence."[259]

With respect to the term "danger," according to the court, this should not be read as a "very serious danger" as that would go beyond what the Refugee Convention and legislation require,[260] although danger to the community is present if the danger is real, and there must be a likelihood of repeating the criminal conduct without the necessity of a causal connection between the conviction and the danger.[261] This general proposition was applied to a person who was involved in a driving accident, causing the death of a pregnant woman, for which he was sentenced to a term of thirty-three months' imprisonment and banned from driving for four years. After his release from prison and in spite of the driving ban, he drove and caused an accident again;[262] these facts resulted in him being a danger to the community,[263] while the seriousness of the offences and his subsequent behaviour outweighed the humanitarian consideration of being with his family.[264] On the other hand, based on expert evidence, it was decided that a person was not a risk to offend and, as such, not a danger to the community even though the crime they were convicted of was murder.[265]

ix) United States

The *Immigration and Nationality Act* states:

> [A]n alien who has been convicted of an aggravated felony (or felonies) for which the alien has been sentenced to an aggregate term, of imprisonment of at least 5 years shall be considered to have committed a particularly serious crime. The previous sentence shall not preclude the Attorney General from determining that, notwithstanding

---

259 *EN & KC*, above note 222 at para 47; see, also, *IH (s 72; "Particularly Serious Crime") Eritrea*, [2009] UKAIT 00012 at para 76, which mentions murder, rape, serious crimes of violence, and public disorder as examples of particularly serious crimes.

260 *EN & KC*, above note 222 at paras 43–45.

261 *Ibid* at paras 45–46.

262 *RY (Sri Lanka) v Secretary of State for the Home Department*, [2016] EWCA Civ 81 at paras 5–10.

263 *Ibid* at paras 49–50.

264 *Ibid* at paras 51–53.

265 *R (on the application of JR (Jamaica)) v Secretary of State for the Home Department*, [2014] EWCA Civ 477 at paras 1 and 17.

the length of sentence imposed, an alien has been convicted of a particularly serious crime.[266]

The first portion of this provision also applies if the aggregate sentence is less than five years.[267] The same statute has defined the meaning of aggravated felony in a long list of crimes, which includes many violent offences, drug offences, and weapons offences but also theft, for which imprisonment of more than one year has been imposed.[268] Conviction has been defined as a

---

266 *Immigration and Nationality Act*, above note 23, s 241(b)(3)(B). This text was the result of three amendments: the *Immigration Act of 1990*, the *AEDPA*, above note 122, and the *Illegal Immigration Reform and Immigrant Responsibility Act of 1996* (*IIRIRA*). (For an overview of the changes, see *Delgado v Holder*, 563 F3d 863 (9th Cir 2009) [*Delgado*], as well as Michael McCarry, "A Statute in Particularly Serious Need of Reinterpretation: The Particularly Serious Crime Exception to Withholding of Removal" (2010) 51 *Boston College Law Review* 209 at 215–21). The second-last sentence of this provision was discussed in *Alaka v Gonzales*, 456 F3d 88 (3d Cir 2006), and *Ali v Achim*, 468 F3d 462 (7th Cir 2006) [*Ali*], where the first court held that the attorney general could only designate aggravated felonies as particularly serious crimes, while the latter did not read the provision that restrictively, meaning that the attorney general could also designate offences with a maximum of less than five years; *Delgado*, *ibid*, agreed with the *Ali* case and also indicated that this power of the attorney general applied both to a general designation as well as to individual cases (for a commentary, see William H. Hains, "Chevron's Ambiguity Hurdle: Delgado v Holder and the Proper Interpretation of the Particularly Serious Crimes Exception to Deportation Relief" (2010) 10 *Brigham Young University Law Review* 81 at 93–100, and McCarry, *ibid* at 232–37); this approach was confirmed two years later in *Delgado v Holder*, 648 F3d 1095 (9th Cir 2011), followed by *Blandino-Medina v Holder*, 712 F3d 1338 (9th Cir 2013).

267 *Guerrero v Whitaker*, 908 F3d 541 (9th Cir 2018).

268 *Immigration and Nationality Act*, above note 23, s 101(a)(43), which lists twenty-one categories of offences; for commentary, see Jennifer M. Chacón, "Unsecured Borders: Immigration Restrictions, Crime Control and National Security" (2007) 39 *Connecticut Law Review* 1827–91. There had been some debate as to whether the listing of these offences was of a categorical nature in the sense of mentioning a generic crime or whether these offences require an assessment of the specific acts in which an offender engaged, the so-called circumstance-specific interpretation. The Supreme Court laid this issue to rest in 2009 in the case of *Nijhawan v Holder*, 129 S Ct 2294 (2009), by saying that, depending on the wording of the offence, either interpretation could be utilized and came to the conclusion that the offence of fraud or deceit in which the loss to the victim or victims exceeds $10,000 (s 101(a)(43)(M)(i)) is a circumstance-specific felony as it requires proof of more than just fraud. Most crimes in this section are specific offences, but there is also a more general one in s 101(a)(43)(F), namely, a crime of violence, which is further defined in 18 USC § 16 as follows: "(a) an offense that has as an element the use, attempted use, or threatened use of physical force against the person or property of another, or (b) any other offense that is a felony and that, by its nature, involves a substantial risk that physical force against the person or property of another may be used in the course of committing the offense." For a discussion of crimes of violence, see, in general, *Hernandez v AG of the United States*, 527 Fed Appx 130 (3d Cir 2013), while for the decision that s (b) was unconstitutional, see *Sessions v Dimaya*, 138 S Ct

formal judgment of guilt of the alien entered by a court or, if adjudication of guilt has been withheld, where-

(i) a judge or jury has found the alien guilty or the alien has entered a plea of guilty or nolo contendere or has admitted sufficient facts to warrant a finding of guilt, and

(ii) the judge has ordered some form of punishment, penalty, or restraint on the alien's liberty to be imposed.[269]

When the statute speaks of felonies, only crimes designated as federal felonies or crimes that encompass all the elements of such felonies are included, not a state felony such as simple drug possession.[270] As well, only convictions are to be considered for this assessment, not dismissed charges.[271]

House arrest with electronic monitoring is considered imprisonment for the purposes of the legislation.[272] According to the jurisprudence, a finding of conviction for a particularly serious crime constitutes a consideration of danger to the community of the United States, and there is no requirement for a separate inquiry into the danger aspect.[273]

Crimes that do not fall within the legislative framework because, for instance, a person was sentenced to less than five years' imprisonment can still be considered to fall within the notion of seriousness by assessing the underlying facts of the conviction, such as the nature of the conviction, the type of sentence imposed, and the circumstances and facts underlying the conviction,[274] as well as whether the type and

---

1204 (2018); a conviction for robbery under California law was not a crime of violence according to *United States v Garcias-Lopez*, 903 F3d 887 (9th Cir 2018).

269 *Immigration and Nationality Act*, above note 23, s 101(a)(48)(A); it goes on to say in s 101(a)(48)(B) that "any reference to a term of imprisonment or a sentence with respect to an offense is deemed to include the period of incarceration or confinement ordered by a court of law regardless of any suspension of the imposition or execution of that imprisonment or sentence in whole or in part."

270 *Lopez v Gonzales*, 127 S Ct 625 (2006); *Berhe v Gonzales*, 464 F3d 74 (1st Cir 2006).

271 *Alaka v Gonzales*, 456 F3d 88 (3d Cir 2006).

272 *Ilchuk v Gonzales*, 434 F3d 618 (3d Cir 2006).

273 *Komarenko v INS*, 35 F3d 432 (9th Cir 1994); *Ahmetovic v INS*, 62 F2d 48 (2d Cir 1995); *Choeum v INS*, 129 F3d 29 (1st Cir 1997); *Kankamalage v INS*, 335 F3d 858, 864 (9th Cir 2003); *Perez v Loy*, 356 F Supp 2d 172 (D Conn 2005); *N-A-M v Holder*, Docket Nos 07-9580, 08-9527 (10th Cir 2009); *Gomez-Sanchez v Sessions*, 887 F3d 893 (9th Cir 2017); for a commentary, see McCarry, above note 266 at 237–41.

274 *Beltran-Zavala v INS*, 912 F2d 1024 (9th Cir 1990); *Al-Salehi v INS*, 47 F3d 390 (10th Cir 1995); *Hamama v INS*, 78 F3d 233 (6th Cir 1996); *Ursu v INS*, 20 Fed Appx 702 (9th Cir 2001); *Perez v Loy*, above note 273; *Bare v Barr*, 975 F3d 952 (9th Cir 2020); it is called the Frentescu approach after the tribunal decision that first enunciated it.

circumstances of the crime indicate that the person will be a danger to the community. Conduct not related to the crimes should not be considered in this context[275] unless it is related to the person's mental condition at the time of the crime.[276] With respect to the specific category of crimes involving selling drugs, the facts to be assessed are the quantity of the drugs; the money paid for the drugs; the involvement of the person in the criminal activity; the absence or presence of violence; the absence or presence of any organized or terrorist organization involvement; and the absence or presence of any adverse or harmful effect as a result of the activity.[277]

The validity of a criminal conviction cannot be examined in a deportation hearing.[278] A single conviction for rape, kidnapping, and battery will lead to *refoulement* even if the event happened ten years earlier.[279]

The following were already considered particularly serious crimes before this legislation came into effect: murder;[280] sexual assault;[281] sexual relations with a minor;[282] assault with intent to murder;[283] trafficking or possession of drugs with the intent to distribute;[284] breaking and entering while carrying a concealed handgun;[285] wilful cruelty toward a child with a deadly weapon;[286] and the shooting of a police officer.[287]

---

275 *Yousefi v INS*, 260 F3d 318 (4th Cir 2001).

276 *Gomez-Sanchez v Sessions*, 887 F3d 893 (9th Cir 2017).

277 *Tunis v Gonzales*, 447 F3d 547 (7th Cir 2006); *Lavira v Attorney General of the US*, 478 F3d 158 (3d Cir 2007); *Solis v Mukasey*, 515 F3d 832 (8th Cir 2008); *Gomes v AG of the United States*, 820 Fed Appx 142 (3d Cir 2020). These factors, with respect to drug offences, were developed as a result of the attorney general's determination in 2002 that all drug-trafficking offences carried a presumption of particularly serious crime, which could be rebutted by a demonstration of extraordinary and compelling factors.

278 *Chammas v INS*, 46 F3d 435 (9th Cir 1994); *Nasrallah v Barr*, 140 S Ct 1683 (2020).

279 *Groza v INS*, 30 F3d 814 (7th Cir 1994); the same was said for conviction for robbery with a weapon in *Tran v INS*, 8 F3d 30 (9th Cir 1993).

280 *Saleh v INS*, 962 F2d 234 (2d Cir 1992); *Abate v INS*, 972 F2d 1336 (9th Cir 1992).

281 *Kassim v INS*, 96 F3d 1438 (4th Cir 1996); *Goh v INS*, 61 F3d 910 (9th Cir 1995).

282 *Gatalski v INS*, 72 F3d 135 (9th Cir 1995).

283 *Gonjaj v INS*, 47 F3d 814 (6th Cir 1995).

284 *Mahini v INS*, 779 F2d 1419 (9th Cir 1986); *Arauz v Rivkind*, 834 F2d 979 (11th Cir 1987); *Ramirez-Ramos v INS*, 814 F2d 1394 (9th Cir 1987); *Martins v INS*, 972 F2d 567 (5th Cir 1992); *Al-Salehi v INS*, 47 F3d 390 (10th Cir 1995); *Crespo-Gomez v Richard*, 780 F2d 932 (11th Cir 1986).

285 *Matty v INS*, 21 F3d 428 (6th Cir 1994).

286 *Mustafa v INS*, 19 F3d 1440 (9th Cir 1994).

287 *Ngyuen v INS*, 991 F2d 621 (10th Cir 1993).

Since 1996, the following crimes have been found to be particularly serious: battery with a dangerous weapon;[288] being a felon in possession of a firearm;[289] aggravated assault;[290] travelling to meet a minor for sexual purposes;[291] burglary;[292] reckless endangerment by firing a gun in the air;[293] stalking;[294] concealment of a dangerous weapon;[295] fraud over $10,000;[296] mail fraud;[297] wire fraud;[298] securities fraud;[299] bank fraud;[300] drug trafficking;[301] aggravated identity theft;[302] use of a false social security card if loss to the victim exceeds $10,000;[303] and tampering with physical evidence.[304] There is some disagreement as to whether state drug offences can amount to aggravated felonies, with some courts being of the opinion that this can only be the case if these offences are punishable as a felony under federal law or the crime contains a trafficking element,[305] while other courts have held that a drug offence that is a felony under state law but is punishable under federal laws only as a misdemeanour is an aggravated felony for immigration purposes.[306]

On the other hand, driving under the influence does not constitute a particularly serious crime because it does not involve the active employment of physical force against the person or property of

288 *Ali*, above note 266.

289 *Bare v Barr*, 975 F3d 952 (9th Cir 2020).

290 *Reyes-Romero v Barr*, 832 Fed Appx 426 (6th Cir 2020).

291 *Yassin v United States AG*, 2021 US App LEXIS 14709 (11th Cir 2021).

292 *Perez v United States AG*, 2019 US App LEXIS 12487 (11th Cir 2019).

293 *Nethagani v Mukasey*, 532 F3d 150 (2d Cir 2008).

294 *Ceren v Barr*, 803 Fed Appx 114 (9th Cir 2020).

295 *Cazares-Zandre v United States AG*, 791 Fed Appx 96 (11th Cir 2019).

296 *Tian v Holder*, Docket No 08-3391 (8th Cir 2009).

297 *Arbid v Holder*, 700 F3d 379 (9th Cir 2012).

298 *Jeudy v United States AG*, 762 Fed Appx 594 (11th Cir 2019).

299 *Kaplun v AG of the United States*, 602 F3d 260 (3d Cir 2010).

300 *Maxi Dinga Sopo v United States AG*, 739 Fed Appx 554 (11th Cir 2018).

301 *Miguel-Miguel v Gonzales*, 500 F3d 941 (9th Cir 2007); *Daas v Holder*, Docket No 06-71898 (9th Cir 2010).

302 *Valerio-Ramirez v Sessions*, 882 F3d 289 (1st Cir 2018).

303 *St John v Ashcroft*, 43 Fed Appx 281 (10th Cir 2002).

304 *Denis v Attorney General of the US*, Docket Nos 09-2113, 09-3520, 10-1390, and 10-1391 (3d Cir 2011). For a general commentary, see Chacón, above note 268 at 1827–91.

305 *Gerbier v Holmes*, 280 F3d 297 (3d Cir 2002); *Aguirre v INS*, 79 F3d 315 (2d Cir 1996); *Cazarez-Gutierrez v Ashcroft*, 382 F3d 905 (9th Cir 2004); *Sunaz v AG of the United States*, 476 Fed Appx 988 (3d Cir 2012); this approach is called the "illicit trafficking element" route.

306 *United States v Hernandez-Avalos*, 251 F3d 505 (5th Cir 2001); *Rodriguez v AG of the United States*, 517 Fed Appx 82 (3d Cir 2013); this approach is called the "hypothetical federal felony" route.

another[307] unless it results in damage or injury,[308] nor is bank fraud with a loss of less than $10,000;[309] transporting or receiving firearms purchased outside the person's state of residence;[310] two state misdemeanour marijuana offences;[311] filing a false tax return;[312] theft by deception under a state law;[313] negligent manslaughter under state law;[314] and embezzlement without intent to defraud.[315]

4) Observations

With respect to the national security provision as part of *refoulement*, two aspects stand out: the role played by legislative provisions in a number of these countries and the different approach with respect to balancing. This can be seen at both the supranational level in Europe and the national level. In Europe, two directives regulate the concept of national security: the Citizenship Directive and the Qualification Directive. While neither defines danger to the security, the first one specifically requires that a proportionality assessment be conducted, which means taking into account the personal conduct of the person concerned, which needs to be weighed against "considerations such as how long the individual concerned has resided on its territory, his/her age, state of health, family and economic situation, social and cultural integration into the host Member State and the extent of his/her links with the country of origin."[316] The CJEU has interpreted both concepts and said in relation to the danger of security that this is "a threat to the functioning of the institutions and essential public services and the survival of the population, as well as the risk of a serious disturbance to foreign relations or to peaceful coexistence of nations, or a risk to military

307 *Leocal v Ashcroft*, 125 S Ct 377 (2004); see, also, *Delgado*, above note 266.
308 *Anaya-Ortiz v Holder*, Docket No 03-74666 (9th Cir 2011).
309 *Alaka v Gonzales*, 456 F3d 88 (3d Cir 2006).
310 *Joseph v Gonzales*, 465 F3d 123 (3d Cir 2006).
311 *Smith v Gonzalez*, 468 F3d 272 (5th Cir 2006); *Bosede v Mukasey*, 512 F3d 946 (7th Cir 2008).
312 *Nugent v Ashcroft*, 367 F3d 162 (3d Cir 2004).
313 *Jobson v Ashcroft*, 326 F3d 367 (2d Cir 2003).
314 *Valansi v Ashcroft*, 278 F3d 203 (3d Cir 2002); *Sotnikau v Lynch*, 846 F3d 731 (4th Cir 2017).
315 *Dalton v Ashcroft*, 257 F3d 200 (2d Cir 2001).
316 Directive 2004/38/EC of the European Parliament and of the Council of 29 April 2004 on the right of citizens of the Union and their family members to move and reside freely within the territory of the Member States, art 28(1).

interests,"[317] while it added to the personal considerations, in the context of a criminal conviction of a person, the circumstances "by reference in particular to the possible penalties and the sentences imposed, the degree of involvement in the criminal activity, and, if appropriate, the risk of reoffending on the one hand, and, on the other hand, the risk of compromising the social rehabilitation of the person."[318] It has also been said that while the 1F exclusion and a criminal conviction can be factors in this balancing exercise, neither is conclusive in this determination.

At the national level, legislation has influenced the interpretation of the danger to the security or related concepts in seven countries but with different purposes in mind. New Zealand has gone the furthest in defining what amounts to security by providing a detailed and lengthy definition of several aspects that can be brought within the parameters of this concept. In the United States, the legislation contains a deeming provision to the effect that involvement in certain terrorist activities is considered reasonable grounds to believe that the danger of the security of the United States is engaged. While Canada has not defined what a danger to the security is, it has included in its legislation a *refoulement* concept, which is somewhere between danger to the security and danger to the community/public order, that a person should not be allowed to remain in Canada based on the nature and severity of the acts committed.

In the United Kingdom and Belgium, the impact of the legislation is less pervasive in that in the United Kingdom the minister responsible for immigration can issue a certificate during an appeal procedure indicating that a person is not entitled to protection because of national security grounds (which is echoed in the New Zealand legislation but only for deportation proceedings), while in Belgium, the legislation is used to limit the power of the executive by requiring that a determination of danger to the security needs to include the following elements: a genuine, present, and sufficiently serious threat affecting one of the fundamental interests of society and no reasoning based on preventative measures or on economic purposes. This language, which is clearly inspired by the Citizenship Directive, can also be found in the legislation of France and the Netherlands.

The issue of balancing presents a confusing picture as it is required in only five countries under discussion, in Belgium, France, Germany,

317 *Land Baden-Württemberg*, above note 39 at para 44.

318 *Ibid* at paras 51 & 52.

the Netherlands, and Canada, the first four by legislation and the latter due to jurisprudence. In the United Kingdom, balancing was found not necessary by legislation, while in New Zealand and the United States, this was determined in the caselaw, in New Zealand explicitly and in the United States implicitly, by not engaging in a risk determination after a finding of danger to the security was established. In Australia, the position is not clear as neither the legislation nor the jurisprudence has addressed this issue, but there are suggestions that the New Zealand position is the correct one.

Some of the other legislative requirements in Europe are reminiscent of the two EU directives and the CJEU jurisprudence in that the threat must be genuine, present, and sufficiently serious, which is mirrored in the legislation of Belgium, France, and the Netherlands and in the jurisprudence in Germany. In common law countries, the jurisprudence has indicated that the level of threat to the security must be substantial (Canada and New Zealand) or serious (United States), while the threat must be an actual threat rather than a possibility (Australia and the United States) and must go beyond the personal safety of individuals (Canada).

On the other hand, while the threat level must be high, it has been said that given the global security situation, it is not necessary that the danger to the security is only a direct threat to the country of refuge but can also be an indirect threat or a security danger outside the country where a refugee is staying (Belgium, Canada, Germany, New Zealand, and the United Kingdom, while implicitly in France and the United States).

The most detailed definition of national security in the immigration context can be found in the legislation of New Zealand, which incorporates the following elements as being connected to national security: espionage; sabotage; subversion; terrorism; organized crime; the international well-being, reputation, or economic well-being of New Zealand; and the safety and stability of the international community. In the United States, the jurisprudence has identified some of these aspects as being part of national security: activities that endanger the lives, property, or welfare of US citizens; compromise the national defence of the United States; or materially damage the foreign relations or economic interests of the United States, while in Canada, a court has said that national security cannot be limited to instances where the personal safety of Canadians is concerned but that it should extend to instances where the integrity of Canada's international relations and obligations is affected. In Germany, it was said that this concept also includes violence committed against bystanders aimed at propagating general insecurity.

In terms of activities that fall within the danger to the security notion, virtually all judgments concluded that terrorism is the prime candidate in this context, although in one case in Canada, the commission of very serious hate crimes had the same result, while assistance in the development of weapons of mass destruction was also held to be a danger to the security. The CJEU has said in certain circumstances that drug trafficking could also reach this threshold.

As with danger to the security, the danger to the community and danger to the public order (the latter in Belgium, France, and the Netherlands) concepts have been subject to legislation, primarily in the determination of the conviction for the particularly serious crime component, which is a requirement of danger to the community. This legislative interpretation, which has been used in seven of the nine countries in the study (but not in Belgium, which repeats the wording of the Refugee Convention, and not in New Zealand, which has not regulated this part of *refoulement*), has two distinct approaches: the first sets out in general the maximum penalty of an offence that can be given in the domestic criminal legislation (Canada and the Netherlands) or the maximum sentencing that has in actuality been imposed (Canada), while the second approach uses a combination of a maximum penalty and a listing of types of offences applicable (Australia, France, Germany, the United Kingdom, and the United States).

Regarding the first, Canada has a dual approach where danger to the community is assumed for offences where the maximum penalty is ten years or more in the criminal legislation or for which an actual sentence of more than six months has been imposed, while in the Netherlands, this is ten months (both of which were decreased from three years and one year, respectively, in recent amendments to their immigration law). The second approach has been used with variations in Australia in that it sets out four general types of offences: violence against persons, drug offences, serious damage to property, and immigration detention offences, in combination with a maximum sentence for life or a fixed term of imprisonment of at least three years. In France, the legislation adds to the general reference to a ten-year maximum penalty for two offences related to terrorism. In Germany, an actual sentence of one year or more must be imposed for offences against life, physical integrity, sexual self-determination, property, or resisting enforcement officers. In the United Kingdom, a sentence of twelve months or more would result in a danger to the community determination, while the minister responsible for immigration can, in addition, specify other offences for which any conviction has the same result; the minister has issued a lengthy list under this provision with offences in areas such as terrorism, organized crime, and drug and human trafficking, part of which has been held ultra vires by the courts. In the United States, the limit is a five-year sentence for aggravated felonies, although the attorney general can declare that lesser sentences in general or in individual cases can amount to a danger to the community, and this power has been upheld by the courts. The US legislation also has a lengthy listing of what amounts to aggravated felonies by specific references to criminal legislation, of which only one small aspect has been held unconstitutional by the Supreme Court.

In Australia, Canada, the Netherlands, and the United Kingdom, foreign convictions with the same severity as domestic convictions are specifically mentioned as being included in the concept of particularly serious crimes, while Canada has also added the mere commission, in addition to a conviction, of serious offences within the danger to the community concept (although this widening of the convention provision has not been applied in practice).

The jurisprudence has added to the understanding of what type of criminality would reach the threshold of a particularly serious crime—murder or manslaughter (Australia, Belgium, France, Germany, the Netherlands, United States); causing death while driving (United Kingdom); shooting a police officer (United States); assault (Australia, Canada, United States); sexual assault (Canada, France, Germany, United States) or attempts to commit sexual assault (United States); stalking (United States); drug trafficking (Australia, Belgium, Canada, France, United Kingdom, United States); armed robbery (Canada); people smuggling (Belgium); kidnapping or hostage taking (Belgium and Germany); hijacking (France); econonomic crimes (United Kingdom) while specific instances of economic crimes have also been given attention, such as fraud (Belgium, Canada, United Kingdom, United States); immigration fraud (Belgium); serious theft (Belgium, United Kingdom); arson (Germany); breaking and entering (Belgium, United States); theft with violence (Belgium); forgery (Belgium and Canada); or tampering with evidence (United States).

On the other hand, the following crimes were not deemed to be serious enough to invoke a danger assessment: negligent manslaughter

(United States); desertion from the Foreign Legion (France); vagrancy (France); driving under the influence (United States); possession of soft drugs (the Netherlands, United States); visa fraud (the Netherlands); small bank fraud (United States); theft (United States); filling a false tax return (United States); and embezzlement without intent to defraud (United States).

In the context of convictions, it should be pointed that where countries have relied on the public order variety of *refoulement* (Belgium, France, and the Netherlands) and where the courts have made it clear that a conviction is not necessary for this type of assessment, in reality most cases have involved a criminal conviction to come to a conclusion regarding a danger to the public order. The only exceptions are terrorist activities (France) and a 1F exclusion for war crimes or crimes against humanity (Belgium and the Netherlands).

With respect to the second requirement for the danger to the community assessment—in what circumstances following a criminal conviction for a particularly serious crime a person can be considered such a danger—the approach in the various countries is generally consistent, with the exception of the United States, where a determination of a particularly serious offence is said to already include a danger assessment, so there is no need for a separate finding in that regard. In the four civil law countries, this approach is very much inspired by the CJEU jurisprudence, which has found its way into both national legislation and jurisprudence.

The judiciary in all countries, except the United States, insist on a separate danger assessment for which a number of elements have been identified, one of which is the fact that the danger must be real (United Kingdom), actual (Belgium), and present and serious (Australia) and must lie both in the present and in the future (Australia, Canada, United Kingdom). This requirement is expressed more precisely as current and persisting in Germany and as a genuine, present, and sufficiently serious threat in Belgium and the Netherlands. An important consideration has been that future danger can be derived from a repetition of crimes and from a risk of recidivism (Australia, Belgium, Canada, France, the Netherlands, United Kingdom). Other factors have also played a role, such as the length of the sentence imposed (Australia); the type of crime that led to the conviction (the Netherlands, specifically with respect to terrorism and torture); aggravating circumstances, such as whether the criminal conduct has been escalating over time (Belgium);

and continuing to consort with the same people, which had led to criminal conviction (France, Australia, Belgium, France, United Kingdom). These factors need to be weighed against any mitigating circumstances, such as rehabilitation (Australia, Belgium, Canada, Germany); lapse of time between conviction and danger assessment (the Netherlands); good behaviour upon release (France); taking counselling (France) or making an effort to integrate into society (Belgium, France); having a stable family and employment situation (France, Germany); and the elapsed time between the last conviction and the danger opinion (Belgium, the Netherlands).

The connection between exclusion and danger to the public has been explored in Belgium and the Netherlands. In Belgium, exclusion (whether in Belgium or in another country) was found to result in danger to the community if the person had committed crimes against humanity with a large number of victims and little evidence of the person's integration into Belgian society. In the Netherlands, the court has stated that there is a presumption in favour of this connection if the crimes have been committed recently and the person has not exhibited any remorse; a lengthy period between the commission of such crimes and the time of assessing danger should usually be resolved in favour of the person unless the person has committed a large number of crimes while being in a powerful position and minimizing their responsibility in those crimes. In the latter situation, the danger to the public does not lie in the risk of recidivism but because the Netherlands had a policy of no safe haven for war criminals and because of the risk that victims of this person might be retraumatized should they run into them.

The issue of balancing the danger that a person represents and the risk they might face upon removal was not a consideration in the common law countries except for Canada, although in this country, the balancing was rather illusory as in most cases it was found that there was no risk when removing a person to the country of origin. In the civil law countries, judges have addressed the issue of risk with different results, even though balancing is required in all of these countries. Because of their jurisprudence, the result of such an exercise has been different. In Belgium, such a balancing exercise was applied on a number of occasions, resulting in a person not being removed despite being a danger to the community, while in Germany, an interim solution was achieved by issuing a deportation order valid for seven years. It was not considered in France and the Netherlands.

Two final comments can be made regarding the danger to the public. First, in the same way that an assessment as to what constitutes a serious crime for the purposes of 1F(b) has undergone a change from an objective and superficial analysis to a more contextual and subjective approach, by taking into account the personal circumstances of the person concerned, the same can be seen in the evolution of the elements of *refoulement* for danger to the public, specifically in determining what constitutes a danger to the public. Second, there appears to be a hardening of government attitudes through either legislating less serious crimes as particularly serious or by being less tolerant of what amounts to a danger to the public. In common law countries, this means that there is no balancing required between the seriousness of the crime and the danger aspects, either by specifically saying so in their legislation or by prevailing before the courts with this approach. In civil law countries, this means that while the CJEU jurisprudence has been rather clear in what constitutes a danger and what personal circumstances should be taken into account, in practice the approach has been less lenient; this is especially clear with the connection made between exclusion and danger in Belgium and the Netherlands.

C. *NON-REFOULEMENT* TO TORTURE OR INHUMAN, CRUEL, AND DEGRADING TREATMENT OR PUNISHMENT

1) Introduction

The Refugee Convention has a self-contained approach with respect to persons who have committed crimes either before coming to the country of refuge or while residing in that country in that they are not entitled to the benefits bestowed on deserving refugees, while in extreme situations, they can also face the severe consequence of *refoulement*. However, it has been recognized that even persons who were involved in serious criminal activity should not be *refouled* to extreme situations affecting life and limb.

These exceptions to *refoulement* are based on three human rights treaties: two international treaties and one European treaty. The two international treaties are the International Covenant on Civil and Political Rights (ICCPR) and the Convention against Torture (CAT) while the regional treaty is the European Convention on Human Rights

(ECHR). The operative section in the ICCPR is article 7, which says: "No one shall be subjected to torture or to cruel, inhuman or degrading treatment or punishment. In particular, no one shall be subjected without his free consent to medical or scientific experimentation." This article has been interpreted by the Human Rights Committee to also include a prohibition against *refoulement*.[319] Similarly, article 3 of the CAT, which has been given further meaning by the Committee against Torture, indicates that "no State Party shall expel, return (*refouler*) or extradite a person to another State where there are substantial grounds for believing that he would be in danger of being subjected to torture." The ECHR, article 3, in very similar wording, stipulates that "no one shall be subjected to torture or to inhuman or degrading treatment or punishment," which has also been developed jurisprudentially as a *non-refoulement* principle.[320] It has been said that the concept of torture can change over time,[321] meaning that what might be considered a form of inhuman treatment at a particular time can become torture depending on the societal values at that time.

This section of the chapter will examine the jurisprudence of the supranational and international institutions charged with interpreting the meaning of the terms "torture" and "cruel, inhuman, or degrading treatment or punishment" in order to determine in which situations *refoulement* of persons with a criminal background can be affected. The four institutions examined below are the Human Rights Committee, the Committee against Torture, the European Court of Human Rights, and the Inter-American Court of Human Rights.[322] Not only will the jurisprudence of these institutions be examined in the context of

319 Kees Wouters, *International Legal Standards for Protection from Refoulement* (Antwerp-Oxford-Portland: Intersentia, 2009) at 359–60.

320 *Ibid* at 187–88; Goodwin-Gill & McAdam, above note 2 at 356.

321 Wouters, above note 319 at 224; Goodwin-Gill & McAdam, above note 2 at 363; Christine Bicknell, "The Council of Europe and the European System" in Malcolm D. Evans & Jens Modvig, *Research Handbook on Torture: Legal and Medical Perspectives on Prohibition and Prevention* (Cheltenham, UK and Northampton, US: Elgar, 2020) at 195; Inter-American Court of Human Rights, *Case of Cantoral Benavides*, Judgment 18 August 2000, Series C No 69 at para 99.

322 The order of the examination will be chronological, starting with the oldest institution first; as such, the order of looking at the jurisprudence will be the European Court of Human Rights first, then the Human Rights Committee, followed by the Committee against Torture, with the Inter-American Court of Human Rights last.

refoulement to these very undesirable situations, the meaning of these terms in other contexts will also be given attention.[323]

The jurisprudence of these institutions not only carries a great deal of weight due to their status as final arbiters in their countries, which have agreed to be bound by their decisions. Their impact goes beyond these boundaries, has an almost global reach, and can be used outside their immediate sphere of influence. This has been specifically recognized by the International Court of Justice[324] and is evident from the fact that another United Nations body, the International Criminal Tribunal for the former Yugoslavia (ICTY), sought a direct connection between human rights jurisprudence and the interpretation of similar concepts in the area of international criminal law.[325]

The national courts of the countries in this study have also provided their views on the meaning of torture and cruel, inhuman, or degrading

---

323 While there are also two African international institutions, which monitor the human rights set out in the *African Charter on Human and Peoples' Rights*, their impact on the development of the notion of torture or other ill-treatment (contained in art 5 of the *Charter*) is still emerging and not substantial yet (see, in general, regarding the African system, Lawrence Murugu Mute, "Ensuring Freedom from Torture Under the African Human Rights System" in Evans & Modvig, *Research Handbook on Torture,* above note 321 at 227–57). During the issuing of Concluding Observations, the African Commission on Human and Peoples' Rights recommended measures to states (e.g., Uganda, Cameroon, Sudan) to prevent torture, including encouraging states to criminalize torture, ratifying the Optional Protocol to the Convention against Torture, and improving inadequate prison conditions. In addressing art 5, the commission has delivered decisions regarding torture (in the case of *Amnesty International, Comité Loosli Bachelard, Lawyers Committee for Human Rights, Association of Members of the Episcopal Conference of East Africa / Sudan*, 48/90, 50/91, 52/91, 89/93, 15 November 1999 at paras 5 and 53–57); prison conditions (in the case of *Huri-Laws / Nigeria, 225/98*, 23 October 2000 at paras 40–41, relying on the jurisprudence of the European Court of Human Rights); punishment by lashes (in the case of *Curtis Francis Doebbler / Sudan, 236/00*, 29 May 2003 at paras 36–44, relying on the jurisprudence of the European Court of Human Rights); and the failing of a state to investigate allegations of torture of human rights defenders in detention (in the case of *Monim Elgak, Osman Hummeida and Amir Suliman / Sudan,* 379/09, 10 March 2015). The second institution, the African Court on Human and Peoples' Rights, has held that anal search performed by state agents in the presence of children amounted to a violation under art 5 (*Lucien Ikili Rashidi v United Republic of Tanzania, Application Nr* 009/2015, 28 March 2019).

324 *Case concerning Ahmadou Sadio Diallo (Republic of Guinea v Democratic Republic of the Congo)*, Judgment, 30 November 2010, ICJ Rep (2010) General List, No 103 at paras 66–67.

325 *Mucić et al (Čelebići Camp)* (IT-96-21), Trial Chamber Judgment, 16 November 1998 at paras 461–67. A similar deference can be found at the regional level, where CJEU, in interpreting art 15(c) of the Qualification Directive, took into account the jurisprudence of the European Court of Human Rights with respect to art 3 of the ECHR; see *M Elgafaji, N Elgafaji v Staatssecretaris van Justitie*, C-465/07, 17 February 2009 at para 44.

treatment or punishment in the context of *refoulement*, and their jurisprudence will be examined as well.[326]

2) International Jurisprudence

a) European Court of Human Rights[327]

i) *General Principles*

While the prohibition in the ECHR pertains to the more serious form of maltreatment, torture, and inhuman and degrading treatment or punishment, some general principles apply to both.

First of all, the prohibition is absolute in the sense that under no circumstances, even in the face of terrorist threats, can a deviation of these rights be allowed, in terms of a proportionality assessment, between the level of maltreatment on the one hand and the level of threat to, for instance, the security of a state on the other.[328] This absolute character applies to both forms of the prohibited behaviour set out in article 3 of the ECHR, not just to torture.[329] The only argument that can be made in this context is a relative one: that the conduct in question does not reach the fairly high threshold of torture or inhuman and degrading treatment of punishment, for instance, during a regular deportation, or where such conduct might be considered appropriate, such as during medical treatment.[330] The level of severity required to fall within the scope of

326 While the countries in question also have in their national legislation a prohibition against torture and other types of inhuman and cruel treatment, the jurisprudence under these instruments, which examines in most cases the behaviour of their national police forces and correctional institutions personnel, does not add significantly to the understanding given to these terms by the international bodies or the national *refoulement* caselaw. Examples of this national legislation are the Eighth Amendment in the *Bill of Rights* in the US Constitution; s 12 of the *Canadian Charter of Rights and Freedoms*, Part 1 of the *Constitution Act, 1982*, being Schedule B to the *Canada Act 1982* (UK), 1982, c 11; s 9 of the *New Zealand Bill of Rights Act 1990*; art 4 of the *Charter of Fundamental Rights of the European Union* (as, for instance, implemented in the United Kingdom in the *Human Rights Act 1998*, Schedule 1, art 3); and the *Crimes Legislation Amendment (Torture Prohibition and Death Penalty Abolition) Bill 2009* in Australia.

327 See, in general, Bicknell, above note 321 at 188–90.

328 Wouters, above note 319 at 307–9; UN Doc A/CN.4/565, *Expulsion of Aliens*, above note 9 at 354–56, paras 567–69; Bicknell, above note 321 at 196; *El-Masri v the former Yugoslav Republic of Macedonia*, 13 December 2012, Application No 39630/09 at para 195; *Mocanu and Others v Romania*, 17 September 2014, Applications Nos 10865/09, 45886/07, and 32431/08 at para 315.

329 Wouters, above note 319 at 311–14; Goodwin-Gill & McAdam, above note 2 at 364–65 and 369.

330 Wouters, above note 319 at 309; see, also, *A and Others v The United Kingdom*, 19 February 2009, Application No 3455/05 at para 126 [*A and Others*]; *A v The Netherlands*, 20 July 2010,

article 3 depends on all the circumstances of a particular case, such as the duration of the treatment and its physical and mental effects.[331]

A second principle, which applies to both types of prohibitions in the convention, is that the suffering can be the result of either a single isolated act or prolonged treatment. As well, whether such conduct reaches the level of suffering required to come within the parameters of article 3 will depend on its context, such as the duration of the treatment, the physical or mental effect on the victims, and the sex, age, and health of the victims.[332]

While the court has examined situations as they applied in the countries for which it had jurisdiction, as well as situations involving *refoulement* to third countries, the approaches taken as to what amounts to torture and inhuman and degrading treatment or punishment are for the most part the same,[333] although in the latter case, a different element needs to be given attention as it is prospective: whether there is a real, personal, foreseeable risk that the maltreatment will take place upon return to the third country.[334]

As well, the prohibition in article 3 is not just directed at state officials; private individuals can also come within its framework, and the state in which the conduct occurs can be held responsible for the actions of such individuals.[335]

Application No 4900/06 at paras 142–43; *Boutagni v France*, 18 November 2010, Application No 42360/08 at paras 44–45.

331 *Muršić v Croatia*, 20 October 2016, Application No 7334/13 at para 97.

332 Wouters, above note 319 at 223 and 226–27; *A and Others*, above note 330 at para 127; *Al-Saadoon and Mufdhi v The United Kingdom*, 2 March 2010, Application No 61498/08 at para 121; *Bazjaks v Latvia*, 19 October 2010, Application No 71572/01 at para 105; *Haidn v Germany*, 13 January 2011, Application No 6587/04 at paras 101–2; *MSS v Belgium and Greece*, 21 January 2011, Application No 30696/09 at para 219 [*MSS*].

333 Wouters, above note 319 at 242–43; Katharina Röhl, "Fleeing Violence and Poverty: Non-refoulement Obligations Under the European Convention of Human Rights" (January 2005) UNCHR Working Paper No 111at 14, online: www.unhcr.org/research/working/41f8ef4f2/fleeing-violence-poverty-non-refoulement-obligations-under-european-convention.html; Goodwin-Gill & McAdam, above note 2 at 373–74.

334 Wouters, above note 319 at 247–64; Röhl, above note 333 at 17–19; Goodwin-Gill & McAdam, above note 2 at 373; Bicknell, above note 321 at 199.

335 Wouters, above note 319 at 225 and 237–38; Bicknell, above note 321 at 198–99; UN Doc A/CN.4/565, *Expulsion of Aliens*, above note 9 at 356, para 570; *Abdolkhani and Karimnia v Turkey*, 22 September 2009, Application No 30471/08 at para 74; *NS v Denmark*, 20 January 2011, Application No 58359/08 at para 70 (the same was said in four other cases involving deportation from Denmark to Sri Lanka decided on the same day).

The spectre of diplomatic assurances has been raised for both types of conduct in the context of *refoulement*. Assurances have traditionally been used in extradition to ensure, for instance, that persons will not face the death penalty when sent to the country requesting extradition. This practice has come into vogue for immigration deportation situations, although primarily to prevent article 3 type of conduct. The court has been reluctant to allow removal in either type of cases, where the country to which a person would be removed has a history of human rights abuses.[336] The additional step of monitoring, which has been offered by states on occasion, has not always mitigated this concern of the court,[337] nor has the fact that such a country is a signatory to human rights treaties.[338] In outlining the obligation to examine diplomatic assurances, the court stated:

> Assurances are not in themselves sufficient to ensure adequate protection against the risk of ill-treatment. There is an obligation to examine whether assurances provide, in their practical application, a sufficient guarantee that the applicant will be protected against the risk of ill-treatment. The weight to be given to assurances from the receiving State depends, in each case, on the circumstances prevailing at the material time.[339]

Last, states also have positive obligations under article 3, which are as follows:

> Firstly, an obligation to put in place a legislative and regulatory framework of protection; secondly, in certain well-defined circumstances, an obligation to take operational measures to protect specific individuals against a risk of treatment contrary to that provision; and, thirdly, an obligation to carry out an effective investigation into arguable claims of

336 Mariagiulia Giuffré, "Deportation with Assurances and Human Rights: The Case of Persons Suspected or Convicted of Serious Crimes" (2017) 15:1 *Journal of International Criminal Justice* 75 at 83–90; UN Doc A/CN.4/565, *Expulsion of Aliens*, above note 9 at 364–70, paras 585–94; *Yuldashev v Russia*, 8 July 2010, Application No 1248/09 at para 85; *Karimov v Russia*, 29 July 2010, Application No 54219/08 at para 101; *Sultanov v Russia*, 4 November 2010, Application No 15303/09 at para 73; *MSS*, above note 332 at para 353.

337 Wouters, above note 319 at 302–3.

338 *Ibid* at 304–7.

339 *Othman (Abu Qatada) v The United Kingdom*, 17 January 2012, Application No 8139/09 at para 187; see, also, European Court of Human Rights, *Guide on the Case-Law of the European Convention on Human Rights* (31 August 2022) at 32–33, online (pdf): www.echr.coe.int/Documents/Guide_EU_law_in_ECHR_case-law_ENG.pdf.

> infliction of such treatment. Generally speaking, the first two aspects of these positive obligations are classified as "substantive," while the third aspect corresponds to the State's positive "procedural" obligation.[340]

The state becomes responsible for the ill-treatment when it fails to take reasonably available measures that could have mitigated the harm or altered the outcome.[341]

ii) Torture

Torture is the most intense and severe form of inhuman treatment, requiring an element of intent, the infliction of such treatment, and attaching a special stigma to deliberate inhuman treatment causing very serious and cruel suffering.[342] It can be of both a physical and a mental nature.[343]

The court has not gone beyond the above description in terms of setting out a general definition of torture but has determined that specific types of conduct amount to torture on a case-by-case basis.

Examples of torture in the jurisprudence have been rape;[344] cutting off an ear while in detention;[345] being in a permanent state of physical pain and anxiety owing to uncertainty of the person's fate together with physical blows during a lengthy interrogation session;[346] hanging with arms tied behind the back and then being suspended by the arms; beatings on the soles of the feet accompanied by blows on the chest; repeated kicking, beating, and striking of the head with a rifle, resulting in severe bruising and injuries to the head, causing brain damage, combined with a significant lapse of time (thirty-six hours) before receiving medical treatment; electric shocks; treatment with cold and hot water and blows to the head while in police custody; being stripped naked and submerged in cold water while being blindfolded; being attached by the arms to ceiling pipes; continuous beating while in detention while also being threatened with hard punishment; physical abuse and sodomy;

---

340 Bicknell, above note 321 at 198; *X and Others v Bulgaria*, 2 February 2021, Application No 22457/16 at para 178.

341 Bicknell, above note, 321 at 198; *O'Keeffe v Ireland*, 28 January 2014, Application No 35810/09 at para 149.

342 Wouters, above note 319; Bicknell, above note 321 at 196–97; Röhl, above note 333 at 13; *Gisayev v Russia*, 20 January 2011, Application No 14811/04 at para 143.

343 Wouters, above note 319 at 222.

344 *Ibid* at 224; *Mucić et al (Čelebići Camp)*, above note 325 at paras 466 and 487–89.

345 *Sadykov v Russia*, 7 October 2010, Application No 41840/02, at para 237.

346 Wouters, above note 319 at 224–25; *Mucić et al (Čelebići Camp)*, above note 325 at paras 465–66; *Gisayev v Russia*, 20 January 2011, Application No 14811/04 at paras 144–46.

and severe beatings by police officers resulting in the death of the applicant's relative.[347]

Domestic abuse involving death threats, bodily injuries, and severe mutilation by former partners or husbands has also been recognized as torture under article 3.[348] The court further held that the involved state's legal system lacked a definition of "domestic violence" and the local authorities failed to lead effective investigations, which violated aspects of article 3.[349]

Furthermore, the court has acknowledged the emotional and psychological impact of human rights violations of victim's family members, largely in the context of enforced disappearances. However, special factors will be considered in respect of the victim's relatives for a separate violation of article 3, which includes the proximity of the family tie, the circumstances of the relationship, the extent to which the family member witnessed the events in question, and the involvement of the applicants in the attempts to obtain information about the fate of their relatives.[350]

iii) Inhuman and Degrading Treatment or Punishment

Inhuman and degrading treatment or punishment is seen as a less severe form of ill-treatment than torture, as intense suffering of either a physical or a mental nature,[351] but it still must reach a certain level of

---

347 Wouters, above note 319 at 224–25; *Mucić et al (Čelebići Camp)*, above note 325 at paras 465–66; *Satybalova and Others v Russia*, 30 June 2020, Application No 79947/12 at para 76; *Lutsenko and Verbytskyy v Ukraine*, 21 January 2021, Application Nos 12482/14 and 39800/14 at paras 79–80.

348 *Tunikova and Others v Russia*, 14 December 2021, Application Nos 55974/16, 53118/17, and 27484/18 at paras 75–76.

349 *Ibid* at paras 100 and 121.

350 *Janowiec and Others v Russia*, 21 October 2013, Application Nos 55508/07 and 29520/09 at para 177.

351 Manfred Nowak, United Nations Special Rapporteur on Torture and Other Cruel, Inhuman, or Degrading Treatment or Punishment between 2004 and 2010, took issue with the distinction between torture and inhuman treatment along a spectrum of severity and instead is of the view that the difference lies in "the intention of the perpetrator and the powerlessness of the victim. Torture constitutes such a horrible attack on the dignity of a human being because the perpetrator of torture deliberately inflicts severe pain or suffering on a powerless victim for a specific purpose, such as extracting a confession or information. Cruel and inhuman treatment, on the other hand, means the infliction of severe pain or suffering without purpose or intention and outside a situation where a person is under the de facto control of another"; see UN Doc, Report of the Special Rapporteur on Torture and Other Cruel, Inhuman or Degrading Treatment or Punishment, 5 February 2010, A/HRC/13/39/Add 5 at 50–51, para 188; see, also, *Dzhabirailova and Dzhabrailova v Russia*, 2 December 2010, Application No 15563/06 at para 123.

severity to set it apart from other forms of harsh treatment or punishment, which are not within the purview of article 3.[352]

The jurisprudence usually does not distinguish between inhuman treatment or punishment and degrading treatment or punishment,[353] although for the latter it has been said that it is present if it can be objectively shown that it was intended to raise in its victims feelings of fear, anguish, and inferiority capable of humiliating them,[354] while as far as the consequences are concerned, it adversely affected the victim's personality in a manner incompatible with article 3.[355] Two examples of degrading treatment are having a gynecological examination while handcuffed and with three male security officers present in the consultation room[356] and the forced shaving of a prisoner's hair without justification.[357]

Other court decisions also relate to the degrading treatment of minors, including an unaccompanied minor living in precarious conditions due to the authorities' failure to execute a judicial placement order[358] and authorities failing to ensure that a minor was looked after by an adult when arresting the parents.[359] Intent to cause this type of suffering may be relevant to a finding of inhuman treatment or punishment, but it is not conclusive, nor is the consent of the victim.[360]

Prohibited ill-treatment was present in situations of severe physical abuse (such as the binding of wrists with wire in such a manner as to cut the skin and the prolonged exposure of the feet to water or snow); sexual abuse; the destruction of homes and property and the subsequent deprivation of livelihood and forced eviction; and particularly bad living conditions, such as in the case of children who were locked inside an extremely filthy house most of the day for almost four years.[361] As well, the disappearance of family members, depending on the

352 Bicknell, above note 321 at 197.

353 Wouters, above note 319 at 222 and 228.

354 *Ibid* at 228 (also indicating that the court has considered the public nature of the humiliation); Röhl, above note 333 at 15; Bicknell, above note 321 at 197; *Dzhabirailova and Dzhabrailova v Russia*, above note 351 at para 123; *MSS*, above note 332 at para 220.

355 *A and Others*, above note 330 at para 127; *Al-Saadoon and Mufdhi v The United Kingdom*, 2 March 2010, Application No 61498/08 at para 121.

356 *Filiz Uyan v Turkey*, 8 January 2009, Application No 7496/03 at paras 32–34.

357 Wouters, above note 319 at 235; *Women's Initiatives Supporting Group and Others v Georgia*, 16 December 2021, Application Nos 73204/13 and 74959/13 at para 60.

358 *Khan v France*, 28 February 2019, Application No 12267/16 at paras 94–95.

359 *Ioan Pop and Others v Romania*, 6 December 2016, Application No 52924/09 at para 65.

360 Wouters, above note 319 at 226; Röhl, above note 333 at 12–13 and 16; *A and Others*, above note 330 at para 127.

361 Wouters, above note 319 at 229–30.

relationship of the family members; the conduct of the authorities when brought to their attention; and the extent to which the victim witnessed the disappearance have increasingly been seen as inhuman treatment.[362] The imposition of the death penalty after an unfair trial with the risk of the sentence being carried out yields the same result.[363] On the other hand, some forcible medical treatment, such as feeding, medicating, and restraining a psychiatric patient, involves suffering but will not reach the article 3 threshold as long as it is done in accordance with generally accepted psychiatric principles.[364]

Most cases have dealt with arrest and detention situations. With respect to arrest, the court has acknowledged that a certain degree of force can be required to subdue a person, but when this force is excessive or disproportionate to what is necessary in the circumstances, then the situation has entered the realm of inhuman or degrading treatment or punishment.[365] A combination of wall standing, hooding, being subjected to continuous loud and hissing sounds, and deprivation of sleep, food, and drink were considered to be inhuman and degrading, as was being held in a cold and dark cell while blindfolded and treated in a way that left bruises on a person's body.[366] While strip searches may be necessary occasionally to ensure prison security or prevent disorder or crime, they must be conducted in an appropriate manner and must be justified; conducting such a search by male staff members of a female applicant stripped naked in a sobering-up centre is not appropriate.[367]

---

362 *Ibid* at 229–30; Röhl, above note 333 at 15; *Sasita Israilova and others v Russia*, 28 October 2010, Application No 35079/04 at paras 105–6; *Tumayeva and Others v Russia*, 16 December 2010, Application No 9960/05 at para 133; *Taymuskhanovy v Russia*, 16 December 2010, Application No 11528/07 at paras 121–24; *Dzhamayeva and Others v Russia*, 21 December 2010, Application No 26980/06 at para 123–25; *Skendžić and Krznarić v Croatia*, 20 January 2011, Application No 16212/08 at para 93.

363 Wouters, above note 319 at 230.

364 *Ibid* at 235.

365 *Ibid* at 230–31; UN Doc, Report of the Special Rapporteur on Torture and Other Cruel, Inhuman or Degrading Treatment or Punishment, above note 351 at 50–51, para 188; *Samüt Karabulut v Turkey*, 27 January 2009, Application No 16999/04 at paras 42–43; *Shchukin and Others v Cyprus*, 29 July 2010, Application No 14030/03 at paras 93–100; *Boris Popov v Russia*, 28 October 2010, Application No 23284/04 at paras 51–56; with respect to force that can be used during demonstrations, see *Timtik v Turkey*, 9 November 2010, Application No 12503/06 at paras 44–54.

366 Wouters, above note 319 at 232; *Mucić et al (Čelebići Camp)*, above note 325 at paras 535–38; *Sashov and Others v Bulgaria*, 7 January 1010, Application No 14383/03 at paras 44–47; *Petyo Petkov v Bulgaria*, 7 January 2010, Application No 32130/03 at paras 39–47.

367 *Wiktorko v Poland*, 31 March 2009, Application No 14612/02 at paras 53–57.

Certain severe conditions of overcrowding in prisons have been held to amount to prohibited conduct as well, such as in circumstances when they took place with a combination of a lack of food, a lack of adequate bedding, limited access to daylight, and unsanitary conditions.[368] Other aspects of prison conditions have also come under the scrutiny of the court, such as for persons on death row, depending on the personal circumstances of the detainee; the length of time of such detention; the type of detention regime during that time; and the exposure to physical or sexual attacks while in detention.[369] The type of discipline used in prisons cannot be excessive, which would be the case if the main purpose were to frighten and humiliate prisoners.[370]

The jurisprudence has also recognized that prisoners are entitled to proper medical treatment while incarcerated.[371] Solitary confinement in

---

368 Wouters, above note 319 at 232–33; *Ramishvili and Kokhreidze v Georgia*, 27 January 2009, Application No 1704/06 at paras 84–88; *Sulejmanovic v Italy*, 16 July 2009, Application No 22635/03 at paras 39–42; *Orchowski v Poland*, 22 October 2009, Application No 17885/04 at paras 119–22; *Roman Karasev v Russia*, 25 November 2010, Application No 30251/03 at paras 49–52; *Veliyev v Russia*, 24 June 2010, Application No 24202/05 at paras 127–30; *Florea v Romania*, 14 September 2010, Application No 37186/03 at paras 51–62; *Bazjaks v Latvia*, 19 October 2010, Application No 71572/01 at paras 113–19; *ID v Moldova*, 30 November 2010, Application No 47203/06 at paras 42–46.

369 Wouters, above note 319 at 233; *Simeonovi v Bulgaria*, 12 May 2017, Application No 21980/04 at para 90.

370 *Davydov and Others v Ukraine*, 1 July 2010, Applications Nos 17674/02 and 39081/02 at paras 262–72; *Bazjaks v Latvia*, 19 October 2010, Application No 71572/01 at para 106.

371 The principle with respect to medical care in detention facilities is expressed as follows in the jurisprudence: "Article 3 of the Convention cannot be interpreted as laying down a general obligation to release a detainee on health grounds or to transfer him to a civil hospital, even if he is suffering from an illness that is particularly difficult. However, this provision does require the State to ensure that prisoners are detained in conditions which are compatible with respect for human dignity, that the manner and method of the execution of the measure do not subject them to distress or hardship of an intensity exceeding the unavoidable level of suffering inherent in detention and that, given the practical demands of imprisonment, their health and well-being are adequately secured by, among other things, providing them with the requisite medical assistance" in *Sławomir Musiał v Poland*, 20 January 2009, Application No 28300/06 at para 86; see, also, *Kaprykowski v Poland*, 3 February 2009, Application No 23052/05 at paras 68–74; *Grori v Albania*, 7 July 2009, Application No 25336/04 at paras 126–33; *Aharon Schwarz v Romania*, 12 January 2010, Application No 28304/02 at paras 89–93; *Andrzej Wierzbicki v Poland*, 19 January 2010, Application No 48/03 at paras 54–64; *Hajol v Poland*, 2 March 2010, Application No 1127/06 at paras 59–64; *Visloguzov v Ukraine*, 20 May 2010, Application No 32362/02 at paras 66–70; *Engel v Hungary*, 20 May 2010, Application No 46857/06 at paras 26–30; *Xiros v Greece*, 9 September 2010, Application No 1033/07 at paras 72–76; *Pakhomov v Russia*, 30 September 2010, Application No 44917/08 at paras 61–63; *Llogvinenko v Ukraine*, 14 October 2010, Application No 13448/07 at paras 77–78; *Petukhov v Ukraine*, 21 October 2010, Application No 43374/02 at paras 89–94; *Dobri v Romania*, 14 December 2010, Application No

itself is not a breach of article 3, nor is prohibiting contact for security, disciplinary, or protective reasons, but complete sensory and social isolation would be a violation, while the same can be said for a lack of sufficient medical care and inappropriate strip or body searches during such confinement.[372] Lifelong detention is not by itself a violation of this article[373] as long as there is a system for consideration of release,[374] which also applies to long-term immigration detention.[375] The detention of a minor in an adult prison would be a violation.[376]

The conditions of asylum seekers have been held to be "degrading" in certain situations. Examples include confining an asylum seeker to a prefabricated cabin for two months without allowing him outdoors or to make a telephone call, and with no clean sheets and insufficient hygiene products;[377] conditions where, for three months, the asylum

---

25153/04 at paras 43–45; *Kozhokar v Russia*, 16 December 2010, Application No 33099/08 at paras 105–16; *Gladkiy v Russia*, 21 December 2010, Application No 3242/03 at paras 65–73; *Colesnicov v Romania*, 21 December 2010, Application No 36479/03 at paras 74–86; *Blokhin v Russia*, 23 March 2016, Application No 47152/06 at para 136.

372 Wouters, above note 319 at 234; *Khider v France*, 9 July 2009, Application No 39364/05 at paras 102–7; *AB v Russia*, 14 October 2010, Application No 1439/06 at paras 99–113.

373 Walter Kälin & Jörg Künzli, *The Law of International Human Rights Protection*, 2d ed (Oxford: Oxford University Press, 2019) at 327; *Iorgov (II) v Bulgaria*, 2 September 2010, Application No 36295/02 at paras 49–52.

374 *A and Others*, above note 330 at para 128.

375 *Ibid* at paras 129–31; see, also, European Court of Human Rights, *Guide on the Case-Law of the European Convention on Human Rights*, above note 339 at 16–17.

376 *Güveç v Turkey*, 20 January 2009, Application No 70337/01 at para 98; *Muskhadzhiyeva and Others v Belgium*, 19 January 2010, Application No 41442/07 at paras 55–63.

377 *MSS*, above note 332 at para 222; the court went on the say at paras 230–31 that in the specific situation of immigration detention in Greece, "the Court notes that, according to the findings made by organisations that visited the holding centre next to the airport, the sector for asylum seekers was rarely unlocked and the detainees had no access to the water fountain outside and were obliged to drink water from the toilets. In the sector for arrested persons, there were 145 detainees in a 110 sq. m space. In a number of cells there was only one bed for fourteen to seventeen people. There were not enough mattresses and a number of detainees were sleeping on the bare floor. There was insufficient room for all the detainees to lie down and sleep at the same time. Because of the overcrowding, there was a lack of sufficient ventilation and the cells were unbearably hot. Detainees' access to the toilets was severely restricted and they complained that the police would not let them out into the corridors. The police admitted that the detainees had to urinate in plastic bottles which they emptied when they were allowed to use the toilets. It was observed in all sectors that there was no soap or toilet paper, that sanitary and other facilities were dirty, that the sanitary facilities had no doors, and the detainees were deprived of outdoor exercise. The Court reiterates that it has already considered that such conditions, which are found in other detention centres in Greece, amounted to degrading treatment within the meaning of Article 3 of the Convention."

seeker was detained without access to any recreational activities and meals;[378] asylum seekers being confined to inadequate conditions in an airport transit zone;[379] and when administrative delays resulted in inadequate living conditions and not receiving state support as required by domestic law.[380]

In the refugee and immigration context, the court has held that expulsion can involve a degree of suffering but must reach a certain level of severity before it becomes objectionable.[381] *Refoulement*, which can be either direct or indirect (the latter being removal to a safe country, which will then carry out the *refoulement*),[382] involves a risk assessment of the fate a person might befall upon return, the assessment of which is often along the same lines as past situations involving inhuman or degrading treatment or punishment, keeping in mind the general situation in the country of return and the personal circumstances of the person to be removed.[383] Article 3 has been applied by the court where it found that there were substantial grounds for believing that a person would be returned to a country with an officially recognized regime of slavery; where a person could be stoned to death for committing adultery; where a person would publicly receive 100 lashes for sexual activity; where a person would be subjected to kicking, intimidation, harassment, and forced labour; where a person would be subject to female genital mutilation;[384] or where the person might be exposed to detention incommunicado, prolonged exposure to the sun at high temperatures, and tying of hands and feet in painful positions.[385] However, in a case involving terrorism offences, the court held that the applicant's extradition did not

378 *Tabesh v Greece*, 26 November 2009, Application No 8256/07 at paras 38–44.

379 *ZA and Others v Russia*, 21 November 2019, Application No 61411/15 at para 195.

380 *NH and Others v France*, 2 July 2020, Application No 28820/13 at para 184.

381 *NS v Denmark*, 20 January 2011, Application No 58359/08 at para 70 (the same was said in four other cases involving deportation from Denmark to Sri Lanka decided on the same day); *Paposhvili v Belgium*, 18 December 2016, Application No 41738/10 at para 174; *Ilias and Ahmed v Hungary*, 21 November 2019, Application No 47287/15 at para 126; see also European Court of Human Rights, *Guide on the Case-Law of the European Convention on Human Rights*, above note 339 at 29–30.

382 *MSS*, above note 332 at paras 342–43 and 365–68; *AL (XW) v Russia*, 29 October 2015, Application No 44095/14 at paras 63–66.

383 *YP and LP v France*, 2 September 2010, Application No 32476/06 at paras 63–65; *N v Sweden*, 20 July 2010, Application No 23505/09 at paras 51–54; a person facing deportation to Afghanistan in a situation where she was about to divorce her husband while being in another relationship would have exposed her to a risk of reprisal amounting to inhuman treatment (at paras 58–62).

384 Wouters, above note 319 at 239–40.

385 *Ibid* at 242.

contravene article 3 as a high threshold for terrorism offences is required to demonstrate that the sentence is grossly disproportionate.[386]

The degree of suffering does not reach the objectionable level where a child is deported as long as they are accompanied by an adult and appropriate arrangements are made upon arrival in the country of destination.[387] The same was said in cases where a person's state of health or life expectancy might diminish sharply due to illness and a lack of resources in the receiving country, such as not being able to receive the same health treatment for HIV/AIDS.[388]

As well, the "mere possibility of ill-treatment on account of an unsettled situation in the receiving country" does not give rise to a breach of article 3.[389] As well, the court has been reluctant to read into article 3 any social or economic rights. For instance, persons not able to regain their original property or employment upon return did not meet the level of inhuman or degrading treatment.[390] The same was said with respect to an obligation to provide everyone with a home or to give refugees financial assistance to enable them to maintain a certain

---

386 *Aswat v UK*, 16 April 2013, Application No 17299/12 at para 58.

387 Wouters, above note 319 at 235–37.

388 UN Doc A/CN.4/565, *Expulsion of Aliens*, above note 9 at 361–63, paras 578–83; Röhl, above note 333 at 21–24; in *N v The United Kingdom*, 27 May 2008, Application No 26565/05, the observation is made at paras 44–45 that

> advances in medical science, together with social and economic differences between countries, entail that the level of treatment available in the Contracting State and the country of origin may vary considerably. While it is necessary, given the fundamental importance of Article 3 in the Convention system, for the Court to retain a degree of flexibility to prevent expulsion in very exceptional cases, Article 3 does not place an obligation on the Contracting State to alleviate such disparities through the provision of free and unlimited health care to all aliens without a right to stay within its jurisdiction. A finding to the contrary would place too great a burden on the Contracting States. Finally, the Court observes that, although the present application, in common with most of those referred to above, is concerned with the expulsion of a person with an HIV and AIDS-related condition, the same principles must apply in relation to the expulsion of any person afflicted with any serious, naturally occurring physical or mental illness which may cause suffering, pain and reduced life expectancy and require specialised medical treatment which may not be so readily available in the applicant's country of origin or which may be available only at substantial cost.

See, also, *Paposhvili v Belgium*, 18 December 2016, Application No 41738/10 at paras 175–93, as well as European Court of Human Rights, *Guide on the Case-Law of the European Convention on Human Rights*, above note 339 at 33–35.

389 *Iskandarov v Russia*, 23 September 2010, Application No 17185/05 at para 127; *Gaforov v Russia*, 21 October 2010, Application No 25404/09 at para 115.

390 Wouters, above note 319 at 240–41.

standard of living,[391] although the court "has not excluded the possibility that the responsibility of the State may be engaged . . . in respect of treatment where an applicant, who was wholly dependent on State support, found herself faced with official indifference in a situation of serious deprivation or want incompatible with human dignity."[392]

a) United Nations Human Rights Committee[393]

i) *General Principles*

Some of the principles developed by the European Court of Human Rights can be detected in the jurisprudence of the Human Rights Committee as well.[394] The prohibition of torture is absolute,[395] even in the

391 *MSS*, above note 332 at para 249.

392 *Ibid* at paras 250–52; the court applied this exception to a person who had been deported from Belgium to Greece where he was homeless and destitute by saying: "The obligation to provide accommodation and decent material conditions to impoverished asylum seekers has now entered into positive law and the Greek authorities are bound to comply with their own legislation. . . . What the applicant holds against the Greek authorities in this case is that, because of their deliberate actions or omissions, it has been impossible in practice for him to avail himself of these rights and provide for his essential needs. The Court attaches considerable importance to the applicant's status as an asylum seeker and, as such, a member of a particularly underprivileged and vulnerable population group in need of special protection. . . . That said, the Court must determine whether a situation of extreme material poverty can raise an issue under Article 3. . . . It observes that the situation in which the applicant has found himself is particularly serious. He allegedly spent months living in a state of the most extreme poverty, unable to cater for his most basic needs: food, hygiene and a place to live. Added to that was the ever-present fear of being attacked and robbed and the total lack of any likelihood of his situation improving. It was to escape from that situation of insecurity and of material and psychological want that he tried several times to leave Greece."

393 For a general overview, see Christof Heyns, Carmen Rueda & Daniel du Plessis, "Torture and Ill Treatment: The United Nations Human Rights Committee" in Evans & Modvig, *Research Handbook on Torture*, above note 321 at 106–27.

394 A number of the principles developed in the jurisprudence were originally stated in general in its "General Comment No. 20: Prohibition of Torture, or Other Cruel, Inhuman or Degrading Treatment or Punishment (Article 7)" 10 March 1992), online: www.ohchr.org/en/resources/educators/human-rights-education-training/general-comment-no-20-prohibition-torture-or-other-cruel-inhuman-or-degrading-treatment-or.

395 Wouters, above note 319 at 402–4; Heyns, Rueda & du Plessis, above note 393 at 111; Goodwin-Gill & McAdam, above note 2 at 364. In this context, the committee has made it clear that a person who has been excluded for 1F reasons is still entitled to the protection of art 7; see *Hamida v Canada*, 11 May 2010, Communication No 1544/2007 at paras 2.4 and 8.5–8.7, as well as Concluding Observations on Portugal, 5 July 2003, UN Doc CCPR/CO/78/PRT at para 12, although an assessment of the particular circumstances will not always lead to a prohibited removal; see *Tarlue v Canada*, 28 April 2009, Communication No 1551/2007 at para 7.4.

face of a public emergency[396] or the "ticking time bomb" scenario;[397] prohibited acts can be committed by both state actors and private individuals;[398] and personal factors such as sex, age, and the person's state of health need to be examined to determine whether persons can be described as victims of prohibited conduct.[399] Not only direct[400] but also indirect *refoulement* is prohibited.[401] As well, both physical and mental suffering are recognized as falling within the notions of torture and cruel, inhuman, or degrading treatment or punishment.[402]

The Human Rights Committee has acknowledged that anguish caused to the victim's family, especially in relation to incommunicado detention and enforced disappearances, can amount to a violation under article 7 of the ICCPR.[403] Examples include anguish and distress caused to the person due to the disappearance and torture of her daughter, including the uncertainty concerning her whereabouts,[404] and emotional suffering caused by state authorities not properly investigating the enforced disappearance of a family member.[405]

While the committee does not in principle disapprove of diplomatic assurances, it requires that they are effective and that they include credible mechanisms for ensuring compliance by the state to which a person is removed.[406] As well, the more systematic the practice of human rights abuses is in a given country, the less likely the risk of mistreatment can be avoided by assurances.[407] If the alleged risk is from non-state actors or foreign states operating in the territory, the receiving state can provide credible assurances and explore internal flight options.[408]

---

396 *Avadanov v Azerbaijan*, 2 November 2010, Communication No 1633/2007 at para 9.3.

397 Concluding Observations on Israel, 3 September 2010, UN Doc CCPR/C/ISR/CO/3 at para 11.

398 Heyns, Rueda & du Plessis, above note 393 at 109–10.

399 Wouters, above note 319 at 382–83.

400 Concluding Observations on Switzerland, 3 November 2009, UN Doc CCPR/C/CHE/CO/3 at paras 15–16; Concluding Observations on Australia, 7 May 2009, UN Doc CCPR/C/AUS/CO/5 at para 19.

401 Wouters, above note 319 at 407.

402 *Ibid* at 381; Heyns, Rueda & du Plessis, above note 393 at 116–17.

403 *Nakarmi v Nepal*, 8 May 2017, Communication No 2184/2012 at para 11.8.

404 *Quinteros v Uruguay*, 15 October 1982, Communication No 107/1981 at para 14; *Sharma et al v Nepal*, 6 April 2018, Communication No 2364/2014 at para 9.1.

405 *Zakharenko v Belarus*, 18 May 2017, Communication No.2586/2015 at para 7.4.

406 *Mohammed Alzery v Sweden*, 25 October 2016, Communication No 1416/2005 at para 11.5; Giuffré, above note 336 at 80–83.

407 Wouters, above note 319 at 399–402; Concluding Observations on Sweden, 7 May 2009, UN Doc CCPR/C/SWE/CO/6 at para 16.

408 General Comment No 36, 3 September 2019, UN Doc CCPR/C/GC/3 at para 30.

ii) Torture

The following have been found to amount to torture by the committee: electric shocks;[409] repeated immersions in a mixture of blood, urine, vomit, and excrement; hooding and handcuffing with a piece of wood thrust in the mouth for several days and nights; extended hanging from hand or leg chains; near asphyxiation; mock amputation; mock execution; threats of torture and violence against friends and family;[410] being held incommunicado for more than three months while being kept blindfolded with hands tied together;[411] incommunicado detention for prolonged periods;[412] and severe and repeated beatings.[413]

Torture was also found to be present in a situation where a person was "handcuffed and assaulted with hosepipes; laid face down on an iron bed, handcuffed and tied by the ankles to the bed, and assaulted with a club and a hose pipe; kept in a dark room for eight days; that during one assault he received an injury to his right eye and bled from his eye; that he was suspended from the roof and beaten, and thereafter fainted; that his head was immersed under water."[414] Moreover, if the use of force by the police becomes excessive, then it may be regarded as a violation of article 7.[415]

In one case, the threshold applied was lower than in the above situations, where a person had been forced to remain standing while hooded for a long period, during which he fell and broke his leg, resulting in permanent physical damage.[416]

The committee has also found a violation of article 7 in cases of gender-based violence. Examples include a minor being forced to continue with pregnancy, subjecting her to a life-threating situation and serious mental suffering;[417] states' obligation to prevent female genital mutilation;[418] and protection of women's reproductive rights.[419]

---

409 *Kirpo v Tajikistan*, 3 December 2009, Communication No 1401/2005 at para 6.2.

410 Wouters, above note 319 at 384.

411 *Mucić et al (Čelebići Camp)*, above note 325 at para 461.

412 *El-Boathi v Algeria*, 16 May 2017, Communication No 2259/2013 at para 7.6.

413 *Iskiyaev v Uzbekistan*, 22 April 2009, Communication No 1418/2005 at para 9.2.

414 *Arachchige v Sri Lanka*, 23 April 2009, Communication No 1432/2005 at n2 and para 9.

415 *Chernev v Russian Federation*, 4 April 2019, Communication No 2322/2013.

416 Wouters, above note 319 at 384, who makes the comment in n139 that in a similar fact pattern in a case before the European Court of Human Rights such conduct was deemed to be inhuman and degrading treatment but not torture.

417 *KL v Peru*, 24 October 2005, Communication No 1153/2003.

418 General Comment No 28, art 3 (The Equality of Rights Between Men and Women), 26 May 2014, UN Doc CCPR/C/21/Rev.1/Add.10 at para 11.

419 *Ibid* at para 20.

iii) Cruel, Inhuman, and Degrading Treatment or Punishment

Most cases decided in this context by the committee involved situations of arrest and detention. The committee has said that arrest or detention by itself is not a breach of article 7 of the ICCPR, but additional factors, such as being severely and systematically beaten during an interrogation, deprivation of food and drink, or the threat of being tortured, will bring such activities within the parameters of prohibited conduct.[420]

Lengthy terms of imprisonment do not amount by themselves to a violation of article 7, nor does being on death row, but if the latter is accompanied by lengthy delays or specific conditions of imprisonment resulting in severe psychological impact on the prisoner, then it will be considered ill-treatment. However, a twenty-hour delay in detention while in an actual death cell after the issuance of a warrant of execution is cruel and inhuman treatment, as is the failure to notify family and lawyers of such a warrant.[421]

Prolonged solitary confinement can also result in a violation of the ICCPR,[422] especially if it is combined with incommunicado detention, such as where a person has been chained to a bed for three-and-a-half months with little clothing or food.[423] Detention in circumstances so crowded that detainees had to sit on excrement while not receiving food or water until being released after fifty hours were found to be unacceptable, as was a situation where a person was deprived of food and drink for four days and was subsequently kept interned under unacceptable sanitary conditions. The same was found for a person who had been forced to stand blindfolded and bound for thirty-five hours while listening to the cries of other detainees being tortured and forced to sit blindfolded and motionless on a mattress for many days.[424]

---

420 Wouters, above note 319 at 382; Heyns, Rueda & du Plessis, above note 393 at 115.

421 Wouters at 319; Kälin & Künzli, above note 373 at 326.

422 Heyns, Rueda & du Plessis, above note 393 at 116.

423 Wouters, above note 319 at 386–87; UN Doc E/CN.4/2006/120, 27 February 2006, Situation of Detainees at Guantánamo Bay at 17, para 53; Concluding Observations on Colombia, 4 August 2010, UN Doc CCPR/C/COL/CO/6 at para 21; Concluding Observations on Rwanda, 7 May 2009, UN Doc CCPR/C/RWA/CO/3 at para 14; regarding incommunicado detention as a violation by itself, see *El Abani v Libya*, 14 September 2010, Communication No 1640/2007 at para 7.2; *Aboussedra v Libya*, 2 November 2010, Communication No 1751/2008 at para 7.2; *McCallum v South Africa*, 2 November 2010, Communication No 1818/2008 at paras 6.2–6.8.

424 *Mucić et al (Čelebići Camp)*, above note 325 at paras 539–40.

Whipping,[425] beating a prisoner over the head so severely that he needed stitches, flogging, and being blindfolded and thrown into a canal resulted in similar findings. Certain methods of handcuffing, hooding, shaking, sleep deprivation, and rubbing salt water into a person's nasal passages while handcuffed to a chair overnight without anything to drink were also violations,[426] as was a severe beating after arrest resulting in broken ribs[427] and being held naked and without provision of elementary personal hygiene items for several days while being administered psychotropic drugs.[428]

Severe overcrowding in prisons[429] and the practice of holding mentally ill persons in regular prisons[430] or in enclosed restraint beds are also seen as problematic.[431] The use of dogs against persons with a phobia, exposure to extreme temperatures, and sleep deprivation for several consecutive days can amount to ill-treatment when combined with torture.[432]

Outside of situations of arrest and detention, both the phenomenon of forced disappearance and the mental suffering of close family members caused by the disappearance of a woman's daughter, combined with the continuing uncertainty concerning her fate or whereabouts, resulted in a finding of inhuman or cruel treatment.[433] Crimes against women, such as forced sterilization, female genital mutilation, honour crimes, and domestic violence, have also been singled out as

425 *Bondonga v Democratic Republic of Congo*, 18 August 2009, Communication No 1481/2006 at para 6.2.

426 Wouters, above note 319 at 386–87.

427 *Dunaev v Tajikistan*, 22 April 2009, Communication No 1195/2003 at para 7.2.

428 *Umarova v Uzbekistan*, 3 November 2010, Communication No 1449/2006 at para 8.3.

429 Heyns, Rueda & du Plessis, above note 393 at 115–16.

430 Draft Concluding Observations on Belgium, 16 November 2010, UN Doc CCPR/C/BEL/CO/5 at paras 18–19.

431 Concluding Observations on Croatia, 4 November 2009, UN Doc CCPR/C/HRV/CO/2 at para 12.

432 UN Doc E/CN.4/2006/120, 27 February 2006, Situation of Detainees at Guantánamo Bay at 17, para 52.

433 Wouters, above note 319 at 381; forced disappearance has been defined with reference to the International Convention for the Protection of All Persons from Enforced Disappearance as well as the Rome Statute in the case of *Benaziza v Algeria*, 16 September 2010, Communication No 1588/2007 at para 9.3; the same case in para 9.6 considers sons to be close family members; see, also, *El Abani v Libya*, 14 September 2010, Communication No 1640/2007 at para 7.3, regarding the definition of disappearance and the consideration of children and spouse as close family members.

prohibitive-conduct.[434] The detention of refugees in regular prisons is also a violation of the same provision,[435] as is the use of excessive force during expulsion proceedings.[436]

With respect to deportation, the committee stated in General Comment 31 that states should not

> extradite, deport, expel or otherwise remove a person from their territory, where there are substantial grounds for believing that there is a real risk of irreparable harm, such as contemplated by arts 6 and 7 of the Covenant, either in the country to which removal is to be effected or in any country to which the person may subsequently be removed.[437]

Regarding the death penalty, the Human Rights Committee has stated, "Considerable progress may have been made towards establishing an agreement among the States parties to consider the death penalty as a cruel, inhuman or degrading form of punishment. Such a legal development is consistent with the pro-abolitionist spirit of the Covenant."[438]

Degrading treatment is the lowest level of suffering contained in article 7 after torture and inhuman treatment, and intense pain and suffering are not required, as is the case for inhuman treatment.[439] Examples of degrading treatment are stripping detainees naked, particularly in the presence of persons of the opposite sex;[440] the beating of a prisoner combined with pushing him with a bayonet and emptying a

---

434 Wouters, above note 319 at 387; regarding female genital mutilation, see Concluding Observations on Cameroon, 4 August 2010, UN Doc CCPR/C/CMR/CO/4 at para 10, and Concluding Observations on Sweden, 7 May 2009, UN Doc CCPR/C/SWE/CO/6 at para 9; regarding corporal punishment, see Heyns, Rueda & du Plessis, above note 393 at 120, while for abortion, see at 124–25.

435 Concluding Observations on Hungary, 16 November 2010, UN Doc CCPR/C/HUN/CO/5 at para 15.

436 Heyns, Rueda & du Plessis, above note 393 at 117.

437 General Comment No 31, The Nature of the General Legal Obligation Imposed on States Parties to the Covenant, UN Doc CCPR/C/21/Rev.1/Add.13, 26 May 2004, at para 12; see, also, Heyns, Rueda & du Plessis, above note 393 at 121–23.

438 General Comment No 36, art 6 (Right to Life), UN Doc CCPR/C/GC/36, 3 September 2019, at para 51; to date, there are no decisions by the Human Rights Committee that states that the death penalty violates art 7 of the ICCPR. However, in its General Comment 36, the Human Rights Committee outlines its opposition to the death penalty; see, also, Heyns, Rueda & du Plessis, above note 393 at 119–20.

439 UN Doc E/CN.4/2006/120, 27 February 2006, Situation of Detainees at Guantánamo Bay at 17, para 51.

440 *Ibid.*

urine bucket over his head; humiliating prisoners by repeatedly placing them in solitary confinement, subjecting them to the cold, and moving them around different cells in a persistent manner; beating a prisoner with rifle butts and refusing medical treatment; detention in a tiny cell combined with assault, theft of personal effects, and the soaking of his bed; and displaying a person in a cage to the press.[441]

c) United Nations Committee against Torture[442]

i) *General Principles*

The CAT contains a prohibition against torture in article 1.1, and, unlike the other two conventions mentioned above, this article provides a detailed description by saying:

> [F]or the purposes of this Convention, torture means any act by which severe pain or suffering, whether physical or mental, is intentionally inflicted on a person for such purposes as obtaining from him or a third person information or a confession, punishing him for an act he or a third person has committed or is suspected of having committed, or intimidating or coercing him or a third person, or for any reason based on discrimination of any kind, when such pain or suffering is inflicted by or at the instigation of or with the consent or acquiescence of a public official or other person acting in an official capacity. It does not include pain or suffering arising only from, inherent in or incidental to lawful sanctions.[443]

Article 16.1 of the convention addresses other forms of ill-treatment and reads in part:

> [E]ach State Party shall undertake to prevent in any territory under its jurisdiction other acts of cruel, inhuman or degrading treatment or punishment which do not amount to torture as defined in article 1, when such acts are committed by or at the instigation of or with the

441 Wouters, above note 319 at 386.

442 See, in general, Felice Gaer, "The Committee Against Torture: Implementing the Prohibition Against Torture" in Evans & Modvig, *Research Handbook on Torture*, above note 321 at 128–53.

443 The last sentence of this article, the lawful sanction portion, has been controversial and has generally not been applied when states tried to rely on it, prompting some commentators to say that it does not serve any useful purpose and should be ignored; see Manfred Nowak, "Challenges to the Absolute Nature of the Prohibition of Torture and Ill-Treatment" (2005) 23:4 *Netherlands Quarterly of Human Rights* 674 at 679–83, and Wouters, above note 319 at 455–57.

consent or acquiescence of a public official or other person acting in an official capacity.

As a result of these articles, the notions of torture and other forms of ill-treatment are set out more narrowly in the CAT than in the ECHR and the ICCPR, as both articles require some form of official involvement, while for torture further limitations are imposed by also requiring a specific intention and a specific purpose.[444] On the other hand, unlike the ECHR and ICCPR, the CAT specifically prohibits *refoulement* to torture in Article 3, including indirect *refoulement*,[445] although this prohibition has been read in by the jurisprudence for the two other instruments.[446] Article 16 does not contain a prohibition against *refoulement*.[447]

The Committee against Torture has provided some guidance as to the interpretation of article 3 by indicating:

> [T]he author must establish that he/she would be in danger of being tortured and that the grounds for so believing are substantial in the way described, and that such danger is foreseeable, personal, present and real. However, when the author has demonstrated that they cannot possibly obtain documentation relating to their allegations, the burden of proof shifts to the state to investigate the allegations. All pertinent information may be introduced by either party to bear on this matter.
>
> The following information, while not exhaustive, would be pertinent:
>
> (a) Whether the State concerned is one in which there is evidence of a consistent pattern of gross, flagrant or mass violations of human rights;
>
> (b) Whether the complainant has been tortured or ill-treated by, at the instigation of or with the consent or the acquiescence (tacit agreement) of a public official or other person acting in an official capacity in the past, and, if so, whether this was in the recent past;
>
> (c) Whether there is medical, psychological or other independent evidence to support a claim by the complainant that the complainant

444 Heyns, Rueda & du Plessis, above note 393 at 110.

445 UN Doc A/CN.4/565, *Expulsion of Aliens*, above note 9 at 350–51, paras 559–61.

446 This article has been applied to a number of specific fact situations; see UN Doc A/CN.4/565, *Expulsion of Aliens*, above note 9 at 340–41, para 541; Wouters, above note 319 at 505–6; Goodwin-Gill & McAdam, above note 2 at 364–65.

447 Wouters, above note 319 at 518–20.

has been tortured or ill-treated in the past, and whether the torture had after-effects;

(d) Whether the State party has ensured that the complainant facing deportation from the territory under its jurisdiction, control or authority has had access to all legal and/or administrative guarantees and safeguards provided by law and, in particular, to an independent medical examination to assess claims that the complainant has previously suffered torture or ill-treatment in the complainant's country of origin;

(e) Whether there is any credible allegation or evidence that the complainant and/or other person's next of kin have been or will be threatened or exposed to reprisals or other forms of sanctions amounting to torture or other cruel, inhuman or degrading treatment or punishment in connection with the communication submitted to the Committee;

(f) Whether the complainant has engaged in political or other activities within or outside the State concerned that would appear to make the complainant vulnerable to the risk of being subjected to torture were the complainant to be expelled, returned or extradited to the State in question;

(g) If returned to the State to which the complainant is being deported, whether the complainant is at risk of further deportation to another State where the complainant would face the risk of being subjected to torture;

(h) Bearing in mind the status of physical and psychological fragility encountered by the majority of complainants, such as asylum seekers, former detainees and victims of torture or sexual violence, which is conducive to some inconsistencies and/or lapses of memory in their submissions, whether there is any evidence concerning the credibility of the complainant;

(i) Taking into account some inconsistencies that may exist in the presentation of the facts, whether the complainant has demonstrated the general veracity of the claims.[448]

---

448 These guidelines were initially part of General Comment No 1, 21 November 1997, UN Doc A/53/44, Annex IX. However, General Comment No 1 has been replaced by General Comment No 4, 8 February 2018, UN Doc CAT/C/GC/4 at paras 48–49. For examples of how these principles are applied, see *TI v Canada*, 3 December 2009, Communication No 333/2007 at paras 7.2–7.4, and *Güclü v Sweden*, 14 December 2010, Communication No 349/2008 at paras 6.2–6.4.

With respect to the restrictive elements in the definition of torture, two have been the subject of interpretation: the concepts of intention and public officials. With respect to intention, it has been said that ttheir term refers to the specific intent of inflicting severe pain and suffering but also includes the knowledge of the torturer that their conduct will have this effect.[449] As well, intent does "not involve a subjective inquiry into the motivations of the perpetrators, but rather must be objective determinations under the circumstances."[450]

With respect to state officials, "acquiescence refers to conduct by state officials when they knew or could have known that acts of torture were occurring but were unwilling to take appropriate steps to address these practices."[451] The issue of state officials has also been addressed in the context of situations of failed states, such as Somalia, or internal armed conflicts where established state authority has been subverted. In such situations, the Committee against Torture examined whether certain groups have effective control over a particular area in a country and whether they exercised quasi-governmental authority.[452] When considering deporting individuals, states are also obligated to consider whether the deportee would be in danger of being subjected to torture or other ill-treatment by both state and non-state actors.[453]

As with the other two conventions, the prohibition against torture in the CAT is absolute.[454] Member states are also required to exercise

---

449 Wouters, above note 319 at 443; UN Doc Report of the Special Rapporteur on Torture and Other Cruel, Inhuman or Degrading Treatment or Punishment, above note 351 at 13–14, para 34.

450 General Comment No 2, 24 January 2008, UN Doc CAT/C/GC/2 at para 9; Goodwin-Gill & McAdam, above note 2 at 367–68.

451 Wouters, above note 319 at 445–49; Heyns, Rueda & du Plessis, above note 393 at 110.

452 Wouters, above note 319 at 449–55; UN Doc A/CN.4/565, *Expulsion of Aliens*, above note 9 at 349–50 at paras 556–58; UN Doc Report of the Special Rapporteur on Torture and Other Cruel, Inhuman or Degrading Treatment or Punishment, above note 351 at 15, para 39.

453 *MKM v Australia*, 10 May 2017, UN Doc CAT/C/60/D/681/2015 at para 8.9; General Comment No 4, above note 448 at para 30.

454 Article 2 of the CAT makes this clear by saying "no exceptional circumstances whatsoever, whether a state of war or a threat or war, internal political instability or any other public emergency, may be invoked as a justification of torture. An order from a superior officer or a public authority may not be invoked as a justification of torture"; see, also, General Comment No 2, 24 January 2008, UN Doc CAT/C/GC/2 at para 5, which goes on to say that

> it emphasizes that *no exceptional circumstances whatsoever* may be invoked by a State Party to justify acts of torture in any territory under its jurisdiction. The Convention identifies as among such circumstances a state of war or threat thereof, internal political instability or any other public emergency. This includes any threat of terrorist

universal jurisdiction over acts of torture and prosecute or extradite alleged offenders present on their territory.[455]

With respect to diplomatic assurances, the Committee against Torture is reluctant to accept them unless strict requirements have been met: they can only be used for states that do not systematically violate the CAT; they can only be used after a thorough examination of the merits of each individual case; and there are clear procedures in place for obtaining and relying on such assurances, including measures of effective monitoring.[456] The Committee against Torture has also stated that assurances "cannot be used as an instrument to avoid the application of the principle of *non-refoulement*, especially in situations where post-expulsion monitoring has not taken place."[457]

> acts or violent crime as well as armed conflict, international or non-international. The Committee is deeply concerned at and rejects absolutely any efforts by States to justify torture and ill-treatment as a means to protect public safety or avert emergencies in these and all other situations. Similarly, it rejects any religious or traditional justification that would violate this absolute prohibition. The Committee considers that amnesties or other impediments which preclude or indicate unwillingness to provide prompt and fair prosecution and punishment of perpetrators of torture or ill-treatment violate the principle of non-derogability.

See, also, Goodwin-Gill & McAdam, above note 2 at 364–65; UN Doc, Report of the Special Rapporteur on Torture and Other Cruel, Inhuman or Degrading Treatment or Punishment, above note 351 at 14, paras 41–42; Jan Doerfel, "The Convention Against Torture and the Protection of Refugees" (2005) 24:2 *Refugee Survey Quarterly* 83 at 92; UN Doc A/CN.4/565, *Expulsion of Aliens*, above note 9 at 351–54, paras 562–65; Wouters, above note 319 at 502–4; the latter two sources mention a case decided by the Committee against Torture indicating that 1F determination would not set aside the absolute character of the prohibition; see, also, Concluding Observations on Israel, 23 June 2009, CAT/C/ISR/CO/4 at para 14, indicating that the necessity or ticking time bomb defence does not apply.

455 *Questions Relating to the Obligation to Prosecute or Extradite (Belgium v Senegal)*, Judgment, 20 July 2012, ICJ Rep (2012) General List, No 133.

456 Concluding Observation on the United States of America, 25 July 2006, CAT/C/USA/CO/2 at para 21; Giuffré, above note 336 at 80–83; Wouters, above note 319 at 496–99, who points out at 500–1 that the fact that a country is a party to human rights treaties is not conclusive on the issue of removal. The United Nations Special Rapporteur on Torture and Other Cruel, Inhuman or Degrading Treatment or Punishment has been of the view that even with such stringent application of assurances the practice of relying on diplomatic assurances should not be used; see Nowak, above note 443 at 687, and UN Doc, Report of the Special Rapporteur on Torture and Other Cruel, Inhuman or Degrading Treatment or Punishment, above note 351 at 66–67, para 243; General Comment No 4, above note 448 at paras 19 & 20; *HY v Switzerland*, 7 September 2017, UN Doc CAT/C/61/D/747/2016.

457 *Tursunov v Kazakhstan*, 8 May 2015, Communication No 538/2013 at para 9.10; European Council on Refugees and Exiles, *ECRE/ELENA Legal Note on Asylum and the UN Treaty System* (Brussels: European Legal Network on Asylum, March 2021) at 26–28, online (pdf): https://ecre.org/wp-content/uploads/2021/03/Legal-Note-8.pdf.

ii) Torture

A former United Nations Special Rapporteur on Torture and Other Cruel, Inhuman or Degrading Treatment has given a comprehensive description of contemporary forms of torture by saying:

> [I]n most cases of torture, victims suffer from brute and unrestrained violence. They were punched and kicked, usually until they passed out; beaten with sticks, truncheons, iron bars, rifle butts, or hammers; flogged with whips or chains; suffocated with plastic bags or gas masks over their head—sometimes chili or similar irritants were added; their skin was burned with cigarettes or hot metal objects; sensitive parts of their bodies, e.g., genitals, were particularly severely beaten or electrocuted. Victims were trampled on their thighs and legs, and had needles forced under their fingernails. Sometimes even shot wounds were intentionally inflicted. The list could be easily extended. The victims are normally handcuffed to a chair or radiator, stripped naked or suspended from the ceiling. In no way is the victim able to protect him or herself.[458]

Rape has also been considered a form of torture,[459] as well as solitary confinement without light and adequate ventilation; hands tied behind the back with arms pulled backward; mock execution; electric shocks

---

458 UN Doc, Report of the Special Rapporteur on Torture and Other Cruel, Inhuman or Degrading Treatment or Punishment, above note 351 at 17, para 51; he goes on to say in the next paragraph that "more sophisticated torture methods are applied with such regularity that they acquired their own names, e.g., 'flying to space' (a person is made to stand on a chair which is eventually kicked away), 'grilled chicken' (a detainee is handcuffed behind the knees and hung upside-down from a pole passed behind the knees and subjected to beatings (also called 'farruj'), 'telephone' (beating with the flat hands on both ears, resulting in temporary or permanent damage to their hearing), 'tiger bench' (the victim is forced to sit motionless on a tiny stool a few centimeters off the ground for a long period of time), 'exhausting an eagle' (the victim is forced to stand on a tall stool and subjected to beatings until exhaustion), 'reversing an airplane' (person has to bend over while holding legs straight, feet close together and arms lifted high). The euphemistic wording only adds to the humiliation and reflects the dehumanisation of the victim."

459 UN Doc, Report of the Special Rapporteur on Torture and Other Cruel, Inhuman or Degrading Treatment or Punishment, above note 351 at 18, para 53; Wouters, above note 319 at 442–43; *Njamba v Sweden*, 3 June 2010, Communication No 322/2007 at para 9.5; Concluding Observations on the Philippines, 29 May 2009, CAT/C/PHL/CO/2 at para 18; Concluding Observations on Cambodia, 20 January 2011, CAT/C/ KHM/CO/2, at paras 15 and 21.

and the threat of being drowned;[460] incommunicado detention;[461] and enforced disappearance.[462]

Although corporal punishment may be permitted by the national law of a state, when a person is deported to a country to be exposed to a sentence of corporal punishment, this punishment has been held to amount to torture.[463] When there are discrepancies between the convention's definition of torture and that incorporated by national law, the Committee against Torture has held that it creates potential loopholes for impunity.[464]

The Committee against Torture has also examined the unique situations of vulnerable groups being subjected to torture, including LGBTQI[465] and persons with disabilities.[466] The Special Rapporteur has drawn an explicit link between discrimination and an enhanced risk of torture and identified specific groups, including women, children, and persons with disabilities.[467]

---

460 Wouters, above note 319 at 443. The practice of water boarding was called torture or cruel, inhuman, or degrading treatment or punishment in Concluding Observation on the United States of America, 25 July 2006, CAT/C/USA/CO/2 at para 24. Prolonged solitary confinement without any aggravating circumstances can amount to inhuman treatment; see UN Doc, Report of the Special Rapporteur on Torture and Other Cruel, Inhuman or Degrading Treatment or Punishment, above note 351 at 62–63, para 234; Concluding Observations on Colombia, 4 May 2010, CAT/C/COL/CO/4 at para 21; Concluding Observations on Israel, above note 454 at para 17; Concluding Observations on Kenya, 19 January 2009, CAT/C/KEN/CO/1 at para 15.

461 Concluding Observations on Yemen, 25 May 2010, CAT/C/YEM/CO/2/Rev.1 at para 12; Concluding Observations on Israel, above note 454 at para 17.

462 Concluding Observations on Yemen, above note 461 at para 13; Concluding Observations on Colombia, 4 May 2010, CAT/C/COL/CO/4 at para 17; Concluding Observations on Honduras, 23 June 2009, CAT/C/HND/CO/1 at para 11; Concluding Observations on Kenya, 19 January 2009, CAT/C/KEN/CO/1 at para 20; Concluding Observations on Ethiopia, 20 January 2011, CAT/C/ETH/CO/1 at para 15.

463 *Rouba Alhaj Ali v Morocco*, 3 August 2016, UN Doc CAT/C/58/D/682/2015 at paras 8.5–8.8.

464 Concluding Observations on the Combined Third to Fifth Period Reports of the United States of America, 19 December 2014, UN Doc CAT/C/USA/CO/3-5 at para 9. Concerned about the United States' definition of psychological torture, the Committee against Torture stated that there are discrepancies between the convention's definition and that incorporated into domestic law, which can create actual or potential loopholes for impunity.

465 Ninth Annual Report of the Subcommittee on Prevention of Torture and Other Cruel, Inhuman or Degrading Treatment or Punishment, 22 March 2016, UN Doc CAT/C/57/4 at paras 48–82.

466 Approach of the Subcommittee on the Prevention of Torture and Other Cruel, Inhuman or Degrading Treatment or Punishment Regarding the Rights of Persons Institutionalized and Treated Medically Without Informed Consent, 26 January 2016, UN Doc CAT/OP/27/2.

467 Seventieth Anniversary of the Universal Declaration of Human Rights: Reaffirming and Strengthening the Prohibition of Torture and Other Cruel, Inhuman or Degrading Treatment or Punishment, 20 July 2018, UN Doc A/73/207 at para 64.

iii) Cruel, Inhuman, or Degrading Treatment or Punishment

The United Nations Special Rapporteur has singled out female genital mutilation[468] and forms of corporal punishment as examples of other modes of ill-treatment. Objectionable corporal punishment includes the use of such practices as judicial sanctions; stoning or public flogging as a penalty for the commission of a crime;[469] disciplinary measures against detainees, such as severe beatings;[470] the infliction of physical and mental suffering, such as severe beatings that were aggravated by the person's particular vulnerability;[471] and severe beatings during arrest.[472] The forceful internment and long-term restraint used in institutions for persons with mental disabilities will also attract the attention of the committee,[473] as will the detention of convicted prisoners on death row, in particular the use of shackles for twenty-four hours a day.[474]

The Special Rapporteur has reported that COVID-19 has caused a deterioration in conditions of detention, including increased use of lethal force and unrestrained police brutality.[475]

d) Inter-American Court of Human Rights[476]

i) General Principles

Article 5.2 of the American Convention on Human Rights (ACHR) says that "no one shall be subjected to torture or to cruel, inhuman, or degrading punishment or treatment." This instrument does not explain these terms, but to establish the scope of this article, the court has

---

468 Report of the Special Rapporteur on Torture and Other Cruel, Inhuman, or Degrading Treatment or Punishment, above note 351 at 54, paras 201–2.

469 *Ibid* at 58–59, paras 216–19.

470 *Ibid* at 59–61, paras 220–28.

471 *Osmani v Republic of Serbia*, 25 May 2009, Communication No 261/2005 at para 10.4.

472 *Keremedchiev v Bulgaria*, 21 November 2008, Communication No 257/2004 at para 9.3.

473 Concluding Observations on Serbia, 19 January 2009, CAT/C/SRB/CO/1 at para 16; Concluding Observations on Bosnia and Herzegovina, 20 January 2011, CAT/C/BIH/CO/2-5 at para 20.

474 Concluding Observations on China, 12 December 2008, CAT/C/CHN/CO/4 at para 34.

475 Lack of Accountability for Torture Worldwide Due to Systemic Denial, Evasion by Public Authorities, Special Rapporteur Tells Third Committee, 12 October 2021, UN Doc GA/SHC/4322.

476 See, in general, Diego Rodríguez-Pinzón, "The Prohibition of Torture and Cruel, Inhuman or Degrading Treatment or Punishment in the Inter-American Human Rights System: Systems, Methods and Recent Trends" in Evans & Modvig, *Research Handbook on Torture*, above note 321 at 203–26.

resorted to the definition of torture under article 2 of the Inter-American Convention to Prevent and Punish Torture,[477] which says:

> [T]orture shall be understood to be any act intentionally performed whereby physical or mental pain or suffering is inflicted on a person for purposes of criminal investigation, as a means of intimidation, as personal punishment, as a preventive measure, as a penalty, or for any other purpose. Torture shall also be understood to be the use of methods upon a person intended to obliterate the personality of the victim or to diminish his physical or mental capacities, even if they do not cause physical pain or mental anguish. The concept of torture shall not include physical or mental pain or suffering that is inherent in or solely the consequence of lawful measures, provided that they do not include the performance of the acts or use of the methods referred to in this article.[478]

The court has recognized that not just persons who have personally suffered torture or ill-treatment are recognized as victims for the purposes of the American convention but also close family members as indirect victims.[479] Following the jurisprudence of the European Court of Human Rights, the Inter-American Court was of the view that certain family members or direct relatives could suffer torture or inhuman treatment, especially in the context of enforced disappearance, based on the reasoning that

> it is possible to understand that the violation of the right to psychic and moral integrity of the next of kin of the victim is a direct consequence, precisely, of that phenomenon, which causes them a severe suffering due to the fact itself, which is increased, among other factors,

---

477 Case of *Tibi v Ecuador*, Judgment of September 7, 2004, Series C No 114 at para 145; see, also, Rodríguez-Pinzón, above note 476 at 207–8.

478 Article 4 of the same instrument says that "the fact of having acted under orders of a superior shall not provide exemption from the corresponding criminal liability," while art 5 sets out the absolute nature of this prohibition of torture by indicating that "the existence of circumstances such as a state of war, threat of war, state of siege or of emergency, domestic disturbance or strife, suspension of constitutional guarantees, domestic political instability, or other public emergencies or disasters shall not be invoked or admitted as justification for the crime of torture. Neither the dangerous character of the detainee or prisoner, nor the lack of security of the prison establishment or penitentiary shall justify torture." See, also, art 27 of the ACHR and Rodríguez-Pinzón, above note 476 at 207 and 223, for the jurisprudence confirming this point.

479 Case of *Juan Humberto Sánchez v Honduras*, Judgment 7 June 2003, Series C No 99 at paras 101–2.

> by the constant negative of the state authorities to provide information regarding the whereabouts of the victim or to start an effective investigation in order to clarify what occurred.[480]

Close family members or direct relatives are considered to be mothers and fathers, sons and daughters, spouses, life partners, or permanent companions.[481] The court has adopted a broad approach as children and siblings of disappeared persons who were not born when the disappearance occurred may still be considered victims as they had to live in an environment of suffering and uncertainty.[482] Other close kin can also be considered victims in the sense of article 5 of the convention, but they have to show that they fall within this class, based on a number of circumstances, such as the closeness of the family relationship, the particular circumstances of the relationship with the victim, the degree to which the family member was a witness of the events related to the disappearance, the way in which the family member was involved in attempts to obtain information about the disappearance of the victim, and the state's response to the steps undertaken.[483]

The court applied these principles to relatives of victims of massacres[484] while leaving open the possibility of extending the circle of victims to other persons, based on the characteristics of the case and

---

480 Case of *Radilla-Pacheco v Mexico*, Judgment of 23 November 2009, Series C No 209 at para 161.

481 Case of *Blake v Guatemala*, Judgment of 24 January 1998, Series C No 36 at para 114; Case of *Tiu Tojín v Guatemala*, Judgment of 26 November 2008, Series C No 190 at para 87; Case of *Anzualdo-Castro v Peru*, Judgment of 22 September 2009, Series C No 202 at para 105; Case of *González et al ("Cotton Field") v Mexico*, Judgment of 16 November 2009, Series C No 205 at paras 415 and 424; Case of *Radilla-Pacheco v Mexico*, Judgment of 23 November 2009, Series C No 209 at para 162; Case of *Chitay-Nech et al v Guatemala*, Judgment of 25 May 2010, Series C No 212 at paras 220–23; see, also, Rodríguez-Pinzón, above note 476 at 224.

482 Case of *Gudiel Álvarez ("Military Journal") v Guatemala*, Judgment of 20 November 2012, Series C No 253 at para 287; Case of *Contreras et al v El Salvador*, Judgment of 31 August 2011, Series C No 232 at para 122.

483 Case of Bámaca Velásquez, Judgment of 25 November 2000, Series C No 70 at para 163; Case of *Escué Zapata v Colombia*, Judgment of 4 July 2007, Series C No 165 at para 119; Case of *Kawas-Fernández v Honduras*, Judgment of 3 April 2009, Series C No 196 at paras 128–29.

484 Case of *Ituango Massacres v Colombia*, Judgment of 1 July 2006, Series C No 148 at paras 260–67; Case of *Vargas Areco*, Judgment of 26 September 2006, Series C No 155 at para 43; Case of *Miguel Castro-Castro Prison v Peru*, Judgment of 25 November 2006, Series C No 160 at para 335; Case of the *Rochela Massacre v Colombia*, Judgment of 11 May 2007, Series C No 163 at para 137; Case of *Escué Zapata v Colombia*, Judgment of 4 July 2007, Series C No 165 at para 106; Case of the *"Las Dos Erres" Massacre v Guatemala*, Judgment of 24 November 2009, Series C No 211 at para 206.

the existence of some special relationship between the next of kin and the victim or the facts of the person in the case.[485]

ii) Torture

The Inter-American Court of Human Rights has considered the human rights violation of enforced disappearance,[486] which is viewed as a continuing, permanent, and multiple offence,[487] as constituting torture. The essential elements are a deprivation of liberty because of acts by the state and a refusal to acknowledge the detention and reveal the fate or the whereabouts of the person involved.[488]

The court said this about the phenomenon of enforced disappearance:

> [W]hen examining an alleged forced disappearance it should be taken into account that the deprivation of liberty of the individual must be understood merely as the beginning of the constitution of a complex violation that is prolonged over time until the fate and whereabouts of the alleged victim are established. In keeping with the above, it is therefore necessary to consider the offense of forced disappearance *in toto*, as an autonomous offense of a continuing or permanent nature with its multiple elements intricately interrelated. Consequently, the examination of a possible forced disappearance should not be approached in an isolated, divided and fragmented manner, considering merely

485 Case of *Ituango Massacres v Colombia*, Judgment of 1 July 2006, Series C No 148 at para 264.

486 Case of *Velásquez Rodriguez*, Judgment of 29 July 1988, Series C No 4 at paras 155–58; Case of *Bámaca Velásquez*, Judgment of 25 November 2000, Series C No 70 at para 165; Case of *La Cantuta v Peru*, Judgment of 29 November 2006, Series C No 162 at para 115; Case of *Radilla-Pacheco v Mexico*, Judgment of 23 November 2009, Series C No 209 at paras 158–59; Case of *Anzualdo-Castro v Peru*, Judgment of 22 September 2009, Series C No 202 at para 86 (this case describes the legal elements of forced disappearance at paras 90–99, including a reference to the Rome Statute at para 95); Case of *Chitay-Nech et al v Guatemala*, Judgment of 25 May 2010, Series C No 212 at paras 94–103; Case of *Vereda la Esperanza and Others v Colombia*, Judgment of 31 August 2017, Series C No 341; Case of *Isaza Uribe and Others v Colombia*, Judgment of 20 November 2018, Series C No 363.

487 Case of *Heliodoro Portugal v Panama*, Judgment of 12 August 2008, Series C No 186 at para 106; Case of *Ticona Estrada et al v Bolivia*, Judgment of 27 November 2008, Series C No 191 at para 62.

488 Case of *Heliodoro Portugal v Panama*, Judgment of 12 August 2008, Series C No 186 at para 110, relying on international instruments, including the Rome Statute; the same analysis was used earlier in Case of *Goiburú et al v Paraguay*, Judgment of 22 September 2006, Series C No 153 at paras 81–85; it has also been said that "forced disappearance constitutes a grave violation of human rights that are non-derogable in character, producing a gross abandonment of the basic principles on which the inter-American system is based"; see Case of *Tiu Tojín v Guatemala*, Judgment of 26 November 2008, Series C No 190 at para 53.

> the detention, or the possible torture, or the risk of loss of life, but rather the focus should be on all the facts presented in the case being considered by the Court.[489]

Corporal punishment by flogging[490] and incommunicado detention involving strict isolation for one year in a crowded cell with other prisoners, without ventilation or natural light, amount to both physical and mental torture.[491]

Mental torture was found to exist where a woman was unlawfully and arbitrarily detained, covered by a hood, and kept handcuffed to a bed in a room with the light on and the radio kept at full volume, preventing her from sleeping. She was also subjected to prolonged interrogations, during which she was shown photographs of individuals who showed signs of torture or had been killed in combat and was threatened that she would be found by her family in the same way. Last, the person interrogating her also threatened to torture her physically or to kill her or members of her family if she did not collaborate. This situation was also found to be physically cruel and inhuman treatment.[492] Rape[493] and violent acts related to the sexual orientation and gender identity of the victim were on the list of specific purposes where sexual violence can constitute torture.[494]

iii) Cruel, Inhuman, or Degrading Punishment or Treatment

According to the court, "intensity of suffering" is the distinguishing factor between torture and cruel, inhuman, or degrading treatment.[495] With respect to prisoners, employing the death penalty by hanging[496] and extensive solitary confinement[497] amount to inhuman treatment, as

---

489 Case of *Heliodoro Portugal v Panama*, Judgment of 12 August 2008, Series C No 186 at para 112; see, also, Rodríguez-Pinzón, above note 476 at 209 and 224.

490 Case of *Caesar v Trinidad and Tobago*, Judgment of 11 March 2005, Series C No 123 at para 88; see, also, Rodríguez-Pinzón, above note 476 at 208.

491 Case of *Cantoral Benavides*, Judgment of 18 August 2000, Series C No 69 at paras 83–105.

492 Case of *Maritza Urrutia v Guatemala*, Judgment of 27 November 2003, Series C No 103 at paras 84–94.

493 Rodríguez-Pinzón, above note 476 at 208.

494 Case of *Azul Rojas Marín and Others v Peru*, Judgment of 12 March 2020, Series C No 402 at para 163.

495 Case of *Caesar v Trinidad and Tobago*, Judgment of 11 March 2005, Series C No 123 at para 50.

496 Case of *Boyce et al v Barbados*, Judgment of 21 November 2007, Series C No 169 at paras 82–85.

497 Case of *Castillo Petruzzi et al*, Judgment of 30 May 1999, Series C No 52 at paras 192–98; Case of *Hilaire, Constantine and Benjamin et al v Trinidad and Tobago*, Judgment of 21 June

do prolonged isolation and being held incommunicado.[498] Deplorable detention conditions, such as poor hygiene and a lack of adequate lighting and ventilation, victims being kept in their jail cells for twenty-three hours a day for weeks or months at a time, prison overcrowding,[499] and denying essential medical treatment,[500] amounted to cruel and inhuman treatment. In an early case, the court ruled that being detained by the police and placed in the trunk of a police car can amount to inhuman treatment even if no physical or other maltreatment occurred.[501] A combination of being captured, detained for approximately three hours, subjected to threats and intimidation, and then witnessing the execution of colleagues resulted in suffering amounting to inhuman treatment.[502]

Another development in detention is a decision by the Inter-American Commission on Human Rights,[503] where the United States was held to be responsible for the inhuman treatment of a detainee for the purposes of interrogation at Guantánamo.[504] Specifically, the commission found that the detainee was subjected to practices amounting to torture and inhuman treatment that included chemical exposure, water boarding, sleep deprivation, force-feeding, and prayer disruptions.[505] The commission also held that detainees should not be transferred when there are

---

2002, Series C No 94 at paras 164–72; see, also, Rodríguez-Pinzón, above note 476 at 222 (which refers to decisions by the commission rather than by the court).

498 Case of *Chaparro Álvarez y Lapo Íñiguez v Ecuador*, Judgment of 21 November 2007, Series C No 170 at paras 116–72.

499 Case of *Loayza Tamayo v Perú*, Judgment of 17 September 1997, Series C No 33 at para 58; Case of *García Asto and Ramírez Rojas v Perú*, Judgment of 25 November 2005, Series C No 137 at para 221; Case of *Miguel Castro-Castro Prison v Peru*, Judgment of 25 November 2006, Series C No 160 at para 315; Case of *Boyce et al v Barbados*, Judgment of 21 November 2007, Series C No 169 at paras 90–102; Case of *Yvon Neptune v Haiti*, Judgment of 6 May 2008, Series C No 180 at paras 131–33; see, also, Rodríguez-Pinzón, above note 476 at 209–10 and 217 for other situations.

500 See Rodríguez-Pinzón, above note 476 at 224.

501 Case of *Castillo Páez*, Judgment of 3 November 1997, Series C No 34 at para 66.

502 Case of the *Rochela Massacre v Colombia*, Judgment of 11 May 2007, Series C No 163 at paras 134–36.

503 The inter-American system has two principal entities: the Inter-American Commission on Human Rights and the Inter-American Court of Human Rights. Both bodies have authority to decide individual complaints concerning alleged human rights violations; the commission also engages in monitoring and promotion of human rights–related activities; see Rodríguez-Pinzón, above note 476 at 204–6.

504 Djamel Ameziane (United States of America), Merits Report of 22 April 2020, Case 12.865, Report No 29/20; see, also, Rodríguez-Pinzón, above note 476 at 224.

505 Djamel Ameziane (United States of America), Merits Report of 22 April 2020, Case 12.865, Report No 29/20 at paras 168–70.

"substantial grounds" to believe that there might be a danger of torture or ill-treatment of detainees, and diplomatic assurances should not be used to circumvent the state's *non-refoulement* obligation.[506]

Threats of torture used during an interrogation are also inhuman treatment,[507] while the same was said about continuous harassment, mistreatment, and intimidation by government officials in response to inquiries about the fate of disappeared persons by their relatives.[508]

A failure to provide adequate health care services, including for persons infected with HIV, can result in a finding of cruel and inhuman treatment,[509] as can the severe harassment of human rights defenders and their families.[510]

With respect to diplomatic assurances, the Inter-American Court of Human Rights has followed the same principles established in other international bodies, including the Human Rights Committee and the European Court of Human Rights.[511] In determining whether a presumed victim would face a real, foreseeable, and personal risk if extradited, the court will examine all the information available, including the relevant conditions in the requesting state, the specific circumstances of the presumed victim, and diplomatic assurances.[512]

3) National Jurisprudence

a) Introduction

The jurisprudence regarding the interpretation of the terms derived from the above international instruments as transposed into national legislation varies in both depth of analysis and quantity of decisions. In this section, only the countries under consideration[513] with sufficient

506 Extension of Precautionary Measures Regarding Detainees in Guantánamo Bay, Cuba, 28 October 2005, PM 259/02 at para 10.

507 Case of *Villagran Morales et al* (The "Street Children" Case), Judgment of 19 November 1999, Series C No 63 at para 165; Case of *Tibi*, Judgment of 7 September 2004, Series C No 114 at para 147; Case of *Baldeón García*, Judgment of 6 April 2006, Series C No 147 at para 119; Case of *Ituango Massacres v Colombia*, Judgment of 1 July 2006, Series C No 148 at para 255.

508 Case of *González et al ("Cotton Field") v Mexico*, Judgment of 16 November 2009, Series C No 205 at para 424.

509 See Rodríguez-Pinzón, above note 476 at 224.

510 *Ibid* at 225.

511 Case of *Wong Ho Wing v Peru*, Judgment of 3 June 2015, Serial No 297 at paras 178–82.

512 *Ibid* at para 167.

513 In Europe, the Qualification Directive only allows *refoulement* of refugees "where not prohibited by the international obligations" according to art 21.2.

caselaw to point to a trend will be examined in detail,[514] namely, Canada, France, the Netherlands, the United Kingdom, and the United States, and in those countries only the jurisprudence that has shed light on the interpretation of these terms.[515]

In Australia,[516] it has been said that regular removal will not amount to inhuman treatment,[517] while the same conclusion was reached for mandatory detention of illegal aliens, even if they were children, unless there is a punitive reason for such detention, such as solitary confinement or inordinately long detention.[518]

In Belgium, a person is entitled to subsidiary protection if that person faces torture or inhuman or degrading treatment or punishment.[519] There was a 2008 decision by the Council of State saying, in general, that a claim of *refoulement* would not prevent a tribunal from determining a 1F allegation as this issue only comes into play when a person becomes a subject of deportation action by the government.[520] At the tribunal level, it has been said that, given that Belgium has incorporated the ECHR into national legislation,[521] the jurisprudence of the European Court of Human Rights should be given a great deal of deference in interpreting the parameters of *refoulement*.[522] In this context, many tribunal decisions were issued in 2010 in the context of removing refugees to Greece, which generally did not see an objection to doing so, but

---

514 Outside the parameters of this study, the Supreme Court of Ireland has indicated that female genital mutilation amounts to inhuman treatment; see *Meadows v Minister for Justice, Equality and Law Reform*, [2010] IESC 3 at para 79.

515 While in Canada there is a large body of caselaw in the context of the Pre-Removal Risk Assessment procedure in s 112 of the *IRPA*, above note 17, in most cases the result is based on a conflation of persecution and human rights violations. In France, virtually all the jurisprudence giving meaning to the concepts under discussion stems from the subsidiary protection principles rather than *refoulement*, while in Belgium and the Netherlands, there is a large body of caselaw under s 3 of the ECHR, but most of it is very factual, with general findings as to the presence or absence of inhuman or degrading treatment.

516 For the legislative provisions regarding *refoulement*, see Ch 1, n87 & n88.

517 *M38/2002 v Minister for Immigration & Multicultural & Indigenous Affairs*, [2003] FCAFC 131 at paras 75–78.

518 *Re Woolleys*, [2004] HCA 49 at paras 78 and 186–89.

519 *Aliens Act*, above note 64, s 48/4.2(b); s 55.4 prohibits removal on those grounds, while s 49/2 provides that persons with such status are entitled to stay in Belgium for one year, which can be renewed annually.

520 CE No 184.647, 24 June 2008.

521 *Aliens Act*, above note 64, s 48/4(2)(b).

522 CCE No 40.761, 24 March 2010.

this line of cases was overtaken by a decision of the European Court of Human Rights in January 2011.[523]

In Germany, the legislation has also incorporated the text of the Qualification Directive regarding the parameters of *non-refoulement*.[524] The jurisprudence of the highest administrative court has addressed, in general terms, the issue of direct and indirect *refoulement*[525] and has relied on article 3 of the ECHR[526] or the jurisprudence of the European Court of Human Rights to give meaning to the terms "torture" and "inhuman and degrading treatment"[527] but has not analyzed these parameters in detail.

In New Zealand, where the legislation includes the humanitarian *refoulement* prohibition,[528] no decisions on the interpretation of the term "torture" or "inhuman or degrading punishment or treatment" have been rendered so far.

b) Canada

The legislation prohibits removal to a risk of torture or cruel and unusual treatment or punishment,[529] which it has not defined, while specifically excluding the following circumstances from its application: if the risk is inherent or incidental to lawful sanctions, unless imposed in disregard of accepted international standards, or if the risk is caused by the inability of that country to provide adequate health or medical

---

523 *MSS*, above note 332.

524 Section 4(1) of the *Asylum Act*.

525 Bundesverwaltungsgericht (Federal Administrative Court), BverwG 10 C 13.07, 2 August 2007.

526 Bundesverwaltungsgericht (Federal Administrative Court), BverwG 10 C 51.07, 5 March 2007.

527 Bundesverwaltungsgericht (Federal Administrative Court), BverwG 1 C 14.04, 7 December 2004, and Bundesverwaltungsgericht (Federal Administrative Court), BverwG 10 C 5.09, 27 April 2010, both dealing with a removal of a PKK (Kurdistan Workers' Party) member to Turkey; more recently, the issue of possible removal to torture was addressed indirectly when this court stated that such a risk presupposes that the authorities of the state to which a person was going to be removed were aware of the specific reasons for the deportation; see Bundesverwaltungsgericht (Federal Administrative Court), BverwG 1 A 3.17, 22 August 2017 at para 38.

528 The *Immigration Act 2009*, above note 111, s 164(4), prohibits removal of refugees and protected persons, the latter defined as persons who might face torture or cruel treatment.

529 *IRPA*, above note 17, s 115(1); however, an exception is made along the same lines as art 33.2 of the Refugee Convention in s 115(2). If a person is found to be within the exception set out in s 115(2), they are still entitled to a Pre-Removal Risk Assessment, according to s 112(1), and entitled to refugee status if a risk exists, but if the person has a serious criminal background, the effect of this assessment will be a stay of removal until the situation in their country of refuge changes for the better in terms of human rights (ss 114(1)(b) & 114(2)).

care.[530] A manual provides the following examples of physical torture: "electric shocks, beatings, suffocation, burns, sexual assault, prolonged denial of sleep," while for mental torture it lists "creating fear in the victim that they will be killed or that reprisals will be taken against a spouse or children; forcing a person to witness events such as the execution or the torture of other detainees or of family members; or depriving a person of human contact through prolonged isolation."[531]

In general, it has been said that under international law the *refoulement* to torture is an absolute prohibition,[532] although regular deportation does not raise the spectre of human rights violations.[533] With respect to diplomatic assurances, the Supreme Court has ruled that the "human rights record of the government giving the assurances, the government's record in complying with its assurances, and the capacity of the government to fulfill the assurances, particularly where there is doubt about the government's ability to control its security forces," should be taken into account.[534]

Female genital mutilation falls within the parameters of this prohibition.[535] The fact that laws in other countries are harsher than in Canada or the fact that prisons in other countries are not of the same standard as those in Canada does not meet the threshold of the prohibition against *refoulement* unless such harsher treatment will result in ill-treatment.[536]

---

530 *Ibid*, s 97(1)(b)(iii) & (iv), which is the section that deals with conferring protection, but it is likely that it will also apply to the *refoulement* section as well; for a discussion of the second limitation, see *Covarrubias v Canada (Minister of Citizenship and Immigration)*, 2005 FC 1193.

531 Immigration and Refugee Board of Canada (IRB), *Interpretation of Convention Refugee and Person in Need of Protection in the Case Law*, Ch 14, "Persons in Need of Protection" (31 December 2020) at 14.4.1.1, online: https://irb.gc.ca/en/legal-policy/legal-concepts/Pages/RefDef.aspx; see, also, more generally, Immigration, Refugees and Citizenship Canada, "Pre-removal Risk Assessments (PRRAs)" (29 May 2020), online: www.canada.ca/en/immigration-refugees-citizenship/corporate/publications-manuals/operational-bulletins-manuals/refugee-protection/removal-risk-assessment.html.

532 *Suresh*, above note 72 at para 75; *Li v Canada (Minister of Citizenship and Immigration)*, 2005 FCA 1, which also addressed the level of risk required for this prohibition to apply.

533 *Canada (Minister of Employment and Immigration) v Chiarelli*, [1992] 1 SCR 711.

534 *Suresh*, above note 72 at para 125, although it said that under Canadian law such *refoulement* could occur under extraordinary circumstances (at para 76); for more details regarding diplomatic assurances, see *Sing v Canada (Minister of Citizenship and Immigration)*, 2007 FC 361 at paras 128–43.

535 *Alexandria v Canada (Minister of Citizenship and Immigration)*, 2004 FC 1616.

536 *Usta v Canada (Minister of Citizenship and Immigration)*, 2004 FC 1525; *Cure v Canada (Minister of Citizenship and Immigration)*, 2005 FC 637; *Ozunal v Canada (Minister of Citizenship and Immigration)*, 2006 FC 560; all three cases were in relation to prison conditions for army

The jurisprudence has indicated that home invasion, threatening notes, telephone threats, muggings, workplace robbery, motor vehicle destruction, and attempted kidnapping are not serious enough to meet the threshold of cruel and unusual treatment or punishment,[537] nor is mistreatment that does not rise to the level of persecution,[538] being slapped without threat of serious physical harm,[539] detention for lengthy questioning,[540] or constant harassment of civilians at military checkpoints.[541] Generally, hazing practices in the military do not fall within this notion either unless they result in very severe consequences.[542]

Outside the area of *refoulement*, it has been said that indefinite immigration detention would amount to cruel and unusual treatment unless the detention or the conditions are accompanied by a meaningful process of ongoing review that considers the context and circumstances of the individual case.[543]

c) France

The risk of torture or inhuman or degrading punishment or treatment is included in the legislation as part of subsidiary protection,[544] and the jurisprudence has examined the contours of these concepts in terms of past victimization rather than in the context of *refoulement*.[545]

---

deserters in Turkey, and in each case, it was held that removal to such conditions would not amount to cruel or unusual treatment or punishment.

537 *Nasso v Canada (Minister of Citizenship and Immigration)*, 2003 FC 1354.

538 *Kharrat v Canada (Minister of Citizenship and Immigration)*, 2005 FC 106; see, also, *Malik v Canada (Minister of Citizenship and Immigration)*, 2005 FC 1707.

539 *Ghazaryan v Canada (Citizenship and Immigration)*, 2011 FC 1036.

540 *Kuzu v Canada (Citizenship and Immigration)*, 2018 FC 917.

541 *Khalifeh v Canada (Minister of Citizenship and Immigration)*, 2003 FC 1044.

542 *Emirbekov v Canada (Minister of Citizenship and Immigration)*, 2001 FCT 391; *Walcott v Canada (Minister of Citizenship and Immigration)*, 2011 FC 415.

543 *Charkaoui v Canada (Citizenship and Immigration)*, 2007 SCC 9 at para 107; for a general discussion of this form of *refoulement*, see IRB, *Interpretation of Convention Refugee and Person in Need of Protection in the Case Law*, above note 531 at 14.5.

544 Section 512-1 of the *CESEDA*, above note 86; see, also, Sibylle Kapferer, "Exclusion Clauses in Europe: A Comparative Overview of State Practice in France, Belgium and the United Kingdom" (supp, 2000) 12 *International Journal of Refugee Law* 195 at 218.

545 In one recent decision, it was said that a finding by the European Court of Human Rights that a person would be subject to torture or inhumane treatment upon return should be taken into consideration by the authorities; see CE, 3 October 2018, 406222.

Crimes against women have been seen as inhuman or degrading treatment in cases of repeated instances of severe wife abuse;[546] serious sexual crimes;[547] a minor forced into prostitution;[548] the fear of becoming the victim of a honour crime;[549] forced marriage;[550] and 100 lashes with a whip for adultery.[551] While undergoing female genital mutilation is inhuman treatment,[552] the risk of a mother having to watch this happen to her daughter is not.[553] Death threats have also been considered to reach the level of violence to fall within the parameters of this form of subsidiary protection.[554]

With respect to inhuman treatment related to criminal justice, it was held that six months' imprisonment for fraud in Jordan did not lead to the operation of this prohibition,[555] or five to six years' imprisonment for desertion in Algeria,[556] or the payment of a fine of €200 for religious desecration in the Comores.[557]

d) The Netherlands

A person can obtain a temporary resident permit if they fear torture or inhuman or degrading treatment or punishment upon removal.[558]

In interpreting this provision, the jurisprudence of the European Court of Human Rights[559] has played a crucial role, while the Dutch

546 CRR, 19 July 2006, 526541, Mme M; CRR, 26 January 2006, 463518, Mlle A; CRR, 2 November 2007, 412955, Mme T ép M Touvier; CNDA, 4 July 2008, 616623, Mlle V; CNDA, 3 April 2008, 584799, Mlle A.

547 CRR, 28 February 2006, 501569, Mlle B; CRR, 28 April 2006, 550589, Mme S épouse T.

548 CRR, 9 March 2006, 548670, Mlle B; CRR, 12 July 2007, 581079, Mlle S.

549 CRR, 16 February 2006, 552561, Mlle M.

550 CRR, 16 February 2006, 552561, Mlle M; CRR, 11 January 2007, 550107, Mlle S.

551 CRR, 9 June 2006, 550721, M.

552 CNDA, 12 March 2009, 638891, Mme D ép K; CNDA, 12 March 2009, 639908, Mlle K.

553 CNDA, 12 March 2009, 638891, Mme D ép K.

554 CRR, 14 February 2007, 540585, H.

555 CRR, 8 November 2005, 522959, N.

556 CNDA, 27 June 2008, 623320, B.

557 CRR, 2 July 2007, 597313, C.

558 Section 29.1(b) of the *Aliens Act*, above note 64.

559 Rb, The Hague, Awb 02/24179, 27 June 2002; Rb, The Hague, Awb 07/31032, 18 September 2007; Rb, The Hague, Awb 07/31755, 15 December 2007; Rb, The Hague, Awb 07/24266, 30 January 2008; Rb, The Hague, Awb 08/196, 22 July 2008; Rb, The Hague, Awb 08/1988, 23 July 2008; Rb, The Hague, Awb 08/34931, 08/34930, 29 April 2009; Rb, The Hague, Awb 09/38004, 2 November 2010; AbRS, 5 July 2010, nr 200908706/1/V1; AbRS, 17 September 2010, nr 200708704/1/V2.

district courts and Council of State have also provided meaning to these terms where novel situations warranted such an approach.

One regulation applies article 3 of the ECHR to a specific situation where Afghani women have adopted a Western lifestyle upon arrival in the Netherlands, which could result in severe difficulties upon return to Afghanistan.[560] In other situations, female genital circumcision is seen as a form of inhuman treatment,[561] while it is possible that, in exceptional circumstances and because of urgent reasons of a humanitarian nature, a removal to a country with a severe lack of medical and social services can amount to a violation of article 3 in the case of a medical condition,[562] as can the lack of housing.[563] The same can be said for removal to another country resulting in detention with deplorable conditions.[564] On the other hand, removal to a country that has suffered an earthquake or other natural disaster does not amount to inhuman or degrading treatment.[565]

e) United Kingdom

The prohibition against *refoulement* based on human rights considerations is set out in the *Immigration Rules*, which say: "A deportation order will not be made against any person if his removal in pursuance of the order would be contrary to the United Kingdom's obligations under the Convention and Protocol Relating to the Status of Refugees or the Human Rights Convention."[566] The implementation of this rule is contained in a government manual[567] that provides guidance with

---

560 *Vreemdelingencirculaire* 2000 (B), arts B8/10; for an interpretation of this section, see Rb, The Hague, Awb 07/12408, 07/12377, 1 April 2009; AbRS, 13 December 2010, nr 201000606/1/V1; AbRS, 11 June 2010, nr 200902991/1/V1.

561 AbRS, 20 April 2009, nr 200806071/1.

562 Rb, The Hague, Awb 01/69244, 14 February 2003; Rb, The Hague, Awb 02/1094, 02/9908, 02/1095, 02/1130, 2 April 2003; Rb, The Hague, Awb 01/57254, 6 August 2003; Rb, The Hague, Awb 02/34687, 02/34688, 26 August 2003, relying on ECHR caselaw; Rb, The Hague, Awb 01/69576, 14 June 2004; Rb, The Hague, Awb 02/60945, 10 February 2005; Rb, The Hague, Awb 05/32958, 05/32947, 25 November 2005, using ECHR cases; Rb, The Hague, Awb 05/38742, 18 July 2007, relying on ECHR caselaw; Rb, The Hague, Awb 06/36045, 15 November 2007; AbRS, 10 July 2009, nr 200901055/1/V3; Rb, The Hague, Awb 08/34130, 15 December 2009.

563 Rb, The Hague, NL 20.15181, NL 20.15183, NL 20.15188, and NL 20.15194, 19 October 2020.

564 Rb, The Hague, 13.706708-10 RK 10/5605, 17 December 2010, in the context of an extradition procedure and relying on ECHR jurisprudence.

565 Rb, The Hague, Awb 10/10927 and 10/10925, 9 April 2010.

566 *Immigration Rules*, above note 116, s 397.

567 Humanitarian Protection in Asylum Claims lodged before 28 June 2022.

respect to the parameters of torture, inhuman treatment, and degrading treatment. The jurisprudence, which has incorporated the judgments of the European Court of Human Rights on every occasion, has also made it clear that the prohibition against *refoulement* under article 3 of the ECHR is absolute,[568] while it also applies to indirect *refoulement*.[569]

Reliance on diplomatic assurances should be used with caution, especially with respect to countries that violate human rights. But in specific situations where a detailed memorandum of understanding between the United Kingdom and another country has been negotiated at the highest level, addressing specific human rights concerns in the country of return, such assurances can be sufficient even if there is no provision for monitoring.[570]

With respect to violations of article 3 of the ECHR, the jurisprudence has addressed issues such as detention conditions and poor medical and living conditions in the country of return. Removal of a person to a prison sentence of life without parole does not violate this article,[571] while bad prison conditions such as overcrowding by themselves do not result in inhuman treatment unless there are "a number of special exacerbating features" related to health, hygiene, sanitation, and medical services.[572] It was found that such conditions were not present in

---

568 *Othman (Jordan) v Secretary of State for the Home Department*, [2008] EWCA Civ 290 at para 14; *Secretary of State for the Home Department v MM (Zimbabwe)*, [2017] EWCA Civ 797 at para 38; see, also, Maria O'Sullivan, *Refugee Law and Durability of Protection: Temporary Residence and Cessation of Status* (New York & Abingdon: Routledge, 2019) at 259–68.

569 *Secretary of State for the Home Department v Nasseri*, [2009] UKHL 23 at para 44; *R (on the Application of Saeedi) v Secretary of State for the Home Department*, [2010] EWHC 705 at paras 94, 139, and 159.

570 *MT (Algeria) & Ors v Secretary of State for the Home Department*, [2007] EWCA Civ 808 at paras 126–32 [*MT & Ors*]; *RB (Algeria) (FC) and another (Appellants) v Secretary of State for the Home Department (Respondent) OO (Jordan) (Original Respondent and Cross-Appellant) v Secretary of State for the Home Department (Original Appellant and Cross-respondent)*, [2009] UKHL 10 at paras 115–17 and 192–93; *QJ v Secretary of State for the Home Department*, SC/84/2009 (SIAC) at paras 25–27; see, also, *BB, PP, W, U & Ors v Secretary of State for the Home Department*, [2015] EWCA Civ 9 at paras 27–42; see, also, Sarah Singer, "'Undesirable and Unreturnable' in the United Kingdom" (2017) 36:1 *Refugee Survey Quarterly* 9 at 14–15.

571 *Wellington R (On the Application of) v Secretary of State for the Home Department*, [2008] UKHL 72 at paras 36, 46, 53, 62, and 89; this was an extradition case.

572 *SH (prison conditions) Bangladesh CG*, [2008] UKAIT 00076 at para 36; see, also, *BB, PP, W, U & Ors v Secretary of State for the Home Department*, [2015] EWCA Civ 9 at paras 20–26. The Humanitarian Protection in Asylum Claims lodged before 28 June 2022, above note 567, states the following at 17:

Bangladeshi[573] or Algerian[574] prisons, but the courts reached the opposite conclusion for Ukraine[575] and Russia.[576]

With respect to persons who have a serious medical condition and cannot receive the same level of medical care in the country of removal compared to the country of refuge, the judiciary has been reluctant to read in a prohibition on those grounds, or, in the words of the House of Lords, such persons "cannot claim any entitlement to remain in the territory of a contracting state in order to continue to benefit from medical, social or other forms of assistance provided by the expelling state. For an exception to be made where expulsion is resisted on medical grounds the circumstances must be exceptional."[577] The parameters of exceptional circumstances were recently clarified by requiring a significant reduction in life expectancy in the country of removal due to the lack of medical facilities in the country that removed the person.[578] However, if a person has been so traumatized by events in the past that return to the country of origin would result in suicide, article 3 can be engaged.[579]

> Prison conditions which are systematically inhumane and life-threatening are contrary to Article 3 of the ECHR. However, even if conditions are not severe enough to meet that high threshold, Article 3 may still be breached if, due to the individual's personal circumstances, detention would amount to inhuman or degrading treatment. This will depend on a combination of the following factors: the likely length of detention; the type and conditions of detention facilities; the individual's age, gender, vulnerability, physical or mental health; any other relevant factors taking all evidence into account. If the sentence or prison regime, irrespective of its severity, is discriminatory or disproportionately applied for reasons of race, religion, nationality, membership of a particular social group or political opinion, the claimant may qualify as a refugee.

573 *SH (prison conditions) Bangladesh CG*, [2008] UKAIT 00076 at para 37.

574 *MT & Ors*, above note 570 at para 173.

575 *TV (Ukraine—prison conditions) Ukraine*, [2004] UKIAT 00222 at para 23; *PS (prison conditions; military service) Ukraine CG*, [2006] UKAIT 00016 at para 100.

576 *Batayav v Secretary of State for the Home Department*, [2003] EWCA Civ 1489 at para 21, and *ZB (Russian prison conditions) Russian Federation CG*, [2004] UKIAT 00239 at para 23.

577 *N v Secretary of State for the Home Department*, [2005] UKHL 31 at para 48; *GS (India) & Ors v The Secretary of State for the Home Department*, [2015] EWCA Civ 40 at para 84; *Secretary of State for the Home Department v MM (Zimbabwe)*, [2017] EWCA Civ at paras 39–43; with respect to mental health problems, it was said that they do not fall within the notion of exceptional; see *KH (Afghanistan)*, [2009] EWCA Civ 1354 at para 3.

578 *AM (Zimbabwe) (Appellant) v Secretary of State for the Home Department (Respondent)*, [2020] UKSC 17 at para 30; the court is disinclined to follow the jurisprudence of the ECHR, which had imposed a stricter standard by requiring a death within a short time; see at paras 31–34.

579 *Y (Sri Lanka) v The Secretary of State for the Home Department; Z (Sri Lanka) v The Secretary of State for the Home Department*, [2009] EWCA Civ 362 at paras 62–65.

The jurisprudence regarding poor living conditions deals with the issue of whether becoming homeless and destitute when deported to another country can amount to inhuman treatment. The House of Lords was of the view that in extreme circumstances the spectre of article 3 can be raised

> when it appears on a fair and objective assessment of all relevant facts and circumstances that an individual applicant faces an imminent prospect of serious suffering caused or materially aggravated by denial of shelter, food or the most basic necessities of life. Many factors may affect that judgment, including age, gender, mental and physical health and condition, any facilities or sources of support available to the applicant, the weather and time of year and the period for which the applicant has already suffered or is likely to continue to suffer privation.[580]

This approach was further refined by the Supreme Court when it said:

> Although one starts with a significant evidential presumption that listed states will comply with their international obligations, a claim that such a risk is present is not to be halted *in limine* solely because it does not constitute a systemic or systematic breach of the rights of refugees or asylum seekers. Moreover, practical realities lie at the heart of the inquiry; evidence of what happens on the ground must be capable of rebutting the presumption if it shows sufficiently clearly that there is a real risk of article 3 ill-treatment if there is an enforced return.[581]

f) United States

A person cannot be removed from the United States if this removal would result in torture as defined by the CAT.[582] The legislation has provided detailed definitions of all aspects related to the concept of torture by saying:

---

580 *R (Limbuela) v Secretary of State for the Home Department*, [2005] UKHL 66 at paras 8 and 59-63; it was decided that for return to Italy, these conditions were not met; see *R (EW) v Secretary of State for the Home Department*, [2009] EWHC 2957 at para 100.

581 *R (on the application of EM (Eritrea) and Others v SSHD (Respondent)*, [2014] UKSC 12; see, also, Asylum Policy Instructions on Humanitarian Protection, above note 120 at 13.

582 *The Code of Federal Regulations*, Title 8, § 208.16(c)(1); § 208.16(c)(4), indicates that such a person is entitled to deferral of removal.

(1) Torture is defined as any act by which severe pain or suffering, whether physical or mental, is intentionally inflicted on a person for such purposes as obtaining from him or her or a third person information or a confession, punishing him or her for an act he or she or a third person has committed or is suspected of having committed, or intimidating or coercing him or her or a third person, or for any reason based on discrimination of any kind, when such pain or suffering is inflicted by or at the instigation of or with the consent or acquiescence of a public official or other person acting in an official capacity. Pain or suffering inflicted by a public official who is not acting under color of law shall not constitute pain or suffering inflicted by or at the instigation of or with the consent or acquiescence of a public official acting in an official capacity or other person acting in an official capacity, although a different public official acting in an official capacity or other person acting in an official capacity could instigate, consent to, or acquiesce in the pain or suffering inflicted by the public official who is not acting under color of law.

(2) Torture is an extreme form of cruel and inhuman treatment and does not include lesser forms of cruel, inhuman or degrading treatment or punishment that do not amount to torture.

(3) Torture does not include pain or suffering arising only from, inherent in or incidental to lawful sanctions. Lawful sanctions include judicially imposed sanctions and other enforcement actions authorized by law, including the death penalty, but do not include sanctions that defeat the object and purpose of the Convention Against Torture to prohibit torture.

(4) In order to constitute torture, mental pain or suffering must be prolonged mental harm caused by or resulting from:

(i) The intentional infliction or threatened infliction of severe physical pain or suffering;

(ii) The administration or application, or threatened administration or application, of mind altering substances or other procedures calculated to disrupt profoundly the senses or the personality;

(iii) The threat of imminent death; or

(iv) The threat that another person will imminently be subjected to death, severe physical pain or suffering, or the administration or application of mind altering substances or other procedures calculated to disrupt profoundly the sense or personality.

> (5) In order to constitute torture, an act must be specifically intended to inflict severe physical or mental pain or suffering. An act that results in unanticipated or unintended severity of pain and suffering is not torture.
>
> (6) In order to constitute torture an act must be directed against a person in the offender's custody or physical control.
>
> (7) Acquiescence of a public official requires that the public official, prior to the activity constituting torture, have awareness of such activity and thereafter breach his or her legal responsibility to intervene to prevent such activity. Such awareness requires a finding of either actual knowledge or willful blindness. Willful blindness means that the public official acting in an official capacity or other person acting in an official capacity was aware of a high probability of activity constituting torture and deliberately avoided learning the truth; it is not enough that such public official acting in an official capacity or other person acting in an official capacity was mistaken, recklessly disregarded the truth, or negligently failed to inquire. In order for a public official to breach his or her legal responsibility to intervene to prevent activity constituting torture, the official must have been charged with preventing the activity as part of his or her duties and have failed to intervene. No person will be deemed to have breached a legal responsibility to intervene if such person is unable to intervene, or if the person intervenes but is unable to prevent the activity that constitutes torture.[583]

The same legislation also allows for the possibility of obtaining diplomatic assurances from the country to which a person who might be subject to torture could be removed, including an assessment of the reliability of such assurances.[584] With respect to the purpose portion of the definition, torture does not have to be based on a specific enumerated ground since it also refers to any reason based on discrimination.[585]

Rape can be torture,[586] as can severe domestic violence[587] and female genital mutilation.[588] Being tied up naked in a painful position for

583 *Ibid*, § 208.18(a).

584 *Ibid*, § 208.18(c).

585 *Zheng v Ashcroft*, 332 F3d 1186 (9th Cir 2003).

586 *Zubeda v Ashcroft*, 333 F3d 463 (3d Cir 2003).

587 *Ali v Reno*, 237 F3d 591 (6th Cir 2001).

588 *Nwaokolo v INS*, 314 F3d 303 (7th Cir 2002); *Mohammed v Ashcroft*, 400 F3d 785 (9th Cir 2005); *Musa v Lynch*, 813 F3d 1019 (7th Cir 2016).

twenty-five days in the hot desert sun while being regularly beaten and whipped until the skin breaks open on the person's back and feet also amounts to torture.[589] Forcible stretching of the legs to a 180-degree position, causing the leg and groin muscles to tear, would also qualify as such,[590] as would 400 lashes with a whip;[591] sustained and severe beatings over a one-month period combined with being burned with cigarettes;[592] threat of assassination;[593] and being beaten, forced to watch a rape, and subjected to a threat that their own wife would be raped.[594] In a situation in Cameroon, a combination of beatings, abduction, and deplorable detention conditions was found to amount to torture.[595]

However, a combination of detention, criminal incarceration, physical abuse, and re-education through labour[596] would not reach this threshold, nor would a severe beating by sticks and belts while in detention for a month[597] or a loss of property.[598] Discrimination with occasional physical violence does not amount to torture.[599] The legislation requires a specific intent on the part of the torturer:

> [F]or an act to constitute torture, there must be a showing that the actor had the intent to commit the act as well as the intent to achieve the consequences of the act, namely the infliction of the severe pain and suffering. In contrast, if the actor intended the act but did not intend the consequences of the act, *i.e.*, the infliction of the severe pain and suffering, although such pain and suffering may have been a foreseeable consequence, the specific intent standard would not be satisfied.[600]

In a specific application with respect to bad prison conditions in Haiti, this meant that although Haitian authorities were intentionally

589 *Nuru v Gonzales*, 404 F3d 1207 (9th Cir 2005).
590 *Chhokar v Gonzales*, Docket No 03-71599 (9th Cir 2005).
591 *Al-Mousa v Mukasey*, 545 F3d 694 (9th Cir 2008).
592 *Al-Saher v INS*, 268 F3d 1143 (9th Cir 2001).
593 *Comollari v Ashcroft*, 378 F3d 694 (7th Cir 2004).
594 *Namo v Gonzales*, 401 F3d 453 (6th Cir 2005).
595 *Tchemkou v Gonzales*, 495 F3d 785 (5th Cir 2007).
596 *Zhou v Gonzales*, 437 F3d 860 (9th Cir 2006).
597 *Kumar v Gonzales*, 444 F3d 1043 (9th Cir 2006).
598 *Jo v Gonzales*, 458 F3d 104 (2d Cir 2006).
599 *Pamphile v Garland*, 854 Fed Appx 408 (2d Cir 2021).
600 *Auguste v Ridge & Ashcroft*, 395 F3d 722 (3d Cir 2005), overruling *Zubeda v Ashcroft*, 333 F3d 463 (3d Cir 2003), which had said that no specific intent was required.

detaining criminal deportees knowing that the detention facilities were substandard, there was no evidence that they were intentionally and deliberately creating and maintaining such prison conditions in order to inflict torture. Detention in a backward prison system does not by itself constitute torture[601] even if the conditions are subhuman and deplorable since they were part of a general situation and not inflicted to cause pain and suffering.[602] The only exception would be made for an HIV-positive, wheelchair-bound double amputee as they would not be able to obtain food or water given their disabilities and the aggressive behaviour of other detainees to obtain nourishment, nor would they be able to obtain any meaningful medical treatment. The basis for this different reasoning is that they would be singled out for torture beyond what was faced by the general prison population.[603] Lengthy periods of solitary confinement without other aggravating circumstances do not amount to torture.[604]

With respect to public officials, it has been held that a village elder in Burkina Faso,[605] a tribal chieftain in Niger,[606] and landlords in Honduras[607] do not fall within the notion of government authorities, nor do insurgents against the Iraqi government that the government could not control[608] or the Revolutionary Armed Forces of Colombia (FARC) for the same reason.[609] A person who might face torture in Somalia can be removed as "Somalia currently has no central government, and the clans who control various sections of the country do so through continued warfare and not through official power."[610]

---

601 *Auguste v Ridge & Ashcroft*, 395 F3d 722 (3d Cir 2005); *Robert v Ashcroft*, Docket No 03-6093-43 (5th Cir 2004); *Toussaint v Attorney General of the US*, 455 F3d 409 (3d Cir 2006); *Pierre v Gonzales*, 502 F3d 109 (2d Cir 2007). The same was said for deplorable conditions in mental hospitals in Mexico in *Villegas v Mukasey*, 523 F3d 984 (9th Cir 2008).

602 *Lavira v AG of United States*, 478 F3d 158 (3d Cir 2007); see, also, *Gonzales v Garland*, 2022 US App LEXIS 8698 (8th Cir 2022).

603 *Lavira, ibid*; however, the *Lavira* case was overruled a year later by *Pierre v Attorney General of US*, 528 F3d 180 (3d Cir 2008), which applied the specific intent standard again to the Haitian situation; see, also, *Jean-Pierre v US Attorney General*, 500 F3d 1315 (11th Cir 2007), and for a Nigerian prison situation, *Eneh v Holder*, Docket No 05-75264 (9th Cir 2010).

604 *Gallina v Wilkinson*, 988 F3d 137 (2d Cir 2021); unusually, the court referred to international jurisprudence to come to this conclusion.

605 *Tun v United States INS*, 445 F3d 554 (2d Cir 2006).

606 *Haoua v Gonzales*, 472 F3d 227 (4th Cir 2007).

607 *Ontunez-Tursios v Ashcroft*, 303 F3d 341 (5th Cir 2002); *Garcia-Milian v Holder*, 755 F3d 1026 (9th Cir 2014); *Fajardo-Paz v Barr*, 776 Fed Appx 539 (9th Cir 2019).

608 *Hadad v Ashcroft*, Docket No 03-4285 (6th Cir 2005).

609 *Tamara-Gomez v Gonzales*, 447 F3d 345 (5th Cir 2006).

610 *D-Muhumed v US Attorney General*, 388 F3d 814 (11th Cir 2004).

Acquiescence by a government does not mean that there has to be official consent or approval or even actual knowledge or wilful acceptance but only that government officials were aware of the torture or remained wilfully blind.[611] A general ineffectiveness on the government's part to investigate and prevent crime will not suffice to show acquiescence.[612] Allowing a rebel group, as part of peace talks, to maintain control over large parts of the country in which they carry out torture could amount to acquiescence,[613] while the same was said where a person had been kidnapped and beaten and then filed five reports with the police, who took no action.[614] On the other hand, general government actions against militant Muslim organizations resulting in the decline of torture committed by such groups would counter an allegation of acquiescence,[615] as would a specific investigation by the government into the activities of an individual.[616] There is also a lack of acquiescence if the government is aware that torture is taking place in its country but is unable to stop it.[617]

A person who faced the death penalty for desertion and the shooting of a superior officer in Ethiopia was found not to face torture as this prohibition does not include pain and suffering inherent in or incidental to lawful sanctions, including the death penalty.[618] However, such sanctions must be imposed by a court and cannot be meted out without judicial involvement, even if it involved desertion during a war.[619] As

---

611 *Zheng v Ashcroft*, above note 585; *Cruz-Funez v Gonzales*, 406 F3d 1187 (10th Cir 2005); *Khouzam v Ashcroft*, 361 F3d 161 (2d Cir 2004); *Ochoa v Gonzales*, 406 F3d 1166 (9th Cir 2005); *Rafiq v Gonzales*, 468 F3d 165 (2d Cir 2006); *Amir v Gonzales*, 467 F3d 921 (6th Cir 2006); *Ornelas-Chavez v Gonzales*, 458 F3d 1052 (9th Cir 2006); *Silva-Regifo v Attorney General of US*, 473 F3d 58 (3d Cir 2007); *Morales v Gonzales*, 478 F3d 972 (9th Cir 2007). It is also not a requirement that a victim would be under the control or custody of public officials in order for the prohibition to operate, according to *Azanor v Ashcroft*, 364 F3d 1015 (9th Cir 2004). For an analysis of this caselaw, see Patricia J. Freshwater, "The Obligation of Non-refoulement Under the Convention against Torture: When Has a Foreign Government Acquiesced in the Torture of Its Citizens?" (2005) 19 *Georgetown Immigration Law Journal* 585 at 594–600.

612 *Garcia-Milian v Holder*, 755 F3d 1026 (9th Cir 2013); *Andrade-Garcia v Lynch*, 828 F3d 829 (9th Cir 2016).

613 *Delgado v Mukasey*, 508 F3d 702 (2d Cir 2007).

614 *Valdiviezo-Galdamez v Attorney General of the US*, 502 F3d 285 (3d Cir 2007).

615 *Purwanto v Gonzales*, 498 F3d 822 (8th Cir 2007).

616 *Menjivar v Gonzales*, 416 F3d 918 (5th Cir 2005); *Miah v Mukasey*, 519 F3d 784 (8th Cir 2008).

617 *Mouawad v Gonzales*, 479 F3d 589 (8th Cir 2007).

618 *Yohanns v Ashcroft*, Docket No 03-60171 (5th Cir 2004).

619 *Nuru v Gonzales*, above note 589.

well, punitive treatment that is feared as retaliation for criminal acts or as part of a system of sanctions lawful in the country of removal may nevertheless constitute torture if that punitive treatment defeated the objective and purpose of the CAT.[620]

4) Observations

The jurisprudence at the international level with respect to the concepts of torture and cruel, inhuman, or degrading treatment or punishment is generally quite consistent, with some minor differences that are at times the result of a different mandate or different fact situation. In terms of mandate, the Committee against Torture is the most limited in that, unlike the definitions in three other authorizing instruments, the definitions of both types of prohibited conduct only fall within the CAT if there is state involvement, except in the specific situation of deportation. In addition, the definition of torture in the CAT has two additional limitations: a particular purpose and the fact that pain and suffering incidental to lawful sanctions do not amount to torture. In practice, it is the state involvement requirement that has set apart the reach of the CAT the most when compared to the ECHR, the ICCPR, and the ACHR. While not exclusive to the CAT, it has been said that torture is not only different from other forms of ill-treatment in terms of the severity of the suffering but also that it needs the mental requirement of intent, the infliction of such treatment.

While only the CAT contains a specific prohibition against *refoulement*, this has been read in by the European Court of Human Rights and the Human Rights Committee with respect to the conventions they administer. The Inter-American Court of Human Rights has interpreted its authorizing instrument only with respect to violations that occurred on the territory of the parties to the ACHR.

All four institutions subscribe to the notion that the prohibition against torture and other ill-treatment is absolute and non-derogable, which is at times expressed as a *jus cogens* norm, especially by the Inter-American Court of Human Rights. Similarly, the three institutions that have addressed the issue of *refoulement* have extended this prohibition to both direct and indirect *refoulement*, while all three in

620 *Tun v United States INS*, 445 F3d 554 (2d Cir 2006); *Gallina v Wilkinson*, 988 F3d 137 (2d Cir 2021).

this context have expressed grave concerns about utilizing diplomatic assurances with countries that have a poor human rights record to deport persons who might otherwise be at risk of ill-treatment. The two United Nations committees have specifically indicated that a person who has been found excluded for 1F reasons is still entitled to a human rights *refoulement* assessment. As well, all four institutions have made it clear that torture is the most severe form of suffering, both physical and mental, followed by inhuman treatment and degrading treatment. The jurisprudence of the four institutions has tended to develop in some isolation from the work done by their equivalent bodies, except for the Inter-American Court of Human Rights, which regularly refers to the caselaw of the European Court of Human Rights.

In terms of the infliction of torture, the jurisprudence of the four institutions is quite similar in terms of acts that amount to torture, especially in interrogations or detentions. One exception to this consistency is forced disappearance, which is seen by the Committee against Torture and the Inter-American Court on Human Rights as torture but as inhuman treatment by the European Court on Human Rights and the Human Rights Committee. While all four institutions have found that solitary confinement and being held incommunicado amount to inhuman treatment, the Committee against Torture and the Inter-American Court of Human Rights have at times elevated such detention conditions to torture, while the Inter-American Court of Human Rights has also considered severe forms of corporal punishment, such as flogging, as torture, and the Committee against Torture believes that such punishments are usually inhuman treatment.

Another difference in the appreciation of a particular fact situation can be seen where a person was forced to remain standing while hooded for a long period, during which he fell and broke his leg, resulting in permanent physical damage. This was considered torture by the Human Rights Committee but inhuman treatment by the European Court of Human Rights. Outside the interrogation and detention situations, all four institutions have considered rape and other forms of sexual violence to be torture.

Mental torture has been accepted in situations of mock execution (Human Rights Committee, Committee against Torture); mock amputation (Human Rights Committee); and threat of torture or ill-treatment against the person (European Court of Human Rights, Human Rights Committee, Inter-American Court of Human Rights) or against the person's family (Human Rights Committee, Inter-American Court of Human Rights).

The Inter-American Court of Human Rights has given special attention to indirect victims of torture. While the European Court of Human Rights, in the context of forced disappearance as inhuman treatment, has made it clear that close family members of disappeared persons are subjected to mental suffering, the Inter-American Court of Human Rights has extended this principle in two directions. First, in addition to close family members or direct relatives, others can also be considered victims based on a number of circumstances, such as the closeness of the family relationship, the particular circumstances of the relationship with the victim, the degree to which the family member was a witness to the events related to the disappearance, the way in which the family member was involved in attempts to obtain information about the disappearance of the victim, and the state's response to the steps undertaken. Second, both categories of victims have been extended to massacres.

With respect to cruel, inhuman, or degrading treatment or punishment, all four institutions have often collapsed these terms and referred to certain situations by employing all of them without a distinction. In particular, the term "cruel," which is not used in the ECHR, or the term "punishment" has rarely been the subject of a separate discussion, while "degrading" has been given a distinct meaning by both the European Court of Human Rights and the Human Rights Committee. Both institutions have indicated that strip searches or other intimate treatment is degrading if carried out in the presence of the opposite sex, while humiliating treatment during detention, such as soaking a prisoner's bed while confining them to a very small cell, theft of their personal effects, and displaying a person in a cage to the press, were found to be degrading by the Human Rights Committee. The European Court of Human Rights came to the same conclusion where a prisoner had his head shaved without justification.

Most decisions regarding inhuman treatment were made in the context of arrest and detention. All four institutions recognize that arrest and detention will at times involve the use of force or unpleasant conditions in a prison, but if a certain threshold is exceeded, then such treatment has entered the realm of the inhuman.

With respect to arrests and interrogations, severe beatings and interrogation techniques combining wall standing, hooding, being subjected to continuous loud and hissing sounds, and deprivation of sleep, food, and drink amounted to inhuman treatment according to the European Court of Human Rights, the Committee against Torture, and the Human Rights Committee, while the latter came to the same conclusion when psychotropic drugs were used.

There is agreement that certain extreme practices in respect to prisoners, such as being subject to the death penalty, lifelong or prolonged detention, or being in solitary confinement, do not necessarily attract negative attention in terms of inhuman treatment, but the following examples would bring into play a consideration of inhuman treatment: a death penalty due to an unfair trial (European Court of Human Rights); the death penalty carried out in an inhumane fashion, such as hanging (Inter-American Court of Human Rights); being on death row for a long time and in very restricted circumstances (European Court of Human Rights, Human Rights Committee, Committee against Torture); no system for consideration of release for lengthy incarceration (European Court of Human Rights, Human Rights Committee); and complete sensory and social isolation during solitary confinement (European Court of Human Rights), combined with being held incommunicado and being chained (Human Rights Committee) or for an extensive period of time (Inter-American Court of Human Rights).

Along the same lines, overcrowding in prisons by itself does not result in a violation of the four human rights treaties but, combined with other aspects, such as a lack of food, a lack of adequate bedding, limited access to daylight, and insufficient sanitary conditions (European Court of Human Rights, Inter-American Court of Human Rights) and exposure to extreme temperatures and sleep deprivation for several consecutive days (Human Rights Committee), will reach the threshold set out in these instruments. It is also recognized that prisoners are entitled to proper medical treatment (European Court of Human Right and Inter-American Court of Human Rights).

Detention in other situations, such as mental hospitals and for immigration purposes, will also be scrutinized by international institutions in cases where these are not done according to internationally accepted principles (European Court of Human Rights regarding mental hospitals), when such detention takes place in regular prisons (Human Rights Committee for both types of detention), or with the extensive use of restraints (Committee against Torture in respect to mental institutions).

Outside the area of arrest and detention, crimes against women, such as sexual abuse (European Court of Human Rights); forced sterilization, honour crimes, and domestic violence (European Court of Human Rights and Human Rights Committee); female genital mutilation (European Court of Human Rights, Human Rights Committee, and Committee against Torture); and destruction of homes or property resulting in subsequent deprivation of livelihood and forced eviction (European Court of Human Rights, Committee against Torture) amount to inhuman treatment, as does a lack of health care services according to the Inter-American Court of Human Rights.

While the above situations have occurred in the country of residence of the complainants, it is recognized in general that the principles developed in that context should also inform the contents of the concept of *refoulement*. The European Court of Human Rights has not hesitated to prohibit *refoulement* to countries that have an officially recognized regime of slavery; where a person could be stoned to death for committing adultery; where a person would publicly receive 100 lashes for sexual activity; and where a person would be subjected to intimidation, harassment, and forced labour. The same court has given a great deal of attention to the issue of *refoulement*, in which the starting point is that the mere possibility of ill-treatment on account of an unsettled situation in the receiving country will not amount to inhuman treatment, nor will it in circumstances where a person's state of health or life expectancy might diminish sharply due to illness and a lack of resources in the receiving country, such as not being able to receive the same health treatment for HIV/AIDS.

On the other hand, this same court has been reluctant to read into article 3 any social or economic rights. The inability of persons to regain their original property or employment upon return does not meet the threshold of inhuman treatment, while the same was said with respect to an obligation to provide everyone with a home or to give refugees financial assistance to enable them to maintain a certain standard of living. However, the court has indicated that there might be an exception with respect to the latter issue in the case of a person who is completely dependent on state support in a situation of serious deprivation incompatible with human dignity.

The national jurisprudence, like the international caselaw, has usually not distinguished between torture and cruel, inhuman, or degrading treatment or punishment, except for the United States, which only applies the prohibition against *refoulement* based on torture. European countries have been heavily influenced by the jurisprudence of the

European Court of Human Rights, either by direct reference in general (Belgium and Germany), by direct reference in specific situations (the Netherlands and especially the United Kingdom), or by applying the principles indirectly without specific reference (France). Even in Canada, a non-European country, reference was made to this jurisprudence in a manual.

With respect to diplomatic assurances, this possibility is set out in the US legislation but has not yet been judicially considered. In Canada and the United Kingdom, such assurances are viewed with caution when received from countries with a poor human rights record, although the judiciary in the United Kingdom allowed removal based on assurances in a detailed memorandum of understanding between the United Kingdom and another country, which was negotiated at the highest level and addressed specific human rights concerns in that country.

In terms of ill-treatment, like the international jurisprudence, the courts have acknowledged that regular removal or even *refoulement* does not always engage the human rights treaties. This was said in general terms in Australia and with more specificity in Canada and France with respect to harsher sentencing or prison conditions in foreign countries compared to their own, while the United Kingdom and the Netherlands followed European jurisprudence very closely in determining that bad prison conditions, such as overcrowding, by themselves do not result in inhuman treatment unless there are a number of special exacerbating features related to health, hygiene, sanitation, and medical services.

In the United States, it was said that a combination of beatings, abduction, and deplorable detention conditions would be torture but that this would not be the case for detention, criminal incarceration, physical abuse, and re-education through labour, nor for a severe beating by sticks and belts while in detention for a month. In the United States, it was also held in a number of cases involving deplorable prison conditions in Haiti, at a level seen as inhuman treatment by international institutions, that this did not amount to torture as the specific intent of inflicting such conditions was not present in respect to the person being *refouled* but that such conditions were applicable to all prisoners in that country.

In Canada, it was also held that home invasion, threatening notes, telephone threats, muggings, workplace robbery, motor vehicle destruction, and attempted kidnapping do not meet the inhuman treatment threshold, while the same conclusion was reached in the Netherlands for removal to a country that has suffered an earthquake or other natural disaster. In the United Kingdom and the Netherlands, some attention was given to the question of whether insufficient medical or social care in the country of origin or destitution could be included in inhuman treatment. It was said that that would only be the case in exceptional circumstances.

Where *refoulement* will result in crimes against women, the spectre of torture or inhuman treatment was raised, especially where a woman would be subject to female genital mutilation (Canada, France, the Netherlands, United States), as would severe wife abuse (France, United States); serious sexual crimes (France, United States); a minor forced into prostitution (France); the fear of becoming the victim of an honour crime (France); forced marriage (France); and 100 lashes with a whip for adultery (France), while forced sterilization is considered in the United States to be a form of torture, but not consistently. In this context, it is interesting to note that being forced to watch a rape was seen as torture in the United States, but watching a daughter undergo female genital mutilation was not considered torture in France.

Death threats were also considered prohibited conduct in France, while the examples of torture in the United States tend to be consistent with the level of such treatment considered in international institutions, such as lengthy, severe, and sustained suffering.

With respect to the issue of state officials, the US jurisprudence is generally consistent with that of the Committee against Torture in that in countries with a lack of central control, they both examine whether other groups exercise effective control and, with respect to the notion of acquiescence, they both require that it applies to state officials who knew about torture in their country or were wilfully blind in that respect and did not take steps to prevent such practices.

D. CONCLUSION

This chapter has examined in what circumstances persons with a criminal background can and cannot be removed. Two aspects of the examination warrant further comment: the relationship between exclusion and the *refoulement* provision in the Refugee Convention; and the relationship between that type of removal of undesirable persons and the application of the absolute prohibition set out in the other human rights instruments.

Before embarking on those two queries, it is useful to establish what is meant by undesirable persons under the Refugee Convention. As indicated at the beginning of this chapter, the sequential distinction between exclusion and *refoulement* in the Refugee Convention is not as strictly applied now as it once was. Taking exclusion and *refoulement* together, the following categories of persons with a criminal background can be subject to removal under the Refugee Convention: persons who have committed crimes against peace, war crimes, crimes against humanity, or acts against the purposes and principles of the United Nations, either inside or outside the country of refuge and either before or after coming to the country of refuge; persons who have committed serious non-political crimes but only outside the country of refuge and come to that country after having carried out such activities; persons who are a danger to the security of the country of refuge, which can manifest itself in acts carried out both inside and outside that country; and persons who are a danger to the public order or community of the country of refuge, both in general and preceded by a criminal conviction inside or outside that country.

In practice, the result of this approach in the Refugee Convention means that the area with the potential for the most crimes, common crimes, also has the possibility of the widest gap, especially in respect to crimes committed in the territory of the country of refuge compared to crimes committed outside that country. While the distinction between serious crimes in 1F(b) and particularly serious crimes in article 33.2 has in most cases been illusory (in spite of the urging of the UNHCR to give meaning to the notion of particularly serious), the requirement of a conviction (which so far has always been a conviction for personal conduct rather than extended liability) and the requirement of a separate danger assessment (except in the United States), which in most cases involves a determination regarding the possibility of recidivism, raise the possibility that a number of people carrying out criminal activities in the country of refuge would not be subject to removal, while persons with a similar background would be excluded. The fact that 1F(b) requires a non-political crime does not alter this equation much because the political exception in this exclusion ground has been severely restricted in practice due to the jurisprudence in the countries under consideration.

However, on the other side of the coin is the fact that for the category of persons who can be subject to *refoulement* for common criminality and for which such a removal is restricted to persons who have been convicted, the spectre of additional punishment, removal, can be raised, resulting in more severe treatment than for persons who have committed similar crimes but are not refugees in the country where they are residing. Against this form of distinct treatment based on a person's status, it can be argued that such an imposition also applies to non-citizens in the immigration area, while for both groups, it has been said that immigration and refugee laws fulfill different purposes than in criminal law in respect to persons with a criminal background. These purposes are primarily related to the fact that immigration and refugee status is a privilege; that citizenship, which can usually be obtained after spending many years in a country without adverse indicators, carries additional benefits; and that immigration law and refugee law also have the collective good in mind in more indirect ways than the general deterrence in criminal law.

However, despite the gap noted between 1F(b) and danger cases, it would appear that persons with the most serious criminal backgrounds would be subject to removal under the Refugee Convention. This conclusion regarding the possibly wide circle of persons who can be subject to removal needs to be tempered by the realization that the provisions of the convention cannot be considered anymore without also considering the application of other human rights instruments.

With respect to the relationship between Refugee Convention's *refoulement* and other human rights protection, the first question can be asked whether, due to the absolute prohibition to removal to torture or cruel, inhuman, or degrading treatment or punishment, the danger to the national security, public order, and community has become obsolete since any finding in that regard would be overruled by human rights protections. Such a comment might be an overstatement for two reasons. The first one is that there are forms of suffering that do not reach the level of the ill-treatment described in international human rights instruments but do amount to persecution as regulated by the Refugee Convention. Persons who fall into the latter category cannot be removed unless they have the criminal background prescribed in articles 32.1 and 33.2 of the convention. Second, the protection based on international instruments is seen as a temporary one, and removal will occur when the substantial risk of ill-treatment has subsided, unless the regular protection of the convention, including its exceptions, can be relied upon.

However, while the human rights protection applies to everyone with a risk of exposure to ill-treatment, it might very well be more meaningful for persons with a criminal background as they, as a group, could typically face this type of risk because they will be seen as criminals upon return and face inhuman treatment in detention conditions, which all international human right institutions have identified as a major concern in their work.

In the relationship between *refoulement* under the Refugee Convention and protection under the human rights instruments, which have generally been addressed in separate proceedings in the national practice and jurisprudence (except in Belgium, New Zealand, and the United States), some thought could be given to how far a risk assessment is required to go as part of the convention's *refoulement* examination process. Given the fact that risk is the only consideration for human rights protection and that two risk assessments would be conducted both at the refugee and the human rights protection stage in the present situation, issues of overlap and time could be of concern. A balancing approach is required in the danger process in Belgium, Canada, France, Germany, and the Netherlands, but a recalibration between the provisions of the Refugee Convention and the human rights treaties in Australia, New Zealand, the United Kingdom, and the United States might be in order.

In examining the nine countries, the general approach with respect to both danger issues under the Refugee Convention and protection granted by international instruments has been fairly similar, with the exception of the United States; as a result of the lower threshold for particularly serious criminality, not using a danger to the community assessment, and only adhering to the more limited form of ill-treatment contained in the CAT, the United States is the least hospitable country for persons with a criminal background.

Finally, whether risk is assessed as part of a danger process, as part of a human rights protection process, or in some combination of the two, it has become clear that the possibility of removing persons with a criminal background to their country of origin has become increasingly difficult for governments that want to ensure that the exclusion and the *refoulement* provisions of the Refugee Convention are enforced.

CHAPTER SEVEN

Alternatives to *Refoulement*

A. INTRODUCTION

When a person cannot be removed because of the risk of torture or cruel, inhuman, or degrading treatment or punishment, but they do not fulfill the requirement to obtain the status of refugee under the Refugee Convention, they are given subsidiary protection status. Since there is an expectation that removal can occur when the human rights situation in the country of removal improves,[1] the benefits of this subsidiary protection status are not the same as with refugee status. Like refugees, they are allowed to stay in the country of refuge, but the rights associated with subsidiary status tend to be fewer, in the sense that while substantive rights, such as the right to education, medical care, and employment, are generally the same,[2] the right to remain in the country of refuge is more conditional than for refugees, which is usually expressed by being granted a permit to stay in the country for a limited time period.[3]

This applies in general to persons with subsidiary status, but such rights are further restricted for persons with a criminal background in that exclusion and at times danger to the security or community

1 See, e.g., the Qualification Directive, art 16.

2 For instance, the rights are the same in Canada (see Intergovernmental Consultations on Migration, Asylum and Refugees, *Asylum Procedures: Report on Policies and Practices in IGC Participating States* (Geneva, December 2015) at 113), online (pdf): www.igc-publications.ch/upload/Asylum_Procedures_Report_2015.pdf; Germany (*ibid* at 198); and the Netherlands (*ibid* at 268) but fewer in Belgium (*ibid* at 79) and the United States (*ibid* at 450–51).

3 This time period (usually with a possibility of extension) is twelve months in Australia (*Asylum Procedures*, *ibid* at 51); one year in Belgium (*ibid* at 79); one year in Germany (*ibid* at 198); five years in the Netherlands (*ibid* at 269); and six months in the United Kingdom (*ibid* at 407).

considerations can also be applied to persons applying for subsidiary status. In such situations, only a suspension on removal until the situation in the country of removal improves is granted,[4] although in some countries this minimal right applies to all persons with subsidiary protection status.[5]

However, the assumption that a situation in a country with serious human rights violations will improve will not always be correct, certainly not in the short term. For that reason, countries have sought other solutions to deal with the conundrum of at times having very serious criminal refugees on their territory whose deportation is prohibited by human right obligations and who are usually not entitled, because of their criminality, to a regular type of immigration status.[6] This chapter will examine the most common devices developed in the countries of interest: the criminal prosecution of criminal refugees, the extradition to their country of origin, long-term detention, and humanitarian solutions.

When assessing the efficacy of those solutions, it should be kept in mind that the population in question differs depending on the type of crimes they have been involved in. For instance, persons who have committed war crimes or crimes against humanity typically will come to a country of refuge to "retire" and will not likely represent a danger to the community, which, while not a consideration for a *refoulement* assessment under the Refugee Convention (which only applies to persons who have obtained refugee status to which they are not entitled due to their exclusion), will not make them good candidates for any type of detention, let alone long-term detention. On the other hand, persons with a

4 Canada (*Asylum Procedures*, above note 2 at 120).

5 *Ibid* at 202 for Germany, at 300 for New Zealand, and at 457 for the United States.

6 A Belgian decision recently mentioned this dilemma and pointed out that this is not something that could be resolved by the judiciary but rather the legislator; see CCE No 230.793, 23 December 2019 at 16. This group of persons is at times referred to as "persons who are undesirable but unreturnable"; see Refugee Law Initiative, School of Advanced Study, University of London (UK), and Center for International Criminal Justice, VU University Amsterdam (the Netherlands), *Undesirable and Unreturnable? Policy Challenges Around Excluded Asylum Seekers and Other Migrants Suspected of Serious Criminality Who Cannot Be Removed* (University of London, 2016), online: https://gtr.ukri.org/projects?ref=AH%2FL015463%2F1. In Belgium, some jurisprudence referred to this phenomenon without offering a solution, such as CCE No 221.222, 18 October 2018; CCE No 230.793, 23 December 2019; and CCE No 264.267, 25 November 2021. For an overview of policies regarding such persons in countries other than the ones discussed in this book, see Maarten Bolhuis & Joris van Wijk, *Study on the Exchange of Information Between European Countries Regarding Persons Excluded from Refugee Status in Accordance with Article 1F Refugee Convention* (VU, Amsterdam & UDI, Oslo, 2015) at 15 (Denmark), at 18–19 (Norway), and at 20–21 (Sweden).

committed terrorist background might continue to present a danger both to the country of refuge and to the country of origin, justifying more strict detention measures. Then there are persons who might have been excluded for either low-level common crimes or for peripheral involvement in such crimes who do not present a danger, nor do they evoke a sense of revulsion for the acts committed, and, as such, might benefit from a certain level of integration into the country of refuge's society.

B. PROSECUTION

Before discussing the attempts of countries to put criminal refugees on trial, it is necessary to discuss the international obligation to prosecute or extradite (the *aut dedere aut judicare* principle), as well as the concept of universal jurisdiction, which is the type of jurisdiction in play in the nine countries of interest in this study.

The obligation to prosecute or extradite refers to the alternate obligation contained in several multilateral treaties designed to secure international cooperation in the suppression of certain kinds of serious criminal conduct. While this obligation is framed in different ways in these treaties, it essentially requires a state, on whose territory a perpetrator of a serious crime is present, to either extradite this person to another state that is prepared to put them on trial or have them prosecuted in its own courts.[7]

There are many multilateral treaties[8] that contain some variation of this duty to prosecute or extradite. These variations can generally be grouped into three categories. The first category contains treaties

7 Robert J. Currie & Joseph Rikhof, *International & Transnational Criminal Law*, 3d ed (Toronto: Irwin Law, 2020) at 21–22, 103–4, and 370–72; see, also, *Questions Relating to the Obligation to Prosecute or Extradite (Belgium v Senegal)* [20 July 2012] ICJ Rep 422 at paras 90–91, 94–95, 114–15, and 120; UN Doc A/69/10, Report of the International Law Commission, Sixty-sixth Session, 5 May–6 June and 7 July–8 August 2014, *The Obligation to Extradite or Prosecute (aut dedere aut judicare): Final Report of the International Law Commission*, 2014; UN Doc A74/10, *Draft Articles on Prevention and Punishment of Crimes Against Humanity, with Commentaries*, International Law Commission, 2019 at 92.

8 M. Cherif Bassiouni & Edward M. Wise, *Aut Dedere, Aut Judicare: The Duty to Extradite or Prosecute in International Law* (Dordrecht/Boston/London: Martinus Nijhoff, 1995) at 7–8 and 75–287, set out over 100 international instruments, divided into twenty-four groups, that contain such an obligation, while a 2010 study for the International Law Commission examined sixty-one treaties; see UN Doc A/65/10, *Report of the International Law Commission*, Sixty-second Session, 3 May–4 June and 5 July–6 August 2010, General Assembly Official Records, Sixty-fifth Session, Supp No 10 at 332, para 337.

stipulating that prosecution can only occur when an extradition request has been refused in the country where the offender is present.[9] The second group is treaties that contain an absolute obligation to prosecute (expressed by the words "shall bring such persons . . . before its courts") but have a choice between prosecution and extradition when an extradition request has been submitted to the state where the person sought is present.[10] The last and most recent category is a hybrid between the first two models in that the obligation to prosecute is a default to extradition, but the obligation to prosecute is framed in a less absolute fashion by requiring that a state "shall submit the case to its competent authorities for the purpose of prosecution."[11]

In this book, the most important international instruments regulating the obligation to prosecute or extradite are the ones dealing with international crimes set out in the exclusion clauses: genocide, war crimes, crimes against humanity, and terrorism. There are very few treaties dealing with common crimes apart from drug and people trafficking. When examining these treaties, it becomes clear that not all manifestations of these crimes are subject to the obligation to prosecute or extradite. This is especially the case with war crimes committed in non-international armed conflicts and crimes against humanity. The 1949 Geneva Conventions only have this obligation in respect to war crimes committed in international armed conflicts, while Protocol II of 1977 regarding non-international armed conflicts does not contain a provision equivalent to the one in the Geneva Conventions. The only way that such an obligation can be made applicable is if activities

---

9 Bassiouni & Wise, above note 8 at 12–14; UN Doc A/CN.4/630, International Law Commission, Sixty-second Session, Geneva, 3 May–4 June and 5 July–6 August 2010, *Survey of Multilateral Conventions Which May Be of Relevance for the Commission's Work on the Topic "The obligation to extradite or prosecute (aut dedere aut judicare),"* Study of the Secretariat, 16 May 2010 at 67–68, paras 132–37; UN Doc A/69/10, above note 7 at 4; all three documents refer to the 1929 Counterfeiting Convention as the first example of this formula.

10 Bassiouni & Wise, above note 8 at 14–15; UN Doc A/CN.4/630, above note 9 at 62–65, paras 127–29; UN Doc A/69/10, above note 7 at 4–5; all three documents refer to the 1949 Geneva Conventions as the prime example of this model.

11 Bassiouni & Wise, above note 8 at 116–19; UN Doc A/CN.4/630, above note 9 at 65–67, paras 130–31; UN Doc A/69/10, above note 7 at 5; UN Doc A74/10, above note 7 at 92–93; these documents show that this formula became prevalent with the anti-terrorism conventions, starting with the 1970 Convention for the Suppression of Unlawful Seizure of Aircraft, as well as with the Convention against Torture; see, also, UNHCR, *The Exclusion Clauses: Guidelines on Their Application* (December 1996); Sibylle Kapferer, *The Interface Between Extradition and Asylum* (November 2003) UNHCR Legal and Protection Policy Research Series PPLA/2003/05 at 7–11, paras 22–32 , online (pdf): www.unhcr.org/3fe84fad4.pdf.

prohibited in the anti-terrorism conventions also amount to acts committed during a non-international armed conflict.[12]

This limitation also applies to crimes against humanity.[13] Unless another treaty imposes a duty to prosecute or extradite for conduct that is addressed in that treaty, no such obligation applies to the crimes amounting to crimes against humanity. Currently, only four international conventions can be used in such a manner: the Genocide Convention, the Torture Convention, the Apartheid Convention,[14] and the Enforced Disappearance Convention. The latter two allow for the easiest transposition as articles 1 and 5, respectively, of these conventions state that the conduct regulated by them is also a crime against humanity if committed in a systematic or widespread fashion, which is assumed for apartheid. The Torture Convention only covers the narrow version of torture (with a specific purpose and state involvement) compared to international criminal law, while its reference to inhuman treatment is not the same as the crimes against humanity of inhumane acts. With respect to genocide, this crime only covers the most egregious forms of crimes against humanity, while the Genocide Convention has the obligation to extradite or prosecute, but the latter only applies in the territory where genocide has taken place.[15]

Because of this limitation in the obligation to prosecute or extradite in the area where the need is the highest, crimes against humanity, and because of its prevalency compared to war crimes in international armed conflict and genocide, attempts have been made to find such an obligation in customary international law. While there are differences of opinion on this issue, the generally accepted view is that such an obligation, especially in respect to crimes against humanity, can now only be found in relation to territorial jurisdiction in that the obligation is only placed on the authorities in the same territory where the crimes have occurred. Such an obligation has not crystallized yet for the type of jurisdiction applicable to the countries examined in this study, which is universal jurisdiction.[16]

12 UN Doc A/69/10, above note 7 at 12.

13 Although see UN Doc A74/10, above note 7, art 10 at 92, which incorporates the same obligation, but this document is not yet finalized.

14 International Convention on the Suppression and Punishment of the Crime of Apartheid of 18 July 1976.

15 Genocide Convention, art 6.

16 UN Doc A/CN.4/L.774, International Law Commission, Sixty-second Session Geneva, 3 May–4 June and 5 July–6 August 2010, *Bases for Discussion in the Working Group on the Topic "The*

The most common type of criminal jurisdiction is based on the principle of sovereignty, that a state is entitled to prosecute crimes that have taken place on its territory—hence the term "territorial jurisdiction." However, international law also recognizes the ability of states to exercise jurisdiction for crimes committed outside its territory provided that there is some link between the state and this exercise of extraterritorial jurisdiction. Such links are found in the nationality of persons belonging to a state that can be further divided in the active nationality or active personality principle, where a state can prosecute crimes committed by its nationals abroad, and in the passive nationality or personality principle, where a state can prosecute a crime abroad where its national has been a victim. Last, a prosecution can be based on universal jurisdiction, present in a situation where the crime is not committed in the state wanting to prosecute, but the link is found where a perpetrator of a crime abroad has subsequently gone to this state. In some instances, this type of jurisdiction has also been used where there is no perpetrator present in the state, but investigations have been undertaken as a result of the serious nature of the crimes committed and for which any country is entitled to initiate a prosecution. This is frequently referred to as absolute jurisdiction or universal jurisdiction *in absentia*.[17] The following crimes have traditionally been seen in customary international law to be the subjects of universal jurisdiction: piracy, genocide, war crimes, crimes against humanity, and torture.[18]

---

obligation to extradite or prosecute (aut dedere aut judicare)," Paper prepared by Zdzislaw Galicki, Special Rapporteur, at 3–4, para 10; UN Doc A/69/10, above note 7 at 16–17; *Questions Relating to the Obligation to Prosecute or Extradite (Belgium v Senegal)* [20 July 2012] ICJ Rep 422 at paras 53–55 (and, more specifically, the Separate Opinion of Judge Abraham at paras 21, 24–25, and 31–19, as well as Dissenting Opinion of Judge ad hoc Sur at para 16).

17 Currie & Rikhof, above note 7, 62–82; UN Doc A/73/10, Report of the International Law Commission Seventieth Session (30 April–1 June and 2 July–10 August 2018), 2018, Annex A, *Universal Jurisdiction*, Report by Charles Chernor Jalloh, 307–11.

18 Currie & Rikhof, above note 7 at 75–77; UN Doc A/73/10, above note 17, 307–8; Council of the European Union, *The AU-EU Expert Report on the Principle of Universal Jurisdiction*, 8672/1/09/ REV 1, 16 April 2009 at 7–8, para 9, added that under treaty law other crimes have also been added: primarily terrorist offences; UN Doc A/65/181, Report of the Secretary-General, *The Scope and Application of the Principle of Universal Jurisdiction*, prepared on the basis of comments and observations of governments, 29 July 2010 at 8–9, paras 27–28, indicates that slavery and crimes against peace could also fall under this type of jurisdiction under customary international law; REDRESS/FIDH, "Extraterritorial Jurisdiction in the European Union: A Study of the Laws and Practice in the 27 Member States of the European Union," December 2010 at 22–23, indicates the types of crimes in the countries of the European Union that are subject to universal jurisdiction.

While the concept of universal jurisdiction is distinct from the obligation to prosecute or extradite, there are some connections between these two notions, explained as follows:

> [T]he establishment of jurisdiction, universal or otherwise, is a logically prior step: a state must first vest its courts with competence to try given criminal conduct. It is only once such competence has been established that the question whether to prosecute the relevant conduct, or to extradite persons suspected of it, arises . . . . [A] state party to one of the treaties in question is not only bound to empower its criminal justice system to exercise universal jurisdiction but is further bound actually to exercise that jurisdiction by means of either considering prosecution or extraditing.[19]

While the obligation to prosecute or extradite is limited to certain crimes in countries that exercise universal jurisdiction, international law certainly permits such countries to go beyond the duty to undertake prosecutions involving crimes against humanity and war crimes in non-international armed conflicts.[20] In Europe, a number of countries have assumed universal jurisdiction to investigate and prosecute crimes other than the ones set out above and at times have also included the possibility of prosecuting crimes not regulated by international law but that are also common crimes.[21]

As a result of the permissive nature of prosecuting international crimes based on universal jurisdiction, sixteen countries in Europe and North America (including the seven countries discussed in this book in those two regions) have instituted investigations and prosecutions based on this type of jurisdiction and other forms of extraterritorial jurisdiction. These include seven of the countries we are examining in this book, resulting in over 100 trials.[22]

---

19 Council of the European Union, *The AU-EU Expert Report*, above note 18 at 10, para 11; see, also, UN Doc A/65/181, above note 18 at 6–8, paras 18–22; UN Doc A74/10, above note 7, art 7 at 87.

20 Currie & Rikhof, above note 7 at 102.

21 For European Union countries, see REDRESS/FIDH, above note 18 at 22, Table 2, second column (of the countries in this study in Europe, only Belgium has this possibility); for an overview of European and African countries, see Council of the European Union, *The AU-EU Expert Report*, above note 18 at 12–14, paras 15–16 and at 20–21, paras 22–23; for a global overview, see UN Doc A/65/181, above note 18 at 27–32, Table 1.

22 These trials resulted in the convictions of 135 persons and twenty acquittals; see Terje Einarsen & Joseph Rikhof, *A Theory of Punishable Participation in Universal Crimes* (Brussels: Torkel Opsahl Academic EPublisher, 2018) 425–515, as well as Máximo Langer & Mackenzie

Since there is not always an obligation to prosecute, prosecutors and investigative judges have the discretion to decide when to investigate or prosecute. In general, a decision to undertake a prosecution will entail a number of factors, usually related to the sufficiency of the evidence and the public interest.[23] With respect to crimes that are subject to extraterritorial jurisdiction, additional factors, such as international obligations and a better-situated forum, either domestically (for instance, before a court where the crime has occurred) or internationally (an international tribunal might have an interest in the case), can play a role as well.[24] At times, the discretion of a prosecutor or investigative judge to make a decision in respect to crimes subject to such jurisdiction is, in addition,

---

Eason, "The Quiet Expansion of Universal Jurisdiction" (2019) 30:3 *European Journal of International Law* 779–817, and Trial International, *Universal Jurisdiction Annual Review*, which has been published between 2014 and 2022. While the United States has carried out only one prosecution in this specific context, it has prosecuted a large number of persons involved in international crimes under its immigration legislation; see Joseph Rikhof, "Prosecutors on the Front Line: A Q&A with Teresa McHenry, Head of the Human Rights and Special Prosecutions Section of the US Department of Justice" (2019) 3 *PKI Global Justice Journal* 41.

23 UN Doc A/65/181, above note 18 at 17, para 71; Public Prosecution Service of Canada, *Public Prosecution Service of Canada Deskbook*, ch 2.3 (2020), online (pdf): www.ppsc-sppc.gc.ca/eng/pub/fpsd-sfpg/fps-sfp/tpd/d-g-eng.pdf (this discretion was confirmed judicially in *Kunlun Zhang v Canada (Minister of Citizenship and Immigration)*, 2006 FC 276, and *Kunlun Zhang v Canada (Attorney General)*, 2007 FCA 201); Federal Prosecution Service, *Prosecution Policy of the Commonwealth: Guidelines for the Making of Decisions in the Prosecution Process*, ch 3 (Australia), online (pdf): www.cdpp.gov.au/sites/default/files/Prosecution-Policy-of-the-Commonwealth_0.pdf); Crown Law, *Solicitor-General's Prosecution Guidelines* (July 2013), ch 5 (New Zealand) , online (pdf): www.crownlaw.govt.nz/assets/Uploads/Prosecution-Guidelines/ProsecutionGuidelines2013.pdf; Crown Prosecution Service, *The Code for Crown Prosecutors* (October 2018), ch 3 (United Kingdom), online (pdf): www.cps.gov.uk/sites/default/files/documents/publications/Code-for-Crown-Prosecutors-October-2018.pdf. Sufficiency of evidence requires a reasonable prospect of obtaining a conviction, while the public interest consideration tends to involve factors such as whether the offence is serious or trivial; any mitigating or aggravating circumstances; the age, intelligence, health, or any special infirmity of the alleged offender, any witness, or victim; the alleged offender's antecedents; the staleness of the offence; the availability and efficacy of any alternatives to prosecution; the attitude of the victim; the likely outcome in the event of a finding of guilt; and the need for deterrence.

24 UN Doc A/65/181, above note 18 at 17, para 71; REDRESS/FIDH, above note 18 at 27–30; Open Society Justice Initiative and Trial International, *Prosecuting International Crimes: A Matter of Willingness*, 2020, examining the practices in Canada, Finland, France, Germany, the Netherlands, Norway, Sweden, and Switzerland, in which prosecutorial discretion is discussed in the individual reports in ch 3 under the heading "Universal Jurisdiction Requirements"; see, also, in the United Kingdom, Crown Prosecution Service, "War Crimes/Crimes Against Humanity Referral Guidelines," under "A. Scoping Exercise" (7 August 2015), online: www.cps.gov.uk/publication/war-crimescrimes-against-humanity-referral-guidelines, and in Germany, Deutscher Bundestag, Drucksache 18/12533, Antwort der Bundesregierung, 30 May 2017, at 4, Answer 15.

made subject to the approval of a higher executive officer, such as the head of a prosecution service or the attorney general.[25]

Apart from legal constraints and the legal complexity of international crimes, a prosecution based on extraterritorial jurisdiction also faces some practical difficulties. The main difficulty is the cost of investigating and mounting a prosecution based on evidence, which for the most part must be collected outside the country.[26] As well, during the investigation, special care needs to be taken with witnesses in terms of obtaining unfettered access through cooperation arrangements with the country where they are located; the manner in which the witnesses are interviewed in light of the different legal backgrounds of the witnesses and the interviewers; the passage of time between crimes and the interviews; and witness protection. Some of these concerns apply to obtaining documents from local and international institutions and may also apply to the trial phase of a criminal proceeding.[27]

As a result of the significant resources required in criminal investigations and prosecutions of international crimes, from both a financial and a human resources perspective, the discretionary factors for determining whether to initiate an investigation or a prosecution are further broken down to set priorities. For instance, in Canada, a number of considerations are taken into account before embarking on a prosecution of a 1F case with criminal investigation potential, including that the allegation must disclose personal involvement or command responsibility and that the evidence pertaining to the allegation must be

---

25 UN Doc A/65/181, above note 18 at 19, para 78; REDRESS/FIDH, above note 18 at 30–31; Open Society Justice Initiative and Trial International, *Prosecuting International Crimes*, above note 24 at ch 4, under the heading "Universal Jurisdiction Requirements."

26 The average costs of two such investigations and prosecutions was estimated in a Canadian report to be around $5 million. See Department of Justice, Corporate Services Branch, Evaluation Division, Crimes against Humanity and War Crimes Program Evaluation, Final Report, August 2016, online: www.justice.gc.ca/eng/rp-pr/cp-pm/eval/rep-rap/2016/cahwc-cchcg/index.html at 57.

27 See, in general, Maarten P. Bolhuis & Joris van Wijk, "Alleged War Criminals in the Netherlands: Excluded from Refugee Protection, Wanted by the Prosecutor" (2015) 12:2 *European Journal of Criminology* 151 at 157–64, and Sarah Singer, "'Undesirable and Unreturnable' in the United Kingdom" (2017) 36:1 *Refugee Survey Quarterly* 9 at 27–29; with respect to witness protection and some resolutions, see REDRESS/FIDH, above note 18 at 46–55; REDRESS/FIDH, "Strategies for the Effective Investigation and Prosecution of Serious International Crimes: The Practice of Specialised War Crimes Units" (December 2010) at 23–24 , online (pdf): www.fidh.org/IMG/pdf/The_Practice_of_Specialised_War_Crimes_Units_Dec_2010.pdf; Open Society Justice Initiative and Trial International, *Prosecuting International Crimes*, above note 24 in the chapter "Witness and Victim Protection."

corroborated and obtainable in a reasonable and rapid fashion.[28] In the Netherlands, factors such as whether another country has jurisdiction over the crimes in question; whether there are cooperation agreements in place with the countries where the witnesses are located; the level of security in the country where an investigation will take place; the level of protection that can be given to the witnesses; how far the rights of the defence can be respected during an investigation; whether the person can be removed; and whether the person is still engaged in criminal activities will be taken into account in deciding whether and when to investigate an international crime.[29]

As a result of the above limitations with respect to investigations and prosecutions, it cannot be expected that many persons who have been excluded and who cannot be removed will face a criminal trial. In the Netherlands, where the most information regarding this relationship is available and where a large number of prosecutions based on extraterritorial jurisdictions have been launched since 2004, eighteen prosecutions were initiated involving twenty-four persons (two involved Dutch nationals), of which all but two were successful.[30] Compared to the almost 1,000 persons who were excluded between 2000 and 2020,[31] the prosecution rate represents less than a quarter of 1 percent of the 1F population, which is unlikely to exceed in any of the other countries in this survey.

---

28 *Canada's Program on Crimes Against Humanity and War Crimes, Tenth Annual Report, 2006–2007*, under the headings "Enforcement in Canada," "Criminal Investigations and Prosecution." Earlier, there had been a longer list of factors for this type of priority setting, which included the credibility of the allegation; the seriousness of the allegation; the seriousness of the crime; whether the person had a military or civilian position; the strength of evidence; the progress of the investigation; the ability to secure cooperation with another country or international tribunal; the likelihood of effective cooperation with other countries; the presence of victims or witnesses in Canada; the presence of victims or witnesses in other countries with easy access; the likelihood of being part of a group investigation in Canada; the likelihood of parallel investigation in another country or by international tribunal; the ability to conduct documentary research to test the credibility of an allegation; the likelihood of continuing offence or danger to the public; the likelihood of a reasonable prospect of fair and real prosecution in other country; whether this is a high-profile case; whether an indictment by international tribunal or extradition request is likely; see *Canada's Program on Crimes Against Humanity and War Crimes, Fifth Annual Report, 2001–2002*, under the heading "Developments Under the Crimes Against Humanity and War Crimes Act."

29 Letter from the Minister of Justice to the President of the House of Commons, 2007–8 Session, 31 200-VI nr 193, 9 September 2008 at 2.1.

30 See above note 22 for the sources for this calculation.

31 See Chapter 5, n680, for the calculation of this number.

C. EXTRADITION

As with prosecution, the obligation to extradite is not universal, and as with prosecution, there are a few limitations in respect to extradition. First, while it is possible under international law to extradite in the absence of a treaty or other formal arrangement, most countries do require a transfer from their country to another pursuant to a bilateral or multilateral instrument.[32] Second, an extradition can only occur at the request of the country where the crime was committed,[33] and an attempt to influence a country to issue such a request by a country where a person is present will raise the spectre of disguised extradition and can result in a finding of abuse of process.[34]

Apart from these procedural difficulties, there is also the same substantive issue that has caused problems when attempts were made to deport a person with a criminal background: a violation of human rights upon arrival in the country that issued the extradition request. Given that in the context of extradition a criminal trial is often contemplated, not only do human rights associated with torture or cruel, inhuman, or degrading treatment or punishment come into play[35] but also the right to a fair trial.[36]

A poignant example of how human rights can prevent the extradition of serious criminals was witnessed in 2008–9 when both the

32 Currie & Rikhof, above note 7 at 531–32.

33 *Ibid*, at 533–37; see, also, UNHCR, *The Interface Between Extradition and Asylum*, above note 11 at 15, para 46.

34 Currie & Rikhof, above note 7 at 564–67; for other issues regarding the interplay of extradition and exclusion, see Geoff Gilbert, "Undesirable but Unreturnable: Extradition and Other Forms of Rendition" (2017) 15:1 *Journal of International Criminal Justice* 55–74.

35 There is some debate as to whether in contemplating the possibly conflicting treaty obligations arising out of human rights instruments and extradition treaties, human rights treaties might give way to extradition obligations (see Kees Wouters, *International Legal Standards for Protection from Refoulement* (Antwerp-Oxford-Portland: Intersentia, 2009) at 30–31, 319, 406–7, 506–7, 565–66), but the better view appears to be that human rights prevail over extradition obligations; see UNHCR, *The Interface Between Extradition and Asylum*, above note 11 at 45–48, paras 123–33; UNHCR, *Guidelines on the Application in Mass Influx Situations of the Exclusion Clauses of Article 1F of the 1951 Convention relating to the Status of Refugees* (February 2006) at 12, para 38; Commission of the European Communities, "The Relationship Between Safeguarding Internal Security and Complying with International Protection Obligations and Instruments," Document COM (2001) 743 (5 December 2001) at 13–14; European Council on Refugees and Exiles (ECRE), "Position on Exclusion from Refugee Status" at 283–84; see, also, Ahorugeze, Case No Ö 1082-09, 26 May 2009, Supreme Court of Sweden at 12.

36 European Convention on Human Rights, art 6; International Covenant on Civil and Political Rights, art 9; American Convention on Human Rights, art 8.

prosecutor of the International Criminal Tribunal for Rwanda (ICTR) and the governments of several European countries attempted to extradite persons involved in the 1994 Rwandan genocide to that country but were unable to do so because of concerns raised by the judiciary.

In 2008, the prosecutor of the ICTR filed five requests to have cases transferred to Rwanda, but in all cases the Trial Chamber and on three occasions the Appeals Chamber prevented this transfer from taking place.[37] In the Trial Chamber, three concerns were identified in relation to the conduct of the trials and subsequent detention conditions: the fact that the judiciary was not independent enough from the Rwandan government; the fact that there was not sufficient witness protection, especially for defence witnesses; and the fact that Rwanda allowed solitary confinement for life as a punishment. At the appeal level, the first concern was dismissed,[38] but a transfer was not allowed based on the latter two problems,[39] which were also the reasons for refusal in two subsequent Trial Chamber decisions.[40] As a result, the prosecutor decided to have the trials take place before the ICTR, resulting in convictions for four of them,[41] while the fifth person was at large.[42]

---

37 *Hategekimana* (ICTR-00-55B-R11bis), Appeals Chamber, Decision on the Prosecution's Appeal Against Decision on Referral under Rule 11bis, 4 December 2008; *Kanyarukiga*, (ICTR-2002-78-R11bis), Appeals Chamber, Decision on the Prosecution's Appeal Against Decision on Referral under Rule 11bis, 30 October 2008; *Munyakazi* (ICTR-97-36-R11bis), Appeals Chamber, Decision on the Prosecution's Appeal Against Decision on Referral under Rule 11bis, 8 October 2008; *Gatete* (ICTR-2000-61-R11bis), Trial Chamber, Decision on Prosecutor's Request for Referral to the Republic of Rwanda, 17 November 2008; *Kayishema* (ICTR-01-67-R11bis), Trial Chamber, Decision on Prosecutor's Request for Referral to the Republic of Rwanda, 16 December 2008.

38 *Munyakazi* (ICTR-97-36-R11bis), Appeals Chamber, Decision on the Prosecution's Appeal Against Decision on Referral under Rule 11bis, 8 October 2008, at paras 27–31.

39 *Munyakazi* (ICTR-97-36-R11bis), Appeals Chamber, Decision on the Prosecution's Appeal Against Decision on Referral under Rule 11bis, 8 October 2008, at paras 20–21 and 45; *Kanyarukiga* (ICTR-2002-78-R11bis), Appeals Chamber, Decision on the Prosecution's Appeal Against Decision on Referral under Rule 11bis, 30 October 2008, at paras 16 and 35–38; *Hategekimana* (ICTR-00-55B-R11bis), Appeals Chamber, Decision on the Prosecution's Appeal Against Decision on Referral under Rule 11bis, 4 December 2008, at paras 30 and 38.

40 *Gatete* (ICTR-2000-61-R11bis), Trial Chamber, Decision on Prosecutor's Request for Referral to the Republic of Rwanda, 17 November 2008, at paras 72 and 95; *Kayishema* (ICTR-01-67- R11bis), Trial Chamber, Decision on Prosecutor's Request for Referral to the Republic of Rwanda, 16 December 2008, at paras 25–29 and 46.

41 *Munyakazi* (ICTR-97-36A-T), Trial Chamber Judgment, 5 July 2010; *Kanyarukiga* (ICTR-02-78), Trial Chamber Judgment, 1 November 2010; *Hategekimana* (ICTR-00-55b-T), Trial Chamber Judgment, 6 December 2010; *Gatete* (ICTR-00-61), Trial Chamber Judgment, 31 March 2011.

42 *Kayishema* (ICTR-01-67-R11bis), Trial Chamber, Decision on the International Criminal Defence Attorneys Association for Leave to Appear as *Amicus Curiae* and Invitation to the Republic of Rwanda to File Submissions, 18 February 2011, at para 1.

The prosecutor also decided that for persons who were arrested after 2010 or who were still at large, he would try again to obtain a transfer to Rwanda.[43] The concern with respect to the sentencing portion was already alleviated because the Special Court of Sierra Leone was able to transfer all eight persons, who had been convicted at that time, to Rwanda in October 2009 after an agreement was reached with the Rwandan government that these persons would not be subject to the solitary confinement for life regime. In 2011 and 2012, both the Trial Chamber and the Appeals Chamber of the ICTR concluded that all impediments with respect to referral to Rwanda had been alleviated.[44]

A similar pattern occurred in Europe. Rwanda had requested the extradition of *génocidaires* from several countries, but in quick succession between October 2008 and May 2009, the courts in Germany, Finland, France, Italy, Switzerland, and the United Kingdom refused to accede to these requests, citing the fair trial concerns, and they all depended heavily on the original ICTR judgments in their reasoning.[45] The UK court refused extradition, partially on the same basis as the ICTR jurisprudence, but they disagreed with it in respect to its assessment on the question of whether the judiciary was sufficiently independent and refused extradition on that basis,[46] in addition to the issue of

---

43 *Uwinkindi* (ICTR-2001-75-R11bis), Trial Chamber, Decision on Government of Rwanda's Request for Extension of Time to File *Amicus Curiae* Brief pursuant to Chamber's Invitation, 1 February 2011, at paras 1–2; *Kayishema* (ICTR-01-67-R11bis), Trial Chamber, Decision on the International Criminal Defence Attorneys Association for Leave to Appear as *Amicus Curiae* and Invitation to the Republic of Rwanda to File Submissions, 18 February 2011, at para 2.

44 *Uwinkindi* (ICTR-2001-75-R11bis), Trial Chamber, Decision on Prosecutor's Request for Referral to the Republic of Rwanda, Rule 11bis of the Rules of Procedure and Evidence, 28 June 2011, at paras 222–25; *Uwinkindi* (ICTR-01-75-AR11bis), Trial Chamber, Decision on Uwinkindi's Appeal Against the Referral of his Case to Rwanda and Related Motions, 16 December 2011, §75; *Kayishema* (ICTR-01-67-R11bis), Trial Chamber, Decision on Prosecutor's Request for Referral to the Republic of Rwanda, 22 February 2012.

45 See *Vincent Brown, aka Vincent Bajinja and others v The Government of Rwanda and The Secretary of State for the Home Department*, [2009] EWHC 770 (Admin) at para 47, and Ahorugeze, Case No Ö 1082-09, 26 May 2009, Supreme Court of Sweden at 14–15.

46 See *Vincent Brown aka Vincent Bajinja and others v The Government of Rwanda and The Secretary of State for the Home Department*, [2009] EWHC 770 (Admin) at paras 119–21. There were three different proceedings in France, while the extradition process in the United Kingdom involved four persons; in the other four countries, there was one proceeding involving one person each. Only in Finland was the person in question charged with genocide after the extradition refusal and convicted two years later.

witness protection.[47] However, this trend was reversed in May 2009 in Sweden, six weeks after the decision in the United Kingdom, when the Supreme Court decided that, based on the evidence provided to it, there was no issue in respect to the problems identified by the United Kingdom in terms of the treatment of witnesses and the independence of the Rwandan judiciary.[48] The European Court of Human Rights, to which the person concerned had appealed, sided with the Swedish government in 2011.[49]

Remarkably, this same scenario was repeated a number of years later when the British court again refused extradition to Rwanda, this time primarily because of the lack of a fair trial due to obstacles for defence witnesses,[50] while courts in other countries saw no problem in doing so.[51] Apart from the nine instances of extradition to Rwanda, this option has been used sparingly for international crimes in the

---

47 See *Vincent Brown aka Vincent Bajinja and others v The Government of Rwanda and The Secretary of State for the Home Department*, [2009] EWHC 770 (Admin) at para 66; see, also, Correspondent's Report, United Kingdom, (2009) 12 *Yearbook of International Humanitarian Law* at 681–82.

48 Ahorugeze, Case No Ö 1082-09, 26 May 2009, Supreme Court of Sweden at 18–20; the court preferred the ICTR assessment regarding the judiciary in Rwanda over that of the UK court at 18. For a commentary, see Correspondent's Report, Sweden, (2009) 12 *Yearbook of International Humanitarian Law* at 646–48.

49 *Ahorugeze v Sweden*, 27 October 2011, Application No 37075/09 at para 95; for an overview of extradition by European countries to Rwanda, see Maarten P. Bolhuis, Louis P. Middelkoop & Joris van Wijk, "Refugee Exclusion and Extradition in the Netherlands: Rwanda as Precedent?" (2014) 12:5 *Journal of International Criminal Justice* 1115 at 1115–28.

50 *Government of Rwanda v Nteziryayo & Ors* [2017] EWHC 1912 (Admin) at paras 365–80; this was the same conclusion reached in a number of cases in France — Manasse Bigwenzare, Claude Muhayimana, Innocent Musabyimana Laurent Serubuga, Félicien Baligira — after which the French authorities laid criminal charges against Muhayimana, who was eventually convicted in December 2021; see the reports by Trial International, above note 22, as well as Nicola Palmer, "International Criminal Law and Border Control: The Expressive Role of the Deportation and Extradition of Genocide Suspects to Rwanda" (2020) 33:3 *Leiden Journal of International Law* 789 at 795–806.

51 The Netherlands extradited four persons: Jean Claude Iyamuremye and Jean-Baptiste Mugimba, both extradited in November 2016; Venant Rutunga, who was extradited in July 2021; and Charles Ndereyehe, whose extradition was approved by the Supreme Court of the Netherlands on 12 April 2022 (see HR, 21/04555), while Jean de Dieu Munyaneza was deported in March 2015. Denmark extradited Emmanuel Mbarushimana in July 2014 and Wenceslas Twagirayezu in December 2018, while Norway did the same with Charles Bandora in 2013 and Eugene Nkuranyabahizi in 2015; and Sweden with Jean-Paul Micomyiza in April 2022. Canada used the deportation option in January 2012 to remove Léon Mugesera and Henri Jean-Claude Seyoboka in November 2016 to Rwanda, while the United States did the same with Marie-Claire Mukeshimana in January 2011, for a total of thirteen persons removed (including four deportations); see sources in above note 22.

countries under consideration: twenty-six times between 2001 and 2020, and all to countries of the former Yugoslavia: Croatia, Serbia, and Bosnia-Herzegovina.[52]

Another variation of extradition can also be utilized: surrender to international tribunals or the International Criminal Court (ICC). While human rights issues, such as a fair trial, will not play as much of a role in the transfer of persons suspected of serious crimes, other limitations will have to be taken into consideration, such as the policy or mandate of these institutions to only pursue persons with the greatest responsibility[53] and the limited number of situations in which such institutions have jurisdiction or have taken actions. For instance, in the case of the ICC, which will soon be the only forum to which such surrender will be possible, only two transfers so far were from countries where persons could have been prosecuted based on universal jurisdiction: Belgium[54] and France.[55] For these reasons, it must be clear that extradition to other countries or international institutions at their request will not result in reducing the number of excluded persons in a country at all.[56]

---

52 There was one extradition from Norway to Serbia in 2008, while three countries extradited persons to Bosnia-Herzegovina: Germany in 2018; Switzerland in 2012, 2015, and 2017; and the United States in 2011 (two persons), 2013, 2015 (two persons), 2016, and 2020. Most persons have been extradited to Croatia: by Australia in 2016; Austria in 2011; France in 2011 (two persons) and 2016; Germany in 2007 (three persons); the Netherlands in 2011, 2016, and 2019; Switzerland in 2001; and the United Kingdom in 2008 and 2009; for sources, see Joseph Rikhof, "Fewer Places to Hide? The Impact of Domestic War Crimes Prosecutions on International Impunity (2009) 20 *Criminal Law Forum* 1 at 26–38, and the report by Trial International, above note 22.

53 See Currie & Rikhof, above note 7 at 246 and 250.

54 Decision of Confirmation of Charges, *Bemba* (ICC-01/05-01/08), Pre-Trial Chamber II, 15 June 2009 at para 2–4.

55 Warrant of Arrest for Callixte Mbarushimana, *Mbarushimana* (ICC-01/04-01/10) Pre-Trial Chamber I, 28 September 2010 at para 8; for issues regarding the ICC and persons who have been excluded, see Emma Irving, "When International Justice Concludes: Undesirable but Unreturnable Individuals in the Context of the International Criminal Court" (2017) 15:1 *Journal of International Criminal Justice* 115–31.

56 The number of people who have been deported for international crimes is higher than is the case with extradition; since 2003, the United States has deported more than 1,000 such persons; see US Immigration and Customs Enforcement (ICE), "ICE Arrests 23 Known or Suspected Human Rights Violators Across the US During Operation Safe Nation" (12 April 2022), online: www.ice.gov/news/releases/ice-arrests-23-known-or-suspected-human-rights-violators-across-us-during-operation, while the number was 160 in Canada between 2008 and 2015 according to *Canada's Program on Crimes Against Humanity and War Crimes*, 12th and 13th reports. For the Netherlands, it is said that between 2008 and 2015 about fifty persons had been deported and about sixty had left the country voluntarily (see Maarten P. Bolhuis, Hemme Battjes & Joris van Wijk, "Undesirable but Unreturnable Migrants in the Netherlands"

D. DETENTION

The question of whether long-term detention can be considered a viable alternative for excluded persons who cannot be removed due to human rights concerns must be assessed within the general issue of whether and in which circumstances detention of refugees or asylum seekers is allowed under international and domestic law and, as such, is different from the discussion of detention conditions addressed in the previous chapter.

While the 1951 Refugee Convention does not specifically speak to the issue of detention, a number of provisions in the treaty can arguably have an impact on it, such as article 31.1, which prohibits the imposition of penalties on refugees "on account of their illegal entry or presence," and article 31.2, which says, "The Contracting States shall not apply to the movements of such refugees restrictions other than those which are necessary and such restrictions shall only be applied until their status in the country is regularized or they obtain admission into another country." In interpreting the convention, the United Nations High Commissioner for Refugees (UNHCR) has indicated that the detention of refugees and asylum seekers is "inherently undesirable," while also saying that if detention must be used, it should only be used in exceptional circumstances, such as in the following situations: to verify identity; to determine the elements on which the claim for refugee status or asylum is based; in cases where asylum seekers have destroyed their travel or identity documents or have used fraudulent documents in order to mislead the authorities of the state; and to protect national security and public order.[57] More recently, the overall goal of ending

---

(2017) 36:1 *Refugee Survey Quarterly* 61 at 68), while in 2020, eighteen persons had left the country (according to the government reporting in "Rapportagebrief for Internationale Misdrijven 2020," 3). However, these numbers do not provide a complete and accurate picture in terms of an alternative remedy for excluded persons who cannot be removed, for at least two reasons: first of all, the above statistics for Canada and the United States do not distinguish between excluded persons and person who have been the subject of other immigration remedies, while the outcome of a deportation in terms of effectiveness in bringing perpetrators to justice is limited, in that most such persons will not face any penal consequences upon return to their country of origin (with the exception of Rwanda, where the four persons mentioned in above note 51 were tried and convicted of serious crimes); as well, an annual deportation rate of about fifty-six persons in the United States and twenty in Canada still would not diminish the number of excluded persons dramatically.

57 UNHCR, *Guidelines on Applicable Criteria and Standards Relating to the Detention of Asylum-Seekers* (February 1999) at 3–5; these grounds were repeated in UNHCR, Excom Conclusion No 44 (XXXVII) 1986 at para (b); (for other, more general ExCom Conclusions regarding detention, see UNHCR, *A Thematic Compilation of Executive Committee Conclusions*, 5th ed

detention for asylum seekers became part of a UNHCR global strategy with the following purposes:

> (1) to end the detention of children; (2) to ensure that alternatives to detention (ATDs) are available in law and implemented in practice; and (3) to ensure that conditions of detention, where detention is necessary and unavoidable, meet international standards by, inter alia, securing access to places of immigration detention for UNHCR and/or its partners and carrying out regular monitoring; and provides for guidance on how to achieve these goals, by defining areas of engagement such as advocacy interventions, awareness raising and campaigning, strengthening partnerships, strategic litigation and monitoring and evaluations.[58]

More general human rights conventions, which address the issue of detention, will also come into play, such as the International Covenant on Civil and Political Rights,[59] the European Convention on Human

---

(January 2010) at 141–45) and replaced in UNHCR, *Guidelines on the Applicable Criteria and Standards Relating to the Detention of Asylum-Seekers and Alternatives to Detention* (2012). See, also, Ophelia Field (with the assistance of Alice Edwards), *Alternatives to Detention of Asylum Seekers and Refugees*, POLAS/2006/03 (April 2006) at 4–6, paras 14–18, online (pdf): www.unhcr.org/protection/globalconsult/4474140a2/11-alternatives-detention-asylum-seekers-refugees-ophelia-field.html; Guy S. Goodwin-Gill, "Article 31 of the 1951 Convention Relating to the Status of Refugees: Non-penalization, Detention, and Protection" in Erika Feller, Volker Türk & Frances Nicholson, eds, *Refugee Protection in International Law: UNHCR's Global Consultations on International Protection* (Cambridge: Cambridge University Press, 2003) at 188–97, 218–19, 221–34; Alice Edwards, "The Optional Protocol to the Convention Against Torture and the Detention of Refugees" (2008) 57:4 *International and Comparative Law Quarterly* 789 at 790–91 and 806–8. The European Union's Asylum Procedures Directive states in art 18 that "1. Member States shall not hold a person in detention for the sole reason that he/she is an applicant for asylum. 2. Where an applicant for asylum is held in detention, Member States shall ensure that there is a possibility of speedy judicial review." The grounds for detention at the national level are, in general, the same with the addition of the risk of absconding; for those grounds in the European Union, including the jurisprudence of the European Court of Human Rights and the Court of Justice of the European Union, see European Asylum Support Office (EASO), *Judicial Analysis: Detention of Applicants for International Protection in the Context of the Common European Asylum System* (2019) at 24–30, online (pdf): https://euaa.europa.eu/sites/default/files/Detention-JA-EN-PDF.pdf; see, also, at the national level, below at n63–71 (with the same legislative provisions as mentioned for Canada, New Zealand, and the United States, while for Australia, it is the same source as is the case for Belgium, France, Germany, the Netherlands, and the United Kingdom, but under the heading "1. Grounds for Detention").

58 UNHCR, *Global Strategy Beyond Detention 2014–2019: Final Progress Report* (4 November 2020) at 6, online (pdf): www.unhcr.org/protection/detention/5fa26ed64/unhcr-global-strategy-beyond-detention-final-progress-report-2014-2019.html; for the approach in the European Union regarding alternative detention, see EASO, *Judicial Analysis*, above note 57 at 34–37.

59 Articles 9.1 and 12.1.

Rights (ECHR),[60] and the American Convention on Human Rights,[61] all of which guarantee that a person shall not be subjected to arbitrary arrest or detention and that a person has the right to movement, while they have also been interpreted to apply outside the criminal context and in situations of refugees or asylum seekers.[62]

In the countries under consideration, the duration of detention is usually limited.[63] In most countries, the maximum detention period is fixed by legislation and can vary from ninety days in France[64] to six months in Belgium,[65] Germany,[66] New Zealand,[67] and the United States,[68] while in the Netherlands, it is eighteen months.[69] Other countries do not have a specified maximum but require regular detention

60 Articles 5.1 and 2.1.

61 Articles 7.2 and 22.1.

62 See Chapter 6, Section E, for the judicial interpretation of these provisions by international human rights courts and tribunals; see, also, UNHCR, *Alternatives to Detention of Asylum Seekers*, above note 57 at 6–16, paras 19–54.

63 See, in general, in the European Union, EASO, *Judicial Analysis*, above note 57 at 37–42.

64 Asylum Information Database (AIDA)/European Council on Refugees and Exiles (ECRE), France, Country Report under "Detention of Asylum Seekers"; "B. Legal framework of detention"; "4. Duration of detention" (8 April 2022), online: https://asylumineurope.org/reports/country/france/detention-asylum-seekers/legal-framework-detention/duration-detention; for more details, see Chloé Peyronnet, "Undesirable and Unreturnable Migrants Under French Law: Between Legal Uncertainty and Legal Limbo" (2017) 36:1 *Refugee Survey Quarterly* 35 at 53–60.

65 Asylum Information Database (AIDA)/European Council on Refugees and Exiles (ECRE), Belgium, Country Report under "Detention of Asylum Seekers"; "B. Legal framework of detention"; "4. Duration of detention" (8 April 2022), online: https://asylumineurope.org/reports/country/belgium/detention-asylum-seekers/legal-framework-detention/duration-detention.

66 With possible extension for a maximum of eighteen months; see Asylum Information Database (AIDA)/European Council on Refugees and Exiles (ECRE), France, Country Report under "Detention of Asylum Seekers"; "B. Legal framework of detention"; "4. Duration of detention" (21 April 2022), online: https://asylumineurope.org/reports/country/germany/detention-asylum-seekers/legal-framework-detention/duration-detention.

67 *Immigration Act 2009*, ss 313 and 323.

68 This is read implicitly into s 241(1)(a) of the *Immigration and Nationality Act*; see Congressional Research Services, *The Law of Immigration Detention: A Brief Introduction* (updated 1 September 2022) at 2.

69 Asylum Information Database (AIDA)/European Council on Refugees and Exiles (ECRE), the Netherlands, Country Report under "Detention of Asylum Seekers"; "B. Legal framework of detention"; "4. Duration of detention" (8 April 2022), online: https://asylumineurope.org/reports/country/netherlands/detention-asylum-seekers/legal-framework-detention/duration-detention.

reviews (Canada)[70] or have detention terminated upon the occurrence of a specific event, such as deportation or granting of a visa (Australia),[71] or when released or directed by the secretary of state (United Kingdom).[72]

If regular detention can only be of limited duration and for limited specific reasons, it will come as no surprise that the judiciary in a number of countries under consideration has expressed serious concerns with long-term detention without the prospect of speedy removal, even in situations of persons with a serious criminal background.

In the United States, the Supreme Court indicated that indefinite detention is not permitted but that a person can only be kept in an immigration hold for a time that is reasonably necessary to bring about a person's removal from the United States.[73] As a result, the *Immigration and Nationality Act* was amended in respect to mandatory detention of terrorists to read:

> An alien detained solely under paragraph (1) who has not been removed under section 241(a)(1)(A), and whose removal is unlikely in the reasonably foreseeable future, may be detained for additional periods of up to six months only if the release of the alien will threaten the national security of the United States or the safety of the community or any person.[74]

In New Zealand, the Court of Appeal was of the view that "detention would be both arbitrary and unlawful under the *Immigration Act* if the purpose of detention could not be fulfilled and the detention was therefore otherwise indefinite or permanent."[75] The court also indicated that a regular review of such a detention would ameliorate an otherwise

---

70 *Immigration and Refugee Protection Act*, SC 2001, c 27, ss 55–57 [*IRPA*]; however, in security cases, these detention reviews can be carried out every six months; see s 82 of the *IRPA*; for a criticism, see Jonathan Porter, "Falling Between the Cracks of Cornerstones: Challenging the Detention of Asylum Seekers on Identity Grounds" in James C. Simeon, ed, *Serious International Crimes, Human Rights and Forced Migration* (London: Routledge, 2022) at 152–75.

71 Intergovernmental Consultations on Migration, Asylum and Refugees, *Asylum Procedures*, above note 2 at 38–41; for a critical assessment, see Satvinder S. Juss, "Detention and Delusion in Australia's Kafkaesque Refugee Law" (2017) 36:1 *Refugee Survey Quarterly* 146 at 149–51, 160–63; Peter Billings, "International Crimes, Refugee 'Prisoner' Swaps and Duplicity in Australia's Refugee Admission" in Simeon, above note 70 at 183–92.

72 *Immigration Act 1971*, s 2(3) of Schedule 3; see, also, *UK Borders Act 2007*, s 36, in respect to detention of convicted criminals; see, also, Singer, above note 27 at 20–22.

73 *Zadvydas v Davis*, 533 US 678 (2001).

74 Section 236A(a)(6).

75 *Zaoui v The Attorney General & Ors*, [2004] NZCA 228 at para 88.

undesirable situation.[76] The *Immigration Act of 2009* allows for detention of a maximum of six months, after which only a judge can authorize further detention and in limited circumstances.[77]

The House of Lords in the United Kingdom reached a similar conclusion, again in the context of a security case, by finding an incompatibility between indefinite detention and the ECHR,[78] while the High Court of Australia was also opposed to indefinite detention but indicated that the fact that the Australian legislation did not contain a maximum period of detention did not make it invalid as long as deportation was carried out within a reasonable time.[79]

The Supreme Court of Canada, relying on UK and US jurisprudence as well as decisions of the European Court of Human Rights, concluded that the special detention provisions in the legislation dealing with security cases that would allow immigration incarceration for long periods were constitutional as they permitted "robust ongoing judicial review of the continued need for and justice of the detainee's detention pending deportation."[80]

In Europe, an EU directive sets out the requirements for detention for the purposes of removal, such as the fact that such a detention should only be employed when no other measures are available; that it should only be applied when there is a risk that the person will abscond or will hamper the removal process; that any detention shall be for as short a period as possible and only maintained as long as removal arrangements are in progress and executed with due diligence; that detention shall be ordered by administrative or judicial authorities; that detention shall be reviewed at reasonable intervals of time; that in cases of prolonged detention periods, reviews shall be subject to the supervision of a judicial authority; and that if it appears that a reasonable prospect of removal

---

76 *Ibid* at paras 110–12.

77 Section 323(2).

78 *A & Ors v Secretary of State for the Home Department*, [2004] UKHL 56 at paras 73, 139, 160, and 239, although this finding was primarily predicated on discrimination in detention treatment between citizen and non-citizens accused of terrorist activities; see, also, Abdi; *Khalaf v Secretary of State for the Home Department*, [2011] EWCA Civ 242, and *Home Office v TR and another*, [2019] EWHC 49 at paras 21 and 50–52.

79 *Re Woolleys*, [2004] HCA 49 at paras 87–96.

80 *Charkaoui v Canada (Citizenship and Immigration)*, 2007 SCC 9 at para 123.

no longer exists for legal or other considerations, the person concerned shall be released immediately.[81]

At the judicial level, the European Court of Human Rights examined the issue of long-term immigration detention in 2009 in the same situation as was considered by the House of Lords five years earlier. The court made a number of important statements in respect to non-criminal detention, including that the ECHR

> does not demand that detention be reasonably considered necessary, for example to prevent the individual from committing an offence or fleeing. Any deprivation of liberty ... will be justified, however, only for as long as deportation or extradition proceedings are in progress. If such proceedings are not prosecuted with due diligence, the detention will cease to be permissible. Detention ... must be carried out in good faith; it must be closely connected to the ground of detention relied on by the Government; the place and conditions of detention should be appropriate; and the length of the detention should not exceed that reasonably required for the purpose.[82]

While the court indicated that there had been no violation of article 3 of the ECHR, in that the long-term detention did not amount to inhumane treatment as the detainees were not without any prospect or hope of release since they could challenge the legality of the detention,[83] there was a violation of article 5, which states in part that "everyone has the right to liberty and security of person" and that "no one shall be deprived of his liberty save in the following cases and in accordance with a procedure prescribed by law: ... (f) the lawful arrest or detention of a person ... against whom action is being taken with a view to deportation or extradition" because the detainees were incarcerated as a result of their terrorist background and not with a view to deporting them.[84]

From the limitations placed by the most senior courts in the countries under review and an influential supranational court, it will be

---

81 Council of the European Union, *Directive on Common Standards and Procedures in Member States for Returning Illegally Staying Third-Country Nationals*, 2008/115/EC (16 December 2008), art 15; art 9 indicates that removal of illegal persons should be postponed if it would violate the principle of *non-refoulement*; for a discussion of the Directive, see EASO, *Judicial Analysis*, above note 57 at 27–28.

82 *A and Others v The United Kingdom*, 19 February 2009, Application No 3455/05 at para 164.

83 *Ibid* at para 131.

84 *Ibid* at paras 170–71.

very difficult to use long-term detention in situations where a person has been excluded but cannot be removed because of human rights concerns, even if such a person would fit the requirement of short-term detention, such as being a flight risk or a danger to the public or national security, the latter of which is already unlikely in the case of persons who have been excluded.[85]

E. HUMANITARIAN SOLUTIONS

It has been recognized in general that for refugees or asylum seekers who cannot be removed for humanitarian reasons and whose situations persist, a more durable solution should be considered. All nine countries have mechanisms whereby a person can be granted a reprieve on removal for humanitarian considerations if no other means of providing solace exits.[86]

In most countries, such a humanitarian solution is granted in exceptional circumstances on a case-by-case basis at the highest level.[87] The following aspects will be taken into account as part of a humanitarian solution: serious hardship a person will face upon removal (Australia, Canada, Germany, the Netherlands, New Zealand); the time a person has been in the country (Germany); the level of integration into the country (Canada, France[88]); compassionate circumstances related to the age, health, or psychological state of the person (Australia); circumstances where exceptional economic, scientific, cultural, or other

85 See Chapter 6, Section D(2)(j), where it was said that only in Belgium and the Netherlands was a connection made at times between danger to the public and exclusion, but only in limited circumstances.

86 The various mechanisms are described in *Asylum Procedures*, above note 2 at 50 for Australia; at 86 for Belgium; at 119 for Canada; at 202–3 for Germany; at 274 for the Netherlands; at 299 for New Zealand; at 423 for the United Kingdom; and at 457 for the United States; see, also, Refugee Law Initiative, *Undesirable and Unreturnable?* above note 6 at 6, and Joris van Wijk & Maarten Bolhuis, "The Removal of Undesirable Asylum Seekers" in Satvinder Singh Juss, ed, *Research Handbook on International Refugee Law* (Cheltenham, UK & Northampton, US: Elgar, 2019) at 414, for more details on some of these countries.

87 Canada is an exception in that humanitarian and compassionate considerations, as set out in s 25 of the *IRPA*, above note 70, have been delegated to lower-level decision makers and become, because of their very frequent use, an almost automatic further step to be assessed by persons under a removal order; as a result, a number of procedures have been developed; see Jennifer Bond, "Unwanted but Unremovable: Canada's Treatment of 'Criminal' Migrants Who Cannot be Removed" (2017) 36:1 *Refugee Survey Quarterly* 168 at 176–77 and 181–83.

88 Peyronnet, above note 64 at 43–44.

contribution benefits the country of refuge (Australia); health reasons (France,[89] the Netherlands); medical condition or age, pregnancy or recent birth of a child, and the presence of relatives who are residents (Belgium); the best interests of the children (Canada); or, more generally, the public interest (Germany, New Zealand).

In Europe, there is an EU directive that regulates the various aspects of long-term residency. It indicates that long-term status should be granted to persons who have resided in a country legally and continuously for more than five years.[90] It also sets out that a condition for granting such status must be that a person has stable and regular resources that are sufficient to maintain himself and the members of their family, without recourse to the social assistance system,[91] while a refusal might be based on the grounds of public policy or public security.[92]

Some countries have a similar policy in place for the regularization of the status of persons who cannot be removed after a lengthy period. In Germany, a person whose deportation has been suspended due to international law or on humanitarian grounds[93] can apply after eight years to become a resident, and this can be granted if the person speaks German, has lived in Germany continuously for at least six years, has adequate resources, has not deceived the authorities on any immigration requirements, and has not engaged in extremist or terrorist activities or committed serious offences.[94]

In the United States, the same result (called cancellation of removal and adjustment of status) can be achieved if the person has been physically present in the United States for a continuous period of not less than ten years; has been a person of good moral character during this period; has not been convicted of a serious offence; can establish that removal would result in exceptional and extremely unusual hardship to

89 *Ibid.*

90 Council of the European Union, *Directive Concerning the Status of Third-Country Nationals Who Are Long-Term Residents*, 2003/109/EC, art 4.1.

91 *Ibid*, art 5.2.

92 *Ibid*, art 6.1, which goes on to say that "the severity or type of offence against public policy or public security, or the danger that emanates from the person concerned, while also having proper regard to the existence of links with the country of residence, should be taken into account as well." The same considerations apply if removal of a long-term resident is considered (art 12).

93 *Residence Act*, s 60(a); this is called the *Duldung* or tolerance provision.

94 *Residence Act*, s 104a(1); with respect to the criterion of non-involvement in terrorist organizations, see Bundesverwaltungsgericht (Federal Administrative Court), BverwG 1 C 19.09, 26 October 2010 at paras 24–32.

the person's spouse, parent, or child; and is a citizen of the United States or a person who has been lawfully admitted for permanent residence.[95] A serious medical condition by itself does not reach the legislative standard of hardship,[96] but an aggregate of factors, such as "the ages, health, and circumstances of the qualifying relative, whether the alien has a child with very serious health issues or compelling special needs in school, and whether the qualifying relative would experience a lower standard of living or adverse country conditions in the country of return," could be sufficient.[97] A serious offence is a crime involving moral turpitude and must be punishable by a sentence of imprisonment of at least one year or longer.[98]

In Canada, persons who are inadmissible for criminality related to security, international crimes, or organized crime are not entitled to humanitarian or compassionate considerations[99] unless the minister is of the view that for public policy reasons, a person can be granted permanent resident status.[100]

In the United Kingdom, a person can be granted a temporary stay (restricted leave) if they have been excluded or as a result of article 33.2 of the Refugee Convention but who cannot be removed from the United Kingdom; this leave is granted for six months but can be renewed, although it is subject to a number of restrictions related to the ability to work, reside, study, and have recourse to public funds.[101] In general, after

95 *Immigration and Nationality Act*, § 240A(b)(1).

96 *Ramirez-Villagomez v United States AG*, 2022 US App Lexis 8303 (11th Cir 2022).

97 *Romero-Jaimes v United States AG*, 2021 US App LEXIS 23344 (11th Cir 2021).

98 *Magassouba v Holder*, 526 Fed Appx 66 (2d Cir 2013).

99 *IRPA*, above note 70, ss 25(1) & 25.1(1); there have been a number of decisions applying these sections: *Betoukoumesou v Canada (Citizenship and Immigration)*, 2014 FC 591; *Sabadao v Canada (Minister of Citizenship and Immigration)*, 2006 FC 292; *Hamida v Canada (Citizenship and Immigration)*, 2014 FC 998; *Aazamyar v Canada (Citizenship and Immigration)*, 2015 FC 99; *Yousif v Canada (Citizenship and Immigration)*, 2019 FC 128; *Guzelian v Canada (Immigration, Refugees and Citizenship)*, 2021 FC 460; and *Rutayisire v Canada (Citizenship and Immigration)*, 2021 FC 970; invariably, these decisions applied the regular principles of complicity for 1F(a) crimes to determine whether the person was entitled to such considerations.

100 *IRPA*, s 25.2(1).

101 Paragraph 339D of the *Immigration Rules* states that excluded persons falling under art 33.2 are not entitled to humanitarian protection; see, also, Home Office, *Restricted Leave* Version 6.0 (19 July 2022) at 5–6, online (pdf): https://assets.publishing.service.gov.uk/government/uploads/system/uploads/attachment_data/file/1092616/Restricted_leave.pdf, while the general restricted leave policy can be found in this manual at 11–28; see, also, Singer, above note 27 at 29–34; challenges against this policy were rejected in *The Queen (on the application of Kardi) v Secretary of State for the Home Department*, [2014] EWCA Civ 934

a long period combined with a number of extensions of the restricted leave, a person can obtain a permission to stay (called indefinite leave to remain or ILR, on the ground of long residence in the United Kingdom) if the person has resided continuously in the United Kingdom and can speak sufficient English and there are no reasons arising out of the public interest not to grant status. The public interest is expressed in the following criteria: age; strength of connections in the United Kingdom; personal history, including character, conduct, associations, and employment record; domestic circumstances; previous criminal record and the nature of any offence of which the person has been convicted; and compassionate circumstances.[102]

Indefinite leave can also be granted in situations not addressed in the *Immigration Rules*, including to persons who have been excluded but are not removable.[103] This policy was based on jurisprudence[104] and sets out three main requirements: length of residence, gravity of conduct, and the extent to which the person has changed. With respect to the length of residence, it is said:

> There is no limit in how often a restricted leave can be extended while for gravity of conduct the approach is that for exclusion and the section 33.2 cases there will almost always be public interest reasons not to grant indefinite leave to remain. This is because even if the adverse behaviour was committed some time ago, the government's view is that such persons are unwelcome here and the UK has international obligations to prevent this country from becoming a safe haven for those who have committed very serious crimes.[105]

[*Kardi*], and MS, R (on the application of) v Secretary of State for the Home Department (excluded persons: Restrictive Leave policy) (IJR) [2015] UKUT 539 (IAC) at paras 119–21 and 130–32 [*MS*] (upheld on appeal in *MS & Anor v The Secretary of State for the Home Department*, [2017] EWCA Civ 1190 [*MS & Anor*].

102 *Immigration Rules*, s 276B.

103 Home Office, *Restricted Leave*, above note 101 at 33–36.

104 *Kardi*, above note 101 at para 32; *MS*, above note 101 at para 144 (suggesting relevant factors such as "whether the applicant has remained blamelessly in the United Kingdom for a lengthy period of time or the prospect of removal of the applicant to his or her home country but also an appraisal of the political circumstances of the home country bearing in mind the international reputation of the United Kingdom which can be in point in these cases, and other case specific issues concerned with the particular circumstances of the original reason for exclusion from the Refugee Convention and the particular circumstances of the applicant and his life in the United Kingdom") and *MS & Anor*, above note 101 at paras 120–23.

105 Home Office, *Restricted Leave*, above note 101 at 34–35; it relies on *MS & Anor*, above note 101, for this statement even though the case itself is not as unequivocal when it says at

Regarding the last requirement, that the person has changed, it is said that just good conduct is not sufficient but that the person has contributed positively to society, so there has been a "lasting and genuine change."[106]

The Netherlands has a long-standing and detailed policy regarding long-term residents with a 1F background (which in the Netherlands means criminality in both the exclusion and *refoulement* stages). The most important part of this policy[107] was the result of a number of decisions by the Council of State,[108] which attempted to resolve the dilemma of persons with a 1F history who could not be removed because of concerns arising out of article 3 of the ECHR[109] by introducing a durability and proportionality test.[110] If a person can fulfill both parts of

---

para 124: "In all cases involving terrorist offences full weight must be accorded to her [secretary of state for the Home Department] view that it is not in the public interest to allow this country to become a safe haven for terrorists and to any other, more specific, aspects of the case requiring a judgement on matters of national security or foreign relations. Particular respect should likewise be paid to any view she may express as to the public acceptability of the grant of ILR to migrants who have committed certain kinds of offending." See, also, *Babar v The Secretary of State for the Home Department*, [2018] EWCA Civ 329 at paras 32–36, and *R (on the application of Gornovskiy) v Secretary of State for the Home Department (extradition and immigration powers)*, [2021] UKUT 321 (IAC) at paras 91–93. For a situation where indefinite restricted leave was granted, see *Ruhumuliza (Article 1F and "undesirable": Rwanda)*, [2016] UKUT 284 (IAC).

106 *Restricted Leave*, above note 101 at 35; see, also, at 35–36. Other considerations related to the public interest, such as the risk of offending or any unlawful stay in the United Kingdom, also play a role, while for persons only subject to an s 33.2 decision, indefinite leave can be granted if they can show that they are no longer a danger to the community.

107 Other parts of the policy were to actively facilitate the relocation of such persons to third countries and to grant a temporary residence permit; see Bolhuis, Battjes & van Wijk, above note 56 at 71–74 & 75, respectively.

108 AbRS, 2 June 2004, nr 200308871/1; AbRS, 9 July 2004, nr 200411181/1; AbRS, 18 July 2007, nr 200701663/1; Letter from the Minister and State Secretary of Justice to the House of Commons, 2007–8 Session, 31 200 VI, Nr 160, 9 June 2008 at 5; Notitie betreffende de toepassing van artikel 1F Vluchtelingenverdrag at 25–27.

109 The Dutch government estimates that as of the end of 2020, sixty-seven persons fall under this category, while eighteen such persons had been removed from the Netherlands; see Rapportagebrief internationale misdrijven 2020, 29 October 2021, 3.

110 Since 2017, this test has been set out in the *Aliens Manual* or *Vreemdelingencirculaire* 2000 (C), art 7.10.2.6, with the following main components: (a) art 3 of the ECHR resists on a continuous basis the removal of an alien to their country of origin and (b) the consequences of denying the alien a residency permit are disproportional in relation to the interest of the state to apply art 1F of the Refugee Convention. There had been a district court decision, which states that this approach should only apply to 1F(a) cases and not 1F(b); see Rb, The Hague, Awb 08/8496, 20 January 2009, but that reasoning was overruled later in the year by the Council of State in AbRS, 9 September 2009, nr 200901146/1.

this test, then they would be entitled to have their status regularized by obtaining a temporary residency permit.[111] This test has been fleshed out by setting out the following requirements to be met in order to come within the parameters of the test:

- the person has found themself for a lengthy period of time in a situation that they cannot be deported because of human rights concerns;
- there is no prospect of change in this situation in the near future;
- departure to a third country despite sufficient efforts by the person concerned has proven to be impossible; and
- the person is in an exceptional situation in the Netherlands.[112]

The government has interpreted the requirement of a lengthy period to be more than ten years from the date of the initial claim to refugee status,[113] which has been deemed to be reasonable by the judiciary.[114]

With respect to an assessment of proportionality, in general the judiciary will give the government a great deal of deference.[115] The fact that a person has almost finished a university education is not a circumstance that would lead to a finding of disproportionality,[116] nor would the fact that they have no right to income or housing during the waiting period;[117] nor a combination of a negative effect on family life; nor the fact that the person has suffered as a result of the accusation of being a war criminal; nor has been in the past a victim of torture; nor has

111 However, if the person cannot show first that the sustainability part of the test applies to them, there is no need to assess the proportionality portion; see AbRS, 21 November 2007, nr 200704604/1; Rb, The Hague, Awb 08/24943, 25 September 2009.

112 Bolhuis, Battjes & Van Wijk, above note 56 at 75–76; AbRS, 18 July 2007, nr 200701663/1; AbRS, 9 September 2009, nr 200901146/1; regarding the prospect of change, see AbRS, 21 November 2007, nr 200704604/1; regarding the requirement of making efforts to find an alternative destination, see AbRS, 5 February 2010, nr 200903826/1, and Rb, The Hague, NL 21.3223, 1 April 2021; the minister needs to assess all of these requirements before making a negative decision according to AbRS, 25 January 2013, nr 201113000/1; *Vreemdelingencirculaire* 2000 (C), art 7.10.2.6.

113 Letter from the Minister and State Secretary of Justice to the House of Commons, 2007–8 Session, 31 200 VI, Nr 160, 9 June 2008 at 5; Notitie betreffende de toepassing van artikel 1F Vluchtelingenverdrag at 26.

114 Rb, The Hague, Awb 08/16875, 17 March 2009; Rb, Den Bosch, Awb 13/9468, 30 December 2013; Rb, Utrecht, Awb 10/18603, 7 March 2014; this is also now specified in the *Vreemdelingencirculaire* 2000 (C), art 7.10.2.6.

115 AbRS, 12 November 2007, nr 200703870/1.

116 *Ibid.*

117 Rb, The Hague, Awb 05/11010, 28 June 2006.

lived in the Netherlands for almost seven years; nor has achieved a high level of integration; and nor has been pursued by the Dutch authorities during that time period.[118] A serious medical condition could play a positive role in this assessment.[119]

As a result of the high standard of the proportionality part of the test, there have been very few instances where a person has been given legal permission to stay in the Netherlands.[120]

F. CONCLUSION

None of the possible solutions attempted by the various governments has been ideal. Prosecutions based on extraterritorial jurisdiction, while possible and successful at times, will remain elusive as an option except in very few cases due to the extensive amount of resources required for this remedy. There has been a suggestion to make this approach more effective by adopting more strategic litigation, which would rely on better cooperation between universal jurisdiction states to determine which cases to investigate and prosecute, as well as in which forum,[121]

118 Rb, The Hague, Awb 06/7531, 21 November 2006; the right to family life as enshrined in art 8 of the ECHR does not affect a negative finding regarding disproportionality; see AbRS, 24 June 2009, nr 200806832/1; Rb, Rotterdam, Awb 09/13852, 21 October 2010; Rb, The Hague, Awb 10/(LJN: BO4158), 16 November 2010.

119 Rb, The Hague, Awb 17/12240, 28 February 2018.

120 According to Bolhuis, Battjes & Van Wijk, above note 56 at 76, this was only the case in ten instances until January 2016. For a discussion of this approach, see Zarif Yakut-Bahtiyar, *Exclusion Clauses of the Refugee Convention in Relation to National Immigration Legislations, European Policy and Human Rights Instruments; Article 1F Versus the Non-refoulement Principle* (Nijmegen: Wolf Legal Publishers, 2016) at 269–71, and Joke Reijven & Joris van Wijk, "Caught in Limbo: How Alleged Perpetrators of International Crimes Who Applied for Asylum in the Netherlands Are Affected by a Fundamental System Error in International Law" (2014) 26:2 *International Journal of Refugee Law* 248 at 264–65.

121 Wolfgang Kaleck, "From Pinochet to Rumsfeld: Universal Jurisdiction in Europe 1998–2008" (2009) 30:3 *Michigan Journal of International Law* 927 at 976–80. Some attempts have already been made in closer coordination in investigations and prosecutions of war crimes cases by improving exchange of information pertaining to investigations and by establishing best practices; for instance, Interpol convened four International Expert Meetings on Genocide, War Crimes, and Crimes Against Humanity between 2005 and 2012, while in 2014, a dedicated unit, the War Crimes and Genocide Sub-directorate, was created to focus on war crimes, genocide, and crimes against humanity. In 2002, the Council of the European Union decided to establish a European network of contact points in respect of persons responsible for genocide, crimes against humanity, and war crimes, which meets on a regular basis (Decision of 13 June 2002, 2002/494/JHA, and Decision 2003/335/JHA of 8 May 2003) and has been supported since 2011 by the Genocide Network Secretariat of Eurojust. There are

while a division of labour in prosecutions between states with territorial and universal jurisdiction, complemented by international institutions in the most egregious cases, has also been contemplated.[122]

However, the fact that there have only been a few cases in universal jurisdiction states should not mean that this effort should be abandoned—rather to the contrary, as it can be expected with the demise of the international institutions in the near future, with the exception of the ICC, that domestic prosecutors will have to increase their efforts in order to give some force to the adage that there can be no impunity for perpetrators of international crimes. As well, even a modest level of prosecutions could very well have a deterrent effect, maybe not on the commission of international crimes[123] but on the choice of a refugee claimant to come to a country that prosecutes international crimes or to remain in such a country.

It should also be kept in mind that not all such persons can be made subject to this remedy as they have already been subject to a conviction and have served their sentence. The jurisprudence in the exclusion 1F(b) area and in the public order or national security context has made it clear that a conviction is not an impediment to using these approaches. On the assumption that prosecution remains available in many cases and governments are willing to investigate and prosecute crimes committed by refugee claimants or refugees, the role of territorial jurisdictions should be clarified. Prosecutions for crimes committed on the territory of the prosecuting agency are much easier to carry out than if committed outside that country. This applies to countries of refuge that have prosecuted persons involved in common crimes or even terrorist offences on their territory before making them subject to a *refoulement* procedure. It also applies in situations of genocide, war crimes, and crimes against humanity, where prosecutions that took place in the country where the crimes were committed have resulted in far more convictions than in the countries that use universal jurisdiction.[124]

---

also cooperation efforts in the exclusion area; see Bolhuis & van Wijk, above note 6 at 36–47, as well as the establishment in Europe of the Exclusion Network in 2017 under the auspices of EASO (as of 19 January 2021, the European Union Agency for Asylum (EUAA)).

122 Rikhof, above note 52 at 51.

123 Mark A. Drumbl, *Atrocity, Punishment and International Law* (Cambridge: Cambridge University Press, 2007) at 169–73.

124 Rikhof, above note 52 at 15–25.

Transferring persons with a criminal background to the territorial jurisdiction of another country is also problematic, primarily because of human rights concerns, whether the result of such a transfer is achieved by deportation or extradition. The solution to this problem is as practical as it is legal since in most cases such a transfer is prohibited if it is because of inadequacies in the trial conducted in the territorial state or the conditions of imprisonment after sentencing. However, countries that want to have a person transferred to a territorial jurisdiction are not entirely powerless in accomplishing that goal, especially if they could obtain more robust assurances, including monitoring. The fact that the Special Court of Sierra Leone was able to transfer all persons convicted under its jurisdiction to Rwanda after concluding a detailed arrangement in respect to prison conditions in that country, and the fact that a number of countries have been able to extradite people to Rwanda, Bosnia-Herzegovina, Croatia, and Serbia, shows that the development of such arrangements is in flux and can be improved upon, especially if some capacity building, in improving the judicial system and prison conditions, accompanies the attempt to obtain assurances. In this context, it seems that the international human rights monitoring institutions are willing to take a softer line with respect to assurances in the extradition context than in the deportation context.

In examining the last two options set out in this chapter, long-term detention and humanitarian solutions, it seems that detention is the least attractive as a result of the limited grounds on which detention can be utilized and even more so as a result of it being very difficult to build a *non-refoulement* policy around it given the uncertainties of continued detentions due to regular reviews.

While humanitarian solutions look useful on the surface, the countries under consideration are reluctant to extend this possibility to persons with a criminal background. When setting out general rules for humanitarian residence for persons who cannot be removed, an exception is frequently made for persons who have committed serious crimes or are a danger to the public order or national security. Even in the Netherlands and the United Kingdom, where a policy is in place to provide a solution for persons with a 1F background, this policy is restrictive in its parameters and even more limited in its application.

There have been attempts to provide solutions to this dilemma of persons who are undesirable but unreturnable (UBUs). In 2016, a policy brief following a two-year research project indicated, with respect to

UBUs, that because of the lack of a coherent policy response, guidance should be provided to states. The first steps would include measures that would "limit the number of allegedly criminal migrants ending up in legal limbo" by either reducing the number of persons considered to be "undesirables" or by increasing the number of those who are returned or removed. The policy brief recognized that despite such measures, some UBUs whose legal status continues to be uncertain will remain. For this group of persons, a balancing test was suggested whereby a state's interests in prolonging the "status of undesirability," such as the level of an acute security threat, the seriousness of the alleged crimes, and the level of responsibility of the individual, would be weighed against the UBU's interests of being removed from the category of "undesirable," especially in relation to the social, psychological, and physical impact of the protracted situation of uncertainty.[125]

Building on the suggested solutions in the policy brief, it might be possible to arrive at a more satisfactory solution when the various approaches discussed above are not applied in isolation from each other, nor from the underlying reason as to why *refoulement* alternatives are needed in the first place: the dilemma of dealing with persons with a criminal background. While during the exclusion phase most persons (at least for 1F(a) and 1F(c) exclusion) have been refused status for complicity-type involvement, and during the *refoulement* stage convictions for crimes constitute most of the cases, the seriousness of the criminality involved moves along a spectrum. This spectrum has not been considered during the humanitarian alternative either because they are excluded altogether in the general application of long-term solutions or because the criminality is a constant to move beyond, as in the Dutch or UK situation.

However, taking the Dutch solution as an example as it is the most sophisticated, it might be fruitful to include in the assessment of long-term solutions not only factors such as the length of time in the country or the exceptional humanitarian situation of an applicant but also the level of involvement of a person in the crimes committed. For instance, having been a low-level member in a criminal organization or having carried out support tasks, which were on the periphery of

---

125 Refugee Law Initiative, *Undesirable and Unreturnable? Policy Challenges*, above note 6 at 5; see, also, David James Cantor et al, "The Emperor's New Clothing: National Responses to 'Undesirable and Unreturnable' Aliens Under Asylum and Immigration" (2017) 36:1 *Refugee Survey Quarterly* 1 at 7–8, and van Wijk & Bolhuis, above note 86 at 415–16.

the commission of international crimes, would not eliminate being subject to this policy but could affect some of its elements, either on the durability side, by requiring less time spent in the country, or on the proportionality side, by requiring less of an effort to seek alternatives for the person's removal or requiring less stringent exceptional circumstances.

This might result in fewer persons whose criminality is on the lower end of the spectrum being held in legal limbo, while the persons with more serious criminality can be made the subject of extradition requests, where a grouping of requests can be envisaged in that assurances of a country are sought specifically to address the main human rights concerns of fair trial and prison conditions for a number of persons from that country rather than on an individual basis. This could be done together with other countries to make the request for such assurances (as well as possible monitoring) more compelling and might eventually serve as an impetus for a more general improvement of the human rights situation in the country in question, thereby obviating the human rights concerns for *refoulement*.

Cases remaining after such an exercise could be investigated and prosecuted either by the countries based on universal jurisdiction or by international institutions. While some countries, such as Canada and the Netherlands, already have some system of priority setting for prosecution purposes, a more robust and cooperative model, taking into account all alternatives for *refoulement*, might result in applying the appropriate remedy to the appropriate level of criminality.

CHAPTER EIGHT

Conclusion

Before drawing some final conclusions from the examination of the international and domestic practices regarding exclusion, *refoulement*, and alternative remedies, it may be useful to recall some of the observations made earlier in the book in respect to the responses to refugees with a criminal background.

In Chapter 2, which examined the historical background of exclusion and *refoulement* provisions, it was clear that the concern with criminality had permeated virtually all discussions related to the rights of refugees. This had begun with legal philosophers, such as Grotius and Vattel, who advocated states' obligations to protect persons fleeing persecution but who were not inclined to extend these rights to serious criminals. Soon after the issue of refugees had become a concern of the international community and international agreements were drawn up to provide protection to displaced persons, criminality in the form of a *refoulement* provision had already found a place in the first comprehensive refugee arrangement, the 1933 Refugee Convention. This convention included exceptions for *non-refoulement* for situations of national security or public order. The first instruments after the Second World War were less concerned with criminality as an exception to *refoulement* than with ensuring that certain criminal elements would not be entitled to any benefit normally associated with refugees in the first place. The drafting of the Refugee Convention brought these two strands of criminality together for the first time by having both an exclusion ground and an exception to the *non-refoulement* provision.

In terms of the types of criminal activities that should limit the benefits to asylum seekers, the basic parameters as sketched out by Grotius and Vattel do not differ that much conceptually from what was considered to be nefarious in later centuries, taking into account the political and legal context of the times when those instruments were conceived. After all, crimes injurious to humankind, destructive to society, or a menace to public security everywhere, as stated by those two scholars, are not far removed from concepts such as national security, public order, crimes against peace, war crimes, crimes against humanity, or acts against the purposes and principles of the United Nations. Similarly, an elucidation of what constitutes a danger to security by a commentator on the 1933 Refugee Convention on the effect of activities that upset the very equilibrium of society resonates quite clearly with the comments made in relation to the 1951 Refugee Convention, that such a concept involves acts of a serious nature directly or indirectly threatening the government, the integrity, the independence, or the external peace of the country.

What changed after the Second World War was, first, the beginning of attempts to provide more detail for those universally known criminal concepts, especially because of the debates related to the 1951 Refugee Convention. Second, because of concerns about *refoulement* to unacceptable situations from a human rights perspective, the limitations on the benefits for refugees were restricted and further clarified.

In the exclusion chapters (chapters 3 to 5), it was noted that both divergent and convergent trends could be detected depending on the subject matter. As an overarching comment with respect to exclusion, it was said that the various concepts in exclusion, including the conceptual definitions of the crimes set out in Article 1F(a), the ancillary notions of complicity in all three clauses, the notion of political crimes in Article 1F(b), and the residual function of Article 1F(c), could be traced to parallel legal movements in other areas of the law, such as international criminal law, extradition law, and domestic criminal law.

While the three exclusion clauses are supposed to serve different criminal activities, it is clear from the language employed, the discussions during the *travaux préparatoires*, and the application by the national refugee tribunals and courts that overlap between them is possible. For instance, serious crimes as a category are to be considered under Article 1F(b), but when these serious criminal activities exceed a particular threshold as established in international criminal law, they can also become Article 1F(a) activities. Similarly, terrorist activities had traditionally been dealt with under Article 1F(b) until 2001, when the United Nations decided that they could also be brought under Article 1F(c), a position adopted at the national level soon after.

With respect to the specific exclusion clauses, Article 1F(a), because of its reference to international instruments in relation to the crimes mentioned—crimes against peace, war crimes, and crimes against humanity—presents a clear invitation to use international criminal law as its source for interpretation. This was already mentioned by the drafters of the Refugee Convention, who wanted this provision set out as broadly as possible to consider the jurisprudence developed after the Second World War and the emerging areas of international humanitarian law and international criminal law. This invitation continues unabated and has been accepted without hesitation at the national level when giving meaning to the *chapeaux* elements of the international crimes and the specific crimes they had to apply in this exclusion provision. It certainly helped that the international institutions had few, if any, differences in interpreting the parameters of the crimes of genocide, war crimes, and crimes against humanity and the underlying crimes of most importance to the national decision makers, such as torture, inhumane acts, persecution, and rape.

In terms of the definition of concepts for Article 1F(b), the drafters did not provide any examples of the type of criminality they thought should be included in this provision, and there was even disagreement in how much minor crimes should be part of this exclusion clause, while the same lack of resolution can be detected in the relationship between extradition and refugee law. In this aspect, the development of international law since 1951 has been more useful than the drafters' debates, especially in making a connection between international extradition law and exclusion law when choosing the appropriate test for determining if a crime is political. The predominance and proportionality test, which was developed originally in extradition law, has been wholeheartedly accepted by all countries in this study. The same thing might and certainly should happen with the emerging definition for terrorism, where consensus is developing at the international and national levels in regard to its two essential elements: the commission of very serious crimes against persons or property with a view to intimidating a population and forcing national or international institutions to do the bidding of groups employing such tactics.

On the other hand, the search for a definition for acts against the principles and purposes of the United Nations has been less successful at the international level. The drafters of the convention only provided some examples of what could constitute Article 1F(c) behaviour, and those were for human rights that did not reach the Article 1F(a) crimes against humanity threshold or were acts contrary to the maintenance of a just peace. The international community has mentioned five activities since the drafting of the convention: hostage taking, torture, forced disappearance, apartheid, and terrorism. But only the last one is in specific connection to Article 1F(c), and then which were only recently also accepted at the national level, as were attacks against peacekeepers. National refugee decision makers were left to find their own meaning for this specific exclusion provision, but they were not able to escape the same dilemma that had occurred at the international level in that their attempts to give meaning to this article overlapped with the activities already prohibited by the two other exclusion clauses. The only advantage of using Article 1F(c) as opposed to Article 1F(b) for terrorist activities was the fact that Article 1F(c) eliminates the need for assessing whether these acts were committed for a political purpose, although this possibility had been greatly reduced already for the Article 1F(b) approach, either by the specific elimination of this exception in a number of terrorism conventions or by finding the exception not applicable on the facts in most of the cases before the refugee decision makers.

Outside the area of defining criminal concepts in the three exclusion clauses, a connection has recently been sought with international criminal law when giving meaning to the various form of extended liability. It is not clear yet how this trend will continue or whether a wholesale transfer of international criminal law concepts to the refugee sphere is desirable. As explained earlier in this book, until 2009, all courts applying the exclusion clause in Article 1F(a) developed the notions of extended liability separately from the developments in this area by international institutions. Some of these extended liability concepts as developed in the national jurisprudence had already incorporated the elements as provided in the international jurisprudence, such as the requirement that aiding and abetting must have a substantial contribution with knowledge of the activities of the organization to which the contribution is made.

The requirements of forms of extended liability, such as aiding and abetting and command responsibility, can easily be transferred from the international to the national level, but legally complex notions, such as joint criminal enterprise or forms of perpetration, might flounder in the face of the unique type of procedures used for exclusion, which are of a more summary character and require less evidence than an international or a national criminal trial. The more practical national equivalent of joint criminal enterprise developed at the domestic level, which is based on a number of factors, such as career path, duration with an organization, the manner of dissociation, and the type of organization, might yield the same result in the specific circumstances of a refugee proceeding without sacrificing the connection to international criminal law.

While in general the connection in extended liability between Article 1F(a) and international criminal law is clearly present and desirable, the same cannot be said for Article 1F(b). From the drafters' comments, the language of the provision itself, without any international reference, and the jurisprudence in the nine countries, it is clear that the connection was sought in this exclusion ground with national criminal law. To preserve some influence from international law regarding the interpretation of the types of extended liability to be employed in this article, reference to transnational law, especially for terrorism and organized crime, would be useful.

The last observation with respect to Article 1F(b) can be made with even more force for Article 1F(c) as the six crimes identified within this exclusion clause have their source in transnational law, with the result that the forms of liability used in the treaties regulating those crimes should be given a great deal of weight in the interpretation of the term "guilty," which is broader than the term "committed" in 1F(a) and 1F(b) and could include the inchoate crimes of attempt, incitement, and conspiracy.

As noted in Chapter 6, when dealing with *refoulement*, the notion of danger to the security has been interpreted in a similar fashion by the countries under consideration in this book by indicating that, while the threat level must be high, given the global security situation, it is not necessary for the danger to the security to be only a direct threat to the country of refuge; it can also be an indirect threat or a security danger outside the country where a refugee is staying. On the other hand, the practice of the judiciary in danger to the community shows divergence in a number of aspects, from determining which approach to employ in the notion of conviction for a particularly serious crime as stipulated in section 33.2 of the convention, to the level of criminality to be construed as particularly serious, to whether or not a risk assessment is required as part of a danger approach, although in the latter case, only the United States strikes a discordant note.

In comparing *refoulement* as set out in the Refugee Convention with exclusion in the same instrument, it is clear that the area with the potential for the most crimes, common crimes, also has the possibility of the widest gap, especially in respect to crimes committed in the territory of the country of refuge compared to crimes committed outside such a country. While the distinction between serious crimes in 1F(b) and particularly serious crimes has, in most cases, been illusory in terms of the gravity of the offence, the requirement of a conviction, which so far has mostly been a conviction for personal conduct rather than extended liability, and the requirement of a separate danger assessment in most countries (which in many cases involves a determination regarding the possibility of recidivism) raise the possibility that many people carrying out criminal activities in the country of refuge would not be subject to removal, while persons with a similar background would be excluded.

With respect to the relationship between Refugee Convention *refoulement* and other forms of human rights protection, as discussed in Chapter 6, the practice of the countries in determining what types of suffering amount to torture or other types of maltreatment has been quite consistent, most likely due to the jurisprudence of the four international or supranational institutions in this area: the United Nations Human Rights Committee, the United Nations Committee against Torture, the European Court of Human Rights, and the Inter-American Court of Human Rights.

In the context of the grafting of human rights protection onto refugee *refoulement*, the question can be asked whether, because of the absolute prohibition of removal to torture or cruel, inhuman, or degrading treatment or punishment, the danger to the national security, public order, and community has become obsolete since any finding in that regard would be overcome by human rights protections. Such a comment might be an overstatement for two reasons. The first is that there are forms of suffering that do not reach the level of the ill treatment described in international human rights instruments but do amount to persecution as regulated by the Refugee Convention. Persons who fall into that latter category cannot be removed unless they have the criminal background prescribed in articles 32.1 and 33.2 of the Refugee Convention. Second, the protection based on international instruments is seen as temporary, and removal will occur when the substantial risk of ill treatment has subsided, unless the regular protection of the Refugee Convention, including its exceptions, can be relied upon.

However, while the human rights protection applies to everyone with a risk of exposure to ill treatment, it might be more meaningful for persons with a criminal background as they, as a group, could typically face this type of risk because they will be seen as criminals upon their return and face inhumane treatment in detention conditions, which all international human right institutions have identified as a major concern in their work.

As a result, whether risk is assessed as part of a danger process, as part of a human rights protection process, or in some combination of the two, it is clear that the possibility of removing persons with a criminal background to their country of origin has become more difficult for governments that want to ensure that the exclusion and the *refoulement* provisions of the Refugee Convention are enforced. In trying to address this problem at the national level, we saw in Chapter 7 that so far none of the possible solutions attempted by the various governments have been ideal.

Prosecutions based on extraterritorial jurisdiction, while successful at times, will remain elusive as an option due to the extensive amount of resources required for this remedy. Transferring persons with a criminal background to the territorial jurisdiction of another country is also problematic, whether the transfer is achieved by deportation or extradition, mostly because of human rights concerns. In examining the last two alternative remedies, long-term detention and humanitarian solutions, it seems that the detention option is the least attractive as a result of the limited grounds on which detention can be utilized but even more so because it is very difficult to build a *non-refoulement* policy around it given the uncertainties of continued detentions due to regular reviews. While humanitarian solutions, such as regularizing the immigration status of persons who cannot be removed for human rights reasons, look useful on the surface, the countries under consideration are reluctant to extend this to persons with a criminal background. When setting out general rules for humanitarian residence for persons who cannot be removed, an exception is frequently made for persons who have committed serious crimes or are a danger to the public order or national security.

Having examined the major trends in jurisprudence with respect to exclusion and *refoulement*, the remainder of this chapter will address two questions of overarching concern: consistency (or lack thereof) in national practice and the problematic issue of the inability to remove serious criminals because of human rights concerns.

In regard to the first issue, as a preliminary point we can ask whether it is desirable to strive for consistency in areas of refugee law that have their source in or are related to concepts of criminal law. While criminal law, at both the international and domestic levels, contains many similar concepts, there are also many differences, especially in the types of behaviour that have been criminalized and the level of punishment ascribed to these types of criminal activities, which in turn reflect, especially at the national level, different societal values and approaches to criminal conduct.

On the other hand, a strong argument can be made that even though exclusion and *refoulement* have connections to criminal law concepts, the purposes of criminal law and refugee law in these areas are not the same. As well, the criminal concepts in refugee law all find their source in one international instrument, the Refugee Convention, which sets out principles that the drafters intended should transcend national interpretations of key criminal concepts. In addition, the fact that this human rights instrument does not have its own monitoring or interpretative oversight body, like other similar instruments do, should be no reason to assume that asylum seekers, as a matter of fair procedure, can expect the same treatment for criminal behaviour no matter where they have made an application for refugee status.

With respect to consistency in exclusion, we noted earlier that the search for the same meaning for various concepts has yielded different results depending on the exclusion clause involved and the specific concept addressed. As a starting principle of interpretation, deference should be given to the international instruments that underlie the exclusion clauses, either directly or indirectly. This is the most obvious for 1F(a), where there is a specific reference to international instruments in respect to the crime under consideration in that clause and to the modes of liability. As there is already a substantial body of international criminal law in respect to both crimes and extended liability, this body of law should be very persuasive in the interpretation of exclusion 1F(a), unless there are important and well-reasoned arguments to come to the opposite conclusion. With respect to the international crimes set out in 1F(a), the national judiciary has been following the international body of law on a regular basis, and this will most likely continue. The same has been done for the concept of acts against the principles and purposes of the United Nations in 1F(c), where reliance has been placed on transnational criminal law for the crimes most often associated with this clause, terrorism and crimes against peacekeepers. With respect to 1F(b), while there has been some lip service paid to the Palermo Convention, which all nine countries have ratified and defines serious crime as a crime with a maximum penalty of at least four years' imprisonment, the jurisprudence in most of the nine countries has opted for a more contextual approach, where several factors related to the perpetrator are taken into consideration to determine what constitutes a serious crime. This approach is different from the methodology used by states in circumscribing the notion of particularly serious crimes during the *refoulement* stage, where the main indicator is still related to a term of imprisonment, either a maximum penalty or as actually imposed.

As to extended liability for the exclusion clause, the approaches there present a more confusing picture. So far, the courts and tribunals have had no difficulty applying the same principles to all three exclusion clauses as a result of the much closer nexus established by the highest courts in the United Kingdom, New Zealand, Canada, and Australia (in chronological order) between international and domestic law and their view that Article 1F(a) complicity is broader than domestic forms of accountability. A more fundamental discussion of forms of liability will be required if 1F(b) and 1F(c) are going to be applied to a broader circle of perpetrators than is presently the case. If some countries that have other types of liability in their domestic criminal statutes than those contained in the Rome Statute are likely to prefer their domestic law over international law for Article 1F(a), this will certainly be the case for Article 1F(b) because of the lack of an international instruments reference and the fact that all nine countries already view their domestic criminal law as the proper source for Article 1F(b) crimes. In Europe, there has been a unifying force for 1F(b) and 1F(c) complicity in that the Court of Justice of the European Union has laid out some basic principles in this regard and hopes that common law countries will take this jurisprudence into account when further developing the parameters of these two exclusion grounds. The general trend in the jurisprudence has been that 1F(a) has the narrowest scope of extended liability, with more forms of liability susceptible to being part of 1F(b) and 1F(c) and with the broadest reach in 1F(c) due to its ability to include inchoate offences. However, an even broader form of extended liability, membership in a nefarious organization (used in the past), has ceased to be a separate type of complicity in all three exclusion grounds, although it can still have a smaller role as a factor in an overall assessment of involvement in exclusion crimes.

In comparing the jurisprudence of the countries examined in this study, it can be seen that despite some differences between the jurisprudence in specific exclusion issues, the trends tend to be moving in the same direction, and it is hoped that domestic courts and tribunals will continue to use exclusion as a powerful means to ensure that all objectives of the 1951 Refugee Convention are met and that they will develop exclusion concepts with an even keener eye to the jurisprudence of their judicial counterparts in other countries than has happened in a few instances in recent years. Perhaps this book can make a small contribution in this regard.

The other area of overarching concern discussed in Chapter 7 was the various ways of dealing with persons with a criminal background who cannot be removed because of human rights concerns. While it has already been noted that none of the four solutions addressing this phenomenon has been very successful, Chapter 7 showed that it might be fruitful to include in the assessment of a long-term solution not only factors such as the length of presence in the country or the exceptional humanitarian situation of an applicant but also the level of involvement of a person in the crimes committed rather than just the type of crime a person has committed. This might result in fewer persons whose criminality is at the lower end of the spectrum being held in a legal limbo, while the persons with more serious criminality can be made the subject of extradition requests. In a situation with a grouping of requests, it can be envisaged that the assurances of a country to which persons are extradited are sought specifically to address the human rights concerns of fair trial and prison conditions for a number of persons from the extraditing country rather than on an individual basis. Cases remaining after such an exercise should be investigated and prosecuted, either by the countries based on universal jurisdiction or by international institutions. A more robust and cooperative model that considers all the alternatives for *refoulement* might result in applying the appropriate remedy to the appropriate level of criminality.

In this context, it should be noted that, in comparing the state of the law between the first edition of this book and now, there has been a hardening of attitudes by governments in respect to persons with a criminal background. While the courts have arrested this development somewhat with respect to complicity, in other aspects governments were given freer rein. Examples can be found, especially in the areas of *refoulement* and persons who are "undesirable but unreturnable," where in the former the notion of particularly serious crime has been expanded, as have the concepts of danger to the security and public, while for the latter, more persons have been extradited, the maximum duration of detention has been increased, and humanitarian solutions have been tightened, both in general and with respect to persons who have been excluded or *refouled* but cannot be removed.

Last, while this book has primarily been a legal treatise, like all legal issues, the question of exclusion, *refoulement*, and alternative remedies takes place against a larger international and domestic political and policy background. The exclusion of suspected war criminals is often seen as part of the larger strategy of the international fight against impunity, while organized crime and terrorism approaches in refugee law mirror or complement criminal attempts to deal with the underlying phenomenon. If the legal responses arising out of refugee law are seen to fulfill a more overarching and consistent purpose, then the same should be required from international and domestic policy makers. The fact that the international situation with respect to the acceptance of refugees has worsened in the last ten years has also influenced the hardening of attitudes against asylum seekers or refugees with a criminal background. But for both situations, it is important not to lose sight of the overarching purpose of the Refugee Convention, respect for the dignity of all persons, no matter in what situations they have found themselves.

Bibliography

Literature

AAGTEN, ANNE. "Migrant Smuggling in the Mediterranean: An Excludable Act Under Article 1F(b) Refugee Convention?" (2018) 2 *Crimmigratie & Recht* 59–75.

ADVIESCOMMISSIE VOOR VREEMDELINGENZAKEN. "Artikel 1F Vluchtelingenverdrag in het Nederlands vreemdelingenbeleid" (The Hague: Adviescommissie voor Vreemdelingenzaken, 2008).

AITCHISON, SHARELLE & MARTIN TREADWELL. "Staged Interpretation of Article 1F(b): 'Serious Non-political Crime Outside the Country of Refuge Prior to [His or Her] Admission to That Country as a Refugee': A Periaktos, Scene Setting Problem?" in James C. Simeon, ed, *Serious International Crimes, Human Rights and Forced Migration* (London, Routledge, 2022) 280–307.

ALLAIN, JEAN. "The *Jus Cogens* Nature of *Non-refoulement*" (2001) 13 *International Journal of Refugee Law* 533–58.

AMNESTY INTERNATIONAL. *Dangerous Deals: Europe's Reliance on "Diplomatic Assurances" Against Torture* (London: Amnesty International Publications, 2010).

ASYLUM INFORMATION DATABASE (AIDA)/EUROPEAN COUNCIL ON REFUGEES AND EXILES (ECRE). Belgium, Country Report.

———. France, Country Report.

———. Germany, Country Report.

———. The Netherlands, Country Report.

ATAK, IDIL & JAMES C. SIMEON. "Human Trafficking: Mapping the Legal Boundaries of International Refugee Law and Criminal Justice" (2014) 12 *Journal of International Criminal Justice* 1019–38.

ATAK, IDIL & FRANÇOIS CRÉPEAU. "Refugees as Migrants" in Cathryn Costello, Michelle Foster & Jane McAdam, eds, *The Oxford Handbook of International Refugee Law* (Oxford: Oxford University Press, 2021) 134–51.

ATWELL, JULIE. "Aviation and International Terrorism" in Ben Saul, ed, *Research Handbook on International Law and Terrorism*, 2d ed (Cheltenham, UK & Northampton, US: Elgar, 2020) 47–59.

BANTEKAS, ILIAS. "The International Law on Terrorist Financing" in Ben Saul, ed, *Research Handbook on International Law and Terrorism*, 2d ed (Cheltenham, UK & Northampton, US: Elgar, 2020) 97–108.

BASSIOUNI, M. CHERIF. *International Extradition: United States Law and Practice*, 6th ed (Oxford: Oxford University Press, 2014).

BASSIOUNI, M. CHERIF & EDWARD M. WISE. *Aut Dedere, Aut Judicare: The Duty to Extradite or Prosecute in International Law* (Dordrecht/Boston/London: Martinus Nijhoff, 1995).

BATTJES, HEMME. "Subsidiary Protection and Other Alternative Forms of Protection" in Vincent Chetail & Céline Bauloz, eds, *Research Handbook on International Law and Migration* (Cheltenham, UK & Northampton, US: Elgar, 2014) 541–61.

BAULOZ, CÉLINE. "The (Mis)Use of International Humanitarian Law Under Article 15(C) of the EU Qualification Directive" in David Cantor & Jean-François Durieux, eds, *Refuge from Inhumanity? War Refugees and International Humanitarian Law* (Leiden & Boston: Brill Nijhoff, 2014) 247–69.

BECKER, HILLKA. "The Application of Article 1F UNCSR in International Protection Decision Making in Ireland in the Context of EU and International Law" in James C. Simeon, ed, *Serious International Crimes, Human Rights and Forced Migration* (London: Routledge, 2022) 202–28.

BEVERSLUIS, ANNELIEKE ET AL. "Once a Criminal, Always a Threat? Investigating Whether the Dutch Practice of Applying Article 1F Refugee Convention Criteria to Article 27 Citizenship Directive Conforms with EU Law" (Migration Law Clinic, University of Amsterdam, July 2016).

BICKNELL, CHRISTINE. "The Council of Europe and the European System" in Malcolm D. Evans & Jens Modvig, eds, *Research Handbook on Torture: Legal and Medical Perspectives on Prohibition and Prevention* (Cheltenham, UK & Northampton, US: Elgar, 2020) 177–202.

BILLINGS, PETER. "Operation Sovereign Borders and Interdiction at Sea: *CPCF v Minister for Immigration and Border Protection*" (2016) 23 *Australian Journal of Administrative Law* 76–101.

———. "International Crimes, Refugee 'Prisoner' Swaps and Duplicity in Australia's Refugee Admission" in James C. Simeon, ed, *Serious International Crimes, Human Rights and Forced Migration* (London: Routledge, 2022) 179–201.

BILLINGS, PETER & REBECCA ANANIAN-WELSH. "Counterterrorism and the Exclusion of Refugees and Refugee-Citizens from Australia" in James C. Simeon, ed, *Terrorism and Asylum* (Leiden & Boston: Brill Nijhoff, 2020) 175–214.

BILLINGSLEY, JAMES. "No Second Chances: The Default Exclusion of Refugee Claimants on Grounds of Serious Criminality: A Case Comment on *Febles v Canada*" (2015) 20 *Appeal: Review of Current Law and Law Reform* 99–119.

BLAKE, NICHOLAS. "Exclusion from Refugee Protection: Serious Non-political Crimes After 9/11" (2003) 4 *European Journal of Migration and Law* 425–47.

BLISS, MICHAEL. "Serious Reasons for Considering Minimum Standards of Procedural Fairness in the Application of the Article 1F Exclusion Clauses" (supp, 2000) 12 *International Journal of Refugee Law* 92–132.

BOAS, GIDEON & PASCALE CHIFFLET. "Suspected War Criminals in Australia: Law and Policy" (2016) 40 *Melbourne University Law Review* 46–86.

BOLHUIS, MAARTEN P., HEMME BATTJES & JORIS VAN WIJK. "Undesirable but Unreturnable Migrants in the Netherlands" (2017) 36 *Refugee Survey Quarterly* 61–84.

BOLHUIS, MAARTEN P., TARA DITZEL & JORIS VAN WIJK. "Vergelijking van 1F-uitsluitingen van Syrische Asielzoekers in Nederland en België" (2020) 8 *A&MR, Tijdschrift voor Asiel & Migrantenrecht* 385–90.

BOLHUIS, MAARTEN P., LOUIS P. MIDDELKOOP & JORIS VAN WIJK. "Refugee Exclusion and Extradition in the Netherlands: Rwanda as Precedent?" (2014) 12 *Journal of International Criminal Justice* 1115–39.

BOLHUIS, MAARTEN P. & JORIS VAN WIJK. "Alleged War Criminals in the Netherlands" (2015) 12 *European Journal of Criminology* 151–68.

———. *Study on the Exchange of Information Between European Countries Regarding Persons Excluded from Refugee Status in Accordance with Article 1F Refugee Convention* (VU, Amsterdam & UDI, Oslo, 2015).

———. "Alleged Terrorists and Other Perpetrators of Serious Non-political Crimes: The Application of Article 1F(b) of the Refugee Convention in the Netherlands" (2016) 29 *Journal of Refugee Studies* 19–38.

BOND, JENNIFER. "Excluding Justice: The Dangerous Intersection Between Refugee Claims, Criminal Law, and 'Guilty' Asylum Seekers" (2012) 24 *International Journal of Refugee Law* 37–59.

———. "Principled Exclusions: A Revised Approach to Article 1(F)(A) of the Refugee Convention" (2013) 35 *Michigan Journal of International Law* 21–78.

———. "The Defence of Duress in Canadian Refugee Law" (2016) 41 *Queen's Law Journal* 408–54.

———. "Unwanted but Unremovable: Canada's Treatment of 'Criminal' Migrants Who Cannot Be Removed" (2017) 36 *Refugee Survey Quarterly* 168–86.

BOND, JENNIFER, NATHAN BENSON & JARED PORTER. "Guilt by Association: Ezokola's Unfinished Business in Canadian Refugee Law" (2020) 39 *Refugee Survey Quarterly* 1–25.

BOND, JENNIFER & MICHELLE KRECH. "Excluding the Most Vulnerable: Application of Article 1F(a) of the Refugee Convention to Child Soldiers (2016) 20 *International Journal of Human Rights* 567–88.

BONNER, DAVID & RYSZARD CHOLEWINSKI. "The Response of the UK Legal and Constitutional Orders to the 1991 Gulf War and Post-9/11 'War on Terrorism'" in Anneliese Baldaccini & Elspeth Guild, eds, *Terrorism and the Foreigner: A Decade of Tension Around the Rule of Law in Europe* (Leiden/Boston: Martinus Nijhoff, 2007) 123–76.

BOSSUYT, MARC J. *Guide to the* "Travaux Préparatoires" *of the International Covenant on Civil and Political Rights* (Dordrecht/Boston/Lancaster: Martinus Nijhoff, 1987).

BOSTOCK, CHANTAL MARIE-JEANNE. "The International Legal Obligations Owed to the Asylum Seekers on the *MV Tampa*" (2002) 14 *International Journal of Refugee Law* 279–301.

BOSTOCK, CHANTAL & JASON CABARRÚS. "Short Shrift to International *Non-Refoulement* Obligations? Australia's Approach to Criminal Deportation" (2020) 32 *International Journal of Refugee Law* 597–622.

BRANÉ, MICHELLE & CHRISTIANA LUNDHOLM. "Human Rights Behind Bars: Advancing the Rights of Immigration Detainees in the United States Through Human Rights Frameworks" (2008) 22 *Georgetown Immigration Law Journal* 147–75.

BRIDDICK, CATHERINE & VLADISLAVA STOYANOVA. "Human Trafficking and Refugees" in Cathryn Costello, Michelle Foster & Jane McAdam, eds, *The Oxford Handbook of International Refugee Law* (Oxford: Oxford University Press, 2021) 553–68.

BURGERS, J. HERMANN & HANS DANELIUS. *The United Nations Convention Against Torture: A Handbook on the Convention Against Torture and Other Cruel, Inhuman or Degrading Treatment or Punishment* (Dordrecht/Boston/London: Martinus Nijhoff, 1988).

CANTOR, DAVID JAMES. *Returns of Internally Displaced Persons During Armed Conflict: International Law and Its Application in Colombia* (Leiden & Boston: Brill Nijhoff, 2018).

CANTOR, DAVID & FARAI CHIKWANHA. "Reconsidering African Refugee Law" (2019) 31 *International Journal of Refugee Law* 182–260.

CANTOR, DAVID JAMES & DIANA TRIMIÑO MORA. "A Simple Solution to War Refugees? The Latin American Expanded Definition and Its Relationship to IHL" in David Cantor & Jean-François Durieux, eds, *Refuge from Inhumanity? War Refugees and International Humanitarian Law* (Leiden & Boston: Brill Nijhoff, 2014) 204–24.

CANTOR, DAVID JAMES ET AL. "The Emperor's New Clothing: National Responses to 'Undesirable and Unreturnable' Aliens Under Asylum and Immigration" (2017) 36 *Refugee Survey Quarterly* 1–8.

CARLIER, JEAN-YVES & DIRK VAN HEULE. "Where Is the Reference? On the Limited Role of Transnational Dialogue in Belgian Refugee Law" in Guy S. Goodwin-Gill & Hélène Lambert, eds, *The Limits of Transnational Law: Refugee Law, Policy Harmonization and the Judicial Dialogue in the European Union* (Cambridge: Cambridge University Press, 2010) 17–34.

CHACÓN, JENNIFER M. "Unsecured Borders: Immigration Restrictions, Crime Control and National Security" (2007) 39 *Connecticut Law Review* 1827–91.

CHENOWETH, ERICA ET AL, EDS. *The Oxford Handbook of Terrorism* (Oxford: Oxford University Press, 2019).

CHETAIL, VINCENT. "Moving Towards an Integrated Approach of Refugee Law and Human Rights Law" in Cathryn Costello, Michelle Foster & Jane McAdam, eds, *The Oxford Handbook of International Refugee Law* (Oxford: Oxford University Press, 2021) 202–20.

COLLOPY, DREE K. *AILA Asylum Primer: A Practical Guide to US Asylum Law and Procedure,* 8th ed (Washington, DC: American Immigration Lawyers Association, 2019).

CHERGUI, HINDE & HELEN OOSTEROM-STAPLES. "The Impact on Immigration and Asylum Law in the Netherlands" in Anneliese Baldaccini & Elspeth Guild, eds, *Terrorism and the Foreigner: A Decade of Tension Around the Rule of Law in Europe* (Leiden/Boston: Martinus Nijhoff, 2007) 266–94.

CLARK, ROGER S. & OTTA TRIFFERER. "Article 26: Exclusion of Jurisdiction over Persons Under Eighteen" in Otto Triffterer, ed, *Commentary on the Rome Statute of the International Criminal Court: Observers' Notes, Article by Article* (Oxford, Munich: Beck/Hart, 1999).

COLE, GEORGIA. "Cessation" in Cathryn Costello, Michelle Foster & Jane McAdam, eds, *The Oxford Handbook of International Refugee Law* (Oxford: Oxford University Press, 2021) 1029–45.

COLEMAN, NILS. "From Gulf War to Gulf War—Years of Security Concern in Immigration and Asylum Policies at the European Level" in Anneliese Baldaccini & Elspeth Guild, eds, *Terrorism and the Foreigner: A Decade of Tension Around the Rule of Law in Europe* (Leiden/Boston: Martinus Nijhoff, 2007) 3–84.

COLLOQUIUM ON CHALLENGES IN INTERNATIONAL REFUGEE LAW. *The Michigan Guidelines on the Exclusion of International Criminals* (2013) 35 *Michigan Journal of International Law* 3–15.

CONGRESSIONAL RESEARCH SERVICES. *The Law of Immigration Detention: A Brief Introduction,* 20 July 2021.

CONTE, ALEX & RICHARD BURCHILL. *Defining Civil and Political Rights: The Jurisprudence of the United Nations Human Rights Committee,* 2d ed (Farnham/Burlington: Ashgate, 2009).

CORRESPONDENT'S REPORT. Belgium, 12 (*Yearbook of International Humanitarian Law* 2009) 486–87.

———. France, 13 *Yearbook of International Humanitarian Law* (2010) 491–92.

———. Sweden, 12 *Yearbook of International Humanitarian Law* (2009) 644–48.

———. United Kingdom, 12 *Yearbook of International Humanitarian Law* (2009) 681–82.

———. United States, 13 *Yearbook of International Humanitarian Law* (2010) 644–46.

COUNCIL OF EUROPE. *Collected Edition of the "Travaux Préparatoires" of the European Convention on Human Rights* (The Hague: Martinus Nijhoff, 1976), vols I–IV.

CROSS, MATTHEW E. "The Standard of Proof in Preliminary Examinations" in Morten Bergsmo & Carsten Stahn, eds, *Quality Control in Preliminary Examination*, vol 2 (Brussels: Torkel Opsahl Academic EPublisher, 2018).

CURRIE, ROBERT J. & JOSEPH RIKHOF. *International & Transnational Criminal Law*, 3d ed (Toronto: Irwin Law, 2020).

CUSTER, MICHAEL. "Punishing Child Soldiers: The Special Court for Sierra Leone and the Lessons to Be Learned from the United States' Juvenile Justice System" (2005) 19 *Temple International & Comparative Law Journal* 449–76.

DANKOFF, JOSHUA. "Advocating Duress and Infancy Exceptions to the Persecutor Bar to Asylum for Former Child Soldiers" (2011) 31 *Children's Legal Rights Journal* 43–60.

DARCY, SHANE. *Collective Responsibility and Accountability Under International Law* (Leiden: Transnational Publishers, 2007).

———. "The Reinvention of War Crimes by the International Criminal Tribunals" in Shane Darcy & Joseph Powderly, eds, *Judicial Creativity at the International Criminal Tribunals* (Oxford: Oxford University Press, 2010) 106–28.

DASTYARI, AZADEH & DANIEL GHEZELBASH. "Asylum at Sea: The Legality of Shipboard Refugee Status Determination Procedures" (2020) 32 *International Journal of Refugee Law* 1–27.

DAUVERGNE, CATHERINE. "The Troublesome Intersections of Refugee Law and Criminal Law" in Katla Franko Aas & Mary Bosworth, eds, *The Borders of Punishment: Migration, Citizenship, and Social Exclusion* (Oxford: Oxford University Press, 2013) 76–90.

———. "Irregular Migration, State Sovereignty and the Rule of Law" in Vincent Chetail & Céline Bauloz, eds, *Research Handbook on International Law and Migration* (Cheltenham, UK & Northampton, US: Elgar, 2014) 75–92.

DE VATTEL, EMER. *The Law of Nations or the Principles of Natural Law Applied to the Conduct and Affairs of Nations and Sovereigns* (1758), translated from French by J Chitty, Esq, based on the 1797 edition.

DEN HEIJER, MAARTEN. "Whose Rights and Which Rights? The Continuing Story of Non-refoulement Under the European Convention on Human Rights" (2008) 10 *European Journal of Migration and Law* 277–314.

DJORDJEVIC, NED. "Exclusion Under Article 1F(b) of the Refugee Convention: The Uncertain Concept of Internationally Serious Common Crimes" (2014) 12 *Journal of International Criminal Justice* 1057–74.

DÖRMAN, KNUT. *Elements of War Crimes Under the Rome Statute of the International Criminal Court, Sources and Commentary* (Cambridge: Cambridge University Press, 2003).

DRUMBL, MARK A. *Atrocity, Punishment, and International Law* (Cambridge: Cambridge University Press, 2007).

DRUMBL, MARK & JASTENE BARRETT, EDS. *Research Handbook on Child Soldiers* (Cheltenham, UK & Northampton, US: Elgar, 2019).

DRUMMOND, CATHERINE. "Different Sources of International Criminal Law and Exclusion: How the Federal Court of Australia in *SRYYY v Minister for Immigration and Multicultural and Indigenous Affairs* Got It Wrong and Why It Matters" (2013) 3 *Oxford Monitor of Forced Migration* 35–42.

DUCHATELIER, MOETSI & CATHERINE PHUONG. "The African Contribution to the Protection of Internally Displaced Persons: A Commentary on the 2009 Kampala Convention" in Vincent Chetail & Céline Bauloz, eds, *Research Handbook on International Law and Migration* (Cheltenham, UK & Northampton, US: Elgar, 2014) 650–67.

DUFFY, AOIFFE. "Expulsion to Face Torture? *Non-refoulement* in International Law" (2008) 20 *International Journal of Refugee Law* 373–90.

DURIEUX, JEAN-FRANÇOIS & JANE MCADAM. "*Non-refoulement* Through Time: The Case for a Derogation Clause to the Refugee Convention in Mass Influx Emergencies" (2004) 16 *International Journal of Refugee Law* 8–24.

DURIEUX, JEAN-FRANÇOIS. "Temporary Protection and Temporary Refuge" in Cathryn Costello, Michelle Foster & Jane McAdam, eds, *The Oxford Handbook of International Refugee Law* (Oxford: Oxford University Press, 2021) 678–94.

DURLAND, LEAH. "Overcoming the Persecutor Bar: Applying a Purposeful *Mens Rea* Requirement to 8 USC § 1101(1)(42)" (2010) 32 *Hamline Law Review* 571–608.

EDWARDS, ALICE. "The Optional Protocol to the Convention Against Torture and the Detention of Refugees" (2008) 57 *International and Comparative Law Quarterly* 789–825.

EGELMAN, ZOË. "Punishment and Protection, Two Sides of the Same Sword: The Problem of International Criminal Law Under the Refugee Convention" (2018) 59 *Harvard International Law Journal* 461–99

EINARSEN, TERJE. "Drafting History of the Convention/New York Protocol" in Andreas Zimmermann, ed, *The 1951 Convention Relating to the Status of Refugees and its 1967 Protocol: A Commentary* (Oxford: Oxford University Press, 2011).

EINARSEN, TERJE & JOSEPH RIKHOF. *A Theory of Punishable Participation in Universal Crimes* (Brussels: Torkel Opsahl Academic EPublisher, 2018).

EUROPEAN ASYLUM SUPPORT OFFICE (EASO). *An Introduction to the Common European Asylum System for Courts and Tribunals: A Judicial Analysis*, August 2016 (as of 19 January 2022, EASO became the European Union Agency for Asylum (EUAA)).

———. *Article 15(c) Qualification Directive (2011/95/EU): A Judicial Analysis*, December 2014.

———. *Compilation of Jurisprudence Exclusion: Articles 12 and 17 Qualification Directive*, 2d ed, 2020.

———. *Ending International Protection: Articles 11, 14, 16 and 19 Qualification Directive (2011/95/EU): A Judicial Analysis*, December 2016.

———. *Ending International Protection, Compilation of Jurisprudence*, 2d ed, 2021.

———. *Exclusion: Articles 12 and 17 Qualification Directive (2011/95/EU): A Judicial Analysis*, January 2016.

———. *Judicial Analysis, Detention of Applicants for International Protection in Context of the Common European Asylum System*, 2019.

———. *Judicial Analysis, Exclusion: Articles 12 and 17 Qualification Directive*, 2d ed, 2020.

———. *Practical Guide on Exclusion for Serious (Non-political) Crimes*, December 2021.

———. *Qualification for International Protection (Directive 2011/95/EU): A Judicial Analysis*, December 2016.

EUROPEAN COUNCIL ON REFUGEES AND EXILES (ECRE). "Position on Exclusion from Refugee Status, PP1/03/2004/Ext/CA, March 2004" (2004) 16 *International Journal Refugee Law* 257–85.

———. "The Impact of the EU Qualification Directive on International Protection" (October 2008).

EUROPEAN LEGAL NETWORK ON ASYLUM (ELENA). "International Course on the Application of Article 1C and Article 1F of the 1951 Convention Relating to the Status of Refugees" (17–19 January 2003).

EVERETT, JENNIFER C. "The Battle Continues: Fighting for a More Child-Sensitive Approach to Asylum for Child Soldiers" (2009) 21 *Florida Journal of International Law* 286–355.

EWI, MARTIN & ANTON DU PLESSIS. "Counter-terrorism and Pan-Africanism: From Non-action to Non-indifference" in Ben Saul, ed, *Research Handbook on International Law and Terrorism*, 2d ed (Cheltenham, UK & Northampton, US: Elgar, 2020) 654–68.

FARMER, ALICE. "*Non-refoulement* and *Jus Cogens*: Limiting Anti-terror Measures That Threaten Refugee Protection" (2008) 23 *Georgetown Immigration Law Journal* 2–43.

FERRIS, ELISABETH. "Internal Displacement and the Right to Seek Asylum" (2008) 27 *Refugee Survey Quarterly* 76–92.

FIDLER, DAVID. "Nuclear, Chemical and Biological Terrorism in International Law" in Ben Saul, ed, *Research Handbook on International Law and Terrorism*, 2d ed (Cheltenham, UK & Northampton, US: Elgar, 2020) 80–96.

FREI, NULA & CONSTANTIN HRUSCHKA. "Caught Between Unworthiness and Exclusion: Asylum Applicants and Refugees Suspected of Terrorism in Swiss Law and Practice" in James C. Simeon, ed, *Terrorism and Asylum* (Leiden & Boston: Brill Nijhoff, 2020) 311–41.

FULLERTON, MARYELLEN. "Terrorism, Torture, and Refugee Protection in the United States" (2011) 29 *Refugee Survey Quarterly* 4–30.

GAER, FELICE. "The Committee Against Torture: Implementing the Prohibition Against Torture" in Malcolm D. Evans & Jens Modvig, eds, *Research Handbook on Torture: Legal and Medical Perspectives on Prohibition and Prevention* (Cheltenham, UK & Northampton, US: Elgar, 2020) 128–53.

GARCIA, MICHAEL JOHN & RUTH ELLEN WASEM. "Immigration: Terrorist Grounds for Exclusion and Removal of Aliens," Congressional Research Service Report for Congress, 12 January 2010.

GERMAIN, REGINA. *AILA Asylum Primer: A Practical Guide to US Asylum Law and Procedure* (Washington, DC: American Immigration Lawyers Association, 2007).

GIL-BAZO, MARÍA-TERESA & ELSPETH GUILD. "The Right to Asylum" in Cathryn Costello, Michelle Foster & Jane McAdam, eds, *The Oxford Handbook of International Refugee Law* (Oxford: Oxford University Press, 2021) 868–82.

GILBERT, GEOFF. "Current Issues in the Application of Exclusion Clauses" in Erika Feller, Volker Türk & Frances Nicholson, eds, *Refugee Protection in International Law: UNHCR's Global Consultations on International Protection* (Cambridge: Cambridge University Press, 2003) 425–78.

———. "Exclusion Under Article 1F Since 2001: Two Steps Backwards, One Step Forward" in Vincent Chetail & Céline Bauloz, eds, *Research Handbook on International Law and Migration* (Cheltenham, UK & Northampton, US: Elgar, 2014) 519–39.

———. "Undesirable but Unreturnable: Extradition and Other Forms of Rendition" (2017) 15 *Journal of International Criminal Justice* 55–74.

———. "Exclusion" in Cathryn Costello, Michelle Foster & Jane McAdam, eds, *The Oxford Handbook of International Refugee Law* (Oxford: Oxford University Press, 2021) 711–26.

GINSBORG, LISA. "The United Nations Security Council's Counter-terrorism ISIL (Da'esh) and Al-Qaida Sanctions Regime" in Ben Saul, ed, *Research Handbook on International Law and Terrorism*, 2d ed (Cheltenham, UK & Northampton, US: Elgar, 2020) 550–63.

GIUFFRÉ, MARIAGIULIA. "Deportation with Assurances and Human Rights: The Case of Persons Suspected or Convicted of Serious Crimes" (2017) 15 *Journal of International Criminal Justice* 75–95.

GLENDON, MARY ANN. *A World Made New: Eleanor Roosevelt and the Universal Declaration of Human Rights* (New York: Random House, 2001).

GÖKŞEN, ELIF. "Proportionality in Refugee Exclusion: An Underestimated Analysis" (2020) 18 *Journal of International Criminal Justice* 1131–56.

GONZÁLEZ, JAVIER GAMARRO. *Estudio sobre los estatutos de protección internacional en América Latina* (Hungarian Helsinki Committee, 2022).

GOODMAN, KARL. "*Negusie v Holder*: The End of the Strict Liability Persecutor Bar" (2009) 13 *New York City Law Review* 143–70.

GOODWIN-GILL, GUY S. *The Refugee in International Law,* 3d ed (Oxford: Oxford University Press, 1999).

———. "Article 31 of the 1951 Convention Relating to the Status of Refugees: Non-penalization, Detention, and Protection" in Erika Feller, Volker Türk & Frances Nicholson, eds, *Refugee Protection in International Law: UNHCR's Global Consultations on International Protection* (Cambridge: Cambridge University Press, 2003) 185–232.

———. "Forced Migration: Refugees, Rights and Security" in Jane McAdam, ed, *Forced Migration, Human Rights and Security* (Oxford & Portland, OR: Hart, 2008) 1–18.

———. "The Search for the One, True Meaning . . ." in Guy S. Goodwin-Gill & Hélène Lambert, eds, *The Limits of Transnational Law: Refugee Law, Policy Harmonization, and the Judicial Dialogue in the European Union* (Cambridge: Cambridge University Press, 2010) 204–41.

———. "*Non-refoulement*, Temporary Refuge, and the 'New' Asylum Seekers" in David Cantor & Jean-François Durieux, eds, *Refuge from Inhumanity? War Refugees and International Humanitarian Law* (Leiden & Boston: Brill Nijhoff, 2014) 433–59.

———. "The Office of the United Nations High Commissioner for Refugees and the Sources of International Refugee Law" (2020) 69 *International & Comparative Law Quarterly* 1–41.

GOODWIN-GILL, GUY S. & JANE MCADAM. *The Refugee in International Law,* 3d ed (Oxford: Oxford University Press, 2007).

———. *The Refugee in International Law,* 4th ed (Oxford: Oxford University Press, 2021).

GOTTWALD, MARTIN. "Asylum Claims and Drug Offfences: The Seriousness Threshold of Article 1F(b) of the 1951 Convention Relating to the Status of Refugees and the UN Drug Conventions" (2006) 10 *International Journal of Refugee Law* 87–117.

GRAHL-MADSEN, ATLE. *The Status of Refugees in International Law,* vol I (Leiden: AW Sijthoff, 1966).

———. *The Status of Refugees in International Law,* vol II (Leiden: AW Sijthoff, 1972).

GROSSMAN, NIENKE. "Rehabilitation or Revenge: Prosecuting Child Soldiers for Human Rights Violations" (2007) 38 *Georgetown Journal of International Law* 323–62.

GROTIUS, HUGO. *The Law of War and Peace in Three Books* (1625), translated into English by Francis W. Kelsey (1925).

GROVER, SONJA. "'Child Soldiers' as 'Non-Combatants': The Inapplicability of the Refugee Convention Exclusion Clause" (2008) 12 *International Journal of Human Rights* 53–65.

GUILD, ELSPETH. "When Border Control Operations Become Crimes Against Humanity" in James C. Simeon, ed, *Serious International Crimes, Human Rights, and Forced Migration* (London: Routledge, 2022) 329–43.

GUNARATNA, ROHAN & GLORIA CHEUNG. "Regional Legal Responses to Terrorism in Asia and the Pacific" in Ben Saul, ed, *Research Handbook on International Law and Terrorism*, 2d ed (Cheltenham, UK & Northampton, US: Elgar, 2020) 669–87.

HAINS, WILLIAM H. "Chevron's Ambiguity Hurdle: *Delgado v Holder* and the Proper Interpretation of the Particularly Serious Crimes Exception to Deportation Relief" (2010) 10 *Brigham Young University Law Review* 81–100.

HAINES, ROGER. "National Security and *Non-refoulement* in New Zealand: Commentary on *Zaoui v Attorney-General (No 2)*" in Jane McAdam, ed, *Forced Migration, Human Rights and Security* (Oxford & Portland, OR: Hart, 2008) 63–92.

HATHAWAY, JAMES. *The Rights of Refugees Under International Law,* 2d ed (Cambridge: Cambridge University Press, 2021).

HATHAWAY, JAMES & MICHELLE FOSTER. *The Law of Refugee Status,* 2d ed (Cambridge: Cambridge University Press, 2014).

HATHAWAY, JAMES & COLIN J. HARVEY. "Framing Refugee Protection in the New World Disorder" (2001) 34 *Cornell International Law Journal* 257–320.

HEYNS, CHRISTOF, CARMEN RUEDA & DANIEL DU PLESSIS. "Torture and Ill Treatment: The United Nations Human Rights Committee" in Malcolm D. Evans & Jens Modvig, eds, *Research Handbook on Torture: Legal and Medical Perspectives on Prohibition and Prevention* (Cheltenham, UK & Northampton, US: Elgar, 2020) 106–27.

HINOJOSA-MARTÍNEZ, LUIS MIGUEL. "A Critical Assessment of United Nations Security Council Resolution 1373" in Ben Saul, ed, *Research Handbook on International Law and Terrorism*, 2d ed (Cheltenham, UK & Northampton, US: Elgar, 2020) 564–87.

HOLBORN, LOUISE W. *The International Refugee Organization: A Specialized Agency of the United Nations: Its History and Work, 1946–1952* (London, New York, Toronto: Oxford University Press, 1956).

———. *Refugees: A Problem of Our Time: The Work of the United Nations High Commissioner for Refugees, 1951–1972,* vol I (Metuchen, NJ: The Scarecrow Press, 1975).

HOLVOET, MATHIAS. "Harmonizing Exclusion Under the Refugee Convention by Reference to the Evidentiary Standards of International Criminal Law" (2014) 12 *Journal of International Criminal Justice* 1039–56.

INDEPENDENT EXPERT PANEL FOR THE LEGAL DEFINITION OF ECOCIDE. *Commentary and Core Text,* June 2021.

INELI-CIGER, MELTEM. "Temporary Protection of Forced Migrants" in Satvinder Singh Juss, ed, *Research Handbook on International Refugee Law* (Cheltenham, UK & Northampton, US: Elgar, 2019) 57–69.

INTERGOVERNMENTAL CONSULTATIONS ON MIGRATION, ASYLUM AND REFUGEES. *Asylum Procedures: Report on Policies and Practices in IGC Participating States (2009)* (Geneva, 2009).

———. *Asylum Procedures: Report on Policies and Practices in IGC Participating States (December 2012)* (Geneva, 2012).

———. *Asylum Procedures: Report on Policies and Practices in IGC Participating States (December 2015)* (Geneva, 2015).

IRVING, EMMA. "When International Justice Concludes: Undesirable but Unreturnable Individuals in the Context of the International Criminal Court" (2017) 15 *Journal of International Criminal Justice* 115–31.

JACKSON, IVOR C. *The Refugee Concept in Group Situations* (The Hague/London/Boston: Martinus Nijhoff, 1999).

JASTRAM, KATE. "Left Out of Exclusion: International Criminal Law and the 'Persecutor Bar' in US Refugee Law" (2014) 12 *Journal of International Criminal Justice* 1183–99.

JOECK, MOLLY. "Canadian Exclusion Jurisprudence Post-*Febles*" (2021) 33 *International Journal of Refugee Law* 54–88.

JOHNS, MELANIE. "Adjusting the Asylum Bar: *Negusie v Holder* and the Need to Incorporate a Defence of Duress into the Persecutor Bar" (2010) 40 *Golden Gate University Law Review* 235–62.

JOHNSTON, JEFFREY G. "Removing the Mask: Disguised Extradition Through Deportation as an Abuse of Process" in Robert J. Currie, ed, *Transnational and Cross-Border Criminal Law: Canadian Perspectives* (Toronto: Irwin Law, 2023) 448–71.

KALECK, WOLFGANG. "From Pinochet to Rumsfeld: Universal Jurisdiction in Europe 1998–2008" (2009) 30 *Michigan Journal of International Law* 927–77.

KÄLIN, WALTER & JÖRG KÜNZLI. *The Law of International Human Rights Protection*, 2d ed (Oxford: Oxford University Press, 2019).

———. "Article 1F(b): Freedom Fighters, Terrorists, and the Notion of Serious Non-political Crimes" (supp, 2000) 12 *International Journal of Refugee Law* 46–78.

KALPOUZOS, IOANNIS. "International Criminal Law and the Violence Against Migrants" (2020) 21 *German Law Journal* 571–97.

KAPFERER, SIBYLLE. "Exclusion Clauses in Europe: A Comparative Overview of State Practice in France, Belgium and the United Kingdom" (supp, 2000) 12 *International Journal of Refugee Law* 195–221.

———. "Article 14(2) of the Universal Declaration of Human Rights and Exclusion from International Refugee Protection" (2008) 27 *Refugee Survey Quarterly* 53–75.

KARP, DAVID A. "Setting the Persecutor Bar for Political Asylum After *Negusie*" (2009) 61 *Florida Law Review* 933–44.

KAUSHAL, ASHA & CATHERINE DAUVERGNE. "The Growing Culture of Exclusion: Trends in Canadian Refugee Exclusions" (2011) 23 *International Journal of Refugee Law* 54–93.

KHODAY, AMAR. "Resisting Criminal Organizations: Reconceptualizing the Political in International Refugee Law" (2016) 60 *McGill Law Journal* 461–509.

KINGSLEY NYINAH, MICHAEL. "Exclusion Under Article 1F" (supp, 2000) 12 *International Journal of Refugee Law* 95–316.

KIRGIS, FREDERIC L. "Custom on a Sliding Scale" (1987) 81 *American Journal of International Law* 146–67.

KLABBERS, JAN. "International Legal Histories: The Declining Importance of *Travaux Préparatoires* in Treaty and Interpretation?" (2003) 50 *Netherlands International Law Review* 267–88.

KOSIŃSKA, ANNA MAGDALENA. "The Problem of Exclusion from Refugee Status on the Grounds of Being Guilty of Terrorist Acts in the CJEU Case-law" (2017) 19 *European Journal of Migration and Law* 425–46.

KRESS, CLAUS & LEONIE VON HOLTZENDORFF. "The Kampala Compromise on the Crime of Aggression" (2010) 8 *Journal of International Criminal Justice* 1179–217.

KWAKWA, EDWARD. "Article 1F(c): Purposes and Principles of the UN" (supp, 2000) 12 *International Journal of Refugee Law* 79–91.

ŁACHACZ, OLGA. "The Application and the Scope of the Refugee Status Exclusion Clause in the Court of Justice of the EU Judgment in the *Lounani* Case" (2017) 1 *European Journal of Public Matters* 97–106.

LAMBERT, HÉLÈNE. "Customary Refugee Law" in Cathryn Costello, Michelle Foster & Jane McAdam, eds, *The Oxford Handbook of International Refugee Law* (Oxford: Oxford University Press, 2021) 241–57.

———. "Protection Against *Refoulement* from Europe: Human Rights Law Comes to the Rescue" (1999) 48 *International and Comparative Law Quarterly* 515–44.

———. *Refugee Status, Arbitrary Deprivation of Nationality, and Statelessness within the Context of Article 1A(2) of the 1951 Convention and its 1967 Protocol relating to the Status of Refugees,* UNHCR Legal and Protection Policy Research Series No 33, October 2014.

LAMBERT, HÉLÈNE, FRANCESCO MASSINEO & PAUL TIEDEMANN. "Comparative Perspectives of Constitutional Asylum in France, Italy, and Germany: *Requiescat in Pace?*" (2008) 27 *Refugee Survey Quarterly* 16–32.

LAMBERT, HÉLÈNE & JANINE SILGA. "Transnational Refugee Law in the French Courts: Deliberate or Compelled Change in Judicial Attitudes?" in Guy S. Goodwin-Gill & Hélène Lambert, eds, *The Limits of Transnational Law: Refugee Law, Policy Harmonization and the Judicial Dialogue in the European Union* (Cambridge: Cambridge University Press, 2010) 35–56.

LANGER, MÁXIMO & MACKENZIE EASON. "The Quiet Expansion of Universal Jurisdiction" (2019) 30 *European Journal of International Law* 779–817.

LAUTERPACHT, ELI & DANIEL BETHLEHEM. "*Non-refoulement* (Article 33 of the 1951 Convention)" in Erika Feller, Volker Türk & Frances Nicholson, eds, *Refugee Protection in International Law: UNHCR's Global Consultations on International Protection* (Cambridge: Cambridge University Press, 2003) 87–177.

LEFEBVRE, CAMILLE & FANNIE LAFONTAINE. "The Exclusion Clause in Canada: Prioritizing Practical Expediency" (2021) 33 *International Journal of Refugee Law* 405–35.

LEGOMSKY, STEPHEN H. "Refugees, Asylum and the Rule of Law in the USA" in Susan Kneebone, *Refugees, Asylum Seekers and the Rule of Law: Comparative Perspectives* (Cambridge: Cambridge University Press, 2009) 122–70.

LERESCU, NICOLE. "Barring Too Much: An Argument in Favor of Interpreting the Immigration and Nationality Act, Section 101(a)(42) to Include a Duress Exception" (2007) 60 *Vanderbilt Law Review* 1875–907.

LI, YAO. *Exclusion from Protection as Refugee: An Approach to a Harmonizing Interpretation in International Law* (Leiden & Boston: Brill Nijhoff, 2017).

LOPER, KELLEY. "Human Rights, *Non-refoulement* and the Protection of Refugees in Hong Kong" (2010) 22 *Journal of Refugee International Law* 404–39.

MANSFIELD, JAMES. "Extraterritorial Application and Customary Norm Assessment of *Non-refoulement*: The Legality of a *Refoulement*: The Legality of Australia's 'Turn-Back' Policy" (2015) 17 *University of Notre Dame Australia Law Review* 17–57.

MANSON, ROBERT L. "Identifying the Rough Edges of the Kampala Compromise" (2010) 21 *Criminal Law Forum* 417–43.

MATHEW, PENELOPE. "Resolution 1373—A Call to Pre-empt Asylum Seekers? (or 'Osama, the Asylum Seeker')" in Jane McAdam, ed, *Forced Migration, Human Rights and Security* (Oxford & Portland, OR: Hart, 2008) 19–62.

———. "Constructive *Refoulement*" in Satvinder Singh Juss, ed, *Research Handbook on International Refugee Law* (Cheltenham, UK & Northampton, US: Elgar, 2019) at 207–23.

———. "*Refoulement*" in Cathryn Costello, Michelle Foster & Jane McAdam, eds, *The Oxford Handbook of International Refugee Law* (Oxford: Oxford University Press, 2021) 899–916.

MAYSTRE, MAGALI. "The Interaction Between International Refugee Law and International Criminal Law with Respect to Child Soldiers" (2014) 12 *Journal of International Criminal Justice* 975–96.

MCADAM, JANE. *Complementary Protection in International Refugee Law* (Oxford: Oxford University Press, 2007).

MCADAM, JANE. "The Refugee Convention as a Rights Blueprint" in Jane McAdam, ed, *Forced Migration, Human Rights and Security* (Oxford & Portland, OR: Hart, 2008) 263–82.

———. "Complementary Protection" in Cathryn Costello, Michelle Foster & Jane McAdam, eds, *The Oxford Handbook of International Refugee Law* (Oxford: Oxford University Press, 2021) 661–77.

MCCARRY, MICHAEL. "A Statute in Particularly Serious Need of Reinterpretation: The Particularly Serious Crime Exception to Withholding of Removal" (2010) 51 *Boston College Law Review* 209–41.

MCKEEVER, DAVID. "Evolving Interpretation of Multilateral Treaties: Acts Contrary to the Purposes and Principles of the United Nations in the Refugee Convention" (2015) 64 *International and Comparative Law Quarterly* 405–44.

MEILI, STEPHEN. "National Constitutions and the Right to Asylum" in Cathryn Costello, Michelle Foster & Jane McAdam, eds, *The Oxford Handbook of International Refugee Law* (Oxford: Oxford University Press, 2021) 883–98.

MERON, THEODOR. *Human Rights and Humanitarian Norms of Customary International Law* (Oxford: Clarendon Press, 1989).

METTRAUX, GUÉNAËL. "The United Nations Special Tribunal for Lebanon: Prosecuting Terrorism" in Ben Saul, ed, *Research Handbook on International Law and Terrorism*, 2d ed (Cheltenham, UK & Northampton, US: Elgar, 2020) 588–99.

MICHEL, NICOLE. "Purpose and Principles of the United Nations: The Way in Which France Applies 1F(c)" in Peter J. van Krieken, ed, *Refugee Law in Context: The Exclusion Clause* (The Hague: T.M.C. Asser, 1999) 294–99.

MORENO-LAX, VIOLETA. "Protection at Sea and the Denial of Asylum" in Cathryn Costello, Michelle Foster & Jane McAdam, eds, *The Oxford Handbook of International Refugee Law* (Oxford: Oxford University Press, 2021) 483–501.

MORSINK, JOHANNES. *The Universal Declaration of Human Rights* (Philadelphia: University of Pennsylvania Press, 1999).

MURPHY, CIAN C. "The Legal Response to Terrorism of the European Union and Council of Europe" in Ben Saul, ed, *Research Handbook on International Law and Terrorism*, 2d ed (Cheltenham, UK & Northampton, US: Elgar, 2020) 614–25.

MUTE, LAWRENCE MURUGU. "Ensuring Freedom from Torture Under the African Human Rights System" in Malcolm D. Evans & Jens Modvig, eds, *Research Handbook on Torture: Legal and Medical Perspectives on Prohibition and Prevention* (Cheltenham, UK & Northampton, US: Elgar, 2020) 227–57.

NETHERLANDS' STATE SECRETARY OF JUSTICE. "Note on Article 1F to Parliament, November 1997" in Peter J. van Krieken, ed, *Refugee Law in Context: The Exclusion Clause* (The Hague: T.M.C. Asser, 1999) 300–12.

NI GHRÁINNE, BRID. "Internally Displaced Persons and International Refugee Law" in Satvinder Singh Juss, ed, *Research Handbook on International Refugee Law* (Cheltenham, UK & Northampton, US: Elgar, 2019) 31–43.

NORTJE, WINDELL & NOELLE QUENIVET. *Child Soldiers and the Defence of Duress Under International Criminal Law* (London: Palgrave Macmillan, 2020).

NOWAK, MANFRED. "Challenges to the Absolute Nature of the Prohibition of Torture and Ill Treatment" (2005) 23 *Netherlands Quarterly of Human Rights* 674–88.

OGG, KATE. "Separating the Persecutors from the Persecuted: A Feminist and Comparative Examination of Exclusion from the Refugee Regime" (2014) 26 *International Journal of Refugee Law* 82–111.

———. "New Directions in Article 1(D) Jurisprudence: Greater Barriers for Palestinian Refugee Seeking the Benefits of the Refugee Convention" in Satvinder Singh Juss, ed, *Research Handbook on International Refugee Law* (Cheltenham, UK & Northampton, US: Elgar, 2019) 358–73.

O'NEILL, WILLIAM. "Conflict in West Africa: Dealing with Exclusion and Separation" in (supp, 2000) 12 *International Journal of Refugee Law* 171–94.

O'NEILL, WILLIAM, BONAVENTURE RUTINWA & GUGLIELMO VERDIRAME. "The Great Lakes: A Survey of the Application of the Exclusion Clauses in the Central African Republic, Kenya and Tanzania" (supp, 2000) 12 *International Journal of Refugee Law* 136–70.

OPEN SOCIETY JUSTICE INITIATIVE & TRIAL INTERNATIONAL. *Prosecuting International Crimes: A Matter of Willingness*, 2020.

O'SULLIVAN, MARIA. *Refugee Law and Durability of Protection: Temporary Residence and Cessation of Status* (Abingdon & New York: Routledge, 2019).

PALMER, NICOLA. "International Criminal Law and Border Control: The Expressive Role of the Deportation and Extradition of Genocide Suspects to Rwanda" (2020) 33 *Leiden Journal of International Law* 789–807.

PAPASTAVRIDIS, EFTHYMIOS. "Maritime Terrorism in International Law" in Ben Saul, ed, *Research Handbook on International Law and Terrorism*, 2d ed (Cheltenham, UK & Northampton, US: Elgar, 2020) 60–69.

PATANÈ, FLAVIA, MAARTEN P. BOLHUIS, JORIS VAN WIJK & HELENA KREIENSIEK. "Asylum-Seekers Prosecuted for Human Smuggling: A Case Study of *Scafisti* in Italy" (2020) 39 *Refugee Survey Quarterly* 123–52.

PEERS, STEVE. "Irregular Migrants: Can Humane Treatment Be Balanced Against Efficient Removal?" (2015) 17 *European Journal of Migration and Law* 289–304.

PEERS, STEVE ET AL. "Institutional Framework" in Steve Peers et al, eds, *EU Immigration and Asylum Law (Text and Commentary)*, 2d rev ed, vol 3, *EU Asylum Law* (Leiden & Boston: Brill Nijhoff, 2015).

PERERA, AMRITH ROHAN. "The Draft United Nations Comprehensive Convention on International Terrorism" in Ben Saul, ed, *Research Handbook on International Law and Terrorism*, 2d ed (Cheltenham, UK & Northampton, US: Elgar, 2020) 120–28.

PEYRONNET, CHLOÉ. "Undesirable and Unreturnable Migrants Under French Law: Between Legal Uncertainty and Legal Limbo" (2017) 36 *Refugee Survey Quarterly* 35–60.

PIOTROWICZ, RYSZARD. "Smuggling and Trafficking of Human Beings" in Vincent Chetail & Céline Bauloz, eds, *Research Handbook on International Law and Migration* (Cheltenham, UK & Northampton, US: Elgar, 2014) 132–47.

PORTER, JONATHAN. "Falling Between the Cracks of Cornerstones: Challenging the Detention of Asylum Seekers on Identity Grounds" in James C. Simeon, ed, *Serious International Crimes, Human Rights and Forced Migration* (London: Routledge, 2022) 148–78.

PUFENDORF, SAMUEL. *On the Law of Nature and Nations, Eight Books* (1672), translated by Basil Kennett (1703).

REDRESS/FIDH. "Extraterritorial Jurisdiction in the European Union: A Study of the Laws and Practice in the 27 Member States of the European Union," December 2010.

———. "Strategies for the Effective Investigation and Prosecution of Serious International Crimes: The Practice of Specialised War Crimes Units," December 2010.

REED-HURTADO, MICHAEL. *The Cartagena Declaration on Refugees and the Protection of People Fleeing Armed Conflict and Other Situations of Violence in Latin America,* UNHCR Legal and Protection Policy Research Series, No 32, June 2013.

REFUGEE LAW INITIATIVE. School of Advanced Study, University of London (UK) and Center for International Criminal Justice, VU University Amsterdam (the Netherlands)*, Undesirable and Unreturnable? Policy Challenges Around Excluded Asylum Seekers and Other Migrants Suspected of Serious Criminality Who Cannot Be Removed* (2016).

REIJVEN, JOKE & JORIS VAN WIJK. "Caught in Limbo: How Alleged Perpetrators of International Crimes Who Applied for Asylum in the Netherlands Are Affected by a Fundamental System Error in International Law" (2014) 26 *International Journal of Refugee Law* 248–71.

RIKHOF, JOSEPH. "Fewer Places to Hide? The Impact of Domestic War Crimes Prosecutions on International Impunity" (2009) 20 *Criminal Law Forum* 1–51.

———. "War Criminals Not Welcome: How Common Law Countries Approach the Phenomenon of International Crimes in the Immigration and Refugee Context" (2009) 21 *International Journal of Refugee Law* 453–507.

———. "Update on Exclusion and Inadmissibility Jurisprudence: New Developments Since the Decisions of the Supreme Court of Canada in *Ezokola* and *Febles*" (April 2017) Canadian Association for Refugee and Forced Migration Studies (CARFMS/ACERMF) Working Paper No 2017/2, online: https://carfms.org/wp-content/uploads/2017/04/CARFMS-WPS-No10-Joseph-Rikhof.pdf.

———. "Prosecutors on the Front Line: A Q&A with Teresa McHenry, Head of the Human Rights and Special Prosecutions Section of the US Department of Justice" (2019) 3 *PKI Global Justice Journal* 41, online: https://globaljustice.queenslaw.ca/news/prosecutors-on-the-front-line-a-qa-with-teresa-mchenry-head-of-the-human-rights-and-special-prosecutions-section-of-the-us-department-of-justice.

———. "Child Soldiers and Asylum—Duality or Dilemma" in Mark Drumble & Jastene Barrett, eds, *Research Handbook on Child Soldiers* (Cheltenham, UK & Northampton, US: Elgar, 2019) 390–408.

———. "Protected Groups in Refugee Law and International Law" (2019) 8:4 *Laws* 25.

———. "Complicity in Exclusion for Terrorist Crimes" in James C. Simeon, ed, *Terrorism and Asylum* (Leiden & Boston: Brill Nijhoff, 2020) 147–74.

———. "Ethnic Cleansing and Exclusion" in James C. Simeon, ed, *Serious International Crimes, Human Rights and Forced Migration* (London: Routledge, 2022) 259–78.

ROBINSON, NEHEMIAH. *The Universal Declaration of Human Rights: Its Origin, Significance, Application, and Interpretation* (New York: Institute of Jewish Affairs, World Jewish Congress, 1958).

RODRÍGUEZ-PINZÓN, DIEGO. "The Prohibition of Torture and Cruel, Inhuman or Degrading Treatment or Punishment in the Inter-American Human Rights System: Systems, Methods and Recent Trends" in Malcolm D. Evans & Jens Modvig, eds, *Research Handbook on Torture: Legal and Medical Perspectives on Prohibition and Prevention* (Cheltenham, UK & Northampton, US: Elgar, 2020) 203–26.

ROMANOV, DAVID. "Recalibrating the Scales: Balancing the Persecutor Bar" (2020) 61 *Boston College Law Review* 385–418.

ROMERO, JOSHUA A. "The Special Court for Sierra Leone and the Juvenile Soldier Dilemma" (2004) 2 *Northwestern Journal of International Human Rights* 8–29.

ROSSI, ELISABETH A. "A Special Track for Former Child Soldiers: Enacting a Child Soldier Visa as an Alternative to Asylum Protection" (2013) 31 *Berkeley Journal of International Law* 392-460.

ROVERSI, ALESSANDRA. "The Evolution of the Refugee Regime and Institutional Responses: Legacies from the Nansen Period" (2003) 22 *Refugee Survey Quarterly* 21–35.

RUSALOV, AKBAR. "Criminals as Refugees: The 'Balancing Exercise' and Article 1F(B) of the Refugee Convention" (2002) 16 *Georgetown Immigration Law Journal* 815–34.

SAMUEL, KATJA. "The Legal Response to Terrorism of the Organization of Islamic Cooperation" in Ben Saul, ed, *Research Handbook on International Law and Terrorism*, 2d ed (Cheltenham, UK & Northampton, US: Elgar, 2020) 639–53.

SAUL, BEN, ED. *Research Handbook on International Law and Terrorism*, 2d ed (Cheltenham, UK & Northampton, US: Elgar, 2020).

SCHABAS, WILLIAM A. "The Unfinished Work of Defining Aggression: How Many Times Must the Cannonballs Fly, Before They Are Forever Banned?" in Dominic McGoldrick et al, eds, *The Permanent International Criminal Court: Legal and Policy Issues* (Oxford: Hart, 2004) 123–44.

SCHLOENHARDT, ANDREAS. "Smuggling of Migrants and Refugees" in Cathryn Costello, Michelle Foster & Jane McAdam, eds, *The Oxford Handbook of International Refugee Law* (Oxford: Oxford University Press, 2021) 535–52.

SCHRIJVER, NICO. "Interpreting the Principles and Purposes of the United Nations" in Peter J. van Krieken, ed, *Refugee Law in Context: The Exclusion Clause* (The Hague: T.M.C. Asser, 1999) 237–46.

SHARPE, MARINA. *The 1969 OAU Refugee Convention and the Protection of People Fleeing Armed Conflict and Other Situations of Violence in the Context of Individual Refugee Status Determination,* UNHCR Legal and Protection Policy Research Series No 30, January 2013.

SIMENTIĆ, JANJA. "To Exclude or Not to Exclude, That Is the Question: Developments Regarding Bases for Exclusion from Refugee Status in the EU" (2019) 20 *German Law Journal* 111–24.

SIMEON, JAMES C. "Complicity and Culpability and the Exclusion of Terrorists from Convention Refugee Status Post-9/11" (2011) 29 *Refugee Survey Quarterly* 104–37.

———. "The Evolving Common Law Jurisprudence Combatting the Threat of Terrorism in the United Kingdom, United States, and Canada" (2019) 8:1 *Laws* 5.

———. "What Is the Future of *Non-refoulement* in International Refugee Law?" in Satvinder Singh Juss, ed, *Research Handbook on International Refugee Law* (Cheltenham, UK & Northampton, US: Elgar, 2019) 189–93.

SINGER, SARAH. "Terrorism and Article 1F(c) of the Refugee Convention: Exclusion from Refugee Status in the United Kingdom" (2014) 12 *Journal of International Criminal Justice* 1075–91.

———. *Terrorism and Exclusion from Refugee Status in the UK: Asylum Seekers Suspected of Serious Criminality* (Leiden & Boston: Brill Nijhoff, 2015).

———. "'Undesirable and Unreturnable' in the United Kingdom" (2017) 36 *Refugee Survey Quarterly* 9–34.

———. "The War on Terror and Refugee Law" in Satvinder Singh Juss, ed, *Research Handbook on International Refugee Law* (Cheltenham, UK & Northampton, US: Elgar, 2019) 374–89.

SINGH JUSS, SATVINDER. "Will Acceptance of a Universally Approved Definition of Terrorism Make Article 1F of the 1951 Refugee Convention More Effective in Excluding Terrorists?" (2006) 2 *Journal of Migration and Refugee Issues* 91–119.

———. "The Notion of Complicity in UK Refugee Law" (2014) 12 *Journal of International Criminal Justice* 1201–16.

———. "Detention and Delusion in Australia's Kafkaesque Refugee Law" (2017) 36 *Refugee Survey Quarterly* 146–67.

SINGH JUSS, SATVINDER & JENI MITCHELL. "Gatekeepers of Asylum: UK Country Guidance, Indiscriminate Violence and Internal Relocation" in Satvinder Singh Juss, ed, *Research Handbook on International Refugee Law* (Cheltenham, UK & Northampton, US: Elgar, 2019) 139–69.

SIVAKUMARAN, SANDESH. "Exclusion from Refugee Status: The Purposes and Principles of the United Nations and Article 1F(c) of the Refugee Convention" (2015) 26 *International Journal of Refugee Law* 350–81.

SLOAN, JAMES. "The Application of Article 1F of the 1951 Convention in Canada and the United States" (supp, 2000) 12 *International Journal of Refugee Law* 222–48.

SOSSAI, MIRKO. "The Legal Response of the Organisation of American States in Combating Terrorism" in Ben Saul, ed, *Research Handbook on International Law and Terrorism*, 2d ed (Cheltenham, UK & Northampton, US: Elgar, 2020) 628–38.

SPIJKERBOER, THOMAS & B.P. VERMEULEN. *Vluchtelingenrecht* (Nijmegen: Ars Aequi Libri, 2005).

STOREY, HUGO. "EU Refugee Qualification Directive: A Brave New World" (2008) 20 *International Journal of Refugee Law* 1–49.

———. "The 'War Flaw' and Why It Matters" in David Cantor & Jean-François Durieux, eds, *Refuge from Inhumanity? War Refugees and International Humanitarian Law* (Leiden & Boston: Brill Nijhoff, 2014) 39–56.

SYMES, MARK. "Exclusion from Asylum on the Basis of Criminality—The United Kingdom's Response and Its Broader International Law Context" in James C. Simeon, ed, *Terrorism and Asylum* (Leiden & Boston: Brill Nijhoff, 2020) 249–74.

TAKKENBERG, ALEX & CHRISTOPHER C. TAHBAZ. *The Collected Works of the 1951 Geneva Convention Relating to the Status of Refugees* (Amsterdam: Dutch Refugee Council Under the Auspices of the European Legal Network on Asylum, 1989), 3 vols.

TAYLOR, SAVITRI. "Exclusion from Protection of Persons of 'Bad Character': Is Australia Fulfilling Its Treaty-Based *Non-refoulement* Obligations?" (2002) *Australian Journal of Human Rights* 83–106.

———. "Australia and the Refugee Convention" in Satvinder Singh Juss, ed, *Research Handbook on International Refugee Law* (Cheltenham, UK & Northampton, US: Elgar, 2019) 238–51.

TIBERGHIEN, FRÉDÉRIC. *La protection des refugies en France* (Aix-en-Provence: Presses Universitaires D'Aix-Marseille, 1988).

TIEDEMANN, PAUL. "The Use of Foreign Asylum Procedure in the German Administrative Court" in Guy S. Goodwin-Gill & Hélène Lambert, eds, *The Limits of Transnational Law: Refugee Law, Policy Harmonization, and the Judicial Dialogue in the European Union* (Cambridge: Cambridge University Press, 2010) 57–84.

TRIAL INTERNATIONAL, *Universal Jurisdiction Annual Review*.

TRIGGS, GILLIAN D. & PATRICK C.J. WALL. "'The Makings of a Success': The Global Compact on Refugees and the Inaugural Global Refugee Forum" (2020) 32 *International Journal of Refugee Law* 283–339.

VAN KRIEKEN, PETER J. "Introduction" in Peter J. van Krieken, ed, *Refugee Law in Context: The Exclusion Clause* (The Hague: T.M.C. Asser, 1999) 1–10.

VAN SLIEDREGT, ELIES. *The Criminal Responsibility of Individuals for Violations of International Humanitarian Law* (The Hague: T.M.C. Asser, 2003).

———. *Individual Criminal Responsibility in International Law* (Oxford: Oxford University Press, 2012).

———. "International Outlaws" (2020) 33 *Leiden Journal of International Law* 535–40.

———. "International Crimes, International Outlaws and the Interface Between ICL and IRL" in James C. Simeon, ed, *Serious International Crimes, Human Rights and Forced Migration* (London: Routledge, 2022) 45–54.

VAN WAAS, LAURA. "The Intersection of International Refugee Law and International Statelessness Law" in Cathryn Costello, Michelle Foster & Jane McAdam, eds, *The Oxford Handbook of International Refugee Law* (Oxford: Oxford University Press, 2021) 152–68.

VAN WIJK, JORIS & MAARTEN BOLHUIS. *Case Management, Identity Controls and Screening on National Security and 1F Exclusion: A Comparative Study on Syrian Asylum Seekers in Five European Countries*" (Oslo: UDI & Amsterdam: VU, 2018).

———. "The Removal of Undesirable Asylum Seekers" in Satvinder Singh Juss, ed, *Research Handbook on International Refugee Law* (Cheltenham, UK & Northampton, US: Elgar, 2019) 403–16.

VON HEBEL, HERMAN & DARRYL ROBINSON. "Crimes Within the Jurisdiction of the Court" in Roy Lee, ed, *The Making of the Rome Statute: Issues, Negotiations, Results* (The Hague: Kluwer, 1999) 79–126.

WAGNER, KRISTEN. "UNHCR's Involvement in the Great Lake Refugee Crisis" (2009) 21 *Pace International Law Review* 365–86.

WALLS, LORI K. "The Persecutor Bar in US Immigration Law: Toward a More Nuanced Understanding of Modern 'Persecution' in the Case of Forced Abortion and Female Genital Cutting" (2007) 16 *Pacific Rim Law & Policy Journal* 227–56.

WALSH, FRANK M. "Navigating the Series of Rocks: Applying the Lessons from the Material Support Bar, *De Minimis*, and Age of Consent Exceptions to the Persecutor Bar" (2010) 22 *Florida Journal of International Law* 227–50.

WATT, ELLA. "International Criminal Law and New Zealand Refugee Status Determinations: A Case Note on *Attorney-General v Tamil X*" (2012) 43 *Victoria University Wellington Law Review* 235–62.

WEERASINGHE, SANJULA. *Refugee Law in a Time of Climate Change, Disaster and Conflict,* UNHCR Legal and Protection Policy Research Series No 40, January 2020.

WEIS, PAUL. *The Refugee Convention, 1951: The* Travaux Préparatoires *Analysed, with a Commentary by the Late Dr. Paul Weiss* (Cambridge & New York: Cambridge University Press, 1995).

WEISBORD, NOAH. *The Crime of Aggression: The Quest for Justice in an Age of Drones and Autocrats* (Princeton & Oxford: Princeton University Press, 2019).

WHITE, KATHRYN. "A Chance for Redemption: Revising the 'Persecutor Bar' and 'Material Support Bar' in the Case of Child Soldiers" (2010) 43 *Vanderbilt Journal of Transnational Law* 191–222.

WITTEN, SAMUEL. "The International Convention for the Suppression of Terrorist Bombings" in Ben Saul, ed, *Research Handbook on International Law and Terrorism*, 2d ed (Cheltenham, UK & Northampton, US: Elgar, 2020) 109–19.

WOOD, TAMARA. "The 1969 OAU Convention Governing the Specific Aspects of Refugee Problems in Africa" in Satvinder Singh Juss, ed, *Research Handbook on International Refugee Law* (Cheltenham, UK & Northampton, US: Elgar, 2019) 16–30.

WOUTERS, KEES. *International Legal Standards for Protection from Refoulement* (Antwerp-Oxford-Portland: Intersentia, 2009).

YAKOOB, NADIA. "Political Offender or Serious Criminal? Challenging the Interpretation of 'Serious, Nonpolitical Crimes' in *INS v Aquirre-Aguirre*" (2000) 14 *Georgetown Immigration Law Journal* 545–85.

YAKUT-BAHTIYAR, ZARIF. *Exclusion Clauses of the Refugee Convention in Relation to National Immigration Legislations, European Policy and Human Rights Instruments: Article 1F Versus the* Non-refoulement *Principle* (Nijmegen: Wolf Legal Publishers, 2016).

ZAGOR, MATTHEW. "Persecutor or Persecuted: Exclusion Under Article 1F(A) and (B) of the Refugees Convention" (2000) 23 *University of New South Wales Law Journal* 164–89.

ZALAR, BOŠTJAN. "Legal Implications of the 'Presumption of Innocence' and the Exclusion Clauses in International Protection Cases: The European Law Perspective" in James C. Simeon, ed, *Serious International Crimes, Human Rights and Forced Migration* (London: Routledge, 2022) 55–75.

ZAMBELLI, P. *The 1995 Annotated Refugee Convention: 1951 Convention Relating to the Status of Refugees* (Scarborough, ON: Carswell, 1994).

ZIEGLER, REUVEN. "International Humanitarian Law and Refugee Protection" in Cathryn Costello, Michelle Foster & Jane McAdam, eds, *The Oxford Handbook of International Refugee Law* (Oxford: Oxford University Press, 2021) 222–39.

ZIMMERMANN, ANDREAS & PHILIPP WENNHOLZ. "Article 1F (Definition of the Term 'Refugee')" in Andreas Zimmermann, ed, *The 1951 Convention Relating to the Status of Refugees and its 1967 Protocol: A Commentary* (Oxford: Oxford University Press, 2011).

Official Documents

League of Nations Documents

Additional Protocol to the Provisional Arrangement and to the Convention Concerning the Status of Refugees Coming from Germany (198 League of Nations Treaty Series 141)

Arrangement concerning the Extension to other Categories of Refugees of certain Measures taken in favour of Russian and Armenian Refugees of 28 June 1928 (89 League of Nations Treaty Series 63)

Arrangement for the Issue of a Certificate of Identity to Refugees from the Saar (1935 League of Nations Official Journal 1681)

Arrangement of 12 May 1926 relating to the Issue of Identity Certificates to Russian and Armenian Refugees (89 League of Nations Treaty Series 47)

Arrangement of 30 June 1928 relating to the Legal Status of Russian and Armenian Refugees (89 League of Nations Treaty Series 53)

Arrangement with Regard to Issue of Certificates of Identity to Russian Refugees (13 League of Nations Treaty Series 237)

Convention concerning the Status of Refugees Coming from Germany (192 League of Nations Treaty Series 59)

Convention for the Prevention and Punishment of Terrorism (16 November 1937) (19 League of Nations Official Journal 23)

Convention of 28 October 1933 Relating to the International Status of Refugees (159 League of Nations Treaty Series 199)

Plan for the Issue of a Certificate of Identity to Armenian Refugees (League of Nations Official Journal, No 7–10, 1924, 969–70)

United Nations Documents

Agreement for United Nations Relief and Rehabilitation Administration, 9 November 1943

Charter of the United Nations, 26 June 1945

Constitution of the International Refugee Organization of 15 December 1946

Convention against Torture and Other Cruel, Inhuman or Degrading Treatment or Punishment of 10 December 1984

Convention for the Protection of All Persons from Enforced Disappearance of 20 December 2006

Convention on Offences and Certain Other Acts Committed on Board Aircraft, Signed at Tokyo on 14 September 1963

Convention on the Prevention and Punishment of Crimes Against Internationally Protected Persons, including Diplomatic Agents, Adopted by the General Assembly of the United Nations on 14 December 1973

Convention on the Prevention and Punishment of the Crime of Genocide of 9 December 1948

Convention on the Rights of the Child of 20 November 1989

Convention for the Suppression of Unlawful Acts against the Safety of Maritime Navigation, Concluded at Rome on 10 March 1988

Convention for the Suppression of Unlawful Seizure of Aircraft, Signed at The Hague on 16 December 1970

Convention on the Safety of United Nations and Associated Personnel, Signed in New York on 8 December 2005

Convention relating to the Status of Refugees of 28 July 1951

Geneva Conventions of 12 August 1949

Global Compact for Safe, Orderly and Regular Migration, UN Doc A/RES/73/195, 11 January 2019

Global Compact on Refugees, UN Doc A/73/12 (Part II), 2 August 2018

International Convention against the Taking of Hostages, Adopted by the General Assembly of the United Nations on 17 December 1979

International Convention against Transnational Organized Crime (Palermo Convention), Adopted by the General Assembly of the United Nations on 15 November 2000

International Convention for the Suppression of Acts of Nuclear Terrorism Adopted by the General Assembly of the United Nations on 13 April 2005

International Convention for the Suppression of Counterfeiting Currency of 20 April 1929

International Convention for the Suppression of the Financing of Terrorism, Adopted by the General Assembly of the United Nations on 9 December 1999

International Convention for the Suppression of Terrorist Bombings, Adopted by the General Assembly of the United Nations on 15 December 1997

International Convention on the Elimination of All Forms of Racial Discrimination of 21 December 1965

International Convention on the Protection of the Rights of All Migrant Workers and Members of Their Families of 18 December 1990

International Covenant on Civil and Political Rights of 16 December 1966

International Covenant on Economic, Social and Cultural Rights of 16 December 1966

International Refugee Organization, *Manual for Eligibility Officers* (Genève: Imprimeries Populaires, 1950)

Protocol against the Smuggling of Migrants by Land, Sea and Air of 15 November 2000

Protocol for the Suppression of Unlawful Acts against the Safety of Fixed Platforms Located on the Continental Shelf, Done at Rome on 10 March 1988

Protocol on the Suppression of Unlawful Acts of Violence at Airports Serving International Civil Aviation, Supplementary to the Convention for the Suppression of Unlawful Acts against the Safety of Civil Aviation, Signed at Montreal on 24 February 1988

Protocol relating to the Status of Refugees of 31 January 1967

Protocol to Prevent, Suppress and Punish Trafficking in Persons, Especially Women and Children of 15 November 2000

Protocols I and II Additional to the Geneva Conventions of 12 August 1949 and of 8 June 1977

Rome Statute of the International Criminal Court of 1 July 2002

Seventieth Anniversary of the Universal Declaration of Human Rights: Reaffirming and Strengthening the Prohibition of Torture and Other Cruel, Inhuman or Degrading Treatment or Punishment, 20 July 2018, UN Doc A/73/207

UN Doc A/51/10, Report of the International Law Commission on the Work of its Forty-eighth Session, Official Records of the General Assembly, Fifty-first Session, Supplement No 10, Chapter II

UN Doc A/51/22, UN Doc A/59/894, UN Doc A/65/10, Report of the International Law Commission, Sixty-second Session, 3 May–4 June and 5 July–6 August 2010, General Assembly Official Records, Sixty-fifth Session, Supplement No 10

UN Doc A/65/181, The Scope and Application of the Principle of Universal Jurisdiction: Report of the Secretary-General Prepared on the Basis of Comments and Observations of Governments, 29 July 2010

UN Doc A/69/10, Report of the International Law Commission, Sixty-sixth Session, 5 May–6 June and 7 July–8 August 2014, "The Obligation to Extradite or Prosecute (*aut dedere aut judicare*)," Final Report of the International Law Commission, 2014

UN Doc A/73/10, Report of the International Law Commission, Seventieth Session, 30 April–1 June and 2 July–10 August 2018, Annex A, Universal Jurisdiction, Report by Charles Chernor Jalloh, 2018

UN Doc A/73/10, Report of the International Law Commission, Seventieth Session, Chapter V, Draft Conclusions on Identification of Customary International Law, 2018

UN Doc A/75/437, 20 November 2020

UN Doc A/810 (1948)

UN Doc A74/10, Draft Articles on Prevention and Punishment of Crimes Against Humanity, with Commentaries, International Law Commission, 2019

UN Doc A/C.3/SR.121

UN Doc A/C.3/SR.122

UN Doc A/C.6/65/L.10, 3 November 2010, Appendix I

UN Doc A/CN.4/565, Expulsion of Aliens, Memorandum by the Secretariat, International Law Commission, Fifty-eighth session, Geneva, 1 May–9 June and 3 July–11 August 2006, 10 July 2006

UN Doc A/CN.4/625, International Law Commission, Sixty-second Session, Geneva, 3 May–4 June and 5 July–6 August 2007, Sixth Report on the Expulsion of Aliens by Mr. Maurice Kamto, Special Rapporteur, 19 March 2010

UN Doc A/CN.4/630, International Law Commission, Sixty-second Session, Geneva, 3 May–4 June and 5 July–6 August 2010, Survey of Multilateral Conventions Which May Be of Relevance for the Commission's Work on the Topic, "The Obligation to Extradite or Prosecute (*aut dedere aut judicare*)," Study of the Secretariat, 16 May 2010

UN Doc A/CN.4/L.682, International Law Commission, Fifty-eighth Session, 1 May–9 June and 3 July–11 August 2006, Fragmentation of International Law: Difficulties Arising from the Diversification and Expansion of International Law, Report of the Study Group of the International Law Commission, Finalized by Martti Koskenniemi, 13 April 2006

UN Doc A/CN.4/L.741, International Law Commission, Seventy-second Session, Geneva, 27 April–5 June and 6 July–7 August 2020, Second Report on General Principles of Law by Marcelo Vázquez-Bermúdez, Special Rapporteur, 9 April 2020

UN Doc A/CN.4/L.747, International Law Commission, Seventy-third Session, Geneva, 18 April–3 June and 4 July–5 August 2022, Fifth report on peremptory norms of general international law (jus cogens) by Dire Tladi, Special Rapporteur, 24 January 2022, pages 82–83, Annex

UN Doc A/CN.4/L.774, International Law Commission, Sixty-second Session, Geneva, 3 May–4 June and 5 July–6 August 2010, Bases for Discussion in the Working Group on the Topic, "The Obligation to Extradite or Prosecute (*aut dedere aut judicare*)," Paper Prepared by Mr. Zdzislaw Galicki, Special Rapporteur

UN Doc A/CONF.2/4
UN Doc A/CONF.2/74
UN Doc A/CONF.2/76
UN Doc A/CONF.2/92
UN Doc A/CONF.2/SR 3
UN Doc A/CONF.2/SR 19
UN Doc A/CONF.2/SR 21
UN Doc A/CONF.2/SR 24
UN Doc A/CONF.2/SR 29
UN Doc A/CONF.183/9
UN Doc A/CONF.183/2/Add.1
UN Doc A/RES/21/2198 (1996)
UN Doc A/RES/50/186 (1997)
UN Doc A/RES/51/120 (1996)
UN Doc A/RES/319(IV)A (1949)
UN Doc E/1618 and Corr.1
UN Doc E/800

UN Doc E/1814
UN Doc E/AC.7/SR 160
UN Doc E/AC. 7/SR 166
UN Doc E/AC.32/5 and Corr.1
UN Doc E/AC.32/L3
UN Doc E/CN.4/2006/120, *Situation of Detainees at Guantánamo Bay*, 27 February 2006
UN Doc E/CN.4/AC.1/39
UN Doc E/CN.4/AC.1/SR.9
UN Doc E/CN.4/AC.1/SR.13
UN Doc E/CN.4/AC.1/SR.25
UN Doc E/CN.4/AC.1/SR. 30
UN Doc E/CN.4/AC.1/SR.31
UN Doc E/CN.4/AC.1/SR.37
UN Doc E/L.82
UN Doc GA/SHC/4322, Lack of Accountability for Torture Worldwide Due to Systemic Denial, Evasion by Public Authorities, Special Rapporteur Tells Third Committee, 12 October 2021
UN Doc Official Records of the Third Session of the General Assembly, Part I, Social, Humanitarian and Cultural Questions, Third Committee, Summary Records of Meetings, 21 September—8 December 1948
UN Doc, "Ombudsperson to the ISIL (Da'esh) and Al-Qaida Sanctions Committee"
UN Doc Report of the Special Rapporteur on Torture and Other Cruel, Inhuman or Degrading Treatment or Punishment, 5 February 2010, A/HRC/13/39/Add.5
UN Doc Resolution ICC-ASP/16/Res.4
UN Doc Resolution ICC-ASP/18/Res.5
UN Doc Resolution RC/Res.5, Annex I, "Amendments to Article 8 of the Rome Statute"
UN Doc Resolution RC/Res.6, Annex I, "Amendments to the Rome Statute of the International Criminal Court on the Crime of Aggression"
UN Doc Resolution RC/Res.6, Annex II, "Amendments to the Elements of Crimes"
UN Doc S/25704, 3 May 1993, The Report of the Secretary General Pursuant to Paragraph 2 of Security Council Resolution 808 (1993)
UN Doc S/RES/731 (1992)
UN Doc S/RES/748 (1992)
UN Doc S/RES/827 (1993)
UN Doc S/RES/955 (1994)
UN Doc S/RES/1269 (1999)
UN Doc S/RES/1373 (2001)
UN Doc S/RES/1377 (2001)
UN Doc S/RES/1493 (2003)
UN Doc S/RES/1566 (2004)
UN Doc S/RES/1624 (2005)
UN Doc S/RES1904 (2009)

UN Doc S/RES 1966 (2010)
UN Doc S/RES/2178 (2014)

UN Doc, "Security Council Committee Pursuant to Resolutions 1267 (1999) 1989 (2011) and 2253 (2015) Concerning Islamic State in Iraq and the Levant (Da'esh), Al-Qaida and Associated Individuals, Groups, Undertakings and Entities"

UN Doc, United Nations Economic and Social Council, Commission on Human Rights, Drafting Committee, International Bill of Rights, First Session, Summary Record of Thirteenth Meeting, 20 June 1947

UN Doc, United Nations Treaty Collection, Text and Status of the United Nations Conventions on Terrorism

UNHCR, *Addressing Security Concerns Without Undermining Refugee Protection: UNHCR's Perspective*, 29 November 2001

UNHCR, *Advisory Opinion from the Office of the United Nations High Commissioner for Refugees (UNHCR) on the Scope of the National Security Exception Under Article 33(2) of the 1951 Convention Relating to the Status of Refugees*, 6 January 2006

UNHCR, *Advisory Opinion from the Office of the United Nations High Commissioner for Refugees (UNHCR) Regarding the International Standards for Exclusion from Refugee Status as Applied to Child Soldiers*, 12 September 2005

UNHCR, *Advisory Opinion on the Extraterritorial Application of* Non-refoulement *Obligations Under the 1951 Convention Relating to the Status of Refugees and its 1967 Protocol*, 26 January 2007

UNHCR, *Alternatives to Detention of Asylum Seekers and Refugees*, Ophelia Field with the assistance of Alice Edwards, POLAS/2006/03, April 2006

UNHCR, *Asylum in the European Union: A Study of the Implementation of the Qualification Directive*, November 2007

UNHCR, *A Thematic Compilation of Executive Committee Conclusions (7th edition)*, June 2014

UNHCR, *Background Note on the Application of the Exclusion Clauses: Article 1F of the 1951 Convention Relating to the Status of Refugees*, 4 September 2003

UNHCR, Brief of United Nations High Commissioner for Refugees as *Amicus Curiae* Supporting Petitioner in the Case of *Daniel Girmai Negusie v Merrick Garland*, US Attorney General, No 21-60314, 4 August 2021

UNHCR, *Commentary on the Refugee Convention 1951 (Articles 2–11, 13–37)*, October 1997 (written by Professor Atle Grahl-Madsen in 1963; republished by the Department of International Protection in October 1997)

UNHCR, *Comments on the European Commission Proposal for a Qualification Regulation—COM (2016) 466*, February 2018

UNHCR, *Conclusions Adopted by the Executive Committee on the International Protection of Refugees, 1975–2007 (Conclusion No 1–114)*, October 2017

UNHCR, *Data Finder*, New Asylum Applications Registered in 2019 Country of Asylum, June 2020

UNHCR, *Eligibility Guidelines for Assessing the International Protection Needs of Asylum-Seekers from Afghanistan*, HCR/EG/AFG/18/02, 30 August 2018

UNHCR, *Eligibility Guidelines for Assessing the International Protection Needs of Asylum-Seekers from Guatemala,* HCR/EG/GTM/18/01, January 2018

UNHCR, *Eligibility Guidelines for Assessing the International Protection Needs of Members of Religious Minorities from Pakistan*, HCR/EG/PAK/17/01, January 2017

UNHCR, ExCom Conclusion No 12 (XXIX) 1978

UNHCR, ExCom Conclusion No 17 (XXXI) 1980

UNHCR, ExCom Conclusion No 44 (XXXVII) 1986

UNHCR, ExCom Conclusion No 55 (XL) 1989

UNHCR, ExCom Conclusion No 82 (XLVIII) 1997

UNHCR, ExCom Conclusion No 94 (LIII) 2002

UNHCR, ExCom Conclusion No 97 (LIV) 2003

UNHCR, ExCom Conclusion No 100 (LV) 2004

UNHCR, ExCom Conclusion No 102 (LVI) 2005

UNHCR, ExCom Conclusion No 103 (LVI) 2005

UNHCR, *ExCom Conclusions on International Protection*

UNHCR, *Factum of the Intervenor, UNHCR, Suresh v the Minister of Citizenship and Immigration; the Attorney General of Canada, SCC No 27790*, 8 March 2001

UNHCR, *Global Strategy Beyond Detention 2014–2019; Final Progress Report*, 4 November 2020

UNHCR, *Global Trends: Forced Displacement in 2021* (Copenhagen, Denmark: UNHCR Global Data Service,16 June 2022), online: www.unhcr.org/62a9d1494/global-trends-report-2021

UNHCR, *Guidance Note on Extradition and International Refugee Protection*, April 2008

UNHCR, *Guidance Note on Refugee Claims Relating to Victims of Organized Gangs*, March 2010

UNHCR, *Guidelines on Applicable Criteria and Standards Relating to the Detention of Asylum-Seekers*, February 1999

UNHCR, *Guidelines on the Applicable Criteria and Standards Relating to the Detention of Asylum-Seekers and Alternatives to Detention*, 2012

UNHCR, *Guidelines on the Application in Mass Influx Situations of the Exclusion Clauses of Article 1F of the 1951 Convention Relating to the Status of Refugees*, February 2006

UNHCR, *Guidelines on International Protection: Application of the Exclusion Clauses: Article 1F of the 1951 Convention Relating to the Status of Refugees*, HCR/GIP/03/05, 4 September 2003

UNHCR, *Guidelines on International Protection No 13: Applicability of Article 1D of the 1951 Convention Relating to the Status of Refugees to Palestine Refugees*, December 2017, HCR/GIP/17/13

UNHCR, *Guidelines on International Protection: Child Asylum Claims Under Articles 1(A)2 and 1(F) of the 1951 Convention and/or 1967 Protocol Relating to the Status of Refugees*, HCR/GIP/09/08, 22 December 2009

UNHCR, *Handbook on Procedures and Criteria for Determining Refugee Status and Guidelines on International Protection Under the 1951 Convention and the 1967 Protocol relating to the Status of Refugees*, HCR/1P/4/Eng/Rev.4

UNHCR, *Intervention Before the Supreme Court of Canada in the Case of Ezokola v Canada (Minister of Citizenship and Immigration)*, 15 December 2012

UNHCR, *Intervention Before the Supreme Court of the United Kingdom in the Cases of Yasser al-Sirri (Appellant) v Secretary of State for the Home Department (Respondent) and DD (Afghanistan) (Appellant) v Secretary of State for the Home Department (Respondent)*, 23 March 2012

UNHCR, *Intervention by the Office of the United Nations High Commissioner for Refugees in the Case of the Minister of Public Safety and Emergency Preparedness v Medhanie Aregawi Weldemariam*, 27 April 2021

UNHCR, *Luis Alberto Hernandez Febles v Minister of Citizenship and Immigration: Factum of the Intervener*, 11 March 2014

UNHCR, *Maritime Interception Operations and the Processing of International Protection Claims: Legal Standards and Policy Considerations with Respect to Extraterritorial Processing,* November 2010

UNHCR, *Note on Diplomatic Assurances and International Refugee Protection*, August 2006

UNHCR, *Note on International Protection (A/AC.96/951)*, 13 September 2001

UNHCR, *Note on the Principle of Non-refoulement,* November 1997

UNHCR, *Note on the Structure and Operation of the KhAD/WAD in Afghanistan 1978–1992*, May 2008

UNHCR, *Procedural Standards for Refugee Status Determination Under UNHCR's Mandate,* 1 September 2005

UNHCR, Refugee Data Finder, Key Indicators, 2022

UNHCR, *Resettlement Handbook*, 2011

UNHCR, *Selected Documents Relating to Detention*, February 2009

UNHCR, *Statement on Article 1F of the 1951 Convention, Issued in the Context of the Preliminary Ruling References to the Court of Justice of the European Communities from the German Federal Administrative Court Regarding the Interpretation of Articles 12(2)(b) and (c) of the Qualification Directive*, July 2009

UNHCR, Submission by the Office of the United Nations High Commissioner for Refugees in the Case of SS and Others v Italy (Appl No 21660/18) Before the European Court of Human Rights, 14 November 2019

UNHCR, *The Exclusion Clauses: Guidelines on Their Application*, December 1996

UNHCR, *The Interface Between Extradition and Asylum*, by Sibylle Kapferer, PPLA/2003/05, November 2003

UNHCR, *The Nationality, Immigration and Asylum Act 2002 (Specification of Particularly Serious Crimes) Order 2004, UNHCR Comments*, November 2004

UNHCR, *UNHCR RSD Procedural Standards Unit 10: Procedures for Cancellation and Revocation of Refugee Status*, August 2020

UNHCR, United Nations High Commissioner for Refugees, States Parties to the 1951 Convention Relating to the Status of Refugees and the 1967 Protocol

UNHCR, United Nations High Commissioner for Refugees, *Cancellation of Refugee Status*, March 2003, PPLA/2003/02

UNHCR, United Nations High Commissioner for Refugees, *Expert Meeting, The Concept of Stateless Persons Under International Law, Summary Conclusions*, Expert meeting organized by the Office of the United Nations High Commissioner for Refugees, Prato, Italy, 27–28 May 2010

UNHCR, *UNHCR Statistical Yearbook 2014*, Chapter 4: Asylum and Refugee Status Determination, 8 December 2015

UNHCR, *Working Paper No 111, Fleeing Violence and Poverty: Non-refoulement Obligations Under the European Convention of Human Rights* by Katharina Röhl, January 2005

UN Human Rights Council, Global Issue of Unaccompanied Migrant Children and Human Rights, UN Doc A/HRC/36/51 (24 July 2017)

UNICEF, Ad Hoc Committee on Refugees and Stateless Persons, A Deadly Journey for Children: The Central Mediterranean Migration Route, 2017

UN Office of Legal Affairs, Codification Division, International Covenant on Civil and Political Rights, New York, 16 December 1966, Procedural History (Audiovisual Library of International Law)

UN Office of Legal Affairs, Codification Division, The Convention against Torture and Other Cruel, Inhuman or Degrading Treatment or Punishment, 10 December 1984, Procedural History (Audiovisual Library of International Law)

United Nations, Universal Declaration of Human Rights of 10 December 1948

United Nations War Crimes Commission, *Law Reports of Trials of War Criminals*, Volume XV, Digest of Laws and Cases (London: His Majesty's Stationary Office, 1949)

United Nations Yearbook on Human Rights for 1948, Yearbook of the United Nations, 1947–48

Regional Governmental Organizations' Documents

African Charter on Human and Peoples' Rights of 26 June 1981

African Charter on the Rights and Welfare of the Child of 11 July 1990

African Union Convention for the Protection and Assistance of Internally Displaced Persons in Africa (Kampala Convention) of 22 October 2009

American Convention on Human Rights of 22 November 1969

Arab Charter of Human Rights on 15 September 1994
Arab Convention on the Suppression of Terrorism, Signed at a Meeting Held at the General Secretariat of the League of Arab States in Cairo on 22 April 1998
ASEAN Convention on Counter Terrorism, Signed at Cebu, Philippines, on 13 January 2007
Association of Southeast Asian Nations (ASEAN), Cha-Am Hua Hin Declaration on the Intergovernmental Commission on Human Rights of 23 October 2009
Bangkok Principles on Status and Treatment of Refugees of 24 June 2001
Cartagena Declaration on Refugees of 1984
Charter of the Association of Southeast Asian Nations of 20 November 2007
Charter of Fundamental Rights of the European Union of 7 December 2000
Convention of the Organization of the Islamic Conference on Combating International Terrorism, Adopted at Ouagadougou on 1 July 1999
Commission of the European Communities, "The Relationship Between Safeguarding Internal Security and Complying with International Protection Obligations and Instruments," Document COM, 5 December 2001 (2001) 743
Council of Europe Convention on the Prevention of Terrorism, Concluded at Warsaw, 16 May 2005
Council of Europe, Committee of Ministers, *Recommendation Rec(2005)6 of the Committee of Ministers to Member States on Exclusion from Refugee Status in the Context of Article 1F of the Convention Relating to the Status of Refugees of 28 July 1951*, 23 March 2005
Council of Europe, Group of Experts on Action Against Trafficking in Human Beings (GRETA), Guidance Note on the Entitlement of Victims of Trafficking, and Persons at Risk of Being Trafficked, to International Protection, June 2020
Council of the European Economic Community, Directive 64/221/EEC of 25 February 1964
Council of the European Union, Council Common Position of 27 December 2001 on the Application of Specific Measures to Combat Terrorism (2001/931/CFSP)
Council of the European Union, Directive Concerning the Status of Third-Country Nationals Who Are Long-term Residents, 2003/109/EC
Council of the European Union, Directive on the Right of Citizens of the Union and Their Family Members to Move and Reside Freely Within the Territory of the Member States, 2004/38/EC
Council of the European Union, Decision 2002/494/JHA of 13 June 2002, Setting up a European Network of Contact Points in Respect of Persons Responsible for Genocide, Crimes Against Humanity and War Crimes
Council of the European Union, Decision 2003/335/JHA of 8 May 2003 on the Investigation and Prosecution of Genocide, Crimes Against Humanity and War Crimes
Council of the European Union, Framework Decision on Combating Terrorism, 2002/475/JHA
Council of the European Union, Framework Decision on the European Arrest Warrant and the Surrender Procedures Between Member States, 2002/584/JHA

Council of the European Union, Joint Position of 4 March 1996 Defined by the Council on the Basis of Article K.3 of the Treaty on European Union on the Harmonized Application of the Definition of the Term "Refugee" in Article 1 of the Geneva Convention of 28 July 1951 Relating to the Status of Refugees, 96/196/JHA, 4 March 1996

Council of the European Union, Qualification Directive, 2004/83/EC

Council of the European Union, Receptions Conditions Directive, 2003/9/EC

Council of the European Union, Regulation Establishing the Criteria and Mechanisms for Determining the Member State Responsible for Examining an Asylum Application Lodged in One of the Member States by a Third-Country National, No 343/2003 (Dublin Regulation)

Council of the European Union, Temporary Protection Directive, 2001/55/EC

Council of the European Union, The AU-EU Expert Report on the Principle of Universal Jurisdiction, 8672/1/09/REV 1, 16 April 2009

European Convention on Extradition, Concluded at Paris on 13 December 1957

European Convention on Human Rights, Concluded at Rome on 4 November 1950

European Convention on the Suppression of Terrorism, Concluded at Strasbourg on 27 January 1977

European Council Decision (CFSP) 2016/1693 of 20 September 2016 Concerning Restrictive Measures Against ISIL (Da'esh) and Al-Qaeda and Persons, Groups, Undertakings and Entities Associated with Them

European Council Implementing Decision (EU) 2022/382 of 4 March 2022, Establishing the Existence of a Mass Influx of Displaced Persons from Ukraine Within the Meaning of Article 5 of Directive 2001/55/EC, and Having the Effect of Introducing Temporary Protection

European Council Regulation (EC) No 2580/2001 of 27 December 2001 on Specific Restrictive Measures Directed Against Certain Persons and Entities with a View to Combating Terrorism

European Council Regulation (EU) 2016/1686 of 20 September 2016 Imposing Additional Restrictive Measures Directed Against ISIL (Da'esh) and Al-Qaeda and Natural and Legal Persons, Entities or Bodies Associated with Them

European Court of Human Rights, Guide on the Case-Law of the European Convention on Human Rights European Parliament and Council of the European Union, Directive 2011/95/EU of 13 December 2011 (recast) (the Qualification Directive)

European Parliament and Council of the European Union, Directive (EU) 2017/541 on Combating Terrorism and Replacing Council Framework Decision 2002/475/JHA and Amending Council Decision 2005/671/JHA, 15 March 2017

European Parliament and of the Council of the European Union, Directive 2008/115/EC of 16 December 2008 on Common Standards and Procedures in Member States for Returning Illegally Staying Third-Country Nationals

European Parliament and of the Council of the European Union, Directive 2013/32/EU of 26 June 2013 on Common Procedures for Granting and Withdrawing International Protection (recast) (Asylum Procedures Directive)
Inter-American Commission on Human Rights, *Report on Immigration in the United States: Detention and Due Process*, OEA/Ser.L/V/II, Doc. 78/10, 30 December 2010
Inter-American Convention Against Terrorism of 3 June 2002
Inter-American Convention on Extradition of 25 February 1981
Inter-American Convention to Prevent and Punish Torture of 28 February 1987
OAU Convention on the Prevention and Combating of Terrorism, Adopted at Algiers on 14 July 1999
OAU Convention Governing the Specific Aspects of Refugee Problems in Africa of 10 September 1969
Organization of American States (OAS), Convention to Prevent and Punish Acts of Terrorism Taking the Form of Crimes against Persons and Related Extortion That Are of International Significance, Concluded at Washington, DC, on 2 February 1971
Protocol on Amendments to the Protocol on the Statute of the African Court of Justice and Human Rights (Malabo Protocol)
Protocol to the African Charter on Human and Peoples' Rights on the Rights of Women in Africa of 11 July 2003
South Asian Association for Regional Cooperation (SAARC) Regional Convention on Suppression of Terrorism, Signed at Kathmandu on 4 November 1987
Treaty of Lisbon of 13 December 2007

National Legislation and Official Documents

Legislation

Australia

Australian Security Intelligence Organisation Act 1979
Charter of the United Nations Act 1945
Crimes Legislation Amendment (Torture Prohibition and Death Penalty Abolition) Bill 2009
Criminal Code Act 1995
Extradition Act 1988
Migration Act 1958
Migration Amendment (Complementary Protection) Bill 2009
Migration Regulations 1994

Belgium

Aliens Act (Law Regarding the Entry, Residence, Settlement and Removal of Aliens) 15 December 1980
Criminal Code, Code Pénal/Strafwetboek, C.Pén./Sw.

Canada

Charter of Rights and Freedoms, Part I of the *Constitution Act, 1982*, being Schedule B to the *Canada Act 1982* (UK), 1982, c 11

Criminal Code, RSC, 1985, c C-46

Extradition Act, SC 1999, c 18

Immigration and Refugee Protection Act, SC 2001, c 27

Immigration and Refugee Protection Regulations

United Nations Act, RSC, 1985, c U-2

France

Code for Entry and Residence of Foreigners and Right of Asylum (CESEDA), Décret n°2006-1378 du 14 novembre 2006

Criminal Code, Code Pénal, C. Pén

Germany

Act on the Residence, Economic Activity, and Integration of Foreigners in the Federal Territory (Residence Act of 2008), 25 February 2008

Asylum Act, AsylVfG 2008, 2 September 2008

Criminal Code, StGB

The Netherlands

Aliens Act 2000, (Vw 2000), 1 April 2001

Aliens Regulation 2000

Criminal Code, Sr

New Zealand

Bill of Rights Act 1990, Public Act 1990 No 109

Crimes Act 1961, Public Act 1961 No 43

Extradition Act 1999, Public Act 1999 No 55

Immigration Act 2009, Public Act 2009 No 51

Terrorism Suppression Act 2002, Public Act 2002 No 34

United Nations Act 1946, Public Act 1946, No 7

South Africa

Refugees Act of 1998, No. 130 of 1998

United Kingdom

Anti-terrorism, Crime and Security Act 2001 (2001 c 24)

Asylum and Immigration Appeals Act 1993 (1993 c 23)

Extradition Act 2003 (2003 c 41)

Human Rights Act 1998

Immigration Act 1971 (1971 c 77)

Immigration, Asylum and Nationality Act 2006 (2006 c 13)

Immigration Rules
Nationality and Borders Act 2022
Nationality, Immigration and Asylum Act 2002 (2002 c 41)
Nationality, Immigration and Asylum Act 2002 (Specification of Particularly Serious Crimes) Order 2004
Terrorism Act 2000 (2000 c 11)
Terrorism Act 2000 (Proscribed Organisations) (Amendment) Order 2000
Terrorism Act 2006 (2006 c 11)
UK Border Act 2007 (2007 c 30)
United Nations Act 1946 (1946 c 45)

United States

Antiterrorism and Effective Death Penalty Act of 1996 (*AEDPA*), 104 PL 132, 110 Stat 1214
Bill of Rights
Child Soldiers Accountability Act of 2008, 110 PL 340, 122 Stat 3735
Code of Federal Regulations, Title 8
Consolidated Appropriations Act, 2008, 110 PL 161, 121 Stat 1844
Exemption of African National Congress from Treatment as Terrorist Organization for Certain Acts or Events Public Act, Public Law 110-257, 110 PL 257, 122 Stat 2426
Illegal Immigration Reform and Immigrant Responsibility Act of 1996 (*IIRIRA*), 104 PL 208, 110 Stat 3009
Immigration Act of 1990, 101 PL 649, 104 Stat 4978
Immigration and Nationality Act, 117 PL 360, 136 Stat 6292
REAL ID Act of 2005, 109 PL 13, 119 Stat 302
Refugee Protection Act 2010 (proposed)
Torture Victim Protection Act of 1991, 102 PL 256, 106 Stat 73
United States Code, Title 18
Uniting and Strengthening America by Providing Appropriate Tools Required to Intercept and Obstruct Terrorism (USA PATRIOT) Act of 2001, 107 PL 56, 115 Stat 272

Official Documents

Australia

Administrative Appeals Tribunal (AAT), *Guide to Refugee Law in Australia*
Department of Immigration and Citizenship, *Annual Report 2006–2007*
Federal Prosecution Service, *Prosecution Policy of the Commonwealth*
Minister of Home Affairs, Direction No 90, entitled "Visa Refusal and Cancellation Under s 501 and Revocation of a Mandatory Cancellation of a Visa Under s 501CA," 8 March 2021

Belgium

2012 Annual Report of the Office of the Commissioner General for Refugees and Stateless Persons

Canada

Canada's Crimes Against Humanity and War Crimes Program, Fifth Annual Report, 2001–2002

Canada's Program on Crimes Against Humanity and War Crimes, Tenth Annual Report, 2006–2007

Canada's Program on Crimes Against Humanity and War Crimes, 12th Report, 2008–2011

Canada's Program on Crimes Against Humanity and War Crimes, 13th Report, 2011–2015

Department of Justice, Corporate Services Branch, Evaluation Division, *Crimes against Humanity and War Crimes Program Evaluation, Final Report,* August 2016

Government of Canada, "Asylum Claims by Year – 2011–2016"

Immigration and Refugee Board of Canada (IRB), *Interpretation of Convention Refugee and Person in Need of Protection in the Case Law.* Chapter 10—Exclusion Clauses—Article 1E, 31 December 2020

Immigration and Refugee Board of Canada (IRB), *Interpretation of Convention Refugee and Person in Need of Protection in the Case Law.* Chapter 11—Article 1F, 31 December 2020

Immigration and Refugee Board of Canada (IRB), *Interpretation of Convention Refugee and Person in Need of Protection in the Case Law.* Chapter 14, Persons in Need of Protection, 31 December 2020

Immigration, Refugees and Citizenship Canada, *Pre-removal Risk Assessments (PRRAs)*

Immigration, Refugees and Citizenship Canada, *Operations Manual, Enforcement 18—Human or International Rights Violations*

Immigration, Refugees and Citizenship Canada, *Operations Manual, Enforcement 28, Ministerial Opinions on Danger to the Public, Nature and Severity of the Acts Committed and Danger to the Security of Canada*

Public Prosecution Service of Canada, *Public Prosecution Service of Canada Deskbook*

Germany

Deutscher Bundestag, *Drucksache 18/12533, Antwort der Bundesregierung,* 30 May 2017

The Netherlands

Aliens Manual (*Vreemdelingencirculaire*) 2000 (B)

Aliens Manual (*Vreemdelingencirculaire*) 2000 (C)

Amendment 2006/22 to the *Vreemdelingencirculaire* 2000 of 2 June 2006
Kamerstuk 19637, Vreemdelingenbeleid, Nr 1808, 14 April 2014
Letter from the Minister of Foreign Affairs to the President of the House of Commons, Reference BZDOC-853412865-43, 22 May 2018
Letter from the Minister of Immigration and Integration to the House of Commons, 2002–3 Session, 19 637, nr 695, 7 November 2002
Letter from the Minister of Immigration and Integration to the House of Commons, 2003–4 Session, 19 637, nr 811, 8 April 2004
Letter from the Minister of Immigration and Integration to the House of Commons, 2003–4 Session, 19 637, nr 829, 23 June 2004
Letter from the Minister and State Secretary of Justice to the House of Commons, 2007–8 Session, 31 200 VI, nr160, 9 June 2008, attaching Notitie betreffende de toepassing van artikel 1F Vluchtelingenverdrag
Letter from the Minister of Justice to the House of Commons, 2006–7 Session, 30 800 VI, nr 12 313, August 2007
Letter from the Minister of Justice to the President of the House of Commons, 2007-8 Session, 31 200 VI nr 193, 9 September 2008
Letter from the State Secretary of Justice to the House of Commons, 1999–2000 Session, 19 637, nr 520, 3 April 2000
Letter from the State Secretary of Justice to the House of Commons, 1997–98 Session, 19 637, nr 295, 28 November 1997
Netherlands Refugee Statistics 1960–2021
Rapportagebrief for Internationale Misdrijven 2015–20

New Zealand

Crown Law, *Solicitor-General's Prosecution Guidelines*
Immigration New Zealand (INZ) Operational Manual
New Zealand Parliament, *Parliamentary Debates (Hansard)*, 3 August 2006

United Kingdom

Crown Prosecution Service, *War Crimes/Crimes Against Humanity Referral Guidelines*
Crown Prosecution Service, *The Code for Crown Prosecutors*
Home Office, *Exclusion (Article 1F) and Article 33(2) of the Refugee Convention*, Version 7.0, 28 June 2022
Home Office, *Humanitarian Protection in Asylum Claims* (lodged before 28 June 2022)
Home Office, *Restricted Leave*
Home Office's *Asylum Policy Instruction: Article 1D of the Refugee Convention: Palestinian Refugees Assisted by the United Nations Relief and Works Agency (UNRWA)*, version 2 (9 May 2016)

United States

Attorney General of the US, Matter of *Negusie*, 28 I&N Dec 120 (AG 2020), Interim Decision #3999, 2020

Department of State, Bureau of Counterterrorism, Foreign Terrorist Organizations

———, Terrorism Exclusion List

Executive Office for Immigration Review (EOIR), Department of Justice, *Immigration Court Practice Manual*

USCIS, *Affirmative Asylum Procedures Manual* of the US Citizenship and Immigration Services, Refugee, Asylum, and International Operations Directorate, Asylum Division, May 2016

USCIS, Jonathan Scharfen, Deputy Director, "Processing the Discretionary Exemption to the Inadmissibility Grounds for Providing Material Support to Certain Terrorist Organizations," 24 May 2007

USCIS, Policy Memorandum PM-602-0096, "Implementation of New Discretionary Exemption Under INA Section 212(d)(3)(B)(i) for Activities and Associations Relating to the Oromo Liberation Front (OLF)," 31 December 2013

USCIS, Policy Memorandum, PM-602-0099, "Implementation of New Discretionary Exemption Under INA Section 212(d)(3)(B)(i) for Activities and Associations Relating to the Eritrean Liberation Front (ELF)," 15 June 2014

USCIS, Policy Memorandum PM-602-0112, "Implementation of the Discretionary Exemption Authority Under Section 212(d)(3)(B)(i) of the Immigration and Nationality Act for the Provision of Certain Limited Material Support," 8 May 2015

USCIS, Policy Memorandum PM-602-0113, "Implementation of the Discretionary Exemption Authority Under Section 212(d)(3)(B)(i) of the Immigration and Nationality Act for the Provision of Insignificant Material Support," 8 May 2015

USCIS, "Terrorism-Related Inadmissibility Grounds (TRIG)—Group-Based Exemptions," 11 November 2019

USCIS, "Terrorism-Related Inadmissibility Grounds (TRIG)—Situational Exemptions," 29 August 2022

US Department of Homeland Security, Immigration and Customs Enforcement, "Human Rights Violations and War Crimes"

US Immigration and Customs Enforcement (ICE), "ICE Arrests 23 Known or Suspected Human Rights Violators Across the US During Operation Safe Nation," 12 April 2022

Table of Cases

JURISPRUDENCE

International Court of Justice (ICJ)

United Nations Committee against Torture (CAT)

United Nations Committee on the Elimination of Racial Discrimination (CERC)

United Nations Human Rights Committee (HRC)

International Criminal Court (ICC)

International Tribunal for the Former Yugoslavia (ICTY)

International Tribunal for Rwanda (ICTR)

Extraordinary Chambers of the Court of Cambodia (ECCC)

Kosovo Specialist Chamber (KSC)

Sierra Leone Special Court (SLSC)

Senegal Extraordinary African Chambers (EAC)

Special Tribunal For Lebanon (STL)

Post-Second World War Jurisprudence

African Commission on Human and People's Rights (ACHPR)

African Court of Human and People's Rights (AfCHPR)

Court of Justice the European Union (CJEU)

European Court of Human Rights (ECtHR)

Inter-American Commission on Human Rights (IACHR)

Inter-American Court of Human Rights (IACtHR)

COUNTRIES

Australia

Austria

Belgium

Canada

Czech Republic

France

Germany

Hong Kong

India

Ireland

Kenya

The Netherlands

Rb, Den Bosch, Awb 08/22199, 1 March 2010....................................... 361

New Zealand

South Africa

Sweden

Switzerland

United Kingdom

United States

Index

About the Author

Joseph Rikhof has received a BCL from the University of Nijmegen, The Netherlands; an LLB from McGill University; a Diploma in Air and Space Law from McGill University; and a PhD from the Irish Centre for Human Rights. He teaches international criminal law as an adjunct professor at the University of Ottawa. He was senior counsel, Manager of the Law, with the Crimes against Humanity and War Crimes Section of the Department of Justice, Canada. He was special counsel and a policy advisor to the Modern War Crimes Section of the Department of Citizenship & Immigration between 1998 and 2002 and a visiting professional with the International Criminal Court in 2005 and served with the Department of Justice from 2002 until his retirement in 2017. He was also a member of the editorial board of the *Philippe Kirsch Global Justice Journal* between 2017 and 2022, where he regularly posted short commentaries on recent developments in international criminal justice.

His area of expertise is in law related to organized crime, terrorism, genocide, war crimes, and crimes against humanity, especially in the context of immigration and refugee law. He has published over sixty articles, as well the books *International and Transnational Criminal Law*, 3d ed (with co-author Robert J. Currie, 2020), and *A Theory of Punishable Participation in Universal Crimes* (with co-author Terje Einarsen, 2018), exploring these research interests, and has lectured on the same topics in North and South America, Europe, Africa, Asia, the Middle East, Australia, and New Zealand.

FSC
www.fsc.org
MIX
Papier | Fördert
gute Waldnutzung
FSC® C083411

Kolibri 360 GmbH
Ferdinand-Jühlke-Straße 7
99095 Erfurt, Deutschland
produktsicherheit@kolibri360.de